S0-AIS-223

WITHDRAWN FROM
MACALESTER COLLEGE
LIBRARY

TEST CRITIQUES: VOLUME X

Daniel J. Keyser, Ph.D.
Richard C. Sweetland, Ph.D.

General Editors

TEST CRITIQUES
Volume X

pro·ed
8700 Shoal Creek Boulevard
Austin, Texas 78757-6897
(512) 451-3246

Copyright © 1994 by PRO-ED, Inc.

All rights reserved. No part of this book
may be reproduced in any form or by any means
without the prior written permission of the publisher.

Printed in the United States of America

LC 84-26895

ISBN 0-89079-596-7

The reviewers participating in each volume of *Test Critiques* are qualified
scholars and test users who are invited to contribute because of their
knowledge of and experience with testing and assessment instruments. The
opinions they express are their own and do not necessarily reflect the opinions
of either the series editors or the publisher.

pro·ed
8700 Shoal Creek Boulevard
Austin, Texas 78757-6897

10 9 8 7 6 5 4 3 2 1   94 95 96 97 98

CONTENTS

ACKNOWLEDGEMENTS

The editors wish to acknowledge the special contributions of our test reviewers, who have done an outstanding job. Our thanks extend from our deep pleasure and gratitude over their participation and the quality of their work. We know many of the contributing reviewers remain as "caught up" in this project as we and are now writing additional reviews for subsequent volumes. Thanks also must go to the test publishers, whose ongoing release of information and materials to the participating reviewers ensures the continuation of this series.

We thank the staff at Westport Publishers who assisted in the compilation of this volume, and Jane Doyle Guthrie, editor and typesetting coordinator.

We also wish to thank the staff at PRO-ED, Inc., now our publisher for this series. We look forward to our ongoing association.

Finally, we want to express our warmest thanks to our readers. It is their use of *Test Critiques* that gives a final validity to this project. It is our sincere desire that *Test Critiques* will consistently have a true application for them.

INTRODUCTION

Test Critiques is a fulfillment of a goal of the editors and a continuation of a task begun with the publication of *Tests: A Comprehensive Reference for Assessments in Psychology, Education and Business* (1983), its *Supplement* (1984), and *Tests: Second Edition* (1986). With the *Test Critiques* series, we believe that we have moved into the final phase of this project—to include those vital parts that were not appropriate for our directory. With succeeding editions of *Tests* and the ongoing *Test Critiques* series, the reader will have a full spectrum of current test information.

When *Tests* was published, a decision was made to leave out important psychometric information relating to reliability, validity, and normative development. Normative data and questions of reliability and validity were considered simply too complex to be reduced to the "quick scanning" desk reference desired. It was also apparent to the editors that a fair treatment of these topics would unnecessarily burden less sophisticated readers. More learned readers were familiar with other source books where such information could be obtained. The editors were aware, however, that a fuller treatment of each test was needed. These complex issues, along with other equally important aspects of tests, deserved scholarly treatment compatible with our full range of readers.

The selections for each volume were in no way arbitrarily made by the editors. The editorial staff researched what were considered to be the most frequently used psychological, educational, and business tests. In addition, questionnaires were sent to members of various professional organizations and their views were solicited as to which tests should be critiqued. After careful study of the survey results, the staff selected what was felt to be a good balance for each of the several volumes of critiques and selection lists were prepared for invited reviewers. Each reviewer chose the area and test to be critiqued, and as can be noted in each volume's table of contents, some reviewers suggested new tests that had not been treated to extensive reviews. As test specialists, some reviewers chose to review tests that they had researched extensively or were familiar with as users; some chose to review instruments that they were interested in but had never had the opportunity to explore. Needless to say, the availability of writers, their timetables, and the matching of tests and writers were significant variables.

Though the reviewers were on their own in making their judgments, we felt that their work should be straightforward and readable as well as comprehensive. Each test critique would follow a simple plan or outline. Technical terms when used would be explained, so that each critique would be meaningful to all readers—professors, clinicians, and students alike. Furthermore, not only would the questions of reliability and validity along with other aspects of test construction be handled in depth, but each critique would be written to provide practical, helpful information not contained in other reference works. *Test Critiques* would be useful both as a library reference tool containing the best of scholarship but also as practical, field-oriented books, valued as a reference for the desks of all professionals involved in human assessments.

It might be helpful to review for the reader the outline for each critique contained in this series. However, it must be stressed that we communicated with each critique writer and urged that scholarship and professional creativity not be sacrificed through total compliance to the proposed structure. To each reviewer we wrote: "The test(s) which you are reviewing may in fact require small to major modifications of the outline. The important point for you to bear in mind is that your critique will appear in what may well become a standard reference book on human assessment; therefore, your judgment regarding the quality of your critique always supersedes the outline. Be mindful of the spirit of the project, which is to make the critique practical, straightforward, and of value to all users— graduate students, undergraduates, teachers, attorneys, professional psychologists, educators, and others."

The editors' outline for the critiques consisted of three major divisions and numerous subdivisions. The major divisions were Introduction, Practical Applications/ Uses, and Technical Aspects, followed by the Critique section. In the Introduction the test is described in detail with relevant developmental background, to place the instrument in a historical context as well as to provide student users the opportunity to absorb the patterns and standards of test development. Practical Applications/Uses gives the reader information from a "user" standpoint—setting(s) in which the test is used, appropriate as well as inappropriate subjects, and administration, scoring, and interpretation guidelines. The section on Technical Aspects cites validity and reliability studies, test and retest situations, as well as what other experts have said about the test. Each review closes with an overall critique.

The reader may note in studying the various critiques in each volume that some authors departed from the suggested outline rather freely. In so doing they complied with their need for congruence and creativity—as was the editors' desire. Some tests, particularly brief and/or highly specialized instruments, simply did not lend themselves easily to our outline.

Instituted in Volume III, an updated cumulative subject index has been included in this volume. Each test has been given a primary classification within the focused assessment area under the main sections of psychology, education, and business. The subject index is keyed either to correspond directly to or be compatible with the classification system used in *Tests*.

It is the editors' hope that this series will prove to be a vital component within the available array of test review resources—the *Mental Measurements Yearbooks*, the online computer services for the Buros Institute database, *Psychological Abstracts*, professional measurement journals, *A Consumer's Guide to Tests in Print* by Hammill, Brown, and Bryant, and so forth. To summarize the goals of the current volume, the editors had in mind the production of a comprehensive, scholarly reference volume that would have varied but practical uses. *Test Critiques* in content and scholarship represents the best efforts of the reviewers, the editors, and the other individuals involved in its production.

TEST CRITIQUES: VOLUME X

H. O'Neal Smitherman, Ph.D.

Assistant to the Vice Chancellor and Director of Institutional Research, The University of Alabama System, Tuscaloosa, Alabama.

ABERRANT BEHAVIOR CHECKLIST

Michael G. Aman and Nirbhay N. Singh. East Aurora, New York: Slosson Educational Publications, Inc.

Introduction

The Aberrant Behavior Checklist (ABC) is an evaluative instrument designed to serve as an index for the effects of drugs or other intervening factors on dysfunctional or inappropriate behaviors. The test consists of 58 items that are rated on a scale of 0 to 3, indicating the existence or absence of each behavior. As the scale is a straightforward checklist of an individual's activity, the task requires no formal training in test administration. The only prerequisite of the individual completing the ABC is that he or she has a good knowledge of the subject.

The test may be completed by family members and friends if the subject lives in the home and by direct-care staff or professional staff if the subject resides within an institution.

The ABC evolved in an effort to provide an instrument that could measure behavior changes due to the effects of drug therapy. Although a number of existing scales were reviewed, the developers (Aman & Singh, 1986) felt these assessments did not measure the effects of various chemical therapies adequately. The authors were influenced by the work of Conners (1969, 1970), Quay (1977; Quay & Werry, 1979, pp. 1–42), Werry (1978), and O'Leary (1981) in assessing psychotherapy and drug effects in children. They attempted to develop a scale that was empirically based, focused on concrete behaviors, nonintrusive, and psychometrically sound.

Test development began by compiling a pool of items representing "problem behaviors" associated with moderately to profoundly retarded individuals. This item pool came from inspection of records in institutions for the mentally retarded, references to other scales in mental retardation and childhood psychopathology, and consultation with direct-care staff in institutions and day-care environments. These methods resulted in a total of 125 items. The items then were applied to a total of 1,465 residents who were rated by direct-care staff on a scale of 0 (not a problem at all) through 3 (the problem is severe in degree). When mildly retarded and nonambulatory individuals were removed from the evaluation, a total of 418 residents remained. Next the developers excluded items that applied to less than 10% of the individuals tested. They factor analyzed the remaining items using a principal factor method and an oblique rotation. This analysis yielded a total of 76 items for the scale.

Next a group of 585 residents was rated. Elimination of mildly retarded and nonambulatory individuals produced a total sample of 509 subjects, and factor

3

analyses yielded five factors. When the factor analyses of the two sets of samples were compared, agreement was reached on all factors except 1 and 4, the "acting-out factors." The disagreements between the two samples appeared to be due to impure items loading on alternate factors.

After removing impure items and dropping those that tended to load on more than one factor, a total of 58 items remained. The ABC's five scale factors include 1) irritability, agitation, crying; 2) lethargy, social withdrawal; 3) stereotypic behavior; 4) hyperactivity, noncompliance; and 5) inappropriate speech (Aman & Singh, 1986).

The ABC consists of two parts: the checklist itself and the scoring sheet. In the copies supplied to this reviewer, the checklist mark-off sheet was a yellow foldout approximately 8½" × 11" containing three pages of written materials. The score sheet was a single-sided sheet of green paper. The first page of the checklist contains basic information about the individual being rated, including his or her name, that of the rater, the subject's living area (unit, villa, ward), the current date, his or her gender, the date of birth, his or her chronological and mental age, his or her IQ and the test used for measuring it, the degree of mental retardation (mild, moderate, severe, profound, or do not know), whether the individual received specialized training, and the subject's medical status (regarding deafness, blindness, epilepsy, cerebral palsy, psychosis, paralysis, and other), plus a place for indicating any medication (and its dosage) that the subject may be taking.

The next section of the checklist provides instructions. In these the respondent is asked to rate the subject's behavior for the last 4 weeks using a 4-point scale for each item: 0 (not at all a problem), 1 (the behavior is a problem but slight in degree), 2 (the problem is moderately serious), or 3 (the problem is severe in degree). Raters are instructed to consider the frequency of the behavior, whether it occurs with all staff, whether it interferes with the subject's development, and the observation of others. The items themselves are broken into sets of 10, and their order appears nonsystematic relative to the factorial scales.

The score sheet contains spaces for the subject's name, the date, the "study phase," and the name of the rater. Next follows a listing of the five subscales. Each subscale is numbered and identified with the key word representing the scale factor. Under each subscale title appears a list of the items that constitute that scale (indicated by their number on the checklist) and accompanying lines for recording the score of each item. Under each column of items the format provides a line for recording the total score for that subscale.

Administration requires the rater merely to respond to the first page of descriptive information and then circle the appropriate rating number corresponding to each checklist item. Participation is straightforward and should be learned easily by any raters. Scoring may be performed by the rater or someone else. The process consists merely of recording onto the score sheet the subject's rating on each item as it corresponds to the subscales. Finally, scores for the five subscales are obtained by adding up the individual item scores within each subscale.

Practical Applications/Uses

Aman and Singh designed the ABC to be a reliable indicator of medication effects on maladaptive behaviors. They emphasize a conscious decision to address "maladaptive behaviors" rather than "prosocial behaviors" (Aman & Singh, 1986). Indeed as the test developed these two attributes appeared to be merely opposite sides of the same coin. As "inappropriate" behaviors are those for which drug therapies or unexpected side effects constitute the primary consideration, changes in aberrant behaviors should be most representative of the effect of chemical intervention.

The ABC appears to be particularly effective in describing and categorizing the behavioral changes that may be associated with drug intervention. The target group for this scale has remained moderately to profoundly retarded, ambulatory individuals. Further, the items appear to adequately represent those aberrant behaviors represented by institutionalized subjects.

The use of this test in "unintended" surroundings would require the development of baseline information prior to its administration for intervention effects; however, the instrument appears to be sensitive enough to measure effects that are not place specific.

Because the ABC is a behavioral rating instrument, it may be completed in any comfortable setting that will accommodate the rater's recording tasks. As indicated earlier, anyone familiar with the subject may complete the checklist, but the developers suggest that the rater know the subject for at least 4 weeks prior to attempting the ABC.

The procedures are straightforward and clearly described. While the checklist presents items in a sequential order, there is no apparent need for rigidly following this sequence. Items requiring further thought may be skipped and returned to later. Experienced raters may finish the ABC in 5 minutes or less. However, new users may require more time.

The scoring of the ABC is clearly presented and easy to follow. Because of the score sheet's uncluttered layout, the process may take 5 minutes or less; it involves merely transferring responses (ratings) from the checklist to the appropriate spaces on the score sheet and then adding up columns for subscale totals.

Neither the manual nor the checklist scoring sheet indicate any availability of computer or machine scoring services; however, the hand-scoring method is so simple that machine scoring would not be necessary. Nonetheless, machine scoring could be developed quite easily, requiring only minor enhancements to any standard scoring technique.

The interpretation of the ABC may be clearly based on objective scores. That is, each subscale has a score associated with it, and this score may be compared following treatment intervention to the same subscale results prior to intervention. Such a comparison would produce a clear difference score, which in turn can be compared to the normalized standard deviations for each subscale. Although a basic knowledge of statistics and psychometric concepts is helpful in understanding the interpretation process for this instrument, the necessary basics for appropriate ABC interpretation could be taught easily.

Technical Aspects

The factor structure of the ABC was appropriately developed with an empirically based process. Further, comparisons have been made between the United States institutions study by Aman, Richmond, Bell, Stewart, and Kissell (1986; reported in Aman & Singh, 1986) and administration of the checklist with a sample from New Zealand. Of the 58 items, 50 produced the same respective factors in both samples except for the subscales on irritability and stereotypic behavior; all subscales loaded heavily on the same respective subscales as those in the original developmental analysis. Further, when mean factor loadings from the original subscale assignment were compared to the United States and New Zealand analyses, the mean factor loadings for all 58 items was .58. Such a high consistency indicates good cross-validation. Further cross-validation comes from the comparisons of randomly selected subgroups within each of the populations under study.

Various forms of psychometric reliability have been addressed in the ABC manual. Internal consistency as measured by Cronbach's (1951) coefficient alpha was calculated for the parent population for each subscale of the ABC. The results indicate coefficient alpha results above .90 on all subscales except inappropriate speech, which produced a coefficient alpha of .86. Similar high results were obtained from the United States population.

Interrater reliability was established through comparisons of the scores for individuals between various raters. Spearman correlation coefficients for pairs of nurses rating residents indicate moderate to high correlations between raters. Average correlations of .63 accounting for 40% of the variance were found.

The developers assessed test-retest reliability by having 13 nurses rate 184 hospital residents initially and then 4 weeks later. Spearman correlations between the two ratings all emerged above .95.

As an indication of criterion group validity, the developers compared scores of institutionalized subjects enrolled in training sessions to those of individuals who had not attended training. Results indicate that subjects attending training produced lower subscale scores in all areas except inappropriate speech. The test authors indicate that this anomaly may have occurred due to less verbal attainment for those individuals who had not attended training sessions. Other comparisons of groups with physical handicaps to non–physically handicapped peers indicated the obvious effect of lack of motility on lower "aberrant behavior" scores.

According to the manual, the ABC also has been compared to the Slosson IQ test, the Fairview Self-help Scale, the Vineland Social Maturity Scale, the Adaptive Behavior Scale, and others. Spearman correlation coefficients between the subscales of the ABC and these instruments indicated that the ABC subscale scores related only marginally to IQ but were moderately related to the Fairview Self-help Scale, the Vineland Social Maturity Scale, and the AAMD Adaptive Behavior Scale Part I. Further, the ABC subscales were unrelated to the total scale score from Part II of the Maladapted Behavior portion of the Adaptive Behavior Scale.

Further confirmation of ABC ratings' validity comes from a comparison of ABC scores and independent behavior observations. For a group of 36 individuals, these comparisons yielded a mean level of agreement of 91.3%, with a range of 77% to 98% across all observers.

Critique

The Aberrant Behavior Checklist is a well-designed tool that performs appropriately in a badly needed area. It provides a consistent methodology for measuring intervention effects and offers a systematic approach to an area that is otherwise difficult to study. The developers have used appropriate and somewhat creative approaches to construction and have followed sound procedures in the development of their subscales.

The manual accompanying the ABC is well written and presents sufficient information to support the soundness of the instrument. The checklist sheet and the scoring sheet are also well designed and provide an uncomplicated presentation of the requirements for administration and scoring.

References

Aman, M.G., & Singh, N.N. (1986). *Aberrant Behavior Checklist manual.* East Aurora, NY: Slosson Educational Publications.

Aman, M.G., Richmond, G., Bell, J.C., Stewart, A.W., & Kissell, R.C. (1986). *The Aberrant Behavior Checklist: Factorial validity and the effect of demographic/medical variables in American and New Zealand facilities.* Manuscript submitted for publication.

Conners, C.K. (1969). A teacher rating scale for use in drug studies with children. *American Journal of Psychiatry, 126,* 152–156.

Conners, C.K. (1970). Symptom patterns in hyperkinetic, neurotic, and normal children. *Child Development, 41,* 667–682.

Cronbach, L.J. (1951). Coefficient alpha and the internal structure of tests. *Psychometrika, 16,* 297–334.

O'Leary, K.D. (1981). Assessment of hyperactivity: Observational and rating methodologies. In S.A. Miller (Ed.), *Nutrition and behavior* (pp. 291–298). Philadelphia: Fauklin Institute Press.

Quay, H.C. (1977). Measuring dimensions of deviant behavior: The Behavior Problem Checklist. *Journal of Abnormal Child Psychology, 5,* 277–288.

Quay, H.C., & Werry J.S. (Eds.). *Psychopathological disorders of childhood* (2nd ed.). New York: Wiley.

Werry, J.S. (1978). Measures in pediatric psychopharmacology. In J.S. Werry (Ed.), *Pediatric psychopharmacology: The use of behavior modifying drugs in children* (pp. 29–78). New York: Brunner/Mazel.

Brian Bolton, Ph.D.
University Professor, Arkansas Research and Training Center in Vocational Rehabilitation, University of Arkansas, Fayetteville, Arkansas.

ACCEPTANCE OF DISABILITY SCALE

Donald C. Linkowski. Washington, D.C.: George Washington University, Department of Human Services, Rehabilitation Counselor Education Program.

Introduction

The Acceptance of Disability Scale (AD Scale; Linkowski, 1987) is a 50-item self-report questionnaire that measures the extent to which an individual with a physical disability has made a satisfactory adjustment to his or her disabling condition. The AD Scale derives from a theory of acceptance of loss formulated by Dembo, Leviton, and Wright (1956) that emphasizes the subjective meaning of the disability to the person, with the associated emotions and values. In-depth discussions of the concept of disability acceptance appear in Linkowski (1969) and Butler and Thomas (1980).

Donald C. Linkowski is a professor in the Department of Human Services at George Washington University, where he has been on the faculty for more than 20 years. He is a nationally recognized authority in rehabilitation counselor education, having served as president of the American Rehabilitation Counseling Association, the National Council on Rehabilitation Education, and the Council on Rehabilitation Education. Professor Linkowski developed the AD Scale in conjunction with his dissertation project at the State University of New York at Buffalo (Linkowski, 1969).

The AD Scale consists of 50 brief statements that refer to the respondent's values and attitudes with respect to physical disablement. Fifteen items embody positive values, while 35 express negative attitudes toward disability. Examples from the AD Scale (reproduced with the author's permission) follow:

9. My disability affects those aspects of life which I care most about.
25. A person with my disability is unable to enjoy very much in life.
34. Personal characteristics such as honesty and a willingness to work hard are much more important than physical appearance and ability.
40. There is practically nothing a person in my condition is able to do and really enjoy it.

Responses to each statement are recorded using a standard 6-point Likert format (I disagree very much, I disagree pretty much, I disagree a little, I agree a little, I agree pretty much, I agree very much). To simplify administration of the instrument, the response format repeats with each statement; hence, there is no separate answer sheet. The entire consumable questionnaire is seven pages in length and requires about 15 minutes to complete.

The AD Scale may be used with adolescents and adults with physical or medical disabilities (as opposed to intellectual or psychiatric disabilities) who read at the fourth-grade level or above. The 50 item responses are summed into a total score, on the assumption that all items measure a common underlying construct, acceptance of disability. However, as discussed below, research has not determined whether there are discriminable facets of the global construct present in the AD Scale item set.

The author has made only very minor revisions in the language and phrasing of the AD Scale items since 1969. Demonstrating its wide popularity and importance in cross-cultural research, the AD Scale has been translated into Hebrew, German, Thai, Japanese, and Mandarin. Students have used it in 25 thesis and dissertation projects, and 25 studies have appeared in refereed rehabilitation and psychology journals.

Practical Applications/Uses

The AD Scale was designed to measure the global construct of adjustment to a physical or medical disability. Linkowski developed his instrument to predict rehabilitation outcomes and counseling with clients with disabling conditions. Its use extends to a variety of rehabilitation settings such as hospitals, rehabilitation centers, and independent living programs, by rehabilitation counselors, psychologists, and other allied health professionals.

The AD Scale can be used appropriately with individuals aged 16 and older who have physical or medical disabilities and language skills at the fourth-grade level or above. Poor readers may receive the inventory items via audiotape. Small group administration of the AD Scale probably offers the most efficient approach, but the measure can be administered individually when warranted. For all practical purposes, this instrument is self-administering, because the instructions are straightforward and the task is easily comprehended. The typical respondent requires between 15 and 20 minutes to complete the AD Scale.

Scoring the AD Scale is a simple clerical matter, requiring only that one assign the numeric values 1, 2, 3, 4, 5, and 6 to the positively phrased items and reverse the values for negatively stated items. The total score is calculated by summing the 50 item scores. Raw total scores range from 50 to 300.

Because no published norms exist yet for the AD Scale, interpretation of the protocol must come from a clinical examination of the responses to the individual items or by locating the average item score with respect to the six anchors of the response format. It would be possible to develop approximate normative translations using the descriptive statistics given in the manual for two small samples of 46 rehabilitation center clients and 55 college students with disabilities (Linkowski, 1987, pp. 2–3).

Technical Aspects

The AD Scale was constructed to measure Dembo et al.'s (1956) concept of acceptance of loss, which was explicated more fully by Wright (1960, 1983). The process of adjustment to loss as outlined by Wright consists of a series of value changes. The four value shifts that characterize individuals who have accepted their disabilities follow:

Enlargement of scope of values—the extent to which a person can see values other than those in direct conflict with the disability.

Subordination of physique—the extent to which a person can deemphasize aspects of physical ability and appearance that contradict his or her disabled condition.

Containment of disability effects—the extent to which a person can restrict his or her handicap to the actual physical impairment, rather than spreading it to other aspects of the functioning self.

Transformation from comparative to asset values—the extent to which a person does not compare him- or herself to others in terms of limitations and liabilities, but rather emphasizes his or her own assets and abilities.

In writing the AD Scale items, Linkowski made no attempt to avoid overlap of the four value areas. In other words, items were not conceptualized as "pure" indicators of the four specific types of value changes postulated by Wright (1960, 1983). The assumption underlying the author's strategy was that the value areas are not independent components of adjustment, but rather related facets of a global construct of disability acceptance.

It is important to emphasize that the two alternative conceptions of the nature of disability acceptance suggested above are not incompatible; that is, the four value areas could overlap to some extent (thus reflecting a shared underlying dimension) and yet also possess some specific meaning in each area. In fact, many psychological domains are organized in this way. For example, the central construct called *general intelligence* underlies any broad sample of ability tests.

Principal factor analyses of the 50 AD Scale items for samples of 46 rehabilitation center clients and 55 college students with disabilities resulted in first principal factors accounting for 48% and 69% of the common variance, respectively. Although these figures, when considered in conjunction with the pattern of item loadings on the first principal factors, do support a global dimension of acceptance of disability, these data do not rule out a possible multiple-factor conception of the construct. It would be necessary to rotate two, three, and four factors and examine the resulting factor patterns carefully before concluding that there is no basis for a multidimensional view of disability acceptance.

Carrying out a thorough factor analysis of the AD Scale would entail an independent evaluation to determine which of the four value areas is measured primarily by each of the 50 items. One could make this assessment by asking a panel of expert judges to allocate each item to one of the four value areas and then calculating the predominant choice, along with figures indicating the extent of agreement for each item.

The 50 items that compose the AD Scale were written by the author and independently evaluated for clarity and relevance to Wright's (1960, 1983) conception of disability acceptance by two authorities in rehabilitation counseling. Statements that the experts judged unclear or not central to the theory of loss were either revised or replaced.

One further test to ensure the discriminant validity of the items involved asking four graduate students in rehabilitation counseling to complete the items as if they were persons with physical disabilities who accepted their disabilities. Each student then completed the items as they thought a nonacceptor of disablement would respond. Those items that did not demonstrate a consistent bipolarity were revised in the development of the final version.

The manual presents only one reliability coefficient for the AD Scale. For the sample of 46 rehabilitation center clients who were in the evaluation and planning stages of their rehabilitation programs when they completed the inventory, the internal consistency coefficient (calculated via the split-half method) was .93. The size of the first principal factor for the sample of 55 college students with disabilities suggests that the internal consistency reliability coefficient would be even higher. The manual reports no test-retest reliabilities.

A variety of correlational evidence supports the validity of the AD Scale (see Butler & Thomas [1980] and Linkowski [1987] for details about the individual studies). First, two demographic variables, gender and education, relate to disability acceptance. Females are typically more accepting of disability than males, and persons with higher levels of education are generally more accepting than those with less education. No reliable relationships have emerged for age, occupation, socioeconomic status, type and nature of disability, race, ethnicity, or religious preference.

However, intensity of religious belief (religiosity) and spiritual well-being do correlate positively with acceptance of disability. Furthermore, self-esteem, satisfaction with social relationships, attitudes toward people with disabilities, and participation in self-help groups are associated with greater disability acceptance. Other variables correlated with acceptance of disability are internal locus of control, perception of improvement as a result of rehabilitation, and realism of expectations held by persons recently disabled. Also, assertion training resulted in improved disability acceptance. These relationships are consistent with theoretical expectations, thus suggesting strongly that the AD Scale is a valid measure of the construct variously characterized as acceptance of loss, adjustment to disability, and acceptance of disability.

Critique

The AD Scale measures a variable that has both theoretical and practical significance in rehabilitation psychology, and all available evidence supports the instrument's reliability and validity. However, additional research must precede the scale's use for clinical assessment. First, a study of the dimensionality of the inventory should be completed using confirmatory factor analysis. Second, norm tables for several different rehabilitation populations are essential. It is possible that some normative data could be retrieved from the published studies and dissertations that have used the AD Scale. Third, test-retest reliability evidence should be collected. Finally, a study to determine if the 6-anchor response format is optimal would be helpful.

In conclusion, the AD Scale presents an important instrument in the field of rehabilitation that requires further psychometric research before it can be recommended without reservation for application in counseling and other service settings.

References

Butler, A.J., & Thomas, K.R. (1980). Disability acceptance. In R. Woody (Ed.), *Encyclopedia of client assessment* (pp. 1060–1067). San Francisco: Jossey-Bass.

Dembo, T., Leviton, G.L., & Wright, B.A. (1956). Adjustment to misfortune—A problem in social psychological rehabilitation. *Artificial Limbs, 3*, 4–62.

Linkowski, D.C. (1969). *A study of the relationship between acceptance of disability and response to rehabilitation.* Unpublished doctoral dissertation, State University of New York at Buffalo.

Linkowski, D.C. (1987). *The Acceptance of Disability Scale.* Washington, DC: George Washington University, Rehabilitation Research and Training Center.

Wright, B.A. (1960). *Physical disability: A psychological approach.* New York: Harper & Row.

Wright, B.A. (1983). *Physical disability: A psychosocial approach* (rev. ed.). New York: Harper & Row.

Mary M. Wellman, Ph.D.

Professor, Department of Counseling and Educational Psychology, Rhode Island College, Providence, Rhode Island.

ACKERMAN-SCHOENDORF SCALES FOR PARENT EVALUATION OF CUSTODY

Marc Ackerman and Kathleen Schoendorf. Los Angeles, California: Western Psychological Services.

Introduction

The Ackerman-Schoendorf Scales for Parent Evaluation of Custody (ASPECT) make up a clinical instrument designed to assist professionals in forming recommendations regarding child custody cases. The ASPECT comprises several standardized scales that measure the ability of both mother and father to be the custodial parent. These scales incorporate the results of most commonly used psychological tests and the clinician's observations and interviews.

The biographic directory of the American Psychological Association states that Marc Ackerman, Ph.D., received his doctorate in clinical psychology from the University of Georgia in 1972. He has been a private practitioner since 1975, a child clinical psychologist at the St. Francis Children's Center since 1973, and the Director of Clinical Training in Psychology at the Wisconsin School of Professional Psychology since 1986. No information was available in the directory or from Western Psychological Services regarding Dr. Schoendorf's background and credentials.

The ASPECT was developed to meet the need for an all-inclusive custody evaluation tool. The manual reports that before 1900, custody automatically was given to the father because he was better able to provide financial support. In the years following, the belief that younger children fared better under their mother's care caused a reversal in ensuing custody decisions in favor of the mother. In the changing social mores of the 1960s, the notion of "the best interests of the child" caused courts to seek reliable guidelines for determining parental and environmental characteristics that serve the best interests of the children involved in the custody dispute. The ASPECT combines the results of psychological testing, interviews, and observations of each parent and the children to provide normative data regarding the suitability of each parent for custody.

The ASPECT has three subscales: Observational, Social, and Cognitive-Emotional. The items were derived from a theoretical and data-based overview of the literature on parenting and individual psychopathology.

The participants in the instrument's standardization were 200 parents seeking a custody evaluation and their children. A psychologist in private practice evaluated each couple, using the ASPECT instrument. Parental ages ranged from 24 to 57 years, with a mean of 34 years, and the children's from 4 months to 17 years. The sample was representative of the United States population, except that par-

13

ents were more well educated than the U.S. norms, suggesting that more knowledgeable and perhaps affluent persons sought legal disposition of their custody issue.

The evaluating psychologist interviewed each parent separately and observed him or her interacting with the children. Each parent was evaluated psychologically with the Wechsler Adult Intelligence Scale–Revised (WAIS-R), the Minnesota Multiphasic Personality Inventory (MMPI), the Rorschach inkblots, and the Wide Range Achievement Test–Revised (WRAT-R) or the Norris Educational Achievement Test (NEAT). Each parent also completed the ASPECT Parent Questionnaire. The couple's children also were interviewed individually and were administered an age-appropriate intelligence test, a projective storytelling test, and a family drawing.

The manual reports that two examiners saw the first 25 families and completed the ASPECT questionnaire in order to establish interrater reliability. In addition, through the use of comparisons of the ASPECT scores and judges' custody determinations for mothers and fathers, the developers determined that separate norms on the ASPECT for males and females were not needed.

The scales were published in February 1992 and, as a new instrument, have not yet undergone any revisions. The ASPECT also has not yet been published in any other language or in braille.

ASPECT materials consist of a 6-page parent questionnaire containing 68 narrative questions, a 3-page answer form filled out and scored by the examiner, a 56-page manual, and optional computer-scoring and interpretation answer sheets. Users can purchase a complete kit, containing 20 parent questionnaires, 10 hand-scored answer forms, a manual, and two prepaid computer answer sheets, from the publisher.

The 68 narrative questions read and answered by both parents pertain to the parent's family of origin and developmental history, substance abuse, legal and medical history, beliefs about custody of their children, self-evaluation of parenting skills, and child-care arrangements. In addition, the questions relate to parental knowledge of the children's developmental history, emotional needs, school performance, social skills, and reaction to the divorce, plus anticipation of their needs in the future. The manual states that parents "with poor reading ability" may have the questions read to them (no reading level for the questions appears). In using the ASPECT, this reviewer has found that the parent must have not only proficient reading skills, but also good independent work habits and organizational skills. In my experience, the questionnaire takes approximately 1 to 2 hours to complete, and it probes sensitive matters. Consequently, some parents become overwhelmed after completing only half the questionnaire and need to have the remaining portion administered orally by the examiner as a structured interview. The examiner needs to be cognizant that structured interviews tend to be more threatening than a nonconfrontational paper-and-pencil format. Thus, the client may not reveal as much clinical information when the structured interview format is used. There are no separate norms for the structured interview format.

The ASPECT manual states that the instrument is designed for parents with children between the ages of 2 and 18. The manual also states that uncooperative parents, same-sex couples, and unmarried cohabiting couples should not be administered the ASPECT, as the results will not be valid. Prior to administration, parents are to be given the Lamb warning (i.e., the statements made by the parents and the results of the evaluation will not be confidential, and a report will be made to the court through the attorneys involved).

In addition to filling out the questionnaire, each parent must be administered the WAIS-R, MMPI or MMPI-2, Rorschach, and WRAT-R or NEAT. Interviews of each parent, observations of each parent interacting with the children, as well as interviews, intellectual assessment, and personality testing of each child are also necessary components of the complete evaluation. Following this, the examiner completes the 56 questions on the ASPECT answer form for each parent and then either calculates the scores for the Observational, Social, and Cognitive-Emotional scales and plots the profile, or mails in the Autoscore computer answer forms in order to receive scores, graphs, and a narrative report on each parent.

In the case of hand scoring, the examiner completes several simple arithmetic calculations in order to obtain raw scores for the Observational, Social, and Cognitive-Emotional scales and a Parental Custody Index (PCI) total raw score. He or she then graphs the raw scores on a profile sheet in order to obtain T-scores and percentiles for each of the four raw scores.

Practical Applications/Uses

The ASPECT is designed to assess parenting abilities and the best environment for children involved in custody disputes. The variables measured are the initial impression of parenting effectiveness created by each parent, the social environment provided by each parent, and each parent's emotional and cognitive capacity for child rearing.

This test's role in custody decisions is to provide standardized norms by which to compare the relative strengths and weaknesses of each parent. The most likely users are psychologists, either in private practice or at outpatient mental health settings, rather than psychiatrists, social workers, or counselors, because it involves the administration, scoring, and interpretation of sophisticated intellectual and personality psychological tests, and usually subsequent court testimony.

Because it requires that the adult desiring custody have an extensive, intimate knowledge of the child or children in question, the ASPECT would not be appropriate for screening suitable foster or adoptive parents who have not yet met and worked with a particular child. This instrument possibly could be used to determine the suitability of foster parents who have cared for a child for some length of time as prospective adoptive parents of that child. When using the ASPECT for this purpose, both mother and father would need to score in an acceptable range, as the child would be living with the two of them in an intact family rather than with either one or the other.

Relatively high functioning and cooperative parents who are engaged in a custody dispute are the most suitable consumers of this instrument. Those with chronic mental illness, such as schizophrenia, or who are cognitively limited, hostile, or sociopathic would be inappropriate subjects because of their potential inability to answer the questions honestly or at all.

Parents whose children are all 2 years old or younger would also be inappropriate consumers, because many of the questions are designed for those with children over the age of 2.

For parents who are bilingual or non–English speaking, presumably a structured interview using the six pages of questions should be used, with the examiner or an interpreter asking the questions in the parents' native language. Similarly, for visually or hearing impaired parents, the questions could be asked orally or in American Sign Language, respectively.

ASPECT testing is to be done individually, most likely in the examiner's office. The clinical expertise required to combine the results and interpretation of the intellectual and personality testing sessions with the interviews and observations, plus the necessary qualifications for court testimony, indicate that a licensed psychologist use the ASPECT. State laws and ethical standards also support such a restriction.

The administration procedures are simple and clearly stated in the manual. The only task is to present the six pages of narrative questions to the examinee, with instructions to read and answer the questions. The user should determine ahead of time if both parents have sufficient reading and organizational skills to complete the questionnaire independently. If not, the questions should take the form of a structured interview. (The manual should elaborate this point more fully.) In either case, the administration takes approximately 1 to 2 hours.

The instructions for scoring are also simple and clearly presented. Examiners can learn to score this test in approximately 20 minutes. Once mastered, the amount of time required to score the ASPECT is about 30 minutes. The only difficulties in scoring may be the use of clinical judgment on the part of the examiner in filling out the answer form, based on the information derived from the questionnaire, interviews, observations, and psychological testing. Fortunately, the authors have provided guidelines for each of the 56 items on the examiner answer sheet. The examiner must rate each parent on a dichotomous (yes/no) scale on the 9 Observational scale items, the 28 Social scale items, and the 19 Cognitive-Emotional scale items. Of these 56 items, 12 are "critical items," which indicate more serious parenting deficits than are reflected by the total PCI or individual subscale scores. Such items are red flags for the user to note and describe in the interpretive section of the report to the court.

Once the 56 items are rated for each parent, simple arithmetic computations determine the raw scores for the three subscales and the PCI. These scores are then graphed on a profile form, which contains equivalent T-scores and percentile ranks for the raw scores.

Services available from the publisher include computer scoring, lengthy narrative interpretation, and color graphs. Although showy and impressive looking, these "extras" are not necessary, and they are costly. Hand scoring is simple and rapid, and it requires no fragile or otherwise unwieldy materials. The interpretation flows easily once the examiner has completed the psychological testing, interviews, observations, questionnaires, and answer forms, so the computer scoring and interpretation is convenient but certainly not necessary.

Interpretation of the ASPECT is based on scores derived from normative data and some measure of internal clinical judgment. The most sophisticated and technical interpretation comes from the psychological testing and interviewing.

As noted previously, for this reason the ASPECT should be used by a highly trained mental health professional, typically a licensed psychologist. Once the user has entered the results of these assessment devices on the answer forms, along with parent questionnaire results and observational data, the interpretation becomes much easier, because it is derived from the data summarized on the answer forms for each parent.

Technical Aspects

The internal consistency of a test measures the extent to which its items reflect similar content. Internal consistency calculated for the ASPECT's total PCI score, using Cronbach's coefficient alpha formula with a KR-21 correction for dichotomous (yes/no) items, yielded a coefficient of .76, indicating a moderate correlation among items. Likewise, the Social scale showed an adequate internal consistency of .72. However, both the Observational and Cognitive-Emotional scales had .0 internal consistency, indicating that the items measure quite different characteristics. The authors point out that the Observational scale has zero internal consistency because it has a small number of items and measures heterogeneous aspects of the appearance and behavior of the parent (Ackerman & Schoendorf, 1992, p. 51). Further, the Social-Emotional scale likely has zero internal consistency because the items reflect different psychological tests and scales that measure different aspects of functioning. Examiners should exercise caution in interpreting these two subscales alone and in conducting a profile analysis.

Interrater reliability also was calculated, based on two raters independently rating 88 participants randomly selected from the pool of 200. The interrater reliability coefficients emerged as follows: total PCI, .96; Social and Cognitive-Emotional scales, .94; Observational scale, .92. It is curious that the last chapter of the manual discusses this random selection procedure, while an earlier chapter states, "The first 25 families were seen by two examiners in order to establish interrater reliability" (Ackerman & Schoendorf, 1992, p. 48). This procedure is not mentioned at all in the psychometric chapter, and one wonder what the results of that calculation of interrater reliability were.

Predictive validity of the total PCI score based on hit rate compared to judges' orders for custody was calculated for two samples, as described in the manual. In Sample 1 ($N = 118$), examiners used the ASPECT when formulating recommendations for judges; in Sample 2 ($N = 24$), examiners either made no recommendation to judges or made recommendations independently of the ASPECT. Both samples yielded a 75% hit rate, and both yielded significant chi square and phi coefficient results. Of 118 cases in Sample 1, the ASPECT results indicated that 56 fathers were the better custodial parent, and in 39 cases (75%) the judge's decision agreed. Similarly, ASPECT results showed that 62 mothers were the better custodial parent, and in 49 cases (74%) the judge's decision agreed. Thus, the predictive validity was equal for both mothers and fathers.

In another study (Ackerman & Kane, 1991) not found in the manual, ASPECT predictions and judges' final orders were compared in 56 cases. Of these, 26 cases were dropped from the sample because there was less than a 10-point difference between mothers' and fathers' scores on the ASPECT, a nonsignificant difference according to the authors. In the remaining 30 cases, the ASPECT results agreed with the judges' orders 90% of the time.

In the manual the authors discuss the notion of whether judges' decisions present the best criterion for predictive validity studies, and they suggest that future longitudinal research investigate the adjustment of children placed in accordance with ASPECT recommendations as opposed to children placed contrary to ASPECT recommendations.

A flyer advertising the ASPECT mailed by Western Psychological Services states that "ASPECT has a 90% hit rate in predicting custody decisions made by judges," but the only hit rate presented in the manual is 75%. The 90% hit rate study is found in a separate publication (Ackerman & Kane, 1991, cited above) furnished by the publisher.

Critique

The items making up the ASPECT relate closely to the current literature on appropriate criteria for custody decisions. Further, the measure uses criteria from many sources (intellectual, personality, and academic achievement tests, interviews and observations), creating a comprehensive database. This comprehensive database can be a liability as well as an asset. Based on this reviewer's dozen years of clinical experience, a complete evaluation of parents and children using all of the tests included in the ASPECT ratings typically would take 40 to 80 hours. This may be fine for psychologists in private practice who have fairly affluent clients willing and able to pay for such an evaluation, but for less financially secure clients or those evaluated through social service agencies, this comprehensive aspect becomes a liability.

Several solutions are possible. First, the psychologist may be able to gather some of the test data from other sources (school psychology evaluations of the children, previous evaluations of the parents, etc.) if such data exist and are accessible. Second, several items in the Cognitive-Emotional scale relating to specific tests could become optional without adversely affecting the scale's internal consistency (which is already zero). Specifically, either the MMPI or the Rorschach, but not both, could be used, as both measure personality functioning. The two items relating to WAIS-R intellectual functioning also could become optional; though this may lower the overall coefficient alpha, it would also save 3 to 7 hours of test administration and scoring. Alternately, the Rorschach and WAIS-R items might be reworded to reflect clinical judgment based on observation, rather than psychometric data.

More detailed discussion of the problems associated with administration of the six-page narrative parent questionnaire should be written into the manual. Not only is the questionnaire long and laborious, but in addition many of the questions relate to emotionally charged situations in the parent's life. As a result, respondents may become bogged down and unable to complete the questionnaire independently, even if their reading skill is high. It is not wise to allow the parent to take the questionnaire home to complete or to administer it in two sessions, as this would allow seeking the advice or knowledge of others and thus invalidate the questionnaire. Therefore, the examiner needs to be vigilant in observing the parent completing the questionnaire and offer assistance by completing the questionnaire as a structured interview if necessary.

Finally, the discrepancy between the hit rate discussed in the manual (75%) and the hit rate advertised in the flyer (90%) is clarified by the Ackerman and Kane (1991) publication, but this study should be added to the manual as soon as possible, so that the test user is not puzzled by the apparent discrepancy.

References

Ackerman, M.J., & Kane, A.W. (1991). *How to examine psychological experts in divorce and other civil actions.* New York: Wiley.

Ackerman, M.J., & Schoendorf, K. (1992). *Manual for the Ackerman-Schoendorf Scales for Parent Evaluation of Custody.* Los Angeles: Western Psychological Services.

Merith Anne Cosden, Ph.D.
Associate Professor of Education, University of California, Santa Barbara, California.

ADDICTION SEVERITY INDEX

A. Thomas McLellan, L. Luborsky, C. O'Brien, and G. Woody. Philadelphia, Pennsylvania: Treatment Research Institute.

Introduction

The Addiction Severity Index (ASI) is a structured questionnaire designed to obtain information on adults entering drug and alcohol treatment programs. Clients are questioned about their problems in seven domains: medical, education/employment, drug abuse, alcohol abuse, legal, social/family support, and psychological. Although many of the items are not directly about substance abuse, the areas covered are often associated with substance abuse problems. The test can be used to describe clients' needs, classify and match clients to treatments, and evaluate performance over time.

The original Addiction Severity Index (ASI) was developed in 1979 by Dr. A. Thomas McLellan and his colleagues at the University of Pennsylvania. The senior author was affiliated with both the Department of Psychiatry at the University of Pennsylvania and the Drug Dependence Treatment Service at the Veterans Administration Hospital. The developers created the ASI as an assessment tool for clients coming into the VA hospital for treatment of substance abuse problems. The assessment was designed so that a trained technician could administer it within a relatively short period of time (30–40 minutes). It was structured to provide both easily coded and quantifiable data for use in research and a clinical picture of the client (McLellan, Luborsky, Woody, & O'Brien, 1980).

The major difference between the ASI and the other scales then available for assessment of substance abuse was the breadth of its coverage. The original ASI provided a profile of client functioning in six areas: 1) chemical abuse, 2) medical, 3) psychological, 4) legal, 5) family/social, and 6) employment/support. The authors of the test felt that clients seeking help with substance abuse problems often had concurrent problems in these areas and that these problems needed to be addressed as part of the clients' treatment.

The ASI underwent several minor revisions from its inception as a clinical research tool at the University of Pennsylvania. The most widely disseminated versions of the scale are the third and fifth editions (the latter is the latest edition). Earlier revisions of the scale are not readily available. The basic format of the test itself has not changed, with the exception that drug abuse and alcohol abuse are now coded separately and an uncoded family history section has been added.

McLellan et al. developed the fifth edition of the ASI in 1990. Items were added to several of the subscales, based on new knowledge about drug and alcohol problems, and a few additions appeared in the section on legal status and alcohol and drug use. The authors made their greatest number of changes in the section on family/social relationships, adding questions to assess more clearly the client's history of social relationships, the family history of drug and alcohol abuse, and the client's typical living situation. These additions did not change the subset of items on which composite test scores, and severity ratings, have been based (McLellan et al., in press).

Although the authors write that the ASI has been translated into nine languages (McLellan et al., in press), the only published study found for review was on a version of the ASI developed in the Netherlands (Hendriks, Kaplan, Limbeek, & Geerlings, 1989). This was not a direct translation of the American ASI; the authors of the Dutch assessment state that they changed some of the questions within each area to better address the needs of their clients, but they do not specify these alterations. Nevertheless, the Dutch ASI maintains many of the core concepts of its American counterpart. Questions are asked within the same domains and follow the same format. In addition, the same methods for calculating composite scores and severity ratings are used.

Other offshoots of the ASI include several scales designed for adolescent substance abusers, such as the Teen Addiction Severity Index (Kaminer, Bukstein, & Tarter, 1991; Kaminer & Frances, 1991) and the Adolescent Drug Abuse Diagnosis instrument (Friedman & Utada, 1989).

The fifth edition of the ASI is a six-page questionnaire. In addition to a cover sheet used to obtain demographic information, the instrument comprises seven sections: 1) medical status, 2) employment/support status, 3) drug/alcohol use, 4) legal status, 5) family history, 6) family/social relationships, and 7) psychiatric status. As noted previously, drug and alcohol use are scored separately. The other subscales receive separate scores, with the exception of family history; the information obtained in this area does not contribute to the aggregate domain scores, but it can be used for clinical or descriptive purposes.

The number of questions in each area ranges from 11 to 27, and all are designed for easy coding of client responses. Users record client responses in spaces provided alongside each question. The order of questions is the same in each section: First, there is a series of objective questions regarding the number, extent, and duration of problem symptoms in an area. Items elicit information regarding symptoms over the client's lifetime (e.g., "How many years over your lifetime have you used alcohol?") as well as within the past 30 days ("How many days in the past 30 have you used alcohol?"). At the end of each section, the respondent is given a 0–4 rating scale and asked to indicate the extent to which he or she currently is bothered by problems in that area and the extent to which he or she feels the need for treatment. The last items in each section allow interviewers to rate their confidence in the validity of the client's information and to provide their own estimates of the severity of the client's problems.

The examiner must ensure that the client understands each of the questions. All questions are read aloud, and the interviewer is allowed to paraphrase questions if the client does not understand the specific language used in the test. It is also the examiner's responsibility to assess whether or not the client is distorting information.

Two sets of scores are obtained for each domain: a Composite Score, which is obtained directly from client responses to a subset of questions in each domain, and a Severity Index, which is based both on the client's responses to the questionnaire and on the interviewer's perception of the client's need for treatment. These scores, used to provide a profile of client needs, can help match clients with treatment programs (McLellan, O'Brien, Kron, Alterman, & Druley, 1980; McLellan, Woody, Luborsky, O'Brien, & Druley, 1983) or assess their progress over time (McLellan, Luborsky, O'Brien, Woody, & Druley, 1982).

Practical Applications/Uses

The ASI was developed as an assessment tool for clients entering drug and alcohol treatment programs. Its designers intended it to be useful for treatment planning, evaluation of client progress, or research.

As a relatively easy test to administer and because of the clinical relevance of the information it provides, the ASI often is used as a screening tool. The breadth of information the ASI yields makes it valuable for individualized treatment planning, particularly when users are faced with diverse client populations.

The ASI commonly is used as a pre- and post-measure of client progress. Professionals can reevaluate their patients at the end of 30 days or more to determine changes in symptomatology. Studies using the ASI to assess treatment effectiveness have compared outcomes for alcohol- and drug-addicted clients, short-term and long-term clients, and clients entering different treatment facilities (McLellan, Luborsky, Woody, O'Brien, & Druley, 1983; McLellan, Woody, et al., 1983). The ASI allows the examiner to assess outcomes across all seven areas of functioning and to consider the interrelationships between outcomes in these areas.

Another application of the ASI groups clients on the basis of characteristics in one or more domains. This allows users to assess treatment effectiveness as a function of client characteristics. Patient classifications also can help match clients to different types of treatment programs (McLellan, O'Brien, et al., 1980). For example, a few studies using Psychiatric severity ratings to classify and match clients have found that clients with low Psychiatric severity scores benefit differentially from certain types of drug and alcohol intervention programs (McLellan, Luborsky, et al., 1983).

Although a promising tool for better understanding the interrelationships between substance abuse and other areas of life functioning, some research has raised the limitations of this scale for identification of client subgroups. Rogalski (1987), using a principal components factor analysis, identified four factors on the ASI that accounted for only 22% of the total variance in a group of 276 VA substance abusers. Clearly, the effectiveness of using a scale such as this to identify client subgroups is a function of the items included on the scale. More work is needed to identify the strengths and limitations of the model on which the ASI is based.

The Addiction Severity Index was developed for use with clients entering chemical dependency treatment programs (McLellan, Luborsky, et al., 1980). The majority of work with this instrument has been with male veteran populations, but data also are available on male and female substance abusers seeking treatment in other types of inpatient and outpatient facilities (McLellan, Luborsky, Cacciola, Griffith, Evans, et al., 1985).

The ASI is intended for use only with adults. McLellan states that the scale is not appropriate for adolescents, as the questions do not cover areas of importance to this age group, such as school or family problems, from the perspective of the adolescent (McLellan et al., in press).

There are other populations too with whom one should use the ASI with caution. Some clients with long histories of substance abuse may have cognitive difficulty understanding all of the test items (McLellan, Luborsky, Cacciola, Griffith, McGahan, et al., 1985). In addition, the scale is not useful with those who want to misrepresent their problems. This is a particular concern for clients attempting to avoid legal action or drug and alcohol treatment (Fureman, Parikh, Bragg, & McLellan, 1990).

Problems arise with interpretation of the scale when clients are first given the ASI after a period of incarceration or inpatient treatment. Both severity ratings and composite scores are based largely on the client's reported symptomatology over the past 30 days; if he or she has been in a controlled setting the month prior to taking the ASI, scores are likely to underrepresent the need for additional treatment (McLellan et al., in press).

As new populations of substance abusers, such as women and the homeless, are being studied, interest has increased in using the ASI with them (e.g., Dritschel & Pettinati, 1989). While at face value the measure may provide valuable descriptive information on these clients, there is still a need for caution in using it with them, as the ASI was not designed to meet the specific needs of these populations.

The ASI is administered individually as a structured interview. It can be administered by a "technician" (i.e., a person who works in a drug and alcohol facility but does not have professional training or licensure) as long as he or she has specific training with the instrument. The key component is fully understanding the intent of the items and being able to communicate that intent to clients.

From 1990 to 1992, Integra, Inc. had a training grant with the National Institute on Drug Abuse (NIDA) through which they developed and implemented workshops for prospective ASI users and trainers. Training conducted through 2-day programs was designed to help clarify the intent of specific items on the ASI and to provide opportunities for role play. Certification as an interviewer could be obtained if the user submitted tapes for a reliability check. A 2-day training now is available through the Treatment Research Institute (current publisher of the ADI).

One can be self-trained to administer the ASI by reviewing the available written materials and tapes. Administration procedures are covered in the *Guide to the Addiction Severity Index* published by the National Institute on Drug Abuse (McLellan, Luborsky, Cacciola, Griffith, McGahan, et al., 1985) and updated in the workbook for the ASI fifth edition (Fureman et al., 1990). The manual provides descriptions of what is intended by each question. Though the intent of each item is clearly stated, the manual is lengthy and somewhat tedious. For technicians unused to conducting formal assessments, some of the ASI questions may appear deceptively easy, when in fact they can be interpreted in several different ways. It is important that the interviewer study the manual before using the ASI and recheck it after the first few interviews. Data on the reliability of interviewers who were formally trained compared to those who were self-trained are not available.

Self-administration of this measure is not advocated. Many of the clients given the ASI may have reading and comprehension problems, as well as limited motivation. The authors noted problems in reliability when responses were obtained in this manner (McLellan, Luborsky, Cacciola, Griffith, Evans, et al., 1985). Clinically it is important to have direct contact with clients at the beginning of treatment, particularly when discussing some of the sensitive areas covered by the ASI.

Prior to the interview, the manual suggests directly addressing the issue of confidentiality. The interviewer also explains the reasons for asking questions in the seven areas the interview covers. Finally, the interviewer instructs the client in how to use the subjective rating scale. On this scale, ranging from 0 (not at all) to 4 (extremely), clients are asked to rate their subjective distress and perceived need for treatment. At the Integra training workshops, interviewers were asked to write these options on a piece of paper and provide it to the respondent at the start of the interview. This procedure is not clear from the manual, but it may be important for obtaining reliable responses.

The questions on the ASI cover both lifetime functioning and the client's behavior over the past 30 days. When conducting follow-up interviews, only those items relating to the last 30 days, or those that would be expected to change cumulatively since the last interview, are administered. Items that reflect occurrences in the past 30 days (e.g., number of days drugs were used in past 30) are circled on the form; items that might change cumulatively (e.g., total number of incarcerations) are asterisked. The abbreviated follow-up interview may be conducted over the phone. The items included in the follow-up allow the interviewer to calculate composite scores; one also can obtain severity ratings, but they are less reliable if based on phone contact rather than personal interview (McLellan, Luborsky, Cacciola, Griffith, Evans, et al., 1985).

The earlier version of the ASI was expected to take from 25 to 30 minutes. With the additional items, the fifth edition runs closer to 50 to 60 minutes (McLellan et al., in press). The client should take the test in one sitting and questions should be asked in the order presented; data on the impact of deviations from this pattern are not available.

The guide to the ASI (McLellan, Luborsky, Cacciola, Griffith, McGahan, et al., 1985) and the workbook for the fifth edition (Fureman et al., 1990) detail the scoring procedures. Both texts contain brief item-by-item descriptions of how to code client responses. The workbook also contains several tables designed to facilitate coding certain types of information; for example, a listing of both medical and street drug names are provided, as are employment codes using Hollingshead categories. Typically the interviewer can code most responses during the interview itself. Subsequent to the interview, however, some information may still need to be checked, particularly when long and complicated histories are obtained.

Two types of aggregate measures are calculated—composite scores and severity ratings. Descriptions of both follow:

Composite scores. The composite scores are used primarily as outcome measures in research. They represent a direct derivation of client responses to key items in each of the following areas: 1) medical status, 2) employment/social support, 3) drug use, 4) alcohol use, 5) legal status, 6) family/social relationships, and 7) psychiatric status. Items to be included in the composite scores were selected initially by removing those that did not appear to be sensitive to change, then intercorrelating the remaining items within each problem area, and next examining the internal consistency of the obtained measures (McLellan, Luborsky, Cacciola, Griffith, McGahan, et al., 1985). The authors felt that all items should have equal weight in determining their relevant composite scores. Thus, they scaled items by adjusting scores to account for initial differences in the range of possible responses to that item. The guide to the ASI provides a description of the method by which each item is weighted (McLellan, Luborsky, Cacciola, Griffith, McGahan, et al., 1985). The items that enter into the composite scored are the same in the fifth edition of the ASI as in prior editions. The resulting scores range from 0 (no problems) to 1 (very serious problems).

One could obtain composite scores for each domain by following the manual's directions. To do the calculations by hand, however, would be time-consuming. A computerized data entry and scoring program for IBM PC–compatible computers is available at minimal cost from the authors. Using this software, a user can score one protocol in approximately 15 minutes.

Severity ratings. After administering the ASI, interviewers are asked to rate their perceptions of the severity of the client's problems. Severity is defined as the client's need for additional treatment (McLellan, Luborsky, Cacciola, Griffith, McGahan, et al., 1985). As with composite scores, a separate severity rating is provided for each of seven domains, and raters use a 0–9 scale. The lowest score reflects the interviewer's perception that the client does not have a problem and that treatment is not needed; a score of 9 indicates that the client has an extreme problem for which treatment is essential.

The manual provides a step-by-step procedure for obtaining severity ratings. These ratings take client responses into account while also tapping the interviewer's clinical perceptions. The first step determines a 2- to 3-point severity range on the basis of client responses to certain items, as indicated in the manual. Next the interviewer selects a final score on the basis of the client's subjective report of problem severity. If the client regards the problem as considerable and feels that treatment is important, the interviewer would select a higher score within the determined range. If the client feels that his or her problems are not serious or do not warrant treatment, the interviewer would select a middle or lower rating. The noted exception to this rule occurs when the respondent fails to report an obvious need for treatment. In these instances severity ratings reflect the interviewer's best knowledge of the client and his or her needs regardless of client ratings. Learning how to obtain reliable severity ratings requires training and practice. After the interview, it may require an additional 30 to 60 minutes to obtain these scores.

In addition to these aggregate scores, certain individual items, such as number of days in the past 30 spent drinking or using drugs, have been used as outcome measures (e.g., McLellan et al., 1982). Often professionals use these in conjunction with composite scores, as the individual items are more easily interpretable.

One also can create a narrative describing a client's history and needs based on the information obtained from the ASI. This can be done informally, or Biomedical Research also markets a program, titled *Computer Assisted Severity Evaluation (C.A.S.E.) Software for the ASI* (Kushner, 1990), which will provide a written report based on ASI data.

Both composite scores and severity ratings reflect a client's need for additional treatment. Severity ratings typically are used to make clinical decisions, and composite scores to evaluate client outcomes or research.

A lack of external referents for particular scores limits interpretation of severity ratings. The manual states that scores of 0–1 reflect no problem, 2–3 slight problems, 4–5 moderate problems, 6–7 considerable problems, and 8–9 extreme problems. Nevertheless, there are no specific directives regarding how high a severity rating must be to warrant intervention. In the few studies that have stratified subjects on the basis of severity ratings, different scores were used for grouping clients. In one study (McLellan, Woody, et al., 1983), alcohol-dependent patients with Psychiatric severity scores of 0–1 were rated low, 2–5 mid, and 6–9 high in severity and grouped accordingly; in the same study, drug-dependent clients with scores from 0–3 were labeled low, those with scores from 4–6 mid, and those with scores from 7–9 high in severity. Further, Legal and Employment severity scores of 4 or less, and Family severity scores of 5 or less, also were used to group clients. Another study (Kosten, Rounsaville, & Kleber, 1983) found that a severity rating of 3 on the Psychiatric scale was the most sensitive and specific in terms of identifying clients with known psychiatric disorders. This would have been considered a mid-level severity rating in the McLellan, Woody, et al. (1983) study. Thus, while higher severity ratings indicate a greater need for treatment, information on the absolute level of severity necessary to warrant certain types of treatment (e.g., inpatient or outpatient) is not available.

Although composite scores also are used to reflect problem severity, they are not considered useful to clinicians as they do not provide specific information that could assist in treatment planning. These scores are valuable for research and evaluation, however, particularly for comparing clients or assessing progress over time.

Until recently norms have not been available for the ASI. As the popularity of the instrument has grown, McLellan and his colleagues have decided to make available, for comparative purposes, scores for different, well-described groups of drug and alcohol patients (McLellan et al., in press). The first set of norms is based on a sample ($N = 885$) of men and women from inpatient and outpatient substance abuse treatment facilities in the Philadelphia area. Mean composite scores and severity ratings are provided for subsamples of these clients, with separate scores available for pregnant, incarcerated, and psychologically ill users, as well as for users served by different types of treatment programs.

Thus, ASI scores serve to describe a client's need for treatment, to provide a profile of his or her strengths and weaknesses, and to assess progress over time. Though higher scores indicate greater need, further research will help to clarify the relationship between severity scores and need for treatment.

Technical Aspects

The original reliability and validity studies of the ASI were conducted on male patients in the Philadelphia VA Hospital Substance Abuse Unit (McLellan, Luborsky, et al., 1980). Subsequent studies have used other populations seeking help for drug and alcohol problems, and most, but not all, subjects in these studies are men. Virtually all research has been conducted on clients seeking help for substance abuse either in inpatient or outpatient settings.

ASI reliability studies have focused on interrater and test-retest reliability. In the first reliability studies (McLellan, Luborsky, et al., 1980), interrater reliability was determined by four staff members, each coding 25 videotaped interviews. Interrater reliabilities of severity ratings ranged from .85 to .92. Reliability coefficients were similar when based on scores obtained 2 and 4 months after the first ratings. The second set of studies assessed interrater reliability for clients from the Philadelphia VA Hospital and two other treatment centers (McLellan, Luborsky, Cacciola, Griffith, Evans, et al., 1985). Reliability was determined for taped interviews of 30 randomly drawn clients. Coefficients fell between .74 and .99 on all scales. In only 11% of instances did judges vary by more than 2 points on a given scale with any client.

The developers addressed test-retest reliability with a sample of 40 patients seeking help for substance abuse at the Philadelphia VA Hospital and at two other treatment centers (McLellan, Luborsky, Cacciola, Griffith, Evans, et al., 1985). Test-retest reliability was determined by conducting a second interview with clients 3 days after their first interview. Clients were told that their first interview was lost and were paid $5.00 to be interviewed again. The authors report that no single item on the interview showed a discrepancy on more than 25% of the interviews, and no single repeated interview showed a discrepancy on more than 10% of the items. Severity ratings from the matched samples had coefficients of concordance of at least .92. The study yielded no differences between composite scores on matched tests. Item differences appeared to be a function of the clients' difficulty in remembering exact numbers, and a reduced sense of problem severity from the first day that treatment was sought.

McLellan et al. also assessed the test-retest reliability of items added to the fifth edition using 100 subjects, both male and female, at the Philadelphia VA Hospital (McLellan et al., in press). Procedures resembled those in the first studies. Reliability coefficients of .83 or higher are reported for all items.

Several studies have examined the concurrent validity of the ASI. The validity of severity ratings has been studied by correlating these scores with scores on other questions related to that problem area (McLellan, Luborsky, et al., 1980). For example, severity ratings for Substance Abuse were correlated with number of times overdosed, total years of regular use of drugs or alcohol, and amount spent on alcohol or drugs per week. Correlations between severity ratings and individual items ranged from .43 to .72 across domains. Using another method for assessing concurrent validity, McLellan, Luborsky, Cacciola, Griffith, Evans, et al. (1985) separated clients into three groups (low, mid, high) on the basis of their severity ratings and looked at between-group differences to items within each area. In general, trends supported distinctions between the groups (i.e., clients in the high Medical group had more hospitalizations than did clients in the mid or low groups). Given that severity ratings derive in part from client responses to questions on the ASI, the relationship between severity ratings and item responses is not surprising.

In a study of opiate addicts in a Connecticut mental health center drug dependency unit, Kosten et al. (1983) correlated five of the ASI severity ratings with scores from assessment instruments ostensibly measuring similar factors. Among the tests studied, the ASI severity ratings for Psychological functioning were correlated with the Beck Depression Inventory (Beck, Ward, Mendelson, Mock, & Erbaugh, 1961); Family/Social severity ratings were correlated with the Social Adjustment Scale (Weissman & Bothwell, 1976); Employment severity ratings were correlated with the Work factor of the same Social Adjustment Scale; Legal severity ratings were correlated with number of days of illegal profit in the past month; and Drug Abuse severity ratings were correlated with scores on the Michigan Alcohol Screening Test (Selzer, 1971), years of opiate use, and number of times opiates were used in the past 30 days. Moderate, significant relationships were found for the Psychological, Family/Social, Employment, and Legal scales. Severity ratings on the Substance Abuse scale did not correlate well with the other substance abuse measures.

McLellan and his colleagues also evaluated the discriminant validity of the ASI's seven subscales. They cited the low correlations among scale scores (Kosten et al., 1983; McLellan, Luborsky, et al., 1980) as evidence of the scales' relative independence of one another. Discriminant validity was determined by correlating ASI scales with instruments thought to measure similar factors and with others considered to measure different factors. The extent to which ASI scores correlated higher with their designated external measures than with other measures was interpreted as an indication of the subtests' discriminant validity. The researchers assessed a number of instruments in relation to ASI subscales. Among these instruments were the Cornell Medical Index (Dudley, 1976) in relation to ASI Medical scores; the Michigan Alcohol Screening Test (Selzer, 1971) in relation to ASI Alcohol scores; the Cohen and Klein Drug Use Scale (Cohen & Klein, 1971) in relation to ASI Drug scores; the Family and Social subscales of the Social Adjustment Scale (Weissman & Bothwell, 1976) in relation to Family/Social ASI scores; and the Beck Depression Inventory (Beck et al., 1961) in relation to ASI Psychological scores. In most instances, ASI subscales correlated more highly with the matched tests than with other measures, but some significant correlations also emerged between ASI subscales and unmatched tests.

Overall, correlations between ASI subscales and other instruments measuring similar factors have been moderate but mixed. This is not unexpected, given the divergent manner in which the developers chose to cover similar domains as well as the differences in scope and specificity of different tests. It must also be noted that virtually all of the measures against which the ASI has been studied also rely on self-report. Little is known about the relationship of ASI scores to data obtained though methods other than self-report.

Critique

The Addiction Severity Index has made an important contribution to our conceptualization of how to assess clients with substance abuse problems. By including education/employment information, legal issues, psychological problems, family/ social history, and medical history in addition to alcohol and drug abuse information in an interview for clients entering drug and alcohol treatment programs, the scale acknowledges the complexity of these clients' problems. These other factors can relate to substance abuse in many ways; problems in some areas may become a prelude to substance abuse, while problems in other areas may emerge as a result of the substance abuse. Nevertheless, the factors assessed through this scale warrant consideration in treatment planning and in evaluation of client outcomes.

Some of the ASI's limitations are endemic to its basic structure. As a self-report scale designed for patients entering drug and alcohol treatment programs, it cannot be expected to stand up well with involuntary clients or those who have reasons for wanting to distort their histories. Further, both composite and severity scores are heavily influenced by client functioning in the past 30 days; thus, the scale is likely to underrepresent need in those who have been recently incarcerated or hospitalized (McLellan, Luborsky, Cacciola, Griffith, McGahan, et al., 1985).

Although the ASI shows promise both as a clinical and research tool, more work must take place to determine its utility and limitations. Rogalski (1987) has questioned the basic model on which the scale was developed; that is, the effectiveness of the scale in defining client groups and evaluating outcomes can only be as strong as the items used to tap those areas. To date, more work has focused on the use of the Psychiatric scale to classify clients than on the other scales. The efficacy of the other subscales in defining client problems and measuring client progress has not been well addressed.

In addition, the use of the ASI with new populations, such as women, is problematic. Current items on the test may not be appropriate, or sufficient, for all clients seeking help with substance abuse. McLellan suggests augmenting the scale with additional items to meet the needs of new types of patients. Although augmenting the questionnaire can provide needed descriptive information about clients, this solution does not address the appropriateness of giving clients severity scores based on items that may not be central to their problems. As the test has gone through its revisions, the authors have taken great care not to change the items that enter into composite scores or severity ratings. This may result, however, in scores that do not accurately reflect the needs of new groups of clients. At the simplest level, one might reconsider the items selected from the test to determine composite scores and severity ratings for different groups of clients, as only a subset of items from the test currently enter into these scores. That is, there may be theoretical or empirical grounds on which to modify the items that determine composite scores or severity ratings in order to more accurately reflect client needs. Determinations of severity would still be limited by the current pool of items, however. Use of the scale with new populations may require that other items be added, and evaluated, for their impact on effectively determining the need for services by these clients.

References

Beck, A.T., Ward, C.H., Mendelson, M., Mock, J., & Erbaugh, J. (1961). An inventory for measuring depression. *Archives of General Psychiatry, 4*, 561–571.

Cohen, M., & Klein, D. (1971). A measure of severity of multi-drug use among psychiatric patients. *International Journal of Pharmacopsychiatry, 6*, 83–89.

Dritschel, B., & Pettinati, H. (1989). The role of female occupation in severity of alcohol-related problems. *American Journal of Drug and Alcohol Abuse, 15*, 61–72.

Dudley, D. (1976). The Cornell Medical Index as an adjunct to paraprofessional analysis of alcohol addiction. *Journal of Studies on Alcohol, 37*, 97–103.

Friedman, A., & Utada, A. (1989). A method for diagnosing and planning the treatment of adolescent drug abusers: The Adolescent Drug Abuse Diagnosis (ADAD) instrument. *Journal of Drug Education, 19*, 285–312.

Fureman, B., Parikh, G., Bragg, A., & McLellan, A.T. (1990). *Addiction Severity Index manual* (5th ed.). Philadelphia: University of Pennsylvania Veterans Administration Center for Studies of Addiction.

Hendriks, V., Kaplan, C., Limbeek, J., & Geerlings, P. (1989). The Addiction Severity Index: Reliability and validity in a Dutch addict population. *Journal of Substance Abuse Treatment, 6*, 133–141.

Kaminer, Y., Bukstein, O., & Tarter, R. (1991). The Teen Addiction Severity Index: Rationale and reliability. *International Journal of the Addictions, 26*, 219–226.

Kaminer, Y., & Frances, R. (1991). Inpatient treatment of adolescents with psychiatric and substance abuse disorders. *Hospital and Community Psychiatry, 42*, 894–896.

Kosten, T., Rounsaville, B., & Kleber, H. (1983). Concurrent validity of the Addiction Severity Index. *Journal of Nervous and Mental Disorders, 171*, 606–610.

Kushner, H. (1990). *Addiction Severity Index Computer Assisted Severity Evaluation Report* [Computer software]. Philadelphia: Biomedical Computer Research Institute.

McLellan, A.T., Kushner, H., Metzger, D., Peters, R., Smith, I., Grissom, G., & Pettinati, H. (in press). The fifth edition of the Addiction Severity Index: Historical critique and normative data. *Journal of Substance Abuse Treatment*.

McLellan, A.T., Luborsky, L., Cacciola, J., Griffith, J., Evans, F., Barr, H., & O'Brien, C. (1985). New data from the Addiction Severity Index: Reliability and validity in three centers. *Journal of Nervous and Mental Disease, 173*, 412–423.

McLellan, A.T., Luborsky, L., Cacciola, J., Griffith, J., McGahan, P., & O'Brien, C. (1985). *Guide to the Addiction Severity Index: Background, administration and field testing results* (National Institute on Drug Abuse Treatment Research Monograph Series). Washington, DC: U.S. Government Printing Office.

McLellan, A.T., Luborsky, L., O'Brien, C., Woody, G., & Druley, K. (1982). Is treatment for substance abuse effective? *Journal of the American Medical Association, 247*, 1423–1428.

McLellan, A.T., Luborsky, L., Woody, G., & O'Brien, C. (1980). An improved diagnostic instrument for substance abuse patients: The Addiction Severity Index. *Journal of Nervous and Mental Disorders, 168*, 26–33.

McLellan, A.T., Luborsky, L., Woody, G., O'Brien, C., & Druley, K. (1983). Predicting response to alcohol and drug abuse treatments: Role of psychiatric severity. *Archives of General Psychiatry, 40*, 620–625.

McLellan, A.T., O'Brien, C., Kron, R., Alterman, A., & Druley, K. (1980). Matching substance abuse patients to appropriate treatments: A conceptual and methodological approach. *Drug and Alcohol Dependency, 5*, 189–195.

McLellan, A.T., Woody, G., Luborsky, L., O'Brien, C., & Druley, K. (1983). Increased effectiveness of substance abuse treatment: A prospective study of patient-treatment "matchings." *Journal of Nervous and Mental Disease, 171*, 597–605.

Rogalski, C. (1987). Factor structure of the Addiction Severity Index in an inpatient detoxification sample. *International Journal of the Addictions, 22*, 981–992.

Selzer, M. (1971). The Michigan Alcoholism Screening Test: The quest for a new diagnostic instrument. *American Journal of Psychiatry, 127*, 1653–1659.

Weissman, M., & Bothwell, S. (1976). The assessment of social adjustment by patient self-report. *Archives of General Psychiatry, 33*, 1111–1115.

Kevin R. Murphy, Ph.D.

Professor of Psychology, Colorado State University, Fort Collins, Colorado.

APTITUDE INTEREST MEASUREMENT

National Computer Systems and the United States Employment Service. Minnetonka, Minnesota: National Computer Systems/PAS Division.

Introduction

The United States Employment Service (USES) has a long history of using ability tests and interest inventories in both vocational counseling and job referral. Two tests, the General Aptitude Test Battery (GATB; U.S. Department of Labor, 1979a) and the United States Employment Service Interest Inventory (USES-II; Droege & Hawk, 1977; U.S. Department of Labor, 1981b) form the foundation of the USES Counselee Assessment/Occupational Exploration System (U.S. Department of Labor, 1981a), which is designed to provide vocational counselors with information about respondents' work-related aptitudes and interests.

Aptitude Interest Measurement (AIM) is a mail-in version of the GATB and the USES-II that is distributed and scored by National Computer Systems. AIM produces a computer-generated narrative report describing an individual's interests and listing occupations that provide either a good or a poor match to the person's aptitudes and interests. This report is designed to offer vocational counselors a starting point for discussing vocational choices with individuals who have completed the GATB and the USES-II.

Both the GATB and the USES-II have been reviewed in previous volumes of *Test Critiques* and elsewhere (Bolton, 1985; Hartigan & Wigdor, 1989; Keesling, 1985; Kirnan & Geisinger, 1986). Although the present review will provide general descriptions of both tests, readers should consult the cited reviews for detailed information on the tests and their historical backgrounds, and for in-depth technical evaluations of the individual tests. This review concentrates on the information provided by AIM to vocational counselors and examinees, and on the likelihood that this information will be useful in making vocational decisions.

Because little research has examined AIM directly, this review will draw on research on the GATB, on the USES-II, and on the underlying occupational structure by which they are linked to highlight the strengths and weaknesses of AIM and the USES Counselee Assessment/Occupational Exploration System. In particular, a look at a recent evaluation of the GATB conducted by the National Academy of Sciences will highlight potential limitations of the norms used to identify aptitude requirements of various occupations, and the review will discuss the implications of this research for AIM.

GATB. The General Aptitude Test Battery includes 12 separately timed subtests for assessing nine aptitudes. There are eight paper-and-pencil tests and four apparatus tests (used in assessing coordination and dexterity); the total GATB requires over 2½ hours to complete and may involve up to 750 items (because several tests are heavily speeded, the number of items attempted varies over examinees). The tests include 1) Name Comparison, a measure of clerical speed and accuracy that asks respondents to compare two columns of names; 2) Computation, a multiple-choice test of simple arithmetic; 3) Three-Dimensional Space, a multiple-choice test of ability to visualize how a flat figure will look when it is bent or rolled in specific ways; 4) Vocabulary, a test in which respondents must identify either a pair of synonyms or a pair of antonyms from a list of four words; 5) Tool Matching, a test requiring respondents to match a stimulus object (a drawing of a tool) to its identical mate in a set of four objects; 6) Arithmetic Reasoning, a set of arithmetic problems expressed verbally; 7) Form Matching, a test that requires respondents to match identical line drawings presented in two randomly organized groups; 8) Mark Making, a speeded test in which the respondent is asked to make the same three pencil marks on an answer sheet as many times as possible; 9) Place, an apparatus test requiring respondents to place cylindrical pegs in a pegboard as quickly as possible; 10) Turn, an apparatus test requiring respondents to turn pegs in a pegboard as quickly as possible; 11) Assemble, an apparatus test requiring respondents to assemble rivets and washers on a pegboard as quickly as possible; and 12) Disassemble, an apparatus test requiring respondents to remove rivets and washers from a pegboard as quickly as possible.

Scores are obtained on nine aptitudes: intelligence, verbal aptitude, numerical aptitude, spatial aptitude, form perception, clerical perception, motor coordination, finger dexterity, and manual dexterity. Hunter (1983a) suggested that these nine scores could be grouped into three composites (cognitive, perceptual, and psychomotor), but other reviewers have questioned the appropriateness of these composites (Hartigan & Wigdor, 1989).

The relationship between scores on the GATB and performance in a variety of jobs has been examined in literally hundreds of studies. Hunter (1983b) reviewed over 500 GATB validity studies and claimed that the GATB is a valid predictor of performance in essentially *all* jobs. A committee of the National Academy of Sciences (Hartigan & Wigdor, 1989) examined the same validity data, together with over 250 more recent studies, and while they questioned Hunter's claim of validity in all jobs, they did conclude that the GATB has consistently shown validity (albeit at a lower level than claimed by Hunter) in most jobs studied. Because scores on the GATB are strongly affected by general ability or intelligence (which appears to be the best single predictor of job performance; see Ree & Earles [1992] for a recent review), it seems reasonable to believe that the battery will provide potentially useful information about the likelihood of success in a wide variety of jobs.

USES-II. The 162 items of United States Employment Service Interest Inventory describe job activities, occupational titles, and life experiences. For each item, the subject indicates Like, Dislike, or Not Sure; only the Like responses are used in calculating interest area scores. The USES-II provides scores indicating the relative strength of an individual's occupational interests in each of the following 12 areas:

Artistic—interest in creative expression of feelings or ideas

Scientific—interest in discovering, collecting, and analyzing information about the natural world and applying scientific research

Plants & Animals—interest in activities involving plants and animals, especially in outdoor settings

Protective—interest in the use of authority to protect people and property

Mechanical—interest in applying mechanical principles to practical solutions

Industrial—interest in repetitive, concrete, or organized activities in a factory setting

Business Detail—interest in organized, clearly defined activities requiring accuracy and attention to detail, usually in an office setting

Selling—interest in bringing others to a point of view through personal persuasion

Accommodating—interest in catering to the wishes of others, usually by providing services for their convenience

Humanitarian—interest in helping others with their mental, social, spiritual, physical, and vocational needs

Leading-Influencing—interest in leading and influencing others through activities involving high-level verbal and numerical abilities

Physical Performing—interest in physical activities that are performed before an audience

Scores for each interest area are reported as T-scores ($M = 50$, $SD = 10$) and also as broad category scores (i.e., 0–34 = Very Low; 35–42 = Low; 43–57 = Average; 58–65 = High; 66–99 = Very High).

Factor-analytic research provides strong support for the 12-factor structure of the USES-II (Brookings & Bolton, 1989). However, this same research suggests that the factors measured by USES-II cannot be linked in any direct way with the factors suggested in other well-known interest taxonomies (e.g., Holland, 1984; Prediger, 1976; Roe, 1956). As a result, it is difficult to sensibly assess the convergence of the USES-II with more well-established inventories, or to determine links between its scores and those on other similar inventories.

Linking aptitudes, interests, and occupations. The key to linking aptitudes, interests, and occupations is the hypothesis that different aptitudes (and different levels of specific aptitudes) are required for success in various jobs, and that a reasonable match between an individual's interests and the nature of a job is required for satisfaction with and adjustment to work (Dawis & Lofquist, 1984). Translating this hypothesis into a workable system for vocational counseling requires developing a taxonomy of jobs that a) reduces the large number of potential job titles (the *Dictionary of Occupational Titles* includes over 12,000) to a manageable number of reasonably homogeneous work groups, b) identifies the interests most or least relevant to each group, and c) identifies the aptitude requirements of jobs within each group. The *Guide for Occupational Exploration* (GOE; U.S. Department of Labor, 1979b) presents such a taxonomy.

In developing the taxonomy that underlies the GOE, researchers applied a combination of judgmental and empirical methods. Occupational analysts assigned all of the occupations in the *Dictionary of Occupational Titles* to one of 12 interest areas corresponding to the factors on the USES-II. These occupations were then grouped into 66 work groups based on analysts' judgments of similarities in the aptitudes, capabilities, and adaptabilities required in the occupations within each group.

The results of GATB validity studies were used to establish Occupational Ability Patterns (OAPs), which represent patterns of aptitude requirements for the occupations within each work group. A set of 66 OAPs were developed covering occupations in 59 work groups (seven groups proved too small or heterogeneous to allow the establishment of OAPs, and a few groups required more than one OAP; U.S. Department of Labor, 1980). These 66 OAPs provide aptitude requirements for 97% of the nonsupervisory occupations in the GOE.

To illustrate the contents and use of OAPs, consider the work group "Quality Control." This group includes over 60 occupations (e.g., Garment Inspector, Pulp-and-Paper Tester), and all require examination of materials, supplies, products, and so forth. The GATB norms for adult examinees in this work group are scores of 80, 85, and 85 on the Form Perception, Motor Coordination, and Manual Dexterity subtests, respectively (scores are expressed on a standard scale with $M = 100$, $SD = 20$). Individual respondents receive a letter grade for this work group, based on a comparison of their scores on the three subtests to the norms that define the OAP for this work group. A respondent with scores above 80, 85, and 85 on Form Perception, Motor Coordination, and Manual Dexterity receives a grade of "H," which indicates aptitude levels similar to or higher than those of successful workers in that set of occupations. Respondents with scores close enough to the norms on these three tests to indicate the possibility of chance differences between their scores and the norms (specifically, within 1 standard error of measurement unit of the norm) receive a grade of "M," which indicates aptitudes close to those who perform satisfactorily in these occupations. Individuals whose GATB scores fall below the level needed to receive a grade of "M" receive an "L," which indicates a low probability of successful performance.

The overall utility of AIM clearly depends on the validity of the groupings of occupations and their linkages to both interests and aptitudes. Research on the validity of the links between occupations and interests and aptitudes will be examined in a later section of this review.

Practical Applications/Uses

Both the USES Counselee Assessment/Occupational Exploration System and AIM are designed to aid vocational counselors and individuals seeking vocational advice. AIM provides a high degree of flexibility, in the sense that it represents a low-cost system for quickly obtaining information about both aptitude levels and interests as well as ability/interest-occupation matches. Although it is designed for computer scoring, provisions for hand-scoring further increase its ease of use. The system is appropriate for vocational counselors in high schools and colleges, plus those in settings such as adult education and employment services.

After completing the GATB and USES-II, both the respondent and the counselor receive narrative reports describing the interests and occupations that provide good and poor matches to the respondent's interest and aptitudes. The narrative report received by respondents a) describes the 12 interest areas measured by the USES-II, b) provides scores (expressed both as standard scores and percentiles based on a same-sex norm group) indicating the relative strength of the respondent's interest in each of the 12 areas, c) offers a clear description of the meaning of both standard and percentile scores, d) lists, in order, work groups for which the respondent indicated very high, high, average, low, and very low interest, and e) shows, for each work group, the respondent's aptitude level (low, moderate, or high). Counselors receive an abbreviated form of this report that lists interest scores and interest and aptitude levels for specific work groups and occupations.

The respondent's report then provides a detailed description (again listed in order of the extent to which work groups match the respondent's interest) of the activities involved in the work groups (and sample occupations) for which the individual has at least an Average level of interest and High, Moderate, or Low aptitude. The respondent is encouraged to discuss the results of the report with his or her counselor and to consider both the aptitude and interest information in making plans for entering an occupation. For example, there are usually some occupations that closely match the respondent's interests but for which the aptitude requirements are quite high. Respondents whose GATB subtest scores fall below the norms established for specific occupations or work groups are encouraged to discuss their plans and aspirations carefully with counselors before entering occupations in which their present predicted level of success is low.

The narrative report received by respondents does a good job explaining what one can and cannot learn from ability and interest tests. In particular, it repeatedly emphasizes that the scores provide a starting point for discussing vocational choice, not a clear statement of what job the respondent should seek. For example, the narrative notes that low interest scores in a particular area do not necessarily mean that a person is unsuited for occupations within that category; low scores might simply reflect unfamiliarity or a lack of experience with activities in that area. Occupations that are highly consistent with the respondent's aptitudes and interests are offered as suggestions, but the respondent also is encouraged to discuss with counselors occupations that seem interesting but poor matches on the basis of test scores.

Technical Aspects

As noted earlier, the technical adequacy of both the GATB and the USES-II have been examined in detail in several previous reviews. On the whole, the GATB presents a reasonably valid and useful measure of work-related aptitudes (Hartigan & Wigdor, 1989; Hunter, 1983b; Kirnan & Geisinger, 1986). Although considerably less research exists on the validity or the usefulness of the USES-II, this inventory also seems technically adequate (Bolton, 1985, 1988; Brookings & Bolton, 1989; Droege & Hawk, 1977).

Although the two instruments used in AIM appear to be technically adequate, this does not necessarily indicate that AIM will provide useful information to counselors or respondents. The key issue in determining the usefulness of AIM is the validity of the links between scores on the GATB and the USES-II and the interest and aptitude requirements of various occupations.

Evidence for the validity of the interest-occupation linkages is relatively thin.

The manuals and reports describing the development of USES-II do not clearly detail how these linkages were established, beyond noting that they were the product of the expert judgment of occupational analysts. The number of analysts, their familiarity with the occupations in each work group, and the methods used determine which interests were most or least relevant are difficult to discern. The USES-II manual claims that the 12 factors measured by this inventory relate directly to Holland's (1984) six categories of vocational interest, but empirical research does not support this claim (Brookings & Bolton, 1989). The validity of the translation of USES-II factors to Holland (1984) categories is critical, because the Holland categories appear to be a primary basis for linking USES-II factors to jobs. In particular, the *Dictionary of Occupational Titles* classifies all of the job titles listed in terms of the most relevant Holland category (the validity of which are not themselves well established), and it seems clear from the descriptions of USES-II development that the Holland codes for jobs constituted an important determinant of the classification of jobs in terms of USES-II factors. Although the USES-II classifications of work groups seem logical and sensible, the evidence that they represent valid statements of the interest requirements of occupations or work groups is not impressive.

The validity of the aptitude requirements of work groups (i.e., the OAPs) has been the subject of some controversy. To understand this controversy, one must consider in greater detail the development of OAPs. The foundation of each OAP is one or more Specific Aptitude Test Batteries (SATB), each of which represents a combination of two to four aptitudes most relevant to specific occupations and their associated cutting scores. OAPs represent combinations of relevant aptitudes and their associated cutting scores for *groups* of occupations whose aptitude requirements have proven relatively homogeneous. To help minimize the instability of SATBs (e.g., as a result of sampling error in small samples, or of minor differences between occupations within work groups), considerable effort has gone into combining the results of multiple SATB studies to develop OAPs for each homogeneous groups of occupations (U.S. Department of Labor, 1980). Nevertheless, the methods used to determine SATBs have been criticized as crude and outdated (Hartigan & Wigdor, 1989; Keesling, 1985).

Hunter (1983a, 1983b) proposed reducing the nine GATB aptitudes to three composites (only two of which are claimed to be broadly relevant to work performance) and to categorize essentially all jobs into five families, based primarily on their complexity. He developed separate regression equations for each of the five families and showed that these equations were broadly predictive of performance. One implication might be that a large number of SATBs could be replaced by a small number of equations involving cognitive, psychomotor, and (for one of the five job families) perceptual composites. Different cutoff scores might still be set for occupations within each family, or cutoff scores might be dropped altogether and the regression equations used to generate predicted performance levels.

A National Academy of Sciences report on the GATB (Hartigan & Wigdor, 1989) supported some of Hunter's recommendations but questioned the utility (especially for vocational choice) of his approach. For example, the authors noted that the equations for all five families yielded virtually identical results and that all were dominated by cognitive factors, which suggests that the same individuals are likely to be qualified (or unqualified) for virtually all jobs at any given level of complexity, depending on their general cognitive ability. This is exactly the position implied by proponents of the use of general intelligence measures in personnel selection, and there is some research support for this position (Ree & Earles, 1992). Nevertheless, this approach is probably not the most useful for vocational counseling. Evidence exists that the quality of placement decisions increases by considering specific as well as general abilities (Hartigan & Wigdor, 1989); it is likely that the same holds true for the quality of vocational advice.

On the whole, the available evidence does not strongly support the use of the SATBs as a foundation for determining occupational ability requirements. As a result, some caution must be observed in interpreting the performance predictions (i.e., grades of "H," "M," or "L" for specific occupations and work groups) contained in AIM. It is likely that the structure of aptitude requirements for jobs in the U.S. economy is less complex than that implied by the existing set of OAPs, but more complex than the five regression equations (involving two or three composite abilities) suggested by Hunter (1983a, 1983b). More research is needed to determine an optimal structure.

Although one must view the OAPs and the predictions of high, moderate, or low performance implied by them with some caution, they probably are not *seriously* in error. Because of the relatively high level of correlation among the GATB subtests, the choice of specific subtests to form SATBs or OAPs may not always be critical; in many occupations, the predictions that would be generated from a variety of composites or combinations (particularly those involving the cognitive subtests) are likely to be similar. However, until the predictions of performance in various work groups can rely on a somewhat firmer footing, users should observe caution in interpreting the aptitude level scores included in the AIM narrative report.

Critique

Vocational counseling should routinely involve consideration of both abilities and interests. AIM is an attractive tool for doing this, based on well-developed ability and interest measures and tied to a comprehensive system of occupational classification (i.e., a set of work groups that represent virtually the entire set of civilian occupations). The AIM reports are clear and informative, and they help reinforce the important notion that testing should be the starting point, not the ending point, for systematic vocational exploration.

Although the individual tests that underlie AIM are both technically adequate, the technical adequacy of the information provided by AIM is somewhat hard to establish. The links between interests measured by the USES-II and various occupations are reasonable but not established empirically in any convincing way. Similarly, the ability requirements of the various occupations are sensible, but there are a number of reasons to question the methods used to established these links. For these reasons, AIM users should be cautious in interpreting test results. Nevertheless, AIM appears to be a useful tool, which should be seriously considered by vocational counselors.

References

Bolton, B. (1985). United States Employment Service Interest Inventory. In D.J. Keyser & R.C. Sweetland (Eds.), *Test critiques* (Vol. III, pp. 673–681). Austin, TX: PRO-ED.

Bolton, B. (1988). Retest reliability of the USES Interest Inventory: A research note. *Measurement and Evaluation in Counseling and Development, 21,* 113–116.

Brookings, J.B., & Bolton, B. (1989). Factorial validity of the United States Employment Service Interest Inventory. *Journal of Vocational Behavior, 34,* 179–191.

Dawis, R.V., & Lofquist, L.H. (1984). *A psychological theory of work adjustment.* Minneapolis: University of Minnesota Press.

Droege, R.C., & Hawk, J. (1977). Development of the U.S. Employment Service Interest Inventory. *Journal of Employment Counseling, 14,* 65–71.

Hartigan, J.A., & Wigdor, A.K. (1989). *Fairness in employment testing.* Washington, DC: National Academy Press.

Holland, J.L. (1984). *Making vocational choices: A theory of vocational personalities and work environments* (2nd ed.). Englewood Cliffs, NJ: Prentice-Hall.

Hunter, J.E. (1983a). *The dimensionality of the General Aptitude Test Battery (GATB) and the dominance of general factors over specific factors in the prediction of job performance* (USES Test Research Report No. 44). Washington, DC: U.S. Employment Service, U.S. Department of Labor.

Hunter, J.E. (1983b). *Test validation for 12,000 jobs: An application of job classification and validity generalization to the General Aptitude Test battery* (USES Test Research Report No. 45). Washington, DC: U.S. Employment Service, U.S. Department of Labor.

Keesling, J.W. (1985). USES General Aptitude Test Battery. In J.V. Mitchell, Jr. (Ed.), *The ninth mental measurements yearbook* (pp. 1644–1647). Lincoln, NE: Buros Institute of Mental Measurements.

Kirnan, J.P., & Geisinger, K.F. (1986). General Aptitude Test Battery. In D.J. Keyser & R.C. Sweetland (Eds.), *Test critiques* (Vol. VI, pp. 150–167). Austin, TX: PRO-ED.

Prediger, D.J. (1976). A world of work map for career exploration. *Vocational Guidance Quarterly, 24,* 259–287.

Ree, M.J., & Earles, J.A. (1992). Intelligence is the best predictor of job performance. *Current Directions in Psychological Science, 1,* 86–89.

Roe, A. (1956). *The psychology of occupations.* New York: Wiley.

U.S. Department of Labor. (1979a). *General Aptitude Test Battery.* Washington, DC: U.S. Government Printing Office.

U.S. Department of Labor. (1979b). *Guide for occupational exploration.* Washington, DC: U.S. Government Printing Office.

U.S. Department of Labor. (1980). *Manual for the USES General Aptitude Test Battery: Section II-A. Development of the occupational aptitude pattern structure.* Washington, DC: U.S. Government Printing Office.

U.S. Department of Labor. (1981a). *A new counselee assessment/occupational exploration system and its interest and aptitude dimensions* (U.S. Employment Service Technical Report No. 35). Washington, DC: U.S. Employment Service.

U.S. Department of Labor. (1981b). *USES Interest Inventory.* Washington, DC: U.S. Government Printing Office.

Daryl Sander, Ph.D.
Professor Emeritus, School of Education, University of Colorado, Boulder, Colorado.

Shayn Smith, Ph.D.
Assistant Director of Career Planning Programs and Testing Director, Counseling and Career Services, University of Colorado, Boulder, Colorado.

ASSESSMENT OF CAREER DECISION MAKING

Vincent A. Harren, Jacqueline N. Buck, and M. Harry Daniels. Los Angeles, California: Western Psychological Services.

Introduction

The Assessment of Career Decision Making (ACDM) is a 94-item, self-report instrument that assesses a student's career decision-making style and progress on three decision-making tasks (adjustment to school, selection of an occupation and of a major). The instrument was developed originally by Vincent A. Harren, whose model of career decision making integrated the work of Tiedeman and O'Hara (1963), and was later refined by Jacqueline N. Buck and M. Harry Daniels.

Three 10-item scales assess the degree to which students utilize rational, intuitive, and dependent career decision-making styles. The Rational Decision-Making Styles scale measures the degree to which one makes decisions deliberately and logically based on available information. High scorers on this scale take responsibility for their decisions. The Intuitive Decision-Making Styles scale measures the degree to which one makes decisions using personal feelings and imagination rather than logical evaluation. Like the rational decision makers, intuitive decision makers take responsibility for their decisions. The Dependent Decision-Making Styles scale measures the degree to which one makes decisions that are influenced by expectations and desires of others. Dependent decision makers most likely will make decisions that lack fulfillment or personal satisfaction.

The ACDM contains three decision-making tasks scales measuring 1) school/ college adjustment, plus commitment to and certainty of 2) occupation and 3) major. The School Adjustment Decision-Making Tasks scale consists of three 8-item subscales that assess 1) satisfaction with school, 2) involvement with peers, and 3) interaction with instructors. The manual reports that "low levels on these factors are primary contributors to withdrawal from school" (Buck & Daniels, 1985, p. 1). The Occupation Decision-Making Tasks scale contains 20 items that assess the degree of commitment and certainty a student feels toward his or her choice of and occupation. A typical item is, "I need to decide on an occupation."

39

The Academic Major Decision-Making Tasks scale contains 20 items that assess the degree of commitment and certainty a student feels toward his or her choice of an academic major. A typical item is, "It's a relief to have decided on a major."

Practical Applications/Uses

The Assessment of Career Decision Making is intended for use by adolescents and adults in high school, community college, college, and university settings. The instrument is not recommended for non-students because of inappropriate item content and a lack of normative data for this population.

The reading difficulty of the ACDM approximates the sixth-grade level. The authors state that "individuals with low verbal skills due to bilingual background or learning disabilities may have difficulty completing the test" (Buck & Daniels, 1985, p. 2). The instrument can be administered to an individual or to a group and can be done so by a trained paraprofessional, although interpretation should be conducted by "a professional with advanced training and experience" (p. 2).

The ACDM contains 90 true/false items that can be answered in 40 minutes. The answer sheet has the items printed directly on it. Individuals use a black-leaded pencil to bubble in their responses.

Users send the completed answer sheets to the publisher for scoring. Although processing may take only 8 hours, postal service may increase turnaround time to up to 6 working days within the United States, longer if outside the U.S. However, users may pay an extra fee and obtain either overnight or 2-day service.

The computerized report for the ACDM has three parts: the Group Summary, which gives summary scores for all students whose answer sheets were submitted for processing, the Counselor's Report, and the Student's Report. The Counselor's Report contains validity considerations that may alert the counselor to interpret scores cautiously. Also included are a summary of empirical results, a narrative report, comparison of individual scales, and an analysis of profile patterns for the Decision-Making Styles scales. The Student's Report summarizes the material reported in the Counselor's Report, but with less technical language. One should interpret the ACDM using the Student's Report in combination with an individual meeting.

Technical Aspects

Internal consistency reliability coefficients of the ACDM are reported to range from .49 to .84 for the Decision-Making Styles scales and from .78 to .92 for the Decision-Making Tasks scales. Test-retest reliability over 2 weeks is reported to range from .66 to .84 when two School Adjustment subscales are excluded, with the two lowest being two of the three subscales of the School Adjustment Scale.

The manual reports a number of studies by the test authors and others that attribute content, criterion-related, and construct validity to the ACDM.

Critique

The process of making a career decision is just as important as the content of that decision. That is why the Assessment of Career Decision Making is a valuable tool to use in conjunction with instruments designed to measure occupational interests. The data concerning reliability and validity are adequate; however, studies reporting predictive validity seem to be absent from the section of the manual that deals with criterion-related validity. It would also strengthen the validity of the instrument if cross-cultural data were available, particularly those showing validity of this instrument for use with major ethnic groups within the school and college population.

The reliability coefficients appear moderately high with the exception of two of the three School Adjustment subscales. Low reliability coefficients are not surprising considering the few items ($N = 8$) comprising each of these three subscales.

The generalizability of the ACDM could be enhanced by broadening normative data to include a wider range of school and college populations. Likewise, it would be desirable to have validity data based on older, part-time, nontraditional students. Nonetheless, this instrument promises to be a useful tool for counselors and others attempting to help young people in career decision making.

References

Buck, J.N., & Daniels, M.H. (1985). *Assessment of Career Decision Making (ACDM) manual.* Los Angeles: Western Psychological Services.

Tiedeman, D.V., & O'Hara, R.P. (1963). *Career development: Choice and adjustment.* New York: College Entrance Examination Board.

Mary Lynn Boscardin, Ph.D.
Assistant Professor of Special Education, University of Massachusetts, Amherst, Massachusetts.

William Hickey, Ed.D.
Special Education Consultant, Amherst, Massachusetts.

THE ASSESSMENT OF PHONOLOGICAL PROCESSES–REVISED

Barbara Williams Hodson. Austin, Texas: PRO-ED, Inc.

Introduction

The Assessment of Phonological Processes–Revised (APP-R; Hodson, 1986b) was designed to assess the phonological systems of highly unintelligible children by identifying phonological features and rules absent in their speech.

During the late 1960s and early 1970s, the acquisition of phonological features was linked to a developmental system of rules (Compton, 1970; Crocker, 1969; Hodson & Paden, 1981; Ingram, 1976; Smith, 1973). Language samples were used initially to analyze phonological competencies, but unfortunately, although usually accurate, they were time-consuming. Often ongoing assessments were necessary to evaluate therapeutical progress, and again, language samples were cumbersome for clinicians with large caseloads. Hodson filled this void by developing the original Assessment of Phonological Processes in 1980. This test evolved from her 1975 doctoral dissertation completed at the University of Illinois at Urbana-Champaign. The primary goal of the test was to provide readily accessible information that could serve as the basis for a remediation program; the second one was to provide a reliable measure of accountability during and after remediation.

The APP-R contains two sets of pictures and five packets of phonological forms in addition to a manual. Black-and-white picture cards are supplied for objects not readily available, which include the 12 multisyllabic words contained both in the multisyllabic screening test and the complete assessment battery. However, examiners are encouraged to use objects for stimuli whenever possible.

Three test protocols are included in the assessment packet: 1) Preschool Phonological Screening Protocol, 2) Multisyllabic Phonological Screening Protocol, and 3) Assessment of Phonological Processes Screening Protocol.

The Preschool and Multisyllabic screening protocols consist of 12 stimulus words. Three criteria determined the word choice on the Preschool protocol: a) the words are labels known by most English-speaking children, b) the words can be elicited by three-dimensional stimuli, and c) the words provide at least four opportunities for occurrences of each of the phonological processes found prevalent in the speech samples of preschool children who are unintelligible. Three criteria also were used for selecting the words on the Multisyllabic protocol: a) the words generally are known by school-aged English-speaking children, b) the words have complex phonetic structures, and c) the words can be elicited by objects or pictures. These screening protocols have designated columns for recording occurrences of prevalent phonological processes, as well as space to record any additional errors. Questions at the bottom of each screening protocol serve as guidelines for determining the need for further assessment.

The full assessment protocol consists of 50 stimulus words, selected to fulfill the following six criteria: a) the words are generally familiar to preschool children and can be elicited spontaneously by three-dimensional stimuli, b) the words provide at least 10 opportunities for each omission and class deficiency phonological process to occur, c) each word assesses more than one phonological process, d) the words include all English phonemes, e) multisyllabic words are assessed as well as monosyllabic ones, and f) the words contain common phoneme clusters (sequences). Each protocol comes with a recording sheet that includes phonetic transcriptions of Standard American English pronunciations for the stimulus words as well as space to record the child's errors.

Analysis sheets for the full assessment list major phonological processes and provide space for recording phonological process occurrences for each stimulus word. A two-sided summary sheet includes space for listing the total number of occurrences of each error type and for recording the percentage-of-occurrence scores for 10 basic phonological processes. The sheets also allow the user to record a phonological deviancy score and a severity interval.

Three major changes, along with several additions, occurred between the 1980 and 1986 versions. Hodson eliminated five stimulus words from the 1980 version due to currency issues and replaced them with more appropriate words having similar phonetic structures and comparable opportunities for occurrences of phonological process, she simplified the analysis forms to reduce the amount of scoring time, and now most children know the 12 words (10 monosyllabic, 2 bisyllabic) selected for the 1986 edition of the Preschool screening test prior to age 3. The new components include: 1) the 12-word (6 five-syllable, 4 four-syllable, 2 three-syllable) Multisyllabic screening protocol for older elementary children (9- to 10-year-olds) containing pictures that can be used with both this protocol and the full assessment, and 2) a formula for calculating severity ratings that allow clinicians to monitor client progress rather than trying to use chronological age cutoff scores. Adaptations have been made for computer analysis (Hodson, 1985) and Spanish-speaking children (Hodson, 1986a).

Practical Applications/Uses

Given the specialized nature of the APP-R, this test should be administered only by ASHA-certified speech/language pathologists. It should appeal to such professionals in several settings: schools, clinics, hospitals, and private practices. The APP-R can be used to gather baseline data about a client's phonological competencies as well as ongoing information during intervention and post-therapy phases, plus it can validate language sample analyses.

As mentioned previously, the APP-R can be administered and scored in a timely manner. For this reason, speech/language pathologists with large caseloads should find the APP-R quite attractive. Users are encouraged, however, to obtain the words in the multisyllabic screening through a conversational sample.

Although designed primarily for use with children who are highly unintelligible, the APP-R could be adapted for some developmentally or physically disabled adults and may have some limited applications with bilingual children. For example, the Spanish version provides an opportunity for users to compare the degree of unintelligibility in the native language with the degree of unintelligibility in the English language for Hispanic children.

The instructions provided for administering and scoring this test are quite clear and include suggestions for eliciting the stimulus words. If a child does not name objects on his or her own, the examiner can name the objects and have the child point to them to display knowledge of the words. If the examiner still cannot elicit the word from the child, the manual then recommends modeling the stimulus words for the child. Because the test relies heavily on the examiner's auditory discrimination skills, it should be administered in a quiet setting, relatively free of distractions. The instructions recommend using high-quality audiotapes for the multisyllabic screening. There is flexibility in the administration sequence and whenever possible one should employ three-dimensional objects to elicit the stimulus words. The APP-R requires approximately 15–20 minutes to administer, however the time does depend on the client's compliance. Guidelines assist the user in transcribing phonological deviations using Standard American English phonetic transcriptions.

Ten omission and class deficiencies were selected for scoring. Examiners use the first four columns of the analysis form to score phoneme omissions. Four different types (syllable reduction, consonant sequence reduction, prevocalic singleton consonant omission, postvocalic singleton consonant omission) are recorded. Omissions are not marked when substitutions occur except in the case of a glottal stop substitution, because the latter is nonstandard in American English. The next six columns are used to score six class deficiencies (stridency, velarization, liquidization of /l/, liquidization of /r, ɝ/, nasalization, gliding). The examiner marks these columns whenever the examinee's response is deficient or does not produce a particular class. Several columns also are provided for marking miscellaneous error patterns not already identified, such as additions (epenthesis), distortions (glottal replacements), and substitutions (stopping, fronting, backing, gliding, vowelization, vowel deviations, metathesis, migration, reduplication, coalescence, affrication, deaffrication, palatalization, depalatalization). Five types of assimilations are scored (nasal, labial, velar, alveolar, other). Hodson notes that although the assimilation columns could be marked for many misarticulations, often another phonological process may predominate. The rule of thumb offered is to mark assimilation columns when an alternative explanation for a substitution does not exist. Three voicing alterations are identified (prevocalic voicing, prevocalic devoicing, postvocalic devoicing). Minimal place of articulation shifts (sibilant distortions, substitutions of anterior stridents for interdental phonemes) are scored when their production is distracting. The last column on the analysis sheet is reserved for marking other error patterns or preferences (e.g., nasalization, ingression for /s/ productions, stridency addition).

After scoring each of the columns, the user totals the check marks and transfers them to the designated lines on the summary form for each error pattern. One derives the percentage-of-occurrence scores for the 10 basic processes by dividing the total number of occurrences by the possible number of occurrences (which are provided on the summary sheet) specified for each of the phonological processes. In some instances, percentage-of-occurrence scores may exceed 100% (e.g., consonant sequence reduction if whole sequences are deleted). Percentage-of-occurrence scores are not derived for miscellaneous processes for obvious reasons. Although adaptations for computer analysis do exist, the manual describes no hardware specifications or details regarding the procedure.

Hodson provides a section to assist with the interpretation of phonological scores. This interpretation is based on a combination of objective scoring and internal clinical judgment. To properly interpret the scores, the examiner must be well trained in phonological analysis and intervention because this particular assessment instrument was designed to be integral to the intervention process.

Professionals can use the overall percentage-of-occurrence scores to identify and target patterns for primary phonological remediation, for follow-up accountability measures, and to calculate a phonological process average score, which in turn translates to a phonological deviancy score. The author added age-compensatory points for children 4 years of age or older to obtain a phonological deviancy score. This addition was intended to provide older children a higher priority in phonological intervention should triage be necessary. Additional points also are added when the child's average score is 15 or greater and he or she demonstrates the backing process a minimum of five times (5 additional points are added). This has the effect of increasing the phonological deviancy score, which in turn increases the severity rating. Hodson provides four severity intervals (mild, moderate, severe, profound) based on the phonological deviancy scores in order to assist with scheduling. Though miscellaneous error patterns are not targeted initially for intervention, they need to be considered when selecting production-practice words.

Technical Aspects

Validity and reliability data do not appear in the APP-R manual. Rather, one finds citations to research articles and dissertations that support the constructs guiding the development of the APP-R (e.g., Dyson & Paden, 1983; Hodson & Paden, 1981; Ingram, 1976; Khan, Dyson, Edwards, Hodson, & Preisser, 1985; Preisser, 1983; Stoel-Gammon & Dunn, 1985). These in-depth studies looked at phonological development in preschoolers and young children. Using chronological age as the basis of comparison, they present examples of typical and atypical phonological rule acquisition. The studies typically conclude with models and recommendations for remediation. None of these studies discuss ranges of severity; the children with atypical phonological development are simply described as highly unintelligible.

Critique

The APP-R test protocols and manuals compliment one another very well in their clarity and facility. The manual is especially helpful because of its attention to terminology, administration and scoring procedures, and the provision of supporting models for therapy and recommendations for disposition. All of these factors allow for a more effective instrument for the assessment of children who are unintelligible.

From a theoretical perspective, the developmental phonology research (e.g., Ingram, 1976) provides the framework for this instrument. The importance of the role that distinctive features play in this research cannot be overlooked. Distinctive features provide the foundation for the development of rules that describe the phonological processes assessed by the APP-R. The developmental phonology research is based partially on Jakobson, Fant, and Halle's (1952) and Chomsky and Halle's (1968) theoretical models of distinctive features. Other such models, however, do exist (Kim, 1975; Ladefoged, 1971; Singh & Singh, 1972). The utility of using other distinctive feature models as the basis for phonological rules has never been thoroughly investigated. Differences in the number and types of features used to describe a phoneme potentially could affect rule development. For example, Chomsky and Halle's (1968) system is based on 13 features that describe the manner of production, whereas Kim's (1975) system is based on 27 acoustic features placed in one of two major categories. The differences in these features may influence the accuracy of phonological rules. Although it has been shown that Chomsky and Halle's (Peltonen, 1975) and Kim's (Boscardin & Kim, 1978) distinctive features systems correlate highly with perceptual judgments, this may not be enough for the purpose of developing phonological rules; there may be other factors to consider. Researchers need to explore alternative distinctive features systems that serve as the foundation for the construction of phonological rules. Reconstruction of phonological rules obviously would affect the conceptual framework of phonological assessment instruments such as the APP-R.

The data on phonological rule acquisition by children from culturally different linguistic backgrounds are still meager. The Spanish version of the APP-R was based on the development of phonological processes by Mexican-American children; it therefore may not apply to Hispanics of other origins or to Latinos. Data were not available or cited for African-American children. Studies cited as lending validity to the APP-R did not mention the racial, ethnic, gender, or socioeconomic class makeup of the children used in the samples. Subjects were discussed only in terms of age and whether or not they possessed typical or deviant phonological systems. Because the sampling for the APP-R is limited, productions should be obtained from phonologically typical peers in a child's linguistic community prior to scoring the APP-R, with particular attention given to both localized and regionalized production of phonemes.

In terms of practical applications, the APP-R is very thorough in its phonemic assessment. The full-scale APP-R's thoroughness, however, may tax the attention limits of a preschool child or the child who has an attention deficit or behavioral disability. In this event, the APP-R should be administered over two or more sittings, especially to incorporate time for phoneme stimulation and spontaneous speech monitoring. Additional time also may be required to review the names of the items beforehand, either through choice or necessity. In some cases quick eye-hand coordination is required to use the suggested method for presenting the three-dimensional stimulus items. It may be difficult initially to find and record responses as the child chooses items from the boxes, and thus administration may require more than the anticipated time proposed. The time needed to record utterances probably improves with practice. Although it would add to the cost of the test, it might be worthwhile to offer the three dimensional-items as a purchase option.

It is imperative that a speech and language clinician administer this test and be well trained in phonetic transcription. To score the APP-R successfully, one must have a good working knowledge of phonological rules and normal phonological development. Hodson does provide the examiner with definitions for the terminology used on the APP-R, accompanied by a discussion of anticipated age acquisition or discontinuation of the omissions and processes she presents. Room for confusion still remains, though, if the clinician is not competent in the use of that terminology or knowledgeable of developmental age norms. Including brief definitions of terminology used and the age of acquisition on the scoring sheets would free the examiner from depending on memory or the manual.

Although videotaping is not mentioned in the manual, it should be encouraged whenever possible. Videotaping provides visual information about a child's non-verbal language that one cannot obtain from an audiotape. The use of nonverbal language by the examinee may have an effect on the perceived level of severity. It should be noted that camera placement and focusing is critical and that the same recommendations supplied for audiotaping should be applied to videotaping.

The APP-R manual overemphasizes priority placement. The severity intervals generated should be used to increase the accuracy of the description of the phonological errors, not to triage clients, particularly in light of PL 94-142 (amended as PL 101-476), which guarantees disabled individuals (0–21 years of age) the right to the level of services necessary to meet their needs. Correlational studies focusing on the relationship between the time needed for therapeutic remediation and degree of severity would have been more beneficial, as they would provide information about what to expect in terms of remediation time. Validity and reliability data did not accompany the severity rating scale presented in the manual, nor were there citations for where one might locate such data. There is no way of knowing if the percentages obtained from the APP-R data analysis actually correlate with the degree of perceived severity. The data very well may be based on the clinical experiences of the author; however, this should be stated.

In summary, the APP-R is a very good instrument for use by ASHA-certified speech and language pathologists. It provides a structured, more focused method for assessing unintelligible speech as opposed to the use of time-consuming language samples that often are not phonologically representative.

References

Boscardin, M.L., & Kim, B.W. (1978, November). *A perceptual basis for the feature differential index for English phonemes.* Paper presented at the annual convention of the American Speech-Language-Hearing Association, San Francisco.

Chomsky, N., & Halle, M. (1968). *Sound pattern of English.* New York: Harper & Row.

Compton, A.J. (1970). Generative studies of children's phonological disorders. *Journal of Speech and Hearing Disorders, 35,* 315–339.

Crocker, J.R. (1969). A phonological model of children's articulation competence. *Journal of Speech and Hearing Disorders, 34,* 203–213.

Dyson, A., & Paden, E.P. (1983). Some phonological acquisition strategies used by two-year-olds. *Journal of Childhood Communication Disorders, 7,* 6–18.

Hodson, B.W. (1975). *Aspects of phonological performance in four-year-olds.* Unpublished doctoral dissertation, University of Illinois, Urbana-Champaign.

Hodson, B.W. (1985). *Computer analysis of phonological processes.* Stonington, IL: PhonoComp.

Hodson, B.W. (1986a). *Assessment of Phonological Processes–Spanish.* San Diego: Los Amigos.

Hodson, B.W. (1986b). *The Assessment of Phonological Processes–Revised.* Austin, TX: PRO-ED.

Hodson, B.W., & Paden, E.P. (1981). Phonological processes which characterize unintelligible and intelligible speech in early childhood. *Journal of Speech and Hearing Disorders, 46,* 369–373.

Ingram, D. (1976). *Phonological disability in children.* New York: Elsevier.

Jakobson, R., Fant, C.G.M., & Halle, M. (1952). *Preliminaries to speech analysis.* Cambridge, MA: MIT Press.

Khan, L., Dyson, A., Edwards, M., Hodson, B., & Preisser, D. (1985, November). *Early phonological development.* Miniseminar presented at the annual convention of the American Speech-Language-Hearing Association, Washington, DC.

Kim, B.W. (1975). Clinical segmental feature system of English syllabic nuclei, semivowels, and consonants. *Journal of the Acoustical Society of America, 27,* 338–352.

Ladefoged, P. (1971). *Preliminaries to linguistic phonetics.* Chicago: University of Chicago Press.

Peltonen, C.D. (1975). *An investigation of the usefulness of the Chomsky-Halle distinctive feature system for predicting perceptual distance between selected English consonants.* Unpublished master's thesis, University of Wisconsin, Milwaukee.

Preisser, D. (1983). *Prevalence of phonological processes in normal two-year-olds.* Unpublished doctoral dissertation, University of Illinois, Urbana-Champaign.

Singh, S., & Singh, K.S. (1972). A self-generating distinctive feature model for diagnosis, prognosis, and therapy. *Acta Symbolica, 3,* 88–99.

Smith, N.V. (1973). *The acquisition of phonology.* New York: Cambridge University Press.

Stoel-Gammon, C., & Dunn, C. (1985). *Normal and disordered phonology in children.* Austin, TX: PRO-ED.

John H. Hoover, Ph.D.
Associate Professor of Special Education, University of North Dakota, Grand Forks, North Dakota.

John Delane Williams, Ph.D.
Professor and Chair, Department of Educational Foundations and Research Methodologies, Center for Teaching and Learning, University of North Dakota, Grand Forks, North Dakota.

ATTENTION DEFICIT DISORDER BEHAVIOR RATING SCALES

Ned Owens and Betty White Owens. Garland, Texas: Ned Owens, M.Ed., Inc.

Introduction

The Attention Deficit Disorder Behavior Rating Scales (ADDBRS; Owens & Owens, 1982) is a screening instrument developed to identify children at risk for a diagnosis of Attention Deficit Disorder (now Attention Deficit-Hyperactivity Disorder; American Psychiatric Association, 1987). The manual clearly indicates that the ADDBRS is intended to convince medical doctors that a diagnosis of ADHD is warranted and to convince parents and teachers that medical intervention will be beneficial:

> [The ADDBRS] is designed specifically to identify behavior that is supportive of a diagnosis of Attention Deficit Disorder. (Owens & Owens, 1982, p. 1)
>
> [The ADDBRS] has been very successful in . . . follow up of students that assists in monitoring medication dosages. (pp. 1–2)
>
> The instruments and procedures used by the licensed professional counselor resulted in obtaining a diagnosis of Attention Deficit Disorder for all of the students referred. The students' family doctors accepted the evaluation and prescribed medication. (p. 2)

There is only one version of the scales, dated 1982. The instrument is published privately by its authors, Ned and Betty Owens of Garland, Texas. Mr. Owens is a licensed M.S.-level counselor; no professional affiliation appears for the second author.

The ADDBRS consists of a photocopied 10-page manual; consumable rating scales and forms for analyzing performance on the Wechsler Intelligence Scale for Children–Revised (Wechsler, 1974) are ordered separately. The "Attention Deficit Disorders Diagnostic Kit" (Owens & Owens, 1982, p. 8) includes the manual, 25 rating scales, and three audiotapes (a general informational tape about ADHD, one that deals with use of psychotropic medication, and an informational piece about learning disabilities). In addition, the materials these reviewers received included informational sheets about intervention, apparently intended for teachers

49

and parents, but these were not described in the manual and it is not clear whether they comprise part of the Diagnostic Kit. Further, materials are photocopied, and some may find them difficult to read.

The instrument is made up of 50 items, divided into the following 5-item scales: Inattention, Impulsivity, and Hyperactivity (primary, or organic, scales), and Anger Control, Academics, Anxiety, Confidence, Aggressiveness, Resistance, and Social (secondary, or emotional, scales). The scales are not defined other than as labels and by inference from item content. No factor analytic or psychometric data are reported; indeed, no studies have been performed (N. Owens, personal communication, August 3, 1992).

Raters use the following modified 5-point Likert scale to rate items:
1. You have not noticed this behavior before.
2. You have noticed this behavior to a slight degree.
3. You have noticed this behavior to a considerable degree.
4. You have noticed this behavior to a large degree.
5. You have noticed this behavior to a very large degree.

No evidence appears of an effort to provide empirical evidence that the scaling process yielded equal-appearing intervals, nor are there instructions regarding a timeframe for responding to behaviors. Quantities or referents are not provided, either in the manual or on the rating scale itself, to clarify and differentiate such terms as *considerable* or *large*.

The profile sheet is misleading in that it shows possible raw scores of 1, 2, 3, and 4, even though one cannot score less than 5 points per scale because the minimum item-value is 1. The "at risk" category starts at 8 raw score points, which means it is very easy to attain. For example, three item scores of 2 would place the child at risk as would one item score of either 4 or 5. In the former case, children potentially would be referred for ADHD despite *no* behavior being observed beyond a slight degree. This contravenes the intent of the *Diagnostic and Statistical Manual of Mental Disorders* (American Psychiatric Association, 1987), where responses meet criteria "only if the behavior is considerably more frequent than that of most people of the same mental age" (p. 52).

Practical Applications/Uses

The ADDBRS was designed to screen students aged 6–16 (Grades 1–9) at risk for a diagnosis of ADHD (though because of the publication date, the term *ADD* appears throughout the manual). A minor but significant point is that although one uses the instrument for screening, the authors refer to the package as a *Diagnostic* Kit, potentially confusing terminology. Though both parents and teachers are targeted as respondents, the scales are to be interpreted by school counselors.

Family members or teachers "who know the child well" (Owens & Owens, 1982, p. 2) complete the ADDBRS ratings. The authors recommend that, when feasible, both parents and the teacher rate the subject separately. This instrument is designed primarily to initiate physician referrals so that ADHD students may be medicated. The authors admonish that ADD is a medical diagnosis, and though they concede that hard signs are often absent, their materials make it clear that they see the disorder as neurological in nature, to be treated via medication. These reviewers have never seen an instrument before so clearly directed to moving from behavioral symptomatology to a physician referral. This ethos permeates all materials in the ADDBRS kit.

Scoring is straightforward and accomplished by summing ratings down offset columns that correspond to the 10 subscales. While this allows for ease in scoring, it also may elicit particular responses from persons desirous of achieving the ADHD diagnosis for a child. The user transfers observed raw scores to a profile form by placing "X's" in the appropriate raw score columns alongside subscales arranged as rows. The profile divides into three subsections by raw score: "normal" (raw score 5–7), "at risk" (8–16), and "very high risk" (17–25). Students who score in the at-risk or very-high-risk ranges on the first three scales are to be referred for medical diagnosis, though the manual does not make this perfectly clear. It appears that ADD without hyperactivity requires at least at-risk scores on the Inattention and Impulsivity scales, while ADD with hyperactivity requires high scores in the afore-mentioned two plus the Hyperactivity scale. It is not clear what one does if students score in the at-risk or very-high-risk categories in the remaining seven scales.

Another level of analysis offered in the ADDBRS is a distinction between primary-organic ADHD and emotional secondary results of the condition. The authors maintain that the first three scales, Inattention, Impulsivity, and Hyperactivity, represent clear evidence for organic or neurological involvement (Owens & Owens, 1982, p. 1). However, users should interpret this with caution because of the well-known problems with diagnosing brain pathology via paper-and-pencil tests or other soft signs (Ysseldyke & Salvia, 1974). In addition, the neurological underpinnings of many cases of ADHD are not well established and organicity remains controversial, as evidenced by wildly divergent rates of applying the diagnosis in the United States versus Great Britain (Rutter, 1989).

The manual is clearly written if somewhat sparse, lacking considerable information that these reviewers would consider necessary before using the ADDBRS (this will be explicated further in the "Critique" section). An interesting feature of the kit is a work sheet for examining the possible ADHD implications of students' WISC-R profiles. (Because the authors published the ADDBRS in 1982 and have not updated it, the manual contains no reference to the Wechsler Intelligence Scale for Children–III.) The potential utility of this approach is enhanced by an averaged WISC-R profile for the 100 students in the norming sample, all of whom presumably evidenced ADHD. Unfortunately, Owens and Owens argue that depressed scores on nearly every subtest reflect possible evidence for ADHD, a stance not supported by their own profile, which appears to be relatively flat (when estimated SE_M is considered), other than possibly a depressed score for Coding. In addition, this analysis is brought into question by reliability problems with subscale interpretation within ability measures (Salvia & Ysseldyke, 1991) and questionable validity of the technique in the specific case of ADHD (Bohline, 1985). At the very least these issues should be addressed in the manual.

Technical Aspects

The ADDBRS manual provides no evidence for reliability. Relatively straight-forward studies of interrater reliability could have been undertaken and reported but evidently were not. Though it impinges on validity issues, the internal consistency of the scales is important in this type of instrument, and these data also do not appear.

Despite the lack of data, these reviewers assume that ADDBRS reliability, if assessed, would be poor, due to at least three factors. First, the referents for the rating points are worded confusingly. We feel this would result in altered scores across administrations; this error variance would decrease resulting stability coefficients. Second, 5-item scales would be relatively unreliable due to their brevity (compared to longer scales). The length of scales is particularly at issue when internal consistency measures are lacking, as is the case with the ADDBRS. Third, oblique evidence for reliability problems emerges in the manual. Owens and Owens imply that teachers, mothers, and fathers consistently attain different scores when rating the same child. These differences would appear as between-rater variability in generalizability-type reliability studies, a source of measurement error unless normed separately (Cardinet, Tourneur, & Allal, 1981). The lack of reliability data prevents the calculation of such important descriptive indices as standard error of measurement.

Minimal information regarding the behavior of the ADDBRS is available. The manual provides a score profile of 100 students, presumably with scores averaged across 100 ADD students. The average scores of the sample fell in the "at risk" rather than "very high risk" range on 9 of the 10 scales. The exception was the Inattention scale, where the sample averaged 18 (of 25 possible) points. The nature of descriptive group scores is not provided; they are probably means, but the manual never states this. More troubling, the authors report no dispersion indices, such as standard deviation, in any form, making it impossible to estimate the variability of attained scores.

Evidence for the utility of the instrument could be presented via discriminative validity. That is, does the ADDBRS discriminate between ADD and matched non-ADD students? Some overlap or false positives would be tolerable on a screening instrument, but clear discrimination would lend credence to the scales' validity. To this point these reviewers have not seen evidence of the assessment of a single student not at risk for ADHD. Thus, the risk for false positives appears immense. The outcome of false positives on such an instrument could be devastating— namely, inappropriate, invasive drug therapy, potentially dangerous and certainly expensive. For a discussion of potential problems with use of psychotropic medication, see Breggin (1991).

Notably, the manual makes no mention of traditional validity measures. The behavior of the scales could be made clear via comparisons to other ADHD measures or to future behavior in school (concurrent and predictive criterion-referenced validity). The integrity of the 10 scales (a construct validity issue) is never addressed, nor is the source of items, though many appear to be paraphrased from DSM-III (American Psychiatric Association, 1980) diagnostic criteria. To our knowledge, the authors plan no update of materials in light of DSM-III-R. Perhaps a more important issue related both to internal consistency reliability and construct validity is the behavior of individual items vis-à-vis the total instrument and subscales. There is no evidence, other than item content, that a fundamental relationship exists between the scales and attention.

The sample for which data were available is not adequately described. Both male (*n* = 77) and female (*n* = 22) students aged 6 to 16 (Grades 1–9) were included, all of whom evidenced near-normal intelligence on average (range = 78–141). The authors do not make it clear how these students came to their attention (source of referrals), but all of them subsequently were diagnosed as ADD by medical doctors, based in part on ADDBRS results. As mentioned, no nonidentified students were included in the sample; thus, when employing the profile in the manual, users compare their students only to an ADHD sample. Unfortunately, no data external to ADDBRS results exists that these students actually evidenced ADHD, as presumably the physicians based their diagnoses in sum or part on ADDBRS results. This presents the consumer with something of a logical tautology.

No useful demographic information appears in the ADDBRS materials. Further, these reviewers noted several other shortcomings of the sample and the means of reporting it. First, Owens and Owens offer no statistical data; means are implied by a figure, but exact means and standard deviations are missing. Second, data would be more useful divided by gender and age (or the manual should spell out the reasons for not doing so).

Critique

An overall theme that pervades the ADDBRS and accompanying documentation is that ADHD is underdiagnosed, implying that more students should be identified and medicated. Most problems associated with the manual relate to this stance. Though underidentification is never argued overtly, the authors write on page 1 of the manual that "there are one or two children in every classroom who suffer from this problem." The ease with which a child can score in the at-risk category reflects a belief in the need for identifying more ADHD students. We wonder if these unstated assumptions do not constitute a fatal flaw, as there is little noncontroversial evidence for underdiagnosis of ADHD in the United States. The suggested use of this instrument and the makeup of its scales contravene the conservative, multifaceted nature of ADHD diagnosis recommended by such authors as Ostrom and Jenson (1988), who state that "school psychologists must proceed very cautiously in attempting to assess and label children as ADD or ADHD, given the state of our present knowledge regarding attention and attention deficits" (p. 260).

Despite the potential strength of emphasizing parental communication, these reviewers find find this instrument so psychometrically weak that we do not recommend use of the diagnostic package. Though the scales evidence myriad shortcomings, we see the possibility of excessive false positives as most problematic.

The diagnostic process outlined by Owens and Owens has potentially negative overtones, and these deserve mention in the overall context of evaluating students for ADHD. Parents and teachers fill out the rating scale, which in turn is interpreted by a counselor. For children thus determined at risk, referral is made directly to the family physician. Nowhere in the scenario outlined in the manual are other professionals, in psychology or special education, for example, brought into the evaluation process. The danger here lies in short circuiting the interdisciplinary or transdisciplinary team procedures so necessary for effective evaluation and programming.

The ADDBRS manual lacks information about the facets of a multidisciplinary, multimethod assessment process, including direct observation (see Luk, 1985, for a review), clinical interviews, and objective measures such as continuous performance tasks (Gordan & Mettelman, 1987) or tests of impulsivity such as the Familiar Figures Matching Test (Kagan, 1965) or Knox's Cube Test (Stone & Wright, 1973). Certainly procedures such as these should be utilized in, at minimum, concurrent validity studies of the ADDBRS.

The authors of the ADDBRS should speak to the complexity of attention and accompanying measurement problems (Ostrom & Jenson, 1988). The nature of attention is not well developed or understood, and the subtlety of these issues should be communicated to users of the scales. As pointed out by Ostrom and Jenson (1988), clinicians should both familiarize themselves with attentional theory and employ multifaceted assessment procedures.

The psychologists who normally would give and interpret ability measures such as the WISC-R are not mentioned. In addition, psychologists and educators may be more conversant with ADHD than a family physician. Of special concern is the manual's total omission of such treatment methods as behavioral intervention, relaxation therapy, or cognitive and other self-monitoring-type treatment programs (Kauffman, 1989). The effect size for behavioral therapy has proven to be as large as that for psychotropic medication in some cases, with fewer side effects (Brown, 1986; Taylor, 1986). Perhaps the most insidious iatrogenic problem with use of medication is the potential change in the child's locus of control. Students may come to believe that they have no control or potential control over their own behavior and thus attribute successes to psychotropic medication and problems to its absence (Whalen & Henker, 1980). None of these significant factors are addressed in the manual or accompanying materials.

The Attention Deficit Disorder Evaluation Scale (ADDES; McCarney, 1989a) presents an example of another ADHD screening instrument in the form of a rating scale. The ADDES reflects many of the characteristics missing in the Owens's scales; this comparison is not intended as a review of the ADDES but rather to demonstrate positive features of a similar instrument.

McCarney uses the following five referent points:
0. Does not engage in the behavior
1. One to several times a month
2. One to several times a week
3. One to several times a day
4. One to several times an hour

Though not perfect, these scale points seem tied to reasonable quantities and thus probably add to the reliability of the ADDES. The technical manual includes much information missing from the ADDBRS. Further, McCarney's scale includes an intervention manual, specifically pegged to the instrument. Intervention materials are available with the ADDBRS Diagnostic Kit, but they are not nearly as specific and data-based as those accompanying the ADDES (McCarney, 1989b).

The idea that ADHD is substantially underidentified, coupled with the manual's omission of both direct behavioral observation and behavioral and cognitive intervention techniques, leaves the ADDBRS materials somewhat dated. The complete lack of reliability and validity information as well as the inadequately defined norming sample render the instrument of questionable utility, even for screening. In the hands of a person not well trained and experienced with a variety of measurement tools and without a multidisciplinary orientation toward diagnosis, the ADDBRS could be too easily misused.

References

American Psychiatric Association. (1980). *Diagnostic and statistical manual of mental disorders* (3rd ed.). Washington, DC: Author.

American Psychiatric Association. (1987). *Diagnostic and statistical manual of mental disorders* (3rd ed. rev.). Washington, DC: Author.

Bohline, D. (1985). Intellectual and affective characteristics of attention deficit disordered children. *Journal of Learning Disabilities, 10,* 604–608.

Breggin, P.R. (1991). *Toxic psychiatry.* New York: St. Martin's.

Brown, G. (1986). Attention deficit disorder. *Current Pediatric Therapy, 12,* 44–48.

Cardinet, J., Tourneur, Y., & Allal, L. (1981). Extension of generalizability theory and its applications in educational measurement. *Journal of Educational Measurement, 18,* 183–204.

Gordon, M., & Mettelman, B.B. (1987). *Technical guide to the Gordon Diagnostic System.* DeWitt, NY: Gordon Systems.

Kagan, J. (1965). Impulsive and reflective children. In J. Krumboltz (Ed.), *Learning and the educational process.* Chicago: Rand McNally.

Kauffman, J.M. (1989). *Characteristics of behavior disorders of children and youth* (4th ed.). Columbus, OH: Merrill.

Luk, S. (1985). Direct observation studies of hyperactive behaviors. *Journal of the American Academy of Child Psychiatry, 24,* 338–344.

McCarney, S.B. (1989a). *The Attention Deficit Disorders Evaluation Scale: School version technical manual.* Columbia, MO: Hawthorne.

McCarney, S.B. (1989b). *The attention deficit disorders intervention manual.* Columbia, MO: Hawthorne.

Ostrom, N.N., & Jenson, W.R. (1988). Assessment of attention deficits in children. *Professional School Psychology, 3,* 253–269.

Owens, N., & Owens, B.W. (1982). *Attention Deficit Disorder Behavior Rating Scales (ADDBRS).* Garland, TX: Ned Owens, M.Ed., Inc.

Rutter, M. (1989). Attention deficit disorder/hyperkinetic syndrome: Conceptual and research issues regarding diagnosis and classification. In T. Sagvolden & T. Archer (Eds.), *Clinical and basic research* (pp. 1–24). Hillsdale, NJ: Erlbaum.

Salvia, J., & Ysseldyke, J.E. (1991). *Assessment* (5th ed.). Boston: Houghton Mifflin.

Stone, M.H., & Wright, B.D. (1973). *Knox's Cube Test: Junior and senior editions.* Chicago: Stoelting.

Taylor, E. (1986). Syndromes of overactivity and attention deficit. In M. Rutter & L. Hersov (Eds.), *Child and adolescent psychology: Modern approaches* (pp. 424–443). Philadelphia: Blackwell Scientific.

Wechsler, D. (1974). *Manual for the Wechsler Intelligence Scale for Children–Revised.* San Antonio, TX: Psychological Corporation.

Wechsler, D. (1989). *Manual for the Wechsler Intelligence Scale for Children–Third edition.* San Antonio, TX: Psychological Corporation.

Whalen, C.K., & Henker, B. (Eds). (1980). *Hyperactive children: The social ecology of identification and treatment.* New York: Academic Press.

Ysseldyke, J.E., & Salvia, J. (1974). Diagnostic-prescriptive teaching: Two models. *Exceptional Children, 41,* 181–186.

Michael H. Mattei, Psy.D.
Staff Psychologist, Napa State Hospital, Napa, California.

Grant Aram Killian, Ph.D.
Adjunct Professor of Psychology, Nova University, Fort Lauderdale, Florida.

William I. Dorfman, Ph.D.
Associate Professor of Psychology, Nova University, Fort Lauderdale, Florida.

AUTOMATED CHILD/ADOLESCENT SOCIAL HISTORY

Mark Rohde. Minnetonka, Minnesota: National Computer Systems/PAS Division.

Introduction

The Automated Child/Adolescent Social History (ACASH; Rohde, 1988a) was developed with the goal of producing an objective, valid, and reliable social history for children or adolescents in a quick and cost-effective manner. The ACASH is a computer-administered structured interview that uses the client's parents or guardians for data input. After thus collecting the information, the clinician may print out a written report or save the document in the computer for word processing. The instrument is intended to gather psychosocial history data on children or adolescents ranging in age from 5 to 19.

The ACASH author, Mark Rohde, earned a master's of education from Arizona State University and a Ph.D. in professional psychology from The Union Institute–Union Graduate School in Cincinnati, Ohio. He is currently in private practice, specializing in family, group, and individual psychotherapy as well as psycho-education, psychological assessment, and substance abuse treatment. His other professional activities have included assessments in school and hospital settings.

Initial work on the ACASH began in May 1982, and it was copyrighted in 1985 and again in 1988. In 1986 the scope of the project expanded to include the construction of behavioral rating scales from specific test items. The manual (Rohde, 1988b) states that these scales would lend themselves to psychometric analysis, thus meeting the author's original goal to produce an objective, valid, and reliable product. At the time of this writing, however, the publisher had abandoned plans to pursue the development and validation of these scales (M. Maruish, personal communication, July 2, 1991).

Initial questions for the item pool came from various sources, including structured interviews (over 20) used in mental health settings, existing automated social history programs (e.g., GOLPH; Giannetti, 1987), client chart reviews, major test instruments such as the Minnesota-Briggs History Record (Briggs, Rouzer,

56

Hamberg, & Holman, 1972), and the *Diagnostic and Statistical Manual of Mental Disorders* (American Psychiatric Association, 1980). Questions also were based on a review of the social history and interviewing literature.

A general criterion for selecting questions was that a given item have behavioral specificity. In the early stages of development, the author felt that such specificity would aid in future development of behavioral rating scales. Although his intent was to develop a theoretically neutral instrument, Rohde later determined that this was not feasible and as such identified the following theoretical orientations as reflected in the test items: psychoanalytic, developmental, and systems theory.

The author conducted field testing as part of initial development. The process involved having a group of clinicians consider the merits and weaknesses of various topic areas and make suggestions regarding questions. Prior to the release of the program two other field trials took place. The first was carried out over several months and resulted in the inclusion of additional items deemed clinically relevant (e.g., questions regarding handicapping conditions, child-parent separations, and parental criminal behavior). The second trial entailed an evaluation of the program by a psychoanalytic psychiatrist, a general psychiatrist, a systemic family therapist, a Rogerian therapist, a behavioral therapist, and a school guidance counselor (Rohde, 1988b). Since its release, no revisions or alternative formats have developed, although several are planned for the near future, including a paper-and-pencil version and the addition of a diagnostic interview (M. Rohde, personal communication, July 3, 1991).

The ACASH operates on the MICROTEST assessment system, a PC-based system consisting of the software, a mechanical scoring box that attaches to the user's computer, a user guide, and a toll-free technical support number. ACASH administrations are ordered and loaded onto the scoring box by telephone from National Computer Systems (NCS). The scoring box contains an internal "clock" that allows the user to score only a fixed number of prepaid administrations.

The hardware required to run the system consists of an IBM-compatible personal computer with a communications port for a printer, DOS 2.1 or higher, one 360K floppy disk drive, and 720K of hard disk space. Use of a separate numeric keypad is recommended but not required. At this time the MICROTEST system is not configured to operate with Apple computers.

The examiner's role in the data-collecting process is minimal. The primary task is to ensure that the respondent (parent or guardian) has the necessary reading (ninth-grade level) and English-language skills to complete the questionnaire. The examiner should provide the respondent with a rationale for using an automated procedure, discuss the confidentiality of the results, and situate him or her in front of the computer. Examiners should stay with respondents while they answer the first two or three items, not only to ensure that they understand the procedure but also to help allay any anxiety over using a computer. Prior to the start of the interview, the examiner boots the program and answers the questions in the first section. At the end of the administration, the program can print out a report or save the results to disk for future access or word processing.

In order to interact with the computer effectively, the individual providing the information must have at least ninth-grade reading ability, recent experience with the client, "good" English skills, and no evidence of psychosis or other mental disorder. The relatively high reading level required likely exerts a negative impact on the clinical utility of this instrument.

The interview itself is divided into six topic or subtest areas: Reason for Referral and Identifying Information; Developmental History–Pre-Natal, Birth and Infancy; Developmental History–Childhood to Present; Educational History; Current Family–Members and Background; and Problem Identification. For each subtest, the computer presents a series of related questions to assess the specific topical areas.

Because the instrument is computer administered, no written answer forms are available or needed. Questions appear on the screen in a multiple-choice format for the most part. The author feels that response options must be limited in order not to overwhelm the respondent with choices. Because of this stipulation, all possible responses cannot be accounted for, which necessitates the "other/don't know/doesn't apply" response option. Any question answered in this manner can be automatically printed at the end of the report to facilitate further assessment efforts.

The ACASH program uses "response-dependent question presentation," commonly referred to as *branching logic*. This response-dependent format means that the questions presented to the respondent will be based in part on the client's age and sex and on the types of responses made to previous questions. For example, if the client is an only child, the program's design prevents inquiry about relationships to siblings or in assessing for sexual abuse, for example, if none is reported, the program proceeds to another topic; if abuse is noted, a series of questions appears regarding when it occurred, who was the perpetrator, the extent of the abuse as well as the child's reaction, and other relevant information.

The presentation of questions also is designed to decrease the likelihood of a response set developing, this by varying as much as possible how items are presented. For example, some questions require descriptive answers, others a simple "yes" or "no."

The ACASH report offers a narrative presentation of the interview data. In addition, the profile presents basic demographic information on the subject as well as sections identifying potentially critical concerns, improbable responses, and reported assets and strengths. One of the goals here is to avoid the awkward language seen in many computer-generated narratives. With this in mind, the ACASH conforms to the rules of English and to the terminology used within the treatment settings it is designed for as much as possible. For example, when the program compiles a report for a school setting, the client is consistently referred to as "the student." The program also addresses respondents by proper title and refers to them with appropriate pronouns.

Practical Applications/Uses

Each section of the ACASH collects information on variables related to the six previously mentioned topic areas. The manual states that the program can be used in outpatient as well as inpatient settings, juvenile justice agencies, and schools. In both outpatient and inpatient settings, its proposed use is to provide the clinician with the data necessary for developing hypotheses about the nature of the presenting problem. The manual suggests using the ACASH prior to hospitalization in order to help decrease the lag time between admission and implementation of treatment. In juvenile justice agencies, proposed uses include facilitating placement of first-time offenders and providing information that might be otherwise unavailable. In school settings the developer claims it is useful as a screening device for placement in alternative programs. According to the manual, appropriate users include psychologists and psychiatrists as well as other mental health professionals or paraprofessionals.

The publishers state that the instrument could be beneficial in monitoring treatment progress and in conducting final outcome evaluations (M. Maruish, personal communication, July 9, 1991). Rohde feels that although the ACASH is a viable instrument, ongoing evaluation regarding its usefulness needs to continue. Areas he identifies for further clarification or exploration include researching its effectiveness in various clinical settings as well as assessing client and professional acceptance. The author believes that this will help fully establish the instrument's clinical utility (M. Rohde, personal communication, July 9, 1991).

The manual makes no specific recommendations regarding appropriate administration settings except to say that respondents should work alone at a computer terminal. The test manual and its supplement, the Quick Reference Guide, outline thorough and clear instructions for administering the ACASH. The instructions also guide the user through the setup procedures, starting with directions for selecting the appropriate subdirectory and "calling up" an on-line administration. This part of the procedure offers menus from which to make the initial selections. The first section of the ACASH is completed by the examiner in about 10–15 minutes and includes such basic information as client demographics and reason for referral.

According to the instructions, respondents should be advised ahead of time that they will be using an automated assessment instrument and should be given a sound rationale for the procedure (the latter to help allay anxiety about using a computer or about being interviewed). The manual advises telling the respondent that the program is simple to use and that help will be available any time a question arises. Although before proceeding the examiner should ensure that the respondent possesses the required language skills, the manual does not specify how to go about this.

Once in front of the computer the respondent follows on-screen directions, which begin with an introduction to the program. This tutorial covers basic keyboard functions and presents sample questions. The examiner should help in completing the first two or three to make sure that the respondent grasps the instructions and is sufficiently comfortable with the process. If both parents are available, they should not complete the ACASH together (increased administration time often results over disagreements about how questions should be answered). Instead, they should answer the questions separately and the results be compared. This procedure is recommended especially when parents are divorced or marital conflict is apparent.

After the completing the assessment questions, a screen message asks the respondent to summon the examiner. At this point the examiner saves the data and can either print a report or access it with a word processor at a later time. If the administration must be interrupted, the program can store the data until both respondent and examiner are ready to resume. Using the ACASH requires minimal computer knowledge of either the examiner or the respondent, and as such it is relatively easy to use. However, due to the nature of the branching logic programming, no alteration of the testing sequence is allowable. The interview will generally require 1 hour to complete, but this time frame will vary depending on the number of reported difficulties as well as the respondent's reading ability.

Scoring is done automatically by the computer once the data are saved, and the printed report is available within minutes. The reliability of the administration procedures, data recording, and output are much higher than with traditional examiner-administered interviews. Unlike the latter, given a fixed set of conditions and data, the computer will administer the same set of questions and record the answers perfectly every time.

Interpretation of the ACASH narrative derives from the examiner's subjective assessment of the report. The manual suggests that the results be compared with the clinical impressions formed independently by the professional. In addition, a copy of the ACASH narrative should be given to the parent or guardian in order to elicit their input and obtain clarification of any ambiguous or unclear data. The manual states that the section on Potentially Critical Concerns may serve as the basis of the "Identified Problems" section of a typical treatment plan. With this in mind, the examiner is further cautioned to verify this information independently before planning treatment strategies. As the manual clearly states, the respondent's perceptions about the client may be distorted (or at the very least subjective) and quite different from those held by other observers. The report is described as recording "the respondent's perceptions at a particular point in time" and therefore not reflective of any "objective or permanent reality." Given the above-mentioned considerations, it becomes clear that proper use of the ACASH information requires a relatively high level of caution and sophistication.

Technical Aspects

Although structured interviews often are not considered psychometric tests, they nevertheless possess characteristics that make them amenable, in part, to psychometric inquiry and study (Haynes & Jensen, 1979). By definition, the ACASH is an automated structured interview and, as such, should be held to the same professional standards as more traditionally defined psychometric instruments. The governing position with regard to computerized interviews is that "all the standards apply with equal force" (American Educational Research Association, American Psychological Association, & National Council on Measurement in Education, 1985, p. 4). As it would be beyond the scope of this review to evaluate the ACASH on every AERA/APA/NCME standard, the focus here will rely on those classified as primary, which according to the *Standards for Educational and Psychological Testing* "are those which should be met by all tests before their operational use and in all test uses" (AERA et al., 1985, p. 2). For a more exhaustive review of which standards the ACASH met, the reader is referred to Mattei (1991).

The utility of a structured interview rests in part on the content-related evidence of validity. According to Anastasi (1982), content validity should be built into an instrument throughout its development. In addition, demonstrating content validity for the prescribed uses of an instrument is the developer's responsibility (AERA et al., 1985). An examination of how Rohde constructed the ACASH shows that the established procedures to build and demonstrate content validity were for the most part followed. The developer specified the domain that the instrument was intended to represent, subject-matter experts were used appropriately, and an assessment of the appropriateness of topics and questions was done using a second set of subject-matter experts. An examination of the ACASH reveals a well-designed instrument, both complete and comprehensive, that adheres to accepted clinical interview content (Korchin, 1976; Lazarus, 1973; Sundberg, Tyler, & Taplin, 1973; Watson, 1951, cited in Bernstein, Bernstein, & Dana, 1974). Because of this, the developer can demonstrate that the instrument's contents are relevant to its proposed use of obtaining social history data.

According to the AERA/APA/NCME *Standards* (1.7), when subject-matter experts have been used, their relevant training, experience, and qualifications should be described (p. 15). Although the manual fails to describe the first set of subject-matter experts, the omission does not negate the evidence indicating that content validity was "built" into the ACASH.

To date, no attempts have been made to obtain reliability and validity estimates for this instrument. Regardless, the manual states that use of the ACASH increases the "accuracy" of placement decisions for first-time offenders in juvenile justice settings and that the report can be used as a screening device for placement in alternative school programs. However, no evidence appears demonstrating the instrument's predictive validity for these recommended uses. The *Standards* (1.23) state that developers must provide evidence of an instrument's differential predictive ability before claiming that it can classify individuals into "specified alternative treatment groups" (p. 18). In addition, all criterion measures must be clearly specified and a "rationale for choosing them as relevant criteria should be made explicit" (AERA et al., 1985, p. 16). The ACASH clearly violates these requirements. Another primary AERA/APA/NCME standard (1.1) states that "evidence of validity should be presented for the major types of inferences for which the use of a test is recommended" (1985, p. 13). Criterion-related studies examining the interview's predictive validity would be needed for the developer and publisher to justify making the aforementioned claims. These studies should identify the outcome criteria and provide scores with which to predict criterion performance. Until evidence can be provided, the developer and publisher should refrain from making claims of this nature.

The manual implies that the ACASH can measure the theoretical construct of "compromised thought process." Although it does not provide a quantified score as a measure of the construct, the program is said to have the ability to detect indicators of compromised or intact functioning. However, no clear construct-related evidence demonstrating convergent or discriminative validity is offered to support this inference. In addition, no evidence appears demonstrating concurrent validity, which makes this claim a violation of AERA/APA/NCME standard 1.8 ("construct-related evidence should be presented to support such inferences"; p. 15). As noted in the *Standards* (5.7), a test developer and publisher should avoid making unsubstantiated claims.

Numerous studies have shown data obtained through interviews subject to considerable errors of measurement (Walsh, 1967; Yarrow, Campbell, & Burton, 1970). These potential sources of error include client bias and an unwillingness to disclose certain types of information. Technically, the ACASH is not a self-report interview; rather, it is considered an inventory of observed behavior (Anastasi, 1982), which is subject to additional sources of error. For example, studies have shown a tendency on the part of parents to present considerably distorted information when interviewed about their children (Sobell & Sobell, 1975; Vaughn & Reynolds, 1951). Wenar and Coulter (1962) found that only 43% of parents interviewed about their child's development gave consistent accounts when interviewed again between 3 and 6 years later. These findings typify the error associated with retrospective data-recall and retrospective data-gathering techniques. Lapouse and Monk (1958) noted that reliability is low on parent interviews covering vague issues such as overactivity but high on easily defined issues such as speech impediments.

Costello, Edelbrock, and Costello (1985) reported that the reliability of parent interview data obtained from an automated interview was substantially higher than that obtained from an automated child interview. One advantage that computer-based interviews have lies in the virtual elimination of error and bias in both inquiry and response recording (Hay, Hay, Angle, & Nelson, 1979). Rohde does note (personal communication, July 9, 1991) that the computer-administered interview has the potential to control for output variance as well as input variance, thus decreasing or eliminating this source of error.

In general, the ACASH manual fails to address the majority of the issues regarding sources of errors. In fact, the manual presents a somewhat skewed perspective of the research by emphasizing studies that have demonstrated the superior reliability of structured as opposed to unstructured interviews. According to the *Standards* (2.1), a developer should provide estimates of reliabilities and standard errors of measurement in sufficient detail to allow users to determine whether an instrument is "sufficiently accurate for the intended use" (AERA et al., 1985, p. 20). No such information exists for the ACASH. In light of this, the manual should inform users of the lack of reliability data and should make clear and detailed statements regarding possible sources of error.

Critique

The ACASH is a well-constructed and useful computer-based interview. It is comprehensive and easy to use, plus the directions presented to the respondent are clear and detailed. In addition, branching logic greatly enhances the administration process. The *Guidelines for Computer-Based Tests and Interpretations* (American Psychological Association, 1986) state that a computer-based instrument should present questions and collect responses in a way which will not cause unnecessary frustration or handicap the test taker's performance. Rohde's programming eliminates unnecessary inquiry through extensive use of branching, and it facilitates performance with the clarity of displays and instructions. Further, at all times during the administration the ACASH respondent may pause to review the instructions. Unlike other automated interviews, such as the Developmental History (Rainwater & Batter Slade, 1988), the ACASH can be interrupted and the data saved until such time as the interview can proceed. This suspension of the interview is accomplished via easily learned keyboard commands, which the manual explains.

One area in which the ACASH appears significantly deficient is in allowing the respondent to change answers. The APA *Guidelines* state that computerized administration should provide test takers with the same amount of editorial control over their responses as they would experience with a traditional format. Unfortunately, due to programming limitations inherent in the branching logic format, an ACASH respondent wishing to change an answer may only back up one question. This very limited editorial capacity may prove unduly frustrating and perhaps lead to an invalid report.

The program provides good test security in that access to client data is restricted. Returning to the ACASH main menu requires system commands only available to the examiner. This maintains security and reasonably assures confidentiality in that a client could not intentionally or accidentally access other clinically sensitive material in the computer. According to the *Guidelines,* procedures to ensure confidentiality and privacy are the responsibility of the developer (APA, 1986). After an administration, some computer-based interviews, such as the Developmental History (Rainwater & Batter Slade, 1988) and the Psychological Social History Report (Rainwater & Silver Coe, 1988), automatically return to the main menu. By not allowing for this to occur, ACASH denies the respondent access to the DOS directory and other information or programs on the computer.

At the time of this writing, compared to other automated social histories the ACASH was rather expensive in terms of start-up costs and the prices of individual administrations. The MICROTEST system proves cumbersome in that it decreases the flexibility of the program; that is, the scoring box must be attached to the computer and effectively limits the use of the software to one machine. This will make the ACASH particularly inconvenient to users who have notebook, laptop, or portable computers, or who operate out of more than one location.

The ACASH does not allow for alterations in the testing sequence or for personal modifications of questions or topics as do some other automated interviews (Rainwater & Batter Slade, 1988; Rainwater & Silver Coe, 1988). Although this feature might increase the program's utility, its effect on content validity would be uncertain. Because this appears to be a trend in computer-based psychological assessments, it should be noted that the ability to customize a program for uses not originally intended carries with it the potential for significant misuse.

The APA *Guidelines* (26) state that computer-generated reports should warn against common errors of interpretation. Both the ACASH manual and the report caution against using data that conflict with the clinician's own perceptions about a client. The manual also warns that items identified in the Potentially Critical Concerns section must be verified independently by other information sources before the examiner can use them to form the basis of the "Problem Section" of a treatment plan. The report itself cautions that it is based solely on the respondent's understanding of the questions presented, and that the data should be used only in the context of a complete evaluation conducted or supervised by a qualified professional. However, despite these warnings, it cannot be said that the ACASH cautions about using the test incorrectly for certain kinds of decisions nor does it specifically warn users about the lack of established validity of the interpretations offered. In fact, suggesting specific uses for the report in school settings, for example, may encourage potential misuse of the instrument. The underlying assumption appears to be that the implied content validity can generalize and serve as evidence of the instrument's predictive validity. As stated by Anastasi (1982), one cannot use evidence for one type of validity as proof of either overall validity or other types of validity. It is in this assumption that Rohde fails to meet the goal of producing a valid instrument. Although the ACASH may be very well suited to make these differential predictions, no acceptable empirical data are offered, and for this reason alone the instrument should not be marketed in its present form.

The author's plan to develop behavioral scales for the instrument would have been a valuable addition to the ACASH, but apparently these plans have been abandoned. In keeping with the goal of producing a valid and reliable instrument, the addition of these potentially validated behavioral scales would greatly enhance the software and, more importantly, set it apart from its competitors in terms of scientific groundedness.

The ACASH approaches meeting the minimal standards necessary to release it for general use. However, of the 17 primary APA standards on which it was evaluated (Mattei, 1991), it failed to meet a full 53%. Although not every standard carries equal weight, the data suggest that the ACASH at present represents the general trend in psychology to develop and use clinical interviews as nonstandardized and subjective outlines for data gathering and assessment.

Empirical investigation regarding the use of case history interviews must assume greater importance. One factor that apparently has hampered efforts is the widespread assumption that self-report measures are inherently invalid and unreliable. Although studies have tended to support this view, some evidence does suggest that carefully designed interviews may be reliably and validly used to measure specific target behaviors (Linehan, 1977; Lucas, 1977). In addition, Haynes and Jensen (1979) have offered guidelines on how research may begin to estimate the validity of interview-derived information.

The clinical interview must be fully recognized as an assessment instrument and, as such, held up to the same standards of reliability and validity required of other assessment tools. With this in mind, psychologists should stop employing procedures that are recommended only by their availability and ease of use. In 1984 Killian, Holzman, Davis, and Gibbon proposed that psychologists had an ethical obligation to use instruments that conformed to at least the original APA standards published in 1966. The present reviewers now propose that as test users, psychologists have an ethical obligation to use instruments constructed in a sound scientific manner and conform to the current professional standards and guidelines discussed previously in this review. Given that test users and developers increasingly are being held accountable by the courts for "defective test design" and "defective validation" procedures, what was once an exclusively ethical issue now emerges as a legal one as well (Smith, 1991).

References

American Educational Research Association, American Psychological Association, & National Council on Measurement in Education. (1985). *Standards for educational and psychological testing.* Washington, DC: American Psychological Association.

American Psychiatric Association. (1980). *Diagnostic and statistical manual of mental disorders* (3rd ed.). Washington, DC: Author.

American Psychological Association. (1986). *Guidelines for computer-based tests and interpretation.* Washington, DC: Author.

Anastasi, A. (1982). *Psychological testing* (5th ed.). New York: Macmillan.

Bernstein, L., Bernstein, R.S., & Dana, R.H. (1974). *Interviewing: A guide for health professionals* (2nd ed.). New York: Appleton-Century-Crofts.

Briggs, P.F., Rouzer, D.L., Hamberg, R.L., & Holman, T.R. (1972). Seven scales for the Minnesota-Briggs History Record with reference group data. *Journal of Clinical Psychology, 28,* 431–448.

Costello, E., Edelbrock, C., & Costello, A. (1985). Validity of the NIMH Diagnostic Interview for Children: A comparison between psychiatric and pediatric referrals. *Journal of Abnormal Child Psychology, 13*(4), 579–595.

Giannetti, R.A. (1987). The GOLPH Psychosocial History: Response-contingent data acquisition and reporting. In J.N. Butcher (Ed.), *Computerized psychological assessment: A practitioner's guide* (pp. 124–144). New York: Basic Books.

Hay, W.M., Hay, L.R., Angle, H.V., & Nelson, R.O. (1979). The reliability of problem identification in the behavioral interview. *Behavioral Assessment, 1,* 107–118.

Haynes, S.N., & Jensen, B.J. (1979). The interview as a behavioral assessment instrument. *Behavioral Assessment, 1,* 97–106.

Killian, G., Holzman, P., Davis, J., & Gibbon, R. (1984). The effects of psychotropic drugs on cognitive functioning in schizophrenia and depression. *Journal of Abnormal Psychology, 93*(1), 58–70.

Korchin, S.J. (1976). *Modern clinical psychology: Principles of intervention in the clinic and the community.* New York: Basic Books.

Lapouse, R., & Monk, M.A. (1958). An epidemiologic study of behavior characteristics in children. *American Journal of Public Health, 48,* 1134–1144.

Lazarus, A.A. (1973). Multimodal behavior therapy: Treating the "BASIC ID." *Journal of Nervous and Mental Disease, 156,* 404–411.

Linehan, M. (1977). Issues in behavioral interviewing. In J.D. Cone & R.P. Hawkins (Eds.), *Behavioral assessment* (pp. 248–277). New York: Brunner/Mazel.

Lucas, R.W. (1977). A study of patients' attitudes to computer interrogation. *International Journal of Man-Machine Studies, 9,* 69–86.

Mattei, M.H. (1991). *Structured clinical interviews: A review and critique of three instruments.* Unpublished professional research project, Nova University, Ft. Lauderdale, FL.

Rainwater, G.D., & Batter Slade, B. (1988). *Developmental History* [Computer program]. Melbourne, FL: Psychometric Software.

Rainwater, G.D., & Silver Coe, D. (1988). *Psychological/Social History Report* [Computer program]. Melbourne, FL: Psychometric Software.

Rohde, M. (1988a). *Automated Child/Adolescent Social History (ACASH)* [Computer program]. Minnetonka, MN: National Computer Systems.

Rohde, M. (1988b). *A guide to the use of the Automated Child/Adolescent Social History (ACASH).* Minnetonka, MN: National Computer Systems.

Smith, S.R. (1991). Mental health malpractice in the 1990s. *Houston Law Review, 28*(1), 209–262.

Sobell, L.C., & Sobell, M.B. (1975). Outpatient alcoholics give valid self-reports. *Journal of Nervous and Mental Disease, 161,* 32–42.

Sundberg, N.D., Tyler, L.E., & Taplin, J.R. (1973). *Clinical psychology: Expanding horizons* (2nd ed.). Englewood Cliffs, NJ: Prentice-Hall.

Vaughn, C.L., & Reynolds, W.A. (1951). Reliability of personal interview data. *Journal of Applied Psychology, 35,* 61–63.

Walsh, W.B. (1967). Validity of self-report. *Journal of Counseling Psychology, 14,* 18–23.

Wenar, C., & Coulter, J.B. (1962). A reliability study of developmental histories. *Child Development, 33,* 453–462.

Yarrow, M.R., Campbell, J.D., & Burton, R.V. (1970). Recollections of childhood: A study of the retrospective method. *Monographs of the Society for Research in Child Development, 35*(5, No. 138).

Jennifer Ryan Hsu, Ph.D.

Associate Professor of Communication Disorders, William Paterson College, Wayne, New Jersey.

BANKSON LANGUAGE TEST–2

Nicholas W. Bankson. Austin, Texas: PRO-ED, Inc.

Introduction

The Bankson Language Test–2 (BLT-2), a revision of the original Bankson Language Screening Test (Bankson, 1977), is a norm-referenced instrument designed to assess three aspects of linguistic knowledge. There are two principal subtests that are intended to assess expressive language abilities related to knowledge of semantics (vocabulary) and knowledge of morphological-syntactic rules. A third, optional subtest is designed to assess aspects of pragmatic knowledge. According to Bankson (1990), the BLT-2 provides a survey of language skills that professionals may use to identify the presence of a language disorder as well as the areas of linguistic knowledge that need further, in-depth testing. The test materials also include a screening test, the BLT-2S, which consists of 20 items selected from the two principal BLT-2 subtests. The screening test is designed to identify children who need further evaluation.

The BLT-2 was developed by Nicholas W. Bankson, Professor and Chair of the Department of Communication Disorders at Boston University. Prior to coming to Boston, he served on the faculty at the University of Maryland, where he developed the Bankson Language Screening Test (BLST; 1977). Bankson's primary work has focused on the area of phonology. He coauthored with John Bernthal both a text on articulation and phonological disorders and the Bankson-Bernthal Test of Phonology (BBTOP). Bankson has conducted numerous workshops in the areas of language and phonology throughout the United States. He is a fellow of the American Speech-Language-Hearing Association and a past president of the Council of Graduate Programs in Communication Sciences and Disorders.

The development of the BLT-2 resulted from the need to update the BLST to reflect contemporary thinking regarding the nature of language (N.W. Bankson, personal communication, July 15, 1992). A goal of the revision became to develop a test that was more linguistically oriented (N.W. Bankson, personal communication, July 15, 1992). The revisions involved some substantial changes. A total of 48 items out of 153 were retained from the BLST. Two entire parts of the 1977 test were eliminated: the Visual Perception and the Auditory Perception subtests. The two principal subtests of the BLT-2, the Semantic Knowledge and Morphological-Syntactic Rules subtests, were revised to include 66 new items. Thus, 58% of the

---

The reviewer would like to thank Jodie Lewis-Guitman, for her assistance in the review of literature pertaining to this test, and Dr. Louis Hsu, for his advice concerning the technical section of this review and for his careful reading of the manuscript.

BLT-2 items are new. In revising the Semantic Knowledge subtest, Bankson reduced the total number of items from 72 on the 1977 version to 42 on the BLT-2. The Colors/Quantity section was eliminated, while the remaining seven sections of the subtest were retained from the original. A total of 30 items were selected from the original Semantic Knowledge subtest and 12 new items were added. Two sections of the revised subtest (Functions and Prepositions) include six items each from the original version; three sections (Body Parts, Categories, and Opposites) include five original items and one new item, respectively; one section (Nouns) retained three original items and added three new ones; and one section (Verbs) contains only new items.

The second principal subtest of the BLT-2 combined the Morphological Rules and Syntactic Rules subtests of the original instrument. A total of 18 items from the original sections were retained and 54 new items were added. The revisions included deleting the Sentence Repetition/Judgement section of the 1977 version and adding sections assessing regular and irregular past tense forms; modal, auxiliary, and copula forms; and questions. In addition, a new format assessed negation. Overall, the revised Morphological/Syntactic Rules subtest was expanded to include a total of 72 items. Finally, the BLT-2 added the assessment of pragmatics in a third section containing six items. The revisions reduced the percentage of semantic items from 47% in the 1977 version to 35% in the 1990 version and increased the percentage of morphological/syntactic items from approximately 30% (18% for morphology and 12% for syntax) in the 1977 version to approximately 60% in the 1990 version. Among the 72 items making up this section in the revised test, approximately 83% are morphology and 17% are syntactic. Removal of the Sentence Repetition/Judgment task eliminated the assessment of knowledge of word order in the revised instrument. The six pragmatic items represent 5% of the total number of items in the 1990 test.

There were two reasons for the removal of the word *screening* from the title. Bankson (1990) reports that users considered that the amount of information provided exceeded that usually obtained from screening instruments. Bankson (1990) also states that inclusion of the word *screening* in the title limited the use of the test as part of state-mandated assessments (p. 1).

As noted previously, the BLT-2 includes a screening test, and it differs substantially from its 1977 predecessor. The number of items has been reduced from 153 to 20. Because the items on the screening test have been selected from the BLT-2, it does not include any of the sections deleted from the 1977 test. Among the 20 items, 7 (35%) match items on the 1977 version while 4 (20%) have been modified and 9 (45%) are entirely new.

The BLT-2 was standardized on 1,108 children residing in 18 states located in the following four geographical regions of the United States: Northeast, North Central, South, and West. According to the manual (Bankson, 1990), the sample was located by selecting a nationwide group of professionals who had recently purchased the BLST and asking them to test 20 to 30 children using the new BLT-2. In addition, a nationwide group of individuals who had participated in the development of other PRO-ED tests also piloted the new test (Bankson, 1990). Finally, the manual states that teams of examiners specifically trained by the author and/or PRO-ED staff administered the test in major census districts considered represen

Table 1

Sections, Tasks, and Directions of the Semantic Knowledge Subtest

Sections	Tasks	Directions
A. Body Parts	Picture naming	To name the body part indicated
B. Nouns	Picture naming	To name the picture indicated
C. Verbs	Picture naming	To tell what the child in the picture is doing
D. Categories	Naming items in a category	To name two items from a category; e.g., "Name two _____" (category name).
E. Functions	Question/answer	To name an item in response to a question; e.g., "What do we wash with?"
F. Prepositions	Picture naming	To name the location of a clown relative to a box
G. Opposites	Naming words	Given a word, to name a word that means the opposite

tative of national demographic characteristics. Bankson (1990) reports that the distribution of the sample on five demographic variables parallels percentages reported in the 1985 volume of the *Statistical Abstract of the United States*. The demographic variables were sex (male or female), residence (urban or rural), race (white, black, or other), geographic region (Northeast, North Central, South, or West), and family income (under $7,499; $7,500–$14,999; $15,000–$49,999; or $50,000 and over). The standardization sample included 162 three-year-olds, 323 four-year-olds, 381 five-year-olds, and 242 six-year-olds (Bankson, 1990).

In the chapter discussing development, Bankson (1990) indicates that the norms for the screening test are included on the test protocol. With the exception of this comment, the manual contains no discussion of the development of the screening form. It appears that the same standardization sample was used for both the screening test and the BLT-2.

The BLT-2 materials include a manual, a picture book, a profile/examiner record booklet, and a screening protocol. The profile/examiner record booklet provides the directions for administering the test as well as space for scoring responses and summarizing results. The two principal subtests, Semantic Knowledge and Morphological-Syntactic Rules, contain 19 sections with six items per section. Subtest One, the Semantic Knowledge subtest, includes seven sections (42 items) assessing expressive vocabulary. Four of the sections involve picture-naming tasks, whereas the remaining three involve naming items in response to a category, a question, or a word. The sections and the types of tasks presented in this subtest are summarized in Table 1. The Semantic Knowledge subtest also includes the option of testing a child's receptive knowledge of any items that he or she fails to name. All sections use pictures to assess receptive knowledge. Because assessing receptive knowledge is optional, users do not score performance in this area.

Table 2

Sections, Subsections, and Tasks of the Morphological-Syntactic Rules Subtest

Section/Subsection	*Task*

H. Pronouns
  1. Subject
  2. Object
  3. Possessive
	Cloze procedure

I. Verb Usage/Verb Tense
  4. Present Progressive
  5. Third Person Singular
  6. Irregular Past Tense
  7. Regular Past Tense
	Cloze procedure

J. Verb Usage/Auxiliary-Modal-Copula	Story followed by cloze procedure or retelling
K. Plurals	Cloze procedure
L. Comparatives/Superlatives	Cloze procedure
M. Negation	Story followed by retelling
N. Questions	Sentence followed by prompt to elicit a question

Subtest Two, Morphological-Syntactic Rules, comprises seven sections assessing expressive knowledge of either grammatical categories or inflectional morphology. The sections and subsections of subtest two are summarized in Table 2. A total of 72 items assesses the child's expressive knowledge of Morphological-Syntactic Rules. Pictorial contexts are provided for all sections. With the exception of subject pronouns, the cloze procedures involve supplying a word or a word and attached ending to complete the sentence. The story tasks involve listening to several sentences and then responding to a prompt from the story with the target word. For example, to elicit use of the copula, the examiner offers a three-sentence story ("Mary is happy. Suzy is happy. They are happy to get new bicycles.") and then instructs the child to retell the story after the prompt "Mary _____." The section assessing negation, which also uses a story-retelling task, may require the child to remember two of the statements from the story. The prompts used in the Questions section (designed to elicit questions) are illustrated in the following example: "Bobby wants to know about the things in the box. What does he say?" (Answer: *What's in the box?*). The prompts themselves are questions, five involving *What* questions and a sixth involving *How.*

The forms targeted by the Pronouns section (H) are indicated by the subsection titles (Subject, Object, Possessive). All of the personal pronouns are targeted except *I* and *its*. With respect to the section I, covering verb usage and tense, it should be noted that the Present Progressive subsection targets *is* or *are* + Verb *-ing,* and the Present Tense subsection targets the third-person singular form of

Table 3

Categories and Behaviors Assessed by the Supplemental Pragmatics Subtest

Category	Behaviors
Q. Ritualizing	Greeting Telling name and address
P. Informing	Responding to questions with relevant information Asking appropriate questions
Q. Controlling	Maintaining eye contact, engaging adult in conversation
R. Imagining	Role-playing

regular verbs. Section J targets the modal *can,* the auxiliary *am,* and four forms of the copula: *is, are, was,* and *were.* Section K, Plurals, targets the regular plural forms *-s* and *-es* and two irregular forms, *men* and *children.* Section L targets the comparative and superlative forms of *big, good,* and *more.* Section M, Negation, targets the negative words *not, don't, can't, won't,* and *doesn't.* Section N, Questions, targets a yes/no question involving the copula *is* and five *Wh-* questions: *who, what, where, why,* and *when.*

The 20th section of the BLT-2, Subtest Three, is the optional assessment of Pragmatics. As indicated in Table 3, four aspects of pragmatic functioning are assessed. The section contains a total of six items, with each function represented by one or two behaviors.

As noted previously, the profile/examiner record booklet includes the directions for administering all items on the three subtests and provides space for recording both the expressive and receptive responses to each item. Raw scores for the expressive responses are summarized for each section (A–R) of the BLT-2. The cover page of the booklet provides space for recording identifying information as well as the total raw scores, percentile ranks, and standard scores for the Semantic Knowledge subtest and the Morphological-Syntactic Rules subtests. Space also appears for recording an Overall Language Quotient as well as scores from other tests. The standard scores, the language quotient, and results from other tests are plotted on a profile located on the lower left-hand section of the cover page. The lower right-hand section provides space for recording interfering and noninterfering conditions that existed during the administration.

The screening test included in the BLT-2 is entitled the Bankson Screen. The manual refers to it as the BLT-2S or the Screener. Of the Screener's 20 items, 9 were selected from the BLT-2 Vocabulary subtest, sections A, B, D, E, and G (see Table 1 for a description), and 11 items were selected from the Morphological-Syntactic Rules subtest, sections H (categories 1 and 3), I (categories 4, 5, and 6), J, M, and N (see Table 2). The BLT-2S protocol, which is printed on a single 8½" x 11" page, includes administration instructions and pictures for each item. Also included are spaces for recording responses and a table for converting raw scores to either standard scores or percentile ranks. The lower right-hand corner of the page provides space for recording these scores and for entering a classification of either "at risk" or "not at risk."

Practical Applications/Uses

The BLT-2 is intended as a norm-referenced survey of expressive abilities that can be used to identify the presence of a language disorder. Although the test assesses three aspects of language, only two, semantics and morphological-syntactic rules, function to identify children whose performance falls below that of their age peers. Bankson (personal communication, July 15, 1992) recommends that the test be used in conjunction with other measures. According to the manual, the BLT-2 also may determine some initial goals or identify areas needing further testing. All three components, the Semantics, Morphological-Syntactic Rules, and Pragmatics subtests, can apply to these purposes. The test is intended to be used when a structured format is needed in the assessment of a child (N.W. Bankson, personal communication, July 15, 1992). The inclusion of a screening test is intended to provide practitioners with an easily administered means of identifying children at risk and in need of further in-depth evaluation.

Bankson (1990) also states that the BLT-2 may be useful in research studies, such as those investigating the relationship between language and other abilities or those determining the overall effects of a particular intervention strategy. Such studies would be limited to results obtained for the Semantics and Morphological-Syntactic Rules subtests, however, because overall scores are obtained only for these two subtests. In addition, the Pragmatics subtest includes only six items. Bankson (personal communication, July 15, 1992) suggests a further application of the BLT-2 as a training tool. He reports that the experience of administering the BLT-2 helps students develop an understanding of the nature of language disorders.

Bankson designed the BLT-2 and the BLT-2S for children between the ages of 3:0 and 6:11 who are capable of following directions to name items, responding appropriately to a cloze procedure, remembering two- to three-sentence sequences as well as comprehending basic sentence structure, and answering questions such as "What does (s)he say?" The test is not appropriate for visually or hearing impaired populations. Furthermore, memory deficits are likely to interfere with performance on this test.

Qualified users of the BLT-2 would include speech-language pathologists, learning disabilities and special education teachers, and school psychologists. Bankson (1990) states that examiners should complete a minimum of three practice administrations before using the instrument. He also states that actual administration and review of the protocols should be done under the supervision of a clinician trained and experienced in the use of language assessment instruments (Bankson, 1990, p. 4). Because administration and scoring is relatively easy and quick, the BLT-2 will appeal to practitioners working in public schools. It also can be used in preschools, speech and hearing clinics, and private practice settings.

The BLT-2 is administered individually with the child seated across a table from the examiner. The test environment should be quiet and free from distractions. The instructions, presented orally, may be repeated and/or paraphrased if the child does not understand. The examiner may point or use vocal inflections and/

or intonation shifts to focus the child's attention on the required response (Bankson, 1990). Because the visual stimuli on a single page may include pictures relevant to several items, some of the pictures may need to be covered to focus the child's attention on the specific picture related to a particular item (Bankson, 1990).

The directions for administering each item of the BLT-2 appear on the profile/ examiner record booklet; general guidelines for administering the test and supplemental directions are presented in the manual. The directions for administering the test are generally clear and easy to understand. Many items include a "cue" designed to elicit the target response. Although the manual mentions that directions for the items "provide examples of how or how not to cue the expected response" (Bankson, 1990, p. 5), the instructions do not mention whether the cues are required or optional. Also, the instructions do not specify whether the test may be administered over several sessions; as the profile/examiner record booklet provides space for recording the number of sessions required to administer the BLT-2, more than one session appears to be an option. Finally, there is no indication of whether the examiner may alter the order of item presentation. Administration of the BLT-2 takes about 30 minutes.

The directions for administering the screening test appear on the test protocol. Because the items come from the BLT-2, the instructions for administration are similar. The stimulus pictures, which are the same as those used in the BLT-2, are conveniently printed on the back of the protocol. Administration time should take approximately 5 to 10 minutes.

Items on the BLT-2 are scored as they are presented by recording a "1" for correct or a "0" for incorrect in the space provided on the profile/examiner record booklet. Target responses and any alternative acceptable responses appear next to the item. The examiner counts number of correct items to yield a total raw score for the three subtests, respectively. The total raw scores for the Semantic Knowledge and Morphological-Syntactic Rules subtests are converted to percentile ranks and standard scores by referring to norms included in the manual (Bankson, 1990). The user then sums the obtained standard scores for the two subtests and converts them to an overall language quotient and an overall percentile rank using a third table provided in the manual (Bankson, 1990). Examples provided illustrate how to score responses and derive transformed scores as well as how to calculate a child's age at the time of testing from the date of birth and the date of testing. The procedures for scoring the results and deriving the transformed scores are easy to understand. Once learned, they should take no more than 5 to 10 minutes to complete.

As mentioned previously, the profile/examiner record booklet provides space for recording the results of other tests, in a section entitled "BLT-2 Equivalent Score." Although it appears that the equivalent score is a language quotient, the directions are not entirely clear. Bankson (1990) states that "when the standard score reported is of a different type from that of the BLT-2 (e.g., stanines, T-scores, etc.), the test score should be converted to a BLT-2 Language Quotient" (p. 9). A conversion formula is provided. The manual would be strengthened by including some examples of tests considered to yield standard scores similar to those of the BLT-2 as well as a discussion of how one converts such scores into a BLT-2 equivalent score. Bankson (1990) also states that "when gross values will do" (p. 10), a table in the manual may be used to convert other scores such as T-scores, Z-scores, stanines, and percentile ranks into BLT-2 quotients. The meaning of the phrase "when gross values will do" is unclear. Furthermore, it is important to note that a comparison between an obtained BLT-2 language quotient and an equivalent score on another test is meaningful only if the same standardization sample is used on both tests. That is, the mean and standard deviation for other tests must be obtained from the same standardization group as the one used on the BLT-2.

The procedures for scoring items on the screening test resemble those used for the BLT-2, but the manual does not discuss them. However, the test protocol includes the target responses, directions for scoring a "1" or a "0," and spaces for total raw score, percentile rank, standard score, and two classification categories: "at risk" and "not at risk." A table printed on the protocol indicates standard score and percentile equivalents for raw scores. Shaded areas on the table identify scores indicating possible "high risk" performance. Experienced clinicians are likely to find the procedures self-explanatory, but novices may need additional guidance in scoring results and arriving at a classification of a child's performance.

In discussing the interpretation of scores obtained from the BLT-2, Bankson (1990) notes that raw scores from different subtests are not comparable. Thus, the standard scores are used to classify a child's performance on the two principal subtests. Categories for interpreting the standard scores include Very Superior, Superior, Above Average, Average, Below Average, Poor, and Very Poor. This classification system then is used to compare a child's performance across the two subtests. The manual indicates that the user should consider marked classification differences on the two subtests (e.g., "above average" on one and "below average" on the other) a "cause for concern and [it] should lead to further evaluation" (Bankson, 1990, p.11). No discussion appears regarding the meaning of obtaining either a "poor" or "very poor" on either one or both of the subtests.

The language quotient enables the user to examine the child's overall language ability (Bankson, 1990). A language quotient derived from the test is described using the seven category names applying to the standard scores. The meaning of this quotient would become somewhat clearer if the manual discussed its derivation as well as the implications of the seven category names applied to the score.

Bankson (1990) notes that the use of age norms (i.e., age equivalent scores or language ages) has been criticized, and thus he advises against drawing on such scores. However, he does provide formulas for converting either the standard scores or language quotients obtained from the BLT-2 into a language age. Bankson (1990) states that these conversions may be used in cases where such scores might be required by state education agencies or local school districts.

Technical Aspects

Bankson (1990) reports only two types of reliability measures for the BLT-2: internal consistency coefficients and standard errors of measurement. With respect to internal consistency, 50 protocols from each yearly interval between 3:0 and 6:0 were randomly selected from the normative sample. Correlations between items were determined for the Semantic Knowledge subtest, the Morphological-Syntactic Rules subtest, and the screening test. Although correlations also are reported for the overall language quotient, it is unclear which scores were correlated with the quotient. Bankson reports that Cronbach's coefficient alpha for the four age groups between 3 and 6 years, respectively, ranged from .93 to .75 for the Semantic Knowledge subtest, .95 to .88 for the Morphological-Syntactic Rules subtest, .86 to .78 for the screening test, and .97 to .91 for the overall language quotient. In general the two principal subtests appear to show good internal consistency for ages 3 to 5 but lower levels for 6-year-olds. The lower internal consistency of the screening test is not surprising, as it combines items from both of the principal BLT-2 subtests. Although the internal consistency on the overall language quotient appears high, it is difficult to interpret the results without more information on exactly which scores were correlated.

Using the reliability coefficients from the internal consistency research, Bankson (1990) calculated standard errors of measurement (SE_m) for the four age groups between 3 and 6 on the Semantic Knowledge subtest, the Morphological-Syntactic Rules subtest, the screening test, and the overall language quotient. All SE_M's were reported to be 1 except for that obtained for the 6-year-olds on the Semantic Knowledge subtest ($SE_M = 2$). The reported SE_M's are rounded to the nearest integer. This could be misleading, as the standard deviation of the standard scores is reported to be only 3 (Bankson, 1990). For example, an SE_M of 1.49 and a standard deviation of 3 imply a reliability coefficient of .75. However, when this SE_M is rounded to 1.0, this implies a reliability coefficient of .89. Thus, the rounding provides only a very rough estimate of the BLT-2's precision of measurement.

Validity of the BLT-2 is discussed in terms of three traditional measures of validity: content, concurrent, and construct. Although Bankson (1990) defines content validity, he does not provide evidence that this type of validity has been satisfactorily attained by the BLT-2. Instead, he advises readers to reexamine the sections of the manual that discuss the construction of the test, keeping content validity in mind (Bankson, 1990, p. 18). Anastasi (1982) states that establishing content validity of a test requires systematic analysis of the behavior domain to be tested to make certain that the items cover all major aspects and in the correct proportions (p. 132). Lieberman and Michael (1986) make essentially the same point in arguing that assessment instruments should include items that 1) sample from a relevant content domain and 2) are representative of the domain. According to the *Standards for Educational and Psychological Testing* (American Educational Research Association, American Psychological Association, & National Council on Measurement in Education, 1985), expert judgments often are used to assess the relationship between parts of a test and the defined universe (p. 10).

Bankson (1990) states that the BLT-2 derives from the perspective that language reflects content (semantics), form (morphologic and syntactic rules), and use (pragmatics). Although this framework represents an accepted view of the components of language (see, e.g., Bernstein & Tiegerman, 1989; Bloom & Lahey, 1978; Lahey, 1988; and Owens, 1988), establishing whether the items of the BLT-2 adequately sample the relevant content domain and are representative of that domain requires a more detailed description of each component of language. Furthermore, the description should include those aspects of linguistic knowledge manifested by children between 3 and 6 years of age. With respect to the Semantic Knowledge subtest, the manual would be strengthened by inclusion of discussion outlining the central aspects of vocabulary that develop between 3 and 6 years of age as well as identifying the categories and specific items that would provide a representative sampling of this domain.

Inspection of Morphological-Syntactic Rules reveals that this subtest does not assess a number of forms and constructions that develop during the 3-to-6 age range. For example, the test does not assess any complex or conjoined constructions nor does it permit analysis of whether the child manifests subject-auxiliary inversion in either yes/no questions or *Wh-* questions. Use of the conjunction *and* to conjoin sentences, use of infinitival forms involving verbs such as *want, go,* and *have,* or use of subject-auxiliary inversion all constitute important developmental milestones occurring during the 3-to-6 age range (see Owens, 1988). Comparing BLT-2 items to those included in procedures for analyzing language samples or in protocols for analyzing elicited imitative responses of children in approximately the same age range reveals that the BLT-2 assesses fewer inflectional morphological and syntactic categories. Furthermore, among those categories included there is a very limited sampling of items. For example, in comparison to Lee's (1974) protocol, the BLT-2 includes only four of the eight categories (viz., personal pronouns, main verbs, negation, and questions) represented on Lee's protocol. In all of the categories assessed by the BLT-2, items are selected from only the first four of the eight developmental levels of Lee's protocol. It should be noted that although the BLT-2 elicits questions, the scoring procedures do not permit analysis of whether the child manifests subject-auxiliary inversion. Inspection of Miller's (1981), Stickler's (1987), and Tyack and Gottsleben's (1977) protocols as well as Lund and Duchan's (1988) worksheets also reveals that the BLT-2 samples fewer categories and has fewer items for those categories included. A comparison of the BLT-2 to the Carrow Elicited Language Inventory (CELI; Carrow, 1974), which is normed on children ranging from 3:0 to 6:11 years of age, reveals that among the 12 grammatical categories included on the CELI, 6 appear on the BLT-2. Comparing the number of items within categories included on both tests reveals that the BLT-2 generally has fewer items. The one exception concerns the plural morpheme *s*. Comparing the items included on the verb protocol of the CELI to items under Verb Tense and Verb Usage on the BLT-2 reveals the differences observed in comparing the BLT-2 with language sample protocols. The CELI and language sample protocols include a greater range of modals, auxiliary forms, and combinations of auxiliary elements than is assessed by the BLT-2. In addition, unlike the BLT-2, all of these tests include infinitival forms. These comparisons suggest that the second principal subtest of the BLT-2 does not have adequate content validity, both in terms of sampling from the entire relevant domain and in achieving representativeness of the domain.

The Pragmatic subtest also samples a limited range of speech act functions. The Let's Talk Inventory for Children (LTIC; Bray & Wiig, 1987), designed for children between 4 and 8, includes a 13-item Feelings category, which is not represented by any items on the BLT-2. Although BLT-2 has a Ritualizing category, it only assesses two aspects of this domain, whereas the LTIC assesses four. Similarly, the

Informing function, which both tests assess, is represented by two items on the BLT-2 and four on the LTIC. The category of Controlling is assessed by 13 items on the LTIC and only a single item on the BLT-2. The BLT-2 does have an Imagining category, which the LTIC does not include. In a summary of Tough's classification system, Chapman (1981) lists four strategies within this category manifested by children between 3 and 7. Only one, role playing, is assessed by the BLT-2. With the exception of the Imagining function, no overlap exists between children's uses of language as described by Tough (cited in Chapman, 1981) and the items included in the BLT-2. Owens (1991) summarizes taxonomies of the illocutionary functions of children's language between ages 2 and 7. Excluding items related to repeating and imitating, only 2 of the 25 items listed by Owens (1991, p. 70, Table 3.2) appear on the BLT-2. Finally, Owens (1991) indicates that expressing feelings, giving reasons, and hypothesizing are intentions that children master after 3 years of age. None of these functions are assessed by the BLT-2. These comparisons suggest that this BLT-2 subtest needs expanding to adequately sample the domain of pragmatic functions that develops between ages 3 and 6.

Concurrent validity of the BLT-2 was investigated by administering it along with the Screening Children with Early Educational Needs (SCREEN; Hresko, Reid, Hammill, Ginsburg, & Baroody, cited in Bankson, 1990) to 22 students ages 3 through 6. Correlations were obtained between the BLT-2, the BLT-2S, and the three subtests of the SCREEN. Bankson (1990) reports the following correlations: BLT-2 Semantic Knowledge subtest and SCREEN Writing, Reading, and Language subtests, .43, .63, and .68, respectively; BLT-2 Morphological-Syntactic Rules subtest and SCREEN Reading and Language subtests, .63 and .74, respectively; BLT-2 Overall Language Quotient and SCREEN Writing, Reading, and Language subtests, .45, .65, and .73, respectively; BLT-2S and SCREEN Writing, Reading, and Language subtests, .51, .61, and .63, respectively. Bankson (1990) indicates that a nonsignificant correlation was obtained between the BLT-2 Morphological-Syntactic Rules subtest and the SCREEN Writing subtest. This suggests that the above correlations were significant, as actual values are reported; however, the manual does not indicate the alpha levels nor does it explicitly state that the obtained values were significant. Because the BLT-2 is described as a diagnostic instrument, it surprises this reviewer that Bankson used a screening instrument to establish the concurrent validity of his test. It is also surprising that he obtained such low correlations between the SCREEN and the BLT-2S, the screening portion of the BLT-2. Unfortunately, no other concurrent validity statistics are reported. Furthermore, the manual reports that BLT-2 predictive validity has not been studied.

Bankson (1990) discusses several findings that he believes support the BLT-2's construct validity. The means and standard deviations for the BLT-2 subtests and the screening test are reported for the four age groups of the standardization sample. As noted by Bankson (1990), the means suggest a progressive improvement in performance as children grow older. However, no information appears concerning the significance of differences in the means for the four age groups. Bankson (1990) reports that correlations between the raw scores on the subtests and age were .54 for Semantic Knowledge, .40 for Morphological-Syntactic Knowledge, .10 for Pragmatic Knowledge, and .45 for the screening test. Although he states that all of the correlations were significant, he does not report the alpha levels. It is important to note that obtaining a significant correlation generally means that the correlation in the population is not zero; confidence intervals, which indicate ranges of population correlations consistent with the data, would have been preferable. Furthermore, a correlation of .10 for Pragmatics means that age accounts for only 1% of the variation in the test scores, and a correlation of .54 for Semantic Knowledge means that age accounts for about 25% of the variation in the test scores. Age accounts for approximately 16% of the variation in the test scores for the Morphological-Syntactic Rules subtest and the screening test. These statistics suggest that a weak relationship exists between age and performance on the subtests of the BLT-2 as well as on the screening test.

The BLT-2 was administered to 26 students across the United States who were classified by their school districts as language delayed (Bankson, 1990). The manual does not indicate how the classification was determined nor does it indicate the age of the children or the severity of the delay. The mean standard scores for the two principal subtests and the screening test as well as the Overall Language Quotient are reported by Bankson (1990) as 1 standard deviation below the respective mean scores for the tests and the quotient for the normal population (i.e., 10 for the subtests and 100 for the language quotient). According to Bankson (1990), "the differences indicate that the BLT-2 distinguishes this group" (p. 19). No statistics appear indicating whether the scores manifested by the language-delayed group differ significantly from those manifested by normal same-age peers.

Bankson (1990) also states that the construct validity of the BLT-2 is supported by the reported relationship between the test and school achievement as indicated by performance on the Screen. Because the Screen is a screening test, it is probably not a true measure of school achievement. The Overall Language Quotient of the BLT-2 also was correlated with the quotient from the Human Figures Drawing Test (Gonzales, 1986), a measure of general aptitude. Bankson (1990) reports obtaining a correlation of .56 that was significant at the .05 level.

According to Bankson (1990), the construct validity of the BLT-2 also is supported by the intercorrelations between the two principal subtests and the results of the item analyses. The intercorrelations, which ranged from .73 to .81 for the four age groups, were significant at the .001 level (Bankson, 1990). It is difficult to assess the meaning of these intercorrelations without a thorough description of the content domain and the theoretical framework underlying the test.

Critique

Both the BLT-2 and the BLT-2S are quick and easy tests to administer and score, features that will appeal to clinicians, especially those with large caseloads. Unfortunately, both tests also have serious shortcomings that will limit their usefulness.

The BLT-2 claims to be "broad based" while at the same time requiring only a small amount of time to administer (Bankson, 1990, p. 1). Thus it attempts to provide a sample of linguistic behavior that can be used for diagnostic decisions, further testing decisions, and treatment selection. However, additional reliability and validity information is needed before the test can be recommended for these purposes. With respect to reliability, both test-retest and interrater reliability evidence is needed. McCauley and Swisher (1984) identify these two types of psychometric data as important for establishing the reliability of language and articulation tests. Without this information, test users do not know to what extent test results are stable and to what extent they will fluctuate over time, nor do they know the degree to which a test taker is likely to receive similar scores if the test is administered or scored by different individuals (McCauley & Swisher, 1984). Both types of reliability information are critical for confidence in diagnostic decisions regarding the presence or absence of an impairment. In addition, information on interrater agreement is important for user confidence in decisions regarding directions for further testing and/or goal selection.

Addressing the issues related to the validity of the test will require both additional information and revision of the instrument. The *Standards for Educational and Psychological Testing* (AERA, APA, & NCME, 1985) state that "content-related evidence of validity is a central concern during test development" (p. 11). As noted previously, content validity has not been established for any of the three BLT-2 subtests. The domain for the semantic subtest needs to be defined. Once this is done, then experts can judge the extent to which the subtest includes relevant categories and an adequate sampling of items. An analysis of the categories and items of the Morphological-Syntactic Rules and the Pragmatic subtests suggests that they lack content validity in terms of both 1) inclusion of all relevant categories and 2) an adequate sampling of items from those categories. Thus, both of these subtests appear to need further revision.

McCauley and Swisher (1984) identify both predictive and concurrent validity studies as important for establishing the validity of language and articulation tests. As noted previously, no studies are reported concerning the BLT-2's predictive validity, and the only evidence for concurrent validity involves correlations with a test that appears to screen for reading, writing, and language problems. The manual does not report any studies comparing performance of 3- to 6-year-old children on the BLT-2 to their performance on well-established diagnostic instruments used for the specific purpose of identifying language-impaired children. This type of comparison would indicate the extent to which the BLT-2 successfully identifies children with such impairments. Another source of this information would be the extent to which the BLT-2 distinguishes between children known to have a language delay and those known to be normal. As noted previously, the manual reports a study of 26 language-delayed children but does not indicate the age of the children, the method used to classify them as language delayed, or the severity of the delay. As results of significance tests also are not reported, the results of the study are virtually uninterpretable.

Deficiencies in the research on concurrent validity also weaken Bankson's (1990) claims regarding the construct validity of the BLT-2. A surprising finding, noted previously, is the apparently weak relationship between age and performance on the BLT-2. The manual only addresses convergent validation, which is the relationship between performance on the test and variables expected to correlate with the test. There are no studies of discriminant validity (i.e., studies of the relationship between test performance and theoretically unrelated variables). (See Anastasi, 1982, for a discussion of the relevance of discriminant validity to construct validity.) Confidence in the results of the BLT-2 will require additional studies establishing both the criterion-related and construct validity of the test.

The manual also needs revision. As noted throughout this review, there are a number of statements that appear vague or unclear. There are also sections, such as the discussion of the interpretation of test scores, that need additional information and elaboration. Finally, there are a number of errors (e.g., use of "months" for "years" on p. 11, use of "bottom" for "right side" in describing Fig. 4.3, and a typographical error on p. 19) that should be corrected.

An important distinction exists between screening and diagnosis. According to Bailey and Wolery (1989), "screening is the process of assessing a large number of children in order to determine which children should participate in a more comprehensive evaluation" (p. 2). Diagnosis is part of a comprehensive, multidisciplinary evaluation that may lead to identifying the etiology of a developmental delay or condition or, at least, to determining whether a child is, in fact, developmentally delayed (Bailey & Wolery, 1989). Clearly screening and diagnostic instruments address very different problems. The rationale presented by Bankson for removing the word *screening* from the name of the BLT-2 (i.e., user comments on the unusual amount of information provided by the test and limited use in state-mandated assessments due to the title) does not adequately address the change in the purpose of the test nor does it discuss the relationship between revisions of the test and its new purpose.

The screening test included in the BLT-2 needs further development before it can be recommended. This development should include reliability and validity studies similar to those recommended for the BLT-2. Of particular importance would be studies on the screening measure's concurrent and predictive validity. An outcome of such studies should be information on the sensitivity and specificity of the instrument (see Bailey & Wolery, 1989; Glaros & Kline, 1988). *Sensitivity* refers to the proportion of language-impaired children correctly identified by an instrument; *specificity* addresses the proportion of normal children correctly identified.

As noted by Bailey and Wolery (1989), it is particularly important to determine the levels of sensitivity and specificity of a screening instrument, as these values have implications for the frequency and types of errors that may occur in the classification of children. Among these errors are false positives and false negatives. False positives refer to children who are identified by the screening instrument as impaired but who manifest normal performance on a follow-up comprehensive diagnostic evaluation (Bailey & Wolery, 1989). The probability of obtaining a false positive is (1 − Specificity). Because this type of error is likely to be detected on retesting, it is not considered as serious as a false negative. The latter occurs when a child who has a problem is not detected by the screening instrument (Bailey & Wolery, 1989). The probability of obtaining a false negative is (1 − Sensitivity). This is the more serious error because a child who needs a complete diagnostic evaluation and intervention will not receive those services. Unfortunately, the BLT-2 manual does not discuss either sensitivity or specificity with regard to the screening test; thus, there is no information on the rates of false negatives or false positives that are likely to occur. In addition, there is very little discussion of the development of the screening test or of the procedures for scoring and interpreting its results.

This reviewer's general conclusion regarding both the screening test and the BLT-2 is that presently these instruments could be used only to confirm results obtained from other assessment tools. However, as screening programs attempt to identify children at risk with maximum efficiency, minimum cost, and minimum errors, it is unlikely that practitioners will want to use more than one such instrument and likely one for which error rates can be determined. With respect to the BLT-2, although it should not be applied as the primary diagnostic tool, practitioners may use the results from its two principal subtests to supplement data from other instruments or to guide selection of additional tests. Practitioners should be extremely cautious in their interpretations of outcomes from the BLT-2, as the reliability and validity information for this instrument is very limited at the present time.

References

American Educational Research Association, American Psychological Association, & National Council on Measurement in Education. (1985). *Standards for educational and psychological testing*. Washington, DC: American Psychological Association.

Anastasi, A. (1982). *Psychological testing* (5th ed.). New York: Macmillan.

Bailey, D.B., & Wolery, M. (1989). *Assessing infants and preschoolers with handicaps*. Columbus, OH: Merrill.

Bankson, N.W. (1977). *Bankson Language Screening Test*. Baltimore, MD: University Park Press.

Bankson, N.W. (1990). *Bankson Language Test–2 (BLT-2)*. Austin, TX: PRO-ED.

Bernstein, D.K., & Tiegerman, E. (1985). *Language and communication disorders in children*. Columbus, OH: Merrill.

Bloom, L., & Lahey, M. (1978). *Language development and language disorders*. New York: Wiley.

Bray, C.M., & Wiig, E.H. (1987). *Let's Talk Inventory for Children*. San Antonio, TX: Psychological Corporation.

Carrow, E. (1974). *Carrow Elicited Language Inventory*. Allen, TX: DLM Teaching Resources.

Chapman, R. (1981). Exploring children's communicative intents. In J. Miller (Ed.), *Assessing language production in children: Experimental procedures* (pp. 111–138). Baltimore, MD: University Park Press.

Glaros, A.G., & Kline, R.B. (1988). Understanding the accuracy of tests with cutting scores: The sensitivity, specificity, and predictive value model. *Journal of Clinical Psychology, 44,* 1013–1023.

Gonzales, E. (1986). *Human Figures Drawing Test*. Austin, TX: PRO-ED.

Lahey, M. (1988). *Language disorders and language development*. New York: Macmillan.

Lee, L. (1974). *Developmental sentence analysis*. Evanston, IL: Northwestern University Press.

Lieberman, R.J., & Michael, A. (1986). Content relevance and content coverage in tests of grammatical ability. *Journal of Speech and Hearing Disorders, 51,* 71–81.

Lund, N.J., & Duchan, J.F. (1988). *Assessing children's language in naturalistic contexts* (2nd ed.). Englewood Cliffs, NJ: Prentice-Hall.

McCauley, R.J., & Swisher, L. (1984). Psychometric review of language and articulation tests for preschool children. *Journal of Speech and Hearing Disorders, 49,* 34–42.

Miller, J.F. (1981). *Assessing language production in children: Experimental procedures*. Baltimore, MD: University Park Press.

Owens, R.E. (1988). *Language development: An introduction*. Columbus, OH: Merrill.

Owens, R.E. (1991). *Language disorders: A functional approach to assessment and intervention*. New York: Macmillan.

Stickler, K.R. (1987). *Guide to analysis of language transcripts*. Eau Claire, WI: Thinking Publications.

Tyack, D., & Gottsleben, R. (1977). *Language sampling, analysis and training: A handbook for teachers and clinicians*. Palo Alto, CA: Consulting Psychologists Press.

Frank Auld, Ph.D.

Professor Emeritus of Psychology, University of Windsor, Windsor, Ontario, Canada.

BECK HOPELESSNESS SCALE

Aaron T. Beck. San Antonio, Texas: The Psychological Corporation.

Introduction

The Beck Hopelessness Scale (BHS; Beck, Weissman, Lester, & Trexler, 1974; Beck & Steer, 1988) is a 20-item scale for measuring negative attitudes about the future. Beck originally developed this scale in order to predict who would commit suicide and who would not. The conceptual basis for the scale derives from the writings of the social psychologist Ezra Stotland (1969).

The author of this measure, Aaron Beck, a professor of psychiatry at the University of Pennsylvania Medical School, is widely known for developing a cognitive theory of depression and for developing a psychotherapy, called *cognitive therapy of depression,* based on this theory. He has extended cognitive therapy to the treatment of anxiety disorders and other psychiatric disorders. Professor Beck is the author of another widely used test, the Beck Depression Inventory, which has become accepted as the definitive measure of clinical depression.

Beck created the first version of the BHS—which he called the Generalized Expectancy Scale—by a) taking 9 items from Heimberg's (1961) test of attitudes about the future and b) creating 11 other items expressing hopelessness. In making use of Heimberg's items, Beck revised them somewhat. In creating the 11 additional items, Beck drew from a pool of pessimistic statements made by psychiatric patients whom clinicians had judged to be hopeless.

Having put together a 20-item scale, Beck then presented these items to a small sample of depressed and nondepressed patients, asking them to give their opinions about the relevance of the items to hopelessness and about the clarity of the statements (see Minkoff, Bergman, Beck, & Beck, 1973).

After the Generalized Expectancy Scale had been used for several years to measure hopelessness in suicide attempters and in patients reporting suicidal ideas, Beck slightly changed the wording of some of the items; the revised scale was named the "Beck Hopelessness Scale."

The participants in the initial study of the reliability and factorial composition of the BHS were 294 psychiatric inpatients who had made recent suicide attempts. This sample included 125 men and 169 women. Of the total sample, 150 were white, 139 were black, and 5 belonged to other racial groups. The average age was 29.9 years. On average, the participants had finished 10.85 years of school. As to marital status, 41.5% were single, 17.3% were married, 31.6% were separated or divorced, 2.7% were widowed, and the rest were unmarried but living together or

82

of unknown status. From this sample Beck et al. (1974) gathered data used to study the internal consistency of the 20-item scale and to compute a factor analysis.

A second study reported by these authors in the same paper focused on whether scores on the BHS correlate with clinicians' ratings of hopelessness. This study made use of data from 23 outpatients "in a general medical practice" and from 62 inpatients who had made recent suicide attempts.

In a third study reported in the same paper, scores on the BHS were correlated with scores on the Stuart Future Test (Stuart, 1962; cited in Beck et al., 1974) and with participants' responses to the pessimism item of the Beck Depression Inventory. These analyses made use of data from 59 depressed patients on the psychiatric unit of the Hospital of the University of Pennsylvania.

The BHS consists of 20 true/false statements, printed on a single 8½" x 11" page. At the top of the page appear the letters "BHS"; the name of the test is not otherwise presented on this sheet. Space is provided for writing the date and the person's name, marital status, age, sex, occupation, and education. A paragraph of instructions at the top of the page (just below the identifying data) tells the participant that the test has 20 items; that he or she should read each statement, one at a time; and that he or she should mark (i.e., darken the circle for) the "T" if the statement "describes your attitude for the past week including today," otherwise mark the "F." The test papers can be scored either by machine or with the help of the transparent template provided by the publishers.

When the participant fills out the questionnaire him- or herself, the examiner should give the test paper to the examinee, then read aloud the instructions that appear at the top of the page. When the examiner wants to present the test orally, the examiner reads a somewhat amplified version of the instructions, then gives the examinee a copy of the questionnaire, saying, "Here is a copy for you so that you can follow along as I read." After reading the first statement the examiner says, "Now, is this statement true or false for you?" The examiner fills out a test paper that he or she has kept.

The BHS is intended for persons 17 years and older. Some research has been done, however, with adolescents as young as 13. The reading level required to understand the items seems to be what one could reasonably expect a grade-school graduate to have attained.

Practical Applications/Uses

A clinician who works with seriously distressed patients, especially with persons who are depressed, would welcome a test that would allow him or her to identify patients who are deeply pessimistic . . . and who might, therefore, be at greater risk of suicide. The BHS was devised to serve this purpose.

It is not likely that a counselor working with high school or college students, or a therapist working in a mental health clinic, would want to use this test routinely or with a majority of clients. The clinician, instead, would want to make use of the test with patients who have given some indication of deep discouragement and pessimism.

The setting in which the BHS is administered should be tranquil, and the lighting should be adequate for reading. The measure does not seem well suited to mass-testing situations.

Any mental health professional might make use of this scale: a psychologist, a social worker, a psychiatrist, a counselor. Although any person who has been trained by a professional to give the test could do the administration, the person interpreting the results should have the background and judgment required to decide the next step if the score is high enough to indicate severe pessimism and hopelessness. Ordinarily, this would require the involvement of a psychologist, a psychiatrist, or a psychiatric social worker.

According to the manual (Beck & Steer, 1988), giving the BHS takes between 5 and 10 minutes when the participant fills out the test paper, and usually about 10 minutes when the examiner reads the items to the examinee.

Scoring is straightforward; one simply adds up each of the items marked in the direction keyed for "hopelessness." Using the scoring template, one counts the number of blackened circles that show up under the circles on the template. That should take the scorer only 2 or 3 minutes. This scale can be scored by machine, but that hardly seems necessary, and the manual does not mention this option.

The user bases his or her interpretation on the total scale score. As the manual states,

> Although cut-off scores should be based upon the clinical decisions for which the instrument is being employed, the CCT [Center for Cognitive Therapy, University of Pennsylvania Medical School] distributes general guidelines for interpretation in which 0 to 3 is within the normal range or asymptomatic, 4 to 8 is mild, 9 to 14 is moderate, and greater than 14 is severe. (Beck & Steer, 1988, p. 5)

Technical Aspects

Normative data. The manual for the BHS presents both the item means and standard deviations and the item-total correlations for persons belonging to seven groups: suicide ideators ($N = 165$), suicide attempters ($N = 437$), alcoholics ($N = 105$), heroin addicts ($N = 211$), persons having the diagnosis "single-episode major depression" ($N = 72$), persons having "recurrent-episode major depression" ($N = 134$), and persons having "dysthymic disorder" ($N = 177$). When we look at the scale mean and standard deviation for each group, as reported in the manual, we are surprised to find that suicide ideators do not differ from suicide attempters; the ideators have a mean of 9.28 on the scale, and the attempters have a mean of 8.86, not significantly different ($t = 0.752$, with 600 degrees of freedom). We notice, too, that those patients suffering from major depression have a slightly higher score than those thinking of or attempting suicide; the mean for those with major depression is 10.28, and that for the suicidal patients is 8.98. Although this is a small difference, it is statistically significant ($t = 2.674, p < .01$). The patients diagnosed as having dysthymic disorder have a mean score of 9.03, not different from that of the suicidal patients but significantly less ($t = 2.232, p < .05$) than the mean of the patients with major depression. The addict groups have considerably lower mean scores on the scale; for the alcoholics, the mean is 4.86, and for the heroin addicts, 3.89.

The manual does not report normative data from samples of presumably normal persons or of neurotic patients who are not depressed (that is, not "dysthymic"). One can assume that such persons would get lower scores than the dysthymic patients, and, indeed, data reported elsewhere in the manual show that this is so.

Reliability. The manual reports KR-20 coefficients (measures of the scale's internal consistency) for each sample described in the preceding section; in the order that the groups were listed at the beginning of that section, the coefficients are .92, .93, .91, .82, .92, .92, and .87. According to Beck and Steer (1988), a study using college students (Durham, 1982) found a lower KR-20 coefficient, .65. Holden and Fekken (1988), however, reported "high test-retest reliabilities" in a sample of 101 female and 48 male undergraduates during a 3-week interval.

The manual states that when 21 patients with mixed diagnoses were tested at the Center for Cognitive Therapy both during an intake evaluation and 1 week later, before beginning their therapy, the correlation between their scores on the two occasions was .69. In another sample of patients from the Center for Cognitive Therapy ($N = 99$), the test-retest reliability over a 6-week span was .66. Both of these test-retest coefficients are statistically significant.

Item analyses making use of data from the seven normative samples showed that every one of the 20 items has a significant correlation with the total score on the scale, in all of the samples. The item-total correlations vary considerably from item to item. The majority of the correlations are greater than .50 (a value that would be considered good for an item correlation).

Content validity. The manual argues that, by adhering to Stotland's (1969) conception of hopelessness, the BHS provides a reasonable representation of negative attitudes concerning the person's future.

Concurrent validity. Beck et al. (1974) examined the relationship between clinical ratings of hopelessness and BHS scores in two samples: a) 23 outpatients in a general medical practice and b) 62 hospitalized patients who had recently attempted suicide. In the general practice sample, the r between the BHS and the ratings of hopelessness was .74; in the suicide-attempt sample, it was .62.

In the seven samples used for the normative study, the correlation between scores on the Beck Depression Inventory and scores on the BHS was computed within each sample, as well as the correlation between the Beck Depression Inventory Pessimism item and scores on the BHS. Correlations between the Depression Inventory and the BHS ranged from .46 to .76 (median of .64), and between the pessimism item and the BHS from .42 to .66 (median of .64). Because hopelessness and depression should be related, it is appropriate that the Hopelessness Scale correlates moderately with the Beck Depression Inventory. The correlation, however, should not be too strong; otherwise, there would be no distinction between "hopelessness" and "depression."

Block (1991) gave a sample of 152 adult psychiatric patients the BHS and the following other tests: the Beck Depression Inventory, the State-Trait Anxiety Inventory, the Self-Report Inventory (O'Brien, 1980), the Self-Rating Depression Scale (Zung, 1965), and three MMPI scales. Block concluded that the relationships among these measures confirm I.H. Gotlib's suggestion that such questionnaires measure general distress, because higher scores express an endorsement of negative affect. Block's research therefore calls into question whether the BHS measures something distinctive.

Discriminant validity. Although the BHS was not designed to discriminate patients with different psychiatric diagnoses, the manual reports some evidence that persons in different diagnostic groups differ in their scores on the measure. Beck, Riskind, Brown, and Steer (1988) found that 199 patients with major depressive disorder had higher mean BHS scores than 48 patients with generalized anxiety disorder or 76 psychiatric patients with mixed nonaffective, nonanxiety diagnoses.

Beck, Steer, Sanderson, and Skeie (1991) reported that the mean BHS scores of 151 patients with panic disorders and 264 patients with other, nondepressive psychiatric disorders were significantly lower those of 485 patients with mood disorders.

Durham (1982) found that the mean BHS score for 99 forensic psychiatric patients was 6.62, for 118 general psychiatric patients was 6.04, and for 197 college students was 2.32. Greene (1981) found a mean score of 4.45 among 396 "randomly selected" Irish adults. Topol and Reznikoff (1982) found that 30 hospitalized, adolescent suicide attempters got higher BHS scores than 35 adolescent psychiatric patients or 35 suburban high school, 13- to 19-year-old students.

From these studies and others like them it appears that depressed and suicidal patients obtain higher BHS scores than other psychiatric patients, and much higher scores than persons who are not psychiatric patients.

Construct validity. To demonstrate that hopelessness adds something to the prediction of suicide intent over and above that which can be made by how depressed the patient is, Minkoff et al. (1973) computed the correlation between the Generalized Expectancy Scale (an earlier version of the BHS) and suicidal intent, with depression (as measured by the Beck Depression Inventory) partialled out; the correlation was .47. The relationship between the depression score and intent, with hopelessness partialled out, was less: .26.

Kovacs, Beck, and Weissman (1975) found that when hopelessness was adjusted for statistically, depression did not relate significantly to suicidal intent in a sample of hospitalized depressed patients ($r = .06$). When, however, the researchers adjusted for depression, hopelessness scores still correlated with suicidal intent ($r = .24$). Wetzel (1976), using the Zung Depression Inventory (Zung, 1965) as the measure of depression, obtained similar findings in a study of 48 suicide attempters, 56 suicide ideators, and 50 psychiatric controls. Dyer and Kreitman (1984) made similar findings in a study of 120 self-poisoners.

Rudd (1990) reported, however, that "contrary to previous findings, depression was a better predictor of suicidal ideation than hopelessness" (p. 16). Rudd's subjects were 737 university students.

If the BHS measures hopelessness, and if psychotherapy is expected to diminish a person's feelings of hopelessness, then the BHS scores should decrease after therapy. Both Blackburn and Bishop (1983) and Rush, Beck, Kovacs, Weissenberger, and Hollon (1982) reported that cognitive therapy aimed at reducing hopelessness did result in lower BHS scores.

Predictive validity. Beck, Steer, Kovacs, and Garrison (1985) reported a 5-year follow-up of 197 patients who had thought about killing themselves but had not recently tried to do so (they had *suicidal ideation*). Of the 197 patients studied, 14 had committed suicide, 34 had died from other causes. However, only 165 of these patients had taken the BHS (the scale had not been given to the first 42 patients in the study); thus the effective size of the sample was 165. Of these 165 patients, 11 had suicided. Ten of the 11 who killed themselves had scores of 9 or more on the BHS. There were also 76 patients with scores of 9 or more who did not kill themselves. Thus the scale identified 10 out of 11 of the eventual suicides, but at the cost of misidentifying about half (76 out of 154, or 49%) of those who did not kill themselves.

Another study, by Beck, Brown, Berchick, Stewart, and Steer (1990), produced similar findings. These authors gave the BHS to 1,958 outpatients at the Center for Cognitive Therapy between 1978 and 1984. Of the 17 who eventually committed suicide, 16 had obtained BHS scores of 9 or higher. Of the 1,941 patients who did not commit suicide, more than half had BHS scores of 9 or higher.

Brittlebank et al. (1990), studying 58 patients who presented at a hospital after an episode of deliberate self-harm, found that the patients who had an additional episode of deliberate self-harm showed significantly higher levels of helplessness and of intropunitive hostility after the index episode than did patients who did not repeat.

Factorial validity. It is of interest to know whether the items in the BHS are expressing a single factor; that is, are they homogeneous. Beck et al. (1974) reported a factor analysis, done by principal axes factoring, of the BHS items, making use of data from 294 suicide attempters. Their first factor was quite strong; a second and a third were quite weak. They described the first factor as "affective," the second as "motivational," and the third as "cognitive." Because the strong internal-consistency indices show that the BHS is quite homogeneous, factoring the items is probably beside the point.

More important is locating the BHS within the factor space of other measures. Block's (1991) study did this, using the Beck Depression Inventory, the State-Trait Anxiety Inventory, the Self-Rating Depression Scale, the Self-Report Inventory, and three MMPI scales. The sample comprised 152 adult psychiatric inpatients. Block's factor analysis, he said, "appeared to confirm I.H. Gotlib's suggestion that such questionnaires measure general distress, as responding endorses negative affect" (1991, p. 1055).

Range and Antonelli (1990), using 308 undergraduates as their subjects, made use of six commonly used inventories: the BHS, the Self-Rating Depression Scale, the Scale for Suicide Ideation (Beck, Kovacs, & Weissman, 1979), the Reasons for Living Inventory (Linehan, Goodstein, Nielsen, & Chiles, 1983), the Suicide Probability Scale (Linehan & Nielsen, 1981), and the Suicide Ideation Questionnaire (Beck et al., 1979). Principal axes factoring yielded four factors, labeled "suicidal/negative ideas," "reasons for living," "self-doubt," and "suicide desire." Only the Survival and Coping Beliefs subscale of the Reasons for Living Inventory and the Suicide Ideation Questionnaire loaded on two factors. The authors concluded that each instrument accounts for unique variance in suicidality. Apparently the BHS measures what a number of other scales do, depressive and despairing thoughts.

Contaminating response sets. Beck took care to avoid an acquiescence response set by balancing items between those keyed "true" and those keyed "false." He did not, however, take account of the social desirability response set in the course of constructing the BHS; accordingly, some critics have contended that responses to the BHS are strongly influenced by the strength of the examinee's tendency to present him- or herself as socially desirable.

Fogg and Gayton (1976) found that subjects' scores on the Edwards Social Desirability Scale (Edwards, 1957) were strongly, and negatively, correlated with scores on the BHS ($r = -.64$). Linehan and Nielsen (1981), studying 196 shoppers at a mall, found a correlation of $-.67$ between the BHS and the Edwards scale. Petrie and Chamberlain (1983), whose measure of social desirability was the Crowne-Marlowe Scale (Crowne & Marlowe, 1960), found a much smaller correlation, $-.30$. Mendonca, Holden, Mazmanian, and Dolan (1983), using the Desirability scale from Jackson's Personality Research Form in a study of 78 subjects, found a correlation of $-.71$.

Using partial correlational techniques to find out whether the BHS relates to suicidal ideation after the effects of social desirability have been taken into account, Cole (1988) found that if the Crowne-Marlowe Scale was used to partial out desirability, the BHS was still related to suicidal ideation.

Ivanoff and Jang (1991), using a stratified random sample of state prison inmates ($N = 126$), found that the BHS and suicidal behavior remained significantly correlated even after social desirability (measured by Edwards's scale) had been partialled out. The partial correlation between the BHS and the Scale for Suicidal Ideation was .55; that between the BHS and a measure called "possible suicidal behavior" was .47.

Critique

On the face of it, the Beck Hopelessness Scale seems to measure pessimism about the future, as its author intended. The questions focus on this topic, and scores on the scale correlate with clinicians' ratings of hopelessness.

The strong internal consistency coefficients show that if a person answers one of the 20 questions pessimistically, he or she likely will give pessimistic answers to the other questions as well. There is also fair stability of the scores on this scale over at least a 6-week period.

The most vexing question about the BHS is this: Does it measure something much different from depression-in-general? We know that scores on the BHS correlate moderately with scores on the Beck Depression Inventory. We know that factor analyses show that various measures of depression and of a feeling that one is not doing well in one's life load on the same factor as the BHS.

Then, as we turn to the practical use of the test, we must ask whether the BHS will help us to predict who will commit suicide and who will not. The superb study by Beck et al. (1985) did indeed show that almost all of those who killed themselves—above 90% of them—had obtained high scores (above 9) on the BHS. But so had half of those patients who did not (in the ensuing 5 years) kill themselves.

If, therefore, one wished to cast a wide net for those who might commit suicide, one could use the BHS in conjunction with measures of suicidal ideation and intent. The data make it clear, however, that the sieve is too fine; it catches too many persons who do not kill themselves.

References

Beck, A.T., Brown, G., Berchick, R.J., Stewart, B.L., & Steer, R.A. (1990). Relationship between hopelessness and ultimate suicide: A replication with psychiatric outpatients. *American Journal of Psychiatry, 147,* 190–195.

Beck, A.T., Kovacs, M., & Weissman, A. (1979). Assessment of suicidal intention: The Scale for Suicide Ideation. *Journal of Consulting and Clinical Psychology, 47,* 343–352.

Beck, A.T., Riskind, J.H., Brown, G., & Steer, R.A. (1988). Levels of hopelessness in DSM-III disorders: A partial test of content specificity in depression. *Cognitive Therapy and Research, 12,* 459–469.

Beck, A.T., & Steer, R.A. (1988). *Beck Hopelessness Scale* (manual). San Antonio, TX: Psychological Corporation.

Beck, A.T., Steer, R.A., Kovacs, M., & Garrison, B. (1985). Hopelessness and eventual suicide: A 10-year prospective study of patients hospitalized with suicidal ideation. *American Journal of Psychiatry, 142,* 559–563.

Beck, A.T., Steer, R.A., Sanderson, W.C., & Skeie, T.M. (1991). Panic disorder and suicidal ideation and behavior: Discrepant findings in psychiatric patients. *American Journal of Psychiatry, 148,* 1195–1199.

Beck, A.T., Weissman, A., Lester, D., & Trexler, L. (1974). The measurement of pessimism: The Hopelessness Scale. *Journal of Consulting and Clinical Psychology, 42,* 861–865.

Blackburn, I.M., & Bishop, S. (1983). Changes in cognition with pharmacotherapy and cognitive therapy. *British Journal of Psychiatry, 143,* 609–617.

Block, P. (1991). Measurement and interrelations of psychiatric symptomatology in inpatients. *Psychological Reports, 68,* 1055–1056.

Brittlebank, A.D., Cole, A., Hassanyeh, F., Kenny, M., Simpson, D., & Scott, J. (1990). Hostility, hopelessness and deliberate self-harm: A prospective follow-up study. *Acta Psychiatrica Scandinavica, 81,* 280–283.

Cole, D.A. (1988). Hopelessness, social desirability, depression, and parasuicide in two college student samples. *Journal of Consulting and Clinical Psychology, 56,* 131–136.

Crowne, D.P., & Marlowe, D. (1960). A new scale of social desirability independent of psychopathology. *Journal of Consulting Psychology, 24,* 349–354.

Durham, T.W. (1982). Norms, reliability, and item analysis of the Hopelessness Scale in general psychiatric, forensic psychiatric, and college populations. *Journal of Clinical Psychology, 38,* 497–600.

Dyer, J.A.T., & Kreitman, N. (1984). Hopelessness, depression, and suicidal intent in parasuicide. *British Journal of Psychiatry, 144,* 137–143.

Edwards, A.L. (1957). *The social desirability variable in personality assessment and research.* New York: Holt, Rinehart & Winston.

Fogg, M.E., & Gayton, W.F. (1976). Social desirability and the Hopelessness Scale. *Perceptual and Motor Skills, 43,* 482.

Greene, S.M. (1981). Levels of measured hopelessness in the general population. *British Journal of Clinical Psychology, 20,* 11–14.

Heimberg, L. (1961). *Development and construct validation of an inventory for the measurement of future time perspective.* Unpublished master's thesis, Vanderbilt University, Nashville, TN.

Holden, R.R., & Fekken, G.C. (1988). Test-retest reliability of the Hopelessness Scale and its items in a university population. *Journal of Clinical Psychology, 44,* 40–43.

Ivanoff, A., & Jang, S.J. (1991). The role of hopelessness and social desirability in predicting suicidal behavior: A study of prison inmates. *Journal of Consulting and Clinical Psychology, 59,* 394–399.

Kovacs, M., Beck, A.T., & Weissman, M.A. (1975). Hopelessness: An indicator of suicidal risk. *Suicide, 5,* 98–103.

Linehan, M.M., Goodstein, J.L., Nielsen, S.L., & Chiles, J.A. (1983). Reasons for staying alive when you are thinking of killing yourself: The Reasons for Living Inventory. *Journal of Consulting and Clinical Psychology, 51,* 276–286.

Linehan, M.M., & Nielsen, S.L. (1981). Assessment of suicide ideation and parasuicide: Hopelessness and social desirability. *Journal of Consulting and Clinical Psychology, 49,* 773–775.

Mendonca, J.D., Holden, R.R., Mazmanian, D., & Dolan, J. (1983). The influence of response style on the Beck Hopelessness Scale. *Canadian Journal of Behavioural Science, 15,* 237–247.

Minkoff, K., Bergman, E., Beck, A.T., & Beck, R. (1973). Hopelessness, depression, and attempted suicide. *American Journal of Psychiatry, 130,* 455–459.

O'Brien, E.J. (1980). *The Self-Report Inventory: Development and validation of a multidimensional measure of the self-concept and sources of self-esteem.* Unpublished manuscript, University of Massachusetts, Amherst.

Petrie, K., & Chamberlain, K. (1983). Hopelessness and social desirability as moderator variables in predicting suicidal behavior. *Journal of Consulting and Clinical Psychology, 51,* 485–487.

Range, L.M., & Antonelli, K.B. (1990). A factor analysis of six commonly used instruments associated with suicide using college students. *Journal of Personality Assessment, 55,* 804–811.

Rudd, M.D. (1990). An integrative model of suicidal ideation. *Suicide and Life-Threatening Behavior, 20,* 16–30.

Rush, A.J., Beck, A.T., Kovacs, J., Weissenberger, J., & Hollon, S.D. (1982). Comparison of the effects of cognitive therapy and pharmacotherapy on hopelessness and self-concept. *American Journal of Psychiatry, 130,* 862–866.

Stotland, E. (1969). *The psychology of hope.* San Francisco: Jossey-Bass.

Stuart, J.L. (1962). *Intercorrelations of depressive tendencies, time perspective, and cognitive style variables.* Unpublished doctoral dissertation, Vanderbilt University, Nashville, TN.

Topol, P., & Reznikoff, M. (1982). Perceived peer and family relationships, hopelessness and locus of control as factors in adolescent suicide attempts. *Suicide and Life-Threatening Behavior, 12,* 141–150.

Wetzel, R.D. (1976). Hopelessness, depression, and suicide intent. *Archives of General Psychiatry, 33,* 1069–1073.

Zung, W.W.K. (1965). A self-rating depression scale. *Archives of General Psychiatry, 12,* 63–70.

Randolph H. Whitworth, Ph.D.
Professor of Psychology, The University of Texas, El Paso, Texas.

BOSTON DIAGNOSTIC APHASIA EXAMINATION, SECOND EDITION

Edith Kaplan and Harold Goodglass. Malvern, Pennsylvania: Lea and Febiger.

Introduction

The Boston Diagnostic Aphasia Examination, Second Edition (including the Boston Naming Test) is the most comprehensive, thorough, and frequently administered of all instruments employed to evaluate aphasia, the organic impairment of language functions. The BDAE is not a single test but a complete battery that includes 29 subtests measuring eight different categories of language functioning. Also included are nine ratings of speech fluency and paraphasias (production of unintended syllables, words, or phrases), resulting in a total of 38 subtest scores (Goodglass & Kaplan, 1983). The Boston Naming Test, although actually published as a separate aphasia test, is included in the manual as a subtest of the complete BDAE (Kaplan, Goodglass, & Weintraub, 1983).

According to the authors, the BDAE is designed to accomplish three general goals: 1) diagnosing the presence and type of aphasic dysfunction, which in turn allows inferences about the cerebral localization of the lesion; 2) measuring the level of performance over a wide range, both to determine the initial level of aphasia as well as to allow evaluation of any change over time; and 3) comprehensively assessing the patient's assets and liabilities in all areas of language function as a guide to therapy and rehabilitation. In order to present a test battery capable of meeting all three goals, the BDAE provides comprehensive measures of the following general categories of language function: language comprehension, naming, oral reading, repetition, automatic speech, reading comprehension, music, and writing. In addition, the first 10 minutes of the BDAE evaluates spontaneous speech. This assessment consists of conversation (usually tape recorded) between the subject and examiner that involves the usual social interactions as well as asking the subject to describe the situation presented in an action picture card. Spontaneous speech is evaluated in terms of such elements as intonation, articulation, phrase length, grammar, informational content, and paraphasias. Scoring of the BDAE is objective and based on normative data of both aphasic patients and normals.

Harold Goodglass (Ph.D., 1951, University of Cincinnati) and Edith Kaplan (Ph.D., 1968, Clark University) have been associated with the Boston Veterans Administration Hospital and the Boston Aphasia Research Center, Boston University School of Medicine, for many years. In their book, *Assessment of Aphasia and Other Disorders* (which includes the BDAE manual and norms), they state that although language disturbance has been observed and described medically for centuries, including the classic works on aphasia by Broca and Wernicke that now bear their names, modern studies of aphasia began with the end of World War II. The war produced large numbers of brain-injured, speech-disabled veterans who required treatment and rehabilitation. In response to these circumstances, a number of manuals on aphasia and aphasia test procedures appeared, including Eisenson's *Examining for Aphasia* (1954), Wepman and Jones's Language Modalities Test for Aphasia (1961), and the Illinois Test of Psycholinguistic Abilities (McCarthy & Kirk, 1966). None of these (nor any other aphasia tests available), however, were viewed by Goodglass and Kaplan as adequate to their needs involving research and treatment of aphasia. The goal in their development of the BDAE was to develop diagnostic and evaluative procedures for aphasia that would provide more insight into the patient's neurological functioning by relating aphasia test scores to aphasic syndromes and, in turn, relate these to neuroanatomical locations. Using a multidisciplinary approach incorporating knowledge and research from neurology, neurosurgery, psychology, speech pathology, and speech therapy, they developed the BDAE, first published in 1972 and revised in 1983.

The original (1972) version of the BDAE derived from data on 207 Boston VA Hospital patients who suffered from various types and severities of aphasia. Each patient was administered the full BDAE, and data were evaluated for type of aphasia, presumed location of brain lesion, and severity of aphasic symptoms. The original normative tables, which consisted of the range, mean, standard deviation, and severity levels for each of the BDAE subtests, came from these data.

In the 11 years after the publication of the original BDAE, a significant increase occurred in knowledge about aphasia, especially as a result of technical advances such as the computerized tomography (CT) scan. In order to account for this increase in knowledge as well as to respond to some criticisms of the original BDAE procedures, the authors revised the BDAE and the second edition appeared in 1983.

The revised BDAE resulted in only very minor changes in either test content or procedure, limited to such minor revisions as a change in ordering of item difficulty. The revision, however, did incorporate a new standardization sample of 242 aphasic patients tested in the Boston VA Center between 1976 and 1982. Normative tables for both the 1972 and the new standardization group appear in the revised BDAE manual. In addition, the revised BDAE presents data on normal controls, which consisted of 147 neurologically normal males, ranging in age from 25 to 85 years.

Because of the length of the BDAE, a number of researchers have attempted to develop shorter versions. The Western Aphasia Battery (Kertesz & Poole, 1974) offers an example of such a shortened battery. It grew out of efforts to develop an instrument using subtests of the BDAE that would generate diagnostic classifications and be suitable for both treatment and research. Using many items taken from the BDAE, the Western Aphasia Battery consists of four oral language subtests that produce five scores based on a rating scale or standardized scores. Test results can provide a measure of the degree of aphasia as well as some indication of the diagnostic subtype, although the accuracy of the latter is limited by the amount of information available due to the brevity of the test.

The original (1972) version of the BDAE was translated into Spanish (Evaluación del Afasia y de Trastornos Similares) by J.B. de Quiros and has been employed extensively in Mexico as well as Central and South America, especially in the diagnosis and treatment of stroke and the dementias. No Spanish language translation of the second edition of the BDAE was available at the time of this writing, however.

The BDAE materials consist of *Assessment of Aphasia and Related Disorders* (2nd ed.) by Goodglass and Kaplan (a 134-page book that includes the BDAE manual), the 32-page Boston Diagnostic Aphasia Examination scoring booklet, 16 test stimulus cards, the 64-page Boston Naming Test, and the 8-page Boston Naming Test scoring booklet. In addition, the user should have a tape recorder available to record the spontaneous speech segment of the test.

Before discussing the individual subtests of the battery in more detail, a brief description of the classification of the aphasic syndromes employed in the BDAE and their behavioral characteristics may prove helpful. The aphasias are acquired disturbances of language that result from insult (vascular damage, trauma, disease, or tumor) to specific regions of the brain, almost invariably the cerebral cortex (Mayeaux & Kandel, 1985). *Fluent/nonfluent* is the major subdivision among the aphasias, based both on the character of the speech output and the location of the brain dysfunction. Nonfluent aphasia refers to language disturbance resulting from damage to the anterior portion of the brain (anterior to the central fissure of Rolando) and is characterized by slow, interrupted, awkwardly articulated speech produced with great effort. Fluent aphasia arises from damage in the posterior portion of the cortex and results in facility in articulation and grammatical construction but difficulty in language comprehension and word finding, plus the production of language with "empty" content.

Of the nonfluent aphasias, *Broca's aphasia* (also called *verbal, expressive,* or *motor aphasia*) is the most common. This disorder results in awkward articulation (even mutism, in severe cases), restricted vocabulary and grammar, but relatively preserved auditory comprehension. It arises from damage to the third frontal convolution of the left hemisphere, also known as the motor and speech association area or, more often, simply Broca's area.

Wernicke's aphasia (also known as *receptive, acoustic,* or *sensory aphasia*) is the most frequently observed of the fluent aphasias. It is characterized by impairment in auditory comprehension but fluently articulated speech, which is often paraphasic or empty in content. The disorder results from damage to the posterior portion of the first gyrus of the left temporal lobe (Wernicke's area).

Anomia (also called *nominal, semantic,* or *amnesic aphasia*) is another fluent aphasia and similar to Wernicke's aphasia. It is characterized by prominent word-finding difficulty in the context of fluent, grammatically well-formed speech, but without the difficulty in auditory comprehension or the production of paraphasias seen in Wernicke's aphasia. Anomia often results from damage to the conjunction of the left temporal and parietal lobes.

Conduction aphasia results from damage to the *arcuate fasciculus,* which connects Broca's and Wernicke's areas. This disorder produces a profound inability to repeat, name, and spell, but verbal fluency remains relatively intact, comprehension is good, and reading aloud and writing also may be impaired.

Global aphasia (also called *total aphasia*) results in impairment to all aspects of language function. Comprehension, naming, and repetition are all poor, and there is a virtual absence of speech. Global aphasia is almost always the result of a large lesion affecting both the anterior and posterior portions of the left hemisphere.

Other aphasic syndromes, while of technical and research interest, occur infrequently and will not be described here.

The BDAE is an individually administered test battery, which, as noted previously, consists of 38 subtests subsumed under eight areas of language functioning. As such, it requires a substantial amount of time to administer, ranging from 1 to 4 hours, depending on the patient's level of functioning. Because it is individually administered and covers such a wide range of language functions, it also requires considerable training on the part of the examiner.

During the first 10 minutes of the BDAE (the evaluation of spontaneous speech), the examiner engages the patient in social conversation, asks questions, and has the patient describe an action picture card, all of which generally is tape recorded for later evaluation. Spontaneous speech then is evaluated for melodic line (intonation), phrase length, articulation, grammatical form, paraphasias, and informational content. Based on this analysis of spontaneous speech, an aphasic severity rating is determined, ranging from 1 (most severe) through 7 (no evidence of aphasia).

Auditory comprehension is the first major category of language function evaluated with the BDAE, and it consists of four subtests. The first subtest, Word Discrimination, requires the patient to point to pictures on a stimulus card in response to words spoken by the examiner. In the second subtest, Body-Part Identification, the patient is asked to point to various parts of his or her body (including left-right discriminations) as requested by the examiner. In the Commands subtest the patient must follow an increasingly complex set of commands, ranging from "make a fist" to "tap each shoulder twice with two fingers while keeping your eyes shut." The fourth and final subtest of this category is Complex Ideational Material, which requires the patient to answer "yes" or "no" to simple questions or to those about paragraphs read aloud by the examiner.

The second major language area assessed by the BDAE is Naming, and it, too, consists of four subtests. Responsive Naming requires the patient to find the correct word in response to a simple question such as "What do we tell time with?" Visual Confrontational Naming requires him or her to provide a name for pictures of various objects. Animal Naming is a test of word generation and requires the subject to name as many different kinds of animals as possible in 90 seconds. The Boston Naming Test is the fourth subtest in this category. This measure requires the person to name drawings of 60 objects, presented in order of increasing difficulty, from a picture of a bed to that of an abacus. If the subject cannot name the picture, the examiner gives a stimulus cue describing it (e.g., for the picture of the toothbrush, the cue is "used in the mouth"). A phonemic cue also may be given when the subject fails to respond, consisting of the first phoneme in the word (e.g., "too" for *toothbrush* in the above example). It might be noted here that the Boston Naming Test very frequently has been used alone or in conjunction with BDAE's spontaneous speech evaluation to diagnose aphasia.

The Oral Reading category consists of only two subtests, Word Reading and Sentence Reading. The patient is asked to read words and sentences of various lengths and difficulties, such as *chair* or *dripping* and "You know how" or "The lawyer's closing argument convinced them."

The Repetition category consists of three subtests. The first, Word Repetition, requires the patient to repeat words spoken by the examiner, from simple (*brown*) to difficult (*Methodist Episcopal*). The other two subtests are High and Low Probability Sentences, wherein the examinee must repeat high probability sentences such as "I got home from work" and low probability ones like "The phantom soared across the foggy heath." In addition to scoring the items as either correct or incorrect, the examiner also rates them for paraphasia.

The Automatic Speech category consists of two subtests. The first, Automatized Sequences, requires the patient to count from 1 to 21, recite the months of the year, and so forth. The second subtest, Reciting, involves reading the patient the first few words to a nursery rhyme (e.g., "Jack and Jill . . .") and then asking him or her to complete it.

The next category, Reading Comprehension, consists of five subtests. The first, Symbol Discrimination, asks the examinee to match letters or words written in different styles. Word Recognition requires that the patient pick the correct printed word from a series of four similar printed words. In the Comprehension of Oral Spelling subtest, the subject must correctly identify a word spelled orally by the examiner (e.g., *on* or the more difficult *whiskey*). Word-Picture Matching requires the person to read a written word and then point to a matching picture. In the last subtest, Reading Sentences and Paragraphs, the patient is asked to read sentences and paragraphs of varying length and complexity and then answer questions about them.

The seventh major category, Music, involves asking the patient to sing a familiar song (e.g., "America") and then rating the performance for melodic line. The Rhythm subtest requires that the person repeat simple rhythms tapped out on the table by the examiner.

The eighth and final category, Writing, consists of seven subtests. The first, Mechanics of Writing, has the subject write his or her name and address (which is provided by the examiner if the examinee cannot recall them). In the next two subtests, Serial Writing and Primer-Level Dictation, the patient must try to write the letters of the alphabet, numbers 1–21, and dictated primer words such as *go* and *baby*. Spelling to Dictation requires that he or she spell more difficult words (e.g., *fight, conscience*) to dictation. Written Confrontational Naming asks the patient to write the names of pictures presented. In Sentences Written to Dictation, the person must write a sentence dictated by the examiner, such as "She can't seen them." For the final subtest, Narrative Writing, the subject is presented with the same action picture stimulus employed in the spontaneous speech evaluation and asked to write as much about it as possible in approximately 2 minutes.

For those who desire an even more complete neuropsychological and neurolinguistic assessment, the authors also list a group of supplementary language and nonlanguage tests (Goodglass & Kaplan, 1983). While these supplements are of interest and value, a description and critique of them would exceed the scope of this review.

Practical Applications/Uses

The Boston Diagnostic Aphasia Examination is essentially a neuropsychological test battery that is confined to the evaluation of language dysfunction. Thus, as with any neuropsychological procedure, it is designed to assess and measure the relationship between brain function and behavior—specifically language behavior in this case. Any thorough neuropsychological evaluation, such as the Halstead-Reitan battery (Reitan, 1969), includes some assessment of aphasia, although most are limited to relatively circumscribed screening tests. The BDAE, however, is designed to measure all areas of language functioning (and dysfunction) in as thorough, comprehensive, and objective manner as possible, in order to determine whether any impairment of language exists and, if so, what type of aphasic disturbance it represents. As with any comprehensive neuropsychological battery, this one attempts to assess not only what functions are impaired but also to evaluate those that are intact or less severely damaged. Based on the type and severity of language impairment found in the examination, the examiner can determine the area of the cerebral cortex likely to have been involved. Finally, based on the test results and interpretation, the user can offer a prognosis for recovery as well as procedures for treatment and rehabilitation.

The design of the BDAE is based on the authors' observations that various components of language may be *selectively* impaired a result of organic brain damage and that this selectivity is a clue to the anatomical organization of language in the brain. This, in turn, leads to a localization of the causative damage (lesion) as well as to an understanding of the functional interactions of the various parts of the language system. Such a diagnostic aim is met by sampling *all* the variables in language functioning that have proven useful in identifying aphasia. The latter approach leads to a very thorough and comprehensive set of subtests and resultant information but also to a test battery that requires a significant amount of time to administer and a high level of professional expertise for both administration and interpretation.

The BDAE was developed in response to a need for a comprehensive aphasia battery in a VA hospital. Initially the majority of those VA patients evaluated had head injuries sustained during the Second World War. Since then, although head trauma patients from the Korean and Vietnam conflicts also have been evaluated, there has been an increase in the evaluation of VA patients with stroke and, as they age, dementia. Although the BDAE initially was developed for use in a VA hospital, it rapidly achieved wide acceptance in the field of neurology and neuropsychology and now is generally considered the most comprehensive and single best aphasia examination available. In addition to its use by neuropychologists and neurologists, the battery is employed by speech pathologists, speech therapists, and vocational and occupational therapists.

Although the number of patients with penetrating head wounds evaluated initially has declined, the incidence of head injuries resulting from other traumas, such as vehicle and industrial accidents, has increased, and the BDAE often is employed in the diagnosis and treatment of these persons. Patients with brain injury as a result of stroke, especially in the left cerebral hemisphere, almost always exhibit some aphasic symptoms, and the BDAE has been use extensively with this group. As the lifespan increases, so does the number of persons with dementia, especially senile dementia of the Alzheimer's type (SDAT or Alzheimer's disease), which is now the most rapidly growing disease in our population. Alzheimer's disease results in cognitive deterioration generally, but it also leads to aphasic symptoms as well, which can be diagnosed with the BDAE.

Prior to the development of the comprehensive Boston aphasia battery, a neuropsychological evaluation usually only reported the presence or absence of aphasia in general terms, such as "expressive aphasia noted." With the arrival of the BDAE, professionals now can perform differential diagnoses of neurological involvement based on the type of aphasic syndromes revealed. This is especially important in the differentiation of the dementias, specifically to differentiate SDAT (Alzheimer's disease) from other dementing conditions such as multi-infarct dementia (caused by numerous small strokes), Parkinson's disease, neurosyphilis, seizure disorders, and so forth, both to rule out treatable conditions and to provide clearly defined groups of SDAT patients for research. Although memory loss has been the primary behavioral dysfunction associated with SDAT, it is also associated with most other dementias as well and differentiation has been difficult, especially in the early stages of the disease. Recent research using the BDAE, either the complete battery or selected subtests, has revealed that different aphasic syndromes emerge in each of the dementias, which allows accurate differential diagnoses among them. For example, two groups of researchers using the BDAE compared SDAT patients with stroke patients and found that SDAT patients had more fluent speech but with poorer comprehension than stroke victims (Appell, Kertesz, & Fisman, 1982; Hier, Hagenlocker, & Schindler, 1985). Another group used the BDAE to accurately differentiate SDAT patients from those with Parkinson's disease (Cummings, Benson, Hill, & Read, 1988), while another study successfully differentially diagnosed SDAT from multi-infarct groups (Powell, Cummings, Hill, & Benson, 1988). In a study by this reviewer, an SDAT patient group, a group of patients with other types of dementias, and a group of age-matched controls were administered the BDAE and it successfully differentiated among them with 95% accuracy (Whitworth & Larson, 1989). From these few studies it is apparent that the BDAE represents a powerful tool in the differential diagnosis of neurological impairment.

As noted previously, a battery as complete and thorough as the BDAE requires significant length and a substantial amount of time to administer. The actual time varies, of course, with the examinee's age, education, health, degree of organic injury, and other variables. In general, the battery will take at least 3 hours or more, although with severely impaired individuals the time may be substantially less. Because of its length and administration time, a temptation may arise among clinicians as well as researchers to administer only some of the subtests or a shortened version of the BDAE. As with any comprehensive neuropsychological test battery, however, one generally pays the price of significantly less information in return for the savings in time and effort. This may be an acceptable bargain in instances that require only limited information, but the practice probably is not recommended when one needs a differential diagnosis of aphasic syndromes.

As with any neuropsychological test battery, the competence of the test administrator is vital to achieving valid results. The BDAE manual and directions for administration are clear, concise, and easy to understand, posing no significant problems for the user. The examiner, however, whether a psychologist, speech pathologist, or technician, should become thoroughly familiar with the administration process and ideally should memorize the procedures and instructions before administering the BDAE professionally. Doing so allows the examiner to focus entirely on the patient, who is often quite impaired, to ensure his or her understanding, concentration, and attention to the tasks presented.

Scoring the BDAE is generally an objective process (usually pass/fail for each item), although a few tasks require examiner judgment, especially those in the spontaneous speech portion of the test. Raw scores are recorded in the 32-page test booklet for each of the 38 subtests. In the 1972 version, raw scores were translated into z-scores measuring severity of aphasia. The second edition of the BDAE translates raw scores into percentiles, also in terms of severity, ranging from 0 (no communication) to 5 (no evidence of aphasia). The transformed percentile scores for each of the subtests (grouped under the major language categories) are then profiled, with the scores for the more severe impairments placed on the left side of the profile and the less severe on the right. The resulting profile then can be evaluated in terms of the impairment to specific categories of language, and it allows the evaluator to note those areas that are spared. This information, in turn, can be interpreted with respect to specific aphasic syndromes.

Interpretation of the BDAE assumes that the user has neuropsychological training as well as knowledge of neuroanatomy. Some training in, or at least considerable knowledge of, speech pathology also is desirable, especially with respect to various aphasic syndromes. To illustrate, assume that a patient has been involved in an automobile accident in which she suffered a concussive head injury. The BDAE, including the Boston Naming Test, is administered and scored. The raw scores are converted to percentiles and profiled. The profile of this patient shows a clustering of scores on the left (more severely impaired) for the categories of Naming, Repetition, and Automatic Speech. Most of the other profiled scores fall to the right (less severe impairment). Looking at this pattern, it would be logical to suspect the presence of a nonfluent (anterior) aphasia, probably Broca's aphasia. This would further suggest that the causative lesion lay in the motor association area of the left anterior frontal brain lobe.

Technical Aspects

As with most neuropsychological tests, the usual technical test construction problems involving measures of reliability and validity are not emphasized in the BDAE. This is not to say that such technical measures are ignored, but rather that a neuropsychological battery presents a different set of reliability and validity problems than, for example, a personality instrument or measure of intelligence. The standard test-retest reliability measures are not appropriate with the BDAE (or other neuropsychological tests) due to common behavior fluctuations, organic factors, and the fact that most aphasics improve with time, which would spuriously lower any test-retest coefficients. The BDAE manual does report internal consistency reliability (Kuder-Richardson) coefficients for all subtests, which range from .68 to .98; with the majority higher than .90, results suggest that the subtests are stable and homogeneous within themselves (Goodglass & Kaplan, 1983).

No criterion-related (predictive or concurrent) validity coefficients for the BDAE are reported, although factor analytic and discriminant analysis evaluations are cited. The lack of criterion-related validity measures can be understood if one considers that the BDAE is a diagnostic test—hence, predictive validity is not appropriate and only concurrent validity would apply. As with most neuropsychological tests, however, demonstrating concurrent validity (i.e., that organically impaired individuals perform differently on the tests than normals), though generally resulting in very high significance levels, really does not reflect the effectiveness or usefulness of the tests. At the present level of development of neuropsychological testing, a 4- or 5-hour test battery that could only distinguish "brain damage" from "no brain damage" or "aphasia" from "no aphasia" would be of questionable value.

To illustrate this point further, although no formal validity coefficients are reported in the manual, the data for the 147 normal controls are quite revealing. With very few exceptions, the mean score for these normals fell within a fraction of 1 point of the *maximum* score possible on all subtests. This, in turn, led the authors to establish cutoff scores (between normals and aphasics) that are very high, within a few points of maximum in most cases. Additionally, in the reviewer's study reported previously, the BDAE differentiated normals from aphasics on 34 of 38 subtests with significance far beyond the .001 level (Whitworth & Larson, 1989). Therefore, though no specific validity data are reported in the manual, the BDAE is very accurate in distinguishing those with aphasia from normals.

For those using the BDAE, however, of more importance than the standard validity coefficients is the test's ability to distinguish among the various types of aphasic syndromes—that is, its efficiency in differential diagnosis. Two questions are relevant here: 1) Is the test battery logically and statistically consistent in its structure (which can be assessed by factor analysis)? and 2) Will it effectively distinguish between the different aphasic syndromes (which is most easily determined by discriminant analysis)? Factor analytic studies of the BDAE, using a Promax rotation procedure, yielded seven different factors. These factors are very like the eight language categories used in the development of the test and described previously, with the exception that two categories combined into a single factor. These results suggest that the logical categorizations of language functions used by the BDAE developers are consistent with the statistical clustering of the subtests and therefore with the behavioral performance of aphasic patients.

Discriminant function analysis is a statistical technique in which linear combinations of predictor variables are combined in order to discriminate among different groups. The BDAE manual reports a discriminant function analysis of 41 cases. Patients representing four categories of the most common aphasic syndromes (Broca's, Wernicke's, anomic, and conduction aphasias) were selected for the study. Six of the BDAE subtests were chosen as predictor variables. The results revealed that 37 of the 41 patients were correctly classified by this procedure, which suggests that the BDAE is quite effective in differentially diagnosing the various types of aphasia.

Critique

In the two decades since it was first published, the BDAE has become the preeminent aphasia battery in the field of neuropsychology. That it has achieved such a dominant position is not surprising, as it embodies all of the qualities that are both necessary as well as desirable in a neuropsychological aphasia test battery. It is comprehensive and measures all relevant aspects of language functioning. It is also very thorough, measuring each area of language function through a wide range of performance. Although test administration requires a high level of training and expertise, scoring is primarily objective and leads to a high level of scoring consistency among administrators. Finally, the test is organized and structured in terms of a logical relationship between language behavior and brain function, which allows the neuropsychologist to make inferences about neuroanatomical involvement from neurolinguistic test data. It thus fulfills all the requirements for a comprehensive, differentially diagnostic aphasia test battery.

As with many neuropsychological batteries, however, the BDAE's very strength is also the source of most criticism. Simply stated, the major criticism of this test battery is that it is too long and takes too much time. Not only does the test require a great deal of the professional's time to administer, score, and evaluate, but it is sometimes very tiring and difficult for the patient, especially if he or she is neurologically and linguistically impaired. Neuropsychological evaluations are frequently difficult for patients, requiring them to perform in their areas of impairment, and this can become very frustrating and lead to emotional distress. Three or four hours of testing for a neurologically impaired patient are simply too much, and two or more sessions are not uncommon to complete this battery. If, as is frequently the case, other neuropsychological tests of cognition, perception, and motor functions are necessary in addition to the BDAE, the testing time (not to mention the expense) becomes a serious problem. For this reason, as noted earlier, the use of only selected subtests or shortened versions of the BDAE may be employed.

From a clinical view, considering the test's length and complexity, it is unlikely that the neuropsychologist would want to routinely administer the BDAE unless a differential diagnosis of aphasia were specifically needed. While the BDAE gives the clinical neuropsychologist a wealth of information about a patient's language functioning, the price paid in time and expense also must be evaluated.

Although the BDAE as a clinical test battery has some limitations, its usefulness and value in neuropsychological research cannot be overestimated. Such research regarding dementia, head injuries, stroke, and neurological disease generally require some measure of language function (and dysfunction). Almost all researchers wanting an evaluation of aphasia presently employ either the full or partial BDAE. In the 20 years since it first was published, the Boston Diagnostic Aphasia Examination has become the standard in the field against which all other aphasia tests are measured.

References

Appell, J., Kertesz, A., & Fisman, M. (1987). A study of language functioning in Alzheimer patients. *Brain and Language, 17,* 73–91.

Cummings, J.L., Benson, D.F., Hill, M.A., & Read, S. (1985). Aphasia in dementia of the Alzheimer type. *Neurology, 35,* 394–397.

Eisenson, J. (1954). *Examining for aphasia.* New York: Psychological Corporation.

Goodglass, H., & Kaplan, E. (1972). *The assessment of aphasia and related disorders.* Philadelphia: Lea & Febiger.

Goodglass, H., & Kaplan, E. (1983). *The assessment of aphasia and related disorders* (2nd ed.). Philadelphia: Lea & Febiger.

Hier, D.B., Hagenlocker, K., & Schindler, A.G. (1985). Language deterioration in dementia: Effects of etiology and severity. *Brain and Language, 25,* 117–133.

Kaplan, E., Goodglass, H., & Weintraub, S. (1983). *Boston Naming Test.* Philadelphia: Lea & Febiger.

Kertesz, A., & Poole, E. (1974). The aphasia quotient: The taxonomic approach to measurement of aphasic disabilities. *Canadian Journal of Neurological Science, 1,* 7–16.

Mayeaux, R., & Kandel, E.R. (1985). Natural language, disorders of language, and other localizable disorders of cognitive functioning. In E.R. Kandel & J.H. Schwartz (Eds.), *Principles of neural science* (2nd ed., pp. 205–229). New York: Elsevier.

McCarthy, J., & Kirk, S.A. (1966). *Illinois Test of Psycholinguistic Abilities.* Urbana: University of Illinois Press.

Powell, A.L., Cummings, J.L., Hill, M.A., & Benson, D.F. (1988). Speech and language alterations in multi-infarct dementia. *Neurology, 38,* 717–719.

Reitan, R. (1969). *Manual for the administration of Neuropsychological Test Batteries for Adults and Children.* Indianapolis: Author.

Wepman, J.M., & Jones, L.V. (1961). *The Language Modalities Test for Aphasia.* Chicago: University of Chicago Press.

Whitworth, R.H., & Larson, C.M. (1989). Differential diagnosis and staging of Alzheimer's disease with an aphasia battery. *Neuropsychiatry, Neuropsychology, and Behavioral Neurology, 1,* 255–265.

Michael H. Mattei, Psy.D.
Staff Psychologist, Napa State Hospital, Napa, California.

Grant Aram Killian, Ph.D.
Adjunct Professor of Psychology, Nova University, Fort Lauderdale, Florida.

William I. Dorfman, Ph.D.
Associate Professor of Psychology, Nova University, Fort Lauderdale, Florida.

BRIEF LIFE HISTORY INVENTORY

Donald I. Templer and David M. Veleber. Buffalo, New York: United Educational Services, Inc.

Introduction

The Brief Life History Inventory (BLHI), first published in 1984 under the name California Brief Life History Inventory, is designed to provide a quick, efficient means of obtaining basic information describing an individual's background and present circumstances. The instrument is intended primarily as a preinterview or prescreening tool and is not meant to replace the more complete social history or intake interview. Prior to a formal assessment, the clinician may use BLHI-obtained data to identify areas of possible concern that require further inquiry. As such, the authors claim that it is not a psychometric instrument but rather a demographic, information sheet (D.I. Templer, personal communication, June 19, 1991).

The first author, Donald I. Templer, earned his Ph.D. in clinical psychology from the University of Kentucky in 1967 and is currently a core faculty member of the California School of Professional Psychology at Fresno. Second author David M. Veleber earned his Ph.D. in clinical psychology from the latter institution in 1981 and currently maintains a private practice in Bethlehem, Pennsylvania, working with children, adolescents, and adults.

The authors developed the BLHI to provide clinicians with a means of obtaining information about an individual's background and present circumstances prior to the initial evaluation. The specific goals were to eliminate two flaws or limitations that the authors felt were present in life history inventories, namely, excessive length of time required to fill out the forms and the creation of undue stress for the respondent by intrusive questions regarding sexual history and difficulties with the law. The authors also stated that traditional life history inventories such as the Minnesota-Briggs History Record (Briggs, Rouzer, Hamberg, & Holman, 1972) have tended to be "insurmountable," especially for persons of low-average intelligence and little education (D.I. Templer, personal communication, June 19, 1991). With this in mind, the BLHI was designed to be used as a brief checklist questionnaire.

Development of this instrument took approximately 1 year. Topics and questions were selected primarily on the basis of what the authors felt would be useful information for the clinician to have prior to the initial interview. According to the second author, "it has never been meant to be comprehensive. It is a quick screen instrument which in the experienced clinician's hands could be used to identify problem areas needing further inquiry" (D.M. Veleber, personal communication, June 17, 1991). According to the authors, no outside subject-matter experts were used in developing the inventory. The only other version of the BLHI is an unpublished Arabic translation currently in use at the University of Alexandria, Egypt.

The adult and student versions of the BLHI can be ordered separately, in packages of 25 questionnaires. Although there is no manual, both the adult and student forms come with a one-page cover letter that briefly describes the inventory. The examiner's participation in the completion process is minimal. The authors advise that he or she assess the client's ability to complete the questionnaire if any reasons suggest potential difficulties. (The cover letter, however, does not include this information.) In a standard administration, the questionnaire may be given to the client by an office worker with instructions to return it through the mail when completed. Clients are instructed to answer the questions as well as possible and advised that they may skip questions of which they feel uncertain or choose not to answer.

The BLHI can be completed by anyone aged 12 and older. According to the authors, a sixth-grade reading and writing level is required to complete the inventory satisfactorily. Both the Student and Adult forms contain three pages of questions and a blank page on which the clinician may summarize relevant findings. The Student Form contains the following major headings: General Information, Present Problems, History, Family Life, Education, and Miscellaneous. Most questions are multiple-choice, although a few require brief written responses. The Adult Form resembles the student version in terms of how questions are answered (multiple-choice, yes/no, brief written answers), but it consists of the following seven sections: General Information, Present Problems, History, Childhood and Relatives, Education, Occupation, and Miscellaneous. On both forms each topic consists of approximately 8 questions except for Present Problems, made up instead of 20 (Adult) or 32 (Student) questions.

Practical Applications/Uses

The BLHI was designed to gather data on a client's presenting problems, family life, work, and substance abuse difficulties. The cover sheet accompanying the test kit claims that it is comprehensive and concise in spite of its length. It also advises that by having a client complete the questionnaire before the initial interview, the clinician learns what matters need further probing. The cover sheet also notes that use of the instrument can lead to a quicker and more accurate diagnosis, overall formulation, and treatment plan.

The General Information section asks for basic demographic data such as name, age, and date of birth. Similar to the Adult Screening Battery (Diston, Faust, & Killian, 1992), the Present Problems section briefly assesses what the authors claim are most of the major mental health symptom categories (e.g., somatic concerns, relationship difficulties, conduct problems, anxiety, depression, educational/occupational difficulties, self-esteem, and suicidality). The History section inquires about past medical and mental health problems and consists of critical items that the authors feel alert the clinician to possible psychosis, neurological involvement, and substance abuse. The Family Life section (Student Form) and the Childhood and Relatives section (Adult Form) present questions related to the respondent's quality of familial relationships. The Education section addresses scholastic functioning, including school performance and conduct. The Adult Form also has a separate section covering occupational history and job satisfaction. Finally, under Miscellaneous, the questions deal with medications the client is taking, illicit drug use, and leisure activities.

The BLHI has been used in hospitals, private practice settings, and child guidance centers for pretreatment screening. It has also been used by select weight-loss clinics. The developers feel that only clinicians qualified to practice independently should administer this inventory, and as such this would include psychologists, psychiatrists, social workers, or other similarly trained professionals. The authors state that although the inventory is not a psychometric instrument, it could be validated empirically. Templer notes (personal communication, June 9, 1991) that the Present Problems section could be expanded to produce a subtest measuring symptom categories, which then could be evaluated in terms of psychometric properties. In addition, he added that the questionnaire could be automated for on-line computer administration. At the time of this writing, the publisher planned to translate the inventory into Spanish and French.

The Student Form is suitable for clients aged 12 to 18, and the Adult Form is intended for those aged 18 and above. The forms may be completed on-site or at home. The cover letter accompanying the test forms adds that the clinician may complete the inventory during the actual interview. This implies that it can be used as an interview outline. Both the Student and Adult forms contain brief directions and a statement assuring that the information provided will be treated confidentially. As noted previously, the respondent is instructed to complete each section of the inventory but is also told that he or she may omit any question. In general, the questions can be answered in less than half an hour. The developers and publisher state that interpretation of BLHI data requires a trained and experienced clinician to decide which areas to focus on during the formal interview. Therefore, the interpretation of the data is based on subjective clinical judgment.

Technical Aspects

At the time of its release in 1984, no attempts had been made to estimate levels of validity and reliability for the Brief Life History Inventory. Since its publication, no studies have been done examining the instrument's effectiveness in what it was designed to do. Unfortunately, self-report inventories traditionally have received little attention in the research literature. This lack is remarkable considering their pervasive use in the practice of mental health. The dearth of research continues even though studies have shown that structured interviews may possess characteristics that make them amenable to psychometric inquiry and study

(Haynes & Jensen, 1979). Perhaps the most well-studied life history inventory has been the Minnesota-Briggs History Record (Briggs et al., 1972), but comparison between the two is not feasible; the Minnesota-Briggs is a lengthy and comprehensive instrument requiring several hours to complete, while the BLHI is four pages long and can be completed in half an hour. Therefore, no hard data pertaining to other life history inventories is directly applicable or generalizable. With this lack of available information, it is difficult for a prospective test user to evaluate the suitability of the BLHI for any of its stated uses.

The *Standards for Educational and Psychological Testing* (American Educational Research Association, American Psychological Association, & National Council on Measurement in Education, 1985) states that "these standards apply primarily to constructed performance tasks, questionnaires [inventories], and structured behavior samples" (p. 4). For these reasons, the evaluation of the BLHI's technical aspects will be based on the AERA/APA/NCME standards related to validity and reliability. As it would be beyond the scope of this review to evaluate the inventory on every standard, the focus will be on those classified as primary, which "are those which should be met by all tests before their operational use and in all test uses" (AERA, APA, & NCME, 1985, p. 2). For a more exhaustive review of which standards the BLHI met, the reader is referred to Mattei (1991).

The BLHI is presented as a quick-screening instrument to be completed before an initial assessment interview. The goal of the inventory is to accurately and comprehensively identify problem areas that require further probing. The developers also identify a second use of the BLHI: to serve as an outline for the initial interview. One of the primary standards states that "evidence of validity should be presented for the major types of inferences for which the use of a test is recommended" (AERA et al., 1985, p. 13). Therefore, the first concern is to assess the evidence supporting use of the BLHI for these purposes.

As with any life history inventory, content validity is of primary importance. According to Anastasi (1982), content validity should be built into an instrument throughout its development. An examination of how the BLHI was constructed shows that the established procedures to build and demonstrate content validity were not followed (AERA et al., 1985). The developers failed to clearly specify the domain represented by the inventory, no subject-matter experts were used to generate questions, and no attempts were made to formally assess the representativeness of the topics or questions included. In addition, during the construction of the instrument, no attempts were made to assess or consider the impact of how the questions were worded. Finally, no demonstration is offered that clearly outlines the content's relevance to its proposed use. Demonstrating content validity for the prescribed uses of an instrument is the developer's responsibility (AERA et al., 1985). Although the authors state that the BLHI is complete, they fail to describe how. Without this knowledge, one cannot determine whether the BLHI contains a representative sample of the questions requisite to a preinterview screen or an outline for an initial assessment interview. For these reasons, it is not possible to say that the BLHI shows evidence of being valid for its defined uses.

The BLHI provides no evidence of construct validity, yet it is proposed as an assessment of multiple constructs. The cover sheet claims that the inventory assesses "virtually every major mental health symptom area" and that it does so in a comprehensive manner. Although the authors may believe this to be true, a cursory review of the DSM-III-R (American Psychiatric Association, 1987) makes it clear that the BLHI fails to address the major symptom categories.

Many studies have shown that the reliability of self-report interview data is quite low (e.g., Walsh, 1967; Yarrow, Campbell, & Burton, 1970). These studies identify possible sources of error, including examiner bias, client bias, and environmental and circumstantial variables such as where the interview is given and under what circumstances the client has come to be interviewed. Other studies have shown that inquiry into sensitive areas such as drug use and sexual difficulties leads to increased distortion of data (Erdman, Klein, & Greist, 1985; Greist, Klein, & Van Cura, 1973; Klein, Greist, & Van Cura, 1975). Possible sources of errors of measurement for the BLHI or any take-home self-report inventory include random response variability and situational variables that result from a lack of standardized administration procedures. The reliability of the data obtained from an interview also can vary in part due to variables such as differences in client-examiner age, race, sex, and social class (Schwitzgebel & Kolb, 1975). Further, the authors' recommendation to use the BLHI as an outline during the initial interview introduces the potential for additional sources of error such as examiner bias. The literature that accompanies the inventory fails to address any possible sources of error. This omission should not lead test users to erroneously assume reliability where none has been shown. Although it is the responsibility of the developer to provide evidence of reliability estimates (AERA et al., 1985), no such information exists.

Critique

The Brief Life History Inventory represents an attempt to provide a structured means of obtaining life history data from an individual. As noted, it is not possible to assess the instrument's content validity for its stated purposes, and, unfortunately, the information provided with the test kit further serves to complicate matters. According to the aforementioned *Standards* (3.16), instructional materials accompanying a test "should facilitate appropriate interpretations" (p. 28). This standard was not met due to the lack of instructional material provided with the test, including a manual.

The BLHI cover sheet suggests that the user consider an individual's responses to specific items as a basis for assessment. Again according to the *Standards* (1.4), a developer making this recommendation should present evidence in a manual supporting this approach or alert the test user to the absence of evidence. The BLHI does neither. In addition, the cover sheet states that the BLHI provides complete and comprehensive information on a client's background and present circumstances, but in fact the inventory does not gather information on topics such as sexual difficulties or criminal record, nor does it cover any topic area in depth; therefore, it is neither complete nor comprehensive. To make this claim is misleading and presents the potential for the data to be interpreted as if it were inclusive. This potential for misuse is not addressed and as such, constitutes a violation of the *Standards* (5.2). A manual should provide the information that a test user needs in order to properly evaluate and use an instrument. This lack of accompanying information severely limits the the usefulness of the BLHI.

Promotional material should be accurate and should avoid making claims that are not supported by the instrument's research base (*Standards*, 5.7). Advertisement for the BLHI states that by using the inventory, the clinician will be able to identify areas that need further probing. This statement implies that the inventory can identify problem areas. Technically, because of the lack of validity estimates, this claim should not be made.

The *Standards* (3.1) state that a test "should be developed on a sound scientific basis" (p. 25). The BLHI apparently was not developed in a scientific manner. Topic areas and questions were selected to a large extent in an arbitrary manner, based on what the authors felt was important. Their basic premise was that existing life history interviews were too lengthy and time-consuming and that the development of an abbreviated version would prove advantageous. No attempts have been made to determine what their inventory actually assesses or if the data obtained are reliable.

Obtaining comprehensive life history data on an individual can be crucial in terms of proper diagnosis and treatment planning. The interview has traditionally been the means of gathering this information, yet research has shown that the process is subject to many forms of error (Morganstern, 1976). Structured self-report inventories were developed with the intention of reducing errors of measurement by providing a standardized procedure to gather life history data. The BLHI represents a modification of this approach, as it is recommended for use as a prescreening instrument before the actual interview. As already noted, no evidence exists to suggest its suitability for this purpose.

The BLHI appears to have been based in part on the assumption that an incomplete structured interview could reliably and validly serve as the basis or foundation for a thorough clinical assessment. The test authors attempted to justify the incompleteness of the instrument with the invalid pretext that an area of inquiry that might (or might not) lead to client discomfort should be omitted from the interview. Although research has shown increased distortion of information given regarding sensitive topic areas such as sexual difficulties (Greist et al., 1973), it would seem that the task of a test developer should be to develop better data-gathering techniques as opposed to doing away with entire lines of questioning. This argument also serves to deflect attention from the fact that the BLHI was developed in an essentially arbitrary and unsystematic manner. As previously noted, the developers chose topic areas and questions based on what they felt was important. Although the vast clinical experience of the senior author qualifies him to be a subject-matter expert, the established procedures for building a content-valid instrument necessitated a more objective approach.

Of the 15 Primary AERA/APA/NCME standards on which Mattei (1991) evaluated the BLHI, it failed to meet a full 80%. Naturally, not every standard is equally weighted in terms of importance and relevance; however, any instrument failing to meet such a significant number of professional standards might be considered questionable in terms of its suitability for any given use.

The BLHI appears to reflect a general view in psychology that clinical interviews are little more than nonstandardized and subjective outlines for data gathering and assessment. As such, its shortcomings may be seen in part as a reflection of the erroneous view that clinical interviewing is a nonscientific, intuitive, and idiosyncratic approach to assessment, excused from the rigorous standards to which other instruments are held. Empirical investigation regarding the use of case history interviews must assume greater importance. One factor that appears to have hampered such efforts is the widespread assumption that self-report measures are invalid and unreliable. Although research has tended to support this view, evidence does exist to suggest that carefully designed interviews may be reliably and validly used to measure specific target behaviors (Linehan, 1977; Lucas, 1977). In addition, Haynes and Jensen (1979) have produced guidelines on how the validity of interview-derived information may begin to be estimated.

The clinical interview must be fully recognized as an assessment instrument and as such held up to the same standards of reliability and validity required of other assessment tools. Until the profession accepts these standards as applicable to the clinical interview, we will continue to see instruments of questionable quality distributed for widespread use. Psychologists should abandon the use of interviews, tests, and procedures that are recommended only by their availability, ease of use, and familiarity. In 1984, Killian, Holzman, Davis, and Gibbon proposed that psychologists had an ethical obligation to use instruments that conformed to at least the original APA standards published in 1966. It is now proposed that as test users, psychologists have an ethical obligation to use instruments constructed in a sound scientific manner and that conform to the current professional standards (AERA et al., 1985).

References

American Educational Research Association, American Psychological Association, & National Council on Measurement in Education. (1985). *Standards for educational and psychological testing.* Washington, DC: American Psychological Association.

American Psychiatric Association. (1987). *Diagnostic and statistical manual of mental disorders* (3rd ed. rev.). Washington, DC: Author.

Anastasi, A. (1982). *Psychological testing* (5th ed.). New York: Macmillan.

Briggs, P.F., Rouzer, D.L., Hamberg, R.L., & Holman, T.R. (1972). Seven scales for the Minnesota-Briggs History Record with reference group data. *Journal of Clinical Psychology, 28,* 431–448.

Diston, L., Faust, J., & Killian, G.A. (1992). Diagnostic Screening Batteries: Adolescent, Adult, and Child. In D.J. Keyser & R.C. Sweetland (Eds.), *Test critiques* (Vol. IX, pp. 154–166). Austin, TX: PRO-ED.

Erdman, H.P., Klein, M.H., & Greist, J.H. (1985). Direct patient computer interviewing. *Journal of Consulting and Clinical Psychology, 53*(6), 760–773.

Greist, J.H., Klein, M.H., & Van Cura, L.J. (1973). A computer interview for psychiatric patient target symptoms. *Archives of General Psychiatry, 29,* 247–254.

Haynes, S.N., & Jensen, B.J. (1979). The interview as a behavioral assessment instrument. *Behavioral Assessment, 1,* 97–106.

Killian, G., Holzman, P., Davis, J., & Gibbon, R. (1984). The effects of psychotropic drugs on cognitive functioning in schizophrenia and depression. *Journal of Abnormal Psychology, 93*(1), 58–70.

Klein, M.H., Greist, J.H., & Van Cura, L.J. (1975). Computers and psychiatry. *Archives of General Psychiatry, 32,* 837–843.

Linehan, M. (1977). Issues in behavioral interviewing. In J.D. Cone & R.P. Hawkins (Eds.), *Behavioral assessment* (pp. 248–277). New York: Brunner/Mazel.

Lucas, R.W. (1977). A study of patients' attitudes to computer interrogation. *International Journal of Man-Machine Studies, 9,* 69–86.

Mattei, M.H. (1991). *Structured clinical interviews: A review and critique of three instruments.* Unpublished professional research project, Nova University, Ft. Lauderdale, FL.

Morganstern, K.P. (1976). Behavioral interviewing: The initial stages of assessment. In M. Hersen & A.S. Bellack (Eds.), *Behavioral assessment* (pp. 51–75). New York: Pergamon.

Schwitzgebel, R.K., & Kolb, D.A. (1975). *Changing human behavior.* New York: McGraw-Hill.

Templer, D.I., & Veleber, D.M. (1984). *Brief Life History Inventory.* Buffalo, NY: United Educational Services.

Walsh, W.B. (1967). Validity of self-report. *Journal of Counseling Psychology, 14,* 18–23.

Yarrow, M.R., Campbell, J.D., & Burton, R.V. (1970). Recollections of childhood: A study of the retrospective method. *Monographs of the Society for Research in Child Development, 35*(5, Serial No. 138).

Russell N. Carney, Ph.D.
Associate Professor of Psychology, Southwest Missouri State University, Springfield, Missouri.

Sharon F. Schattgen, Ph.D.
Director, Project Construct National Center, University of Missouri, Columbia, Missouri.

CALIFORNIA ACHIEVEMENT TESTS, FIFTH EDITION

CTB/McGraw-Hill. Monterey, California: CTB/McGraw-Hill.

Introduction

The California Achievement Tests, Fifth Edition (CAT/5), represent a nationally standardized, broad-spectrum achievement test battery designed for Grades K through 12. Published in spring 1992, the CAT/5 measures basic skills in the areas of reading, language, spelling, mathematics, study skills, science, and social studies. It is available in three formats: the Basic Skills Battery, the Complete Battery, and the Survey Tests. All test formats yield norm-referenced scores. Additionally, the Basic Skills Battery and the Complete Battery provide curriculum-referenced scores so that users can obtain estimates of student mastery over various objectives. Further, four "assessment options" are, or soon will be, available: the Performance Assessment Component, the Listening and Speaking Checklist, the Writing Assessment, and the Test of Cognitive Skills, 2nd Edition (TCS/2).

As detailed in an earlier volume of *Test Critiques* (Bunch, 1985), the California Achievement Tests have been in existence since 1943, and subsequent editions were published in 1950, 1957, 1970 (Forms A and B), 1977 (Forms C and D), and 1985 (Forms E and F). A central reason for revising standardized achievement tests is to improve their content validity by updating the alignment of test items with current school curriculum and instructional practices.

An additional reason for revision/renorming that has received a good deal of attention over the last few years is the old-versus-new-norms controversy, wherein students appear to score higher on older (vs. newer) normed tests. Several years ago, Cannell (1987) noted that all 50 states were reporting their students' mean performance as above the national average in academic achievement. This seemingly contradictory phenomenon was dubbed the "Lake Wobegon Effect," after the popular radio program in which Garrison Keillor told stories about a community where "all the women are strong, all the men are good-looking, and all the children are above average." As was the case with several prominent standardized achievement tests (e.g., Linn, Graue, & Sanders, 1990), older CAT norms (i.e., 1977) produced higher user scores than did newer norms (i.e., 1985).

While test makers tended to explain the phenomenon as due to an actual increase in school achievement (Airaisian, 1989), a variety of other explanations were proposed—including the notion that norm-referenced tests are indeed sensitive to instruction (Shepard, 1990). That is, after tests have been in the schools for a period of time, the tests' content makes its way increasingly into the curriculum, which produces improved performance on the part of current test-takers in comparison to the original norm group. If nothing else, the controversy over the Lake Wobegon Effect has served to underscore the need for the frequent revision and renorming of standardized achievement tests and for increased test security.

The CAT/5 (1992) is the successor to the well-received CAT Forms E and F (1985). The areas covered by the newer test are similar to those in the 1985 edition, which provides continuity for school systems wishing to measure achievement trends over time. While building on the prior edition, the CAT/5 differs significantly in terms of development, where a more integrated approach was taken. Test developers worked "in concert," rather than independently in their specific content domains, in an effort to integrate content in a logical manner. For example, a science passage might be used in a language test. This approach was taken to match current instructional trends toward a more integrated curriculum. Test items on the CAT/5 are more broadly based than those on the previous edition. Thus, norm-referenced scores in the various domains should represent more global measures.

As previously stated, the CAT/5 is a comprehensive set of multilevel achievement batteries that measure the basic skills taught in elementary and secondary schools. The three primary configurations of this test (Basic Skills Battery, Complete Battery, and Survey Tests) measure the same content with overlapping items as well as with items of closely matched difficulty. The configurations differ in the number of items and the level of specificity of the scores they provide.

The Basic Skills Battery (only Form A is available) provides both norm-referenced and curriculum-referenced results for Reading, Spelling, Language, Mathematics, and Study Skills. The Complete Battery has two parallel forms, A and B, and offers the same norm- and curriculum-referenced data as the Basic Skills Battery, plus Science and Social Studies at Grade 1 and above. Subtests in both of these batteries contain from 24 to 50 items. The Survey Tests provide norm-referenced scores for the same content areas as the Complete Battery. Fewer items per subtest (e.g., 20) are required in the Survey Tests configuration, as curriculum-referenced scores are not reported. Thus, testing time for the Survey Tests is less than for the Complete/Basic Skills Battery, but measurement error is, as *Technical Bulletin I* (CTB/Macmillan/McGraw-Hill, 1992) notes, greater.

There are 13 overlapping levels of the CAT/5. The Basic Skills and Complete Batteries are available for Levels K through 21/22 (beginning of the Kindergarten year through the end of the Grade 12 year). The Survey Battery was developed for Levels 12 through 21/22 (the latter part of the Grade 1 year through the end of the Grade 12 year).

For each of the three configurations of the CAT/5, items are of the two-, three-, four-, or five-option, multiple-choice type, with the vast majority being four-choice. Within subtests there is a range in item difficulty, but on the average about 50% of examinees in the standardization group answered each item correctly.

A specific test booklet accompanies each level of the CAT/5; booklets for Kindergarten through Grade 3 are scorable, while those for Grades 4 through 12 are used with answer sheets. At all levels, the test booklets are easy to read and use, with legible type and graphics and attractively formatted pages. Answer sheets and examiner's manuals are also easy to use. At the primary grade levels, the examiner reads both directions and items aloud to students, while at the upper elementary and secondary grade levels, he or she reads only the directions.

Normative scores are reported for each of the content areas covered by a particular configuration as well as for subject areas. For example, in addition to an overall Reading score, students also obtain scores for Vocabulary and Comprehension. These scores are based on all items in the respective subtest. A score also is reported for the Total Battery, which derives from the Reading, Language, and Mathematics items. The curriculum-referenced information yielded by the Complete and the Basic Skills Batteries is based on at least four items per objective.

Locator tests serve to match students in the same grade with different levels of the CAT/5 and consist of 20 multiple-choice vocabulary items and 20 multiple-choice mathematics items. To give students experience in taking a standardized test, practice tests present about 15 multiple-choice items covering the various subtests.

The publishers of the CAT/5 offer three performance-based enhancements that users can administer in conjunction with the multiple-choice components. The Performance Assessment Component consists of three modules for Grades 4/5, 6/7, and 8/9, covering Reading and Language Arts, Mathematics, Science, and Social Studies. (At the time of this writing, additional levels for Kindergarten through Grade 3 were under development.) For each content area, 12 to 25 constructed-response items require students to use higher order thinking skills to arrive at answers they write directly in the test booklet. Responses can be scored locally or by the publisher. Scores are reported in six broad skill categories ("integrated outcomes").

Additional performance-based options offered to the CAT/5 user are the Listening and Speaking Checklist, as well as the Writing Assessment. The Listening and Speaking Checklist measures "important oral language proficiencies" that are not routinely assessed in instructional or testing programs. The three checklists cover Grades K–3, 4–8, and 9–12. Though the Listening and Speaking Checklists are designed to be scored by the teacher, the results can be sent to the publisher for incorporation into reporting systems. The Writing Assessment, which is based on either an independent or a reading-related prompt, evaluates students' writing via actual writing samples (Grades 2 through 12). The samples are scored, either locally or by the publisher, as a function of the reader's overall impression and/or on discrete elements.

A final assessment option is the Test of Cognitive Skills, 2nd Edition (TCS/2), a test of academic aptitude for Grades 2 through 12. By combining scores from the TCS/2 and the CAT/5, "anticipated achievement scores" can be produced that compare the student's level of achievement to that of others of the same age, grade, and academic aptitude.

Practical Applications/Uses

The CAT/5 is designed to measure academic achievement in the basic skills taught in schools. As previously noted, the battery can be used to assess students' learning in reading, language, spelling, mathematics, study skills, science, and social studies.

Test users are primarily public and private elementary and secondary educators who want to know how their students compare to a national sample and, in the case of the Basic Skills and Complete Batteries, which specific skills their students have mastered. Results yielded by the CAT/5 also can be used to identify students for further testing for possible placement in special programs (e.g., gifted and talented, special education) and to evaluate the effectiveness of educational programs (e.g., Chapter 1). Though most likely used by professional educators in school-related settings, these tests could be employed by clinicians or clients with training in administering and using such measures who need general or specific information about a client's levels of academic achievement.

Because it was developed for and standardized with students in Kindergarten through Grade 12, the CAT/5 would be inappropriately given to students outside this range. All levels provide fall and spring norms, so students can take these tests at the beginning and/or conclusion of the academic year. (Level 11 for first grade also provides winter norms.) Additionally, the publisher can produce braille and large-type editions for visually impaired examinees.

A group-administered test battery, the CAT/5 is designed to be given by teachers (assisted by proctors) in the regular classroom environment. The examiner's manuals provide clear and comprehensive instructions, including checklists to assist in planning for testing, directions for administering the tests, and guidelines for processing completed tests. These very specific directives make administration quite easy, although the examiner must read them carefully.

In general, the tests must be given according to the prescribed procedures, although examiners may, when reading directions aloud, substitute familiar terms for those that students may be unaccustomed to using. Examiners may change the order of presentation of the subtests if they so desire.

The CAT/5 is not primarily a speeded test. There are, however, time limits for each subtest, so some students may not complete all of the items. The working time allowed for the subtests ranges from 14 to 50 minutes. Administration of the Complete Battery, for example, requires a minimum of 1½ to a maximum of 5¼ hours' working time, depending on the level used.

Booklets for Levels K and 10 through 13 (Kindergarten through Grade 3) and answer sheets for Levels 14 through 21/22 (Grades 4 through 12) are available in both computer-scorable and hand-scorable formats. (This is true for all configurations except the Basic Skills Battery, for which there are no hand-scorable books.) If answer booklets/sheets are computer scored by the publisher, a vast array of standard and custom reporting options are available, all of which provide individual results for every student and summary data for classrooms, buildings, and districts. In general, these reports are attractively formatted, easy to read, and present typical norm-referenced scores (e.g., national percentiles, normal curve equivalents, scale scores, grade equivalents), plus, for the Complete and Basic Skills Batteries, objective-referenced information. As mentioned earlier, if the CAT/5 is administered in combination with the TCS/2, anticipated achievement scores are available, thereby providing a way to estimate the degree to which a student is achieving in accordance with expectations for comparable students.

One innovative example of a computer-generated report is the Multiple Assessment Profile, which presents information from the multiple-choice component of the CAT/5 and up to 11 of its various enhancements (e.g., Listening and Speaking Checklist, Writing Assessment, TCS/2) to provide an overall picture of a student's or group's performance. In addition, software support for generating additional reports and planning and managing instruction is available from the publisher.

The examiner accomplishes hand scoring quickly and easily by means of either stenciled keys or answer sheets with self-contained keys. Manual scoring, however, yields only a limited number of reporting options relative to the wide variety of computer-generated possibilities, although the hand-scoring report forms allow for efficient organization and presentation of individual and classroom data. Number correct scores are converted to scale scores and then to other normative scores using tables provided in the norms book, and objective mastery results are estimated using information on the answer booklet/sheet and one of the hand-scoring forms.

Scores yielded by the CAT/5 are explained and interpreted in two publications, the *Test Coordinator's Handbook* and the *Class Management Guide*. The handbook is designed primarily for test directors and curriculum supervisors, while the guidebook is written with classroom teachers in mind. These documents were not available for review at the time of this writing; however, earlier versions suggest that the new editions will serve as excellent resources for the CAT/5 user. For example, the *Test Coordinator's Handbook* (CTB/McGraw-Hill, 1986b) for CAT Forms E and F provides a thorough explanation of each type of score reported and gives detailed information about how to use each of the report forms. In addition, the *Class Management Guide* (CTB/McGraw-Hill, 1986a) for Forms E and F contains a helpful section on describing standardized test results to parents. Both manuals offer appropriate advisements and caveats about the interpretation and use of test scores.

To further facilitate usability of results, each of the computer-generated individual student reports prepared by the publisher includes explanations of the specific scores presented. This feature should be especially helpful to parents and students who are not familiar with measurement terminology.

Technical Aspects

A thorough description of content development comprises Part 2 of the *CAT/5 Technical Bulletin 1* (CTB/Macmillan/McGraw-Hill, 1992). As outlined there, the developers' approach to determining the educational objectives to be measured was quite thorough and included reviews of textbook series, instructional programs, state and district curriculum guides, and norm- and criterion-referenced tests. Information gleaned from these reviews was categorized into broad areas, which then served as the structure for the CAT/5.

As mentioned earlier, an integrative approach guided the development of the CAT/5 to reflect the more cross-disciplinary curriculum of today's classroom. In particular, the batteries reflect trends toward "a more holistic approach to language arts" and "literature-based instruction." Descriptive information regarding the tests' content appears in item classification tables in the *Class Management*

Guide and the *Test Coordinator's Handbook.* Professional item writers—many with teaching experience—developed the CAT/5 items. Items were carefully edited, and vocabulary difficulty, plus passage difficulty and length, were monitored closely using well-known readability formulas. Later, during tryout, participating teachers were asked to comment on the appropriateness of the items. Another review of the entire test involved curriculum experts as well as teachers. It is evident that the test developers were especially sensitive to the issue of bias. Thoughtful procedures were followed to avoid items that might exhibit gender, ethnic, or racial bias. These efforts included both internal and external reviews, as well as empirical analyses using statistical procedures.

New items (as well as anchor items from the Benchmark format of the Comprehensive Tests of Basic Skills, Fourth Edition [CTBS/4], used for linking purposes) were administered to representative samples of students during the winter of 1991. The resultant tryout data were analyzed using the three-parameter item response theory (IRT) model. (The three-parameter model incorporates item difficulty, item discrimination, and the probability of a correct response by a very low-scoring student.) Items were selected for the final versions of the tests based on data yielded by the tryouts (e.g., IRT item parameters, fit of the item to the three-parameter IRT model) as well as other types of information (e.g., bias ratings, match with content). Thus, item selection involved choosing those items with the best statistical characteristics within content considerations. These items then were administered in spring 1991 to a second sample in order to obtain data for use in scaling and equating. This second administration was a necessary follow-up to the initial tryout, in that it involved larger samples, occurred in the spring rather than the winter, and likely avoided the theoretical possibility of bias in parameter estimates due to "capitalization on chance."

During the test construction phase, the various configurations and forms of the CAT/5 were matched closely in terms of content and statistical properties to ensure that they would yield equivalent scores. During the norming stage, the three-parameter IRT model was used for scaling and equating. All test levels except K are "vertically" linked. The Benchmark tests from the CTBS/4 and inter-level linkage tests were used to establish the score scale and link the items in the successive test levels. According to the *CAT/5 Technical Bulletin 1,* "Approximately half the items in each inter-level linkage test are from the lower of the two levels being linked, and the other half are from the upper level" (p. 35). The developers used adequate numbers of examinee responses to accomplish the linking. The final step in this process involved linearly transforming the scale so that all scores (across the entire grade span measured by the CAT/5) range from 1 to 999.

The use of IRT scaling and equating was advantageous for at least two reasons. First, these models allow for items in different tests or test levels to be calibrated (placed on the same scale); use of calibrated item parameters in test scoring results in equated scores. Second, IRT scores are based on the relationship of an examinee's overall pattern of responses to the parameters associated with each test item (rather than simply the number of correct responses, which does not take into account each item's characteristics), resulting in more accurate measurement.

National standardization took place during the winter, spring, and fall of 1991. The winter standardization (only Level 11 at Grade 1) took place during January and involved 4,161 students. The fall standardization (all levels except Level 10 at K and Level 11 at Grade 1) was completed in October. The spring standardization (all levels except Level 10 at Grade 1) took place in April. Overall (Grades K through 12), sample sizes per level for the spring and fall standardizations ranged from 3,541 to 11,306. More specifically, sample sizes at the various levels for Grades 1 through 8 ranged from 9,198 to 11,306.

The developers utilized a stratified random sampling procedure to ensure that all socioeconomic and minority groups were fairly represented. Stratification variables included geographic region (Northeast, Midwest, Southeast, West), community type (urban, suburban, rural, large urban), and socioeconomic status. In the end, public school districts, Catholic dioceses, and private non-Catholic schools were sampled in a stratified manner. Participating schools were asked to test all students who normally would be tested.

According to the *CAT/5 Technical Bulletin 1*, "a reliable test is one that produces scores that are expected to be relatively stable if the test is administered repeatedly under similar conditions" (CTB/Macmillan/McGraw-Hill, 1992, p. 43). The most direct measure of this would entail estimates of test-retest score reliability, compiled by testing the same sample of students on two separate occasions and then correlating their scores. The stronger the correlation coefficient, the more reliable the test (over time). At the time of this review, test-retest reliability data were unavailable for the CAT/5, but a test-retest reliability study was planned for spring 1993. The test-retest reliability of the previous CAT (1985) was satisfactory. Wardrop (1989) observed that test-retest reliabilities over a 2½-week period were greater than or equivalent to the reported internal consistency (KR-20) estimates.

Another significant indicator of test score reliability is internal consistency. One measure of this, the Kuder-Richardson formula 20 (KR-20), efficiently produces a reliability estimate based on a single administration of the test. KR-20 reliabilities for the CAT/5 spring 1991 sample are provided in Tables 5 and 6 of the *CAT/5 Technical Bulletin 1* (pp. 49–53) for each of the tests in the test battery. For the Survey (Form A), KR-20 values ranged from .59 to .90, with most falling in the .70s and .80s. For the Complete Battery (Form A), KR-20 values ranged from .65 to .95, with most in the .80s and .90s. As would be expected, the longer tests composing the Complete Battery (e.g., 40 vs. 20 items per test) tended to produce greater KR-20 reliability estimates. All in all, the reliability estimates seem satisfactory for instruments of this nature. The technical bulletin also reports standard errors of measurement for subtests and total scores, and adequately explains and emphasizes this important concept.

Because there are two forms of the CAT/5 (A and B), alternate forms reliability estimates should be reported, representing the correlation between Form A and Form B administered to the same sample. Although unavailable at the time of this review, estimates should be provided in the next edition of the technical bulletin.

The forthcoming test-retest and alternate forms reliability estimates are important measures of the CAT/5's reliability. As Standard 2.6 of the *Standards for Educational and Psychological Testing* (American Educational Research Association, American Psychological Association, & National Council on Measurement in Education, 1985) states, "Coefficients based on internal analysis should not be interpreted as substitutes for alternate-form reliability or estimates of stability over time unless other evidence supports that interpretation in a particular context" (p. 21).

Finally, because objective mastery results are reported, the technical bulletin should report estimates of the reliability of these mastery classification decisions. (It is likely that decision reliability estimates will be quite low, given the small number of items used to measure each objective.) The publishers do, however, utilize confidence intervals to report objective mastery data for an individual student, so users are given some information about the reliability of mastery classifications.

Content validity is of utmost importance for an achievement test. That is, does the test measure what it is supposed to measure? Content validity is built into a test through the careful selection of items. As indicated earlier, the CAT/5 authors developed educational objectives in a very thorough manner, and item writers worked "in concert" so that their items better reflected the more integrated curriculum of today's schools. Though item classification tables were not available for examination at the time of this review, the previous edition of the CAT (1985) appears to have had excellent content validity, and that will likely be the case for the CAT/5.

According to *Technical Bulletin 1*, the CAT/5 was designed to measure "students' understanding of the broad concepts developed by all curricula as opposed to being content specific to any particular instruction program" and to "demonstrate students' skills in applying information" (CTB/Macmillan/McGraw-Hill, 1992, p. 5). Because of this broad content base, the publisher considers the new tests to be more accurate representations of curriculum domains and, therefore, more content valid.

No information concerning construct validity or criterion-related validity (either concurrent or predictive) appeared in the *CAT/5 Technical Bulletin 1*. These reviewers hope that both of these validity matters will be addressed in future publications.

A final issue that concerns a test's validity for particular groups is that of bias. Part 5 of the *CAT/5 Technical Bulletin 1*, titled "Bias Studies," begins by defining test bias as occurring when the test is "measuring different things for different groups" (CTB/Macmillan/McGraw-Hill, 1992, p. 25). After describing the concept of bias in some detail, the bulletin lists the procedures utilized to reduce potential bias in their battery. As mentioned earlier, efforts included careful internal and external bias reviews, as well as an empirical analysis by way of studies utilizing a procedure suggested by Linn and Harnisch (1981). The bulletin provides a table of ethnic bias ratings for both the Survey, Form A (Levels 12 through 21/22) and for the Complete Battery, Form A (Levels 10 through 21/22). The editors were "required to produce final tests that had average bias ratings better than the pool of on-level tryout items" (p. 21).

Critique

At the time of this writing (September 1992), only a subset of the CAT/5 materials were available for examination. In particular, the *Class Management Guide: Using Test Results* and the *Test Coordinator's Handbook* were still in production, as were several of the assessment options. Thus, in producing this review, we relied heavily upon the *CAT/5 Technical Bulletin 1*, the publisher's 1992 catalog, sample CAT/5 tests (Form A), reviews of previous CAT editions, and personal communication with representatives of CTB/McGraw-Hill.

As an achievement battery, the CAT/5 has several notable strengths. First, the entire test development process was carried out in a very thorough and professional manner. Efforts to achieve content validity were first-rate. Indeed, the developers appear to have selected items that do reflect the current instructional trend toward the integration of various skills across the curriculum. Their use of vertical equating is commendable, as is the presence of locator tests.

Second, the variety of test configurations, the assessment options, and the types of score reports allow test consumers to choose the arrangement that best suits their needs. In particular, the Performance Assessment Component promises to be a valuable tool.

The *CAT/5 Technical Bulletin 1* and other ancillary documents are highly readable and easy to use. Though the new edition of the *Class Management Guide* was unavailable at the time of our writing, we would note that reviews of previous versions of the guide (e.g., Airasian, 1989; Bunch, 1985) have given it high praise in terms of its clarity and helpfulness.

Finally, the test developers have made significant efforts to reduce potential bias in their tests through internal and external reviews and through statistical analysis.

In fairness, it should be noted that several of the criticisms that follow may be made regarding the majority of standardized achievement tests. First, previous reviewers of the 1977 and 1985 CAT (Rogers, 1985; Wardrop, 1989) have observed that the number of "first-choice" schools that elected not to participate in the norming process were not reported. Although we have not seen documentation regarding this figure for the CAT/5, perhaps a forthcoming publication will provide this information.

A second issue of concern regards producing mastery scores based on four items per area. Such a limited sampling tends to yield a score with a large standard error of measurement, making the reliability and validity of the mastery score rather suspect. Previous reviewers (e.g., Bunch, 1985) have made this same point.

Finally, the issues of construct and criterion-related validity need more coverage. In particular, Messick (1989) and others have advanced the argument that all validity is in reality construct validity. Regarding construct validity, Airasian (1989) noted a "substantial overlap" between the California Achievement Test and the Test of Cognitive Skills. As these are companion instruments, this seems somewhat natural; however, Standard 1.8 in the *Standards for Educational and Psychological Testing* (AERA, APA, & NCME, 1985) suggests that if the test is purported to be a measure of a specific construct (e.g., achievement), then it "should be distinguished from other constructs" (e.g., ability) (p. 15). According to the developers of the CAT/5, the test items have become more global in nature. Consequently, the test itself may have become even more similar to the Test of Cognitive Skills. Increased discussion of this issue would be appreciated.

In conclusion, despite the concerns listed above, the CAT/5 appears to be an excellent achievement test battery that represents the state of the art in terms of test development practices. It will likely enjoy the popularity that previous editions have attained and will serve school districts, and the children who are their raison d'etre, well.

References

Airasian, P.W. (1989). California Achievement Tests, Forms E and F. In J.C. Conoley & J.J. Kramer (Eds.), *The tenth mental measurements yearbook* (pp. 126–128). Lincoln, NE: Buros Institute of Mental Measurements.

American Educational Research Association, American Psychological Association, & National Council on Measurement in Education. (1985). *Standards for educational and psychological testing*. Washington, DC: American Psychological Association.

Bunch, M.B. (1985). California Achievement Tests, Forms C and D. In D.J. Keyser & R.C. Sweetland (Eds.), *Test critiques* (Vol. III, pp. 111–124). Austin, TX: PRO-ED.

Cannell, J.J. (1987). *Nationally normed elementary achievement testing in America's public schools: How all fifty states are above the national average*. Daniels, WV: Friends for Education.

CTB/Macmillan/McGraw-Hill. (1992). *CAT/5 technical bulletin 1*. Monterey, CA: Author.

CTB/McGraw-Hill. (1986a). *CAT (Forms E and F) class management guide: Using test results*. Monterey, CA: Author.

CTB/McGraw-Hill. (1986b). *CAT (Forms E and F) test coordinator's handbook*. Monterey, CA: Author.

Linn, R.L., Graue, M.E., & Sanders, N.M. (1990). Comparing state and district test results to national norms: The validity of the claims that "everyone is above average." *Educational Measurement: Issues and Practice, 9* (3), 5–14.

Linn, R.L., & Harnisch, D. (1981). Interactions between item content and group membership in achievement test items. *Journal of Educational Measurement, 18,* 109–118.

Messick, S. (1989). Validity. In R.L. Linn (Ed.), *Educational measurement* (3rd ed., pp. 13–103). New York: Macmillan.

Rogers, B.G. (1985). California Achievement Tests, Forms C and D. In J.V. Mitchell, Jr. (Ed.), *The ninth mental measurements yearbook* (pp. 243–246). Lincoln, NE: Buros Institute of Mental Measurements.

Shepard, L.A. (1990). Inflated test score gains: Is the problem old norms or teaching the test? *Educational Measurement: Issues and Practice, 9*(3), 15–22.

Wardrop, J.L. (1989). California Achievement Tests, Forms E and F. In J.C. Conoley & J.J. Kramer (Eds.), *The tenth mental measurements yearbook* (pp. 128–133). Lincoln, NE: Buros Institute of Mental Measurements.

Oliver C.S. Tzeng, Ph.D.
Professor of Psychology, Indiana University–Purdue University at Indianapolis, Indianapolis, Indiana.

CALIFORNIA MARRIAGE READINESS EVALUATION

Morse P. Manson. Los Angeles, California: Western Psychological Services.

Introduction

As indicated by its title, the California Marriage Readiness Evaluation (CMRE) was designed to evaluate certain areas of probable maladjustment or conflict in premarital couples. The test follows a relatively simple, objective, and comprehensive approach for providing individuals with counseling prior to marriage.

Manson (1965) offered two major reasons for the development of this measure. First, the distressing trends in divorce and family disruption in contemporary society indicated the need for effective tools in counseling premarital couples confronted with various relationship problems. Second, he shared the general belief that the vulnerability of unsuccessful, especially early, marriage derived primarily from a lack of preparation and communication skills. Thus, the author developed the CMRE to serve three useful functions: 1) to identify a couple's strengths and weaknesses (including specific problems) in the premarital relationship, 2) to identify similarities and differences between their perceptions and expectations, and 3) to evaluate issues and concerns that may not be relevant to marriage readiness but are important to satisfying marriages.

The CMRE measures three domains of marriage readiness, and each domain further contains two to three subscales: Personality (Character Structure, Emotional Maturity, Marriage Readiness), Interpersonal Compatibility (Marriage Motivation and Compatibility), and Preparation for Marriage (Family Experiences, Dealing with Money, and Planning Ahead). As the instrument emerged from a clinical and counseling approach, its measurement domains, subscales, and items were all constructed on the basis of the author's subjective experiences from therapeutical or clinical settings.

The Personality domain and its three subscales are purported to determine the level of effectiveness and satisfaction of a marital relationship. The Preparation for Marriage domain and its three subscales are designed to deal with money and the ability to plan ahead in order to ensure a smooth marriage. The Interpersonal domain and its two subscales are used to understand the motivation to embark upon a marriage in reference to physical, emotional, and cultural compatibilities between two individuals.

The eight subscales are measured by a total of 110 statements (items). The respondent judges each statement true or false as applied to his or her relation-

120

ship with the other individual. As an example, an item such as "I have been gainfully employed for the last two years or more" would be scored for Character Structure; "Children are a nuisance" would be scored for Character Structure, Emotional Maturity, and Dealing with Money; and "We enjoy talking to each other" would be scored for Compatibility. At the end of the test, five open-ended statements (e.g., "I am most worried about . . .") elicit subjects' inner feelings, thoughts, or "projective" information. The entire test takes about 30 minutes to complete and can be used with individuals having relatively low reading levels.

Each item is scored into more than one subscales. Consequently, 239 different scores are generated from the 110 test items. The various combinations of these item scores yield 12 different measures about marriage readiness in correspondence with the eight subscales, three major measurement domains, and overall test. The test (raw) scores of each subject on these measures are further summarized graphically on a profile, so that each subject's readiness can be characterized in terms of four discriminatory levels, ranging from *minimum readiness, fair readiness, good readiness,* to *maximum readiness.*

Practical Applications/Uses

Each subject's CMRE profile is intended to aid in identifying traits, characteristics, behaviors, symptoms, signs, and trends of relationship patterns. Specifically, for counselors or clinicians, the profile should serve as a means of gaining an overall understanding of the attitudes, values, habits, and motivations of each subject. Such information should provide leads for further investigation in the therapeutic setting. Patterns of responses across all subscales and major categories may signal certain potential difficulties that serve to contraindicate marriage at a certain time and to a specific person.

The response patterns of each individual also can be used to compare with those of the potential spouse. Marked differences in responses or discrepancies in profile patterns would indicate important areas where the clinicians should raise questions.

In general, profiles with all areas scored as "good readiness" or "maximum readiness" identify the individual as mature, prepared, and willing to meet the responsibilities of a long-term commitment relationship. Profiles falling in the "minimum readiness" or "fair readiness" levels indicate immaturity, unreadiness, and unwillingness to face the responsibilities of married life, even though the individual may be currently in a relationship. All "fair readiness" or "minimum readiness" patterns should be interpreted with caution, because they may represent individual weaknesses or those of the relationship itself.

All CMRE subscales and measurement domains are considered equally important. Thus different patterns of readiness across different individuals should be interpreted with reference to the different personality configurations of all individuals. For example, a relatively mature and stable young person might show immaturity in the handling of money or planning ahead, perhaps due to limited experience and training, but show good potential for growth and development in the subcategories and/or major categories in which he or she is deficient.

Thus, the user can compare profiles of individuals with those of their partners in order to assess the readiness and compatibility of the couple before marriage. Specifically, "danger signals" can be detected in terms of low scores, marked discrepancies in scores between the couple, strong doubts or uncertainties about each other, and limited knowledge or understanding of each other. If many items cannot be answered or if many questions are raised in answering the questionnaire, the individuals may feel that they are not yet ready for marriage.

Technical Aspects

Since its publication over 25 years ago, the CMRE has received very little evaluation in the research community from both the application and test construction perspectives. The major weaknesses seem related to issues of theoretical foundations, measurement properties, and empirical statistical evidence in the development of a scientific instrument for measuring intimate relationships.

At the theoretical level, this scale was not built on any prevailing theories of love and intimate relations (for a comprehensive description and evaluation of some 30 theorizations of love development, maintenance, conflict, and dissolution, see Tzeng, 1991). Consequently, the three major domains and eight subscales were intuitively constructed without theoretical postulations and justifications.

At the measurement level, no quantitative indices such as reliability and validity measures have been attempted. Many measurement issues remain unaccounted for, such as the representativeness of the entire item pool for marriage considerations, the response format of individual items, multiple scorings for an individual item, internal consistency among markers for each subscale, construct validity of individual subscales, and the discriminability of score profiles between couples ready and unready for marriage. In comparisons with other existing measures for love and intimate relationships, this scale is much too intuitive (primitive) to fulfill the requirements of measurement properties (for a summary description of over 26 measurement scales on love and intimate relationships, see Tzeng, in press).

Finally, at the statistical evidence level, the CMRE lacks normative data (profiles and scores of representative norm groups) for users to compare results with. Thus, the utility of the resulting profile is strictly limited to speculation and inference. Marriage counselors should treat these profiles as only a device for stimulating clients' active participation in the interviewing process.

Critique

Overall, the California Marriage Readiness Evaluation is poorly constructed, without reasonable considerations and logical linkage across issues on the theoretical foundations, measurement properties, and statistical evidence of marriage development. Consequently, for the development of love and marriage research, it can only be considered as an initial protocol of measurement that desperately needs improvement, revision, and further evaluation to become a sophisticated measurement tool in the future.

References

Manson, M.P. (1965). *California Marriage Readiness Evaluation: Manual.* Los Angeles: Western Psychological Services.

Tzeng, O.C.S. (1991). *Theories of love development, maintenance, and dissolution: Octagonal cycle and differential perspectives.* Westport, CT: Praeger.

Tzeng, O.C.S. (in press). *Measurement of love and intimate relations: Theories, scales, and applications for love development, maintenance, and dissolution.* Westport, CT: Praeger.

Julian Fabry, Ph.D.
Counseling Psychologist, Omaha, Nebraska.

CANTER BACKGROUND INTERFERENCE PROCEDURE FOR THE BENDER GESTALT TEST

Arthur Canter. Los Angeles, California: Western Psychological Services.

Introduction

The Canter Background Interference Procedure (BIP) for the Bender Gestalt Test is an adaptation of the method originally designed by Wertheimer to measure an individual's visual perceptual tendencies to reproduce geometric configurations. Lauretta Bender, a psychiatrist, pioneered the use of her visual-motor gestalt test with a wide variety of clinical groups at Bellevue Hospital in New York City (Bender, 1938). The assessment was used in the evaluation of cortical functioning. Although she produced a manual, it included no reliability, validity, or systematic data analysis, largely because no systematic scoring procedure had been developed.

The BIP was developed in order to assist in the evaluation and diagnosis of various cerebral pathological states. At the time of its inception, no predictive validity studies on the effectiveness of diagnosing organic brain damage existed. The Bender Gestalt had relied on the clinical acumen of the clinician rather than on objective assessment to judge pathological levels of performance. Arthur Canter of the University of Iowa was frustrated with this lack of objectivity in scoring and evaluating an examinee's performance. Inadvertently he found that a coffee stain on a piece of graph paper strained the performance of a neurosurgical patient. This began Canter's study of interference effects that eventually produced the current method.

The assessment begins with the administration of the Bender Gestalt under the standard method in which the subject copies nine geometric designs (identified as A and 1–8) onto an 8½" x 11" sheet of white paper. After a short delay with some other activity (i.e., the administration of an IQ test or further interviewing), the test is readministered using a sheet of paper configured with intersecting sinusoidal lines, which provide background "noise" or interference to the examinee. Upon completion, the examiner compares the subject's performance on both administrations after scoring the assessments via the Pascal-Suttell criteria (1951). Specially constructed tables for the standard and BIP methods are used to classify the results into an organic, borderline, or nonorganic category.

The BIP manual gives detailed instructions on the administration, scoring, and determination of various scores and diagnoses. Specific attention is paid to "false positives and negatives" in categorizing a person's performance.

Practical Applications/Uses

The BIP was developed to identify individuals with mild to severe organic brain dysfunctioning. In addition, this assessment was designed to differentiate normals from organics, organics from psychotics, and organic psychotics from nonorganic psychotics.

The test can be administered by technicians (i.e., psychometrists) and para-professionals as well as professionals. It can be used in clinics and hospitals where this type of assessment is needed.

As noted previously, directions for administering and scoring this assessment are contained in the manual. The exercises provided allow novice users to compare their scorings with those of the author.

The BIP can be administered within 20 minutes. However, the author strongly recommends that one do so after some interviewing activity and the standard administration. The procedure can comprise part of a neuropsychological battery or be given by itself. As with other appraisal techniques, the user should address a referral question as well as obtain a biopsychosocial history that includes hospital admissions, accidents, and the use of medications, alcohol, and drugs.

Canter recommends the BIP for individuals 15 years of age or older, although Adams and Kenny (1982) found it effective with 12- to 16-year-olds who were labeled as having cerebral dysfunctioning. These researchers discovered an 81% "hit rate" within this age group, whereas they found only a 60% rate in a 6- to 11-year-old group of cerebrally dysfunctioning children.

Scoring criteria using the Pascal-Suttell (1951) method are available within the manual, and specific, detailed examples appear for each Bender Gestalt configuration. The user obtains scores for the standard as well as the BIP administration and can post them on a convenient form included in the BIP materials. Scores for each configuration are tallied and the difference between the standard and the BIP forms are established. Subtracting the BIP Summary Score from the Standard Summary Score yields the Difference Score (D-score). A table is entered in the manual using the Standard score to determine the "Base Level." With the D-score the user then enters a two-way table to determine the subject's classification (i.e., "C" = organic brain disorder; "B" = borderline or equivocal results; "A" = no organic brain disorder).

The manual and subsequent research hit rates suggest that 84% of organic and 95% of nonorganic brain-damaged patients can be identified by this method. Tsai and Tsuang (1981) have suggested using the BIP primarily when some other methods have yielded normal results as a way to avoid unnecessary CT scanning for psychiatric patients.

Canter indicates that certain diagnostic problem areas exist for the BIP in evaluating certain organic disorders. He notes that the procedure seems to miss convulsive disorders where there is no brain damage, especially left temporal lobe focal pathology and diffuse arteriosclerotic disease with minor CNS damage (see also Delaney, 1982; McKinzey, Curley, & Fish, 1985). The BIP also has been known to yield an organic picture for persons with bipolar disorder in the manic phase, for elderly patients with a history of depressive illness who have been treated with electroconvulsive therapy, and for "process" schizophrenics with a history of long hospitalizations (Canter, 1976, p. 10).

Subtle or residual defects that do not necessarily interfere with cognition or visuomotor coordination under ordinary circumstances can be appraised with this procedure. Canter (1976) has suggested that residual defects in rehabilitated individuals who have recovered from organic brain damage as well as mildly diffuse organic states that may have accompanied drug abuse, toxicity, or endocrine dysfunction can be identified utilizing the BIP.

Technical Aspects

The BIP manual (Canter, 1976, p. 12) indicates that interrater reliability for the procedure ranges from .86 to .96. The document also presents a study involving a 30-minute test-retest reliability investigation on the error scores for the standard administration. The results indicate a correlation of .88. A correlation of .57 was determined for the D-score on the BIP, but Canter (1976) states that 90% of the individuals were still classified as they had been previously.

The author maintains that the proportion of nonorganics correctly identified is approximately 95% (Canter, 1976, p. 16). Within the manual, the author cites a number of studies comparing the BIP classification with actual diagnoses or classification accuracy. Heaton, Baade, and Johnson (1978) state that this procedure accurately classified 84% of organics. Song and Song (1969) used the BIP to separate organic mental retardates from a nonorganic "cultural-familial" retarded group. Canter and Straumanis (1969) reported that they correctly classified 14 of 16 senile and 16 of 17 healthy elderly persons by means of the BIP. The procedure also identified all 16 nonschizophrenic organic patients, 13% of short-term hospitalized schizophrenics, and 24% of long-term hospitalized schizophrenics (Canter, 1971). Positive results also seem to have been found with hebophrenic or "process" schizophrenics.

In a study of various diagnostic methods (BIP, EEG, brain scan, and skull X ray) for brain-damaged individuals, Krop and Cohen (1972) reported that the BIP correctly classified 70%; the EEG hit 61%, the standard Bender 56%, the skull X ray 45%, and the brain scan 42%.

Further results of various research projects suggest that the difference scores (D-score) between the standard administration and the BIP probably are not affected by the artifacts of intelligence (Yulis, 1969). Although the degree of difference found varied considerably between right and left hemiplegics, they still fell within the organic range when compared to non-brain-damaged controls (Nemec, 1977).

Critique

The Canter Background Interference Procedure appears to be an adequate neuropsychological assessment in evaluating nonorganic individuals as well as some organic individuals within a variety of pathological groups. It apparently is not so useful with children under the age of 13, nor with epileptics.

Along with the advantages of ease of administration, nonthreatening nature, and some significant supporting research, the BIP offers low distortion probability unless a subject has knowledge of the procedure (Canter, 1976, p. 11). As noted previously, the assessment also has the flexibility of utilization within a battery or alone as a screening instrument. Further research may enhance this instrument's utility in clinics and hospitals where a brief assessment is required instead of more costly investigations.

References

This list contains text citations and suggested additional reading.

Adams, J., & Canter, A.H. (1969). Performance characteristics of school children in the BIP Bender Test. *Journal of Consulting and Clinical Psychology, 33*, 508.

Adams, J., & Kenny, T.J. (1982). Cross-validation of the Canter Background Interference Procedure in identifying children with cerebral dysfunction. *Journal of Consulting and Clinical Psychology, 50*(2), 307–309.

Adams, J., Kenny, T.J., & Canter, A.H. (1973). The efficiency of the Canter Background Interference Procedure in identifying children with cerebral dysfunction. *Journal of Consulting and Clinical Psychology, 40*, 489.

Bender, L.A. (1938). A visual motor gestalt test and its clinical use. *American Orthopsychiatric Association Research Monographs* (No. 3).

Canter, A.H. (1963). A background interference procedure for graphomotor tests in the study of deficit. *Perceptual and Motor Skills, 16*, 914.

Canter, A.H. (1966). A background interference procedure to increase sensitivity of the Bender Gestalt Test to organic brain disorder. *Journal of Consulting Psychology, 30*, 91–97.

Canter, A.H. (1968). BIP Bender Test for the detection of organic brain disorder: Modified scoring method and replication. *Journal of Consulting and Clinical Psychology, 32*, 522–526.

Canter, A.H. (1971). A comparison of the Background Interference Procedure effect in schizophrenic, non-schizophrenic and organic patients. *Journal of Clinical Psychology, 27*, 473–474.

Canter, A.H. (1976). *The Canter Background Interference Procedure for the Bender Gestalt Test: Manual for administration, scoring and interpretation.* Los Angeles: Western Psychological Services.

Canter, A.H., & Straumanis, J.J. (1969). Performance of senile and healthy aged persons on the BIP Bender Test. *Perceptual and Motor Skills, 28*, 695–698.

Delaney, R. (1982). Screening for organicity: The problem of subtle neuropsychological deficit and diagnosis. *Journal of Clinical Psychology, 38*(4), 843–846.

Heaton, R.K., Baade, L.E., & Johnson, K.L. (1978). Neuropsychological test results associated with psychiatric disorders in adults. *Psychological Bulletin, 85*, 141–162.

Krop, H., & Cohen, E. (1972, April). *Predictive validity of the BIP Bender Test.* Paper presented at the annual meeting of the Southeastern Psychological Association, Atlanta.

McKinzey, R.K., Curley, J.F., & Fish, J.M. (1985). False negatives, Canter's Background Interference Procedure, the Trailmaking Test and epileptics. *Journal of Clinical Psychology, 41*(6), 812–820.

Nemec, R.E. (1978). Effects of controlled background interference on test performance by right and left hemiplegics. *Journal of Consulting and Clinical Psychology, 46*, 294–297.

Pascal, G.R., & Suttell, G.J. (1951). *The Bender Gestalt Test: Its quantification and validity for adults.* New York: Grune & Stratton.

Song, A.Y., & Song, R.H. (1969). The Bender Gestalt Test with the Background Interference Procedure on mental retardates. *Journal of Clinical Psychology, 25*, 69–71.

Tsai, L., & Tsuang, M. (1981). How can we avoid unnecessary CT scanning for psychiatric patients? *Journal of Clinical Psychiatry, 42*(12), 452–454.

Whitworth, R.H. (1984). Bender Visual Motor Gestalt Test. In D.J. Keyser & R.C. Sweetland (Eds.), *Test critiques* (Vol. I, pp. 90–98). Austin, TX: PRO-ED.

Yulis, S. (1969). The relationship between the Canter Background Interference Procedure and intelligence. *Journal of Clinical Psychology, 25*, 405–406.

Chester I. Palmer, Ed.D.
Professor of Mathematics, Auburn University at Montgomery, Montgomery, Alabama.

COLLEGE-LEVEL EXAMINATION PROGRAM GENERAL EXAMINATIONS

The College Board. New York, New York: The College Board.

Introduction

The College-Level Examination Program (CLEP) is the most widely accepted credit-by-examination program in the United States; about 2,800 colleges and universities award credit for at least some of the CLEP examinations, including nearly three quarters of all accredited institutions of higher education. The Program, which is administered by the College Entrance Examination Board (the "College Board"), consists of three sets of tests: 5 General Examinations, covering the areas of English Composition (two test versions, one with essay and one without), Humanities, Mathematics, Natural Sciences, and Social Sciences and History; 30 Subject Examinations, each intended to test the content of one to three specific college courses; and 2 Education Assessment Series (EAS) tests, constructed as parallel to the General Examinations in English Composition and Mathematics, and intended not for awarding credit but for assessing groups of college students at any point from admission to the end of the general education portion of their programs. This review discusses only the General Examinations, although much of the discussion of the English Composition and Mathematics examinations also applies to the EAS examinations.

The General Examinations are intended to allow students to obtain credit for courses normally required in the general education portion of a college program. According to the College Board, "each of the five General Examinations covers material taught in courses that most students take as requirements during their first two years of college" (1992, p. 1). The registration brochure explains that "three or six semester hours of credit are usually awarded for satisfactory scores on each General Examination" (The College Board, 1991, p. 5). All the College Board publications are careful to indicate, however, that the amount and kind of credit offered for a particular test or score are determined by the college involved and not by the CLEP program. The five General Examinations are administered as separate tests, not as a battery; that is, a student may choose to take any number and combination of them. The tests are administered at about 1,200 participating institutions of higher education, each of which sets its own examination schedule (except for the General Examination in English Composition with Essay, which at present is offered only four times per year; there are plans to offer it eight times per year in the future). Students must register at least 4 weeks before the testing date. The Program makes a number of accommodations available for candidates with disabilities. Score reports are provided to the candidate and to one institution requested at the time of registration; transcript service is available for 20 years. Score reports of candidates receiving special accommodations indicate that the test administration was nonstandard (The College Board, 1990b, "Overview," pp. 8–9).

CLEP General Examinations are constructed under the direction of committees of faculty members who are knowledgeable in the content area that the examination covers. For new tests or major revisions of existing ones, curriculum surveys gather information regarding course content at many institutions. The test committee has the principal responsibility for the development of the test specifications and the preparation and selection of items. The tests are then given to students at an appropriate level from a variety of colleges and universities. The results of such administrations allow the developers both to study the statistical properties of the test itself and its items, and to develop the scale for scoring the test (The College Board, 1990b, "Overview," pp. 10–11).

The CLEP General Examinations have a long and complex history. The initial forms were first developed in 1963, and at that time, all sections had a multiple-choice format. In 1972 all the tests other than English Composition were revised. In 1978 all five tests were revised; in addition, the English Composition test became available in two versions, one all multiple-choice, the other half multiple-choice and half a single essay. Finally, in 1986 the English Composition test was again revised; the new test was again offered in two versions, one with and one without an essay section. Over the years, the time limits changed a number of times, and all the tests had multiple forms and editions. The history of the scaling and equating of the various tests and forms is also very complex. In general, scores are reported on a scale set with a mean of 500 and standard deviation of 100 in the original reference group of last-semester college sophomores tested in 1963; the Mathematics test was rescaled in 1972. A detailed discussion of these issues is available in the "Overview" section of the *College-Level Examination Program Technical Manual* (The College Board, 1990b). For simplicity, and because it is unlikely that many students will present scores from before 1986, this review will discuss only the latest versions of the tests. It should be noted, however, that the technical manual indicates that a revised edition of the examination in Social Sciences and History is due in 1992. In addition, the test developer informed this reviewer that new versions of the English Composition and Mathematics examinations will be available in fall 1994.

The College Board publishes two excellent sources of information regarding the CLEP General Examinations; both in fact cover the Subject Examinations also. The *Official Handbook for the CLEP Examinations* (The College Board, 1992) is an outstanding guide for both students and professionals. In addition to general information on the program, the book offers detailed information about each test, including the format (number of sections and number and type of questions), the content (coverage by topic and by taxonomic level), a list of suggested readings, and a set of 20 to 40 sample questions prepared by the committee that developed the examination. The 1992 handbook replaced the earlier but similar *College Board Guide to the CLEP Examinations* (The College Board, 1990a). Professionals also may wish to consult the previously mentioned technical manual, which is outstanding as well. It begins with an overview section that discusses the history of the program and test development, administration, and scoring; it also offers suggestions regarding the development of an institutional CLEP policy and summarizes the recommendations of various learned organizations regarding policies for awarding academic credit for CLEP examinations. The overview is followed by a Test Information Guide for each examination. Each Guide contains a detailed history of the particular test, information regarding the test similar to that in the handbook, reference data on student performance in terms of both raw scores and scaled scores, and information on item statistics and test reliability, validity, and speededness. The presentations could serve as models in presenting technical information concisely but clearly; for the General Examinations, the Guides are each only 11 to 15 pages long.

Practical Applications/Uses

The principal use of the CLEP General Examinations is the granting of credit for part or all of the general education components of a college program. Accordingly, this use will be considered first, and other possible uses later.

In evaluating the use of a test for college credit, there are two principal considerations. The first is test content: Exactly what material does the test cover, and at what level? The user must then decide whether the coverage is worthy of college credit at a particular institution. For the General Examinations, the content may not need to match closely any particular course(s) as long as it adequately meets institutional expectations regarding general education. Assuming that the content is acceptable, users then must select the cutoff score for granting credit. Both of these issues will be discussed in detail below.

The following brief summaries of test content are based on more detailed information available in both the CLEP handbook and the technical manual. Each test is given in two separately timed sections and each is formula scored, using the usual correction for guessing.

The English Composition Examination covers only composition; it does not include research skills or literature. Section I of the examination contains 55 items covering grammar, usage, and clarity of expression. On the version including an essay, Section II requires a single argumentative essay. On the version without essay, Section II contains 40 items covering organization, argumentation, and emphasis. Each section has a time limit of 45 minutes. Essays are scored holistically, each by at least two readers; the technical manual details the grading process. This reviewer's English consultant thought the items excellent, with content corresponding to a rigorous course in English composition.

New versions of the English Composition Examination (both with and without essay) are scheduled for initial administration in fall 1994. The developer provided this reviewer with an early draft of the proposed new content specifications, which of course could change during the development process. However, according to current plans, the major difference is that the new version will give substantially less weight to work at the sentence level and more weight to work within the context of extended passages of text. Thus, the current, all multiple-choice version gives weights of 73% to work at the sentence level and 27% to work with extended passages, compared with planned weights of 55% and 45% on the new version;

the current version with essay gives weights of 50% to work at the sentence level and 50% to the essay, compared with planned weights of 30% for work at the sentence level, 20% to work with extended passages, and 50% to the essay. No items were available for examination at the time of this review.

The Humanities Examination covers literature (50%) and fine arts (25% visual arts, 15% music, 10% other). About 50% of the items are at the level of factual information, 30% involve recognitions of techniques, and 20% involve interpretation of presumably unfamiliar material. Each section has a time limit of 45 minutes and contains 75 items; each topic area appears in both sections. In addition to the overall Humanities score, the examination yields subscores for Literature and for Fine Arts; however, these subscores are not intended for the granting of credit in the separate areas. (Beginning July 1, 1993, subscores no longer will be reported.) This reviewer's humanities consultant thought the items good, the coverage extremely broad, and the level appropriate.

On the Mathematics Examination, Section I, with a time limit of 30 minutes, contains 40 items covering basic skills and concepts in arithmetic (30%), algebra (35%), geometry (15%–20%), and data interpretation (15%–20%). Section II, consisting of 50 items with a time limit of 60 minutes, covers college topics, including sets and logic (20%), real numbers (30%), functions and graphs (20%), probability and statistics (15%), and other algebraic topics (15%). In the overall score, Section I is weighted one third and Section II is weighted two thirds. In addition to the overall Mathematics score, separate subscores are reported for the two sections. (Beginning July 1, 1993, subscores no longer will be reported.) In general, the questions are well constructed. Some of the items use the "quantitative comparison" format, in which candidates are instructed to answer "A if the quantity in Column A is greater; B if the quantity in Column B is greater; C if the two quantities are equal; D if the relationship cannot be determined from the information given" (*Handbook*, p. 76). The reviewer dislikes the inherent complexity of such questions but agrees that such items often do have desirable statistical characteristics.

The developers have undertaken a new version of the Mathematics examination, scheduled for initial use in fall 1994. At the time of this writing, the content specifications were not complete, and thus this reviewer cannot give any details regarding possible changes in the new version.

Each section of the Natural Sciences Examination contains 60 items and has a time limit of 45 minutes. Section I (50% of the test) covers biological sciences, and Section II (also 50%) covers natural sciences. About 40% of the items require only factual knowledge, 20% require interpretation and comprehension of information presented on the test, and 40% cover applications of principles, with an emphasis on nonquantitative applications. Separate subscores are reported for biological and physical sciences, but again they are not intended for the granting of credit in particular subjects. (Beginning July 1, 1993, subscores no longer will be reported.) The reviewer's science consultant thought the items generally of high quality. He considered that for an examination covering general science courses for non–science majors, the items often reflected surprisingly high expectations for both factual information and analytic ability.

The Social Sciences and History Examination covers history (35%), sociology (25%–30%), economics (15%–20%), political science (15%–20%), and social psychology (3%–5%). Notice that, perhaps surprisingly, psychology receives very little emphasis. Each section has a time limit of 45 minutes; Section I contains 65 questions and Section II contains 60 questions, but each topic area appears in both sections. Separate subscores are reported for History and for Social Sciences, but these subscores are not intended for granting credit in the separate areas. (Beginning July 1, 1993, subscores no longer will be reported.) The reviewer's social science consultant thought the items good and at an appropriate level, but considered some of them dated. (Recall that a new edition of this test is currently in preparation.)

Overall, then, the CLEP General Examinations represent carefully constructed tests, each closely matching its published specifications. The extent to which the content of the examinations agrees with institutional expectation for general education will of course vary from campus to campus. Confidential inspection copies of actual tests are available from the developer for local review. In general, the English Composition examination and the Natural Sciences examination cover rather standard courses, likely to be found on most campuses and taken by many students. The Mathematics examination covers rather standard material, but material that usually is taught in courses taken by relatively few students. The Social Sciences and History examination covers relatively standard material, but material that is often spread across a wide variety of courses; the major areas are world history, U.S. history, sociology, economics, and political science. The Humanities examination contains a relatively standard section on literature, but the section on fine arts is not like any standard course. If institutions do decide to grant credit for some or all of these examinations, they must exercise care in choosing course equivalents. As an example, students majoring in sciences should probably not receive any credit toward a degree for the examinations in Mathematics and in Natural Sciences, both of which are clearly intended for non–science majors. (There are CLEP subject examinations in mathematics and science for which credit would probably be appropriate for science majors.) Thus, institutions offering credit should be careful to communicate to potential students which examinations are helpful in particular curricula.

Although it is certainly possible to quarrel with some of the individual items, overall item quality appears more than satisfactory, ranging from good to outstanding. For users who are in sympathy with the choice of test content, these tests are excellent measurement instruments.

It is now necessary to consider the selection of cutoff scores appropriate for granting credit. The College Board does not recommend specific cutoff scores, but the overview chapter of the technical manual does suggest a process for institutions to follow in setting cutoff scores. The method involves a combination of reviewing national data and recommendations and conducting local test administrations for setting standards. This reviewer agrees that such a process is desirable and would provide the required information but doubts that many institutions actually have implemented such steps.

In fact, the technical manual also provides information regarding the recommendations of various learned groups regarding cut scores. The American Council on Education (ACE) recommends that up to 6 semester hours of credit be given for a score of 421 or above on each of the CLEP General Examinations (Whitney &

Malizio, 1987). The summary of the ACE recommendations in the technical manual does not give specific cutoff scores, but recommends the range of 421 to 500. (These scores correspond to the 25th and 50th percentiles of the performance of second-semester sophomores at a variety of colleges and universities in 1963 for four of the tests and in 1972 for the Mathematics test.)

In the absence of local performance data, it is very difficult to evaluate the appropriateness of any particular cut score. As an example of some of the complexities, consider the history of group performance on the General Examination in Mathematics (all the information below comes from the technical manual). In the 1972 reference group of second-semester sophomores at 21 institutions, the 25th percentile of the scores was 424 and the median score was 497. Any proposed use of this information in setting a local cut score is subject to a number of concerns: How many of these students had taken college mathematics at all? For those who had taken college mathematics, which courses did they take, and how recently? Some such information is available in the technical manual and shows the importance of such considerations; on the 1963 Mathematics examination, in the reference group of last-semester college sophomores, engineering, mathematics, and physical science majors averaged 609, while education majors averaged 437. In 1978, the test was administered to students completing introductory-level college mathematics courses at 27 institutions; this time the 25th percentile score was only 396 and the median score was 446. One might expect that students just completing an appropriate course should score higher than the general population of second-semester sophomores, but in fact they scored noticeably lower. Why? The most probable explanation is that the population of students completing a general mathematics course is very different from that of college students at large; for example, it probably contains no mathematics, science, or engineering majors. In fact, at most institutions, students taking general mathematics courses tend to be low-performance students in mathematics. All these issues underline the usual caution that performance data must be interpreted with respect to the population from which they were derived. There are just too many variables involved here for anyone to make a reasonable choice of cut scores just from the national reference data—even before consideration of issues such as the representativeness of the institutions in the reference group. (Although, in fact, institutions rarely worry much about such issues when granting transfer credit, at least from accredited institutions, so it is not clear how important an issue this may be.)

It is true that it is somewhat easier to interpret the reference data for some of the other tests; but only for the English Composition test, where course work is far more uniform, does it seem reasonable to rely on the national data in setting cutoff scores. This reviewer strongly endorses the recommendation of The College Board that institutions conduct local studies for the purpose of establishing appropriate cutoff scores. The developer provides tests free, or at reduced rates, for such local studies (The College Board, 1990b, "Overview," p. 18).

Although these tests are intended primarily for granting college credit, other uses are certainly possible. An institution that requires students to elect courses in various areas of the curriculum could reasonably use the tests to provide exemptions from some such requirements even without offering credit. The technical manual suggests the possibility of using these tests for course placement ("Overview," p. 18). Obviously, local judgments of content are also important here, but at first glance, only the English Composition and Mathematics tests seem well suited for such use. The set of five tests would make a good instrument for measuring general education, although it is possible to take exception to the choice of topics in Mathematics for many students and in Natural Sciences for some. Because testing time for the five exams totals 7½ hours, however, using them as a general education test would require heroic efforts of the students; on the other hand, some kind of matrix sampling, such as randomly assigning each student to one of the five tests, would allow institutional assessment within a reasonable amount of student time. Note that for a less comprehensive look at student outcomes, CLEP offers the EAS Examinations in English Composition and in Mathematics. The EAS exams are intended for group assessment and provide content coverage parallel to that of the CLEP General Examinations on the same subjects. Each EAS exam requires 45 minutes of testing time, and the optional essay requires another 45 minutes.

Technical Aspects

There is little point in an extensive review of the technical aspects of these tests. In general, the technical work is at the very high level one would expect from a well-established program run by a leading testing organization.

It is difficult to calculate a meaningful reliability for the English Composition Test with Essay because it has only one essay; on the other tests, the lowest reliability is .895 and the highest .948. Standard errors of measurement for the scaled scores range from 18 to 26 points.

The CLEP General Examinations are quite difficult for their intended populations. In the 1978 reference population of students completing relevant college courses, the mean formula score was 32% in Natural Sciences, 33% in Mathematics, 37% in Social Sciences and History, 44% in Humanities, and 46% in English Composition. On each section of the Mathematics and Natural Sciences examinations, substantial numbers of students (14%–33%) scored in the chance range. Because these tests are intended to make a yes/no decision on credit, the reliability of the scores is far more important for those near the cutoff point than in other regions of the score distribution; for example, there is no point in distinguishing performance worth a grade of A from that worth a grade of B. Unfortunately, all multiple-choice tests suffer from the problem that high scores are generally more reliable than low ones, provided, as seems likely, that low-scoring candidates guess on more questions than high-scoring candidates. These tests are all too difficult for optimal discrimination at the cutoff score, at least for cutoff scores in the range of the ACE recommendations (421–500), although by varying amounts. For the recommended range of cutoff scores, the required formula scores are 33% to 49% of the total available score in English Composition, 31% to 49% in Humanities, 19% to 37% in Mathematics, 26% to 41% in Natural Sciences, and 27% to 45% in Social Sciences and History. Thus all of the tests, especially Mathematics, would be improved with somewhat easier questions, so that a higher formula score would be required to pass; nevertheless, all the tests have sufficient items to provide generally satisfactory measurement, even at these cutoff scores. The tests are mildly speeded, with the not-reached score variance representing about 10% of the total score variance.

Critique

The CLEP General Examinations are technically sound tests. They are all well constructed in accordance with published specifications. Many institutions, relying on the unquestioned competence of the test developer and the recommendations of groups such as the ACE, have probably developed policies for granting credit with very little consideration of either the extent to which the test content meets local expectations or of the desirability of setting cutoff scores in accordance with local standards. Despite the quality of the tests themselves, development of an appropriate institutional policy requires some careful consideration; indeed, the nature of the General Examinations, and the type of reference data available, may well make it more difficult to formulate a reasonable policy for the five General Examinations than for the much larger number of subject examinations, which are more closely tied to specific courses. The College Board states that "setting a fair and adequate CLEP policy cannot be done hurriedly. It should be a time-consuming, thoughtful process" (The College Board, 1990b, "Overview," p. 20). Institutions willing to engage in that process may find the CLEP General Examinations useful tools for offering students the opportunity to receive credit by examination.

References

The College Board. (1990a). *College Board guide to the CLEP examinations* (rev. ed.). New York: Author.

The College Board. (1990b). *College-Level Examination Program technical manual.* New York: Author.

The College Board. (1991). *CLEP: Making learning pay. Information for candidates and registration form, 1991–92.* New York: Author.

The College Board. (1992). *Official handbook for the CLEP examinations.* New York: Author.

Whitney, D.R., & Malizio, A.G. (Eds.). (1987). *Guide to educational credit by examination* (2nd ed.). New York: American Council on Education/Macmillan.

Chester I. Palmer, Ed.D.

Professor of Mathematics, Auburn University at Montgomery, Montgomery, Alabama.

COLLEGE-LEVEL EXAMINATION PROGRAM SUBJECT EXAMINATIONS IN MATHEMATICS: COLLEGE ALGEBRA, TRIGONOMETRY, COLLEGE ALGEBRA AND TRIGONOMETRY, CALCULUS WITH ELEMENTARY FUNCTIONS

The College Board. New York, New York: The College Board.

Introduction

As described in the preceding review of the College-Level Examination Program General Examinations, the CLEP tests make up the most widely accepted credit-by-examination program in the United States. About 2,800 colleges and universities award credit for at least some of these examinations, including about three fourths of all accredited institutions of higher education. Within the program's three sets of tests are the 5 General Examinations (English Composition, Humanities, Mathematics, Natural Sciences, and Social Sciences and History), 30 Subject Examinations (each intended to test the content of one to four specific college courses), and a pair of tests in the Education Assessment Series (English Composition and Mathematics) for assessing the general education level of groups of college students. This review discusses only the four subject examinations in mathematics: College Algebra, Trigonometry, College Algebra and Trigonometry, and Calculus with Elementary Functions. Some of the discussion of test construction and scaling, however, also applies to the other subject exams.

CLEP tests are administered at about 1,200 participating institutions of higher education. Each institution sets its own examination schedule except for the General Examination in English Composition with Essay, which is offered only four times per year. Students register with the institution where they will be tested at least 4 weeks before the testing date. A number of accommodations are available for candidates with disabilities. Score reports are provided to the candidate and to one institution requested at the time of registration, and a transcript service is available for 20 years. Score reports of candidates receiving special accommodations indicate that the test administration was nonstandard (The College Board, 1990b, "Overview," pp. 8–9).

Developers construct the CLEP subject examinations under the direction of faculty committees knowledgeable in the content area that the examination covers. For new tests, or major revisions of existing tests, curriculum surveys provide a means to gather information regarding course content at many institutions. The test committee has the principal responsibility for the development of the test

136

specifications and the preparation and selection of items. The tests then are taken by students from a variety of colleges and universities who are completing appropriate courses. The results of such administrations enable developers both to study the statistical properties of the test and its items and to establish the scale for scoring the test, which for a new test is set to mean 50 and standard deviation 10 in the reference group. For new forms of existing examinations, scores may be equated to those on previous forms (The College Board, 1990b, "Overview," pp. 10–12). Three of the four current subject examinations in mathematics are relatively old tests; the development of the present forms for the College Algebra, Trigonometry, and College Algebra and Trigonometry tests took place in 1979. Although the content of these courses has changed little since then, the data on student performance were at the time of this writing substantially outdated. The College Algebra test is currently being redeveloped, with a new version due in fall 1994. The Calculus with Elementary Functions test was last revised in 1986, but a new edition will be available beginning in fall 1993.

CLEP scores normally have correlations with course grades in the range of .30 to .70. For the four subject tests in mathematics, the correlations tend toward the high end of this range (.58–.64), as one might expect; mathematics is a relatively easy subject to examine in standardized multiple-choice format. Given the variability in grading standards between institutions and between instructors within institutions, it would be interesting to know how much higher these correlations would be if computed within institution or within instructor. More detailed information on the development and scaling of CLEP subject examinations is available in the *College Level Examination Program Technical Manual* (The College Board, 1990b, "Overview," pp. 10–15).

The College Board publishes two excellent sources of information regarding the CLEP Subject Examinations; both also cover the General Examinations. The *Official Handbook for the CLEP Examinations* (The College Board, 1992) represents an outstanding guide for both students and professionals. In addition to general information on the program, the book provides detailed information about each test, including the format (number of sections and number and type of questions), the content (coverage by topic and by taxonomic level), a list of suggested readings, and a set of 20 to 40 sample questions prepared by the committee that developed the examination. The 1992 handbook replaced the earlier but similar *College Board Guide to the CLEP Examinations* (The College Board, 1990a). Professionals also may wish to consult the technical manual (The College Board, 1990b), which is generally outstanding. This manual begins with an overview that discusses the history of the program and test development, administration, and scoring; it also offers suggestions about developing an institutional CLEP policy and summarizes the recommendations of various learned organizations regarding policies for awarding academic credit for CLEP examinations. The overview section is followed by a Test Information Guide for each examination. Each Guide contains a detailed history of the particular test, information regarding the test similar to that in the CLEP handbook, reference data on student performance (in terms of both raw scores and scaled scores), and information on item statistics and test reliability, validity, and speededness. The presentations could serve as models in presenting technical information concisely but clearly; for most examinations, the Guides run only 10 to 16 pages. Unfortunately, the information in the Guides for the mathematics tests is not always correct; detailed comments for each test appear below.

Practical Applications/Uses

CLEP subject examinations are intended for the purpose of granting course credit in one or more specific college courses. For the mathematics subject examinations, Calculus with Elementary Functions is designed to cover two courses, and each of the other examinations covers a single course.

In considering the use of these tests in granting course credit, there are two principal considerations: appropriateness of content and establishing cutoff scores. The College Board (1990b) recommends that users should, "if possible, conduct local standard-setting administrations" ("Overview," p. 18). This reviewer believes that such local administrations, although desirable, are less important for the subject examinations in mathematics than for the general exams. Unlike the latter, the subject examinations in mathematics all cover courses that are relatively standard on most campuses; thus, the national reference data do provide a reasonable guide to setting a cut score. (Of course, there are also practical considerations. It would be reasonable for institutions to conduct local studies of those CLEP tests that many students present, and rely on the national data for other CLEP tests.) The College Board (1990b) carefully refers to the results of its scaling administrations as "reference data" instead of "norms" because "institutions participate in CLEP studies on a voluntary basis and it is difficult to ascertain the representativeness of the samples" ("Overview," p. 6). As part of its analysis of the performance of the reference group, the College Board tabulates the average examination score obtained by students who receive each letter grade in the course. The American Council on Education (ACE) has recommended that, in the absence of local studies, colleges give credit to students who attain a score at least equal to that made by students who received grades of C in the course (Whitney & Malizio, 1987). For these tests, that recommendation sets cut scores of 45 in College Algebra, 50 in Trigonometry, 45 in College Algebra and Trigonometry, and 47 in Calculus with Elementary Functions. This method of setting cut scores seems reasonable, at least for institutions where expectations are not especially high or low by national standards, although the reference data for three of the tests (all but Calculus with Elementary Functions) were collected in 1979 and appear somewhat dated at the time of this writing; institutions with unusual expectations should conduct local standard-setting administrations. The publisher provides tests free, or at special rates, for such administrations (The College Board, 1990b, "Overview," p. 18).

All the mathematics subject examinations are constructed in a multiple-choice format, with five possible answers to each question. All are formula-scored as the number right minus one fourth the number wrong, thus incorporating the usual correction for guessing. All are administered in two separately timed sections, each with a time limit of 45 minutes. For each test, only a total score is reported. The current Calculus with Analytic Geometry examination also is available with an optional 90-minute free-response section, which is locally graded.

Technical Aspects

Because these tests are intended to make a yes/no decision on credit, the reliability of the scores is far more important for those near the cutoff point than those in other regions of the score distribution; for example, there is no point in distinguishing performance worth a grade of A from that worth a grade of B. Unfortunately, all multiple-choice tests suffer from the problem that high scores are generally more reliable than low scores, provided, as seems likely, that low-scoring candidates guess on more questions than high-scoring candidates. The fact that different institutions may set different cut scores is an additional complication. The discussions of the individual tests assume that institutions are most likely to set cut scores in the general area of the ACE recommendations.

College Algebra. The College Algebra test covers the contents of a relatively standard course in college algebra, including polynomials, factoring, algebraic fractions, and radicals (25%); linear and quadratic equations, inequalities, and graphs (20%); functions, including exponential and logarithmic functions (20%); theory of equations (10%); and other topics, notably sets, complex numbers, systems of equations, matrices, and determinants (25%). Approximately 50% of the questions are routine and 50% are nonroutine. The test puts relatively low weight on complex computations, both arithmetic and algebraic, and on word problems. Individual items are generally appropriate and well constructed.

Each section of the test contains 40 questions. Overall, the test is mildly speeded; 80% of the students reached 36 to 40 questions on each part. The reliability of the overall score is satisfactory—.91 on one form of the test and .89 on the other; the standard error of the scaled score is about 3 points. Although overall this test seems a satisfactory instrument, it is much too difficult for optimal discrimination at the cut score; the formula score required to attain the ACE-recommended cut score is, depending on form, only 23 to 24 of a possible 80. Even A students have an average formula score of only about 40.

A new version of the College Algebra examination is currently under development, scheduled for initial administration in fall 1994. At the time of this review, the content specifications were not yet complete, and thus no details are possible regarding possible changes in the new edition.

The Test Information Guide for this test contains several small errors, but they are unlikely to present serious problems for the user.

Trigonometry. The Trigonometry examination covers the content of a relatively standard trigonometry course, but with very heavy emphasis on the circular functions and their definition, relationships, and identities (50% of the content). The remaining topics include trigonometric equations and inequalities (10%), graphs of trigonometric functions (10%), triangles (10%), and miscellaneous topics including inverse trigonometric functions and polar form of complex numbers (20%). About 60% of the problems are routine and 40% are nonroutine. Individual items generally appear very good.

Each section contains 40 questions. Overall, the test is mildly speeded; 80% of the students reached 36 to 39 questions on each part. The reliability of the overall score is .92, which is very good; the standard error of the scaled score is about 3 points. Although generally this test seems a satisfactory instrument, it is somewhat too difficult for optimal discrimination at the cut score; the formula score required to attain the ACE-recommended cut score is 32 of a possible 80.

College Algebra and Trigonometry. The College Algebra and Trigonometry test is a single instrument consisting of one section from the College Algebra test and one section from the Trigonometry test. (The content specifications for those tests are reviewed above.) Only an overall score is reported. Candidates seeking credit in two separate courses are advised to take the two separate examinations.

Each section contains 40 questions. The test is slightly speeded; on a preliminary version, which had 45 questions per section, on each section 80% of the students completed 41 to 43 questions. The reliability of the overall score is .92, which is very good; the standard error of the scaled score is about 3 points. Although in general this test seems satisfactory, it is too difficult for optimal discrimination at the cut score; the formula score required to attain the ACE-recommended cut score is, depending on form, 28 to 30 of a possible 80.

The Test Information Guide for this test contains several minor errors unlikely to confuse the user, plus one major error: The content specifications are given only for the College Algebra section, not for the Trigonometry section.

Calculus with Elementary Functions. According to The College Board, this test is intended to cover the content of a year or two semesters of calculus. Unfortunately, the coverage falls well short of these statements. (For those who are familiar with the College Board Advanced Placement Examinations, this test is a converted version of the less demanding AB test, not the more demanding BC test.) The content outline for the test calls for coverage of elementary functions and limits (20%), differential calculus (40%), and integral calculus (40%). The test contains a surprising number of questions on topics in elementary functions that generally would be covered in a precalculus course; the form examined by this reviewer contained seven such questions, forming 16% of the test. The coverage of differential calculus is quite comprehensive, including treatment of trigonometric, inverse trigonometric, logarithmic, and exponential functions. In general, this part of the test has a strong emphasis on curve sketching and little emphasis on limits and on word problems except for those involving position, velocity, and acceleration. The treatment of integral calculus is much less comprehensive. The only applications covered are mean value on an interval, area between curves, and volumes of solids of revolution; the test does not cover arc length, work, moments, or center of mass. The only techniques of integration covered are algebraic substitution and parts; trigonometric substitution and partial fractions are omitted. The test does not cover polar coordinates, sequences and series, or Taylor's theorem. It seems unlikely that this coverage represents two semesters (or even two quarters) at most institutions; the topic outline for this test provides little assurance that students passing it would be adequately prepared for a third calculus course. Most institutions granting two units of credit for this test should give credit for one precalculus course and one calculus course, not two calculus courses, and should rely on a local test for granting credit in the second calculus course. Given the test specifications, individual items are appropriate and well constructed.

The test provided for review contained 44 questions, 23 in the first section and 21 in the second. The test is very slightly speeded. The reliability of the overall score is adequate (.87); the standard error of the scaled score is about 3.4 points. Although generally this test seems a satisfactory instrument, it is much too difficult for optimal discrimination at the cut score; the formula score required to attain the ACE-recommended cut score is approximately 13 or 14 of a possible 45. Even A students have an average formula score of only about 25 or 26.

As indicated above, a new edition of this test will appear in fall 1993. There are two principal differences between the current and new editions: the new version will permit (but not require) the use of a scientific, nongraphing calculator, and it will not contain an optional free-response section. The content specifications for the new edition are the same as for the current one; indeed, the CLEP handbook indicates that the sample questions for the current edition also will be appropriate for the new edition (p. 369). The test developer provided this reviewer with an examination copy of the new edition. Although the questions are all new, the revised edition is very similar to its current counterpart. Only two meaningful changes are apparent: the new edition contains 45 questions (25 on the first section and 20 on the second section), and it has only 3 precalculus questions, compared with 7 on the current edition. (Many of the calculus questions do also require substantial knowledge of elementary functions, especially trigonometric functions.) No technical data were available for the new edition as the scaling administration had not yet occurred. Based on information from the Advanced Placement program, however, the new edition likely will resemble the old edition in difficulty and reliability.

Critique

The CLEP subject examinations in mathematics generally are well-constructed tests. Three of the four (College Algebra, Trigonometry, and College Algebra and Trigonometry) are well suited to their intended purpose of offering credit for a single college mathematics course. The cutoff scores for credit recommended by the ACE represent reasonable standards for most institutions; some may wish also to conduct local standard-setting administrations. The existing forms of these three tests, plus the student reference data, were developed in 1979 and were somewhat dated at the time of this writing. Fortunately, a new version of the College Algebra examination is currently under development; users should hope that the new exam will have questions that are, on the average, easier than those on the present forms, with a corresponding increase in the formula score required to pass. It is disturbing that the schedule for test development shows no additional versions of the Trigonometry or College Algebra and Trigonometry examinations until at least the year 2000. If the developer intends to continue offering these examinations, it would be desirable at least to collect new reference data. (Recall that the cutoff scores for credit recommended by ACE are based on the performance of students receiving a grade of C, and thus they presumably would change if new reference data were available.) The fourth examination, Calculus with Elementary Functions, is well constructed but shows inadequate content for its announced coverage of two semesters or a year of calculus. Institutions should examine the content very carefully before making decisions regarding the credit to offer to students taking that test.

References

The College Board. (1990a). *College Board guide to the CLEP examinations* (rev. ed.). New York: Author.

The College Board. (1990b). *College-Level Examination Program technical manual.* New York: Author.

The College Board. (1992). *Official handbook for the CLEP examinations.* New York: Author.

Whitney, D.R., & Malizio, A.G. (Eds.). (1987). *Guide to educational credit by examination* (2nd ed.). New York: American Council on Education/Macmillan.

James A. Moses, Jr., Ph.D.

Clinical Associate Professor of Psychiatry and Behavioral Sciences, Stanford University School of Medicine, and Coordinator, Psychological Assessment Unit, Veterans Administration Medical Center, Palo Alto, California.

COMMUNITY-ORIENTED PROGRAMS ENVIRONMENT SCALE

Rudolf H. Moos. Palo Alto, California: Consulting Psychologists Press, Inc.

Introduction

The Community-Oriented Programs Environment Scale (COPES; Moos, 1974b, 1988) is a multidimensional, categorical, impressionistic, self-report measure of social climate, completed by patients or staff in community-based treatment programs. The questionnaire consists of 100 brief declarative statements to which the respondent answers "true" or "false."

Three forms of the COPES are available for comparison of real, ideal, and expected social climate features of community-oriented treatment settings. Items for the Real Form (Form R) are phrased in the present tense and completed by patients and staff familiar with the community-oriented treatment setting of interest. The Expected Form (Form E) items, phrased in the future tense, would be applicable to persons entering a new community-oriented treatment environment or to those about to undergo a significant change in the established treatment program. The Ideal Form (Form I) phrases the items conditionally, and it describes what an ideal community-oriented treatment program might be like.

A Short Form (Form S) of the COPES also is available for use in settings where administration time is limited or where the user needs only a brief overview of the treatment setting's social climate a preliminary assessment or screening procedure. Form S consists of the first 40 items of Form R. Four items from each of the 10 COPES subscales appear in Form S.

The COPES has been validated in several British Commonwealth countries, including Great Britain (Fischer, 1977, 1979; Moos, 1974c, chapter 10), Australia (Manning & Lees, 1985; Packer & Wright, 1983), and Canada (Brill, 1979). The COPES also has been translated into several non-English languages—French (Cote, LeBlanc, & Trudeau-LeBlanc, 1985), Italian (Burti, Glick, & Tansella, 1990), and Hebrew (Meier, 1983)—and validated in overseas countries (France, Italy, Israel) where subjects speak these languages natively.

The COPES items have not been revised since the original appearance of the test (Moos, 1974a), but the author has written a revised manual (Moos, 1988). This second edition of the manual provides additional recommendations for program design, planning, and evaluation using the COPES, both singly and in combination with other Social Climate Scales. The literature review also has been updated in the revised manual. This additional experimental and clinical material provides considerable supplementary information to basic and applied social scientists who use the COPES in their work.

Considerable empirical and theoretical work taking place in recent years has clarified the dimensional structure of the COPES and its relationship to other social climate and environmental variables. This work is fully reviewed only in the revised manual. Although the original COPES manual still suffices for test administration and scoring, Moos (1988) strongly encourages those who use the COPES to study and implement the guidelines presented in the revised test manual.

The author of the COPES, Rudolf H. Moos, received the B.A. with honors (1956) and the Ph.D. (1960) degrees from the University of California, Berkeley. Thereafter he served as a postdoctoral fellow at the University of California, San Francisco for 2 years. He is a Diplomate in Clinical Psychology of the American Board of Professional Psychology (1965), a recipient of the Hofheimer Award for Research from the American Psychiatric Association (1975), a Department of Veterans Affairs (DVA) Career Scientist (since 1981), and a fellow of numerous learned societies. He has held a faculty position in the Department of Psychiatry and Behavioral Sciences at Stanford University since 1962 (Professor since 1972), and at the DVA Medical Center, Palo Alto, California, he directs both the Center for Health Care Evaluation and the Program Evaluation and Resource Center. He had published 12 books and 270 book chapters, manuals, literature reviews, and professional research articles through January 1988. Dr. Moos is best known for his pioneering work on the development and implementation of the social ecological approach to classification, description, evaluation, and consultation.

Development of the initial COPES item pool began using a variety of techniques. Moos and his colleagues initially asked clients and staff members in community-oriented treatment facilities to adapt some of the inpatient-oriented items from the Ward Atmosphere Scale (WAS; Moos, 1989) to describe their community-oriented programs. The researchers also developed items based on observational information they obtained about community-oriented treatment programs. Information elicited through structured interviews was used to supplement and refine the other sources of programmatic characteristic analysis. The tricategorical social ecological model that has guided development of all of the Social Climate Scales primarily determined the emphasis in content and wording of each of the COPES items. Each item had to explicitly define a characteristic of a *relationship, personal growth,* or *system maintenance* social ecological dimension. (More will be said of the social ecological model in the next section of this review.)

Moos published the initial Form A of the COPES in 1972. The initial item pool was consensually sorted into categories by three independent judges. Analysis of social desirability was performed to identify and eliminate items with a high social desirability content. The 130 items that remained after this process comprised Form B of the COPES. This version was administered to 373 clients and 203 staff members in 21 community-oriented treatment programs. The programs sampled included "nine day-care centers, two mixed-sex residential centers, one men's and one women's residential program, two rehabilitation centers, three community care homes, a residents' workshop, and two adolescent residential centers"

(Moos, 1988, p. 15). The clientele and treatment orientations of these programs were intentionally diverse, so that the COPES item content would apply to describing a wide variety of community-oriented treatment programs.

The final Form R (Real Form, for describing current treatment program) consists of 100 items, divided into 10 subscales. This form was developed from Form B by selecting items that met several stringent psychometric criteria. First, each subscale had to show adequate internal consistency. This criterion requires that the items of the scale measure a common theoretical dimension or construct and that they relate to each other consistently and complementarily. Next, each item had to correlate more highly with the COPES subscale to which it was assigned than with any of the other subscales. This criterion ensures that the item is dimension-specific. To eliminate items that would characterize only atypical programs, items selected for final scale inclusion had to be endorsed by less than 80% of the respondents. Ninety-five percent of the items included met this criterion for program members or staff or members of both groups. Items on each COPES subscale also had to be approximately evenly divided between true and false responses in the scored direction to control for generalized positive or negative response bias. Items selected for the final form of the scale could not correlate significantly with a social desirability response scale. Developers typically apply this exclusion criterion in this type of scale construction to prevent biased responding, which gives a conventionally favorable, stereotyped social impression regardless of the objective characteristics of the program described.

Instructions for Form R (Real Form) are relatively straightforward, directing respondents to mark each item "true" if the statement is definitely or primarily true or "false" if the statement is definitely or primarily false as it applies to their current view of the community-oriented treatment program. For Form E (Expected Form), the respondent answers "true" or "false" to the same item content statements phrased in the future tense; that is, what he or she thinks a new unit about to be entered "will be like" or what the current unit may be like after some anticipated change in the program occurs. For Form I (Ideal Form) the respondent is asked to describe what he or she thinks an ideal unit "would be like." The COPES is recommended for self-report group administration in the usual case, with an assurance of individual response anonymity to encourage candor in descriptions of the unit rather than defensive or socially desirable response tendencies (some individuals may fear a penalty if they criticize the program or the treatment staff).

The COPES materials consist of a four-page reuseable question booklet and a special two-sided answer sheet designed for the COPES and the WAS. On the answer sheet the respondent records the Social Climate Scale administered, the form of the COPES completed (Form R, Form E, or Form I), his or her name (or identification code), age, sex, hospital or program, years-months-days of participation in the program described, lifetime duration of living or working in mental hospitals (years-months-days), exact job title if a staff member, date of test administration, and other miscellaneous information. A worked example is given for true and false responses to questions. Numbered boxes that correspond to each question are horizontally divided in half. Respondents indicate "true" by marking an X in the top half of the box and "false" by marking an X in the bottom half.

The profile sheet for plotting the COPES profile can be used with any of the 10 Social Climate Scales. The program rated is indicated in addition to the Social Climate Scale type, the scale form, the normative group used to convert raw scores to standardized scores, and the date of administration. The legend of the profile has boxes to indicate the scaled score and the subscale title acronym for the appropriate Social Climate Scale completed. Moos designed the profile with a range of 4 standard deviations below the mean through 5 standard deviations above the mean (T-scores 10 through 100), which is sufficient to characterize even extreme outliers as well as typical programs.

Separate COPES norms are provided in the test manual for program members (patients) and staff respondents for American and British samples on Form R. For Form S (short form of Form R) and Form I, norms appear for American normative samples only. Form E preliminary norms derive from an American normative sample only. Each of these normative groups will be discussed in turn.

Form R: American normative sample. The American normative sample consists of 54 community-based treatment programs. In a core sample of 32 programs, both members and staff were tested with Form R. In another 22 programs the researchers used members only. The 54 program sample consisted of the following:

> 2 rehabilitation workshops, 2 partial hospitalization programs, 11 halfway houses, and 17 day-care centers. These programs were administered by the Department of Veterans Affairs (DVA); state county, psychiatric, and general hospitals; and private organizations. The additional 22 programs in which members only were tested were all DVA programs, including 20 foster homes, 1 outpatient support group, and 1 patient-run self-help unit. A total of 779 members and 357 staff compose this normative sample. (Moos, 1988, p. 8)

For more details of the sample characteristics, see chapter 10 of *Evaluating Treatment Programs* (Moos, 1974c).

These normative data are reported separately for each COPES subscale in samples of program members and staff. Mean data for each reference group appear in addition to standard deviation values for programs (averaged data) and individuals. The variability of individuals is necessarily greater than the variability of averaged data for programs. Provision of both measures of variability allows one to compare programs as well as individuals to the central tendency standard (for data summary, see Moos, 1988, p. 9).

Form R: British normative sample. The British normative sample consists of 209 responding program members and 74 staff respondents. Central tendency and variability descriptive statistics are provided only for individual respondents in this sample. The researchers obtained these norms from 20 community-oriented treatment programs in the United Kingdom.

> This sample includes 2 psychiatric day hospitals in major teaching hospitals in London and 18 halfway houses in the United Kingdom, most of which were located in the south of England. Three of the halfway houses were administered by the Borough of London. The remaining 15 houses were all relatively small and were administered by a privately endowed foundation. (Moos, 1988, pp. 9–10)

Moos points out in the COPES manual that the sampling characteristics of the American and British normative samples were systematically different and therefore the two samples are not directly comparable.

Form S: American normative sample. The mean and standard deviation data for Form S derive from the same programmatic samples reported for Form R. Program member norms are based on the sample of 54 programs, while staff norms come from the subsample of 32 programs.

Form I: American normative sample. Characteristics of this sample beyond descriptive statistics do not appear in the test manual. Moos provides separate central tendency and variability data for program members and staff on Form I, plus separate measures of variability for individuals and programs within each respondent category. The staff members sampled were 252 individuals from 26 programs, and the program members were 618 individuals from 47 programs.

Form I: Preliminary British norms. Moos (1988) refers to his earlier work (1974c, chapter 10) to note that preliminary data were collected on Form I in a sample of 19 British community-oriented treatment programs. The data were not sufficiently representative for routine use to report in the manual. The interested reader is referred to the original source for details.

Form E: Preliminary American norms. In another exploratory study, Moos (1988, p. 13) reports preliminary data on 118 unspecified prospective community-oriented program members about to enter one of five such programs. He provides scale-wise individual mean and standard deviation data for these individuals and encourages extension of these norms to well-specified groups on a local application basis until generally applicable norms can be developed.

Practical Applications/Uses

Like the other Social Climate Scales, the COPES is based on a tricategorical social ecological model that has been developed and extensively validated by Moos and his colleagues. The theoretic basis for this work comes from the formulations of Henry Murray (1938), the first social theorist to emphasize the complementary roles of individual needs and environmental press as codeterminants of complex social perception and behavior. The social ecological model of Moos and his colleagues postulates the three general categories of Relationship, Personal Growth, and System Maintenance dimensions. The COPES measures these dimensions in community-oriented programmatic settings with 10 subscales. Moos (1988, pp. 2–3) describes the COPES subscales and dimensions as follows in the revised test manual:

RELATIONSHIP DIMENSIONS

Involvement—how active members are in the day-to-day functioning of their program

Support—how much members help and support each other; how supportive the staff is toward members

Spontaneity—how much the program encourages the open expression of feelings by members and staff

PERSONAL GROWTH DIMENSIONS

Autonomy—how self-sufficient and independent members are in decision making and how much they are encouraged to take leadership in the program

Practical Orientation—the degree to which members learn practical skills and are prepared for release from the program

Personal Problem Orientation—the extent to which members are encouraged to understand their feelings and personal problems

Anger and Aggression—how much members argue with each other and with staff, become openly angry, and display other aggressive behavior

SYSTEM MAINTENANCE DIMENSIONS

Order and Organization—how important order and organization are in the program

Program Clarity—the extent to which the members know what to expect in the day-to-day routine of the program and the explicitness of program rules and procedures

Staff Control—the extent to which the staff uses measures to keep members under necessary controls

The COPES is used primarily in clinical and consultative settings for multidimensional programmatic analysis and evaluation. Enhancement of social skill learning in community-oriented treatment programs requires accurate information concerning the program's members and staff perceptions about the social options, goals, limits, and contingencies in their treatment setting. Also important to the assessment of program member and staff motivation and satisfaction is information about the specific areas of perceived congruence and discrepancy between their real program and an idealized one. The COPES is well suited to make such information explicitly and dimensionally clear.

Comparison of program members and staff on Form R can show the degree to which agreement or disagreement exists between staff and program members in their perception of specific aspects of the actual program. Desired change can be evaluated for staff or program members through comparison of Form R and Form I. This analysis is used to assess the degree of real versus ideal goal discrepancy separately for each subgroup. When Forms R and I are compared, it is customary to subtract the score on Form R from the score on Form I. A higher Form I than Form R subscale score would yield a positive difference score with this method, reflecting a desire for increase in that social environmental feature. A negative difference score, conversely, would indicate a desire for decrease in that experienced dimension. Discrepancies on the order of 1 to 2 raw score points are considered interpretable, given the small standard deviation of the COPES subscales as a group that approximate this range. By means of such discrepancy measures the user can compare program member and staff satisfaction across programs. Such information may aid in evaluating the respondent characteristics that can be matched to program characteristics to optimize both treatment effectiveness and the assignment of staff and patients to various community-oriented programs.

Similarly, users can evaluate at baseline the degree of expected programmatic change by administering COPES Forms E and R before the alteration. Form R could be readministered after the change took place to compare perceptions of the new program (retest with Form R) with pre-change expectation (Form E) and experienced (pre-change Form R) ratings. Such comparisons can provide a useful measure of experienced programmatic change that supplements impersonal descriptions of the program in its various phases. Comparison of pre- and post-change expectations and outcome could prove useful in evaluating efforts to prepare program members and staff for change and to facilitate their adjustment and reduce their stress during the change period.

Professional qualifications for program consultants who use the COPES are not explicitly stated in the manual. One would expect that a qualified consultant would have completed graduate-level training in a mental health specialty and possess at least a journeyman's level of working knowledge in psychometric theory and statistics. A professional psychologist would be the preferred consultant to a community-oriented treatment program using the COPES as a measure of programmatic description or evaluation.

The COPES is suitable for administration in a wide variety of community-oriented treatment settings. The American normative database is widely representative of a variety of community-oriented treatment modalities. The more selective nature of the British normative sample limits its generality to the types of programs sampled. The manual specifies no minimal age for COPES administration, but the sixth-grade reading level required for independent completion of the scale and the nature of the item content suggests that it is not appropriate for use before age 11, and it probably is best suited for use with adolescent and adult members of community-oriented treatment programs.

The COPES typically is self-administered as a self-report measure. Moos recommends anonymous response to encourage candor on the part of both program members and staff. Cox (1977) has reported that respondents tend to answer questions of this kind more conservatively when they are individually identified than when they respond anonymously. Administration should take place in a quiet, well-lighted, well-ventilated room, with adequate working space for each respondent. A proctor should be present during the session to answer questions, encourage task orientation, and prevent response discussion among respondents. Unsophisticated subjects may require more supervisory assistance, particularly explanation of unfamiliar words. Such subjects should be tested in smaller groups to individualize attention in order to ensure valid test results. Simple restatements of word meanings are allowable, but the proctor must be careful not to influence respondents.

The proctor should read the directions aloud while respondents read them silently and follow the examples. Lead pencils with erasers should be provided so that no one uses a pen. Subjects who have difficulty answering questions as definitely true or false should be advised to respond affirmatively if they believe the statement is true "most of the time." Anyone still uncertain about the response to a given question should be encouraged to guess as an alternative to nonresponse. The COPES as a whole, and particularly Form S, is relatively short, so that an incomplete protocol is a threat to test reliability and hence validity. Answer sheets therefore should be checked for completeness of demographic information and responses to all test questions as the test forms are collected.

In most situations administration of the COPES is straightforward and poses no difficulty for the proctor or respondents who can read at a sixth-grade level. For program members who cannot read at this level, as is not uncommon with socio-culturally disadvantaged or bilingual clients, Moos (1987, p. 23) recommends the use of tape-recorded or computerized instructions. In community-oriented settings the proctor might simply read the questions aloud to the respondents, as the audiovisual and electronic devices suggested typically are not available. If the program member has an especially low or generally impaired level of functioning, personal interviewing by a mental health professional and simplification of the language of some items may be necessary to ensure response validity and item comprehension.

Each form of the COPES typically requires 15 to 20 minutes to complete. Forms I and E are available from the publisher for noncommercial use. If more than one form of the COPES is to be administered to the same person, the author recommends administration of the two forms at separate sittings to keep the descriptions disjoint and objective.

Scoring of the COPES is a clerical task. Subscale items are arranged in columns on the answer sheet. One places the clear plastic scoring template over the answer sheet and counts the number of answer marks (X's) that show through the circular openings. These subscale raw scores then are entered in boxes below the response portion of the sheet. The raw scores are translated into scaled scores using tables provided in a series of appendices in the test manual for a variety of American normative groups.

Raw scores for program members may be translated to *averaged* standard scores for members of whole programs on Forms R and S. Such norms allow one to compare individual perceptions on various COPES dimensions for a given program with those of larger groups of program members whose individual perceptions have been averaged to obtain a consensual view. Raw scores for program staff may be translated to standard scores based on *averaged* norms for program members or on alternative *averaged* norms for program staff for Forms R and S. In this way the *modal* response trends of staff can be compared with typical response patterns of patients and other staff members to highlight overall similarities and differences between the programmatic evaluations of the groups. Separate raw score tables allow translation of *individual* raw scores to standard scores for program members and for program staff on each COPES subscale.

Scoring and profiling of the COPES results for a single individual should require only about 10 minutes for an experienced user. No mention is made in the manual about automated scoring, but an administration and scoring program would be relatively easy to develop once the relevant normative database had been chosen for profile plotting. This could be done in a menu format. Development of such a program would be time- and cost-effective, particularly when one considers that relatively large samples probably would be generated from many community-oriented treatment programs.

Interpretation of the COPES typically is normative. Differences in profile elevations between groups or between forms for the same group or individual are interpreted as clinically relevant when the difference approaches 1 standard deviation. A valuable tool for users would be a tabular report of standard error of measurement and standard error of difference statistics with ipsative numerical criteria for determination of statistically significant score differences or elevations above or below the mean of the profile at various levels of probability. Currently one must infer significance levels through impressionistic comparison of the mean profile differences for one's program groups with the extensive tabular summaries in the manual, but nonchance differences are difficult to ascertain. One should note that real-ideal difference scores of as little as 1 or 2 mean raw score points are significant due to the small standard deviation values of the COPES subscales. The operational definition of such decision-making criteria thus could prevent the inexperienced COPES user from overlooking subtle but important individual differences between subscales on profile or interform comparisons.

The COPES profile interpretation examples that the test manual provides (Moos, 1988, pp. 23–28) illustrate the use of Form R for comparison of program members and staff in three community-based treatment programs. Analysis of each program reveals specific areas of agreement and disagreement in the perception of members and staff and highlights the different treatment models in facilities serving adolescent and adult clients.

The staff-versus-member level of analysis of the COPES for the adolescent example program is carried to additional levels in the examples that follow to illustrate similarities and differences between members and staff in perception of actual and idealized versions of the program. In a comparison of mean raw scale scores for staff and members on Form I, one notes agreement on desire for strong emphasis on Relationship dimensions, with varying levels of congruence on the Personal Growth and System Maintenance dimensions.

In the third phase of the example analysis, Moos compares the real (Form R) versus ideal (Form I) mean raw score discrepancies of the members and staff in the adolescent program for each subscale of the COPES profile. The Form R score is subtracted from the Form I score to lessen the frequency of negative values in these analyses. A score of 0 on this phase of the analysis shows exact congruence between actual and idealized descriptions of the program. Positive difference scores using the recommended format (Form I greater than Form R) show a desire for greater emphasis on or expression of that social climate dimension in the actual program. Negative difference scores show that the social climate dimension is expressed to a greater degree than desired in the actual program and that the respondents would like to see that aspect of the program lessened.

Analysis and imitation of the models presented in the manual is essential to initiate COPES users, but it is not sufficient to master the technique. As an initial step one might wish to reanalyze the profiles presented in the test manual from the data only, once the worked examples have been studied. Reproducing details of the analysis after learning to recognize key features of it can be a quite different process. Demonstrated modification of key features of the programs to analyze how these changes would affect the nature of the program as a whole also would be useful as an interpretive exercise. Finally, an analysis of programs well known to the interpreter to see how the COPES operationally redefines and refines one's understanding of social climate dimensions in familiar circumstances also would be instructive.

Moos (1988, pp. 28–31) cites several illustrative examples from the literature in which the COPES has been used successfully to evaluate modifications in treatment program structure and to prospectively plan and evaluate improvement in program characteristics. Schneider, Kinlow, Galloway, and Ferro (1982) studied COPES pre-post change scores in resident and staff satisfaction with a social learning program that was modified to more closely match an idealized theoretical model. They found that the changes based on the COPES analysis were successfully implemented. Similar results were reported by Phillips, Coughlin, Fixsen, and Maloney (1979).

Serial comparisons of traditional psychiatric inpatient treatment programs with community-based residential treatment center programs have been studied extensively using the COPES by Ryan and colleagues (Bell & Ryan, 1984, 1985; Ryan & Bell, 1985a, 1985b; Ryan, Bell, & Metcalf, 1982). (For an overview of these studies, see Moos, 1988, pp. 30–31.) An important finding from this series of studies showed that a community-based treatment program for schizophrenics emphasizing "vocational, social, and community living skills" in addition to patient autonomy, self-responsibility, and independence was more effective than traditional inpatient treatment programs or an insight-oriented community program supplemented with "patient self-help groups and rehabilitation services" (Moos, 1988, p. 30). Outcome measures used to determine degree of therapeutic success included program dropout and symptomatic relapse rates, and follow-up employment status. It is consistent with self-management theory and research that the self-generated behavior change generalized more effectively and that it was more productive of adaptive behavior change than were insight-oriented or supportive therapy modalities (Kanfer & Schefft, 1988).

Program evaluation using the COPES as a baseline and follow-up instrument to identify areas of desirable change, plan specific programmatic alterations, and evaluate the outcome of those changes has been implemented successfully in a variety of facilities (cf. Bakos et al. 1979; Friedman, 1982; Friedman, Jeger, & Slotnick, 1982; Moos, 1973, 1974c [chapter 11]; Shinn, 1982; Shinn, Perkins, & Cherniss, 1980).

It is important to note that these dimensional theoretical constructs are *perceived* aspects of the social ecological system and that COPES ratings reflect desire for change in the experience of the social climate. Matching desired and actual program characteristics may be quite important to the clarification of program perception and the optimization of program staff and member motivation and coordinated goal striving. It is entirely another matter, however, to determine whether these changes relate to the rate of treatment progress or the effectiveness of treatment outcome. The COPES can be used to address such questions when measures of social climate are tied to behavioral outcome measures and issues of social climate are included as prospective variables that may influence treatment process and outcome. Excellent examples of the use of the COPES in the evaluation of alcoholism treatment program design and treatment outcome evaluation appears in Moos, Finney, and Cronkite (1990). One also can consult this text for numerous additional examples of worked profile analyses with varied treatment programs.

Technical Aspects

Form R reliability. Reliability is the statistical criterion for the accuracy of measurement of a psychometric instrument. A test cannot be theoretically or clinically useful if it is not reliable. Several key indices of reliability have been established for COPES Form R. The first and perhaps most basic of these involves the internal consistency of each of the Form R subscales. To the degree that the items of a test or subscale correlationally group together to measure a single common dimension, they meet the criterion of internal consistency. Internal consistency is statistically limited by the number of items in the subtest studied. That is, the longer a test, the more reliable it tends to be. Ideally the internal consistency of a test should approximate 0.80, which value reduces statistical measurement error to a practical minimum (Nunnally, 1978).

In a sample of program members from 21 settings, the split-half internal consistency values using the Kuder-Richardson formula 20 for the 10 COPES Form R subscales ranged from 0.62 (Autonomy) to 0.82 (Anger and Aggression); the mean internal consistency value was 0.79 for program member respondents. Comparable internal consistency values for staff respondents from the same sample of programs ranged from 0.64 (Support, Practical Orientation) to 0.89 (Autonomy). The mean internal consistency value for staff respondents was 0.78. All Form R internal consistency values fall within acceptable limits, given the relatively short subscale lengths. Most of the values are near optimal level. The COPES Form R subscales thus meet stringent criteria for internal consistency.

The manual does not report the method of splitting the COPES Form R item pool for each subscale, but it probably involved an odd-even item number division of each subscale. Nunnally (1978) recommends that internal consistency values optimally should be calculated by means of Cronbach's coefficient alpha because it is the mean of all possible split-half values for a given item pool and thus gives the best overall estimate of internal consistency. This statistic would be useful to calculate and report in a sample of at least 300 cases, as results from such an analysis should generalize to a comparably composed sample of any size (Nunnally, 1978).

A related statistical item-analytic criterion is the average correlation of each of the subscale items of Form R with the total subscale score. When calculating these statistics, it is customary to eliminate the item of interest from the subscale total to eliminate correlational inflation. The resulting item-remainder subscale correlational value provides a measure of the relationship of the item to the other items on the subscale. These correlational values should be moderate rather than high. If the item-remainder values are moderate, then each item will make a substantial contribution to the overall subscale. Item-remainder values that are too high suggest item redundancy.

Average item-subscale correlational values for Form R fall in the desirable moderate range. Analysis of the values for program members from a sample of 21 programs shows a range of average item-subscale correlations from 0.38 (Autonomy) to 0.53 (Order and Organization). Comparable data for staff show a range of 0.43 (Practical Orientation) to 0.53 (Order and Organization). The COPES Form R subscales meet this criterion of item complementarity as well.

Item specificity on Form R also has been investigated by comparing the average correlation of items with subscales to which they are *not* assigned to the correlation of the same items to subscales where they *are* assigned. In this measure of discriminant validity, items should show low correlations with scales to which they are not assigned. This criterion assures that COPES Form R items are not simply measuring some sort of generalized performance-level dimension across scales independent of the specific target constructs for which each of the subscales has been designed. As expected the average correlation of each of the COPES Form R items with non-target scales is consistently low. The range of these correlations in the sample of 21 programs for program member respondents varied from 0.10 (Anger and Aggression, Staff Control) to 0.16 (Involvement, Spontaneity); the mean correlational value was 0.13. The correlational variation on these measures for staff respondents was similarly low, from 0.10 (Practical Orientation) to 0.16 (Involvement, Personal Problem Orientation); the mean value was 0.14 for staff respondents.

Because Moos designed the COPES scales to measure complementary but distinct measures of the community-based therapeutic environment, logically they should have moderate but not high intercorrelations. They also should measure patient and staff perceptions in complementary ways if the scoring for these two groups of program participants is valid. The correlational analyses of the COPES subscales meets these expectations well. For program staff ($N = 203$), the interscale correlations range from 0.02 (Anger and Aggression with Practical Orientation) to 0.46 (Personal Problem Orientation with Autonomy; Anger and Aggression with Personal Problem Orientation). For program members ($N = 373$), the interscale correlations range from 0.01 (Practical Orientation with Anger and Aggression) or -0.01 (Program Clarity with Staff Control) to 0.50 (Involvement with Support). The correlations of the COPES subscales are typically in the moderate range. Only the Relationship dimensions (Involvement, Support, Spontaneity) show moderate intercorrelations with each other across program member and staff samples.

The temporal stability of a test is measured test-retest reliability. This standard is important to establish because one must be certain that test results are reproducible across administrations. Establishing reliability standards for retest ensure that nonchance deviations from these standards may be attributed to real change and not to error variance. Unfortunately Moos does not provide values in the test manual for the retest reliability of the individual COPES subscales. These values would help the user calculate standard error values (measurement error due to chance alone) for each of the subscale measures if he or she wished to evaluate some specific aspect of the program. Ideally those values would be included in the test manual as well for each of the subscales of the test.

As an alternative Moos (1988) provides retest stability coefficients for the COPES profile as a whole. The profile is highly stable for members across varying time intervals, but only moderately so for staff beyond 1 year. This is a remarkable finding for the patient samples in particular, because the perception of the reference programs that maintained a consistent treatment philosophy remained essentially unchanged, even though different respondents completed the baseline and follow-up evaluations for some programs over longer time intervals.

For specific profile stability statistics, the interested reader is referred to the COPES manual (Moos, 1988, p. 19, Table 9). Data for these comparisons come from a variety of sources, which are cited in the test manual with the summary statistics. For program member respondents, the mean profile stability coefficient ranged from 0.81 at 4–6 months, through 0.90 at 16 months, to 0.98 at 24 months for the samples cited. The extremely high 24-month retest coefficient was based on only one program, but the program members had changed during the test-retest interval. Clearly the COPES can reflect enduring characteristics of the program if its treatment philosophy remains stable even though the specific respondents change.

For staff respondents, the mean profile stability coefficient ranged from 0.81 at 4–6 months, through 0.64 at 16 months, to 0.60 at 24 months. The 24-month retest value may be biased as it also is based on only one program. Clinicians or researchers who plan to use the COPES for applied or basic research should consult the original sources of reliability research cited in the test manual.

These data indicate high profile stability across programs and retest intervals for program member respondents, but less stable retest findings for program staff as the intertest interval increases. These results represent a mixture of data across programs in which the COPES was administered different numbers of times. Some of the data, particularly for patients, may reflect frequent retesting of similarly diagnosed samples who are treated very similarly by staff and who experience the program in much the same way over member generations. Why the staff should experience the program as more variable than the members over time is a question worth investigating rigorously, particularly in situations where the same programs are studied a given number of times over a given period. The moderate intraclass retest profile correlations for staff in the current analyses suggest that variability in staff perceptions of community-oriented programs should be viewed conservatively until the basis of the variability can be clarified.

Overall the question of retest reliability with COPES Form R is easy to address methodologically, but it requires additional elaboration and study. Basic and applied investigators who employ the COPES in retest studies of programmatic change are advised to conduct their own studies of retest reliability with control groups of program members to assess retest effects. Publication of a variety of such studies would be useful to clarify and cross-validate retest effects on this test in varied samples and for different intertest intervals. The usual optimal retest period for an untreated group is approximately 2 weeks. Investigation of such shorter interval retest effects is necessary to supplement the long-term stability studies overviewed above.

Form I reliability. In a sample of 15 programs, item-to-subscale correlations for COPES Form I were moderate, ranging from 0.35 to 0.55. Split-half internal consistency coefficients for Form I subscales ranged from 0.70 (Program Clarity) to 0.88 (Personal Problem Orientation). The manual does not report retest values at the subscale level for Form I. Profile stability coefficients based on data from Ryan et al. (1982) showed average profile correlational retest values of 0.81 at 4 months, 0.86 at 8 months, and 0.82 at 12 months for program members. For staff, the profile stability retest coefficients ranged from 0.91 at 4 months, 0.90 at 8 months, to 0.89 at 12 months. These analyses should be replicated at these and longer intervals and reported at the subscale and profile levels. Comparison of the relative reliabilities of Forms R and I on the same samples over the same retest intervals also would be of value.

COPES factor structure. Three analyses of the COPES subscale factor structure have found different dimensional structures. The factor solutions of Kohn, Jeger, and Koretzky (1979) and Schwartz (1981) did not closely fit the tripartite social ecological theoretical model on which Moos based his Social Climate Scales, including the COPES. In an analysis of COPES data from five alcoholism treatment programs, however, Fischer (1977) produced a three-factor solution that rather closely matched the theoretical model (for a summary, see Moos, 1988, p. 20). Moos (1988) rightly noted that results of factor analysis may be affected by sampling characteristics, factorial extraction, and rotation methods. He cautioned against seeking "the" factor solution that will be definitive as an empirical basis for theory building. This is a reasonable precaution. On the other hand, it is important to perform rigorous statistical tests of the theoretical model through such multivariate methods as confirmatory factor analysis and to cross-validate them with social ecological and other empirical analyses so that the theoretical model can be refined and modified to better characterize different classes of treatment environments. Large data sets with sufficient variability to model representative community-based treatment programs should continue to be studied with factorial methodology *as one method among many* to test and refine the social ecological model. Confirmatory factor analytic modeling in which two- and three-factor solutions are prospectively tested would be of particular value in this respect to evaluate their relative merits as dimension reduction and modeling methods.

An extensive empirical literature supports the construct, concurrent, and predictive validity of the COPES. Construct validity in this case refers to the degree to which hypotheses about social ecological attributes of programs derived from the theoretical model on which the COPES is based are upheld by empirical test. Construct validity is not established in any one study but rather gradually accumulates as the volume and range of objective empirical evidence about a measure increases. Concurrent validity refers to the degree to which dimensions of the COPES empirically match other known behavioral or psychometric variables that can serve as objective criteria of a specific behavior pattern obtained at the same time the COPES is administered. Predictive validity refers to the degree to which scores obtained on the COPES at one time can be used to predict behavioral outcomes at some future time.

This review will briefly overview only key trends in this literature due to space limitations. The interested user is referred to the primary sources and extensive literature summaries by Moos, Clayton, and Max (1979) and Moos and Spinrad (1984), as well as the updated summary in the COPES test manual (Moos, 1988, chapter 7). The conceptual overview of the COPES literature that follows is abstracted from the latter source. For discussion of issues in research and consultative applications of the COPES, the test author recommends consulting Cronkite, Moos, and Finney (1984) and Moos (1984, 1985a, 1985b, 1987).

Moos (1988, chapter 7) has organized the empirical COPES literature into three broad categories. This review will follow his model so that the interested user can transfer easily from this overview to Moos's detailed summary and also to the primary sources. The first major application area for the COPES is *treatment program description and comparison*. Dimensional information from COPES analysis of a program can help provide more a thorough and accurate description of program characteristics than is usually obtained through impressionistic observation (Otto & Moos, 1973). Moos et al. (1990) found the COPES useful for objectively and accurately identifying distinguishing features of alcohol abuse treatment programs that differed in therapeutic philosophy. Perhaps more important was their finding that facilitation of interpersonal relationships and emotional expression were unrecognized but important contributory social variables that helped bring about alcoholism recovery. The COPES also has been used successfully to characterize similarities and effective treatment parameters among therapeutic community programs for primarily nonalcoholic substance abusers (cf. Bell, 1983; DeLeon, Schwartz, Wexler, Jainchill, & Rudie, 1980).

Other applications of the COPES to analysis of community-based treatment programs have included dimensional analysis of behavior modification programs (Milby, Pendergrass, & Clarke, 1975), medical rehabilitation programs (Greenwood, Marr, Roessler, & Rowland, 1980; Schmidt, 1981/1982), and skilled nursing facilities (Dennis, Burke, & Graber, 1977; Jelinek, 1974; O'Donnell, Collins, & Schuler, 1978; Pino & Howard, 1984; Pino, Rosica, & Carter, 1978; Shadish, Straw, McSweeny, Koller, & Bootzin, 1981). In modified interview form, the COPES methodology has been used effectively to evaluate community-based treatment and residential centers for developmentally disabled people with mild to moderate mental retardation (Packer & Wright, 1983; Pankrantz, 1975; Willer & Intagliata, 1981, 1984).

Particularly important in this series of dimensional programmatic studies was a cluster-analytic typological investigation of prototypical American and British community-based treatment programs, which produced a COPES profile typology (see Moos, 1988, pp. 39–42, for detailed descriptions and modal profiles). The six COPES modal profile program types were Therapeutic Community, Relationship-Oriented, Action-Oriented, Insight-Oriented, Control-Oriented, and Disturbed Behavior. The results of the cluster-analytic study closely resembled those of a related study with the Ward Atmosphere Scale (WAS) as reported by Moos (1989). This is a predictable result, because the WAS and the COPES measure comparable dimensions for inpatient and outpatient treatment facilities, respectively.

The second major area of empirical validational research in which the COPES has been used involves *"program climate"* analysis. Variables investigated in this regard have included urban versus rural program setting (Redmon, Cullari, & Spates, 1982), program size, degree of program member participation in decision making and self-determination, age of program staff, and presence or absence of staff professional education or training. In an integrative summary of trends, Moos (1988, p. 46) concluded that

> smaller and better staffed programs with younger members and staff are more involving and supportive and place more emphasis on personal problem orientation and the open expression of anger. These programs tend to downplay the System Maintenance dimensions, especially staff control. Programs in which staff are better educated and in which members are allowed to make more decisions for themselves place more emphasis on autonomy, whereas programs in which formal evaluations occur frequently are lower on autonomy.

Studies of staff roles with the COPES suggest that professionally trained staff should be primarily responsible for the development of program structure planning, whereas nonprofessional staff are most helpful in patient skill-learning enhancement, particularly in assisting members to learn to be more independent and adaptive at personal problem solving.

The third broad area of validational study with the COPES has been in the area of *treatment process and outcome studies.* Program members who perceived their program as strong on the Involvement, Support, Autonomy, Practical and Personal Problem Orientation, Order and Organization, and Program Clarity dimensions had high morale (Fairchild & Wright, 1984). Segal and Aviram (1978) found that an idealized set of program characteristics based on a COPES analysis was the best predictor of social adaptation within their community-based treatment program, but that this effect did not extend to coping competence in the community.

Program dropout rates as criterion outcome measures to be predicted by COPES variables have produced positive predictive findings of relationships between social ecological variables and attrition rates in alcoholism and substance abuse rehabilitation programs (Bell, 1985; Friedman & Glickman, 1987; Patton, 1977; Moos, Mehren, & Moos, 1978). Null results also have been reported, but considerably less frequently (Hall, Bass, Hargreaves, & Loeb, 1979). Otto and Moos (1974) found that patient expectations of the program were a powerful mediating variable in dropout rate prediction. Expectations unmet by the program related significantly to increased dropout rate, whereas expectation-experience congruence in the program led to favorable programmatic adjustment.

In substance abuse rehabilitation programs for adolescents, member ratings of the program as high in Spontaneity and staff ratings of the program as high on Organization and Practical and Personal Problem Orientation resulted in more frequent client reports of lessened drug use (Friedman & Glickman, 1986; Friedman, Glickman, & Korach, 1986). Program Clarity with well-defined Personal Problem Orientation was associated with posttreatment reduction in substance abuse and improved vocational adjustment, whereas patients in a comparison program that lacked these features were significantly less well adjusted on the outcome measures at 2-year follow-up (Bale et al., 1984).

Similarly, Fischer (1979) found that key predictors of posttreatment alcohol sobriety duration and relapse severity included high COPES ratings on indices of program clarity, personal problem orientation, and anger expression. Cronkite and Moos (1978) and Moos et al. (1990) found that COPES social ecological dimensions were as effective in predicting alcohol dependence treatment outcome as traditional social and demographic predictor variables.

Critique

The COPES has been proven to be an accurate, thoroughly validated, widely applicable, modifiable, cross-culturally sensitive descriptive and predictive measure of key social ecological dimensions for community-based treatment facilities. Although originally designed to evaluate psychiatric units, its sensitivity and accuracy also have proven useful in a variety of medical units. The COPES becomes particularly valuable when combined with the Ward Atmosphere Scale (WAS) and other Social Climate Scales in various treatment settings where clients move from inpatient (WAS applicable) to outpatient (COPES applicable) settings. Through joint use of these measures one can evaluate the same or similar dimensions across settings and phases of the patient's treatment program. The generality of the COPES findings suggests that the social ecological model upon which the test is based is itself a robust descriptive and predictive general model for social system analysis.

Work with the COPES in the area of alcohol dependence and other substance abuse disorder treatment has been particularly valuable in specifying the nature of the social portion of the bio-psycho-social model governing these addictive syndromes. Many relevant social treatment variables that interact with a given set of biologic and psychologic treatments have been isolated and investigated as predictive and mediational variables affecting treatment outcome. These variables typically have been unclearly defined and inconsistently managed therapeutically. Sex differences (Cronkite & Moos, 1984) have proven important predictors of response to treatment environment perception and response. Not surprisingly, psychiatric diagnosis plays a significant role in response to treatment program characteristics, and type and severity of psychiatric diagnosis have been shown to impact adjustment to community-based treatment environments of various types (cf. Coulton, Holland, & Fitch, 1984; Lehman & Ritzler, 1976).

The COPES provides a methodology for dimensionally analyzing which social ecological variables are important in programmatic adjustment and treatment outcome. The power of the COPES as a descriptive and predictive device has increased since it has been used in conjunction with other demographic, diagnostic, psychometric, and social ecological indices. The results of COPES analysis are specific as well as sensitive to programmatic change. They also are temporally stable even when program respondents change, as long as the program itself remains consistent in its treatment model.

This reviewer would like to see more formal study of COPES reliability at the subscale and profile levels. The longer term retest stability of the measure should be replicated with larger samples. Ipsative tables for comparison of profile elevation levels beyond chance variation for different significance values would be useful, to avoid overlooking small but significant variations in profile change and misinterpreting chance variation as treatment effect.

The establishment of profile stability does not obviate the need to establish the specific retest reliability of the COPES subscales. The degree of chance variation in these measures will determine the limits of reliable change scores that are critical to evaluating treatment effectiveness in pre- versus posttreatment analyses. Internal consistency of the COPES subscales also should be optimally estimated through calculation of Cronbach's coefficient alpha, which remains to be reported.

Users particularly would welcome more work with the COPES in combination with the WAS to evaluate the parameters of transition from inpatient to outpatient care and the variables that predict community tenure and quality of adjustment in various disorders. Routine use of the COPES in transitional living programs such as day hospital programs and halfway houses would be particularly valuable. Much more systematic work with the COPES in a variety of substance abuse and dual diagnosis programs is warranted given the excellent and powerful specific initial results with those populations. In the case of dual-diagnosis patients, work should investigate the role of each diagnosis alone in comparison samples and then contrast these effects with the dual-diagnosis group for each comparison pair to note interaction effects of psychiatric and substance abuse diagnosis on treatment program response and outcome.

Moos has written the current COPES manual for use in research and clinical or consultative applications, but more specific and detailed work is needed for clinical applications in specific populations. Recent works such as Moos et al. (1990) address clinical and consultative issues in great detail and have begun to meet this need. Continued such systematic empirical work with an applied focus that develops the applications of the test for clinical populations is strongly encouraged. Ongoing development of a parallel literature that clarifies the psychometric basis of the COPES and its relationship to a variety of other applied and theoretical measures also is needed to fully realize its potential.

Consideration of the burgeoning literature on this outstanding measure shows these needs being jointly addressed by the test author, by his colleagues, and by many independent professional users of the COPES. Its continued development and systematic application doubtless will contribute substantially to the optimization of patient care delivery and evaluation for community-based treatment settings.

References

Bakos, M., Bozic, R., Chapin, D., Gandrus, J., Kahn, S., Mateer, W., & Neuman, S. (1979). *Group homes: A study of community residential environments.* Cleveland, OH: Architecture Research Construction.

Bale, R., Zarcone, V., Van Stone, W., Kuldau, J., Englesing, T., & Elashoff, R. (1984). Three therapeutic communities: Process and outcome in a prospective controlled study of narcotic addiction treatment. *Archives of General Psychiatry, 41,* 185–191.

Bell, M. (1983). The perceived social environment of a therapeutic community for drug abusers. *International Journal of Therapeutic Communities, 4,* 262–270.

Bell, M. (1985). Three therapeutic communities for drug abusers: Differences in treatment environments. *Journal of the Addictions, 20,* 1523–1531.

Bell, M., & Ryan, E. (1984). Integrating psychosocial rehabilitation into the hospital psychiatric service. *Hospital and Community Psychiatry, 35,* 1017–1023.

Bell, M., & Ryan, E. (1985). Where can therapeutic community ideals be realized? An examination of three treatment environments. *Hospital and Community Psychiatry, 36,* 1286–1291.

Brill, R. (1979). *Development of milieus facilitating treatment* (Final Report No. 4). Montreal: University of Montreal, Groupe de Recherche sur l'Inadaptation Juvenile, Shawbridge Youth Center Research Project.

Burti, L., Glick, I.D., & Tansella, M. (1990). Measuring the treatment environment of a psychiatric ward and a community mental health center after the Italian reform. *Community Mental Health Journal, 26,* 193–204.

Cote, G., LeBlanc, M., & Trudeau-LeBlanc, P. (1985). *La cité des prairies: L'expérience des unités d'intervention externes.* Quebec: University of Montreal, Centre International de Criminologie Comparée.

Coulton, C.J., Holland, T.P., & Fitch, V. (1984). Person-environment congruence and psychiatric patient outcome in community care homes. *Administration in Mental Health, 12,* 71–88.

Cox, G. (1977). *Environmental study of the Memphis Correctional Center.* Memphis, TN: State Technical Institute, Correctional Research Evaluation Center.

Cronkite, R., & Moos, R. (1978). Evaluating alcoholism treatment programs: An integrated approach. *Journal of Consulting and Clinical Psychology, 46,* 1105–1119.

Cronkite, R., & Moos, R. (1984). Sex and marital status in relation to the treatment and outcome of alcoholic patients. *Sex Roles, 11,* 93–112.

Cronkite, R., Moos, R., & Finney, J. (1984). The context of adaptation: An integrative perspective on community and treatment environments. In W.A. O'Connor & B. Lubin (Eds.), *Ecological approaches to clinical and community psychology* (pp. 189–215). New York: Wiley.

DeLeon, G., Schwartz, S., Wexler, H., Jainchill, N., & Rudie, W. (1980, September). *Therapeutic communities for drug abusers: Studies of the treatment environment.* Paper presented at the annual convention of the American Psychological Association, Montreal.

Dennis, L., Burke, R., & Garber, K. (1977). Quality evaluation system: An approach for patient assessment. *Journal of Long-Term Care Administration, 5,* 28–51.

Fairchild, H., & Wright, C. (1984). A social-ecological assessment and feedback intervention of an adolescent treatment agency. *Adolescence, 19,* 263–275.

Fischer, J. (1977). Alcoholic patients' perception of treatment milieu using modified versions of the Ward Atmosphere Scale (WAS) and Community-Oriented Programs Environment Scale (COPES). *British Journal of Addiction, 72,* 213–216.

Fischer, J. (1979). The relationship between alcoholic patients' milieu perception and measures of their drinking during a brief follow-up time period. *International Journal of the Addictions, 14,* 1151–1156.

Friedman, A.S., & Glickman, N.W. (1986). Program characteristics for successful treatment of adolescent drug abuse. *Journal of Nervous and Mental Disease, 174,* 669–679.

Friedman, A.S., & Glickman, A.W. (1987). Residential program characteristics for completion of treatment by adolescent drug abusers. *Journal of Nervous and Mental Disease, 175,* 419–424.

Friedman, A.S., Glickman, N.W., & Kovach, J.A. (1986). The relationship of drug program environmental variables to treatment outcome. *American Journal of Drug and Alcohol Abuse, 12,* 53–69.

Friedman, S. (1982). Consultation for self-evaluation: Social climate assessment as a catalyst for programmatic change in mental health treatment environments. In A. Jeger & R. Slotnick (Eds.), *Community mental health and behavioral ecology: A handbook of theory, research and practice* (pp. 187–196). New York: Plenum.

Friedman, S., Jeger, A., & Slotnick, R. (1982). Social ecological assessment of mental health treatment environments: Towards self-evaluation. *Psychological Reports, 50,* 631–638.

Greenwood, R., Marr, J., Roessler, R., & Rowland, P. (1980). The social climate of a rehabilitation center: Implications for organizational development. *Journal of Rehabilitation Administration, 4,* 20–24.

Hall, S., Bass, A., Hargreaves, W., & Loeb, P. (1979). Contingency management and information feedback in outpatient heroin detoxification. *Behavior Therapy, 10,* 443–451.

Jelinek, R. (1974). *A methodology for the evaluation of quality of life and care in long-term facilities.* Springfield, VA: U.S. Department of Commerce. (NTIS No. PB-236725)

Kanfer, F.H., & Schefft, B.K. (1988). *Guiding the process of therapeutic change.* Champaign, IL: Research Press.

Kohn, M., Jeger, A., & Koretzky, M. (1979). Social-ecological assessment of environments: Toward a two-factor model. *American Journal of Community Psychology, 7,* 481–495.

Lehman, A., & Ritzler, B. (1976). The therapeutic community inpatient ward: Does it really work? *Comprehensive Psychiatry, 17,* 755–761.

Manning, N., & Lees, J. (1985). *Australian community care: A study of the Richmond Fellowship.* Canterbury, England: University of Kent.

Meier, R. (1983). The impact of the structural organization of public welfare offices on the psychosocial work and treatment environments. *Journal of Social Service Research, 7,* 1–18.

Milby, J., Pendergrass, P., & Clarke, C. (1975). Token economy versus control ward: A comparison of staff and patient attitudes toward ward environment. *Behavior Therapy, 6,* 22–29.

Moos, R. (1972). Assessment of the psychosocial environments of community-oriented psychiatric treatment programs. *Journal of Abnormal Psychology, 79,* 9–18.

Moos, R. (1973). Changing the social milieus of psychiatric treatment settings. *Journal of Applied Behavioral Science, 9,* 575–593.

Moos, R.H. (1974a). *Community-Oriented Programs Environment Scale, Form R* (test form). Palo Alto, CA: Consulting Psychologists Press.

Moos, R.H. (1974b). *Community-Oriented Programs Environment Scale manual.* Palo Alto, CA: Consulting Psychologists Press.

Moos, R.H. (1974c). *Evaluating treatment environments: A social ecological approach.* New York: Wiley.

Moos, R.H. (1984). Context and coping: Toward a unifying conceptual framework. *American Journal of Community Psychology, 12,* 5–25.

Moos, R.H. (1985a). Creating healthy human contexts: Environmental and individual strategies. In J.C. Rosen & L.J. Solomon (Eds.), *Prevention in health psychology* (pp. 366–389). Hanover, NH: University Press of New England.

Moos, R.H. (1985b). Evaluating social resources in community and health care contexts. In P. Karoly (Ed.), *Measurement strategies in health psychology* (pp. 433–459). New York: Wiley.

Moos, R.H. (1987). *The Social Climate Scales: A user's guide.* Palo Alto, CA: Consulting Psychologists Press.

Moos, R.H. (1988). *Community-Oriented Programs Environment Scale manual* (2nd ed.). Palo Alto, CA: Consulting Psychologists Press.

Moos, R.H. (1989). *Ward Atmosphere Scale manual* (2nd ed.). Palo Alto, CA: Consulting Psychologists Press.

Moos, R.H., Clayton, J., & Max, W. (1979). *The Social Scales: An annotated bibliography* (2nd ed.). Palo Alto, CA: Consulting Psychologists Press.

Moos, R.H., Finney, J.W., & Cronkite, R.C. (1990). *Alcoholism treatment: Context, process, and outcome.* New York: Oxford University Press.

Moos, R.H., Mehren, B., & Moos, B. (1978). The Salvation Army alcoholism treatment program: A case study. *Journal of Studies on Alcohol, 39,* 1267–1275.

Moos, R.H., & Spinrad, S. (1984). *The Social Climate Scales: An annotated bibliography update.* Palo Alto, CA: Consulting Psychologists Press.

Murray, H.A. (1938). *Explorations in personality: A clinical and experimental study of fifty men of college age.* New York: Oxford University Press.

Nunnally, J.C. (1978). *Psychometric theory* (2nd ed.). New York: McGraw-Hill.

O'Donnell, J., Collins, J., & Schuler, S. (1978). Psychosocial perceptions of the nursing home: A comparative analysis of staff, resident, and cross-generational perspectives. *Gerontologist, 18,* 267–271.

Otto, J., & Moos, R. (1973). Evaluating descriptions of psychiatric treatment programs. *American Journal of Orthopsychiatry, 43,* 401–440.

Otto, J., & Moos, R. (1974). Patient expectations and attendance in community treatment programs. *Community Mental Health Journal, 10,* 9–15.

Packer, J., & Wright, J. (1983). *I like where I live: An evaluation of models of group home style living.* Brisbane, Australia: Queensland Department of Health, Intellectual Handicap Services.

Pankrantz, L. (1975). Assessing the psychosocial environment of halfway houses for the retarded. *Community Mental Health Journal, 11,* 341–345.

Patton, M. (1977). *Environments that make a difference: An evaluation of Ramsey County Corrections Foster Group Homes.* Minneapolis: University of Minnesota, Center for Social Research.

Phillips, E., Coughlin, D., Fixsen, D., & Maloney, D. (1979). *Youth care: Programs and progress.* Boys Town, NE: Father Flanagan's Boys Home, Department of Youth Care.

Pino, C.J., & Howard, S. (1984). Sex differences in environmental perceptions, activities and behavior mapping in well aged housing residents. *Journal of Gerontological Social Work, 6,* 3–17.

Pino, C., Rosica, L., & Carter, T. (1978). The differential effects of relocation on nursing home patients. *Gerontologist, 18,* 167–172.

Redmon, W., Cullari, S., & Spates, C.R. (1982, August). *Quality of life in community residences for the mentally ill.* Paper presented at the annual meeting of the American Psychological Association, Washington, DC.

Ryan, E., & Bell, M. (1985a). *Psychoanalytic inpatient treatment with and without social rehabilitation: A comparison of two treatment milieus and their outcome.* West Haven, CT: West Haven Veterans Administration Medical Center.

Ryan, E., & Bell, M. (1985b). *A rehabilitation program for persons with schizophrenia: Process and outcome.* West Haven, CT: West Haven Veterans Administration Medical Center.

Ryan, E., Bell, M., & Metcalf, J. (1982). The development of a rehabilitation psychology program for schizophrenics: Changes in the treatment environment. *Rehabilitation Psychology, 27,* 67–85.

Schmidt, A. (1982). Application of the social ecological approach to compliance with hemodialysis treatment (Doctoral dissertation, University of Windsor, Canada, 1981). *Dissertation Abstracts International, 43,* 917B.

Schneider, K., Kinlow, M.R., Galloway, A.N., & Ferro, D.L. (1982). An analysis of the effects of implementing the teaching-family model in two community based group homes. *Child Care Quarterly, 11,* 298–311.

Schwartz, S.A. (1981). Dimensions of the Community Oriented Programs Environment Scale (COPES): A hypothesis testing factor analysis. *Multivariate Experimental Clinical Research, 5,* 67–72.

Segal, S., & Aviram, U. (1978). *The mentally ill in community-based sheltered care: A study of community care and social integration.* New York: Wiley.

Shadish, W., Straw, R., McSweeny, A.J., Koller, D., & Bootzin, R. (1981). Nursing home care for mental patients: Descriptive data and some propositions. *American Journal of Community Psychology, 9,* 617–633.

Shinn, M. (1982). Assessing program characteristics and social climate. In A.J. McSweeny, R. Hawkins, & W. Fremouw (Eds.), *Practical program evaluation in youth treatment* (pp. 116–143). New York: Thomas.

Shinn, M., Perkins, D., & Cherniss, C. (1980). Using survey-guided development to improve program climates: An experimental evaluation in group homes for youths. In R. Stough & A. Wandersman (Eds.), *Optimizing environments: Research, practice and policy* (pp. 124–135). New York: Environmental Design Research Association.

Willer, B., & Intagliata, J. (1981). Social environmental factors as predictors of adjustment of de-institutionalized mentally retarded adults. *American Journal of Mental Deficiency, 86,* 252–259.

Willer, B., & Intagliata, J. (1984). *Promises and realities for mentally retarded citizens: Life in the community.* Baltimore, MD: University Park Press.

Alan C. Bugbee, Jr., Ph.D.
Director of Educational Systems, The American College, Bryn Mawr, Philadelphia.

COMPUTER ANXIETY INDEX (VERSION AZ), REVISED

Matthew Maurer and Michael R. Simonson. Ames, Iowa: ISU Research Foundation, Iowa State University.

Introduction

The Computer Anxiety Index (CAIN) is a 26-item scale designed to measure computer-related anxieties by tapping the respondent's feelings toward computers and their use. The subject indicates how he or she feels about each statement by selecting one of six options, ranging from "strongly agree" to "strongly disagree." The resulting score shows degree of anxiety toward computers. This instrument is intended to identify individuals, primarily students, who have a great deal of computer anxiety so that anxiety may be reduced.

Although the CAIN may be given and utilized independently, it is presented as a part of the Standardized Test of Computer Literacy (STCL; Montag, Simonson, & Maurer, 1984), which assesses areas of general computer literacy. The intended audience is students taking a first course in computer literacy (e.g., Introduction to Data Processing) or a similar beginning course in high schools, colleges, business schools, and universities.

The CAIN is included in the STCL because "it has been demonstrated that cognitive computer literacy competencies are difficult for extremely computer anxious students to acquire" (Montag et al., 1984, p. 5). The CAIN attempts to measure one of the prerequisites for computer literacy—a positive, anxiety-free attitude about computers and their use. The authors believe that this attitudinal prerequisite conjoins with skills in three requisite areas: computer applications, computer systems, and computer programming. Thus they present this attitude scale along with their test of computer literacy. Although the CAIN was not necessarily developed as part of an overall scheme to assess the components of computer literacy, from the manual and the reprint of an article contained within it, one can reasonably assume that the developers produced it simultaneously with (and perhaps dependent on) the STCL. In fact, the manual presents what the CAIN measures, computer attitudes, as one of the four sections of the computer literacy test (Montag, Simonson, & Maurer, 1984, p. 7). The STCL/CAIN manual (p. 17) identifies 9 Attitudinal Computer Literacy Competencies in addition to 70 cognitive Computer Literacy Competencies (25 in computer systems, 25 in computer applications, and 20 in computer programming). Although a larger picture could be presented about the STCL in general, this review focuses only on the CAIN. Any discussion of the cognitive aspects of the STCL will appear in terms of how it relates to the CAIN.

164

The CAIN seems to have developed originally as master's thesis work (Maurer, 1983; Montag, 1984), presumably under the direction of co-author Michael R. Simonson, Ph.D., a faculty member of the institution granting the degree. The manual (Montag et al., 1984, p. 3) reports that the entire STCL, of which the CAIN makes up a part, took 2 years to develop. The CAIN takes the form of a 6-point Likert-type scale. The target of its assessment, computer anxiety, is defined as "the fear or apprehension felt by individuals when they used computers, or when they considered the possibility of computer utilization" (Simonson, Maurer, Montag-Torardi, & Whitaker, 1987, p. 238).

Following conventions for this type of scale development (Likert, 1932/1974), the authors produced a large number of statements believed to represent a person's feelings about computers. The manual reports (p. 46) that "the second step in the design of the CAIN was to pilot test these items in a manner similar to the one described for the verification of the achievement items [for the Standardized Test of Computer Literacy]." From the description of that process, one can infer that the authors administered the items to two pilot groups, one consisting of people who were computer literate, the other of people who were not. The results of this (these?) pilot test(s) were used to select the items that proved the best discriminators between computer literate and non–computer literate subjects. The authors produced a revised version of the CAIN and tested it, though the manual does not say whether the same groups were used for the second trial. The results guided the next revision, which yielded the present 26-statement scale. (See Henerson, Morris, & Fitz-Gibbon, 1978, for a discussion of the process used to construct this type of summated rating scale.) Although all materials refer to the current edition of the CAIN as Version AZ, Revised, there is no mention of what it was revised from. Perhaps the master's thesis version (Maurer, 1983) was the original and the commercial version is the revised one.

The CAIN consists of a single, two-sided, heavy stock sheet of paper, titled "Computer Opinion Survey (Version AZ), Revised," with accompanying machine scorable answer sheets. The manual states (p. 5) that this name is intended "to minimize the possibility of answer bias," which might result by calling it an anxiety test. The front side of the sheet gives instructions for filling in the test form and presents several demographic questions (name, sex, grade in school, birthdate) plus two questions on computer literacy. The first asks if the subject has ever taken a course in computer literacy and/or programming and allows a "yes" or "no" response. The second question, answered only if the response to the preceding was "yes," asks for the total number of semesters of computer course work the subject has completed. The possible responses range from "less than a full semester" to "nine semesters." Neither the form nor the manual addresses how to count course length in other than semesters (i.e., quarters, non-academic courses, etc.).

The reverse side of the sheet presents instructions and the 26 statements of the scale. The response choices for each are "strongly agree," "agree," "slightly agree," "slightly disagree," "disagree," and "strongly disagree." The CAIN assigns these choices values 1 though 6 and has respondents fill in the appropriate values on their answer sheets.

As is the case with most attitude scales, the examiner has little to do in the process of administration. There are no instructions for the examiner to read to the students, and only six sentences appear on how to administer the test, two of which relate to scoring and results. The extent of the examiner's participation would appear to be providing the materials that students need (test sheet, optically scorable answer sheet, and soft lead pencil) and seeing that they respond to all of the statements on the scale.

The CAIN is intended to identify students with computer-related anxiety, primarily so the anxiety can be controlled and/or eliminated as part of their becoming computer literate. In effect, it is a diagnostic tool. Although not identified as age related, beyond describing the target audience as students, the development sample comprised college students in teacher education. The subjects for its normative studies were junior high school and college students, computer professionals, teachers, and computer users. The manual does state, however, that the Standardized Test of Computer Literacy (STCL), of which the CAIN makes up a part, is "used with students in senior high schools, industrial or business training programs, and universities who have taken their first, and often only, course in computer literacy" (p. 4). Thus, users can assume that the CAIN developers had a specific age group in mind.

This implicit target age group seems in keeping with the language level for the CAIN's statements. The manual provides no information about expectations for subjects' reading levels, although, as with age levels, one can infer that they should have at least high-school reading ability. The materials offer no information or instructions on answering questions about statement or word meanings within the scale. Also, no allowance is made for presenting the statements verbally, again verifying the assumption of subjects' reading ability.

Practical Applications/Uses

The CAIN attitude scale measures a single trait or construct, computer anxiety, as defined above. With possible scores ranging from 26 to 156, it is designed so that the higher the score, the more anxious the individual is about computers. The manual provides no information, however, on the apparent underlying continuum of computer anxiety or at what point a subject's feelings toward computers no longer present a concern. This continuum seems one-sided in that it extends from no aversion towards computers to an extreme dislike of them. Although some of the statements might imply a liking of computers, the authors have not addressed this idea clearly. They provide no mid-point for either the responses (i.e., there is no uncertain option) or the scale.

The materials offer no information on how scores are assigned. It would seem incorrect to assume that the response to each statement corresponds to the value of the response option selected. That is, while the response "strongly agree" has a value of 1 on the scale, it would be illogical for all responses of "strongly agree" to indicate little or no aversion to computers as not all statements are unidirectional. Because some of the statements are favorable toward computers and some are unfavorable, a "strongly agree" response would not necessarily indicate lack of computer anxiety. If this was not taken into account, it would necessarily produce circular triads, the inconsistency of responses, highly undesirable in a scale. (See A.L. Edwards [1957/1974] for information on this concept.)

The CAIN is intended as a diagnostic tool to identify computer-related anxiety so that the latter can be reduced, eliminated, or made positive. This is done because "research has demonstrated that when anxiety is reduced, achievement tends to improve" (Montag et al., 1984, p. 5). Apparently the measure has not been used or even considered for any other purpose. Appropriately, the intended audience covers persons without computer experience who will be getting information (in courses, seminars, workshops, etc.) intended to make them "computer literate." Computer literacy, the focus of the test (Standardized Test of Computer Literacy) the CAIN shares the manual with, is defined as "an understanding of computer characteristics, capabilities, and applications, and the ability to implement this knowledge in the skillful, productive use of computer applications suitable to individual roles in society" (Montag et al., 1984, p. 7). Though the CAIN seeks to assist in the accomplishment of this goal, it need not, however, be limited thus. The developers probably could expand the age range it covers, with perhaps a version for younger students. It would make a useful tool in business situations that involve computers, perhaps in assessing personnel who will become drawn into computer use or a similar activity. It may have real value in research, such as in assessing the relationship of computer-related anxiety with performance on computerized testing. As the authors mention and as other research has shown (e.g., Bernt, Bugbee, & Arceo, 1990; Cambre & Cook, 1984), students' feelings about computers can affect their performance. The CAIN provides a means to follow this further, especially in the current attempts to computerize a wide range of national assessment and licensure examinations.

Scoring is included in the price ($.50/student) of the answer sheet. The results are reported for each student and for the group of students. As previously mentioned, the range of scores runs from 26 to 156; other than this, the manual provides no information on the scoring or score reporting of individual or group performance. Assuming that a table appearing in the manual (Montag et al., 1984, p. 24) represents the group report, that document will show number of scores in group (*N*), group mean score, standard deviation, low score, and high score. The manual does not mention if any interpretive information accompanies individual or group scores.

Technical Aspects

As mentioned previously, the Computer Anxiety Index appears to have grown out of a student's master's thesis (Maurer, 1983). Although the manual refers to this source throughout, little technical information from it appears. The manual proper (Montag et al., 1984) provides no statistical information on the CAIN beyond two tables and one figure. The first table (p. 24) shows the means, standard deviations, and ranges of six norm groups (*N* = 614), listed as college students, junior high, teachers, professionals, users, and others. The college students group consists of 111 freshman, sophomores, and juniors at Iowa State University. Junior high subjects are mostly students in the eighth grade. The teachers come "from all grade levels" (nothing indicates whether this means from kindergarten teachers to graduate school professors or some reduced set). "Professionals" ($n = 67$) refers to "people in business and industry who were formally trained in computer skills." It is not clear whether this refers to programmers, systems analysts, and so forth, or to "computer literate" persons. The users group ($n = 122$) comprises subjects in business who use computers routinely, but apparently without formal training. The group of "others" ($n = 25$) presents subjects who did not fit into any of the other five groups. This table apparently came directly from the aforementioned thesis.

The second table (p. 25) shows raw scores converted to percentiles. As mentioned earlier, because this scale seems to demonstrate only degrees of computer-related anxiety, it is unclear what these percentiles would mean interpretively, if anything. Would students with raw scores of 58 and percentile ranks of 50 be only half afraid of computers or would they be neutral (neither positive nor negative about computers)?

The one figure (p. 26), also taken intact from Maurer's thesis, shows the distribution of CAIN scores grouped into 5.2-point intervals. Apparently this presents the distribution of scores from the normative group, as the same number (614) of scores appear in both tables.

Users find the only other technical information provided in the manual's bibliography. These seven pages (pp. 31–37) list reference books, papers, and articles, some of which concern technical aspects of testing. It is interesting to note that the manual cites only two of the works listed in the bibliography (the two previously mentioned theses of Maurer, 1983, and Montag, 1984). This is the extent of the manual's information about reliability, validity, and norming.

Fortunately, bound together with the manual is a copy of an article on the development of the CAIN and the STCL (Simonson et al., 1987), which provides the technical information about the CAIN. The reported reliability of the 26-item version that emerged from pilot testing was an alpha coefficient of .94. Nothing appears on the data used to calculate this coefficient.

The article also reports that the 26-item version was evaluated for test-retest reliability. An unspecified number of college students in a teacher education course completed the scale twice over a 3-week session, yielding a coefficient of .90. This is the extent of the information provided on the CAIN's reliability.

Validity was determined by comparing the CAIN scores of 110 teacher education students with their scores on a state-trait anxiety scale and on rating scales based on observations of the students in their first laboratory situation. This concurrent validation method derived from assumptions that the computer anxiety measured by the CAIN was also measurable by the state part of the State-Trait Anxiety Index (STAI) when the subjects were seated at a computer (the state of anxiety). The authors also had two raters observe the subjects during a 2-hour session following the administration of the STAI. Raters judged the students in terms of the level of anxiety they displayed. The anchors on the 3-point rating scale were "computer anxious," "neutral," and "computer comfortable." The rating for each student came from averaging the two ratings together. The reported interrater reliability for the two judges is .85. No information is provided on the point values assigned to these scale ratings or how the raters made their decisions. For example, were all ratings based on one observation by each rater during the 2-hour period, or were ratings made at the end of a 2-hour period of continuous monitoring?

The relationship of the CAIN with the STAI score is reported as .32. The relationship between the CAIN and observational rating is reported as .36. Both of these scores are significant at the .01 level with 108 degrees of freedom. No information appears regarding the relationship between the STAI and the observational rating.

The article reprint accompanying the manual reports that the CAIN normative data was obtained from 1,943 students in six states, which differs from the norm group data reported in the manual (p. 24) and discussed earlier in this review. One cannot tell which norm groups apply to the CAIN as it is presented. Because no information is included on how the CAIN is scored and what information is provided to the user, the user cannot identify how any normative data are used.

A subset of this normative group (n = 67) took both the CAIN and the STCL to examine the relationship between computer anxiety and computer literacy. This study was in keeping with the premise underlying the inclusion of the CAIN with the achievement parts of the STCL: "cognitive computer literacy competencies are difficult for extremely computer anxious students to acquire. . . . when anxiety is reduced, achievement tends to improve" (Montag et al., 1984, p. 5). The results of this showed significant correlation, at the .05 level, between the overall computer achievement score and the CAIN score (r = -.27). In terms of the STCL's and the CAIN's relationship, the hypothesis that students with higher CAIN scores tend to have lower achievement scores is demonstrated. The authors, however, point out that this is a relatively weak relationship despite its statistical significance, and they imply that further research should occur.

Although there is no description of the 67 students within this subsample of the normative study, one can infer that they are the same 67 students listed (p. 49, Table 4) as Formally Trained Computer Users for the CAIN. It is interesting to note that this group has the lowest mean score (46.28) of all normative groups. In fact, this group has a very significantly lower mean than any of four other groups. Assuming that the CAIN was administered prior to computer literacy training (one of the basic recommendations in the manual), this would point to an a priori difference in anxiety among groups, which perhaps would predispose this group toward fulfilling the desired outcome. That is, the significant relationships between the CAIN and the STCL may have been due to the sample used rather than the treatment. This *selection* threat to the internal validity of this quasi-experiment (see Cook & Campbell, 1979, p. 53; and Campbell & Stanley, 1963, pp. 5, 12, 15) calls the value of this finding into question.

Critique

The Computer Anxiety Index is a Likert-type, summated ratings attitude scale posing as a test. The manual seems uncertain about which one it is and uses both terms indiscriminately throughout. The manual does imply (p. 42), however, that the CAIN is a criterion-referenced test because nine computer attitude "competencies" have been identified. As pointed out in another review of the CAIN (Edwards, 1989, p. 766), this is not a criterion-referenced test. Although its development incorporated some features of criterion-referenced test development, the methods used in item selection and scale building are those of an attitude scale applied to different groups. Because, as previously noted, no information is provided with it beyond individual and group scores, the CAIN is not really a norm-referenced test, either.

This reviewer is uncertain why the authors seem to be trying to present a perfectly good Likert-type attitude scale as a criterion-referenced or norm-referenced test. Perhaps because the measure grew out of a master's thesis, they felt it needed to be larger to become commercially viable. Nonetheless, the CAIN offers a useful means of measuring student attitudes towards computers. To be useful to the tune of $.50 a copy, however, it needs to be much more than it is.

Another problem with the CAIN concerns the level to which it is aimed—senior high school, business or industrial training programs, and college students. When it was constructed, this age range and the instrument's language level were probably appropriate. However, in current use of computers in schools, it may be more appropriate to aim now at much younger students for their first course in computer literacy. Though it would be premature to state that all or most students have exposure to computers before senior high school, American education seems headed in that direction, albeit slowly. Thus, the CAIN may be obsolete as a useful tool because it applies to a group that either no longer exists or is rapidly becoming extinct: senior high school or college students with no computer experience and, consequently, adults in industrial and/or business training programs with no computer experience.

For the CAIN to be used in the manner its authors intended, at the very least a version for lower educational levels must be developed. Further, as mentioned earlier, the language level (now aimed at high school students) must be written to a more appropriate level for first-time computer users—elementary and/or junior high school. Perhaps two versions would be appropriate.

The Computer Anxiety Index (Version AZ), Revised is a well-assembled, unidimensional, age-specific, summated rating scale for measuring a subject's degree of anxiety about using computers and/or about computers themselves in a course-taking situation. If appropriately revised, it could be useful in assessing the relationship of people's attitude about computers vis-à-vis their performance on computers in testing situations, for example. This use could produce results quite different from situations in which subjects are taking a course to learn about computers. This would shift the scale's current focus on improving attitudes toward computers as an end in itself to one of assessing interaction with computers when the issue of interest is not the computer itself but rather what it is used to achieve (i.e., a medical diagnosis, a test result, etc.). The CAIN has useful possibilities, but its authors first must bring it up to date, to reflect the different and changing demographics of groups experiencing their first exposure to computer use.

References

Bernt, F.M., Bugbee, A.C., & Arceo, R.D. (1990). Factors influencing student resistance to computer administered testing. *Journal of Research on Computing in Education, 22,* 265–275.

Campbell, D.T., & Stanley, J.C. (1963). *Experimental and quasi-experimental designs for research.* Chicago: Rand McNally.

Cambre, M.A., & Cook, D.L. (1984, April). *Computer anxiety: Definition, measurement, and correlates.* Paper presented at the annual meeting of the American Education Research Association, New Orleans.

Cook, T.D., & Campbell, D.T. (1979). *Quasi-experimentation.* Boston: Houghton Mifflin.

Edwards, A.L. (1974). Circular triads, the coefficient of consistence, and the coefficient of agreement. In G.M. Maranell (Ed.), *Scaling: A sourcebook for behavioral scientists* (pp. 98–105). Chicago: Aldine. (Reprinted from *Techniques of attitude scale construction,* 1957, pp. 66–72, 76–81. New York: Appleton-Century-Crofts)

Edwards, R. (1989). Standardized Test of Computer Literacy and Computer Anxiety Index (Version AZ), Revised. In J.C. Conoley & J.J. Kramer (Eds.), *The tenth mental measurements yearbook* (pp. 765–768). Lincoln, NE: Buros Institute of Mental Measurements.

Henerson, M.E., Morris, L.L., & Fitz-Gibbon, C.T. (1978). *How to measure attitudes.* Beverly Hills, CA: Sage.

Likert, R. (1974). The method of constructing an attitude scale. In G.M. Maranell (Ed.), *Scaling: A sourcebook for behavioral scientists* (pp. 233–243). Chicago: Aldine. (Reprinted from "A technique for the measurement of attitudes," *Archives of Psychology,* 1932, 140, 44–53)

Maurer, M.M. (1983). *Development and validation of a measure of computer anxiety.* Unpublished master's thesis, Iowa State University, Ames.

Maurer, M.M., & Simonson, M.R. (1984). *Computer Opinion Survey (Version AZ), Revised.* Ames, IA: Iowa State University.

Montag, M., Simonson, M.R., & Maurer, M.M. (1984). *Test administrator's manual for the Standardized Test of Computer Literacy and Computer Anxiety Index.* Ames, IA: Iowa State University.

Simonson, M.R., Maurer, M., Montag-Torardi, M., & Whitaker, M. (1987). Development of a standardized test of computer literacy and a computer anxiety index. *Journal of Educational Computing Research, 3,* 231–247.

Jerry B. Hutton, Ph.D.

Professor of Psychology and Special Education, East Texas State University, Commerce, Texas.

CONNERS' PARENT AND TEACHER RATING SCALES

C. Keith Conners. North Tonawanda, New York: Multi-Health Systems, Inc.

Introduction

The Conners' Parent and Teacher Rating Scales were designed to rate the problem behaviors of children and adolescents ages 3 through 17. The instrument consists of two versions—the Conners' Teacher Rating Scales (CTRS) and the Conners' Parent Rating Scales (CPRS)—with two forms for each. The CTRS is available with 28 and 39 items (CTRS-28; CTRS-39), and the CPRS is comprised of two forms, one with 48 items (CPRS-48) and the other with 93 (CPRS-93). All four versions provide four rating options for each item, and the informants rate the behaviors by marking how much the child has been bothered by "this problem" within the past month (not at all, just a little, pretty much, or very much). Three of the scales (CPRS-48, CTRS-39, and CTRS-28) award 0 to 3 points to the ratings, while the CPRS-93 applies 1 to 4 points for the four options. Information collected through the administration of the Conners' Rating Scales has been used in research and clinical practice to characterize the behavior of children and adolescents.

The Conners' Rating Scales are promoted by the author as useful for screening behavior problems, evaluating the effectiveness of interventions and remedial programs, and studying factors associated with childhood psychopathology. One or more variants of the Conners' Rating Scales have been reported in the research literature since 1969. Most studies have used the CTRS-39. Over 400 references to the scales are listed in the manual (Conners, 1990).

C. Keith Conners, a professor in the Department of Psychiatry, Duke University Medical Center, has contributed to the literature on hyperactivity in children for over 20 years. His early research focused on the use of behavior rating scales and the effects of drug therapy on hyperactivity in childhood (Conners, 1969, 1970, 1971, 1973). In the 1970s, authors cited Conners' behavior rating scales in the assessment of hyperactivity (Cantwell, 1975; Ross & Ross, 1976), and the abbreviated questionnaires, consisting of 10 items, enjoyed widespread use. This reviewer recalls finding informally duplicated variants of the abbreviated teacher rating form in school districts throughout Texas over the past several years. The form has been favored by physicians for help with the diagnosis and drug monitoring of hyperactivity, the hyperkinetic syndrome, minimal brain dysfunction (MBD), attention deficit disorder (ADD), and now, attention deficit hyperactivity disorder (ADHD). Two forms of the abbreviated version, Conners' Abbreviated Symptom

172

Questionnaire (ASQ), are available from Multi-Health Systems, Inc.: one for teachers (ASQ-T) and one for parents (ASQ-P). Drug efficacy studies first applied the ASQ (Sprague & Sleator, 1973).

The Conners' Rating Scales have been published since 1989 by Multi-Health Systems, Inc., and several other publishers also distribute the scales. Prior to that time, the scales were used primarily in research and in informal clinical applications. The commercial publication of the scales has increased their availability and has provided for the widespread use of the norms. As noted in the manual, the scales enjoy international application and are "among the most widely used assessment instruments for childhood problem behaviors in the world" (Conners, 1990, p. 1). The Conners' Rating Scales have been used with children in Australia (Holborow & Berry, 1986), Brazil (Brito, 1987), Hong Kong (Luk, Leung, Lee, & Lieh-Mak, 1988), Spain (O'Leary, Vivian, & Nisi, 1985), and Germany (Sprague & Sleator, 1977).

Table 1 compares a few of the features of the Conners scales. All contain some items related to hyperactivity and share some of the original items developed for the CTRS-39. Also, all scales have a conduct problem dimension. Some differences are noted for the age span covered by the specific scales. For example, the CTRS-39 applies to a narrower range (4 to 12 years) of children than the CTRS-28 (3 to 17 years). The situation is similar for the two forms of the parent version. In the manual, the author recommends that the CTRS-28 and CPRS-48 be used because the norms derive from the same groups of children (Goyette, Conners, & Ulrich, 1978). However, the longer teacher form (CTRS-39) has a very large sample.

Almost anyone may administer the Conners' Rating Scales due to the ease of administration. However, interpretation of results should be reserved for individuals who realize the "limitations of such screening and diagnostic procedures" (Conners, 1990, p. 7), and prospective users are advised to familiarize themselves with the *Standards for Educational and Psychological Testing* (American Educational Research Association, American Psychological Association, & National Council on Measurement in Education, 1985). Informants can complete the scales in from less than 10 minutes for the shortest scale (CTRS-28) to about 30 minutes for the longest (CPRS-93).

Practical Applications/Uses

The Conners' Rating Scales may be used to screen children for possible behavior problems, to evaluate the results of medication or other treatment or remedial programs, or to study the psychopathology of children and adolescents. School psychologists may find the scales beneficial, particularly as they can be used by teachers and parents to systematically rate their observations of a target child's conduct problems. Their ratings, along with other assessment data, could help establish a special education eligibility diagnosis. Physicians may wish to continue their use of the Conners' Rating Scales because of the instrument's sensitivity to the effects of drug therapy on hyperactive behavior. School counselors could benefit from having parents and teachers rate a target child's behavior from their perspectives. Counseling interventions thus may result in improved behavioral interventions in school or home.

Table 1

A Comparison of the Conners' Rating Scales

CTRS-39	CTRS-28	CPRS-93	CPRS-48
Informants			
Teachers	Teachers	Parents	Parents
Items			
39	28	93	48
Scales			
Anxious-Passive	Conduct Problem	Antisocial	Anxiety
Asocial	Hyperactivity	Anxious-Shy	Conduct Disorder
Conduct Problem	Hyperactivity	Conduct	Hyperactivity
Daydream-	Index	Disorder	Index
Attention	Inattentive-	Hyperactive-	Impulsive-
Problem	Passive	Immature	Hyperactive
Emotional-		Learning	Learning Problem
Overindulgent		Problem	Psychosomatic
Hyperactivity		Obsessive-	
Hyperactivity		Compulsive	
Index		Psychosomatic	
		Restless-	
		Disorganized	
Ages			
4–12 years	3–17 years	6–14 years	3–17 years
Norms			
9,583 (1982)	578 (1978)	683 (1970)	578 (1978)

Regardless of the professional using the scales, the user should collect data from many if not all the adults who have observed the target child over a period of time. As with the adage "Two heads are better than one," so are observations made in different settings by different people. As noted by Barkley (1988), the Conners scales should be given at least twice before the pre- and posttest assessment periods when used to assess treatment or intervention effects to compensate for the possible practice effects some have reported for the scales. Children tend to have more favorable ratings on the posttest even without intervention.

The subjects for the CTRS-39 were taken from the Canadian data, composed of ratings on 9,583 children (Trites, Blouin, & Laprade, 1982). Because the reference group is Canadian, practitioners in the United States or other countries may wish to take that into consideration. Although the data pool for CTRS-39 is quite substantial, one might be better advised to seek out normative groups more representational of the children who will be evaluated. In contrast, the normative data for the CTRS-28 and the CPRS-48 were taken from a different sample, based upon the work of Goyette et al. (1978). Although the author does not describe any of the normative samples satisfactorily in the manual, separate norms are given according to gender and age groupings on the CTRS-28, CTRS-39, and CPRS-48.

The use of three-part carbonless response forms facilitates scoring the Conners' Rating Scales. The informant circles one of four options for each item. As the circles transfer automatically to the second sheet, it is important that the informant not erase when wishing to change an answer. Changes can be made by writing an X over the incorrect circle and marking another option. The third sheet in the group is a profile form, on which the examiner may transfer the raw scores from page 2. Along each side of the profile form appear the standard scores (T-scores), enabling the examiner to inspect the standard scores for each of the scales without referring back to tables in the manual. The manual provides examples of scoring as well as case studies to aid in interpreting the profiles.

Administration, scoring, and interpretation of the Conners' Rating Scales also may be accomplished through computer software. Unfortunately, this software uses a counter system, which limits the number of times the program may be used. However, the manual states that the software requires only single floppy disk drive (either 5.25" 360K, 5.25" 1.2MB, 3.5" 720K, or 3.5" 1.44MB), and by contacting the test publisher, the user may find appropriate versions for use within local area networks (LANs).

From this reviewer's perspective, the hand-scoring profile forms are easy to use, time efficient, and expedient. If one wants to prevent the informant from scoring and profiling the responses, the profile sheet can be removed before the informant does the ratings and reattached later for scoring purposes. Another consideration with regard to the computerized version is interpretation. Although computer printouts may help the novice examiner, interpreting the Conners' Rating Scales is not complex and the manual is helpful in this regard. Also, if computer interpretations are available, it may be tempting to use them without integrating other assessment results.

The interpretation of the Conners' Rating Scales derives from a straightforward hypothesis. With the reference or normative group representing children "not specifically identified as having a diagnosable behavior problem" (Conners, 1990, p. 26), high standard scores (T-scores) suggest a problem and low ones indicate an absence of problems, at least from the perspective of the informant. However, interpretation may be more difficult for some children, particularly those rated differently by different informants.

Conners provides a step-by-step sequence for interpreting the rating Scales. The six steps include consideration for the source of the ratings and the context in which the child is being rated, inspection of relative strengths and weaknesses, individual item analysis, integration with other sources of information, and the development of a remedial or intervention strategy. By following these interpretation steps, discrepancies between the ratings may be clarified and understood.

The manual provides a table for interpreting the T-scores. Because these scores have a mean of 50 and a standard deviation of 10, the more a child's standard score deviates from the average, the more extreme the behavior. The author designates increments of one half a standard deviation to delimit the various levels. The average range is defined as 45 to 55, whereas the slightly above average or slightly below average range either increases or decreases 5 points from the average range limits. At the extreme ends of the table fall those scores considered very much above average (T-score = above 70) or very much below average (T-score = below 30).

Users may consider T-scores at 65 and above as clinically significant. A T-score of 70 or greater should serve as a cutoff when screening children for problems. Conner notes that different cutoffs may be established when one suspects that cultural differences systematically increase or decrease ratings. Rater bias as well as systematic cultural influences may indeed affect the levels of problem behaviors identified when using the Conners norm group for comparison. Separate norms are not available for North American children with an African-American, Latino or Hispanic, Asian, Pacific Islander, or Native American heritage.

Although the author recommends the use of the CPRS-48 and CTRS-28 because they use the same norm group, he notes that the CPRS-93 may be preferred in clinical settings. The CPRS-93 advantage stems from the increased number of items rated by the parent. The user can conduct an item analysis by looking at items grouped under as many as 25 different problem areas, from problems of eating, sleeping, speaking, and keeping friends, to restlessness, lying, stealing, fire-setting, and overassertiveness. A disadvantage of the CPRS-93 arises from the lack of norms for the Hyperactivity Index. The other three forms each contain the 10-item Hyperactivity Index, and norms are used to convert raw scores into T-scores.

Technical Aspects

A review of the technical aspects of the Conners' Rating Scales is difficult due to the multiplicity of studies employing one or more variants of the scales. As noted in the manual, some studies used modified versions and others failed to identify whether they employed a long- or short-form version. In addition, the research spans over 20 years. The author notes that "unfortunately, the lack of investigator consistency has plagued this instrument (probably because of its world-wide circulation in a research form) far more than other competing instruments used to also measure child problem behaviors" (Conners, 1990, p. 37). With the publication of the Conners' Rating Scales, future research is likely to be more consistent in the use and description of the scales.

Descriptions of the standardization groups are difficult to find in the manual, and the available information is incomplete. Interested researchers may have to go back to some of the original studies for additional information. The parent scales were developed using two separate groups. The first one (CPRS-93) was developed on a sample of 683 children (Conners, 1970), and the second (CPRS-48) used a sample of 578 (Goyette et al., 1978).

Similarly, the teacher scales used two different samples for norming. The longer form (CTRS-39) has one of the largest samples (N = 9,583) ever employed in the development of a behavior rating scale (Trites et al., 1982). The CTRS-39, the author's original scale (Conners, 1969), was employed first to measure the effects of drug trials. The shorter form (CTRS-28) shares the subject pool reported for the CPRS-48 (Goyette et al., 1978).

Information regarding test-retest, internal consistency, and interrater reliability is presented in the manual. Test-retest reliability studies are reported for the CTRS-39 and CPRS-93. Reliability coefficients range from .72 to .91 on the various scales of the CTRS-39 for a 1-month interval. Studies reporting the test-retest reliability for the Hyperactivity Index show stability over 2 weeks (.89; Zentall & Barack, 1979) and 1 month (.86; Epstein & Nieminen, 1983). Reliability coefficients for the CPRS-93 with a 1-year interval range from .40 for the Psychosomatic factor to .70 for the Immature-Inattentive and Hyperactive-Impulsive factors (Glow, Glow, & Rump, 1982). No test-retest data appear for either of the short forms, CTRS-28 or CPRS-48.

Internal consistency coefficients, using Cronbach's alpha coefficient, are mostly within reasonable limits for the CTRS-39. Edelbrock, Greenbaum, and Conover (1985) reported an average reliability coefficient of .94 for the various scales. Another study indicated that alpha coefficients ranged from .61 on Daydreaming to .95 on Hyperactivity (Trites et al., 1982). The Hyperactivity Index of the CPRS-48 is reported to have an alpha coefficient of .92 (Sandberg, Wieselberg, & Shaffer, 1980). The manual does not report internal consistency studies for the CTRS-28 or the CPRS-93.

Studies of interrater reliability using the CTRS-39 range from strong reliability (.94; Epstein & Nieminen, 1983) to weak (.39; Kazdin, Esveldt-Dawson, & Loar, 1983). Using the CPRS-48, Goyette et al. (1978) reported a mean correlation coefficient of .51 for the ratings made by mothers and fathers. Conners (1973) reported an average coefficient of .85 for mother-father correlations when using the CPRS-93. Comparisons of ratings made by teachers and parents have yielded lower correlations (.24 to .49) when the two short-form versions have been used (Glow, 1979; Goyette et al., 1978).

As noted in the manual, the validity of an instrument is established through the accumulation of evidence employing various methodologies (Campbell & Fiske, 1959). The Conners' Rating Scales have been used in hundreds of clinical and experimental studies, and in general, these studies do indeed support the validity of the scales.

The CTRS-39 has proven sensitive to behavioral change during drug trials (Werry & Sprague, 1974), effective as a screening instrument for hyperactivity, inattentiveness, and defiance or conduct problems (Glow & Glow, 1980; Kazdin et al., 1983; Schachar, Sandberg, & Rutter, 1986), and capable of predicting hyperactivity at later ages (Gillberg & Gillberg, 1983). Significant correlations have been reported between scores on the CTRS-39 and other child behavior rating scales (Campbell & Steinert, 1978; Edelbrock et al., 1985). One study showed that the short form (CTRS-28) is a valid screener for children's behavioral disorders (Stein & O'Donnell, 1985).

A few studies have employed the CPRS-93. Significant correlations were obtained when comparing the CPRS-93 ratings of children with Quay and Peterson's scales of the Behavior Problem Checklist (Campbell & Steinert, 1978). The CPRS-93 discriminates between groups of boys with ADD, specific learning disabilities, and matched "normal" controls (Kuehne, Kehle, & McMahon, 1987). As noted earlier, the CTRS-39, CTRS-28, and CPRS-48 each include a Hyperactivity Index. Several studies have reported results supporting the validity of this index (Boyle & Jones, 1985; Margalit, 1983; Porter & Omizo, 1984; Sandoval, 1977; Wynne & Brown, 1984). Few if any validity studies are reported specifically for the CPRS-48.

Several factor analytic studies of the Conners' Rating Scales have been reported (Cohen, 1988; Cohen & Hynd, 1986; Conners, 1969; Moehle & Fitzhugh-Bell, 1989; Trites et al., 1982; Werry, Sprague, & Cohen, 1975). As the manual notes, some studies have found certain differences in the factor structures. Typically, the most robust factors include a conduct problem and hyperactivity/inattention. Some have suggested that the factors proposed by Conners (1990) may vary, depending on the types of children being assessed. Moehle and Fitzhugh-Bell (1989) concluded that their results support the continued use of the revised CTRS (CTRS-39) in the assessment of child behaviors in clinical populations.

Critique

C. Keith Conners is recognized as one of the pioneers in the use of behavior rating scales for assessing child behavior problems. His work has resulted in hundreds of studies using one or more forms or variants of the Conners' Rating Scales. The extensive clinical and experimental use of the scales, the inconsistent description of which scales are being used, and the modifications of items from one scale to the next contribute to some confusion for users who must select the most psychometrically sound instrument. The publication of the scales by Multi-Health Systems is likely to contribute to more consistency in the application and reporting of clinical and research results.

The clinical and research history of the scales provides a strength. Unfortunately, the scales' other strengths are more difficult to assert. The manual needs to address the standardization groups for each of the scales in a clear manner, giving more attention to demographic characteristics; currently it does not enable one to determine the representativeness of the samples. Further, some authorities believe that samples over 15 years old are out of date. The CTRS-39 norms, which were established more recently than those for the other three forms, are over 10 years old. Another consideration is the size of the standardization sample. The CTRS-39 sample is unusually large (N = 9,583), but the samples for the other three forms are too small if one accepts 1,000 as a minimal sample size for standardization purposes.

Most of the research reporting on the psychometric properties of the Conners scales uses the CTRS-39, but much less work is reported for the other three scales, particularly the two short forms. The manual reports positive findings related to reliability and validity, but the numbers of subjects and levels of significance are not routinely reported, leaving one the task of referring back to the original work for that information. It would be practical for the manual to include tables with more a complete listing of information so that the reader can formulate judgments regarding reliability and validity.

Because so much has been written about the Conners' Rating Scales, it is fitting to mention some views given by other writers. Guevremont, DuPaul, and Barkley

(1990) presented an overview of the assessment of ADHD in children, noting that the CPRS-48 has psychometric properties that are "quite satisfactory" and can be "quite useful in evaluating treatments" (p. 58). They also state that the 28-item version (CTRS-28) of the revised CTRS-39 is "well normed and yields scores for factors relevant to the assessment of ADHD" (p. 60). They conclude that the CTRS "primarily assesses dimensions of conduct problems and may not be as sensitive to other domains of child psychopathology" (p. 60).

Barkley (1988) reviewed the Conners' Rating Scales and observed that the original CPRS (CPRS-93) contains items that primarily assess conduct problems or externalizing disorders, and they consider the scales to have adequate concurrent validity. The revised CPRS (CPRS-48) also assesses conduct problems, with the proportion of internalizing items reduced from the original. The authors note that investigators may prefer the CPRS-48 because norms are provided for a wider age range and are reported by gender. The CPRS-48 has not been studied as thoroughly as the original version, and additional research "would seem useful to establish its discriminant, concurrent, construct, and predictive validity" (Barkley, 1988, p. 119).

Regarding the original CTRS (CTRS-39), Rutter et al. (1988) noted that it is the most widely used rating scale in research on child psychopathology to date. Somewhat different factor structures have been identified by various investigators, but reliability information has been well established. The scale has weak interrater reliability, however.

Discriminant, construct, and concurrent validity are well established for the CTRS-39, according the review by Barkley (1988), but predictive validity is weak. Regarding the short version (CTRS-28), although test-retest reliability has been established, information is not available regarding interrater or internal consistency reliability. Also, though construct and concurrent validity are acceptable, data do not appear concerning the discriminant and predictive validity of the CTRS-28. Rutter et al. (1988) seem to prefer the CPRS-48 and CTRS-28 to the longer forms, and it appears that their review of the soundness of the short forms is based largely on the more extensive research done on the longer forms and their variants.

Hammill, Brown, and Bryant (1992) have reported ratings of over 250 tests or assessment instruments performed by a consumer's guide review board, relying upon operationally defined criteria for judging various aspects regarding norms, reliability, and validity. The standards developed from a review of positions recommended by a variety of writers in the field of psychometrics. Not one of the Conners' Rating Scales measure up to the standards used by Hammill et al. (1992). The recency of the norms for the CTRS-28 and CPRS-48 were rated acceptable, but overall ratings suggest that the Conners scales are "not recommended" (Hammill et al., 1992, pp. 28, 63–64).

In summary, the Conners' Rating Scales have resulted in several hundred studies of child psychopathology and they continue to be used in clinical and experimental research. Years of modifications of items and the lack of a manual and adequately described normative groups have resulted in a somewhat confusing picture for these scales. Nevertheless, the cumulative data appear encouraging, and it is suggested that the Conners' Rating Scales will continue to be preferred by many clinicians and researchers. However, the norms need to be updated for the CTRS-39 and CPRS-93, and expanded and described for the CTRS-28 and CPRS-48. Further, reliability and validity studies should be reported for the two short forms, CTRS-28 and CPRS-48; it is probably not defensible to grant favor to the short forms on the basis of their parents, the longer forms. Nevertheless, Dr. Conners is to be commended for not only stimulating the use of behavioral rating scales in the study of child psychopathology, but also for influencing others in developing scales for similar uses.

References

American Educational Research Association, American Psychological Association, & National Council on Measurement in Education. (1985). *Standards for educational and psychological testing.* Washington, DC: American Psychological Association.

Barkley, R.A. (1988). Child behavior rating scales and checklists. In M. Rutter, A.H. Tuma, & I.S. Lann (Eds.), *Assessment and diagnosis in child psychopathology* (pp. 113–155). New York: Guilford.

Boyle, M.H., & Jones, S.C. (1985). Selecting measures of emotional and behavioral disorders of childhood for use in general populations. *Journal of Child Psychology and Psychiatry and Allied Disciplines, 26,* 137–159.

Brito, G.N. (1987). The Conners' Abbreviated Teacher Rating Scale: Development of norms in Brazil. *Journal of Abnormal Child Psychology, 15,* 511–518.

Campbell, D., & Fiske, D. (1959). Convergent and discriminant validation by the multitrait-multimethod matrix. *Psychological Bulletin, 56,* 81–105.

Campbell, S.B., & Steinert, Y. (1978). Comparison of rating scales of child psychopathology in clinic and nonclinic samples. *Journal of Consulting and Clinical Psychology, 46,* 358–359.

Cantwell, D.P. (Ed.) (1975). *The hyperactive child.* New York: Spectrum.

Cohen, M.J. (1988). The Revised Conners' Parent Rating Scale: Factor structure replication with a diversified clinical sample. *Journal of Abnormal Child Psychology, 16,* 187–196.

Cohen, M.J., & Hynd, G.W. (1986). The Conners' Teacher Rating Scale: A different structure with special education children. *Psychology in the Schools, 23,* 13–23.

Conners, C.K. (1969). A teacher rating scale for use in drug studies with children. *American Journal of Psychiatry, 126,* 884–888.

Conners, C.K. (1970). Symptom patterns in hyperkinetic, neurotic, and normal children. *Child Development, 41,* 667–682.

Conners, C.K. (1971). Recent drug studies with hyperkinetic children. *Journal of Learning Disabilities, 4,* 14–19.

Conners, C.K. (1973). Rating scales for use in drug studies with children. *Psychopharmacology Bulletin* [Special issue: Pharmacotherapy with Children], *9,* 24–84.

Conners, C.K. (1990). *Conners' Rating Scales manual.* North Tonawanda, NY: Multi-Health Systems.

Edelbrock, C., Greenbaum, R., & Conover, N.C. (1985). Reliability and concurrent relations between the teacher version of the Child Behavior Profile and the Conners' Revised Teacher Rating Scale. *Journal of Abnormal Child Psychology, 13,* 295–303.

Epstein, M.H., & Nieminen, G.S. (1983). Reliability of the Conners' Abbreviated Teacher Rating Scale across raters and across time: Use with learning disabled students. *School Psychology Review, 12,* 337–339.

Gillberg, I.C., & Gillberg, C. (1983). Three-year follow-up at age 10 of children with minor neurodevelopmental disorders: I. Behavioral problems. *Developmental Medicine and Child Neurology, 25,* 438–449.

Glow, R.A. (1979). Cross-validity and normative data on the Conners' Parent and Teacher Rating Scales. In K.D. Gawdow & J. Loney (Eds.), *Psychosocial aspects of drug treatment for hyperactivity*. Boulder, CO: AAAS Westview Press.

Glow, R.A., & Glow, P.H. (1980). Peer and self-rating: Children's perception of behavior relevant to hyperkinetic impulse disorder. *Journal of Abnormal Child Psychology, 8*, 471–490.

Glow, R.A., Glow, P.H., & Rump, E.E. (1982). The stability of child behavior disorders: A one year test-retest study of Adelaide versions of the Conners' Teacher and Parent Rating Scales. *Journal of Abnormal Child Psychology, 10*, 33–60.

Goyette, C.H., Conners, C.K., & Ulrich, R.F. (1978). Normal data on revised Conners' Parent and Teacher Rating Scales. *Journal of Abnormal Child Psychology, 6*, 221–236.

Guevremont, D.C., DePaul, G.J., & Barkley, R.A. (1990). Diagnosis and assessment of attention deficit hyperactivity disorder in children. *Journal of School Psychology, 28*, 51–78.

Hammill, D.D., Brown, L., & Bryant, B.R. (1992). *A consumer's guide to tests in print* (2nd ed.). Austin, TX: PRO-ED.

Holborow, P., & Berry, P. (1986). A multinational, cross-cultural perspective on hyperactivity. *American Journal of Orthopsychiatry, 56*, 320–322.

Kazdin, A.E., Esveldt-Dawson, K., & Loar, L.L. (1983). Correspondence of teacher ratings and direct observations of classroom behavior of psychiatric inpatient children. *Journal of Abnormal Child Psychology, 11*, 549–564.

Kuehne, C., Kehle, T.J., & McMahon, W. (1987). Differences between children with attention deficit disorder, children with specific learning disabilities, and normal children. *Journal of School Psychology, 25*, 161–166.

Luk, S.L., Leung, W.P., Lee, P.L., & Lieh-Mak, F. (1988). Teachers' referral of children with mental health problems: A study of primary schools in Hong Kong. *Psychology in the Schools, 25*, 121–129.

Margalit, M. (1983). Diagnostic application of the Conners' Abbreviated Symptom Questionnaire. *Journal of Clinical Child Psychology, 12*, 355–357.

Moehle, K.A., & Fitzhugh-Bell, K.B. (1989). Factor analysis of the Conners' Teacher Rating Scale with brain-damaged and learning-disabled children. *Psychology in the Schools, 26*, 113–125.

O'Leary, K.D., Vivian, D., & Nisi, A. (1985). Hyperactivity in Italy. *Journal of Abnormal Child Psychology, 13*, 485–500.

Porter, S.S., & Omizo, M.M. (1984). The effects of group relaxation training/large muscle exercise and parental involvement on attention to task, impulsivity, and locus of control among hyperactive boys. *Exceptional Child, 31*, 54–64.

Ross, D.M., & Ross, S.A. (1976). *Hyperactivity: Research, theory, and action*. New York: Wiley.

Sandberg, S.T., Wieselberg, M., & Shaffer, D. (1980). Hyperkinetic and conduct problem children in a primary school population: Some epidemiological considerations. *Journal of Child Psychology, Psychiatry and Allied Disciplines, 21*, 293–311.

Sandoval, J. (1977). The measurement of hyperactive syndrome in children. *Review of Educational Research, 47*, 293–318.

Schachar, R.J., Sandberg, S., & Rutter, M. (1986). Agreement between teachers' ratings and observations of hyperactivity, inattentiveness, and defiance. *Journal of Abnormal Child Psychology, 14*, 331–345.

Sprague, R.L., & Sleator, E.K. (1973). Effects of psychopharmacologic agents in learning disorders. *Pediatric Clinics of North America, 20*, 719–735.

Sprague, R.L., & Sleator, E.K. (1977). Methylphenidate in hyperkinetic children: Differences in dose effects in learning and social behavior. *Science, 198*, 1274–1276.

Stein, M.A., & O'Donnell, J.P. (1985). Classification of children's behavior problems: Clinical and quantitative approaches. *Journal of Abnormal Child Psychology, 13*, 269–279.

Trites, R.L., Blouin, A.G., & Laprade, K. (1982). Factor analysis of the Conners' Teacher

Rating Scale based on a large normative sample. *Journal of Consulting and Clinical Psychology, 50,* 615–623.

Werry, J.S., & Sprague, R.L. (1974). Methylphenidate in children: Effect of dosage. *Australian and New Zealand Journal of Psychiatry, 8,* 9–19.

Werry, J.S., Sprague, R.L., & Cohen, N.M. (1975). Conners' Teacher Rating Scale for use in drug studies with children—an empirical study. *Journal of Abnormal Child Psychology, 3,* 217–229.

Wynne, M.E., & Brown, R.T. (1984). Assessment of high incidence learning disorders: Isolating measures with high discriminant ability. *School Psychology Review, 13,* 231–237.

Zentall, S.S., & Barack, R.S. (1979). Rating scales for hyperactivity: Concurrent validity, reliability, and decisions to label for the Conners' and Davids' abbreviated scales. *Journal of Abnormal Child Psychology, 7,* 179–190.

George Domino, Ph.D.
Professor of Psychology, University of Arizona, Tucson, Arizona.

CREATIVITY CHECKLIST
David L. Johnson. Wood Dale, Illinois: Stoelting Company.

Introduction

The Creativity Checklist (CCh), according to its author, is "an objective, self-report, eight-item instrument developed specifically to identify overt creativity observed by at least one other person" (Johnson, 1979, p. 1).

The CCh consists of a two-sided page; the first side defines eight characteristics of the creative person (fluency, flexibility, independence, etc.), and the reverse side looks quite a lot like a classroom grade sheet, with spaces for the names of up to 26 pupils and nine columns, labeled 1 through 8 plus a total, where the respondent rates each child on each of the eight definitions using a 5-point scale (consistently, frequently, occasionally, seldom, never). Thus, contrary to its title, the CCh is not a checklist but an observational recording device, and it is not a self-report but is to be filled out by an observer who wishes to record his or her evaluations of eight aspects presumably related to creativity.

No information is available on the history, background, and developmental procedures used for the CCh. The copyright date is given as 1979, and the earliest technical report cited in the manual and presumably using the CCh carries a date of 1975. The CCh was first reviewed in *The Ninth Mental Measurements Yearbook*, which was published in 1985. Thus the CCh has been around for some 17 years and apparently has not undergone the kinds of revisions and data gathering one would expect nor has it appeared in research reports in the literature.

The CCh, despite the author's definition, is a recording schedule on which observers, presumably classroom teachers in primary grades, can record their observations for each of the eight identified dimensions of creativity, using the previously mentioned 5-point scale. The schedule is not used to record one's own behavior nor is anything checked.

The recording form itself is quite simple and, as Dwinell (1985) indicated, the typical reaction is "Is this all there is?" Even with this simplicity, it is an awkward form to fill out; the eight dimensions are defined on the first page but not on the reverse where the actual ratings are made. Thus the observer either has to memorize the eight dimensions or continuously flip back and forth.

There is no information given as to the age group for which the CCh is intended, but a couple of studies cited in the Validity section of the "Instruction Manual" assessed children in primary grades.

The respondent-observer's task, then, is to rate each child on each of the eight dimensions and then add up the numbers for a total score, which can range from a low of 8 to a high of 40. The only table given in the one-page manual seems to indicate that total scores can go as low as 0, which of course they cannot.

Practical Applications/Uses

If the CCh were supported by the necessary reliability and validity evidence, by appropriate norms, and by the other accoutrements of a legitimate test, a number of possibilities would present either for research usage (e.g., for the identification of potentially creative children), curricular applications (e.g., to monitor changes made in classroom procedures designed to enhance creativity), or other applications of substantial import (e.g., in the assessment and/or identification of potentially creative minority children who typically do not do well on traditional measures). Currently, however, this reviewer can only echo the conclusion of Hawthorne (1985) that the CCh "in its present state does not appear to be a viable instrument" (p. 414).

This form is designed for an observer to rate "each person's social interactions in a given setting" (Johnson, 1979, p. 1) along eight dimensions, presumably related to creativity. These dimensions are preference for complexity, fluency, flexibility, resourcefulness, constructional skill, ingenuity, independence, and self-confidence. The intended rater is a classroom observer, including the teacher; no specifics are given, but presumably the CCh was developed for use in primary grades where the children do a fair amount of interacting. Potentially the rating also could be used with older children, high school or college students, and adults in work settings, if the proper observational opportunities prevailed.

On the one hand, little psychological skill is required to complete the form—any minimally trained person can rate a child or children on the eight dimensions—and so the form could be used with unsophisticated raters such as college students, aides, playground monitors, and so forth, much as a medical degree is not required to use a scalpel. However, to obtain meaningful ratings involves an astute and well-trained observer, one who knows what to look for and what not to be influenced by; the manual provides no instruction on how to achieve this.

The CCh instruction manual presents no normative data, does not describe any standardization samples, gives no information on any samples that might have been used in development, does not explicitly indicate age ranges for which the CCh might be appropriate, and does not consider children who might have developmental, physical, emotional, or other handicaps, except to cite a study of 18 "white children" that included 5 subjects with "visual-perceptual problems." No information appears regarding whether the form could be adapted for use with non-English-speaking observers or to observe children who present assessment challenges, such as blind children.

The CCh as an observational schedule could be utilized in any setting where observations can be made—obviously the classroom, but also the playground, the cafeteria, the assembly hall, and so on. As the definition of the CCh includes "social interactions in a given setting," the observations presumably must be limited to such interpersonal give and take. The degree to which these limits might or might not influence the obtained ratings is not considered, yet studies of creativity in adults certainly show that creative persons differ in many ways in how they partake of such social interactions.

The respondent who does the observations presumably should be trained, but the instruction manual does not address this issue other than to indicate that one in-service training session is usually sufficient to maintain adequate intercoder reliability. No information is given as to what such an in-service session might cover or how it would be carried out. There are no useful guidelines given for the prospective observer other than the statement that CCh users should "periodically check reliability."

The manual states that the CCh typically requires less than 15 minutes for the coding to be recorded, depending, of course, on the number of children assessed. No mention is made of how long the actual observation period should be, nor what should one look for, nor how the looking translates into the coding system.

Because the CCh is not a test in any sense of the word, there are no templates or scoring procedures, and no scores are generated. Once each child has been rated on the eight dimensions, the eight numbers are added to obtain a "total score." What to do with these scores is left to the imagination of the observer, save for the inclusion of a table that lists five levels of creativity (high to very low) and the "total scores" associated with each. As far as can be judged, the table is based solely on the author's predilection rather than on any normative data.

The author provides no interpretive guidelines for this schedule except for the one table, which appears totally unrelated to any empirical data. For example, no guidelines suggest what can be said about a child who is rated in a particular range of creativity, nor on the appropriateness or inappropriateness of giving equal weight to each of the eight dimensions, nor about whether the dimensions are psychometrically independent and represent basic aspects of creativity, nor on "profile" interpretation (e.g., what does it mean if a child is rated low on preference for complexity but high on resourcefulness?).

Technical Aspects

The CCh instruction manual contains one paragraph headed "Reliability," which exhorts the user to sample a number of settings where creativity may be observed, to use the CCh with care, to reduce bias and maintain high reliability, and to establish baseline criteria. All of these are worthwhile goals, but they are neither clearly defined nor is the user instructed on how they might be achieved. How is high reliability maintained? How is intercoder reliability computed? Should the observer just be concerned with the reliability of the total scores or also with the reliability of the eight rated dimensions? How does one compute baseline criteria?

More critically, the section on reliability gives absolutely no empirical evidence that the author has investigated the reliability of the CCh. No correlation coefficients are documented based on actual data, nor is anything like test-retest reliability mentioned. As Hawthorne (1985) indicated, inter- and intrarater reliability data are critical for any observation-based instrument, and Johnson reports no such data.

The validity section consists of three paragraphs reporting on three studies, all of which are inadequate, appear to be classroom projects done by students of the author using samples of convenience, and "available" as technical reports (several efforts by this reviewer to obtain these reports met with failure).

For the first study, the manual states that "Johnson (1975) reported that different school district studies yielded an overall positive mean correction ($r = .51$)" between the CCh and another coding instrument. There is no explanation, however, of what a "mean correction" is, nor why a mean correction is expressed as a correlation coefficient, nor whether the reported r is in fact a standard Pearson correlation coefficient between two coding systems that presumably code the same behavior, nor how many children and observers participated. Other basic information needed to judge the adequacy of this study is also lacking.

The second reported study consisted of 18 children whose CCh scores (for some reason changed to "ranks") were correlated with the WISC Similarities subtest, with an obtained coefficient of .62. If the CCh is supposed to codify creativity, this is a rather sizeable correlation with a subtest from a measure of *intelligence*, and it strongly suggests that the teachers' ratings of creativity were unduly influenced by academic achievement and/or intelligence. In other words, though it is inadequate evidence, it offers evidence against the validity of the CCh.

A third study compared the CCh ratings of seven school band members with their scores on a locus of control scale. The author does not indicate why there should be a relationship between these two variables, but the reader simply is told that the results supported the prediction of a negative association.

No evidence appears (nor are the issues even discussed) regarding whether the eight dimensions of the CCh are basic to creativity or regarding the implications of adding the eight together to derive a total score. Several of the dimensions are actually "multidimensional." For example, the first is "observed sensitivity or preference for complexity." Are these two aspects being equated? Is the author saying that sensitivity is the same as preference for complexity? Or is the observer being instructed to judge either one?

There are no tables of norms, no correlation matrices, no descriptive statistics, and no mention of halo effect, gender differences, and so forth. In short, as there are no data reported on the CCh, even the title of "Instruction Manual" is misleading.

Critique

As a psychologist particularly interested in tests, I become personally excited when I discover a test like the CPI, the WAIS, the Rotter Locus of Control scale, for I much admire the author's theoretical richness, the ingenuity with which theory is translated into item, and the years of work that culminate in a useful, laudable instrument. And then there are "tests" like the CCh, which seem to ignore even the most elementary aspects of test construction, let alone the guidelines embodied in documents like the *Standards for Educational and Psychological Testing* (American Educational Research Association, American Psychological Association, & National Council on Measurement in Education, 1985).

The reviewers of the CCh in *The Ninth Mental Measurements Yearbook* (Dwinell, 1985; Hawthorne, 1985) were most kind and concluded that "publication of the CCh appears to be premature" and that "there is no reason to recommend" the CCh over unaided observation. I shall not be so kind. The measurement and assessment of creativity is still in its infancy and does not need products like the CCh.

References

American Educational Research Association, American Psychological Association, & National Council on Measurement in Education. (1985). *Standards for educational and psychological testing.* Washington, DC: American Psychological Association.

Dwinell, P.L. (1985). Creativity Checklist. In J.V. Mitchell, Jr. (Ed), *The ninth mental measurements yearbook* (pp. 412–413). Lincoln, NE: Buros Institute of Mental Measurements.

Hawthorne, L.W. (1985). Creativity Checklist. In J.V. Mitchell, Jr. (Ed), *The ninth mental measurements yearbook* (pp. 413–414). Lincoln, NE: Buros Institute of Mental Measurements.

Johnson, D.V. (1979). *Creativity Checklist instruction manual.* Wood Dale, IL: Stoelting.

Ann H. Stoddard, Ed.D.

Professor of Education, University of North Florida, Jacksonville, Florida.

CULTURE FAIR INTELLIGENCE TEST

Raymond B. Cattell and A.K.S. Cattell. Savoy, Illinois: Institute for Personality and Ability Testing, Inc.

Introduction

The Culture Fair Intelligence Test (CFIT) is designed to measure individual intelligence while minimizing the influence of cultural learning, social climate, and educational level. The tests may be administered individually or in a group setting, using nonverbal items that involve perception of relationships in shapes and figures. There are three scales: Scale 1 (eight subtests), for 4- to 8-year-olds and retarded institutionalized adults; Scale 2 (four subtests), for 8- to 12-year-olds and unselected adults; and Scale 3 (four subtests), for upper high school students, college students, and selected adults (e.g., graduate students, business executives, and highly gifted adults). Raymond Cattell, prominent personality theorist and psychologist and one of the CFIT authors, recognized that pictorial tests reflect cultural influences to a degree, while other tests that claim to avoid culture completely, such as performance tests, tend also to avoid measuring intelligence (Cattell, Feingold, & Sarason, 1941).

Work on the CFIT began in the late 1920s and resulted in the 1930 publication of the Cattell Group and Individual Intelligence Tests. Five years later, several scales were revised to reflect a nonverbal format in an attempt to diminish the influence of verbal fluency. During a 26-year span, the CFIT was revised and refined three separate times (1940, 1949, 1961), resulting in four subtests retained today, an alteration of the format including four subtests at two difficulty levels, the development of a new item pool, and adjustments of the difficulty level and sequencing of items. Additionally, norm samples were expanded to achieve a preferred national sampling representation.

The CFIT has been used in 23 foreign countries. No translations have been needed because of the test's nonverbal approach. The Spanish edition includes translations of the instructions as well as modified translations of the test booklets and answer sheets to coincide with the instructions. Research indicates that U.S. immigrant groups do not show great differences between first and later testings, and that the *g* saturation is as good on the CFIT as on other standard tests.

As the CFIT Scale 1 differs from Scales 2 and 3, the three will be discussed separately when required. Scale 1 is not entirely culture free, due to the "difficulty of obtaining a sufficiency of tests in the new perceptual test medium that would [command] the sustained interest of young children and meet other requirements special to this age group" (Cattell, 1950, p. 4). Scale 1 is composed of eight 12-item subtests: Substitution, Classification, Mazes, Selecting Named Objects, Following

Directions, Wrong Pictures, Riddles, and Similarities. Further, these subtests can be grouped to abbreviate the full-length CFIT: The Group Test Abbreviated Form covers subtests that can be given in a group situation (1, 3, 4, and 8, and sometimes 2); The Fully Culture Fair Test Form covers subtests that are culture free without the loss of reliability (1, 2, 3, and 8); and The Short Time Form uses all of the subtests (1 through 8) but adjusts the time allocated to complete them.

The Scale 1 subtests are relatively easy to answer. In Substitution, test takers must underline or mark a drawing similar to the provided example. For example, if there is a square drawn under a train, the examinee must draw a square under each train pictured on the page. The Classification test requires examinees to place six cards correctly in the spaces. In Mazes, the test taker must draw a line from the mouse to the cheese in 90 seconds. In the Selected Named Objects subtest, examinees must draw a line under the designated object(s) in 12 tries, beginning with underlining one object in item 1 and increasing to five objects by item 12. In Following Directions, the examinee must do whatever the examiner says, after the direction has been repeated. Directions increase from doing three things to doing four things that require decision-making skills by the 12th try. During the administration of Wrong Pictures, 12 pictures are shown containing errors, and the test taker must point to each error. In Riddles, examinees must select the correct answer from a group of three or four options. For example, the examiner might say, "A horse, a goat, a cow, or a dog. What is it that has four legs and says 'moo'?" Finally, in Similarities, test takers must find the object in a row of five that is identical to the first object in the row.

Scales 2 and 3 are very similar in structure, but differ in level of difficulty. Four subtests make up both scales, and each subtest is composed of 12 to 13 items. The incomplete Progressive Series requires examinees to select the response that best continues the series from the choices provided. The Classification subtest differs between Scales 2 and 3. In Scale 2, the test taker must select the one figure that is different from the other four, whereas in Scale 3 he or she must correctly identify two figures that are different from the other three. In the Matrices subtest, examinees must complete the design provided at the left of each row. The Conditions or Topography subtest necessitates selecting from among five choices the single figure that duplicates the conditions given in the far-left box. In each instance, examples are provided so that the task stipulations are well defined to the examinee.

The answers for Scale 1 are recorded in the consumable booklet and monitored by the examiner. The scores for each subtest and remarks are tabulated on the front of the test booklet, along with demographic data. The back page is used to record the child's behavior during an individual administration of the CFIT. Space for logging IQ, mental age, and chronological age also is provided. There are separate answer sheets for Scales 2 and 3, Forms A and B. Space appears on both the answer sheets and test booklets for test scores and remarks along with demographic data.

Practical Applications/Uses

The CFIT provides data for assessing the general mental capacity factor, g, in both research and clinical work. The test authors state that approximately 135 research projects were conducted from 1980 through 1989, and data from some of these projects were available for this review. International studies (in several Western countries, plus China, Pakistan, and Mexico) completed by many researchers focus on numerous areas of intelligence testing. Areas of possible use for the CFIT appear essentially unlimited. The test could be applied in any situation with a need for a measure of intellectual potential that includes an assessment of a) racial ability structure, b) deviant behavior characteristics, c) creative thinking abilities, d) effects of computer-assisted instruction, e) cultural differences, and f) correlations with other intelligence tests. In addition, the lower end of the age range (4–8 years) suggests possibilities of using the instrument in an educational setting for placement and selection as well as in clinics and counseling centers. The CFIT findings at the upper level (high school and adults) certainly could be applied appropriately to advising and planning postsecondary education and prevocational or vocational experiences.

New areas of research using the CFIT are organized under the following headings: timed and untimed age trends, cultural differences, foreign use of CFIT, direct validity, and concrete validity in both educational and industrial settings. The test authors report that while a more extensive standardization is in progress, the original samples show "no significant differences from one to another at any age level, while the age plots from 3½ through 12 show internal consistency and smooth progression" (Cattell, 1950, p. 11).

The standardization for Scale 1 was based on 400 cases, combining middle-class American and British samples. For Scale 2, the standardization group comprised 4,328 male and female subjects from varied regions of Britain and the United States. Scale 3 norms are based on a standardization group of 3,140 American high school students (equally divided among freshmen, sophomores, juniors, and seniors) and young adults in a stratified job sample.

Individual studies with subjects from China, Germany, Pakistan, Micronesia, and Hong Kong, underprivileged black children, foreign students in the United States, Job Corps enrollees, and high school dropouts were conducted to provide insight into the use of the CFIT in the following areas: timed and untimed age trends, cultural differences, foreign use of the CFIT, and direct validity and concrete validity in industrial and educational settings. The studies dealing with concept validity showed a tendency for the CFIT to load higher on the general intelligence factor than on the achievement factor. Research focusing on concrete validity revealed that only 25%–50% of variance in achievement scores accounted for intelligence, whereas if personality and motivation measures had been included, prediction of job success would be greater.

The instructions for administering Scale 1 are brief but detailed, whereas those for Scales 2 and 3 are very detailed and precise. The manuals list all introductory remarks for the examiner and describe the general considerations for the test setting. Because Scale 1 addresses young children, it is recommended that two sittings be used, if necessary, to avoid examinee fatigue. All three scales are timed, and verbatim instructions for Scale 2 and 3 are required. In the case of Scale 1, children are not to be corrected, but they should be reminded to continue and move on to the next item.

From descriptions in the manuals, the CFIT can be administered in any setting appropriate for clinical and research assessment. Desks should be widely spaced and a quiet atmosphere with few distractions should be considered. The manual stresses that time limits must be adhered to and instructions must be presented exactly as printed.

Although the manuals do not identify specific credentials for the examiner, they do refer to "psychologists." It appears that no special technical skills are required of the examiner other than complete familiarity with the directions, test sequence, and timing. With younger children in groups of more than 25, an assistant familiar with the test should be used to help monitor test-taking behavior. The manuals do suggest that any departure from the instructions could seriously affect the results and render the norms inappropriate. At the end of the session, test booklets should be collected quickly to prevent changes in responses.

The amount of time necessary for the administration of each CFIT scale is indicated specifically in the manual. Scale 1 requires 22 minutes; however, with instructions and preparation, the actual test time fluctuates between 40 and 60 minutes for the full form and about half that for the short form. Scales 2 and 3 require 12½ minutes; with instructions, that time increases to approximately 20 to 30 minutes.

The ease of scoring for all scales of the CFIT is a major strength. Two types of scoring are available, one for the answer sheet and one for the answers recorded directly in the test booklet. Specific directions for using the scoring key appear on the key. The score for each subtest can be recorded on the front of the booklet or on the answer sheet, along with demographic data for the examinee. (Space for comments also is available.) Raw scores must be transformed to a normalized standard score IQ before test results can be interpreted. Tables are available to handle the conversion to IQs and percentile ranks.

Interpretation is based on objective scores, a relatively simple and clear process. The normalized standard score IQ permits comparison with other intelligence instruments, while the percentile rank is useful when relating the scores to parents.

Technical Aspects

One of the most impressive aspects of the CFIT is the amount of validity and reliability data presented in the technical manual. For Scale 1, factor analyses of direct concept, or construct, validity of the subtests and the total test reveals a range of respectable values, .64 to .84 for the subtests and .95 for the total test. Correlations were reported using the Binet IQ and the Goodenough Draw-A-Man test. On Scales 2 and 3, concept and concrete validities were conducted using samples of 522 to 702 males and females. Coefficients for concept validity ranged from .81 to .92 for the short form. Coefficients for concrete validity ranged from .66 to .70, which are somewhat low, for the short form and full test. The majority of the studies rely upon comparatively small samples, generally less than 200 subjects. There appear to be no problems inherent in the missing information about the subjects used for the validity estimates. High school students, school dropouts, white-collar workers, semiskilled workers, culturally different students, urban and rural subjects, and subjects from foreign countries, all ranging in age from 4 to 60 years, made up the population used in the validity studies.

Reliability coefficients for Scale 1 using three separate homogeneity coefficients ranged from .91 to .94. One test-retest study yielded an *r* of .80. Subtests tended to present lower coefficients, ranging from .59 to .69. Reliability coefficients for Scales 2 and 3 looked to consistency over items, .85 to 87; consistency over parts, .80 to .82; and consistency over time (immediate to 1 week), .82 to .84. The number of subjects used in each study ranged from a high of 3,999 to a low of 402, the majority of them being public school students.

With regard to norms, the manual reports that Scale 1 was "normed" on a population of 400 American and British subjects; Scale 2, a population of 4,328 American and British subjects; and Scale 3, a sample of 3,140 subjects from the high school and young adult population. The manual does not provide a clear description on the normative groups. It does not state whether the population includes rural, urban, or representation of different geographic areas of this country. Hopefully, as the authors promise, future editions of the CFIT will publish results of an expanded norm population.

Critique

The CFIT appears to be a well-designed instrument for measuring the general mental capacity factor, *g*, in children and adults with items that are culture free, though the test authors admit that Scale 1 is not completely culture free. In his review of the CFIT, Koch (1984) states that to produce a "pure culture fairness" test is nearly impossible at best. The difficulty in constructing a purely culture-fair test is centered around the answer to the question, "Whose culture?" Although the CFIT has been used throughout the world, its limits appear in the selection of samples from Western and industrialized countries and few, if any, from undeveloped and developing countries or from Asian, African, or South American cultures. In these latter areas, culture tends to differ from the Western world in many aspects, especially in decision-making skills, concept of cooperation, socialization, and lifestyles. Nonetheless, the CFIT represents one of the few standardized instruments available in the area of culture-fair intelligence assessment.

The measure has a number of strengths, including its ease of administration, scoring, and interpretation. The technical manual distinctly describes the measures of abstract reasoning and relation-perceiving abilities and provides an adequate assessment of the general intelligence factor, consistent with the idea that the CFIT measures "fluid" intelligence. Although the manual suggests that the CFIT is used to compare ability structures and factors among groups and levels, to identify characteristics of deviant behavior, to determine dogmatism, stress, and academic achievement, and to identify intellectually gifted students, it is possible that some of these applications extend beyond the intended dictates of reliability and validity considerations. The scales do seem to provide important information on examinees' abstract-reasoning abilities when the interpretation of results is limited to the CFIT's intended purpose. In addition, the use of four to eight subtests (instead one or two) to assess *g* is a plus for the CFIT.

Koch (1984), in an earlier critique, cites specific factors that he feels would improve the CFIT. He lists dated drawings, elaborate oral instructions, the printing quality, and inadequate norming, and calls for a "large scale revision" that should enhance the CFIT. No changes have occurred since that time.

The internal consistency reliability coefficients, taken with correlations from eight other respectable intelligence tests, suggest that the CFIT does indeed tap an ability construct much like the component of Spearman's *g*. However, as Koch (1984) cites, one problem is that the general ability concept has been surrounded by controversy the past 20 years. If one thinks of intelligence as sets of intelligence or multiple intelligence, as does Gardner (1983) in his *Frames of Mind*, then the CFIT is extremely limited in the measurement of total mental capacity (if, indeed, any test truly does this). Nonetheless, the CFIT as a global manifestation of mental ability provides some insight into how individuals think as well as into possibilities for reforming educational practices to achieve academic success and understanding. The CFIT, along with other measures, can be used to identify gifted students and to predict success in academic performance of students.

In summary, the CFIT has been and still remains one of the primary instruments for the measurement of intelligence using culture-fair test items. The scales are efficient and easy to administer, score, and interpret, generating information that is reliable and useful for a variety of purposes. The CFIT has fared well relative to most culture-fair scales. Its continued competitiveness will depend largely on whether the publishers will develop a means to update and expand the norms, especially for Scales 2 and 3. They might also consider Koch's (1984) recommendation of 10 years ago that would bring the CFIT into the technological age. His innovative suggestions included the use of the microcomputer for administration with high resolution graphics, voice synthesizers, and internal clocks. Today the use of laser discs and CD-ROM, computer scoring, and printouts for interpretation and percentile ranks should be considered.

References

This list includes text citations and suggested additional reading.

Cattell, R.B. (1950). *Handbook for the individual or groups: CFIT.* Champaign, IL: Institute for Personality and Ability Testing.

Cattell, R.B. (1973a). *Measuring Intelligence with the Culture Fair Tests: Manual for Scales 2 and 3.* Champaign, IL: Institute for Personality and Ability Testing.

Cattell, R.B. (1973b). *Technical supplement for CFIT, Scales 2 and 3.* Champaign, IL: Institute for Personality and Ability Testing.

Cattell, R.B., Feingold, S.N., & Sarason, S.B. (1941). A culture free intelligence test: II. Evaluation of cultural influences on test performances. *Journal of Educational Psychology, 32,* 81–100.

Gardner, H. (1991). *Frames of mind.* New York: Basic Books.

Koch, W.R. (1984). Culture Fair Intelligence Test. In D.J. Keyser & R.C. Sweetland (Eds.), *Test critiques* (Vol. I, pp. 233–238). Austin, TX: PRO-ED.

Nenty, H.J. (1986). Cross-cultural bias analysis of Cattell Culture Fair Intelligence Test. *Perspectives on Psychological Researchers, 9*(1), 1–16.

Paspalanova, E., & Shtetinski, D. (1985). Standardization of the CF 2A intelligence test of Cattell for Bulgarian population. *Psychology* (Bulgaria), *5,* 12–22.

Smith, P. (1986). Application of the information processing approach to the design of a nonverbal reasoning test. *British Journal of Educational Psychology, 56,* 119–137.

Smith, A., Hays, J., & Solway, K. (1977). Comparison of the WISC-R and Culture Fair Intelligence Test in a juvenile delinquent population. *Journal of Psychology, 97,* 119–182.

Thomas, E.C., & Holcomb, H. (1981). Nurturing productive thinking in able students. *Journal of General Psychology, 104*(1), 69–79.

Zoref, L., & Williams, P. (1980). A look at content bias in IQ tests. *Journal of Educational Measurement, 17,* 313–322.

Debra Steele Johnson, Ph.D.
Assistant Professor of Psychology, University of Houston, Houston, Texas.

CURTIS INTEREST SCALE

James W. Curtis. Murfreesboro, Tennessee: Psychometric Affiliates.

Introduction

The Curtis Interest Scale (Curtis, 1959a) was developed to aid in identifying individuals' vocational interest patterns. The scale assesses preferences to perform tasks encountered in 10 different occupational fields and provides a graphic display of the relative strength of individuals' interests in these occupational fields.

James Curtis developed this scale to provide a quick and simple method of assessing vocational preferences. He sought to develop a scale that would require little time to administer and score in comparison to other vocational preference measures. Curtis received both his B.A. (1938) and M.A. (1939) in psychology from the University of Kentucky, in Lexington, Kentucky, and describes himself as having a focus in industrial/organizational psychology (personal communication, September 1992). Now retired, he was a private consultant and a faculty member at various colleges during his active career. He was a member of the American Psychological Association (1942–73) as well as the Illinois Psychological Association, and he remains an emeritus member of the Midwest Psychological Association.

Only one form of the Curtis Interest Scale is available, and the scale has not been revised since its appearance in 1959. The three-page manual provides little information on how the instrument was developed. For example, the manual does not indicate how items were developed or whether they were selected from a larger pool, and no information is provided on what norms or criteria were used in scale development. The manual reports that the selection of the 10 occupational fields was based on the job placements of several thousand clients of an Illinois vocational rehabilitation agency during an 8-year period (Curtis, 1959b) and further indicates that these 10 fields reflected 95% of the requests received for trainees or employees. However, it fails to indicate how or why specific job applicant requests were categorized into these 10 fields. In addition, the manual provides no specific information on how job placements were tracked or how specific tasks were determined to reflect jobs in each occupational field. No specific information appears regarding the characteristics of the client population; thus, it is unclear whether the results obtained for these subjects would generalize to other populations. An addition to the manual provides vocational interest profiles that typify members of 13 different occupations (Curtis, 1964): accountants, actors, assembly workers, civil engineers, electrical engineers, mechanical engineers, farmers, lab

195

technicians, psychologists, sales engineers, salesmen, seminarians, and teachers. However, the text does not indicate how these profiles were determined.

Practical Applications/Uses

The Curtis Interest Scale consists of a four-page booklet containing 55 statements. The statements are organized into five sets of 10 statements that reflect the 10 occupational fields, and one set of five items that address how much responsibility an individual prefers. The test taker ranks the 10 statements within each set according to how much he or she prefers to perform the task described, writing a number between 1 (least preferred) and 10 (most preferred) in a box to the left of each statement. The occupational fields assessed are applied arts, business, computation, direct sales, entertainment, farming, interpersonal, mechanics, production, and science. The remaining set of five statements indicates five levels of responsibility; the test taker selects the one level that best indicates his or her preference for responsibility by placing an X in the box to the left of the choice. This scale is intended for adults and students at or above the ninth-grade level and has been written for appropriate use with trade school students or semi-skilled workers as well as for college students and professionals.

The Curtis scale can be administered individually or in groups. The manual provides clear, simple instructions for administration and scoring. Moreover, the scale is self-administering and hand scored, requiring little or no specialized expertise or equipment. The measure presents examinees with simple instructions and a simple response format (i.e., ranking tasks from 1 to 10). Although untimed, the scale usually requires 6 to 8 minutes to complete. Scoring is accomplished by summing the rankings across the five sets of statements for each occupational field (e.g., a ranking of 9 in each set for Business would produce a score of 45). Scores for each occupational field then are marked on a graph on the back page of the scale booklet and appropriate lines are drawn to produce either a profile or a bar graph. The desired level of responsibility is indicated in a section below the graph by circling a number between 1 (high) and 5 (low), based on the examinee's response to the last set of statements. Although the manual does not address this, scoring requires between 5 and 10 minutes.

On one level, scale interpretation is easy and requires little sophistication. That is, a graph is produced indicating occupational preferences and the desired level of responsibility. Further, the manual indicates that a "theoretically average interest" would produce a score between 20 and 25; 30 or above indicates a primary interest, and 24 through 29 indicates a secondary interest. A score of 15 indicates rejection of that field. Further, one can compare scores obtained to responses from individuals employed in these fields as indicated by Table 1 in the manual. Responses from employees are presented for their own field as well as for other fields that the sample ranked high.

Unfortunately, some of the issues relating to scale development arise again here. That is, no information is provided on how jobs were categorized into these 10 fields or how task statements were determined to be related to these fields. In addition, no explanation appears regarding how the data in Table 1 were obtained. The latter indicates a mean score for samples of employees within an occupational field. More than one job was sampled for each occupational field according to the manual, and some types of jobs are indicated for each field. However, while information is given regarding how many members of an occupational field were sampled, this information is not broken down into specific jobs. Further, sample sizes for occupational fields range widely, from a minimum of 50 to a maximum of 600 employees. It is not clear that these numbers are sufficient to adequately sample a given field, especially given that one cannot tell how many different jobs are represented in the different fields. For example, commercial artists, draftsmen, and advertising layout employees are listed as jobs in the applied arts field, but it is not clear that this list is inclusive and if not, what the boundaries of this field are. Thus, more information is needed before one could rely heavily on the information provided in Table 1. Similarly, when one compares an individual's scores with those in the typical profiles of employees in 13 occupations, many of the same issues arise, and these concerns constrain one's reliance on the information.

Technical Aspects

The manual reports reliability data from a study of 140 individuals retested after 6 weeks. The manual reports test-retest reliabilities, using Pearson correlation coefficients, between .81 and .88 for the 10 occupational fields. However, the manual also reports that test-retest reliabilities might be inappropriate because an individual's interest patterns are expected to be dynamic. No explanation appears for why one might expect interest patterns to be dynamic. An explication of the author's reasoning would be helpful, especially given that interest patterns remained stable at least over a short period (i.e., 6 weeks). No other reliability data are provided, although information on the relatedness of the statements within each occupational field would be helpful. It would also be helpful if the manual indicated to what extent the occupational fields were distinct and nonoverlapping in terms of the task statements describing them.

Another aspect of the scale to note relates to its response format. That is, each set of statements is ranked from 1 to 10, forming an ipsative scale; to the extent that some statements are ranked high, others are forced to receive lower rankings. Thus, on this interest scale, an individual could not score high on all occupational fields. Rather, lack of consistency in an individual's responses or lack of differentiation between tasks would result in average scores across the occupational fields. It would be helpful if the manual described why this format was chosen rather than other alternatives (e.g., a forced-choice format between pairs of statements or Likert scales). Moreover, it would helpful if the implications of this choice were addressed in the manual.

Validity data are provided, indicating the interest scores reported by members of different occupational fields. Although described in Table 1 and discussed briefly above, it would be helpful to have more information on the author's criteria for including different jobs in the 10 occupational fields, sampling, and data collection procedures used, as well as more complete data on similarities and differences between profiles for different jobs within each occupational field. One other concern relates to how adequately the occupational fields defined in 1959 reflect current occupational fields and to what extent the jobs included in those fields adequately represent current positions. Additional validation research would be helpful in clarifying these issues.

Critique

This scale was developed in 1959. Some research has been done examining its characteristics, but more work is needed before it represents a viable tool for the researcher or counselor. A search of the literature revealed no research either using or examining this scale. Further, to the author's or test publisher's knowledge, no research of this type has been conducted since the scale's development (J.W. Curtis, personal communication, September 1992).

Most critical is the need to define the occupational fields (or redefine them to reflect current fields) and the jobs that represent them, prior to determining which task statements best reflect and differentiate among the defined occupational fields. Once such conceptual definitions are provided, a more comprehensive assessment of reliability and validity needs to be performed. Further, documentation of conceptual definitions and research addressing reliability and validity must include more specific information on samples, procedures used, and so forth. The Curtis Interest Scale is obviously quick and easy to administer and score. However, it is unclear how one interprets an individual's scores. The current manual does not provide sufficient information on scale development or scale characteristics to enable either a clear understanding of the occupational fields assessed or a clear interpretation of the vocational interest patterns obtained.

References

Curtis, J.W. (1959a). *Curtis Interest Scale*. Murfreesboro, TN: Psychometric Affiliates.
Curtis, J.W. (1959b). *Curtis Interest Scale manual*. Murfreesboro, TN: Psychometric Affiliates.
Curtis, J.W. (1964). *Curtis Interest Scale profile*. Murfreesboro, TN: Psychometric Affiliates.

Edward E. Gotts, Ph.D.

Director of Psychology, Madison State Hospital, Madison, Indiana.

DEMENTIA RATING SCALE

Steven Mattis. Odessa, Florida: Psychological Assessment Resources, Inc.

Introduction

The Dementia Rating Scale (DRS) is a formal testing procedure designed to measure the mental capacity or status of persons with known limitations of brain function due to degenerative conditions such as dementia of the Alzheimer's type. Because of its focus on degenerative conditions, the scale most likely will be used with elderly subjects to determine whether they are senile and, if so, how severe their loss of mental capacity is. Yet dementia also can appear in younger persons (i.e., "presenile dementia"), so the DRS is applicable in some instances for persons younger than 65. One critical concern with degenerative dementias is how rapidly the changes are taking place that will make the person less able to function independently, without supervision and protection by others. The DRS addresses this concern by permitting comparisons of performances on repeated occasions over the course of degenerative change.

Steven Mattis, Ph.D. completed his doctoral studies in clinical psychology at Columbia University in 1965. A specialist in neuropsychology, he has worked with children as well as adults and with rehabilitation-type neurological patients and psychiatric ones. For some years he was affiliated with the Albert Einstein College of Medicine and the Montefiore Hospital and Medical Center in the Bronx, where he held appointments as Associate Professor of Neurology and Chief Psychologist. He since has moved to New York Hospital and Cornell University's downstate campus, where he serves as Associate Professor of Clinical Psychology. Dr. Mattis is a past president of the American Psychological Association's Division 40, Clinical Neuropsychology.

Dr. Mattis and his colleagues undertook to develop the Dementia Rating Scale because existing standardized tests such as the Wechsler Adult Intelligence Scale and the Wechsler Memory Scale (i.e., the versions in use during the early 1970s) were too difficult for demented patients and thus often would produce no useful information. That is, these other tests had insufficient floor to differentiate among persons with varying severities of dementia; test results might show them all equally impaired, whereas it was apparent that some were more impaired than others. The earliest citation of the DRS referenced in the administration manual is 1973. Research on the characteristics of the instrument continues to the present time, although its publication in 1988 as a commercially distributed test may be viewed as one milestone or end point in the process of its development.

The development of the DRS took place during a study of Alzheimer's disease in persons already exhibiting dementia. The author and his colleagues searched

199

for items that could assess the general cognitive abilities of this population, even at advanced stages of decline. Those cognitive functions specifically sampled were attention, memory, language, reasoning, motor, and construction (reproduction) tasks. Items thus located were of the kinds typically used by neuropsychologists, neurologists, and neurosurgeons. After assembling a pool of items, the developers submitted them to a team of neuroscience professionals to review for "comprehensiveness, clarity, and brevity" (Mattis, 1988, p. 23). The team's suggestions led to minor revisions of the pool. Mattis et al. then arranged the items in an order representing "a logical and easily administered sequence" that could be given either in an office or at the bedside (Mattis, 1988, p. 23). Studies with the scale during its development typically sampled elderly persons from both mentally impaired and normal populations.

Since that time the DRS has remained essentially unchanged. It is available in a single form, designed for administration in English. Although use with other language groups would be possible for many of the items, those involving the reading or recognition of words or printed text are all produced in English. Thus the language barrier would require preparing an alternate set of stimulus cards as well as translating the test administration procedures.

Someone first hearing the instrument's name, Dementia Rating Scale, might expect an observational procedure or a set of structured tasks through which a clinician gains information needed to grade or rate the quality of a subject's responses. In actuality, the items are more typical of those used in interviews and direct tests of performance; the scoring consequently does not require the administrator to make differentiating ratings, as such. The DRS consists of five subscales— Attention, Initiation/Perseveration, Construction, Conceptualization, and Memory— represented by 36 tasks of varying length (i.e., some call for a single response, while others call for multiple responses). In general the tasks are grouped and presented within their respective subscales in the order noted above for the subscales. An exception to this is that the author has interspersed some attention items with the memory tasks as "fillers" or ways of creating a delay between the original presentation of a memory task and a later test of how well the information has been retained.

Attention tasks include repeating a series of numerals in the order presented (i.e., digit span) and in reverse (i.e., digit span backwards), and performing two simple motor actions simultaneously upon command. Easier items then follow, such performing a single simple motor action on command. The first four subscales apply this testing strategy of presenting more difficult or challenging tasks first. If the person successfully responds to the initial tasks presented, then he or she automatically receives credit for the later tasks and testing on that subscale is discontinued. Because even the more difficult DRS items normally are passed by nearly all nonimpaired elderly persons, failure on the early items of a subscale gives an advance indication of possible cerebral impairment. Older persons who are not in fact impaired thus are screened with minimal testing effort and duration.

For *Initiation/Perseveration*, the examinee first is asked to think of and name as many items as possible that he or she might encounter in a particular familiar environmental setting, all within a specified time limit. Next he or she must identify by name specific items visible at the time in the immediate environment. Following this, tasks involve repeating a series of syllables, performing simple movements (repetitively alternating positions with one hand while simultaneously performing the opposite position with the other hand), and copying simple designs or patterns that appear on the DRS Stimulus Cards. The examinee is directed to do the latter with a pencil in a designated area of a plain sheet of paper.

Construction tasks resemble in many respects the copying tasks for the Initiation/Perseveration subscale, as do their scoring rules. The first five Construction tasks all call for copying of this type, followed by the direction to write one's name on the paper. (Similarities noted between the Construction tasks and some Initiation/Perseveration tasks will be discussed later in this review.)

The *Conceptualization* subscale begins with the examiner presenting a series of eight stimulus cards, each displaying three geometric forms or line drawings that always appear as a horizontal row. The examinee is directed to study the three "designs" and to state which two "are the same" or "most alike." Three of the eight arrays involve a match (i.e., two of the three forms are identical) and five involve a similarity between two of the forms. After presenting the last card, the examiner returns to the beginning of the series and presents all again, now asking which form is "different" or does not "belong." The manual seems to require a correct verbal labeling of the basis of the similarity or the distinction that sets the odd form apart. In a conversation with this reviewer, the author clarified that credit also is to be given for correct pointing responses and that the test was standardized and normed following this approach. This is an important point, because it means that someone whose expressive language was impaired but who still conceptualized adequately could receive credit for a correct identification. The examiner next presents pairs of objects verbally while asking the examinee to identify ways that they are "alike" or "the same." Responses are graded for both abstractness and relevance, such that a relevant but less abstract reply receives less credit than an abstract similarity. At this point the subscale may be discontinued if the respondent has received enough points.

If continuing with the Conceptualization subscale, the following kinds of tasks are given: "Name three things that people [eat, wear, etc.]." The examiner then repeats the examinee's three replies while asking how they are alike or the same. (*Note:* If the examinee cannot supply the three things requested, the examiner prompts by giving three answers of the appropriate type and saying "_____, _____, and _____ are things people _____." This is done only if the examinee cannot name three things or explain what people do with them, and only for the first of the three items of this type in the task. If the second of the items is missed, the third is not presented, and the examiner proceeds to another task.) The examiner next names three things and asks which one does not belong or fit, and finally names two objects and asks, in a multiple-choice format, whether both are (abstract choice) or (concrete choice) or (incorrect choice). Scores are assigned as 2 for abstract, 1 for concrete, and 0 for incorrect. There are four such items in this task, and it is the author's practice and intent that the multiple-choice responses be presented in a randomized order from item to item; however, the administration booklet and response form unfortunately may lead the examiner to present them all in an identical multiple-choice order (i.e., abstract-concrete-incorrect) and thereby generate a potential order-bias effect. Again, as in an earlier remark, the standardization and norming call for the examiner to administer these items as intended by the DRS author and as confirmed by his personal communication with this reviewer.

At the end of the Conceptualization subscale appear two memory problems that are presented at that point but not scored until later in the Memory section when their recall is requested. If the examinee performs the second of these, the response is scored for Conceptualization also. These memory items ask the examinee to read aloud a sentence (i.e., a simple declarative statement) that appears in boldface type and to remember it because it will be requested later. The administration manual does not indicate that adapted testing is permitted with illiterates or those who are too visually impaired to read; however, the author in personal communication clarified that under these circumstances one may present the sentence orally to an examinee to score for recall later in the usual manner. Immediately after this the examiner asks the examinee to make up a sentence using two specified words and to remember the sentence in anticipation of being asked later to repeat it. Next the examinee is asked a series of personal and informational orientation questions covering time, place, and current governmental officials. Two filler or distraction tasks follow and are scored as a part of the Attention subscale. Immediately following these, the examiner asks the subject to recall the sentence read earlier and to then recall the sentence that he or she made up using the two specified words.

Another Attention task appears next in order to set up another Memory task. The examinee is asked to read from a stimulus card a list of five words four times (i.e., rehearsal) "so that you will remember each word." This is followed directly by a test of recognition: Pairs of words (one from the list of five words and one not from the list) are presented on each of five test cards and the examinee is asked to pick the one from the list just read. Obviously, illiterates will need an adapted form of this task, although the situation is not covered in the testing procedure. However, experienced neuropsychological examiners will understand how to make the necessary adaptation while assistants or technicians will require instruction in allowable methods of adapted administration.

After this test of recognition of words previously rehearsed, a final problem is presented, scored once more for Attention. The examiner presents two stimulus cards simultaneously, each containing four simple but abstract designs, one in each quarter of the card and surrounded by a frame. The figures on the two cards are identical but they appear in different locations or quarters of each card. The examinee is asked to point out on the card nearer him or her the same design to which the examiner is pointing on the other card. All four figures are presented for matching a total of four times, offered in a randomized order within each of the practice trials. It should be noted that examiner does not prompt or cue the examinee to anticipate recall of the figures later. Immediately following the last of these four practice series, the examiner administers the figural recognition task. It consists of four items, each appearing on a separate stimulus card that depicts, in a side-by-side format, two figures bounded by frames. One of these was among the four practice figures matched earlier and one is a similarly constructed figure that was not among the set of four. As each of the four test cards is exposed, the examinee is asked to choose or point to the one that was matched during practice.

As stated previously, the examiner's role on the Γ   so much that of observer and rater as that of test administrator. A   nt of rating is only sometimes present, as when the examiner must   value to a particular response based on scoring criteria stated in the m   any items, on the other hand, simply are scored as "pass" or "fail" and   no examiner discrimination of variations of response quality.

Though used primarily with the elderly, it v   pear to be only a short step to extend the use of the DRS to persons of any   suspected of having a dementia, whether static or progressing. In the same sense the scale could be used to assess diminished cognitive functioning in persons experiencing severe temporary states of cognitive dysfunction. The validity of such extensions of use, nevertheless, has yet to be established.

Normal elderly individuals achieve nearly perfect scores while the test proves difficult for demented persons. The test materials include an individual scoring form for recording the results of each DRS examination. Where attention tasks are interspersed with other subscale tasks (i.e., when they appear outside of their own subscale), it is necessary to have a convenient method of drawing these scores together with the remainder of the Attention subscale. The DRS accomplishes this by assigning a discriminable symbol to each of the subscales and then printing that symbol next to each task score on the Scoring Form. The examiner, thus, needs only to scan through the Memory subscale section to find the balance of the attention tasks, as labeled by their symbol. All of the remaining scoring is of adjacent tasks that appear entirely within the subscale section to which they are assigned. The cover page of the Scoring Form provides space for identifying information on the examinee and for summarizing the scores. Here the five subscale raw scores are recorded and their sum is designated as the DRS Total Score. In a column next to these raw scores, the examiner records, based on a table of cutoff scores in the manual, whether examinee's performance is above ("+" or normal) or below ("–" or demented) relative to normal elderly persons. Two final columns provide space for recording, for known/suspected demented persons, how raw scores compare to a known sample of demented persons. These scores can be expressed in both percentile and non-normalized T-score form. No profile of subscales is plotted as such, although this is depicted implicitly in the T-score column without the additional graphic representation.

Practical Applications/Uses

The DRS is targeted specifically to detect the presence of dementia and to differentiate among levels of dementia. If it accomplished just the former of these objectives, it would be a "screening" instrument only, but its ability to differentiate among severity levels makes it more akin to psychological tests that measure degree or strength of a trait or quality. Because dementia is a condition of diminished mental performance affecting the higher cognitive processes in particular, the DRS accomplishes its assessment objectives by measuring performance in five areas that call upon a person's cognitive abilities: attention, initiation/perseveration, construction, conceptualization, and memory. By means of these evaluations and their sum, the DRS Total Score, the examiner obtains a sample of relevant cognitive performance overall and in the five designated areas. The DRS is constructed to show its principal sensitivity within the below-normal range, with all nondemented persons expected to obtain scores near the scale's ceiling or maximum possible scores. As with other tests that have a similar purpose of classification—in this case classifying subjects as demented versus nondemented—cutoff scores are empirically established to optimize the detection of the condition while not incorrectly including in the affected classification those whose performance is normal. In addition, the DRS provides separate norms for demented individuals, making it possible to decide for persons within the affected class how advanced their condition of mental loss may be. Interpretation is not limited, however, to the issues of dementia detection and grading. The examiner also can use variations among the five subscales' standard scores to inquire into whether the process of cognitive loss has uniformly affected performance in the five areas assessed or whether some areas of better functioning still exist.

Given the foregoing, it is apparent that the DRS will be used principally in those clinical service and research settings that work with persons who have or may have dementia. These can include general hospital and specialized neurological services, nursing homes, freestanding psychiatric facilities, rehabilitation programs, home-based services for the elderly, and similar settings. Professionals in neurology, neuroscience, neuropsychology, and allied fields represent the most likely users. The occupational groups include physicians, psychologists, and those who work under their licenses or supervision. Although use of the DRS has focused strongly on dementia of the Alzheimer's type, it presents an instrument to consider with dementias of other known etiology and with the presenile dementias. Moreover, this scale might well prove useful in the evaluation of persons whose cerebral functioning is affected temporarily by acute conditions. These latter types of applications nevertheless would require careful study of the DRS's effectiveness in detecting and grading the degree of severity of groups that differ from those included in the norming sample.

All professional neuropsychological evaluation calls for some degree of adaptation in order to accurately assess impaired persons, illiterates, those with sensory deficits, persons with reduced coordination, those who tire easily, or those who readily give up or become frustrated. That is, any test that aims to sample a particular mental function or process may be standardized for presentation in a way to which an impaired or limited person cannot respond competently, for reasons unrelated to the mental process in question. The neuropsychologist's challenge in such a case becomes administering the same task in an only slightly altered manner that enables the person to avoid failing because of item-format-related variance and instead to succeed in demonstrating the mental function competence in question. For example, it may be legitimate to test an illiterate subject by reading aloud an item that normally is read by the examinee. Naturally, if the question of ability to read is the one being answered, that would rule out this adaptation. Neuropsychologists must routinely make decisions to engage in adapted testing, but they often can safeguard against errors arising from loss of exact standardization by keeping their focus on the specific psychological function or process about which an inference is desired. Moreover, their testing adaptations often will be made within an extended battery of tests that provide redundancy, overlap, and so forth, that support an internal consistency analysis of case materials. If one were using only the DRS, any adaptations would need to be limited correspondingly to those that preserve the original intent of the tasks regarding the psychological functions that they sample. Some of the adaptations that users can make without undermining the DRS's standardization were discussed with Dr. Mattis, the test's author, and appear in the Introduction section of this review.

The DRS is administered individually face to face, in a setting as free of distraction as the examiner can manage. Attention, memory, and to a lesser extent initiation/perseveration tasks could be adversely affected even with normals in a noisy setting or one with many people moving about in a distracting manner. The scale should be administered by a licensed professional or an assistant who is trained and supervised to go beyond simple administration and recording of responses. Only persons of these qualifications will be able to conduct adapted testing as needed as well as observe and describe in detail any unusual or signifi-cant behaviors that indicate the need for additional assessment or that permit inferences about why the examinee is having difficulty. Thus, it is not the de-mands of administering the scale in its standardized form but rather the other inevitable demands of neuropsychological assessment with seriously impaired persons that suggest someone above a technician level should be responsible for administering, observing, and recording with the DRS.

Generally, administration of this instrument is fairly direct and clearly pre-sented in the manual. There are some exceptions, however, that this reviewer discussed with both the author and the publisher's representative, John A. Schinka, Ph.D. These conversations permit clarification here of how to proceed with the few problematic portions of the test's administration:

1. In the Conceptualization subscale, the first task (*V*) appears to ask for a verbal response but also can be read as if it calls for any response designating identity/similarity and then oddity. The directions to the examiner can be supplemented as follows: "Accept either a verbal or a pointing response; if the examinee both points and states a response verbally, and the verbal response is imprecise or even erroneous, the pointing response should take precedence." In the latter instance, questions to clarify the examinee's intent would encourage pointing as a means of final designation of answer choice.

2. Directions for Conceptualization task *X* also could be expanded beneficially. For example, when the examinee names the three objects requested by the exam-iner in the first part of the item, it is these same three things that are to be repeated by the examiner in presenting the second part of the item. This procedure is to be followed three times as three different items are presented.

3. For task *Z* of the Conceptualization subscale, the examiner should offer the multiple-choice answer options in a randomized order rather than in the pre-printed order.

4. At the end of the Conceptualization subscale, Memory task *AA* is presented. If, as is permissible, the sentence is read aloud to the examinee, he or she should be asked to repeat it: "Say the sentence back to me after I read it to you." The examinee should be allowed to look at the printed sentence while hearing it so that any recognizable visual information may assist later recall. Later, when pre-senting task *AF* of the Memory subscale, the examiner would say, "Remember the

sentence I read to you earlier and asked you to remember? Say it to me now." On the other hand, if examinee claims to have some reading ability but it is quite limited, a better approach at point *AA* in the exam would be to say, "We're going to read this sentence together. You follow the words while I point to them and read them out loud. Now you say the sentence that I just read." At that point the examiner should tell the examinee to remember the sentence. Within this mode of administration, the examiner would begin task *AF* with "Remember the sentence that we read together?"

5. The foregoing approach likewise would be used when presenting the words printed on stimulus card *21* and appearing in the test sequence at point *AH*. The required four rehearsals should be accomplished for *AH*. Note, however, that *AH* is scored as an Attention subscale item, even though it appears within the Memory subscale; this adapted presentation for the Memory subscale is not to be confused with correct responding when scoring the Attention subscale. (More will be said of this later.) This memory task is tested at point *AI*, for which rewording may not necessarily be required.

With the preceding suggestions, the DRS should be relatively easy to administer to normal elderly persons. The more seriously impaired the examinee, however, the more difficult and challenging the administration becomes. The difficulty is not a function of the test items but of examinee characteristics. The examiner will need to use encouragement and occasional prodding as well as reassurances to keep some examinees working. Alertness to the examinee's potential emotional and physiological distress also should be emphasized, as many demented persons are physically fragile.

The time required for test administration is also a function of the examinee's degree of impairment, with more impaired persons requiring longer to complete the examination. Although the DRS manual does not specify the time needed for testing, the publisher's catalog suggests a range of 15–45 minutes for administration plus scoring. Based on this reviewer's somewhat limited experience with the DRS, this estimate appears reasonable. Normal or minimally impaired persons easily could be tested and scored within a 15-minute period. For demented persons, the testing time will increase but remains quite variable across subjects. From the perspective of the usual amount of time required for administering neuropsychological tests, the DRS is exceedingly brief. In this sense, it should be less stressful to the elderly persons asked to participate in the procedure.

Scoring instructions are clear and easy to follow, and the process, which is not difficult, can be learned within as little as 1 hour by an experienced test administrator. If every item and task within the protocol is attempted, scoring on average should not take more than 15 minutes. Some points, nevertheless, deserve mention:

1. In the Initiation/Perseveration subscale, an examinee can demonstrate atypical behavior for some items either by not persisting long enough to produce the requested number of responses or by failing to keep track and instead producing more than the number requested. When the criterion for scoring such tasks is stated as, for example, "four repetitions" (see tasks *G* and *H*), too few and too many repetitions can be problematic. Thus, in scoring, it would be well to view "four repetitions" as meaning "exactly four repetitions." Similarly, for tasks *I*, *J*, and *K*, the examinee who has difficulty stopping when asked to do so would

appear to present problems of perseveration. Yet on task *O*, the examiner is cautioned to disregard the number of repetitions during copying!

2. When scoring task *X*, the examiner must remember that the score is not based on the examinee's list of three responses to each item, but rather is based only on a final response to the inquiry of how the three named things are alike. This point is somewhat ambiguous in the manual but clarified by inspecting the scoring form.

3. Finally, if it is necessary to give an adapted administration of task *AH* (e.g., to a person with limited reading skills), assistance given on the first "reading" would appear to preclude giving credit for that trial. However, if the list then is repeated correctly on any subsequent trial(s), it would seem appropriate to award a point for each such completed repetition. This, admittedly, is an extrapolation from the test protocol, but it is representative of the kinds of extrapolations that neuropsychologists typically must make when engaging in adapted testing. Such adapted methods can be validated empirically by internal consistency analysis methods and by reviewing the discriminating power of individual tasks when presented in the standard manner and in an adapted manner. In the absence of such studies, clinical judgment must be used.

To summarize, most DRS scoring is completed easily by following the directions in the manual and entering scoring decisions on the scoring form. In tasks that pose difficulty, such as those considered above, not all issues can be resolved conclusively; some will require exercising prudent clinical judgment in relation to the reasons that the various tasks have been included within the DRS.

After each item is evaluated and assigned points, scoring is completed by summing the points associated with each subscale symbol. After recording these scores on the face of the scoring form, the examiner also records there the appropriate normative information (obtained from the manual) corresponding to the raw scores.

Interpretation of the DRS should emerge first from the normative data–based cutoff scores and the percentiles and T-scores obtained from the scale manual. Second, the examiner should make extensive behavioral observations of performance difficulties, peculiarities, notable compensations, and so forth, and use these findings for the qualitative interpretation of the test record (to the extent warranted by his or her clinical acumen). The DRS manual articulates the former approach to interpretation, which is of course all that the scale itself purports to measure. Yet one would expect that users experienced in the neurosciences will resort to the qualitative method of interpretation as a complement to the normative one. Because the qualitative interpretive method depends on the extent of the examiner's training and clinical experience database, no further remarks will ensue here on that approach.

The examiner uses Table 2 in the manual to determine the cutoff scores that compare the examinee to normal elderly persons. Generally one interprets scores that fall below the cutoff points as indicating the presence of subnormal performance suggestive of dementia. Obvious cases of dementia can be expected to obtain DRS Total Scores and subscale scores that all register below cutoff levels. Suppose, however, that some of an individual's subscale scores exceed the assigned cutoffs (i.e., they are in the "+" range). Rather than hastily concluding that a nonuniform drop in performance indicates dementia, the experienced examiner would consider as many alternate hypotheses as the subject's history might suggest. It is in such cases also that the use of qualitative data becomes important, as a means of avoiding the error of treating the score as an ultimate datum. Thus, decisions about the presence of dementia become fairly straightforward and easy to make if performance falls below all relevant cutoffs, but mixed results require more interpretive judgment. Also, because these norms apply to the elderly, it may well be the case that DRS use with presenile dementias would call for an even more elevated set of cutoff scores, as younger normals might be expected to produce a score distribution on these tasks that would more closely approach the error-free level. Thus, these cutoffs may not be demanding enough relative to younger impaired persons.

Table 4 in the manual serves to interpret the meaning of scores falling within the demented range as to degree of severity. It is important to note that as many as 8% to 10% of persons known to have dementia of the Alzheimer's type scored above the DRS Total Score cutoff for concluding that they were demented (i.e., they were false negatives). Thus, despite behavioral deterioration, cognitive functioning for some individuals still may remain above the critical level when measured by the DRS. This may not be entirely a function of measurement error, but rather may reflect a longer preservation of intellectual abilities in some individuals who are becoming demented (e.g., previously bright persons might continue to perform in the measured respects at above cutoff levels). As misclassification based on individual subscales is even more likely, the examiner is cautioned about approaching their interpretation in isolation from other data.

The manual does not suggest specific score ranges for early, mild, or moderate degrees of dementia, although admittedly there might not be a strong consensus on the external indicators by which one might validate such distinctions. However, on page 21 of the manual, Mattis cites findings that support using the DRS to differentiate mild from moderate cases of dementia, commenting that subscale analysis is beneficial for this purpose. Nevertheless, the following rationale may prove useful for distinguishing mild from moderate degrees of dementia. First, the cutoff scores in the DRS manual's Table 2 have been placed between the raw scores falling at or nearest 2 standard deviations below the means for the normal elderly sample. This is true for the Total Score and the five subscales. Second, the usually accepted meaning of moderate impairment is about 1 standard deviation below the level of mild impairment. Accordingly, if cutoffs were set at about 3 standard deviations below the means listed in Table 1 of the DRS manual, the results would appear to correspond to a commonly agreed upon standard for classifying someone as moderately impaired. This would result in the following approximate cutoffs: Total Score, below 116; Attention, below 30; Initiation/Perseveration, below 26; Construction, below 4, but as this is the present cutoff, below 3; Conceptualization, below 29; and Memory, below 17. Comparing these cutoffs to the normal elderly subjects in DRS manual Table 2, the number of false positives thereby would be significantly reduced for Total Score, Attention, and Construction, but with little or no improvement for the remaining subscales in discriminating power. In the absence of other guidelines in the manual, users might try the foregoing for goodness of fit—yet with the healthy skepticism that leads to a search for cutting scores that correspond best to the clinical distinction of mild versus moderate impairment within the particular population being studied.

Technical Aspects

Dr. Mattis and his colleagues assembled and judged the pool of items used in constructing the DRS by rational (i.e., not empirical) methods. This approach leaves open the question of how well these five subscales represent important and somewhat independent sources of variation in performance among the elderly and those with dementia in particular. In personal communication, Dr. Mattis told this reviewer that recent factor analytic studies have indicated that the variation produced by respondents to the item pool can readily be accounted for or explained by a smaller number of factors than five. The details of these findings were not available to this reviewer, but the study's conclusion appears quite reasonable in view of the similarity of tasks assigned to different subscales in the DRS. For example, as noted previously, construction (reproduction by copying) tasks appear in both the Initiation/Perseveration and Construction subscales, and seem similarly difficult in some instances. Although studies of reliability and some studies of validity do not address the preceding issue, concurrent examination of convergent and discriminant validity instead can illuminate the adequacy of a rationally assigned subscale structure.

All of the published studies of the DRS through 1988 appear to be cited in the scale manual. A search for subsequent studies failed to turn up additional citations, including those mentioned by the author in personal communication. Hence, appraisal of the DRS's psychometric properties is covered in the manual about as thoroughly as is possible. A summary of the evidence reported in the manual follows below.

Test-retest reliability coefficients were computed over a 1-week interval (i.e., short-term stability coefficient) with a group of 30 patients having senile dementia of the Alzheimer's type (Coblentz et al., 1973), yielding the following: Total Score, .97; Attention, .61; Initiation/Perseveration, .89; Construction, .83; Conceptualization, .94; and Memory, .92. All of these appear acceptable indications of reliability for their respective constructs; even Attention is not problematic, as variations in attention are expected to be considerable even among normals, resulting in lower reliability. Split-half reliability for DRS Total Score was .90 among 25 elderly persons with organic mental disorders (Gardner, Oliver-Muñoz, Fisher, & Empting, 1981). A final component of the reliability investigation was the internal consistency method. Among persons with Alzheimer's-type dementia, alpha internal consistency coefficients were found to range from .75 to .95 (Vitaliano, Breen, Russo, et al., 1984). No reliabilities are reported for normal elderly persons using any of the foregoing methods of estimation. In the single study of test-retest reliability, small improvements in mean scores were found for Total Score and all subscales, while all standard deviations became smaller over the 7-day intertest interval (Coblentz et al., 1973), revealing a small practice effect over short intervals even in a demented population.

Coblentz and others (1973) further investigated the DRS for validity in relation to some commonly used indicators of cerebral functioning: Wechsler Adult Intelligence Scale (WAIS; Wechsler, 1955) and the Paired Associate Learning (PAL) subtest of the Wechsler Memory Scale (WMS; Wechsler, 1945). Their sample included 11 normals and 20 persons with organic mental disorders, all in the age range 58–71 years. The DRS correlated .75 with the WAIS Full Scale scores among patients and .86 for a select patient group whose PAL Total Scores were at least 1 standard deviation below the mean. The normals, whose WAIS scores exceeded 85 and whose PAL scores were normal, all scored over 140 on the DRS, a result that is congruent with other findings for normals with the DRS (Butters, Wolfe, Martone, Granholm, & Cermak, 1985; Granholm, Wolfe, & Butters, 1985; Moss, Albert, Butters, & Payne, 1986).

Chase and associates (1984) also studied a mixed group of healthy elderly adults and age-matched Alzheimer's patients. DRS Total Score, WAIS Full Scale IQ, and WMS Memory Quotient were 30%–45% lower for the patients than the normals, and mean cortical glucose metabolism (i.e., as assessed by positron emission tomography) was reduced by 30% in the Alzheimer's group compared to normals. Correlations between the DRS and other measures were WAIS, .67; WMS, .70; cortical glucose metabolism, .59.

The ability of the DRS to identify dementia also was tested in the previously cited study by Vitaliano, Breen, Albert, et al. (1984). These researchers found that large and statistically reliable differences existed among normal, mildly demented, and moderately demented subjects. Further, all of the subscales differentiated between individuals with mild versus moderately severe dementia, while only some of the subscales detected differences between normals and mildly demented individuals (i.e., true for Initiation/Perseveration, Construction, and Memory). DRS Total Scores in this same study (Vitialano, Breen, Albert, et al., 1984) also correlated with practical indicators of functioning: basic activities of daily living, .76, and independence as manifested in recreation and reading, .56.

Another aspect of the ability of the DRS to identify dementia concerns whether the established cutoff scores effectively differentiate among different groups. Montgomery and Costa (1983a) included patients of the following classifications: depressed, psychological disorders, and dementia. For the DRS Total Score cutoff of 123, classification revealed that no depressed patients scored below this level, and only 12% of psychologically disordered patients did. By contrast, 36% of patients with focal (i.e., more circumscribed) brain injuries dropped below the cutoff, and fully 62% of dementia patients obtained such scores.

The preceding evidence suggests that the DRS Total Score and the five subscale scores are generally quite reliable. Validity indicators also favor the test's stated purposes of detecting the presence of dementia and evaluating changes as dementia progresses from mild to moderately severe levels. Moreover, the DRS appears to differentiate accurately among dementia, focal brain lesions, and functional mental and emotional disorders. Admittedly the samples in these studies have been uniformly small, as have the two studies used to establish DRS norms (Coblentz et al., 1973; Montgomery & Costa, 1983b). Further, as noted previously, there is also a need to examine subscale structure.

Critique

As Dr. Mattis has communicated to this reviewer, the DRS has received fairly wide acceptance and adoption in clinical settings. This is understandable in view of the scale's ease of administration and scoring and the economy of examiner time it affords. In this last respect it is clearly preferable from a perspective of patient effort and stress as well, as persons undergoing the changes of dementia may find longer formal testing procedures taxing and they often are physically compromised as well. It is prudent as well as considerate to stress the dementia patient as little as necessary for purposes of diagnosis and care planning. A positive finding of dementia with the DRS does not necessarily terminate neuropsychological assessment, however. Further testing may be needed to clarify a variety of other issues relative to care, supervision, and structure needed. Certainly some appraisal will be required of the person's reactions to intellectual and adaptive loss, whether expressed in frustration, denial, depression, fearfulness, or other ways.

Having said the foregoing, it must also be acknowledged that research to date with the DRS is fairly limited for an instrument that has been in use in its present essential form for about 19 years. Consequently, the user must not become overly dependent on the accuracy of available norms. Additional guidelines are needed in the manual regarding uses of the DRS to differentiate among persons with varying degrees of dementia, because at present it provides no specific rules or criteria for cutting scores except for separating normals from demented individuals. False positives (i.e., persons incorrectly called demented) from the DRS Total Score cutoffs would appear to run about 5%, which is not especially problematic so long as caution is exercised in such labeling in the absence of corroborative findings. False negatives (i.e., demented persons incorrectly classified as normal) exceed 8% relative to the DRS Total Score, based on a reanalysis completed of Table 4 in the DRS manual. False negatives are greater than this when evaluated by the subscales, ranging from 11.5% for Memory up to 21.2% for both Initiation/Perseveration and Construction. The rate of false negative cases was even greater in a study by Montgomery and Costa (1983b), in which 38% of demented persons were not identified by the DRS Total Score cutoff. Therefore, users should apply considerable caution when test scores exceed the cutoff to avoid missing the presence of dementia. The examiner should rely on other kinds of information regarding declining performance to guard against the tendency to dismiss as normal anyone whose DRS Total Score exceeds 122 points. Perhaps additional research on the factor structure of the DRS and the elimination of tasks that do not contribute to the effective detection of dementia may improve the instrument's discriminating power.

Finally, as noted earlier in this review, the examiner who can rely on an extensive experiential database of neuropsychological patients will obtain much additional information from the DRS and will be able to engage in adapted testing and internal consistency analysis. For persons lacking this background, a chapter by Mattis (1976) in which he makes numerous references to the DRS will afford valuable guidance on neuropsychological methods of assessment and inference.

References

Butters, B., Wolfe, J., Martone, M., Granholm, E., & Cermak, L.S. (1985). Memory disorders associated with Huntington's disease: Verbal recall, verbal recognition and procedural memory. *Neuropsychologia, 23,* 729–743.

Chase, T.N., Foster, N.L., Fedio, P., Brooks, R., Mansi, L., & Di Chiro, G. (1984). Regional cortical dysfunction in Alzheimer's disease as determined by positron emission tomography. *Annals of Neurology, 15*(Suppl.), 170–174.

Coblentz, J.M., Mattis, S., Zingesser, L., Kasoff, S.S., Wisniewski, H.M., & Katzman, R. (1973). Presenile dementia: Clinical aspects and evaluation of cerebrospinal fluid dynamics. *Archives of Neurology, 29,* 299–308.

Gardner, R., Oliver-Muñoz, S., Fisher, L., & Empting, L. (1981). Mattis Dementia Rating Scale: Internal reliability study using a diffusely impaired population. *Journal of Clinical Neuropsychology, 3,* 271–275.

Granholm, E., Wolfe, J., & Butters, N. (1985). Affective arousal factors in the recall of thematic stories by amnesic and demented patients. *Developmental Neuropsychology, 1,* 317–333.

Mattis, S. (1976). Mental status examination for organic mental syndrome in the elderly patient. In L. Bellak & T.B. Karasu (Eds.), *Geriatric psychiatry: A handbook for psychiatrists and primary care physicians* (pp. 77–121). New York: Grune & Stratton.

Mattis, S. (1988). *Dementia Rating Scale manual.* Odessa, FL: Psychological Assessment Resources.

Montgomery, K.M., & Costa, L. (1983a). *Concurrent validity of the Mattis Dementia Rating Scale.* Paper presented at a meeting of the International Neuropsychological Society, Lisbon.

Montgomery, K.M., & Costa, L. (1983b). *Neuropsychological test performance of a normal elderly sample.* Paper presented at a meeting of the International Neuropsychological Society, Mexico City.

Moss, M.B., Albert, M.S., Butters, N., & Payne, M. (1986). Differential patterns of memory loss among patients with Alzheimer's disease, Huntington's disease, and alcoholic Korsakoff syndrome. *Archives of Neurology, 43,* 239–246.

Vitaliano, P.P., Breen, A.R., Albert, M.S., Russo, J., & Prinz, P.N. (1984). Memory, attention, and functional status in community-residing Alzheimer type dementia patients and optimally healthy aged individuals. *Journal of Gerontology, 39,* 58–64.

Vitaliano, P.P., Breen, A.R., Russo, J., Albert, M.S., Vitiello, M., & Prinz, P.N. (1984). The clinical utility of the Dementia Rating Scale for assessing Alzheimer patients. *Journal of Chronic Disabilities, 37,* 743–753.

Wechsler, D. (1945). A standardized memory scale for clinical use. *Journal of Psychology, 19,* 87–95.

Wechsler, D. (1955). *Wechsler Adult Intelligence Scale.* San Antonio, TX: Psychological Corporation.

Ann H. Stoddard, Ed.D.
Professor of Education, University of North Florida, Jacksonville, Florida.

DETROIT TESTS OF LEARNING APTITUDE–PRIMARY (SECOND EDITION)

Donald D. Hammill and Brian R. Bryant. Austin, Texas: PRO-ED, Inc.

Introduction

The second edition of the Detroit Tests of Learning Aptitude–Primary (DTLA-P:2) is designed to measure cognitive abilities in children aged 3 through 9. The 100-item test samples 15 cognitive behaviors that are categorized into six subtests and one total General Mental Maturity score. The items sample developed behaviors (attention, linguistics, and manual dexterity) that fall into the center of Anastasi's (1980) continuum. The test presently has four major uses: a) to inventory the relative strengths and weaknesses among developed mental abilities, b) to identify children who are significantly deficient in general mental ability, c) to make predictions about a child's future performance, and d) to serve as a research tool investigating the intellectual functioning of young children, especially aptitude, intelligence, and cognitive behavior.

Donald D. Hammill and Brian R. Bryant have been involved with testing and some aspect of its correlates since 1974. Hammill, experienced in the effectiveness of linguistic training, is president of PRO-ED, Inc. in Austin, Texas, and a prolific, distinguished author of many journal articles, widely used textbooks, and tests in language and learning. Bryant, a graduate of and faculty member at the University of Texas, serves as director of research at PRO-ED and has coauthored several texts in addition to the DTLA-P:2, including the Diagnostic Achievement Battery, the Diagnostic Achievement Tests for Adolescents, and the Gray Oral Reading Tests–Revised.

The DTLA-P:2 evolved from the original DTLA and the first edition of DTLA-P. The significant difference between the older versions and this new edition lies in its ability to contrast scores within the ability areas or domains, plus three other changes: withdrawing instructions from the picture book, reducing the number of items, and lowering basals and ceilings.

The DTLA-P:2 was standardized on 2,095 children in two separate phases, 1985 and 1990. Thirty-six states and two Canadian provinces were included in the sample, each site representing demographic characteristics similar to those of the nation as a whole. The second phase, which used 619 children, accommodated the elimination of 200 cases in the first phase due to the lack of item scores.

The new test contains six subtests: *Verbal*, in which items involve the knowledge of words and their use; *Nonverbal*, using items that do not require reading, writing, or verbalization; *Attention-Enhanced*, emphasizing concentration and short-term memory; *Attention-Reduced,* emphasizing long-term memory; *Motor-Enhanced,* in which items involve complex manual dexterity; and *Motor-Reduced,* in which items require oral or pointing responses. *General Mental Ability* is a combined score of all 100 items.

The test materials include a picture book, a response form, and a profile/examiner record form. Examinees are asked to point to objects, to repeat a phrase or sentence, to draw a line under or to an object, or to draw an object. Fifteen different cognitive behaviors are included in the six subtests: Articulation, Conceptual Matching, Design Reproduction, Digit Sequence, Draw a Person, Letter Sequence, Motor Directions, Picture Fragments, Oral Directions, Object Sequence, Picture Identification, Sentence Imitation, Symbolic Relations, Visual Discrimination, and Word Opposites and Word Sequences. Space for profiling scores is included on the profile/examiner's record form. A scan of the scores gives a clue to the strengths and weaknesses within the identified six cognitive areas. Space also is available to include other test results and anecdotal remarks.

Basically this test is not difficult to take or to administer. The response form accompanies the picture book and answers are recorded by the examiner on the profile form. There are no optional or alternate forms of DTLA-P:2. The manual does contain valuable information about the examiner's qualifications, cautions about test interpretation, and guidelines for sharing test results.

Practical Applications/Uses

The DTLA-P:2 is an individually administered test of general mental ability for children from 3 years to 9 years, 11 months of age. The three domains that make up the GMA score are language, attention, and manual dexterity, with each domain comprised of two sections: Verbal and Nonverbal; Attention-Enhanced and -Reduced; and Motor-Enhanced and -Reduced. Educators and psychologists use the DTLA-P:2 to identify children below their peers in important abilities, to detect strengths and weaknesses among children's developed mental abilities, to make judgments about children's future performances, and to assess aptitude, intelligence, and cognitive behavior for research studies. Its most appropriate users are school psychologists and counselors who consult with teachers regarding cognitive behavior relative to language, attention, and manual dexterity or regarding deficiencies in general mental ability. The DTLA-P:2 can provide potentially helpful information for teachers who want to identify strengths and weaknesses of cognitive behavior, make recommendations for further assessment, or offer suggestions for appropriate interventions or placement. The instrument is not appropriate for diagnostic classification. In fact, the test authors note that test results provide merely observations of "performance level at a given time under a particular situation" (Hammill & Bryant, 1991, p. 32); they serve as aids to clinical judgment. Despite these limitations, DTLA-P:2 is applicable to all students in the age range specified who can function in a regular classroom and pre-K programs, as well as in some special education classrooms.

The demographic characteristics of the 2,095 children used in the standardization study were based on the *Statistical Abstract of the United States.* As noted previously, the sample population represented 36 states in four geographic regions of the United States and two provinces in Canada. Although a high percentage of the sample was white (78%), four other racial and ethnic groups were represented. Gender was equally represented, as well as urban and rural residences. Approximately 75% of the sample was 5 through 8 years old.

To be qualified to administer the DTLA-P:2, the examiner needs formal training in basic assessment plus an understanding of test statistics and the procedures governing administration, scoring, and interpretation. Helpful also is specific information about mental ability evaluation and supervised practice in using mental abilities instruments. The manual lists nine basic procedures to ensure reliable administration of the DTLA-P:2. Familiarity with all components of the packet is essential because the test is designed to be given without reference to the manual during administration. The other procedures to be followed deal with rapport, responsiveness to examinee fatigue and/or interest loss, creating a comfortable and nondistracting environment, offering consistent praise and encouragement and avoiding specific phrases such as "that's good" and "very good" when reflecting on the accuracy of the child's response, positioning oneself to ensure secure setting, and repeating items if they do not involve short-term memory.

The entire test can be administered in 15 to 45 minutes, depending on the child's age and ability. Timing is important. If the child does not respond within 10 seconds, encouragement for response is recommended. If no response occurs, then the item is scored as incorrect. It generally takes only one session to complete the DTLA-P:2. However, for some children and inexperienced examiners, several sessions are needed.

The DTLA-P:2 is administered individually. The examiner shows the child pictures from the picture book and asks specific questions about the material. The manual provides clear directions for administering each item as well as sample responses, making the test easy to complete. It also furnishes information on what answers are considered correct and incorrect. For example, when the examinee responds to Picture Identification, the examiner is cautioned to ignore speech problems, dialectical influences, and mispronunciations.

Scoring the DTLA-P:2 items require rather uncomplicated decisions for the examiner, and scoring time is minimal because in most cases the response is either correct or incorrect. Since the test is administered individually, scoring can occur as questions are asked. On the profile/examiner record form's space for anecdotal remarks, the examiner records the examinee's physical behavior or signs of fatigue. Incorrect responses are recorded as 0; correct responses, 1. Each item contributes to one total and three subtest scores. However, when testing, 1 or 0 goes only in the GMA column. When the testing is complete, the examiner goes back and fills in the subtest items. The total score and subtest scores are totaled and transferred to the front of the profile/examiner record form. Totals are then converted to standard scores, percentiles, stanines, and age equivalents.

To reduce test time, only points, basals, and ceilings are used. Testing begins with the item that corresponds to the child's age. For example, age 5 begins with item 50. If the child misses eight consecutive items (ceiling), the examiner returns to the entry point and tests downward until eight consecutive items are answered correctly. This point establishes a basal. There are three alternative procedures to using the basal and ceiling to determine the examinee's raw score.

A software scoring and report system has been developed for the DTLA-P:2, for Apple IIe, IIc, and IIGS computers as well as IBM PCs and compatibles. Input includes demographic data and the option of subtest scores or the item scores. The latter option lets the computer conveniently tally the raw scores, then convert them to standard scores, percentiles, and age equivalents. The program also permits comparative analysis for intra-ability discrepancies and allows input from achievement tests to determine aptitude-achievement discrepancy analysis. The printout describes the DTLA-P:2 and gives the examinee's scores as well as a profile of performance. Also included is a description of various intraindividual discrepancy analyses.

Using the software system's printout requires no interpretation by the examiner. At this point, recommendations can be made. The test authors point out that the standard scores present the most accurate indication of the examinee's performance. An appendix in the manual provides tables for converting raw scores to quotients and to age equivalents for those need that information for administrative purposes. Because age equivalents are problematic, the use of standard scores and percentiles are recommended when reporting results to parents and other professionals. To help with score interpretation, each subtest is discussed in detail. Information is provided on how one should analyze high and low scores, as well as on contrasting analysis between subtest domains. Guidelines also assist in intra-ability discrepancy analyses and interpreting the quotients. Caution in interpreting test results is based on certain limitations: a) concern for the test reliability that has a true variance of only 40%; b) the diagnostic issue; c) the aptitude-treatment hypothesis used to make instructional inferences; and d) situational and student error.

Technical Aspects

The test manual reports reliability on three estimates: content sampling, time sampling, and standard error of measurement. To determine internal consistency, 50 protocols were selected from the normative sample. Using Cronbach's coefficient alpha method, it was determined that the mean coefficients were in an acceptable range, .90, significant at $p < .05$. When time sampling was used to determine the stability of DTLA-P:2 over time, two studies using two different sets of children were conducted. In both studies correlation coefficients obtained in the test-retest situation ranged from .89 to .95, indicating evidence of stability reliability, significant at the .001 level. The standard error of measurement is provided for raw scores and quotients. The SE_M ranged from 1 to 3 on the raw scores and from 3 to 7 on the quotients. Based on the confidence with which the DTLA-P:2 quotient (standard) score can be interpreted accurately, one might assume that the larger SE_M (7) in the area of nonverbal abilities for 3-year-olds cannot be interpreted as accurately as the GMA (3) of the 8-years-olds.

The issue of validity is evidenced by means of content validity, criterion-related validity, and construct validity. Using Salvia and Ysseldyke's (1988) classification system, as well as different theories of intellect, the DTLA-P:2 test items demonstrate that the content and abilities they measure are identifiable in terms of behaviors according to Das (1972), Horn and Cattell (1966), Jensen (1980), and Wechsler (1974). Item selection responded to criticism of the 1986 version of the DTLA-P and to item analysis to determine the appropriateness of the changes. Three studies were conducted to determine criterion-related validity. Using three different sets of students who were administered the Woodcock-Johnson Psycho-Educational Battery, the Scholastic Aptitude Scale, the Kaufman Assessment Battery for Children, and the WICS-R, the results showed a range of criterion-related validity of nonsignificance at $p < .05$ to .72, the median being .49. These coefficients provided evidence of acceptable criterion-related validity. Five separate studies were conducted to determine construct validity: age differentiation, interrelationships among values, relationship to school achievement, group differentiation, and item validity. The resulting coefficients ranged from highly significant ($p < .001$) to those with only sufficient magnitude ($p < .05$). Relationship with school achievement was determined using the Wide Range Achievement Test–Revised, Woodcock-Johnson Psycho-Educational Battery, Daberon Screening for School Readiness, and the Iowa Tests of Basic Skills. Concurrent validity was investigated by McGhee in 1991 and has not been published.

The DTLA-P:2 also controlled for bias. Two studies provided evidence that the test contains little or no gender bias and no nonwhite bias. Bias was found, however, regarding use of the English language. Thus it was recommended that the DTLA-P:2 should not be administered to non-English speakers and given only with caution to examinees who speak English poorly.

Critique

The DTLA-P:2 appears to be an excellent instrument for assessing cognitive abilities in young children. The test authors provide an admirable example for test construction, based both on considering major theories of mental ability testing and on a normative sample that represents not only four geographic regions but also four minority groups: Black, Hispanic, Native American, and Asian. These two factors alone enhance the generalizability of the DTLA-P:2. Among the instrument's strengths are its studies on reliability and validity, its ease of use and scoring, and the test's practicality. Although classroom teachers might be able to administer the test after becoming familiar with the manual, two factors jeopardize their assuming the task. The first is time, as the test must be conducted individually, and the second is accuracy of interpreting test scores and behavior during the testing if classroom teachers lack the examiner qualifications. The software program does print out two readings, a brief form and a long form, and both are very helpful to educators. If classroom teachers are going to be responsible for the administration of DTLA-P:2, it is recommended that the long form summary report be used because it describes the total GMA and each subtest in detail and rates the scores from below average to above average.

In sum, the DTLA-P:2 is relevant and could be useful when one makes decisions about examinees based on assessment of their psychological assets and deficits relative to language, attention, and manual dexterity. Furthermore, the test results could prove helpful when making judgments about an examinee's future performance, especially when such decisions could make a difference in his or her life. The DTLA-P:2 provides some clue as to the examinee's capacity to process information and to respond to some of the intellectual requirements of the educational environment.

References

Anastasi, A. (1980). Abilities and the measurement of achievement. *New Directions for Testing and Measurement, 5*, 1–10.

Das, J.P. (1972). Patterns of cognitive ability in nonretarded and retarded children. *American Journal of Mental Deficiency, 77*, 6–12.

Hammill, D.D., & Bryant, B.R. (1991). *Detroit Tests of Learning Aptitude–Primary* (2nd ed.). Austin, TX: PRO-ED.

Horn, J.L., & Cattell, R.B. (1966). Refinement and test of the theory of fluid and crystallized general intelligences. *Journal of Educational Psychology, 56*(5), 253–270.

Jensen, A.R. (1980). *Bias in mental testing.* New York: Free Press.

McGhee, R. (1991). *Concurrent validity of the Detroit Tests of Learning Aptitude–Primary: Second Edition.* Unpublished manuscript. Austin, TX: PRO-ED.

Salvia, J., & Ysseldyke, J.E. (1988). *Assessment in special and remedial education.* Boston: Houghton Mifflin.

Wechsler, D. (1974). *Wechsler Intelligence Scale for Children–Revised.* San Antonio, TX: Psychological Corporation.

Peggy VanLeirsburg, Ed.D.
Teacher, Elgin Public Schools, Elgin, Illinois.

DETROIT TESTS OF LEARNING APTITUDE–3

Donald D. Hammill. Austin, Texas: PRO-ED, Inc.

Introduction

The third edition of the Detroit Tests of Learning Aptitude (DTLA-3) contains 11 subtests that measure a variety of developed abilities. These different, but interrelated, mental abilities are termed *developed abilities,* replacing the familiar psychometric categories of intelligence, aptitude, and achievement. Depending on the needs of the test user, the DTLA-3 reportedly can measure general cognitive functioning (intelligence), predict future success (aptitude), or show mastery of particular content and skills (achievement) (Hammill, 1991).

Developed in 1935, the original DTLA had 19 subtests and tapped a wide variety of abilities, such as verbal, motor, reasoning, number, and time and space relationships, for individuals between the ages of 4 and 19. The authors, Baker and Leland, assessed different mental abilities standardized on the same population. Intraindividual strengths and weaknesses then could be studied; prior to that time, mental ability measures yielded only a single score. Although the DTLA was recognized as a potentially useful tool, criticism was made uniformly of its statistical characteristics. Silverstein (1978), for example, lists unreliable standardization procedures, inadequate test-retest reliability, and low intercorrelations between subtests. No validity data were presented in the early DTLA manual.

The DTLA-2, developed by Hammill in 1985, attempted to answer the criticism of the previous version's statistical aspects. Stehouwer (1985) described the DTLA-2 as statistically sound, with appropriate levels of reliability, validity, and standardization data. The purpose of the DTLA-2, like that of its predecessor, was to focus on the intraindividual strengths and weaknesses of children and adolescents through the use of subtests that assessed learning aptitude. Silverstein (1989) reported that the DTLA-2, from a psychometric perspective, appeared vastly superior to the original measure.

Four changes were made in the 1991 DTLA–3. The first was a reduction in the four "domain composites." The following composites were retained: Verbal vs. Nonverbal, Attention-Enhanced vs. Attention-Reduced, and Motor-Enhanced vs. Motor-Reduced. The Cognitive domain composite, Conceptual vs. Structural, was deleted because it failed to demonstrate usefulness in most diagnostic senses. A second change in the new edition involved deleting three subtests (Oral Directions, Conceptual Matching, and Word Fragments) and adding new ones titled Basic Information, Picture Fragments, and Story Sequences.

The third change introduced theory-based composites relating to current ideas of intelligence and information processing. A discussion of theory-driven composites may benefit professionals exploring the relationship of these constructs to areas such as behavior and achievement. The final new feature in the DTLA-3 is the Optimal Composite. Derived by adding the four largest standard scores on the subtests, it is the best estimate of general mental ability when inhibiting factors are suppressed (Hammill, 1991).

The DTLA-3, like its predecessors, has only one form and is suitable for individual administration to persons aged 6 through 17. The complete kit includes the examiner's manual, response forms, examiner record booklets, the profile/summary form, a picture book for story sequences, a picture fragments flipbook, a picture book for design sequences (also including story construction, design reproduction, and symbolic relations), a group of cubes with designs, and numerical tiles.

The 11 subtests that make up the DTLA-3 require the examinee to answer questions, draw pictures, and manipulate design blocks. Descriptions of the subtests follow (adapted from Hammill, 1991):

1. *Word Opposites:* Measures a highly complex vocabulary ability. The examinee must give the opposite of a stimulus word spoken by the examiner.

2. *Design Sequences:* Measures visual discrimination and memory for nonmeaningful graphic material. The examinee is shown a picture for 5 seconds and must arrange cubes to reproduce the design sequence.

3. *Sentence Imitation:* Measures auditory memory related to spoken syntax and grammar. The examinee must repeat a sentence spoken aloud by the examiner in a normal manner.

4. *Reversed Letters:* Measures short-term visual memory and attention, spatial ability, and eye-hand coordination as it relates to handwriting. The examiner says a series of letters at the rate of one per second, and the examinee must write each letter in the series in reversed order.

5. *Story Construction:* Measures the ability to conceptualize and orally express a cogent story appropriate to presented pictures. The examinee is shown a picture and told to make up a story about its contents.

6. *Design Reproduction:* Measures attention, manual dexterity, short-term memory, and spatial relations. The examiner shows the examinee a picture of a geometric form, then removes it, and the examinee must draw the form from memory.

7. *Basic Information:* Measures knowledge of commonly known facts. The examinee gives oral answers to such questions as, "What is the greenhouse effect?"

8. *Symbolic Relations:* Measures nonverbal reasoning ability. The examinee is shown a visual problem involving a series of geometric or line drawings in which one design is missing. He or she must select the missing design from among six pictured possibilities.

9. *Word Sequences:* Measures auditory attention span for unrelated words. The examiner says a series of unrelated and isolated words, and the examinee must repeat the series.

10. *Story Sequences:* Measures organizational and conceptual ability. The examinee is shown a series of cartoon-like pictures that, if put in a particular order, produce a meaningful, humorous story. The examinee indicates the story order by placing numbered chips under the pictures.

11. *Picture Fragments:* Measures closure or "gestalt" functions. The examinee is asked to say aloud the names of common objects depicted in pictures with varying elements missing.

Composite scores are generated from raw scores on the DTLA-3. Combining the standard scores of the subtests in various clusters results in 16 composite scores grouped into the following four sets:

1. *General Mental Ability:* Total of all standard scores on the 11 subtests. For most subjects, this score probably reflects the best estimate of *g*, or general intelligence, on the widest array of developed abilities.

2. *Optimal Level Composite:* Total of the four largest standard scores and used to estimate potential. Potential relates to the highest level of performance an individual is capable of when inhibiting factors are disregarded.

3. *Domain Composites:* Total of six composites that deal with language, attention, and manual dexterity. The Language, or linguistic, domain includes the contrasting Verbal and Nonverbal composites; the Attention domain contrasts the Attention-Enhanced and Attention-Reduced composites; and the Motor composite contrasts the Motor-Enhanced and Motor-Reduced composites.

4. *Theoretical Composites:* Total of eight composites that relate to the hypothetical systems currently espoused by theorists to explain intelligence. The test battery's subtests are assigned to composites that represent Horn and Cattell's fluid and crystallized intelligence, Das's simultaneous and successive processes, Jensen's associative and cognitive levels, and Wechsler's verbal and performance scales.

The composite scores that one can derive from the DTLA-3 were designed to give more information than that of a single intelligence score. The interpretation of such scores may allow for a hierarchy of assessment relative to an individual. Diagnosis may occur at the level of a single item, subtest, and/or composite performance.

Practical Applications/Uses

The DTLA-3 has four principle uses: 1) to determine strengths and weaknesses among developed mental abilities; 2) to identify subjects significantly below their peers in important abilities; 3) to predict future performance; and 4) to serve as a measurement device in research studies investigating aptitude, intelligence, and cognitive behavior (Hammill, 1991). These broad purposes form the basis for most testing situations within educational settings and private practices. The DTLA-3 provides insights into individual strengths and weaknesses, which can be helpful in program planning. For example, subjects with weak auditory attention and strong motor ability may profit from instructional planning including a "hands-on" approach (Stehouwer, 1985). Vocational assessment can derive from the DTLA-3 by comparisons of strong and weak individual abilities (e.g., high scores in manual dexterity may be matched with a future profession requiring such a strength).

Hammill (1991) urges that all examiners using the DTLA-3 have formal training in assessment, including knowledge of basic testing statistics and the general procedures involved in administering and interpreting standardized tests, plus specific information about mental ability evaluation.

Testing time may vary due to the fact that only a few of the subtests have set time limits. The manual suggests actual administration time to be from 50 minutes to 2 hours. Although the DTLA-3 often is completed within one session, some subjects may require several sessions to produce optimal performances.

Five of the 11 subtests have entry points related to the age of the examinee; the other six begin with item 1. The use of basals and ceilings permits a bit of time saving, though all items on Design Sequences, Reversed Letters, Story Construction, and Story Sequences are administered. The manual provides specific instructions for the administration of each subtest. When scoring takes on a more subjective nature, specific scoring criteria are given for each item, thereby reducing subjectivity in scoring.

An individual's test performance is recorded on the profile/summary form, which contains the following sections:

Section I: Identifying information
Section II: Record of the DTLA-3 subtest scores
Section III: Profile of DTLA-3 subtest scores
Section IV: Workspace for computing composites
Section V: Record of other test scores
Section VI: DTLA-3 characteristics
Section VII: Administration conditions
Section VIII: Interpretations and recommendations
Section IX: Profile of DTLA-3 composites and other test scores

The DTLA-3 may be scored via computer software. The user must enter only demographic data and raw scores for the program to produce standard scores, percentiles, composite quotients, and a summary report. The DTLA-3 yields five types of scores: raw scores, subtest standard scores, composite quotients, percentiles, and age equivalents.

Interpretation of scores is clearly and thoroughly explained. However, a strong basic knowledge of testing statistics is necessary for sophisticated interpretations. Discussion relative to conducting intra-ability discrepancy analyses suggests that "scatter" profiles, demonstrated by numerous strengths and weaknesses, may be associated with organicity, learning disabilities, or attentional deficits. Such a clinical analysis, while a valuable tool, may become contaminated if composite comparison is not limited. Incorrect interpretation, in the case of diagnosis, could be extremely unprofessional. The manual warns that tests do not diagnose; their results are merely observations. The DTLA-3 may be helpful in individual diagnosis, but "great caution should be taken about making instructional inferences" (Hammill, 1991, p. 55).

Technical Aspects

Care was taken to ensure appropriate norming procedures for the DTLA-3. Between 1989 and 1990, a total of 2,587 subjects from 36 states were tested. The characteristics of this sample with regard to sex, residence, race, ethnicity, and geographic area very closely match demographic data for the general U.S. population for 1990. No mention is made, however, of matching for handicapping conditions. For example, no percentage of learning disabled, deaf, or mentally handicapped subjects in the norming group are listed and matched to a like group in the general population.

The manual reports reliability of the DTLA-3 in two ways. The first method discussed is internal consistency, investigated by the use of Cronbach's alpha for dichotomously scored items. Fifty subjects at each age level (from 6 through 17) were randomly selected from the normative sample to serve as subjects for the analysis. Internal consistency reliabilities were derived for the composites using Guilford's formula. Coefficients resulting from the two types of calculations are reported in table form. For the subtests, the coefficients reported range from .70 to .97, with the majority in the .80s and .90s. The manual reports "that 86% of the alphas reach .80, criterion for acceptable reliability; 34% attain .90, the optimal level" (Hammill, 1991, p. 66). The alphas reported for the composite scores are even higher, ranging from .86 to .97. The table of reliability coefficients for both the subtests and the composites displays a remarkably acceptable range of internal consistency.

Reliability was also studied using a test-retest method. However, the sample included only 34 children residing in Austin, Texas, who were tested within a 2-week interval. The reliability coefficients reported for the subtests range from .77 to .96; coefficients for the composites are reported from .81 to .96. Taken at face value, these statistics of reliability are of sufficient magnitude to allow confidence in the test scores' stability over time. However, the sample size and demographics do not allow one to generalize the conclusions to any other tested group.

The manual discusses three types of validity—content, criterion, and construct— as they relate to the DTLA-3. Content validity, or whether items on a test cover a representative sample of the behavior domain to be measured, must be built into the test as it is conceptualized and written (Anastasi, 1988). Hammill (1991) offers four demonstrations of content validity for the DTLA-3. First, the manual presents an extremely detailed rationale for the formats and items of each subtest. Second, the contents of subtests are discussed as parallel to Salvia and Ysseldyke's (1988) listing of behavior usually measured by tests of aptitude and intelligence. Third, the subtests and composites are shown to be identifiable with currently popular theories of intellect. Fourth, item analysis procedures used to choose items during test construction support content validity and were distributed between 15% and 85% for acceptability.

Several studies were undertaken to examine the criterion-related validity of the DTLA-3. Presumed to measure mental ability, the DTLA-3 should correlate with tests that are known or presumed also to test mental ability. Hammill reports that 76 individuals from the standardization sample were also given the WISC-R and 25 had been given the PPVT-R. The magnitude of the correlation coefficients provide evidence of criterion-related validity, with all coefficients significant at $p < .05$. However, again it must be pointed out that the sample used is quite small. All subjects were either enrolled in special education or being screened for such placement.

Construct validity examines the underlying traits of a test and the extent to which they reflect the theoretical model on which the test is based. Developers of the DTLA-3 examined five construct issues. First, the age differentiation of the norming sample was examined as it related to the distribution of general mental ability and chronological age. Second, the values for the subtests and composites were measured to ensure correlation, as all are measuring general mental ability. Third, the subtests were examined to ensure that they correlated well with other measures of academic performance because the DTLA-3 measures those constructs. Fourth, factor analysis was used to discover whether the DTLA-3 measures similar yet discrete traits. Last, items of every DTLA-3 subtest were measured to determine whether the relation to the total subtest was sufficiently high to ensure the measurement of similar traits. The resulting reported coefficients make a case for strong construct validity.

The manual reports studies completed by the test authors and for content, criterion-related, and construct validity. The studies reported suggest that validity is acceptable; indeed, highly acceptable. However, caution must be interjected at this point. The subjects chosen often are from a specific location or population, and the numbers sampled are quite small. The validity of the DTLA-3 must be further researched on larger and more random samples. Stehouwer (1985) suggested the use of a multitrait-multimethod matrix to support construct validity claims for the DTLA-2. This suggestion also could be applied for strengthening the construct validity claims for the DTLA-3.

Critique

The DTLA-3 is an individually administered measure of different but interrelated developed mental abilities. Although the purpose of this test has remained the same through two earlier editions, the norming procedures as well as reliability and validity evidence have vastly improved from the first edition to the current, 1991 DTLA-3.

As noted previously, however, no normative data are reported for subjects with handicapping conditions. This information should be included due to the diagnostic nature of the DTLA-3. Claims of testing strengths and weaknesses, neurological impairment, and learning disability need to be grounded in comparative normed information. Further, sample stratification for age was not equalized. For example, 164 subjects were sampled for age 6 and 337 subjects were age 10. Sound test score interpretation may be less valid at age 6 due to the small number in the norm group.

Data for reliability and validity studies are encouraging, yet based on specific and limited samples. Further and more random selection studies would be beneficial to strengthen the high correlations claimed for both reliability and validity. Cross-validation studies are reported for the DTLA-3 that are a welcome addition to the data regarding the test's statistical soundness.

The DTLA-3 battery may be used by professionals who have a sound basis in standardized test administration and knowledge of basic test statistics. This professional group may include psychologists, diagnosticians, special educators, speech/language pathologists, and others interested in determining "the psychological constitution of examinees" (Hammill, 1991, p. 9). Given these requirements, the manual is quite descriptive regarding the theory on which the DTLA-3 is based. Individual testing time may range from 50 minutes to 2 hours, and more than one session may be necessary. Scoring and interpretation is easy yet time-consuming without the use of the computer program. The manual provides specific instructions for giving and interpreting each subtest. Consumers of the DTLA-3 must decide if the subtest and composite scores will yield the information necessary to diagnose a specific individual. Such information may be necessary and helpful enough to warrant the amount of time involved administering and interpreting this test battery.

The testing profile of an individual is considered an observation of behavior on a given day, at a certain time, during a specific testing situation. When used to make judgments about an individual, test scores thus must be taken with a grain of salt. These cautions are refreshingly stated in the DTLA-3 manual. Test users are informed that test results can make a contribution to diagnosis, but practical decisions rest with the skill and experience of the examiner.

In future reprints of the manual, an error should be corrected on page 11 in the description of the Story Sequences subtest. Fine motor skill is required on the part of the *examinee* to manipulate the chips, not the *examiner.*

In summary, the DTLA-3 shows potential as a diagnostic device in specific situations in the hands of knowledgeable examiners. The technical information has improved a great deal since the original DTLA. However, reliability over time, criterion-related validity, and construct validity studies should be expanded and enlarged to permit confidence in the battery's statistical soundness and thus strengthen its overall usefulness.

References

Anastasi, A. (1988). *Psychological testing* (6th ed.). New York: Macmillan.

Hammill, D. (1991). *Detroit Tests of Learning Aptitude–3: Examiner's manual.* Austin, TX: PRO-ED.

Salvia, J., & Ysseldyke, J.E. (1988). *Assessment in special and remedial education.* Boston: Houghton Mifflin.

Silverstein, A.B. (1978). Detroit Tests of Learning Aptitude. In O.K. Buros (Ed.), *The eighth mental measurements yearbook* (pp. 214–215). Highland Park, NJ: Gryphon Press.

Silverstein, A.B. (1989). Detroit Tests of Learning Aptitude. In J.C. Conoley & J.J. Kramer (Eds.), *The tenth mental measurements yearbook* (pp. 235–236). Lincoln, NE: Buros Institute of Mental Measurements.

Stehouwer, R.S. (1985). Detroit Tests of Learning Aptitude–2. In D.J. Keyser & R.C. Sweetland (Eds.), *Test critiques* (Vol. II, pp. 223–230). Austin, TX: PRO-ED.

Jeffrey B. Brookings, Ph.D.

Professor of Psychology, Wittenburg University, Springfield, Ohio.

EATING DISORDER INVENTORY–2

David M. Garner. Odessa, Florida: Psychological Assessment Resources, Inc.

Introduction

The Eating Disorder Inventory–2 (EDI-2; Garner, 1991) is a 91-item, self-report measure of behaviors, feelings, and other "symptoms" associated with bulimia and anorexia nervosa. The first version of the EDI, published in 1984 by David M. Garner and Marion Olmsted of the University of Toronto, consisted of 64 items scored on eight subscales (described below). The impetus for developing the EDI arose from the realization that the few published assessment devices available at that time did not reflect the growing awareness of eating disorders as multi-faceted, multiply determined problems.

Professor Garner, affiliated now with Michigan State University, authored the EDI-2, which includes the original 64 items and an additional 27 items allocated to three "provisional" subscales. The EDI-2 is thus a longer version of its predecessor rather than a revision per se. In fact, the most important change is the expanded clinical sample that now comprises the normative database for the 64 "core" items. That is, whereas the original EDI clinical sample consisted of only 215 female anorexia nervosa patients from the Clarke Institute of Psychiatry and Toronto General Hospital, the updated sample includes 782 female patients from the Toronto General Hospital and an additional 107 female patients from two Michigan eating disorder programs.

The EDI-2 test booklet consists of a cover page containing demographic items and questions related to weight and dieting (e.g., current weight, highest past weight), followed on the next three pages by the 91 EDI-2 items. Some items refer specifically to eating behavior (e.g., feelings after overeating, thoughts about dieting); others relate more to overall psychological and emotional well-being (e.g., communicating effectively with others, meeting parental expectations). The examinee responds to each item on a separate answer sheet using a 6-point scale: Always (A), Usually (U), Often (O), Sometimes (S), Rarely (R), or Never (N). (Ordinarily the provision of a separate answer sheet would mean that the item booklets are reusable. On the EDI-2, however, the examinee responds to the demographic and weight/dieting items directly on the booklet, and it cannot be reused.) Profile forms allow comparisons of examinees' 11 subscale scores with the patient and female college student norms.

An optional form for use in conjunction with the EDI-2 is the EDI Symptom Checklist (EDI-SC), a self-report index of specific eating symptoms (e.g., binge eating, purging, use of laxatives and diuretics). The EDI-SC includes several items related specifically to the DSM-III-R (American Psychiatric Association, 1987) eating disorder criteria; examiners are cautioned that the EDI-SC is only an *aid* to diagnosis, however, and should not be used as the sole basis for diagnosis.

The 64 items that comprised the EDI—and appear in the EDI-2 as items 1–64—are scored on eight subscales:

1. *Drive for Thinness* (7 items): Excessive fear of weight gain, preoccupation with weight and dieting.

2. *Bulimia* (7): Frequent bouts of bingeing (i.e., uncontrollable overeating) and thoughts about bingeing.

3. *Body Dissatisfaction* (9): Dissatisfaction over the size and shape of regions of the body of most concern to those having eating disorders (e.g., stomach, hips).

4. *Ineffectiveness* (10): Feelings of insecurity, worthlessness, and inadequacy.

5. *Perfectionism* (6): High expectations for personal performance and achievement.

6. *Interpersonal Distrust* (7): Feelings of alienation, avoidance of close relationships.

7. *(Lack of) Interoceptive Awareness* (10): Inability to identify accurately one's own emotional states and bodily sensations related to eating and hunger.

8. *Maturity Fears* (8): Desire to retreat or "regress" to the relative safety and security of childhood.

Items on the Drive for Thinness, Bulimia, and Body Dissatisfaction subscales are concerned directly with eating- and weight-related behaviors and problems; the remaining five subscales assess general psychological problems assumed to have clinical relevance to eating disorders.

The final 27 items on the EDI-2 are scored on three "provisional" subscales:

1. *Asceticism* (8 items): Belief in the virtue of self-discipline, control of bodily urges, self-denial, and so forth.

2. *(Lack of) Impulse Regulation* (11): Tendency toward impulsivity, self-destructiveness, recklessness, and so forth.

3. *Social Insecurity* (8): Perceptions of self-doubt and insecurity in social relationships.

These subscales are considered provisional because a) the items comprising them are new, relative to the 64 items contained in the eight original EDI subscales; b) the norms for these subscales are based on a small clinical sample of only 107 female patients; and c) item-total correlations for Asceticism and (Lack of) Impulse Regulation were lower than those reported for the eight core subscales. Despite these problems, the provisional subscales were retained in the final version of the EDI-2 because, according to Garner (1991), they identified a small but distinct subgroup of eating disordered patients.

Practical Applications/Uses

The primary purpose of the EDI-2 is to assist clinicians in a) assessing patient symptomatology, b) planning treatment, and c) evaluating the effectiveness of clinical interventions. In nonclinical settings, the inventory may be used by high school or college counselors as a screening device for identifying individuals with "subclinical" eating problems or those at risk for developing an eating disorder. Finally, the EDI-2 is used frequently as a predictor or outcome measure in research studies of eating disorders, in both clinical and nonclinical populations.

Garner (1991) cautions that the EDI-2 is *not* a diagnostic instrument, but it does provide directly relevant information for evaluating and treating individual patients. For example, comparisons of patient subscale profiles with the norms for eating-disordered and normal control samples helps clarify the nature and severity of the problems presented by individual patients and provides direction for treatment planning. Also, because the EDI-2 is multidimensional, pretest/posttest comparisons can be used to assess the effectiveness of specific, targeted interventions (e.g., changes in Body Dissatisfaction subscale scores in response to cognitive behavioral treatment of body image distortion).

To use the EDI-2 as a screening device, Garner (1991) recommends a two-stage process. Those whose scores exceed a predetermined cutoff on the Drive for Thinness subscale—which has demonstrated clinical relevance—are interviewed to determine if they meet the diagnostic criteria for an eating disorder. Alternatively, individuals with elevations on specific subscales may be reassessed periodically to detect the evolution of subclinical eating problems into full-blown eating disorders.

In addition to its assessment and screening uses, the EDI-2 is enjoying increased popularity among researchers. There are several reasons for its popularity: It is relatively easy to administer and score, it has adequate psychometric properties (described below), and the norms are much improved over the 1984 edition. Also, because the EDI-2 is multidimensional, it is sensitive to a broader array of etiological factors and treatment effects than are unidimensional measures such as the Eating Attitudes Test (Garner & Garfinkel, 1979).

The EDI-2 is appropriate for males and females, as young as 11 years of age. Garner cautions, however, that the validity of the three provisional subscales for "younger children" (i.e., under 12) has not been established.

Administration of the EDI-2 does not require a trained examiner, although clarification of examinee questions about specific items presupposes some knowledge of the test and the variables it is intended to measure. The test can be administered individually or in groups. Completion time for the EDI-2 is about 20 minutes, and the EDI-SC requires an additional 5–10 minutes. The EDI-2 manual (Garner, 1991) contains detailed directions for administering the test and specific suggestions for encouraging candid responses.

The computer version of the EDI-2 (available for IBM PCs or compatibles) includes a scoring subroutine, but hand-scoring the paper-and-pencil version is quite simple also, thanks to the design of the test materials. Attached to the underside of the answer sheet is a carbon page—not visible to the examinee— that translates item responses into item scores and indicates the subscale on which each item is scored. Thus, it is a simple clerical task to calculate raw scores for the 11 subscales by summing the item scores. The test manual provides tables for converting raw subscale scores to percentile ranks for patient (anorexia nervosa, restricting and bulimic subtypes; bulimia nervosa) and nonpatient (female and male college students, female and male high school students, 11- to 18-year-old females) groups.

Although the *mechanics* of scoring the EDI-2 items are straightforward, the item scoring scheme itself has been the source of some controversy. Examinees respond to the EDI-2 items on a 6-point scale, but item responses are assigned scores ranging from 0 to 3, thus condensing the range for each item from 6 to 4 points.

That is, the most extreme response in the "symptomatic" direction ("Always" or "Never," depending on item phrasing) is assigned a score of 3, the adjacent response receives a 2, a score of 1 is assigned to the next adjacent response, and the three most extreme "asymptomatic" responses are scored 0.

The rationale for this scoring procedure is that for any particular item, responses in the asymptomatic direction (e.g., responding "Never," "Rarely," or "Sometimes" to an item about frequency of eating binges) reflect an absence of pathology. Therefore, an examinee selecting any of these three options should receive a score of 0 for that item.

Ollendick and Hart (1986) scored the EDI items on both the 4- and 6-point item scales. They reported that a) the mean internal consistency reliabilities for the eight EDI scales were higher for the 6-point scale (.82) than for the 4-point version (.74), and b) the two systems produced equivalent results in terms of differentiating bulimic patients from matched controls. Garner and Olmsted (1986) pointed out that Ollendick and Hart's conclusions were based on a sample consisting of only 12 bulimic women, whereas the recommended EDI scoring procedure is supported by a much larger clinical database, and Garner (1991) concluded that there are insufficient data to recommend use of an alternative scoring system. However, the relative utility of the two scoring systems is an empirical question that should be addressed more systematically.

Interpretation of EDI-2 protocols involves inspecting patient profiles for overall elevation and dispersion of the 11 subscales, identifying elevations in specific subscales, and comparing patient subscale profiles with the normative data. Each interpretive procedure requires examiner training and experience, as well as background in the etiology and symptomatology of eating disorders.

Overall profile elevation and dispersion are important because even a relatively low subscale score (e.g., at the 35th percentile on Drive for Thinness) may be clinically relevant if scores on the other subscales are uniformly low (e.g., at the 10th percentile). Elevations on specific subscales, particularly Drive for Thinness, may have important implications as well. For example, Garner, Olmsted, Polivy, and Garfinkel (1984) reported that 75% of female subjects scoring greater than 14 on EDI Drive for Thinness had current or past eating disorders. It was suggested that this score might be used as a cutoff for identifying "weight-preoccupied" women, but Garner (1991) concludes that too much profile variability across populations exists to justify recommending a universal cutoff score.

Profile comparisons are facilitated by shaded regions on the profile form, which represent 68% confidence intervals (i.e., – 1 standard error of measurement) for the eating disorder and nonpatient comparison groups on the 11 subscales. The test manual reports standard errors of measurement and 95% confidence intervals, along with five illustrative case studies to help examiners interpret EDI-2 profiles.

Technical Aspects

The initial EDI item pool consisted of 146 items generated by clinicians who were conversant with the empirical literature on anorexia nervosa and had clinical experience treating the disorder (Garner & Olmsted, 1984). Then, to maximize the criterion-related validity and internal consistency reliability of the subscales, the following item selection criteria were applied: 1) each item had to differentiate significantly between the patient and control samples; 2) for each item, correlations with total scores on the "target" subscale had to exceed correlations with the other subscales; and 3) all subscale internal consistency reliabilities (i.e., alpha coefficients) had to exceed .80. The EDI-2 manual provides no information on the item generation and selection processes used to construct the provisional subscales. Nineteen of the 64 original EDI items and 6 of the 27 provisional subscale items are phrased negatively to control for acquiescence response set.

Internal consistency reliabilities (i.e., alpha coefficients) for the eight original EDI subscales ranged from .83 to .93 for 155 eating disorder patients (Garner & Olmsted, 1984) and from .80 to .92 for the updated patient sample ($N = 889$; Garner, 1991). Mean item-total correlations for the two samples were .63 and .60, respectively.

Comparable alpha coefficients have been reported for patient samples completing German (Thiel & Paul, 1988) and Swedish (Norring & Sohlberg, 1988) versions of the test. Internal consistency reliabilities for nonpatient male and female samples tend to be somewhat lower, in part because of range restriction effects.

Internal consistency reliabilities for the provisional subscales are considerably lower (mean alphas = .76 and .68 for the eating disorder and nonpatient samples), as are the item-total correlations (mean rs = .44 and .37, respectively). The Asceticism subscale is particularly problematic; for the nonpatient sample, the alpha coefficient was only .44 and the mean item-total correlation .14.

The following mean test-retest reliabilities have been reported for three nonpatient samples: .84 for a 1-week retest interval, .85 for a 3-week interval, and .58 for an interval of 1 year (see Garner, 1991). Test-retest data for the provisional subscales are not available.

As noted previously, a criterion-keying strategy was used to select items for the original EDI subscales; that is, the authors retained only items that differentiated significantly between patient and control samples. Consequently, considerable supportive evidence exists for the inventory's criterion-related validity. In Garner, Olmstead, and Polivy's (1983) study, for example, anorexia nervosa patients (restricting and bulimic subtypes) scored significantly higher than did female controls, male controls, and recovered anorexia nervosa patients on all eight EDI subscales. Gross, Rosen, Leitenberg, and Willmuth (1986) reported similar findings. In addition, there is evidence (summarized in the EDI-2 manual) that several of the EDI subscales—particularly Drive for Thinness, Bulimia, and Ineffectiveness—are sensitive to patient improvement resulting from treatment (e.g., individual psychotherapy, residential treatment, drug therapy).

Studies of the factorial validity of the original eight EDI subscales have yielded mostly positive results. Welch, Hall, and Norring (1990) conducted an item factor analysis of the 64 EDI items for 271 female eating disorder patients. They concluded that eight factors, corresponding to the EDI subscales, best represented the inventory's dimensionality. Raciti and Norcross's (1987) factor analysis of responses from 268 female college freshmen provided additional evidence for the eight a priori dimensions, as did Brookings and Wilson's (1990) joint confirmatory factor analysis of the EAT and EDI for 149 female college undergraduates. However, Welch, Hall, and Walkey's (1988) study produced a three-factor solution that replicated across three different nonpatient samples (female college students, student nurses, aerobic dance class enrollees).

Garner et al.'s (1983) study provided evidence for the convergent validity of the EDI. Anorexia nervosa patients' scores on the subscales correlated significantly (*r*s ranging from .43 to .68) with clinicians' ratings of them on the corresponding dimensions. In support of the concurrent validity of the test, all eight EDI subscales correlated significantly with the Eating Attitudes Test (Garner & Garfinkel, 1979) and seven correlated with the Restraint Scale (Herman & Polivy, 1975), a measure of dieting behavior. The largest EDI correlate of these tests was Drive for Thinness. Finally, the EDI subscales were correlated as predicted with a number of body image measures, including actual/ideal weight discrepancy and ideal body size estimation (see Garner, 1991, for a summary).

Despite these positive findings, problems remain. First, the EDI-2 manual reports only meager evidence for the convergent and discriminant validity of three of the original EDI subscales: Perfectionism, Interpersonal Distrust, and Maturity Fears. Second, support for the validity of the three provisional subscales—Asceticism, Impulse Regulation, and Social Insecurity—is equally scant. Finally, data are lacking for the discriminant validity of all of the EDI subscales.

Critique

In an earlier review of the EDI (Eberly & Eberly, 1985), two principal criticisms of the test were that the normative samples were too small and that the validity of the test for clinical use had not been established. Regarding the first criticism, the revised manual (Garner, 1991) includes samples that are much larger and more representative of the various populations for which the test purportedly can be used.

With respect to the second criticism, the validity of the test as an adjunct to clinical assessment and intervention remains an issue. For example, the Bulimia, Drive for Thinness, and Ineffectiveness scales appear to be sensitive indicators of the severity of eating disorder symptoms and their responsiveness to treatment, but support for the other "core" subscales is much weaker.

The absence of data on the influence of method variance on the concurrent validity coefficients is troublesome as well. The EDI-2, as a self-report measure, is susceptible to distortion resulting from response sets, which may spuriously inflate correlations between the EDI-2 subscales and other self-report scales. Consequently, multitrait-multimethod studies should assess method variance in EDI responses; to date no such studies have occurred.

A final problem is that the justification for adding the EDI-SC and the provisional subscales to the original EDI is weak. Regarding the EDI-SC, the EDI-2 manual (Garner, 1991) states that "addition of selected EDI-SC items may improve the discrimination of the EDI and may add information relevant to diagnosis" (p. 11). However, the document provides no guidance as to which items are to be selected and how one would use them as adjuncts to diagnosis. Further, the provisional subscales were retained on the test, despite their psychometric deficiencies, because they identified a group of eating-disordered patients "who report the kind of disturbed functioning that has been related to poor prognosis" (Garner, 1991, p. 28). However, the manual furnishes little descriptive information on this patient group and no indication of how the provisional subscale scores should be used to identify them.

Despite these problems, the EDI-2 has much to recommend it as a predictor or outcome measure in studies of eating disorders. First of all, the new manual includes considerably more data than did the first on the inventory's psychometric properties, and the evidence is mostly positive, particularly for the original EDI scales. Secondly, studies of the factor structure of the original EDI subscales indicate that, for the most part, the authors successfully developed distinct, factorially valid subscales. Finally, the popularity of the EDI has produced a sizeable database spanning a variety of subject populations, so that the strengths and weaknesses of the test are increasingly well known.

In summary, the EDI-2 is a useful tool for assessing individual differences in eating disorder symptomatology and is recommended for studies that require a multidimensional, self-report instrument. Although evidence exists for the clinical utility of three of the original EDI subscales, support for the remaining subscales (particularly the provisional ones) and the EDI-SC is weaker. In fact, the most useful feature of the EDI-2, relative to the EDI, is not the addition of the provisional subscales or the EDI-SC, but the expanded database presented in the EDI-2 manual.

References

American Psychiatric Association. (1987). *Diagnostic and statistical manual of mental disorders* (3rd ed. rev.). Washington, DC: Author.

Brookings, J.B., & Wilson, J.F. (1990, May). *Joint confirmatory factor analysis of the Eating Disorder Inventory and Eating Attitudes Test*. Paper presented at the annual meeting of the Midwestern Psychological Association, Chicago.

Eberly, C.C., & Eberly, B.W. (1985). A review of the Eating Disorder Inventory. *Journal of Counseling and Development, 64*, 285.

Garner, D.M. (1991). *The Eating Disorder Inventory–2 professional manual*. Odessa, FL: Psychological Assessment Resources.

Garner, D.M., & Garfinkel, P.E. (1979). The Eating Attitudes Test: An index of the symptoms of anorexia nervosa. *Psychological Medicine, 9*, 273–279.

Garner, D.M., & Olmsted, M.P. (1984). *The Eating Disorder Inventory manual*. Odessa, FL: Psychological Assessment Resources.

Garner, D.M., & Olmsted, M.P. (1986). Reply to Ollendick and Hart. *American Journal of Psychiatry, 143*, 805–806.

Garner, D.M., Olmsted, M.P., & Polivy, J. (1983). Development and validation of a multidimensional eating disorder inventory for anorexia nervosa and bulimia. *International Journal of Eating Disorders, 2*, 15–34.

Garner, D.M., Olmsted, M.P., Polivy, J., & Garfinkel, P.E. (1984). Comparison between weight-preoccupied women and anorexia nervosa. *Psychosomatic Medicine, 46*, 255–266.

Gross, J., Rosen, J.C., Leitenberg, H., & Willmuth, M.E. (1986). Validity of the Eating Attitudes Test and the Eating Disorders Inventory in bulimia nervosa. *Journal of Consulting and Clinical Psychology, 54*, 875–876.

Herman, C.P., & Polivy, J. (1975). Anxiety, restraint, and eating behavior. *Journal of Personality, 84*, 666–672.

Norring, C., & Sohlberg, S. (1988). Eating Disorder Inventory in Sweden: Description, cross-cultural comparison, and clinical utility. *Acta Psychiatrica Scandinavica, 78,* 567–575.

Ollendick, T.H., & Hart, K.J. (1986). Reply to Garner and Olmsted. *American Journal of Psychiatry, 143,* 680–681.

Raciti, M.C., & Norcross, J.C. (1987). The EAT and EDI: Screening, interrelationships, and psychometrics. *International Journal of Eating Disorders, 6,* 579–586.

Thiel, A., & Paul, T. (1988). Entwicklung einer Deutschsprachigen version des Eating Disorder Inventory (EDI). *Zeitschrift fur Differentielle und Diagnostische Psychologie, 4,* 267–278.

Welch, G., Hall, A., & Norring, C. (1990). The factor structure of the Eating Disorder Inventory in a patient setting. *International Journal of Eating Disorders, 9,* 79–85.

Welch, G., Hall, A., & Walkey, F.H. (1988). The factor structure of the Eating Disorder Inventory. *Journal of Clinical Psychology, 44,* 51–56.

Mary Lynn Boscardin, Ph.D.
Assistant Professor of Special Education, University of Massachusetts, Amherst, Massachusetts.

William Hickey, Ed.D.
Special Education Consultant, Amherst, Massachusetts.

THE EFFECTIVE SCHOOL BATTERY

Gary D. Gottfredson. Odessa, Florida: Psychological Assessment Resources, Inc.

Introduction

The Effective School Battery (ESB) was designed to assess what its author refers to as "school climate in secondary schools." Structured to include the whole school in the assessment process, the battery's purpose is to provide information that enables participants to recognize strengths and weaknesses, develop improvement plans, and evaluate improvement projects (either planned, in progress, or completed).

The ESB resulted from 5 years of research on school climate by Gary Gottfredson and the Center for Social Organization of Schools at Johns Hopkins University. The original data came from students in 58 schools and teachers in 56 of those same schools who completed the questionnaires in spring 1981. The sample schools were primarily urban, with large minority populations. New items were written and subjected to item analysis in spring 1982, and the final version emerged in spring 1983.

The ESB comprises a Student and a Teacher Inventory, each with its own 8-page booklet of questions and scannable answer sheet. Although the battery uses both inventories to develop a profile measuring a school's climate, the inventories can be administered separately for a school's own purpose. The battery is designed for use with secondary students and faculty. The Student Inventory reading level is upper fifth grade.

The measures of student characteristics, intended to evaluate student conduct, divide into four areas: social background, peer relations, attitudes and psychosocial development, and self-reported behavior. These areas reportedly were determined by school personnel as important to the implementation of educational and school improvement programs. Gottfredson addressed the measures of teacher characteristics believing that most improvement projects are aimed at teachers (e.g., classroom management or changes in teacher attitudes), and therefore he considered it important to assess the teachers' perceptions and attitudes about various aspects of school life to improve the chances of success for any change agenda.

The Student Inventory is divided into the following parts: 1) What About You? (asks for descriptive data about the student); 2) How Do You Spend Your Time? (asks about time spent in and out of school); 3) Your School (asks students' views on how the school works); and 4) What Do You Think? (pools students' opinions to develop what Gottfredson calls a psychosocial scale). This fourth part further divides into six areas: Safety, Respect for Students, Planning and Action, Fairness, Clarity, and Student Influence. The Student Inventory also has been translated into Spanish.

The Teacher Inventory comprises a dozen parts: 1) Background Information (asks for descriptive information about the staff); 2) Involvement of Parents (looks at parent-teacher interaction and community involvement); 3) Classroom Management and Teaching Practices (asks about rewards and grading practices); 4) Resources (inquires about availability for instruction); 5) Job Satisfaction (addresses whether teachers like their jobs); 6) Training and Other Activities (looks at committee work and in-service); 7) Interaction with Students (asks how and to what extent respondents are involved with students); 8) School Rules (seeks opinions on clarity and enforcement of school rules); 9) How Different Groups Get Along (asks about race relations within the school and between groups); 10) Personal Safety (addresses both school/classroom issues and personal experiences); 11) Your Opinions (looks at attitudes toward race and authority); and 12) School Climate (seeks information about staff morale and relations with administration and other teachers). This last part is further divided into the following areas: Safety, Staff Morale, Planning and Action, Smooth Administration, Resources for Instruction, School Race Relations, Involvement of Parents and the Community, Student Influence, and Use of Grades as a Sanction.

Much of the research on which the ESB is reported to be based was derived from the National Institute of Education (1978; cited in Gottfredson, 1984) Safe School Study (i.e., many of the items were taken from instruments used in that study). In addition, the author notes the inclusion of instruments suggested by Fox and associates (1974; cited in Gottfredson, 1984), the School Initiative Evaluation questionnaires (Grant, Grant, Daniels, Neto, & Yamasaki, 1979; cited in Gottfredson, 1984), and "a number of other instruments used in major social surveys or for individual assessments" (Gottfredson, 1984, p. 17).

Each of the ESB inventories uses a separate answer sheet on which respondents fill in the appropriate circles following the questions. Users send completed answer sheets to an optical scanning service, licensed by the publisher, where they are read and the results are transferred to profile forms. Scores result from averaging the total participant responses on any given item rather than compiling individual views. In assessing the organization's climate, the use of averaging across many different reports was determined to be a secure, dependable way of assessing a school as opposed to individual views. No names appear on the answer sheets to ensure anonymity.

The profile sheets provide a summary of each school's climate and are intended to be self-interpreting. When the entire ESB is used, there will be four profile sheets: one pair representing the school's psychosocial climate and the other representing the school population (one from each pair is based on teacher reports and the other on student reports).

Profiles are presented as a table, with the vertical axis representing the areas measured and the horizontal axis indicating the rating of the scores, running on a continuum from Very Low on the left to Very High on the right. The scores are plotted on these profiles for the school districts by the scanning service. Interpretation of the profile (considered self-explanatory) is left to the districts, to determine what areas need to be addressed.

Practical Applications/Uses

The ESB is intended to provide schools with the information necessary to improve their organization by using the feedback from the students and faculty. The materials note that users also should include information such as standardized achievement test scores, disciplinary records, data about staff turnover and student retention rates, the kind of community the school is in, evidence about the attendance of both students and staff, budget information, and the experience and enthusiasm of the faculty and administration when planning improvements. However, how to incorporate and utilize this additional information is left to the discretion of the users.

Two ESB profiles show scores for nine psychosocial climate scales based on teacher reports and six psychosocial climate scales based on student reports; two others show scores for seven kinds of teacher characteristics and twelve different student characteristics. The profiles are designed to allow users to compare one school to any other school(s). They are also expected to help schools establish priorities for improving school programs and overall school effectiveness.

The guidelines for the administration of the Teacher Inventory recommend giving it at a staff meeting to allow time to explain its purposes and uses and to accommodate questions. However, the inventory also can be completed by the teachers individually in a setting other than a group. The Student Inventory offers two administration options for schools: Students can respond in their classrooms or in a large group, and in either case the school can use nonprofessional staff as monitors. The Student Inventory requires between 25 and 50 minutes to complete, depending on the reading level and ability of participating students.

In addition to the inventories, the ESB includes a Survey Coordinator's Manual for the person chosen to plan and coordinate the administration of the battery. Materials also include the ESB manual, essentially designed to explain the development of the instrument and its uses.

As noted earlier, a licensed scoring service reads the survey answer sheets with an optical scanner and provides copies of the completed profiles to the schools. Additional statistical analysis also can be completed if requested prior to sending the forms to the service.

The analysis of the ESB derives from objective scoring. The interpretation of the profiles is intended to be easily comprehensible to administrators, teachers, parents, and school board members alike. The author recommends choosing an individual to interpret the results and present the findings to the interested group (e.g., school board or administration personnel).

Technical Aspects

Gottfredson used two types of reliability measures for the ESB: 1) the "homogeneity" coefficient (an estimate using an alpha coefficient), which is an index of how well the items composing the scales (i.e., Safety, Planning and Action, Morale, etc.) measure whatever they measure at a given point in time, and 2) test-retest reliability, which is based on the correlating scores obtained from the same individuals or schools over time.

A low homogeneity coefficient would indicate that the scale did not measure the construct well, whereas a high one would mean the scales did measure the construct reasonably well. The test author applied the homogeneity coefficient to determine the reliability of the scales measured on a single occasion. In this case they were used to measure the usefulness of each scale used in the Student and Teacher Inventories drawn from a large sample of mostly urban schools.

To obtain test-retest reliability, scores from 1981 were compared to the same schools and individuals in 1982 and 1983. Based on this comparison, Gottfredson determined that retest reliability measures the effect of change. In this case, if the reliability coefficient is high then the characteristic is resistant to change; that is, something is preventing change from occurring or nothing has been done to allow it to occur. Retest reliability was established using a random half-sample of the students in the same school with a 1-year interval between administrations.

Because of the newness of the instrument, the author used a variety of methods to assess its validity. One used readers' impressions of the item content in each measure, another examined earlier research of closely related measures, and a third examined the correlates of measures from efforts and intervention strategies used to implement change.

Critique

The Effective School Battery addresses two areas: the organizational climate of a school and the characteristics of the students and teachers who work there. The test should appeal to those who subscribe to "grass roots" approaches, as it gives users the opportunity to determine how to interpret the results for their own particular situation. Regretfully, there is no guide to assure users that they will make, or are making, appropriate decisions and choices, nor is there certainty that they will have a clear picture of what it is that they are supposed to achieve.

ESB items derived from National Institute of Education (NIE, 1978) Safe School Study data, the School Initiative Evaluation questionnaire (Grant et al., 1979), and a number of other instruments (not listed in the manual). Nevertheless, it has not been clearly demonstrated that the measures used are indicative of an effective school, primarily because the author has not clearly defined the term *effective.* Gottfredson has determined that certain indices can measure certain characteristics, but whether these, when combined, will provide for an effective school is open to question by users of the instrument.

It should also be noted that, although students from other ethnic and cultural groups are represented in the schools' statistics, a major portion of the comparisons represented in tables are of African Americans and Caucasians, and male and female students and teachers. This may not provide an adequate representation for understanding the student body of today because of the present and continued growth of multicultural populations, especially in our urban areas. Demographers anticipate that 38% of students under 18 will be non-white (Hispanic, African American, Native American, and Asian) by the year 2000.

Although Gottfredson designed the ESB for secondary schools, with further research and modifications it should be possible to assess elementary schools in the same way. It may also be possible to combine some of the items in this survey and, with the research on the effects of community influences and multiculturalism, develop an instrument that will assess school culture.

The author provides a rationale for the use and purpose of the ESB and states the importance of including other information to obtain a more complete picture of the school or district, but he does not show why or how to incorporate that additional information. The literature on effective schools, dating from the late 1960s to the present, uses a variety of measures and characteristics to assess whether a school is or is not effective. The inclusion of this information might prove beneficial to potential users of this instrument.

Recognizing that the ESB alone will not determine what constitutes an effective school today, it would be helpful in any future revision to incorporate the areas measured as part of the school climate with those of the more revealing and influential process associated with a school's culture. The author suggests that changes will occur from the knowledge this instrument provides. While true to a point, at present it will not help users to understand how schools and communities become successful at fostering change and maintaining that environment for an effective school. The ESB is outcome oriented and does not focus enough on the current practices and processes a school uses to enact policy.

This instrument relates more to recognizing the attitudes and behaviors that aid or detract from attempts to change and improve schools, and thus it becomes more of a needs assessment for identifying what and whose attitudes to address before attempting to improve a school. This differs from what the effective schools literature has targeted for change. In their review of the literature, Purkey and Smith (1983) identified five common characteristics found in effective schools: 1) strong leadership by the principal or other staff, 2) high expectations by staff for student achievement, 3) clear goals, 4) an academic emphasis for the school and an effective school-wide staff training program, and 5) a system of monitoring student progress. Only two studies in their review found order and discipline important. The ESB leaves it up to the user to determine whether or not the results are effective, and thus it is not a complete guide to developing what the literature refers to as an effective school (Cohen, 1982; Edmonds, 1979; Purkey & Smith, 1983).

In summary, this instrument would be a very good investment to aid a school or district in assessing aspects associated with change. As a needs assessment, the ESB would be very effective at stimulating communication through the use of common terminology and points of reference. A more appropriate title then would be "A School and Program Needs Assessment Battery." In addition, the ability to interpret the school profiles by professionals and lay people alike provides a very positive means for drawing more interested parties into the process, and it allows participants to take ownership for the analysis and development of plans for improvement.

References

This list includes text citations and suggested additional reading.

Cohen, M. (1982). Effective schools: Accumulating research findings. *American Education, 18*(1), 13–16.

Edmonds, R. (1979, October). Effective schools for the urban poor. *Educational Leadership,* pp. 15–27.

Gottfredson, G.D. (1984). *The Effective School Battery: Users manual.* Odessa, FL: Psychological Assessment Resources.

Lezotte, L.W. (1984). *School effectiveness research: A tribute to Ron Edmonds.* (ERIC Document Reproduction Service No. ED 017 472)

Neufield, B., Farrar, E., & Miles, M.B. (1983). *A review of effective schools research: The message for secondary schools.* Cambridge, MA: Huron Institute. (ERIC Document Reproduction Service No. ED 228 241)

Purkey, S.C., & Smith M.S. (1983). Effective schools: A review. *Elementary School Journal, 83*(4), 427–452.

Purkey, S.C., & Smith, M.S. (1985). School reform: The district policy implication of the effective schools literature. *Elementary School Journal, 85*(3), 353–389.

Rutter, M., Maugham, B., Mortimore, R., Ouston, J., & Smith, A. (1979). *Fifteen thousand hours: Secondary schools and their effects on children.* Cambridge, MA: Harvard University Press.

David O. Herman, Ph.D.
Psychologist, New York City Public Schools, New York, New York.

EXPRESSIVE ONE-WORD PICTURE VOCABULARY TEST–REVISED

Morrison F. Gardner. Novato, California: Academic Therapy Publications.

Introduction

The Expressive One-Word Picture Vocabulary Test–Revised (EOWPVT-R), like its predecessor, is a brief, individually administered children's test of expressive vocabulary. It is called "expressive" to distinguish it from measures of receptive vocabulary; the format requires the child to name each of a series of pictures. It is called a "one-word" test presumably because most of the stimulus pictures can be named with a single word. In fact all of the pictures do illustrate a single object or concept, even if more than one word is sometimes needed to define them (e.g., Statue of Liberty). Thus no complex definitions or explanations are called for.

According to the manual for the EOWPVT-R (Gardner, 1990), the test results should provide an estimate of a child's verbal intelligence through his or her vocabulary, one aspect of what the child has learned from the environment and from formal education. The test's described uses include measuring a child's expressive language functioning, determining readiness for kindergarten, and grouping children for various instructional purposes. The author properly points out that test performance may be influenced by speech and auditory defects, bilingual status, auditory processing problems, and a host of behavioral characteristics such as attention span, impulsivity, self-confidence, and problems in concentration.

The EOWPVT-R is a 1990 revision of the Expressive One-Word Picture Vocabulary Test, originally published in 1979. The goals of the revision were to eliminate dated content, try out and add new items, improve some of the existing drawings, update the standardization data, increase the size of the stock on which the pictures are printed, and make several minor changes in the format of the norms tables, size of the record form, and the like. In all the length of the test has been reduced from 110 to 100 items. The age range remains unchanged: 2 years, 0 months through 11 years, 11 months.

Besides the book of stimulus pictures, the test materials consist of the manual and record forms. The EOWPVT-R may be administered in Spanish using the same set of pictures but with a separate Spanish record form.

Practical Applications/Uses

The EOWPVT-R appears to measure a complex verbal function that is not as yet fully explicated. The author's discussion of the uses and purposes of the test helps and, as far as a reviewer can tell from the test materials, is accurate as far as it goes. The instrument is not merely a vocabulary test. A number of items require more than recognizing an object and speaking its name; these call for the ability to abstract common elements from a group of objects and to retrieve a word for the abstraction. For example, one of the plates shows an electronic keyboard, a trumpet, a violin, and a saxophone, and the examinee's task is to recognize them collectively as musical instruments. Thus the test content gives some support to the author's contention that the test measures "how a child thinks" and may be used to estimate verbal intelligence.

At the same time, the range of verbal ability that the EOWPVT-R samples is rather narrow for a measure of intelligence. Consider, for example, that most psychologists would be reluctant to use only the Vocabulary subtest of a Wechsler scale as a short-form measure of Verbal IQ, though some might use it to give a rough indication. If only for this reason, one should avoid using scores on this test as stand-alone measures of verbal intelligence. To its credit the manual explicitly notes that one should make inferences concerning general ability with caution.

The procedures for administering the test are not difficult and should not require special training for examiners experienced in administering individual ability examinations. Further, the artwork gives clear representations of the intended objects and concepts. Testing begins with four unscored sample items and then, in most cases, moves to an item marked as appropriate for the child's chronological age. If the child does not answer eight consecutive items correctly, the examiner works backward from the starting place until eight consecutive correct answers are recorded. All items below this point are assumed to have been passed. Testing continues until the child has given six consecutive wrong answers. Testing time is said to vary from about 7 minutes for young children who respond to relatively few items, to about 15 minutes for older and more able children.

The manual does not present explicit directions for scoring responses as right or wrong, but it strongly implies that only the word printed on the record form for each item is acceptable. (For some items an alternate word or two is given.) For several of the items, answers not specifically noted on the record form would be easy to defend. It would be helpful to know, for example, that using more inclusive scoring rules has little effect on test scores. According to the author, however (M.F. Gardner, personal communication, November 9, 1992), all of the acceptable answers shown on the record form are based on the actual responses of children tested during the development of the test. Unless children's responses to these items show marked geographic variation, the list of acceptable answers may be less restricted than it first appears.

The Spanish version of this test deserves a few comments. The items are presented in the same sequence as on the English edition, which is to say in approximate order of difficulty for native speakers of English in the United States. The manual properly notes that some of the concepts are out of difficulty order for Spanish-speaking children and suggests that examiners administer all items on the test but score according to the usual rules involving basal and ceiling levels. In the absence of empirical data, this is probably good advice, yet this procedure will tend to yield slightly higher scores for Spanish-speaking youngsters than if the items were presented in the Spanish order of difficulty.

The manual notes that many Spanish words have regional variants; nearly half the items have anywhere from two to six alternate acceptable responses. The author clearly has been sensitive to the variations in vocabulary and word usage that characterize spoken Spanish, and to their implications for test fairness. The directions for administering the test to Spanish-speaking children wisely emphasize that examiners must not only be fluent in the language but also aware of regional variations in both word usage and word sounds.

Raw scores on the EOWPVT-R may be transformed through the norms tables to age equivalents and to several types of within-age-group converted scores: standard scores (mean of 100, standard deviation of 15), scaled scores (mean of 10, standard deviation of 3), percentile ranks, and stanines. The within-age norms are presented separately for each 2-month band between 2 and 12 years.

Technical Aspects

Many of the items for the original 1979 test evolved from parents' responses to a questionnaire from the author concerning words that their children used and the ages when they used them. Attention was given to avoiding bias of various sorts and to including words from all areas of the United States. The new items tried out for possible inclusion in the revision were picked according to the same requirements.

Gardner carried out the pilot testing of new and existing materials for the test revision on the same sample used for norms development: 1,118 children residing in the San Francisco Bay Area, about evenly divided by sex. The samples at ages 2 and 3 years have fewer than 100 children in each, but the eight samples from ages 4 to 11 years have between 105 and 137 children.

Traditional methods guided the selection of content for the final scale. Difficulty values for each year of age helped place the items in appropriate age groups. Item-total correlations and another discrimination index were used to screen out inadequate items. Once the content was set, Gardner prepared frequency distributions of raw scores separately for each 4-month age band of the sample. The medians of these distributions were smoothed across age groups, and the smoothed values were used to adjust the original raw score distributions. The adjusted distributions then were normalized and transformed to standard and scaled scores for the norms tables.

The size of the sample should be adequate for standardization purposes as long as evidence indicates that the selected group resembles the national population in important ways. Unhappily the manual offers no data on the socioeconomic or ethnic makeup of this combination tryout/standardization sample. The author has indicated that the ethnic makeup of the EOWPVT-R standardization sample did resemble that of children in the San Francisco Bay Area at the time of testing (M.F. Gardner, personal communication, November 9, 1992). Socioeconomic data on the sample are still lacking, however, and users still have no assurance that the sample gives fair representation of children-in-general in the United States, or even in the Bay Area. For this reason users should be cautious about interpreting standard scores on the EOWPVT-R as estimators of children's verbal intelligence.

Internal consistency reliability was estimated through the Kuder-Richardson formula 20, separately at each year of age in the standardization sample. The median of the 10 coefficients was .90. Corresponding standard errors of measurement are presented in terms of both standard and scaled scores. The manual does not report test-retest stability.

Empirical evidence of validity takes the form of correlations of scaled scores on the EOWPVT-R and other tests of verbal ability. These include portions of the Wechsler Preschool and Primary Scale of Intelligence—Revised (WPPSI-R), the Wechsler Intelligence Scale for Children—Revised (WISC-R), the Peabody Picture Vocabulary Test—Revised (PPVT-R), and others. Correlations emerge mostly in the .40 to .50 range, though the correlation with the WPPSI-R "overall" IQ was .69 (presumably the Verbal rather than the Full Scale IQ). Correlations are about .60 with the PPVT-R and the author's own Receptive One-Word Picture Vocabulary Test. Some of the correlational samples encompass broad age ranges, but computing the statistics from within-age scaled scores avoided spuriously overestimating the relationships.

It is unfortunate that the validity tables omit the supporting means and standard deviations in these correlational studies. Such data would tell something of the ability levels of the samples, but also, more importantly, would provide evidence of the quality of the test's standardization sample—and its norms. It would have been reassuring to know that the mean and standard deviation of EOWPVT-R scaled scores were close to those of, say, the WISC-R Vocabulary subtest for the group of children given both tests, for this would indicate how closely the test's standardization sample resembled an independent, well-defined, and carefully selected standardization sample in terms of a relevant measure.

The correlation of test scores with gender is given as .02 for the full standardization sample, indicating that boys and girls score about the same on the test as a whole.

Critique

The author has taken appropriate steps and pains to select the content of this brief measure of expressive vocabulary, and the artwork illustrates the objects and concepts clearly. Internal consistency is good, and correlations with other tests of verbal ability indicate substantial criterion-related validity. All that is missing is norms that clearly reflect the performance of a well-defined and representative standardization sample. In their absence the meaning of the EOWPVT-R norms remains uncertain, which makes the instrument undesirable as an estimator of verbal intelligence.

Some users may be able to work with local norms for the EOWPVT-R once they have accumulated enough data and experience with the test. But until then it should be considered primarily a measure of vocabulary and one possible component of a clinician's or school psychologist's battery.

References

Gardner, M.F. (1990). *Manual for the Expressive One-Word Picture Vocabulary Test—Revised.* Novato, CA: Academic Therapy Publications.

Rona Preli, Ph.D.
Assistant Professor, Graduate School of Education and Allied Professions, Fairfield University, Fairfield, Connecticut.

Janet F. Carlson, Ph.D.
Assistant Professor, Graduate School of Education and Allied Professions, Fairfield University, Fairfield, Connecticut.

FAMILY ADAPTABILITY AND COHESION EVALUATION SCALES III

David H. Olson, Joyce Portner, and Yoav Lavee. St. Paul, Minnesota: Family Social Science, University of Minnesota.

Introduction

The Family Adaptability and Cohesion Evaluation Scales III (FACES III) is the third version in a series of FACES scales developed by David Olson and his colleagues to assess family cohesion and family adaptability, the two major dimensions of the circumplex model. The latter is a conceptual clustering of concepts from family theory and the family therapy literature. It proposes that three dimensions—cohesion, adaptability, and communication—characterize family functioning. Extremes on any dimension will distinguish families likely to have difficulty coping with situational and developmental stress.

Dr. David H. Olson is a professor in the Family Social Science Department at the University of Minnesota. He has written over 100 articles and book chapters on various topics related to marriage and family life, has authored 20 books, and has developed instruments used for research and clinical work with couples and families.

Olson initially developed the circumplex model with Douglas Sprenkle and Candyce Russell in 1979. Their model is organized by two central dimensions—cohesion and adaptability. *Cohesion* assesses the degree to which family members are connected within the family in terms of emotional bonding. *Adaptability* refers to the extent to which the family system is flexible and able to change in terms of its power structure and role relationships in response to situational and developmental stress. The developers hypothesized both dimensions as related to family functioning in a curvilinear manner. Optimal functioning exists among families who achieve moderate rather than extreme levels of cohesion and adaptability.

The original FACES, developed in 1978 as the dissertation work of Joyce Portner and Richard Bell, was designed to measure the functioning of both "normal" and nonnormative families, regardless of symptomatology. The authors constructed the 111-item self-report scale specifically to measure the two major dimensions of the circumplex model.

FACES II appeared in the spring of 1981, a shorter instrument with "simple" sentences that users could administer to children and those with limited reading ability. Additionally, the developers sought to 1) reduce the number of double negatives, 2) provide a 5-point response scale, 3) drop the individual autonomy/ independence scale to cohesion, and 4) develop a scale with two empirically reliable and valid independent dimensions. The 50 items of the initial FACES II were reduced to 30, with 2–3 items for each of the 14 content areas. The final 30-item scale contained 16 cohesion items and 14 adaptability items. The eight cohesion dimensions were Emotional Bonding, Family Boundaries, Coalitions, Time, Space, Friends, Decision Making, Interest, and Recreation. The six concepts for adaptability were Assertiveness, Leadership, Discipline, Negotiations, Roles, and Rules.

FACES III, developed in 1985, is a 20-item self-report instrument that was designed to improve the reliability, validity, and clinical utility of FACES II. Additional objectives of the revision involved 1) shortening the instrument to be administered under perceived and ideal conditions, 2) developing two empirically independent orthogonal dimensions, 3) eliminating negative items for scoring ease and to compare and establish norms, 4) rewriting the ideal version to make it more understandable, 5) developing items relevant for a variety of family forms, and 6) producing specific norms for adults across the life cycle. The 20-item scale has 10 cohesion items and 10 adaptability items. Two items correspond to each of the six concepts related to cohesion: emotional bonding, supportiveness, family boundaries, time, friends, and interest in recreation. There are correspondingly two items for each of the five concepts related to adaptability: leadership, control, discipline, roles, and rules.

The test authors report that FACES III is based on a normative sample of 2,453 adults across the life cycle, including 412 adolescents. It is unclear from the literature provided by the authors how they obtained their normative sample and to what extent the demographics of the sample represent the U.S. population.

The authors report that the inventory accounts for cultural and ethnic diversity, basing this claim on the hypothesis that families who operate at the extremes of the circumplex model will function well as long as all family members are satisfied. Family satisfaction is measured by having the members complete FACES III twice. The first time members respond to how they perceive their family. On the second administration, they respond based on how they would like their families to be ideally. FACES III uses a 5-point Likert response scale: 1 = almost never, 2 = once in a while, 3 = sometimes, 4 = frequently, and 5 = almost always. Responses to the items are recorded directly on the FACES III questionnaire.

The manual (Olson, Portner, & Lavee, 1985) does not specify administration guidelines, and it is not clear who should administer the test or how the instrument should be presented to the participants. The examiner will need to devise a format for presenting the materials to ensure consistency and clarity.

The authors do state that FACES III may be administered to either small groups (individuals, couples, families) or to large groups such as classes. Respondents read the statements and decide for each how frequently the described behavior occurs in their family on the scale from 1 (almost never) to 5 (almost always). The test may be administered to children over the age of 12 or persons with seventh-grade reading ability.

Upon completion of the FACES III, two scores are obtained, one for cohesion and one for adaptability. These may be computed as individual scores, couple scores, or family scores. The results are used then to classify the family into one of 16 family types, based on the relevant cutting points provided by the test authors. After locating the appropriate classification, the profile may further include identifying the family as *balanced, midrange,* or *extreme.* This classification refers to the family's level of functioning.

FACES III apparently can be duplicated for research purposes. Although the instrument is copyrighted, the test authors assure permission to reproduce it after prospective users submit a completed abstract of the proposed research. Upon completion of the study, a report and summary should be sent to the FACES III authors.

Practical Applications/Uses

FACES III has been used in clinical practice and research settings. Regarding the latter, it is noteworthy that much of the extant literature addresses validation of the instrument (e.g., Alexander, Johnson, & Carter, 1984; Edman, Cole, & Howard, 1990; Fristad, 1989; Hampson, Hulgus, & Beavers, 1991; Schmidt, Rosenthal, & Brown, 1988). Unfortunately, some researchers have assumed that the model upon which FACES III is predicated—the circumplex model—is itself valid.

When used in conjunction with scales assessing family communication, such as the Marital Communication scale of the ENRICH Inventory (Olson, Fournier, & Druckman, 1982), FACES III may have the potential for enhancing the development of therapeutic objectives for family treatment. It may prove valuable in therapeutic or educational settings where family functioning is at issue or where such functioning bears relevance to the treatment goal, such as with underachieving schoolchildren (e.g., Masselam, Marcus, & Stunkard, 1990). The scales' clinical utility appear to lie in the conceptual, rather than measurement, domain.

Mental health professionals from a variety of disciplines may be inclined to use FACES III, with the common denominator being an interest or specialization in family treatment. Clinicians such as marriage and family therapists, psychologists, and social workers would comprise some of the potential users. In research applications, persons from family studies programs or psychology or sociology departments may find the instrument workable for their settings.

As noted previously, the types of subjects to whom FACES III may be administered include members of families, approximately 12 years of age and older. The authors also encourage survey completion by as many family members as possible, though it is not clear why. No method of generating a legitimate family score is provided, as will be discussed in greater detail subsequently. FACES III is not appropriate for use with persons from linguistically diverse backgrounds or for those with limited English proficiency.

The authors developed a "Couple Version" from the FACES III items, and they include it in the FACES III manual. However, no psychometric data appear on the reliability and validity of this form. The Couple Version apparently was developed simply by modifying the original FACES III items through rewording. The legitimacy of this procedure is questionable, as it assumes that the original set of items function similarly for couples and families.

Anyone affiliated with family treatment or research can distribute and collect the questionnaire, as no special training is required to administer it. Although the manual does not specify standardized directions for administration, informal instructions follow logically from the obvious task at hand. In research applications, however, it is essential to develop a standard set of directions as well as a standard set of briefing and debriefing guidelines. As noted earlier, such guidelines would be useful in clinical applications as well. In either setting, the user must ensure that respondents understand the task and directions and should provide an opportunity for specific questions. Although not specified in the test manual, participants will need approximately 10 to 15 minutes to complete the survey.

Scoring is straightforward, consisting of simple addition of the ratings (numbers) given to odd- and even-numbered items for cohesion and adaptability, respectively. Scoring is done by hand, and each response form takes only about 5 minutes to score.

Although the interpretation of FACES III is based on objective scores, the user encounters several difficulties. The scales are designed to measure family functioning, though the data obtained come from individual family members. Obtaining accurate and consistent information about units of people is an ongoing issue in family studies/family therapy research. The authors of FACES III confront the same difficulty. Although a family or couple score may be obtained by calculating the mean, the test authors recognize the many limitations of mean scores so obtained. They also provide a formula for calculating a discrepancy score; however, it is unclear how this formula more accurately provides a family portrait representing all the members. The test authors report low correlations among family members' reports on the scales, which further complicates obtaining a representative and accurate profile. They further state that the FACES III has been adapted for use by clinicians. But again, correlations between the scores of clinicians and family members are low, making difficult the interpretation of "actual" family functioning.

A recent evaluation of FACES III (Green, Harris, Forte, & Robinson, 1991) has raised questions about the validity of the Adaptability scale and the curvilinear nature of the Cohesion scale. Inconsistent findings among research studies utilizing FACES III further contributes to the difficulty in interpreting the results.

The examiner using FACES III should be trained in family therapy or family studies. Clinicians, researchers, or academics knowledgeable in family dynamics would be capable of properly interpreting the scales' results.

Technical Aspects

Overall, information provided regarding the scales' psychometric properties and normative sample is extremely limited. Further, some of the information presented is misleading or incomplete. The burden of validation, particularly concurrent validation, has been largely left to other researchers and those in practice (e.g., Green et al., 1991).

Regarding construct validity, the test authors discuss a factor analytic procedure implemented during the development of the previous edition of the scales. Thus, the item pool for FACES II (consisting of 50 items, 30 of which were retained in the final version of FACES II) was administered to some 2,400 individuals. A factor analysis of the 30 items retained to form FACES II was conducted, limiting the factors to two. The results for 20 of the items—those used to form FACES III— are presented as Table 4 of the test manual, entitled "Factor Analysis of FACES III" (Olson et al., 1985, p. 21). The factor loadings for Cohesion are relatively clean, with all items loading at least .39 (.50 on average) on the Cohesion factor, and no item loading more than – .16 on the second factor, Adaptability. The factor loadings for Adaptability, however, are considerably lower, averaging only .38 and extending no higher than .48. As well, several items load at least – .20 on the other factor, Cohesion. These values, however, appear to represent an improvement over earlier versions of the instrument (i.e., FACES II), in which the Adaptability factor retained items with factor loadings as low as .10.

The table also lists the correlation coefficients of individual items and their respective factor. The latter information, sometimes termed the *item/total scale correlation*, represents a form of content validation. For the Cohesion factor, these values range from .51 to .74, with a mean value of .60; the values for the Adaptability factor are lower, ranging from .42 to .56 and averaging .48. The test authors refer to these levels as high correlations, when "moderate" would more aptly apply.

The authors do not address content validity specifically, although considerable attention to these matters appears needed. Several items on the Adaptability factor appear to tap hierarchical dimensions of the family, rather than "adaptability" per se. Although the authors cite relevant literature in justifying the use of the Cohesion and Adaptability dimensions, they give no information about the procedures used in developing the item pool or about the assessment of the items' suitability for use on the scales.

Scant attention is given to FACES III reliability, although the test manual does present some reliability information on earlier versions of the scales. For FACES III, internal consistency reliabilities are addressed specifically for Cohesion ($r = .77$), Adaptability ($r = .62$) and the total scale ($r = .69$), using a sample size of 2,412. The test authors recognize the lack of congruence between ratings made by individual family members or between family members and clinicians. They note that low to moderate correlations occur for a variety of scales of this sort, with average coefficients hovering in the .40s. Some of the FACES III correlations fall in this range, but many are well below it, with values as low as .13 and .21 reported for mother/adolescent and father/adolescent pairs, respectively, on the Adaptability scale. Despite levels of statistical significance and the fate of other scales, these values are meaningless. The test authors suggest that these findings point up the need to obtain data from as many family members as possible. Again, the reasoning behind this recommendation is unclear, as to do so would seem merely to neutralize disparate ratings rather than improve the viability of results.

A table in the test manual lists the norms and cutting points for FACES III. Very little information is provided regarding the "national survey" apparently used to develop the norms. The total number in this sample is given as 2,453, which is slightly higher than the total sample size given earlier (2,412). It is not clear whether these two samples are one and the same.

Critique

Several problems exist with the FACES III, such as the extent to which the scales are valid (e.g., Green et al., 1991). The test authors have responded to recent inconclusive research regarding the validity of the Adaptability scale by relabeling the scale as "flexibility" (Olson, 1991a, 1991b). Overall the myriad revisions and reformulations reflect a poorly developed instrument. Psychometric properties were not addressed adequately during the original test development, although the test authors do appear to be attempting to correct such deficiencies as field-based researchers inform them of these issues. Along similar lines, research has often cut both ways, attempting validation of FACES III and the circumplex model in a single undertaking. The model and the instrument are often used interchangeably.

A particularly troublesome weakness is the incomplete and sometimes misleading presentation of information relating to technical aspects, such as test development specification, development of the original pool of items, and the psychometric rationale for reducing the length of the original scale. Further, disclosure of norming procedures is essential, as is information regarding the characteristics of the individuals comprising the standardization sample. Average test users will not be able to determine the appropriateness of the instrument for their purposes from the information provided. There are many other departures from acceptable testing standards as specified in the *Standards for Educational and Psychological Testing* (American Educational Research Association, American Psychological Association, & National Council on Measurement in Education, 1985).

Regarding conceptual and theoretical issues, the Adaptability scale appears to measure the power structure within families rather than the members' ability to change. The Adaptability scale may in fact have more utility as a measure of constructs from the structural and strategic schools of family therapy rather than as a measure of the circumplex model. Traditional tests of validity might greatly benefit the further development of the Adaptability scale. The questions raised about the curvilinear nature of the Cohesion scale further complicate the use and interpretation of FACES III. Again, further tests of validity might be of benefit in the development of the Cohesion scale.

Although the instrument reportedly has been adapted for use by clinicians, the test authors provide little information about the validity and reliability of the revised scales except to report low correlations between the scores of clinicians and the scores of family members. For the scale to assist clinicians in their therapeutic work with families, greater elaboration is needed.

In the family studies and family therapy fields, few instruments adequately test systemic concepts. That FACES III attempts to do so is itself laudable. It remains an issue, however, how this or any instrument can produce a profile of family functioning when the respondents are individual family members.

References

Alexander, B.B., Johnson, S.B., & Carter, R.L. (1984). A psychometric study of the Family Adaptability and Cohesion Evaluation Scales. *Journal of Abnormal Child Psychology, 12,* 199–208.

American Educational Research Association, American Psychological Association, & National Council on Measurement in Education. (1985). *Standards for educational and psychological testing.* Washington, DC: American Psychological Association.

Edman, S.O., Cole, D.A., & Howard, G.S. (1990). Convergent and discriminant validity of FACES-III: Family adaptability and cohesion. *Family Process, 29,* 95–103.

Fristad, M.A. (1989). A comparison of the McMaster and circumplex family assessment instruments. *Journal of Marital and Family Therapy, 15,* 259–269.

Green, R.G., Harris, R.N., Jr., Forte, J.A., & Robinson, M. (1991). Evaluating FACES III and the circumplex model: 2,440 families. *Family Process, 30,* 55–73.

Hampson, R.B., Hulgus, Y.F., & Beavers, W.R. (1991). Comparisons of self-report measures of the Beavers systems model and Olson's circumplex model. *Journal of Family Psychology, 4,* 326–340.

Masselam, V.S., Marcus, R.F., & Stunkard, C.L. (1990). Parent-adolescent communication, family functioning, and school performance. *Adolescence, 25,* 725–737.

Olson, D.H. (1991a). Commentary: Three-dimensional (3-D) circumplex model and revised scoring of FACES III. *Family Process, 30,* 74–79.

Olson, D.H. (1991b, November). *Three-dimensional (3-D) circumplex model: Theoretical and methodological advances.* Paper presented at the NCFR Theory Construction and Research Methodology Workshop, Denver.

Olson, D.H., Fournier, D.G., & Druckman, J.M. (1982). *ENRICH.* Minneapolis, MN: PRE-PARE-ENRICH.

Olson, D.H., Portner, J., & Lavee, Y. (1985). *FACES III: Family Adaptability and Cohesion Evaluation Scales.* St. Paul, MN: Family Social Science, University of Minnesota.

Schmidt, K.D., Rosenthal, S.L., & Brown, E.D. (1988). A comparison of self-report measures of two family dimensions: Control and cohesion. *American Journal of Family Therapy, 16,* 73–77.

Ron D. Cambias, Jr., Psy.D.
Staff Psychologist, Children's Hospital, New Orleans, Louisiana.

FAMILY APPERCEPTION TEST

Wayne M. Sotile, Alexander Julian III, Susan E. Henry, and Mary O. Sotile. Los Angeles, California: Western Psychological Services.

Introduction

The Family Apperception Test (FAT; Sotile, Julian, Henry, & Sotile, 1991) is a thematic apperceptive technique "designed specifically to evoke associative material that may be evaluated in terms of family systems variables" (Sotile et al., 1991, p. 1). The FAT follows in a long succession of thematic apperception tests, most notably the Thematic Apperception Test (TAT; Murray, 1971) and the Children's Apperception Test (CAT; Bellak & Bellak, 1980). The FAT differentiates itself from other apperceptive techniques through its focus as a family assessment instrument using single subjects.

The first author, Wayne Sotile, Ph.D., obtained his doctorate in clinical psychology from the University of South Carolina and completed his medical psychology training at Duke University Medical Center in Durham, North Carolina. He is a former member of the faculty of the Bowman Gray School of Medicine. For the past 14 years, he has co-directed Sotile Psychological Associates and has served as director of psychological services for the Wake Forest Cardiac Rehabilitation Program. The author of numerous professional papers and publications, he recently has published *Heart Illness and Intimacy: How Caring Relationships Aid Recovery* (Sotile, 1992).

Alexander Julian III, Ph.D., is a clinical and consulting psychologist in Charlotte, North Carolina. He earned a degree in clinical psychology from the University of South Carolina in 1979 and has a background of working with troubled youngsters and families in both mental health and private psychiatric settings. At present, he is a consultant at several psychiatric facilities and maintains a private practice that emphasizes assessment and treatment of children, adolescents, and dysfunctional families. He is the principal developer of the Family Apperception Test (Julian, 1985) and the educational videotape "Teaching Children Responsibility" (Julian, 1990). In addition, he has invented and marketed a number of educational game products for children, including the "WanderMap" (c. 1986) and the board game "Master of the Mountain" (c. 1991).

Susan Henry, Ph.D., earned her doctorate in school psychology from the University of South Carolina in 1978. Presently she is a school psychologist employed as director of assessment in the Charlotte-Mecklenburg School System in North Carolina. She also maintains a private practice and has held previous positions as a pupil assessment specialist, program specialist for a behaviorally-emotionally handicapped program, and student services specialist. She has published and presented on a number of diverse topics, including testing in the school system, cross-cultural issues, and other school-related topics.

Mary Owen Sotile, M.A., graduated from the University of North Carolina and obtained a master's degree in counseling from Wake Forest University. For the past 14 years, she has co-directed, along with her husband, Sotile Psychological Associates, a multifaceted private practice specializing in medical psychology and marital and family therapy. She and her spouse frequently collaborate in both research and clinical projects regarding various aspects of health psychology.

Unfortunately, no information regarding the development of the FAT stimulus cards or scoring system is presented in the manual. Such information ideally should appear in any future editions of the FAT. No other forms of the test have been developed (e.g., for Spanish-speaking subjects, specific minority groups, etc.).

The theoretical rationale of the FAT derives from general family systems theory; no individual school of family systems thinking predominates. The test authors utilized the following four systemic variables as guidelines for developing the FAT: conflict, conflict resolution, limit setting, and relationship patterns. Relationship patterns encompass the quality of relationships (ally vs. stressor), boundaries, and dysfunctional circularity (i.e., a repetitive sequence of maladaptive relating among family members). The FAT departs from a more individual, psychodynamic focus through assessment of family systems variables from single subjects.

The FAT kit consists of the manual, stimulus cards, and 100 scoring sheets. A relatively brief manual covers the test's purpose and description, testing procedure, theoretical rationale, scoring, reliability and validity, guidelines for interpretation, and four case examples.

Twenty-one 8½" × 11" black-and-white charcoal drawings make up the FAT stimulus pictures. All pictures may be given to a particular subject and are not grouped by sex. The test pictures portray scenes concerning family life. For example, Card 1 shows a dinner scene, with a man, a woman, and three children seated around a table. The adults are conversing, and one child is eating. This card pulls for conflict within the family and issues regarding relationships and boundaries.

Each scoring sheet consists of a section for recording brief demographic information (i.e., the subject's name or I.D. number, date administered, age, and position in family), with rows of scoring categories (outlined below) and columns pertaining to each of the 21 stimulus cards. Each scoring category has a corresponding circle pertaining to a particular stimulus card, which is to be darkened if that scoring category applies to the response given to the particular card. Use of such scoring sheets paves the way for possible future computer-scoring of FAT protocols. In the right-hand margin are spaces for keeping track of scores for each of the scoring categories. A Total Dysfunctional Index also can be computed by adding scores from categories suggestive of family dysfunction. However, due to lack of standardization, this index possesses little meaning at the present time.

The FAT scoring system addresses the following major scoring categories:

1. *Obvious Conflict:* the presence of conflict in stories, encompassing a) family conflict, b) marital conflict, c) other conflict, and d) absence of conflict.

2. *Conflict Resolution:* how conflict is resolved, including a) positive resolution and b) negative or no resolution.

3. *Limit Setting:* how limits are set by parents and subsequently obeyed by children, including a) appropriate/compliance (i.e., parents set appropriate limits and children comply with them), b) appropriate/noncompliance, c) inappropriate/compliance, and d) inappropriate/noncompliance.

4. *Quality of Relationships:* the levels of stress between family members, viewing the following as either allies or stressors: a) mothers, b) fathers, c) siblings, d) spouses, and e) others.

5. *Boundaries:* entails consideration of the following factors: a) enmeshment, b) disengagement, c) mother/child coalition, d) father/child coalition, e) other adult/child coalition, f) open system, and g) closed system.

6. *Dysfunctional Circularity:* repetitive unresolved events within the family or repetitive themes to more than one stimulus card.

7. *Abusive Remarks:* remarks involving a) physical abuse, b) sexual abuse, c) neglect/abandonment, and d) substance abuse.

8. *Unusual Responses:* distortions of figures, themes, emotions; denial of obvious aspects of a picture; illogical, primary process thinking; severe injury or death of a central character; or homicidal/suicidal themes.

9. *Refusal:* no response, or incomplete response, to a particular card.

An additional optional scoring category is described as follows:

10. *Emotional Tone:* the presence of one or more of the following emotions in a particular story: a) sadness/depression, b) anger/hostility, c) anxiety/fear, d) happiness/satisfaction, and e) other emotions (e.g., shame, guilt, jealousy).

Practical Applications/Uses

The FAT is most appropriate for use by clinicians in the evaluation of children and adolescents regarding emotional/adjustment problems, especially as these problems may relate to family systems variables. Although research on the instrument's psychometric properties was conducted with subjects aged 6 to 15, the test authors report that the FAT is clinically useful with older adolescents and adults as well (Sotile et al., 1991). Unfortunately, no research to date has been conducted to demonstrate the usefulness of the FAT with these latter populations.

Although several FAT stimulus cards appear to portray black figures, most scenes comprise white, middle-class characters. Therefore, the FAT's ability to elicit identification between minority subjects and the stimulus picture figures remains questionable until proven otherwise by research. Unless a test presents stimulus picture figures with which subjects can identify, the ability of the subject to identify with those pictures may be compromised (Lubin & Wilson, 1956). Furthermore, such lack of cultural relevance may decrease the verbal fluency of minority subjects (Costantino & Malgady, 1983), thereby calling the validity of the test into question (Anderson & Anderson, 1955).

The FAT is administered individually in any quiet, well-lit room free from distractions. Although not stated in the manual, subjects presumably should have no acute sensory or neuropsychological deficits. The manual states that responses should be recorded verbatim on a separate piece of paper. Although recording by hand may save time, this method is less efficient than audiotaping, as demonstrated by TAT research comparing machine recording with recording by hand

(Baty & Dreger, 1975). Also, recording by hand may interfere both with building rapport and with the flow of responses should the examiner need to interrupt the subject in order to clarify or repeat what the subject had said.

The examiner begins administration with a set of instructions similar to those given with the TAT (i.e., encouraging the subject to tell a story), with certain prescribed inquiries should the subject give an incomplete story. The examiner may choose to administer the entire set of 21 cards if the formal FAT scoring system is to be utilized or an abbreviated set for informal scoring. If opting for the formal scoring system, all 21 cards should be presented in numerical sequence. Preliminary research has demonstrated that several FAT cards (5, 7, 11, and 12) may prove to be a suitable brief form due to their ability to discriminate between clinic and nonclinic subjects (Eaton, 1988; Lundquist, 1987). However, more research is needed to establish further the psychometric properties of an FAT short form.

While the manual states that 30 to 35 minutes is sufficient for administering the FAT, this seems overly optimistic. A more realistic period would fall in the neighborhood of 45 to 60 minutes.

Scoring may be conducted through the formal FAT scoring system or through informal analysis of test data. Use of the formal system entails perusing each story and then darkening a circle on the answer sheet corresponding to each of the scoring system categories listed above (e.g., Family Conflict, Positive Resolution, etc.). For example, if a subject tells a story about a son who argues about not doing his homework and his parents respond by telling him to go to his room, and the son subsequently runs away, the user would mark the following scoring categories: Family Conflict, Negative Resolution, Appropriate/Noncompliance, Mother as Stressor, Father as Stressor, and Anger/Hostility. Scoring that involves a determination of the presence versus absence of specific categories greatly diminishes scoring subjectivity and likely increases the interrater (or scorer) reliability of the FAT.

One possible source of confusion arises in scoring multiple categories. Some specific categories automatically are scored consequent to the scoring of another category. For example, if Other Conflict is scored, the Other Stressor category also is scored. Conversely, when certain categories are scored, no score is entered for others. For example, if Other Conflict is scored, no score is entered for the Limit Setting category. Scoring multiple categories may led to some confusion but is almost inevitable when scoring projective test data. Sums of scores can be computed for each scoring category and for the Total Dysfunctional Index when using the formal FAT scoring system.

The manual clearly presents the scoring instructions as well as examples to illustrate scoring for each category. Depending on the complexity and length of responses, the estimated time required for scoring the FAT would range between 20 and 60 minutes. Obviously, proficiency in scoring would increase with experience and affect the length of time required.

Interpretation involves either clinical judgment or use of the FAT formal scoring system. However, both forms invite criticism in an age when the trend with regard to apperceptive techniques has headed toward more objective scoring methods. As neither clinical intuition nor the formal scoring system are based on an objective process using normative data (at least as yet for the formal system), examiners leave themselves open to the criticism that they may misinterpret stories told to stimulus pictures.

The manual provides guidelines for interpretating subject protocols through use of the FAT scoring system. An outline provided in the manual covers the following broad areas: a) the validity of the protocol, b) the extent of conflict, c) the location of conflict, d) the typical family process involved, e) the quality of relationships in the family, f) the systemic aspects of family relationships, g) the indications of extreme maladjustment, and h) the particular story themes that may provide clinically useful material (Sotile et al., pp. 21–22). For each part of the outline, the test authors make suggestions regarding specific categories to examine for analysis. Through the use of such an outline, one can formulate hypotheses concerning the subject's family system.

Informal analysis of FAT protocols includes using general concepts from the scoring system and/or using preliminary descriptions of frequent card themes that are listed in the manual as a guide to interpretation (p. 22). This approach also may be implemented when using selected portions of the FAT as a brief assessment or as a strategic means for engendering therapeutic discussion.

Interpretation of the FAT is relatively complex and would require a clinician with at least basic knowledge of family theory in addition to training in child/adolescent psychopathology and psychological testing on at least a master's degree level. Interpretation, as with any test, should not take place in isolation but in comparison with data from other sources, such as clinical interviews and behavior rating scales. Until standardization occurs, the formal FAT scoring system acts simply as guidelines for interpretation, not as objective indices per se.

Technical Aspects

The reliability and validity of the FAT were assessed through five master's theses (Buchanan, 1987; DeChatelet, 1988; Eaton, 1988; Gingrich, 1987; Lundquist, 1987). These theses each were submitted through the Master of Education in Counseling program at Wake Forest University. All five studies utilized a pool of data comprising 104 clinical subjects from two South Carolina State Department of Mental Health clinics and 83 nonclinical subjects obtained through solicitations of civic groups and teachers.

Interrater (scorer) reliability was assessed by two separate studies. Gingrich (1987) compared two scorers' assessments of 22 clinic and 22 nonclinic subjects' protocols using a preliminary version of the FAT scoring system. Using Cohen's kappa coefficient for determining agreement between raters, statistically significant agreement was found for almost every scoring category regardless of group membership (i.e., clinic vs. nonclinic). Moderate to substantial agreement was found on 7 of the 10 categories tested. This study resulted in modifications of the FAT scoring system that then led to the current version.

In a second study, DeChatelet (1988) compared the amount of agreement of three raters' assessments of 44 clinic and 39 nonclinic subjects' protocols. A statistical modification of Cohen's kappa was employed, allowing measure of agreement among more than two raters. Results indicated statistically significant agreement for all nine major FAT scoring categories. Moderate to substantial agreement was found on 6 of the 9 categories. Thus, both studies lend support for the scorer reliability of the FAT.

No other reliability studies to date have been conducted with the FAT. Suggestions for improving the reliability of this instrument are as follows: As pointed out in the manual (p. 16), the DeChatelet (1988) study could be improved by differentiating interrater reliability for clinic versus nonclinic protocols. The interrater reliability also could be improved by assessing the discrete scoring categories composing the nine major scoring categories (e.g., the Positive Resolution and Negative/No Resolution categories of the Conflict Resolution major category). Such a study obviously would require a great number of subjects to ensure a sufficient number of responses to submit for analysis. Next, as also mentioned in the test manual (p. 16), the test-retest reliability of the FAT has not been assessed. Although test-retest reliability for personality instruments, especially using long intervals of time, may be confounded by true changes in psychological functioning, such reliability needs to be established to ensure the accuracy of the instrument. Finally, a measure of internal consistency, using Kuder-Richardson formula 20, ideally would be established.

The validity of the FAT was assessed through three separate studies. In the first study, Lundquist (1987) compared the frequency of conflict responses to the FAT between clinic and nonclinic populations. Twenty-two clinic and 22 nonclinic subjects were matched according to sex, race, age, and grade. A chi square analysis of subjects' responses revealed that the clinic group responded with a greater number of conflict responses than the nonclinic group, thus supporting the ability of the FAT to discriminate between clinic and nonclinic samples. Furthermore, a chi square analysis identified four individual cards (5, 7, 11, and 12) that differentiated significantly between clinic and nonclinic groups. This study paved the way for a later study of the validity of a FAT shortened form (Eaton, 1988).

In the second study, Buchanan (1987) examined the construct validity of the FAT by comparing protocols from 24 clinic and 24 nonclinic subjects. Subjects were matched according to age, grade, race, and sex. The clinic group included subjects whose primary psychiatric diagnoses involved various adjustment disorders, conduct disorders, oppositional disorder, and parent-child problems. A multivariate analysis of variance comparing clinic and nonclinic protocols across the 34 discrete scoring variables of the FAT identified 11 comparisons significant at or beyond the .05 level. Four of the 34 categories could not be included for analysis due to the low frequency of responses. All 11 comparisons had higher means in the direction expected; for example, the clinic sample demonstrated higher mean scores for family conflict, viewing parents as stressors, and disengagement. This study demonstrated the ability of the FAT to differentiate between psychiatric groups undergoing treatment from nonclinical groups not undergoing treatment.

Finally, in the third study, Eaton (1988) examined the construct validity of the FAT, the shortened version, and the Total Dysfunctional Index. Eaton basically expanded upon the Buchanan (1987) study by comparing the protocols of 28 clinic and 28 nonclinic subjects using a refined, final version of the FAT scoring system. Subjects were matched according to sex, age, race, and parental marital status. The clinic group included children and adolescents with diagnoses of adjustment disorder, conduct disorder, oppositional disorder, attention deficit disorder with hyperactivity, and parent-child problems. Due to the low frequency of responses for some scoring categories, Eaton (1988) combined several scoring categories, resulting in a total of 30 categories for examination.

A multivariate analysis of variance of the group means for each scoring category yielded 19 statistically significant between-group comparisons (three scoring categories were disregarded for analysis due to too few responses). Of the 19 significant comparisons, all group means fell in the expected direction (i.e., for scoring categories suggesting greater dysfunction, clinic group means were higher; for scoring categories suggesting greater functionality, nonclinic group means were higher). These results again provide evidence of the FAT's ability to discriminate between clinic and nonclinic groups.

Eaton (1988) also examined the ability of the shortened version of the FAT (cards 5, 7, 11, and 12) to differentiate clinic and nonclinic samples. Due to the few number of responses for some scoring categories, only 20 scoring categories were subjected to analysis. A multivariate analysis of variance yielded eight significant between-group comparisons. Again, group means fell in the expected direction, thus lending tentative support for the validity of a FAT short form.

Finally, Eaton (1988) examined the validity of the Total Dysfunctional Index. For both the FAT short and long forms, clinic groups produced significantly higher scores than the nonclinic groups (long form: $F = 37.87$, $p < .001$; short form: $F = 24.37$, $p < .001$). These results provide support for the Total Dysfunctional Index as a measure of overall family dysfunction.

Suggestions for further assessing the FAT's validity include those presented in the manual (p. 20): using a greater number of subjects, matching subjects according to intelligence level, and ascertaining validity for scoring categories that have not yielded sufficient numbers of responses for analysis. Also, despite the fact that the domains addressed through the FAT's scoring system represent key concepts of family theory, no formal content validation procedures were employed. This point is a minor criticism, however, given the "face validity" of the scoring domains and preliminary support for the FAT's construct validity. Further studies supporting the construct validity of the FAT may make the lack of any preliminary content validation study a moot point. Once standardization of the instrument is completed, other suggestions would include criterion-related validity studies using other apperception or family assessment instruments (e.g., the Roberts Apperception Test for Children [RATC; McArthur & Roberts, 1982], the Family Environment Scale [Moos & Moos, 1986], or the former Beavers-Timberlawn Family Evaluation Scale [B-TFES; Lewis, Beavers, Gossett, & Phillips, 1976]). Muha (1977) examined the efficacy of the Roberts Apperception Test and the B-TFES in discriminating between clinic and nonclinic families, demonstrating that both instruments were individually effective in such a discrimination and even more effective when combined, as shown by discriminant function analyses. One RATC measure, Reliance on Others, also was found to correlate significantly with 12 of the B-TFES scales. This study serves as an example of the kind of criterion-validation research that investigators might conduct using the FAT.

Further suggestions include validation studies with various minority populations and populations whose primary language is other than English (e.g., blacks,

Hispanics, Asians, etc.). Also, validation studies with older adolescents and adults will be necessary to support the test authors' claims that the FAT has been found clinically useful with these populations. Finally, a study on the relative effectiveness of the FAT and other apperception tests in discriminating clinical from nonclinical samples is recommended. Such research would demonstrate the relative effectiveness of the FAT with regard to other available instruments.

Critique

The Family Apperception Test addresses the need to integrate the assessment of family systems variables into therapists' work with individual clients. The richness and complexity of factors influencing behavior and maladjustment are lost when one considers only individual or intrapsychic processes. The FAT distinguishes itself as the first apperceptive technique designed to assess family systems variables via single subjects.

Despite its promise, the FAT is currently in the early stages of development. The test authors hope that publication at this point will foster research and lead to the instrument's eventual standardization (W.M. Sotile, personal communication, April 13, 1992). The strengths of the FAT include a scoring system based on key concepts from family systems theory, promising early evidence for reliability and validity, clinical experience suggesting utility with adults as well as with children, and preliminary support for a shortened version and dysfunctional index that discriminate clinical from nonclinical samples. The test's limitations include a lack of evidence for clinical utility with minority populations and those whose primary language is other than English, a lack of normative data (which results in examiners' subjective interpretation of test data, unfortunately common for projective instruments), and a need for further research regarding its psychometric properties (especially criterion-related validation studies, once standardization of the FAT takes place).

The 1980s witnessed the publication of thematic apperception tests that approximated conventional psychometric standards (American Educational Research Association, American Psychological Association, & National Council on Measurement in Education, 1985). Tests like the Michigan Picture Test–Revised (MPT; Hutt, 1980), Roberts Apperception Test for Children (RATC; McArthur & Roberts, 1982), Tell-Me-A-Story (TEMAS; Costantino, Malgady, & Rogler, 1988), and the Children's Apperceptive Story-Telling Test (CAST; Schneider, 1989) were developed and met at least minimum standards of reliability, validity, and standardization. The development of such psychometrically sound apperceptive techniques marked a new era and perhaps the death knell for the less psychometrically robust TAT and CAT.

Although now in its infancy, the FAT promises to follow in the footsteps of these newer instruments. However, the present lack of normative data diminishes seriously clinicians' prudent use of the test. In the meantime, only a subjective analysis of test data can be conducted, albeit with family systems guidelines. Such subjective interpretation, though, leaves the examiner open to criticism that he or she may be projecting as much as the subject. Therefore, the FAT can be recommended only for research purposes until standardization takes place.

References

This list includes text citations and suggested additional reading.

American Educational Research Association, American Psychological Association, & National Council on Measurement in Education. (1985). *Standards for educational and psychological testing.* Washington, DC: American Psychological Association.

Anderson, H., & Anderson, G. (1955). *An introduction to projective techniques.* Englewood Cliffs, NJ: Prentice-Hall.

Baty, M.A., & Dreger, R.M. (1975). A comparison of three methods to record TAT protocols. *Journal of Clinical Psychology, 31*(2), 348.

Bellak, L., & Bellak, S. (1980). *A manual for the Children's Apperception Test* (7th ed.). Larchmont, NY: C.P.S.

Bowen, M. (1978). *Family therapy in clinical practice.* New York: Aronson.

Buchanan, S.M. (1987). *A comparison of clinic and non-clinic children on the Family Apperception Test.* Unpublished master's thesis, Wake Forest University, Winston-Salem, NC.

Cambias, R.D., Jr., Killian, G.A., & Faust, J. (1992a). Children's Apperceptive Story-Telling Test (CAST). In D.J. Keyser & R.C. Sweetland (Eds.), *Test critiques* (Vol. IX, pp. 66–79). Austin, TX: PRO-ED.

Cambias, R.D., Jr., Killian, G.A., & Faust, J. (1992b). Roberts Apperception Test for Children: Supplementary Test Pictures for Black Children. In D.J. Keyser & R.C. Sweetland (Eds.), *Test critiques* (Vol. IX, pp. 431–437). Austin, TX: PRO-ED.

Cambias, R.D., Jr., Killian, G.A., & Faust, J. (1992c). TEMAS (Tell-Me-A-Story). In D.J. Keyser & R.C. Sweetland (Eds.), *Test critiques* (Vol. IX, pp. 545–560). Austin, TX: PRO-ED.

Costantino, G., & Malgady, R. (1983). Verbal fluency of Hispanic, black and white children on TAT and TEMAS, a new thematic apperception test. *Hispanic Journal of Behavioral Sciences, 5*(2), 199–206.

Costantino, G., Malgady, R., & Rogler, L.H. (1988). *TEMAS (Tell-Me-A-Story) manual.* Los Angeles: Western Psychological Services.

DeChatelet, M.P. (1988). *A study of the interrater reliability of the Family Apperception Test utilizing three raters.* Unpublished master's thesis, Wake Forest University, Winston-Salem, NC.

Eaton, C.B. (1988). *The Family Apperception Test: A study of the construct validity of a long and short form.* Unpublished master's thesis, Wake Forest University, Winston-Salem, NC.

French, J. (1985). Michigan Picture Test–Revised. In D.J. Keyser & R.C. Sweetland (Eds.), *Test critiques* (Vol. III, pp. 447–453). Austin, TX: PRO-ED.

Friedrich, W.N. (1984). Roberts Apperception Test for Children. In D.J. Keyser & R.C. Sweetland (Eds.), *Test critiques* (Vol. I, pp. 543–548). Austin, TX: PRO-ED.

Gingrich, N.E. (1987). *Interrater reliability of the Family Apperception Test: A preliminary study.* Unpublished master's thesis, Wake Forest University, Winston-Salem, NC.

Guerin, P.J., Jr. (Ed.). (1976). *Family therapy: Theory and practice.* New York: Gardner.

Haley, J. (1978). *Problem-solving therapy.* San Francisco: Jossey-Bass.

Hutt, M.L. (1980). *The Michigan Picture Test–Revised.* New York: Grune & Stratton.

Julian, A. (1985). *Family Apperception Test: Test pictures.* Los Angeles: Western Psychological Services.

Julian, A. (Producer/Director). (1990). *Teaching children responsibility* [Film]. Charlotte, NC: Feedback Services.

Kline, P. (1986). *A handbook of test construction: Introduction to psychometric design.* New York: Methuen.

Lewis, J.M., Beavers, W.R., Gossett, J.T., & Phillips, V.A. (1976). *No single thread: Psychological health in family systems.* New York: Brunner/Mazel.

Lubin, N.M., & Wilson, M.O. (1956). Picture test identification as a function of "reality" (color) and similarity of picture to subject. *Journal of General Psychology, 54,* 31–38.

Lundquist, A. (1987). *A projective approach to family systems assessment: A preliminary validity study of the Family Apperception Test.* Unpublished master's thesis, Wake Forest University, Winston-Salem, NC.

McArthur, D.S., & Roberts, G.E. (1982). *Roberts Apperception Test for Children manual.* Los Angeles: Western Psychological Services.

Minuchin, S. (1974). *Families and family therapy.* Cambridge, MA: Harvard University Press.

Moos, R.H., & Moos, B.S. (1986). *Family Environment Scale manual* (2nd ed.). Palo Alto, CA: Consulting Psychologists Press.

Muha, T.W. (1977). *A validation study of the Roberts Apperception Test as a measure of psychological dysfunction in families.* Unpublished doctoral dissertation, California School of Professional Psychology, Los Angeles.

Murray, H.A. (1971). *Thematic Apperception Test manual.* Cambridge, MA: Harvard University Press.

Obrzut, J., & Cummings, J. (1983). The projective approach to personality assessment: An analysis of thematic picture techniques. *School Psychology Review, 12*(4), 414–420.

Schneider, M. (1989). *CAST: Children's Apperceptive Story-Telling Test manual.* Austin, TX: PRO-ED.

Sotile, W.M. (1992). *Heart illness and intimacy: How caring relationships aid recovery.* Baltimore: Johns Hopkins University Press.

Sotile, W.M., Julian, A., III, Henry, S.E., & Sotile, M.O. (1991). *Family Apperception Test manual.* Los Angeles: Western Psychological Services.

Von Bertalanffy, L. (1968). *General systems theory.* New York: Braziller.

Karen M. O'Brien, Ph.D.
Assistant Professor of Counseling Psychology, University of Kansas, Lawrence, Kansas.

Steven D. Brown, Ph.D.
Professor of Counseling Psychology, Loyola University, Chicago, Illinois.

FAMILY INVENTORY OF LIFE EVENTS AND CHANGES

Hamilton I. McCubbin, Joan Patterson, and Lance Wilson. St. Paul, Minnesota: Family Social Science, University of Minnesota.

Introduction

The Family Inventory of Life Events and Changes (FILE) assesses the cumulative stressors and life changes experienced by members of a family in order to provide an index of family stress and to identify families vulnerable to crisis. The FILE is also described as having predictive uses; namely, to predict the psychological and physical health status of family members. In general, it was designed to assist professionals in the assessment of the family's vulnerability and resources and to aid in the identification of appropriate interventions (McCubbin & Patterson, 1983, 1991).

The theoretical basis for the development of the instrument has its roots in psychobiological stress research and family stress theory. McCubbin and Patterson (1983) incorporated the construct of "pile-up" (multiple life changes within a short period of time) in Hill's (1958) ABCX family crisis model. Hill's model proposed that "A (the stressor event) interacting with B (the family's crisis-meeting resources) interacting with C (the definition the family makes of the event) produces X (the crisis)" (Hill, 1958, p. 141). McCubbin and Patterson expanded this model to a double ABCX model (aABCX), suggesting that in addition to examining the stressor event, the cumulative stressors experienced by members of the family during the past year should be considered because cumulative stress may increase a family's vulnerability to a single stressful event.

The first version of this inventory (FILE, Form A) was developed by McCubbin, Wilson, and Patterson in 1979 and used both with families who experienced a chronic illness among one of their members and with rural families. The 171 items on the inventory were chosen to reflect substantive changes (either positive or negative) experienced by families that would require adjustment in typical family interactions. Clinical experience and research with families and individual life changes inventories provided direction for the selection of the items. Further, items that reflected life events typically experienced by families at different stages in the family life cycle were included. Finally, the items were categorized as follows: family development, work, management, health, finances, social activities, law, and extended family relationships.

The initial version of the FILE was reduced to a 71-item questionnaire (Form C) in 1981 by McCubbin, Patterson, and Wilson in order to facilitate use of the inventory in applied settings. A factor analysis of these items with families who had a chronically ill child resulted in nine subscales: Intra-Family Strains, Marital Strains, Pregnancy and Childbearing Strains, Finance and Business Strains, Work-Family Transitions and Strains, Illness and Family Care Strains, Family Losses, Family Transitions In and Out, and Family Legal Strains. Several infrequently occurring items that did not load on any scale were retained for conceptual reasons.

Thus, the most recent version of the FILE is a 71-item self-report inventory that lists normative and nonnormative events (positive and negative changes) that the family may have experienced. The authors designed the inventory for completion by one or both adult members of the family independently. However, depending on the purpose of the testing, couples may complete the measure collaboratively. The respondent determines which (if any) of the 71 events listed occurred to any family member or the family as a whole during the last year and responds by checking "yes" or "no." The inventory takes approximately 10 minutes to complete and is appropriate for individuals with average reading abilities (McCubbin & Patterson, 1991).

Practical Applications/Uses

The FILE is intended to provide an index of the amount of cumulative stress a family is experiencing. The test authors suggest that the inventory may be used by family therapists and family life educators in a variety of settings. They clearly encourage the use of FILE as an assessment tool, an initial screening test, or a means of generating discussion of stressors and significant family issues. The authors state that using the FILE may

> (1) identify some of the major stressors and daily hassles that chip away at the family's flexibility and resiliency; (2) foster the family's own awareness of what stressors, strains, and hardships they have been struggling with; and (3) encourage the family to look at all these demands and the impact they may have on the family unit. (McCubbin & Patterson, 1983, p. 292)

The inventory seems best suited for use with traditional families although the authors imply that it is appropriate with single parents and cohabiting couples. The inventory can be administered in a variety of settings and requires only the respondent(s) and a pencil. It is important that the individual administering and interpreting the inventory be familiar with the theory underlying the inventory as well as the normative data and present the results in a manner consistent with the inventory's intent. The instructions for administration and scoring are clearly written, and the inventory can be administered and scored in approximately 15 to 20 minutes.

The FILE is hand scored on the questionnaire. Several possible scoring mechanisms allow tailoring the use of the inventory to the needs of the family and the practitioner. The test authors recommend using weighted standardized scores developed to account for the relative importance and intensity of the life events listed on the inventory. The recommended scoring procedures result in a "Family-Couple Readjustment Score" or a "Family Readjustment Score." The Family-Couple Readjustment Score consists of the sum of the weights from the items endorsed by either adult member of the family when the inventory was completed individually. The Family Readjustment Score is identical to the preceding except that the measure is completed by the adult family members together.

Three additional scoring procedures are available. A "Family Life Events Score" may be computed in which adult members complete the inventory together. Each item endorsed receives a score of 1. Subscale scores and a total score are computed by summing the endorsed items. The "Family-Couple Life Events Score" is computed when both members complete the inventory separately. Both questionnaires are examined and each item endorsed by either or both partners receives a score of 1. The endorsed items are then summed to compute subscale and total "pile-up" scores.

Finally, a "Family-Couple Discrepancy Score" may be computed. The adult family members complete the FILE separately, then the responses are examined for discrepancies. Each discrepancy (where one adult endorsed the item and the other failed to) receives a score of 1. The scores are then added to generate the subscales and total pile-up scores. It is important to note that the latter method of scoring does not result in the typical index of family stress, but can be used, according to the test authors, to assess communication as well as over- and understatements of family stress between partners.

The interpretation of this inventory derives from normative data and clinical judgment of the counselor or educator. Normative data were collected from 2,280 married subjects across the seven stages of the family life cycle (Olson et al., 1982). The test authors believe that the degree of family stress should be evaluated only on the basis of a comparable stage of the life cycle. Thus, the Total Family Pile-Up Score is compared with the normative data for families in the same stage of the family life cycle. The normative data locate the family in a high-stress, moderate-stress, or low-stress category. Normative data were not collected for the subscale scores, as research has found that the subscale scores lack reliability due to the wide variance of life events experienced by families. To summarize, the FILE is not complicated and, with preparation, easily can be administered, scored, and interpreted appropriately.

Technical Aspects

Very little reliability and validity information was available for this instrument. A sample of 322 families with a chronically ill child yielded an internal consistency estimate (Cronbach's alpha) of .72 for a Total Family Pile-Up Score (McCubbin & Patterson, 1991). Additional analyses resulted in an overall reliability coefficient of .81 with another sample of 2,740 individuals (McCubbin & Patterson, 1991). However, the internal consistency estimates for the subscales were lower, ranging from .16 to .72 according to the tables provided in the manual (McCubbin & Patterson, 1991). Thus, the test authors recommend that the Total Family Pile-

Up Score be used as opposed to the individual subscales. Finally, a study by Olson et al. (1982) reported in the test manual investigated test-retest reliabilities with a sample of 150 individuals. The participants were predominantly single, with a mean age of 23. Subjects completed the inventory 4 to 5 weeks after the initial administration and most responded to the inventory for their family of origin. Analysis of the Pearson correlations suggest relatively stable responses for the Total Family Pile-Up Score ($r = .80$) and the subscales (.64 to .84).

Validity evidence was provided by several investigations. McCubbin and Patterson (1991) reported that the same factor structure for the inventory was replicated in two independent samples of adults ($N = 1,330$ and $N = 1,410$). Further, the Total Family Pile-Up Score of the original measure correlated significantly and inversely with decline in health status of children with cystic fibrosis (Patterson & McCubbin, 1983). The test authors also correlated the nine subscales and the Total Family Pile-Up Score of the revised instrument with the Family Environment Scales (FES; Moos, 1974). As expected, the total score of the FILE related significantly and inversely to several FES scales, including Family Cohesion, Independence of Family Members, and Family Organization. A positive correlation was noted between the Total Family Pile-Up Score and family conflict as measured on the FES. Other investigators have found that the total score of the FILE related negatively to variables of family cohesion, adaptability, and positive affect toward children with a sample of first-married ($N = 106$) and remarried ($N = 108$) families (Waldren, Bell, Peek, & Sorell, 1990). These researchers also found that remarried families experienced more stress than first-married families. However, this relationship was not significant when years of marriage, education, and church attendance were entered as covariates in the analyses. Finally, McCubbin and Patterson (1983, 1991) reported that a discriminant analysis revealed differences between low- and high-conflict families in the Total Family Pile-Up scores and several subscales with a sample of families who had a child diagnosed with either cerebral palsy or myelomeningocele.

Critique

The FILE is an attractively packaged instrument with clear theoretical underpinnings. The face validity of the instrument as well as the ease in administration and scoring seem to provide counselors and family life educators with a useful descriptive indicator of family stress.

Unfortunately, psychometric data are meager and often presented confusingly in the manual (McCubbin & Patterson, 1991) and other publications (e.g., McCubbin & Patterson, 1983). For example, although the test authors recommend using the weighted scores (i.e., Family-Couple Readjustment or Family Readjustment scores) for interpretive purposes, reliability estimates are consistently presented for undefined "Total Family Pile-Up scores." It is unclear whether these are weighted or unweighted scores and whether they were obtained from individual or consensus judgments of couples (see prior description of scoring). Our best guess from an inspection of tables is that these are consistently the unweighted scores (either Family Life Event or Family-Couple Life Event scores). Thus, if we are correct, no reliability data are presented for the scores that the test authors favor. If we are incorrect, the test authors need to be much clearer about the scores for which reliability data are available in future publications.

The authors indicate, in various publications (McCubbin & Patterson, 1983, 1991), that the FILE has several uses: a) to assess the current level of family stress and vulnerability to crisis, b) to predict health and mental health status of individual family members, c) to assess resources available to family members, d) to suggest appropriate interventions, e) to foster awareness among family members about current stressors, and f) to encourage families to look at their stressors and how they impact on family functioning. Unfortunately, little validity evidence exists that would support any of these uses.

No evidence appears in the published literature that these reviewers could locate to suggest that families who take the FILE are more aware of the stressors impinging on them than those who do not (item "e," above) or that such families spend more time or energy discussing or acting upon their stressors (item "f," above). There is also no evidence that we could find suggesting that FILE scores relate as would be expected to criterion indices of family vulnerability to single life events or to other indices of family stress (item "a," above), or that scores or patterns of scores are differentially associated with intervention effectiveness (item "d," above). Finally, resources are not assessed on the FILE nor could we find any suggestions or evidence on how resources could be assessed or predicted from FILE scores (item "c," above).

Some evidence does suggest that the undefined Total Family Pile-Up scores on the original 171-item version of the FILE relate modestly to changes in pulmonary functioning (McCubbin & Patterson, 1991) and health status (Patterson & McCubbin, 1983) of children with cystic fibrosis, but no evidence indicates that the current version of the FILE has similar validity for this or other changes in health or mental health status (item "b," above). There is also evidence that FILE total and scale scores relate to scores on the FES, but construct validity evidence provided by these findings is weak, as the theory underlying the development of the FILE makes no specific predictions of how family stress should relate to FES scale scores.

Suggestions regarding how to interpret levels of family stress on the basis of weighted scores (McCubbin & Patterson, 1991) also lack validity evidence. Cutoff scores to identify levels of family stress (low, medium, and high) on the basis of weighted scores were derived from scores obtained from 2,280 married persons at different stages of the family life cycle. Scores falling at least 1 standard deviation above the mean for this normative sample are considered to indicate high levels of family stress, while scores within 1 standard deviation of the mean indicates moderate stress, and those below 1 standard deviation of the mean suggest low stress. No other evidence is provided to validate these cutoffs, and interpretative descriptions are provided of families at each level of stress without data confirming the accuracy of these descriptions. For example, families scoring 1 standard deviation below the normative mean (low-stress families) are described as "unburdened by life changes and strains," "poised to seek stimulating life experiences," and as having "uneventful, possibly even mundane" lives (McCubbin & Patterson, 1991, pp. 93–94). However, publications neither describe how these descriptions were obtained (e.g., were norm-group families given standardized self-descriptive checklists along with the FILE, or were these descriptions simply derived from clinical experience?) nor provide any evidence to validate the accuracy of these interpretative descriptions.

As stated previously, future publications also should describe the samples used in psychometric studies more thoroughly. The cursory sample descriptions provided in extant publications on the FILE give these reviewers the impression that the measure is best suited for the assessment of traditional families and the types of stressors that impinge on them.

Finally, analysis of the type of stressors experienced by families at various stages in the family life cycle may enhance the usefulness of the inventory. McCubbin and Patterson (1983) argue that it is critical to compare families with normative data that accurately represent their current developmental stage because different stressors may be more typical at various stages of the family life cycle. They provided the example that the death of a family member is more likely during the later stages of the life cycle than at earlier stages. However, the authors have yet to devise a means to incorporate in the scoring procedures whether the stressors experienced by a family member are typical for a given stage in the family life cycle (i.e., the weights assigned to the stressors are identical despite life-cycle stage). An examination of this point and further clarification of the development of the weights assigned to each stressor in the scoring procedures would be helpful.

To conclude, the FILE was carefully designed from a clear and consistent theoretical model of family stress. This instrument is embedded in a rich nomological network that has yet to be even partially tapped by construct-oriented validation research. Even more troublesome is the lack of practical, criterion-oriented validation of its most basic stated uses. A good deal of rudimentary psychometric work needs to be completed before we could recommend the FILE for anything other than routine screening of the number and types of life events that the families seen by clinicians and family life educators experience. We would caution users not to overinterpret score meanings in terms of family vulnerability or member health risks, and we definitely would urge extreme caution in drawing implications about family characteristics and functioning on the basis of the normative data provided in the manual. However, it is our hope that this review stimulates both theoretically and practically oriented validity investigation on the FILE because this instrument has the potential to contribute to the advancement of theory and to benefit users in a variety of clinical settings.

References

Hill, R. (1958). Generic features of families under stress. *Social Casework, 49,* 139–150.

McCubbin, H.I., & Patterson, J.M. (1983). Stress: The Family Inventory of Life Events and Changes. In E. Filsinger (Ed.), *Marriage and family assessment: A source book for family therapy* (pp. 275–297). Beverly Hills, CA: Sage.

McCubbin, H.I., & Patterson, J.M. (1991). FILE: Family Inventory of Life Events and Changes. In H.I. McCubbin & A.I. Thompson (Eds.), *Family assessment inventories for research and practice* (pp. 81–96). Madison, WI: Family Stress, Coping and Health Project, University of Wisconsin.

McCubbin, H.I., Patterson, J., & Wilson, L. (1981). *Family Inventory of Life Events and Changes (FILE) Form C.* St. Paul, MN: Family Social Science, University of Minnesota.

McCubbin, H.I., Wilson, L., & Patterson, J. (1979). *Family Inventory of Life Events and Changes (FILE) Form A.* St. Paul, MN: Family Social Science, University of Minnesota.

Moos, R.H. (1974). *Family Environment Scales and preliminary manual.* Palo Alto, CA: Consulting Psychologists Press.

Olson, D.H., McCubbin, H.I., Barnes, H., Larsen, A., Muxem, M., & Wilson, M. (1982). *Family inventories: Inventories used in a national survey of families across the family life cycle.* St. Paul, MN: Family Social Science, University of Minnesota.

Patterson, J., & McCubbin, H. (1983). The impact of family life events and changes on the health of a chronically ill child. *Family Relations, 32,* 255–264.

Waldren, T., Bell, N.J., Peek, C.W., & Sorell, G. (1990). Cohesion and adaptability in post-divorce remarried and first married families: Relationships with family stress and coping styles. *Journal of Divorce and Remarriage, 14,* 13–28.

Norman D. Sundberg, Ph.D.

Professor Emeritus, Department of Psychology, University of Oregon, Eugene, Oregon.

FAMILY SATISFACTION SCALE

David H. Olson and Marc Wilson. St. Paul, Minnesota: Family Social Science, University of Minnesota.

Introduction

The family is the basic unit of society, evocative of strong emotional, social, and political feelings and ideas. Yet social scientists seem to have produced few psychometric instruments about how gratifying or disturbing family life is. David Olson and Marc Wilson, in the introductory material that this reviewer will call the "manual" of the Family Satisfaction Scale (dated 1982, but distributed still in 1992), state, "While it may seem surprising, we have found no other published literature which empirically or theoretically investigates the construct of family satisfaction." (There have been, however, widely used measures of marital satisfaction for a long time; e.g., the Locke-Wallace scale, 1959.) In recent years a few compendia of family measurement procedures have been published (Jacob & Tennenbaum, 1988; Touliatos, Perlmutter, & Straus, 1990).

The Family Satisfaction Scale grew out of an extensive program of research led by David Olson, Professor of Family Social Science at the University of Minnesota. Olson's circumplex model (Olson, Russell, & Sprenkle, 1989), strongly influenced by general systems theory, has two basic dimensions, Cohesion and Adaptability, to which a third is added, Communication. The model leads to a number of hypotheses, of which the following is central: Balanced families, that is, those showing moderate cohesion (neither emmeshed nor disengaged) and moderate adaptability (neither rigid nor chaotic), function best across the life cycle (Olson, 1989). Over more than two decades using the circumplex model, Olson and his associates developed a large set of family and marital inventories and rating scales (available through the Family Inventory Project, Family Social Science, University of Minnesota). Most prominent among these is FACES (Family Adaptability and Cohesion Evaluation Scales), a 20-item self-report inventory concerning the two primary dimensions of the model. Research and clinical work with families, however, showed that gathering information about cohesion and adaptability did not capture the character of families sufficiently. Olson came to the conclusion that, even if families are at the extremes on the circumplex model, "they will function well as long as all family members are satisfied with these expectations" (1989, p. 21). Thus, it is not enough to describe a family's location on the circumplex structure; one must also have a measure of satisfaction with that location.

The Family Satisfaction Scale was built to reveal how well people liked the cohesion and adaptability of their family. (The third element in the circumplex model, communication, is covered by separate measures.) The scale consists of 14 items, selected by factor analysis so that there is one item each from the eight Cohesion subscales (Emotional Bonding, Family Boundaries, Coalitions, Time, Space, Friends, Decision-Making, and Interests and Recreation) and the six Adaptability subscales (Assertiveness, Control, Discipline, Negotiation, Roles, and Rules). Subjects choose one of five possibilities, ranging from "dissatisfied" to "extremely satisfied," in response to questions like these paraphrased ones: "How satisfied are you with the amount of time your family spends together?" "How satisfied are you with your family's way of making decisions?" Presumably the test administrator defines what "family" refers to—whether family of origin, current family, extended family, and so forth. (Note that present-time phrasing calls for state rather than trait characteristics.) Scoring is simple—the sum of the 1 to 5 weights given each of the 14 items. No mention is made of what to do with omitted items.

Practical Applications/Uses

The purposes of the Family Satisfaction Scale are mentioned only briefly in the "manual" but references are made to both research and clinical usage. The authors recommend that the total score be used for research projects, but surprisingly they state that the somewhat less reliable subscales for cohesion and adaptability may be used primarily for clinical purposes. The "manual" does not discuss clinical interpretation. (Olson, 1989, does give some clever and interesting illustrations of basic circumplex family types from movies, such as the rigidly disengaged family in "Ordinary People" and the chronically enmeshed situation in "Who's Afraid of Virginia Woolf?") Olson (1989) discusses the Family Satisfaction Scale only briefly, indicating that it is probably more sensitive to change than the basic circumplex dimensions of cohesion and adaptability. There is also very little discussion of family satisfaction in general and the Family Satisfaction Scale in particular in the major reference to the circumplex model (Olson et al., 1989). There are clinical examples of assessment and treatment of addicted families, sexual abusing families and other dysfunctional families, but the model is complex, and there is never a clear delineation of how satisfaction enters into the clinical picture alone. Cases are discussed only in the larger context of the model.

This reviewer's survey of recent articles on the Family Satisfaction Scale revealed only a few studies. For instance, Mathis and Tanner (1991) showed that later life couples (aged 51–79 years) were more satisfied with their families than those in the national sample; older people also showed an extreme amount of adaptability and flexibility. Daley, Sowers-Hoag, and Thyer (1990) questioned the validity of the family satisfaction construct, finding only a weak association between that measure and a validated measure of family discord. Using another measure of family satisfaction, some research (Harter, Neimeyer, & Alexander, 1989) indicates that reports from different members of a family triad may have different predictive power. Information about the differentiation of perspectives by different family members is much needed; the combining of husbands' and wives' scores for the scale's norms (see "Technical Aspects" section of this review) may cover up some important discrepancies. In the circumplex group (Olson & Wilson, 1982; Olson et al., 1989), there is little or no recognition of other measures that might be related to the Family Satisfaction Scale, such as their own and others' communication scales, adjustment measures, Moos's Family Environment Scale, and others in the literature (Jacob & Tennenbaum, 1988; Touliatos et al., 1990).

Technical Aspects

Though the Family Satisfaction Scale items were based on the two circumplex dimensions, the "manual" states that the total score is most valid. The authors indicate that the scale is one dimensional, all items loading more than .50 on the first principal component in the factor analysis. The authors also report a Cronbach alpha reliability coefficient of .92, and the eight cohesion items and six adaptability items show alphas of .85 and .84, respectively. The test-retest reliability coefficient over a 5-week period for the total score was .75.

The "manual" reports norms for the Family Satisfaction Scale based on a national survey of 1,026 couples of various ages and 412 adolescents. Husband and wife norms were so similar that they were combined, and the adolescent norms are kept separate from the parents. Percentile equivalents are given for raw scores. On parental norms, raw scores of 42 to 53 cover the middle half of the percentile distribution (25–75 percentiles); thus the typical adult in the family says on this scale that she or he is somewhat more than generally satisfied with family life. No figures are given for disturbed families. The "manual" mentions nothing about social desirability or indications of test-taking attitude.

Critique

In conclusion, the Family Satisfaction Scale is a short, easily given procedure that has not been treated as a test in its own right but as an adjunct to the larger circumplex model. It has good reliability with normal samples, but as a state measure it is likely to be affected by therapy and changing situations. A genuine, up-to-date manual for the test is sorely needed. The authors also need to clarify just how the test is administered and the intended meaning. Because the items are obvious and easily fakeable, considerable care must be given to test-taking attitude. Little work has been done on validity, especially using external criteria, both concurrent and predictive. Although this scale and the circumplex model in general have remained rather isolated from other similar efforts, a great deal of credit should go to the authors for having aimed consistently at developing that rare phenomenon in applied social science—a close relationship between theory, research, and practice in an important area of social science.

References

Daley, J.G., Sowers-Hoag, K., & Thyer, B.A. (1990). Are FACES-II "family satisfaction" scores valid? *Journal of Family Therapy, 12,* 77–81.

Harter, S., Neimeyer, R.A., & Alexander, P.C. (1989). Personal construction of family relationships: The relation of commonality and sociality to family satisfaction for parents and adolescents. *International Journal of Personal Construct Psychology, 2,* 123–142.

Jacob, T., & Tennenbaum, D.L. (1988). *Family assessment: Rationale, methods and future directions.* New York: Plenum.

Locke, H.J., & Wallace, K.M. (1959). Short marital adjustment and prediction tests: Their reliability and validity. *Marriage and Family Living, 21,* 251–255.

Mathis, R.D., & Tanner, Z. (1991). Cohesion, adaptability, and satisfaction of family systems in later life. *Family Therapy, 18,* 47–60.

Olson, D.H. (1989). Circumplex model of family systems VIII: Family assessment and intervention. In D.H. Olson, C.S. Russell, & D.H. Sprenkle (Eds.), *Circumplex model: Systemic assessment and treatment of families* (pp. 7–49). New York: Haworth.

Olson, D.H., Russell, C.S., & Sprenkle, D.H. (Eds.). (1989). *Circumplex model: Systemic assessment and treatment of families.* New York: Haworth.

Olson, D.H., & Wilson, M. (1982). Family satisfaction. In D. Olson et al. (Eds.), *Family inventories.* St. Paul, MN: Family Social Science, University of Minnesota.

Touliatos, J., Perlmutter, B.F., & Straus, M.A. (Eds.). (1990). *Handbook of family measurement techniques.* Newbury Park, CA: Sage.

James A. Moses, Jr., Ph.D.

Clinical Associate Professor of Psychiatry and Behavioral Sciences, Stanford University School of Medicine, and Coordinator, Psychological Assessment Unit, Department of Veterans Affairs Medical Center, Palo Alto, California.

FINGER LOCALIZATION TEST

Arthur L. Benton, Kerry deS. Hamsher, Nils R. Varney, and Otfried Spreen. New York, New York: Oxford University Press.

Introduction

The Finger Localization Test (FLT) is a three-part, 60-item test of a subject's ability to identify the specific fingers on each hand touched by the examiner with and without visual cueing, and the ability to identify the specific pairs of fingers on one hand touched by the examiner without visual cueing. Two equivalent forms of the test are available, in which the right and left hand sequences are reversed. (For a listing of the items for FLT Form B, see Benton, Hamsher, Varney, & Spreen, 1983, p. 86, Table 9–1.) Ten trials are administered with each of the subject's hands for each of three test conditions: single finger recognition with the patient's tested hand visible, single finger recognition with the patient's tested hand concealed from view, and finger pair recognition with the patient's tested hand concealed from view.

The hand being tested must be held in the palm-up, fingers-separated position on the table during administration in all three test conditions. If the patient cannot hold his or her hand in this position due to sensorimotor deficit (e.g., spastic hemiplegia following stroke), or if he or she cannot feel the test stimulus due to peripheral tactile sensory loss, then the hand affected in one of these ways cannot be tested with the FLT. The patient may respond by indicating the finger or pair of fingers touched in each condition by pointing to a specific finger on a line drawing of a palm-up hand. Alternatively the patient may identify the finger touched by calling off a number that corresponds to the finger on the manual diagram for the hand being examined (fingers are numbered consecutively on the diagram for each hand: 1 = thumb, 2 = index finger, 3 = middle or long finger, 4 = ring finger, 5 = little finger).

Head (1920) was the first investigator to report formally that *unilateral* impairment of the ability to recognize fingers by touch is a sign of contralateral parietal lobe disease. Gerstmann (1924, 1927, 1930) subsequently reported a syndrome of *bilateral* finger localization that involved impairment in recognition extending to the fingers of the examiner as well as those of the patient. He identified variants of the finger localization deficit in which the patient could not name the fingers, show them on verbal command, or localize them after tactile stimulation. The

Gerstmann syndrome, characteristic of a lesion of the left angular gyrus (in the inferior parietal lobe, near the temporo-parietal border), was defined by a symptom complex of finger agnosia, agraphia, acalculia, and right-left disorientation. This syndrome still is recognized in clinical neurology, and its early discovery suggested the value of finger localization deficit as a contributory sign of specific, perhaps focal neurologic disease.

Subsequent work by a variety of investigators showed many dimensional variants and syndrome subtypes of the finger localization deficit syndrome. Benton (1959) produced a complex dimensional classification schema for finger agnosic disturbance "according to the nature of the stimulus (verbal or nonverbal, visual or tactile, single or multiple), the nature of the required response (verbal or nonverbal), and the extent of the impairment (bilateral or unilateral)" (Benton et al., 1983, p. 84). Ettlinger (1963) composed a battery of 12 tests to objectively classify and analyze the variants of the finger localization deficit or "finger agnosia" syndrome. Benton (1959) emphasized that trends in the literature at that time favored the development of tests of finger localization deficit that allowed subjects to identify the fingers without naming them as an integral component of the response. This feature allows for the administration of the test to aphasic as well as nonaphasic patients and removes the element of language from the key functional system that is involved in test performance. The FLT was developed according to these language-free test response principles.

The principal author of the FLT, Arthur L. Benton, Ph.D., received the A.B. degree (1931) and the A.M. degree (1933) from Oberlin College, and later his Ph.D. from Columbia University (1935). He began his career as an assistant in psychology at Oberlin College (1931–33), Columbia University and New York State Psychiatric Institute (1934–36), and Cornell University Medical College (1936–39), where he subsequently served as a staff psychologist. Benton was appointed an attending psychologist at New York Hospital–Westchester Division and a psychologist in the Student Personnel Office of the City College of New York from 1939 to 1941. He served on active duty in the U.S. Navy during and after the Second World War (1941–46). Later he was appointed Associate Professor of Psychology at the University of Louisville Medical School and Chief Psychologist at the Louisville Mental Hygiene Clinic and the Louisville General Hospital (1946–48). From 1948 to 1958 he served as Professor of Psychology and Director of the Graduate Training Program in Clinical Psychology at the University of Iowa. For two decades, from 1958 to 1978, he was Professor of Psychology and Neurology at the University of Iowa. Dr. Benton has continued to coauthor theoretical and research papers and books since 1978, when he became Professor Emeritus at the University of Iowa.

Benton's fundamental contributions to the field of clinical neuropsychology have been extensively and internationally acknowledged. He has received both honorary Doctor of Science (Cornell College, 1978) and Doctor of Psychology (University of Rome, 1990) degrees, as well as numerous other honors and awards, including the Distinguished Service Award of the Iowa Psychological Association (1977), the Distinguished Professional Contribution Award from the American Psychological Association (1978), the Outstanding Scientific Contribution Award of the International Neuropsychological Society (1981), the Samuel Torrey Orton

Award from the Orton Dyslexia Society (1982), the Distinguished Service and Outstanding Contributions Award from the American Board of Professional Psychology (1985), and the Distinguished Clinical Neuropsychologist Award from the National Academy of Neuropsychology (1989).

Benton is a past president of the American Orthopsychiatric Association (1965–66) and the International Neuropsychological Society (1970–71). He served as the Secretary-General of the Research Group on Aphasia for the World Federation of Neurology from 1971 to 1978. He has been a lecturer or visiting scholar at the University of Milan (1964), the Hôpital Sainte-Anne, Paris (1968), the Hadassah-Hebrew University Medical School, Jerusalem (1969), the Free University of Amsterdam (1971), the University of Helsinki (1974), the University of Melbourne (1977), the University of Minnesota Medical School (Baker Lecturer, 1979), the University of Victoria, British Columbia (Lansdowne Scholar, 1980), and the University of Michigan (1986). He also served as Directeur d'Études Associé, École des Hautes Études, Paris (1979), and as a visiting scientist at the Tokyo Metropolitan Institute of Gerontology (1974).

Dr. Benton has authored, coauthored, or edited 12 books and monographs, approximately 150 professional journal articles, and 22 historical reviews in the area of clinical neuropsychology and behavioral neurology. He is recognized as a pioneer and a leading authority in the area of clinical neuropsychology.

The standardized, commercially published version of the FLT appeared with the clinical manual for this and other tests in the Benton-Iowa Neuropsychological Test Battery (Benton et al., 1983). The coauthors of this clinical manual with Dr. Benton are Kerry deS. Hamsher, Ph.D. (Associate Professor of Neurology, University of Wisconsin Medical School); Nils R. Varney, Ph.D. (Staff Neuropsychologist, Department of Veterans Affairs Medical Center, Iowa City, Iowa); and Otfried Spreen, Ph.D. (Professor Emeritus, Department of Psychology, University of Victoria, Victoria, British Columbia, Canada).

Practical Applications/Uses

Administration of the FLT is straightforward. For Part A, "Identification of single fingers—hand visible," the examiner instructs the patient by saying, "I am going to touch different fingers on your hand; you tell me which finger I touch. You can name the fingers, if you wish, or you can point to it on this card" (Benton et al., 1983, p. 85). The examiner touches each of the patient's fingers on one hand with the pointed tip of a pencil for 2 seconds per trial if the patient has normal tactile sensation in the hand tested. If there is sensory loss or the patient is inattentive to task, the finger touch stimulation time may be extended to 3 or 4 seconds. The examiner must confirm that the patient has felt the tactile sensory stimulus on each trial. The patient is free to see the finger touched during the first part of the FLT. The fingers are touched for each hand in a fixed order presented on the answer sheet. Each finger is touched on two different trials for each hand, which produces 10 trials for each hand during Part A.

Part B, "Identification of single fingers—hand hidden," is administered next. During this portion of the examination, the patient's hand being tested must be concealed from his or her view; only tactile cues serve as the basis for finger localization. The examiner faces the patient across a table with a three-sided, slanted-top box between them. The top of the box slants downward toward the patient and the back of it is open on the examiner's side. An opening in the patient's side of the box is covered by a small curtain through which the patient places the hand to be tested. The fingers of that hand are concealed from the patient's view by the box and the curtain. The response card, which presents a line drawing of a hand with numbered fingers corresponding to the hand being tested, is placed on top of the box so that the patient can use it to make response choices. The test apparatus and procedure are illustrated in the test manual (Benton et al., 1983, p. 88).

The directions for Part B go as follows:

> "Now put your (right, left) hand under this curtain. You won't see me touching your finger but you will feel it." Guide the patient's hand, palm up, into the box; have him extend and slightly separate the fingers and insure that the posture is comfortable for him. "Tell me which finger I touch. You can name the finger or point to it on this card or call the number of the card." (Benton et al., 1983, p. 85)

As in Part A, the order of administration is indicated on the answer sheet, and two trials are administered for each finger of each hand. All trials of one hand are completed before the other hand is tested.

In Part C, "Identification of two simultaneously touched fingers—hand hidden," instructions to the patient are, "Now I am going to touch two of your fingers at the same time. Tell me which fingers I touch. Again, either name the fingers or point to them on the card or call their numbers on the card" (Benton et al., 1983, p. 86). The answer sheet lists the order of administration for touching pairs of fingers. All possible pairs are represented, except 4-5 (ring-little); the two central pairs of fingers (2-3 and 3-4) are repeated twice in the series, probably because they are the most likely combination to be confused among normals. The order of trials varies from one hand to the other, but the frequency of specific pairs and trials is the same for each hand. Ten trials are given for each hand on this part of the FLT as on the other two sections.

Benton and his colleagues advise that the examiner may indicate correct responses on the answer sheet with a checkmark or "plus," but that incorrect responses should be specifically noted by number. On part C, the patient must correctly identify *both* fingers touched to receive credit. Scoring is a clerical task. Separate scores for the right and left hands are summed for each of the three sections of the FLT and for the test as a whole. A total score based on the number of correct responses across all three parts of the test also is computed.

The FLT was normed on 104 hospitalized control patients (64 men, 40 women) without a past or present history of brain-related neurologic or psychiatric disorder. The age range was 16–65 years and the educational range was 5–16+ years. Examination of a demographic breakdown that cross-classifies subjects by age and educational level shows 24–28 subjects in the age range 16–45 for educational levels 8–11 or 12 years. The sample size is 16 for the group of subjects aged 46–55 with educational level in the range 8–11 years. The distribution of subjects in other demographic categories shows cell loadings of less than 10 subjects, and in some cases as small as a single subject. Two cells are empty (age 56–65, educational levels 12 and 13+ years). Normative results for the FLT in specific demographic groups should be not used clinically for reference groups with fewer than 15 subjects, as noted for the samples above, as individual differences are likely to play too great a biasing role in determining the reference group mean value. Overall test result values should be generalized with caution beyond the limits of the predominantly high-school-educated and young-to-middle-aged sample that formed the majority of the FLT normative reference group.

Thirty percent (31/104) of the medical control patients in the FLT reference sample earned perfect total scores of 60 points, and another 30% earned nearly errorless total scores in the range of 58–59 points. Sixty percent of the normative sample made two errors or less on the FLT as a whole. The mean total FLT score for the normative sample was 57.5 points (*SD* = 2.7). The central tendency and variability descriptive statistics for the normative sample of men (*M* = 57.4, *SD* = 2.7) and women (*M* = 57.7, *SD* = 2.6) were virtually identical to each other and to the total group values. Although the authors concluded on the basis of inspection of their cross-tabulated results for age and educational level that there was no apparent effect of either variable on FLT performance level, they had very few subjects at any age with either 13 or more years of education (8 total) or 5–7 years of education (12 total). The value of age and particularly educational level corrections to adjust the accuracy and sensitivity of FLT thus remains moot.

Based on these results, it is apparent that the FLT constitutes a relatively easy task for adults with a wide variety of demographic characteristics, even for those ill with non-neuropsychiatric disorders. In the normative sample, 82% of all errors made on the FLT occurred on Part C. The error rate among the medical control patients was only 0.3% in Part A, 2.0% in Part B, and 10.1% in Part C.

The test manual presents a summary of performance level cutoff values and associated percentile values for the categorization of FLT total score levels (Benton et al., 1983, p. 90, Table 9-3). These ratings should be considered descriptive performance level trends; values and labels for categorization of performance patterns that follow should be used for clinical categorization of FLT performances. Scores of 54–60 (12–85+ percentile) are rated as normal, those in the 51–53 range (6–7 percentile) are borderline, those in the 48–50 range (1–5 percentile) are moderately defective, and those in the 0–47 range (below first percentile) are severely defective.

Benton et al. (1983, pp. 88–89) also have identified a number of "performance patterns" or disjoint descriptive error pattern categories that are useful for classifying FLT score profile patterns:

A. *Normal.* Total score = 51–60, single-hand scores = 25–30, right-left difference of 0–3 points.

B. *Borderline.* Total score = 49–51; one single-hand score = 23–24 and one single-and score = 26–27, right-left difference = 0–3 points.

C. *Bilateral symmetric defect.* Single-hand scores = less than 26, right-left difference = 0–3 points.

D. *Bilateral asymmetric (right hand) defect.* Single-hand scores = less than 26; right-hand score 4 or more points lower than left-hand score.

E. *Bilateral asymmetric (left hand) defect.* Single-hand scores = less than 26; left-hand score 4 or more points less than right hand score.

F. *Right unilateral defect.* Right-hand score 4 or more points less than left-hand score of 26 or higher.

G. *Left unilateral defect.* Left-hand score 4 or more points less than right-hand score of 26 or higher.

AR. *Normal right hand.* Right-hand score = 26–30; left hand not tested.

AL. *Normal left hand.* Left-hand score = 26–30; right hand not tested.

BR. *Borderline right.* Right-hand score = 25; left hand not tested.

BL. *Borderline left.* Left-hand score = 25; right hand not tested.

(F). *Right-hand defect.* Right-hand score less than 25; left hand not tested.

(G). *Left-hand defect.* Left-hand score less than 25; right hand not tested.

An overview of developmental trends in tactile finger localization appears in the test manual (Benton et al., 1983, pp. 89–93). For numerical trends in the data across the developmental period from age 3 through 12 years, the interested reader should see especially Tables 9-7 and 9-8 on performance patterns of preschool and school-aged children. The present review will note only general trends in this literature (adapted from Benton et al., 1983), as the FLT is not recommended for use with young children. Visual identification of specific fingers originates between ages 3 and 5 years in normal preschool children. By age 4 approximately 60% of normal children can point to one of their fingers that they have seen the examiner touch. Identifying the finger touched on a picture of a hand is mastered by only half of normal preschoolers by age 5. Normal children aged 6 find the tactile identification of fingers touched (FLT, Part B) to be difficult (average children mean FLT total score = 38.6; superior children mean FLT total score = 44.5). Only by age 9 is this task performed with relatively few errors by children of average ability (mean FLT total score = 50.9) and superior ability (mean FLT total score = 52.2) levels. As expected there is a gradual and monotonic increase in the level of the FLT task as a function of age between 6 and 12 years. The curve reaches approximate maximal preadolescent developmental asymptote by age 9 years. The 9-year-old still experiences considerable difficulty with Part C of FLT, producing an error rate of 37.5%—approximately four times as frequent as the rate in adult medical controls.

Exploratory work by Clawson (1962) examined the level of performance of age- and intelligence-level-matched groups of brain-injured, emotionally disturbed, and normal control children aged 8–13 years on the version of Benton's finger localization measure that was available at that time. Eighty percent of the neurologically impaired children scored at a level below the 10 percentile for normal and emotionally disturbed children on the instrument. Benton et al. (1983) note that Clawson's samples were relatively small, so her conclusions are necessarily tentative. They certainly should be replicated.

Technical Aspects

The primary FLT validational study was performed in a sample of 61 neurologic patients with brain disease (reported by Benton et al., 1983, pp. 93–95). Twenty of these cases had bilateral hemispheric disease, mostly of a diffuse degenerative disorder type; a few of them suffered from multifocal lesions such as brain metastases. Nineteen patients in the neurologic sample had unilateral right-hemispheric lesions, predominantly cerebrovascular syndromes. No patient with a right-hemispheric lesion was aphasic. Twenty-two of the cases had unilateral left-hemispheric lesion syndromes, predominantly due to cerebrovascular disease. Of these 22 left-hemispheric lesion cases, 15 were not aphasic and 7 were aphasic. The age range of the sample was 18–64 years; other demographic descriptive statistics are not reported. All patients were tested with FLT on both hands.

In a summary of trends drawn from a distribution of lesion locus by FLT error pattern (Benton et al., 1983, pp. 93–94, and Table 9-10), Benton and his colleagues offer a number of general conclusions. More than half (57%) of the 61 subjects sampled showed an abnormal performance pattern of types B through F in the classification schema summarized in the last section of this review. Failure on the FLT was considerably greater in patients with lesions of both cerebral hemispheres (70%) and in aphasic patients (86%) than in those without aphasia who presented with a unilateral hemispheric lesion (42%–47%). Fifty-five percent of patients with bilateral hemispheric disease and 57% of patients with aphasia showed bimanual FLT impairment. This pattern was uncommon in nonaphasic patients with a lesion of only one cerebral hemisphere (11%–13% incidence). In patients with a lesion of one cerebral hemisphere only, the most common pattern of FLT deficit was impairment with only the hand contralateral to the side of the lesion.

Gainotti, Cianchetti, and Tiacci (1972) reported that for right-handed patients with unilateral cerebral lesions, a greatly increased rate of bilateral finger localization deficit appeared when the patient was demented or aphasic. In unilateral left-hemispheric-lesioned cases that were "mentally deteriorated," the incidence of this deficit was 33% (10/30), whereas in nondeteriorated cases it was only 10% (6/58). Aphasic disorder due to a unilateral left-hemispheric lesion was associated with bilateral finger localization deficit in 38% of cases (13/34). In nonaphasic cases, a unilateral left-hemispheric lesion syndrome was found in only 6% of cases (3/54) with bilateral finger agnosia. In unilateral right-hemispheric lesion cases, bilateral finger localization deficit was noted in 45% (10/22) of the cases. In nondemented cases with right-hemispheric lesions, the rate of bilateral finger localization deficit was only 4% (2/52). Other investigators have reported confirmatory results that link dementia or aphasia with bilateral impairment of finger localization ability (Benton, 1959, 1962; Poeck & Orgass, 1969; Sauguet, Benton, & Hécaen, 1971).

In subsequent work Gainotti and Tiacci (1973) found significantly greater incidence of unilateral finger localization deficit in patients with lesions of the right cerebral hemisphere than in those with lesions of the left cerebral hemisphere. This finding was not replicated in the sample of Benton et al. (1983), but their sample size (N = 61) was considerably smaller than that of Gainotti and Tiacci (1973; N = 176—99 left-hemisphere lesion cases, 77 right-hemisphere lesion cases).

Benton et al. (1983, p. 96) report FLT error score results for a sample of 20 mixed brain-damaged patients chosen at random who were not otherwise demographically or diagnostically described in a tabular summary. They note that Part A of the FLT is passed by a high percentage (87.5%) of this sample and is not of apparent differential diagnostic value in adult samples because it is too elementary for them, at least as long as tactile sensory, visual-perceptual, and visual-spatial skills are reasonably well spared. Further analysis of their table shows that approximately half of their random sample of brain-damaged patients passed Part B of the FLT without error and that 70% of them made an average of two or less errors across pooled trials for each hand. No subject made an errorless performance in Part C, and there was a very wide and relatively even range of error scores from 1–9 errors with each hand, so that no clear criterion for establishment of a cutting score could be assigned to these data empirically.

Critique

The Finger Localization Test is a relatively brief, standardized, quantified measure of a specific sensory skill that is sensitive and specific for classifying unilateral and bilateral variants of the finger localization deficit syndrome. Benton et al. (1983) emphasize the importance of distinguishing between FLT syndromes that involve unimanual versus bimanual impairment. The unimanual finger localization deficit syndromes are associated with specific, higher order contralateral parietal lobe sensory dysfunction. The bimanual finger agnosic syndromes, however, are commonly associated with dementing and aphasic disturbance, and examiners should administer the FLT in such cases as part of the clinical workup, to better define the deficit syndrome. Benton and his colleagues acknowledge that while the presence of bilateral finger localization deficit suggests the likelihood of an associated dementing or aphasic disorder, numerous patients with each of these disorders do not show the finger localization disturbance. Conversely, a "pure" Gerstmann syndrome including bilateral finger agnosia is occasionally found in nondemented, nonaphasic patients with focal lesions in the posterior parietal area of the left hemisphere (Benton, 1992).

The functional systems underlying the finger localization disturbance and its relationship to syndromes of aphasia and dementia remain to be clarified dimensionally. These analyses should proceed along dimensional pattern-of-performance rather than simply level-of-performance lines. That is, subsequent investigators should study known parameters of intellectual, memorial, and linguistic functioning relative to finger localization disturbance rather than global syndromes such as dementia or aphasia that are present or absent as elements of the clinical syndrome. Use of recent theoretical and empirical findings from experimental cognitive psychology may be invaluable as sources of empirically testable functional system models.

More work is warranted to extend the FLT normative database in most of the age and educational level demographic categories reported in the test manual (Benton et al., 1983, p. 90, Table 9-2). Both college-educated and grade-school-educated subjects have been minimally sampled at all age levels, and subjects aged 56 and older also have been sampled minimally as a group. The need for demographic corrections for age and educational level to improve the sensitivity of the FLT should be reconsidered once the expanded sample has been composed.

Reliability studies are needed to establish internal consistency and test-retest indices for the FLT. Reliability is a psychometric standard of accuracy of measurement, and one type of reliability does not substitute for another variety. Internal consistency is best estimated by coefficient alpha, a statistic that provides a quantified measure of the degree to which the items of an itemized test correlate with each other to form a unified or "internally consistent" measure of a single theoretical dimension or construct. If the index of internal consistency is low, the items are not systematically related to each other, and one is not justified in adding them to develop a summary measure such as a scale score. Ideally the value of coefficient alpha approximates .80, a value that reduces the statistical error of measurement to a practical minimum (Nunnally, 1978). This value should be used as an ideal standard in a diagnostically heterogeneous sample for the FLT total score (60 items), and the summary right- and left-hand scores (30 items each). The reliability of a measure is directly proportional to its length. For these summary measures, the FLT has enough items to warrant use of this stringent standard of internal consistency. Internal consistency standards for unimanual, 10-trial subscales of each part of the FLT, however, should be somewhat liberalized. A standard of .70 is suggested as a rigorous yet reasonable standard value for a measure of this length. The internal consistency of both forms of the FLT should be established independently.

A measure of test-retest reliability also is needed for this test, to show that changes in FLT scores over time are due to nonchance variation in finger localization ability and not to statistical error of measurement. The standard procedure for such demonstration involves administration of the same form of the test to a normal sample of subjects twice, with an intertest interval of approximately 2 weeks. The retest reliability correlational value for the two testings should meet or exceed .80. Either form of the FLT could be used for this purpose, as they are essentially identical in their central tendency and variability characteristics.

The normative work on development of finger localization ability in children is intriguing and potentially important for the analysis of "soft" signs of neurologic disorder that may signal mild neurologically based cognitive deficit such as learning disability. With regard to this matter, Benton (1979) notes that research on concurrent findings of specific reading disability and finger localization difficulty have been inconsistent. In contrast, Benton et al. (1983) note the growing evidence that the presence of finger localization difficulty in kindergartners (age 5 years) is a valid predictor of later reading ability (Fletcher, Taylor, Morris, & Satz, 1982; Lindgren, 1978; Satz & Friel, 1973, 1974; Satz, Taylor, Friel, & Fletcher, 1978).

More normative work also is needed on the relevance and applicability of various portions of the FLT to the developmental and educational competence of children at various age levels. Perhaps parts of the FLT are too difficult for children at a given developmental level, but now sufficient evidence has accumulated on FLT developmental trends to design clinical and special educational studies that can clarify the discrete cognitive elements of the developing *functional systems* involved in such complex behaviors as reading and tactile finger localization. Conflicting reports in the literature most likely result from too global a level of analysis, in which variants of a disorder, such as reading disability, are multiply determined in different subsyndromes but grouped together for analysis because of a single emergent property, such as the difficulty with reading.

All of these complex behaviors, including finger localization, are multiply determined. Analysis of the dimensional elements of functional systems (Luria, 1980) in the manner that Benton and his colleagues have analyzed the functional systems underlying finger localization is necessary. Logical, hypothesis-driven relationships among parameters and associated syndromes must be investigated rationally, and such analysis requires dimensional understanding. This is as true of the analysis of adult syndromes as it is of the analysis of developmental disorder in children.

References

Benton, A.L. (1959). *Right-left discrimination and finger localization: Development and pathology.* New York: Hoeber-Harper.

Benton, A.L. (1962). Clinical symptomatology in right and left hemisphere lesions. In V.B. Mountcastle (Ed.), *Interhemispheric relations and cerebral dominance* (pp. 253–263). Baltimore: Johns Hopkins Press.

Benton, A.L. (1979). The neuropsychological significance of finger recognition. In M. Bortner (Ed.), *Cognitive growth and development.* New York: Brunner/Mazel.

Benton, A.L. (1992). Gerstmann's syndrome. *Archives of Neurology, 49,* 445–447.

Benton, A.L., Hamsher, K.deS., Varney, N.R., & Spreen, O. (1983). *Contributions to neuropsychological assessment: A clinical manual.* New York: Oxford University Press.

Clawson, A. (1962). Relationship of psychological tests to cerebral disorders in children. *Psychological Reports, 10,* 187–190.

Ettlinger, G.E. (1963). Defective identification of fingers. *Neuropsychologia, 1,* 39–45.

Fletcher, J.M., Taylor, H.G., Morris, R., & Satz, P. (1982). Finger recognition skills and reading achievement: A developmental neuropsychological perspective. *Developmental Psychology, 18,* 124–132.

Gainotti, G., Cianchetti, C., & Tiacci, C. (1972). The influence of hemispheric side of lesions on non-verbal tasks of finger localization. *Cortex, 8,* 364–381.

Gainotti, G., & Tiacci, C. (1973). The unilateral forms of finger agnosia. *Confina Neurologica, 35,* 271–284.

Gerstmann, J. (1924). Fingeragnosie: Eine umschriebene Störung der Orientierung am eigenen Körper. *Weiner Klinische Wochenschrift, 37,* 1010–1012.

Gerstmann, J. (1927). Fingeragnosie und isolierte Agraphie: Ein neues Syndrom. *Zeitschrift für Neurologie und Psychiatrie, 108,* 152–177.

Gerstmann, J. (1930). Zir Symptomatologie der Hirnlasionen im Uebergangsgebiet der unteren Parietal- und mittleren Occiptalwindung. *Nervenarzt, 3,* 691–695.

Head, H. (1920). *Studies in neurology.* London: Oxford University Press.

Lindgren, S.D. (1978). Finger localization and the prediction of reading disability. *Cortex, 14,* 87–101.

Luria, A.R. (1980). *Higher cortical functions in man* (2nd ed.). New York: Basic Books.

Nunnally, J.C. (1978). *Psychometric theory.* New York: McGraw-Hill.

Poeck, K., & Orgass, B. (1969). An experimental investigation of finger agnosia. *Neurology, 19,* 801–807.

Satz, P., & Friel, J. (1973). Some predictive antecedents of specific learning disability. In P. Satz & J. Ross (Eds.), *The disabled learner.* Rotterdam, The Netherlands: Rotterdam University Press.

Satz, P., & Friel, J. (1974). Some predictive antecedents of specific reading disability: A preliminary two-year follow-up. *Journal of Learning Disabilities, 7,* 437–444.

Satz, P., Taylor, H.G., Friel, J., & Fletcher, J. (1978). Some developmental precursors of reading disabilities: A six-year follow-up. In A.L. Benton & D. Pearl (Eds.), *Dyslexia.* New York: Oxford University Press.

Sauguet, J., Benton, A.L., & Hécaen, H. (1971). Disturbances of the body schema in relation to language impairment and hemispheric locus of lesion. *Journal of Neurology, Neurosurgery, and Psychiatry, 34,* 496–501.

Jean Powell Kirnan, Ph.D.

Assistant Professor of Psychology, Trenton State College, Trenton, New Jersey.

HILSON PERSONNEL PROFILE/SUCCESS QUOTIENT

Robin E. Inwald. Kew Gardens, New York: Hilson Research, Inc.

Introduction

The Hilson Personnel Profile/Success Quotient (HPP/SQ; Inwald 1988a, 1988b) is designed as a measure of general career success for use in a variety of occupations. The instrument is based on the success quotient theory (SQT) of Robin Inwald, the test's author, which proposes that successful behaviors demonstrate a consistency over time and situation. Reminiscent of biodata theory, which derives from the hypothesis that the best predictor of future performance is past performance, the HPP/SQ measures successful behaviors in past academic, work, social, and interpersonal experiences and combines these with self-perceptions of drive, confidence, and commitment. The earlier one demonstrates these behaviors, the greater one's likelihood of future success.

The HPP/SQ measures five personality traits that the author proposes make a successful employee. These five traits are measured in separate scales and also combined to derive a Success Quotient, or total score, that measures overall potential for success in the workplace. Three of these scales are broken down further into subcategories or content areas. The author's "best judgment" was used in the construction of the items and in determining their relevance for the different scales. This initial draft was then pretested on a group of 50 nonrandomly selected individuals. Items were revised to better fit the author's impression of these individuals' measures on the different scales. The five scales are described as follows:

1. *Candor* (16 items): Measures decisiveness and willingness to be honest about faults. A low score here could indicate that other scores are inflated because of a desire to appear perfect.

2. *Achievement History* (33 items): Measures past achievement on jobs and in school. High scores indicate academic/work success.

3. *Social Ability* (40 items): Measures the extent to which the applicant is extraverted, social, and outgoing. High scores indicate a popular, social person. They also may indicate "people oriented" individuals who are concerned with gaining the approval of others. This category breaks down into content areas of Extraver-

---

The reviewer gratefully acknowledges the assistance of Jennifer DeNicolis. Her diligence and insights contributed significantly to the review.

sion, Popularity, and Sensitivity to Others. Individuals may score high or low on each of these subcategories, which combine to form Social Ability.

4. *"Winner's" Image* (28 items): Measures the subcategories of Self-Confidence and Competitive Spirit. High scores in these two areas indicate a person confident in him- or herself, who thrives on competition.

5. *Initiative* (33 items): Measures the ability to start as well as complete projects. High scores indicate a hard-working, goal-driven individual. Initiative includes content areas of Drive, Preparation Style, Goal-Orientation, and Anxiety about Organization. (Some confusion exists in later tables of the test manual with regard to this scale. Preparation Style is referred to there as PS, yet when first referenced in the manual it is referred to as PR.)

The HPP/SQ normative base consists of a sample of 985 entry-level city agency job applicants. In addition to these normative data, separate occupational norms were compiled for a variety of occupations, ranging from CEOs to juvenile detention administrators. The separate occupations were then compared to the normative group.

Although descriptive statistics as to the ethnic and gender composition of the normative group are not provided directly, one can calculate them by comparison of the sample sizes reported in a number of tables. Because this is the comparison group for HPP/SQ scores, there is evidence for concern regarding its representativeness for certain occupational groups. For example, of the 985 subjects in the sample, 31% are female. Of these 309, 88% are black, 8% are Hispanic, and 3% are white. Similarly in the male sample, 58% are black, 21% are Hispanic, and 19% are white.

The publisher addresses the disproportionate number of minorities in a separate report entitled "Additional Notes on the Development of the HPP/SQ" (Inwald, n.d.-a), but this information should be integrated into the test manual. In these research notes, the justification for the large percent of minorities is both confusing and unconvincing. First, no percentages are given; the text simply states that there is a disproportionate number of blacks and Hispanics. Further, it states that Hispanics are the fastest growing segment of the population and will represent a larger percentage of the work force in the future. Although undoubtedly true and supported by U.S. census data, this assertion ignores the fact that the sample here is largely black and not Hispanic. The report further states that the sample is representative of entry-level populations in urban areas, "where the most pre-employment testing is likely to be conducted." This may or may not be true, with the relocation of so many large organizations to suburban settings. Additionally, for several of the occupations cited in the manual—CEOs, sales representatives, psychologists, and computer programmers—even at entry-level positions, the proportion of minorities would be much lower than in the normative group.

Also, the samples for many of the occupational groups are extremely small (one third of the occupations had a sample size of 10 subjects or less). These should not be reported as aggregate data. The statement is made that an individual's results can be compared to occupational norms to see how he or she scores relative to persons who are "already known to be 'successful' in that occupation" (Inwald, 1988a). It is unclear how the author determined that these individuals were in fact successful in their reported occupations. However, a later reference in the manual to three samples (CEOs, sales professionals, and personnel administrators) who were tested while attending a professional convention states that it is reasonable to assume individuals attending such conventions are "successful" (Inwald, 1988a, p. 69). This presents a rather dubious definition of success, and one is still left with the question of how success was defined in the other samples.

The HPP/SQ consists of a Hilson Personnel Profile test booklet and a separate Scantron answer sheet. The answer sheet has space for over 300 true/false answers, although the test consists of only 150 questions. The answer sheet also provides space to record the applicant's name, agency, sex, and race. The test booklet contains the actual questions, which are presented in a true/false format.

The test items tap into a variety of experiences, both past and present, in the areas of work, school, social, and interpersonal behaviors, experiences, and tendencies. They include perceptions of parents and comparison of self to relevant peer groups. Many items refer to school experiences, some specifying high school and others simply referring to "school." It is unclear whether the reference to school refers to one's most recent experience or to school in general. Some of the items refer to childhood. As the test is designed for use with an adult population, one would expect a broad age range, and questions such as these may be difficult to respond to or appear "irrelevant" to older examinees. A few items are confusing as they use conjunctions to join two statements; the respondent may have difficulty responding if one statement is true but the other is not. One item may be objectionable as it implies that heterosexual tendencies ("boy-crazy") present the "right" answer.

The format offers a nice mix of positively and negatively worded items, which should aid in reducing "yea-saying" or "nay-saying" tendencies. One does develop a sense of redundancy as many items ask similar questions. For example, one item inquires if the respondent scored above a stated score on the SAT. A later item asks if the respondent has scored above a different stated score on the SAT, and the stated scores only differ by 50 points. Some of the phrases used, such as "walks of life," "boy-crazy," and "hustler," are catchy, but they might not be understood in the same way by all applicants, and this could cause confusion. Most of the items are potentially verifiable and thus lend to the presumed honesty in an applicant's responses.

As the HPP/SQ is a personality test and not an intelligence measure, the items do not have a difficulty level in regards to percent responding correctly. The manual does state that the items on the test have been calculated to be on a sixth-grade reading level.

Practical Applications/Uses

The HPP/SQ may be administered on a group or individual basis. No special conditions are required aside from the usual suggestions of a comfortable environment, free from distractions. The instructions for the test administrator warn that answer sheets missing the demographic information of sex, race, and age will not be processed.

Although the test is untimed, the approximate testing time is reported as 20 to

30 minutes. Instructions for filling out the answer sheet appear in the test booklet, but examiners are asked to read the instructions aloud to applicants whenever possible. The examiner may answer questions regarding the definitions of words, but no additional interpretation of items should be provided.

The HPP/SQ is entirely computer scored. Once completed, answer sheets are sent to Hilson Research in New York. Scoring keys are not released, in an effort to preserve their integrity. As same-day scoring is promised, turnaround time would depend mainly on the mailing time to and from Hilson Research. The manual describes another method of receiving score results as the "Hilson Research Remote System Software." When using this scoring option, the true/false answers are either read by a scanner or manually keyed into a computer and sent to Hilson Research by modem. The manual reports turnaround time for this method as "6–10 seconds." Once the test is scored, Hilson Research returns a four-part printout of the applicant's results, which can be sent either through the mail or by computer if the test is scored via modem.

The first part of the printout is the Narrative Report, describing the applicant's strengths and weaknesses on the Candor, Achievement History, Social Ability, "Winner's" Image, and Initiative scales. These traits and statements are standardized and somewhat general, but can help to identify occupations and areas in which the applicant would be successful.

The next section of the printout, the Scale Profile, provides users with information on how examinees scored on the different scales and on the total test in relation to other individuals. T-scores as well as a graphical display are presented. The manual provides guidelines with regard to identifying high and low scores. Hilson Research also can provide a local or occupational norm graph with information on how the individual performed with respect to the organization or his or her occupation. These norm graphs also can appear in the printout. The Scale Profile is designed to provide comparative information on a given respondent relative to other individuals tested with the HPP/SQ, and instructions are given for its interpretation.

The third section of the printout, the Content Area Profile, depicts how the individual scored on content areas within the scales. In other words, the scales are broken into their smaller subcategories. For instance, Social Ability divides into Extraversion, Popularity, and Sensitivity to Others. This part of the printout graphs how the individual performed compared to others in these subcategories.

The last part of the printout contains a listing of how the examinee answered each of the questions, which allows an employer to verify the accuracy of the scoring.

Score guidelines indicate how to interpret an individual's scale scores both relative to others and relative to self, in order to identify the greatest areas of strength and weakness.

The manual states that Hilson Research will retain a user's test information on computer files. These data may be retrieved to calculate separate norms for a particular organization. Alternatively, an organization may request ASCII data files of scores and demographic information, which might be used for local validation studies.

Hilson Research also has published a shorter (50-item) version of this instrument for students, called the Mini-HPP/SQ. The latter is supposed to identify strengths and personality characteristics for future reference in the workplace and identify areas that need improvement so they can be worked on. The questions are a subset of the original HPP/SQ and consist of items concentrating on school activities and some personality characteristics. The wording of the questions is almost identical to those in the original, with a few exceptions: some items were changed from positive to negative, and in one or two that questioned both school and work activities, the part of the question discussing work was deleted. Certain concerns noted for the original HPP/SQ also apply to the Mini-HPP/SQ. Some of the items are ambiguous or confusing, and some contain statements joined by conjunctions that could leave one part of the answer true and one part of it false. Also, the test could be administered to high school or college students; if the student is in college, though, it is difficult to determine whether the questions should be answered about high school or about college.

The Mini-HPP/SQ presents instructions on the first page for filling out the answer sheet. The sheet consists of 50 spaces to fill in true/false answers, plus an area for recording the student's name, sex, age, and race. There are also spaces to fill in the student's school, year in school, course he or she is being tested in, grade point average, and SAT scores. It is stated that this information is needed for statistical purposes only.

Students may hand score their own tests, and they can see the results immediately. The manual describes what are considered high and low scores for the subcategories and the total, and what high and low scores in each of these areas indicate. Attached to the answer sheet is a scoring sheet, with space for subtotals and Success Quotient scores. The subcategories for the Mini-HPP/SQ resemble those for the original HPP/SQ: Candor (CA) and Achievement History (AH) assess the same dimensions measured in the original, Popularity/Leadership (PO) is very similar to Social Ability in the original, Competetive Spirit (CO) assesses the same trait as "Winner's" Image, and Drive (DR) measures the same trait as Initiative. As with the HPP/SQ, the Mini-HPP/SQ yields a total score, called a Success Quotient, which measures the likelihood of success in the workplace.

Technical Aspects

The reliability of the HPP/SQ was addressed using both internal consistency and test-retest techniques. Internal consistency was measured in two separate samples (931 entry-level city agency job applicants and 340 employees from various businesses) and was comparable across both. Coefficient alphas ranged from .76 to .83 for the five scales. A lower correlation was obtained initially for the Candor scale, but the scale was revised immediately through the deletion of poor items and the addition of stronger ones. This boosted the correlation to .80 for this scale. It is unclear if the normative sample responded to the original or the revised Candor scale items.

Test-retest reliability was assessed in a sample of 100 entry-level job applicants tested both during application and 4 to 6 weeks later. These correlations ranged from .74 to .84 for the five scales. Intercorrelations between the five scales are low, indicating that they are measuring unique traits. A separate research report provides reliability coefficients for the separate content areas. As noted previously with regard to demographic information, this data should be incorporated into the manual.

The evidence for validity of the HPP/SQ is presented via three different techniques: comparison to scores on other psychological tests, factor analysis results, and validity studies. A sample of 497 entry-level applicants completed the HPP/SQ, the MMPI (Minnesota Multiphasic Personality Inventory) and the IPI (Inwald Personality Inventory). A second sample of 76 entry-level job applicants completed both the HPP/SQ and the CPI (California Psychological Inventory). Intercorrelation matrices between the scales on these instruments revealed a pattern of divergent and convergent validity that would be expected. Scales measuring diverse traits showed no relationship, while those measuring similar traits showed strong correlations. For example, the Candor scale on the HPP/SQ correlated –.40 with the MMPI Lie scale, –.53 with the IPI Guardedness scale, and –.38 with the CPI Good Impressions scale. The manual refers to the above analyses as demonstrating concurrent validity. It may be more accurate, however, to refer to this as simply construct validity, as the term *concurrent* implies one of the criterion-related methods of demonstrating validity.

A factor analysis of the five scales was conducted separately for two samples: a sample of 931 entry-level job applicants and a sample of 455 individuals employed in various organizations. In the job applicant sample, a single factor was extracted that accounted for 47% of the variance. The author (Inwald, 1988a) states that this is evidence that the HPP/SQ measures a single construct of successful career attitudes and behavior patterns. In the second sample, two factors were extracted: one containing all four of the major scales (Achievement History, Social Ability, "Winner's" Image, and Initiative) accounted for 41% of the variance, and the second, composed of Candor and Initiative, accounted for 22% of the variance. It may prove interesting to subject the individual items to a factor analysis to determine if the five scales are in fact measuring five unique characteristics and if the items are identified correctly with the given scales.

The manual refers to a number of validity studies designed to demonstrate a relationship between the HPP/SQ and actual success on the job. These are disturbing because of the small sample sizes and a concurrent experimental design (job incumbents were used to respond to the HPP/SQ). For example, the manual devotes five pages to the discussion of a validity study with a sample size of 49 conducted for a national security company. Other studies cited, also with small samples, include administrative assistants ($N = 7$), computer programmers ($N = 3$), psychologists ($N = 13$), sales professionals ($N = 30$), CEOs ($N = 8$), and personnel administrators ($N = 132$).

By not assessing job applicants, the results of the concurrent design may not be applicable in selection. Although several of the items on the HPP/SQ are historical in nature and responses should not change over time, still, many others assess current self-perceptions in work and personal situations. Certainly, someone who is currently successful will respond in a more favorable manner to these items. One must ask, "Does the HPP/SQ predict success, or does success predict one's responses to the HPP/SQ?"

A final section in the manual provides a series of individual HPP/SQ profiles along with a narrative description of the individual respondent. Again, these are all concurrent administrations of the HPP/SQ. If the instrument is to be used in selection, some predictive validation work must be conducted.

Some of these concerns have been addressed in ongoing research by the publisher. Although not part of the manual, the publisher provided this reviewer with a number of research reports detailing the use of the HPP/SQ with a variety of occupational groups. These can be divided into two types: additional studies reporting profiles of individuals currently on the job, and studies utilizing the test in a predictive fashion.

A study of police administrators (Inwald & Brockwell, 1988d) with a sample of 76 convention attendees provides a profile of this occupational group identifying the scales on which they scored high, low, or average relative to the normative group described in the manual. With this larger sample size, this type of concurrent study is a good start to identifying the "profile" for a group. However, comparison to the normative group of 900 applicants would be problematic. As already discussed, this group is heavily minority and made up of applicants. Maybe *any* job incumbents will differ from this applicant pool. For example, it is noted that the Candor scale is higher here than in the normative applicant pool. Perhaps a sample of concurrent employees can be more honest, in that no decision rides on their test scores. Applicants for a job are more likely to attempt to portray themselves in the best light possible, even if that means stretching the truth a bit.

Two other studies establish normative information for juvenile detention administrators (Inwald & Brockwell, 1988c) and adult correctional administrators (Inwald & Brockwell, 1988b). Differences in scales between these occupations and between each occupation and the normative sample are noted. In these studies of current employees, the profiles usually make sense regarding the scales on which the job incumbents score high or low. These concurrent studies, and those presented in the manual, are unclear as to the intended use of the resulting occupational profiles: to identify characteristics of individuals in a given occupation, or to identify *successful* individuals in an occupation. The former suggests the profiles are useful in career counseling, while the latter intention suggests their use in selection. The use of the profiles in selection would not be appropriate on the basis of the evidence provided. For example, the study of police administrators assumes that a) the convention attendees are successful, b) the profile of these administrators differs from other applicants for the job, and c) the answers given by the administrators at the time of testing would be the same responses given when they are applying for these positions.

A study of the relationship between training success and the HPP/SQ with a sample of 448 law enforcement trainees *was* conducted in a predictive fashion (Inwald & Patterson, 1989). All were administered both the HPP/SQ and the IPI, although these measures were not used in selection. The instruments differentiated successful and nonsuccessful trainees, as defined by completion of the training program in the academy. The utility of the instrument is difficult to gauge in this sample, as the base rate was high—76% were successful. The fact that some selection technique was used obviously reduced the number of failures. This is the type of study that should be included in the manual and repeated to demonstrate cross-validation.

Additional studies of police (Inwald, 1990), sales personnel (Inwald & Kaufman, n.d.), and sales representatives (Inwald & Brockman, 1988a) were conducted in a predictive fashion. Again, this type of predictive design dispels many of the concerns raised in the concurrent research.

All studies suggesting occupational profiles should be cross-validated. In a separate research report, the author notes that "the sample size here may be responsible for an increase in classification accuracy due to the ability of customized prediction equations to capitalize on idiosyncrasies of a small sample" (*Hilson Research Abstracts*, n.d., p. 3). This statement is correct, yet it understates the problem. Any model will capitalize on the pecularities of the sample on which it is developed. This is why cross-validation is required even when large samples of several hundred are used. The problem is compounded when small samples are utilized in developing a predictive model.

Critique

The manual does not present the HPP/SQ in its best light. Numerous clerical errors and incorrect references detract from the instrument. For example, the manual refers the reader to Appendix A for occupational norms, but there is no Appendix A. However, under Section IV, a subsection designated as "A. Norms" does exist, and one assumes that this is the section referred to. A reference is made on page 7 of the manual to "Figure 3," but again, there is no Figure 3. It appears that the information referred to is on page 9, but the information is not labeled.

The publisher should update the manual to include the findings from the various research reports. The manual presents only concurrent research, yet many subsequent studies of a predictive design have been conducted and provide evidence for the use of the HPP/SQ as a selection and placement tool. Information on the ethnic composition of the normative sample and the reliabilities for the subcontent areas also should be added.

Suggestions for future research include modifications to the normative sample and cross-validation of the profiles. The normative sample should be larger and representative of the occupations for which this instrument will be used. Perhaps the high percent of minorities is appropriate for occupations in corrections, security, and police work, but this should be documented.

Occupational profiles must be cross-validated. In a more recent concurrent study of 95 administrative employees at a health-care accounts receivable management company, equations were developed using the different HPP/SQ scales to predict employee success. In this study, the author called for the cross-validation of the equations (Inwald, n.d.-b). Obviously the publisher is aware of the need for cross-validation, and it can be the anticipated course for future research.

In conclusion, the HPP/SQ presents a tool that can be used in career counseling and assessing a candidate's strengths and weaknesses relative to various occupational groups. Its potential as a selection instrument is suggested in predictive validity studies that, unfortunately, are not included in the manual. Continuation of an already vigorous research program and expansion into cross-validation studies will doubtless demonstrate its utility in a variety of occupations.

References

Hilson research abstracts. (n.d.). New York: Hilson Research.

Inwald, R.E. (1988a). *Hilson Personnel Profile/Success Quotient manual.* New York: Hilson Research.

Inwald, R.E. (1988b). *Hilson Personnel Profile/Success Quotient test booklet.* New York: Hilson Research.

Inwald, R.E. (1990). *Use of the HPP/SQ and HCSI to predict supervisory ratings* (Research Abstract). New York: Hilson Research.

Inwald, R.E. (n.d.-a). *Additional notes on the development of the HPP/SQ.* New York: Hilson Research.

Inwald, R.E. (n.d.-b). *The HPP/SQ as a predictor of adult work performance.* Manuscript submitted for publication.

Inwald, R.E., & Brockwell, A.L. (1988a). *Predicting sales representative performance using the HPP/SQ.* Manuscript submitted for publication.

Inwald, R.E., & Brockwell, A.L. (1988b). *Success quotient profiles of juvenile and adult correctional administrators.* Manuscript submitted for publication.

Inwald, R.E., & Brockwell, A.L. (1988c). *Success quotient profiles of juvenile detention administrators.* Manuscript submitted for publication.

Inwald, R.E., & Brockwell, A.L. (1988d). *Success quotient profiles of law enforcement administrators.* Manuscript submitted for publication.

Inwald, R.E., & Kaufman, J.C. (n.d.). *Job type and performance classifications of managers and sales personnel using the HPP/SQ* (Research Abstract). New York: Hilson Research.

Inwald, R.E., & Patterson, T. (1989). *Use of psychological testing to predict success of law enforcement trainees.* New York: Hilson Research.

Lizanne DeStefano, Ph.D.
Associate Professor of Educational Psychology, University of Illinois at Urbana-Champaign, Champaign, Illinois.

Deborah L. Winking, Ph.D.
Associate Evaluator, North Central Regional Educational Laboratory, Oak Brook, Illinois.

THE INSTRUCTIONAL ENVIRONMENT SCALE

James E. Ysseldyke and Sandra L. Christenson. Austin, Texas: PRO-ED, Inc.

Introduction

The Instructional Environment Scale (TIES; Ysseldyke & Christenson, 1987) is not a norm-referenced test, but rather a qualitative scale used to gather descriptive information on the nature of a student's instructional environment. The TIES is designed to gather data on 12 interrelated components of effective instruction: Instructional Presentation, Classroom Environment, Teacher Expectations, Cognitive Emphasis, Motivational Strategies, Relevant Practice, Academic Engaged Time, Informed Feedback, Adaptive Instruction, Progress Evaluation, Instructional Planning, and Student Understanding. Each component is considered a principle of effective instruction, which one should take into account when describing a student's instructional environment. Because the 12 components are regarded as representing the key elements related to achievement, the authors argue that educational personnel must consider these components and make decisions about how best to deliver, manage, or assure the presence of each.

To develop a framework and context for the scale, the authors reviewed literature pertaining to predictors of positive academic outcomes for regular education, at risk, and special education students. Research on school effectiveness, teacher effectiveness, instructional effectiveness, student cognition, teacher decision making, models of school learning, and instructional psychology was included. Most of the literature was correlational in nature, and several large-scale experimental studies were reviewed.

As a product of the comprehensive literature review, Ysseldyke and Christenson developed a list of over 100 factors found to be correlated with positive academic outcomes. These factors were screened and selected for potential inclusion based on the following criteria: a) factors that were repeatedly mentioned in the literature as important for improving academic progress, b) factors that were easily observable, or c) factors that were supported by empirical documentation in model teaching programs. These factors were used to develop potential scale items describing the way in which instruction was planned, delivered, and evaluated for an individual student. Initial versions of the TIES consisted of 200 statements describing classroom instruction. This list was too long, too laborious to complete, and redundant. Through extensive piloting of the long scale in school settings, items were omitted, combined, or reworded. Redundant items, items requiring excessive interviewing, and situationally based or content-unique items were eliminated. On the basis of the pilot studies, the authors reduced the initial version of the scale from 200 to 107 to 81 to 45 and finally to 40 items.

As the list of items was being finalized, several formats, including checklists, rating scales, narrative recordings, and frequency counts, were considered. A qualitative rating scale, indicating how characteristic each component is for an individual student, was chosen. Four categories (very much like, somewhat like, not much like, not at all like) were selected.

In order to realistically represent the complexity of the classroom environments, the 40 selected items were organized into components representing the essential components of instruction. After piloting, the 22-component scale was reduced to a 12-component scale. Pilot studies of the final revision of the scale were conducted in suburban elementary schools over a 6-month period; however, detailed explanations of the schools used, characteristics of settings, and students within these settings (necessary to fully appreciate the content analysis and field testing that resulted in the final product) are not reported.

The authors contend that while the 12 components describe characteristics of a student's instructional environment, they do not evaluate the quality of instruction for a student. They hypothesize that how the components are combined or delivered during teaching—due to the synergistic effect—describes the quality of instruction for an individual student. Thus, the kinds of decisions being made in the 12 areas and the interrelationships among the components influence the quality of instruction for individual students. The TIES relies on multiple data sources and data collection strategies. Persons administering the scale gather data using three methods: interviewing the student's teacher, observing the student in a classroom setting, and interviewing the student.

The TIES is organized into four parts: the Data Record Form, the Instructional Rating Form, the Summary/Profile Sheet, and Descriptors. The four-page Data Record Form is used to record data obtained through observation and interviews. One page of the form consists of seven teacher interview questions and space to record the teacher's responses to each of those questions, two pages are used to record data obtained by observation, and the last page presents a list of student interview questions with space to record responses. The Data Record Form captures information essential to completing the Instructional Rating Form.

The Instructional Rating Form contains a detailed list of factors to consider in rating each of the 12 components of the student's instructional environment. The Likert-type rating scale ranges from "Very much like the student's instruction" to "Not at all like the student's instruction." The four-page rating form is considered similar to a test protocol and as such may be placed in the diagnostician's assessment file.

The two-page Summary/Profile Sheet, which provides an inventory of the student's instructional environment under certain conditions at a point in time, is used to specify the student's instructional needs and document action to be taken to address the identified needs. This sheet is a summary of potential instructional interventions and as such is meant to be placed in the student's cumulative file.

The Descriptors, which appear in Appendix 1 of the TIES manual, are detailed lists of factors that comprise each of the 12 components. They are used to identify specific ways to intervene in a student's instruction.

Practical Applications/Uses

Ysseldyke and Christenson cite two major purposes for using the TIES: a) to systematically describe the extent to which a student's academic or behavior problems are a function of factors in the instructional environment, and b) to identify starting points in designing appropriate instructional interventions for individual students. They also list several secondary purposes, such as prereferral intervention, consultation, IEP development, environment contrast, teacher training, progress monitoring, and research.

The authors also go to some lengths to describe inappropriate use of the scale. The TIES was designed as a means of documenting and describing instruction as it occurs for an individual student. This individual focus limits the scale's utility. Despite its representation of classroom instruction, the TIES was not designed as a teacher evaluation scale and should not be used as such. Further, this instrument is not norm referenced; because there are so many factors, including student characteristics, that influence the qualitative nature of the instructional environment for an individual, the TIES should not be used to evaluate or compare schools, teachers, or school districts.

Although the TIES does not require rigid administration procedures, specific guidelines must be considered and followed in order to reliably describe a student's instructional environment. Professionals who conduct assessments, compile assessment data, or are part of a multidisciplinary assessment or child study team (e.g., school psychologists, school counselors, teacher consultants, special educators, teachers, school social workers, clinical psychologists, and educational diagnosticians) may be qualified to use the TIES. Users must have training in or knowledge of the components of effective instruction and must be familiar with the content of the Descriptors that define and illustrate each of the 12 components.

Administration of the TIES requires six steps:

1. conducting a classroom observation and completing the middle two pages of the Data Record Form;
2. interviewing the student and completing page 4 of the Data Record Form;
3. interviewing the student's teacher and completing page 1 of the Data Record Form;
4. deciding if additional data are needed and, if so, gathering them;
5. completing the Instructional Rating Form and the Summary/Profile Sheet; and
6. providing feedback to the teacher and the student.

The process is flexible in that the order and number of interviews and observations will vary. The user should plan the observation and interview schedule on an individual basis after considering factors such as the purpose of the assessment, time constraints, teacher preference, and the complexity of the case. It may be that multiple assessments (e.g., over time, across instructional settings) are necessary to capture an accurate description of instruction for an individual student.

Due to the qualitative nature of the TIES, the user must be able to integrate information from various sources in order to make summary judgments regarding relevant features of the instructional environment. In this sense scoring and interpretation occur simultaneously. The process involves making integrative judgments on a 4-point scale, evaluating each of the 12 components in terms of the degree to which it characterizes the student's learning environment (i.e., from "Very much like the student's instruction" to "Not at all like the student's instruction"). The Instructional Rating Form describes each component and provides prompts to users regarding the critical factors to consider when rating each component. After conducting classroom observations and teacher and student interviews, the examiner must read the description of the factors that comprise each component and select the point on the Likert scale that typifies the student's instructional environment.

The integration of multiple data sources results in informed summary judgments regarding each component. The examiner is encouraged to consider all data sources and is cautioned that no one source is more important than any other when determining which rating best fits the instructional interaction. The authors label this task of triangulation of multiple data sources as *blending*. The interpretation section of the examiner's manual guides examiners through the process of blending observational and interview data. Guidelines for scoring include a discussion of the characteristics of ordinal scaling and the mindset that facilitates triangulation, as well as four sample vignettes where blending techniques were used to arrive at summary judgments.

Following scoring, ratings from the Instructional Rating Form are transferred to the Summary/Profile sheet. Lines then drawn to connect the component ratings create a graphical representation of peaks and valleys in the student's instructional environment. Ratings of 1 or 2 suggest areas that may be interfering with the student's instructional progress; ratings of 3 and 4 point out areas that enhance the student's instructional progress. The Summary Profile sheet can be used to discuss instructional needs with the teacher and may be placed in the student's permanent file.

The graphical representation of ratings for the 12 components contributes to the easy interpretation of the TIES for teachers and practitioners. However, the authors caution that while interpretation is not difficult, the task does require good consultative skills and should be approached carefully. Their guidelines regarding the best presentation of results to teachers focus on the student's instructional needs and *not* on teacher strengths and weaknesses.

Technical Aspects

Because the TIES is a qualitative scale used to gather descriptive information and not a norm-referenced instrument, the primary technical concerns addressed by the authors are limited to interobserver agreement and content validity. Other considerations of technical rigor that can be used to support the strengths of qualitative instruments (such as measures to ensure social and discriminant validity) are not reported.

Interrater reliability was calculated by computing intraclass correlations using procedures outlined by Shrout and Fleiss (1979). Twenty-eight observers watched tapes of each of two teachers instructing a small group of elementary-age students. Observers completed the observation record form and were given copies of completed teacher interviews and student interviews. They scored the instructional situation that they viewed on the basis of observation tapes and interview data. Intraclass correlations were computed.

The specific method of intraclass correlation used was a one-way analysis of variance with random effects. The intraclass correlation was estimated by

$$ICC(1,1) = \frac{\text{MS Tapes} - \text{MS Residual}}{\text{MS Tapes} + (K-1)\text{MS Residual}}$$

where K was the number of judges (28) rating each target student. The obtained reliability coefficients for each TIES component ranged from .83 (Cognitive Emphasis, Motivational Strategies) to .96 (Academic Engaged Time, Informed Feedback, Student Understanding), with an average of .93. The reliabilities meet criteria specified for use of a scale in screening and instructional planning (Salvia & Ysseldyke, 1985).

Critique

The Instructional Environment Scale represents a refreshing movement away from a "pathology"-based approach toward learning problems. As opposed to emphasizing what is "wrong" with the child, this instrument focuses on the dynamic exchange between teacher, materials, and student that occurs in the learning environment. This environmental perspective of educational needs is supported in psychological, educational, and special education research and practice. The approach was theoretically conceptualized by Bandura (1978) as a reciprocal exchange between cognitive and environmental influences. Subsequent research in special education has resulted in an assessment strategy as a methodology for ecological inventories that involves the documentation of *environmental* antecedents and consequences to behaviors occurring in educational or other contexts (Snell, 1983). One of the greatest contributions of the TIES may be that it offers practitioners a *systematic* approach to categorizing, labeling, and describing the educational milieu for individual students. As such, it legitimatizes shifting the focus of remediation from being solely child-centered toward the interaction of the individual with environment, materials, and delivery of instruction.

The qualitative approach provides a database that results in a richer understanding of the learning environment of the individual student. Essentially the administrator of the TIES becomes involved in a "micro" case study of a bounded system. The system, as authors are careful to point out, is the instructional environment of a *single* student, not the class as a whole nor the teacher exclusively. Although some qualitative evaluators maintain that it takes years of training to become an effective observer, recent research in responsive evaluation has supported the effectiveness of techniques that train parents, teachers, and others in the use of qualitative techniques for specific evaluative purposes (DeStefano, Maude, Crews, & Mabry, 1992).

The methodology employed in the TIES is grounded in this movement toward wider use of qualitative data-gathering techniques. The TIES manual provides administrators with instruction and guidelines for specific observation and interview activities. Further, techniques for effective observation and interview appear in both the manual and the rating forms (e.g., written cues that focus the observer's attention on the target student and on relevant indicators are presented directly on the observation form). In addition, examiners are urged to conduct a simplified form of member checks (Lincoln & Guba, 1985); that is, to verify information gathered through interview and to clarify ambiguous observations.

Although the examiner is guided through the process of interviewing and observing, the final task of interpreting qualitative data presents the user with unique problems inherent in qualitative methods, including synthesizing the data derived from various sources and condensing relatively large amounts of data for the purpose of interpretation. In sum, theoretical discussions of methods, guidelines for interview and observation, teaching examples and vignettes, and the data collection instruments exemplify sound techniques for qualitative inquiry and present them in a useful format for practitioners. However, ultimately the responsibility for triangulation of data and interpretation falls on the individual administering TIES, a responsibility that can be overwhelming even for the experienced qualitative researcher. In this sense (and in all situations where a "human instrument" is used as the assessment device) caution must be exercised in interpreting results, especially in cases that involve high-stakes decisions for individual students.

Specialized techniques are designed to combat the potential criticism of drawing conclusions from a snapshot view of a single point in time (i.e., an isolated instructional observation). Although space on the scoring form accommodates only one observation, the user is instructed to conduct as many as necessary to provide a clear picture of the instructional environment. A strength of the methodology lies in its focus on rich description of the instructional setting and the attention to multiple perspectives. The equal attention given to student perceptions (as evidenced in the interview process) is a welcome departure from the traditional view of students as passive recipients of learning. In addition to providing a rich source of data that is not tapped in other assessments, inclusion of student perceptions may serve to provide those who typically have not succeeded in school with feelings of empowerment regarding improvement of their own learning capabilities. Second, the student interview protocol advises interviewers to refer to the specifics of the instructional setting observed and if necessary to present the student with actual products of his or her work completed during the session. This technique helps to remind the student of what happened during the observation, helps build rapport, facilitates reliable responding during the interview, and ensures that both the examiner and student are referencing the same instructional session.

Although the flexibility of the interview techniques is sufficient to accommodate individual needs, the manual should provide the interviewer with further instruction to increase the validity of responding with diverse populations. Standard interview procedures may need to be modified based on the language development of the student assessed. For example, initially a set of similar questions may be asked in various ways to determine if the student has a reliable response pattern or an accurate yes-no response. This information is important, given the obvious implication for validity of data if the TIES is administered to individuals without a reliable communication system. Techniques such as spending time with the student, using pictures, or engaging in role play also may be necessary to gain trust, depending on individual student differences and accompanying behavioral, emotional, or learning problems. The importance of individualizing interview techniques cannot be ignored if examiners are to seriously consider student input as valuable data in the total assessment process.

The TIES presents an essentially proactive response to educational problems, an approach consistent with the current climate of educational thought that supports serving students with special needs in regular environments whenever possible (Lilly, 1988). Used as intended, this scale serves as a powerful prereferral tool. The diagnostic profile targets educational interventions that can be used in the regular classroom, thereby prompting users to exhaust alternative strategies before referring the student to special education. Illustrating this commitment to solving problems within the context of regular education adaptations, a supplemental text was compiled to complement the TIES: *Strategies and Tactics for Effective Instruction* (Algozzine & Ysseldyke, 1992). This reference tool serves as a guide to proactive instructional planning.

In cases where the student already has been targeted for special education services, the TIES may be employed as a systematic method for satisfying the observational requirement of initial IEP development as well as the yearly evaluation mandated under PL 94-142. Used on a formative basis, the TIES captures valuable qualitative data with which to supplement the traditionally quantitative data used to make educational placement decisions.

From a content perspective, the TIES offers a wealth of information to the evaluator or educational consultant; however, psychometrically the instrument lacks precision. Following identification in the literature, numerous indicators of effective instruction were organized into 22 and finally 12 components that the authors state comprise effective instructional environments. In order to present empirical evidence of construct validity, it would be helpful to provide information (via statistical or social validation techniques) regarding the extent to which each of the indicators relates to the component, as well as the extent to which each component relates to the construct of "effective instructional environment."

Measures of discriminant validity also would provide powerful evidence of the scale's adequacy for measuring instructional environment. Just as we are interested in combinations of components that comprise effective instruction, it is also important to be assured that the absence of those components relates to the opposite outcome (i.e., ineffective instruction). Exploration of discriminant validity could include low or insignificant correlations of components with others thought to be irrelevant to effective instruction, as well as observations of various instructional sessions to determine factors that are absent and those that are present in instructional settings judged to be effective and ineffective.

Although content validity was explored through the literature, and the components admittedly seem intuitively related to some notion of effective instruction, the absence of factor analysis raises questions regarding whether the scale is truly measuring the construct of "learning environment" for which it was designed. If one is to assume that statistical tests of psychometric properties were not pursued given the qualitative nature of the scale, techniques of social validation could have been employed to lend strength to claims that the 12 components in fact comprise effective instructional environments. The process of social validation allows one to consider the perceptions of both researchers and practitioners in the field in rating the importance, relevance, or utility of each of the instructional components. Likewise other methods of social validation use focus groups of experts and practitioners to assist in defining and refining the content of each of the components cited in the literature. Application of these techniques would lend credibility to the scale and perhaps contribute to feelings of ownership by the teachers and clinicians for which the instrument is targeted.

Finally, sufficient detail is unavailable regarding the pilot studies that served as the basis of content validity. Although the authors report that "use" of the instrument in school settings resulted in narrowing of descriptive statements and actual numbers of components, the examiner has no data describing the types of schools or individual students with which the instrument was piloted.

Attention to interobserver agreement provides more than adequate evidence that given an instructional scenario, different observers would agree on the instructional environment components in place in that situation. The stability of responses across similar instructional settings for an individual, however, is not explored. Although test-retest reliability in the traditional sense is not an issue when considering the dynamic exchanges that occur between teacher, student, and materials in a single instructional session, some measure of consistency or stability across observations is desirable. As noted previously, though the scoring protocol is designed to accommodate only a single observation, the authors advise users to conduct as many observations as necessary to provide a clear picture of the instructional environment. Tests of stability of scoring components across similar instructional settings for the same student are necessary to ensure that placement decisions made are not based on an anomaly; that is, a single combination of instructional components unlikely to occur again. Sound decision making requires some confidence in the degree of stability of profiles obtained from similar instructional-setting observations of the same individual.

Additional cautions to users involve the potential misuse of this instrument. The first caution underscores a concern cited by authors: use of the TIES as a teacher evaluation tool. Extreme care must be exercised in presenting results to teachers to avoid misinterpretation of the assessment as an evaluation of instructor competence or as a critique of teacher behavior, either of which could potentially undermine use of results in the classroom. Second, the manual's inclusion of a section describing teacher training as a secondary TIES use sends conflicting messages of purpose to potential users. Although the authors adamantly insist that the scale not be used as a teacher evaluation tool, the section on teacher training and the close link between teacher training and evaluation in the minds of many educators may result in the application of the TIES for the very purpose that the authors claim to guard against.

The potential flexibility with which the instrument can be administered and the rich descriptive data that result promise to make the TIES an essential tool for regular educators, special educators, and administrators. Additionally, the detailed descriptive information provided on the 12 components of effective instructional environments and their basis in research provides the resource teacher or clinician with a valuable desktop reference. The case study approach by definition promotes a "description" before "diagnosis" orientation, which prompts decision-makers to look at alternatives. First and foremost, the holistic process for analyzing instructional environments and interviewing teachers supports an interdisciplinary approach and cooperation among professionals. By facilitating dialogue in the form of teacher interview and presentation of results, the TIES discourages fragmenting the student into a discrete "set of problems" and instead focuses attention on relevant aspects of the education process for a *unique* individual. Unanswered questions regarding the stability of ratings across similar observations, lack of attention to issues of social and discriminant validity, and unclear discussion of characteristics of the pilot population are all cause for caution when using this instrument in making decisions with likely long-term impact on individual students. However, involving teachers in the process as examiners and interviewees has multiple positive effects, including increasing validity of the process and increasing ownership for results, thereby increasing the chance for positive change for individual students.

References

Algozzine, B., & Ysseldyke, J. (1992). *Strategies and tactics for effective instruction.* Longmont, CO: Sopris West.

Bandura, A. (1978). The self system in reciprocal determinism. *American Psychologist, 33,* 344–351.

DeStefano, L., Maude, S., Crews, S., & Mabry, L. (1992). Using qualitative evaluation methods to identify exemplary practices in early childhood education. *Early Education and Development, 3*(2), 173–187.

Lilly, S. (1988). The regular education initiative: A force for change and general and special education. *Education and Training in Mental Retardation, 23*(4), 253–257.

Lincoln, Y., & Guba, E. (1985). Naturalistic inquiry. Beverly Hills, CA: Sage.

Salvia, J., & Ysseldyke, J.E. (1985). *Assessment in special and remedial education* (3rd ed.). Boston: Houghton Mifflin.

Shrout, P.E., & Fleiss, J.L. (1979). Intraclass correlations: Uses in assessing rater reliability. *Psychological Bulletin, 86*(2), 420–428.

Snell, M.E. (1983). *Systematic instruction of the moderately and severely disabled.* Columbus, OH: Merrill.

Ysseldyke, J.E., & Christenson, S.L. (1987). *The Instructional Environment Scale: A comprehensive methodology for assessing an individual student's instruction.* Austin, TX: PRO-ED.

Lucille B. Strain, Ph.D.
Professor of Education and Coordinator of the Graduate Reading Program, Bowie State University, Bowie, Maryland.

INTEGRATED ASSESSMENT SYSTEM

Roger Farr and Beverly Farr. San Antonio, Texas: The Psychological Corporation.

Introduction

The Integrated Assessment System (IAS; Farr & Farr, 1990, 1991) is designed for the assessment of abilities and skills in the language arts. In its entirety, the IAS comprises the "Language Arts Performance Assessment" and the "Language Arts Portfolio," each containing a number of related components. Together, these provide a means for developing and assessing students' use of a variety of thinking strategies in reading and writing, as well as a framework for collecting and maintaining a record of student performance. The IAS fosters integration of several important elements in language arts development. It encourages integration not only in use of thinking, reading, and writing abilities but in instructional and assessment procedures as well. Particularly designed to accommodate needs in classrooms where whole language and literature-based instructional approaches are used, it also can be used advantageously in more traditional instructional situations. Published in 1990, the Language Arts Performance Assessment and the Language Arts Portfolio of the IAS are complementary, although each can be applied independently of the other.

Siblings Roger and Beverly Farr are the authors of the IAS. Dr. Roger Farr is Professor of Education, director of the Center for Reading and Language Studies, and Associate Dean for Research and Graduate Development at Indiana University in Bloomington, Indiana. He also serves as part-time associate director of the ERIC Clearinghouse in Language Arts. Distinguished in the fields of reading, research, and evaluation in reading, Dr. Farr is widely known for his numerous publications. Among these, he is the author of the Metropolitan Achievement Test: Reading (1986), the coordinating editor of the Iowa Silent Reading Tests (1972), and a senior author in the area of measurement and evaluation for the *Language Arts Programs* published by Harcourt Brace Jovanovich. In 1970 his research monograph, *Reading: What Can be Measured?* (1969), was selected as one of the 20 outstanding books in education by Pi Lambda Theta. He also has coauthored two texts, *Reading: What Can be Measured?* (Farr & Carey, 1986) and *Teaching a Child to Read* (1979). Distinguished as an educational leader, Farr was president of the International Reading Association (IRA) from 1979 to 1980 and a member of its board of directors from 1974 to 1977. He has chaired many IRA committees, including the Committee on Evaluation of Tests and the Committee on the National Assessment of Educational Progress. His editorial experiences include service on the editorial advisory boards of *Reading Research Quarterly, Early Years, Research and Creative Activity,* and the *Journal of Re-*

search and Development in Education. Acclaimed for his services and achievements in education, Farr has received numerous awards and honors, including the 1984 IRA William S. Gray Award for Outstanding Lifetime Contributions to the field of reading. He was elected to the IRA Hall of Fame in 1986 and selected as the Outstanding Teacher Educator in 1988.

Dr. Beverly Farr received her doctorate from Indiana University, Bloomington, Indiana, and is associated with the Far West Educational Laboratory in San Francisco, California.

Materials included in the Language Arts Performance Assessment are the reading passages and writing activities, response forms, directions for administering, a scoring guide, scoring rubrics, and a training package for scoring. These materials are described as follows:

Reading passages and guided writing activities. Each reading passage is contained in a separate, colorful, illustrated booklet designed for a specific grade level (1–8). Whether containing an original story or informational piece or a selection from children's literature, all reading passages present high-interest, thought-provoking material. Throughout the series are selections representative of realistic fiction, poetry, plays, and expository writing. All reading passages are printed in a grade-appropriate typeface and size. For all levels except Grade 1, a reading passage and a writing activity together comprise a "prompt," so called because their purpose is to elicit student response. At Grade 1, a single student booklet is used as a prompt.

Each guided writing activity is integrated with the specific reading passage it accompanies. Writing tasks are designed to encourage a process approach to writing. That is, students are led through a step-by-step process of planning, writing, editing, and revising their work before producing a final draft of the type of writing required in the task. Activities focus on major types of writing, such as information reports, story endings, persuasive essays, character analyses, letters, pattern stories, directions, newspaper stories, and feature articles. Except for Grade 1, each guided writing activity is contained in a separate booklet.

Response forms. Response forms for students to use in writing their final drafts are provided for each guided writing activity. These forms facilitate maintenance of a systematic record of students' writing. On each form, spaces are designated for the student's name, ID number, sex, school, grade, district, date completed, name of teacher, and prompt number. Spaces also are designated for recording a grade for each of the three dimensions specified in the scoring rubric (set of scoring guidelines).

Directions for administering. Accompanying each reading/writing prompt are general directions for administering all prompts and specific directions for administering the given prompt. Attention focuses on the nature of the reading/writing prompts and their unique features that allow assessment to "mirror" instruction, yield diagnostic insights, allow for flexible use, and permit a high degree of collaboration and teacher-student interaction. Specific steps and their sequences in administration are described and explained. Also provided are annotated lists of related literature and children's literature appropriate to the topic of a given prompt.

Scoring guides. Scoring guides are designed to show how students' responses to the reading/writing prompts should be scored. In six major sections, each scoring guide provides general information: terminology, the general scoring rubric and the scale to be used, factors to consider while scoring and how to handle scoring inconsistencies, unique features of a particular prompt and how to interpret the scoring rubric for that prompt, model student papers, a sample student paper to provide practice in scoring, suggestions for interpreting student performance, and a discussion of additional instructional insights that might be gained from student responses.

Scoring rubrics. A scoring rubric, the set of scoring guidelines used to rate a student's response, is included for each reading/writing prompt. Although the general guidelines are the same for all prompts, specific modifications apply for each individual prompt.

Training package for scoring. A kit is provided containing all materials needed for scoring responses to the reading/writing prompts along with details for holistic scoring. Also contained in the kit are materials essential for staff development activities related to the uses of the IAS.

Included in the Language Arts Portfolio are a videotape and viewer's guide, a teacher's manual, student portfolios, and a portfolio storage box. These materials are described as follows:

Videotape and viewer's guide. Narrated by Dr. Roger Farr, the videotape and viewer's guide provide an introduction to the concept of portfolio assessment and specific suggestions for use of the IAS. Viewers are instructed in means for initiation and maintenance of portfolios, as well as offered suggestions for sharing results of portfolio assessment with parents and administrators.

Teacher's manual. Contained in a three-ring binder that permits adding or deleting material, the teacher's manual provides information on portfolio assessment generally and the Language Arts Performance Assessment specifically.

Individual student portfolios. Individual portfolios are provided for the collected writings of students. Information pertinent to record keeping is printed on each folder in order to facilitate orderly organization of the materials placed inside by the student.

Portfolio storage box. As the name suggests, this is a sturdy box provided for storage and easy retrieval of students' individual portfolios.

Packages of materials are available from the publisher either for examination or for classroom use. An examination package (specimen kit) includes one reading passage, one guided writing activity/blackline master, one response form, one copy of directions for the response form, one copy of the directions for administration, and one copy of a passage-specific scoring rubric. A complete package of materials in the Language Arts Performance Assessment suitable for classroom use contains 25 of each of three reading passages, one set of each of three guided reading activities/blackline masters, one copy of the directions for administering, three packages of 25 response forms each, and one copy of directions for using the response forms.

Practical Applications/Uses

The purposes served by the IAS relate closely to the goals of instruction in the language arts sought in classrooms in which holistic and literature-based approaches are used. Students are challenged and directed to use a variety of higher order thinking strategies in their reading and writing activities. Relationships are drawn between students' prior experiences and knowledge and the topics about which they are reading and writing. Students are encouraged to read a variety of materials, including children's literature and expository selections, and led to use metacognitive strategies in assessing their reading and writing performances. In their written tasks, students are led through a process of planning, writing, revising, and editing before producing a final draft. Thus, they are encouraged to develop a sense of "ownership" of their written products, and they become active participants in evaluating their progress.

The scoring system of the Language Arts Performance Assessment yields evidence of students' abilities to use their comprehension of reading passages in their writing tasks. Scores range from a low of 1 to a high of 4 for each of three dimensions of performance. The "Response to Reading" dimension reflects comprehension of a passage, taking into account the amount and accuracy of information used from the passage and its relevance to the assigned task. The "Management of Content" dimension pertains to the student's ability to organize content, maintain focus, and develop a finished product according to a logical plan. The final dimension, "Command of Language," focuses on the grammar and usage characterizing the student's work. It takes into consideration the nature of the student's sentence structure and variety of sentences used, word choices, and the like.

Each scoring rubric for the reading/writing activities provides clear descriptions of characteristics to consider in evaluating the student's performance in each of the defined dimensions. Guidelines for a score at any of the levels (1 through 4) are clearly drawn so that a scorer can assess a response objectively. Each scoring rubric is presented on a single page, thereby simplifying its use.

The IAS Portfolio includes several types of materials essential for organizing and maintaining students' work and for helping teachers become skilled in the use of portfolios generally and the Language Arts Performance Assessment in particular. Printed materials are included for preparation of student portfolios, and instructions are given for organizing and maintaining the portfolios. By means of the videotape and viewer's guide, users receive an introduction to developing many important concepts related to portfolio assessment. Teachers are helped to realize ways by which portfolio assessment can be initiated and the results shared with parents and administrators. The concept of portfolio assessment as well as specifics related to its use can apply in any situation in which language-arts development is sought.

The IAS offers a means for providing evidence of students' performances over a period of time. This collection of evidence can be used to augment the information gained from traditional test scores. It also can help students, parents, and others concerned gain a meaningful view of a student's progress.

Results of students' performances on the IAS aid in clarifying the direction that instruction should take in a given situation. These results can clearly indicate the objectives and procedures that educators should implement in a particular classroom. In this way, relationships between instruction and assessment become practically identifiable.

Use of the IAS serves to provide students and teachers with clear concepts of relationships between reading and writing. At the same time, the role of higher order thinking strategies in reading and writing become clear. Because of this, the IAS can be used to supplement both instruction and assessment in traditional language arts curricula. In situations in which specific skills and basic levels of thinking tend to be overemphasized, use of the IAS facilitates achieving an appropriate balance with some of the broader aspects of the language arts.

The IAS is designed to be administered by classroom teachers in any of the grade levels 1 through 8. Directions for administration are easily understood, and scoring guides simplify scoring procedures. The time required for administration is appropriate in terms of class periods, varying from one to three or four periods.

The IAS can be used to encourage collaboration within a classroom. As students compete only with their own previous performances, they are encouraged to share ideas and assistance in a number of ways.

For best results, the Language Arts Performance Assessment and the Language Arts Portfolio are used together, comprising the complete IAS. Each, however, also can be applied independently, depending on the needs in a particular instructional situation.

Technical Aspects

Important information pertinent to understanding the technical aspects of the IAS is available in the preliminary technical report (Farr & Farr, 1991). According to this report, development of the IAS began in the summer of 1989 and continued through the 1989–90 school year. Prompts (reading passages and guided writing activities) were written by the authors of IAS and a team of experienced writers at Indiana University and then field tested in each grade level 1 through 8. Three sequential stages marked development of the prompts: actual writing of the prompts and scoring rubrics, a small-scale tryout of the prompts and scoring rubrics, and a large-scale field test of the prompts and rubrics.

Several factors were considered in the development of guidelines for determining the nature of the reading passages and guided reading activities. It was decided that the reading passages would represent a number of text types or genres of interest and appeal for students at a given targeted grade level. The difficulty of the passages would be appropriate to a wide range of student abilities at each specific grade level. Passages would be longer than those typically found on standardized tests, yet short enough to complete within a single class period. Some of the passages would include multiple selections, in order to give students an opportunity to integrate and synthesize information across sources.

Similarly, the guided writing activities were designed in light of several factors. Instead of being "pure" measures of writing performance, the guided writing activities would focus on a student's ability to use reading material to accomplish a writing task. Thus, the reading/writing prompts would be organized according to "written products" rather than according to modes of writing (e.g., narration, description, explanation, and persuasion). Based on a survey of leading language arts programs, the types of writing to be included in the guided writing activities would represent the types of writing usually implemented at each grade level.

Each prompt would be designed to elicit a cluster of higher order thinking skills rather than a single isolated skill at a time.

As in determining the nature of the reading/writing activities, several factors were taken into consideration in selecting the thinking strategies that the prompts would elicit. Leading language-arts instructional programs and curriculum guides were examined to determine current trends in development of thinking skills. Based on the findings, a determination was made to elicit critical-thinking and problem-solving skills by the prompts.

The IAS scoring system was designed to serve the dual purpose of measuring both reading comprehension and writing performances. Research supporting "discourse synthesis" (drawing on existing texts to produce new texts) formed the major basis of the scoring system.

The advantages and disadvantages of commonly used methods of scoring writing samples (holistic, analytic, and primary trait) were given careful attention. A number of language-arts curriculum specialists were consulted regarding the most effective types of scoring for the reading/writing prompts. The majority of specialists consulted preferred some type of analytic scoring, which offered the advantage of providing information for planning and evaluating instruction more effectively than would a single overall score. This evidence, along with consideration of the intended audience (classroom teachers), led to the decision to utilize an analytic scoring system for the IAS. Further considerations led to the adoption of a 4-point scale as opposed to a 6- or 8-point scale. It also was decided that evaluation would take place on three dimensions rather than on a larger number. The adopted scoring system could be easily learned and efficiently implemented in typical classroom situations.

Names of the school districts participating in the small-scale tryout and the large-scale field tests are published in the preliminary technical report (Farr & Farr, 1991, pp. 6–7). School districts represented a cross-section of U.S. regions. In addition to geographic diversity, participating school districts also represented students with a variety of ethnic and cultural differences and differences in abilities. Convergent and discriminative validity data from the field tests showed coefficients of correlation ranging from .81 to .94 (Farr & Farr, 1991). Coefficients of reliability determined by the Pearson and Spearman formulas were comparably high.

Final drafts of all students' writings were scored by two readers to verify the scoring system's interrater reliability. When the two scores for a paper differed on any of the relevant dimensions by 2 or 3 points, a third reader resolved the discrepancy. The number and percent of exact agreement among scorers and the resolutions of discrepancies among scores for each dimension on all prompts are presented in Table XX of the preliminary technical report (Farr & Farr, 1991). The table shows a high percentage of perfect agreement among scorers of the prompts.

Critique

Although the concept of portfolio assessment is not new, its potential for assessing development in the language arts is unrealized by many teachers. In a discussion of portfolio assessment with this reviewer, a group of classroom teachers brought to light several generally held misconceptions and unanswered questions: "What is there to learn about using portfolios? They are only collections of students' work"; "Portfolio assessment does not contribute to accountability"; "Portfolio assessment requires more time than I can afford to give to it"; "It is a problem to keep the contents of portfolios in order and to get kids to use them properly"; "What should be put into portfolios?"

The IAS offers clarification for such misconceptions and answers questions such as those the teachers expressed. The IAS presents a tool for purposeful collections of student writing over periods of time. Not only does it provide a place to keep students' work, but it also provides a conceptual framework for an important aspect of development and assessment in the language arts—the integration of reading and writing, and the integration of instruction and assessment. Because of its flexibility, the IAS accommodates varying time allocations in classroom situations.

The IAS is an authentic test reflecting several principles important in assessing student performance in the language arts. It offers a means for testing reading and writing performance in situations analogous to instructional situations, as recommended by authorities in the field of reading evaluation (Ekwall & Shanker, 1988).

The IAS presents reading passages of high interest and meaning as well as of sufficient length to encourage exercising higher order thinking skills. Tasks are realistic and relevant to the achievement of objectives sought in classrooms that utilize holistic and literature-based approaches. The IAS provides for continuity in assessment by allowing for the development of performance patterns over time. It also encourages students to reflect on their own accomplishments and progress, thereby strengthening their metacognitive skills. The multidimensional nature of this instrument gives students opportunities for wide reading and for integrating their reading and writing activities.

The principle that evaluation should be a cooperative process, involving all persons affected by the evaluation, is well supported by the IAS. Students are involved in their own assessment and made aware of their progress or lack of it. The IAS provides concrete evidence that users can readily share with parents, administrators, or others as may be required. Collaboration is encouraged between student and teacher and among students.

Assessment occurs in terms of objectives when the IAS is used. Outcomes are clearly indicated, as are directions for each activity. Both students and teachers are encouraged to remain aware of the objectives providing direction for each activity and for the assessment of that activity.

Because the IAS focuses specifically on the integration of reading and writing and requires students to use results of reading in their writing, it offers a creditable approach to the measurement of reading comprehension generally and of certain higher order thinking skills specifically. Students are required to become aware of and use the available cue systems in the text. At the same time, they are given an opportunity to utilize their background knowledge about a topic in detecting assumptions not explicitly stated in the text. Results of the IAS can yield some information about students' retrieval and production strategies.

The structure of the IAS and its mode of administration go far to relieve students of the anxiety of test taking. They are encouraged to see themselves as authors, responsible for their products. Further, the process of planning, writing, revising, and editing prior to making a final draft relieves students of the urgency to write perfectly in a limited amount of time the first time around.

Effective use of the IAS requires appropriate staff development, and provisions are made for this through the materials, strategies, and procedures included in the system. One valuable such resource is the videotape, which provides viewers with information essential to effective portfolio assessment. Another is the teacher's manual, which provides specific answers to the kinds of questions teachers are likely to raise regarding portfolio assessment.

Because the IAS authors took into consideration the various types of students typically found in classroom groups, the content of the materials is suitable regardless of student differences. This makes it easy for classroom teachers to administer and score the results of this assessment.

It is widely recognized that no one test is sufficient for assessing student performance completely in any given instance. A variety of factors can impinge upon this performance at any given time. This fact often has been ignored in the dependence placed on conventional tests for revealing the nature of students' performances. According to Hayes (1991, p. 230), "any symbol or percentage means little unless supported be clear, specific responses that provide the student or parent with a basis for interpretation." The graphic and concrete evidence available from use of the IAS can augment information achieved from conventional test scores.

Many other major criticisms of traditional types of paper-and-pencil tests are offset through use of the IAS. While many traditional tests fail to reflect the full range of students' cultural backgrounds, learning aptitudes, background knowledge, and other pertinent factors, the IAS takes all of this into account, allowing individuals to interact with the reading/writing prompts in their own individual ways. The IAS focuses on a range of behaviors often neglected by other means of assessment, in this way becoming an important supplement to other forms of assessment in use in particular situations.

The authors of the IAS are singularly qualified to provide a means of assessment commensurate with the objectives and procedures characteristic of holistic and literature-based approaches applied in a growing number of classrooms. Many of the principles and guidelines for effective assessment were developed through the research of Dr. Roger Farr, and many of the materials and procedures essential in holistic and literature-based programs have been designed by him. Thus one would expect that the IAS would represent the best that is known for assessing some of the higher abilities and skills that are often slighted in conventional reading and writing assessments. At the same time that the IAS fulfills a major need in classrooms that utilize modern approaches to developing reading and writing abilities, it has potential for improving the assessment and development of these skills in classrooms that take more traditional approaches to language arts instruction.

References

This list includes text citations and suggested additional readings.

Barr, R., & Sadow, M.R. (1988). *Reading diagnosis for teachers*. White Plains, NY: Longman.
Durkin, D. (1966). *Children who read early: Two longitudinal studies*. New York: Teachers' College Press.

Ekwall, E., & Shanker, J.L. (1988). *Diagnosis and remediation of the disabled reader.* Boston: Allyn & Bacon.

Farr, R. (1969). *Reading: What can be measured?* Newark, DE: International Reading Association.

Farr, R. (1979). *Teaching a child to read.* New York: Harcourt, Brace, Jovanovich.

Farr, R., & Carey, R.F. (1986). *Reading: What can be measured?* Newark, DE: International Reading Association.

Farr, R., & Farr, B. (1990). *Integrated Assessment System: Examination kit.* San Antonio, TX: Psychological Corporation.

Farr, R., & Farr, B. (1991). *Integrated Assessment System: Preliminary technical report.* San Antonio TX: Psychological Corporation.

Harp, B. (1987). Why are your kids writing during reading time? *The Reading Teacher, 41,* 88–90.

Hayes, B.L. (1991). *Effective strategies for teaching reading.* Boston: Allyn & Bacon.

Heller, M.F. (1991). *Reading-writing connections.* White Plains, NY: Longman.

Hull, G.A. (1989). Research on writing: Building a cognitive and social understanding of composing. In L.B. Resnick & L.E. Klopper (Eds.), *Toward a thinking curriculum: Current cognitive research* (pp. 104–128). Washington, DC: Association for Supervision and Curriculum Development.

Loban, W. (1976). *Language development: Kindergarten through grade 12.* Urbana, IL: National Council of Teachers of English.

Shanahan, T. (1988). The reading-writing relationship: Seven instructional principles. *The Reading Teacher, 41,* 636–647.

Tierney, R.J., & Pearson, P.D. (1983). Toward a composing model of reading. *Language Arts, 60,* 568–580.

Kenneth W. Wegner, Ed.D.

Professor of Counseling Psychology, Boston College, Chestnut Hill, Massachusetts.

INTEREST DETERMINATION, EXPLORATION AND ASSESSMENT SYSTEM–ENHANCED VERSION

Charles B. Johansson. Minnetonka, Minnesota: National Computer Systems/PAS Division.

Introduction

The Interest Determination, Exploration and Assessment System–Enhanced Version (IDEAS; Johansson, 1990) is a 128-item interest inventory designed to measure interest preferences of 7th- through 12th-grade students and adults. Modeled after the 25 basic interest scales of the Career Assessment Inventory (CAI) also developed by Johansson, the items for the 16 IDEAS scales were drawn from the same item pool. Students and adults can complete the inventory, score and plot their profiles, and interpret their results in less than an hour. Johansson also suggests various methods of converting IDEAS scores into six theme scores similar to Holland's theoretical vocational R-I-A-S-E-C model, which is used in many career exploration systems. This further facilitates the test takers' exploration and discussion of the world of work.

Dr. Charles Johansson completed his doctoral studies at the University of Minnesota, where he worked with David Campbell on the development of the Strong Interest Inventories (SII). He currently is director of the Office of Measurement Services at University of Minnesota. In addition to providing test scoring services for the university, the office also supplies elementary and secondary schools with achievement, aptitude, and interest inventory materials and services. Dr. Johansson has published over 50 journal articles and the following inventories: the CAI, Exploring Career Options (ECO), and IDEAS. He also coauthored the Temperament and Values Inventory (TVI) and the Word and Number Assessment Inventory (WNAI).

The original IDEAS inventory was developed in 1977 in response to a demand for a shortened, self-scoring version of the CAI. After 12 years of use, a decision to update was made in 1989. The 1989 standardization group was composed of 1,700 students in Grades 7–9, 2,891 students in Grades 10–12, and 900 adults. Due to base-rate differences between genders, the manual provides separate norms for males and females. Roughly equal numbers of males and females were used. Although racial information appears for only 1,900 sample members, minorities are represented in the norms. The subjects in the norm groups were participants in the research on the enhanced Career Assessment Inventory (Johansson, 1986).

Since its first publication in 1977 there had been suggestions for improving

309

IDEAS. The 1990 enhanced IDEAS was revised in response to the feedback from test administrators. These revisions included increasing the diversity of students in the norm sample, adding an adult norm group, altering the format of the IDEAS test booklet to accommodate the addition of two new scales, updating both scales and items where necessary, designing a more contemporary cover, and including procedures to convert IDEAS scale scores to fit to the Holland (1985) R-I-A-S-E-C vocational themes.

There is no evidence of the availability of the IDEAS in languages other than English. Although designed for self-administration, IDEAS could be completed orally by a handicapped person and scored and interpreted by an administrator.

The enhanced IDEAS is contained within a self-scoring, 128-item paper-and-pencil booklet. The items consist of work activities, occupations, and school subjects related to 16 broad interest areas. The eight-item scales are related to the Holland themes as follows: Mechanical/Fixing, Protective Services, and Nature/Outdoors (Realistic); Mathematics, Science, and Medical (Investigative); Creative Arts and Writing (Artistic); Community Service, Educating, and Child Care (Social); Public Speaking, Business, and Sales (Enterprising); and Office Practices and Food Service (Conventional). The test taker reads the item and indicates if he or she would like very much/like somewhat/indifferent/dislike somewhat/dislike very much by circling a corresponding response option (L, l, I, d, D).

Hand scoring is easy, as the circled responses on page 1 are transposed automatically onto a carbonless copy score sheet on page 3. Thus, each letter circled response on page 1 corresponds directly to an encircled numerical weight for that response on page 3. Page 2 of the booklet faces page 3 and lists specific directions for tallying the response weights for each scale. Simple addition is required for scoring purposes. After this has been completed, the weighted raw score total for each of the 16 scales is plotted on an appropriate norm profile (Grade 7–9, 10–12, or Adult) in the booklet. The profile for each norm group is complete with scale headings, possible range of raw scores, and standard scores. Page 4 lists specific directions for transferring scores and correctly plotting profiles. Administration, scoring, and profiling require approximately 40–50 minutes.

The test booklet also contains a take-home section for further use. These materials include a second copy of the profile for the examinee to complete, a guide to understanding the profile's standard scores, a brief description of each of the 16 career fields to aid in better understanding scores, and lists of courses and occupations related to each scale, with page references to the *Occupational Outlook Handbook* (OOH; U.S. Department of Labor, 1988) and *Dictionary of Occupational Titles* (DOT; U.S. Department of Labor, 1975).

The administrator's role is fairly simple. In group administrations it consists of reading the directions and being available for questions. The format permits administration in groups, individually, or as a take-home exercise. After administration, the guidance counselor should play a more direct role in 1) ensuring that the student has correctly scored and interpreted his or her results, 2) helping the student with further investigation of vocational reference materials, and 3) explaining the use of the theme codes in relation to Holland's model.

The age group for which IDEAS was designed falls into three categories. For the students in Grades 7–9, the age level is 12–14 years; for Grades 10–12, the ages are 15–18. The adult norms apply to anyone over 18. The IDEAS reading level is sixth grade and up. Users also must have the ability to add the weights for eight items per scale and follow simple instructions.

Practical Applications/Uses

According to the manual, the goals for the updated version of the IDEAS were to develop 1) a short, easy to administer inventory; 2) a modest number of scales that would be comprehensive, easily interpreted, reliable, and valid; 3) a non-biased inventory across gender and racial differences; 4) a simple, easy to understand inventory that simultaneously was a valid psychometric instrument; and 5) a common linkage with other related resources organized according to Holland's R-I-A-S-E-C model. The variables measured in IDEAS are summarized by the 16 basic interest scales' titles. Obtained scores across these variables reflect one's relative interest in these areas. For example, a high raw score of 30 on the Creative Arts scale suggests a substantial amount of interest in the artistic career field.

The purpose of IDEAS was to help "provide information about people's current preferences—the results are like a snapshot of their vocational likes and dislikes" (Johansson, 1990, p. 1). As such, it is similar to other interest inventories used to aid people in the career decision-making process. IDEAS is designed to be useful for beginning career exploration, helping students think about their future educational or vocational plans in response to their inventory profile, and assisting adults in reassessing their present interests.

The original design and primary setting for using IDEAS is the public schools (Grades 7 and up). Thus teachers and guidance counselors make up the typical professionals users of this inventory. With adult norms the enhanced IDEAS may become more common in social service and employment agencies, particularly in school dropout or correctional programs where an instrument with a low level of reading difficulty is appropriate.

IDEAS was designed for both males and females, ages 12 and up. The standardization sample includes members of both white and non-white groups. IDEAS would be inappropriate for those for whom English is not a first or second language, who lack basic mathematical and reading abilities, or who have less than a sixth-grade level of mental functioning/ability. There is no evidence to suggest that the inventory could not be adapted to other subjects outside of the standardization sample. As indicated previously, the content of the test is appropriate for the physically handicapped, but assistance in administration and interpretation would be required.

IDEAS would be best administered "in an environment that is as non-threatening and demystified as possible" (Johansson, 1990, p. 20). Because the instrument is a simple self-scored interest inventory, test takers need not be in a classroom or a group testing environment. Although it would be helpful to have someone familiar with IDEAS to answer any questions (especially for younger students), this is not technically necessary. Examiners need no specific qualifications beyond competency in the general procedures of administering, scoring, and interpreting tests. The administration procedures as described in the manual are simple and straightforward.

Clear directions appear for scoring IDEAS, a task that on the average would take 10–15 minutes. There appears to be one potential difficulty in scoring. If an individual chooses to change a marked response, the directions say to blacken in that circle and recircle the new selection. However, if one chooses to revert back to the original response, this will create a mess on the carbonless scoring page underneath. Thus, administrators are instructed to encourage subjects to give their first impression and work at a steady pace without going backward and changing responses.

After responding to the 128 items on page 1, examinees proceed to page 2, which explains the scoring procedures. (Although adults may choose to continue at their own pace, it is suggested that scoring instructions be read aloud to students.) The scoring process involves transferring a circled weight for each item response to an adjacent box. Total scores are obtained by adding the weights for each of the eight items, then posting the totals at the bottom of the page. These total scores are then transferred onto the appropriate norm profile on page 5, 6, or 7. Page 3 may be removed from the booklet to facilitate accurate transfer of scores in plotting the profile. Individuals should complete the information at the top of their profile for future reference (name, age, grade, etc.), and then mark an X over their raw scores in the column for each scale on the profile. The outside margins of the profile contain reference marks for standard scores and indicate if they are at the "high interest" (above 60), "average interest" (40–60), or "low interest" (below 40) levels. These standard scores for each scale are then transferred onto another profile on page 13, which individuals can keep for their own records. Pages 9–12 are also for the test taker to keep. They include brief descriptions and interpretations of each of the 16 scales, some examples of occupations that typically would have high scores on that scale, a summary of how to correctly interpret one's profile, and a reference chart for further investigation using the DOT and OOH. For individuals who wish to correlate their IDEAS scores with Holland's types, three procedures are described in the manual's Appendix I. No machine- or computer-scored version of IDEAS exists, as the inventory was designed for self-administration and immediate feedback. However, one may use the Holland theme scale scores obtained as input for one of the career search systems (e.g., DISCOVER or SIGI) if available in the school or agency.

The interpretation of the IDEAS scales derives from objective scores rather than clinical or internal judgment. The interpreter should be prepared to assist examinees in understanding the meaning of high, average, and low scores, and in applying their results to career exploration. Thus the interpreter should be a trained counselor, or at least have completed courses in testing and career development.

Technical Aspects

The items for both the original and enhanced versions of IDEAS were drawn from the same pool of 370 items used to construct the enhanced CAI (Johansson, 1986). The procedure for developing scales involved performing a cluster analysis on intercorrelated items and selecting the "best" eight items to form each of 16 clusters. The sample used to develop items consisted of 2,000 students in 100 schools who took the CAI in 1989. The larger sample used in the norming process included 1,893 students (white, black, Hispanic, Asian, American Indian, etc.) in Grades 7–12 in 14 states, plus 3,510 other similar students and adults (for whom race information was not available). The items selected for a scale had to correlate at least .30 with each other. The cross-validation procedure demonstrated that the selected items correlated with their respective scales in the range of .54 to .88, varying with subjects' age level and gender. The 1990 enhanced IDEAS has 16 scales, two more than the original, and some scale titles and their item content differ slightly from the original edition. Minor item changes were also made to reduce reading and understanding requirements to the sixth-grade level.

The IDEAS scales were standardized by scoring the items for the larger normative sample described above. The raw score means and standard deviations were then converted to standard scores, with a mean of 50 and standard deviation of 10 for each scale.

Although the manual provides separate norms by gender, the profiles in the test booklet represent composite samples of males and females. Appendix C of the manual suggests that the reason for providing only composite norms to the examinee was to avoid reinforcing the idea that females and males differ in career outlooks. The gender differences reported indicate that males tend to respond more positively to items representing Holland's Realistic types, and females to items representing Artistic, Social, and Conventional types. The only minority versus Caucasian differences appeared in a tendency for minority group members to mark "like very much" or "like somewhat" to more items. The manual suggests that the counselor interested in discussing separate gender norms should make a transparency of the norms graphs in Appendix C to use as an overlay on the counselee's profile in the IDEAS test booklet. These might help in discussions of nontraditional gender-related interests with the client. For example, if a female scored above the 75th percentile for her gender on the Mechanical/Fixing scale, she might be encouraged to explore that area further. The gender-specific norms bar graphs of the middle 50% range of scores indicate minimal overlap for students in Grades 7–9 and 10–12 on the Mechanical/Fixing, Protective Services, Office Practices, Child Care, and Food Services scales. However, the adult norms bar graphs overlap considerably more (except for the Protective Services scale).

The manual presents evidence for content, construct, and concurrent validity. Content validity was built into the item selection process described above. Items had to correlate at least .30 with each other to be included in a scale. Consequently, the scale internal consistencies across gender, race, and grade level range from .83 to .93. These correlations appear satisfactorily high, particularly for eight-item scales.

Construct validity was determined by correlating the IDEAS scales with similarly named scales on the enhanced version of the CAI and the Strong Interest Inventory (SII). These intercorrelations are reported to be .92 or higher with the CAI scales and .80 or above with the SII scales. The high intercorrelations with the CAI scales are not surprising, as the IDEAS scales are essentially shorter versions of those on the CAI. Unfortunately, the manual does not report the actual intercorrelations, so it is not possible to tell which "similar-named" scales were used for these comparisons. Other evidence for construct validity appears in the IDEAS scale intercorrelations reported in the manual's Appendix F. A major purpose of these intercorrelations was to test the fit of the scales into the six Holland vocational themes. For example, the Mechanical/Fixing, Protective Services, and Nature/Outdoors scales logically fit the Holland Realistic theme and should have high positive correlations with each other. In contrast, these scales should show lower intercorrelations with those representing the Social theme (Community Services, Educating, and Child Care). In general this holds true, but some IDEAS scales show inconsistencies. The IDEAS Medical scale utilizes items from both the Medical Science and Medical Services scales of the CAI. As these two CAI scales derive from different Holland themes on the CAI (Investigative and Social), the IDEAS Medical scale correlates almost equally well with other scales from both themes. The manual explains that the IDEAS Medical scale was placed in the Investigative theme because of its higher correlation with the Science scale. Similarly, the Food Service scale (Conventional theme) also appears strongly related to other scales placed in the Investigative, Artistic, and Enterprising categories.

Concurrent validity was demonstrated by using data from over 100 samples of students and adults in career programs and occupations who had taken the CAI. Because most of the IDEAS items were selected from the CAI, the CAI answer sheets were scored using the 16 IDEAS keys. The difference between the highest and lowest mean occupational scores for each scale was about 2 standard deviations. Groups most related to each scale had a standard score of about 60, while those least related averaged around 40. Appendix G of the manual lists examples of high and low occupational groups for each scale. In general, the occupations listed for the high end of each scale appear to logically fit that interest area.

Appendix H of the manual provides test-retest reliability correlations for three samples ($N = 54, 31$, and 42) over 1-week to 30-day intervals. These range from .77 to .95 across the 16 scales, with median correlations of .86 to .91 for the three time periods. One criticism of this data is that it did not include any junior high students.

The evidence for validity and reliability presented in the manual was difficult to evaluate and was sometimes confusing. Construct validity correlation ranges were reported, but not the actual correlations or scales of the CAI and SII that were compared with the IDEAS scales. The concurrent validity section of the manual reports general information on over 100 samples of students and adults, but the actual mean scores of these groups do not appear in Appendix G. In fact, Appendix G indicates that not all occupational groups had taken the same forms of the CAI. Thus actual means were used for 8 of the 16 IDEAS scales, but estimated means were used for 8 other scales in the concurrent validity studies. This was necessary because one or more items from those scales were not included in the earlier version of the CAI (Johansson, 1980). In effect, the manual does not indicate that IDEAS has been used *directly* with *any* training or occupational groups to determine concurrent validity (although its correlations with similar SII scales does support some external concurrent validity). Although no evidence of predictive validity is presented, one hopes such studies will appear in the future.

Appendix I of the manual describes three methods of converting IDEAS scale scores to Holland themes. The first procedure simply requires listing the standard score for the one IDEAS scale that correlates highest with each of the six Holland themes from the CAI. The second method uses the average of the scores on the two or three IDEAS scales placed within each of the theme groups. The third method requires calculating a multiple regression equation for each theme. For three theme scores (R, I, and C), using single IDEAS scale scores would produce essentially the same results as averaging or using the regression equation method. For the other three themes, the complexity (and potential error) of calculations by individuals using the second and third methods may not be worth the effort. It would be interesting to see a comparative study of whether or not the three methods would produce the same rank order (highest to lowest) of the theme scales. Holland's and other approaches to career exploration use only the two or three highest theme scores to identify relevant occupations. Thus, if there are no major differences between the three methods in rank order of theme scales, then the first method would seem to have the advantage of simplicity of derivation and interpretation in the counseling situation. Perhaps a better approach to resolving the problem of choosing between the three methods would be to develop Holland theme scales for IDEAS via the same procedures used in developing them for the CAI.

Critique

The current and previous versions of IDEAS have been reviewed by others. Weeks (1985) criticized the 1980 edition as too brief and simplistic, with inadequate information provided on the socioeconomic, educational, ethnic, and geographic characteristics of the normative samples. This information has been included in the manual for the latest edition. Weeks also cited some minor item clarity and scoring procedure problems, which appear to have been corrected in the current edition as well. Overall, IDEAS is praised for its technical qualities and potential for use as a research instrument, or for discussing general interest areas with persons having interests in occupations not requiring a college education.

Swanson (1987) relayed five major concerns regarding the 1980 version. First, the original manual provided an impressive amount of information, but not in sufficient detail for a full understanding or evaluation of IDEAS. The 1990 edition provides more information but still lacks the detail to evaluate the validity data. Swanson's second concern related to the representation of the scales on IDEAS, questioning why only 14 scales were chosen from the potential 22 on the CAI. A similar question could be asked now as to why only 16 scales were chosen for the 1990 edition. One could conclude that limiting the number of scales attempts to prevent an overemphasis on one or another of the six Holland types. Additionally, only 9 of the current 16 scales have the same names as the 1980 version, and only 8 have the same item content. The reasons for the renaming and revisions of previous scales is not clear in the manual.

Swanson's third criticism focused on the area of potential scoring and profiling errors mentioned by Weeks (1985). The suggestion of close supervision or an audit of these procedures by the administrator is probably still valid for the current edition. Her fourth concern about the inadequacy of discussion of Holland's theory still holds true for the 1990 IDEAS. Although Holland is referenced, the administrator would have to consult Holland (1985) and the CAI (Johansson,

1986) to understand the rationale for grouping the IDEAS scales under the six Holland themes. The fifth criticism relates to the issues surrounding the use of combined gender versus separate gender norms. Johansson's response was to include both in the 1990 IDEAS manual, but separate-gender interpretations are only available if the interpreter constructs transparent overlays as suggested in the manual.

A recent review was compiled by Bauernfeind (1991) on the 1990 version of IDEAS. He and four other testing authorities collaborated in the review. These panelists gave overall ratings to IDEAS ranging from 6 to 9 (on a scale of 1 to 10, with 10 being highest). Most of their minor criticisms focused on item content and scoring procedures. The major criticisms centered on inadequate technical information on norm groups and lack of occupational criterion group norms with which to compare an individual's scores. Several panelists thought it was a very useful instrument and that Johansson had responded well to critics' and users' suggestions for improving the original edition.

Most of the criticisms generated by the present writer and other reviewers of IDEAS center on the adequacy of information in the manual for evaluating the technical data and development rationale for the instrument. For the test specialist, questions arise repeatedly as to the specific criteria for selecting the particular items on each scale and why only some of the current 25 broad interest area scales on the CAI were chosen for IDEAS.

After 35 years in the field of psychometrics, this reviewer also has qualms about the validity of eight-item scales, despite evidence of good reliability. It is difficult to believe that an eight-item scale is comprehensive enough to measure an interest domain. Although format and time required to administer, score, and profile the inventory may have been major concerns, no rationale is specified for limiting the scales to only eight items.

The question of what constitutes an adequate and comprehensive number of scales continues to be debated. The other inventories in common use today with Grade 7–12 students have 6 to 10 general interest theme scales. It may be that Holland's six themes are more easily understood and interpreted by students at the middle school level, and further research may suggest reducing the number of scales on IDEAS and increasing the number of items per scale.

Obviously the most objective method of evaluating an inventory is in terms of how well it meets the author's goals. The goal of constructing an easy to administer, short measure has been well met. Users who require an instrument that can be administered during a 50-minute class period will find IDEAS fits this criterion. The goal of developing a number of scales that are reliable, valid, easy to interpret, and comprehensive has been met to varying degrees. The scales are reliable and have good content and construct validity. More work needs to be done on concurrent and predictive validity, although IDEAS is probably adequate for use in generalized career exploration. Ease of interpretation and comprehensiveness are debatable (depending on the user's purposes or the evaluator's criteria), but again this inventory is probably adequate in these respects. The author seems to have addressed the issues of gender and racial bias appropriately in developing the 1990 IDEAS items. There are both combined and separate-gender norms, and it appears that minorities are adequately represented in both. Care also was taken in the development stage to make the inventory items simple and understandable at the sixth-grade reading level, yet the items were reported to be almost equally valid with older subjects. The last goal of linking IDEAS with resource materials organized according to Holland's six themes was accomplished by selecting two or three scales to represent each theme and providing methods for converting scales to theme scores. As indicated previously, this goal might be better accomplished by developing Holland theme scales directly from the IDEAS item content.

Overall, the 1990 IDEAS has a strong theoretical and technical background, and the current inventory and manual are much improved over the originals. IDEAS shows good potential for use in the career exploration process and in research to fill the information gaps cited above. Most criticisms might also be resolved by providing more specific and comprehensive technical data in the manual.

References

Bauernfeind, R.H. (Ed.). (1991). CSCGI report: Interest Determination, Exploration and Assessment System. *AMECD Newsnotes, 26*(2), 6–10.

Holland, J.L. (1985). *The Self-Directed Search.* Odessa, FL: Psychological Assessment Resources.

Johansson, C.B. (1980). *Manual for IDEAS: Interest Determination, Exploration and Assessment System.* Minneapolis, MN: National Computer Systems.

Johansson, C.B. (1986). *Manual for Career Assessment Inventory–Enhanced Version.* Minneapolis, MN: National Computer Systems.

Johansson, C.B. (1990). *Manual for IDEAS–Enhanced Version.* Minneapolis, MN: National Computer Systems.

Swanson, J.L. (1987). Interest Determination, Exploration, and Assessment System. In D.J. Keyser & R.C. Sweetland (Eds.), *Test critiques* (Vol. VI, pp. 253–259). Austin, TX: PRO-ED.

U.S. Department of Labor. (1975). *Dictionary of occupational titles* (4th ed.). Washington, DC: Author.

U.S. Department of Labor. (1988). *Occupational outlook handbook* (Bulletin 2300). Washington, DC: Author.

Weeks, M.O. (1985). Interest Determination, Exploration, and Assessment System. In J.V. Mitchell, Jr. (Ed.), *The ninth mental measurements yearbook* (pp. 698–699). Lincoln, NE: Buros Institute of Mental Measurements.

Patricia M. Hargrove, Ph.D.

Professor of Communication Disorders, Mankato State University, Mankato, Minnesota.

INVENTORY OF LANGUAGE ABILITIES AND INVENTORY OF LANGUAGE ABILITIES II

Esther H. Minskoff, Douglas E. Wiseman, and J. Gerald Minskoff. Ridgefield, New Jersey: Educational Performance Associates.

Introduction

The Inventory of Language Abilities (ILA) and the Inventory of Language Abilities II (ILA-II) were developed as companions to the MWM Program for Developing Language Abilities (MWM; Minskoff, Wiseman, & Minskoff, 1971). As screening instruments designed to identify potential language learning disabilities in children, these inventories are not standardized tests; rather, they are checklists developed to focus classroom teachers' attention on the social and academic behaviors associated with language learning disabilities. Additionally, the ILA and ILA-II are designed to assist classroom teachers in the treatment of language learning disabilities. Both inventories are coded to identify treatment activities from the MWM.

The authors of the ILA and ILA-II, Esther H. Minskoff, Douglas E. Wiseman, and J. Gerald Minskoff, have doctorates in special education and considerable experience as educational consultants and administrators in education, with emphasis in learning disabilities. They developed the ILA to assess students from kindergarten through second grade. The ILA-II, an extension of ILA, was designed for Grades 3 through 5. (In the directions for the ILA-II, the authors claim, however, that it can be used with junior and senior high school students with learning disabilities.)

The organization of the ILA and ILA-II is based on the subtests of the Illinois Test of Psycholinguistic Abilities (ITPA; Kirk, MacCarthy, & Kirk, 1968). Despite this organizational linkage, the items from ILA and ILA-II clearly have not been derived directly from the ITPA. The ILA and ILA-II are self-contained, 16-page pamphlets, each of which contains instructions, an inventory, and a profile. Both inventories consist of 11 checklists corresponding to the 12 subtests of the ITPA. (The final checklist combines two subtests.) Each checklist contains 12 descriptors that represent behaviors that students with language impairment might display on the specified subtest of the ITPA. Behaviors sampled in the checklists include interactions with peers, writing skills, and language arts skills.

Teachers complete an inventory for each child by noting if the child's behavior conforms to behaviors on the checklist. The results of the checklists are transferred 1) to an individual profile and 2) to a classroom profile, which is provided in

318

addition to the pamphlet. The individual profiles highlight each student's strengths and weaknesses; the classroom profile presents a summary of the scores of the students in the class.

Practical Applications/Uses

The ILA and ILA-II were designed to identify students who should be referred for diagnostic evaluations for language learning disabilities and to permit teachers to design appropriate activities for students who display language learning problems. To identify students with potential language learning disabilities, the classroom teacher determines whether items on the checklists represent the students in question. Behaviors the classroom teachers are asked to evaluate include a) listening skills, b) following directions, c) communication breakdowns, d) ability to function in the classroom, e) play behavior, f) quality of responses, g) ability to follow rules, h) syntactic and morphological skills, i) ability to interpret pictures and writing, j) discourse skills, and k) ability to express intentions. The authors provide a single criterion level for all 11 subtests—a problem with more than 50% of the items on any checklist is considered indicative of impaired skills in that area.

To serve as a treatment guide, teachers merely refer to the items marked on the checklist. Each item is assigned a code that corresponds to treatment activities as in the MWM Program for Developing Language Abilities; thus, classroom teachers have a means of improving the student's language-based weaknesses in the absence of further assessment.

The nature of the items on the ILA and ILA-II checklists limits their application to the classroom and their administrators to classroom teachers or individuals with a thorough knowledge of the students' academic and social interaction skills. However, the use of the ILA and ILA-II need not be limited to identification and treatment issues. For example, the information in the inventories could assist in sensitizing classroom teachers to the ramifications of language impairment (i.e., in-service training). Additionally, the checklist items have the potential to assist teachers in making decisions regarding the readiness of students to be mainstreamed.

All procedural, scoring, and interpretation instructions for the ILA and ILA-II appear on two pages in the manual. The procedures are quite straightforward, and teachers are encouraged to create contexts to elicit behaviors for which they cannot provide a definite response. The items on the checklist are clearly written, and classroom teachers should encounter little difficulty in their interpretation.

Scoring instructions also are clearly written, and scoring procedures are quite simple. Items that apply to the student are checked and the number of checks then are tallied at the bottom of each checklist. The authors provide guidelines for scoring alterations when items are inappropriate because of curricular or individual differences. Nevertheless, a serious problem exists with the scoring system. Teachers are required to make decisions regarding the student's academic or social skills but are provided with only the descriptor from the checklist to assist in making the decision. Although for some cases the student decisions may not be difficult, in others the skill level may be less obvious. For example, it is not clear how "impaired" a child's performance must be before it warrants a check: Does the child make the error 10% of the time? 30%? 70%? Teachers are required to develop their own criteria, and this, of course, could create reliability problems.

Like the administration and scoring instructions, the interpretation of the IPA and IPA-II is straightforward. Scores are transferred to a profile and the results are graphed. Teachers should experience little difficulty identifying possible language learning problems or remedial activities. There are, however, serious questions whether the recommended interpretations are valid because of the aforementioned weaknesses in scoring and the questionable procedure of assessing, classifying, and treating disability based on performance on a single test.

Technical Aspects

Standardization, reliability, and validity data are not provided with either of the two inventories (ILA or ILA-II). It should be noted that Minskoff et al. (1971) clearly state that neither the ILA nor the ILA-II are tests; rather, they are identified as instruments for focusing classroom teachers' attention on linguistically basic social and academic behavior.

Critique

The ILA and ILA-II were developed for two purposes: to identify potential language-learning problems and to suggest treatment activities appropriate to an individual student's weaknesses. Because the authors provide no normative, reliability, or validity data for the inventories, neither the ILA nor the ILA-II appear to be useful for their intended purposes. The authors should not be freed from all "psychometric responsibility" merely by claiming their measure is not a test. Despite this disclaimer, Minskoff et al. (1971) recommend using the instruments in a test-like manner—screening potential language learning disabilities. Consumers need data describing the effectiveness of the ILA and ILA-II.

A second problem with the inventories stems from the fact that their organizational framework is based on the ITPA, because use of either the ILA or the ILA-II implies acceptance of the ITPA approach to language-learning disabilities. The ITPA view of language-learning disabilities and testing language has been subjected to considerable criticism (e.g., Lahey, 1988; Prutting, 1979) and currently is not enjoying widespread acceptance among professionals concerned with language impairment. The controversial theoretical underpinnings also make the decision to use either the ILA or the ILA-II as a description of a student's performance or a treatment guide questionable.

Despite the above-mentioned limitations, the inventories' emphasis on social and academic behaviors is excellent, and the authors should be commended for their emphasis on interactive/social communication skills long before the pragmatic approach to language impairment took hold. Although these well-written checklists may have many potential uses, test administrators should not use them as the major source of information when making decisions about disability or the treatment of disability.

References

Kirk, S.A., McCarthy, J.J., & Kirk, W.D. (1969). *The Illinois Test of Psycholinguistic Abilities.* Urbana: IL: University of Illinois Press.

Lahey, M. (1988). *Language development and language disorders* (2nd ed.). New York: Wiley.

Minskoff, E.H., Wiseman, D.E., & Minskoff, J.G. (1971). *MWM program for developing language abilities.* Ridgefield, NJ: Educational Performance Associates.

Prutting, C.S. (1979). The Illinois Test of Psycholinguistic Abilities (ITPA), Revised Edition. In F.L. Darley (Ed.), *Evaluation and appraisal techniques in speech and language pathology* (pp. 162–165). Reading, MA: Addison-Wesley.

Allan L. LaVoie, Ph.D.

Professor of Psychology, Davis & Elkins College, Elkins, West Virginia.

THE JESNESS INVENTORY

Carl F. Jesness. North Tonawanda, New York: Multi-Health Systems, Inc.

The Jesness Inventory (JI; Jesness, 1991) was designed to measure 11 characteristics relevant to the classification of delinquents. The JI scales are Social Maladjustment, Value Orientation, Immaturity, Autism, Alienation, Manifest Aggression, Withdrawal, Social Anxiety, Repression, and Denial, plus a summary scale, the Asocial Index. The first three scales were devised by a criterion-based item selection process, the next seven were based on standard analytic procedures including cluster analysis, and the last was calculated by regression analysis from the scores on the first 10 scales; it indicates the severity of delinquency. The 155 true/false items have been written at a simple reading level so they would be comprehensible when read to 8-year-olds. Jesness has been criticized for his outdated norms and inadequate manual (e.g., Butt, 1978), but at the same time his test has been usefully applied to screening problems. He designed it to be used with disturbed children ages 8 to 18 as well as experimentally with adults. A Spanish version is available, as are several computer interpretation or reporting programs (though none were examined for this review).

Administration and scoring of the JI entails a simple, straightforward process, with a self-administering questionnaire and a set of transparent scoring templates. Interpretation is not so simple, however, as the manual contains only brief descriptions of scale score extremes. The prototype interpretations provided were based on procedures and criteria not available from the manual (Weintraub, 1972). In addition, the JI works closely with the Jesness Behavior Checklist (1984) and with a classification scheme called *I-levels* (Interpersonal Maturity), of which there are nine. The I-level classification uses scores from the Checklist and the JI, and manipulates them by computer analysis to arrive at the likeliest categorization of each client. The procedure has been criticized (Bornholt & Rosenthal, 1987); it also has been extensively revised (Jesness & Wedge, 1984, 1985; Jesness, 1986, 1988, p. 19).

Carl F. Jesness earned his Ph.D. in educational psychology in 1955 from the University of Minnesota. He was heavily influenced by Paul Meehl (C.F. Jesness, personal communication, November 10, 1992), who taught a year-long course on the MMPI and later helped to supervise Jesness's internship. After earning his doctorate Jesness spent 2 years in a clinical internship at a Veterans Administration hospital. He next worked in a mental health center as a clinical psychologist and then moved to the California Youth Authority, first as a clinician and then as a researcher. His research work there involved the classification of delinquents as well as attempts to assess the most effective treatment modalities. Before retiring in 1985, Jesness was for 3 years the chief of the CYA research bureau.

Practical Applications/Uses

To date the JI has been used primarily in developmental studies, the main goals of which have been to screen for delinquency (an odd goal, given that the JI was developed in the California Youth Authority system where the courts sent clients already categorized; in fact, the definition of delinquency in the manual depends on the child being taken from the home and referred to the CYA by law enforcement agencies [Jesness, 1988, p. 20]), to assist in classifying the degree of delinquency, and to help determine whether therapeutic interventions would assist. It was not one of the goals that the JI should try to predict recidivism (Jesness, 1988, p. 27).

Jesness also set out to develop an instrument that could be used to assess progress through the system; that is, to monitor clinical change (Jesness, 1988, p. 3). Throughout the manual one finds tension between these goals: to reliably classify delinquents and to monitor change. If the classification is truly reliable, it should lead to the same result time after time. And if it measures change, it will lead to different results from time to time. Jesness attempted unsuccessfully to reconcile these different goals: for example, "the ideal compromise between stability and sensitivity to change remain [*sic*] a matter of judgment" (Jesness, 1988, p. 21), and later, "validity of the Asocial Index should be limited by this low stability [$r = .26$], yet in most instances its predictive validity appears to be fairly high" (p. 27). His success would have been much easier to judge had he defined his goal a little more exclusively, and the potential applications would have been clearer.

One set of uses does not get addressed in any detail in the JI manual. Real world needs require that a child be classified in several ways (e.g., institutional security risk, therapeutic intervention most likely to be successful, degree of community risk, recidivism potential, psychological comorbidity, educational level, family functioning level, etc.); where does the JI fit into a comprehensive battery? In the manual we see relationships with the California Psychological Inventory, but not with any other standard instruments such as the MMPI, the Wide Range Achievement Test–Revised, and the projective tests required by some state agencies. It remains unclear whether the JI would comprise a useful part of a standard battery, or whether it would be completely redundant.

Technical Aspects

The main issues here are reliability, validity, and other qualities of the JI scales such as score independence and classificatory efficiency. Reliability can be summarized fairly easily. The individual scale scores have modest internal consistency, averaging about .74 based on almost 2,000 subjects. Test-retest stability is lower, with the average for 536 subjects over 1 year being .61, and for 131 subjects over 8 months, .56. A small sample of 57 delinquents was tested on consecutive days with two instruction sets, completely anonymous the first day and with the expectation that the classification board would see their scores the second day. Despite the dramatic change in instructions, 44 subjects received the same delinquent classification on both days, and only three scales showed significant differences.

Validity as always is a difficult question and must be based on the cumulative research. From the manual it is very difficult to reach meaningful conclusions, as Jesness (1988) has mixed together the data from the initial development studies with the data from the cross-validation studies. He says that "the entire development described here serves as a cross-validation of the three empirical scales" (Jesness, 1988, p. 20). This position is hard to defend and in any case should not have been claimed as it deviates from standard practice. To claim cross-validation, one must not revise items or make other changes in mid-stream, as Jesness has done.

Regarding validity, the goals must be clarified. For example, to determine whether the JI validly identifies delinquency, one can compare scores with various categories of delinquent acts, age of onset of delinquent acts, or changes in development corresponding to delinquencies. Several studies speak to this question, including the large-scale studies of LeBlanc, which generally find orderly relationships between externally defined delinquencies and various scale scores. Martin (1981) compared scores across four groups: 80 controls, 77 adolescents who had shown minor acting out, 70 institutionalized but not adjudicated youth, and 70 adjudicated youth. The biggest differences emerged on the Social Maladjustment scale and on the Asocial Index ($p < .001$). Note that this was not a predictive study; Martin reported that the results encourage the use of the JI for presentence planning, as the Asocial Index provides a useful baseline for comparison with others in placement or treatment situations. LeBlanc et al. (1991) report that all JI scales were significantly different in the predicted direction as a function of age of onset of delinquency: the earlier the onset, the more disturbed the JI profile.

Munson and Revers (1986) used the JI to monitor progress of delinquent girls in a treatment program and compared their scores with a large matched control sample. Several scales successfully distinguished the treatment from the control clients, but only the Asocial Index significantly discriminated at all age levels.

A similar study was conducted by Roberts, Schmitz, Pinto, and Cain (1990). They examined treatment effects in a small sample of conduct-disordered youth and found that the Asocial Index did not reflect significant changes. Seven of the other scales did.

Craighead (1991) used the JI to assist with differential diagnosis of depression, anxiety, and conduct-disordered subtypes. His review indicates that about 20%–30% of adolescents diagnosed as depressed also will be conduct disordered and that their response to treatment procedures will differ from the nondepressed or the non–conduct disordered. Curry and Craighead (1990) report that in a sample of psychiatric inpatient adolescents, the Social Maladjustment scores correlated highly with depression scores ($r = .68$, $n = 63$, $p < .001$) and with attributional style for positive events ($-.46$, $< .001$). Further, the mean score on Social Maladjustment is significantly higher than reported for nondelinquents.

Friesen and Wright (1985) compared the JI scores with scores on the Carlson Psychological Survey, producing results that provide modest evidence of convergent validity. For example, 50 male adolescents incarcerated in a detention center took both questionnaires. The correlation between Alienation on the JI and Antisocial Tendencies on the Carlson was .57 ($p < .001$); between Asocial Index scores and Antisocial Tendencies, the correlation was negative and nonsignificant. The

Carlson Chemical Abuse scale correlated with a number of the JI scales, including Social Maladjustment (.30, < .05), Value Orientation (.35, < .01), and Social Anxiety (–.25, < .05).

In summary, these classification studies indicate that the JI typically performs as expected in differentiating delinquents and that its scales correlate appropriately with other measures.

The dimensionality of the JI has been addressed in several studies. Typical results find three dimensions (Woodbury & Shurling, 1975; Wunderlich, 1985). Based on item-level analysis of more than 400 juveniles referred for treatment, Wunderlich found that the items formed three second-order factors: Mistrust, Social Pessimism, and Hypersensitivity.

Critique

The accumulated evidence seems to point to several clear conclusions. First, the JI can distinguish accurately between delinquents and nondelinquents, as well as among degrees of severity, from mild acting out to severe criminal behavior. There is no evidence that it can do so predictively, but that is the clear implication of the developmental studies performed to date.

The scales have adequate internal consistency. Score stability is also adequate for test-retest purposes. In longitudinal studies delinquents receiving treatment tend to improve their JI scores in appropriate ways.

In a few studies, the JI scales have formed patterns indicative of subtypes of delinquency. For example, Social Maladjustment scores may prove useful in identifying a subgroup of delinquents who are depressed and hence require different treatment than those who are acting out.

Much remains to be determined about the JI scales. Particularly interesting questions include how well it predicts delinquency in a random sample of normal subjects, how it will fit into a battery of other classification tests, and how various specific treatments may affect scores on each of the several scales. Until these questions are answered, it would probably be wise to use the JI as an experimental measure.

References

Bornholt, L.J., & Rosenthal, D.A. (1987). Classification procedures for differential treatment. *British Journal of Clinical Psychology, 26*, 155–156.

Butt, D.S. (1978). The Jesness Inventory. In O.K. Buros (Ed.), *The eighth mental measurements yearbook* (pp. 876–878). Highland Park, NJ: Gryphon Press.

Craighead, W.E. (1991). Cognitive factors and classification issues in adolescent depression. *Journal of Youth and Adolescence, 20*, 311–326.

Curry, J.F., & Craighead, W.E. (1990). Attributional style in clinically depressed and conduct disordered adolescents. *Journal of Consulting and Clinical Psychology, 58*, 109–115.

Friesen, W.J., & Wright, P.G. (1985). The validity of the Carlson Psychological Survey. *Journal of Personality Assessment, 49*, 422–426.

Jesness, C.F. (1984). *Manual for the Jesness Behavior Checklist.* Palo Alto, CA: Consulting Psychologists Press.

Jesness, C.F. (1986). Validity of Jesness Inventory classification with nondelinquents. *Educational and Psychological Measurement, 46*, 947–961.

Jesness, C.F. (1991). *The Jesness Inventory manual.* Toronto: Multi-Health Systems.

Jesness, C.F., & Wedge, R.F. (1984). Validity of a revised Jesness Inventory I-level classification with delinquents. *Journal of Consulting and Clinical Psychology, 52,* 997–1010.

Jesness, C.F., & Wedge, R.F. (1985). *Jesness Inventory classification system.* Palo Alto, CA: Consulting Psychologists Press.

LeBlanc, M., McDuff, P., Charlebois, P., Gagnon, C., Larrivee, S., & Tremblay, R.E. (1991). Social and psychological consequences, at 10 years old, of an earlier onset of self-reported delinquency. *Psychiatry, 54,* 133–147.

Martin, R.D. (1981). Cross-validation of the Jesness Inventory with delinquents and nondelinquents. *Journal of Consulting and Clinical Psychology, 49,* 10–14.

Munson, R.F., & Revers, M.P. (1986). Program effectiveness of a residential treatment center for emotionally disturbed adolescent females as measured by exit personality tests. *Adolescence, 21,* 305–310.

Roberts, G., Schmitz, K., Pinto, J., & Cain, S. (1990). The MMPI and Jesness Inventory as measures of effectiveness on an inpatient conduct disorders treatment unit. *Adolescence, 25,* 989–996.

Weintraub, S.A. (1972). The Jesness Inventory. In O.K. Buros (Ed.), *The seventh mental measurements yearbook* (pp. 202–203). Highland Park, NJ: Gryphon Press.

Woodbury, R., & Shurling, J. (1975). Factorial dimensions of the Jesness Inventory with black delinquents. *Educational and Psychological Measurement, 35,* 979–981.

Wunderlich, R.A. (1985). Dimensions of delinquency. *Educational and Psychological Measurement, 45,* 101–108.

James A. Moses, Jr., Ph.D.

Clinical Associate Professor of Psychiatry and Behavioral Sciences, Stanford University School of Medicine, and Coordinator, Psychological Assessment Unit, Department of Veterans Affairs Medical Center, Palo Alto, California.

JUDGMENT OF LINE ORIENTATION

Arthur L. Benton, Kerry deS. Hamsher, Nils R. Varney, and Otfried Spreen. New York, New York: Oxford University Press.

Introduction

Judgment of Line Orientation (JLO; Benton, Hamsher, Varney, & Spreen, 1983) is a 30-item, standardized, objectively scored, quantitative psychometric measure of visual-spatial perceptual ability that is hierarchically organized by item difficulty level. Two different versions of the test (Forms H and V) are commercially available, consisting of the same 30 items organized in a "slightly" different order between forms. A.L. Benton (personal communication, April 27, 1992) has noted that "the difference [between the two JLO forms] consists of minor changes in placement among the easier items and minor changes in placement among the more difficult items. Thus the two versions are simply the same test items in slightly different orders of presentation." He also mentioned parenthetically that the two forms were given the letter designations "H" and "V" in recognition of the contributions of Dr. Hamsher (to Form H) and Dr. Varney (to Form V) during the development of these variant forms of JLO. Order of item difficulty typically increases gradually in each JLO form.

Disturbance of visual-spatial perception generally has been recognized as a specific, dissociable symptom of brain disease, particularly of the right cerebral hemisphere, for approximately a century. For an overview of diagnostic issues and a list of references to the historical literature on this clinical problem, the interested reader is referred to Benton et al. (1983, pp. 44–45). Evaluation of visual-spatial disturbance in the presence of visual-perceptual disorder associated with cerebral hemispheric disease has become a key feature of any complete analysis of higher cortical functions. JLO can play an integral part in assessing this perceptual ability.

The developmental origin of JLO began with experimental rather than clinical work in the area of visual-spatial perception. Fontenot and Benton (1972) showed that right-handed, neurologically normal subjects could make more accurate spatial discrimination judgments of visual stimuli that were presented very briefly tachistoscopically in their left visual field than those that were presented in the right visual field. This experimental demonstration preliminarily suggested the dominance of the right cerebral hemisphere for visual-spatial perception. Warrington and Rabin (1970) presented a visual-spatial line slope comparison task to groups of neurologic patients with lateralized cerebral lesions. The patients with left-hemispheric lesions performed comparably to the controls, whereas the patients with right-hemispheric lesions performed the task with a significantly higher error score than the other groups. The greatest impairment of visual-spatial perception was associated with lesions of the right parietal area.

Benton, Hannay, and Varney (1975) increased the complexity of the Warrington and Rabin (1970) experimental paradigm by briefly presenting single lines at fixed angles and pairs of lines at differing angles through a tachistoscope for 300 milliseconds. After this presentation the subjects were required to identify from memory the slopes of the lines on a multiple-choice array of sloped lines. Relative to the lower performance limit of the control group, none of the left-hemispheric-lesioned patients performed the task defectively, but 59% of the right-hemispheric-lesioned patients fell below this level of performance.

Benton and his colleagues attempted to make this experimental task into a procedure for the clinical assessment of visual-spatial function in neurologic patients. When they presented the same stimuli to patients without time constraints, however, the same visual-spatial discrimination task alone did not prove sufficiently difficult to distinguish between patients with and without visual-spatial deficit. Most patients made very few or no errors.

In an ingenious alteration of the task, Benton and his colleagues halved the length of the directional lines and varied their distance from the origin of the imaginary circle center from which the directional rays originated. This procedure produced a task of comparable difficulty to the tachistoscopically presented original version of the spatial discrimination task and did not require a time-limited stimulus exposure so that it could be used conveniently as a bedside examination task. It remained for Benton, Varney, and Hamsher (1978) to standardize and norm the revised procedure with shortened directional lines, which became the final, commercially available form of JLO.

The principal author of JLO, Arthur L. Benton, Ph.D., received the A.B. degree (1931) and the A.M. degree (1933) from Oberlin College, and subsequently the Ph.D. degree from Columbia University (1935). He began his career as an assistant in psychology at Oberlin College (1931–33), Columbia University and New York State Psychiatric Institute (1934–36), and Cornell University Medical College (1936–39), where he later served as a staff psychologist. He was appointed as an attending psychologist at New York Hospital–Westchester Division and as a psychologist in the Student Personnel Office of the City College of New York from 1939–41. He served on active duty in the U.S. Navy during and after the Second World War (1941–46). Subsequently he was appointed as Associate Professor of Psychology at the University of Louisville Medical School and as Chief Psychologist at the Louisville Mental Hygiene Clinic and the Louisville General Hospital (1946–48). From 1948 to 1958 he served as Professor of Psychology and Director of the Graduate Training Program in Clinical Psychology at the University of Iowa. For the next two decades (1958–78) he then served as Professor of Psychology and Neurology at the University of Iowa. Dr. Benton has continued to coauthor theoretical and research papers and books since 1978, when he became Professor Emeritus at the University of Iowa.

Benton's fundamental contributions to the field of clinical neuropsychology have been acknowledged extensively and internationally. He has received honorary Doctor of Science (Cornell College, 1978) and Doctor of Psychology (University of Rome, 1990) degrees, as well as numerous other honors and awards, including the Distinguished Service Award of the Iowa Psychological Association (1977), the Distinguished Professional Contribution Award from the American Psychological Association (1978), the Outstanding Scientific Contribution Award of the International Neuropsychological Society (1981), The Samuel Torrey Orton Award from the Orton Dyslexia Society (1982), the Distinguished Service and Outstanding Contributions Award from the American Board of Professional Psychology (1985), and the Distinguished Clinical Neuropsychologist Award from the National Academy of Neuropsychology (1989).

Benton is a past president of the American Orthopsychiatric Association (1965–66) and the International Neuropsychological Society (1970–71). He served as the Secretary-General of the Research Group on Aphasia for the World Federation of Neurology from 1971 to 1978. He has been a lecturer or visiting scholar at the University of Milan (1964), Hôpital Sainte-Anne, Paris (1968), Hadassah-Hebrew University Medical School, Jerusalem (1969), Free University of Amsterdam (1971), University of Helsinki (1974), University of Melbourne (1977), University of Minnesota Medical School (Baker Lecturer, 1979), University of Victoria, British Columbia (Lansdowne Scholar, 1980), and the University of Michigan (1986). He also served as Directeur d'Études Associé, École des Hautes Études, Paris (1979) and as a visiting scientist at the Tokyo Metropolitan Institute of Gerontology (1974).

Benton has authored, coauthored, or edited 12 books and monographs, approximately 150 professional journal articles, and 22 historical reviews in the area of clinical neuropsychology and behavioral neurology. He is recognized as a pioneer and a leading authority in the area of clinical neuropsychology.

The standardized, commercially published version of JLO appeared with the clinical manual for this and other tests in the Benton-Iowa Neuropsychological Test Battery (Benton et al., 1983). Coauthors of this clinical manual with Dr. Benton are Kerry deS. Hamsher, Ph.D. (Associate Professor of Neurology, University of Wisconsin Medical School); Nils R. Varney, Ph.D. (Staff Neuropsychologist, Department of Veterans Affairs Medical Center, Iowa City, Iowa); and Otfried Spreen, Ph.D. (Professor Emeritus, Department of Psychology, University of Victoria, Victoria, British Columbia, Canada).

Practical Applications/Uses

JLO is a specific measure of visual-spatial perceptual competence that can be valuable as a technique to separate the effects of a visual field defect from a visual-spatial disorder. Presence or absence of a central homonymous visual field defect is not predictive of spatial perception as measured by JLO (Benton et al., 1983). The JLO technique serves as an objective measure of the degree of visual-spatial disturbance, which otherwise may be difficult to evaluate clinically independent of a visual field defect.

The JLO items appear on a set of 35 stimulus cards. The first 5 cards are practice items; the remaining 30 present the formal test items. All of the test cards are contained in a single spiral-bound booklet. Title cards separate the card sections for practice items and test items to keep them distinct. Each JLO item consists of facing cards in the booklet. On the upper card appear two unlabeled directional lines, which the patient must match to an array of numbered standard reference lines below, on the lower facing card. The lower directional reference card (the same for every item) consists of 11 numbered lines that point from 0 degrees (horizontal left ray) through 180 degrees (horizontal right ray) relative to their central circular origin at equal 18-degree intervals. Each of these directional reference lines is 1½ inches long, as is each of the lines for the five initial practice items. It was this sort of direct matching task that proved relatively easy even for clinical samples, so it is used as an introductory technique to explain the task to the patient who may have significant visual-spatial difficulty.

The 30 actual test items that follow the practice items have directional rays only *half* as long as the numbered directional reference lines to which they must be spatially compared. An additional source of difficulty is introduced by systematically varying the distance of the line segments from their point of origin. On the JLO answer sheet, the combination of line segments is indicated for each item to aid the examiner in performing a qualitative analysis of the patient's specific types of errors. Line segments closest to their point of origin are labeled "L" (for low, in the closest ¾-inch segment to the origin). Line segments in the furthest ¾-inch segment relative to the origin are labelled "H" (high) segments. Line segments in the intermediate ¾-inch segment on a directional ray are labeled "M" (middle) segments; they appear at an intermediate distance, ¼ inch from the extremes of each of the L and H segments. JLO test items consist of pairs of lines presented in eight combinations: HH (two distal segments), MM (two intermediate segments), LL (two proximal segments), and five mixed distance combinations—HL, LH, HM, MH, and LM. Many of the "mixed items," in which the lines are at different distances from the point of origin, present contrasting spatial directional cues that may be challenging for even the spatially competent individual to resolve.

The JLO test booklet should be placed so that the reference lines on the lower card (nearer the patient) lay flat on the table and the stimulus items on the upper card (nearer the examiner) remain at about a 45-degree angle from horizontal, toward the patient. All of the JLO stimuli should be held completely within the patient's sighted visual field. The patient should be allowed to hold and position the test card booklet so that it is most easily seen and the stimuli are glare-free.

Directions for administering the JLO are extensive, highly structured, and precise, and the examiner must follow them verbatim. As a result they are reproduced here directly from the test manual for clarity and completeness of explanation (Benton et al., 1983, pp. 46–47):

> The examiner should begin with practice item A, point to the lines on the upper stimulus page, and say: *"See these two lines? Which two lines down here* (pointing to the response card) *are in the same direction as the two lines up here?"* *"Tell me the number of the lines."* If the patient supplies the correct answers, say *"that's right"*, and proceed with practice item B. If the patient is aphasic or otherwise shows a tendency to misstate the numbers while pointing to correct response-choices, say instead: *"Show me these lines down here. Point to them."* If the patient does not

understand the task continue by using your hand to cover the line in position 6 (vertical ray) and, pointing to the other line (in position 1—horizontal left ray), say *"Let us just look at this line. Which line down here* (pointing to the response-choice display) *points in the same direction as this one* (pointing to the stimulus line) *and is also in the same position? That is, it's on the same side of the page as this line up here?"* Record the response on the record sheet where it is labeled A'. Correct the patient if he still supplies the wrong answer and proceed, using these extended instructions, by covering the other line (in position 1) and pointing to the line in position 6. After demonstrating the line in position 6, again supply the correct answers if it is not given on the second trial (A'). Continue with practice item B. If the patient again gives the wrong answers for this practice item, follow up with the extended instructions using single lines (trial B'). Continue with this cycle of instructions until the patient gives two correct responses on the practice items on the first trial.

To be scored correct, both elements of an item must be answered correctly; no partial credit is assigned for successful identification of only one item element on JLO. If the patient fails to master the two correct item criterion in the five practice trials, the test is discontinued and a severely defective spatial orientation score is assigned.

To rule out extraneous, nonperceptual sources of failure on JLO, the examiner must establish that the patient is alert, attentive to the task and to the examiner, and able to reply in a task-relevant manner. By means of these criteria the examiner can ensure that a severely defective score assigned on the basis of failure on the practice items alone is not due to other causes, such as inattention, confusion, or auditory comprehension difficulty. Failure to master the JLO practice items at the two-item criterion level for reasons *other* than visual-spatial perceptual difficulty would be grounds for discontinuing the test. It also should suggest other directions for supplementary assessment to determine the cause of the performance difficulty, using procedures appropriate to the patient's area of apparent cognitive or sensory-perceptual deficit. No statement about the patient's visual-spatial ability would be possible on the basis of failure on the JLO sample items *unless* causes of failure other than visual-spatial perceptual deficit could be excluded as bases of the performance failure.

If the five practice items are completed successfully, the examiner presents instructions for the actual test items while the cover card stating "test items" overlays the first creditable JLO test item. The patient is told, "Now we are going to do more of these, except now the lines which you see up here *(pointing to the upper page)* will be shorter, because part of the line has been erased. Tell me *(show me)* which two lines down here are pointing in the same direction as the lines up here" (Benton et al., 1983, p. 47). No feedback on performance accuracy is provided to the patient for the creditable test items. General, nonspecific statements of encouragement are permissible to maintain optimal task motivation. Although no time limit applies to JLO administration, the test authors recommend encouragement of forced guessing at the preferred choice alternatives if the patient delays for more than 30 seconds on any item. Benton and his colleagues also recommend verbatim recording of patient responses for later qualitative analysis, not simply recording "correct" or "incorrect" as a performance-level evaluation of response accuracy.

Scoring the JLO is a clerical task. One point is assigned for each completely correct test item, in which the spatial orientation of both line elements of the stimulus are correctly matched to the numbered directional reference line array. The initial five sample items are not credited. The possible range of scores on JLO is 0 to 30 points. Actuarial analysis of the demographic effects of age and sex on JLO performance required minor score corrections for these factors to equalize mean score distributions across the normative age range and sex categories. With these corrections, only one set of interpretive range diagnostic categorization rules is needed for JLO clinical interpretation.

The JLO was normed on a composite sample of 137 subjects (65 men, 72 women) who were demographically cross-classified by age and sex. The age breakdown was stratified in three broad ranges: 16–49 years (27 men, 31 women), 50–64 years (17 men, 26 women), and 65–74 years (21 men, 15 women). Small but consistent declines of 1 to 2 points are seen across the age categories in both sexes. The women also score approximately 2 points lower than the men on JLO in all three age groups. These demographic trends have been adjusted actuarially in the corrected JLO scoring system by means of a series of demographic corrections for age and sex. To correct for demographic bias, if a subject is aged 50 to 64 years, 1 point is added to the JLO total raw score. Three points are added if the subject is aged 65 to 74 years, and 2 additional points are added if the subject is a woman of any age.

Benton et al. (1983, p. 50) have assigned descriptive labels and percentiles to JLO *corrected* total score ranges for clinical use. These normative and descriptive interpretative guidelines are reproduced here for reference. Total corrected scores in the range 29–30 (86+ percentile) are rated as superior; 27–28 (72 percentile), high average; 25–26 (56 percentile) and 23–24 (40 percentile), average; 21–22 (22 percentile), low average; 19–20 (9 percentile), borderline; 17–18 (4 percentile), moderately defective; and 0–16 (1.5 percentile and below), severely defective. For clinical screening purposes, JLO corrected raw scores of 19 or less are rated as test failures and indicate significant visual-spatial dysfunction.

Professional qualifications for an examiner to administer and score the JLO are not stated explicitly in the test manual. One would expect that a qualified JLO administrator would be either a multidisciplinary mental health professional with clinical patient care responsibility or a trained technician. Those who interpret the JLO results in clinical practice should be specialist clinicians with at least a master's degree in a professional discipline such as clinical neuropsychology or behavioral neurology that provides thorough training in understanding and analysis of "brain-behavior relationships." Experimental researchers in human neuropsychology and related disciplines also could make productive use of JLO results in theoretical studies of visual-spatial and related perceptual processes.

JLO was validated clinically in a study with two samples of 50 patients each who had medically confirmed, unilateral brain lesions of the left or the right cerebral hemisphere. The test manual reports the results of the study in detail (Benton et al., 1983, pp. 49–52). The two groups of subjects were demographically similar in age but not educational level. The left-hemispheric (LH) group had a mean age of 52 years (range = 20–74, *SD* unreported), and the right-hemispheric (RH) group had a mean age of 54 years (range = 22–72, *SD* unreported). The mean LH group educational level was 12 years (range = 6–16, *SD* unreported), but the mean RH group educational level was only 10.7 years (range = 8–16, *SD* unreported).

No *t* test comparison statistics of the groups for comparability of these demographic variables is reported in the test manual's discussion of the study. It is difficult to estimate whether the mean educational levels in particular significantly differed without knowledge of the standard deviation statistics. The demographic comparability of these groups of subjects on age and educational level variables therefore remains uncertain. This is an important issue, as both variables are known to influence performance level strongly on a wide variety of cognitive measures of higher cortical function integrity. Their relative influence on JLO performance should be determined by correlational studies. In the absence of demographic comparison statistics between the lateralized lesion samples, the results for each sample should be treated separately and not necessarily comparably.

The two lateralized lesion groups also differed remarkably in linguistic competence. Seventy-eight percent of the left-hemispheric-lesioned patients were aphasic, but no right-hemispheric-lesioned patients were. Vascular disease predominated as the primary diagnostic entity in both lateralized lesion groups (LH: 62%, RH: 56%), followed by brain tumors and other "space occupying lesions" (LH: 26%, RH: 42%). The unihemispheric-lesioned cases were subdivided where possible into regionally focal lesion groups by radiographic and surgical operative criteria. Patients were divided into "prefrontal, perirolandic, posterior, and indeterminate" categories for analysis. These cases were subdivided further into subgroups of cases with and without (homonymous) visual field defects. Presence or absence of a central visual field defect was not related to performance level on JLO. A summary of subgroup performance trends shows no failures in the prefrontal lesion group (*n* = 4 cases), a 13% failure rate in the perirolandic lesion group, a 75% failure rate in the posterior lesion group, and a 63% failure rate in the "indeterminate" (overlapping focal zones, multifocal, or very large lesion) cases. For details of lesion locus, neuroanatomical categorization, and statistical breakdown of results by lesion subgroup, see Benton et al. (1983, pp. 49–52).

Benton and his associates also carried out an analysis of JLO results by type of lesion (vascular vs. neoplastic) and found null results. This is not surprising, as one would expect the psychometric results to be quite heterogeneous within each lesion group depending upon the extent, chronicity, locus, and specific nature of the disease process. Subsequent investigators may wish to attempt more detailed syndrome analytic studies to follow up on this initial exploratory study. It is also important to note that Benton et al. (1983, p. 52) emphasized that all of their patients in this study were cooperative and fully able to comprehend the JLO task. They stress the importance of clinically differentiating between JLO failure due to dementia, confusion, or lack of patient cooperation and failure due to selective difficulty with spatial perception alone. Careful attention to the patient's qualitative performance and testing the limits to determine the cause of his or her cognitive difficulty is a painstaking and critical process in JLO administration, requiring considerable examiner experience, clinical judgment, and sensitivity.

Investigators who may wish to replicate and extend this validational study should note that acute, unilateral, nonhemorrhagic, occlusive stroke is a well-lateralized, criterion neurologic syndrome, but brain tumor and cerebral mass lesions are not always suitable as criterion cases for lesion-lateralization effect studies (for a discussion, see Damasio & Geschwind, 1985, pp. 8–9). The cerebral tumor volume commonly produces considerable physical pressure within the brain and skull, a "mass effect," that may cross the midline to affect both cerebral hemispheres structurally and functionally. Physiological effects such as brain edema and abnormal metabolic alteration associated with the neoplasm also can disrupt function of both cerebral hemispheres to differing degrees, depending on the locus, acuteness, and malignancy of the lesion. Lateralized lesion findings associated with subjects in which brain tumors and other mass lesions are sampled (which are part of both lateralized lesion groups in this study) should be considered preliminary at best. This study should be replicated with sizeable samples of strongly lateralized lesion criterion cases (preferably acute, unilateral, single event, occlusive strokes) in which these effects have been experimentally controlled rigorously.

Damasio (1985, p. 281) suggested that JLO appeared most closely associated with lesions of the right parietal-occipital area. The lateralizing value of JLO in syndrome analysis also should be studied systematically in lateralized lesion patient groups as a function of lesion chronicity. Longitudinal repeated measures studies of recovery patterns in focal lesion cases would be particularly instructive to study empirically, particularly now that basic JLO validity and reliability studies have been completed.

The findings of two recent studies that employed JLO are particularly instructive in this regard, as they highlight the importance of individual differences and the need for a variety of parametric investigations to clarify test patterns in various syndrome variant and diagnostic groups. Mehta, Newcombe, and Damasio (1987) studied elderly patients (age M = 65 years) with old penetrating head wounds that had been sustained during wartime, many decades prior to the time of assessment with JLO. The JLO total scores of both left- and right-hemispheric-lesioned patients emerged within normal limits. Although the JLO mean performance level of the left-hemispheric-lesion group fell significantly below that of the controls, the mean JLO total score level of the right-hemispheric-lesion group was comparable.

An experimentally well-controlled follow-up study to the Mehta et al. (1987) investigation has been completed by Hamsher, Capruso, and Benton (1992). Hamsher and his colleagues studied only patients with unilateral cerebrovascular accidents, some of whom were seen in a rehabilitation unit (some sampling details are courtesy of A.L. Benton, personal communication, April 27, 1992). All subjects studied were right-handed. Hemispheric unilaterality of all lesions was radiographically and neurologically documented. The samples were relatively large to lessen individual difference bias (24 left-hemispheric lesions, 17 aphasic; 30 right-hemispheric lesion cases, none aphasic; and 30 control cases). All groups were matched for mean age (range 58–65 years across groups) and mean educational level (M = 11 years across groups, variability statistics unreported).

Hamsher et al. (1992) demonstrated the expected performance decrement of right-hemispheric-lesioned patients on JLO (63% defective performance rate with

JLO age-corrected score cutoff value of 19) relative to controls (no control cases performed defectively). Of the left-hemispheric cases, however, 24% (4/17) of the aphasic patients performed defectively on JLO, while none of the nonaphasic left-hemispheric cases performed defectively. This finding was unexpected, and it raises the question of the role of verbal mediation in a subject's evaluation of alternatives in the JLO multiple-choice response format, wherein close differential visual discriminations are required.

The degree of deviation from the correct response in the failing aphasic cases would be of interest to note in an item analysis of their performances, to see if their responses were at least partially correct (uncreditable under JLO formal scoring, but notable in qualitative analysis). Also of interest is the difficulty of the perceptual task. Errors might occur more readily when the portions of the JLO directional rays were at different lengths from the origin and thus gave conflicting visual-spatial cues that might be resolved by means of verbal mediation. These speculations may be of value to clinicians and future researchers in conducting item pattern analysis beyond summary score performance-level analysis.

JLO mean performance level decrement has proven sensitive to cognitive deficit in dementia, although it is not typically specific (32% incidence in a diagnostically mixed sample of patients with dementia) for this generic differential diagnostic question (Eslinger, Damasio, Benton, & Van Allen, 1985). Two patients with visual agnosia following resolution of cortical blindness performed adequately on JLO (scores of 22, 25) as well as on measures of visual-form discrimination and mental (visual-spatial) rotation, but they could not perform "figure-ground discrimination, visual integration, facial discrimination, and constructional tasks" (Mendez, 1988, p. 1754).

An elegant study by Gur and others (1987), using regional cerebral blood flow measurements as a criterion variable, showed that a modified version of JLO performance differentially activated function of the right cerebral hemisphere while verbal tasks differentially activated function of the left cerebral hemisphere in normals. These differential task response patterns were absent in patients with unilateral cerebral infarctions. Gur et al. (1987) concluded that patients with right-hemispheric cerebral infarcts (RCI) were best identifiable as functionally deficient relative to the control group on the JLO task, whereas left-hemispheric infarct (LCI) patients were deficient in performance level relative to controls on both verbal analogy and JLO (nonverbal) tasks. In a summary of complex trends, Gur and his colleagues (1987) concluded that

> the side of a stroke also affected the magnitude of asymmetry of hemispheric CBF (cerebral blood flow) increase produced by cognitive activation. . . . RCI patients had a normal activation pattern for the verbal task (increased left hemispheric activation) and relative bilateral reduction in overall activation for the spatial task. LCI patients showed reduced activation for both tasks. (p. 779)

They considered their results to be preliminary due to small sample size ($N = 15$), but their experimental controls were rigorous and their results are theoretically consistent with clinical syndrome data.

In a subsequently reported study with normal volunteers, Deutsch, Bourbon,

Papanicolaou, and Eisenberg (1988) also used regional cerebral blood flow as a criterion measure of cerebral activation. In this study the researchers employed JLO, "mental rotation of three-dimensional cube arrays, and a fragment puzzle (visual closure) task" as putative dependent measures of right-hemispheric functioning. JLO and the three-dimensional plane "mental rotation" task performances were related to increased physiological (blood flow) activation of the right cerebral hemisphere. The rotational task showed a somewhat stronger right-hemispheric effect than did JLO, although both measures were significant at very high statistical levels. There also was a highly significant blood flow activation effect for the right *frontal* region on both the rotational and JLO tasks only. Deutsch et al. (1988, p. 449) associated this effect with (nonverbal) attentional focusing that is required to process visual-spatial reasoning tasks. The right-hemispheric increased lateral cerebral blood flow effect on visual-spatial tasks was significantly greater in women than in men. This sex difference was maintained at rest and on all three of the experimental tasks. This finding replicated previous findings in other studies but was not theoretically explainable.

Sandson, Daffner, Carvalho, and Mesulam (1991) studied a case of extremely well-documented multifocal infarction of the left medial thalamic area "as well as several tiny foci . . . involving the white matter of both hemispheres" (p. 1300) that produced a complex left frontal-lobe executive dysfunction syndrome, dysnomia, a verbal retrieval memory deficit, *and* borderline performance on JLO (20/30) at 3-month follow-up evaluation. Unfortunately only part of the JLO test could be given to the patient during the acute phase of her illness (3/10 designs correct), and she was not examined with this measure at 8-month follow-up. In the presence of a thalamo-frontal executive and memorial dysfunction syndrome such as this, one cannot rule out impulsive guessing, distractibility, perseveration, naming/verbal encoding difficulty, or failure to retrieve partial visual solutions from short-term nonverbal memory as a basis for the poor JLO performance. There also was evidence of bilateral petechial lesioning in both hemispheres. The role of JLO in this interesting syndrome-analytic case therefore is moot.

Technical Aspects

It is important to quantitatively demonstrate that a test has reliable, or statistically accurate and reproducible, findings. No test can serve as a valid measure of a behavioral or theoretical construct or dimension if it is not also reliable. One aspect of reliability involves internal consistency. This statistical criterion quantitatively measures the degree to which the items of a test correlationally group together to measure a common dimension or variable. A common method of determining internal consistency involves sampling random halves of the test, such as odd and even items, and then statistically correlating these two half-tests with each other to estimate the similarity of item content in the test as a whole. Standard statistical formula corrections are used to estimate the reliability of the original-length test when the split-half method of internal consistency estimation is applied. The reliability of a psychometric measure relates directly to its length, and one would not wish to artifactually underestimate the reliability of the measure by splitting and comparing halves of the item pool as two shorter subtests without correction. The value that reduces error of measurement to a practical minimum is generally taken to be .80 for internal consistency measures.

Internal consistency based on corrected split-half reliability of JLO Form H in a sample of 40 adult subjects was reported to be .94, and the comparable value for Form V in a sample of 124 adult subjects was .89. In a composite sample of 164 adult subjects, the corrected split-half reliability of JLO was .91. The data from the two forms were blended in the composite adult sample analysis because the item content across JLO forms is equivalent. These are exceptionally high internal consistency values. Such analyses demonstrate that JLO measures a unitary psychometric construct or dimension because the items all correlate highly with each other.

According to some authorities, particularly Nunnally (1978), however, the ideal estimator of internal consistency is not the classical split-half method of item sampling but rather Cronbach's coefficient alpha statistic, because it is the mean of all possible split-half values for an item pool. Any single split-half value may be unpredictably biased upward or downward from this mean value. Nunnally also recommends computation of coefficient alpha in a sample of approximately 300 subjects, as values based on such a sample will generalize to a sample of essentially any size that is similarly composed. If the requisite sample could be composed and analyzed, the internal consistency results for JLO based on Nunnally's recommendations would be definitive. Although this is an ideal psychometric standard, it is clear from available evidence that JLO is a reliable measure with sound internal consistency. The additional study would be useful, however, to demonstrate the general parametric trends in the population with this measure.

Another important aspect of reliability is the demonstration that a test is temporally stable. One must be able to reproduce testing results from one session to another over a relatively brief interval during which no substantive objective change occurs in the behavioral variable to be measured. Demonstration of such test-retest reliability is necessary to assert that changes in the test score over time are due to treatment, practice, or other systematic effects and not to chance variation alone. A relatively brief, preferably standardized period of time, often about 2 weeks, is chosen between test and retest sessions to allow for random or minor situational fluctuations in behavior, mood, attention, and so forth; the latter should account for minor performance-level variation but not affect the overall test score if the results are accurate and stable. The test and retest scores are correlated to estimate their congruence.

Forms H and V of JLO were administered serially to a sample of 37 adults with unreported demographic or diagnostic characteristics over an intertest interval ranging from 6 hours to 21 days. The mean JLO summary scores on the two test administrations were very similar (23.1 and 23.5 points). The test authors noted that no mean practice effect emerged due to retesting in their adult sample. The JLO cross-form test-retest reliability correlation coefficient for adults was .90, and the standard error of measurement for adults was 1.8 points (Benton et al., 1983, p. 46).

The cross-form retest reliability of JLO is very high. Without demographic and diagnostic descriptions of the population sampled, however, the generalizability of these results is unknown. These reliability figures should be considered tentative until rigorously controlled studies of JLO reliability can be performed and reported in the literature. JLO very likely has quite high retest reliability, but the statistical limits of this presumption and the effects of retesting, particularly the retest practice effect, as yet remains unknown in specific clinical diagnostic and control groups.

Developmental trends in JLO performance among boys ($n = 153$) and girls ($n = 162$) aged 7 to 14 years also have been reported by Lindgren (1977) and by Lindgren and Benton (1980). The corrected split-half reliability value for JLO in a mixed-age sample of children ($n = 315$) was reported as .84. It should be noted that 94 children in the sample were tested twice and inclusion of their test and retest scores in the internal consistency sample calculations may have biased the results. The retest stability (long-term reliability) values for the 94 children who were retested are not reported in the test manual.

A steady although not entirely uniform increase in JLO overall accuracy score occurs across the childhood age range for both sexes. Lindgren and Benton (1980) found a relatively small correlation of verbal intelligence, as measured by a pro-rated form of the Wechsler Intelligence Scale for Children–Revised, with JLO total score in these children (range = $-.09-.42$; median correlational value = $+.15$). This mean value explains only about 2% of the variance in JLO, which is negligible. JLO thus was shown to measure a skill that is not attributable to verbal (or general) intelligence alone as a global performance level measure. For details of the age distribution and sampling procedures, see Benton et al. (1983, pp. 52–53).

Critique

JLO shows high retest reliability and a temporally stable total score. It also is an internally consistent, accurate measure. Replication of the retest reliability of JLO in demographically comparable, matched sets of men and women across a strati-fied age range of normal subjects remain to be completed, however. Replications of the initial JLO reliability studies, indeed all studies, should report full demo-graphic and test score characteristics of the samples, including mean, variability, standard error, and range statistics, so that the generalizability of the results to clinical and experimental samples can be determined objectively. Coefficient al-pha should be used in calculating internal consistency values for JLO in a mixed diagnostic sample of 300 or more subjects.

In both validity and reliability studies, the two alternate-order forms of JLO should be studied separately to test their relative differences, if any exist. In some published studies, data from the two forms are pooled, yet the two forms of the test also are presented as separate versions. Whether the item order between the two forms would affect the relative difficulty of the test as a whole is not known. The description of the interform item-ordering differences as relatively minor, however, suggests that systematic differences between the forms would not be suspected on theoretical grounds.

Validation studies of JLO to date have been quite impressive; the test shows excellent initial concurrent validity against physiological (cerebral blood flow) measures in normals. In patients with brain lesions, JLO sensitivity and specific-ity to right-hemispheric perceptual deficit are less clear, though. The effects of aphasia, aphasic subtype, and chronicity of lesion have produced varying results in the exploratory studies reviewed above. Controlled experimental studies designed to systematically evaluate variants of these parameters *and* their interactions remain to be reported. Conflicting results across studies seem due to unsystematic sampling on these and possibly other unspecified variables.

Systematic studies of the construct validity of JLO relative to other, well-established measures of visual perception and nonverbal cognition also are needed to establish its convergent and divergent validities. There is reason for optimism that careful study of demographic and diagnostic variables in relation to JLO performance in experimental and clinical studies will show logical and consistent patterns of performance that likely may be complex and interactive, but as yet the experimental explication of these relationships has only begun.

References

Benton, A.L., Hamsher, K.deS., Varney, N.R., & Spreen, O. (1983). *Contributions to neuropsychological assessment: A clinical manual.* New York: Oxford University Press.

Benton, A.L., Hannay, H.J., & Varney, N.R. (1975). Visual perception of line direction in patients with unilateral brain disease. *Neurology, 25,* 907–910.

Benton, A.L., Varney, N.R., & Hamsher, K.deS. (1978). Visuospatial judgment: A clinical test. *Archives of Neurology, 35,* 364–367.

Damasio, A.R. (1985). Disorders of complex visual processing: Agnosias, achromatopsia, Balint's syndrome, and related difficulties of orientation and construction. In M.M. Mesulam (Ed.), *Principles of behavioral neurology* (pp. 259–288). Philadelphia: Davis.

Damasio, A.R., & Geschwind, N. (1985). Anatomical localization in clinical neuropsychology. In J.A.M. Fredericks (Ed.), *Handbook of clinical neurology: Clinical neuropsychology* (Vol. 45, pp. 7–22). Amsterdam: Elsevier.

Deutsch, G., Bourbon, T., Papanicolaou, A.C., & Eisenberg, H.M. (1988). Visuospatial tasks compared via activation of regional cerebral blood flow. *Neuropsychologia, 26,* 445–452.

Eslinger, P.J., Damasio, A.R., Benton, A.L., & Van Allen, M. (1985). Neuropsychologic detection of abnormal mental decline in older persons. *Journal of the American Medical Association, 253,* 670–674.

Fontenot, D.J., & Benton, A.L. (1972). Perception of direction in the right and left visual fields. *Neuropsychologia, 10,* 447–452.

Gur, R.C., Gur, R.E., Silver, F.L., Obrist, W.D., Skolnick, B.E., Kushner, M., Hurtig, H.I., & Reivich, M. (1987). Regional cerebral blood flow in stroke: Hemispheric effects of cognitive activity. *Stroke, 18,* 776–780.

Hamsher, K., Capruso, D.X., & Benton, A. (1992). Visuospatial judgment and right hemisphere disease. *Cortex, 28*(3), 493–495.

Lindgren, S.D. (1977). *Spatial perception in children.* Unpublished doctoral dissertation, University of Iowa, Iowa City.

Lindgren, S.D., & Benton, A.L. (1980). Developmental patterns of visuospatial judgment. *Journal of Pediatric Psychology, 5,* 217–225.

Mendez, M.F. (1988). Visuoperceptual function in visual agnosia. *Neurology, 38,* 1754–1759.

Mehta, Z., Newcombe, F., & Damasio, H. (1987). A left hemisphere contribution to visuospatial processing. *Cortex, 23,* 447–461.

Nunnally, J.C. (1978). *Psychometric theory* (2nd ed.). New York: McGraw-Hill.

Sandson, T.A., Daffner, K.R., Carvalho, P.A., & Mesulam, M.M. (1991). Frontal lobe dysfunction following infarction of the left-sided medial thalamus. *Archives of Neurology, 48,* 1300–1303.

Warrington, E.K., & Rabin, P. (1970). Perceptual matching in patients with cerebral lesions. *Neuropsychologia, 8,* 475–487.

James E. Jirsa, Ph.D.
School Psychologist, Madison Metropolitan School District, Madison, Wisconsin.

KAUFMAN BRIEF INTELLIGENCE TEST

Alan S. Kaufman and Nadeen L. Kaufman. Circle Pines, Minnesota: American Guidance Service.

Introduction

The Kaufman Brief Intelligence Test (K-BIT; Kaufman & Kaufman, 1990b) is a multipurpose intelligence screener which assesses verbal (Vocabulary) and non-verbal (Matrices) factors in individuals from 4 to 90 years of age. The K-BIT can usually be administered and scored in under 30 minutes by a wide variety of technicians, paraprofessionals, and professionals.

Alan S. Kaufman, Ph.D., and Nadeen L. Kaufman, Ed.D., the test's authors, are familiar to clinical and educational assessment professionals, especially those associated with the evaluation of child, adolescent, and adult intelligence. The Kaufmans have coauthored the Kaufman Assessment Battery for Children (K-ABC; 1983a, 1983b), the Kaufman Test of Educational Achievement (K-TEA; 1985a, 1985b), and the AGS Early Screening Profiles: Cognitive/Language Profile (1990a); currently they are working on the standardization of the Kaufman Adolescent and Adult Intelligence Test (KAIT). The Kaufmans collaborated on the revision of the Wechsler Intelligence Scale for Children (with David Wechsler) and on the standardization of the WISC-R and the McCarthy Scales of Children's Abilities.

In addition to over 100 articles and chapters in the intelligence assessment literature, Alan Kaufman authored the classic 1979 reference volume, *Intelligent Testing With the WISC-R*, and, in 1990, *Assessing Adolescent and Adult Intelligence*. Dr. Kaufman received his Ph.D. under Robert Thorndike at Columbia University and is currently Research Professor at the University of Alabama.

Nadeen Kaufman has published widely in the area of intelligence assessment and is a certified teacher and school psychologist with graduate degrees from Columbia University. At this time she is Adjunct Associate Professor of School Psychology at the University of Alabama.

Early development of the K-BIT began with item writing and tryouts during 1984–86, followed by a national tryout in 1986–87 and a national standardization study in 1989. The latter process resulted in a sample of 2,022 individuals ages 4 to 90 at 60 locations nationwide. The initial standardization plan called for 100 subjects at yearly intervals from ages 4 through 10; 150 subjects ages 11–12 through 17–19; 200 subjects ages 20–34; 150 ages 35–54; and 100 subjects ages 55–90. This plan would have provided a total of 1,750 subjects, but as the target numbers were surpassed at all age levels except one (15–16), the actual number tested exceeded the plan by 272 subjects. Most subjects in the standardization study (59%) came from the 7- to 19-year-old age groups.

Table 1

Final K-BIT Standardization Sample Composition

Stratification Variable	Percent in K-BIT Sample	Percent in U.S. Population
Gender		
Female	50.4	49.6
Male	49.6	50.4
Geographic Region		
Northeast	15.2	19.3
North Central	24.6	24.3
South	37.3	35.3
West	22.9	21.1
Parental Education Level		
< Grade 8	6.4	7.4
Grades 9 to 11	12.1	10.4
High school graduate	37.0	40.3
College/tech 1–3 years	24.7	19.6
College graduate & more	19.8	22.3
Ethnic Group		
Black	14.8	14.7
Hispanic	9.4	9.8
Other	3.8	3.1
White	72.0	72.4

Standardization testing was designed to match U.S. census data as closely as possible, using the stratification variables of gender, geographic region, socio-economic status (subject or parent education level), and ethnicity. Each variable was compared within age groups, generally consisting of ages 4–6, 7–19, 20–44, and 55–90. The final standardization sample is compared to U.S. population figures in Table 1 (adapted from Kaufman & Kaufman, 1990b, pp. 49–50), which demonstrates the close congruence of the sample to the population figures.

As the number of subjects at each grade level was relatively small, the authors report that the Angoff-Robertson method (Angoff & Robertson, 1987) of data aggregation was used to develop subtest standard score norms. According to the K-BIT manual, this method of score construction produces a more stable metric by combining data from all "ages into a single distribution after adjusting raw scores at successive ages for differences in mean, variability, and distribution" (Kaufman & Kaufman, 1990b, p. 52).

The K-BIT materials consist of a spiral-bound manual, individual test records or protocols, and an easel that contains all test stimuli. The easel is constructed with a large-diameter binder, allowing easy page turning with minimal effort. In addition, each of the subtests are indicated by large plastic tabs along the lower edge of the preceding page, which aids greatly in the quick location of and smooth transition from one test to another. Following the title page for each subtest is a "Remember Page," which provides useful information such as administration pointers, appropriate probes, scoring guidelines, any special or unique instructions, and the correct starting points tied to age. Although the easel format is very common among educational assessment instruments, the K-BIT version nonetheless can be considered a model of the type. It is physically easy to work with, well designed with good materials, and logically laid out and presented. Illustrations and printing are clear, dark, and smudge-resistant.

The K-BIT consists of two subtests, Vocabulary and Matrices. Vocabulary Part A is comprised of 45 expressive vocabulary items, administered to all ages and requiring the respondent to provide a verbal label for a variety of objects pictured sequentially on the easel pages. Vocabulary Part B is made up of 37 definition items, administered to individuals 8 years and older and limited to 30 seconds per response. The examinee must provide a label after exposure to two clues, a descriptive phrase and an incomplete spelling of the word. Both clues for a specific word are presented on the same easel page facing the subject. The Vocabulary tests measure factors such as general word knowledge/information, verbal concept formation and expression, verbal conceptualization, and language development. Scoring well on these factors is associated primarily with the exposure to formal schooling and specific cultural opportunities.

The Matrices subtest consists of 48 increasingly difficult multiple-choice visual analogy items requiring the individual to select a meaningful (people, objects, etc.) or abstract (dots, drawings, etc.) response to complete a partial pattern shown. This process reflects such intellectual components as nonverbal reasoning, the ability to handle multiple variables in a flexible problem-solving situation, level of general intelligence, and understanding relationships.

According to some sources (e.g., Horn & Cattell, 1966), the Vocabulary components of the K-BIT measure crystallized intelligence, while the Matrices subtest assesses fluid thinking or intelligence.

The record form, printed on recycled paper, measures 11" × 17" before folding; the two vertical folds result in a six-page document, with each page measuring approximately 5½" × 11". This is a rather unusual dimension, but it works well in practice. The front page contains the usual student identification data and places to compute age and record all scores. Provision also is made to enter an occupation for older individuals. The three K-BIT subtests are presented on separate inside pages, contributing to efficient administration. Examiner comments are entered on another page, and the last page contains a Score Profile.

The profile resembles those associated with other Kaufman assessment materials (e.g., K-TEA), and it allows the display and plotting of standard scores, bands of error, and the derivation of percentile ranks and standard deviations. Filling in the profile can be a somewhat tedious chore and in most cases probably would be done only as an aid in explaining scores to parents. However, the completed profile tends to present a "busy" appearance, and its contribution to clarity and understanding on the part of individuals not used to dealing with numbers and graphs is problematical. Of greater potential use for reporting K-BIT results is a three-page reproducible form provided in the manual entitled "K-BIT Report to Examinees and Parents." This document explains the test, provides an example from each subtest, discusses scores with respect to error or measurement ranges, compares verbal/nonverbal areas, and provides space to recommend specific additional testing if appropriate. Not only does this approach present results within an explanatory framework, but it gives the parent or examinee something to take with them and refer to again at some later point—a definite advantage.

The 8½" × 11" K-BIT manual is spiral-bound, so it lays flat and provides easy access to data in the various tables. This manual is well organized and clearly written, plus it offers a wealth of norming and technical information.

All K-BIT materials arrive in (and easily can be stored in) an angle-cut box, which keeps individual items within easy reach.

Practical Applications/Uses

The K-BIT manual repeatedly stresses that this instrument was developed for screening; it should not be used to provide diagnostic data for placement decisions or neuropsychological interpretations. Although the K-BIT yields standard scores with the same mean (100) and standard deviation (15) as those associated with the Wechsler and Kaufman intelligence scales, the manual emphasizes that "this equality is intended only to facilitate score comparisons between the K-BIT and more thorough intelligence batteries; it does not imply that the K-BIT may substitute for a comprehensive measure of a child's or adult's intelligence" (Kaufman & Kaufman, 1990b, p. 1).

Within the general framework of screening then, K-BIT promotional materials as well as the manual suggest the following potential uses for the instrument with individuals from ages 4 through 90:

1. Screening individuals who may require further assessment
2. Estimating the intelligence of large numbers of institutionalized adults (prisons, group homes, etc.)
3. Screening to provide a quick intelligence estimate as part of a more extensive evaluation
4. Reevaluation of the intellectual status of individuals previously evaluated in a more thorough manner
5. Providing useful information in vocational or rehabilitation settings
6. Testing job applicants
7. Educational diagnostic screening
8. Screening to identify potentially talented or gifted students
9. Large-scale screenings to identify possible high-risk students
10. Research applications

Because all test stimulus materials are contained on individual easel pages, it would be possible to adapt the K-BIT for some vision-impaired students by using a full-page magnifier. However, the use of the K-BIT with this population is constrained by two factors. First, some items are timed (the Definition part of the Vocabulary subtest), and vision-impaired individuals may require more than the 30 seconds allowed. Second, individuals with limited vision are not identified in the manual as included in the standardization sample.

The K-BIT is an easily administered individual assessment instrument. The manual claims that "valid scores can be obtained by examiners who lack formal training in individual intellectual assessment" (Kaufman & Kaufman, 1990b, p. 4). However, the manual also strongly suggests that individuals lacking formal assessment training receive K-BIT training from a qualified person, presumably someone possessing the formal measurement credentials. Such training, at a minimum according to the manual, should include the essentials of standardized administration (reading instructions exactly as provided), the importance of providing only the allowed cues and prompts, and the importance of attaining and maintaining rapport with the subject. In addition, it is recommended that a new examiner's first two or three K-BIT administrations be closely observed.

Administration time for the K-BIT is reported to range from 15 to 30 minutes, shorter for younger children because they are not given the Definitions portion of the Vocabulary subtest and longer for adults. Experience suggests that the 30-minute time can be expanded significantly when evaluating highly gifted adolescents. Such students generally will not reach a ceiling on any subtest, and they usually tend to closely examine the more difficult Matrices items for longer periods before responding than do their more average age mates.

The guidelines for administering the K-BIT subtests are clearly presented in the manual. All subtest items are grouped in units, which are identified on the record form. This grouping of items allows the easy application of the basic discontinue rule, which states that any subtest may be ended when the respondent fails all items within a particular unit. Beginning points for each subtest and sample items for Vocabulary Definition and Matrices also are clearly identified on the record form and on the examiner side of the easel. Numerous examples of specific administration problems appear in the manual, which should respond adequately to a wide range of examiner questions.

The scoring instructions and process also are clearly presented in the manual. Because the scoring procedure is completely dichotomous (correct responses = 1, incorrect responses = 0) and objective, the user can master it very quickly. Scoring and recording all K-BIT data, following a practice administration or two, could be accomplished consistently in less than 10 minutes.

Raw scores for each subtest usually are obtained by subtracting the number of errors from the ceiling item. The exception to this general rule arises when an examinee passes fewer than two items in the first unit begun at the age-appropriate level. The manual thoroughly explains and illustrates this situation. The sums of raw scores for Vocabulary (Expressive Vocabulary + Definitions) and Matrices are converted to standard scores through age-referenced tables. The standard scores then are summed to enter another table that enables the examiner to determine the composite standard score. National percentiles corresponding to the standard scores and descriptive categories all are entered on the front of the record form. Bands of error (selected from confidence levels from 68 through 99) also are entered for each of the three major standard scores. The final table provides standard score differences by age required for statistical significance (either $p < .05$ or $p < .01$) between Vocabulary and Matrices.

The manual makes a clear distinction between K-BIT administration, scoring, and interpretation, emphasizing that the latter is the responsibility of an individual with advanced training and experience in this particular area. K-BIT interpretation consists basically of four operations: obtaining standard scores for the two subtests and the composite; attaching bands of error to each of the three standard scores; converting the standard scores to percentiles and descriptive performance categories; and determining the significance of the differences, if any, between the standard scores. The process is simple, straightforward, and aided both by good organization and by the provision and placement of the required tables in the manual. The manual cautions users about overinterpreting standard score differences, given the single-subtest format of the K-BIT.

Technical Aspects

Three aspects of reliability are addressed in the K-BIT manual: internal consistency of subtest and composite scores, stability over time, and measurement error.

Internal consistency, demonstrated by split-half reliability coefficients, represents the extent to which K-BIT standard scores can be associated with measurement of a single factor, skill, or trait. Using individuals in the standardization sample for 14 age groups, split-half reliability coefficients were produced by correlating odd and even item raw scores from the Vocabulary and Matrices sections. These correlations then were corrected for half-test length by the Spearman-Brown formula. All reliability estimates from the Vocabulary subtest were above .89 (high = .98). The Matrices range was from .74 (age 5) to .95 (ages 55–90), and the Composite range was from .88 (age 5) to .98 (ages 55–90). Total sample (N = 2,022) reliabilities were Vocabulary, .93; Matrices, .88; and Composite, .94. Thus K-BIT internal consistency appears very good.

A total of 232 individuals between the ages of 5 and 89 in four studies were tested twice with the K-BIT to establish test-retest reliability. Test-retest reliabilities for four age groups (5–12, 13–19, 20–54, and 55–89) ranged from .80 (age group 13–19, Matrices) to .97 (age group 20–54, Vocabulary). Mean test-retest reliabilities were Vocabulary, .94; Matrices, .85; and Composite, .94 (average time between tests = 21 days; range = 12–145 days).

In general, the test-retest findings are commensurate with the split-half correlation coefficients and in both cases the reliability values tend to increase with age. Taken together, the data presented in the manual support a conclusion of very good reliability for the K-BIT standard scores.

Standard errors of measurement (SE_Ms), or the degree of uncertainty surrounding an individual's "true" score, are derived from reliability data. Because K-BIT reliability is very good, SE_Ms are low, averaging approximately 4 points throughout the instrument's age range for Vocabulary and Composite, and slightly over 5 points for Matrices. An individual's obtained score of 90, for example, is banded with the appropriate SE_M, for example 4, which is presented as 90 ± 4. This means that the chances are 68% (± 1 standard deviation from the mean) that the "true" score lies within the range from 86 to 94.

Test validity refers to the extent to which an instrument does what it says it can do. Validity then is more correctly viewed as a process rather than as a single or aggregate outcome. Essentially, validity encompasses the selection of the particular subtests to be used in a given test, an analysis of items used in the subtests, and an examination of the final form of the instrument.

As it was necessary that a logical relationship exist between the K-BIT and a

Table 2

Comparison of Construct Validity Data: K-BIT and WISC-R

WISC-R	K-BIT								
	Vocabulary			*Matrices*			*Composite*		
Verbal IQ	.78[1]	.83[2]	.86[3]	.48[1]	.62[2]	.77[3]	.77[1]	.79[2]	.89[3]
Performance IQ	.54	.58	.78	.50	.70	.77	.63	.69	.84
Full Scale IQ	.75	.77	.86	.56	.72	.82	.80	.81	.92

[1]Adapted from Kaufman & Kaufman (1990b), p. 66
[2]Adapted from Prewett (1992), p. 26
[3]Jirsa (1992)

number of longer test batteries, the subtests selected needed to be commensurate with the following established standards: the Verbal/Performance split (Wechsler, 1974, 1981, 1989); the Verbal/Perceptual-Performance difference associated with the work of McCarthy (1972); the Achievement/Mental Processing dichotomy (Kaufman & Kaufman, 1983b); and the proposed distinction between fluid and crystallized intelligence associated with other major assessment systems (Kaufman & Kaufman, in press; Thorndike, Hagen, & Sattler, 1986; Woodcock & Johnson, 1989). It is highly unlikely that any recognized or experienced authority would seriously challenge the appropriateness of the Vocabulary and Matrices subtests of the K-BIT. The abilities measured by these kinds of subtests constitute major portions of a large number of widely used assessment instruments.

Item selection for the K-BIT derived from a series of pilot studies that were followed by national tryouts in 1986 and 1987. The 150-item K-BIT resulting from this process was further reduced by a series of statistical procedures, including item analysis, reliability analysis, and bias analysis. Following a reordering of items based on tryout and the analysis of data, the final 130-item form of the K-BIT emerged.

The manual provides very detailed and specific information regarding 20 validity studies involving the K-BIT. A total of 249 examinees participated in construct validity studies using the K-ABC, the WISC-R, and the WAIS-R. Concurrent validity studies involved 336 examinees using the Test of Nonverval Intelligence and the Slosson Intelligence Test. An additional 397 examinees participated in concurrent validity projects using measures of achievement: the K-TEA (Brief and Comprehensive forms) and the WRAT-R. The manual reports a single construct validity study using the WISC-R with students between the ages of 6 and 15 ($N = 35$). Prewett (1992), testing students ages 7 to 16 referred for evaluation in an urban setting, found consistently higher correlations between the two instruments. Finally, this reviewer administered the K-BIT and the WISC-R to a total of 21 middle school students with an age range from 11.3 to 14.10. Data from these three sources appear in Table 2.

The correlational data provided in Table 2 indicate a range of variance accounted for from 23% (Kaufman & Kaufman [1990b], Matrices and Verbal IQ) to

Table 3

Comparison of K-BIT and WISC-R Means and Standard Deviations

	Kaufman and Kaufman[1]		*Prewett*[2]		*Jirsa*[3]	
	$\overline{X}$	SD	$\overline{X}$	SD	$\overline{X}$	SD
K-BIT						
Vocabulary	106.0	13.7	74.2	14.9	98.8	17.1
Matrices	104.1	12.8	78.9	16.2	103.2	21.0
IQ Composite	105.5	12.1	74.4	15.0	101.1	19.7
WISC-R						
Verbal IQ	110.2	17.5	77.1	14.0	104.9	21.1
Performance IQ	109.9	16.3	87.2	15.6	111.3	22.6
Full Scale IQ	111.4	16.5	80.6	14.3	108.7	22.9

[1]Adapted from Kaufman & Kaufman (1990), p. 66
[2]Adapted from Prewett (1992), p. 26
[3]Jirsa (1992)

Table 4

K-BIT and WISC-R IQ Score Differences

	Source and Outcome	
Comparison	*Prewett (1992)*	*Jirsa (1992)*
K-BIT Composite IQ and WISC-R Full Scale IQ	$t(34) = 4.03; p < .01$	$t(20) = 3.83; p < .001$
K-BIT Matrices and WISC-R Performance IQ	$t(34) = 3.98; p < .01$	$t(20) = 2.53; p < .05$
K-BIT Vocabulary and WISC-R Verbal IQ	$t(34) = 2.01;$ n.s.	$t(20) = 2.57; p < .05$

84% (Jirsa [1992], Composite IQ and Full Scale IQ). In general, these data support the construct validity of the K-BIT. Table 3 provides a comparison of measures of central tendency from the same sources as identified in Table 2. In all instances, K-BIT IQ scores are lower than WISC-R scores. Prewett (1992) and Jirsa (1992) provide the information found in Table 4 regarding the magnitude of these differences.

The major problem associated with these identified differences between K-BIT and WISC-R IQ scores, as pointed out initially by Prewett (1992) and substantiated here, is the possible overidentification of students requiring a full assessment. "For instance, it appears likely that students suspected of mental retardation because they obtained a K-BIT score lower than 70 will often score above 70

Table 5

K-BIT and WISC-R Summary Score Comparison by IQ Range

| | | $\overline{X}$ IQ | | |
IQ Range*	N	K-BIT Composite	WISC-R Full Scale	Difference
≤ 79	1	50.0	52.0	2.0
80–119	13	94.6	99.6	5.0
≥ 120	7	120.5	133.8	13.3

*Range assignment dependent upon WISC-R Full Scale IQ.

on the WISC-R if their K-BIT score was less than 6 points lower then 70" (Prewett, 1992, p. 27). The Jirsa (1992) data suggest that the K-BIT scores could be 7 points lower than 70 and still lead to an overidentification of MR students needing a more complete evaluation.

Although the overall correlations between K-BIT and WISC-R scores are generally high, mean score differences are significant and the degree of difference seems to depend, at least partially, on the population of examinees. Prewett's (1992) sample consisted of students referred for a psychoeducational evaluation; the Kaufman and Kaufman (1990b) students were characterized as "normal" children; the Jirsa (1992) sample included students referred for reassessment M-Teams, general nonexceptional education academic/learning difficulties, and intellectually gifted students. Table 5 provides mean score differences related to three WISC-R Full Scale categories.

The score discrepancy then seems to vary with IQ level. In the most extreme case in the Jirsa (1992) dataset, a student earned the following scores:

WISC-R		K-BIT	
Verbal IQ	= 147	Vocabulary	= 122
Performance IQ	= 139	Matrices	= 108
Full Scale IQ	= 147	Composite IQ	= 117

Critique

The K-BIT is a well-constructed and meticulously developed instrument packaged in an extremely efficient and user-friendly manner. Given the very small numbers in the Kaufman and Kaufman (35), Prewett (35), and Jirsa (21) correlational and mean score difference tables, a definitive judgment regarding the efficacy of the K-BIT is not warranted. However, in order for this instrument to begin to build user confidence, a great deal of additional data will need to be accumulated and published regarding performance by different groups.

Based on the evidence to date, and given that it falls far short of a reliable or representative sample of any population, it nonetheless appears that the K-BIT would be used most appropriately to reconfirm previously established IQ levels in the middle of the distribution. It would not be appropriate, at this time, to use the K-BIT as a screening instrument for the identification of academically or intellectually gifted students.

Until and unless adequate data exist that describe the relationship between the WISC-R and the K-BIT when used with a variety of populations, a prudent examiner should exercise caution in the use and interpretation of the K-BIT.

References

Angoff, W.H., & Robertson, G.J. (1987). A procedure for standardizing individually administered tests, normed by age or grade level. *Applied Psychological Measurement, 11,* 33–46.

Horn, J.L., & Cattell, R.B. (1966). Refinement and test of the theory of fluid and crystallized intelligence. *Journal of Educational Psychology, 57,* 253–270.

Jirsa, J.E. (1992). [WISC-R/K-BIT correlational data]. Unpublished data. Madison, WI: Research and Evaluation, Madison Metropolitan School District.

Kaufman, A.S. (1979). *Intelligent testing with the WISC-R.* New York: Wiley.

Kaufman, A.S. (1990). *Assessing adolescent and adult intelligence.* Boston: Allyn & Bacon.

Kaufman, A.S., & Kaufman, N.L. (1983a). *Administration and scoring manual for the Kaufman Assessment Battery for Children.* Circle Pines, MN: American Guidance Service.

Kaufman, A.S., & Kaufman, N.L. (1983b). *Interpretive manual for the Kaufman Assessment Battery for Children.* Circle Pines, MN: American Guidance Service.

Kaufman, A.S., & Kaufman, N.L. (1985a). *Manual for the Kaufman Test of Educational Achievement, Brief Form.* Circle Pines, MN: American Guidance Service.

Kaufman, A.S., & Kaufman, N.L. (1985b). *Manual for the Kaufman Test of Educational Achievement, Comprehensive Form.* Circle Pines, MN: American Guidance Service.

Kaufman, A.S., & Kaufman, N.L. (1990a). *AGS Early Screening Profiles: Cognitive/Language Profile.* Circle Pines, MN: American Guidance Service.

Kaufman, A.S., & Kaufman, N.L. (1990b). *Manual for the Kaufman Brief Intelligence Test.* Circle Pines, MN: American Guidance Service.

Kaufman, A.S., & Kaufman, N.L. (in press). *Manual for the Kaufman Adolescent and Adult Intelligence Test.* Circle Pines, MN: American Guidance Service.

McCarthy, D. (1972). *McCarthy Scales of Children's Abilities.* San Antonio, TX: Psychological Corporation.

Prewett, P.N. (1992). The relationship between the Kaufman Brief Intelligence Test (K-BIT) and the WISC-R with referred students. *Psychology in the Schools, 29,* 25–27.

Thorndike, R.L., Hagen, E.P., & Sattler, J.M. (1986). *Stanford-Binet Intelligence Scale: Fourth Edition.* Chicago: Riverside.

Wechsler, D. (1974). *Manual for the Wechsler Intelligence Scale for Children–Revised.* San Antonio, TX: Psychological Corporation.

Wechsler, D. (1981). *Manual for the Wechsler Adult Intelligence Scale–Revised.* San Antonio, TX: Psychological Corporation.

Wechsler, D. (1989). *Manual for the Wechsler Preschool and Primary Scale of Intelligence–Revised.* San Antonio, TX: Psychological Corporation.

Woodcock, R.W., & Johnson, P. (1989). *Woodcock-Johnson Psycho-Educational Battery–Revised: Tests of Cognitive Ability.* Allen, TX: DLM Teaching Resources.

Julie A. Larson, Ed.D.

Education Specialist, Child Evaluation and Treatment Program,
University of North Dakota Rehabilitation Hospital and Clinic,
Grand Forks, North Dakota.

John Delane Williams, Ph.D.

Professor and Chair, Department of Educational Foundations and
Research Methodologies, Center for Teaching and Learning,
University of North Dakota, Grand Forks, North Dakota.

KEYMATH REVISED: A DIAGNOSTIC INVENTORY OF ESSENTIAL MATHEMATICS

Austin J. Connolly. Circle Pines, Minnesota: American Guidance Service.

Introduction

KeyMath Revised (Connolly, 1988) is a individually administered instrument designed to provide a comprehensive assessment of a student's understanding and application of important mathematics concepts and skills. It consists of 13 threads of content (or strands), each of which is measured by a separate subtest. These subtests assess content in three areas—Basic Concepts, Operations, and Applications. Basic Concepts subtests include Numeration, Rational Numbers, and Geometry. Operations subtests include Addition, Subtraction, Multiplication, Division, and Mental Computation. Applications subtests include Measurement, Time and Money, Estimation, Interpreting Data, and Problem Solving.

Each subtest within the KeyMath Revised contains three or four domains of nearly equal instructional importance. With this representation the instrument can provide reliable data that will give valuable information in regard to instructional alternatives.

Four levels of diagnostic information about a student's performance emerge, which the examiner can use to identify strengths and weaknesses. These four levels include Total Test, Area, Subtest, and Domain. The KeyMath Revised serves for a variety of reasons, including assessment for general instruction, assessment for remedial instruction, contribution to a global assessment, pre- and posttesting, and curriculum assessment.

Austin J. Connolly, author of this diagnostic inventory, resides in Broomfield, Colorado. He holds a doctorate in education from Colorado State College (University of Northern Colorado). Connolly's extensive classroom teaching encompasses elementary, secondary, and university instruction as well as special education. His development of the KeyMath Revised spanned nearly 6 years.

Initial development work took place from 1981 to 1983 for the revised test. The original KeyMath had its beginnings in a 1962 dissertation by one of the original

350

authors. During this time a content framework emerged. Essential features were balanced in the importance of content among strands as well as the specification and balance of content at the domain level. The instrument was tested originally on educable mentally handicapped (EMH) students.

KeyMath Revised differs in content from the original in several ways:

1. There are 13 instead of 14 subtests.

2. A Rational Numbers subtest was introduced to expand coverage from fractions to include decimals and percentages.

3. A single subtest including both time and money content replaces separate subtests in the original.

4. The Mental Computation subtest was expanded beyond mental computation chains.

5. A new subtest was developed to assess the ability to estimate.

6. A new subtest was added to measure the ability to organize and interpret quantitative data.

7. A new subtest on Problem Solving was added.

In response to requests from users of the original KeyMath, the author developed alternative forms A and B. Further, the total number of test items increased from 209 in the original to achieve the depth of material needed to support content-domain structure.

In the spring of 1984 the item tryout edition of the KeyMath Revised was administered to more than 600 students. The purpose of this study was to assess item difficulty, clarity, artwork, item stems and directions, and so on. The revised version was administered to students representative of the U.S. student population in Grades K–9. It was standardized in fall 1985 and spring 1986. The fall total sample included 873 students in Grades K–8 at 22 test sites in 16 states; the spring sample involved 925 students in Grades K–9.

The KeyMath Revised is comprised of two forms, A and B, each containing 258 items presented in two free-standing test books. Easel 1 of each form contains the subtests of Basic Concepts and Operations areas; Easel 2 of each form contains the Applications area subtests. The easel kit is designed to facilitate a smooth presentation. As the student looks at one side of the easel, the examiner views the other side, where the directions appear. Each form of the test has a separate 12-page test record, the cover of which provides space for background information, plus a summary of total test, area, and subtest scores.

Although the easels contain instructions, reading the manual is essential before administering the KeyMath Revised. Each chapter describes important components about the test. Further, several portions of the manual are devoted to appendices, the most widely used of which are those that contain the norms and interpretive tables.

Available as a supplementary component, the Report to Parents provides a means of communicating a student's test results to his or her parents.

Another option to the KeyMath Revised test kit is the KeyMath Revised–Assist (automated system for scoring and interpreting standardized tests). This microcomputer package provides automatic conversion, profiling, and record management.

The examiner is responsible for establishing an appropriate testing atmosphere. The area should be comfortable and free from distractions, and the manual strongly recommends that testing be done with examiner and student on adjacent sides of the table.

Examiners may include a broad range of regular and special education teachers, classroom aides and other paraprofessionals, and those with special psychometric training. Interpretation requires an understanding of derived scores, measurement error, and levels of confidence, plus the ability to ascertain a student's strengths and weaknesses.

The KeyMath Revised effectively assesses the elementary grades from Kindergarten through Grade 9. There are two keys to a successful administration. The examiner first needs a familiarity with the test organization, items, and scoring procedures. Then, after a thorough review of the materials and when the examiner is completely comfortable with testing procedures, he or she must establish and maintain rapport with the examinee. The manual provides very elaborate examples of how to score the test.

Typically children in primary grades will complete the test in 30–40 minutes. Older students may take 40–50 minutes. The KeyMath Revised works to identify the student's "critical range." This critical range is delineated by the basal level (that point at which the preceding easier items are assumed to be mastered) and the ceiling level (that point at which more difficult items are assumed to be too difficult).

Practical Applications/Uses

Educators could find the KeyMath Revised a great asset to their scope and sequence work in math. The information and breakup of the concepts is done in a very beneficial way, and the test requires almost no reading or writing skills. The information yielded includes total test performance, area performance in content, operations, and total test performance, plus a metric supplement is available to assess students' metric measurement skills.

The procedure of recording information is very easy and quickly accomplished by professionals. The first step involves computing the child's chronological age (CA), followed by scoring the various domains. The basal and ceiling are then computed, with the computation of the total raw score following next. The examiner then selects the appropriate norms, which are given by grade and fall and spring administration. Next, the scaled scores are obtained, which include percentile ranks, grade and age equivalents, and stanines and normal curve equivalents. The last step is to compute the score profile.

The original KeyMath Test was found to be a valid instrument for use with learning disabled (LD) students (Cruise, Dalton, Pemberton, & Wilkins, 1979; Tinney, 1976). It could be used to obtain achievement levels before and after instruction in order to obtain a gross measure of the progress made by each student and by each group between test administrations. Greenstein and Strain (1977) administered the KeyMath Revised to a group of learning disabled adolescents and found it a very positive tool to use with them. They noted that LD performance was quite distinct in terms of types of computational errors made on the tests.

Technical Aspects

As a revision of KeyMath (Connolly, Nachtman, & Pritchett, 1971), which originated in the authors' dissertations (Connolly, 1968; Nachtman, 1962; Pritchett, 1965), the newer version has a lengthy history of tryout, use, and thought by Dr. Connolly. The standardization sample consisted of 1,798 students in Grades K–9, and care was taken to represent the general population in terms of gender, socioeconomic status, race, and ethnicity.

Reliability was assessed using alternate forms, split-half, and the Rasch model (Lord, 1980). Alternate-forms reliabilities range from .53 to .80 for the subtests, from .82 to .85 for the area tests, and from .88 to .92 for the total test. Split-half reliabilities are shown by subtest and by grade. While these coefficients generally are higher than the alternate forms coefficients, the split-half reliabilities for some subtests in Grades K and 1 are low. For example, Division shows a split-half reliability of only .18 for the spring administration in kindergarten (.38 for the fall). Rational Numbers for Grade 1 shows a split-half reliability of only .24. The split-half reliabilities for the total test on two different samples were .97 and .99, respectively. The Rasch model item response theory reliability estimates generally are acceptably high, with a total test reliability of .95 to .99. A notable exception emerges in Mental Computation at the kindergarten level, with reliabilities of .10 (fall) and .16 (spring).

Connolly (1988) discusses the content validation process in the KeyMath Revised manual. Construct validity is assessed in a number of ways. Developmental change is expected to follow in a prescribed manner, including increasing means on subtests, measures of internal consistency (intercorrelations), and correlations with other tests. The construct validity of the test seemingly would have been enhanced by factorial studies.

Most of the data on KeyMath Revised in relation to other tests in fact relates to KeyMath. Some weaknesses can be noted. First, KeyMath Revised was in fact a major revision. Some subtests retained the same name; others were changed. One astonishing correlation occurs in Division with KeyMath Revised: $r = .01$ for Grade 1. While later grades yield higher correlations, Division was seemingly a problem area on either the original KeyMath or the revised version or both. Correlations were found among the KeyMath Revised and the Iowa Tests of Basic Skills (ITBS; Hieronymous & Hoover, 1978) mathematics subtests. Correlations run from .19 (KeyMath Revised Division to ITBS Mathematics Computation) to .70 (KeyMath Revised Rational Numbers to ITBS Mathematics Concepts).

In general, the manual is very complete and is a massive revision from the original test (339 pages, compared to the original's 53 pages). Although the necessary data are shown, the size may seem to keep some users from more than a perfunctory perusal.

Critique

KeyMath Revised is basically a sound instrument appropriate for its intended purposes, which include assessment for general instruction, assessment for remedial instruction, contribution to global assessment, curriculum assessment, and research. Not all of these uses are of equal interest; perhaps one of the major uses, assessment for remedial instruction, may be KeyMath Revised's weakest area. Whereas the total test and the area tests (Operations and Applications) generally show suitable reliability, some of the subtests do not. In particular, the subtests are less reliable for younger persons and lower grades. In the hands of a knowledgeable user who is an advocate for children, this problem may be minimal. In the hands of a person wishing to use the test as a basis for retention in Kindergarten and Grade 1 (where retention is most likely to take place), the psychometric properties of the KeyMath Revised would lend toward inappropriate decision making. As Connolly could rightly state that retention at a grade level was not the intervention intended by his test, perhaps this comment then is directed more to test abusers than to test users. Used appropriately, as a diagnostic test to intervene with remedial instruction, the test's shortcomings at the lower ages are not serious. In general, if the intent of users correspond to the intent of the author, KeyMath Revised is a very valuable tool.

References

Connolly, A.J. (1968). *An instrument of measurement to appraise the arithmetic abilities of educable mentally retarded children ages 13 through 16.* Unpublished doctoral dissertation, Colorado State College, Greeley.

Connolly, A.J. (1988). *KeyMath Revised: A Diagnostic Inventory of Essential Mathematics.* Circle Pines, MN: American Guidance Service.

Connolly, A.J., Nachtman, W., & Pritchett, E.M. (1971). *KeyMath Diagnostic Arithmetic Test.* Circle Pines, MN: American Guidance Service.

Cruise, R.M., Dalton, J.M., Pemberton, N., & Wilkins, E.M. (1977). *An analysis of school achievement for Woodcock Reading Mastery Tests and KeyMath arithmetic tests of adolescents in a psychiatric hospital.* Berrien Springs, MI: Andrews University. (ERIC Document Reproduction Service No. ED 237 562)

Greenstein, J., & Strain, P.S. (1977). The utility of KeyMath Diagnostic Arithmetic Test for adolescent learning disabilities students. *Psychology in the Schools, 14,* 275–282.

Hieronymous, A.N., & Hoover, H.D. (1978). *Iowa Tests of Basic Skills.* Chicago: Riverside.

Lord, F.M. (1980). *Applications of item response theory to practical testing problems.* Hillsdale, NJ: Erlbaum.

Nachtman, W.R. (1962). *An instrument of measurement to appraise the quantitative abilities of the educable mentally retarded child.* Unpublished doctoral dissertation, Colorado State College, Greeley.

Pritchett, E.M. (1965). *An instrument of measurement to appraise the arithmetic abilities of educable mentally retarded children ages six through nine.* Unpublished doctoral dissertation, Colorado State College, Greeley.

Tinney, F.A. (1976). The KeyMath Diagnostic Arithmetic Test: Use with learning disabled students. *Journal of Learning Disabilities, 8,* 315.

Diane J. Tinsley, Ph.D.
Senior Counseling Psychologist and Adjunct Associate Professor, Southern Illinois University, Carbondale, Illinois.

LEARNING AND STUDY STRATEGIES INVENTORY

Claire E. Weinstein, David R. Palmer, and Ann C. Schulte. Clearwater, Florida: H&H Publishing Company, Inc.

Introduction

The Learning and Study Strategies Inventory (LASSI; Weinstein, 1987) is a diagnostic instrument designed to assess a set of competencies (strategies and skills) students need to manage and monitor their own learning in a variety of contexts. The LASSI has been developed within a cognitive or educational psychology frame of reference, in which numerous definitions of learning styles and strategies have been proposed. Weinstein and MacDonald (1986) defined effective learning strategies as any cognitive, affective, or behavioral activity that facilitates encoding, storing, retrieving, or using knowledge. They also described knowledge acquisition, comprehension monitoring, active study strategies, and support strategies as four basic categories of the more general construct of learning strategy. However, there is no specific correspondence between this classification system and the constructs measured by the LASSI. Mayer's (1988) definition of learning strategies as behaviors intended to influence how the learner processes information is a good working definition for the focus of the LASSI items.

Claire E. Weinstein, Ph.D., principal developer of the LASSI, received her graduate degree in educational psychology from the University of Texas at Austin in 1975 with specialties in learning, learning theory, and cognitive psychology (American Psychological Association, 1989). The other two primary developers of the inventory, Ann C. Schulte, Ph.D., and David R. Palmer, Ph.D., have both been associated with the Cognitive Learning Strategies Project at the University of Texas at Austin. Schulte received her Ph.D. in educational psychology in 1983 from the University of Texas at Austin, at which time she joined the faculty in the School Psychology Program at the University of North Carolina at Chapel Hill. Her specialties include educational measurement and evaluation (APA, 1989). Palmer is employed at the University of Texas at Austin.

Weinstein (1987) indicates use of the LASSI can improve students' retention by providing information about their study patterns that can establish a meaningful and useful basis for remediation. She describes the LASSI as a useful counseling tool in orientation programs, developmental education programs, and learning assistance programs. It also can be used as a brief pre-post intervention achievement measure for students participating in counseling and educational programs.

Because the LASSI user's manual (Weinstein, 1987) is vague about many as-

355

pects of the instrument's development, this reviewer obtained additional information from Weinstein, Zimmerman, and Palmer (1988). Development began in the late 1970s, 9 years prior to the publication of the manual by H&H Publishing. Shulte and Weinstein (1981) reviewed study skills instruments and found inconsistent definitions of these skills. The reliability of existing subscales was often low, and good study practices had not been validated. No measure had been validated for use as a diagnostic tool. The available instruments could be faked easily, and most items dealt with consistent study techniques and not with learning styles directly. The authors decided to develop an instrument that would focus on active learner behaviors that promote effective learning.

Cognitive Learning Strategies Project investigators at the University of Texas at Austin collected 645 items from a number of sources, including other instruments, and divided them into 19 categories. A preliminary and second pilot test were performed prior to a series of field tests conducted between 1982 and 1985. In the process, the investigators changed the original true/false item response format to a 5-point Likert format, with response alternatives ranging from "not at all typical of me" to "very typical of me." They reduced the original 19 categories to 14 and subsequently to 10.

During the development phase, the investigators eliminated items that focused on behavior or experiences that could not be changed and, therefore, were not useful for remediation (e.g., "My parents read to me as a child"). Also eliminated were compound items, items that did not correlate with cumulative GPA at a confidence level of .10, and items that correlated .50 or greater with a measure of social desirability. Subsequently, new items were added to the instrument, however, so the relations of specific items or scales in the published version of LASSI to GPA and social desirability are unknown.

Three forms of the LASSI are available. The 77-item college form (LASSI) is available both in a paper-and-pencil and an electronic (E-LASSI) format, with identical items (Weinstein, Palmer, & Shulte, 1987). The E-LASSI is available for Apple II, IBM PC, and PC-compatible computers (Holland & Holland, 1988). One 5¼-inch disk can hold up to 200 E-LASSIs. A 76-item high school form (LASSI-HS) was modified from the LASSI to reflect a secondary school vocabulary level and the learning tasks and demands of a high school environment (Weinstein & Palmer, 1990). The publisher did not provide information to this reviewer about the latter instrument, but Eldredge (1990) has reviewed it.

The current LASSI versions provide scores on 10 scales that measure five personal factors related to school achievement (i.e., Attitude, Motivation, Time Management, Anxiety, and Concentration) and five metacognitive factors related to school achievement (e.g., Information Processing, Selecting Main Ideas, Study Aids, Self-Testing, and Test Strategies). Pintrich and Johnson (1990) further subdivided the five personal factor scales into those dealing with motivation (i.e., Attitude, Motivation, and Anxiety) and self-management (i.e., Time Management and Concentration).

All of the LASSI and E-LASSI scales have eight items except the five-item Selecting Main Ideas. Most of the LASSI-HS scales also have eight items, except for the seven-item Time Management scale and the five-item Selecting Main Ideas. The authors offer no explanation for including fewer items on these scales.

About half of the items are stated negatively. Item content appears to overlap within scales (e.g., LASSI items 22 and 42) and between scales (e.g., LASSI items 1 and 29). This redundancy lengthens the time needed for test completion, and it may affect students' use of this instrument by stimulating factors such as boredom or fatigue.

Practical Applications/Uses

The LASSI can be used by a wide range of helping professionals, including secondary and post-secondary school educators, guidance counselors and student personnel workers, community mental health counselors, and counseling psychologists. It can be used to document change in the learner and examine the success of an intervention designed to improve learning abilities; to increase students' self awareness and responsibility for their own learning; and to provide diagnostic information needed in developing specific interventions. High school teachers and counselors can administer the LASSI-HS and discuss students' results individually or in small groups, to help them plan their transition and adjustment to high school. The college version can be used in a similar way to help high school seniors prepare for the transition to college or post-secondary training.

College personnel can administer and interpret LASSI results as part of a freshmen orientation program or other developmental outreach programs in the area of study skills, tutoring programs, course scheduling, or residence hall programming. Student services outreach offices might have the E-LASSI available for students who report academic difficulties. Learning centers and learning labs might make the instrument available as a diagnostic tool for students requesting help in learning to learn more effectively.

College counselors, career planning specialists, and community mental health counselors can use the LASSI as a self-exploration tool in individual and group counseling with displaced homemakers and other nontraditional, older students entering college or other post-secondary training programs. Greater numbers of academically underprepared students are enrolling in community colleges and universities, and university personnel want to increase their ability to meet these students' unique needs. The use of LASSI could help such individuals gain a stronger sense of responsibility and self-confidence about their abilities as learners. Learning style also can be described as a more general personality variable that may relate to the selection of an academic major, and, subsequently, a career choice (Green & Parker, 1989), so the exploratory use of LASSI may be useful in career-planning activities.

Staff development programs for secondary and post-secondary school educators might use the LASSI to teach participants more about what students learn and how they go about learning (Weinstein, 1987). Studies such as that of Clift, Ghatala, Naus, and Poole (1990) document the need for such training. Researchers generally distinguish between class-related processes or procedures and the cognitive strategies that facilitate task performance. Although the teachers reported awareness of study strategies, their descriptions of them focused mostly on teacher-directed activities rather than teaching students metacognitive strategies (i.e., why, when, and how strategies should be used). The teachers' definitions of strategies seem to disregard the role of student initiation and control of the strategic activity. Investigations such as this one tend to support continued use of the LASSI by researchers investigating relations between theory and practice in cognitive and educational psychology.

Weinstein (1987) indicates that as the LASSI employs a self-report format, it does not require special administration procedures or specially trained personnel. The inventories may be administered individually or in a group, generally in about 25–30 minutes (including about 10 minutes for students to hand score their responses). Test administration directions and scoring procedures are summarized in the introductory inventory booklet. The individual LASSI items seem clear, and the instrument appears user friendly. The LASSI packet includes a cover/instruction sheet and two-part carbonless forms that the user separates from the booklet and sets aside until after completion of the assessment. All three forms of the inventory can be self-administered and self-interpreted.

The inventory booklet contains a two-part carbonless answer sheet and a profile chart. The ratings given to negatively worded items are reversed, and the ratings are summed to obtain raw scale scores. These raw scores are converted to percentiles for each scale. The authors recommend against summing the 10 scale scores to obtain a total score.

Each of the 10 scales is given a three-letter code indicating a strategy or method category. For example, ATT is the abbreviation for attitude and interest; SMI, for selecting main ideas and recognizing important information. The items are fairly concrete and specific, and no other interpretive explanations for the categories appear on the student's copy of the hand-scored profile or the electronically scored computer-generated profile form. The forms do provide the statement that students can use these percentile ranks to compare their scores to other college students' scales. The self-scoring form also indicates that a LASSI user's manual is available; the computer-generated profile sheet provides the name, address, and telephone number of the test publisher. In the manual, the prescriptions to help students improve their skills are very literal restatements and slight elaborations of scale items, so it does not seem that the LASSI developers require that any specifically trained psychometrists or other professionals must help students understand their results.

Each scale score is compared to "national norms." Information about the LASSI norms is relatively limited; the normative sample seems to consist of 880 entering freshmen from a large Southern university. Inadequate information appears about the median age, age range, gender, cultural/ethnic background, and geographic representation of the sample.

Eldredge (1990) indicated that norms for LASSI-HS are available for Grades 9 through 12 and were developed on a sample of 2,616 high school students in a mid-sized city in the southwestern United States. The students are described in general terms as having been selected to reflect a range of ethnic backgrounds, economic conditions, and academic achievement levels; a more specific description of the normative sample was not available.

The scoring process for E-LASSI is totally automated. The brochure also indicates that the program generates and stores three types of reports: a graph of each student's study strategies profile, a listing of the students with their percentile ranks on the 10 LASSI scales, and an alphabetical roster of the students who took the inventory. Only the graph of the student profile is available on the demonstration disk, which can be used for five administrations of the instrument.

Weinstein (1987) indicates that students who score above the 75th percentile compared to the norm group often do not need to work to improve their skills on that scale. She recommends that students who score between the 50th and 75th percentile should consider interventions to improve those learning and study skills. Students scoring below the 50th percentile may not succeed in an academic setting without improvements. These general recommendations do not take into account the wide range of demands on students in different environments, their general ability, or the amount of specific content knowledge that they already have about the particular learning situation.

Technical Aspects

The manual (Weinstein, 1987) inadequately summarizes the reliability of the LASSI. Coefficient alpha internal consistency reliabilities range from .68 for the Study Aids scale to .86 for the Time Management scale, with a median reliability of .81. All but the Study Aids scale have internal consistency reliabilities of .72 or higher. The sample from which these data were obtained is not clear. Reliability is as much a function of the sample as it is the instrument, so this oversight reduces the usefulness of these data.

Test-retest reliability was assessed for a 3-week interval using a sample of 209 students from an introductory communications course at a large Southern university (Weinstein, 1987). These values ranged from .72 for the Information Processing scale to .85 for the Time Management and Concentration sales. The median test-retest reliability was .795.

Eldredge (1990) reported the reliabilities for the LASSI-HS are inferred from the college version without sufficient detail, and that validity has not been established.

Olejnik and Nist (1992) reported internal consistency and 10-week retest reliability estimates for a sample of 264 first-quarter first-year college students enrolled in a developmental studies program. The mean SAT Verbal score of the sample was 389 (i.e., 1.1 standard deviations below the mean), indicating the students were low average when compared to the SAT normative sample. The investigators provided students with a 10-week period of instruction between test administrations. Olejnik and Nist reported alpha internal consistency coefficients that were slightly lower than those reported in the user's manual. Their test-retest reliabilities ranged from .37 (Study Aids) to .57 (Time Management), a full 25 points lower than those reported in the manual. However, the type of student investigated and the incorporation of the intervention may account for the discrepancy.

Weinstein (1987) reports using three different approaches to examine the validity of the LASSI. She indicated that an undefined number of professors, advisors, developmental educators, counselors, and learning center specialists who have used the LASSI on a trial basis provided testimonials. These opinions, however, do not constitute evidence of validity. Scale scores on the LASSI also have been compared to scores on other tests or subscales measuring similar factors. These tests and subscales are not named, and no data are provided documenting these comparisons. Finally, some of the scales have been validated against unnamed performance measures. No evidence of validity is reported for the inventory beyond these general statements. In short, Weinstein (1987) essentially provides no evidence to substantiate the LASSI's validity.

The LASSI has enjoyed some research use despite the lack of demonstrated validity. Olejnik and Nist (1992) examined the instrument's factor structure using both exploratory and confirmatory factor analysis. They used two independent samples of college freshmen from a large Southeastern university ($N = 264$; $N = 143$). The first sample was used to estimate reliability and to identify the structural measurement model. The second was used to test the proposed model through confirmatory factor analysis. They reported that a three-factor solution provided the best fit to the measurement model. These factors, labeled Effort-Related Activities, Goal Orientation, and Cognitive Activities, were interrelated. The strongest relation occurred between the Effort-Related and Cognitive Activities factors; the Goal Orientation factor had a much weaker relation to the other two. Both the exploratory and confirmatory factor analyses indicated that the inventory is multidimensional, thus supporting Weinstein's view that a single index is inappropriate.

The LASSI also has been used in intervention studies, two of which are summarized here for purposes of illustration. McKeachie, Pintrich, and Lin (1985) evaluated introductory cognitive psychology courses designed to teach learning strategies to anxious students, minority students, and student athletes. The course was offered in the fall of 1982 with 113 students enrolling; in the winter semester, 80 students enrolled. Most were freshmen, about equally balanced across gender. The investigators obtained several self-report measures at the beginning and the end of the semester, including an early version of the LASSI and measures of test anxiety, need for cognition, locus of control, and expectancies for success and failure. They also collected GPAs in courses following the class. The investigators interpreted the modest correlation between scores on the LASSI posttest and later GPA (.38; $p < .001$) as indicating a transfer of learning to subsequent courses. These results reveal little about the validity of the LASSI.

Nist, Mealey, Simpson, and Kroc (1990) investigated the cognitive and affective growth of regularly admitted and developmental study students and they evaluated LASSI's predictive utility by examining the subjects' grades in subsequent content area courses. The subjects were 71 regularly admitted students from the University of Arizona and 168 developmental study students from the University of Georgia. All subjects completed the LASSI as a pre- and posttest measure and participated in an 8-week study strategy instruction. Although the results indicated both cognitive and affective growth for both samples, the LASSI was predictive of GPA and class achievement only for the regularly admitted students. These authors concluded that more research is needed before the LASSI can be used with special at-risk populations.

Critique

Conceptually the LASSI can be viewed as a diagnostic instrument or as a structured educational intervention. The authors emphasize the former, but it is clear that using the instrument in that manner cannot be advocated yet. The LASSI may have face validity, but virtually no evidence of external validity is available. The manual makes brief reference to broad, vaguely described comparisons, but information is needed to document its reliability and its criterion-related and construct validity.

An alternative is to use the LASSI to stimulate student development rather than to measure student status. An earlier section of this review identified a number of potential uses for this inventory as a self-awareness instrument by a wide range of professionals. This reviewer believes that the LASSI taps important constructs that can help students organize information about themselves and improve their ability to cope in a wide range of academic and other post-secondary training environments. Individuals can interpret their scores in an idiographic manner to learn about their relative strengths and weaknesses, without giving any particular attention to norm group scores. However, potential users of the LASSI are cautioned to assess subjects' understanding of the items and the relevance of the instrument to their goals. Also, it is important to consider whether a ceiling effect would limit the usefulness of the instrument in differentiating the individual's relative strengths and weaknesses across the 10 scale scores.

On balance, however, it appears that the test developers' emphasis on practical application has taken precedence over their efforts to establish reliability and validity. Despite its potential, this reviewer cannot recommend use of the LASSI for purposes other than pure research until its reliability and validity have been established.

References

American Psychological Association. (1989). *Directory of the American Psychological Association*. Washington, DC: Author.

Clift, R.T., Ghatala, E.S., Naus, M.M., & Poole, J. (1990). Exploring teachers' knowledge of strategic study activity. *Journal of Experimental Education, 58,* 253–263.

Eldredge, J.L. (1990). Learning and Study Strategies Inventory–High School Version (LASSI-HS). *Journal of Reading, 34,* 146–149.

Green, D., & Parker, R.M. (1989). Vocational and academic attributes of students with different learning styles. *Journal of College Student Development, 30,* 395–400.

Holland, J.W., & Holland, P.N. (1988). *E-LASSI's user's manual.* Clearwater, FL: H&H.

Mayer, R.E. (1988). Learning strategies: An overview. In C.E. Weinstein, E.T. Guetz, & P.A. Alexander (Eds.), *Learning and study strategies: Issues in assessment, instruction, and evaluation* (pp. 11–22). San Diego, CA: Academic Press.

McKeachie, W.J., Pintrich, P.R., & Lin, Y.-G. (1985). Teaching learning strategies. *Educational Psychologist, 20,* 153–160.

Nist, S.L., Mealey, D.L., Simpson, M.L., & Kroc, R. (1990). Measuring the affective and cognitive growth of regularly admitted and developmental studies students using the Learning and Study Strategies Inventory (LASSI). *Reading Research and Instruction, 30,* 44–49.

Olejnik, S., & Nist, S.L. (1992). Identifying variables measured by the Learning and Study Strategies Inventory (LASSI). *Journal of Experimental Education, 60*(2), 151–159.

Pintrich, P.R., & Johnson, G.R. (1990). Assessing and improving students' learning strategies. In M.D. Svinicki (Ed.), *The changing face of college teaching* (pp. 83–91). San Francisco: Jossey-Bass.

Schulte, A.C., & Weinstein, C.E. (1981, April). Inventories to assess cognitive learning strategies. In C.E. Weinstein (Chair), *Learning strategies research: Paradigms and problems.* Symposium conducted at the annual meeting of the American Educational Research Association, Los Angeles.

Weinstein, C.E. (1987). *LASSI user's manual.* Clearwater, FL: H&H.

Weinstein, C.E., & MacDonald, J.D. (1986). Why does a school psychologist need to know about learning strategies? *Journal of School Psychology, 24,* 257–265.

Weinstein, C.E., & Palmer, D.R. (1990). *Learning and Study Strategies Inventory–High School Version (LASSI-HS).* Clearwater, FL: H&H.

Weinstein, C.E., Palmer, D.R., & Schulte, A.C. (1987). *Learning and Study Strategies Inventory.* Clearwater, FL: H&H.

Weinstein, C.E., Zimmerman, S.A., & Palmer, D.R. (1988). Assessing learning strategies: The design and development of the LASSI. In C.E. Weinstein, E.T. Goetz, & P.A. Alexander (Eds.), *Learning and study strategies: Issues in assessment, instruction, and evaluation* (pp. 25–40). San Diego, CA: Academic Press.

Steven C. Russell, Ph.D.

Associate Professor of Education and Communication Disorders, Departments of Special Education and Communication Disorders, Bowling Green State University, Bowling Green, Ohio.

LEARNING DISABILITY EVALUATION SCALE

Stephen B. McCarney. Columbia, Missouri: Hawthorne Educational Services, Inc.

Introduction

The Learning Disability Evaluation Scale (LDES; McCarney, 1988a) is an individually completed instrument with particular application to the referral and screening process involved in determining a learning disability. This scale, which relies on the classroom observations of a teacher or some other person charged with instructional responsibilities, attempts to characterize the observed difficulties of a particular student in those academic areas (listening, thinking, speaking, reading, writing, spelling, and mathematical calculations) most commonly examined when evaluating for a learning disability. Raw scores are converted to standard scores, subscale scores for each of the areas, and a Learning Quotient.

Accompanying LDES materials include a "Pre-Referral Checklist" (McCarney, 1988b), a "Pre-Referral Intervention Strategies Documentation" form (McCarney, 1989), a technical manual, the Learning Disability Evaluation Scale rating form (McCarney, 1988a), and the *Learning Disability Intervention Manual, Revised Edition* (McCarney & Bauer, 1989). Though advertised as included, "The Parent's Guide to Learning Disabilities" was not available with the specimen kit provided for this review.

The author of the LDES, Stephen B. McCarney, Ed.D., is presently the president and chief executive officer of Hawthorne Educational Services, Inc. He serves as the director of research there as well. Dr. McCarney has held faculty positions at both the University of Florida and the University of Missouri. His professional background includes experience as a teacher of students with learning and behavior problems, a consultant offering workshops and inservices, and a coordinator of university training in the area of behavior problems. He has authored or co-authored a number of educational assessment instruments, including the Behavior Evaluation Scale–2, the Attention Deficit Disorders Evaluation Scale (ADDES), the Emotional or Behavior Disorder Scale (EBDS), the Early Childhood Behavior Scale (ECBS), the Transition Behavior Scale (TBS), the Adaptive Behavior Evaluation Scale (ABES), the Gifted Evaluation Scale (GES), the Preschool Evaluation Scale (PES), and the Teacher Evaluation Scale (TES), among others.

The development of the LDES grew out of a number of concerns regarding the status of assessment practices as they relate to the identification of students most appropriately served by special education for a learning disability. These concerns included the growing awareness that many of the typically used assessment instruments lacked the technical adequacy needed for such decision making; practitioners' lack of an informal means to verify a suspected learning disability in the void created by the technical inadequacy of the more commonly used assessment instruments; and the need to employ direct observation of academically relevant tasks in the determination of a learning disability. Using the definition of learning disability provided in Public Law 94-142, the LDES was developed to accommodate these concerns and needs.

As discussed by McCarney (1988a) in the technical manual for the LDES, the development of the scale consisted of several steps, including development of items, field testing those items, standardization procedures, and measures of reliability and validity (which will be discussed in a later section of this review). Educational diagnosticians and special education personnel were used in the initial phases of development to identify educationally relevant "indicators which are most commonly found to represent students with learning disabilities" (McCarney, 1988a, p. 9). From those supplied, an item pool of 97 indicators was constructed for further analysis. These items were returned to the original participants and further refined in terms of wording, appropriateness, and completeness for representing those students typically identified as learning disabled. This step resulted in the selection of 89 items, which McCarney then assigned to the most appropriate of the seven areas identified in PL 94-142 as characteristic problem areas for students with learning disabilities (listening, speaking, reading, writing, spelling, mathematical calculation, and thinking).

The next step involved field testing the items with elementary and secondary classroom teachers in Missouri. Each participant conducted two evaluations of randomly selected classroom students. This randomization was not to "include or exclude any student for any reason (e.g., identified handicapped, gifted, someone they wanted to refer, etc.)" (McCarney, 1988a, p. 9). It is noted, however, that one of these randomly selected students was to represent the "typical or average student" and one was to represent a student "having academic or related difficulties in the classroom." Following receipt of the responses to this step, four analyses of the field testing were completed including "(a) a principal components analysis with varimax rotation of the interitem correlations for the entire instrument, (b) a principal components analysis of each of the logically defined subscales, (c) an item analysis of each logical subscale, and (d) a determination of the reliability of each logical subscale" (McCarney, 1988a, p. 10). These procedures allowed for analyses of the items and grouping them into subscales. These analyses resulted in the elimination of one item, yielding an 88-item scale with items clustered around the seven characteristic areas of learning disability.

The next step in the development of the LDES was to provide normative standardization of the instrument: "the normative sample . . . included 1,666 students from 19 states which adequately represented the four major geographical regions of the United States" (McCarney, 1988a, p. 13). To obtain this sample, the author had 414 regular education teachers (representing an "unselected sample") evaluate, using the LDES, students randomly selected from their classes. Data presented in the technical manual provide the user with information related to numbers of students evaluated at various ages (from 4 years, 6 months through 18+ years), numbers of teachers evaluating at each age level, number of states and school districts represented, and demographic characteristics of the students evaluated, including breakdown by sex, residence, race, geographic area, and parent occupation. The author attempted to utilize a standardization sample that would approximate the characteristics of the general population as reported in the 1980 *Statistical Abstract of the United States.*

Again, the previously noted four analyses used during field testing were performed here on the results of the evaluations of these 1,666 students. The seven subscales of the LDES were supported by the principal components analysis with varimax rotation of the interitem correlations for the entire instrument. The principal component analysis of items within each subscale indicated a general homogeneity, though "subscales could be broken down into even finer categories" (McCarney, 1988a, p. 17). An analysis of the distribution of responses to items indicated a high variation in item scores. This assisted in substantiating the usefulness of each of the items in differentiating between individuals. Finally, an analysis was completed of the correlations of items within a subscale and the subscale total score. All items met the minimum acceptable criterion of .3 to assure confidence that the items within a subscale are measuring the same thing and that the items will assist in discriminating between individuals scoring high on a subscale and those scoring low on that same subscale. Item/subscale correlations ranged from .57 to .86, with two items outside this range at .40 (item 81 on the Writing subscale) and .48 (item 78 on the Reading subscale). The author justified keeping these items within the stated subscale due to their perceived appropriateness for that subscale.

The evaluation form used for the LDES is a folded, three-panel document, resulting in six pages. A technical manual accompanies the evaluation form, providing information on the rationale for use of the evaluation scale, development and technical characteristics, administration and scoring, interpretation and use of the LDES, and tables for converting raw scores to subscale standard scores and sum of subscale standard scores to learning quotients. The complete LDES evaluation kit, as indicated above, also includes several other components (e.g., "Pre-Referral Learning Problem Checklist," etc.). Though not part of the complete kit, the "Computerized LDES Quick Score" and *Computerized Learning Disability Intervention Manual* are available for use on the Apple II.

The LDES evaluation form begins with a page for summary information concerning the student being evaluated, general information regarding the student's participation with the observer, and a profile summary to record standard scores for each of the seven subscale areas and Learning Quotient information. An important note is included on this page, directing the respondent to page 5 for instructions before using the scale.

Pages 2 through 4 present the 88 item statements, divided into the seven subscale areas (Listening, 7 items; Thinking, 17 items; Speaking, 9 items; Reading, 14 items; Writing, 14 items; Spelling, 7 items; and Mathematical Calculations, 20 items). Examples of items include "Does not hear all of what is said (e.g., misses word endings, misses key words such as 'do not,' etc.)" (Listening); "Has difficulty classifying (e.g., does not recognize similarities, differences, etc.)" (Thinking); "Has a limited speaking vocabulary" (Speaking); "Does not know all the letters of the alphabet" (Reading); "Does not use appropriate subject-verb agreement when writing" (Writing); "Spells words correctly in one context but not in another (e.g., can spell the word on a quiz but not in a sentence, cannot spell the word from dictation but can spell it correctly in a sentence, etc.)" (Spelling); and "Fails to correctly solve math problems requiring regrouping (borrowing and carrying)" (Mathematical Calculations).

Each statement is rated on a 3-point scale, where 1 = rarely or never, 2 = inconsistently, and 3 = all or most of the time. This scale repeats at the top of each page. Each subscale section ends with space for a raw score and a subscale standard score. At the end of the seventh area, space also is provided for a sum of subscale standard scores and a quotient score.

Page 5 of the LDES form presents a guide for the observer rating the student and includes directions pertaining to who should complete the form and how completion should be accomplished. Page 6 of the LDES form allows the individual completing the form space to make comments or suggestions.

Practical Applications/Uses

According to McCarney (1988a), the LDES was designed to accomplish seven specific purposes. First, the LDES was developed so that teachers with direct instructional responsibility in the classroom would have an objective method to describe relevant classroom behaviors. Second, the LDES was developed to report those behaviors commonly associated with a learning disability. Third, the LDES was constructed to report observed behaviors by categorizing them into the seven areas characteristic of a learning disability as defined by PL 94-142 (i.e., thinking, listening, speaking, etc.). These three purposes allow the user to screen for a learning disability.

Fourth, the LDES was standardized in order to allow users to compare individual learning problems with those of a national sample. Fifth, McCarney indicates that the LDES was designed to add information to the assessment procedure. These two purposes intend to allow users to obtain a measure of learning disability for individual students and may aid in the diagnosis of a learning disability.

Sixth, the LDES was designed to aid professionals in the development of individualized educational plans by furnishing information useful for constructing goal statements and objectives. And seventh, the LDES was developed to furnish "the basis for program planning by identifying specific academic and behavioral characteristics which are in need of improvement" (McCarney, 1988a, p. 5). These two purposes intend to allow the user to "develop goals and objectives for the IEP, . . . identify instructional activities for identified problem areas, and . . . document entry points, progress which occurs as a result of interventions, and identify exit points from special service delivery" (McCarney, 1988a, p. 5).

As may be obvious, the most appropriate setting for the LDES is a school or learning environment. Because the items center on expected academic and behavioral performance, and the goal is to screen for or determine a learning disability based on observations related to that academic and behavioral performance, the LDES should be used only in those contexts that require such performance. The LDES will be employed most often by education professionals; few others will have observed the subject in the educational contexts that would make rating with the LDES appropriate.

This scale is appropriate for those children and youth aged 4 years, 6 months to 19 years who are suspected of having a learning disability. Administration is completed rather simply by a teacher or teachers who have had relevant observational experiences with the student to be rated. McCarney indicates that this criterion is not dependent on a specific amount of experience with the student to be rated, though the rating is more likely to be made accurately by those professionals who have had ample opportunity to observe the performance of the student and who have engaged in instructing him or her. It is suggested that the typical elementary teacher will have little difficulty in completing the evaluation scale. Where elementary schools are departmentalized, as well as at the secondary level where teachers typically observe and work with students in particular disciplines or areas, teachers should rate only those areas of the LDES in which they have made observations. Collaboration among professionals is encouraged for subscales where one individual may have only partial knowledge. "Guessing should never be used to complete a rating and no items may be left blank" (McCarney, 1988a, p. 26). Professionals should rate students based on their typical performance, and "the student should not be given a 'performance' test in order to determine if he/she can successfully perform the items" (McCarney, 1988a, p. 26).

Many of the items included on the LDES are developmental. Hence, as some students being rated will not have acquired a particular skill, either through development or through instruction, respondents should indicate those items that are not within a student's ability. Because students are compared to their age mates, this avoids unduly penalizing them (as their age mates probably also will not yet exhibit the skills either). This is useful to point out to those completing the LDES, so that they do not become concerned about potentially penalizing students in rating them on skills not yet introduced or developmentally attained.

As indicated previously, the LDES uses a 3-point rating scale (rarely or never/ inconsistently/all or most of the time) for each of the evaluation items. The technical manual that accompanies the LDES provides a detailed description of each of these ratings, and it is important for raters to become quite familiar with the definitions for each degree of rating so that they may be applied as objectively, consistently, and accurately as possible.

Although the author indicates the time needed to complete the LDES is approximately 20 minutes (including scoring), it seems clear that this will depend on the familiarity of the professional(s) completing the form with the student being rated as well as on the number of professionals who must collaborate on completing the rating form. McCarney advises that completion of the form in one sitting is not necessary; therefore the rating and scoring could be completed in as little as 20 minutes or over the course of several days if multiple sittings and professionals are involved.

Scoring procedures are clearly outlined in the technical manual that accompanies the LDES. In fact, a sample protocol that has been completed also appears in this manual, illustrating raw scoring, conversion to standard scores, sum of subscale standard scores, and conversion to a Learning Quotient. Furthermore, an example of the LDES profile that summarizes this information also is included. Once mastered, the scoring procedure probably would take no more than 10 minutes. As noted earlier, a computerized LDES "quick score" is available for the Apple II.

A section in the technical manual describes the interpretation and use of raw scores, subscale standard scores, the Learning Quotient, and the LDES profile. Interpretation is based on scores achieved, and the level of difficulty in interpreting the results rests primarily with a thorough reading of the technical manual.

Technical Aspects

The coefficient alpha formula for internal consistency reliability, "a derivation of the Kuder-Richardson Formula 20 with similarity to Hoyt's procedure" (Mc-Carney, 1988a, p. 18), was used here to establish the reliability of the LDES subscales. Subscale reliability values ranged from .88 for Listening and Speaking to .97 for Mathematical Calculations, with the standard error of measurement for each subscale ranging from 1.19 for Spelling to 2.17 for Mathematical Calculations. Average item discrimination ranges from .71 for Thinking to .84 for Spelling.

Also as a measure of internal consistency reliability, correlation coefficients were computed for the intercorrelations between LDES subscales. Correlation coefficients between subscales ranged from .57 (Listening and Mathematical Calculations) to .86 (Writing and Spelling), and all were significant at the .001 level. Further, a principal components analysis of the LDES also is presented in the technical manual to support the scale's logical structure. Loadings of .25 or greater are presented in a factor-loading matrix with the varimax rotated solution for the five factors with reasonable interpretations.

McCarney also presents information in the technical manual regarding test-retest reliability. Randomly selected students ($n = 93$, representing all 13 age levels from 4 years, 6 months to 18+ years) from the standardization sample ($N = 1,666$) were rated a second time by teachers ($n = 47$). Thirty calendar days had elapsed between ratings. The result of a Pearson product-moment correlation was $r = .98$ ($p < .01$, $n = 93$).

Interrater reliability figures also are presented to examine stability when an individual is rated by more than one teacher. Students ($n = 272$), again randomly selected from the standardization sample ($N = 1,666$), were rated by "sets of two educators [111 pairs], with equal knowledge of the students" (McCarney, 1988a, p. 22). Pearson product-moment correlation coefficients were calculated for this interrater reliability, and results ranged from .96 to .98 across all age levels.

No other reliability information appears, and independent studies of LDES reliability were not found.

In order to validate use of the LDES, three types of validity data are presented: content, criterion-related, and construct. Content validity for the LDES was provided by the detailed stages involved in the development of the instrument, as described earlier in this review.

In brief, McCarney used the educational diagnosticians and special education personnel, plus the multiple steps involved in arriving at the final items, in order to ensure including the most critical items characteristic of students with a learning disability.

For the purpose of providing criterion-related validity data, the author compared the LDES ratings completed by the primary instructor of randomly selected students (n = 71, representing all age levels from 4 years, 6 months through 18+ years) with performance scores (earned within the previous 3-month period) on the Wechsler Intelligence Scale for Children–Revised (Wechsler, 1974), the Peabody Individual Achievement Test (Dunn & Markwardt, 1970), and the Woodcock Reading Mastery Tests (Woodcock, 1973). Previously, each of these students had been identified as having a learning disability and, at the time of this comparison, was receiving service in special education. The LDES and the WISC-R were compared on the Listening, Thinking, Reading, and Mathematical Calculations subscales, resulting in correlation coefficients of .63, .61, .46, and .53, respectively. All correlation coefficients were significant at the .001 level. The LDES and the PIAT were compared on the Reading, Spelling, and Mathematical Calculations subscales, producing correlation coefficients of .39, .63, and .56, respectively. The correlation coefficient for Reading was significant at the .05 level, while both the Spelling and Mathematical Calculations correlation coefficients were significant at the .001 level. The LDES and the Woodcock Reading Mastery Tests were compared on the Reading and Spelling subscales, with resulting correlation coefficients of .59 and .65, respectively. Both were significant at the .001 level.

Evidence of construct validity is represented by examining the diagnostic validity of the LDES, the subscale interrelationships, and the item validity. Specifically, diagnostic validity was studied by rating regular class students (n = 92, representing all age levels from 4 years, 6 months to 18+ years) randomly selected from the normative sample (N = 1,666) and comparing their ratings to those of learning disabled students (n = 92). These students, both learning disabled and regular, were selected from 11 of the school districts that participated in the scale's standardization. Regular class students had a mean subscale standard score of 10, while the mean subscale standard score for the learning disabled students ranged from 5 (on the Reading, Writing, and Spelling subscales) to 7 (on the Thinking and Speaking subscales). The mean total Learning Quotients were compared, with the learning disabled group having a mean of 76 and the regular students a mean of 98. McCarney also reports that raw score mean differences were statistically significant at the .001 level between the two groups.

The interrelationship between subscales also was investigated to support the construct validity of the LDES, and intercorrelations appear above in the discussion regarding the scale's reliability. McCarney indicates that this high degree of correlation supports the use of the LDES to measure for a learning disability, and further indicates that the results of the principal components analysis support the seven subscales as distinct.

Item validity is supported by examining the discriminating power of the items on the scale, subscale scores, and total scale scores by employing a point-biserial correlation technique. Median coefficients for discriminating powers range from .41 (Writing) to .73 (Listening). The ranges of the coefficients for each subscale's discriminating powers also are presented: Listening, .69–.77; Thinking, .30–.81; Speaking, .28–.82; Reading, .31–.61; Writing, .32–.64; Spelling, .37–.74; and Mathematical Calculations, .65–.79.

No other information regarding the scale's validity is presented in the manual, nor were any independent studies of LDES validity found.

Critique

This reviewer located only one external review of the LDES, reported in Hammill, Brown, and Bryant (1992). There the reviewers categorized the evaluation as an achievement scale, which appears most logical as the items on the LDES are achievement related. The scale is given an overall rating of unacceptable and not recommended, primarily due to the unacceptable evaluation of the instrument's reliability. Although the types of scores offered for each subscale were determined to be good, the size of the sample populations, the demographics provided for the standardization sample, and the recency of the standardization were all found generally acceptable. All of the subscales were found unacceptable in the areas of internal consistency, stability, and overall reliability. One of the subscales (Writing) and the Learning Quotient were found unacceptable in the area of validity, with the remaining subscales found generally acceptable. This review, however, did not distinguish between those assessment instruments recommended for referral and screening purposes versus those recommended for other purposes, such as placement. If this had been the case, the review might have resulted in a different rating.

Salvia and Ysseldyke (1991) assert that assessment is employed in an educational setting to make certain types of decisions: referral, screening, classification, instructional planning, and evaluation of pupil progress. They further indicate that these decisions are made concerning three potential problem areas: academic, behavior, and/or physical. The Learning Disability Evaluation Scale appears to meet criteria for the purposes of referral and screening in the area of academics.

This determination is based on several factors. First is the need for instruments to meet a higher degree of reliability for decisions at the classification level. As indicated by Salvia and Ysseldyke (1991), to make "important educational decisions, such as tracking and placement in a special class . . . the minimum standard [for reliability coefficients] should be .90. When the decision . . . is a screening decision, such as the recommendation that a child receive further assessment. . . . we recommend a .80 standard [for reliability coefficients]" (p. 142). As LDES reliability coefficients fall in the .88 to .97 range, it seems most prudent to consider the scale for referral and screening purposes. Second, it seems apparent from a close examination of the items themselves that the best use of this scale is for referral and screening purposes; the items do not constitute a complete picture of the student, and, as such, find their greatest usefulness in aiding the educational professional in identifying those students who would benefit from more in-depth assessment and evaluation. Third, most states, while using the seven potential problem areas as characteristic of a learning disability, require more data than that available from an administration of the LDES in order to place a student in a learning disability classroom. Finally, for the purposes of instructional planning and the subsequent evaluation of that instruction, most educational professionals would require more in-depth information relative to a particular student's academic strengths and weaknesses.

For these reasons, the present reviewer believes that this scale best serves educational professionals interested in students with potential learning disabilities as a referral and screening tool. This does not lessen the scale's contribution to available assessment resources. First, it must be recognized that the LDES does provide educational professionals with a more formal means of assessing their observation of a particular student, and, as such, it serves a valuable purpose in the referral and screening process. Furthermore, such a formal means of evaluating one's observations gives the multifaceted assessment team valuable information in order to better focus the efforts of their task, a more detailed and specific assessment of the potential for a learning disability.

It would have been most helpful had McCarney included in the technical manual more descriptive information related to the participants involved in the development of the LDES. No information appears about the educational professionals who participated in developing the items or in standardizing the scale. Further, though information is provided about the large normative sample ($N = 1,666$), none is offered relative to the specific samples used to examine the scale's reliability and validity (e.g., the learning disabled students; the regular students). These pieces of information would help users fully understand the scale's reliability and validity for referral and screening purposes.

References

Dunn, L.M., & Markwardt, F.C. (1970). *Peabody Individual Achievement Test.* Circle Pines, MN: American Guidance Service.

Hammill, D.D., Brown, L., & Bryant, B.R. (1992). *A consumer's guide to tests in print* (2nd ed.). Austin, TX: PRO-ED.

McCarney, S.B. (1988a). *The Learning Disability Evaluation Scale* (including the technical manual). Columbia, MO: Hawthorne Educational Services.

McCarney, S.B. (1988b). *Pre-referral checklist.* Columbia, MO: Hawthorne Educational Services.

McCarney, S.B. (1989). *Pre-referral intervention strategies documentation.* Columbia, MO: Hawthorne Educational Services.

McCarney, S.B., & Bauer, A.M. (1989). *Learning disability intervention manual* (rev. ed.). Columbia, MO: Hawthorne Educational Services.

Salvia, J., & Ysseldyke, J.E. (1991). *Assessment* (5th ed.). Boston: Houghton Mifflin.

Wechsler, D. (1974). *Wechsler Intelligence Scale for Children–Revised.* San Antonio, TX: Psychological Corporation.

Woodcock, R. (1973). *Woodcock Reading Mastery Tests.* Circle Pines, MN: American Guidance Service.

Donald I. Templer, Ph.D.

Professor of Psychology, California School of Professional Psychology, Fresno, California, and Supervisory Psychologist, Nevada Department of Prisons, Indian Springs, Nevada.

LEITER RECIDIVISM SCALE

Russell Grayton Leiter. Wood Dale, Illinois: Stoelting Company.

Introduction

It is common knowledge to forensic and mental health professionals that the prediction of recidivism translates into issues of public safety, human suffering, and the many millions of dollars that incarceration costs. Any instrument that purports to help in such decision making represents hope. It also requires careful scrutiny.

The Leiter Recidivism Scale (Leiter, 1975) actually consists of nine scales: Instability, Age-Time Ratio, Social Immaturity, (lack of) Social Control, (lack of) Vocational Adjustment, Personality Dynamics, Abnormal Authority Reaction, (lack of) Institutional Adjustment, and Offense Level. The Instability scale score is determined from numbers of juvenile and adult incarcerations, escapes, probation violations, and placements in mental hospitals and in schools for mental defectives. Age-Time Ratio is based on the percentage of one's life in correctional institutions. Personality Dynamics refer to the adequacy of one's intellectual, interpersonal, and mental health resources. The nature of the other six scales can be understood by their titles.

Total score is based on the weighted score of the nine scales. Factor analysis yielded four factors: personality, time, crime, and institutional adjustment. Some normative-like information is provided, specifically means and standard deviations and frequency distributions of the recidivists and nonrecidivists, but not for the combined groups.

Practical Applications/Uses

For most of these scales the clinician is instructed to make a rating of 1 to 10 with the guidance of some representative statements. The manual asserts these statements had been given an ordinal position on the scale according to the frequency of their appearance in the histories of the recidivists and nonrecidivists. As an example, the Personality Dynamics scale statements that yield a score of 7 are "Emotional attitudes fluctuate widely"; "Poorly controlled hostility, guilt and anxiety"; "Impulsive, suggestive"; "Epilepsy." The statements for a score of 3 are "Discharged from the Armed Services for ineptitude" and "Illegally wore a uniform."

The clinician is encouraged to obtain all information from inmate records, but he or she may interview the inmate if the necessary information is not otherwise available.

The author maintains that this instrument should be applied by a clinical psychologist, preferably one seasoned in working with forensic populations. The manual states, "Trained objectivity is the principle qualification for the examiner. This will insure that the instructions for the application will be faithfully adhered to and that no attempt will be made to outguess the statistically determined classification" (Leiter, 1975, p. iii). Unfortunately, as noted in the "Critique" section of this review, the psychometric precision of the instrument and objectivity of scoring leave much to be desired.

Technical Aspects

Validation of the Leiter Recidivism Scale was based on 306 inmates who were paroled from the Ohio Penitentiary in 1953–55. They were followed up in 1970, and 204 of these inmates had committed a second offense. Discriminant analysis correctly classified 79.2% of the recidivists, 94.2% of the nonrecidivists, and 83.9% of the total number of inmates released on parole. Further evidence of validity is provided by correlations analyses. All of the scales correlated positively with each other, with correlations ranging from .35 to .79. Their correlations with recidivism ranged from .37 to .63. The full scale score correlated .67, and the multiple correlation was .73. The manual states that "the psychologist will be on safe ground if he recommends incarceration for individuals making a recidivism score of .560 or higher, and probation for individuals scoring below .560" (Leiter, 1975, p. 19).

Critique

Although these correlations and the discrimination described in the manual are impressive, the Leiter Recidivism Scale does have psychometric limitations. One of them is that the manual states nothing about cross-validation. Further, there is an apparent dearth of published material in the psychological literature since the publication of the 1975 manual.

Another problem is that interrater reliability was not reported. This is an especially important issue in view of the clinical judgment required in deciding what information in the records is equivalent to the representative statements given in the manual. What is the equivalent of having epilepsy? What is the equivalent of illegally wearing a uniform? Furthermore, there is not good quantitative support in the manual for the representative statements always assessing a greater than nominal ordering. How do we know that being an epileptic is worse than illegally wearing a uniform? In fairness to the scale, however, the examples chosen by the present reviewer were those that reflect least favorably upon this tool. The vast majority of examples that could have been given seem much more reasonable.

Other questions that remain unanswered by the manual are the suitability of all aspects of the Leiter Recidivism Scale in the 1990s, the estimated average time for the clinician to perform the ratings, and the availability of the necessary information in various forensic situations.

In conclusion, the Leiter Recidivism Scale is an instrument with promise. It is both worthy of and needs more research. The scale probably can be used in its present form and stage of development for the prediction of recidivism. It should, however, be used with caution and with full realization of its limitations. At the very least it can be viewed as a way of systemically obtaining and integrating a wide variety of information prior to parole and probation decisions.

References

Leiter, R.G. (1975). *Manual for the Leiter Recidivism Scale.* Chicago: Stoelting.

Bill Kozar, Ph.D.

Associate Professor and Director, Motor Behavior Laboratory, Boise State University, Boise, Idaho.

LINCOLN-OSERETSKY MOTOR DEVELOPMENT SCALE

William Sloan. Wood Dale, Illinois: Stoelting Company.

Introduction

The Lincoln-Oseretsky Motor Development Scale was constructed to evaluate the motor ability of children ages 6 to 14 years. The scale contains 36 items, measuring both gross and fine motor abilities such as finger dexterity, static balance, eye-hand coordination, rhythm, and speed of movement. Both unilateral and bilateral tasks are included, resulting in 53 items to be scored. Each item is individually administered.

The aim of this test, as stated by the author (Sloan, 1954), is to measure motor development over the 9-year age range covered. The present revision was undertaken to make the items more suitable for American children and to follow more closely the testing and scoring procedures used in the United States. Specifically, the intent was to select items that could be scored reliably and objectively, presented little chance of injury to the subjects, did not require elaborate equipment, minimized cultural bias, and correlated quite well with age. Sloan also sought to arrange items in order of difficulty and arrive at tentative norms for boys and girls ages 6 to 14.

In 1955 when this scale was published, very little empirical work was available on American children specifically within this age group. This scale is a rather thorough revision of the English translation of the Portuguese version of a motor ability test published by the Russian N. Oseretsky in 1931. Sloan developed the original version of the Lincoln Adaptation of the Oseretsky test in 1948. All but one of the 36 items on the Lincoln-Oseretsky Scale come from Oseretsky's original instrument. A number of other revisions and adaptations of the original Oseretsky test have been published, both before and since Sloan's 1955 revision (Berk, 1957; Bialer, Doll, & Winsberg, 1974; Bruininks, 1978; Cassel, 1949; Fredericks, Baldwin, Doughty, & Walter, 1972; Kerchner & Dusewicz, 1970; Rutter, Graham, & Yule, 1970; Yule, 1967).

Oseretsky's original test contained 85 items divided into six subtest categories. However, the rationale for the items included to measure the six subtest categories was far from clear. Sloan recognized that while motor skills are quite specific, Oseretsky proposed that test items such as throwing a ball and finger movements measured what he called *dynamic manual coordination*. Clearly throwing a ball is primarily a gross motor skill, while finger movements involving transcribing arcs using the index fingers and thumbs of opposite hands falls more into a fine motor category. Research indicates that fine and gross motor skills are minimally correlated, and thus the underlying motor abilities must be quite different. Sloan also sought to reduce the intellectual component in many items, as he felt this confounded the basic variables involved in the test performance. However, he recognized that the cognitive, affective, and motor domains interact continuously, and knowledge of each is necessary for an adequate understanding of the whole child. Sloan also realized that motor development has significant effects on the other domains and therefore scores from this scale can be used in combination with measures from the other domains to clarify the overall development of a child.

Practical Applications/Uses

The packet supplied for the Lincoln-Oseretsky Scale provides everything needed for testing except for a stopwatch. Sheets for recording scores are straightforward and are packaged separately from the tracing mazes and circles. The manual (Sloan, 1954) indicates that two small wooden boxes are supplied; however, the boxes provided to this reviewer were made of heavy-weight paper and may not last as long as wooden boxes with repeated use. The tasks in the scale and scoring system are such that minimum training would be needed to administer the test. The final score, which is the sum of all individual items, is easily computed. The user can compare this final score to the percentile norms provided in the manual.

The scale items are arranged in order of difficulty, which should challenge the subject and help maintain an appropriate level of motivation and effort. However, the length of the test (approximately 1 hour) does present potential fatigue and attention problems. Test administrators are directed to take precautions in providing enough rest between items and to be sure the subject focuses on and understands the task directions, demonstration, and requirements.

Despite advances in the study of motor development, the Lincoln-Oseretsky Scale probably can still be used as a research instrument to further our knowledge of motor development. The 1-hour administration time per child makes it difficult to use in situations where a large population may need to be tested in a short period of time. However, in certain settings and despite its age, the scale still can be of value as *one part* of the overall assessment of a child's development. This relies on the assumption that one is still using the concept of age-appropriate behavior and that some other test or scale is used to measure several of the gross movements that the Lincoln-Oseretsky Scale does not include.

Technical Aspects

The norms presented were obtained on 380 boys and 369 girls ages 6 to 14. Subjects came from small towns in the Midwest and were selected solely on the basis of grade and age level. These same subjects and scores were used in selecting the items for the finished scale. The author acknowledges the limitation this presents and suggests that further research is needed to provide further normative data. Normative data are presented separately for boys and girls as well as combined (in Tables 2, 3, and 4, and Figures 14, 15, and 16 in Appendix A, rather than in Figures 1, 2, and 3 as stated in the manual). The procedure used assumed that all abilities being measured are normally distributed over the entire age range. Several examples are given where this is not the case. The figures also suggest that the scale may not discriminate ability level in boys beyond age 12, especially beyond the 90th percentile, and in girls beyond the 50th percentile in ages 13 and 14.

Reliability coefficients (split-half) employing the same scores used in the development of the scale are also in the manual. The author recognizes and points out that this may well result in an artificially inflated reliability measure. However, a study conducted by Carey (1954) obtained reliability coefficients that were near the .96 and .97 (for males and females, respectively) reported in the manual. Once again the author suggests that further reliability assessments, such as test-retest, be done to determine performance stability over a 1-month period.

Validity measures presented in the manual suffer from the same problems as those for reliability. No cross-validation sample data appear. Validity coefficients for total score and age of .87 and .88 (for males and females) are presented. Validity is also claimed in terms of the scale measuring a comprehensive area of motor ability, identification of a homogeneous general factor of maturation, and low but positive correlations with two other tests of motor ability.

Critique

The Lincoln-Oseretsky Motor Development Scale was published to be used primarily as a research tool, for further revising and strengthening the scale and for increasing knowledge about child development. The manual notes the scale's shortcomings in terms of norms, reliability, and validity. The author also makes several suggestions for further research, such as shortening the 1-year age intervals and perhaps extending the scale beyond the 14th year. Although some of the research Sloan suggested has been undertaken, much more remains to be done.

A scale such as this one has two purposes, to identify a number of motor abilities in children and to track changes in these abilities over time. The Lincoln-Oseretsky instrument does indeed track changes over time, but a question remains regarding what motor abilities are being measured, as the abilities are essentially test defined. This problem is one that continues to plague motor development researchers (Bruininks, 1978; Krus, Bruininks, & Robertson, 1981; Rarick, Dobbins, & Broadhead, 1976). Keogh and Sugden (1985) indicate that not enough systematic work has been done to make the identification of children's movement abilities very promising.

The convergence of scores for boys and girls as they get older seems to indicate that this scale does not measure strength and power. None of the items measure running speed, agility, catching, striking, and kicking, all generally considered important measures of motor development. In addition, there is very little rationale provided for the scoring system used. The maximum possible score on any item is 3 points. Sixteen tasks are scored 3-2-1-0, 15 are scored 3-0, and 5 are scored 3-2-0. A justification for these differences in scoring the tasks needs to be made, for an unexpected and unjustified weighting of some items may result.

Finally, reference is made several times to the subject passing if he or she performs the task according to the instructions and "does not make any unnatural facial grimaces." The idea that such facial involvement *may* indicate muscular incoordination lacks scientific substantiation.

References

Berk, R.L. (1957). A comparison of performance of subnormal, normal, and gifted children on the Oseretsky tests of motor proficiency. *Dissertation Abstracts, 17,* 1947–1948.

Bialer, L., Doll, L., & Winsberg, B.G. (1974). A modified Lincoln-Oseretsky Motor Development Scale: Provisional standardization. *Perceptual and Motor Skills, 38,* 599–614.

Bruininks, R.H. (1978). *The Bruininks-Oseretsky Test of Motor Proficiency.* Circle Pines, MN: American Guidance Service.

Carey, R. (1954). *A comparative study of the Lincoln adaptation of the Oseretsky tests of motor proficiency with other selected motor ability tests.* Unpublished doctoral dissertation, University of Indiana, Bloomington.

Cassel, R.H. (1949). The Vineland adaptation of the Oseretsky tests. *Training School Bulletin Monographs, 46*(3–4).

Fredericks, H.D.B., Baldwin, V.L., Doughty, P., & Walter, L.J. (1972). *The Teaching Research Motor-Development Scale.* Springfield, IL: Thomas.

Keogh, J., & Sugden, D. (1985). *Movement skill development.* New York: Macmillan.

Kerchner, K.M., & Dusewicz, R.A. (1970). K.D.K.-Oseretsky tests of motor development. *Perceptual and Motor Skills, 30,* 202.

Krus, P.H., Bruininks, R.H., & Robertson, G. (1981). Structure of motor abilities in children. *Perceptual and Motor Skills, 52,* 119–129.

Rarick, G.L., Dobbins, D.A., & Broadhead, G.D. (1976). *The motor domain and its correlates in educationally handicapped children.* Englewood Cliffs, NJ: Prentice-Hall.

Rutter, M., Graham, P., & Yule, W. (1970). *A neuropsychiatric study in childhood.* London: Spastics International Medical Publications.

Sloan, W. (1954). *Manual for the Lincoln-Oseretsky Motor Development Scale.* Wood Dale, IL: Stoelting.

Yule, W. (1967). A short form of the Oseretsky test of motor proficiency. *Bulletin of the British Psychological Society, 20,* 29A–30A.

Jim C. Fortune, Ed.D.
Professor of Educational Research, Virginia Polytechnic Institute, Blacksburg, Virginia.

John M. Williams, Ph.D.
Research and Evaluation Specialist, Appalachia Educational Laboratory, Charleston, West Virginia.

MANAGEMENT APPRAISAL SURVEY

Jay Hall, Jerry Harvey, and Martha S. Williams. The Woodlands, Texas: Teleometrics International.

Introduction

The Management Appraisal Survey (MAS; Hall, Harvey, & Williams, 1986) first appeared in 1967 to serve as a companion scale to the Styles of Management Inventory. The authors stated that the purpose of the survey was to obtain a subordinate's assessment of his or her manager's management practices. The survey can be used independently of the Styles of Management Inventory to provide feedback to managers regarding how their subordinates perceive their management.

The scale was based on the conceptual framework proposed by Blake and Moulton (1968, 1978, 1985)—the managerial grid, a model of management behavior relating production concerns with people concerns. Hall et al. (1986) assigned five names to their management styles. These and a description of the way the authors characterized each style through scores of concern appear in Table 1.

The Task, Country Club, and Impoverished management styles are classified by Hall et al. as styles built upon conflicts of belief. Middle of the Road management exemplifies a compromise of beliefs. Team Management is said to represent integrated beliefs. Hall et al. (1986) recognized the low likelihood that any one manager could be characterized by any one of these styles all of the time.

Scaling of the management styles along the two continua of concern was accomplished with four generic management components: management philosophy, planning and goal setting, implementation, and performance evaluation. Each of the four component area scales is composed of three items that describe five slightly different situations for subordinates to consider in rating the tendencies of their managers.

It is difficult to see the psychometric reasoning behind this approach to scaling. First, the equalization of item representation of content areas across these apparently widely different management components is disturbing. Is performance evaluation equally important in rating the concern dimensions of managers as management philosophy? Are there other important areas of management not even considered in the MAS?

Second, these reviewers found it difficult to read all the text around each item,

379

Table 1

Management Styles and Concern Ratings in the Managerial Grid

Management Style	Low Concern	Compromise Concern	High Concern
Task	People		Production
Country Club	Production		People
Impoverished	People and Production		
Middle of the Road		People and Production	
Team			People and Production

then jump back and forth to the scale below, marking letter responses in the little boxes provided below each item. There are also a few spelling and grammatical errors still remaining in the item text after three republications of the Management Appraisal Survey. Further, it proved to these reviewers difficult to read the fairly complex wording and grammatical style used to write the scale items. Use of this scale to gain subordinate estimates of managerial ratings must provide some real literacy challenges in many industries.

Third, the situations described in many of the items are themselves composed of multiple psychological constructs that are poorly defined. Hall et al. force raters to form their own definition of terms such as *unique, necessary,* and *frequently,* plus many other ambiguous phrases, as they attempt to decide where their manager might fit in the relativistic scenarios described by the Management Appraisal Survey.

In addition to these psychometrical defects, many of the item stems and response selections contain the words *may, assuming, suppose,* and so forth, which makes it nearly impossible to use a simple linear scale from 1 to 10 to rate a manager in the complex situations described in the MAS.

Practical Applications/Uses

The Management Appraisal Survey asks subordinates of managers to read each descriptive situation before rating their manager along a 10-point continuum ranging from "completely characteristic" to "completely uncharacteristic." Subordinates are asked to rate first the description that is most like their manager and place the letter corresponding to the choice along the 10-point continuum. Next, the rater is asked to choose the description least like the manager and place that on the continuum. After these two steps, the rater must place the remaining three choices somewhere else along the continuum between the first two selected anchor points.

The degree of being characteristic or not characteristic is scaled in the mind of the subordinate rater. The authors of the MAS suggested that, if the subordinate was unfamiliar with the management situation presented in the item stem, their scaling should be based on what they think their manager might do.

Both of the present reviewers completed this scale for their own managers in a higher education setting. Completion of the scale took from 30 minutes to an hour. Use of the rating scale seemed to depend heavily on what the rater thought about his manager as opposed to what was known or had been experienced.

Selection of some of the descriptors of managerial behavior appeared quite arbitrary to these reviewers. For example, for one component description, the reviewers' manager appeared to operate like response option "A" during salary adjustment negotiation, like option "C" during class-scheduling time, and like option "D" during time to approve professional development plans. The reviewers' manager never appeared to behave like options "B" or "E," so it was difficult to logically place those choices on the scale with the other options.

Scoring the MAS took as much time as completing the scale. The entire scoring process appeared to be unduly complex. The type of scaling that occurred during the process failed to fit the reviewers' understanding of standard scaling models. The grids that provided qualitative feedback on each of the four scale components in terms of too much or too little of a given management style may prove to be helpful. However, the basis for determining whether a manager has too little or too much of a characteristic appeared to depend on the responses of a poorly defined norm group. This interpretive weakness was first identified by Korman (1978) and remains unrectified today.

Technical Aspects

The authors of the MAS provided normative conversion tables for each management component and for the overall assessment of managerial style. Norms are expressed in terms of T-scores and are based on "24,186 persons rating their immediate superiors" (Hall et al., 1986). Nothing is said in the MAS about the skills of these persons with regard to assessing the context in which they did the norming assessment, nor is anything said about the managers rated by the norming group. Reliability information presented in the MAS manual is equally vague.

Critique

In keeping with Korman (1978), this review summary will end briefly and to the point. The Management Appraisal Survey does not appear to meet the spirit, letter, or intent of the unwritten psychometric "laws" governing the construction, validation, and use of measurement scales.

References

This list includes text citations and suggested additional reading.

Bernardin, H.J. (1989). Management Appraisal Survey. In J. Connelly & J. Cramer (Eds.), *The tenth mental measurements yearbook* (pp. 457–459). Lincoln, NE: Buros Institute of Mental Measurements.

Blake, R.R., & Moulton, J.S. (1964). *The managerial grid: Vol. I.* Houston, TX: Gulf Publishing.

Blake, R.R., & Moulton, J.S. (1978). *The managerial grid: Vol. II.* Houston, TX: Gulf Publishing.

Blake, R.R., & Moulton, J.S. (1985). *The managerial grid: Vol. III.* Houston, TX: Gulf Publishing.

Hall, J., Harvey, J.B., & Williams, M.S. (1986). *Management Appraisal Survey.* The Woodlands, TX: Teleometrics International.

Korman, A.K. (1978). Styles of Leadership and Management. In O.K. Buros (Ed.), *The eighth mental measurements yearbook* (p. 1763). Highland Park, NJ: Gryphon Press.

Thornton, G.C. (1989). Management Appraisal Survey. In J. Connelly & J. Cramer (Eds.), *The tenth mental measurements yearbook* (pp. 457–459). Lincoln, NE: Buros Institute of Mental Measurements.

Janet F. Carlson, Ph.D.

Assistant Professor, Department of Counseling and Psychological Services, State University of New York, College at Oswego, Oswego, New York.

Rona Preli, Ph.D.

Assistant Professor, Graduate School of Education and Allied Professions, Fairfield University, Fairfield, Connecticut.

MARRIAGE ADJUSTMENT INVENTORY

Morse P. Manson and Arthur Lerner. Los Angeles, California: Western Psychological Services.

Introduction

The Marriage Adjustment Inventory (MAI) is a 157-item self-report instrument that addresses commonly occurring marital problems. Clients are asked to decide whether each problem is present or absent in their marriage, and, if present, whether the husband, wife, or both spouses experience the stated problem. The resultant evaluative scores are intended to indicate the severity of maladjustment in marriage.

The MAI was developed primarily for use by clinicians, to identify problems and initiate conversation about areas of concern in troubled marriages where partners have difficulty communicating. The test authors developed the inventory items by consulting with clinically trained professionals (marriage counselors, psychotherapists, psychiatrists, and social workers), males and females seeking marriage counseling, the relevant professional literature, and other sources. Initially they generated 600 items. From these the authors selected 157 items, although it is unclear how they decided to retain test items. The MAI then was administered to a standardization sample of 237 (120 males, 117 females). Although the test authors report the demographic characteristics of the standardization sample, it is unclear how the sample was selected. The authors reportedly asked the sample respondents to rate their marriage as "very happy," "happy," "average," "unhappy," or "very unhappy." The investigators then administered the MAI. The scores obtained by the respondents became the norms for the final three categories or groupings: happily adjusted (very happy, happy), average adjusted (average), and unhappily adjusted (unhappy, very unhappy). The test was published in 1962 and has undergone no revisions or restandardizations.

The MAI is completed by both marital partners. Each spouse completes the instrument independently, indicating for each item whether it applies to "self," "spouse," or "both." (An item is simply left blank if it does not apply.) The inventory items cover a wide range of difficulties applicable to troubled marriages, including disagreements on money, children, religion, expression of anger, and sexual relations. Responses are recorded directly on the response booklet, requiring the respondent to darken appropriate circles. Responses are scored on the response booklet also.

The directions for administration are specified in the MAI manual and printed on the front page of the record form as well. The written directions are simple and clearly stated, instructing respondents to read each statement and decide if the problem exists in their marriage. If the item does describe a problem area, the appropriate circle is darkened to indicate who has the problem.

The completed MAI provides scores on 12 clusters or scales: Family Relationships, Dominance, Immaturity, Neurotic Traits, Sociopathic Traits, Money Management, Children, Interests, Physical, Abilities, Sexual, and Incompatibility. Cluster scores correspond to concerns that the test authors suggest are "frequently noted as influencing the tranquility of marriages" (Manson & Lerner, 1962, p. 1).

Practical Applications/Uses

Although the MAI originally was developed primarily for use in clinical practice, such use is no longer appropriate, given the instrument's technical limitations and lack of theoretical congruity with any recognized school or system of family therapy. Thus, its use presently is restricted to selected research applications, such as those that may contribute to establishing its psychometric features. However, using the MAI items as an adjunctive measure—as part of a structured interview, screening procedure, or problem checklist—may be useful in the clinical domain purely as a means of gathering information, but not to generate meaningful scores or classify respondents' levels of adjustment. Although the test authors greatly overstate the inventory's usefulness when describing its purposes and uses, their earliest characterization of the inventory as an approach to generate discussion of marital problems appears to hold.

Mental health professionals working with married couples may be inclined to use the MAI, modified in one of the ways mentioned above. Clinicians such as marriage and family therapists, psychologists, and social workers would represent some of the potential users. Researchers interested in exploring the technical features of the MAI perhaps would come from family studies programs or psychology or sociology departments.

The subjects to whom the MAI typically is administered are (distressed) couples with at least sixth-grade reading ability. (The test authors do not indicate how the reading level of the test was ascertained.) The manual does not specify age requirements, but persons above the age of 18 would seem to be appropriate test takers. With minor modifications, the items also may be used with unmarried partners, both heterosexual and same-sex. The MAI is not appropriate for persons with limited English proficiency or those with visual impairments.

No special training is required to administer the inventory. However, it is advisable in clinical settings for the administrator to be part of the therapy team, especially if one of the suggested procedural modifications is used (e.g., if the instrument is used as a structured interview or problem checklist). Users may administer the MAI individually or in groups, although the latter may prove inappropriate for some of the modified approaches, such as the structured interview. In addition to standardized directions for administration, the test manual contains some appropriate caveats regarding potential client reactions, the proper setting in which to administer the inventory, and the absolute necessity of confidential treatment of responses. Although not specified in the manual, the time needed to complete the inventory will be about 30–45 minutes.

Scoring is straightforward, consisting mostly of counting and adding the number of responses (i.e., problems) recognized as existing in one's self, one's spouse, and the H-W (husband-wife) unit. Values from these three components are added to yield a total scale score. These four scores comprise the "evaluative scores." In addition, the 12 "cluster scores" are obtained by counting the number of responses in each column marked as self, spouse, or H-W unit. By comparing evaluative scores with the mean scores of the three adjustment groups from the normative sample, the clinician makes a determination of adjustment as "happy," "average," or "unhappy." From there, conversions to percentile equivalents are possible by using a conversion table provided in the test manual. Scoring is done by hand, and each record form takes about 15–20 minutes to score completely.

Test interpretation is based on objective scores, resulting from survey completion. However, the test authors note that the results alone may not provide a sufficient understanding of the responses. The clinician may need to explore certain areas further with the spouses or look more closely at the test items in cases where a large disparity in scores emerges.

The MAI gives the clinician a score indicating the level of maladjustment for couples experiencing marital problems. The items specify the types of problems the couple is facing. Morse and Lerner hypothesize that this information is useful to the clinician in initiating communication between spouses in treatment and identifying areas of concerns and goals for therapeutic intervention. This would suggest that the instrument is useful to those professionals clinically trained to do therapeutic work with couples.

Technical Aspects

No information is provided regarding reliability and validation of the MAI. As suggested earlier, information concerning the development of test specifications and standardization procedures is very limited. Overall, the size of the sample used to standardize the MAI is inadequate, consisting of a total of 237 individuals, and demographic information is provided only for a limited number of variables— marital status, age, educational level, and occupation.

The procedures used to establish the cutting scores for the three levels of adjustment assume a type of concurrent validity. A simple rating on a single item by the respondents in the standardization sample served as the established criterion of comparison. The assumption that this procedure is valid compromises the validity of interpretive procedures as well, because the derived adjustment category is used to convert scores to percentile equivalents and to compare cluster scores.

Critique

In its present form, the MAI has virtually no clinical utility and very limited research viability. Overall, many of the inventory's major weaknesses stem from its age, which gives rise to many departures from contemporary standards of good testing practices and perhaps other aberrations, such as the lack of theoretical grounding. Although the test authors note the "limited technical studies" and caution that "the inventory should not be considered a finished clinical tool" (p. 8), this acknowledgment does not diminish the number and severity of these deficiencies. Likewise, the test authors suggest future directions for research on the MAI. These suggestions indicate that the test authors knew what was lacking in the instrument at the time of its publication, but that does not in any way mitigate the shortcomings.

Pronounced weaknesses and restrictions in the clinical utility of the MAI stem from the lack of information about its psychometric properties, such as validity and reliability. By today's standards, these omissions are grave; by 1962 standards, the omissions may have been more understandable or at least more common. (However, even at that time, the earliest set of guidelines for psychological tests, termed *recommendations*, was available from the American Psychological Association [1954].)

There are many other departures from current standards of testing practice, as specified in the *Standards for Educational and Psychological Testing* (American Educational Research Association, American Psychological Association, & National Council on Measurement in Education, 1985), such as a lack of relevant citations from the literature, an inadequate standardization sample, aged norms, and others. Again, at the time of the instrument's publication, testing standards were less well articulated and less fully developed, but in today's market the weaknesses are striking.

Regarding theoretical issues, the MAI was constructed independent of any theoretical orientation to couples therapy despite its intended use by clinicians. The lack of grounding in a theoretical orientation limits considerably its utility for assessment and intervention with couples in therapy.

The phrasing of the items comprising the MAI is negative and potentially blaming. Spouses are to identify the problem and "who has it," contrary to acceptable approaches to couples therapy. The linear framework opposes standard techniques wherein couples issues are conceptualized as mutually maintained, and this may perpetuate the blaming, critical stance, and perception with which couples often enter treatment.

Similarly, the negative phrasing would work against eliciting any areas of couple strength and compatibility. In addition to the identification of problems, information on couples' strengths is vital to obtaining a balanced picture of functioning. Based on its publication date, the MAI may have preceded the test authors' awareness of the theoretically grounded approach to couples work. Certainly its design lacks fit with contemporary thought in the field of marital therapy. By virtue of the instrument's design, responding couples can only be maladjusted. The instrument serves simply to identify the extent of maladjustment, despite the test authors' claim that the MAI reveals positive as well as negative aspects of the relationship so that "constructive, healthy psychological-sexual-social relationships may be encouraged" (Manson & Lerner, 1962, p. 1). The test authors further state that the MAI will identify "patterns of behaviors." It is entirely unclear how the instrument can accomplish this aim, as to do so would require measuring those complex actions and reactions that characterize a couple's interactions.

On a somewhat more positive note, many of the individual items comprising the MAI appear to have relevance for couples today. Similarly, the problem areas it identifies apply to contemporary marital relationships. Thus, the inventory may be useful as part of an interviewing or screening technique—without scoring or interpreting the items or resultant scales—and in this way serve as a very early starting point for therapeutic endeavors. Using the inventory as a problem checklist may extract preliminary information about couples that can be useful in subsequent clinical explorations. To some extent, the test authors suggest that such a less formal view of the data may be clinically meaningful, as they recommend a review of individual responses and responses to the various problem areas.

The MAI is an aged measure, in need of considerable reworking. With revision and updating, many of the technical inadequacies could be rectified, although its theoretical limitations may be remedied less easily. This is a little known instrument that has not enjoyed particularly wide circulation, perhaps in part due to the nature and number of its limitations. In its present form, it is probably best viewed as a candidate for research (on the instrument itself), although some clinical utility possibly may result from using the items as part of a structured interview, screening procedure, or problem checklist.

References

American Educational Research Association, American Psychological Association, & National Council on Measurement in Education. (1985). *Standards for educational and psychological testing.* Washington, DC: American Psychological Association.

American Psychological Association. (1954). *Technical recommendations for psychological tests and diagnostic techniques.* Washington, DC: Author.

Manson, M.P., & Lerner, A. (1962). *The Marriage Adjustment Inventory: Manual.* Los Angeles, CA: Western Psychological Services.

Harold Takooshian, Ph.D.

Associate Professor, Social Science Division, Fordham University, New York, New York.

MASLACH BURNOUT INVENTORY, SECOND EDITION

Christina Maslach and Susan E. Jackson. Palo Alto, California: Consulting Psychologists Press, Inc.

Introduction

The Maslach Burnout Inventory, Second Edition (Maslach & Jackson, 1986) assesses psychological burnout in human service professionals. This 22-item inventory does not yield a single burnout score, but operationally defines burnout as three separate scores that cannot be combined. These three factorially derived scales are Emotional Exhaustion (EE, 9 items), Depersonalization (DP, 5 items), and Personal Accomplishment (PA, 8 items). EE comprises the drained feeling that one no longer has energy to give to others. DP describes one's negative, cynical attitudes toward one's clients, a callous or even dehumanized perception that they somehow deserve their troubles. PA, low in burnout, represents a high self-regard for oneself and one's own work. These three scores are continua, on which the MBI rates people as high, moderate, or low in burnout compared to colleagues in their own human service profession.

It is no wonder that present-day society is so concerned over burnout and its assessment. "More people are disabled today as a result of stress than at any other time in our history" (Schultz & Schultz, 1990, p. 539). As of 1992, job stress was ranked as one of the 10 leading U.S. health risks (Quick, Murphy, & Hurrell, 1992). Media reports estimate that some one third of U.S. workers today are experiencing burnout or preburnout symptoms. A Blue Cross/Blue Shield survey found that fully 84% of U.S. workers describe stress as a major factor in their work. Overall, some 80% of all U.S. hospital admissions are for stress-related disorders—headaches, internal pain, skin rash, allergy, arthritis, even some cancers. Just two such disorders (coronary disease and ulcers) accounted for $45 billion in U.S. health care costs in 1 year.

The term *burnout* did not exist in the psychological literature before 1974, yet society quickly understood and embraced the term. Earlier terms like *stress* or *tension* actually can be positive as well as negative, a source of increased motivation, even exhilaration, or personal growth. Such positive aspects are termed *eustress* (Selye, 1956). Not so with burnout—a totally negative concept, with nothing positive about it. Conceptually it seems best to view stress and burnout as separate constructs, in which external stress, if constant, leads to internal burnout. Whereas therapy for stress might seek to channel rather than reduce it, the only aim of therapy for burnout is to reduce it, either by prevention or remediation.

Christina Maslach, the senior author of the MBI, completed her doctoral training at Stanford in 1971. Among her current professional pursuits she is a consultant, a professor of psychology at Berkeley, and a director of Consulting Psychologists Press. Susan E. Jackson, coauthor of the MBI, completed her doctoral training with Maslach at Berkeley in 1982. At present she is a professor in the Stern Business School of New York University.

Maslach's writing about the emotional exhaustion of human service workers began back in 1973, with a presentation to the American Psychological Association on what she first termed *detached concern* (Maslach, 1973; see Maslach, 1982, pp. 7–8). She had switched to the more pithy term *burnout* by 1976, publishing a seminal article entitled "Burned-out" that extended the notion beyond health and social service workers to lawyers, government staff, and other professionals. Since 1976, she has become a preeminent authority on burnout, with a steady stream of publications on its many aspects—the concept and its assessment, causes, consequences, and treatment. It seems the term actually was coined in 1974 by another psychologist, Herbert Freudenberger, who wrote an article called "Staff Burnout" for his special issue of the *Journal of Social Issues*. Freudenberger's was indeed a prescient article, which went beyond introducing his new concept to suggest 10 preventive measures to avoid burnout. Since then, Freudenberger too has authored a book (Freudenberger & Richelson, 1980) and many articles on burnout, focusing mainly on at-risk factors (dedication, commitment, routinization) and treatment techniques. (Interestingly, Freudenberger and his citers consistently hyphenate *burn-out*, while Maslach and her citers do not.)

The first edition of the MBI released in 1981 was cautiously subtitled the "research edition," to be used for group but not individual diagnosis. Still, independent reviewers found that 1981 version highly reliable and valid compared to other measures of organizational stress, as in the government-published, comparative review of stress-related inventories by Jones and DuBois (1987). This second (1986) edition is a further improvement in at least two ways. First, the same 22 items are now rated only on "frequency"; previously they were rated on "intensity" as well. The double-ratings were clumsy and somewhat correlated (median $r = .56$), so dropping intensity has halved completion time while, if anything, probably enhanced validity. Second, the normative base has been greatly expanded, to a total of some 11,067 service-providers in six fields: 4,163 in teaching (K–12), 635 in postsecondary education, 1,538 in social service, 1,104 in medicine, 730 in mental health, and 2,897 in other professions (law, policework, probation, clergy, library science, agency administration).

The test format is four pages printed on two 8½" × 11" sheets. Two pages ask 15 simple demographic questions (but not one's name) that might interest a researcher, such as job history, ethnicity, religion, education, and occupation. Page 3 contains the somewhat wordy instructions for completing the 7-point Likert-type scale (0 = never, 6 = every day). Page 4 presents the entire 22-item scale, with three empty spaces for later entry of scores. All MBI items are simple one-sentence statements of this sort: "I feel totally drained after a day at work" (EE), "I am no longer concerned about the welfare of my recipients" (DP), or "I do a lot of good in my job" (PA).

The test form is titled "Human Services Survey" rather than "Burnout Inventory" in order to "minimize the reactive effects" of this ominous term (Maslach & Jackson, 1986, p. 4). The test is entirely self-administered and requires no specific training, though the manual wisely suggests some precautions—safeguarding the respondent's anonymity, guaranteeing privacy for any feedback, and using an administrator outside the respondent's supervisory chain of command.

Practical Applications/Uses

A practitioner or researcher in a human services organization might find many ways to use the MBI. These probably are described most clearly in Maslach's (1982) dated but detailed book, *Burnout: The Human Cost of Caring*, where she reviewed four areas: risk factors, effects, treatment, and prevention. Risk factors can be identified with the MBI, studying who burns out based on diverse predictors—demographic (age, sex, ethnicity, family, education), personality (self-esteem, need for approval, commitment level, motivation, hostility, fear), and organizational (lack of feedback, caseload, level of demands, support, co-worker behavior, policies and procedures). The MBI can document some effects of burnout on oneself (physical and mental pathology, substance abuse) and on others (impaired family life and service to clients). The inventory can monitor various treatment methods by oneself or the organization (training, diversions, support, procedural changes). Finally, the instrument might be used to prevent burnout before it becomes a problem (early detection and skills training to avert the syndrome).

The MBI is an unusual test in several ways, so it is important to distinguish what it cannot do from what it can. First, the format is deliberately anonymous, not asking for a name on the otherwise thorough 15-item face sheet; thus it is designed for group but not individual assessments. Second, the MBI is a transparent instrument, containing none of the embedded methodological scales common in most personality tests (acquiescence, social desirability, lie, malingering); it relies on the veracity of respondents (Maslach & Jackson, 1986, p. 4) and is thus easy to fake (low or high) for whatever reason. Third, the inventory provides a diagnosis of current functioning in a specific job rather a prognosis of future job functioning, so, unlike most industrial tests, it cannot be used for preemployment prediction of success in future roles. Finally, the wording of MBI items limits the assessment to specific human service professions, while excluding the countless blue-collar or corporate occupations that also face burnout—assembly-line workers, managers, executives, secretaries, salespeople, and so on.

The ideal practical application of the MBI is to chart patterns of burnout levels across organizational departments or across time. One example of this would lie in testing before and after an organizational intervention to document impact. Another would be internal research to profile risk factors in large organizations, that is, which demographic or psychographic groups are experiencing most or least burnout.

The MBI is designed for human service workers and teachers who are even minimally literate. The manual presents tabular normative data on a group that is both large (*N* = 11,067) and diverse in many ways (sex, race, age, education). It is unclear how representative this normative group is, as the researchers did not themselves systematically collect the data; rather, they cumulated the raw data collected by some 100 independent investigators in Canada and the U.S. who apparently used the MBI prior to 1986 (the manual acknowledges them by name with thanks). Because diversity alone does not make a group a probability sample, the norms must be used advisedly.

The MBI manual offers two large norm tables. One presents a high/moderate/ low range on each of the three scales (EE, DP, PA) for six occupational groups (K–12 teaching, postsecondary teaching, social service, medicine, mental health, and "other"). A second table presents the mean and standard deviation for the three scales based on five demographics: sex, race, age, marital status, and education. The manual's many normative breakdowns are indeed important, as even casual perusal of these tables reveals that group scores can vary considerably, in notable ways. For example, blacks report much lower EE (mean = 17.8) than whites (23.1) or Asians (25.0), and both EE and DP correlate negatively with age (DP under age 30 = 9.4, over age 50 = 5.3), the same variations found in the first edition (Maslach, 1982, pp. 57–62). There is little variation by sex or education.

This reviewer suggests that examiners make certain to distribute the instructions page face-up, as one quarter of his college student test takers did not notice these instructions until after completing the scale on the reverse side; most notably, the necessarily generic term *recipient* in 7 of the 22 items may seem odd to respondents until they have seen it defined in the instructions. Otherwise, the simplicity of words and sentences make this a suitable test for any literate adult. The publisher's catalog description of the MBI estimates "usually 20–30 minutes" to complete the inventory, the manual estimates about 10 to 15 minutes (p. 4), and this reviewer's college respondents averaged 5.2 minutes.

Hand scoring could not be simpler. With a single template that fits over the test sheet, the process takes barely 40 seconds to extract the three scores for EE, DP, and PA. Interpretation too is simple. Table 2 in the manual gives the means and standard deviations for all three scales for six service occupations. Moreover, Table 1 offers three bands—high/moderate/low—for these same occupations. Thus in a matter of seconds the examiner can chart a three-score burnout profile of a person, as well as compare him or her with the normative mean scores on categories of age, sex, race, education, and marital status.

Technical Aspects

Is burnout an internally consistent trait? The MBI manual carefully tested internal reliabilities for its three scales using a large and diverse sample ($N = 1,316$), with resulting reliabilities that are adequate if not impressive for such brief scales: $\alpha = .90$ for EE (standard error of measurement = 3.8), .79 for DP ($SE_M = 3.2$), and .71 for PA ($SE_M = 3.7$).

Is burnout stable over time? The MBI evidence is less cogent on this question. With a small sample of 53 social work students and administrators, test-retest correlations over a 2- to 4-week interval were $r = .82$ for EE, .60 for DP, and .80 for PA. A larger sample of 248 teachers over a 1-year interval found similarly significant, if modest correlations: $r = .60$ for EE, .54 for DP, and .57 for PA.

The MBI is not available in alternate forms designed to retest the same individual. Since 1986, the second edition offers a Form Ed specifically for teachers rather than human service workers. This form is identical in wording and layout to the original MBI, except for the seven items using the word *recipient;* this becomes *student* in Form Ed. With this, the 1986 manual now incorporates a self-contained five-page section by Richard L. Schwab on "Burnout in Education" (pp. 18–22). Thus, the MBI manual can offer no alternate forms reliability, as the two versions of the scale cannot test the same individual.

The manual reports near-identical internal reliabilities for Form Ed ($N = 462$ teachers): $\alpha = .90$ for EE, .76 for DP, and .76 for PA.

The inventory items have the simple structure most recommended for easy translation for cross-cultural use (Brislin, 1980)—short sentences containing short words. Indeed, to the extent that burnout is certainly a global problem, the MBI's availability in other languages would be useful. This reviewer could locate independent researchers who, happily, offer careful translations (and occasionally norms) for the MBI for cross-national use—in Afrikaans (Odendal & Van Wyk, 1988), Dutch (Van der Ploeg, Van Leeuwen, & Kwee, 1990), Italian (Curci, Beltrami, Pederzoli, & Mari, 1987; Sirigatti & Stefanile, 1988; Sirigatti, Stefanile, & Menoni, 1988), and Swedish (Arnetz, Andreasson, Strandberg, & Eneroth, 1986)—as well as for English-speakers in Britain (Firth, McIntee, McKeown, & Britton, 1985), Australia (Pierce & Molloy, 1989), and New Zealand (Green & Walkey, 1988).

The validity of the MBI has been examined in several different ways, with generally good results. For criterion validity, how much does the MBI correlate with on-the-job activity, current and future? For the former, the manual reports five studies on three service professions: policework, medicine, and social service. Using peer ratings, for instance, one's co-worker satisfaction rating correlated $r = -.16$ with EE, -.41 with DP, and .40 with PA. Using self-ratings, too, 43 physicians reported varied amounts of direct contact with patients ($r = .31$ with EE) and amount of feedback they received on their work (-.44 with DP, .38 with PA). Using behavior, 142 police officers rated by their wives varied in their insomnia (.24 with EE), drinking (.24 with EE), number of friends (-.22 with DP), and use of tranquilizers (-.18 with PA). Evidence of predictive criterion validity (forecasting future job behavior) is not offered in the MBI manual; rather, the authors hope independent investigators will undertake this, and even suggest a series of specific longitudinal and other studies they feel should be done (pp. 15–17, 20–22).

For construct validity, how much is the MBI measuring three genuine indicators of burnout? The only direct evidence offered in the manual is the factorial results used to develop the three-factor scale, based on an original sample of 1,025 and a cross-validation sample totalling 2,545. The factor structure seems clear, with items generally loading low on the other two factors (typically in the .10s) and high on their own factor (median loadings of .65 for EE, .62 for DP, and .53 for PA). The manual does not tell what percentage of the MBI's total scale variance is explained by these three factors. Happily, the three scales show modest correlations, indicating they are separate, yet related constructs: $r = .52$ EExDP, -.22 EExPA, -.26 DPxPA. Fortunately, abundant independent research has used the MBI, generally supporting its validity. Independent factor-analytic studies impressively corroborate the three-factor composition among diverse groups of U.S. social workers (Koeske & Koeske, 1989), human service managers (Lee & Ashforth, 1990), teachers (Gold, 1984), British nurses (Firth et al., 1985), diverse New

Zealanders (Green & Walkey, 1988), and Australian schoolteachers (Pierce & Molloy, 1989). Comparing the MBI with other tests, a study of 146 university employees found that MBI burnout scores were highest for hardy, Type-A workers and lowest for non-hardy Type-B workers (Nowack, 1986). The MBI correlated positively with Pines's Tedium Scale (Corcoran, 1986). Many independent studies have successfully validated MBI scores with relevant job behaviors in teachers (Belcastro, Gold, & Hays, 1983; Corcoran, 1986; Gold, 1984; Gold, Roth, Wright, & Michael, 1991), student teachers (Gold & Michael, 1985), physicians (Arnetz et al., 1986; Rafferty, Lemkau, Purdy, & Rudisill, 1986), nurses (Firth et al., 1985), psychotherapists (Van der Ploeg et al., 1990), college students (Powers & Gose, 1986), and even mothers (Pelsma, Roland, Tollefson, & Wigington, 1989).

This reviewer is pleasantly surprised by the consistency of the validity findings because the MBI makes no effort to distinguish the many, very different sources of stress in one's job. For instance, hospital physician A may greatly enjoy patient contact, while dreading any contact with administrators and feeling only lukewarm toward frequent contact with colleagues; physician B may dread patient contact, while enjoying interaction with other physicians and feeling neutral toward hospital administrators. These two physicians' MBI scores make no attempt to sort out the very different feelings that a human service worker likely has toward her or his job—variegated feelings toward clients, co-workers, supervisors, or the employer. Such intensely mixed feelings are common among many service occupations (teaching, policework, social work), yet MBI items muddle these stressors together rather than distinguishing them. One would expect such global burnout scores to contain error variance that would act to lower validity coefficients.

Critique

Although the MBI has established itself as a uniquely reliable and valid measure of burnout, it has its limitations compared to other personnel tests, some of these already noted.

Because it is anonymous, it cannot be used for individual counseling. It contains no methodological scales, relying instead on the good intentions of the test taker, a fact bemoaned by some MBI users (such as Arthur, 1990). Because it measures a person's current job attitudes, it cannot be used for preemployment screening, like most personnel tests can. The MBI norms in the manual may not be sufficiently detailed or representative for some users. Not least of all, the MBI is limited to assessing human service professionals, excluding the huge number of other workers in the labor force who seem just as prone to burnout—blue-collar and white-collar workers, farmers, and so on. How often do we hear of high stress among managers, secretaries, salespeople, computer staff, assembly-line workers? The MBI is not geared to assessing their burnout.

One frequent criticism of the MBI, at least among researchers, is that it "is not a theory-driven instrument" (Hargrove, 1989, p. 474; Sandoval, 1989), leaving burnout a vague construct that has been operationalized but still lacks a crisp, precise definition. Interestingly the MBI authors themselves agree with this. They note that "much of the work that has been done on burnout has been atheoretical . . .

[and] it is essential to have more theory-driven research. Thus we urge researchers to utilize a more clearly-specified theoretical framework in their future work" (Maslach & Jackson, 1986, p. 17). Indeed, for better or worse, the main body of the MBI manual devotes an equal amount of space (four pages) to suggest future possible studies as it does to summarize past studies of validity. Still, there are two points to be made here about this criticism of too little theory.

First, practitioners may well be unconcerned about the lack of theory undergirding the MBI. A review of the independent empirical literature using the MBI in highly diverse nations and populations finds it an unquestionably valid, reliable instrument that correlates with myriad indicators of job performance and well-being. Second, even for theorists, this too-little-theory criticism of the MBI also can be viewed as a strength. Because the scale is so psychometrically sound, theorists might use it to test hypotheses deduced from their own theoretical viewpoint. For instance, Meier (1983) used Badura's social learning paradigm to define burnout as "expect[ing] little reward and considerable punishment from work because of a lack of valued reinforcement, controllable outcomes, or personal competence" (p. 899). Others have argued for a "process model," that EE is the essence of burnout, with high DP and low PA as common but theoretically separate consequences of it (Koeske & Koeske, 1989), though there is as yet little path-analytic or other causal research to verify this process model. Another fertile though unplowed source of theoretical underpinning is the very parallel social psychological work of Zimbardo (1969), on "depersonalization," "deindividuation," "dehumanization." Indeed, Maslach was a doctoral student assisting in Zimbardo's noted mock-prison study of depersonalization around 1971, when their collaboration led to marriage (Maslach, 1982, pp. xiv–xv). The copious MBI literature makes no explicit connection with Zimbardo's broader social psychology theories of depersonalization (Maslach, 1982, pp. 167–184), but it well could.

This reviewer hopes the MBI might be redesigned and shortened in its third edition. Currently, the three MBI scales are three different lengths (9, 5, and 8 items), haphazardly arrayed into 22 items. In contrast to the elegance of, say, the Eysenck Personality Questionnaire, which symmetrically interweaves its four scales, the MBI does not; four of the first six items tap EE, while four of the last six tap PA, with no apparent reason. Frankly, it appears the inventory also could be easily shortened by 50%. For example, item 8 alone (asking if one feels burnt out) correlates .84 with the full nine-item EE scale. An ideal revision of this inventory might be three uniformly brief (perhaps four-item) scales presented as every third of 12 items, allowing the addition of a brief methodological scale or two (acquiescence, malingering, lie, or social desirability).

What other measures of burnout are available besides MBI? There are several to consider, none as well researched as MBI yet all with respectable records of reliability and validity and all easily found in the literature. The Job Burnout Inventory (JBI), for example, is a 15-item survey developed by Ford, Murphy, and Edwards (1983), based on the idea that too "little attention has focused on job burnout . . . in private sector occupations such as managers, executives, engineers, technicians, clericals, scientists, etc." (p. 996). The JBI is highly suitable for these fields as well as for service professionals, with the hope of eventually expanding further to blue-collar workers, the military, and homemakers (p. 1005). The Tedium Measure is reviewed by Stout and Williams (1983), along with a few related measures of burnout. The Tedium Scale was developed by a colleague of Maslach's (Pines) in 1981, also to assess more broadly than just the service professions (Arthur, 1990; Corcoran, 1986). The Staff Burnout Scale was developed by Jones in 1980, also with a good record of reliability and validity (Arthur, 1990).

To the extent that job stress and burnout are costly problems in organizations worldwide, interest in measuring burnout will continue to increase in coming years. Those drawn to better understanding burnout in their human service organization can turn with confidence to the Maslach Burnout Inventory, which, since its introduction in 1981, has remained the best researched instrument to quantify burnout. MBI validity and reliability have been amply confirmed in more than a decade of research both by the authors and by independent researchers in several countries. Still, for those put off by its current limitations—such as easy fakeability and inappropriateness for blue-collar and most white-collar workers, as well as for individual counseling—there are at least a half dozen alternative instruments that are less scrutinized but equally adequate and easy to administer.

References

Arnetz, B., Andreasson, S., Strandberg, M., & Eneroth, P. (1986). Lakarnas arbetsmiljo. (Physicians' work environment.) *Stressforskningsrapporter, 187,* 144.

Arthur, N.M. (1990). The assessment of burnout: A review of three inventories useful for research and counseling. *Journal of Counseling and Development, 69,* 186–189.

Belcastro, P.A., Gold, R.S., & Hays, L.C. (1983). Maslach Burnout Inventory: Factor structure for samples of teachers. *Psychological Reports, 55,* 1000–1003.

Brislin, R.W. (1980). Translation and content analysis of oral and written material. In H.C. Triandis and J.W. Berry (Eds.), *Handbook of cross-cultural psychology: Vol. 2. Methodology* (pp. 389–444). Boston: Allyn & Bacon.

Corcoran, K.J. (1986). Measuring burnout: A reliability and convergent validity study. *Journal of Social Behavior and Personality, 1,* 107–112.

Curci, P., Beltrami, F., Pederzoli, L., & Mari, M. (1987). La sindrome del burnout e l'assistenza psichiatrica. (Burnout syndrome and psychiatric assistance.) *Rivista Sperimentale di Freniatria e Medicina Legale delle Alienazioni Mentali, 111,* 195–209.

Firth, H., McIntee, J., McKeown, P., & Britton, P.G. (1985). Maslach Burnout Inventory: Factor structure and norms for British nursing staff. *Psychological Reports, 57,* 147–150.

Ford, D.L., Murphy, C.J., & Edwards, K.L. (1983). Exploratory development and validation of a perceptual job burnout inventory: Comparison of corporate sector and human services professionals. *Psychological Reports, 52,* 995–1006.

Freudenberger, H.J. (1974). Staff burn-out. In H.J. Freudenberger (Ed.), *The free clinic handbook* [Special issue]. *Journal of Social Issues, 30*(1), 159–165.

Freudenberger, H.J., & Richelson, G. (1980). *Burn-out: The high cost of achievement.* Garden City, NY: Anchor.

Gold, Y. (1984). The factorial validity of the Maslach Burnout Inventory in a sample of California elementary and junior high school classroom teachers. *Educational and Psychological Measurement, 44,* 1009–1016.

Gold, Y., & Michael, W.B. (1985). Academic self-concept correlates of potential burnout in a sample of first-semester elementary school practice teachers: A concurrent validity study. *Educational and Psychological Measurement, 45,* 909–914.

Gold, Y., Roth, R.A., Wright, C.R., & Michael, W.B. (1991). The relationship of scores on the Educators Survey, a modified version of the Maslach Burnout Inventory, to three teaching-related variables for a sample of 132 beginning teachers. *Educational and Psychological Measurement, 51,* 429–438.

Green, D.E., & Walkey, F.H. (1988). A confirmation of the three-factor structure of the Maslach Burnout Inventory. *Educational and Psychological Measurement, 48,* 579–585.

Hargrove, D.S. (1989). Maslach Burnout Inventory, Second Edition. In J.C. Conoley & J.J. Cramer (Eds.), *The tenth mental measurements yearbook* (pp. 473–475). Lincoln, NE: Buros Institute of Mental Measurements.

Jones, J.W., & DuBois, D. (1987). A review of organizational stress assessment instruments. In L.R. Murphy & T.F. Schoenborn (Eds.), *Stress management in work settings* (pp. 47–66). Washington, DC: National Institute for Occupational Safety and Health.

Koeske, G.F., & Koeske, R.D. (1989). Construct validity of the Maslach Burnout Inventory: A critical review and reconceptualization. *Journal of Applied Behavioral Science, 25,* 131–144.

Lee, R.T., & Ashforth, B.E. (1990). On the meaning of Maslach's three dimensions of burnout. *Journal of Applied Psychology, 75,* 743–747.

Maslach, C. (1973, August). *"Detached concern" in health and social service professions.* Paper presented at the annual meeting of the American Psychological Association, Montreal.

Maslach, C. (1976). Burned-out. *Human Behavior, 5*(9), 16–22.

Maslach, C. (1982). *Burnout: The human cost of caring.* Englewood Cliffs, NJ: Spectrum.

Maslach, C., & Jackson, S.E. (1986). *Manual: Maslach Burnout Inventory.* Palo Alto, CA: Consulting Psychologists Press.

Meier, S.T. (1983). Toward a theory of burnout. *Human Relations, 36*(10), 899–910.

Nowack, K.M. (1986). Type A, hardiness, and psychological distress. *Journal of Behavioral Medicine, 9,* 537–548.

Odendal, F.J., & Van Wyk, J.D. (1988). Die taksering van die sindroom uitbranding. (Assessment of the burnout syndrome.) *South African Journal of Psychology, 18*(2), 41–49.

Pelsma, D.M., Roland, B., Tollefson, N., & Wigington, H. (1989). Parent burnout: Validation of the Maslach Burnout Inventory with a sample of mothers. *Measurement and Evaluation in Counseling and Development, 22*(2), 81–87.

Pierce, C.M., & Molloy, G.N. (1989). The construct validity of the Maslach Burnout Inventory: Some data from down under. *Psychological Reports, 65,* 1340–1342.

Powers, S., & Gose, K.F. (1986). Reliability and construct validity of the Maslach Burnout Inventory in a sample of university students. *Educational and Psychological Measurement, 46,* 251–255.

Quick, J.C., Murphy, J.R., & Hurrell, J.J. (Eds.). (1992). *Stress and well-being at work.* Washington, DC: American Psychological Association.

Rafferty, J.P., Lemkau, J.P., Purdy, R.R., & Rudisill, J.R. (1986). Validity of the Maslach Burnout Inventory for family practice physicians. *Journal of Clinical Psychology, 42,* 488–492.

Sandoval, J. (1989). Maslach Burnout Inventory, Second Edition. In J.C. Conoley & J.J. Cramer (Eds.), *The tenth mental measurements yearbook* (pp. 475–476). Lincoln, NE: Buros Institute of Mental Measurements.

Selye, H. (1956). *The stress of life.* New York: McGraw-Hill.

Schultz, D.P., & Schultz, S.E. (1990). *Psychology and industry today* (5th ed.). New York: Macmillan.

Sirigatti, S., & Stefanile, C. (1988). Per una scala di misurazione del burnout. (A scale for measuring burnout.) *Bollettino di Psicologia Applicata, 187–188,* 29–32.

Sirigatti, S., Stefanile, C., & Menoni, E. (1988). Per un adattamento del Maslach Burnout Inventory. (Toward an Italian version of the Maslach Burnout Inventory.) *Bollettino di Psicologia Applicata, 187–188,* 33–39.

Stout, J.K., & Williams, J.M. (1983). Comparison of two measures of burnout. *Psychological Reports, 53,* 283–289.

Van der Ploeg, H.M., Van Leeuwen, J.J., & Kwee, M.G. (1990). Burnout among Dutch psychotherapists. *Psychological Reports, 67,* 107–112.

Zimbardo, P.G. (1969). The human choice: Individuation, reason, and order versus deindividuation, impulse, and chaos. In W.J. Arnold & D. Levine (Eds.), *Nebraska symposium on motivation* (pp. 237–307). Lincoln: University of Nebraska.

Robert J. Drummond, Ed.D.

Program Director, Counselor Education, University of North Florida, Jacksonville, Florida.

MEASURES OF PSYCHOSOCIAL DEVELOPMENT

Gwen A. Hawley. Odessa, Florida: Psychological Assessment Resources, Inc.

Introduction

The Measures of Psychosocial Development (MPD), comprising an objective self-report assessment based on the theory of Erik Erikson, are used to assess personality development in adolescents and adults. The MPD underwent a series of refinements from the 1980 version to the current 1988 edition, which is the subject of this review.

The MPD was authored by Gwen A. Hawley. In constructing the test, Hawley attempted to write and select stage-specific items that reflected as closely as possible Erikson's developmental theory. The author also decided to have as separate scales the favorable and unfavorable attributes associated with each of the eight stages, resulting in 16 one-dimensional scales. Because Erikson included diverse subconstructs for each stage, an attempt was made to select items here that would represent all facets of a stage. Initially the items were generated from detailed definitions of each of the eight negative and eight positive scales. A total of 225 items were developed and presented in random order to a panel of five judges to determine the items' content validity. Of the 112 items eventually included on the MPD, 94 (83.9%) were agreed upon by the majority of the judges. The remaining 18 items were selected to adequately cover the 16 domains and to balance each scale with an equal number of items. Hawley (1988) states that the items were arranged on the test in "an appropriate psychological order," one that moved from the more objective items first to the more personal last (p. 14).

The MPD has an eighth-grade reading level and has been used with high school and college students and with adults up to 86 years (Hawley, 1988, p. 2). At the time of this writing, no special forms have been developed for visually impaired or other groups with handicaps, or for various cultural or ethnic groups such as Spanish-speaking individuals.

The MPD format consists of self-descriptive items, sometimes just a single adjective, other times a phrase containing a number of words. The items are presented in a test booklet. Individuals taking the test are asked to react to each statement on a 5-point scale, ranging from "very much like me" to "not at all like me." Test takers record their answers on a separate answer sheet. The MPD can be self- or examiner administered, individually or in groups. The directions appear on the front cover of the test booklet. If the test is going to be self-scored by the examinees, a trained examiner should be present.

Table 1

Scales Included on the MPD

Positive Scales	Negative Scales	Resolution Scales
P1 Trust	N1 Mistrust	R1 Trust vs. Mistrust
P2 Autonomy	N2 Shame & Doubt	R2 Autonomy vs. Shame & Doubt
P3 Initiate	N3 Guilt	R3 Initiative vs. Guilt
P4 Industry	N4 Inferiority	R4 Industry vs. Inferiority
P5 Identity	N5 Identity Confusion	R5 Identity vs. Identity Confusion
P6 Intimacy	N6 Isolation	R6 Intimacy vs. Isolation
P7 Generativity	N7 Stagnation	R7 Generativity vs. Stagnation
P8 Ego Integrity	N8 Despair	R8 Ego Integrity vs. Despair
TP Total Positive	TN Total Negative	TR Total Resolution

The MPD scales are listed in Table 1. Each subtest (Trust, Autonomy, etc.) contains seven items, each scored on a 5-point scale (0 to 4). The two-part answer sheet can be separated to expose the second sheet, which contains the blocks of items summed to get the score for each of the scales. Separate four-page profile forms are available for males and females, each including separate norms for individuals aged 13–17, 18–24, 25–49, and 50+ years. The raw scores for each scale can be plotted (each column represents a scale) and then translated into T-scores or percentile ranks presented in columns on the outside of the profile.

Practical Applications/Uses

The MPD is an interesting theoretical and practical instrument. The measures present an excellent tool for teaching Erikson's theory and for conducting research studies on it. The test provides an index of both the negative and positive poles of the eight stages as well as an attempt to investigate the resolution of each stage.

The test also can be valuable to clinicians. The measure it provides of adolescent and adult personality in the developmental framework of Erikson's theory can help clinicians understand the dynamics of client behavior.

Hawley (1988) states that, in addition to a measure of overall psychosocial health based on Erikson's criteria and measures of the eight positive and eight negative stage attitudes, the MPD provides estimates of the degree of resolution for the stage conflict (p. 2).

The author sees the test as a useful addition to a battery of personality tests for gaining a more detailed description of the examinee's personality dynamics as well as a general personality measure to assess his or her developmental stages. Developmental, clinical, consulting, and educational psychologists along with guidance and counseling professionals might find this test valuable in a variety of contexts.

Although the author states that the MPD would be sensitive to differences in overall psychosocial adjustment, the examiner needs to recognize that the test was not originally designed for use with clinical populations or normed on any population other than a "normal" one. Future research efforts with clinical populations classified by DSM-III-R (American Psychiatric Association, 1987) categories possibly could determine whether the test has validity for other than normal populations. A breakdown of the MPD normative sample's demographic characteristics is offered by gender, ethnic group, marital status, education, and region of residence. About two thirds of the sample were females, 92% were white, 52% were single, 55% had more than 12 years' education, and about two thirds lived in the South.

As noted previously, the MPD can be administered individually or in a group, either by the examinee him- or herself or with ease by a secretary, teacher, or trained proctor. The directions for taking the test appear on the test booklet; the general instructions for administering the MPD are discussed in the manual. The directions emphasize the importance of responding to each item. The MPD takes from 15 to 20 minutes for most respondents to complete.

The directions for scoring the MPD are described in the test manual. Each row represents a scale and consists of seven items. Each option to each item has a value of 0 to 4. The numerical values for the items are summed to arrive at the scale scores and then recorded in the appropriate spaces on the scoring sheet. The scoring procedures are simple and require little time to learn. Once familiar with the procedure, it would only take an examiner about 2 minutes to score the MPD. At present computer scoring is not available from the test publisher, but a scoring program would be easy to create if machine-scoring answer sheets were available for the MPD or a computer-administered form was available.

The interpretation of the MPD is norm referenced. The author provides guidelines for interpreting the scores and scales. Detailed descriptions of high scores are presented for the eight Positive and eight Negative scales but not the eight Resolution scales or the Total Positive, Total Negative, and Total Resolution scales. Hawley presents three case studies to illustrate how the test could be interpreted. Individuals with a background in educational and psychological testing and personality theory should have little trouble interpreting this test.

Technical Aspects

Information on the reliability and validity of the MPD is presented in the test manual. Test-retest coefficients, based on 108 adolescents with an interval of 2 to 13 weeks between testing, range from a low of .67 on Inferiority (N4) to a high of .91 on Total Negative (TN) and Identity vs. Identity Confusion (R5). The median coefficient was .82. Cronbach's alphas were computed on a sample of 372 adolescents, producing coefficients that ranged from a low of .65 on Trust (P1) to a high of .84 on Industry (P4), with a median coefficient of .74.

Multitrait-multimethod analysis is used to support the construct validity of the MPD. The intercorrelations of the scales using the test-retest data are presented along with the test-retest reliability coefficients and are designated as the monotrait-monomethod comparison. Hawley also presents correlations with the Inventory of Psychosocial Development (IPD; Constantinople, 1966, 1980) and the Self-Description

Questionnaire (SDQ; Boyd, 1966). The coefficients between similar scales on the IPD and the MPD measured by different methods ranged from .46 to .78, and on the MPD and the SDQ from .28 to .65 (monotrait-heteromethod comparison). The intercorrelations among the scales on the MPD are presented as well as the correlations among the MPD and other scales having neither trait nor method in common (heterotrait-heteromethod comparison). Hawley (1988) concludes that when the results from the monomethod-heteromethod cross-comparisons were studied, the revealing hierarchy of values met the Campbell and Fiske requirements consistently, with the exception of some heterotrait/same pole values for the negative scales that exceed the validities (p. 19).

The age trends for each of the MPD scales also were studied to determine age groupings for normative purposes and to provide additional evidence of the test's construct validity. The author concluded that the majority of the MPD Positive and Resolution scales showed an age trend of increasing scores through age 25, a leveling off of scores between ages 30–40, followed by a downward decline of scores in the 50+ age group. The age groupings were decided upon partly from the data on the means and standard deviations by age and partly from Erikson's theory. Four age groups were selected for calculating the norms: 13–17 (adolescents), 18–24 (young adults), 25–49 (adults), and 50+ (upper aged adults). Hawley reports that large gender differences were found on some scales such as Intimacy, and therefore separate norms were developed for males and females.

Critique

The MPD has potential as a useful assessment instrument for workers in the helping professions. The measures could serve as a valuable addition to other instruments in studying psychosocial development and developmental stages across the life span. Although easy to administer and score, a computerized scoring and interpretation system might enhance the MPD's value. The profile sheet could be embellished by including a brief description of the scales on one side and the specific age/gender profile on the other.

More work is needed to document the instrument's validity and reliability. Only two studies have been reported on the reliability of the test, both with relatively small numbers of individuals and both utilizing adolescents. If the author is going to report norms at different age levels, there needs to be more evidence of the reliability of the MPD across the age span. As the coefficients are used to judge the instrument's construct validity, larger samples across the four age groupings would provide more reliable evidence of construct validity. Comparing the MPD against tests that have not been widely used and have established validity and reliability presents only partial documentation. In looking at the heteromethod, possibly using some established subscales from other widely applied personality tests would be in order. It would be interesting to see the correlations between the scales on the MPD and the Marlowe-Crown Social Desirability Scale. The correlations between the MPD scales appear moderate, suggesting that the scales overlap. A question that needs to be revisited concerns whether the test has bipolar or one-dimensional scales. An individual could score high on both the negative and positive scales representing a stage. The manual presents no factor analytic information on the structure of the MPD items or scales. No means and standard deviations by gender and age level appear in the manual, although marked differences are reported by gender on certain scales. The author should present the standard error of measurement along with the means and standard deviations by gender for each of the four age groups for each scale and indicate where there are significant differences between the means.

The MPD has not been widely used in published studies as yet. This reviewer located only one study in Psych Scan and one in ERIC. Additional studies when reported in the literature might provide a better picture of the MPD's validity as a measure of psychosocial development.

The MPD has promise. This reviewer has found it useful in counseling individuals and understanding the dynamics of their psychosocial development, plus it is a good tool with which to teach Erikson's theory in educational psychology and appraisal classes. This reviewer has used it in a number of research studies, and the instrument has added an interesting dimension to the findings. Helping professionals should be cautious in their use of the MPD, however, until more evidence of its reliability and validity are demonstrated over the entire age span.

References

American Psychiatric Association. (1987). *Diagnostic and statistical manual of mental disorders* (3rd. ed. rev.). Washington, DC: Author.

Boyd, R.D. (1966). *Self-Description Questionnaire*. Madison, WI: University of Wisconsin.

Constantinople, A. (1966, 1980). *Inventory of Psychosocial Development (scales for stages 7 and 8)*. Unpublished manuscript.

Hawley, G.A. (1988). *Measures of Psychosocial Development: Professional manual*. Odessa, FL: Psychological Assessment Resources.

Ann H. Stoddard, Ed.D.

Professor of Education, University of North Florida, Jacksonville, Florida.

MEMORY ASSESSMENT SCALES

J. Michael Williams. Odessa, Florida: Psychological Assessment Resources, Inc.

Introduction

The Memory Assessment Scales (MAS; Williams, 1991) offer a newly developed battery of memory function tasks designed to assess three areas of cognitive function: a) attention, concentration, and short-term memory; b) learning and immediate memory; and c) memory following a delay. The MAS is intended for use specifically with normal and clinical populations. Using an examiner-respondent approach, the MAS provides exploration in the association of verbal and nonverbal tasks, using recall, recognition, and delayed formats.

The MAS consists of 12 subtests based on seven memory tasks. Five of the subtests involve repeated assessment of learned information. The subtests are List Learning, Prose Memory, List Recall, Verbal Span, Visual Span, Visual Recognition, Visual Reproduction, Names-Faces, Delayed List Recall, Delayed Prose Memory, Delayed Visual Recognition, and Delayed Names-Faces Recall. Even though the MAS specifically measures three areas of cognitive function pertinent in the assessment of memory, it also assesses recognition, intrusions during verbal learning recall, and retrieval strategies. Although the MAS is easy to administer, the time needed to do so varies with the respondent's performance on each task. For example, there are six allowable trials for the List Recall subtest. Time is determined for its administration by whether the respondent recalls all items on the first or the sixth trial.

The test author, J. Michael Williams, Ph.D., has several research interests in the area of assessment of memory functions and neuropsychological deficits. In 1987 he developed the Cognitive Behavior Rating Scales, a questionnaire constructed to assess cognitive and behavioral deficits in brain-injured patients. Williams developed the MAS over a 9-year period, from 1981 to 1990. Because of the complexity of the assessment of memory functions, the MAS was developed with two major considerations. First, the scales are designed to accommodate the various clinical situations and restrictions encountered in practice (e.g., bedridden patients), to provide easy transport of materials, and to make scoring procedures direct and easily calculated. Second, Williams designed the normative tables to facilitate the accuracy of professional opinions and decisions.

The MAS test materials consist of the stimulus card set, the record form, and the professional manual. The card set, in a convenient hardback loose-leaf folder, contains the following, in order of administration: Visual Span stimulus card, stimulus and distractor cards for the Visual Recognition task, stimulus and distractor cards for the Visual Reproduction task, and five series of 10 stimulus cards each for the Names-Faces task.

Descriptions of the MAS subtest item types follow here, in the order of their administration:

1. *List Learning.* This subtest consists of 12 common words, 3 for each of four categories (birds, cities, colors, and countries), that assess recall in six trials.

2. *Prose Memory.* The content of this subtest is a short story that the respondent is required to recall and answer nine questions about.

3. *List Recall.* This subtest requires the recall of words presented in List Learning. The respondent is asked to recall the words within semantic categories, as encouraged by the examiner. The respondent also is asked to select the words from a printed list of 24 words.

4. *Verbal Span.* The respondent is required to repeat a series of numbers, ranging from two to nine single digits. Two trials are presented for each series, and the subtest is discontinued after failure on both trials for a series. This procedure is then repeated, with the requirement that the subject repeat the numbers in reverse order. This subtest represents an auditory memory task.

5. *Visual Span.* The examiner points to a series of stars in specified sequences, and the respondent is asked to repeat the process. This subtest is a nonverbal analogue of the Verbal Span subtest.

6. *Visual Recognition.* This task requires recognition memory for geometric (nonverbal) designs. Five trials call for a "like/unlike" recognition response, and five require recognition of design from alternatives.

7. *Visual Reproduction.* With two trials that include an accompanying distractor task, the respondent is required to reproduce a geometric design.

8. *Names-Faces.* This subtest requires the respondent, in two trials, to learn the names of individuals who are portrayed in photographs and then accurately associate the names with the faces (verbal/nonverbal association).

9. *Delayed List Recall.* The respondent is required to recall spontaneously the words presented in the List Learning subtest. He or she also is asked to recall the words within semantic categories.

10. *Delayed Prose Memory.* In this subtest, details of the story presented in Prose Memory must be recalled. The score, however, is based on the nine questions about the story.

11. *Delayed Visual Recognition.* Out of 20 printed geometric designs, the respondent is required to identify the 10 designs presented earlier in the Visual Recognition subtest.

12. *Delayed Names-Faces Recall.* This subtest requires the respondent to recognize the correct names of individuals portrayed in the photographs presented earlier in the Names-Faces subtest.

The appropriate populations for the MAS are adults aged 18 through 90 years, both healthy individuals as well as brain-injured or diseased persons. Although participants should have normal or corrected vision and hearing, exceptions are made for brain-damaged or diseased subjects, as well as those suspected of or known to have neuropsychological deficits.

Practical Applications/Uses

The MAS is designed to describe an examinee's patterns of strengths and weaknesses in memory abilities. It is potentially useful in clinical, research, and educational situations. The instrument also is ideal in individual testing for guidance and educational placement purposes and for making educational recommendations. In clinical situations, psychologists can use the MAS to examine neurosurgery patients in an office, research laboratory, or at bedside. In addition to these applications, the MAS can be used for neuropsychological assessment, vocational assessment, and gerontological evaluation.

The entire MAS can be administered in a single session of approximately 1 to 1½ hours. The time needed for instructions, examples, and the 12 tests, plus ample rest breaks, varies according to the number of trials that the respondent needs. Even though the designs for Visual Recognition are shown for only 15 seconds, the respondent's answers are not timed. The manual provides straightforward directions for administering each subtest. Though the author recommends that a qualified psychologist administer and score the MAS, a trained person with a background in psychological testing can administer and score it as well. On the other hand, interpretation requires professional training in neuropsychology, clinical psychology, or the psychological theories and principles of memory functioning.

The examiner should be very familiar with the testing procedures and directions, practicing at least twice prior to actual testing, to ensure that the standardized procedures are followed precisely. It is recommended that the test environment be comfortable, quiet, and free from distraction. It is preferable that no interruptions occur during the administration.

A professional should require only a few minutes to learn how to score the MAS. Directions as well as cautions for scoring each subtest are explicit, and one should encounter no difficulty in following the directions, as examples are provided in the manual. Scoring involves several steps. Appendix A in the manual has an illustration of a completely scored MAS record form and includes the subtest profile, verbal process scores, summary scales, and a sample of background information, referral information, behavioral observations, and test situations. Scoring is not intricate, based on the precise details that must be followed exactly. For example, in the List Learning subtest, the number of words correctly remembered for each of the trials is added. The Intrusion score is determined by recording the number of words included that were not in the learning list. The Clusters score is indicated by an asterisk when words belonging to the same semantic category are recalled consecutively. The List Clustering is derived by adding all of the times the respondent clustered words and then dividing by the total words correctly recalled. If the scorer is very familiar with the subtests, scoring can be done after each subtest, reserving completion of the composite scores for after the administration of the test.

The MAS was designed to answer questions about a subject's fundamental level of cognitive ability and about the diagnosis of memory disorder resulting from brain injury or illness. The MAS subtests permit the examiner to analyze and evaluate performances in terms of short-term, verbal, and nonverbal (figural, visual-spatial) memory abilities in a recall and recognition format. For accurate interpretation, appropriate normative tables are critical. The normative tables, using normative data for U.S. census–matched samples, compare individuals by age and education. Poor scores suggest general memory impairment or are at least a function of "nuisance" variables known to affect performance.

Interpretation of the MAS scores is not difficult for an examiner familiar with the principles of memory functioning. Individuals with less training and knowledge, by using the tables and case studies carefully, should be able to make minimal interpretations of scores derived from the subtests. The extensive norms are helpful in this regard. Low motivation and anxiety also are taken into consideration when interpreting the MAS scores, and the examiner should determine what each of these inconsistencies indicates.

Technical Aspects

Technical characteristics of the MAS are summarized in the manual and reported in detail. The manual provides meticulous information from actual field administration of the MAS, such as subgroup means, standard deviations, validity data, generalizability coefficients, and standard errors of measurement.

Normative data were collected using 843 subjects recruited through newspaper advertisements and announcements to local community groups. Of the total sample, 677 scores were used for all subtests.

Subjects without a history of neurological disease or chronic substance abuse participated in the norming process. Using a random stratified sampling procedure, a subsample of 467 subjects was selected to reflect the "distribution of the U. S. population, classified by age and gender and by age and education characteristics" (Williams, 1991, p. 19). Regression analysis examining the influence of demographic characteristics on the MAS scores was used to determine two additional groups: age decade ($N = 843$) and age and education ($N = 843$), which was divided into four separate age groups—18–49 years, 50–59 years, 60–69 years, and 70+ years. These four groups were subdivided into three groups according to education: less than 12 years, high school products, and post–high school education.

The test author reports four types of validity for the MAS: convergent, discriminant, factorial, and group differentiation. Convergent and discriminant validity were determined by correlating the MAS scores of the 677 subjects who were administered every subtest. Three predictions about the patterns and correlation results were supported: short-term memory and attention were highly correlated, subtests of verbal memory were highly correlated, and scores from the Names-Faces subtest were moderately correlated with visual and verbal memory subtests.

To demonstrate factorial validity, analyses were derived from 471 normal and 52 neurologically impaired subjects. The normal sample revealed a two-factor solution when looking at immediate memory and marker variables. The variables of Verbal Comprehension and Perceptual Organization, inferred to be general memory and intelligence factors, accounted for 27.9% of the variance, whereas the attention/concentration factor accounted for 22.8% of the variance. Analysis of the neurologically impaired sample yielded a three-factor solution. Perceptual Organization, Visual Span, Visual Reproduction, and Immediate Visual Recognition accounted for 23.9% of the variance. Verbal Span and Visual Span accounted for 23.8% of the variance. List Recall, Immediate Prose Recall, and Immediate Names-Faces accounted for 18.8% of the variance. The manual discusses the factor analysis further in detail.

Group differentiations were conducted by comparing the MAS normative sample to 110 subjects with known neurological impairment from five different medical settings across the United States. Results showed that the neurologically impaired scored lower than the normal group on all MAS subtests and summary scores. This finding corresponds to predicted patterns for the impaired group.

Because some of the subtests do not lend themselves well to traditional internal consistency statistics, reliability coefficients were reported as generalizability coefficients. Three normative bases were computed for all scores except Verbal Process Scores. These were omitted because of the nature of their dichotomous scoring. The test-retest method was used, the time interval being approximately 6 months. Thirty subjects from the standardization sample were used, ranging in age from 20 to 89 years. Coefficients for the MAS subtests ranged from .70 to .95 across the three normative bases. Other coefficients were Summary Scale, .86 to .95; and Global Memory Scale, .90 to .95. In each instance, the coefficients indicated that the MAS showed consistently high levels of generalizability for the three normative bases.

For the drawings, two studies of interexaminer reliability were conducted, one sample being psychology professors and graduate students who had no formal training in the administration of the MAS, and the second being examiners ($N = 10$) who had experience in the administration and scoring of the MAS. Generalizability coefficients for the first group were .95 for Drawing A and .96 for Drawing B; coefficients for the second group were .98 for A and .99 for B.

The standard error of measurement was calculated for the MAS subtests, Summary Scores, and Global Memory Score and across the three normative bases. Standard deviations for the subtests, Summary Scales, and Global Memory Score were 3, 15, and 15, respectively. Across the the normative groups, the $SE\hat{}_M$ ranges were as follows: Subtests, .67 to 1.64; Summary Scores, 4.24 to 5.61; and Global Memory Score, 3.35 to 3.67. Significant differences between the Global Memory Score and IQ, differences among Summary Scores, and differences among subtests scores were obtained and calculated at the .05 level of confidence.

Critique

The MAS provides a direct measure of adults' memory abilities. Its strengths include its ease of administration and scoring, and the card set (in a stable looseleaf binder) that facilitates application in various testing situations. From a research point of view, the MAS has proven its utility as an instrument that distinguishes between the memory impaired and normal individuals. Also among the scale's assets are its development based on theories of and research in memory functioning, its emphasis on memory functioning variables, and its potential applications in the clinical setting for the neurologically impaired. An additional positive feature lies in the technical support provided through research studies. This reviewer's lone concern relates to the generalizability studies that used a low number of subjects. Although the coefficients were high and in line with expectations, one would feel more comfortable with the results if a larger sample were used.

There is a wealth of normative information available in the MAS for a number of age-education groups; it is therefore possible to compare populations using the three bases. The test samples also use two distinct types of content formats, the verbal items and the drawings. Again, as the MAS was designed with ease of application in mind, it is practical to use it in many different clinical/medical settings where a more complex assessment would be out of the question.

In sum, the MAS is capable of providing good information on memory functioning. Caution should be exercised in score interpretation, using well-trained personnel or a psychologist with a background in the principles of memory functioning. Although the MAS appears to be well validated for its intended use, it may have competition with the Wechsler Memory Scale–Revised if the latter has verified the validity and reliability studies with larger samples.

References

This list includes text citations and suggested additional reading.

Cermak, L.S. (1982). *Human memory and amnesia*. Hillsdale, NJ: Erlbaum.

Larrabee, G.J., Kane, R.L., Schuck, J.R., & Francis, D.J. (1985). Construct validity of various memory testing procedures. *Journal of Clinical and Experimental Neuropsychology, 7*, 239–250.

Mayes, A.R. (1986). Learning and memory disorder and their assessment. *Neuropsychologia, 24*, 25–39.

Squire, L.R. (1986). Mechanisms of memory. *Science, 232*, 1612–1619.

Wechsler, D. (1987). *A manual for the Wechsler Memory Scale–Revised*. San Antonio, TX: Psychological Corporation.

Williams, J.M. (1991). *Memory Assessment Scales: Professional manual*. Odessa, FL: Psychological Assessment Resources.

Daryl Sander, Ph.D.

Professor Emeritus, School of Education, University of Colorado, Boulder, Colorado.

Shayn Smith, Ph.D.

Assistant Director of Career Planning Programs and Testing Director, Counseling and Career Services, University of Colorado, Boulder, Colorado.

MILWAUKEE ACADEMIC INTEREST INVENTORY

Andrew R. Baggaley. Los Angeles, California: Western Psychological Services.

Introduction

The Milwaukee Academic Interest Inventory (MAII) is a self-report instrument that assesses a student's interest in six major fields of academic study. The instrument was developed by Andrew R. Baggaley in 1963, and no revision has been reported since.

The MAII is designed for use with college freshman and sophomores and college-bound high school students. The inventory contains 150 items, which the respondent marks as true, false, or undecided, and it can be completed in 20–30 minutes. No reading level of the items is reported.

The author obtained the six major field variables used in the MAII by "criterion keying." The instrument was administered to 858 freshmen entering the University of Wisconsin at Milwaukee. Two and a half years later, 313 of these students remained at the university. The percentage of "true" responses for students in a particular field then were compared to the group's percentage of "true" responses. Items showing a difference significant at the 10% level were included for a particular field variable. The six "field variables" and the academic areas they encompass follow:

Physical Science—physics, chemistry, mathematics, engineering (112 items)

Healing Occupations—medicine, medical technology, pharmacy (41 items)

Behavioral Science—psychology, sociology, anthropology, social work (47 items)

Economics—economics, commerce (91 items)

Humanities–Social Studies—political science, history, philosophy, languages, journalism (65 items)

Elementary Education (112 items)

Practical Applications/Uses

The Milwaukee Academic Interest Inventory is designed to help college freshmen and sophomores and college-bound high school students assess their interests in selected major fields of study.

Although students mark "true," "false," or "undecided" for each of the 150 items, they are cautioned not to answer "undecided" to too many. The manual suggests scoring the answer sheet only if the respondent has marked "true" or "false" to at least 125 of the 150 items. A scoring key is used to obtain raw scores for each of the six major academic fields, then raw scores are converted to stanine scores.

A discriminant interpretation graph allows the user to plot a respondent's answer patterns relative to those of students majoring in 19 different areas (i.e., accounting, biology, business administration, chemistry, communications, elementary education, engineering, English, French, history, marketing, mathematics, medical technology, nursing, political science, prelaw, psychology, sociology, speech).

Technical Aspects

As noted previously, the Milwaukee Academic Interest Inventory originally was given to 858 freshman entering the University of Wisconsin at Milwaukee in the 1950s. A search of the registrar's records 2½ years later indicated 313 of those students were still enrolled at the university. Their fields of concentration were "criterion keyed" with the items in the instrument, resulting in the six fields previously mentioned. According to Baggaley, this process truly reflects the predictive validity of the MAII.

The manual reports Baggaley's cross-validation studies using the MAII with students at two different universities who indicated their intended major at the time. Results showed modest levels of concurrent validity for the instrument.

The manual presents correlations between MAII fields and scale scores on the Kuder Preference Record (Vocational), plus correlations between MAII scales and scores on the Strong Vocational Interest Blank. Most of the reported correlations indicate relationships between scales that support construct validity.

Alpha reliability coefficients derived from entering college freshmen ($N = 185$) range from .72 to .93. Test-retest reliability over 3 months ($N = 50$) ranges from .85 to .94.

Two factor analyses were done on the 150 MAII items using 382 high school juniors and 2,660 university freshmen. Results suggested the interest item variables of Commercial vs. Nurturant interests and Natural Science vs. Social Studies interests. The discriminant interpretation graph of 19 fields of concentration resulted from these factor analyses.

Critique

Although this inventory shows much promise, it could be improved by providing users with more data pertaining to criterion-related validity, utilizing criteria such as grades in courses or persistence in fields of academic interest. Predictive validity data are especially needed, as users might wish to know the probability of success in future employment or specialized training leading to specific occupations.

Because counseling clients often find the interpretation of stanine scores confusing, the test developer might wish to explore the use of percentile ranks or a T-score, both of which are more easily interpreted and commonly used.

The items of the inventory are easily understood and appear quite transparent to those taking the inventory. Thus anxiety related to test taking may be reduced at the possible cost of "fakeability" among respondents.

The Milwaukee Academic Interest Inventory deserves to be used, especially in research endeavors that will strengthen its claims for validity. It is easily administered, can be readily hand scored, and is capable of stimulating career-field exploration among the students who take it.

References

Baggaley, A.R. (1973). *Milwaukee Academic Interest Inventory manual.* Los Angeles: Western Psychological Services.

Norman Abeles, Ph.D.

Professor of Psychology and Director, Neuropsychological Laboratory and Psychological Clinic, Michigan State University, East Lansing, Michigan.

Daniel M. Spica, Ph.D.

Psychologist, Hillside Hospital, Long Island Jewish Medical Center, Glen Oaks, New York.

MINI INVENTORY OF RIGHT BRAIN INJURY

Patricia A. Pimental and Nancy A. Kingsbury. Austin, Texas: PRO-ED, Inc.

Introduction

The Mini Inventory of Right Brain Injury (MIRBI) is primarily a paper-and-pencil test designed to assess neurocognitive impairment implicating the right cerebral hemisphere. Based on Pimental's classification system describing disorders of processing (Pimental & Kingsbury, 1989b), the manual lists six main applications for the inventory: a) to identify patients exhibiting deficits in functional domains known to be compromised by right-brain injury; b) to rate the severity of injury to the right cerebral hemisphere; c) to assess specific deficits based on the authors' classification system; d) to describe right-hemispheric strengths and weaknesses in service of treatment planning; e) to track improvement of right hemisphere recovery from treatment; and f) to facilitate, as a standardized device, research of right-hemisphere brain injury (Pimental & Kingsbury, 1989a).

This test evolved from a dissertation by the senior author, Patricia A. Pimental, who is currently Director of Psychological Services and Assistant Professor in the Department of Physical Medicine and Rehabilitation at the University of Illinois College of Medicine in Chicago. The second author, Nancy Kingsbury, is a speech pathologist at the Department of Otolaryngology–Head and Neck Surgery at the University of Illinois College of Medicine.

Until recently, there has been considerably more public focus on the brain's left rather than right hemisphere. In fact, the right hemisphere often has been called the "silent" hemisphere. As Lezak (1983) points out, the left hemisphere has been described as the dominant hemisphere in both right- and left-handed individuals. It is common to associate the left hemisphere with verbal functions while associating the right with nonverbal functions, though there are exceptions to these generalizations. Neuropsychologists have long acknowledged the contribution of the right hemisphere to a wide array of functions. However, few if any efforts have taken place to create a test battery dedicated solely toward the screening of right cerebral impairment. The MIRBI attempts to fill this gap.

The test is normed on 30 right-brain-injured adults, and comparisons are made with 13 left-brain-injured adults and 30 normal control participants. The right-brain-injured standardization sample consists of 40% females and 60% males, with a mean age of 63.9 and 11.7 years of education, respectively. The mean days of post-onset brain injury was 157.7. Eleven of the right-brain-injured patients had right anterior brain damage, while another 11 were classified as having right posterior brain damage. Eight patients had right subcortical brain damage. The 30 normal participants were matched for age, education, and sex with the right-brain-injured sample. Excluded from the sample were individuals with serious vision or hearing problems, mental retardation, major psychiatric problems, difficulty with English as a second or nonnative language, and medical problems secondary to alcoholism.

The MIRBI is designed for adults, and the manual states no age limit. The authors do point out that there is a need to collect another standardization sample, which should contain a larger number of African-American participants as well as Hispanic participants who are fluent in English as a first or second language.

The inventory consists of an examiner's manual, the test booklet, and a report form designed to share results with other professionals. Materials needed are a pencil, paper, a caliper, and a quarter. There are no time limits, and testing time is expected to range from 15 to 30 minutes. Examiners need to be familiar with the test manual. Because this is a screening device, the authors suggest that the test can be administered by a range of examiners who have experience in test administration. In addition to neuropsychologists and clinical psychologists, appropriate examiners may include specially trained nurses, audiologists, rehabilitation specialists, neurologists, physical therapists, and others.

The entire inventory is composed of 27 items, 5 of which require subjective examiner ratings. All patients should receive every item, presented in the following order:

Visual Processing
 1. Visual Scanning (2 items)
 2. Integrity of Gnosis (3 items)
 3. Integrity of Body Image [neglect] (1 item—examiner observation)
 4. Visuoverbal Processing
    a) Reading (2 items)
    b) Writing (3 items)
 5. Visuosymbolic Processing [reverse serial sevens] (1 item)
 6. Integrity of Praxis (1 item)

Language Processing
 7. Affective Language (2 items)
 8. Higher Level Language Skills [abstraction, humor, expressive abilities] (8 items)

Emotion and Affect Processing
 9. Affect (1 item—examiner observation)

General Behavior and Psychic Integrity
 10. General Behavior (3 items—examiner observation)

Examiners interested in spot checks can obtain a Right-Left Differentiation Subscale Score, which consists of 10 items.

The front and back cover of the test booklet include the summary and profile sheet. There is space provided for pertinent patient information, a record of scores, a section for the Right-Left Differentiation Subscale Score, and a section providing the MIRBI severity profile. Severity ranges from profound (0–7) to normal (38–43). Intermediate categories are severe, moderate-severe, moderate, mild-moderate, and mild.

The MIRBI report form is an additional sheet that provides a brief identification section and a screening summary, which the examiner can complete by circling the relevant performance level and relevant right-hemisphere syndrome description of relevant disorders. In addition, there is a section for listing relative strengths and specific long- and short-term treatment goals.

Practical Applications/Uses

The purposes of this test are to evaluate the strengths and weaknesses of specific skill areas. According to the authors, the MIRBI measures disorders of visual processing, language processing, and emotion and affect, as well as disorders of general behavior and psychic integrity. The test, while a screening measure, is designed to aid in the overall diagnostic effort. Since the MIRBI is a relatively new test, there is as yet no information on possible other uses. It is certainly possible, however, that tests of right-hemisphere functioning could be used to assess aspects of normal aging (LaRue, 1992). At this point in the MIRBI's development, it would appear that it is most useful for post-acute inpatients who have suffered brain impairment. The emphasis on treatment planning and monitoring in the list of primary uses suggests that this inventory serves best as a tool facilitating the transition from secondary to tertiary care for brain-injured patients. Thus, the greatest utility would be for hospital and trauma rehabilitation settings rather than outpatient settings. However, further use of this instrument is needed to evaluate specific advantages and disadvantages. Certainly neuropsychologists, clinical psychologists, and rehabilitation specialists will be most interested in this new test.

At the authors' recommendation, this individually administered assessment should be administered by health professionals (not necessarily mental health professionals) familiar with the attributes of brain-impaired individuals. The directions for administration are unambiguous, and the actual spoken instructions are scripted in the test booklet. Test administration is purposely designed to be easy. These reviewers do foresee problems, however, in some of the inventory's subjective rating systems suggesting more precision than is reasonable for a variety of examiners (with varying levels of expertise and in a variety of clinical settings). For example, general expressive abilities must be rated as fluent and grammatical 0%–50%, 50%–70%, 70%–90%, or 90%–100% of the time. This problem may be compounded by the requirement of a number of subjective ratings; they make up 4 of the 10 items contributing to the Right-Left Differentiation Subscale Score. The manual recommends that all subsections generally be administered in the order given in the test booklet. Except for a spot check on the Right-Left Differentiation Subscale, the inventory should be administered in its entirety.

Instructions for scoring are designed to be simple, and items on subsections are scored as either correct, partially correct, or incorrect. However, scoring procedures are not always straightforward. For example, in the single-item section labeled "Integrity of Body Image," the examiner is asked to identify left unilateral neglect, operationally defined as "He/she is not able to utilize perceptual cues from the left side of the body and to integrate these with environmental cues from the left side of the body" (Test Booklet, p. 4). The manual does not further elaborate on this criterion. Also, subjective ratings that require a judgment on the regularity with which a patient understands conversational language may be difficult to anchor precisely within the 0%–50%, 50%–70%, 70%–90%, or 90%–100% categorizations. Similar doubts arise (although to a lesser degree by virtue of their binary scoring nature) regarding the remaining subjective ratings in the inventory, such as the tests of "Psychic Integrity" that require judgments of impulsivity, distractibility, and the extent of eye contact (0 or 1 point).

Nevertheless, the hand-scoring process takes only a few minutes of tallying, converting to percentages, and transferring the data to the summary profile tables on the outside of the examination booklet. Three types of scores are derived from the raw data: section percentage scores (percent correct), the Right-Left Differentiation Subscale score, and the Overall Severity Rating score. It should be noted that the percentage scores reflect the proportion of correct earned points for that subsection, and two thirds of the scores have a ceiling of 3 or less points. For example, for the Emotional and Affect subscale percentage score, only 1 point is possible, which is then divided by 1 to produce the percentage score. Therefore, only 0% or 100% is possible for that subscale percentage score. Furthermore, the *same item* is used (and divided by 1) for a separate subscale percentage score called Affect.

The Right-Left Differentiation Subscale Score, derived from 10 of the 27 test items (11 possible points), is intended to provide the truly discriminating aspect of the inventory insofar as distinguishing hemispheric asymmetries of impairment. The Overall Severity Rating score provides a summary of the total points received on the entire test.

Interpretation of the MIRBI appears two-staged: first, the Right-Left Differentiation Subscale Score is obtained, then a global rating of severity is gained from the MIRBI Overall Severity Profile score. Unfortunately, although the authors contend that Overall Severity Rating score provides the examiner "with the severity level of the patient's right hemisphere involvement" (Pimental & Kingsbury, 1989a, p. 30), it includes items that many neuropsychologists would consider nonspecific to right-hemisphere processing (e.g., visual scanning, expressive and receptive language, reverse serial sevens, general agitation, etc.). Moreover, no effort was made to standardize the severity ratings according external criteria. This last point may ultimately undermine the integrity of the MIRBI as a psychometric device; because the level of impairment severity of the standardization sample was not assessed or reported, users have no assurance that the inventory did more than discriminate the more impaired patients from the less impaired ones, irrespective of lesion site.

The Right-Left Differentiation Subscale Score was intended as a simple cutting score: one interprets 9 points or less (out of 11 possible) as indicative of right-brain injury. The Severity Profile is based solely on a normal probability plot (without validation) and, as mentioned above, classifies the patient with one of the following labels: Profound, Severe, Moderate-Severe, Moderate, Mild-Moderate, Mild, Normal. These reviewers suggest that some effort should have been made to confirm that these ratings reflect clinically relevant phenomenology.

Despite the authors' caveats in a two-paragraph section titled "Tests Don't Diagnose," the two primary MIRBI scores could invite liberal interpretation of a) what side of the brain is malfunctioning (Right-Left Differentiation Subscale Score) and b) what is the extent of damage (Severity Profile score). As may be apparent already from the fact that the Right-Left Differentiation Subscale Score employs only 10 of the test questions, this scoring system allows for a scenario wherein a patient may miss a *perfect* score on the inventory by only 2 points— such as by failing to sound sufficiently "happy" on command (item 14) and failing to make eye contact to the examiner's satisfaction (item 27)—and still obtain a rating on the differentiation subscale suggesting "a strong probability of right brain damage." This judgment then could be combined with a severity rating of "Normal." Such a contradictory system seems problematic.

Technical Aspects

The manual points out that a 63-item MIRBI was administered to 50 patients with documented right-hemisphere lesions from 18 pilot sites. Initial summary statistics provided data with regard to means, frequencies, and percentages. For the early phase of standardization, the standardized alpha was .91. Item analysis was performed, as was a frequency table for each item to determine percent failure for each. After selecting items considered most sensitive to right-brain injury, 27 were chosen for the final MIRBI. Following this, 30 patients with a diagnosis of right-brain damage (of unspecified severity) were studied (along with matched normals and left-brain-damaged subjects). The independent variable was total points correct, and comparisons between the groups were made. The effects of days post-onset of brain injury, age, education, and sex were partialed out, after which the data were analyzed to assess differences between the groups based on total MIRBI score using a two-way ANCOVA [sex (male, female) group (right, normal, left) × (age as covariant)] with total MIRBI points as the dependent variable. The manual reports a borderline significant difference between right-brain-injured female and left-brain-injured female groups.

At the time of this writing, the MIRBI stands incompletely validated and standardized. The manual identifies a need to collect further standardization samples and points out that as the true range of severity of the right-brain-injured patients is not available, the standardization of the MIRBI may not be a representative sample of right-hemisphere-impaired adults. Although a total score of 38–43 points is interpreted as normal, 37 points or below indicate a brain injury and a Right-Left Differentiation Subscale Score of 9 points or below (11 points possible) indicates right-brain damage. Though data from one set of participants (13 left brain injured, 30 right brain injured, 30 normals) were used to find these cutting scores, the scores were not applied to a second patient validation sample to determine discriminant validity. Thus, a diagnostic accuracy of 99.97% is reported in the MIRBI manual, though this figure represents the subjects used to derive the classification cutting scores.

Another major concern has to do with whether the MIRBI actually assesses right-hemisphere impairment. The authors assure the reader that they fulfilled requirements of content validity "through an extensive and careful survey of the literature on right brain injury and subsequent right hemisphere deficit syndromes prior to item selection" (Pimental, 1989, p. 29). Nevertheless, some neuropsychologists may question whether the visual scanning tasks, asking patients the name of their middle finger, left hand astereognosis without right hand trials, reading, and so on tap skills truly specific to the right hemisphere. To many neuropsychologists, the suitability of these items may remain an empirical question.

The procedures used to develop the MIRBI cannot fully shed light on this topic because no effort was made to control for severity of cerebral dysfunction in the right- and left-brain-damaged groups. It is still possible that the MIRBI measures severity of brain damage exclusively. In fact, there is a reported selection bias away from severe left-hemisphere impairment; in selecting the 13 left-brain-lesioned individuals, subjects exhibiting aphasia greater than "moderate" were rejected to avoid any confounding effects of expressive and receptive language difficulties. This is an understandable choice, but as a result, variance in the items contributing to the right-left differentiation and severity profile scores may reflect the degree of task difficulty or nonspecific pathology irrespective of etiology. The apparently strong ceiling effect for normal controls further diminishes the opportunity to address this concern.

An additional but more minor concern is that the manual reports interrater reliability range on the items from $r = .65$ to $r = .87$. The fact that these coefficients were calculated from only two raters on only four patients makes these results somewhat difficult to interpret.

Critique

Historically psychologists have reserved some amount of "leeway" for screening devices, rationalizing that the time saved by a particular measure does much to counterbalance the potential misclassification of signs and symptoms and, further, that these misclassifications can be corrected in subsequent assessments (provided the screening device errs towards overinclusiveness). Perhaps the determination of how much leeway to grant a measure is best done by individual professionals considering their specific applications and circumstances.

In the case of the Mini Inventory of Right Brain Injury, the device is thought provoking to the extent that it attempts a somewhat systematic assessment of functional domains seldom tested in bedside examinations (i.e., comprehension and generation of affective prosody, understanding humor, etc.). Regardless of the lateralizing implications of these behavioral deficits, assessing these functions could provide potentially useful descriptive information for caregivers and families of brain-injured persons.

The advent of the MIRBI marks a beginning for incorporating novel questions into an easily administered screening device; perhaps with further development, refinement, and additional standardization, such a device eventually may be marketed.

References

LaRue, A. (1992). *Aging and neuropsychological assessment*. New York: Plenum.

Lezak, M.D. (1983). *Neuropsychological assessment*. New York: Oxford University Press.

Pimental, P.A., & Kingsbury, N.A. (1989a). *Mini Inventory of Right Brain Injury manual*. Austin, TX: PRO-ED.

Pimental, P.A., & Kingsbury, N.A. (1989b). *Neuropsychological aspects of right brain injury*. Austin, TX: PRO-ED.

Nancy E. Abrams, Ph.D.
Consultant, Personnel Management and Measurement, Fairport, New York.

MINIMUM ESSENTIALS TEST

William K. Rice, Jr., Thomas R. Guskey, Carole Lachman Perlman, and Marion F. Rice. Coralville, Iowa: The American College Testing Program.

Introduction

The Minimum Essentials Test (MET) is designed for the measurement of minimum competence in the basic skills of reading, language, mathematics, and writing, and the application of these to life situations. It is a component of the Comprehensive Assessment Program, which is a package of tests designed for the evaluation of student growth from kindergarten through adulthood. The MET may be used on its own or as part of the total Comprehensive Assessment Program.

The Minimum Essentials Test was developed by William K. Rice, Jr. of the Chicago Public Schools, Thomas R. Guskey of the University of Kentucky, Carole Lachman Perlman of the University of Illinois at Chicago, and Marion F. Rice of the Chicago Public Schools. John W. Wick of Northwestern University and Jeffrey K. Smith of Rutgers University served as program authors. The test was developed in response to the growing place in school curricula for basic skills. These programs have arisen as a reaction to the complaint of many employers that new high school graduates lack the basic skills necessary for many types of work.

The authors began by developing a list of basic skills objectives and using them as the basis for the test plan. They derived the objectives from reviews of the literature and reviews of minimum competence standards developed by various states and local school districts, as well as from interviews with public school curriculum specialists and personnel executives in business and industry. Unfortunately, neither of the test manuals contains the objectives.

Based upon these objectives, the authors developed approximately 800 test items with a reading level of sixth grade or lower and a vocabulary level of sixth to ninth grade. The authors do not indicate, however, what method they employed to measure these levels. The items went through a series of tryouts and revisions. According to the test manuals, extensive analyses including internal consistency, item difficulty, point-biserial correlations, correlations with other tests, and Rasch analyses were done as part of this process, but results are not presented anywhere in any of the manuals. Neither is there any information on the test's degree of speededness. In addition to the series of item tryouts and pilots, the test was reviewed by a panel of educators and content specialists; however, the size and composition of the panel are not reported.

Three alternate forms of the MET were developed. The teacher's manual contains a description of the item types in each form. There are some differences in the numbers of items by type in the various forms. No information is presented (i.e., alternate form intercorrelations or item analyses) to indicate why these forms should be considered parallel. As no empirical data appear for Forms B and C, this reviewer will limit all comments to Form A of the test, for which normative data are provided.

The test manuals are quite confusing on the subject of norms. The teacher's manual (Rice et al., 1981) reports that in 1979 and 1980 the test was standardized on a nationwide sample of 157 school districts (141 public and 16 nonpublic) covering 528 schools. It also states that the test was administered at 35 military bases. The technical manual (American Testronics, 1981), which actually contains the norms, reports that the standardization was done in the fall of 1979 with students ($N = 16,787$) from 56 school districts. Two problems arise in reviewing these materials: It is unclear whether the normative sample included 56 or 157 school districts, and the manuals do not indicate whether the samples from the military bases, mentioned in the teacher's manual, are included in the norms. Because of these discrepancies, it is difficult to evaluate the norming sample.

The MET has been designed to evaluate the basic skills of students in Grades 8–12 as well as those of adult examinees. Materials consists of a reusable test booklet and a machine- or hand-scorable answer sheet. The test is suitable for group administration.

The test consists of three separately timed sections: Basic Skills, Life Skills, and an optional writing test. The Basic Skills test presents 74 four-option multiple-choice items, administered with a 45-minute time limit. The Life Skills section is made up of 50 four-choice multiple-choice items covering seven content areas; this section also has a 45-minute time limit. These items require the test taker to apply the basic skills to situations drawn from life experiences. The optional writing test presents the test taker with a series of three cartoon drawings that tell a story. He or she must write a paragraph describing the story in 20 minutes.

The Basic Skills test consists of 24 reading, 26 language, and 24 mathematics items. Items have been classified into the following learning objective areas: *Reading*—literal comprehension, inferential comprehension, main idea, and context clues; *Language*—capitalization, punctuation, and grammar; and *Mathematics*—addition, subtraction, multiplication, and division of whole numbers, fractions and decimals, percents, and fraction/decimal conversions. An overall Basic Skills score is produced, as well as separate scores in reading, mathematics, and language.

The Life Skills test consists of 7 communication (e.g., letter writing), 26 finance (e.g., balancing a checkbook), 7 government and law (e.g., interpreting a lease agreement), 7 health, safety, and nutrition (e.g., interpreting directions for taking medicine), 9 occupation (e.g., completing job applications), and 9 transportation items (e.g., interpreting schedules). Some items cover more than one content and/or skill area. For this portion of the test, only an overall Life Skills score is produced.

Practical Applications/Uses

The MET was designed for educators in school districts. The manuals discuss a number of uses for the test, including the following:

1. Identification of students in grades below high school in need of remediation in specific basic skill areas or the application of those skills, which would enable a school district to make an early identification of students in need of remediation in this area;
2. Use as one criterion for graduation from high school, in districts where there is a desire to ensure that all graduates possess basic skills;
3. Evaluation of the effectiveness of a school district's curriculum in the basic skills and application areas covered by the test;
4. Evaluation of success in teaching basic skills in a specific class or school building; and
5. Use as a final examination for a basic skills course.

Although the authors do not discuss the use of the test by employers, this is possible. Employers might use the MET as a portion of the selection process to ensure that new employees possess job-related basic skills. It also could be used to identify those employees in need of remedial basic skills training that would improve job performance. These applications deserve some consideration in light of the growing problems of employers in identifying workers who possess the necessary basic skills.

The content of the MET is equally appropriate for students in Grades 8 through 12 and adults. Norms, however, are presented only for Grades 8 through 12, and there is no indication that this test would be appropriate for younger students. No instructions appear for administering this test to disabled students or adults; therefore, the MET should not be used with these groups.

The test administration instructions are well written and especially easy to follow. The directions include detailed guidance for preparation as well as for the actual administration. This includes assembly of test materials, scheduling, proctor instructions, and physical room layout. The test administration script is particularly easy to follow, with the words said to the students printed in a different color than the rest of the text.

The MET can be administered to groups of any size, providing sufficient proctors are available, and little expertise is required. The basic skills and life skills sections each are given with 45-minute time limits. The optional writing test has a 20-minute limit.

The basic and life skills tests can be scored either by machine or by hand. Hand scoring these portions is very simple, with clear instructions provided. The answer key provided lists the answers to each question. The raw score is calculated by the sum of correct answers. Easy-to-use national norm tables appear in the technical manual.

Machine scoring is available from the test publisher, and either class lists or student labels can be produced. The following scores are provided: raw score, percent correct, percentiles (based both on national and local district norms), stanines (based both on national and local district norms), and normal curve equivalents. In addition, each test user has the option of determining a criterion score (i.e., a score that represents minimal acceptable performance). Students falling below this criterion score would be identified on the machine-generated report. The test manual provides the test user with some guidance on the establishment of the criterion score(s).

The optional writing test is designed to be scored by teachers using holistic scoring; that is, raters quickly read the passage and determine a score based on an overall impression of the piece. The raters do not follow a key, but rather base their assessment on an overall judgment of the quality of the writing using a 4-point rating scale. Because of this approach to scoring, the passages must be rated by more than one teacher, preferably three or more. Because the passages produced by the test takers are brief, scoring this portion of the test by each rater can be done quite quickly.

Interpretation of MET scores should be made in light of the particular use being made of the test. Both test manuals contain clear explanations to aid in the interpretation of percentile, stanine, and normal curve equivalent scores.

Technical Aspects

The MET authors based their test validation strategy on content validation, the process of developing objectives and linking the test content to the objectives. Unfortunately, the test manuals do not contain the objectives, so the initial content validation of the instrument cannot be evaluated. In order for a test user to establish content validation documentation, that user would have to develop objectives or job analysis information and link the test items to the information. The test manual does contain item categorization information to indicate the type and measurement intent of each item. This information would be helpful in the linkage process.

The technical manual reports subtest intercorrelations by grade level, which gives some insight into the independence of each of the scores. The correlations range from .35 between Mathematics and Reading, to .64 between Mathematics and Language, to .66 between Reading and Language. One would expect a lower correlation between the Mathematics and Language tests, especially given the fact that Mathematics does not contain word problems. The Life and Basic Skills tests correlate between .72 and .78. This suggests a high degree of overlap between what is being measured on the two tests, perhaps indicating that there is little difference between possessing the basic skills and being able to apply them to life situations.

No item analyses are presented. A test user has no information on the qualities of the individual items or how they were selected.

This reviewer was unable to identify any published construct or criterion-related validation studies on this test. There is no evidence of any studies of the relation between scores on this test and comparable achievement tests measuring similar basic skills.

The technical manual reports KR-20 reliabilities (measurements of the tests' internal consistency) for each of the separate scores except Writing by grade level for the norming sample. These range from .84 to .95, an acceptable result. No other forms of reliability are reported. The authors report no reliability for criterion score decision. They report neither test-retest nor alternate forms reliability. No interrater reliabilities are presented for the optional writing test.

In addition, the test manuals present no information on the performance on the test by various subgroups. Although the authors claim that the items were written to be free of ethnic and sex stereotyping, they present no information on how this was done and what the score differences were across groups.

In the technical manual, all statistical analyses reported are based on the nationwide norming sample of 56 school districts ($N = 16,787$ students in Grade 8 through 12). The sample appears to have been carefully selected to be representative on variables such as percentage of families living below the poverty level, size of district, and geographic distribution. The sample was composed of 12.3% black and 4.8% Hispanic students. No information is provided on the gender makeup of the sample. It should be noted that in the largest cities in the sample, such as New York, Chicago, Baltimore, and Los Angeles, the schools were supplied by the archdiocese; no public schools were included from these largest cities.

Critique

The Minimum Essentials Test has been designed to meet an important need in the field of education. The authors also have taken care to address ease of administration. Unfortunately, the test has some significant technical limitations, primarily caused by a lack of or a discrepancy in information:

1. The validation of the test is very weak. In order for a school district or employer to use the test, based on content validation alone, the district would have to link objectives/curriculum to the test. Although this normally would be done by a test user, the process is hampered by lack of the original objectives on which the test is based.

2. The test materials indicate that three alternate or parallel forms of the test exist. This is an important consideration for test users who expect to use the test with some frequency. However, the materials present no information, neither statistical nor content, to support that these forms are parallel. In fact, the content information would seem to indicate that they are not parallel, because of somewhat different numbers of items by type. This reviewer must conclude that there is only one useable form of the test, Form A, for which normative and other data are presented.

3. Very limited statistical analyses are presented, and the only reliability information that appears concerns internal consistency. No item statistics are presented, and no information on subgroup test performance is available.

4. Because of the conflicting information concerning the norming samples, this reviewer is uncomfortable in making any conclusions on the technical soundness of the sample. Care should be used in employing these norms.

If a school district wanted to use the MET, that district would need to link the local school curriculum to the content of the test to establish the instrument's validity. The test appears to be most useful as a criterion-referenced measure, so that the local school district would need to establish criterion scores and not rely on the norms.

References

American Testronics. (1981). *Minimum Essentials Test technical manual and norms.* Iowa City, IA: American Testronics.

Rice, W.K., Guskey, T.R., Perlman, C.L., Rice, M.F., Smith, J.K., & Wick, J.W. (1981). *Minimum Essentials Test teacher's manual.* Iowa City, IA: American Testronics.

Jane C. Duckworth, Ph.D.
Professor of Counseling Psychology, Ball State University, Muncie, Indiana.

Eugene E. Levitt, Ph.D.
Professor of Clinical Psychology, Institute of Psychiatric Research, Indiana University School of Medicine, Indianapolis, Indiana.

MINNESOTA MULTIPHASIC PERSONALITY INVENTORY–2

J.N. Butcher, W.G. Dahlstrom, J.R. Graham, A. Tellegen, and B. Kaemmer. Minneapolis, Minnesota: University of Minnesota Press/Distributed exclusively by National Computer Systems/PAS Division.

Introduction

The original Minnesota Multiphasic Personality Inventory (MMPI) was developed to help clinical and research users in assigning psychodiagnostic labels to their patients and subjects. The restandardized version, the MMPI-2, has been designed to retain the most valuable traditional features of the test while addressing contemporary concerns. Many test users felt that the original MMPI, first published in 1943 by Hathaway and McKinley, had become outdated and was in need of revision. The MMPI-2 is the result of almost 10 years of work to modernize the inventory. The revisors of the original, Butcher, Dahlstrom, Graham, Tellegen, and Kaemmer, (1989), changed it in three ways.

First, 70 items in the original MMPI have been edited. Most of the changes were minor; only four items were substantially rewritten. In addition, 90 items were deleted for a variety of reasons (see Levitt, 1990).

A second change affected the normative group. The new standardization sample was designed to match as closely as possible the major characteristics of the U.S. population as shown in the 1980 census.

The third major change is the use of so-called uniform T-scores to report scale results instead of the conventional T-scores used in the original MMPI. The use of uniform T-scores means that all scales now have essentially the same range and distribution, whereas with the original linear T-scores the distributions of the scales varied. In addition to these three changes, new scales have been added that will be described later in this review.

The MMPI-2 is made up of 567 items, compared to 550 in the original. Because the item order has changed, it is possible to score the 4 validity scales and 10 clinical scales—the so-called Basic Profile—from the first 370 items. Only 13 of these items in the original MMPI do not appear in MMPI-2 and no items have been added. Items 371–567 provide data for supplementary scales.

424

The appropriate examinee age for the revised inventory is 18 years and older, and the overall test is written at an eighth-grade reading level. In contrast to the original MMPI, the MMPI-2 should not be used with adolescents; an adolescent version of the test, the MMPI-A, has been developed for this population. Average test-taking time for most individuals is 60 to 90 minutes. The test is scored by either scoring keys or computer to form the Basic Profile. Brief descriptions of the MMPI-2 Basic Scales follow:

VALIDITY SCALES

L (Lie) Scale—15 items reflecting common human faults to which most people are willing to admit.

F (Infrequency) Scale—60 items that are answered in the keyed direction by less than 10% of the standardization group for the original MMPI.

K (Correction) Scale—30 items designed to reveal the test taker who attempts to present him- or herself in the best possible light.

? (Cannot Say)—the number of items that have been left unanswered; reported as a raw score.

CLINICAL SCALES

Scale 1 (Hypochondriasis)—32 items that reflect a person's preoccupation with physical problems.

Scale 2 (Depression)—57 items concerned with feelings of depression and malaise.

Scale 3 (Hysteria)—60 items dealing with specific physical complaints along with a denial of concern about the physical problems.

Scale 4 (Psychopathic Deviate)—50 items reflecting antisocial acts and feelings as well as hostility and/or anger.

Scale 5 (Masculine-Feminine Interests)—56 items that measure stereotypic masculine or feminine interests.

Scale 6 (Paranoia)—40 items that indicate feelings of suspiciousness and wariness of other people's motives.

Scale 7 (Psychasthenia)—48 items concerned with feelings of anxiety and concern, and obsessive ruminations.

Scale 8 (Schizophrenia)—78 items that reflect feelings of alienation, differentness, confusion, and bizarre sensations.

Scale 9 (Mania)—46 items that show excessive energy, psychomotor acceleration, and imperturbability.

Scale 0 (Social Introversion-Extraversion)—69 items measuring social shyness, the preference for solitary pursuits, and a lack of social assertiveness.

In addition to these 14 scales, the Harris-Lingoes Subscales of the clinical scales and Wiener-Harmon Subtle-Obvious Subscales can be scored as with the original MMPI. Each of these sets of scales has its own profile form. The MMPI-2 profile forms use the 65 T-score level to separate normal from abnormal, in contrast to the original which used 70 T-score points.

Eighteen new scales have been added to the MMPI-2 assessment battery (see Butcher, Graham, Williams, & Ben-Porath, 1990). Three of these are validity scales: The Back F scale (F_b), so called because its items appear on the back of the score sheet, consists of 40 items that were endorsed in the pathological direction by less than 10% of the MMPI-2 standardization sample. The Variable Response Inconsistency Scale (VRIN) and the True Response Inconsistency Scale (TRIN) are patterned after Greene's Carelessness Scale (Greene, 1978) and are based on inconsistency in responding to pairs of items.

Fifteen so-called content scales can be scored from MMPI-2 items. These generally follow the pattern of the Content Scales developed by Wiggins (1966) and are highly correlated with corresponding Wiggins scales among subjects in the MMPI-2 standardization sample. Coefficients range from .69 to .92 for males, .75 to .92 for females. Most of these content scales use labels much like those of the Wiggins scales, such as Depression, Fears, Health Concerns, Anger, and Social Discomfort. Four scales do not follow the Wiggins pattern: Work Interference, Negative Treatment Indicators, Obsessiveness, and Type A. However, each has substantial correlations with Wiggins scales: Work Interference, Negative Treatment Indicators, and Obsessiveness with Depression and Poor Morale, and Type A with Manifest Hostility.

Overall, the intercorrelations between MMPI-2 content scales and corresponding Wiggins content scales are as high as the internal consistency coefficients for the former and almost as high as their test-retest correlations. Because the Wiggins scales remain relatively intact in the MMPI-2 (Levitt, 1990), the contribution of the new content scales is problematic. Butcher (1990) suggests that the new content scales can be used in treatment planning, but no evidence for their utility is presented. Ben-Porath, Butcher, and Graham (1991) found that several content scales helped to differentiate major depressives from schizophrenics. Schill and Wang (1990) reported that the MMPI-2 Anger scale had significant correlations with 7 of 11 other anger indices for men and 5 of 11 for women in a small sample of college students.

Practical Applications/Uses

The original MMPI was the most widely used personality test in the world. MMPI-2 may also become as widely used, though early evidence suggests that many clinicians are staying with the original at least for the present (Webb & Levitt, 1992).

As was true for the MMPI, the revised inventory may be useful in psychiatric hospitals, mental health clinics, college counseling centers, and similar agencies as well as widely employed in personality research. Research on the MMPI-2 has began to be published, and the body of literature involving it is slowly growing.

Psychologists are the primary users of the MMPI, but psychiatrists, psychiatric social workers, and psychiatric nurses are acquainted with it and its utility.

Technical Aspects

The validity and reliability of the MMPI-2 is based in part on the validity and reliability of the original inventory. For the latter, each of the scales has its own validity and reliability because of the different behaviors and emotions each scale was designed to measure. As a whole, however, the test was found reasonably effective for its original task of diagnosing mental and emotional problems. Test-retest reliabilities for the validity, clinical, supplementary, and content scales are listed in the MMPI-2 manual (Butcher et al., 1989) and range from .67 (Scale 6, Paranoia) to .92 (Scale 0, Social Introversion-Extraversion). Most of the reliability coefficients are .75 and above. Validity measures reported in the manual (Butcher et al., 1989) relate the validity, clinical, supplementary, and content scales to the total number of recent life changes, a social readjustment rating scale, and partner ratings on an adjustment scale. Research on the accuracy of the MMPI-2 in diagnoses in clinical settings is just starting to be published. In general, the validity and clinical scales of the MMPI-2 seem to be doing about as good a job as the corresponding scales of the original MMPI. Information regarding the accuracy of the new scales developed for the MMPI-2 may take awhile, as most researchers appear to be concentrating on the clinical scales.

Several books designed to help with interpreting the MMPI-2 have already appeared (Butcher, 1990; Graham, 1990; Greene, 1991; Keller & Butcher, 1991; Lewak, Marks, & Nelson, 1990). These are based on assumptions of face validity of the items as research evidence to date is lacking.

Critique

There are advantages to a new version of a widely used personality test. Any test, even the assessment standard of personality evaluation, needs revision after 50 years of use. Items become dated and norm groups developed many years ago need to be revised to more closely fit the current testing population. The authors of the MMPI-2 have made neccesary changes, and the test is thus more relevant for today. In addition to updated items, a positive feature of the MMPI-2 is the addition of new scales that explore areas not assessed previously by the MMPI, though their value remains to be demonstrated.

Some of the changes that are advantages also present disadvantages. The new norm group, albeit more representative of today's population, is still biased by being heavily weighted with professional people who have more education than the general U.S. population: 45% of the normative subjects are college graduates. A norm group with this level of education is more like private psychotherapy patients and less representative of clients from state hospitals and publicly funded mental health centers.

Another disadvantage of the MMPI-2 is that a respondent's Basic Scale profile may be different from his or her profile on the original MMPI. The use of uniform T-scores for the MMPI-2 clinical scales has affected the eight clinical scales differently. Some scales have been lowered by this transformation (e.g., Scales 2, 4, and 8), while others have been raised (e.g., Scales 3 and 6). This means that profiles based on the same raw scores for the eight clinical scales could show different profile patterns for the two tests. Other MMPI-2 scales have been affected by the new education level. Most men will score 10 T-score points lower on the present Scale 5 than on the original MMPI. One implication is that the vast body of information about the original MMPI may not be relevant to MMPI-2.

As a way of dealing with the changes that have come about because of the uniform T-scores and the new normative group, Caldwell (Adler, 1990) has suggested that the MMPI-2 test user plot raw scores from MMPI-2 on both the old test profile and the new MMPI-2 profile. This tactic will provide a clearer view of the discrepancies between the two reports and can help the clinician to decide which one to interpret for the most accurate assessment of an individual's problems.

Publication of MMPI-2 has resulted in a crisis for many users of the test, a situation that includes both a problem and an opportunity. MMPI-2 presents a problem with profile interpretation and an opportunity to better assess personality through a modernized instrument. As more MMPI-2 research is published and professional users become better acquainted with it, its potential for accurate assessment may be realized.

References

Adler, T. (1990, April). Does the "new" MMPI beat the "classic"? *APA Monitor*, pp. 18–19.

Ben-Porath, Y.S., Butcher, J.N., & Graham, J.R. (1991). Contribution of the MMPI-2 content scales to the differential diagnosis of schizophrenia and major depression. *Psychological Assessment, 3*, 634–640.

Butcher, J.N. (1990). *The MMPI-2 in psychological treatment.* New York: Oxford University Press.

Butcher, J.N., Dahlstrom, W.G., Graham, J.R., Tellegen, A., & Kaemmer, B. (1989). *Minnesota Multiphasic Personality Inventory (MMPI-2): Manual for administration and scoring.* Minneapolis: University of Minnesota Press.

Butcher, J.N., Graham, J.R., Williams, C.L., & Ben-Porath, Y.S. (1990). *Development and use of the MMPI-2 content scales.* Minneapolis: University of Minnesota Press.

Graham, J.R. (1990). *MMPI-2: Assessing personality and psychopathology.* New York: Oxford University Press.

Greene, R.L. (1978). An empirically derived MMPI carelessness scale. *Journal of Clinical Psychology, 34*, 407–410.

Keller, L.S., & Butcher, J.N. (1991). *Assessment of chronic pain patients with the MMPI-2.* Minneapolis: University of Minnesota Press.

Levitt, E.E. (1990). A structural analysis of the impact of MMPI-2 on MMPI-1. *Journal of Personality Assessment, 55*, 562–577.

Lewak, R.W., Marks, P.A., & Nelson, G.E. (1990). *Therapist's guide to the MMPI and MMPI-2.* Muncie, IN: Accelerated Development.

Schill, T., & Wang, S. (1990). Correlates of the MMPI-2 anger content scale. *Psychological Reports, 67*, 800–802.

Webb, J.T., & Levitt, E.E. (1992, March). *After two years: A comparison of the clinical use of MMPI-1 and MMPI-2.* Paper presented at the annual convention of the Society for Personality Assessment, Washington, DC.

Wiggins, J.S. (1966). Substantive dimensions of self-report in the MMPI item pool. *Psychological Monographs, 80*(22, Whole No. 630).

James A. Moses, Jr., Ph.D.

Clinical Associate Professor of Psychiatry and Behavioral Sciences, Stanford University School of Medicine, and Coordinator, Psychological Assessment Unit, Department of Veterans Affairs Medical Center, Palo Alto, California.

MOTOR IMPERSISTENCE TEST

Arthur L. Benton, Kerry deS. Hamsher, Nils R. Varney, and Otfried Spreen. New York, New York: Oxford University Press.

Introduction

Clinical investigators have noted for approximately a century that the inability to sustain a voluntary movement continuously for a relatively short period of time is a valid sign of brain disease. This syndrome has been called *motor impersistence* (MI; for historical overview and the clinical syndrome-analytic development of the MI concept, see Benton, Hamsher, Varney, & Spreen, 1983). The MI sign has been demonstrated through a variety of sustained elementary motor behaviors chosen by different investigators. Joynt, Benton, and Fogel (1962) developed their standardized Motor Impersistence Test (MIT) to quantitatively assess the MI syndrome based on the procedures and findings of two well-controlled, empirical studies by Berlin (1955) and Fisher (1956).

The MIT tasks consist of eight elementary motor acts: 1) keeping the eyes closed continuously for 20 seconds, 2) continuously protruding the tongue beyond the lips (while blindfolded) for 20 seconds, 3) protruding the tongue beyond the lips (with the eyes open) for 20 seconds, 4) continuous visual focus on a stimulus in one or the other lateral visual field at eye level while keeping the head facing directly forward for 30 seconds, 5) keeping the mouth open continuously for 20 seconds, 6) continuously looking straight ahead while the examiner horizontally moves a finger at eye level from the side position in line with the patient's ear (out of the peripheral visual field) into the patient's peripheral visual field on one or the other side of the head, 7) continuously looking in the opposite direction while the examiner touches one finger at a time of the patient's hand in the unseen visual field and requires the patient to identify the finger touched, and 8) saying the syllabic blend "ah" for as long as possible (maximal uninterrupted period measured in seconds) (Benton et al., 1983, pp. 127–130).

The principal author of the standardized MIT, Arthur L. Benton, Ph.D., received the A.B. degree (1931) and the A.M. degree (1933) from Oberlin College, followed by the Ph.D. degree from Columbia University (1935). He began his career as an assistant in psychology at Oberlin College (1931–33), Columbia University and New York State Psychiatric Institute (1934–36), and then Cornell University Medical College (1936–39), where he subsequently served as a staff psychologist. He was appointed as an attending psychologist at New York Hospital–Westchester Division and as a psychologist in the Student Personnel Office of the City College of New York from 1939 through 1941. He served on active duty in the U.S. Navy during and after the Second World War (1941–46). From there he was appointed Associate Professor of Psychology at the University of Louisville Medical School and Chief Psychologist at the Louisville Mental Hygiene Clinic and the Louisville General Hospital (1946–48). In the decade 1948–58 he served as Professor of Psychology and Director of the Graduate Training Program in Clinical Psychology at the University of Iowa. From 1958 to 1978 he was Professor of Psychology and Neurology at the University of Iowa. Dr. Benton has continued to coauthor theoretical and research papers and books since 1978, when he became Professor Emeritus at the University of Iowa.

Benton's fundamental contributions to the field of clinical neuropsychology have been acknowledged extensively and internationally. He has received honorary Doctor of Science (Cornell College, 1978) and Doctor of Psychology (University of Rome, 1990) degrees, as well as numerous other honors and awards, including the Distinguished Service Award of the Iowa Psychological Association (1977), the Distinguished Professional Contribution Award from the American Psychological Association (1978), the Outstanding Scientific Contribution Award of the International Neuropsychological Society (1981), The Samuel Torrey Orton Award from the Orton Dyslexia Society (1982), the Distinguished Service and Outstanding Contributions Award from the American Board of Professional Psychology (1985), and the Distinguished Clinical Neuropsychologist Award from the National Academy of Neuropsychology (1989).

Benton is a past president of the American Orthopsychiatric Association (1965–66) and the International Neuropsychological Society (1970–71), and served as the Secretary-General of the Research Group on Aphasia for the World Federation of Neurology from 1971 to 1978. He has been a lecturer or visiting scholar at the University of Milan (1964), Hôpital Sainte-Anne, Paris (1968), Hadassah-Hebrew University Medical School, Jerusalem (1969), Free University of Amsterdam (1971), University of Helsinki (1974), University of Melbourne (1977), University of Minnesota Medical School (Baker Lecturer, 1979), University of Victoria, British Columbia (Lansdowne Scholar, 1980), and the University of Michigan (1986). He also served as Directeur d'Études Associé, École des Hautes Études, Paris (1979) and as a visiting scientist at the Tokyo Metropolitan Institute of Gerontology (1974).

Benton has authored, coauthored, or edited 12 books and monographs, approximately 150 professional journal articles, and 22 historical reviews in the area of clinical neuropsychology and behavioral neurology. He is recognized as a pioneer and a leading authority in the area of clinical neuropsychology.

The standardized, commercially published version of the MIT appeared with the clinical manual for this and other tests in the Benton-Iowa Neuropsychological Test Battery (Benton et al., 1983). Coauthors of this clinical manual with Dr. Benton are Kerry deS. Hamsher, Ph.D. (Associate Professor of Neurology, University of Wisconsin Medical School); Nils R. Varney, Ph.D. (Staff Neuropsychologist, Department of Veterans Affairs Medical Center, Iowa City, Iowa); and Otfried Spreen, Ph.D. (Professor Emeritus, Department of Psychology, University of Victoria, Victoria, British Columbia, Canada).

Practical Applications/Uses

The directions for administration and scoring of the MIT, precise, rigorous, and detailed, are reproduced here for the reader's reference by permission of Dr. Benton:

> The battery consists of eight tests requiring the maintenance of a movement or posture (Table 12-5). [*Note:* This table appears in Benton et al., 1983, p. 136 and provides a facsimile of the MIT administration and scoring form.] The administration and scoring of each test are as follows:
>
> *1. Keeping eyes closed* The patient is instructed to close his eyes and keep them closed. He is judged to have terminated his response if, at any time prior to the end of the trial, any part of the eyeball becomes visible. Fluttering of the lids is not counted as long as the lids remain closed. Two 20-second trials are given and the total score is the sum of seconds over which performance is sustained, a perfect score being 40. Verbatim instructions to the patient are as follows:
>
> *"This is the first thing we are going to do. I want you to close your eyes and keep them closed, until I tell you to open them. Ready, close your eyes.* (First trial of 20 seconds). *Now, you can open them. We will do it again. When I tell you to, close your eyes and keep them closed. Ready, close your eyes.* (Second trial of 20 seconds). *Now you can open them."*
>
> *2. Protruding tongue (blindfolded)* For this task, the patient is blindfolded and told to stick out his tongue and keep it out. He is judged to have terminated his response if, prior to the end of the trial, the tongue is retracted to a point posterior to the outer edge of the upper lip. Two 20-second trials are given, and total score determined in the same manner as on task 1. Verbatim instructions to the patient are as follows:
>
> *"Now this time I want you to stick your tongue out and keep it out, like this. I am going to put this mask over your face like this so that you cannot see.* (Examiner adjusts blindfold). *There, is that OK? Remember, stick your tongue out and keep it out until I tell you to stop. Ready, stick your tongue out.* (First trial of 20 seconds). *Stop. Now we are going to do this one more time. Ready, stick out your tongue and keep it out.* (Second trial of 20 seconds). *Stop."*
>
> *3. Protruding tongue (eyes open)* The same procedure as for task 2 is followed except that the patient is not blindfolded. Verbatim instructions to the patient are as follows:
>
> *"Now we are go do the same thing; this time I will take the mask off so that you can see.* (Examiner removes blindfold). *Remember, stick out your tongue and keep it out. Ready, stick out your tongue.* (First trial of 20 seconds). *Stop. Now we are going to do this one more time. Ready, stick out your tongue and keep it out.* (Second trial of 20 seconds). *Stop."*
>
> *4. Fixation of gaze in lateral visual field.* With his head fixed in the midline position, the patient is instructed to look at the examiner's finger and to keep looking at it, as the examiner extends a finger vertically at approximately a 45 degree angle in the horizontal plane of the patient's right visual field for 30 seconds. The procedure is repeated in the patient's left visual field. Each time the patient looks away from the examiner's finger, one point is scored and the patient is reminded to keep looking at the finger. A point is not scored if, in the examiner's judgment, the patient makes eye movements directed at different points on the examiner's finger. Total score is the number of instances

of looking away from the stimulus. A score of zero indicates perfect performance. Verbatim instructions to the patient are as follows:

"I want you to keep your head in this position. (Examiner adjusts patient's head so that it is in the midline position). *I am going to hold up a finger, and I want you to look at it and keep looking right at it until I tell you to stop. Ready, go."* After 30 seconds, examiner says, *"Now I am going to hold up a finger on the other side. Look at my finger and keep looking right at it until I tell you to stop. Ready, go."* (Second trial of 30 seconds).

5. Keeping mouth open The patient is instructed to open his mouth and keep it open. He is judged to have terminated his response if, prior to the end of the trial, the mouth returned to its pretrial position. Two 20-second trials are given, total score being determined in the same manner as on task 1. Verbatim instructions to the patient are as follows:

"Now when I tell you to, open your mouth and keep it open (Examiner demonstrates) *until I tell you to stop. Ready, open your mouth.* (First trial of 20 seconds). *Stop. Now we are going to do this once more. Ready, open your mouth and keep it open.* (Second trial of 20 seconds). *Stop."*

6. Central fixation during confrontation testing of visual fields The patient is instructed to look at the examiner's nose and to keep looking at it while the examiner gradually brings a finger around the side of the patient's face, from a point in line with the patient's ears, until the finger has reached a point in a 45 degree angle in the horizontal plane of the patient's right or left visual field. Patient is told to tell examiner when he first sees the finger out of the corner of his eye. Each time the patient looks away from the examiner's nose, a point is scored. A point is not scored if, in the examiner's judgment, the patient engages in eye movements directed at different points on the examiner's nose. Each time the patient looks away from the examiner's nose, he is reminded to keep looking at it. Two trials of 20 seconds each are given for each visual field. Fields are tested in alternate order, beginning with the finger in the patient's right visual field. Total score is the number of points scored on all four trials. Verbatim instructions to the patient are as follows:

"When I tell you to begin, I want you to look right at my nose and **keep looking at it.** *While you are doing that I am going to bring my finger around the side of your face, like this* (Examiner demonstrates) *and you tell me when you first see my finger out of the corner of your eye. But keep looking at my nose all the time until I tell you to stop. Ready, go."* After each vacillation, examiner says, *"Keep looking at my nose."* After the first trial of 20 seconds in the right visual field, examiner says, *"Now, we are going to do the same thing with my finger on the other side. Keep looking at my nose, but tell me when you first see my finger out of the corner of your eye. Ready, go."* The same instruction is repeated through two further trials, in the right visual field and the other in the left visual field.

7. Head turning during sensory testing The patient is instructed to state which finger is being touched while the examiner touches each of the patient's fingers in random order. He is told to turn his head away and *not* look at his hand until told that the task is over. One point is scored if, in the examiner's judgment, the patient looks at his hand after the presentation of the stimulus and prior to the ensuing stimulus. A point is not scored if the patient turns his head but looks only at the examiner. After each scored response, the patient is reminded not to look at his hand. If, as occasionally happens, the patient asks the examiner what he should call each finger, he is told to call them whatever he thinks is appropriate, i.e., he is not instructed in the correct labeling of his fingers. No penalty is attached if the patient incorrectly names a finger. Two trials on each hand are given, with the hands tested alternately, beginning with the right. Total score is the number of points scored over the four trials. A perfect score is zero; poorest score is 20. Verbatim instructions to the patient are as follows:

"This time, you will put this (right) hand on the table. (Examiner demonstrates with fingers extended, palms down). *I am going to touch each one of your fingers and you tell me each time which one I have touched. While we are doing this, I want you to look over there.* (Examiner points to wall to patient's left), *and don't look at your hand until I tell you that we have finished. OK, here we go."* (If patient does not turn his head, examiner reminds him to do so).

After one trial with the right hand, the examiner says, *"Done. Now, we will do the same thing with your other hand. Turn your head away and do not look at your hand until I say we are finished. Here we go."* The same procedure is followed through a total of two trials with each hand.

8. *Saying "ah."* After a demonstration, the patient is instructed to take a deep breath and say "ah," holding it as long as he can. The response is judged to have terminated when there is a cessation or interruption of phonation. The continuation of expiration following such a break is not scored, nor is the resumption of voiced speech once it was interrupted. Total score is the sum in seconds of the response on two trials. Verbatim instructions to the patient are as follows:

"Here is the last thing we are going to do. When we begin, I want you to take a deep breath and say 'ah.' Like this, I'll show you. (Examiner takes breath, produces "ah" for five seconds.) *But I want you to say 'ah' as long as you can. OK, whenever you are ready, take a deep breath and say 'ah' as long as you can."* After first trial, examiner says, *"We will do this once more. Whenever you are ready, take a deep breath and say 'ah' as long as you can."* (Benton et al., 1983, pp. 127–130)

The MIT was normed for clinical use on a sample of 106 adult medical and surgical control patients hospitalized in the University of Iowa Hospitals, Iowa City, at the time of testing for treatment of a variety of physical disorders that did not involve brain dysfunction. No control patient in the adult normative sample had a history of neurologic disorder, psychiatric disorder, or mental deficiency. The mean age of the MIT adult normative sample subjects was 44.5 years, and their mean educational level was 10 years (Benton et al., 1983, p. 130). Variability statistics and other demographic information about the sample, such as sex of subjects, were not reported as part of the descriptive presentation in the test manual. Eighty-four percent (89/106) of the MIT adult normative control group subjects performed errorlessly on all of the eight subtests. Fourteen percent (15/106) of them performed defectively on only one subtest. One patient in the MIT adult normative sample failed two subtests and one failed three. Based on these findings, Benton et al. (1983, p. 130) defined two MI syndrome performance levels based on defective MIT performance: Failure on two or three of the eight subtests was categorized as "moderate impersistence," while failure on four or more subtests was described as "marked impersistence."

Benton et al. (1983, pp. 130–131) also present objective, standardized deficit performance rating criteria to use with the adult norms for each of the MIT subtests, paraphrased here for ready reference:

1. *Keeping eyes closed.* Impersistence is defined for this measure by a total eye closure period of 35 seconds or less across two 20-second trials. This performance level corresponds to the second percentile of the adult normative sample.

2. *Protruding tongue (blindfolded).* Any imperfect performance on either of the two trials presented on this task is a sign of MI. This criterion ranks at the fourth percentile of the adult normative group.

3. *Protruding tongue (eyes open).* Any imperfect performance on this task also is defined as a sign of MI. This task was performed errorlessly by every patient in the adult normative sample.

4. *Fixation of gaze in lateral visual fields.* Two or more occurrences of the failure to maintain fixed lateral gaze defines the MI criterion for this measure. This score ranks at the second percentile of the adult normative sample.

5. *Keeping mouth open.* Any imperfect performance on either trial is the criterion for MI on this measure. This performance level ranks below the first percentile of the adult normative sample.

6. *Central fixation during confrontation testing of visual fields.* An error score of 3 or more points (visual focus deviations from the central visual fixation point) defines the MI sign criterion for this measure. This performance level corresponds to approximately the fourth percentile of the adult normative group.

7. *Head turning during sensory testing.* Failure to perform without error on any trial of this task is a sign of MI. This criterion level of performance ranks at the second percentile in the adult normative sample.

8. *Saying "ah."* Sustained pronunciation of this syllabic blend sound for 17 seconds or less is a sign of MI. This level of performance ranks at the sixth percentile in the adult normative sample.

MIT normative data for children aged 5–11 years were reported by Garfield (1963, 1964). Ten boys and 10 girls were sampled at each age level. The children were selected from the Department of Pediatrics at the University of Iowa Hospitals, Iowa City. All children who volunteered as control subjects for the MIT pediatric normative sample were free of acute illness of any kind, had no medical restrictions on their activity level, and had no known history or current medical evidence of neurologic disease or trauma. The children were of average mean intellectual ability level and presented a wide, generally representative range of cognitive performance level on the Wechsler Intelligence Scale for Children intelligence quotient (mean = 102, range = 80–119).

The MIT protocol was modified slightly for subtest 4, "fixation of gaze in lateral visual fields." On this measure the children were required to fixate their gaze for 20 seconds rather than the standard 30 seconds. There is a clear developmental trend in the mastery of the MIT tasks with age. Use of the adult standards for the MI syndrome shows that all 5-year-olds in the control sample demonstrated MI, with failure on two or three of the eight MIT measures. In the age range 6–9 years, approximately half the control samples of children meet adult criteria for MI. By age 10–11 the child control samples are performing at the adult level on MIT measures except for tasks 6 ("central fixation during confrontation testing of visual fields") and 8 ("saying 'ah'"). Detailed tabular analyses of the level of performance on MIT summary indices by age, developmental normative trends on each of the MIT subtests, and frequency of moderate and marked impersistence by age levels appear in the manual (Benton et al., 1983, p. 132, Tables 12-2 through 12-4). Benton and his colleagues note that 90% of 5-year-olds in the normative sample performed within normal limits on at least three MIT subtests. All of the normative sample children aged 6–7 met this criterion. By ages 8–11 all of the normative sample children performed within normal limits on at least four of the MIT subtests.

MIT total score performance level cutoff scores for *moderate impersistence* are defined by Benton et al. (1983, p. 132, Table 12-4) as 6 error points at age 5, 5 error points at ages 6–7, 4 error points at ages 8–9, and 3 error points for ages 10–11. MIT total scores associated with *marked impersistence* are 7 or more points at age 5, 6 or more points at ages 6–7, 5 or more points at ages 8–9, and 4 or more points at ages 10–11.

Technical Aspects

MIT performance levels and patterns have been investigated in brain dysfunctional samples of adults and children, mental retardates, and schizophrenics. Each of these lines of research will be considered in turn.

Brain dysfunctional adults. Joynt et al. (1962) reported an MI rate of 23% in their sample of 101 patients with brain disease affecting one cerebral hemisphere (48 cases with left-hemispheric lesion, 34 cases with right-hemispheric lesion) or both cerebral hemispheres (19 cases with bilateral lesions). They reported no consistent difference in MI syndrome occurrence as a function of cerebral lesion laterality (26% incidence with bilateral lesions, 19% with left-hemispheric lesions, 26% with right-hemispheric lesions). Marked impersistence occurred in 6% of the patients with left cerebral lesions, in 15% of the patients with right cerebral lesions, and in 16% of the patients with bilateral or diffuse cerebral lesions.

Levin (1973b) investigated MI in a sample of 32 patients with unilateral hemispheric lesions only. He reported an incidence of 22% for both moderate and marked impersistence in his sample, but he found no association between severity of motor impersistence and lesion laterality. Both Joynt et al. (1962) and Levin (1973b) incidentally reported normative trends showing patients demonstrating the MI syndrome to be somewhat older than those patients who were impersistence free, but the association between occurrence of MI and age was not consistent, strong, or classificationally disjoint at any reported age level.

Early work on MI syndrome analysis by Berlin (1955) and Fisher (1956) was well controlled and served as a basis for Benton et al.'s development of the standardized MIT measures. Berlin and Fisher associated MI with right-hemispheric brain disease, but Fisher equivocated on the possibility of MI occurrence in the presence of unilateral left-hemispheric brain disease. Ongoing controversy about the laterality of lesion as a correlate of MI continues to be a problematic clinical issue. The issues of patient fatigability, MI test task, chronicity of brain lesion, lesion laterality (and locus), patient inclusion/selection criteria, cognitive deficit severity and type, and change in the MI syndrome with time since onset have been discussed cogently by DeRenzi, Gentilini, and Bazolli (1986) as factors that may influence conflicting results among studies that deal with MI syndrome analysis.

Rigorous syndrome-analytic work by Kertesz, Nicholson, Cancelliere, Kassa, and

Black (1985) reported a strong association of MI with unilateral right-hemispheric disease. In this study patients with unilateral hemispheric disease and control subjects were carefully matched for age and educational level. Normal control patients had no past history of brain injury, brain disease, or neurologic symptomatology. All normal and neurologic subjects in the study were right-handed. Patients with lateralized lesions also were matched for lesion size. Patients with right-hemispheric lesions showed significantly more MI deficit than those with left-hemispheric lesions and controls. Patients with unilateral left-hemispheric lesions did not show more MI than controls on any of 11 Kertesz Battery MI tasks (many similar to MIT tasks) or on the total Kertesz MI summary index. Severe MI symptomatology was associated with a lesion of the right cerebral hemisphere significantly more often than with a lesion of the left hemisphere. Larger lesions in the right hemisphere also were associated with greater severity of behavioral deficit on the Kertesz MI tasks. Lesion size was not significantly associated with MI deficit among left-hemispheric-lesion subjects. The greatest severity of MI deficit occurred with relatively large, midhemispheric lesions that were cortical or subcortical (defined as deep to the insula). Statistical comparisons of anterior versus posterior lesion locus as a factor that might influence MI symptom severity were not statistically significant. There also was not any significant sex difference in the occurrence or severity of MI.

Hier, Mondlock, and Caplan (1983a) used only timed maintenance of eye closure up to 30 seconds as their measure of MI. They found in a sample of 41 patients who had suffered unilateral right-hemispheric strokes that their single measure of MI was associated with severity of hemiplegia and with larger stroke lesion size. They noted an association of MI with right parietal lesions, whereas Kertesz et al. (1985) reported no such association. In associated work Hier, Mondlock, and Caplan (1983b) reported that rate of recovery from MI was relatively slow, as was improvement of the neurologic signs of hemianopia, hemiparesis, and sensory extinction with double simultaneous stimulation. Stroke patients with hemorrhagic lesions tended to recover more rapidly than did patients with cerebral infarcts.

The occurrence of MI in Alzheimer's disease (AD) has been reported recently by Lopez, Becker, and Boller (1991). Like Benton et al. (1983), these researchers noted the frequently reported association of MI with dementia. They made use of a brief battery of MI tasks in addition to a 16-test battery that was designed to evaluate patients in seven key cognitive areas: temporal orientation, short-term memory, expressive language (word finding, naming), receptive language (auditory comprehension), visual-motor speed/vigilance, visual construction, and visual perception. They found severe MI symptomatology in approximately 10% (16/166) of their AD patients with moderate or severe dementia. AD patients with and without MI did not differ in performance level on *any* of the seven cognitive domains tested. Although MI was associated with more severe brain dysfunction in AD, clearly it was not redundant with other dimensional measures of specific cognitive function.

Syndrome analyses of the cognitive and behavioral correlates of MI have produced important results that are useful for syndrome analysis of the basis of MI symptomatology. Carmon (1970) speculated that proprioceptive disturbance might be contributory to MI symptomatology. Levin (1973a) subsequently demonstrated the role of faulty proprioceptive feedback in patients with MI, but only in those with lesions of the right cerebral hemisphere. Rosenbaum, Fischer, Leavell, and Alexander (1992) used an unstandardized set of MI measures to examine cognitive correlates of the MI syndrome in 15 patients with a recent (within 6 weeks of onset) unilateral right-hemispheric stroke. They found that audioverbal attentional measures (Digit Span forward and backward) were *not* correlated with their measures of MI, but that attentional tasks with a motor component (Corsi Block Tapping forward but not backward; Rotary Pursuit acquisition and savings measures) did correlate significantly with their MI index. These researchers concluded that MI that appears in the acute phase of recovery following unilateral right-hemispheric stroke may be related in part to motoric dysfunction and not to global attentional difficulty. In this finding their results are consistent with Levin's (1973a), as defective proprioceptive feedback to the motor system would disrupt motor performance independently of global attentional deficit. These results challenge the hypothesis of primary attentional deficit as a basis for the MI syndrome advanced by Joynt et al. (1962) and supported by the findings of Kertesz et al. (1985).

The importance of testing for MI as a specific behavioral syndrome in clinical settings has been emphasized in a case report by Rosse and Ciolino (1986). These researchers showed presence of the MI syndrome clearly with formal testing in a patient with right-hemispheric brain damage who had been evaluated incorrectly by rehabilitation staff members and who was considered simply uncooperative or poorly motivated to work toward his own recovery goals. The course of his care was facilitated once his deficits were properly understood as related to his neurologic disability.

Brain dysfunctional children. Garfield (1963, 1964) compared the performance of 25 children with brain disease to 25 children with normal brain function. Their mean age was 8.5 years and their mean intellectual level on the Wechsler Intelligence Scale for Children was 94 (range = 80–111). The neurologically impaired children were required to show spastic or flaccid paralysis of the arms or legs related to the brain lesion to substantiate the neurologic diagnosis unequivocally. No child was included in the neurologic sample if the motor deficit precluded performance of the MIT tasks. The two samples of children were matched individually for age, sex, and intelligence level on the Wechsler Intelligence Scale for Children.

As expected, the neurologically impaired children showed a significant performance-level decrement on six of the eight MIT measures relative to their matched control peers. The strongest intergroup differences occurred on MIT subtests 2 and 3 (protruding tongue while blindfolded and with eyes open), 4 (lateral visual field gaze fixation), and 6 (central visual field gaze fixation). The least significant differences between the groups occurred on MIT measures 1 (keeping eyes closed on command) and 7 (prevention of head turning during tactile finger identification). Garfield (1963, 1964) reported that use of pediatric norms for the MIT with an impersistence criterion of two or more failed subtests correctly identified 68% (17/25) of the neurologically impaired children as brain dysfunctional. The base rate of MI in a larger group of 140 normal control children was only 3% (4/140). MI thus was identified as a strong and specific sign of brain dysfunction in neurologically impaired children who show paralytic motor signs in the extremities. The MIT thus appears particularly useful with this subgroup of neurologically impaired children. The strength of the finding may relate to the severity and locus of the lesions producing paralysis of this kind. These preliminary results should be replicated. The relative sensitivity of MIT tasks to prediction of brain dysfunction in other groups of neurologically impaired children with cognitive but not motor deficit also should be explored systematically.

Incidental support for Garfield's findings is reported by Rutter, Graham, and Yule (1970). They noted that five of seven (71%) children in the age range 9–10 years who showed evidence of brain dysfunction on neurologic examination also showed motor impersistence on age-adjusted MIT norms. Incidence of MI also was somewhat elevated in a mixed sample of children with reading disability (20/108, 19%), whereas it occurred in only 5% of their control sample. Motor impersistence has a very low base rate in samples of normal children reported to date, but its relevance to prediction of cognitive or sensorimotor deficit in specific groups of neurologically dysfunctional children remains to be clarified. The studies by Garfield exemplify the type of investigation needed. Performance-level studies on small samples such as that reported by Rutter et al. (1970) are useful as exploratory syndrome investigations but now should be superseded by well-controlled, relatively large-scale parametric empirical studies to test the sensitivity and specificity of the MIT tasks.

Stone and Levin (1979) used a pediatric MI examination methodology similar to that of Garfield (1964) to study a diagnostically mixed sample of 13 children with "developmental delay." Six of the children had clear neurologic deficit; the other seven did not. Ages ranged from 36 to 66 months. Language development functional level as measured with the Denver Developmental Screening Test (DDST) was at 17 months for three subjects. The remainder of the children attained DDST scores ranging from 21 to 64 months. The pediatric MI measures used in this study were the most generally applicable ones attempted for evaluating neurologically impaired children. Measures of stereognosis and graphesthesia also were employed in addition to those tapping MI. The authors noted that MI performance was not related to performance on the Peabody Picture Vocabulary Test, a nonverbal measure of general intelligence. There also was no clear hierarchy of item difficulty among the MI items for this small, diagnostically mixed sample of children.

Schworm and Birnbaum (1989) studied a sample of hyperactive children and found that they were distinguished from a sample of nonhyperactive, learning disabled children by greater MI, increased talking, and nonsystematic task searching.

Mentally retarded children. Benton, Garfield, and Chiorini (1964) compared the MIT performance levels of moderately mentally retarded children (mean IQ = 52) to those of intellectually normal same-age peers and to those of normal younger children of the same mental age as the retardates. As expected the retarded children showed grossly impaired MIT performance overall relative to their intellectually normal peers. The relative rates of failure among the retarded subjects varied with the difficulty levels of the MIT tasks. On tongue protrusion, 38% of the retardates failed the task, whereas 90% of them could not say "ah" for 20 seconds.

Comparison of the moderately retarded children with younger normals of the same *mental* age revealed much more selective MI deficits among the retarded group. These two groups differed significantly on only two MIT tasks: keeping the eyes closed and saying "ah" continuously. A few of the retarded children showed marked impersistence that was atypical for the group as a whole and that therefore could not be accounted for by the relatively low mental age of these children.

Rutter et al. (1970) studied a sample of 9- to 10-year-old mildly to moderately retarded children from the Isle of Wight. Subjects in their sample showed intelligence quotients on the Wechsler Intelligence Scale for Children in the range of 51–85. These researchers used the fifth percentile of the normal sample as a deficit criterion for MI identification. Twenty-three percent of their subjects showed MI according to this criterion.

Finally, Garfield, Benton, and MacQueen (1966) reported significantly greater MI among retarded children with proven brain damage than in children with the nonneurologic syndrome of cultural-familial retardation, even though the two groups of children were matched for chronological age and intelligence level.

Schizophrenia. Domrath (1966) reported moderate MI (failure on two to three tasks) in 15% of his sample of 60 schizophrenics (9/60) as compared to an incidence of only 3% (2/60) in a sample of controls. None of the schizophrenics he studied showed marked impersistence (failure on four or more tasks). One should consider that at the time Domrath wrote, he had available only the first edition of the *Diagnostic and Statistical Manual of Mental Disorders,* and that diagnosis based on those criteria typically were not reliable. Results of his study should be considered exploratory until they have been replicated using currently available, reliable DSM-III-R psychiatric diagnostic criteria for schizophrenia (American Psychiatric Association, 1987).

Critique

Specification of the incidence, nature, and clinical correlates of motor impersistence depends considerably on how the syndrome is operationally defined. Little standardization of MI examination technique has appeared in the literature since Benton and his collegues introduced their MIT methodology. Each author tends to develop another set of MI measures for evaluation of the syndrome as each new study is implemented. Some of these behavioral syndrome-analytic measures are quite thorough, while others have been limited to a single MI measure. Unfortunately very brief and unstandardized MI examination techniques are particularly prone to unreliability, and a measure must be reliable if it is to be accurate and valid.

Even the MIT has produced inconsistent results on studies of interrater reliability (Bell, Lewis, Diller, & Bell, 1971; Garfield, 1964; Rutter et al., 1970). Benton et al. (1983) have raised the question of whether different measures of MI may be differentiable as disjoint syndrome subtypes, so that global MI summary indices may be inappropriate. The possibility that different aspects of the MI syndrome or different MI subsyndromes are combined in the current MIT scoring procedures may account for the inconsistency of MIT scoring findings across studies. To date these issues remain to be resolved empirically.

The use of nonstandard and noncomparable MI measures across studies is unfortunate, because the results of studies that purport to measure the same MI syndrome but that vary greatly in their scope and methodology of examination commonly produce conflicting results that cloud analysis of the syndrome. Differences in measurement technique often are difficult or impossible to separate from differences in clinical syndrome findings. Clearly conclusions about MI syndrome analysis should be limited to the measurement methods employed, and these methods should be as thorough as possible. The best controlled and most thorough lesion correlation study of MI to date has been that of Kertesz et al. (1985), but he did not make use of the MIT procedures published shortly before his research was conducted. The Kertesz et al. (1985) study should be replicated using the MIT measures as the MI syndrome criteria. These two MI batteries have many similar tasks, and a replication study using the MIT should produce results similar to those of the original Kertesz et al. (1985) study if those findings are reliable and valid.

Current evidence suggests that MI incidence is associated with right- more so than left-hemispheric lesions, that it is commonly noted in dementing syndromes, and that it is associated with a more protracted and less successful rehabilitation course (Ben-Yishay, Diller, Gerstman, & Haas, 1968). Studies of MIT interrater reliability are of the foremost importance in a variety of clinical groups, given the concerns about this issue that the test authors have raised. Nearly a decade has passed since they wrote the test manual and noted these concerns, and to date this important work has been overlooked. One hopes that reliability studies will be carried out by clinicians and researchers in acute treatment and rehabilitation settings where neurologic patients are seen. The incidence of MI in chronic schizophrenia and other nonneurologic psychiatric disorders defined by reliable psychiatric diagnostic criteria remains to be investigated.

Extremely thorough and useful methodology for studying the anatomical and behavioral correlates of one index of MI was modeled by Hier et al. (1983a). These researchers produced lateral and medial cerebral hemispheric lesion maps to show the locus of the lesions primarily associated with selected neurologic signs and with failure on various psychometric measures. They also published individual lesion diagrams and behavioral syndrome-analytic patterns on all of their psychometric and behavioral measures for each of their patients. They then reported the frequency of each deficit in their sample and intercorrelated the measures to define syndrome clusters. Unfortunately these investigators used only one index of MI: the ability to keep the eyes closed on command (to a maximum of 30 seconds).

An ideal study of MI would combine the lesion locus–analytic methods of Kertesz et al. (1985) with the lesion and sign correlation methodology of Hier et al. (1983a) together with a thorough measure of MI such as Benton et al.'s (1983) MIT procedures. To date research has not combined the radiographic lesion analysis with thorough syndrome analysis and thorough behavioral MI analysis in a single study.

At present Benton et al.'s (1983) MIT procedure offers the only available methodology for analyzing MI that is standardized, well normed, and suitable for use with adults and children. Questions about its interrater reliability and its clinical correlates remain to be clarified, so its use is probably best classified as experimental at this point. The association of the MIT with lateralized brain dysfunction and with regional areas within each hemisphere has produced conflicting results in the literature. The resolution of such issues first requires the demonstration of psychometric characteristics of validity and reliability. Well-controlled experimental studies of patients with unilateral cerebral lesions, preferably stroke patients in the acute phase of their illness, are needed to investigate syndrome-analytic issues. The MI syndrome–analytic studies of Levin (1973a) and of Rosenbaum et al. (1992) exemplify the sort of parametric work needed to analyze the basis of the MI syndrome. Such analyses of the behavioral and cognitive correlates of MI may be more productive for understanding the neuroanatomic and neurophysiologic bases of the MI syndrome than are lesion correlation studies, which have produced conflicting results on lesion laterality and intrahemispheric lesion locus findings to date.

References

American Psychiatric Association. (1987). *Diagnostic and statistical manual of mental disorders* (3rd ed. rev.). Washington, DC: Author.

Bell, D.B., Lewis, F.D., Diller, L., & Bell, B.W. (1971). Puzzling impersistence of the Motor Impersistence Test. *Proceedings of the 79th Annual Convention of the American Psychological Association, 6,* 623–624.

Benton, A.L., Garfield, J.C., & Chiorini, J.C. (1964). Motor impersistence in mental defectives. *Proceedings of the International Congress on the Scientific Study of Mental Retardation,* 746–750.

Benton, A.L., Hamsher K.deS., Varney, N.R., & Spreen, O. (1983). *Contributions to neuropsychological assessment: A clinical manual.* New York: Oxford University Press.

Ben-Yishay, Y., Diller, L., Gerstman, L., & Haas, A. (1968). The relationship between impersistence, intellectual function and outcome of rehabilitation in patients with left hemiplegia. *Neurology, 18,* 852–861.

Berlin, L. (1955). Compulsive eye opening and associated phenomena. *Archives of Neurology and Psychiatry, 73,* 597–601.

Carmon, A. (1970). Impaired utilization of kinesthetic feedback in right hemisphere lesions: Possible implications for the pathophysiology of "motor impersistence." *Neurology, 20,* 1033–1038.

DeRenzi, E., Gentilini, M., & Bazolli, C. (1986). Eyelid movement disorders and motor impersistence in acute hemisphere disease. *Neurology, 36,* 414–418.

Domrath, R.P. (1966). Motor impersistence in schizophrenia. *Cortex, 1,* 474–483.

Fisher, M. (1956). Left hemiplegia and motor impersistence. *Journal of Nervous and Mental Disease, 123,* 201–213.

Garfield, J.C. (1963). *Motor impersistence in normal and brain-damaged children.* Unpublished doctoral dissertation, University of Iowa, Iowa City.

Garfield, J.C. (1964). Motor impersistence in normal and brain-damaged children. *Neurology, 14,* 623–630.

Garfield, J.C., Benton, A.L., & MacQueen, J.C. (1966). Motor impersistence in brain-damaged and cultural-familial defectives. *Journal of Nervous and Mental Disease, 142,* 434–440.

Hier, D.B., Mondlock, J., & Caplan, L.R. (1983a). Behavioral abnormalities after right hemisphere stroke. *Neurology* (Cleveland), *33,* 337–344.

Hier, D.B., Mondlock, J., & Caplan, L.R. (1983b). Recovery of behavioral abnormalities after right hemisphere stroke. *Neurology* (Cleveland), *33*, 345–350.

Joynt, R.J., Benton, A.L., & Fogel, M.L. (1962). Behavioral and pathological correlates of motor impersistence. *Neurology, 12*, 876–881.

Kertesz, A., Nicholson, I., Cancelliere, A., Kassa, K., & Black, S.E. (1985). *Neurology, 35*, 662–666.

Levin, H.S. (1973a). Motor impersistence and proprioceptive feedback in patients with unilateral cerebral disease. *Neurology, 23*, 833–841.

Levin, H.S. (1973b). Motor impersistence in patients with unilateral cerebral disease: A cross-validation study. *Journal of Consulting and Clinical Psychology, 41*, 287–290.

Lopez, O.L., Becker, J.T., & Boller, F. (1991). Motor impersistence in Alzheimer's disease. *Cortex, 27*, 93–99.

Rosenbaum, J., Fischer, R.S., Leavell, C.A., & Alexander, M.P. (1992, August). *The nature of motor impersistence: Reconsidering attentional and motoric components.* Paper presented at the annual meeting of the American Psychological Association, Washington, DC.

Rosse, R.B., & Ciolino, C.P. (1986). Motor impersistence mistaken for uncooperativeness in a patient with right-brain damage. *Psychosomatics, 27*, 532–534.

Rutter, M., Graham, P., & Yule, W. (1970). *A neuropsychiatric study in childhood.* London: Spastics International Medical Publications.

Schworm, R.W., & Birnbaum, R. (1989). Symptom expression in hyperactive children: An analysis of observations. *Journal of Learning Disabilities, 22*, 35–40.

Stone, N.W., & Levin, H.S. (1979). Neuropsychological testing of developmentally delayed young children: Problems and progress. *Journal of Learning Disabilities, 12*, 66–69.

Howard E.A. Tinsley, Ph.D.

Professor of Psychology and Director, Counseling Psychology Program, Southern Illinois University, Carbondale, Illinois.

NEO PERSONALITY INVENTORY–REVISED

Paul T. Costa, Jr. and Robert R. McCrae. Odessa, Florida: Psychological Assessment Resources, Inc.

Introduction

The revised NEO Personality Inventory (NEO PI-R; Costa & McCrae, 1992) provides measures of five major domains of normal adult personality: Neuroticism, Extraversion, Openness, Agreeableness, and Conscientiousness. The authors view these domains as representing the most basic emotional (Neuroticism), interpersonal (Extraversion), experiential (Openness), attitudinal (Agreeableness), and motivational (Conscientiousness) dimensions underlying the traits identified in natural language and psychological questionnaires. Each domain is further defined in terms of six facet scales, which offer a more fine-grain analysis of specific traits within each of the domains (see Table 1). The five domain scales and 30 facet scales are represented as "a comprehensive assessment" of adult personality (Costa & McCrae, 1992, p. 1).

The NEO PI-R test manual has been updated to provide information about the added facet scores. It continues to provide information on the NEO Five-Factor Inventory (NEO-FFI), a 60-item version of the NEO PI-R that provides scores for the five domains only. The authors recommend use of the NEO-FFI when the time available for testing is limited and one needs information only on global aspects of personality. This review focuses exclusively on the NEO PI-R.

The five-factor model grew out of what has been described as the lexical tradition (Digman, 1990). This work began with an analysis of the trait adjectives used in English and other languages to characterize individuals. Thousands of such words were found, and Cattell (1946) suggested these represented an exhaustive list of personality traits. Research to refine and reduce this list of traits through factor analysis led eventually to Tupes and Christal's (1961) and Norman's (1963) findings that five factors appeared to provide an adequate model for organizing these terms. Digman (1990) reviews the research that led to the development and validation of the five-factor model.

Leong and Dollinger (1990) recently reviewed the NEO Personality Inventory, describing the development and theoretical underpinnings of the instrument and reviewing the evidence pertaining to its validity. The NEO PI-R was developed from the NEO PI by adding facet scales for the Agreeableness and Conscientiousness domains and replacing 10 of the original items measuring the Neuroticism, Extraversion, and Openness domains. Leong and Dollinger's review is still current in most respects, and I attempt to minimize redundancy in this review. A more complete understanding of the NEO-PI-R will be gained by reading both this review and that of Leong and Dollinger.

Table 1

Domains and Facets of the NEO PI-R

Domain/Facet	High Scorer	Low Scorer
Neuroticism		
Anxiety	Apprehensive, fearful, prone to worry, nervous, tense, jittery	Calm, relaxed, do not dwell on potential problems
Angry Hostility	Angry, frustrated, bitter	Easygoing, slow to anger
Depression	Feelings of guilt, sadness, hopelessness, loneliness. Easily discouraged.	Seldom experience these feelings. Not necessarily cheerful or light-hearted.
Self-Consciousness	Uncomfortable around others, sensitive to ridicule, prone to feelings of inferiority	Less disturbed by awkward social situations
Impulsiveness	Unable to control craving and urges	More easily resist temptations, high tolerance for frustration
Vulnerability	Unable to cope with stress; dependent, hopeless, panicked in emergency situations	Capable of handling difficult situations
Extraversion		
Warmth	Affectionate, friendly, like people, forms close attachments	More formal, reserved, distant in manner
Gregariousness	Enjoys company of others	Loners, do not seek (may avoid) social stimulation
Assertiveness	Dominant, forceful, socially ascendant	Prefer to let others do talking
Activity	Rapid tempo, vigorous movement, sense of energy, keeps busy	Leisurely and relaxed in tempo, but not sluggish or lazy
Excitement-Seeking	Craves excitement and stimulation, likes bright colors, noisy environments	Little need for thrills, prefers life that high scorers find boring
Positive Emotions	Laugh easily and often, cheerful, optimistic	Less exuberant and high-spirited

Table 1 *(Cont.)*

Domain/Facet	High Scorer	Low Scorer
Openness		
Fantasy	Vivid imagination, active fantasy life, daydreams	More prosaic, keeps mind on task at hand
Aesthetics	Deep appreciation for art and beauty, moved by poetry, music, and art	Insensitive to and uninterested in art and beauty
Feelings	Experiences deeper, more differentiated emotional states, feel emotions more intensely	Blunted affect, does not believe feelings of much importance
Actions	Prefer novelty and variety to familiarity and routine	Find change difficult, prefer to stick with tried-and-true
Ideas	Intellectually curious, enjoys philosophical arguments, open to ideas	Limited curiosity; narrowly focused on limited topics
Values	Readiness to reexamine social, political, and religious values	Accepts authority and honors tradition
Agreeableness		
Trust	Believe others honest, well-intentioned	Cynical, skeptical, assume others dishonest or dangerous
Straightforwardness	Frank, sincere, ingenious	Manipulate through flattery, craftiness, or deception
Altruism	Concerned for others' welfare; generous, considerate, helpful	Self-centered, reluctant to get involved in others' problems
Compliance	Defers to others, inhibit aggression, forgives and forgets	Aggressive, competitive rather than cooperative, freely expresses anger
Modesty	Humble, self-effacing	Conceited, superior, arrogant
Tender-Mindedness	Sympathetic, moved by others' needs	Hardheaded, rational, less moved by appeals to pity

Continued

Table 1 *(Cont.)*

Domain/Facet	High Scorer	Low Scorer
Conscientiousness		
Competence	Capable, sensible, prudent, effective, well-prepared	Low opinion of abilities; feel unprepared, inept
Order	Neat, tidy, well-organized	Unable to organize, unmethodical
Dutifulness	Adhere strictly to ethical principles, scrupulously fulfill moral obligations	More casual about ethical matters; somewhat undependable or unreliable
Achievement Striving	High aspiration, works hard, diligent, purposeful, sense of direction	Lackadaisical, aimless, lacks ambition, perhaps lazy; not driven to succeed
Self-Discipline	Motivated to get job done	Procrastinate, easily discouraged and eager to quit
Deliberation	Thinks carefully before acting, cautious, deliberate	Hasty, speaks or acts without considering consequences, spontaneous

Note: Reproduced by special permission of the publisher, Psychological Assessment Resources, Inc., 16204 North Florida Avenue, Lutz, Florida 33549, from the NEO Personality Inventory by Paul Costa and Robert McCrae. Copyright 1978, 1985, 1989, 1992 by PAR, Inc. Further reproduction is prohibited without permission of PAR, Inc.

Two versions of the NEO PI-R are available. Form S (for self-reports) consists of 240 items, which are answered using a 5-point scale. Form S is self-administered and considered appropriate for men and women 17 years of age or older. Form R, written in the third person, contains 240 parallel items to be completed by a peer, spouse, or expert. Costa and McCrae (1992, p. 41) refer to the two versions as parallel forms and recommend using Form R as a source of independent information to validate or supplement Form S self-reports. Both forms require sixth-grade reading ability. No time limits are specified for either form, but most respondents require 30 to 40 minutes to complete the NEO PI-R. Older respondents and those with limited reading skills may take longer. For research purposes, the NEO PI-R has been translated into Arabic, Chinese, Czechoslovak, Dutch, French, German, Hebrew, Japanese, Norwegian, Polish, Portuguese, and Swedish.

The NEO PI-R is intended for use with normal individuals; those suffering from disorders that will interfere with their ability to complete a self-report measure in a reliable and valid manner should not be asked to complete this inventory. With special arrangements, however, it can be administered to individuals affected by a variety of physical and psychological disorders. The presence of an examiner is desirable to answer questions that occur, but it is not required. Individuals who are visually impaired or have poor reading skills need the assistance of an examiner to complete the NEO PI-R.

Both Form S and Form R begin with instructions for completing the hand-scoring answer sheet, and then provide directions for the machine-scoring answer sheet on page 2. The 240 items appear on pages 3–8. Form R is available in separate forms for females and males. The questionnaire booklets are laid out in a clear, attractive manner. The contrast of the blue (Form S) or green (Form R) print against the white background, the font size and type used, and the spacing between items make the NEO PI-R test booklets quite easy to read.

As alluded to above, two answer sheets are available with the NEO PI-R. The hand-scoring sheet is a two-part carbonless form, designed for use with either Form S or Form R. Spaces appear at the top of the answer sheet for name, sex, date, and ID number; whether the person being rated is "yourself," "male," or "female"; the initials and age of the person being rated; and the NEO Form (S or R) used. The manual cautions examiners to ensure that the person being rated can be identified correctly by the initials and/or from the name of the rater. Three validity-check items appear at the bottom of the answer sheet. Respondents indicate whether they tried to answer the questions honestly and accurately on a 5-point Likert scale ranging from "strongly disagree" to "strongly agree." Questions asking whether they responded to all of the statements and entered their responses in the correct areas are answered "yes" or "no." Most of the space on the hand-scoring answer sheet is devoted to 240 boxes containing the item number and the initials SD, D, N, A, and SD, which signify responses of "strongly disagree," "disagree," "neutral," "agree," and "strongly agree," respectively.

The hand-scoring answer sheet is uncluttered and visually easy to understand. The answer sheet does not instruct examinees whether to circle, blacken, or draw a line through the letters to signify their responses, but the test booklet provides clear directions about how to record answers. Respondents should experience no difficulty in using the hand-scoring answer sheet.

The machine-scoring answer sheet is a 8½ × 11 scannable form that can be used with either Form S or Form R. The front side presents instructions for marking the form and requests demographic information. Spaces for recording responses to the NEO PI-R items and the three validity-check items are provided on the reverse of the form. The completed machine-scored answer sheets must be sent to the publisher for scoring and interpretation.

The NEO PI-R may be administered either individually or in groups as in a classroom setting. Both forms are essentially self-administering and do not require administration by formally trained professionals. Administration by a teacher, secretary, undergraduate research assistant, or other assistant not highly versed in test administration becomes feasible once familiarity with the test is acquired. It seems unlikely that significant problems will occur during the administration of the test.

There are two profile forms available for Form S and one for Form R. Each profile sheet provides norms for males on one side and for females on the other.

The grey sheet provides college-aged norms for Form S and the white sheet provides adult norms. The college-aged norms should be used with individuals 17–20 regardless of whether they attended or are enrolled in college. The sex of the respondent determines the side of the profile sheet to use. The green form provides adult norms for profiling Form R ratings, and again, the sex of the individual being rated determines which side of the profile sheet to use.

Columns for the five domain scores appear at the left of the profile sheets. Columns for the 30 facets appear to the right, clustered in groups of six with a space between each group. Each column lists raw scores from 0 through the highest score obtainable. Profiling an individual's scores proceeds in three steps: the raw scores from the answer sheet are transcribed to the spaces at the top of the columns; the number in each column that corresponds to the raw score is marked with an X; and the Xs for the domain scores and for the facet scores within a domain are connected with a straight line.

Practical Applications/Uses

Costa and McCrae (1992) describe a wide variety of potential applications for the NEO PI-R in counseling psychology, clinical psychology, psychiatry, behavioral medicine, health psychology, vocational counseling, industrial/organizational psychology, educational research, and other research in general. The authors caution repeatedly that their suggestions are best regarded as hypotheses, a caution this reviewer underscores. They conscientiously remind readers of the speculative, hypothesis-generating nature of their remarks, but practical experience suggests that some readers will overlook these cautions and interpret the remarks as empirically verified summaries. The authors have provided references where findings bear upon suggested applications, but even in these instances the references are often to a single study. It must be emphasized that an extensive program of research is needed to clarify the appropriate uses and limitations of the NEO PI-R.

Costa and McCrae's (1992) suggestions for research vary in quality, possibly as a function of their area of expertise. The extensive, detailed suggestions regarding potential relations between scores on the NEO PI-R facet scales and DSM-III-R (American Psychiatric Association, 1987) personality disorders are clear and seem to outline a potentially fruitful body of research. Their suggestions for using the NEO PI-R in research on the prognosis for therapy and on the selection of optimal treatment approaches highlight important and potentially productive areas of research. Practitioners may find it beneficial to investigate some of these hypotheses in their own work, but the most exciting prospect to this reviewer was the potential benefits that will accrue if programs of research are established to examine these suggestions.

In contrast, some of the authors' suggestions seem implausible. For example, they suggest that the NEO PI-R will assist clinicians in the rapid development of empathy because it provides so much information about the client's personality. Research has failed to document any such benefits with other tests. At another point, the authors argue that individuals who score high on a test assessing interest in sales but low on Extraversion may not understand the nature of the work. I wonder whether the authors understand the nature of interest inventories, for obtaining a high score on an empirically keyed interest measure does not imply an understanding of the nature of an occupation.

This reviewer found Costa and McCrae's (1992) suggestions regarding vocational counseling, industrial/organizational psychology, and educational research to be weak. Important behavioral medicine and health psychology issues related to vocational psychology are not mentioned (e.g., issues pertaining to the debilitating effects of occupational stress and burnout).

Several writers have identified issues in vocational psychology that can be illuminated by research applications of the NEO PI-R (e.g., Brown, 1993; Dawis & Lofquist, 1993; Tenopyr, 1993; Tinsley, 1993). Brown (1993) and Dawis and Lofquist (1993) articulate theoretical justifications for hypotheses about the relations between scores on Neuroticism and job satisfaction, between scores on Conscientiousness and employee satisfactoriness, and between scores on Openness and job turnover and willingness to relocate. Tinsley (1993) postulates relations between the personality and adjustment styles hypothesized by the theory of work adjustment as crucial to work adjustment and scores on the Self-Consciousness and Vulnerability facets of the Neuroticism domain, the Activity facet of the Extraversion domain, and the Deliberation, Order, and Self-Discipline facets of the Conscientiousness domain.

Two dimensions have been identified that underlie the relations among occupations: an orientation toward things versus people, and an orientation toward data versus ideas (see Prediger & Vansickle, 1992). The NEO PI-R may be used to further elaborate these important distinctions among occupations. Extraversion and Agreeableness are both interpersonal dimensions that should bear some relation to the orientation toward people versus things dimension. Openness should be related to the orientation toward data versus ideas, with high Openness related to a preference for dealing with ideas.

For hand scoring, the top stub and top page of the answer sheet are removed to view the responses on the second page. Spaces for summing the domain scores are provided along the right-hand margin of the second sheet. The items are arranged in the test booklet so that they form 30 rows of eight items each on the answer sheet. Each row corresponds to one of the facet scores, and the response options appear as numeric values (4, 3, 2, 1, and 0, or the reverse for negatively worded items). Scoring merely requires summing the numeric values for the eight items in each row. After the 30 facet scores have been calculated, the domain scores are determined by summing the scores for the six facets pertaining to each domain. The user records the domain scores in clearly marked boxes in the lower right-hand corner of page 2 of the hand-scoring answer sheet.

The instructions for scoring are clear, and untrained assistants should be able to learn to score the test with minimal training. Self-scoring is feasible if directions are provided. It should take 5 minutes or less to score each test once one achieves a basic familiarity with the scoring procedures.

The manual cautions administrators to be sure that all items have been answered. If missing responses are discovered after the respondent has left, the examiner must determine whether the NEO PI-R may be validly scored and interpreted. The inventory should not be scored if 41 or more responses are missing; unanswered items should be assigned the neutral response when fewer than 41 responses are missing. Facet scores should be interpreted cautiously when more than three responses are missing from a scale. A response to a validity-check item that indicates the person did not answer the questions honestly and accurately or did not enter responses in the correct spaces invalidates formal scoring of the NEO PI-R. When this occurs, counselors should discuss the test with the respondent to determine the reason for this response.

Once the initial scoring is done, the hand-scoring answer sheet should be checked for three potential response styles, the presence of which invalidates formal scoring and interpretation of the NEO PI-R. Acquiescence is scored by counting the total number of "agree" and "strongly agree" responses across all items; 150 or more "agree" and "strongly agree" responses signifies that a strong acquiescence bias may have influenced the results. This cutoff point is based on research by Costa, McCrae, and Dye (1991), who found that 99% of the respondents in a large volunteer sample agreed or strongly agreed with fewer than 150 items. Nay saying is indicated by a paucity of "agree" or "strongly agree" responses; the endorsement of 50 or fewer items as "agree" or "strongly disagree" indicate a nay saying response bias. The authors recommend a visual inspection of the answer sheet to determine whether random responding occurred. Item response patterns diagnostic of random responding include endorsement of "strongly disagree" to more than 6 consecutive items, "disagree" to more than 9 consecutive items, "neutral" to more than 10 consecutive items, "agree" to more than 14 consecutive items, and "strongly" agree to more than 9 consecutive items. Finally, problematic answers to the validity item about answering honestly and accurately are highlighted in a grey box at the bottom of the answer sheet to draw attention to the questionable validity of the NEO PI-R responses.

With regard to the machine-scoring services available through the publisher, special arrangements can be made to obtain scoring without the accompanying interpretive reports if the user contacts the publisher before ordering the testing materials. This feature may be especially attractive for research applications of the NEO PI-R.

Interpretation of the NEO PI-R requires professional training in psychological testing and measurement and familiarity with the material and procedures described in the test manual. Specific applications of the test results may necessitate specialized training in an area such as counseling psychology, industrial/organizational psychology, or psychiatry.

Appendices B through E of the manual provide NEO PI-R means, standard deviations, and percentiles for adults (Forms S and R) and college students (Form S). As noted previously, college-aged norms should be used for all individuals 17 to 20 regardless of whether they are in or have attended college. Young adults, aged 21 to 30, are in a transitional period. Although adult-aged norms generally should be used for these individuals, using college-aged norms with respondents in this age range may sometimes be appropriate. It is important the test user carefully describe the comparison group used.

A one-page form labeled "Your NEO Summary" is available for providing feedback to respondents. This form presents a very brief description of scores on each of the five domains. The summary is laid out in grid fashion, with five rows corresponding to the five domains and three columns describing T-scores ≥ 56, T-scores from 45–55, and T-scores $\leq$ than 44.

The NEO PI-R profile sheets contain colored bands that span the profile form and descriptors on the left margin to aid interpretation. The descriptors are "very low" (T-scores from 20 to 34), "low" (T-scores from 35 to 44), "average" (T-scores from 45 to 55), "high" (T-scores from 56 to 65), and "very high" (T-scores from 66 to 80). However, Costa and McCrae (1992) caution against using cutoff points to categorize individuals and thinking about NEO PI-R scores as indicating personality types. Each scale represents a continuous dimension, and most individuals will show some combination of traits that might be most characteristic of persons at each extreme. Although the decision rules or cutoff points may be needed for certain applications of the test, the authors caution that those rules are valid only for the special purpose for which they are developed. Categorical trait or type interpretations should not replace the dimensional interpretations for which the test was designed.

A preliminary surface-level interpretation of the NEO PI-R requires no clinical judgment, but users need to understand basic measurement concepts such as the use of T-scores and the distinction between idiographic and nomothetic interpretation. The manual provides clear statements of the meaning of the five domains and the 30 facets, and illustrates profile interpretation with four case studies. The manual provides a reasonable amount of information for beginning the process of learning to interpret the NEO PI-R. Table 1 lists the facets assigned to each domain and the abbreviated descriptors of high and low scores taken from the revised manual (Costa & McCrae, 1992, pp. 16–18).

Technical Aspects

The NEO PI-R has gone through several revisions, with development of the facet scales for Agreeableness and Conscientiousness and minor revisions to the Neuroticism, Extraversion and Openness domain scales just completed in 1992. Sufficient time has not elapsed to allow for evaluation of the long-term stability of these scores on the test, nor for the thorough documentation of validity of portions of the NEO PI-R. Therefore, NEO PI-R users must take care to note the exact version of the inventory used when reviewing research evidence pertaining to the reliability and validity of the instrument. Leong and Dollinger's (1990) thorough review of the reliability and validity of the NEO PI is still current, and Costa and McCrae (1992) and McCrae and Costa (1990) also provide detailed coverages, so the present review provides a synopsis and a more psychometrically oriented evaluation of selected portions of the evidence.

Costa and McCrae (1992) report internal consistency (coefficient alpha) and test-retest reliabilities for the NEO PI-R. Coefficient alpha reliabilities are reported for 1,539 respondents who completed Form S and 277 respondents who completed Form R. The internal consistency reliability of the domain scores ranged from .86 (Agreeableness) to .92 (Neuroticism) for Form S and from .89 (Openness) to .95 (Agreeableness) for Form R. These high values would indicate needless item redundancy in scales measuring a single construct, but they can be regarded as quite satisfactory given that each NEO PI-R domain score incorporates six facets.

The reliabilities for the 30 Form S facet scores range from a low of .56 (Tender Mindedness) to a high of .81 (Depression), with a median of 71. For Form R, the facet scale reliabilities range from a low of .60 (Actions) to a high of .90 (Trust), with a median of .78. By domain, the median reliabilities of the Form S (and Form R) facet scales are .76 (.81) for Neuroticism, .73 (.78) for Extraversion, .715 (.705) for Openness, .70 (.815) for Agreeableness, and .67 (.78) for Conscientiousness. The 12 facet scales added in the latest revision (i.e., those for the Agreeableness and Openness domains) generally have lower internal consistency reliabilities than the 18 original facet scales.

Only five Form R facet scales have reliabilities below .70, and four of those are .69. The exception is the previously mentioned low of .60 for the Actions facet. The internal consistency reliabilities of the following 13 Form S facet scales are below .70: Self-Consciousness (.68), Activity (.63), Excitement Seeking (.65), Feelings (.66), Actions (.58), Values (.67), Compliance (.59), Modesty (.67), Tender Minded-ness (.56), Competence (.67), Order (.66), Dutifulness (.62), and Achievement Striv-ing (.67). These values indicate that a majority of the facet scales possess some factor complexity. Lower internal consistency reliabilities would begin to become alarming, but the degree of factor complexity reflected in these values may have the facilitative effect of allowing stronger relations of NEO PI-R facet scores with external criteria.

Costa and McCrae (1992) cite retest reliability as important in documenting that an instrument purporting to measure a trait does measure enduring dispositions, but their documentation in the manual of the stability of the domain and facet scale scores on the NEO PI-R is inadequate. The authors briefly summarize Form S stability coefficients for the Neuroticism, Extraversion, and Openness domain scales from 6-year and 3-year longitudinal studies, and for Form R from a 7-year longitudinal study. These stability coefficients ranged from .63 to .83 across studies. This reviewer found more detail about the 6-year Form R stability coefficients for a sample of 167 respondents in an earlier work. Costa and McCrae (1988) report the stability coefficients for spouses' ratings of men were Neuroticism, .77; Extra-version, .78; Openness, .82. The stability coefficients of the facet scales ranged from .62 to .76 for Neuroticism, from .65 to .78 for Extraversion, and from .71 to .83 for Openness. For spouses' ratings of women, the stability coefficients of the domains (and facets) were .86 (.70 to .82) for Neuroticism, .77 (.63 to .77) for Extraversion, and .78 (.65 to .73) for Openness. These stability coefficients would indicate good stability for Form R spousal ratings for a briefer period, and they are quite good for a 6-year period.

Another important shortcoming is the absence of Form S–Form R equivalency coefficients. The authors caution professionals against assuming that observer ratings are interchangeable with self-reports, but they also claim that "for use in research on groups, ratings on Form R may often be successfully substituted for self-reports on the NEO PI-R" (Costa & McCrae, 1992, p. 31). The manual provides no evidence in the section labeled reliability to substantiate the equivalence of Form S and Form R domain and facet scores. The authors discuss a study that examined the correlations between three pairs of observers for the domain and facet scales in the section on validity. Self (Form S)/peer (Form R) correlations were .36, .44, .53, .41, and .40 for the N, E, O, A, and C domains, respectively. The range and median correlations for the facets, by domain, were .25 to .35 (me-dian = .30) for Neuroticism, .28 to .50 (median = .40) for Extraversion, .35 to .52

(median = .375) for Openness, .16 to .47 (median = .305) for Agreeableness, and .26 to .42 (median = .34) for Conscientiousness. The authors interpret these values as supporting the validity of the NEO-PI-R, but they also provide strong evidence that Forms S and R should not be used as parallel forms.

Costa and McCrae (1992) cite three investigations of the factor structure of the NEO PI-R. Analyses have been performed on the items and on the facet scores, and on subsamples of men, women, whites, non-whites, young adults (21 to 29), and older adults (30 to 64). The authors conclude that all of these analyses yield support for the five-factor model and for the assignment of the facet scores to their specific domains.

The manual reports in detail only the results of a components analysis of the 30 facet scores based on 500 men and 500 women in the normative sample. Each facet score in this analysis loaded highest on the component associated with its own domain, and all loadings were .44 or higher. Eleven scales were revealed to possess some factor complexity, including Angry Hostility, Impulsiveness, Assertiveness, Activity, Excitement-Seeking, Fantasy, Feelings, Trust, Altruism, Competence, and Self-Discipline. As noted by the authors, this complexity is consistent with theoretical expectations. The eigenvalues and percent of variance accounted for by each component (not reported in the manual) are 3.92 (13.1%), 3.32 (11.1%), 2.59 (8.6%), 3.36 (11.2%), and 3.78 (12.6%) for the N, E, O, A, and C components, respectively. The five-component solution explains only 56.6% of the variance in facet scores. One interpretation of these results is that 34% of the variance in NEO PI-R facet scores is random error variance. Given that the last component extracted accounted for 8.6% of the variance, a more plausible interpretation is that statistically important factors were not extracted.

Leong and Dollinger (1990) aptly summarized the evidence pertaining to the validity of the NEO PI 2 years ago, and the picture has not changed since then. Most directly relevant and unambiguously interpretable is the evidence pertaining to concurrent validity between the NEO PI-R and other self-report measures based on the five-factor model, and the agreement between scores on the NEO PI-R Form S and ratings based on a 40-minute interview using the corresponding five factors from the California Q Set. Additional investigations of the convergent validity of the NEO PI-R have examined the relation of NEO PI scores to scores on other personality scales, such as the Buss-Durkee Hostility Inventory, California Q Set, Eysenck Personality Inventory, Guilford-Zimmerman Temperament Survey, Interpersonal Style Inventory, Minnesota Multiphasic Personality Inventory, Myers-Briggs Type Indicator, Personality Disorders Scales, Personality Research Form, Profile of Mood States, Stait-Trait Personality Inventory, and Sensation Seeking Scale. Other construct validity studies have examined relations among scores on the NEO PI-R and scores on measures of coping (i.e., Ways of Coping Scale), semantic complaints (Cornell Medical Index), sense of well-being and self-esteem (Twenty Statements Test), interpersonal relations (Interpersonal Adjective Scales), and vocational interests (Self-Directed Search). The relation of NEO PI-R scores to social desirability (Marlowe-Crowne Social Desirability scale) and antecedents from childhood experiences (retrospective recollections of parents) have been examined. The ability of NEO PI-R self-report measures to predict open-ended or projective criteria has been studied for criteria such as ego development level (using a sentence completion technique), moral judgment (Defining Issues Test), ego identity (interview-based ratings), divergent thinking (imagining unusual and creative consequences), self-concept (Twenty Statements Test), and grades in an undergraduate personality course. In general, the results of the validity studies show moderate to strong correlations in the theoretically predicted direction. Costa and McCrae (1992) and Leong and Dollinger (1990) provide concise summaries of this body of evidence.

Costa and McCrae (1992) summarize results from two investigations that provide evidence of the validity of the 12 newly added facet scales. One study correlated these facets with 116 scales from 12 personality inventories. Five correlations are reported for each facet. All of the 60 correlations reported appear to be consistent with theoretical expectations. Many (27%) of these correlations are .50 or greater, and most (75%) are .40 or greater. Nevertheless, the validity coefficients for the recently developed facets (median = 43) are somewhat lower than for the established facets (median = 51). In a second study the facets were correlated with the 300 items of the Adjective Check List, and the seven largest correlates were reported for each NEO PI-R facet. The results are consistent with theoretical expectations, as indicated in the following, which provides one correlate of each of the 12 new developed facets: Trust (Trusting), Straightforwardness (- Complicated), Altruism (Generous), Compliance (- Headstrong), Modesty (- Show-off), Tender-Mindedness (Sympathetic), Competence (Efficient), Order (Organized), Dutifulness (- Careless), Achievement Striving (Ambitious), Self-Discipline (Organized), and Deliberation (- Hasty) (see Costa & McCrae, 1992, p. 49).

Critique

This reviewer agrees with Leong and Dollinger (1990) that the NEO PI-R is one of the best instruments available for the assessment of normal adult personality. The instrument is especially welcomed because it was developed and provides adequate norms for adults as opposed to college students. The diversity of information provided by the 5 domain and 30 facet scores ensures its applicability in a great variety of research and applied situations. It is easy to complete, essentially self-administering, and brief enough to be included in a battery with other scales, questionnaires, and tests. A good beginning has been made in documenting the internal consistency and convergent and discriminant validity of the NEO PI-R domain scores and the original 18 facet scores. Evidence is available substantiating the stability of the Form R Neuroticism, Extraversion, and Openness domain scores and the facets of these domains.

Despite this optimistic assessment, there is still work to be done. The 12 new facet scales offer an important addition to the instrument, but psychometrically they appear less sound than the original 18 facet scales. The information provided by Costa and McCrae (1992) suggest that the newly added scales are adequate, but they are less internally consistent and have lower convergent and discriminant validity coefficients than the original facet scales. Their stability has yet to be established.

The sufficiency of five dimensions in accounting for the reliable variance underlying the NEO PI-R is not settled convincingly by the evidence reported in the manual. This issue is more of theoretical and psychometric interest than of practical interest, for the NEO PI-R presents an innovative, insightful view of adult personality, which has many potentially important applications. Nevertheless, the authors should soften their claims that the instrument "allows a comprehensive assessment of adult personality" (Costa & McCrae, 1992, p. 1) or provide more definitive documentation.

The authors need to take a less ambiguous stance regarding the use of NEO PI-R Forms S and R as parallel forms. Costa and McCrae (1992) refer to the forms as parallel (p. 3), they suggest that information from Form R may be substituted for self-ratings (p. 31), and they discuss the development of Form R as an alternative to Form S under the heading "Parallel Forms" (Costa & McCrae, 1992, p. 41). On the other hand, the authors do not actually claim that Forms S and R are parallel, and they caution users against assuming "that observer ratings are interchangeable with self-reports" (Costa & McCrae, 1992, p. 31). The evidence presented in the manual demonstrates unambiguously that Forms S and R are not parallel forms.

I regard the above criticisms as relatively minor and conclude, as did Leong and Dollinger (1990), with "an enthusiastic recommendation for use in research and for thoughtful use in applied settings" (p. 537).

References

American Psychiatric Association. (1987). *Diagnostic and statistical manual of mental disorders* (3rd ed. rev.). Washington, DC: Author.

Brown, S.D. (1993). Contemporary psychological science and the theory of work adjustment: A proposal for integration and a favor returned. *Journal of Vocational Behavior, 43,* 58–66.

Cattell, R.B. (1946). *The description and measurement of personality.* Yonkers, NY: World Book.

Costa, P.T., Jr., & McCrae, R.R. (1988). Personality in adulthood: A six year longitudinal study of self reports and spouse ratings on the NEO Personality Inventory. *Journal of Personality and Social Psychology, 54,* 853–863.

Costa, P.T., Jr., & McCrae, R.R. (1992). *NEO PI-R professional manual.* Odessa, FL: Psychological Assessment Resources.

Costa, P.T., Jr., McCrae, R.R., & Dyer, D.A. (1991). Facet scales for agreeableness and conscientiousness: A revision of the NEO Personality Inventory. *Personality and Individual Differences, 12,* 887–898.

Dawis, R.V., & Lofquist, L.H. (1993). From TWA to PEC. *Journal of Vocational Behavior, 43.*

Digman, J.M. (1990). Personality structure: Emergence of the five-factor model. *Annual Reviews of Psychology, 41,* 417–440.

Leong, F.T.L., & Dollinger, S.J. (1990). NEO Personality Inventory. In D.J. Keyser & R.C. Sweetland (Eds.), *Test critiques* (Vol. VIII, pp. 527–539). Austin, TX: PRO-ED.

McCrae, R.R., & Costa, P.T., Jr. (1990). *Personality in adulthood.* New York: Guilford.

Norman, W.T. (1963). Toward an adequate taxonomy of personality attributes: Replicated factor structure in peer nomination personality ratings. *Journal of Abnormal Social Psychology, 66,* 574–583.

Prediger, D.J., & Vansickle, T.R. (1992). Locating occupations on Holland's hexagon: Beyond RIASEC. *Journal of Vocational Behavior, 40,* 111–128.

Tenopyr, M.L. (1993). Construct validation needs in vocational behavior. *Journal of Vocational Behavior, 43,* 84–89.

Tinsley, D.J. (1993). Extensions, elaborations, and construct validation of the theory of work adjustment. *Journal of Vocational Behavior, 43,* 67–74.

Tupes, E.C., & Christal, R.E. (1961). Recurrent personality factors based on trait ratings. *USAF ASD Technical Report, 61–97.*

Cynthia Russo Silverman, Psy.D.
Psychologist, Boca Raton, Florida.

Grant Aram Killian, Ph.D.
Adjunct Professor of Psychology, Nova University, Fort Lauderdale, Florida.

William Joseph Burns, Ph.D.
Professor of Psychology, Nova University, Fort Lauderdale, Florida.

THE NEONATAL BEHAVIORAL ASSESSMENT SCALE

T. Berry Brazelton. London, England: MacKeith Press. U.S. Distributor—J.B. Lippincott Company.

Introduction

The Neonatal Behavioral Assessment Scale (NBAS; Brazelton, 1973, 1984) is an instrument that investigates the behavioral capacities of neonates at not less than 37 weeks gestation or more than 30 days after birth. The NBAS is designed as an interactive assessment of the normal, healthy, full-term newborn in which the examiner facilitates the best performance over a series of trials. In the process, the infant's inborn characteristics as well as his or her adjustment to labor, delivery, and new environment during the first month of life are assessed. The exam provides a means of assessing the newborn's attempt at homeostasis, the organization of inner and outer stimuli, as well as his or her sociability with caregivers. A major underlying consideration throughout the exam is the newborn's use of states of consciousness as a means of controlling impinging stimuli and regulating homeostasis. Specifically, the pattern of state changes is measured during the exam, and variability of state becomes a hallmark in a healthy neonate's adaptive functioning. According to Brazelton (1978), state becomes the infant's first line of defense against impinging stimuli. Obtaining best performance becomes a reflection of the baby's capacity to organize responses via state behavior.

T. Berry Brazelton, M.D., author of the NBAS, graduated from Columbia University School for Physicians and Surgeons in 1943 and accepted a medical internship in New York City. In 1945 he moved to Boston to serve as a medical resident at Massachusetts General Hospital before undertaking pediatric training at Children's Hospital. His interest in child development then led to training in child psychiatry at the Massachusetts General Hospital and James Jackson Putnam Children's Center from 1947 to 1950. Dr. Brazelton is presently Clinical Professor of Pediatrics at Harvard Medical School and founder of the Child Development Unit (a training and research center) at the Children's Hospital in Boston. He has published 18 books and more than 180 articles on child development. In 1989 Brazelton was appointed to the National Commission on Children by the presi-

457

dent, Senate, and House of Representatives, and he is a national cosponsor of Parent Action, a grassroots organization for parents.

The development of the NBAS came from the author's early work with infants some 30 years ago. Working as a pediatric intern, he noticed behavioral differences among neonates (Brazelton, 1978). The ability of the baby to shape the infant-caregiver dyad was tremendous. Based on the early works of Graham and associates in 1956 and Prechtl and Beintema in 1964 (cited in St. Clair, 1978), Brazelton utilized neonates' states of consciousness in the timing of maneuvers. The pattern of states appeared to be important characteristics of newborns during the period of adjustment to the extrauterine environment. The resulting formalized evaluation, originally titled the Cambridge Newborn Behavioral and Neurological Scales (Brazelton & Freedman, 1971), eventually became the Neonatal Behavioral Assessment Scale (Brazelton, 1973). The development of the scale involved the work of Freedman, Horowitz, Robey, Sameroff, and Tronick. The collaborators came from diverse backgrounds, including anthropology, pediatrics, developmental psychology, and psychiatry. Together with Brazelton, the group developed this comprehensive clinical interactive tool.

There is no comprehensive standardization study available to date for the NBAS. Silverman (1991) has argued for additional reliability studies as well as long-term predictive validity data. The importance of such studies cannot be ignored. According to Kline (1986), test scores from clearly defined samples representative of the population at large are the only basis for comparison. Consequently, if individuals are to compare test scores, only when there is a standardized sample large enough can we trust the results from various research projects. The variability from site to site might be due to cultural differences rather than differences in babies. Because the newborn is influenced by various interuterine and environmental factors, Als, Tronick, Lester, and Brazelton (1977) question the meaningfulness of collecting normative data on such a sample to be used for comparative purposes. They believe it is more important to examine the behavior of the newborn from a particular culture rather than to imagine a baby's behavior might be representative of the U.S. population on the whole. Needless to say, both researchers and clinicians who use the NBAS are forced to adapt their method to a scale not undergoing standardization procedures.

In an effort to explore the effect of background variables of neonatal behavior on a sample of 221 normal newborns, Lancioni, Horowitz, and Sullivan (1980) completed a study utilizing the Neonatal Behavioral Assessment Scale with Kansas Supplements (NBAS-K) and believe the NBAS-K provided for a more individualized infant assessment based on modal or average scores representative of the typical performance across newborns rather than the best performance measured with the NBAS. Their analyses of data are from the first 3 days of life with a subset of 106 infants later retested at 2 weeks and again at 1 month of age. The background variables included age and education of parents, number of previous births, number of pregnancies, length of labor, time since last feeding, birth weight, and current weight at time of exam. The results of those analyses suggest that the background variables selected had minimal influence on performance. Interpretations of the test results are inadequate, however, if one uses the criteria suggested by Kline (1986) recommending a sample size of 500 to reduce statistical error and stratified sampling.

The NBAS has undergone five revisions in the last 20 years. A preliminary version was developed in 1971 by Brazelton and Freedman (the previously mentioned Cambridge Newborn Behavioral and Neurological Scales) but was never published. The administration of items and a definition of neonatal behavioral states and elicited responses were described in an unpublished manual, which gave suggestions for grouping items in a meaningful fashion for purposes of interpretation.

In 1973 Brazelton and his colleagues published a more comprehensive version of the scales through *Clinics in Developmental Medicine*. Entitled the Neonatal Behavioral Assessment Scale (NBAS), this instrument overlapped the 1971 version with a few important exceptions. The 1973 revision suggested an order of administration of the items and general procedure, taking into account the appropriate states in which the assessment of each behavior can be made. Photographs clearly depicting the neonate in six states were included: a) deep sleep, b) light sleep, c) drowsy, d) alert, e) eyes open, and f) crying. Scoring definitions, examiner training requirements, and early research with the scale also were described. The 1973 edition consisted of 27 behavioral items and 20 reflex items intended to score a full-term (40 weeks gestation) normal Caucasian infant as he or she relates to inner and outer stimuli. The 27 NBAS behavioral items, which measure the infant's interactional capacities with his or her caregiver as scored on a 9-point scale, include response decrement to light, rattle, bell, and pinprick; orientation to inanimate visual, inanimate auditory, animate visual, animate auditory, and combined animate visual and auditory stimuli; alertness; general tonus; motor maturity; pull to sit; cuddliness; defensive movement; consolability; peak of excitement; rapidity of buildup to a higher state of arousal; irritability; activity; tremulousness; startle; lability of skin color; lability of states; self-quieting activity; hand-mouth facility; and number of smiles.

Sullivan modified the NBAS and called it the Neonatal Behavioral Assessment Scale with Kansas Supplements (NBAS-K). He asked trained examiners to score infants' behavior in a standard manner looking for best performance and to score their "modal" or average scores on consolability, orientation, and defensive maneuvers (Horowitz, Sullivan, & Linn, 1978). In addition, Sullivan wrote scoring definitions for five additional scales: orientation to inanimate visual and auditory stimuli, quality of infant's alert responsivity, examiner persistence, general irritability, and reinforcement value of infant's behavior. Horowitz et al. (1978) reported that the NBAS-K provides for a more individualized infant assessment based on the modal or average scores achieved with healthy full-term babies. For a modal score to be assigned, at least three to four trials of an item is preferred (Brazelton, 1984).

Investigators conducted research on the stability and structure of the NBAS-K to determine if modal scores were more predictive of a newborn's performance than best scores. A study conducted by Lancioni et al. (1980) reported modal scores did not demonstrate higher correlations over the first 3 days of life than best scores. In addition, there are times when a modal score is difficult to obtain. Disorganized neonates may not be accessible for repeated item administrations. Best scores reflect the neonate's attempt at organization of inner and outer stimuli as well as the amount of facilitation necessary to produce optimal behavior (Brazelton, 1984). Modal scores may be useful as additional information in determining the newborn's performance.

In 1982, Als, Lester, Tronick, and Brazelton developed an instrument to systematically assess the behavior of the preterm infant and document patterns of developing organization. The development of the scale was based on the belief that preterm infants developed quite differently from full-term infants. The new research instrument, called the Assessment of Preterm Infants Behavior (APIB), assessed the neonate when he or she was without medical aids, in a room temperature of 72–80 degrees Fahrenheit. The rationale for developing the APIB was that preterm infants had difficulty maintaining the state of alertness necessary for appropriate administration of the NBAS. In addition, the criteria for scoring term infants' responses were never appropriate for preterm infants. The latter demonstrate an inadequate intake of stimuli, a motor system with unsuccessful inhibition of responses, and autonomic nervous system exhaustion. Detailing changes over a relatively short period of time is helpful in understanding the preterm infant's communication and may lead to adaptations in the environment. Interested readers should refer to Als et al. (1982) for more detailed description of the instrument.

Despite the fact that the ABIP is more time-consuming than the NBAS, it has the advantage of being appropriate for preterm or term infants. Because the NBAS items are included within the ABIP, the two scoring systems can be compared in the same infant. Burns, Deddish, and Hatcher (1982) studied the usefulness of the NBAS with preterm infants at 33 to 40 weeks postconception. Their results support that the NBAS is not an appropriate scale for use with preterm infants. Although the scale did reflect the babies' immature organizational systems, there was a need to adjust the administration of items as the result of decreased responsiveness. These authors thus argue that the NBAS should not be used as a clinical instrument for preterm infants. The APIB is designed to assess the way infants attempt to differentiate and modulate their systems, and it offers a complete description of the specific behaviors these infants use in their efforts to maintain stability. "The continuous identification of the thresholds of balance and stress is the key feature of this examination" (Als, 1984, p. 31).

According to the manual, the second edition of the NBAS (Brazelton, 1984) was developed specifically to a) restate the original purposes of the scale, b) clarify the definitions, c) embellish the training techniques, d) summarize the current research applications, and e) add an inanimate visual and auditory item to the basic scale. Nine supplementary items are included in the 1984 addition and deemed an optional tool, especially with fragile babies. These items, based on APIB items and the NBAS-K, include a) quality of alert responsiveness, b) cost of attention, c) examiner persistence, d) general irritability, e) robustness and endurance, f) regulatory capacity, g) state regulation, h) balance or motor tone, and i) reinforcement value of the infant's behavior. An additional set of modal scores have been added to the 1984 version on items such as orientation, consolability, and defensive maneuvers. Horowitz et al. (1978) argue that modal or average scores can predict a baby's functioning under a normal home situation better than can "best performance" scores. In both editions of the NBAS manual, however, Brazelton and his colleagues recommend using "best performance" scores as the most accurate reflection of infant status. Because a newborn infant is in the midst of an adjustment to birth, the use of optimal rather than modal performance scoring is preferred. "Best performance" scores are interpreted in the context of the amount of effort the examiner and newborn invest in their interactions with each other during the administrations. Although the scores were not designed to predict functioning under home conditions, these scores are considered a good estimate of developmental newborn status. Therefore, modal scores may be used as additional information alongside optimal scores as a way of assessing functioning at home.

The 1984 NBAS package contains an audiovisual tape by Brazelton ("Neonatal Behavioral Assessment Scale"), a test manual that includes the basic background for the NBAS, scoring guidelines, and a data summary sheet, and a set of guidelines for using the NBAS with newborns and their families. There is also a testing kit of equipment necessary to complete the assessment: a) a shiny red ball, b) a flashlight (batteries not included), c) a rattle, d) a bell, e) a tactile probe, and f) a portable carrying case. The package also contains eligibility requirements for professionals wishing to become certified as NBAS-trained examiners and a list of NBAS training centers. The manual provides a description of the test, its development and uses, reliability and validity information, normative data, instructions for administration, scoring, and interpretation, methods for data analysis and prediction studies, suggestions for using the NBAS in research, criteria for selecting scale scores, descriptive criteria for identifying states, and photographs of typical infant responses to NBAS items.

The 20 NBAS reflex items are each scored on a 4-point scale from 0 to 3. Most healthy full-term babies obtain an average score of 2 on these items. The tonic neck reflex, ankle clonus, and nystagmus may receive either a 0, 1, or 2, all considered within normal limits. Brazelton suggests if three elicited scores are deviant, the infant should be referred for a complete neurological exam following the NBAS. There are two global behavioral scales—attractiveness and need for stimulation. The attractiveness dimension measures the infant's organized response capacity, integration of behavior, and positive feedback to the examiner. These factors contribute to the neonate's social attractiveness to the extrauterine environment. "Need for stimulation" refers to the baby's use of and need for stimulation to help organize his or her responses. Both items are rated 0 to 3, with 0 being infants in need of external help to organize and 3 measuring optimal self-organization. The NBAS now contains 28 behavioral items instead of the earlier 27. All of the original behavioral and reflex items are included in the 1984 version.

The manual suggests that scoring can be done at the end of the administration to minimize the examiner's distractibility from the overall flow of infant responsivity. The exam itself usually takes about 20 to 30 minutes. There is a suggested order of administration, although Brazelton suggests that one must follow the infant's availability in order to assure that he or she gives the best performance. Throughout the manual and on the scoring sheets, the state required for each item to be administered is listed in parentheses. Examiners must follow the proper state for each item administered or delay the item if the infant is not in the necessary state. After the administration is completed, scoring usually adds about 15–20 minutes to the total exam. The examiner makes a check mark in the appropriate box on the score sheet for the 28 behavioral items (using a 9-point scale).

There are some difficulties with the interpretation of scoring, and the scale does not have a uniform scoring system. Some items are considered optimal at 9, while others are optimal scored at 5. No summary score can be derived because items are deemed optimal at different points. Instead, clustering for data analysis those items that interact in similar ways and describe global functions in the baby takes place (Lester, Als, & Brazelton, 1982). The clusters are a) habituation, b) orientation, c) motor performance, d) range of state, e) regulation of state, f) autonomic regulation, and g) reflexes. It is also suggested that the examiner write a paragraph at the end of the behavior scoring sheet overall performance, major state fluctuations, and any additional comments relative to the assessment.

The NBAS can be used in a number of settings (hospital, outpatient clinic, home setting), although environmental conditions such as noise level and room temperature must remain standardized. Any deviations from these conditions should be reported on the score sheet. The exam begins ideally when the infant is asleep, midway between feedings. At least two exams on different days are recommended in order to avoid making conclusions on the basis of chance variations. Examiners are more likely to draw erroneous conclusions on the basis of a single exam. Administration takes place ideally on day 3 or 4, when the infant is free of the stress of delivery, and again on day 9 or 10, when the baby is at home. Brazelton (1978) points to "the maximum predictive validity of the scale in the pattern of recovery reflected in repeated assessment over the first few weeks of life rather than in any one assessment" (p. 8). He goes on to say that the scale was not designed for neonates of less than 37 weeks gestation or more than 30 days old. At 1 month after birth, some of the reflexes have all but disappeared.

Detailed information regarding precise methods for administration are clearly outlined in the manual and presented in a user-friendly fashion. The examiner plays an integral part in the administration of the NBAS, as he or she is the extrauterine environment to which the neonate responds. Because the score is based on clinical judgment, examiners must be trained in order to make these judgments. Brazelton has recommended that all researchers and clinicians, regardless of professional background, participate in the training at one of the three specified training centers before using the scale in either a clinical or research project. After an initial acquaintance with the use of the scale (assessing and scoring), new examiners are advised to participate in a 2-day training session to ensure interrater reliability. It is quite time-consuming to learn to administer the NBAS and rather expensive (at the time of this writing, the fee for the Brazelton-Based Consultation with Infants and Families Training Program is $950.00; if the trainer travels to the examiner's site, travel and lodging expenses are additional costs to the trainee).

Practical Applications/Uses

According to the manual, the Brazelton Neonatal Behavioral Assessment Scale is used primarily in research settings and in clinical practice as an interactional tool between newborn and examiner. However, despite the author's warning that the NBAS is not a normative test for infant development, the scale continues to be used as a test. For example, it is used in 500 research centers in the United States, 15 in Europe, and 10 in Asia to help parents understand and attach to their new babies. "The NBAS is not, at present, a tested clinical tool" (Brazelton, 1984, p. 103). Nevertheless, the NBAS does offer a trained examiner the descriptive status of a neonate. Full-term newborns respond in such a way during the exam that their observable physiological reactions, social responsivity, and motor and cognitive skills are scored as reflecting their ability to meet the demands of the environment.

Several studies involving cross-cultural comparisons with the NBAS have been reported, and the search for developmental differences at birth within different cultures has been cited (Brazelton, Koslowski, & Tronick, 1971; Keefer, Tronick, Dixon, & Brazelton, 1982; Kestermann, 1981). Numerous studies have focused on prenatal and perinatal factors associated with NBAS scores in different parts of the world (Brazelton, Tronick, Lechtig, Lasky, & Klein, 1977; Dunlop, 1982; Saco-Pollitt, 1981), exploring factors such as maternal nutrition and parity, drug condition during labor and delivery, and correlations between birth weight and attitude. Certain cross-cultural research has investigated nutrition and teenage childbearing in Puerto Rico and the United States (Lester, Garcia-Coll, & Sepkoski, 1982), and some has compared a typical pattern of fetal growth among normal-size infants born to teenage and older mothers in Puerto Rico (Lester, Garcia-Coll, Valcaicel, Hoffman, & Brazelton, 1986). Included in the latter study was the use of supplementary NBAS items. The findings suggest that the NBAS supplementary items do provide qualitative aspects of neonatal behavior based on the examiner's subjective impressions, but that they do not add predictive information for groups of at-risk infants. Overall, it is important to note that the NBAS itself may not be sensitive to the performance of at-risk infants because it was designed for assessing full-term babies (Brazelton, 1973, 1984).

The NBAS studies of Gomes-Pedro, Bento de Almedia, Silveria da Costa, and Barbosa (1984) and Choi and Hamilton (1986) have investigated, in Portugal and Korea, respectively, the effects of early contact on the behavior of newborn infants and on maternal attitudes towards the newborn. These studies illustrate that early contact with newborns facilitates caring maternal feelings in mothers toward them.

Although sample sizes in all of the studies discussed have been criticized as less than adequate (Kline, 1986) and limited to particular areas in a given country, many sources of variability in neonatal performance have been explored. There is a need to utilize a broader sample of neonates from different cultures in order for valid conclusions to be drawn. Based on the notion that the standardization of context, such as room temperature and noise level, has been a critical concept in Brazelton's (1973, 1984) instruction manual, DeVries and Super (1978) have selected those items on the NBAS that are most sensitive to contextual influences and argue that caution should be used when drawing conclusions about cross-cultural research. In particular they believe that there are differences in the standardization of testing procedures based on differences in contextual variations. They studied the effects of home versus hospital, and tested infants and maternal beliefs about neonatal vulnerability within four regions of Africa. They propose that the NBAS findings obtained in cross-cultural research may be better viewed as indications of cultural bias rather than infant performance. Brazelton does not address this issue in the 1984 NBAS manual.

The effects of prenatal alcohol exposure and maternal narcotic addiction has been documented widely. The NBAS has been used to assess newborn performance in a number of studies. Early investigations of the effects of neonatal narcotic withdrawal suggest that the Brazelton scales are sensitive to many signs of narcotic withdrawal. Addicted newborns showed deficits in state control and interactive ability with an increased irritability and tremulousness in response to a stimulus (Chasnoff, Burns, & Schnoll, 1983; Kron, Kaplan, Finnegan, Litt, & Phoenix, 1975; Soule, Standley, Copans, & Davis, 1974; Strauss, Lessen-Firestone, Starr, & Ostera, 1975; Strauss, Starr, Ostera, Chavez, & Stryker, 1976). Babies who were delivered by mothers using PCP have been found to show significant changes on the NBAS compared with mothers withdrawing from polydrug use (Chasnoff, Burns, Hatcher, & Burns, 1983). Classic signs of withdrawal were not found in polydrug exposed babies, although significant changes in levels of consciousness, hypotonicity, and hyperreflexia were reported (Chasnoff, Burns, Hatcher, & Burns, 1983; Chasnoff, Hatcher, & Burns, 1982; Chasnoff, Schnoll, Burns, & Burns, 1984; Rogan et al., 1986). Methadone-exposed infants measured with the NBAS exhibited deficits in interactive behavior within the first 3 days of life (Finnegan, 1984). In a study by Jeremy and Hans (1985) involving methadone-exposed neonates, NBAS scores were reported during the first week of life and again at 4 weeks. Findings during the first week of life are consistent with other reports in the literature; by 1 month, the problems in neurobehavioral functioning largely have disappeared. The study suggests that methadone does not continue to interfere with neurobehavioral functioning on a long-term basis.

The NBAS also has been utilized in the evaluation of the effects of cocaine on pregnancy and the newborn (Chasnoff, Burns, & Burns, 1987; Chasnoff, Burns, Schnoll, & Burns, 1985; Chasnoff, Griffith, MacGregor, Dirkes, & Burns, 1989). On the NBAS, infants exposed to cocaine exhibited significantly more irritability, tremulousness, and state control as compared with a control group or with infants whose mothers used methadone. One study (Chasnoff et al., 1987) reported a significant increase in the rate of sudden infant death syndrome for cocaine-exposed infants as compared to narcotic-addicted infants.

Additionally, the NBAS has been used in studies relating intrauterine alcohol exposure to infant behavior with special emphasis on the response decrement items (Ernhart et al., 1985; Streissguth, Barr, & Martin, 1983). Varying amounts of alcohol ingestion during different periods in gestation were studied as well (Coles, Smith, & Falek, 1987; Coles, Smith, Fernhoff, & Falek, 1985; Coles, Smith, Lancaster, & Falek, 1987; Smith, Coles, Lancaster, Fernhoff, & Falek, 1986).

Other research has used the NBAS to compare the behavioral responses of infants whose mothers smoked 15 or more cigarettes a day compared to those of nonsmoking mothers (Saxton, 1978). The study failed to show statistically significant difference in overall infant behavior. One limitation in using the NBAS is that there are frequently numerous interpretations of a specific score and scoring is somewhat suggestive of these meanings. Studies examining caffeine ingestion during pregnancy have shown that lower levels of caffeine may affect the infant when socially interactive demands are made. Increased caffeine levels may produce spontaneous and noninteractive behaviors (Emory, Konopka, Hronsky, Tuggey, & Dave, 1988).

Research with neonates exposed in utero has significant implications for future mother-infant interactions. Tronick (1987) discusses some limitations of the Brazelton scale in respect to such research, offering the opinion that NBAS scores are not reflective of any one specific behavior but rather an integration of multiple causative factors. He goes on to suggest that additional assessments be utilized in the study of teratogenic effects on the newborn as well as repeated NBAS exams.

Numerous studies have been undertaken to document the scale's usefulness as an interventional tool for educating parents and health care personnel about newborn behavioral abilities. Several suggest that teaching parents about the abilities of their newborns through a demonstration of the NBAS fosters early positive interactions (Anderson & Sawin, 1983; Beal, 1989; Golas & Parks, 1986; Meyers, 1982; Szajnberg, Ward, Krauss, & Kessler, 1986; Widmayer & Field, 1981; Worobey & Belsky, 1982). However, Belsky (1985) cautions that some of these studies have used confounding interventions such as videotaping, which may have created results due to experimenter effects (Widmayer & Field, 1980). He goes on to suggest that extra contact with the examiner also may have contributed to the positive findings. Beal (1986) cautions restraint as well when reviewing research that implies long-term beneficial effects of early intervention with the NBAS, and she reviews those studies that demonstrate short-term positive effects of NBAS demonstrations during the first year of life. Worobey and Brazelton (1986) suggest that one NBAS-based intervention may not produce a lasting positive effect on a family, but believe it offers an important first step toward developing a feeling of mastery in the parents. It is the opinion of Nugent and Brazelton (1989) that interventions with the NBAS during the early period of newborn development will enhance a positive reciprocal communication in the family with long-term consequences. They suggest that psychological benefits derive from utilizing the NBAS within the family system.

Infant temperament also has been the subject of NBAS research. Such characteristics as infant irritability, activity level, sucking, eye contact, and so on have been thought to influence caregiver behavior during the newborn period and have been assessed using the NBAS (Aleksandrowiez & Aleksandrowiez, 1974; Crockenberg, 1981; Crockenberg & Acredolo, 1983; Crockenberg & McClusky, 1986; Jones & Lenz, 1985; Osofsky, 1976; Osofsky & Danzger, 1974; Penman, Meares, Baker, & Milgrom-Friedman, 1983; Worobey, 1986a, 1986b). These investigators found temperament to be related to NBAS findings. However, the generalizability of many of these studies are limited by small sample size, inclusion of high-risk infants, and possibly a general patterning of maternal perception rather than a true measurement of inherited traits.

The role of obstetric medication on neonatal behavior has been evaluated by the NBAS in a number of studies (e.g., Aleksandrowiez & Aleksandrowiez, 1974; Kuhnert, Linn, Kennard, & Kuhnert, 1985; Muhlen, Pryke, & Wade, 1986; Standley, Soule, Copans, & Duchouny, 1974). Although the studies report neonatal effects for the heavily medicated group of infants as measured by the NBAS, there are methodological difficulties. A wide range of drugs is reported within each group, as well as varying susceptibility to drugs among the mothers tested. Subject loss also posed a problem with this research: Babies could not be assessed because they were taken to special care nurseries. The authors agree that behaviors produced by obstetrical medication may affect the interaction between infant and caregiver, which may in turn affect subsequent infant development.

Several investigators have attempted to study the effects of tactile stimulation on the behavior of preterm infants. The specific effects of stimulation have varied across studies and must be viewed with caution. As noted, the scale was designed to be used with full-term infants (Brazelton, 1973, 1984), and Brazelton believes that the supplementary items should be used when assessing preterm infants with the NBAS. Burns et al. (1982) conducted a study using the NBAS to determine the response characteristics of preterm infants born at 32 to 40 weeks postconceptual age. Their results indicate that the NBAS without modification presents an inappropriate tool with preterm infants. Perhaps the APIB is the better scale for such studies, as it was designed for preterm infants.

Despite the good evidence to the contrary, many researchers have chosen to use the NBAS with preterm infants. Because of the small sample size in these studies, it is very difficult to interpret the results (see Field, 1979; Leijon, 1982; Paludetto et al., 1982; Paludetto, Rinaldi, Mansi, Andolfi, & Del Giudice, 1984; Scafidi et al., 1986). Scanlon, Scanlon, and Tronick (1984) attempted to describe the behavior of the extremely premature neonate using a modified version of the NBAS. These investigators state that the examination was a forerunner of the APIB, and the use of the APIB is supported with preterm infants. Forty-five infants were enrolled in the study. Als (1986) describes the theoretical framework underlying the development of the APIB and its appropriateness for use with the preterm infant as well as at-risk infants and healthy full-term infants.

Regarding special populations of high-risk infants, NBAS studies reported include hydrocephalic infants, jaundiced infants, the effects of maternal anemia on infant behavior, pulmonary hypertension in the neonate, preterm infants with intracranial hemorrhage, neonates with seizures, infants of multi-risk families, and full-term but underweight infants (Als, Tronick, Adamson, & Brazelton, 1976; Anderson et al., 1989; Aylward, Lazzara, & Meyer, 1978; Emory, Tynam, & Dave, 1989; Escher-Graub & Fricker, 1986; Frances, Self, & McCaffree, 1984; Greene, Fox, & Lewis, 1983; Hofheimer, Poisson, Strauss, Eyler, & Greenspan, 1983; Murphy, Scher, Klesh, & Guthrie, 1988; Osofsky, 1974; Vaughn, Brown, & Carter, 1986).

The NBAS has been used in nursing practice to identify infants that have shown suspect behavior during the administration of routine nursing care similar to the NBAS assessment. The NBAS results have been consistent with nursing observation of infant behavior (Maloni, Stegman, Taylor, & Brownell, 1986). The NBAS also has been used as a teaching technique for neonatal nurses, who then can educate parents regarding their newborn's capacities (Gibbs, 1981).

Several studies have documented maternal reactions to various modes of delivery and the impact of mother-infant interactions following delivery. No significant differences were found for mother-infant interaction regardless of delivery method (Gottlieb & Barrett, 1986; Kochanevich-Wallace, McClusky-Faucett, & Meek, 1987; Leijon, Finnstrom, Hedenskog, Ryden, & Tylleskar, 1979). Caution should be exercised when interpreting these results, as sample sizes are less than adequate in all of the studies.

Mental health personnel and researchers would be the most likely candidates to administer the NBAS. Administration and scoring of the scale is open to any individual who has undertaken the training program set up by Brazelton and his colleagues. Scoring can take up to 15 minutes at the end of the exam. As previously described, the examiner is an interactive participant in the evaluation, attempting to draw out the neonate's best performance. Because the scale does not set a fixed order of administration, the examiner must be sensitive to the infant's cues. Brazelton (1984) reports that examiners can be trained to an 85%–90% level of interrater reliability agreement, which can be maintained for up to 2 years without retraining. The scoring criteria presented in the manual are explicit. Brazelton (1984) recommends that the trainee work with at least 20 to 25 babies before training begins in order to master the ability to understand neonate behavioral cues.

Clopton and Martin (1985) argue that the reported percent of interrater agreement may be inflated due to four problems: 1) the predominant use of a few scores, such as midway scores, and the rare use of others, such as extreme scores of 1 or 9; 2) the practice of allowing a difference of 1 point to be counted as agreement, when several items function as 3-point scales; 3) the subjective administration of the decrement items; and 4) the fact that translation to a prior scale does not produce high interrater reliability. Clopton and Martin believe interrater reliability should be reported as exact agreements and that the actual percentage of agreement between trained observers is probably less than 85%. Interrater reliability is an important feature of a good test, and Brazelton does not address the issue of this type of inflation in the manual.

The manual suggests three training films to view as part of the training phase. These films describe the scale in detail and illustrate the performance of various infants. The manual also recommends that the trainee witness a live demonstration by a certified examiner. There is a 2-day reliability training workshop as well, which is conducted by a certified trainer from one of the seven training centers. This phase of training, which serves to bring the trainee to the percent level of reliability agreement, presents a discussion of administration and scoring issues, a demonstration by the trainer, and joint scoring by both examiner and trainee. The trainee must administer the scale to two babies while the examiner and trainee independently score the scaled items. The manual cautions that no more than two babies should be examined in one day since observational powers tend to diminish as fatigue sets in. The examiner must test the infant at least twice over the first few weeks of life in order for a pattern of recovery to be established, which is more meaningful than a single examination.

The 1984 NBAS manual describes the order of administration in great detail. Although there is no fixed item sequence, as noted previously, grouping the items as suggested ensures a sequence of stimulation for the baby that in turn reflects his or her coping mechanism in the face of increasing stress.

The instructions for scoring each item are presented clearly in the manual. Scoring is done by hand immediately following the exam. (There is, however, a computer-generated scoring method for the Lester, Als, & Brazelton [1982] cluster system.) With 48 items, scoring can be quite cumbersome. The individual item scores are not independent, nor do they have equal intervals. Further, NBAS items cannot be transformed into traditional summary scores, although a number of statistical analyses have been performed over the years. Popular approaches have been item comparisons, reduction of the items to several subscales, factor analytic approaches, a priori clusters, and Lester et al.'s (1982) cluster system. For an excellent review of the various scoring systems, see Als et al. (1982). They suggest that there are three drawbacks to the item-by-item comparisons: the items are not independent, the differences arising in a post hoc analysis may be due to chance, and the reported differences may not be greater than the reliability of the examiner. In looking at the reduction of items to various subscales, the main disadvantage is that the items cannot be combined because of differing optimal ranges of performance. In factor analytic methods, sample sizes are often too small and factors are compared at different points in time, a problem because the factors may not be measuring the same variables. Als et al. (1982) recommend a priori clustering of scale items in four areas (physiological organization, motoric processes, organization processes, and interaction organization) and scaling functioning along three points (superior, average, and worrisome). Judgments in scoring here are based on clinical experience with the scale, "not . . . on a frequency distribution of a 'representative' sample" (Als et al., 1982, p. 19).

A priori clustering does provide a description and assessment of overall behavioral competencies in the newborn and adequately deals with the problems of nonlinearity of items (Als et al., 1977). However, Maier et al. (1983) argue that a priori scores are not sensitive to subtle differences among neonates as the result of a limited 3-point scale. Brazelton (1984) feels strongly that babies should not be given a single summary score because they are in a state of rapid change. He recommends the use of Lester et al.'s (1982) scoring method, which clusters the individual NBAS items to describe seven global functions. Their method combines the 28 behavioral items into six clusters and the seventh is the total number of deviant reflex scores. The seven clusters are habituation, orientation, motor performance, range of state, regulation of state, autonomic regulation, and reflexes. Curvilinear scale items are recorded as linear. Gyurke (1988) conducted research that compared the scoring procedures of the Als (1978), Lester et al. (1982), and Jacobson, Jacobson, Fein, and Schwartz (1984) clusters. "Both Als' and Lester's systems recode midpoint optimal scores to high scores without reference to empirical data" (Gyurke, 1988, p. 203). In comparing the three methods, Gyurke found that all three scoring approaches detected differences on items assessing motor maturity and orientation clusters.

Technical Aspects

The disadvantage of the Neonatal Behavioral Assessment Scale continues to be its lack of adequate representative normative samples and standardization scores with statistical properties. There have been no comprehensive standardization studies published to date. Interpretation is based on clinical judgment concerning the behavior that makes up a given score; thus clinical experience with babies and a knowledge of infant development are necessary tools for understanding the meaning of a given score.

Although Brazelton never intended the NBAS to be used as a test, it is defined as one according to the three categories of test instruments outlined in the *Standards for Educational and Psychological Testing* (American Educational Research

Association, American Psychological Association, & National Council on Measurement in Education, 1985): "constructed performance tasks, questionnaires, and to a lesser extent, structured behavior samples" (p. 4). The NBAS falls into the category of structured behavior samples and therefore must be considered a test.

Standardization in the information given to test users is a necessity if reasonable decisions are to be made about test performance. Because the NBAS is defined as a test according to the *Standards*, adherence to the rules that define construction and evaluation of tests is a major consideration. The NBAS fails to provide the standardized information needed for reasonable comparability of infants' performance. Despite the fact that it was never designed as a test, this review will consider its psychometric properties because it falls under the AERA/APA/NCME definition of a test.

According to Standard 6.3, "when a test is to be used for a purpose for which it has not been previously validated, or for which there is no reported claim for validity, the user is responsible for providing evidence of validity" (AERA, APA, & NCME, 1985, p. 42). Brazelton and his colleagues have clearly stated in 1973 and 1984 manuals that the NBAS is not intended to be used as a test. Test users, therefore, must bear the responsibility for using the NBAS inappropriately.

A psychological test must be reliable and valid if it is to be described as a good test (Kline, 1986). Reliability is a necessary but not sufficient prerequisite for validity. The NBAS has questionable reliability and validity based on the AERA/APA/NCME standards. The two methods reported in the manual and utilized in the studies under review address test-retest reliability and interrater reliability. The characteristics of a reliable test are that it yields the same score for individuals over time (test-retest reliability) and that two independent examiners observe the same stimuli and scores consistently (interrater reliability or agreement). High test-retest reliability is associated with good predictive validity because the observed behavior is viewed as stable across time (Jacobson et al., 1984). The test-retest reliability for the NBAS utilizing the Pearson r with repeated exams report low to moderate day-to-day stability (Horowitz et al., 1978; Kaye, 1978; Sameroff, 1978). The Pearson r reflects the relative standing of an individual score within a group on two successive occasions. In a sample of 44 Kansas and Israeli infants, Horowitz et al. (1978) reported correlations from .20 to .50. Sameroff (1978) and his colleagues demonstrated that individual items, factors, and clusters of newborns tested over two sessions demonstrated instability across 2 days. Their analysis was based on a sample of 35 infants who were tested on two consecutive occasions. Kaye (1978) tested 42 neonates at Day 2 and again at 2 weeks of life to explore the stability of various factor scores by "smoothing" them over several sessions. He averaged normalized scores over related items and then averaged over several independent exams. In addition, he obtained scores from the Boston Lying-In Hospital. Kaye concluded that there were no significant correlations between any factors across administrations.

In the 1984 manual, Lester (1984) discusses the method of assessing test-retest reliability on the NBAS. It serves to identify the number of items measuring stable or variable performance in an individual across exams rather than assessing an individual's score within a group on repeated exams. Horowitz and Brazelton (1973) reported data on 60 neonates tested on the third to fourth day of life and again at 1 month of age. Test-retest reliability was computed by using the number of items for which there was an agreement divided by the number of agreements plus the number of scores for which there was a disagreement. Two scores that were identical or within 1 scale score point of each other were considered an agreement. A second level was calculated by determining if two scores were within 2 points of each other, in order to consider low reliability as a function of wide disagreements. A mean test-retest stability was reported at .592 for the first level and .783 at the second level. Nunnally (1978) believes reliabilities of .70 or higher will suffice if basic research is being conducted. Brazelton's test-retest reliability measures do not meet these standards at the first level according to Nunnally.

In the 1984 manual, Lester (1984) suggests that the standard psychometric properties of the Pearson *r* will yield low to moderate test-retest reliability because the method is not a useful measure of day-to-day stabilities in an individual neonate's performance across time. Brazelton (1984) acknowledges that the test-retest characteristics of the NBAS are poor, but he does not offer another measurement of reliability in the manual that would be sensitive to sources of error, including subjectivity of scoring and personality maturation over time. Although many studies under review have been conducted to estimate the test-retest reliability of the NBAS, Nunnally (1978) states that test-retest designs can be used only if three criteria are met: the repeated measurements are independent, no significant development occurs between the tests, and the temperament of the neonate does not change over time. Considering the tremendous growth and development within the neonatal period, another means of assessing reliability should be considered. Nunnally suggests using measures of internal consistency that are based on the average correlation among the sampling of situational factors that accompany the administration of items. He believes the items should correlate highly with one another. Internal consistency measured by coefficient alpha is necessary to support the ideal that clusters include items strongly correlating with each other. As Nunnally (1978) points out, internal consistency should be the major aim of all test constructors.

Jacobson et al. (1984) reviewed the three methods most frequently used to reduce NBAS data: factor analysis (Sameroff, 1978); clusters (Als, Tronick, Lester, & Brazelton, 1979); and Lester clusters (Lester, Als, & Brazelton, 1982). Their study analyzes the problems related to each method. Because in the 1984 manual Brazelton and his colleagues strongly recommend using the Lester clusters, it is important to review the data here. Jacobson et al. found while reviewing the Lester clusters that every item is included in each cluster, including items not found to relate consistently to the others (e.g., consolability). In addition, as the authors point out, the optimal midpoints were chosen without reference to objective empirical criteria. Although the Lester et al. approach offers advantages over the other methods, the psychometric properties of these clusters have not been reviewed extensively with respect to reliability or validity. Jacobson et al. evaluated the Lester clusters, comparing their within- and between-cluster correlations in a sample of 162 newborns. Motor items and range of state showed little internal consistency when recorded as Lester et al. recommend. Jacobson et al. constructed a revised set of clusters from NBAS data that exhibited greater internal consistency (see the Jacobson et al. article for an excellent review of the distributional and psychometric properties of the clusters). These latest findings should be included in a revised edition of the manual.

Osofsky and O'Connell (1977) conducted a study based on 328 newborns, performing a factor analysis on the behavioral items of the NBAS to provide reliability and validity data. Two main factors that appear to represent stable clusters across different socioeconomic, racial groups, geographic locations, and examiners are responsivity and reactivity, suggesting that items correlate highly with one another and are stable across groups. The items appear to exhibit internal consistency reliability.

Asch, Gleser, and Steichen (1986) examined the variability of certain observed cluster scores and the relative size of potential sources of measurement error, such as the examiner and an independent rater, and the occasion of testing. Appreciating sources of error of measurement is a concern in the construction of tests. Not to address measurement error is inconsistent with a primary AERA/APA/NCME standard (2.3), which specifically states that

> Each method of estimating a reliability that is reported should be defined clearly and expressed in terms of variance components, correlation coefficients, standard errors of measurement, percentages of correct decisions, or equivalent statistics. The conditions under which the reliability estimate was obtained and the situations to which it may be applicable should also be examined clearly. (AERA, APA, & NCME, 1985, p. 20)

Contributions to errors of measurement when reporting reliabilities in the manual are not delineated, although the goal in any reliability study reported is to estimate the magnitude of error in the scores obtained. Asch et al. (1986) conclude that when observed scores are averaged, the size of measurement error diminishes. For most of the clusters on the NBAS, three occasions with two raters per occasion are necessary to obtain minimum acceptable generalizability. In the 1984 manual, Lester (1984) urges the use of profile on recovery curves, which is a method for computing patterns of change over three NBAS exams. The procedure (outlined in the manual) is in line with the Asch et al. (1986) recommendations for averaging over scores and thereby reducing measurement error. The language utilized in the manual when discussing the method, however, is technical and may make utilizing the proposed formula difficult.

Training on the NBAS focuses on achieving examiner reliability in scoring and administration. Two observers are required to achieve an interrater agreement level of 90% by procuring the same performance and scoring it within 1 point of each other. The manual has explicit scoring criteria that are well defined. The degree to which two observers can achieve consistency in scoring is a measure of reliability when examining this scale. Als et al. (1977) stated that they could train individuals to produce reliability of 85% after 2 days. In this regard, reliability of the NBAS has been established, as all of the studies reviewed have reported an interobserver reliability coefficient of at least .85, which meet Nunnally's (1978) standards for basic research.

Problems arise, however, upon closer examination of the process of achieving the reliability criterion—that is, by reaching 100% agreement on 20 elicited reflex items and a difference of 2 points or less on 2 of the 28 observed behavioral items on the scale. Dipietro and Larson (1989) caution, however, that an illusion of reliability exists because reliability is based on interobserver scoring methods and not on elicitation of performance. These investigators examined a sample of 100 neonates and found consistent examiner differences although interrater agreement was maintained throughout the testing. They suggest that the behavioral style of the examiner has an effect on the irritable responding of the neonate during the interactive portion of the exam. It may interfere with longitudinal predictability in neonatal development as well. Kaye (1978) states that the agreement between examiners concerning a specific observed behavior tells us nothing about the adequacy of the scale for assessing performance as a reliable characteristic of neonates. Perhaps there are underlying reactions of testers that cause them to score neonates in a similar way. Sameroff (1978) believes that handling techniques must be monitored during the examiner training period so that the level of stimulation a newborn receives is the same across examiners. The significance of the interrater reliability of the scales is questionable; raters scoring differently by 1 score point may still be considered reliable when in fact there may be error variance.

Lester (1984) utilized repeated NBAS cluster scores with two preterm infants at 3, 5, and 7 weeks after birth. They were followed up at 18 months of age and tested with the Bayley Scales of Infant Development (BSID), a well-standardized, reliable, and valid assessment of children's developmental status from 2 months to 2½ years. The profile curves computed from the NBAS were strongly related to 18-month outcome scores on orientation, motor, and two state clusters in a multiple regression analysis. All predictor scores were statistically significant, ranging from 0.42 to 0.63.

Sostik and Anders (1977) conducted a study investigating whether the NBAS predicts 10-week performance on the BSID, and they examined the relationship between early temperament and performance on both scales. Their study utilized 18 full-term infants. The results indicated that the prior Brazelton scoring and neonatal state control were predictive of Bayley mental quotients at 10 weeks. NBAS-identified temperamental intensity and distractibility at 2 weeks correlated later with the BSID 10-week results. However, the Brazelton dimensions did not relate to Bayley motor scale performance at all.

Walters, Vaughn, and Egeland (1980) demonstrated the predictive validity of the NBAS components, especially for the neonate's orienting ability. One hundred neonates were administered the NBAS at 7 and 10 days after birth and subsequently observed in the Ainsworth and Wittig (1969) strange-situation procedure at age 1. Results showed that infants classified as anxiously attached/resistant presented signs of unresponsiveness and motor immaturity at age 1.

The only long term follow-up study to date (Tronick & Brazelton, 1975) compares the predictive value of the NBAS with a standard neurological exam developed in the nationwide collaborative study sponsored by the National Institute for Nervous Disease and Stroke. The investigators studied 53 neonates who were deemed neurologically suspect by the standard neurological assessment. The NBAS was administered twice and a behavioral prediction was made, based on the sum of scores from the two neonatal exams and on the curve of recovery implied by the results. The infants were followed at 4, 8, and 12 months, and again at 2, 4, 6, and 7 years of age. The predictive validity of the respective exams was measured against the 7-year outcome. The NBAS achieved a hit rate of 12 out of 15 children detected as suspect for neurological abnormalities, without including as many normal newborns in the suspect category as did the neurological exam (30 out of 38). The NBAS results indicated a lower false-alarm rate, while both exams were comparable in detecting children who were suspect for later neurological abnormalities. Although there appears to be a correlation between early and later performance, the results of the predictive validity studies should be viewed with caution in light of the small sample sizes used.

Critique

Since its conception 20 years ago, the Neonatal Behavioral Assessment Scale remains one of the most widely used scales in research. Brazelton and his colleagues' original aim, to offer a view of the healthy newborn seen in a social context, based on the way the neonate engages the caregiving environment and regulates internal control, has been achieved. The importance of assessing an infant's behavioral repertoire as early as possible through the changing matrices of states of consciousness has been established and met with success. Indeed, early intervention with the NBAS offers a strength that sets this instrument apart from other neonatal scales. The NBAS remains an excellent vehicle to enhance communication between caregiver, newborn, and researcher, as discussions about the newborn's ability begin while the exam is in process. By modeling constructive ways of interacting with the newborn during the exam, the assessment process promotes early therapeutic interventions. Although the available studies have methodologic flaws that prohibit drawing firm conclusions about positive effects of NBAS-based interventions, we know that parents are learning about their newborn's communication cues at the earliest level. Clinician and parent can begin to discuss their beliefs about the newborn's social availability and organization because they are uncovering these signals together, interpreting changes in skin color, sleeping, and crying behavior. The relative ease with which the NBAS can be administered, the explicit scoring criteria in the manual, and the simple testing kit make it a desirable instrument. However, the requisite training to achieve reliable administration and scoring is costly and time-consuming for the average clinician. Because multiple evaluation sessions are recommended over the first month as opposed to a single session, cost and time constraints are apparent.

Although the NBAS was never intended to be used as a test, it has been critiqued here as one because of the large volume of research utilizing it in this way, and as such its psychometric properties fall short of today's standards. There is a lack of normative data on which to compare the neonate's functioning. Standardization studies should be conducted, making it possible to compare a newborn's scale score with that of the general population of newborns and rendering the interpretation of the score meaningful based on stratified samples. The lack of independence between clusters reported in the studies reviewed is a related difficulty that will have to be addressed. As set forth in *Standards for Educational and Psychological Testing* (AERA, APA, & NCME, 1985),

> Tests and testing programs should be developed on a sound scientific basis. Test developers should compile the evidence bearing on a test, decide which information is needed prior to test publication or distribution and which information can be provided later, and conduct any needed research. (Standard 3.5, p. 25)

If we are to view the NBAS as a test, then it does not comply with this primary standard. Basic research concerning normative data should have been conducted prior to publication of the manual.

Although predictive validity studies have met with some success based on small sample sizes, few long-term validation studies have been completed. Additional long-term validation studies should be incorporated into the manual to support its scientific claims. However, despite limited evidence of validity, the NBAS does comply with Standard 1.11 regarding the descriptions provided of subject samples and the statistical analyses used to determine the degree of predictive accuracy. Another primary standard (1.2) the test developers of the NBAS have complied with states that "if validity for some common interpretation has not been investigated, the fact should be made clear, and potential users should be cautioned about making such interpretations" (AERA, APA, & NCME, 1985, p. 13). Horowitz and Linn (1984) caution that significant correlations reported account for small measures of outcome variance because environmental variables have not been included in combination with NBAS measures. However, subsequent studies have demonstrated predictive validity when correlating NBAS scores with later scores on the BSID. Thus, one should view the evidence for predictive validity cautiously at this time.

The test-retest designs reported to assess the NBAS are inappropriate. In the manual, Lester (1984) questions the value of test-retest reliability on the NBAS using a Pearson r strategy. Another means of assessing reliability therefore should be considered, such as measures of internal consistency. AERA/APA/NCME Standard 2.6 specifies that "coefficients based on internal analysis should not be interpreted as substitutes for alternate-form reliability or estimates of stability over time unless other evidence supports that interpretation in a particular context" (1985, p. 21), and the NBAS does not comply. There appears to be insufficient evidence supporting test-retest reliability of the NBAS, and its validity needs further substantiation as well by long-term prediction studies. Certainly there has been evidence to justify substituting internal consistency reliability over test-retest reliability in the literature reported (Nunnally, 1978).

Because newborn behavior changes rapidly over the first month of life, it is not likely that high test-retest reliability will occur for neonatal assessments such as the NBAS. The measures of interrater reliability are high, but Clopton and Martin (1985) have suggested that subtle differences in examiner style as well as the 1-point difference in scoring may introduce substantial error variance into scoring the scale. Despite the large body of research focused on the NBAS, conclusions about its reliability cannot be drawn at this time.

The NBAS appears to meet acceptable standards for basic research at this time

(Nunnally, 1978), although it is not a clinically tested tool, as Brazelton will confirm. It does not proport to be a well-standardized instrument, and caution must be exercised when administering the scale in clinical practice as well as in research. Those using the NBAS would benefit from a comprehensive normative data study, long-term predictive validity data, and additional reliability studies based on the internal consistency reliability model described in Nunnally (1978). Generalizations to the population at large cannot be made until more appropriate test designs are established. If refined in terms of its psychometric properties, the NBAS might be used to define individual characteristics in a more meaningful way.

References

This list includes text citations and suggested additional reading.

Ainsworth, M., & Wittig, R. (1969). Attachment and exploratory behavior of one year olds in a strange situation. In B. Fuss (Ed.), *Determinants of infant behavior.* New York: Barnes & Noble.

Aleksandrowiez, M.K., & Aleksandrowiez, O.R. (1974). The molding of personality. *Child Psychiatry and Human Development, 5*(4), 231–241.

Als, H. (1978). Assessing an assessment: Conceptual considerations, methodological issues and a perspective on the future of the Neonatal Behavioral Assessment Scale. In A.J. Sameroff (Ed.), *Organization and stability of newborn behavior: A commentary on the Brazelton Neonatal Behavioral Assessment Scale* (Monographs of the Society for Research in Child Development, 43[5–6, Serial No. 177], pp. 14–28).

Als, H. (1984). Newborn Behavioral Assessment. In W. Burns & J. Lavigne (Eds.), *Progress in pediatric psychology* (pp. 1–46). Orlando, FL: Grune & Stratton.

Als, H. (1986). A synactive model of neonatal behavioral organization: Framework for the assessment of neurobehavioral development in the premature infant and for support of infants and parents in the neonatal intensive care environment. *Physical and Occupational Therapy in Pediatrics, 6*(3–4), 3–53.

Als, H., Lester, B., Tronick, E., & Brazelton, B. (1982). Manual for the Assessment of Preterm Infants' Behavior (APIB). In H.E. Fitzgerald, B.M. Lester, & M.W. Yogman (Eds.), *Theory and research in behavioral pediatrics* (Vol. 1). New York: Plenum.

Als, H., Tronick, E., Adamson, L., & Brazelton, T.B. (1976). The behavior of the full-term but underweight newborn infant. *Developmental Medicine and Child Neurology, 18,* 590–602.

Als, H., Tronick, E., Lester, B.M., & Brazelton, T.B. (1977). The Brazelton Neonatal Behavioral Assessment Scale (BNBAS). *Journal of Abnormal Child Psychology, 5*(3), 215–229.

Als, H., Tronick, E., Lester, B.M., & Brazelton, T.B. (1979). The Brazelton Neonatal Scale (NBAS). In H.J. Osofsky (Ed.), *Handbook of infant development.* New York: Wiley.

American Educational Research Association, American Psychological Association, & National Council on Measurement in Education. (1985). *Standards for educational and psychological testing.* Washington, DC: American Psychological Association.

Anderson, C.J., & Sawin, D.B. (1983). Enhancing responsiveness in mother-infant interaction. *Infant Behavior and Development, 6,* 361–368.

Anderson, L.T., Coll, C.G., Vohr, B.R., Emmons, L., Brann, B., Shaul, P.W., Mayfield, S.R., & Oh, W. (1989). Behavioral characteristics and early temperament of premature infants with intracranial hemorrhage. *Early Human Development, 18,* 273–283.

Asch, P.A., Gleser, G.C., & Steichen, J. (1986). Dependability of Brazelton Neonatal Behavioral Assessment cluster scales. *Infant Behavior and Development, 9,* 291–306.

Aylward, G.P., Lazzara, P., & Meyer, A. (1978). Behavior and neurological characteristics of a hydranencephalic infant. *Developmental Medicine and Child Neurology, 20,* 211–217.

Beal, J.A. (1986). The Brazelton Neonatal Behavioral Assessment Scale: A tool to enhance parental attachment. *Journal of Pediatric Nursing, 1*(3), 170–177.

Beal, J.A. (1989). The effect on father-infant interactions of demonstrating the Neonatal Behavioral Assessment Scale. *Birth, 16*(1), 18–22.

Belsky, J. (1985). Experimenting with the family in the newborn period. *Child Development, 56,* 407–414.

Brazelton, T.B. (Ed.). (1973). Neonatal Behavioral Assessment Scale [Special issue]. *Clinics in Developmental Medicine, 50.*

Brazelton, T.B. (1978). The remarkable talents of the newborn. *Birth and the Family Journal, 5*(4), 187–191.

Brazelton, T.B. (Ed.). (1984). *Neonatal Behavioral Assessment Scale* (2nd ed.). London: Spastics International Medical Publications.

Brazelton, T.B., & Freedman, D.G. (1971). Manual to accompany Cambridge Newborn Behavior and Mental Scales. In G.B.A. Stoelings & J.J. Van Der Werff Ten Bosch (Eds.), *Normal and abnormal development of brain and behavior.* Leiden, The Netherlands: Leiden University Press.

Brazelton, T.B., Koslowski, B., & Tronick, E., (1971). Neonatal behavior among urban Zombians and Americans. *Journal of the American Academy of Child Psychiatry, 15*(1), 97–107.

Brazelton, T.B., Tronick, E., Lechtig, A., Lasky, R.E., & Klein, R.E. (1977). The behavior of nutritionally deprived Guatemalan infants. *Developmental Medicine and Child Neurology, 19,* 364–372.

Burns, W.J., Deddish, R.B., & Hatcher, R.P. (1982). Developmental assessment of premature infants. *Developmental and Behavioral Pediatrics, 3*(1), 12–17.

Chasnoff, I.J., Burns, K.A., & Burns, W.J. (1985). Cocaine use in pregnancy: Perinatal morbidity and mortality. *Neurotoxicology and Teratology, 9,* 291–293.

Chasnoff, I.J., Burns, W.J., Hatcher, R.P., & Burns, K.A. (1983). Phencyclidine: Effects on the fetus and neonate. *Developmental Pharmacology Therapeutics, 6,* 404–408.

Chasnoff, I.J., Burns, W.J., & Schnoll, S. (1983). Perinatal addiction: The effects of maternal narcotic and non-narcotic substance abuse on fetus and neonate. *National Institute on Drug Abuse Research Monograph Series, 49,* 220–226.

Chasnoff, I.J., Burns, W.J., Schnoll, S.H., & Burns, K.A. (1985). Cocaine use in pregnancy. *The New England Journal of Medicine, 313*(11), 666–669.

Chasnoff, I.J., Griffith, D.R., MacGregor, S., Dirkes, K., & Burns, K.A. (1989). Temporal patterns of cocaine use in pregnancy. *Journal of the American Medical Association, 261*(12), 1741–1744.

Chasnoff, I.J., Hatcher, R., & Burns, W.J. (1982). Polydrug and methadone-addicted newborns: A continuum of impairment. *Pediatrics, 70*(2), 210–273.

Chasnoff, I.J., Hatcher, R., Burns, W.J., & Schnoll, S. (1983). Pentazocine and tripelennamine (t's and blue's): Effects on the fetus and neonate. *Developmental Pharmacology Therapeutics, 6,* 162–169.

Chasnoff, I.J., Schnoll, S.H., Burns, W.J., & Burns, K.A. (1984). Maternal neonarcotic substance abuse during pregnancy: Effects on infant development. *Neurobehavioral Toxicology and Teratology, 6,* 277–280.

Choi, E.S., & Hamilton, R.K. (1986). The effects of culture on mother-infant interaction. *Journal of Obstetric, Gynecologic and Neonatal Nursing, 15*(3), 256–261.

Claire, K.L. (1978). Neonatal assessment procedures: A historical review. *Child Development, 49,* 5–26.

Clopton, N., & Martin, A.S. (1985). A criticism of interrater reliability procedures for the Brazelton Neonatal Behavioral Assessment Scale. *Physical and Occupational Therapy in Pediatrics, 4*(4), 55–65.

Coles, C.D., Smith, I.E., & Falek, A. (1987). Prenatal alcohol exposure and infant behavior: Immediate effects and implications for later development. In *Children of alcoholics* (pp. 87–105). Binghamton, NY: Haworth.

Coles, C.D., Smith, I.E., Fernhoff, P.N., & Falek, A. (1985). Neonatal neurobehavioral characteristics as correlates of maternal alcohol use during gestation. *Alcoholism: Clinical and Experimental Research, 9*(5), 454–460.

Coles, C.D., Smith, I.E., Lancaster, J.S., & Falek, A. (1987). Persistence over the first month of neurobehavioral differences in infants exposed to alcohol prenatally. *Infant Behavior and Development, 10,* 23–37.

Crockenberg, S., & Acredolo, C. (1983). Infant temperament ratings: A function of infants, mothers, or both? *Infant Behavior and Development, 6,* 61–72.

Crockenberg, S., & McClusky, K. (1986). Change in maternal behavior during the baby's first year of life. *Child Development, 57,* 746–753.

Crockenberg, S.B. (1981). Infant irritability, mother responsiveness, and social support: Influences on the security of infant-mother attachment. *Child Development, 52,* 857–865.

DeVries, M., & Super, C.M. (1978). Contextual influences on the Neonatal Behavioral Assessment Scale and implications for its cross-cultural use. In A. Sameroff (Ed.), *Organization and stability of newborn behavior: A commentary on the Brazelton Neonatal Behavioral Assessment Scale* (Monographs of the Society for Research in Child Development, 43[5–6, Serial No. 177], pp. 92–100).

DiPietro, J.A., & Larson, S.K. (1989). Examiner effects in the administration of the NBAS: The illusion of reliability. *Infant Behavior and Development, 12,* 119–123.

Dunlop, K.H. (1982). Neonatal behavior in an urban working-class Mexican population: Relationships with drug condition and parity. *Interamerican Journal of Psychology, 15*(2), 79–95.

Escher-Graub, D.C., & Fricker, H.S. (1986). Jaundice and behavioral organization in the full-term neonate. *Helvetica Paediatrica Acta, 41,* 425–435.

Emory, E.K., Konopka, S., Hronsky, S., Tuggey, R., & Dave, R. (1988). Salivary caffeine and neonatal behavior. *Psychopharmacology, 94,* 64–68.

Emory, E.K., Tynam, W.D., & Dave, R. (1989). Neurobehavioral anomalies in neonates with seizures. *Journal of Clinical and Experimental Neuropsychology, 11*(2), 231–240.

Ernhart, C.B., Wolf, A.W., Linn, P.L., Sokoi, R.J., Kennard, M.J., & Filipovich, H.F. (1985). Alcohol-related birth defects: Syndromal anomalies, intrauterine growth retardation, and neonatal behavioral assessment. *Alcoholism: Clinical and Experimental Research, 9*(5), 446–453.

Field, T. (1979). Visual and cardiac responses to animate and inanimate faces by young term and preterm infants. *Child Development, 50,* 188–194.

Finnegan, L.P. (1984, April). *Effects of maternal opiate abuse on the newborn.* Paper presented at the 68th Annual Meeting of the Federation of American Societies for Experimental Biology, St. Louis, MO.

Fitzgerald, H.E., Lester, B.M., & Yooman, M.W. (Eds.). (1982). *Theory and research in behavioral pediatrics: Vol. 1.* New York: Plenum.

Frances, P.L., Self, P.A., & McCaffree, M. (1984). Behavioral assessment of a hydranencephalic neonate. *Child Development, 55,* 262–266.

Gibbs, R.M. (1981). *Clinical uses of the Brazelton Neonatal Behavioral Assessment Scale in nursing practice* (Adapted from a presentation sponsored by the Johnson & Johnson Baby Products Co. and given at the NAPNAP First Annual Nursing Conference on Pediatric Primary Care, Feb. 27–Mar. 1, 1980, Washington, DC). Washington, DC: NAPNAP.

Golas, G.A., & Parks, P. (1986). Effects of early postpartum teaching on primiparas: Knowledge of infant behavior and degree of confidence. *Research in Nursing and Health, 9,* 209–214.

Gomes-Pedro, J., Bento de Almedia, Silveria da Costa, C., & Barbosa, A. (1984). Influence of early mother-infant contact on dyadic behavior during the first month of life. *Developmental Medicine and Child Neurology, 26,* 657–664.

Gottlieb, S., & Barrett, D.E. (1986). Effects of unanticipated cesarean section on mothers, infants, and their interaction in the first month of life. *Developmental and Behavioral Pediatrics, 7*(3), 180–185.

Greene, J.G., Fox, N.A., & Lewis, M. (1983). The relationship between neonatal characteristics and three-month mother-infant interaction in high-risk infants. *Child Development, 54,* 1286–1296.

Gyurke, J.S. (1988). An examination of the effectiveness of multiple summary scoring procedures of the BNBAS in detecting group differences. *Infant Mental Health Journal, 9*(3), 201–208.

Hofheimer, J.A., Poisson, S.S., Strauss, M.E., Eyler, F.D., & Greenspan, S.I. (1983). Perinatal and behavioral characteristics of neonates born to multi-risk families. *Developmental and Behavioral Pediatrics, 4*(3), 163–170.

Horowitz, F.D., & Brazelton, T.B. (1973). Research with the Brazelton neonatal scale. In T.B. Brazelton (Ed.), Neonatal Behavioral Assessment Scale [Special issue], *Clinics in Developmental Medicine, 50.*

Horowitz, F.D., & Linn, P.L. (1984). Use of the NBAS in research. In T.B. Brazelton (Ed.), *Neonatal Behavioral Assessment Scale* (2nd ed.). London: Spastics International Medical Publications.

Horowitz, F.D., Sullivan, J.W., & Linn, P. (1978). Stability and instability in the newborn infant: The quest for elusive threads. In A.J. Sameroff (Ed.), *Organization and stability of newborn behavior: A commentary on the Brazelton Neonatal Behavioral Assessment Scale* (Monographs of the Society for Research in Child Development, 43[5–6, Serial No. 177], pp. 29–45).

Jacobson, J.L., Jacobson, S.W., Fein, G.G., & Schwartz, P.M. (1984). Factors and clusters for the Brazelton scale: An investigation of the dimensions of neonatal behavior. *Developmental Psychology, 20*(3), 339–353.

Jeremy, R.J., & Hans, S. (1985). Behavior of neonates exposed in utero to methadone as assessed on the Brazelton scale. *Infant Research and Development, 8,* 323–336.

Jones, L.C., & Lenz, E.R. (1985). Father-newborn interaction: Effects of social competence and infant state. *Nursing Research, 35*(3), 149–153.

Kay, K. (1978). Discriminating among normal infants by multivariate analyses of Brazelton scores. *Monographs of the Society for Research in Child Development, 43*(5–6).

Keefer, C.H., Tronick, E., Dixon, S., & Brazelton, T.B. (1982). Specific differences in motor performance between Gusii and American newborns and a moderation of the Neonatal Behavioral Assessment Scale. *Child Development, 53,* 754–759.

Kestermann, G. (1981). Assessment of individual differences among healthy newborns on the Brazelton scale. *Early Human Development, 5,* 15–27.

Kline, P. (1986). *A handbook of test construction.* New York: Methuen.

Kochanevich-Wallace, P.M., McCluskey-Faucett, K.A., & Meek, N.E. (1987). Method of delivery and parent-newborn interaction. *Journal of Pediatric Psychology, 13*(2), 213–221.

Kron, R.E., Kaplan, S.L., Finnegan, L.P., Litt, M., & Phoenix, M.D. (1975). The assessment of behavioral change in infants undergoing narcotic withdrawal: Comparative data from clinical and objective methods. *Addictive Diseases: An International Journal, 2*(2), 257–275.

Kuhnert, B.R., Linn, P.L., Kennerd, M.J., & Kuhnert, P.M. (1985). Effects of low doses of meperidine on neonatal behavior. *Annals of Analgesia, 64,* 335–342.

Lancioni, G.E., Horowitz, F.D., & Sullivan, J.W. (1980). The NBAS-K 1: A study of its stability and structure over the first month of life. *Infant Behavior and Development, 3,* 341–359.

Leijon, I. (1982). Assessment of behavior on the Brazelton scale in healthy preterm infants from 32 conceptional weeks until full-term age. *Early Human Development, 7,* 109–118.

Leijon, I., Finnstrom, D., Hedenskog, S., Ryden, G., & Tylleskar, J. (1979). Spontaneous labor and elective induction—A prospective randomized study. *Acta Paediatrica Scandinavica, 68,* 553–560.

Lester, B.M., (1984). Data analyses and prediction. In T.B. Brazelton (Ed.), *Neonatal Behavioral Assessment Scale* (2nd ed.). London: Spastics International Medical Publications.

Lester, B.M., Als, H., & Brazelton, T.B. (1982). Regional obstetric anesthesia and newborn behavior: A reanalysis towards synergistic effects. *Child Development, 53,* 687–692.

Lester, B.M., Garcia-Coll, C.G., & Sepkoski, C. (1982). Teenage pregnancy and neonatal behavior: Effects in Puerto Rico and Florida. *Journal of Youth and Adolescence, 11*(5), 385–402.

Lester, B.M., Garcia-Coll, C.T., Valcaicel, M., Hoffman, J., & Brazelton, T.B. (1986). Effects of atypical patterns of fetal growth on newborn (NBAS) behavior. *Child Development, 57,* 11–19.

Maloni, J.A., Stegman, C.E., Taylor, P.M., & Brownell, C.A. (1986). Validation of infant behavior identified by neonatal nurses. *Nursing Research, 35*(3), 133–136.

Maier, R.A., Jr., Prinn, S.M., Nagy, J.N., Halmes, D.L., & Slaymaker, F. (1983). A methodological note on the use of a priori cluster scores for the Brazelton Neonatal Behavioral Assessment Scale (BNBAS). *Infant Behavior and Development, 6,* 299–303.

Meyers, B.J. (1982). Early intervention using Brazelton training with middle-class mothers and fathers of newborns. *Child Development, 53,* 462–471.

Muhlen, L., Pryke, M., & Wade, K. (1986). Effects of type of birth anaesthetic on Neonatal Behavioral Assessment Scale scores. *Australian Psychologist, 21,* 253–271.

Murphy, T.F., Scher, M.S., Klesh, K.W., & Guthrie, R.D. (1988). Easy neurobehavioral abnormalities in infants with persistent pulmonary hypertension of the newborn. *Infant Behavior and Development, 11,* 159–167.

Nugent, K.J. (1980, February/March). *The Brazelton Neonatal Behavioral Assessment Scale: Implications for intervention.* Paper presented at the NAPNAP First Annual Nursing Conference on Pediatric Primary Care, Washington, DC.

Nugent, K.J., & Brazelton, T.B., (1989). Preventive intervention with infants and families: The NBAS model. *Infant Mental Health Journal, 10*(2), 84–99.

Nunnally, J.C. (1978). *Psychometric theory* (2nd ed.). New York: McGraw-Hill.

Osofsky, H.J. (1974). Relationships between prenatal medical and nutritional measures, pregnancy outcome, and early infant development in an urban poverty setting. *American Journal of Obstetrics and Gynecology, 123*(7), 682–690.

Osofsky, J.D. (1976). Neonatal characteristics and mother-infant interaction in two observational studies. *Child Development, 47,* 1138–1147.

Osofsky, J.D., & Danzger, B. (1974). Relationships between neonatal characteristics and mother-infant interaction. *Developmental Psychology, 10*(1), 124–130.

Osofsky, J.D., & O'Connell, E.J. (1977). Patterning of newborn behavior in an urban population. *Child Development, 48,* 532–536.

Paludetto, R., Mansi, G., Rinaldi, P., DeLuca, T., Corchia, C., DeCurtis, M., & Andolfi, M. (1982). Behavior of preterm newborns reaching term without any serious disorder. *Early Human Development, 6,* 357–363.

Paludetto, R., Rinaldi, P., Mansi, G., Andolfi, M., & Del Giudice, G. (1984). Early behavioral development of preterm infants. *Developmental Medicine and Child Neurology, 26,* 347–352.

Penman, R., Meares, R., Baker, K., & Milgrom-Freedman, J. (1983). Synchrony in mother-infant interaction: A possible neuro-physiological base. *British Journal of Medical Psychology, 56,* 1–7.

Rogan, W.J., Gladen, B.C., McKinney, J.D., Carreras, N., Hardy, P., Thullen, J., Tinglestad, J., & Tully, M. (1986). Neonatal effects of transplacental exposure to PCB's and DDE. *Journal of Pediatrics, 109,* 335–341.

Saco-Pollitt, C. (1981). Birth in the Peruvian Andes: Physical and behavioral consequences in the neonate. *Child Development, 52,* 839–846.

Sameroff, A.J. (Ed). (1978). Organization and stability of newborn behavior: A commentary on the Brazelton Neonatal Behavioral Assessment Scale. *Monographs of the Society for Research in Child Development, 43*(5–6, Serial No. 177).

Saxton, D.W. (1978). The behavior of infants whose mothers smoke in pregnancy. *Early Human Development, 44,* 363–369.

Scafidi, F.A., Field, T.M., Schanberg, S.M., Bauer, C.R., Vega-Lahr, N., Garcia, R., Poirer, J., Nystrom, G., & Kuhn, C. (1986). Effects of tactile/kinesthetic stimulation on the clinical course and sleep/wake behavior of preterm neonates. *Infant Behavior and Development, 9,* 91–105.

Scanlon, K.B., Scanlon, J.W., & Tronick, E. (1984). The impact of prenatal and neonatal events on the early behavior of the extremely premature human. *Developmental and Behavioral Pediatrics, 5*(2), 65–73.

Silverman, C.R. (1991). *The Neonatal Behavioral Assessment Scale (NBAS): A review and critique.* Unpublished doctoral dissertation, Nova University, Ft. Lauderdale, FL.

Smith, I.E., Coles, C.D., Lancaster, J., Fernhoff, P.M., & Falek, A. (1986). The effect of volume and duration of prenatal exposure on neonatal physical and behavioral development. *Neurobehavioral Toxicology and Teratology, 8,* 375–381.

Solkoff, N., & Matuszak, D. (1975). Tactile stimulation and behavioral development among low-birthweight infants. *Child Psychiatry and Human Development, 6*(1), 33–37.

Sostik, A.M., & Anders, T.F. (1977). Relationships among the Brazelton neonatal scale, Bayley infant scales and early temperament. *Child Development, 48,* 320–323.

Soule, B.A., Standley, K., Copans, S.A., & Davis, M. (1974). Clinical uses of the Brazelton Scales. *Pediatrics, 54*(5), 583–586.

St. Clair, K.L. (1978). Neonatal assessment procedures: A historical review. *Child Development, 49,* 280–292.

Standley, K.A., Soule, B.A., Copans, S.A., & Duchouny, A. (1974). Local regional anesthesia during childbirth: Effect on newborn behaviors. *Science, 186,* 634–635.

Standley, K.A., Soule, B.A., Copans, S.A., & Klein, R.P. (1978). Multidimensional sources of infant temperament. *Genetic Psychology Monographs, 98,* 203–231.

Strauss, M.E., Lessen-Firestone, J.K., Starr, R.H., Jr., & Ostera, E.M., Jr. (1975). Behavior of narcotics-addicted newborns. *Child Development, 46,* 887–893.

Strauss, M.E., Starr, R.H., Jr., Ostera, E.M., Jr., Chavez, C.J., & Stryker, J.C. (1976). Behavioral concomitants of prenatal addiction to narcotics. *Journal of Pediatrics, 89*(5), 842–846.

Streissguth, A.P., Barr, H.M., & Martin, D.C. (1983). Maternal alcohol use and neonatal habituation assessed with the Brazelton scale. *Child Development, 54,* 1109–1118.

Szajnberg, N., Ward, M.J., Krauss, A., & Kessler, D.B. (1986). Low birth weight prematures: Preventative intervention and maternal attitude. *Child Psychiatry and Human Development, 17,* 152–165.

Tronick, E., & Brazelton, T.B. (1975). Clinical uses of the Brazelton neonatal assessment. In B.Z. Friedlander, G.M. Sterritt, & G.E. Kirk (Eds.), *Exceptional infant 3: Assessment and intervention.* New York: Brunner/Mazel.

Tronick, E.Z. (1987). The Neonatal Behavioral Assessment Scale as a bio-marker of the effects of environmental agents on the newborn. *Environmental Health Perspectives, 74,* 185–189.

Vaughn, J., Brown, J., & Carter, J.P. (1986). The effects of maternal anemia on infant behavior. *Journal of the National Medical Association, 78*(10), 963–968.

Walters, E., Vaugh, B.E., & Egeland, B.R. (1980). Individual differences in infant-mother attachment relationships at age one: Antecedents in neonatal behavior in an urban, economically disadvantaged sample. *Child Development, 51,* 208–216.

Widmayer, S.M., & Field, T.M. (1980). Effects of Brazelton demonstrations on early interactions of preterm infants and their teenage mothers. *Infant Behavior and Development, 3,* 79–89.

Widmayer, S.M., & Field, T.M. (1981). Effects of Brazelton demonstrations for mothers on the development of preterm infants. *Pediatrics, 67*(5), 711–714.

Worobey, J. (1986a). Convergence among assessments of temperament in the first month. *Child Development, 57,* 47–55.

Worobey, J. (1986b). Neonatal stability and one-month behavior. *Infant Behavior and Development, 9,* 119–124.

Worobey, J., & Belsky, J. (1982). Employing the Brazelton scale to influence mothering: An experimental comparison of three strategies. *Developmental Psychology, 18*(5), 736–743.

Worobey, J.W., & Brazelton, T.B. (1986). Experimenting with the family in the newborn period: A commentary. *Child Development, 57,* 1298–1300.

John Delane Williams, Ph.D.

Professor and Chair, Department of Educational Foundations and Research Methodologies, Center for Teaching and Learning, University of North Dakota, Grand Forks, North Dakota.

Jole A. Williams, Ph.D.

Licensed Psychologist, North Star Psychological Services, East Grand Forks, North Dakota.

OARS MULTIDIMENSIONAL FUNCTIONAL ASSESSMENT QUESTIONNAIRE

Center for the Study of Aging and Human Development. Durham, North Carolina: Center for the Study of Aging and Human Development, Duke University.

Introduction

The OARS Multidimensional Functional Assessment Questionnaire (OMFAQ) was originally developed per a federal agency's request to assess alternative strategies to institutionalizing frail older adults. The first form appeared in 1972, and its usage to date has far outstripped the initial objective. The OMFAQ consists of two main parts: Part A, which focuses on individual functioning in five areas (social, economic, mental and physical health, and activities of daily living), and Part B, which focuses on 24 different areas of service usage. The two parts are interwoven in the interview schedule for better interviewing flow.

The OMFAQ was completed in 1975 and revised in 1988. The 48-page questionnaire is published in the present "manual," which is actually a hardback book (Fillenbaum, 1988). A variety of people were involved in the development of the OMFAQ, most of whom would be called gerontologists from a variety of disciplines. Notably, contributors included George Maddox, David Dellinger, and Gerda Fillenbaum.

The initial (and continuing) work on the OMFAQ was far more multidisciplinary than is typical. Physicians, economists, systems analysts, planners, sociologists, and psychologists participated at the inception of the program in 1972. A large probability sampling of older adults made in Cleveland, Ohio, was used for the early version of the instrument. A major intent was to apply the OMFAQ in policy planning regarding elderly Americans. George Maddox was a major influence on the OMFAQ; he wrote the foreword to Tannenbaum's (1988) text as well as a chapter on the use of the OMFAQ in Burstein, Freeman, and Rossi's 1985 *Collecting Evaluation Data.*

The Duke OARS is a "package" in the sense that many different areas of functioning are assessed; the assessment is completely reproduced in Fillenbaum (1988). In that Duke University holds the copyright (1975) but presumably does not actually continue to publish the test, permission to copy the test needs to be secured from them. Most researchers who have used this instrument in the past undoubtedly remember many pages of copied materials as being the OARS, which points to a difference between the OMFAQ and many other commercial products. The major use of the OARS assessment has been in research regarding the elderly; hence the users generally have been sophisticated professionals and researchers who either personally had some contact with personnel at the Duke University Center for the Study of Aging and Human Development or were working with someone who had. Thus the OMFAQ has become a venerable test to gerontological researchers but without the nice attache case or attractively presented commercial product. The intended or unintended effect would keep legitimate users in some degree of contact with the university. Although some might prefer to avoid this contact, it can prove beneficial for both the user and the Center for the Study of Aging and Human Development.

As mentioned earlier, the printed OMFAX is a 48-page appendix in Fillenbaum's (1988) publication. Buying the book would seem to be absolutely necessary, even for the experienced user, because it contains technical data, history of the test, administration instructions, and the questionnaire itself. Also included are the entire instructions for inputting raw data into an SPSS-X data file, together with transformations. The program seems to have been written so that users familiar with the older SPSS system could adjust to SPSS-X with a minimum of difficulty.

The OMFAQ, which can be administered in 45 minutes, anticipates that some (or many) of the questions will be answered by an informant rather than the subject of interest. The 101 questions vary from simple to relatively complex, and many have multiple parts. The right side of the questionnaire serves for computer coding purposes; the term *card* (as in *IBM card* or *punchcard*) is used. Given that the update took place in 1988, this usage is curious. Very few modern researchers have seen punchcards even as late as 1983 or so, when IBM PCs and other computer accessory equipment came into prominence. Indeed most computer centers might be hard pressed even to know where to send punchcards to get them read. (The authors could have easily used the word *line* rather than *card*.)

In that this is a questionnaire rather than a test, the interviewer must ascertain how well the elder respondent will be able to communicate the desired information. In some settings, staff can both help in this determination and serve as a confidant. Therein lies a problem; the most knowledgeable confidant may simply not be knowable to the interviewer, and valuable information may not be obtained. In that it is clearly intended that the data be processed via computer, getting information back will require some computer sophistication, just as administering the questionnaire will require both good human relating skills and a certain degree of investigativeness to acquire the desired information.

It would seem that there are sufficiently strong expectations of the potential user—some degree of computer expertise, surely interviewing skills (including locating an appropriate and knowledgeable informant), and sufficient professional and psychometric experience to use the instrument—that their number might be limited. In fact, many persons interested in gerontology have had some experience with the OMFAQ (which they often refer to as "the Duke OARS"), and they can serve as an additional resource to the potential user.

The OMFAQ inquires about social services resources (9 questions), economic resources (6 questions), mental health (6 questions), physical health (16 questions), and activities of daily living (15 questions), plus several questions ask an informant to make assessments regarding the focal person. Part B addresses services assessment (a single question with 24 parts). The number of questions is a bit misleading; *one* of the six questions on mental health is actually a 10th item in the Short Portable Mental Status Questionnaire; another "item" is a 15-item test of psychiatric functioning.

Practical Applications/Uses

This questionnaire originally was designed for research and for public policy formation. Despite the enormous amount of research that has been conducted on the OMFAQ, Fillenbaum (1988) is silent on usage of the instrument with individuals. This is not to preclude such assessments, but rather to ensure that such usage would occur within the OARS model.

Professionals concerned with gerontology in the variety of helping professions, researchers, and policy researchers comprise the intended audience of the OMFAQ. Users also are expected to be knowledgeable regarding transformation matrices, as it is through them that the appropriate service usage can be traced to persons who would be suitable users of such services.

The OMFAQ clearly was designed to assess functioning, service usage, and needs of older persons; presumably it also could be used to assess younger persons involved in some form of likely institutionalization (such as a nursing home). Because the OMFAQ addresses policy/research issues, one need not restrict it to persons with reduced functioning in some area; it would be appropriate for (and has been used with) the well elderly, too.

The OMFAQ is most assuredly *not* an instrument for which a professional could simply read the manual and then go out and administer it. If the prospective user has not previously administered some form of mini mental status examination, then he or she should acquire some degree of instruction/experience in this area. As portions of the Minnesota Multiphasic Personality Inventory (MMPI) are used, familiarity with personality testing (specifically the MMPI) would be recommended. Actually, it would be best for a potential user to become involved with a multidisciplinary/interdisciplinary team already practiced in administering the OMFAQ. Alternatives could include attending workshops on its administration and uses. Administering the OMFAQ obviously is not limited to a single profession but would include a variety of human services–oriented persons who also have an interest in gerontology.

Working within a team would help smooth over some of the difficulties that otherwise might ensue. When do you seek the information from the target person, and when do you seek the information from a confidant? Though a relatively simple process for the seasoned interviewer, this can be baffling to a person new both to gerontology and to the use of the OMFAQ.

The 21-page directions for administration (written by Service & Heron, 1988) are detailed and should provide the basis for using the questionnaire. It is suggested that one apply these instructions in combination with specific training in administration. Service and Heron indicate that the questionnaire takes about 45 minutes to administer. Learning how to do this in 45 minutes is best accomplished by observing someone who does so smoothly. Parts A and B can be administered separately from one another, and a special guide is available (within the Service and Heron chapter) for such purposes. The OARS staff continues to provide training once each month on the administration (and meaning) of the OMFAQ.

As noted early in this review, ratings occur for each of five areas in Part A: social resources, economic resources, mental health, physical health, and activities of daily living. The interviewer marks the appropriate response on the following 6-point Likert-type scale:

1 = Excellent
2 = Good
3 = Mildly impaired
4 = Moderately impaired
5 = Severely impaired
6 = Totally impaired

This judgment also can be made by a trained person who has access to the questionnaire and who has not seen the subject. The OMFAQ is not an open-ended questionnaire, but rather specific questions are asked and answers limited to specific categories; often the respondent must choose one answer among several options. The most complete information is sought in every case, even if occasionally that might seem excessive. Decisions have to be made as to the reliability of the subject. A preliminary questionnaire (actually a 10-item mini mental status) is given at the beginning of the assessment. Four or more items missed may indicate that the subject cannot give correct information. Specific instructions guide the process in marginal cases. Choosing an acceptable informant is also described, and four levels of acceptability are included (the intent being to select an informant both reliable and knowledgeable regarding the content to be addressed). A separate institutional form (reproduced in Fillenbaum's text) is used for persons residing in a nursing home or similar facility.

Service needs are assessed in Part B and are an integral part of the questionnaire. Indeed, one of these reviewers was involved in a research study addressing possible gender differences in service needs (and usage) among widows and widowers (Barresi & Williams, 1988).

The OMFAQ is presumed to be put into an SPSS-X package by the potential user. Coding for each line together with the construction of variables, including a final summated rating, is possible from the printed program in the text.

Scoring the OMFAQ emphasizes the importance of both training on the instrument and familiarity with the functioning of older persons. On the basis of specific items from the questionnaire, the interviewer makes an overall judgment for each area of functioning on the 6-point scale described previously (from excellent to completely impaired). This decision process does not have a definite algorithm as is typical of most psychometric devices, but rather is done in a "gestalt" manner, based on the answers to specific questions. Clearly, then, the examiner who tries to use the OMFAQ without accessing practiced professionals and without attending specific workshops on the instrument is likely to generate different meanings from the questionnaire than those who have been through training.

Some tests (such as the Stanford-Binet Intelligence Scale, Fourth Edition) lend themselves to "objective" interpretation from scale scores; others, such as the Rorschach, lend themselves to clinical interpretation (though those with scoring systems such as Exner's might claim objective scores). The OMFAQ falls in neither category. Rather, a clinical interpretation of impairment is possible through seeing the objective reporting of answers to a series of questions. Experienced interviewers/ interpreters here do not need sophisticated backgrounds in administering tests such as the Rorschach or the Stanford-Binet, but they do need considerable experience in understanding the needs of the elderly; they also need sufficient interaction in a team setting with other persons involved in OMFAQ administration/ interpretation so that they generate the same meanings.

Technical Aspects

Fillenbaum's (1988) manual briefly but succinctly addresses some aspects of reliability and validity in chapter 2. Regarding validity, the author emphasizes criterion validity—or as others might term it, predictive validity. The 6-point summative rating was correlated to an objective in some measure for Economic (r_s = .68); the rating in Mental Health was correlated to ratings made by geropsychiatrists (r_s = .67), Physical Health to ratings made by physicians assistants (r_s = .82), and Self-Care Capacity to ratings made by physical therapists (r_s = .89). It should be noted that these reliabilities on the scale values ranged from .662 to .865. In addition to the subjective interpretation of a summative rating, ratings can be assigned by a least squares regression process (following a factor analysis into multidimensional scales within most of the five areas). The scale that survived in the Economic area would be suspect in some quarters. Instead of assessing some sense of objective need, it actually assesses perceived economic need.

Critique

The OARS Multidimensional Functional Assessment Questionnaire (OMFAQ) is impressive because it is an attempt to look at functioning in a multivariate way. Until the advent of the OARS in 1975, there had been no systematic attempt in one instrument to look at interrelated areas of functioning. It began as, and has continued to evolve as, a relatively sophisticated instrument in that its primary use is to collect data for research purposes rather than to serve as a screening and evaluation device for the myriad potential service providers to the elderly.

Herein appears a difficulty, however, that needs to be articulated. The OMFAQ was designed to elicit data for program planning and research, not to evaluate "Mr. or Mrs. Elderly American" for personal decisions regarding competency or placement. If at times the instrument has accomplished that end, that is fortunate, but the expectation that it should is unwarranted. A test or instrument is developed purposefully and should be used to measure what it was intended to measure. It is within that context that the instrument is valid. If an assessment tool is used for purposes other than the intended ones, its validity for these unanticipated applications should be called into question.

In practice the OMFAQ often is used by people without specific training either in the questionnaire's administration or in the intent of its questions. Because of its length, sometimes only selected parts are used. What this selective approach suggests is that users have recognized the value of the instrument but have a need for something that doesn't currently exist: a screening device that looks at the five areas of Part A (social, economic, mental and physical health, and activities of daily living).

Instead of having to use the whole instrument, there appears to be a need for a "pop-out" subtest index. This could be conceptualized in much the same way as was done on the Wechsler Memory Scale–Revised (WMS-R). Subtests yielded raw scores that were then weighted, and related subtest weighted scores were summed to produce various indexes, each with a mean of 100 and a standard deviation of 15. The downside of such an approach is the loss of multidisciplinary flavor.

Development of such a companion instrument to the OMFAQ could serve at least two purposes. It would stop the current inappropriate usage and it could provide a needed device that the persons who know subjects best could legitimately administer and use to determine needed services, current levels of functioning, and areas requiring further investigation.

References

Barresi, C.M., & Williams, J.D. (1988, November). *Gender differences in unmet service needs in widowhood*. Paper presented at the annual meeting of the Gerontological Society of America, San Francisco.

Burstein, L., Freeman, H., & Rossi, P. (Eds.). (1985). *Collecting evaluation data*. Beverly Hills, CA: Sage.

Fillenbaum, G.G. (1988). *Multidimensional functional assessment of older adults: The Duke older Americans resources and services procedures*. Hillsdale, NJ: Erlbaum.

Older Americans Resources and Services Program, Duke University Center for the Study of Aging and Human Development. (1988). *OARS Multidimensional Functional Assessment Questionnaire and services supplement* (rev. ed.). Durham, NC: Author.

Service, C., & Heron, B. (1988). Administration of the OARS Multidimensional Functional Assessment Questionnaire. In G.G. Fillenbaum, *Multidimensional functional assessment of older adults* (pp. 61–81). Hillsdale, NJ: Erlbaum.

Deborah L. Winking, Ph.D.
Associate Evaluator, North Central Regional Educational Laboratory, Oak Brook, Illinois.

Lizanne DeStefano, Ph.D.
Associate Professor of Educational Psychology, University of Illinois at Urbana-Champaign, Champaign, Illinois.

OCCUPATIONAL APTITUDE SURVEY AND INTEREST SCHEDULE, SECOND EDITION

Randall M. Parker. Austin, Texas: PRO-ED, Inc.

Introduction

The Occupational Aptitude Survey and Interest Schedule, Second Edition (OASIS-2) is designed to assist 8th- through 12th-graders in self-exploration, vocational exploration, and career development by providing them with information regarding their relative aptitudes and interests in several areas related to the world of work. Although the OASIS-2 cannot predict occupational success, it can be used to assist students in organizing their search for occupational information.

This second edition of the survey (Parker, 1991) contains several changes from the first (Parker, 1983). The updated manual includes recent research findings, and modifications were made to bring the technical characteristics of the OASIS-2 into conformity with test reviewers' recommendations. The student booklet has been reformatted to be more readable, plus two additional examples have been added to the instructions and the item drawings improved. A computer-scored answer sheet was made available as well as a newly formatted hand-scored answer sheet. The profile form has been reformatted to include confidence levels and interpretive information, and new norms tables and interpretive information now appear in the manual.

The OASIS-2 is made up of two separate instruments: the Aptitude Survey (AS), designed to measure vocationally and educationally important developed abilities, and the Interest Schedule (IS), designed to encourage self-exploration, vocational exploration, and career development. The interpretation of both by a trained professional can assist students in developing vocational understanding, goal setting, organizing a purposeful career search, and decision making for career attainment. Descriptions of the OASIS-2 components follow:

1. *Interest Schedule (IS)*. The IS is comprised of 240 items scored on a 3-point Likert scale anchored by "like," "neutral," and "dislike." Each item is assigned to one of 12 scales, and each scale is made up of 20 items. Of the 20 items for each scale, 10 are occupational titles and 10 are job tasks within occupational areas. The 12 scales covered by the IS are Artistic (ART), Scientific (SCI), Nature (NAT), Protective (PRO), Mechanical (MEC), Industrial (IND), Business Detail (BUS),

Selling (SEL), Accommodating (ACC), Humanitarian (HUM), Leading-Influencing (LEA), and Physical Performing (PHY).

2. *Aptitude Survey (AS).* The AS is made up of five subtests, most of which have similar or identical counterparts on other vocational tests such as the General Aptitude Test Battery (GATB; U.S. Department of Labor, 1970):

a. The *Vocabulary* subtest is designed to measure verbal ability. Each of the 40 items consists of a vertical listing of four words. The examinee is required to identify two words in the list that have the same or opposite meanings. There is a 9-minute time limit.

b. The *Computation* subtest, designed to measure numerical aptitude, requires subjects to solve 30 arithmetic and algebra problems presented in a multiple-choice format with five alternatives. Calculators are not permitted, and there is a 12-minute time limit for the task.

c. In the *Spatial Relations* subtest, subjects are asked to determine which one of four three-dimensional objects can be constructed from folding a two-dimensional object. This subtest contains 20 items and has an 8-minute time limit.

d. The fourth subtest, *Word Comparison*, requires the examinee to inspect 100 pairs of words, numbers, or nonsense syllables and determine whether they are alike or different. A similar task was included as a measure of clerical aptitude on the Minnesota Clerical Test (Andrew, Paterson, & Longstaff, 1961).

e. *Making Marks* requires the examinee to draw three lines in the form of an asterisk in each of a series of 160 boxes as quickly as possible as a measure of motor coordination. This subtest has two separately timed sections of 30 questions each.

Practical Applications/Uses

The purpose of the OASIS-2 according to its author is to assist 8th- through 12th-grade students in self-exploration, vocational exploration, and career development. Parker is careful to caution that OASIS-2 results do not predict the occupation students will or should select for their life's work. On the contrary, the instrument is designed to assist adolescents in the early stages of the career development process. The OASIS-2 may provide the impetus for a purposeful occupational search, the goal of which is career attainment. As young people often have limited vocational experience and knowledge of the world of work, the author advises caution in overinterpreting results when counseling students.

Both the Interest Schedule (IS) and the Aptitude Survey (AS) have specific administration and scoring procedures. Parker prescribes exact adherence to the procedures presented in the examiner's manual in order to facilitate administration, assure reliability and validity, and maintain the conditions under which both instruments were standardized and normed. The general instructions for administering both instruments dictate that each examinee have two sharp pencils, a student test booklet, and an answer sheet. A sufficient number of proctors should be stationed in the examination room to facilitate administration to large groups. (The desired ratio is one proctor for every 30 students.) It is suggested that administrators and proctors take and score the IS and AS themselves prior to attempting a group testing session as a way to gain insight into the testing process and the nature of the individual items. Reserve materials should be organized in advance and made available to students at each testing site so that defective materials can be replaced immediately.

The OASIS-2 offers hand-scored and computer-scored formats for both the Interest Schedule and the Aptitude Survey. The directions for use of answer sheets and scoring methods vary slightly based on the format selected. The test administrator must determine in advance whether to utilize the hand- or computer-scored option.

Because the Interest Schedule is untimed and there are no right or wrong answers, "cheating" is not an issue in this portion of the OASIS-2. Students may use dictionaries and other aids, and proctors should feel free to define words and explain unfamiliar terminology. Students are given instructions and examples for completing personal information on the answer sheet. Student booklets are handed out to each respondent and the test administrator reads through the sample items to provide an example of each response option. Students are instructed that the test is untimed, but they are encouraged to work as quickly as possible. Most finish the IS in 30 minutes, but everyone should be encouraged to complete the instrument within 45 minutes. Proctors should gauge the progress of the group by assessing whether the majority have finished the first half of the items referring to job titles (#1–120) in 10 minutes and last half referring to job activities (#121–240) in 20 minutes. Students having difficulty finishing may need special assistance.

For the Aptitude Survey (AS), student seating should be arranged in a manner that discourages cheating. Dictionaries and reference materials are not permitted. Time limits allotted for each AS subtest must be strictly adhered to in order to preserve the conditions under which test norms were developed (a stopwatch should be utilized if possible). The total time allotted is 35 minutes, divided across the five subtests: 9 minutes for Vocabulary, 12 minutes for Computation, 8 minutes for Spatial Relations, 5 minutes for Word Comparison, and 1 minute for Making Marks. Students receive answer sheets and instructions for completing the required personal information on the sheet. They are told that the test is designed to help them with their future career plans, that they should work carefully and quickly, and that there is no penalty for guessing. The scripts provided for each of the five subtests include sample questions of each type found within the subtest. The examiner reads these scripts and completes the sample question(s) at the beginning of each new subtest. Following completion of the sample question(s), students are instructed to begin the test. At the end of the prescribed time period for each subtest, the examiner says "Stop." This procedure is followed until all five aptitude subtests are completed.

If the user has elected to use the computer-scored Interest Schedule (IS), the answer sheets may be sent to the publisher for scoring. Scoring the IS by hand takes approximately 3 to 5 minutes per student and requires familiarity with the layout of the answer sheet, including the configuration of rows and columns on each side. For each row, the number of "Likes" is totaled and recorded in the blank space labeled "L," followed the number of "Neutrals" in the blank space labeled "N." (It is helpful to use a straightedge to align one's eyes with the responses in each row.) Once "Likes" and "Neutrals" are recorded for all 48 rows, the scorer begins the calculation of raw scores for each of the 12 interest scales. For the Artistic scale, for example, one records the number of "Likes" and "Neutrals" for rows 1, 13, 25, and 37 on the scoring form provided in the student booklet. The number of "Likes" for the four rows is added and the result put in the box marked "Sum." The sum is then multiplied by 2 and recorded in the box at the bottom of the sheet marked "Add." The addition step (but not the multiplication) also is followed for the items marked "Neutral." Finally, the "Like" and "Neutral" sums are added and the total is entered in the box marked "ART Raw Score." Raw scores for the remaining 11 interest scales are calculated in the same way.

Raw scores for each of the 12 interest scale areas are transferred to the student profile. Percentile ranks and stanine scores are determined and entered on the profile by using the appropriate column in the manual's Appendix for females, males, and total norm group. Where there were no significant differences between males and females on a scale (i.e., ART, SCI, NAT, PRO, IND, SEL, and LEA), only total norm group percentiles are provided. The remaining scales (i.e., MEC, BUS, ACC, HUM, and PHY) differentiate between male, female, and total norm group in the reporting of percentile ranks because significant mean differences exist between males and females on these scales. For these five scales, the scorer is advised to record scores for all three norm groups regardless of the examinee's gender. As a final step, the scorer plots the student's profile using the same-sex scores for the five scales where differences exist and total norm group scores for the seven scales where no sex differences exist. The Interest Schedule examiner's manual provides an example of a completed scoring form, answer sheet, and student profile.

As with the Interest Schedule, the administrator must decide in advance whether to utilize the hand- or computer-scored option for the Aptitude Survey (AS). (However, subtest 5, Making Marks, is always administered using a separate hand-scored answer sheet; there is no option of computer scoring this subtest.) Hand scoring uses clear plastic scoring keys provided in the AS kit. The raw score for each subtest is determined by counting the number of correct items. No correction is made for guessing and only one response is allowed per item. The Making Marks subtest is scored by counting the number of marks made in the boxes during two 30-second time periods. Each box is counted that contains three lines that roughly approximate the examples shown in the trial section. Boxes with two or fewer lines are not counted. Finally, the General Ability raw score is determined by adding the raw scores obtained for Computation and Vocabulary.

The AS student profile is completed by transferring the raw scores obtained on the five subtests plus the General Ability score. The administrator uses the Appendix in the AS examiner's manual to determine the percentile rank and stanine score associated with each raw score and then records them in the appropriate blanks on the student profile sheet. As a final step, the student's profile is plotted using the stanine scores recorded. For each subtest score, the examiner darkens a box 1 stanine above and 1 stanine below the obtained stanine score, creating bands that correspond to the level of confidence within in which subtest scores would fall if a student was retested. The examiner's manual provides an example of a completed student profile sheet.

After all scoring is complete, a meeting must be arranged with the student to interpret the OASIS-2 results. Parker stresses that the single most important feature of a career assessment should be a thorough, sensitive interpretation of results. This interpretation, the author states, can take place individually or in a group situation and requires 1 hour. The interpretation session should be conducted by a professional with training, certification, and experience in tests and measurement. The author suggests that interpretation be provided by a teacher or counselor with a master's degree.

The interpretation sections of the AS and IS materials are identical except for the addition of a discussion of sex fairness and rank ordering of the 12 scale scores to simplify presentation in the Interest Schedule examiner's manual. Parker points out that the care taken to construct a gender-fair interest survey proves useless if gender bias enters into the interpretation of results to students. Assistance is provided to students in understanding the emphasis on same-sex comparisons for the five scales (i.e., MEC, BUS, ACC, HUM, and PHY) where significant differences exist between males and females. Although same-sex comparisons provide the most valid and meaningful results for these scales and are used in plotting the student profile, other sex and total group norms may be presented and discussed.

General steps for interpreting the OASIS-2 include 1) advising students that the OASIS-2 will not predict the type of work they should do and that performance on both the AS and IS may change over time and with experience; 2) asking for examinees' reaction to the test to assist the professional in understanding individual attitudes toward tests and feelings about themselves; 3) allowing students to scan their student profiles without pressing an interpretation; 4) describing the national norm group, the stanine band of scores, and the level of confidence placed on the stanine band; 5) encouraging involvement and being sensitive to the students' test results; 6) allowing students to express their feelings and not adopting the position of defending the results; 7) always interpreting results in a way that encourages exploration and never stating them in negative or limiting terms; and 8) asking students to summarize what test results mean to them to check for distortions in their understanding. Example cases are provided in both the AS and IS examiner's manuals as well as in the resource guides that describe vocational options and assist in career exploration.

Technical Aspects

The OASIS-2 was originally standardized on a quota and purposive sample ($N = 1,398$) of 8th- to 12th-grade students in 11 states. The present norm group consists of 1,505 students in 8th through 12th grade in 13 states. Evidence is provided in tables that the norm group characteristics are representative of the nation for region, gender, race, and domicile based on U.S. census data. Consumers of the test also are encouraged to develop local norms where useful.

For the Interest Schedule, a principle components analysis was conducted to test the hypothesis that 12 interest factors could be identified from data representing a large group of males and females ($N = 1,221$). Results indicated that 12 components or factors were extracted corresponding to the 12 subscales. Although degree of separation of the factor loadings of the MEC and IND interest scales was not marked in the analyses, both of these interest scales had primary loadings on separate factors.

The five subtests of the Aptitude Survey were developed through factor analytic studies of the General Aptitude Test Battery (GATB; U.S. Department of Labor, 1970). Through additional factor analysis, abilities represented in the GATB were reduced to five factors. This five-factor solution accounted for 73% of the total variance. Eigenvalues and cumulative percent variance accounted for are presented in the examiner's manual. The following labels were assigned to the five factors: Manual Dexterity, Perceptual Aptitude, Numerical Aptitude, Spatial Aptitude, and Verbal Aptitude.

The RELATE program (Veldman, 1967) was used to determine whether factor matrices obtained from new samples could be rotated into agreement with the original factor matrix. A hypothetical target matrix was formulated toward which the new factor matrix is rotated. The rotation procedure described in the examiner's manual was applied to a correlation matrix of eight GATB subtest scores obtained from 2,649 airmen. Results support close alignment between the hypothesized target matrix and the rotated matrix. Additionally, the rotation procedure was performed on GATB data obtain from a sample of 93 clients with handicaps at the University of Texas Job Readiness Clinic. Again the five factors could be rotated into close alignment with the five factors accounting for 87.2% of the variance. Based on these rotation procedures, the author reports some degree of confidence in the stability or factor invariance of the five-factor solution.

The majority of studies reported that provide evidence of the OASIS-2's validity and reliability involve both the Interest Schedule and the Aptitude Survey, and as such the two will be discussed together. In instances where differences exist in the technical aspects of the AS and the IS, explanation will be provided.

Data on intercorrelations among the AS subtests was reported to demonstrate evidence of construct-related validity. With the exception of correlations between the Vocabulary and Computation subtests and between the Computation and Word Comparison subtests, the correlations are low, although statistically significant at the .05 level. These results are used to show that each subtest measures a fairly separate aspect of behavior within the domain of aptitude.

Their relationship to other tests purporting to measure the same construct also was explored to provide further evidence of AS and IS validity. One study examined correlations between the OASIS-2 Aptitude Survey and GATB scores of 59 rehabilitation clients (mean age = 29.4) referred for psychological evaluation. Additionally, 147 students enrolled at a large Southern community college provided the sample for a study designed to determine if a relationship existed between learning style and the dichotomous academic attribute of decision of college major. A discriminant stepwise analysis showed that decision of academic major discriminated among Accommodating and Science scores on the OASIS-2 Interest Survey and Numerical Aptitude scores on the OASIS-2 Aptitude Survey ($p < .05$). Those students labeled "assimilators" on the Learning Styles Inventory received the highest Numerical Aptitude scores and were most decisive in selecting a major. Other studies (Parker & Green, 1987) provide evidence that community college students in mechanical engineering scored significantly higher on AS General Ability and Verbal Ability subtests and significantly higher on IS Mechanical, Science, and Physical Performing scales as compared to other academic majors. Similar hypothesized differences were also found in the IS scale scores of business and humanities majors. Quan (1984) found that students with learning disabilities and nondisabled students differed on occupational aptitudes as measured by the OASIS-2 and the Test of Practical Knowledge (TPK).

Evidence of convergent validity was provided using correlations of the OASIS-2 Aptitude Survey and two frequently used achievement tests, the Iowa Tests of Educational Development (ITED) and the the SRA Achievement Series subtests. Correlations between similar subtests (e.g., AS Vocabulary and ITED Reading) are reported as high (+.68), while subtests measuring different constructs (e.g., AS Making Marks and ITED Reading) are reported as low (-.01). Similar correlation coefficients were obtained with similar and dissimilar subtests of the SRA Achievement Series.

Alpha and test-retest reliability are reported for the Interest Survey. Alpha coefficients ranged from .78 to .94. The coefficients reported indicate item homogeneity and unidimensionality as well as sufficient reliability for stimulating vocational exploration through professional interpretation of results. Standard error of measurement scores also are reported for each of the stanine scores, which provide a range within which the score will fall 68% of the time if retested. Probabilities that scores will not vary more than ±1 standard deviation on retest were calculated. These probabilities, reported as a confidence interval on the profile sheet, range from 91% to 98% for the 12 scales. Test-retest reliabilities reported with a 2-week time interval on data obtained from 54 junior high and high school students yielded reliability coefficients ranging from .66 to .91.

Four types of reliability measures employed in the development of the Aptitude Survey include alpha, split-half, alternate forms, and test-retest reliability. Alpha reliabilities reported for Vocabulary and Computation range from .70 to .94. Split-half reliabilities for the Spatial Relations subtest range from .70 to .92. Word Comparison and Making Marks were developed with separately timed, alternate forms; alternate forms reliabilities ranged from .85 to .94. Test-retest reliability was determined on a sample of 54 junior high and high school students applying the same procedure and 2-week time interval as used for determining the stability of the Interest Schedule.

Internal consistency of AS items was determined and the relationship among items and the total scale score was explored. An item analysis was conducted following the administration of the Aptitude Survey to 273 junior high and high school students in rural Texas. Item-total correlations were computed, and items with correlations belows .20 were routinely omitted based on Nunnally's (1967) assertion that item-total correlations "above .20 are usually considered good." Item-total correlations and item difficulty levels are provided in the AS examiner's manual for the Vocabulary, Computation, and Spatial Relations subtests. Item difficulty level information was utilized to determine the order of the items in the three tests. Item analyses were not appropriate for the speeded tests (i.e., Word Comparison and Making Marks); instead, these subtests were constructed through a series of pilot tests designed to determine the time limits for each subtest that produced maximum reliability.

Critique

The OASIS-2 represents a standardized effort toward the development of an instrument that will assist young people in the often confusing and difficult task of career exploration and selection. Important improvements from the previous edition include the introduction of a computer-scored form that facilitates administration and scoring for large groups, and the addition of confidence levels to the student profile sheet to assist in the meaningful interpretation of scores.

The OASIS-2 serves as a useful tool for career development and counseling programs, to encourage thoughtful self-examination of goals and interests as well as career exploration on the part of high school students. Though career development is a complex process that spans a lifetime, the OASIS-2 could provide structure and impetus for an organized search to young people beginning the process.

The author emphasizes careful and sensitive interpretation by a trained professional as the key to providing useful results that are expansive, "open doors" for students, encourage career exploration, and discourage stereotyping and student self-perceptions of limitations. There is obvious merit in actively engaging students in the process of self-reflection focusing on interests, strengths, and career goals. Increasing student awareness of options and providing a structure for organizing the overwhelming task of a career search is likely to result in more informed career decisions.

Normative procedures are thorough and well explained. Care was taken to make important improvements in the composition of the original norm group, which increases the instrument's representativeness and relevance to the population of students in Grades 8 through 12. Test consumers who are not well versed in the use of standardized instrumentation will find useful the explanation of norms and standardization in the examiner's manuals. The text provides a discussion of the purpose of norms, the representativeness of the norm group on important characteristics in comparison to the U.S. census figures for those characteristics in the larger population, and the usefulness of developing local norms to compare students with others most like them.

In addition, the author reports evidence of numerous studies that provide factor analytic information, relate the IS and the AS to similar and dissimilar instruments, explore the internal consistency of items, and offer data on the expected effects of retesting students. The technical information sections of the AS and IS manuals present a careful discussion of construct-related validity and reliability issues. The reader is provided with straightforward discussions of various methods available to determine reliability and validity of standardized instruments as well as a rationale for the methods chosen to validate the OASIS-2. The many citations from measurement literature lend support for the types of analyses conducted.

While one strength of the OASIS-2 lies in its ability to survey interests and aptitudes of large numbers of students in a standardized manner, concerns emerge in the area of stability of preferences over time. Because preferences and interests vacillate and develop through experience, especially in the case of adolescents, results of the Interest Schedule may vary considerably over time. In addition, lack of prior knowledge of job types and job activities within job types may result in responses based on faulty or vague notions of what tasks actually involve. It may be useful therefore to utilize the OASIS-2 in conjunction with a career survey course or internship program to provide hands-on exposure and experience in occupations so more reliable preferences may be formed and indicators of aptitude may be observed.

Although the AS manual provides an extensive explanation of the survey's development, one may take exception with the author's conclusion of a five-factor solution derived from the original 12 GATB subtests. The factor analysis yields eigenvalues for the first two factors of 3.66 and 2.36, which account for 50.2% of the variance, and an eigenvalue of .98 for Factor 3. The remaining two factors have eigenvalues of less than 1.00. Pedhazur (1982, p. 596) provides a discussion of the confusion in interpretation of eigenvalues under 1.00. For this reason, a three-factor solution may be more plausible than the five-factor solution reported by Parker.

Although item-total correlations were reported in the moderate range, these reviewers found it difficult to interpret these values because item difficulty information is not reported in table form but only summarized in the text.

The results of numerous studies are offered to provide evidence of construct-related validity, and many show agreement between the OASIS-2 and other instruments that purport to measure aptitudes and interests. These are important. Studies are cited that determine a relationship between decisiveness in choosing a college major and high scores in specific aptitude areas. However, limited information is available regarding the consequential validity of the instrument with the groups on which it was normed. Powerful evidence to potential consumers of this instrument includes studies that determine the number of high school seniors who enter and experience success in fields related to the results of the OASIS-2.

Parker seeks to find additional support for construct validity of the AS through research on the relationships between OASIS-2 Aptitude Survey and other tests measuring the same constructs. Parker, Chan, and Carter (1990) report significant canonical correlations between the OASIS Aptitude Survey and the GATB for a sample of 59 clients in a rehabilitation center. Their correlation coefficients obtained in relating the OASIS-2 to other tests are confusing and incidental, given the fact that the comparison group used was different from the group on which the AS was normed. There are a number of problems in interpreting these results due to obvious differences in age, experience, and self-perceptions of rehabilitation clients versus the typical high school student. Therefore, high and moderate correlations between the GATB and the OASIS-2 obtained from samples other than those on which the test was normed provide ambiguous evidence of the instrument's construct validity.

Although reporting confidence levels directly on the student profile offers a useful addition to this newer version of the OASIS, the information that confidence levels provide regarding the assurance that a score will not vary by more than 1 stanine if the student were retested may be misleading given the test-retest information reported in the examiner's manual. The data provided reveal high to moderately high reliability coefficients for retest after a 2-week interval. Although the author uses this to conclude that the Interest Schedule scales and the Aptitude Survey are relatively stable over time, much evidence exists indicating that interests and preferences change markedly with experience. It is highly likely that a high school student will experience many activities that will affect his or her attitudes and preferences toward work. More information is needed regarding the stability of interests over intervals greater than 2 weeks.

In conclusion, the OASIS-2 represents an improvement over the original version, but it still could profit from investigation of its relationship with career success and satisfaction. Additional validity studies are needed using the population for which the test is designed, and a reexamination of the five-factor structure of the Aptitude Survey is warranted.

References

Andrew, D., Paterson, D., & Longstaff, H. (1961). *Minnesota Clerical Test*. San Antonio, TX: Psychological Corporation.

Nunnally, J. (1967). *Psychometric theory*. New York: McGraw-Hill.

Pedhazur, E. (1982). *Multiple regression in behavioral research* (2nd ed.). New York: Holt, Reinhart & Winston.

Parker, R.M. (1983). *Occupational Aptitude Survey and Interest Schedule*. Austin, TX: PRO-ED.

Parker, R.M. (1991). *Occupational Aptitude Survey and Interest Schedule, Second Edition*. Austin, TX: PRO-ED.

Parker, R., & Green, D. (1987). Construct validity of the OASIS Interest Schedule. *Educational and Psychological Measurement, 47,* 755–757.

Parker, R., Chan, F., & Carter, H. (1990). Concurrent validity of the OASIS Aptitude Survey. *Educational and Psychological Measurement, 50,* 209–212.

Quan, H. (1984). The relationship among occupational goal, interests, aptitudes, and practical knowledge of learning disabled adolescents. (Doctoral dissertation, University of Texas at Austin, 1984). *Dissertation Abstracts International, 45,* 2078A.

U.S. Department of Labor. (1970). *General Aptitude Test Battery*. Syosset, New York: National Learning Corp.

Veldman, D. (1967). *FORTRAN programming for the behavioral sciences*. New York: Holt, Rinehart & Winston.

Jane L. Swanson, Ph.D.

Associate Professor of Psychology, Southern Illinois University, Carbondale, Illinois.

OCCUPATIONAL STRESS INVENTORY (RESEARCH VERSION)

Samuel H. Osipow and Arnold R. Spokane. Odessa, Florida: Psychological Assessment Resources, Inc.

Introduction

The Occupational Stress Inventory (OSI) is a 140-item instrument designed to measure three domains of occupational adjustment in employed adults: occupational stress, psychological strain, and coping resources. Fourteen specific scales measure characteristics of the individual or of the environment related to stress, strain, or coping.

The OSI was developed by Dr. Samuel H. Osipow and Dr. Arnold R. Spokane, both counseling psychologists who are eminent researchers in the area of career psychology. Dr. Osipow is Professor of Psychology at the Ohio State University, past president of the Division of Counseling Psychology of the American Psychological Association, founding editor of the *Journal of Vocational Behavior,* and past editor of the *Journal of Counseling Psychology.* Dr. Spokane is a professor of counseling psychology at Lehigh University and has authored numerous publications in career psychology, including a recent book entitled *Career Intervention.*

According to Osipow and Spokane (1987), the OSI was developed for two primary reasons: to develop general measures of stressors that would be applicable across occupational levels and environments, and to provide measures to operationalize a theoretical model that integrates sources of work environment stress, the resultant psychological strains, and available coping resources.

Development of the OSI began with a review of theoretical models regarding occupational stress. Based on this review, the authors developed a model to describe the process of occupational stress, consisting of the three domains of occupational stressors, psychological strain, and coping resources. The model posited by Osipow and Spokane (1984) focuses on the perceptions an individual has of occupational stress; that is, subjective levels of stress are of greater interest and relevance than objective levels of stress. Further, given equal levels of perceived stress, the amount of strain an individual experiences is moderated by the amount of coping resources available. Within this conceptual model, the authors defined facets for each of the domains, again based on a review of available literature: five social roles and one nonsocial aspect were identified as sources of stress, four types of symptoms or responses were identified as comprising psychological strain, and four sets of behaviors were identified as coping resources. These facets then were used to generate a pool of items for initial development of the OSI.

Items were selected from the pool based on their face validity and compiled into the first version (Form E-1) of the OSI (Osipow & Spokane, 1981).

The psychometric characteristics of Form E-1 then were evaluated in two samples: 2-week test-retest reliability with 31 employed adults, and internal consistency with 201 employed adults. Based on data from the latter sample, changes were made to some OSI items: 23 items were reworded, 2 were replaced, and some were deleted to give all of the scales an equal number (10) of items. The resultant inventory (Form E-2) is the current version of the OSI, and consists of 140 items and 14 scales.

The OSI can be viewed as consisting of three independent instruments. The previous version in fact was packaged as three separate entities and entitled Measures of Occupational Stress, Strain, and Coping (Osipow & Spokane, 1981, 1983); the current version (the OSI) is presented as consisting of three subsections: the Occupational Roles Questionnaire (ORQ), measuring the domain of occupational stress (previously titled the Occupational Environment Scales); the Personal Strain Questionnaire (PSQ), measuring the domain of psychological strain experienced by an individual; and the Personal Resources Questionnaire (PRQ), measuring the domain of coping resources. Each subsection contains a number of specific scales, which each consist of 10 items. The OSI components are described as follows (Osipow & Spokane, 1987):

1. The *Occupational Roles Questionnaire* (ORQ) consists of six scales measuring an individual's perceptions of stress resulting from work-related roles:

a. *Role Overload*—extent to which job demands are perceived as exceeding personal and workplace resources, and the perceived ability to accomplish what is expected at work.

b. *Role Insufficiency*—perceived appropriateness of an individual's background (training, skills, and experience) for the job requirements.

c. *Role Ambiguity*—perceived clarity of work priorities, expectations, and evaluation criteria.

d. *Role Boundary*—extent to which conflicting role demands and loyalties are experienced at work.

e. *Responsibility*—amount of responsibility the individual feels for the performance and welfare of other people at work.

f. *Physical Environment*—amount of exposure to extreme physical conditions or environmental toxins.

2. The *Personal Strain Questionnaire* (PSQ) consists of four scales measuring various types of strain or symptoms that result from work-related stressors:

a. *Vocational Strain*—extent to which the individual is experiencing problems with work quality or performance.

b. *Psychological Strain*—presence of psychological or emotional problems.

c. *Interpersonal Strain*—perceived disruption in interpersonal relationships.

d. *Physical Strain*—complaints about physical illness or poor self-care habits.

3. The *Personal Resources Questionnaire* (PRQ) consists of four scales measuring various aspects of coping behavior:

a. *Recreation*—use and enjoyment of recreational activities.

b. *Self-care*—involvement in personal activities that reduce stress.

c. *Social Support*—perceived support and help from others.

d. *Rational/Cognitive Coping*—use of cognitive skills in response to stress.

All 140 items across the three measures are contained in one booklet, with the 10 items for each scale presented consecutively (i.e., items 1 through 10 belong to Role Overload, 11 through 20 belong to Role Insufficiency, etc.). The items were constructed with a 5-point Likert-type scale to assess frequency of occurrence (rarely or never, occasionally, often, usually, most of the time). Approximately one fourth of the items are worded in a negative direction and reverse scored. The estimated reading difficulty of the items is the seventh-grade level.

Two paper-and-pencil forms of the inventory are available: Form HS, consisting of a reusable test booklet and an expendable hand-scored answer sheet, and Form I, consisting of an integrated expendable test booklet and answer sheet that allows computer scoring by the test publisher. In addition, a version of the OSI is available on computer diskette, which allows for integrated computerized administration, scoring, and profile reporting. Form HS is structured so that subsections may be administered separately. The profile form accompanying Form HS has preprinted raw scores and T-score conversions to facilitate normative interpretation of results.

Practical Applications/Uses

One of the original reasons for developing the OSI was to provide measures for testing the authors' theoretical model (Osipow & Spokane, 1984), and the authors continue to recommend only research use at this time. However, they also advise that clinical use might be warranted in situations in which either local norms exist or the research norms clearly apply to the population; data for the research norms were drawn primarily from professional, managerial, and technical employees. The manual clearly states that the OSI should *not* be used for purposes of "selection, retention, promotion, job performance evaluation, or compensation," and should be used to identify "occupationally induced stress for the benefit of an individual *voluntarily* [italics added] taking the test" (Osipow & Spokane, 1987, p. 3).

As a research instrument, the OSI has a great deal of potential. The scholarly literature on work-related stress has expanded rapidly in recent years, yet issues related to the measurement of stress continue to plague researchers: A number of instruments exist to measure stress, strain, and coping, but often scales are developed for a specific study, constraining generalizability across studies and across occupations. Osipow and Spokane's (1984) conceptualization of stress, strain, and coping as three independent but interrelated constructs is shared by other scholars (Lazarus, DeLongis, Folkman, & Gruen, 1985). The OSI offers an integrated instrument with psychometric promise that may prove useful in furthering stress-related research.

In addition to its use as a research instrument, the OSI also shows promise for applied settings. The manual suggests using the OSI 1) as a screening instrument to determine the goals and benefits of individual treatment; 2) to assess an organization's milieu, whether to simply describe an organization or as a precursor to its redesign; 3) in counseling, education, and development, such as to facilitate marital or family discussion; 4) in career counseling, providing additional information for occupational choice or change; and 5) as an outcome measure to assess the effectiveness of organizational or individual interventions. Though all of these suggestions are feasible, each is qualified by a warning in the manual that the OSI has not yet been validated for these purposes. Unfortunately, many test users may not heed the warnings and may use the instrument for purposes for which it was not intended or is not yet ready. Because the instrument currently *is* being used by a wide variety of individuals and organizations, the authors intend to evaluate more closely whether these are appropriate uses (A.R. Spokane, personal communication, October 11, 1992).

A prime example of an applied use of the OSI is as a tool for individual or group clinical work. Work-related stress is a primary issue for many clients, whether in private practice settings, community mental health agencies, or employee assistance and human resource programs. In these contexts, the OSI could provide an efficient indication of a client's overall level of stress in normative terms. Perhaps more importantly, the inventory could help pinpoint specific sources of stress, specific symptoms or strains resulting from stress, and specific individual coping resources that could be mobilized or strengthened. Examining a client's OSI profile of stress, strain, and coping scores could assist in defining the direction of counseling regarding work-related stress.

Administration of the OSI appears to be straightforward and would require little instruction to subjects or training of administrators. The manual estimates an administration time of 20 to 40 minutes, which seems reasonable given that the items are brief and concise and presented at a seventh-grade reading level. Because the test booklet and answer sheet are clearly organized and labeled, the OSI could be given without an administrator present.

As mentioned earlier, the OSI can be hand scored (Form HS) or computer scored (Form I). Hand scoring seems relatively easy and begins with removing the first page of a two-page attached form; responses made by the test taker on the first page are duplicated on the second. The second page differs from the first in that the items that should be reverse scored are indicated so that the examiner can properly sum them into scale scores. Scores for each column (the 10 items per scale) are totaled, providing raw scores. Two sources of error are possible in hand scoring, computational errors and overlooking the reverse-scored items; the frequency or impact of these possible errors is unknown.

The raw scores then are converted to T-scores as they are transferred to the profile sheet (Form HS), through the computer scoring process (Form I), or by consulting the manual. T-scores were developed separately for men and women, although the manual contains no discussion of whether or how men and women differ, or why separate-sex norms were necessary. Percentile scores also appear in the manual.

On the Occupational Roles Questionnaire and the Personal Strain Questionnaire, T-scores above 70 indicate a strong probability of high stress and strain. Scores of 60 to 69 indicate mild levels of stress and strain, 40 to 59 fall within the normal range, and scores below 40 indicate an absence of stress and strain. Interpretation of the Personal Resources Questionnaire scales occurs in the opposite direction of the ORQ and PSQ scales; that is, high scores are indicative of adaptive responses. Scores of 30 or below indicate a significant lack of coping resources, 30 to 39 point to a mild lack of resources, 40 to 59 indicate average resources, and higher scores evidence more well-developed coping resources.

The OSI manual offers guidelines for interpreting the 14 scales on the profile as a set. First, the average elevation of scores within each subsection of scales (ORQ, PSQ, and PRQ) should be considered and compared across subsets; for example, is the average stress score (ORQ) higher or lower than the average strain score (PSQ)? Second, within each subset, individual scales provide information about specific aspects and should be interpreted individually; for example, what type of strain is highest for the individual? It also is recommended that the OSI be used in conjunction with other assessment devices (such as measures of vocational interests, abilities, personality, etc.) to provide a comprehensive view of the client. The manual contains several case studies to provide interpretive illustrations for users.

Technical Aspects

Reliability of Form E-2 was estimated by computing internal consistency coefficients in a sample of 549 working adults. Alpha coefficients for the three subsections were .89 for the ORQ, .94 for the PSQ, and .88 for the PRQ. Coefficients for individual scales ranged from .71 (Responsibility, Vocational Strain, and Recreation) to .90 (Role Insufficiency). Similar results were reported by Alexander (1983; cited in Osipow & Spokane, 1987) in a sample of 155 physicians. Test-retest reliability is not reported for Form E-2. Two-week test-retest reliability coefficients for Form E-1 in a sample of 31 employed adults were .90 for the ORQ, .94 for the PSQ, and .88 for the PRQ; coefficients for individual scales ranged from .56 to .94. Given the number of items from Form E-1 that were modified, replaced, or deleted for Form E-2, updated test-retest reliability information is needed.

Intercorrelations among the total scores and the 14 individual scale scores provide preliminary validity evidence for the instrument, based on unidentified samples ranging in size from 610 to 757 subjects. As predicted, the correlation between the PSQ and the PRQ was negative (-.24), as was the correlation between the ORQ and the PRQ (-.25); in other words, as coping resource scores increase, perceptions of stress and strain decrease. Scales within the ORQ and PSQ had relatively low intercorrelations, suggesting that the scales were measuring different constructs, whereas scales within the PSQ had higher intercorrelations, suggesting that more overlap exists among what these scales measure.

The manual describes four types of studies that provide further validity information for the OSI: 1) analyzing the factor structure underlying the OSI scales, 2) calculating relations between the OSI and other theoretically related variables, 3) examining changes in OSI scores before and after interventions, and 4) testing the theoretical model underlying the OSI.

First, confirmatory factor analyses were conducted separately on the three subsections of the OSI, using three presumably overlapping samples. The analysis of the ORQ ($n = 549$) provided clear evidence of the predicted six factors, corresponding to the six scales. On the other hand, results for the PSQ ($n = 353$) and PRQ ($n = 419$) each produced five factors that were somewhat different from those predicted, and the fifth factor in each analysis was uninterpretable. Further, many of the items assigned to specific scales did not load on any factor, calling into question the underlying structure of the PSQ and PRQ. For example, only 7 of the 10 items on each of the four PRQ scales had loadings greater than .35; only one of the five factors, Social Support, showed any factorial purity. Some of the PSQ scales fared even worse: 5 of the 10 Vocational Strain items did not have factor loadings greater than .20, and 4 of the 10 Interpersonal Strain items did not have factor loadings greater than .30. Items from the Vocational Strain, Interpersonal Strain, and Physical Strain scales showed loadings greater than .35 on three of five factors. Although not discussed in the manual, the authors concluded elsewhere (Osipow & Spokane, 1984) that the PSQ perhaps should be used as a unidimensional measure rather than as separate subscales.

Based on a second confirmatory analysis by Alexander (1983; cited in Osipow & Spokane, 1987), the test authors concluded that "there was substantial agreement between the scales of the OSI and the patterns of factor loadings" (Osipow & Spokane, 1987, p. 10). However, an examination of the table presented in the manual again revealed significant discrepancies in the scale structure. For example, the ORQ Responsibility items did not emerge as a separate factor, and analysis of the PSQ items resulted in four factors with considerable overlap between and within factors. Analysis of the PRQ items produced the most factorial purity of the three subsections of the OSI.

Because factor analysis techniques can reveal the internal structure of an instrument, they provide the most fundamental evidence regarding an instrument's validity. In the case of the OSI, although the manual concludes that the two sets of factor analytic results are strongly supportive of the structure underlying the OSI, examination of these results reveal some discrepancies that need further attention. For example, if items do not load on any factors or load on several, perhaps they should be revised or discarded; if they load on factors other than those corresponding to their assigned scales, perhaps they should be reassigned. Further, a factor analysis of all 140 OSI items together, rather than separately by subsection, is necessary to examine the interrelations of the three theoretical domains measured by the instrument.

For the second type of validity evidence, relations between the OSI and other theoretically related variables, the manual presents a summary of 14 correlational studies that "provide moderate to strong support of the concurrent validity of the OSI" (Osipow & Spokane, 1987, p. 10). For example, a study by Higgins (1985; cited in Osipow & Spokane, 1987) reported strong and predicted relations between PSQ scales and Maslach Burnout Inventory scales: strain was positively related to Emotional Exhaustion and Depersonalization and negatively related to Personal Accomplishment. The third type of validity evidence consists of two treatment studies that suggest that "the PSQ and PRQ are sensitive outcome measures of treatment effects" (Osipow & Spokane, 1987, p. 13). For example, Higgins (1986) reported that PSQ scores decreased significantly for individuals in two stress-reduction interventions, but not for those in a control group. Fourth, studies of the OSI model (Osipow & Spokane, 1984) provide evidence of the validity of the OSI instrument. The manual discusses nine such studies, which use the OSI to test propositions of the model. For example, Osipow and Davis (1988) reported that coping buffered the relation between stress and strain, as predicted.

Finally, the authors provide a listing of future directions for validity studies, including relations of stress, strain, and coping with work-related behaviors and mental and physical health, studies including samples of blue-collar workers, interventions with well-adjusted workers, and person-environment fit and stress. In addition to these suggestions, further validation of the OSI would be evidenced by finding differential stress scale scores across occupations or work environments that should differ in predictable ways, and differential strain and coping scale scores for individuals who differ on personality or demographic variables. Finally, a crucial type of validity evidence is a comparison of the OSI to other measures of stress, strain, and coping (Bernardin, 1985) via multitrait-multimethod analyses (Campbell & Fiske, 1959).

A primary reason that this version of the OSI is considered a research edition is because of the limited normative information. The normative data used to determine the T-score conversions were based on a sample of 909 working adults, primarily in technical, professional, and managerial positions; 130 different occupations were represented. The manual provides a brief demographic description of the normative sample, unfortunately omitting the racial-ethnic composition. A goal for future versions of the OSI is to develop separate norms by occupation (Osipow & Spokane, 1984, 1987).

Critique

To evaluate the current status of the OSI, it is important to weigh what is known about the instrument with what is still unknown. On the whole, the balance tips in favor of the OSI as a research instrument, though considerably more work is needed to establish it as a clinical tool.

In general the manual is clearly and concisely written, offering a good illustration of how material should be organized and presented in a test manual. Enough information is presented for both the casual reader and the psychometric specialist to become well informed. For example, the basic results of the factor analyses appear in the text, and more complete results (factor loadings for 140 items) are available in an appendix. Further, the manual is refreshing in that the authors are straightforward in their claims for the instrument, clearly and repeatedly stating the limitations of the OSI. Some test authors would claim suitability for clinical use based on data available in this manual, which would be premature.

On the other hand, the manual clearly needs to be revised, particularly because it is dated relative to the age of the instrument. A revised manual should include expanded and updated psychometric information, such as the missing evidence of reliability and validity noted earlier. In addition, although the current norms are based on a relatively large and heterogeneous sample, they could benefit from updating; presumably the authors as well as independent researchers have added to the normative base since the manual was published in 1987. A further concern about the current manual is that a majority of the studies offered as evidence of the OSI's validity are unpublished graduate student theses and dissertations. Because these studies are not easily accessible, the test user cannot make an independent evaluation of their quality or conclusions. Often only the most relevant results are reported in the manual, resulting in incomplete information.

In fairness to the test authors, these concerns about the manual are not unusual at this stage in the development of an instrument, considering that the amount of research conducted with the OSI undoubtedly has increased since the manual was published. According to the authors, the instrument and the manual are currently being revised. Goals of the revision include a) adding a fourth set of scales to measure family resources and support, b) rewording some of the items on the current instrument, c) collecting more extensive test-retest reliability data, d) collecting a larger and more representative norm group, e) adding some experimental supplemental scales, and f) updating the manual and supportive materials (A.R. Spokane, personal communication, October 11, 1992).

A final area that might be addressed in a revised manual is updated information about the status of the instrument's theoretical underpinnings. The theoretical model and definitions of the constructs to be measured during development of the OSI were drawn from literature published in the 1960s and 1970s. How has the scholarly literature, independent of the use or validation of the OSI, supported the theoretical model? Have there been new trends in the literature that might affect how the OSI is viewed? How would the model or the OSI be different if developed today?

As compared to previous reviews of the OSI (Bernardin, 1985; Murphy, 1985; Yanico, 1985), progress clearly has been made in further development of the instrument. Some issues raised in earlier reviews have been corrected; for example, Bernardin's (1985) criticisms of the manual seem to have been directly addressed in the current version. However, some issues raised in earlier reviews continue to be problematic, such as Yanico's (1985) observation that "high scorers" were not defined in the manual's interpretive descriptions.

Perhaps the most serious omission yet to be addressed relates to Bernardin's (1985) review. He suggested that it is incumbent upon the developers of a new instrument to demonstrate that something different is being measured and noted the existence of other frequently used measures of role overload and role ambiguity (as also is true of strain symptoms and of coping resources). Convergent and discriminant validity of an instrument typically is demonstrated through the use of conjoint factor analysis, as suggested by Murphy (1985), and multitrait-multimethod analyses, as suggested by Bernardin (1985). However, to date no such analyses of the OSI and related measures have been conducted, and they remain essential in providing psychometric justification for the use of the OSI.

In summary, the OSI offers a brief, integrated measure of occupational stress, strain, and coping resources. Its strengths include a theoretical base, provision of normative data, and measures that are not limited to specific occupational groups or levels. At the present time, the OSI seems to be at a critical juncture in its development. Initial evidence suggests that the instrument holds much promise, and the direction of future research on the OSI seems clearly defined. Given the reputation of the test authors and their careful work thus far, they are likely to continue to build a psychometrically sound and useful instrument.

References

Bernardin, H.J. (1985). Measures of Occupational Stress, Strain, and Coping. In J.V. Mitchell Jr. (Ed.), *The ninth mental measurements yearbook* (pp. 946–948). Lincoln, NE: Buros Institute of Mental Measurements.

Campbell, D.T., & Fiske, D.W. (1959). Convergent and discriminant validation by the multitrait-multimethod matrix. *Psychological Bulletin, 56,* 81–105.

Higgins, N. (1986). Occupational stress and working women: The effectiveness of two stress-reduction programs. *Journal of Vocational Behavior, 29,* 66–78.

Lazarus, R.S., DeLongis, A., Folkman, S., & Gruen, R. (1985). Stress and adaptive outcomes: The problem of confounded measures. *American Psychologist, 40,* 770–779.

Murphy, K.R. (1985). Measures of Occupational Stress, Strain, and Coping. In J.V. Mitchell, Jr. (Ed.), *The ninth mental measurements yearbook* (pp. 948–949). Lincoln, NE: Buros Institute of Mental Measurements.

Osipow, S.H., & Davis, A.S. (1988). The relationship of coping resources to occupational stress and strain. *Journal of Vocational Behavior, 32,* 1–15.

Osipow, S.H., & Spokane, A.R. (1981). *Measures of Occupational Stress, Strain, and Coping (Form E-1).* Columbus, OH: Marathon Consulting and Press.

Osipow, S.H., & Spokane, A.R. (1983). *Manual for Measures of Occupational Stress, Strain, and Coping (Form E-2).* Columbus, OH: Marathon Consulting and Press.

Osipow, S.H., & Spokane, A.R. (1984). Measuring occupational stress, strain, and coping. In S. Oskamp (Ed.), *Applied Social Psychology Annual, 5,* 67–87.

Osipow, S.H., & Spokane, A.R. (1987). *Manual for the Occupational Stress Inventory (Research Version).* Odessa, FL: Psychological Assessment Resources.

Yanico, B.J. (1985). Occupational Environment Scales, Form E2. In D.J. Keyser & R.C. Sweetland (Eds.), *Test critiques* (Vol. II, pp. 535–542). Austin, TX: PRO-ED.

James A. Moses, Jr., Ph.D.
*Clinical Associate Professor of Psychiatry and Behavioral Sciences,
Stanford University School of Medicine, and Coordinator,
Psychological Assessment Unit, Department of Veterans Affairs
Medical Center, Palo Alto, California.*

PANTOMIME RECOGNITION TEST

*Arthur L. Benton, Kerry deS. Hamsher, Nils R. Varney, and
Otfried Spreen. New York, New York: Oxford University
Press.*

Introduction

The authors of the Pantomime Recognition Test (PRT) describe their instrument as "an objective, standardized procedure for assessing a patient's ability to understand meaningful, nonlinguistic pantomimed actions. The test requires the patient to point to drawings of objects whose pretended uses are shown in a series of videotaped pantomimes" (Benton, Hamsher, Varney, & Spreen, 1983, p. 64). Because the PRT was designed primarily to evaluate patients who have an aphasic disorder and possibly an associated apraxic disturbance, the linguistic and voluntary movement features of the administration and response modalities have been intentionally simplified. These methods specify the functional system required for task performance more clearly and make it possible to separate specific perceptual pantomime recognition deficit from commonly associated disorders of naming, auditory comprehension, and voluntary movement.

The PRT items are recorded in color on a standard ¾-inch videocassette tape. The test can be administered with a standard videocassette player attached to a color television monitor. The PRT initially presents 4 unscored practice items that are followed by the 30 scored test items. Each PRT item is separated from the next by 7 seconds of blank tape to allow time for patient response. The four initial practice items were chosen to introduce and demonstrate the stimulus and response requirements of the PRT. As the sample items were the easiest tasks developed for the test, they proved suitable for task introduction but not for syndrome analysis. Aphasic patients, the primary intended clinical PRT test group, typically could perform the PRT sample items without error.

Accompanying the videotaped pantomimes is a 31-page response choice booklet. Each page presents four line drawings as response alternatives for each pantomimed action presented on the videotape. The patient interprets the pantomimed action for each item by pointing to the response alternative that depicts the object associated with the pantomimed action. All items used in the PRT are common, familiar objects. The four response alternatives for the sample items are presented on the first page of the response booklet, labeled "P" (practice) to distinguish it

507

from response choice cards for the scored test items. The remainder of the pages are numbered to correspond to the test item order on the answer sheet.

Each of the 30 test items presents four types of response choices; one alternative is correct and the other three are incorrect "foils." The *correct choice* (e.g., a violin) shows the line drawing of the object whose use is simulated in the videotaped pantomime action. The *semantic foil* choice shows a line drawing of an object in the same logical conceptual class of objects as the correct choice (e.g., a trombone). A *neutral foil* is a correct choice for another PRT item and therefore is an object suitable use in pantomime (e.g., a gun). The *odd foil* alternative consists of an object that cannot be used for pantomime (e.g., an anchor). Specification and limitation of the possible PRT error types enhances syndrome analysis when patient performance is defective.

The inability to correctly interpret pantomimed actions has been recognized as a specific symptom of brain dysfunction since Finkelnburg clinically described the first recognized case in 1870 (for a brief historical overview of associated syndrome-analytic issues, see Benton et al., 1983, p. 63, and Duffy & Liles, 1979). Pantomime recognition deficit has been demonstrated reliably in a subset of patients with aphasic disorder and in patients with severe dementia. Severity of aphasic disorder is not associated directly with the presence of pantomime recognition deficit.

Benton and his colleagues point to the importance of investigating pantomime recognition deficit as a higher order nonlinguistic syndrome in aphasic patients because it can better define the nature and range of the patient's communication disorder across linguistic and nonlinguistic dimensions. In their review of Varney's work (1978, 1982), Benton et al. (1983) noted a strong association between pantomime recognition deficit and reading comprehension difficulty, plus a secondary association between pantomime recognition deficit and auditory comprehension and naming deficit. Ferro, Santos, Castro-Caldas, and Mariano (1980) have replicated these findings. Benton and his colleagues also indicate that the presence and severity of pantomime recognition deficit may be of value for predicting the rate and extent of recovery from aphasia. However, the necessary and sufficient neurologic deficits for emergence of pantomime recognition deficit remain unclear to date.

The principal author of the PRT, Arthur L. Benton, Ph.D., received the A.B. degree (1931) and the A.M. degree (1933) from Oberlin College, followed by the Ph.D. degree from Columbia University (1935). He began his career as an assistant in psychology at Oberlin College (1931–33), Columbia University and New York State Psychiatric Institute (1934–36), and then Cornell University Medical College (1936–39), where subsequently he served as a staff psychologist. He was appointed as an attending psychologist at New York Hospital–Westchester Division and as a psychologist in the Student Personnel Office of the City College of New York from 1939 to 1941. He served on active duty in the U.S. Navy during and after the Second World War (1941–46), and next was appointed as Associate Professor of Psychology at the University of Louisville Medical School and as Chief Psychologist at the Louisville Mental Hygiene Clinic and the Louisville General Hospital (1946–48). From 1948 to 1958 Benton served as Professor of Psychology and Director of the Graduate Training Program in Clinical Psychology at the University of

Iowa and then, for the next two decades (1958–78), as Professor of Psychology and Neurology. He has continued to coauthor theoretical and research papers and books since 1978, when he became Professor Emeritus at the University of Iowa.

Benton's fundamental contributions to the field of clinical neuropsychology have been acknowledged extensively and internationally. He has received honorary Doctor of Science (Cornell College, 1978) and Doctor of Psychology (University of Rome, 1990) degrees, plus numerous other honors and awards including the Distinguished Service Award of the Iowa Psychological Association (1977), the Distinguished Professional Contribution Award from the American Psychological Association (1978), the Outstanding Scientific Contribution Award of the International Neuropsychological Society (1981), The Samuel Torrey Orton Award from the Orton Dyslexia Society (1982), the Distinguished Service and Outstanding Contributions Award from the American Board of Professional Psychology (1985), and the Distinguished Clinical Neuropsychologist Award from the National Academy of Neuropsychology (1989).

Benton is a past president of the American Orthopsychiatric Association (1965–66) and the International Neuropsychological Society (1970–71). He served as the Secretary-General of the Research Group on Aphasia for the World Federation of Neurology from 1971 to 1978 and has been a lecturer or visiting scholar at the University of Milan (1964), Hôpital Sainte-Anne, Paris (1968), Hadassah-Hebrew University Medical School, Jerusalem (1969), Free University of Amsterdam (1971), University of Helsinki (1974), University of Melbourne (1977), University of Minnesota Medical School (Baker Lecturer, 1979), University of Victoria, British Columbia (Lansdowne Scholar, 1980), and the University of Michigan (1986). He also served as Directeur d'Études Associé, École des Hautes Études, Paris (1979) and as a visiting scientist at the Tokyo Metropolitan Institute of Gerontology (1974).

Benton has authored, coauthored, or edited 12 books and monographs, approximately 150 professional journal articles, and 22 historical reviews in the area of clinical neuropsychology and behavioral neurology. He is recognized as a pioneer and a leading authority in the area of clinical neuropsychology.

The standardized, commercially published version of the PRT appeared with the clinical manual for this and other tests in the Benton-Iowa Neuropsychological Test Battery (Benton et al., 1983). Coauthors of this clinical manual with Dr. Benton are Kerry deS. Hamsher, Ph.D. (Associate Professor of Neurology, University of Wisconsin Medical School); Nils R. Varney, Ph.D. (Staff Neuropsychologist, Department of Veterans Affairs Medical Center, Iowa City, Iowa); and Otfried Spreen, Ph.D. (Professor Emeritus, Department of Psychology, University of Victoria, Victoria, British Columbia, Canada).

Practical Applications/Uses

Administration of the PRT is straightforward and could be performed easily by a trained technician or a multidisciplinary professional. Interpretation of the PRT results, however, should be limited to a professional formally trained in behavioral neurology, neuropsychology, speech pathology, or a related field that provides a basis for thoroughly understanding brain-behavior relationships, particularly syndrome analysis of neurolinguistic cognitive deficit. Neuropsychologists, speech pathologists, and behavioral neurologists with experimental interests in the analysis of aphasia and related disorders also could make use of the PRT effectively in their work.

The patient taking the PRT sits at a table with the response booklet open on the table in plain view. The color television monitor should be positioned 4 to 6 feet in front of the patient, optimally tuned for picture clarity and free from glare. The examiner should ensure that the patient is wearing glasses if they are needed. The response booklet is opened first to the page of practice items. The examiner then directs the patient's attention to the television monitor and plays the first pantomime from the videotape. Pointing to the response booklet, the examiner says "Which one of these things was the man pretending to use? Point to it down here." If the patient responds correctly, the examiner should continue with the remaining practice items. If he or she fails to respond, however, or responds incorrectly or inappropriately (e.g. naming, imitation, etc.), the examiner points to the correct response and says "He was pretending to use this one, the comb" (Benton et al., 1983, pp. 64–65). The authors advise that several repetitions may be necessary for the patient to understand the correct response procedure. Aphasic patients with auditory comprehension problems may require minor modifications (simplification of instructions or response demonstration most probably) to clarify the task administration and response requirements.

One judges the patient's testability with the PRT from his or her performance on the practice items. If the patient is unimpaired or makes only one error on the four practice items, the examiner proceeds with the full 30-item PRT administration. If the patient makes two or more errors on the practice items, however, the PRT is discontinued. Such consistent failure on these very elementary items offers evidence that either the patient has a severe deficit in pantomime recognition or a severe auditory comprehension problem exists that precludes a valid administration of the PRT. If this level of PRT performance decrement occurs, the patient's auditory comprehension ability should be examined further with an appropriate measure such as the Token Test to distinguish the specific reason for PRT failure.

Scoring the PRT is a clerical task. Patient responses are recorded on the answer sheet in columns arranged by response type (correct choice, semantic foil, neutral foil, odd foil; see Benton et al., 1983, p. 66, for a facsimile of the scoring sheet), and the total number of responses of each type is tallied for each category. The examiner assigns 1 point for each correct response; no credit is allowed for erroneous responses. With a four-item multiple-choice test such as the PRT, one could expect 7–8 responses to occur correctly by chance in the 30-item series. The nonchance or "effective" PRT total score range therefore is 8–30 points.

The test manual presents frequency distributions of PRT scores for samples of 30 hospitalized inpatient medical controls without history or current symptoms of brain disease (21 men, 9 women) and 105 demographically and diagnostically unspecified aphasic patients (Benton et al., 1983, p. 67). The sample of medical controls had an age range of 38–60 years and an educational range of 8–16 years; associated descriptive statistics for these demographic variables were not reported. Eighteen of 30 control patients (60%) achieved perfect or nearly perfect PRT performances, scoring in the range of 29–30 points. Their mean PRT score was 28.7 points (range = 26–30). Only two of 30 controls (7%) scored as low as 26 points. Based on these findings, PRT total scores of 25 and below are classified as defective. It is typical to rate scores below approximately the fifth percentile of normal performance as defective on the Benton-Iowa series of tests (Benton et al., 1983). Because the PRT total score of the lowest scoring control subjects ranked at the seventh percentile, the cutting score for abnormal PRT performance was assigned as the total score value just below this level.

Technical Aspects

The only clinical group on which PRT group data have been validated are patients with aphasic disorder. The manual reports PRT results for a sample of 105 aphasic patients whose linguistic disorder arose from a unilateral lesion of the left cerebral hemisphere. The aphasic syndrome subtypes of these patients are not reported; the severity of their linguistic disorder is described as "clinically evident" (Benton et al., 1983, p. 65). Perfect or near perfect PRT total scores were obtained by 31.4% (33/105) of these subjects, and an additional 31 of them (29.5%) scored in the range of 26–28 points. Nearly 61% scored in the normal range. The defective performances of the remaining aphasic subjects varied widely in severity level. Ten of these patients performed in the mildly defective range (total scores of 24–25), while 17 of them performed in the severely defective range (total scores of 10–19).

Analysis of error types in patients performing defectively also is instructive. Benton and his colleagues noted that most PRT errors made by their aphasic patients who performed defectively overall on the PRT were in the semantic category rather than in the neutral or odd categories. They suggested that the predominance of PRT semantic errors probably was due

> to a semantically vague understanding of the significance of the pantomimed actions rather than to confusion or complete lack of understanding. An analogy can be drawn between their responses in interpreting the nonverbal messages from pantomimed actions and their imprecise understanding of verbal messages when they fail to make correct choices among objects within the same category, e.g. knife for fork, crayon for pencil. (Benton et al., 1983, p. 68)

Varney and Benton (1982) reported more errors of the semantic type than of the other error types *combined* in 36/40 (90%) of their cases with defective-range PRT total scores. Their four patients who did not show a predominance of semantic errors among the incorrect responses were severely impaired in pantomime recognition ability. The investigators noted, however, that other aphasic patients comparably impaired in pantomime recognition ability did show the usual semantic error predominance. The trend toward semantic errors among this sample of aphasic patients is clear, but the relationship of PRT error type to specific aphasic disorder subtype remains to be clarified.

The patterns of defective PRT performance among patients with specific syndromes of cortical and subcortical dementia also remain to be identified empirically. Varney (1982) has made a preliminary investigation of this issue, raising the question of whether defective PRT performance among aphasic patients might be simply a performance-level deficit associated with generalized cognitive deficit. He made use of age-corrected scores from the Wechsler Adult Intelligence Scale (WAIS) Block Design subtest as a nonlinguistic estimator of cognitive performance ability that was differentiable from the linguistic deficit. He found a wide range of Block Design performance levels (range = 0–14 scaled score points on a scale with $M = 10$ and $SD = 3$) in his sample of aphasics with impaired PRT performance. Five of his 18 defectively scoring PRT aphasics produced Block Design scores in the average to above average range (10–14 scaled score points), while 17/18 (94.4%) of them could not pass a simple reading comprehension test. Clearly PRT performance was tied to at least one aspect of linguistic performance as Benton et al. (1983) have reported. Although PRT failure was associated with poor nonverbal cognitive performance level on the WAIS Block Design subtest in the majority of Varney's aphasic cases (13/18, 72.2%), a sizeable minority of them performed normally on this measure. Depending on the type of aphasic deficit and the patient's cognitive strategy, the defective performances on Block Design also could reflect impaired verbal mediation of the task, which would be consistent with the linguistic deficit hypothesis of PRT deficit advanced by Benton et al. (1983). Refined syndrome analyses of aphasic deficit and performance errors and strategies among both clinical and normal groups will be necessary to clarify the construct validity of PRT more clearly.

Reliability is the psychometric term for measurement accuracy. To date the test-retest and internal consistency reliability statistics for PRT have not appeared in the literature. Both are important psychometric characteristics to establish for any new test, as the instrument cannot be valid if it is not reliable. These two types of reliability estimate different aspects of error variance that affect the measurement accuracy of the test as a whole. The internal consistency measure of reliability estimates the degree of error due to item sampling. To the degree that test items coalesce to measure a common construct or behavioral dimension, they meet the criterion of internal consistency. This quality may be demonstrated by use of split-half reliability, in which the odd and even items of the test are separated into two subsets and correlated with each other. A better measure of internal consistency, however, is Cronbach's coefficient alpha statistic, which provides the mean of all possible split-half values for an item pool. The ideal value for coefficient alpha is approximately .80, which reduces error variance to a practical minimum (Nunnally, 1978). In a diagnostically and demographically representative sample of 300 or more cases that are heterogeneously composed, the obtained value of coefficient alpha should generalize to a sample of any size assembled according to similar criteria.

The other psychometric accuracy measure that remains to be calculated for PRT is its test-retest reliability. Demonstration of temporal stability is necessary to show that results on PRT are reproducible from one administration to another. To meet this criterion the PRT should be administered to relatively large samples of neurologically normal and/or symptomatically stable neurologically impaired patients twice, with approximately a 2-week intertest interval. The investigators should take care to tap a widely representative sample within each group, showing considerable diagnostic and demographic variability. A narrow range of demographic or diagnostic variability on characteristics that affect cognitive test performance level (e.g., age, educational level, intelligence level, and linguistic competence) could artifactually limit the range of the reliability statistic as well as give a spurious result. Again a retest reliability value in the range of .80 or higher would be desirable to show that the PRT performance is minimally affected by extraneous, extratest variability that is diagnostically irrelevant. With establishment of this standard, one could attribute more confidently a change in PRT scores to clinical improvement or decline, which is diagnostically important to tracking the patient's clinical course.

Critique

The Pantomime Recognition Test is a rigorously constructed, standardized, objective measure of a complex nonlinguistic skill, and it has great potential relevance to the analysis of aphasic disorder. The test appears to have an association with linguistic deficit or aphasic disorder subtypes in a sizeable minority of aphasic cases. The relationship of the PRT to aphasic disturbance apparently is not related simply to severity of linguistic disturbance as a performance-level phenomenon. Systematic empirical investigation of the relationship of PRT performance to specific linguistic parameters, particularly those that are visually mediated such as reading comprehension, remains as an important but incomplete aspect of the construct validation of the PRT as a syndrome-analytic measure.

The authors should expand the PRT normative database to allow for empirical assessment of the relative effects of age, intelligence, educational level, and sex differences on PRT performance among normal volunteers and hospitalized, non-neurologically impaired medical controls. PRT performance in specific aphasic subgroups with well-defined linguistic characteristics is necessary to work out the specific linguistic correlates of PRT deficit. Some very insightful, initial exploratory work has been accomplished and reported by Benton and his colleagues, but much additional effort will be necessary to systematically investigate the potential and the limitations of the PRT technique. The relationship of PRT performance to cognitive deficit in syndromes of cortical and subcortical dementia remains to be explored almost in its entirety. The correlates of pantomime recognition ability in normal controls and analysis of the functional system underlying pantomime recognition deficit in neurologic patients, particularly those with aphasic syndromes, also must be explicated.

Basic internal consistency and retest reliability studies of the PRT probably should precede further extensive work on the technique's validity, although much work on construct and concurrent validation of the method is needed. Establishing the dimensional relationship of the PRT to other tests of known reliability and validity, particularly Benton and Hamsher's Multilingual Aphasia Examination, Goodglass and Kaplan's Boston Diagnostic Aphasia Examination (see review in this volume), and the WAIS or WAIS-R, certainly would be well advised. Systematic study of the sensory modality of deficit performance (auditory vs. visual) as suggested by Benton et al. (1983) is important in studying the PRT. Work along these lines to date has been largely level-of-performance oriented; subsequent studies should be more refined to investigate the parametric relationships *among* linguistic and cognitive parameters that may clarify the necessary and sufficient skills required by PRT performance and the ways in which they become dysfunctional in various aphasic and dementing syndromes. The reasons why the majority of patients without defined aphasic disorder do *not* have difficulty with PRT is a complementary problem to explain in the syndrome analysis of the test. Its dimensional construct validity as yet remains relatively little understood.

The clinical syndromatic analysis of the nonlinguistic correlates of aphasic disturbance has a long history, but the parametric empirical investigation of these behavior patterns is a relatively recent development. The PRT has operationally defined an important aspect of this class of variables that appears relevant to the study of aphasia and dementia. The role of the right cerebral hemisphere in pantomime recognition seems relatively neglected in initial exploratory studies of the PRT, and the role of focal lesions of each cerebral hemisphere should be investigated with regard to PRT performance. More importantly, the range of well-defined cognitive and linguistic skills considered primarily mediated by functional systems of each cerebral hemisphere and the sensory modalities through which they are processed also must be investigated systematically if we are to solve the riddle of pantomime recognition.

References

Benton, A.L., Hamsher, K.deS., Varney, N.R., & Spreen, O. (1983). *Contributions to neuropsychological assessment: A clinical manual*. New York: Oxford University Press.

Duffy, R., & Liles, B.Z. (1979). Finkelnburg's 1870 lecture on aphasia with commentary. *Journal of Speech and Hearing Disorders, 44*, 156–168.

Ferro, J., Santos, M., Castro-Caldas, A., & Mariano, G. (1980). Gesture recognition in aphasia. *Journal of Clinical Neuropsychology, 3*, 277–292.

Nunnally, J.C. (1978). *Psychometric theory*. New York: McGraw-Hill.

Varney, N.R. (1978). Linguistic correlates of pantomime recognition in aphasic patients. *Journal of Neurology, Neurosurgery, and Psychiatry, 41*, 564–568.

Varney, N.R. (1982). Pantomime recognition defect in aphasia: Implications for the concept of asymbolia. *Brain and Language, 15*, 32–39.

Varney, N.R., & Benton, A.L. (1982). Qualitative aspects of pantomime recognition in aphasia. *Brain and Cognition, 1*, 132–139.

Victor L. Willson, Ph.D.
Professor of Educational Psychology, Texas A&M University, College Station, Texas.

Luisa Guillemard, M.S.
Lecturer, Texas A&M University, College Station, Texas.

PAR ADMISSIONS TESTING PROGRAM

Carol A. Long. Seekonk, Massachusetts: Richard D. Irwin, Inc.

Introduction

The PAR Admissions Testing Program is intended to assess potential enrollees for certificate and diploma, non–degree-granting career and vocational programs in the United States. The Aptitude Test is intended to screen potential students for achievement in five areas: basic information of facts and terms, reading, writing, computation, and problem solving. Both English and Spanish versions are available, but norm and validity data are provided only for the English version. The Personal Inventory is intended to assess personal and social factors that may inhibit or assist potential students in entering or remaining in their chosen programs. A counseling questionnaire is intended for use with students without initial problems who are at risk for dropping out.

The publisher states that the PAR instruments are compatible with U.S. federal guidelines for assessment with Title IV (Act unspecified). The wording of the manual implies that use of the tests is required by the U.S. government:

> All potential enrollees for certificate and diploma, nondegree-granting career and vocational programs should be tested with the *PAR Aptitude Test* (40 basic skills questions) as well as the *Personal Inventory* (factors which affect drops) *not* just ability-to-benefit students. . . .

> In addition, DOE will require all students, no matter the program, who receive Title IV funds to be enrolled with a minimum of 24 on the *PAR Admissions Aptitude Test.* (Long, 1992, p. 7)

The actual interpretation is that if the tests are used, a specific cutoff score must be used.

The publisher requires independent test administrators to be registered with the publisher. It is not clear whether these persons must be independent of the institution using the test.

The PAR Aptitude Test is a derivative of the APL test, developed in the early 1970s by the Adult Performance Level Project at the University of Texas–Austin and funded by the U.S. Office of Education. The American College Testing Program later worked with the APL project to improve and validate the APL. This effort was ultimately abandoned and the items placed in public domain, where-

515

upon they were used by both the preceding and the present publishers. The current publisher states that the earlier versions have been modified, listing 1986–87 as the revision date for the aptitude measure.

The author discusses no history for the Personal Inventory self-esteem measure. The Counseling Questions component appears to have been developed specifically to focus on student skills performance and self-assessment in relation to dropping out of an educational training program. No other counseling issues, such as personal or economic problems, are considered.

The Aptitude Test (English version) has two forms, Form B and Alternate Form. The items on the two forms are quite similar, although not identical, and are slightly rearranged in location on the tests. All are four-option multiple-choice items. Identification of facts and terms is measured with six items, reading with nine, computation with nine, writing with eight, and problem solving with eight. Both forms have the same item-by-subject-matter distribution. Students respond on a separate answer sheet but may write in the booklet; neither may be reused. The Spanish version is available only for the Alternate Form, and the answer sheet is also written in Spanish. Items in both forms are extremely easy. Writing items ask for knowledge of basic grammar usage, ability to select an appropriate budget list, how to read a prescription on a pill bottle, or where to answer on a printed form. Problem Solving involves skills such as deciding where to get information, selecting a phone number from a list appropriate to the problem posed in the stem, or selecting the most appropriate answer to a posed situation or condition; some Problem Solving items are simple information items. A punch-out answer key is provided for test administrators. The Spanish version has a number of irritating typographical and grammatical errors in both the tests and the manual, although the items generally have been adequately translated (not literally but substantively).

The Personal Inventory is a single-sheet 20-item test, with each item answered "yes" or "no." The questions are oriented toward either social relationships, current feelings, or self-concept. The scoring is listed as low, average, or high self-esteem. A score of 90 or above (from 100 possible points) indicates high self-esteem; 65–85 is average and 60 or below is low. Both English and Spanish versions are available. The translation of the English items into Spanish is generally adequate, although at least three of the items appear to have been translated literally, resulting in unclear or changed meanings. These changes might be sufficient to alter a subject's self-concept score.

Counseling Questions is intended for use with students who are considering or have initiated dropping the program they are enrolled in. It asks them only questions related to their academic skills and to either potential or past tutoring efforts. The Spanish version should be attempted only by someone who is fluent in Spanish, so that the exact translation of the items will be unimportant in comparison with the meaning of the questions.

The three instruments are intended for adult or age-mature adolescents who are seeking post–high school training; they are intended particularly for prospective students who have not completed secondary education or a GED, called *ability-to-benefit students*. These students, it is assumed, may not function well with more demanding achievement tests. Scores are recorded by the independent test administrator directly on the answer sheet in the five skill areas along with a total score. Only the total score is used in selection decisions, although the profile is reviewed in the Counseling Questions assessment.

The difficulty level of the Aptitude Test is extremely low. A bright middle school youngster would have no trouble passing the cutoff recommended in the test manual. The reading ability requirement is at about the middle school level. The separate, nonreusable answer sheet is straightforward and clearly printed.

The Personal Inventory has a low reading difficulty and easily enables respondents to answer "yes" or "no" to each question on the nonreusable sheet.

The Counseling Questions measure is completed by the independent test examiner, who reads the items aloud to the student. The questions are clearly stated.

Practical Applications/Uses

The PAR Aptitude Test provides minimal evidence for basic skills of persons seeking training in a trade or vocational field. Although the test yields skill area scores and even references them in the counseling component, the publisher provides no basic data on these scores. Without any supporting evidence, it is quite doubtful that the writing skill score has anything to do with writing adequate sentences or text. Computation is the most content-related of the five areas, while the Problem Solving items are questionable compared to problem solving as it is widely discussed in psychology. Knowing who is least likely to be able to help you with your income taxes is one item purported to test problem solving; more likely this is simple knowledge. Most of the items are at this level. In the absence of factor analytic and concurrent validity support, the subtests have little validity and might better be ignored.

The total score for the Aptitude Test does provide an indicator of general achievement. Whether it is sufficient to discriminate between those who can benefit from instruction and those who cannot depends on the supporting evidence presented by the publisher and is discussed later in this review. The use of the test for selection for technical training appears unwarranted, as the level of performance demanded appears to be far below what one might expect in any modern technical field.

The self-esteem measure (Personal Inventory) has no apparent psychological validity to these reviewers. The statements are worded in ways that may confuse many test takers. The requirement that all answers but 2 of the 20 items match those on the key to receive a high self-esteem label is unsupported by empirical or theoretical bases. Labeling someone as having low self-esteem with a score below 65 is even more troublesome and may do significant harm. Without substantial psychological and psychometric evidence, this instrument should not be used, on the basis of potential harm to test takers according to American Psychological Association ethical standards for the use of psychological tests.

With its focus on dropping out in relation only to education skills, the Counseling Questions instrument ignores the other common personal reasons for dropping. These might be picked up in the last question, which may be the best reason to give the test: It asks if there is anything the training program personnel might do to help the student complete the program. The level of counseling training required to use the device is not specified, although it is suggested that someone in the institution's administration should give it. A good counselor might make the instrument into a useful springboard for assisting a student with difficulties.

High school dropouts, high school graduates, and GED recipients are the groups most likely to encounter this test as they seek training in trade or technical postsecondary schools. The test is not appropriate for blind students but as noted previously has an unevenly translated Spanish version that can be used with Spanish monolinguals.

Administration instructions provided in the manual are clear. The time limit for the test is quite generous—50 minutes for the Aptitude Test and 15 for the Personal Inventory (self-esteem measure). Spanish instructions are provided for the Spanish version.

Scoring the Aptitude Test is straightforward and accomplished using a scoring template that fits over the individual scoring sheets. A single sheet can be scored in less than 20 seconds. The Personal Inventory is scored against a key given in the manual. There is no scoring for the Counseling Questions instrument.

Interpreting the total score on the Aptitude Test is easy; there appears little justification in attempting to interpret the subtest scores, as no norms are available and the content validity is questionable. No interpretation of the Personal Inventory appears to these reviewers to be warranted without evidence for validity. The Counseling Questions open-ended items will yield interpretable results for persons with school counseling training, but the usefulness of interpretation by administrators will depend on their knowledge of students, the counseling process, and their ability to use the device beyond its narrow intent.

Technical Aspects

All technical analyses for the Aptitude Test were conducted on the total score only, and subtest scores are not addressed. The Aptitude Test exhibits moderate internal consistency reliability for the total score (.86). The manual notes that only marginal students were assessed, but in a previous section of the document the sample is represented as students from six technical career schools selected from a volunteer sample of 20+ schools from over 500 schools contacted. Only if all or most students from these schools were tested are the reliability results interpretable. The manual inconsistently and interchangeably uses the term KR-21 or KR-20 in text and tables. Norms were not developed from these data but from a subsequent validation study. Internal consistency reliability in the second sample was also .86. The coefficient from a third sample of cosmetology students was .84.

The Personal Inventory or self-esteem measure has a reported KR-20 reliability of .95. No reliability was reported for Counseling Questions, although that appears unnecessary for its intended use as an aid in a counseling session.

Concurrent validity was examined by relating GPA (grade point averages) to total score on the Aptitude Test for students from the 12 institutions who returned data from among the 250 institutions contacted. The publishers note that many schools do not manage student grade information, making difficult the accumulation of validity data. The sample's 813 subjects were classified as dropped, enrolled, and graduated. The three groups differed by one half standard deviation (dropped to enrolled) and about one third standard deviation (enrolled to graduated), with graduated scores highest. The validity coefficient between Aptitude score and GPA was .24, based on 515 students. No evidence for between school grade and test differences was presented, although this might account for some or most of the validity correlation. A g-study is appropriate here.

A second validity study was performed with 429 students from 14 cosmetology schools in the eastern U.S. A validity coefficient with school grades was reported as .317. The publisher argues that this is range-restricted because all students had already been selected. Again, no between school differences were analyzed.

A third study involved 23 schools with 1,108 students from over 50 trade areas. The resulting validity coefficient was .388.

Means from the three validity studies and original data exhibit small variation around an Aptitude score of 29, with the standard deviation about 5. An aggregated norm table and summary statistics for all samples are reported. The mean and standard deviation are reported for use under federal guidelines for cutoff scores, resulting in a cutoff of 24 for acceptance to programs. On the norm tables, this represents about the 13th percentile. Unfortunately, it is somewhat difficult to understand the norm sample, as it is comprised of students in various stages, with only a small sample of dropped students (129). They represent perhaps the best evidence for validity, as a cutoff score of 24 would have eliminated almost 29% while eliminating only 11% of the enrolled and 9% of the graduated students in that study. The modest validity evidence reported in the manual is evidently an improvement over previous versions of the test.

No validity evidence is presented for the Personal Inventory. Means and standard deviations for the six schools of the first study show large variance in means from school to school. Further, there is also no validity information for the Counseling Questions component.

Critique

Any test used to select or exclude individuals must exhibit properties consistent with the standards set by the American Educational Research Association, the American Psychological Association, and the National Council on Measurement in Education (1985). The Aptitude Test appears to these reviewers to be at best a marginal assessment device. Its content validity is questionable as either an aptitude or basic skills achievement test, and its reliability is below the .90 standard commonly espoused for individual decisions. On the other hand, some supporting concurrent validity evidence is presented, although the validity coefficients are still questionable due to technical reasons. If the publisher wishes to continue using this test in the career and trade education field, the dated and content-unsupported items currently on the test make this unwarranted. A decision-oriented test can no longer be based on a brief screening device developed over 20 years ago. Test development has advanced on all fronts, including the sophistication of item development. The populations to be addressed, such as high school dropouts seeking technical training, can be assessed directly and easily in most population centers. Specific skills (such as writing and problem solving) should either be measured directly or measured so that concurrent validity with direct measures is adequate, and such analyses have been conducted for decades in the basic skills testing area. Further, with a better set of items, specific profile analyses might assist students in a true career guidance function. Although such analyses might be conducted with the current test, the expected low reliability of the subtests would probably prevent meaningful results.

Use of the Personal Inventory measure is not recommended until adequate construct validity is presented. The potential for significant psychological damage from inappropriate interpretation of scores exists.

The Counseling Questions instrument is fairly innocuous, although it could be improved to better detect the reasons for a student's imminent or actual dropping out if it is to serve these subjects.

While the current version of this assessment device is an improvement over earlier versions, at least in relation to previous reviews, the PAR Admissions Testing Program does not appear to currently meet professional standards of batteries used to make educational decisions in other areas of postsecondary education. Its use is questionable to these reviewers without significant improvements and revisions.

References

American Educational Research Association, American Psychological Association, & National Council on Measurement in Education. (1985). *Standards for educational and psychological testing.* Washington, DC: American Psychological Association.

Long, C.A. (1992). *User's manual: PAR Admissions Testing Program.* Homewood, IL: Richard D. Irwin.

Elaine M. Justice, Ph.D.

Associate Professor of Psychology, Old Dominion University, Norfolk, Virginia.

PARENT AS A TEACHER INVENTORY

Robert D. Strom. Bensenville, Illinois: Scholastic Testing Service, Inc.

Introduction

The Parent as a Teacher Inventory (PAAT) is a 50-item assessment of attitudes and expectations for parents of children ages 3 to 9 (Strom, 1984, 1993). Its major purpose is to assess parental characteristics that affect the parent-child interaction and have implications for children's self-concept and learning abilities.

The PAAT asks respondents to indicate on a 4-point scale their agreement or disagreement with statements concerning their expectations of their child, and their emotional and behavioral responses to their child's behavior. The 50 items on the scale are grouped into subsets related to five areas of parent-child interactions: Creativity (attitudes that encourage or discourage creative expression by the child), Frustration (dissatisfaction with child rearing), Control (feelings concerning the necessity of regulating the child's behavior), Play (understanding the role of play in child development), and Teaching-Learning (feelings concerning the ability to foster learning for the child). Subset groups were chosen based on the hypothesis that these aspects of the parent-child relationship might support or inhibit the child's attainment of educational goals.

The PAAT was developed by Robert D. Strom at Arizona State University beginning in 1972. An initial version of the test (Form A) was field tested on a sample of 124 parents participating in a ESEA Title I Parent and Child Education (PACE) project in Tucson, Arizona (Slaughter, 1974). Internal reliability for this sample was .76. The PAAT was revised based on these data. Form B includes 23 revised items and a subset structure that maximizes the correlations between the item and subset total (Strom, 1984).

Another revision of the PAAT materials recently has been completed (Strom, 1993). The inventory itself is very similar to the 1984 version, although seven items were modified. Six of these involved minor word changes, while one item (#35) was rephrased more substantially. No data are provided, however, on the basis for these changes. The demographic questionnaire, parental profile, and inventory manual also have been revised (Strom, 1993).

A major use of the PAAT has been to investigate cultural differences in child-rearing attitudes. The PACE study (Slaughter, 1974) involved Mexican-American,

---

This review was written based on a draft of the 1993 edition of the PAAT test and manual provided to the reviewer by Dr. R.D. Strom. The revised materials are available from Scholastic Testing Service as of October 1993.

Native-American, and African-American participants, and testing in both English and Spanish. Subsequent studies cited in the inventory manual include samples from different racial, ethnic, and socioeconomic groups in the United States, as well as cross-cultural studies conducted in over a dozen other countries (Strom, 1993).

It is important that the inventory be administered in the respondent's native language. Scholastic Testing Service publishes the inventory in English and Spanish, plus the 1993 manual indicates that foreign language translations into Arabic, French, German, Greek, Italian, Serbo-Croatian, Turkish, and some Native-American and Australian aboriginal languages may be obtained from the author (an international data bank of studies using the PAAT is maintained at Arizona State University [Strom, 1984]). More recently, a signed version for use with deaf parents has been developed (Strom, Daniels, Wurster, & Jones, 1985). Further, response sheets have been designed that allow the assessment of parents who cannot read or write (Strom & Hill, 1979).

As noted, the PAAT is composed of 50 statements to which the parent is asked to respond on a 4-point scale: "strong yes," "yes," "no," or "strong no." Respondents are instructed to circle a "strong yes" or "strong no" if there is no doubt about their answer; otherwise, they should select "yes" or "no." There is no time limit for completion.

A PAAT Inventory Identification Form serves to obtain demographic information on the child, respondent, and family circumstances. The revised version of this form (Strom, 1993) has been simplified from the previous version (Strom, 1984). The respondent is asked to indicate the name of the child for whom the PAAT is being completed and the child's age, sex, and any exceptionality (e.g., mentally retardation, giftedness). A question is included asking the respondent's relationship to the child. In addition to mother and father, grandmother and grandfather are options. Respondents also are asked questions concerning their sex, age, marital status, employment, income, education, and ethnic group, along with an indication of how much time they spend playing and talking with the child.

The format of the PAAT allows it to be administered individually or in a group. The written directions on the inventory simply state the the respondent will read some statements about his or her child and should circle one answer for each statement. The involvement of the examiner is limited to making sure that all items have been completed.

The PAAT was developed for parents with children between 3 and 9 years of age. Although no minimum reading level is indicated, the language is simple and probably understandable to individuals with seventh- or eighth-grade reading ability. At least one study assessed parents who were illiterate by using tape recordings of the inventory items and a response sheet that presented large and small smiling and frowning faces (Strom & Hill, 1979).

The PAAT Profile is designed to provide feedback to parents concerning their strengths and weaknesses in the five areas of parent development assessed. The cover sheet identifies and defines each of the five areas (Creativity, Frustration, etc.), and explains that the individual's response to each question has been rated as highly favorable, slightly favorable, slightly unfavorable, or highly unfavorable.

When the PAAT has been used as a pretest-posttest measure to assess the effects of some intervention, both pre- and posttest performances are indicated to illustrate changes in attitudes. The remainder of the profile presents the items grouped by area, with indications of the respondent's answer to each question.

Practical Applications/Uses

The PAAT appears to have three major applications: a) assessing parental attitudes for the purpose of providing feedback, b) measuring change in parental attitudes following parent education programs, and c) examining the relation between parental attitudes and child development.

Practitioners working with parents individually or as part of parental education programs may find the PAAT helpful in identifying participants' expectations and beliefs about parenting. Parental expectations associated with less positive child development outcomes can be identified and guidance provided to improve parent-child relations.

The PAAT may be particularly helpful for practitioners working with families from diverse cultural and ethnic backgrounds. It has been widely used to examine parental attitudes across cultures, for immigrants from different ethnic groups, and for parents of handicapped and gifted children (Rees, Strom, Goldman, Daniels, & Wurster, 1984; Strom & Johnson, 1989; Strom & Slaughter, 1978; Strom et al., 1986). Strom and his colleagues argue that understanding cultural differences in beliefs and expectations about child rearing is critical to helping parents foster child development. Parental intervention programs then can be based on the participants' current, culturally influenced beliefs and attitudes.

For individuals implementing parent education programs, the PAAT can provide an important measure of change. Pretest and posttest PAAT responses can help assess changes in attitudes and behavior toward those associated with more positive child outcomes. Strom and his colleagues have used the PAAT to establish a normative profile of parental beliefs and expectations for a particular group that then was used as a basis for parental intervention (Rees et al., 1984).

The PAAT also provides a self-report measure of parental attitudes that can be related to child outcomes. The PAAT was developed based on a review of the literature to reflect dimensions of parenting that had been found to affect child development. Thus, parental attitudes expressed on the PAAT would be expected to influence parent-child interactions and, in turn, the child's development. An initial study by Strom, Hathaway, and Slaughter (1981) found that maternal attitudes towards creativity, control, and teaching-learning correlated significantly with children's scores on subscales of the McCarthy Scales of Children's Abilities. Overall, the control subset score was the best predictor of children's performance.

As noted previously, the PAAT was developed for parents of three- to nine-year-olds, but it also can be used with other caregivers interacting with children in this age range, such as grandparents. One study in which mothers, fathers, and teachers of preschool children completed the inventory found a similar factor structure for all three groups (Thornburg, Gray, & Ispa, 1989).

An advantage of the PAAT is that it can be administered in virtually any setting, either individually or in groups. Minimal examiner training is necessary, but he or she should be fluent in the language of the parent. Although all instructions are written, the examiner should be able to clarify them if necessary. Completion of the inventory takes approximately 30 minutes.

The PAAT manual provides instructions for both manual and computer scoring. Each item receives a numerical value of from 1 to 4, with higher values indicating a more desirable response. A "strong yes" is the most desirable response for 23 of the items, while a "strong no" is most desirable for the remaining 27. The key provided for manual scoring indicates the scoring of each item. After some practice, scoring individual protocols should not require more than 10 minutes.

Scores for the items in each subset are totaled to provide a subset score ranging from 10 to 50. Subset scores are totaled to obtain a total inventory score ranging from 50 to 200. For research purposes or when larger numbers of protocols are being scored, computer scoring is recommended. Instructions for this are based on use of the Statistical Package for the Social Sciences (SPSS-X). Methods for handling reversed scoring of indicated items are described. Coding of the information on the parent identification questionnaire is included, along with columns designated for additional variables of research interest.

The PAAT can be interpreted on either an individual or group basis. For feedback to parents, the data are transferred to the Parent Profile, which groups items for each subset and indicates the parent's responses as more or less favorable. Feedback sessions then can focus on areas in which change is needed to foster positive child development. When parents participate in parent education programs, answers prior to and following the program can be indicated and feedback provided on changes.

Interpretation of PAAT scores for groups is based on mean item, subscale, and total inventory scores. The manual suggests that item scores above 2.5, scale scores above 25, and total inventory scores above 125 are considered favorable. Scores below these values are considered unfavorable. However, the PAAT materials provide no empirical basis for these cutoffs.

Technical Aspects

Although Strom and his colleagues have examined the reliability of the PAAT in a variety of language, cultural, and socioeconomic samples, the revised manual does not report reliability data in detail. Alpha coefficients for the initial version of the inventory (Form A) are reported at .76 for the pretest and .81 for posttest. More recent studies, presumably using the current version of the inventory, are cited with a summary statement indicating that similar alphas had been obtained. Although test-retest reliability is reported to be .80 to .90, no studies are reviewed in the manual.

The five subsets of items on the PAAT came from a review of the literature that identified parental beliefs and expectations related to child development. They were not derived through factor analysis. This is particularly problematic because subset scores have been used to differentiate among cultural and ethnic groups. An initial factor analytic study by Thornburg, Ispa, Gray, and Ponder (1983) found evidence for six factors in the PAAT that were conceptually different from the five subsets. A more recent study, in which maternal and paternal responses to the inventory were analyzed separately, supported a five-factor structure for both parents and also for teachers who were included in the study (Thornburg et al., 1989). Additional support for the use of the subsets as independent dimensions of parenting is needed.

The construct validity of the PAAT has been examined in two studies that examined the relation of parental PAAT responses to observed parental behaviors (Johnson, 1975; Panetta, 1980). Although both of these studies are unpublished, a detailed description of Johnson's (1975) research appears in the 1984 PAAT manual, and Panetta's (1980) work is described in the current edition (Strom, 1993).

Johnson (1975) observed parental behavior in 30 Mexican-American families. Parental behavior was scored as positive or negative for each item appearing on the PAAT. Thus, the parent's expressed behavior was compared to the observed behavior for each item. Thirty-eight of the 50 PAAT items were observed in the homes; the remaining 12 items, 4 of which came from the Control subset, were not observed in any of the homes. Results indicated that parental PAAT responses and observed behavior on the 38 items was consistent 68% of the time.

Panetta (1980) examined the relation between parental attitudes and behaviors for low-income Mexican-American and Anglo mothers at two points during a parental education program. Assessment of attitudes and observations of behaviors were conducted after 6 weeks and at the end of the 6-month program. Consistency was 75% and 85% for the two assessments.

The above studies suggest that parental responses on the PAAT are related to differences in parental behavior that might affect the parent-child interaction. The validity of this hypothesis has been examined in studies of the relation between PAAT scores and specific aspects of child development. A study by Papadales (1982) found that higher scores on the Creativity, Play, and Teaching-Learning subsets were related to higher prereading skills ($p < .01$) on the Metropolitan Reading Test. Parents with a higher PAAT total score, higher scores on the Play subset, and lower scores on the Control subset had children with higher quantitative skills on the Metropolitan Test. A study by Strom, Hathaway, and Slaughter (1981) also found significant relations between maternal PAAT subset scores and children's performance on several subscales of the McCarthy Scales of Children's Abilities.

Critique

The PAAT provides an objective, self-report measure of parental attitudes that can be useful in a variety of ways. It has the advantage of a wealth of previous research conducted in multiple languages, social groups, and cultures. There is evidence of the measure's reliability and some indication of construct and predictive validity. However, additional research and information is needed in several areas.

For practitioners using the PAAT for parental feedback and education, a major disadvantage is that the inventory manual provides no normative data that would characterize the beliefs and attitudes of individuals from different socioeconomic, ethnic, and racial backgrounds. For example, a person working with Mexican-American parents would not find norms indicating the average subset and total scores for parents of that ethnic background. Although such data are available for specific samples in some published reports, many studies are unpublished dissertations or technical reports. Although a lack of factor analytic studies on the PAAT would make using normative data tentative, it is difficult to fully utilize the inventory to respond to ethnic, cultural, and socioeconomic differences without it. Research to establish norms for carefully selected normative groups is needed.

For researchers, several fundamental questions arise concerning the PAAT. The first pertains to the inventory's factor structure. Despite caveats that the subset scores should not be used as independent dimensions (Strom, 1984), many of the studies using the PAAT compare group means on the subset scores. One recent study (Thornburg et al., 1989) suggests that a five-factor structure may be appropriate; however, factor patterns across cultural groups and social classes need to be examined.

Additional research also is needed on the construct and predictive validity of the measure. Only two studies, both unpublished, have examined the relation between PAAT scores and observed parental behaviors. Such studies are critical to the instrument's usefulness as a basis for developing parental education programs and for researchers seeking a valid measure of parental behavior.

Perhaps the clearest deficiency in the PAAT literature is the lack of a critical review of previous research findings. Although a computer bank is maintained of studies using the PAAT (Strom, 1984), no attempt has been made to summarize the usefulness of the measure across studies. The PAAT has been widely used, particularly by Strom and his colleagues, but many of the studies are unpublished. In published studies, differences in samples, cultures, and research questions make comparison difficult.

The conclusion to be drawn at this point is that, pending additional research, researchers and practitioners should be cautious in interpreting the subsets of the PAAT and in inferring their relation to parental behavior and child outcomes.

References

This list includes text citations and suggested additional reading.

Johnson, A. (1975). An assessment of Mexican-American parent child-rearing feelings and behaviors. *Dissertation Abstracts International, 36*(5), 2614A. (University Microfilms No. 75-25-374)

Panetta, S. (1980). An exploration and analysis of parental behaviors which may be related to a child's problem solving abilities. *Dissertation Abstracts International, 41*(7), 2928A. (University Microfilms No. 80-28-343)

Papadales, R. (1982). *The relationship between parental attitudes and children's academic readiness for first-grade entry.* Unpublished master's thesis, Virginia Polytechnic Institute and State University, Blacksburg.

Rees, R., Strom, R., Goldman, R., Daniels, S., & Wurster, S. (1984). A comparison of child-rearing attitudes of parents of handicapped and non-handicapped children. *Journal of Instructional Psychology, 11*(2), 89–103.

Slaughter, H. (1974). *Title I final summary project report for the Parent and Child Education Program.* Tucson, AZ: Research Department, Tucson Public Schools.

Strom, R.D. (1984). *Parent as a Teacher Inventory manual.* Bensenville, IL: Scholastic Testing Service.

Strom, R.D. (1989). Evaluating parent success: Parent As A Teacher Inventory. In C. Carlson & H. Grotevant (Eds.), *Family assessment: A guide to methods and measures* (pp. 67–70). New York: Guilford.

Strom, R.D. (1990). Parental assessment. In J. Touliatos, B. Perlmutter, & M. Straus (Eds.), *Handbook of family measurement techniques* (pp. 413–414). Newbury Park, CA: Sage.

Strom, R.D. (1993). *Parent as a Teacher Inventory manual.* Bensenville, IL: Scholastic Testing Service.

Strom, R.D., Daniels, S., Wurster, S., Betz, M.A., Graf, P., & Jansen, L. (1986). A comparison of West German and guestworker parent's childrearing attitudes and expectations. In G. Kurian (Ed.), *Parent-child interaction in transition* (pp. 157–170). New York: Greenwood.

Strom, R.D., Daniels, S., Wurster, S., & Jones, E. (1985). Deaf parents of normal hearing children. *Journal of Instructional Psychology, 12*(3), 121–126.

Strom, R.D., Hathaway, C., & Slaughter, H. (1981). The correlation of maternal attitudes and preschool children's performance on the McCarthy Scales of Children's Abilities. *Journal of Instructional Psychology, 8*(4), 139–145.

Strom, R.D., & Hill, J. (1979). Determining a parent curriculum. *Journal of American Indian Education, 19*(1), 23–30.

Strom, R.D., & Johnson, A. (1989). Hispanic and Anglo families of gifted children. *Journal of Instructional Psychology, 16*(4), 164–172.

Strom, R.D., & Slaughter, H. (1978). Measurement of childrearing expectations using the Parent as a Teacher Inventory. *Journal of Experimental Education, 46*(4), 44–52.

Thornburg, K.R., Gray, M.M., & Ispa, J.M. (1989). Parent as a Teacher Inventory: Factor analyses for fathers, mothers, and teachers. *Educational and Psychological Measurement, 49,* 689–695.

Thornburg, K.R., Ispa, J.M., Gray, M.M., & Ponder, H. (1983). Parent as a Teacher Inventory: A statistical factor analysis. *Journal of Experimental Education, 5*(4), 200–202.

Michael D. Franzen, Ph.D.

Associate Professor of Behavioral Medicine and Psychiatry and Director of Neuropsychology, West Virginia University School of Medicine, Morgantown, West Virginia.

PEDIATRIC EXTENDED EXAMINATION AT THREE

J.A. Blackman, M.D. Levine, and M. Markowitz. Cambridge, Massachusetts: Educators Publishing Service, Inc.

Introduction

The Pediatric Extended Examination at Three (PEET) represents an attempt to provide a standardized developmental screening instrument for an age group that falls between the most frequently screened age groups, infants and pre-schoolers. Three-year-old children are developing at a quick rate, and the early detection of developmental problems not present at infancy but with important implications for academic and personal achievement is an extremely important issue. The PEET samples skill areas such as Gross Motor, Language, Visual–Fine Motor, Memory, and Intersensory Integration. The procedure includes a physical examination and an observational scoring system for the child's conversational speech and general behavior. The instrument is intended for examinees between the ages of 3 and 4 years.

The PEET was the first in a series of observational instruments that developed out of the Brookline Early Education Program. The general thrust of the program was to investigate the effects of providing school-based services to the families of children under the age of 5. The PEET was partially developed from the materials in the Pediatric Examination of Educational Readiness, which was expanded to include aspects of general health and behavior.

The authors of the PEET hold academic positions in departments of pediatrics and psychiatry and are generally involved in developmental and early educational research. The initial data regarding the PEET was gathered using physicians who were completing fellowships in pediatrics; however, the PEET is recommended for use by other health care personnel, mainly nurses and psychologists. The manual (Blackman, Levine, & Markowitz, 1986) recommends that a health care professional administer the physical examination aspect of the PEET, but that other individuals can administer the remaining portions in a team effort.

PEET administration involves a scoring protocol, a stimulus booklet, a piece of cloth with a set of buttons, a set of pictures, a set of blocks, and a few common objects not included in the test materials (e.g., unlined paper, a penny, a pencil). The examiner provides instructions to the child, encourages compliance, and records the responses.

The items are designed to sample behavior appropriate to the age group of

528

3½ to 4 years. Due to the variability in children's developmental attainment, the items may be administered to older children as well as to those down to age 3.

The PEET subtests, containing a few items each, tap a set of observable behaviors in ways designed to be challenging and fun to children. The Gross Motor subtest, for instance, requires examinees to perform a long jump, to throw and kick a ball, to walk a line forward and backward, and to stand and jump on one leg. Some of the items on a particular subtest require more that the named skill and therefore are summed on more than one subscale. For example, the "following instructions" item on the Language subtest also contributes to scores on the Memory and Sequencing subscales. (The scoring protocol contains a task analysis chart, which simplifies the subscale summing process.) Additionally, the extent of "initial adaptation and reaction during assessment" is scored using a behavioral observation system. A Global Language Rating Scale allows the examiner to make semistandardized observations of the child's conversational speech. Cutoff scores on the scoring protocol are available for the five subtests as well as the nine subscales derived from the task analysis. The cutoff scores are meant to indicate areas of possible concern for further serial observation rather than areas of specific diagnostic delays. Because development may be independent for the various areas tested, no overall score is produced.

Practical Applications/Uses

Because the PEET requires a physical exam as part of the procedures, the instrument is most appropriate for the clinician working on a team that includes a physician. For example, a psychologist in an outpatient pediatrics clinic or otherwise involved in evaluating preschool children would find the PEET applicable to his or her work. Professionals working in early educational intervention projects also may find this assessment useful.

The PEET is administered individually in a quiet setting free from distraction. The parent can be present during the examination, but he or she should be warned against answering for the child. The examiner needs to elicit the child's best performance and should encourage and reward his or her cooperation and effort. The amount of time required can vary across children, but most children can be tested in a single session of 35 or 40 minutes.

Scoring the PEET involves assigning accuracy scores to the subject's behavioral performance. The manual presents the instructions for scoring. Each of the items is reduced to one of three scores: Level One, Two, or Three, where One represents the best performance. Because scoring requires qualitative judgments, the manual recommends that the user receive training from someone experienced in the test's use.

Interpretation of the PEET requires an examiner who is experienced in child development. The norms used in determining the cutoff scores were derived from a sample of 201 middle-class children. Because development, especially in language skills, can vary greatly from one community to another, the manual recommends that users develop local norms. In general PEET results should be used only to identify possible areas for further evaluation or for serial observations.

Technical Aspects

The interscorer reliability of the PEET was examined in a sample of 62 children for whom a second observer also scored performances. The data were collected in the children's preschool. Agreement as to whether possible concerns existed in the various developmental areas averaged 96%. Correlation coefficients between scorers on individual items ranged from .60 to .80. In addition, Cronbach's coefficient alpha was calculated for the three channels of Auditory-Verbal Communication (.73), Visually-Directed Manipulation (.69), and Spatial-Somatic Integration (.73). Examination of validity involved comparing scores from the PEET to appropriate scores from the McCarthy Scales of Children's Abilities in the overall sample of 201 children. Here the resulting correlation coefficients were less robust, with values ranging from .26 to .63 (Blackman, Levine, Markowitz, & Aufseer, 1983).

Critique

The PEET fills an important gap in the screening field, namely the evaluation of development in 3- to 4-year-old children. Studies to date using the PEET are sparse but promising. In order to more rigorously evaluate this instrument, the results of the procedure should be compared to subjects' eventual development. Additionally, children could be evaluated as to whether the identification of problems using the PEET resulted in effective interventions. For now, the PEET may be useful in pediatric outpatient settings as a clinical screen or a research instrument.

References

Blackman, J.A., Levine, M.D., & Markowitz, M. (1986). *Examiner's manual: Pediatric Extended Examination at Three.* Cambridge, MA: Educators Publishing Service.

Blackman, J.A., Levine, M.D., Markowitz, M.T., & Aufseer, C.L. (1983). The Pediatric Extended Examination at Three: A system for diagnostic clarification of problematic three-year-olds. *Developmental and Behavioral Pediatrics, 4,* 143–150.

Patricia McCarthy, Ph.D.
Associate Professor of Counseling and Student Personnel Psychology, University of Minnesota, Minneapolis, Minnesota.

PERSONAL PROBLEMS CHECKLIST FOR ADOLESCENTS

John A. Schinka. Odessa, Florida: Psychological Assessment Resources, Inc.

Introduction

The Personal Problems Checklist for Adolescents (PPC) is a 240-item, paper-and-pencil measure designed to identify current problems in everyday life. These problems are categorized within 13 broad topical areas: Social and Friends, Appearance, Attitudes and Opinions, Parents, Family and Home, School, Money, Religion, Emotions, Dating and Sex, Health and Habits, Job, and Crises. The PPC was developed for use in counseling and psychotherapy settings. According to its author, the purposes of the checklist are

> to provide the client with a means of surveying common problems that might apply to his/her situation; to help establish rapport by providing an efficient and comprehensive method of communicating problems in ordinary conversational terms; to prepare clients for more formal testing procedures by initiating them to paper-and-pencil responses; and, to provide written documentation of presenting problems consistent with community standards of care. (J.A. Schinka, personal communication, July 21, 1992)

The developer of the PPC, Dr. John A. Schinka, is a staff psychologist at the Haley Veterans Administration Medical Center in Tampa, Florida. Dr. Schinka began development of the first of nine problem checklists 16 years ago while he was a psychotherapist in private practice. He created the checklist to facilitate data gathering during initial interviews with adult clients; it was also intended to be prophylactic (i.e., client written responses to a comprehensive list of problems could help prevent certain types of legal liability on the part of the therapist). Dr. Schinka's Personal Problem Checklist for Adults became popular locally as his supervisees and colleagues began to use it in their clinical work. This popularity grew as the author began to receive requests from other professionals for copies of the instrument. Eventually he was contacted by Psychological Assessment Resources, Inc., with whom he has since published nine checklists. These consist of separate child, adolescent, and adult forms of the Personal Problems Checklist, a Personal History Checklist, and a Mental Status Checklist.

Schinka developed the Personal Problems Checklist for Adolescents by first generating 800 items that represent a comprehensive array of problems commonly experienced by adolescents. Next he used a rational approach to sort these items into topical areas, eliminating any duplicate items. He also eliminated items

531

with low base rates (i.e., those representing problems likely to be experienced by relatively few respondents). The author then rewrote items to meet his stated criteria of brevity, common language wording, and no offensiveness to respondents. He gave this draft of the PPC to a panel of seven experts, doctoral-level clinicians, who evaluated it with respect to the appropriateness of the topical areas and individual items for an adolescent population. Based on their comments, Schinka further revised the PPC, modifying some items, adding some, and deleting others. He submitted this second draft of the checklist to the evaluation of another panel of five experts. Some of these experts also administered the checklist to their adolescent clients. Based on the experts' responses, Dr. Schinka arrived at the final, 240-item adolescent version. Currently the PPC is published only in English; however, it could be translated into other languages and read to visually impaired and illiterate respondents.

The Personal Problems Checklist for Adolescents is a self-report measure contained within a four-page booklet. The first page requests demographic information—respondent name, age, and gender, and the current date. This is followed by brief, clear directions that ask respondents to check all of the problems they are currently experiencing and to circle those that are the worst or are currently causing the most difficulty. A visual example of how to complete an item is included. The directions include a reminder that there are no right or wrong answers and request that respondents answer as honestly as possible. Respondents are informed that they can write down any problems not listed within the checklist. Confidentiality is specified by a statement that their answers will be discussed only with the doctor or counselor.

The next three pages of the booklet contain the 240 items, grouped within the 13 topic areas: Social and Friends (20 items), Appearance (14 items), Attitudes and Opinions (12 items), Parents (22 items), Family and Home (24 items), School (22 items), Money (12 items), Religion (14 items), Emotions (24 items), Dating and Sex (18 items), Health and Habits (20 items), Job (20 items), and Crises (18 items).

The PPC is intended for adolescents ages 13 to 17. It requires approximately 10 to 20 minutes to complete and can be administered to individuals who are literate and of low average intelligence or higher. Items are concisely and simply worded, ranging from 2 to 10 words per item, and are behaviorally stated rather than relying on labels or vague terms. Because no particular knowledge of test construction or psychometric skills is necessary to administer the PPC, it can be administered easily by a variety of personnel (e.g., receptionists, secretaries, paraprofessionals, etc.). However, interpretation and discussion of answers with respondents should be done by professional counselors/psychotherapists.

The PPC is not scored per se, as it was designed primarily to gather information. The 13 problem areas are not domain scales and should not be viewed as subscales; they merely represent topical areas of basic adolescent functioning. Furthermore, there is a fair amount of overlap between items in the various areas. For example, relationship issues comprise part of several of the categories. The 240 individual items should be considered nominal or categorical data; therefore, they typically would not be scored, other than perhaps to tally the total number of items endorsed.

Practical Applications/Uses

The PPC has utility for a variety of individuals and settings. It would be appropriate for normal or neurotic adolescents with low average intelligence or higher. Item wording is relevant for both male and female respondents. The PPC would not be appropriate for children or adults; as mentioned earlier, Schinka has developed separate checklists for these populations to represent their typical experience. Further, the PPC would not be appropriate for psychotics or individuals with low intelligence. These subjects would have difficulty reading and/or understanding the items.

The potential usefulness of the PPC is most apparent for counselors and psychotherapists engaged in either inpatient or outpatient individual, couple, family, or group therapy. Thus, clinical, counseling, and school psychologists, school guidance counselors, social workers, marriage and family therapists, and group specialists might use it in their professional practice. The PPC can quickly generate a comprehensive picture of the types of problems being experienced by an adolescent, as well as indicate those causing the individual most concern. This type of information can assist therapists in initial problem assessment, goal setting, and treatment planning. It would also help therapists determine in what areas an adolescent client might need referral to other agencies or helping professionals. The PPC might be administered at both the beginning and completion of therapy to determine which areas are no longer problematic for the client. It might also be administered periodically throughout therapy to indicate any significant changes; this may be especially useful with less verbal clients.

As mentioned earlier, the PPC can assist a therapist in determining whether to administer more formal diagnostic tests, and it provides clients practice in test taking. It may help focus the client on problem areas in need of discussion, it may indicate problem areas an adolescent is uncomfortable verbally disclosing, and it may help generate conversation in therapy. Finally, the PPC contains "duty to warn" problem areas such as potential harm to oneself or others (e.g., suicide), allowing the therapist to pursue any endorsed items further with the client and to inform the appropriate individuals and agencies as necessary. The PPC also provides a certain element of "protection" for the therapist with regard to duty-to-warn issues if the client does not endorse items of this type.

In addition to its utility in therapeutic settings, the PPC also might be useful in educational settings. For example, junior and senior high school teachers could administer it to generate a broad psychosocial profile of their students. The teachers could consult with school counselors or school psychologists in interpreting their students' responses. The PPC can be administered either individually or in group settings, and it is suitable for classrooms.

Although not originally developed as a research instrument, the PPC might serve in empirical studies. In fact, some investigators have sought permission from the author to use the PPC in their research (J.A. Schinka, personal communication, July 21, 1992). For example, it could be used to gather normative data about the prevalence of certain problems among different subgroups of adolescents. Responses to the PPC could be correlated with other psychosocial indices (e.g., measures of adolescent depression, self-esteem, etc.). Factor analytic techniques could be used to determine possible subscales on the PPC, thus making data reporting more manageable and useful.

The manner in which the PPC is administered is fairly flexible. The sequence of the items can be altered, and items themselves may be deleted (e.g., those pertaining to school would not be relevant for dropouts). Because the test contains so many items, it might be administered in sections over two or more sessions.

The PPC resembles other types of checklists (e.g., the Inventory of Common Problems, Hoffman & Weiss, 1986; the Mooney Problem Checklist, Mooney & Gordon, 1950) that are not scored and provide no summary data from which to draw inferences. Therefore, there are no directions for scoring the PPC. Responses should be examined and interpreted "qualitatively," based on internal clinical judgment. Types of problems and "most important" items should be noted. One major purpose of this qualitative assessment would be to determine which problem areas need additional information from the respondents. This type of interpretation can be done by an experienced professional in approximately 15 minutes. Experienced professionals here include master's- and doctoral-level individuals with some knowledge and training in psychological theory (e.g., personality theory, psychopathology, developmental theory, systems theory, etc.).

The PPC does not have a manual. However, it is sent from the publisher with a cover sheet (Psychological Assessment Resources, Inc., 1992) that describes the population for whom it is appropriate, its intended uses, the length of time to complete the checklist, an overview of its content, and brief suggestions for how to interpret responses.

Technical Aspects

Because the PPC was not designed to be a scale or test instrument, assessments of its psychometric properties have not been done. An examination of the checklist suggests that it has face validity. The rational process that Schinka used to develop items and topical areas and his submission of two drafts of the checklist to panels of expert judges provide support for content validity. There is no information about other types of validity and no data on test-retest reliability or internal consistency. According to the author (J.A. Schinka, personal communication, July 21, 1992), some of the items probably are not reliable; however, his intent was not to develop a psychometrically sound scale, but rather to develop stimulus items to generate initial information about adolescent client problems.

Critique

The Personal Problems Checklist for Adolescents is a comprehensive paper-and-pencil survey of 240 problems currently concerning an individual. Developed through rational methods and expert judges' evaluations, it is intended primarily for use in therapy settings during intake (initial interview) procedures. The individual problems can be categorized within 13 topic areas. Respondents endorse all problems that currently concern them and indicate those of greatest concern.

The PPC can be administered easily and completed fairly quickly. It can be quickly and easily interpreted by a trained professional. It has potential applicability in therapeutic settings for diagnosis (problem-identification), rapport building, and for "providing written documentation of presenting problems consistent with community standards of care" (Psychological Assessment Resources, Inc., 1992). It also may be useful in educational settings and in empirical investigations. It seems most appropriate in applied settings where a relationship between the respondent and interpreter can be established or where one already exists.

The PPC appears to cover the major problems commonly experienced by adolescents. Items are worded clearly and concisely, in nonsexist language, and include problems in behavior, cognitions, and affect. The PPC seems to have adequate face and content validity. Other types of validity and reliability have not been established, but these psychometric properties seem more critical for measures intended to be formal instruments or scales. Because PPC was intended primarily to be an initial screening tool in therapy, reliability and types of validity are less relevant.

There are a few potential limitations to the PPC. First, although instructed to be honest, respondents may not answer truthfully (e.g., they may fail to endorse items about substance use/abuse). Trained professionals are expected to be aware of this possibility and to follow up in certain areas even when not endorsed by the respondent. Second, some of the problems may be more relevant to older adolescents (e.g., items concerning jobs/work). Therefore, some sections of the PPC might not be administered to all respondents, or respondents should be informed that some items may not pertain to them. Third, the number of items and the reading level of the PPC would probably prove to be very challenging for socioeconomically disadvantaged adolescents. They may need to have the checklist read to them and/or complete it in more than one session. Fourth, the PPC seems to be based on certain value positions that might not be endorsed by all cultural groups. For example, most items in the dating and sex area seem oriented towards heterosexuality; items in the religion area seem restricted to organized religion and church and do not incorporate some of the current broader perspectives on spirituality. Therefore, potential users of the PPC should screen the instrument to determine whether all of the items are appropriate for their population.

The final limitation of the PPC involves the statement in the directions concerning confidentiality. In this reviewer's opinion, the statement is somewhat misleading. Respondents are told that their responses will be discussed only with their doctor or counselor. In actuality, an adolescent's parents/guardians have a legal right to this information. Furthermore, if adolescents endorse items suggesting harm to themselves or to others, then the therapist may be legally and ethically mandated to reveal this information to other people. Perhaps limits to confidentiality need to be discussed with the respondent prior to administering the PPC.

In summary, the PPC appears to be a useful tool for surveying the concerns of adolescents. It is easily administered, it can be adapted to fit the unique needs of the populations with whom it is used, and it can enhance several aspects of the therapeutic relationship.

References

Hoffman, J.A., & Weiss, B. (1986). A new system for conceptualizing problems of college students: Types of crises and the Inventory of Common Problems. *Journal of American College Health, 34,* 259–266.

Mooney, R.L., & Gordon, L.V. (1950). *The Mooney Problem Checklist manual.* San Antonio, TX: Psychological Corporation.

Psychological Assessment Resources, Inc. (1992). *Personal Problems Checklist for Adolescents cover sheet.* Odessa, FL: Author.

James A. Moses, Jr., Ph.D.

Clinical Associate Professor of Psychiatry and Behavioral Sciences,
Stanford University School of Medicine, and Coordinator,
Psychological Assessment Unit, Department of Veterans Affairs
Medical Center, Palo Alto, California.

PHONEME DISCRIMINATION TEST

Arthur L. Benton, Kerry deS. Hamsher, Nils R. Varney, and
Otfried Spreen. New York, New York: Oxford University
Press.

Introduction

The Phoneme Discrimination Test (PDT) offers a series of 30 sequential pairs of nonmeaningful identical or similar speech-sound phonemic blends, presented on an audiocassette by a male reader. The lower register and typically greater resonance of a male voice should make the PDT items easier to discriminate for patients with high-frequency hearing loss, particularly those who are elderly. The subject must distinguish whether the two phonemic blends presented for each item are the same or different. Ten PDT items contain a single syllable; the other 20 are composed of two syllables.

PDT item presentation has been structured carefully both to control for guessing and to highlight details of the basic linguistic auditory comprehension process. Half of the PDT items differ in one phonemic element; the other half of the item pairs are identical. Phonemic pair differences on PDT are those "primarily involving vowels and liquid consonants" (Benton, Hamsher, Varney, & Spreen, 1983, p. 99). *Liquid* is the term used by phoneticians for certain consonants that have a tonal or flowing quality, such as m, n, l, or r. To control for perseverative response bias to series of items as "same" or "different," the test authors have systematically arranged the order of the same and different phonemic pairs in the PDT. Within each group of 10 sequential items on the test (1–10, 11–20, 21–30), five items present the same phonemic pairs and five items present different phonemic pairs.

Benton et al. (1983) emphasize that the PDT presents only a sampling of the range of possible phonemic discriminations. They recommend against qualitative item error analysis to identify specific phonemic discrimination deficit subtypes, as the range of phonemic discriminations tested is not sufficient for this type of auditory comprehension differential diagnosis. The PDT is effective as a phonemic level-of-performance measure, but it was not designed to serve as a measure of pattern of performance.

Phonemic discrimination presents the most elementary unit of linguistic auditory comprehension, as syllables are the most elementary units of meaningful discourse. Partial failure to understand language at the phonemic or syllabic level

537

could cause misunderstanding of related words, in a manner similar to the auditory comprehension problems of a patient with a hearing loss who often confuses words that have a similar sound element. More pervasive impairment of phonemic comprehension would preclude understanding speech at all. When one hears an unfamiliar foreign language, it is said that one does not even hear the speech sounds spoken; the utterance appears much like a melodic auditory blur. By contrast, hearing a new word in a familiar language may lead one to ask to have the word repeated, or to try to "sound it out" (phonemically or syllabically analyze it) to try to relate its elements to familiar words. The PDT is designed as a screening device to evaluate this ability to comprehend and discriminate similar phonemic sounds.

The principal author of the PDT, Arthur L. Benton, Ph.D., received his A.B. (1931) and A.M. (1933) degrees from Oberlin College, followed by his Ph.D. from Columbia University (1935). He began his career as an assistant in psychology at Oberlin College (1931–33), Columbia University and New York State Psychiatric Institute (1934–36), and Cornell University Medical College (1936–39), where he subsequently served as a staff psychologist. After appointments as an attending psychologist at New York Hospital–Westchester Division and as a psychologist in the Student Personnel Office of the City College of New York from 1939 to 1941, he went on to active duty in the U.S. Navy during and after the Second World War (1941–46). Subsequently he was appointed as Associate Professor of Psychology at the University of Louisville Medical School and as chief psychologist at the Louisville Mental Hygiene Clinic and the Louisville General Hospital (1946–48). From 1948 to 1958 Benton served as Professor of Psychology and Director of the Graduate Training Program in Clinical Psychology at the University of Iowa, and then, for the next two decades (1958–78), as Professor of Psychology and Neurology. He has continued to coauthor theoretical and research papers and books since 1978, when he became Professor Emeritus at the University of Iowa.

Benton's fundamental contributions to the field of clinical neuropsychology have been acknowledged extensively and internationally. He has received honorary Doctor of Science (Cornell College, 1978) and Doctor of Psychology (University of Rome, 1990) degrees, along with numerous other honors and awards, including the Distinguished Service Award of the Iowa Psychological Association (1977), the Distinguished Professional Contribution Award from the American Psychological Association (1978), the Outstanding Scientific Contribution Award of the International Neuropsychological Society (1981), The Samuel Torrey Orton Award from the Orton Dyslexia Society (1982), the Distinguished Service and Outstanding Contributions Award from the American Board of Professional Psychology (1985), and the Distinguished Clinical Neuropsychologist Award from the National Academy of Neuropsychology (1989).

Benton is a past president of both the American Orthopsychiatric Association (1965–66) and the International Neuropsychological Society (1970–71). He served as secretary-general of the Research Group on Aphasia for the World Federation of Neurology from 1971 to 1978. He has been a lecturer or visiting scholar at the University of Milan (1964), Hôpital Sainte-Anne, Paris (1968), Hadassah-Hebrew University Medical School, Jerusalem (1969), Free University of Amsterdam (1971), University of Helsinki (1974), University of Melbourne (1977), University of Minnesota Medical School (Baker Lecturer, 1979), University of Victoria, British Columbia (Lansdowne Scholar, 1980), and the University of Michigan (1986), plus Directeur d'Études Associé, École des Hautes Études, Paris (1979) and a visiting scientist at the Tokyo Metropolitan Institute of Gerontology (1974).

Benton has authored, coauthored, or edited 12 books and monographs, approximately 150 professional journal articles, and 22 historical reviews in the area of clinical neuropsychology and behavioral neurology. He is recognized as a pioneer and a leading authority in the area of clinical neuropsychology.

The standardized, commercially published version of the PDT appeared with the clinical manual for this and other tests in the Benton-Iowa Neuropsychological Test Battery (Benton et al., 1983). Coauthors of this clinical manual with Dr. Benton are Kerry deS. Hamsher, Ph.D. (Associate Professor of Neurology, University of Wisconsin Medical School); Nils R. Varney, Ph.D. (staff neuropsychologist, Department of Veterans Affairs Medical Center, Iowa City, Iowa); and Otfried Spreen, Ph.D. (Professor Emeritus, Department of Psychology, University of Victoria, Victoria, British Columbia, Canada).

Practical Applications/Uses

The PDT should be administered in a quiet room, free from ambient sound. The items are presented on an audiocassette tape that is commercially available from Oxford University Press with the other test materials. The tape player used should be of good commercial quality with less than 5% distortion and minimal background noise. The volume should be adjusted so that the patient can attend and respond optimally to the auditory stimuli presented.

The examiner plays audiotaped items sequentially for the patient. The manual stipulates no standardized instructions to the patient; the examiner simply asks the patient to listen to the audiotaped sounds and indicate whether they were exactly the same or different in any way. The items are presented on the tape at a moderate rate, approximately one phonemic sound per second within each pair, with several seconds of silence between items to allow for patient response. The items on the tape are not numbered.

Same and different phonemic blends are indicated with diacritical marks as well as parenthetical scoring codes (S = same, D = different) on the PDT answer sheet, a facsimile of which appears in the test manual (Benton et al., 1983, p. 99). The manual does not indicate whether the tape may be stopped between items to allow the patient extra time to respond. In the case of patients with significant auditory comprehension difficulty or increased response latency, this procedure seems advisable both to ensure that the patient does not become confused and to encourage maximal task cooperation and motivation.

If one has reason to question whether the patient understands the nature of the PDT auditory discrimination task and the manner of response, Benton and his colleagues recommend using a variety of screening methods to test the reliability and accuracy of the patient's response. They make use of visual stimuli with auditory commands for this screening task, a valuable procedure as a screening method for assessing the validity and reliability of alternative methods of response. Before the test is begun, the examiner presents the patient of questionable response ability with a series of pairs of objects and asks "Are these the same or different?" Benton et al. state that the series they generally use goes as follows: pen and paper, paper and paper, paper and book, pen and pen, and book and book (1983, p. 100). The authors recommend that the examiner pay close attention to the manner in which the patient answers these response-modality, testing-the-limits questions. If he or she can produce a reliable response verbally, then the preferred response method is to say "same" or "different" for each pair of items presented. If the accuracy of the spoken verbal response is questionable but the patient can read, then he or she can indicate the choice by pointing to one of two large-print cards with the words *same* or *different* on them. If the patient cannot speak or read reliably, as is often the case in aphasic syndromes, then he or she may nod vertically for "yes" and horizontally for "no" to indicate same and different sounds, respectively. Benton et al. (1983, p. 100) note that confusion or perseverative response on either "same" or "different" response choices to all items in the series may occur in aphasic patients. The PDT is invalidated in such cases, the patient cannot respond meaningfully in either modality.

Scoring the PDT is a clerical task, awarding 1 point for each correct response. The user calculates separate scores for number and type of correct responses and the number and type of errors. The number of "same" and "different" responses are calculated separately within both correct and error response categories. This cross-categorical scoring allows for important qualitative analysis of response patterns and response bias. Because the PDT is a two-choice task, a random response pattern would produce 15 correct responses by chance alone. The "effective range" (beyond chance) of the test therefore is 15–30 points. Some response patterns suggest response bias and receive special discussion in the test manual. Benton et al. (1983, p. 100) note that

> if most of the errors occur on the *same* items, it is possible that the performance is invalid, and that the patient was attending to nonrelevant features of the stimuli. [The examiner also should] note whether more than 20 errors are made. These performances are significantly poorer than would be expected on a chance basis and probably reflect confusion about the required same-different responses.

The PDT was normed preliminarily on a sample of 30 medical patients who were hospitalized at the time of testing. They presented no current or past evidence of brain disease or psychiatric disorder and their hearing ability fell within normal limits. No patient was over age 65, but the sample is not described otherwise, either diagnostically or demographically, in the test manual. Ninety percent of the normative sample earned PDT scores of 25–30; the remaining 10% scored in the range of 22–24 points. Based on these preliminary findings, the test authors tentatively set the PDT total score impairment cutoff at 22 points. PDT total scores of 21 points or less are rated as defective.

Technical Aspects

The test authors carried out and reported a multigroup, criterion-related, exploratory validational study of the PDT as part of the test development process. They compared the performance of the preliminary sample of control patients using the standard audiotaped version of the PDT with samples of nonaphasic patients with unilateral lesions of the right cerebral hemisphere ($n = 16$), aphasic patients with unilateral lesions of the left cerebral hemisphere ($n = 100$), and another group of control patients ($n = 89$) who were administered the PDT items aurally by a confronting examiner rather than by the standard audiotape method. As the diagnostic and demographic characteristics of these samples do not appear in the test manual, the generalizability of the results (particularly for the small right-hemispheric lesion group) is unclear.

Using the "21 points and below" PDT total score impairment criterion showed that 94% (15/16) of the nonaphasic patients with unilateral right-hemispheric lesions were correctly classified by PDT total scores within normal limits. Seventy-six percent of the aphasic patients with unilateral left-hemispheric lesions showed defective performances (total score range = 13–21 points) on the PDT. The PDT scores of 17% (17/100) of these aphasic patients were noted by the test authors as in the total score range of 13–18 points, which approximates the chance level of performance and indicates severe phonemic auditory comprehension deficit. None of the normal controls who completed PDT in the "live-voice" condition showed defective PDT total scores.

As a refinement of the foregoing study, the test authors validated the PDT total score performance level against the normal versus impaired performance-level outcome on the Aural Comprehension of Words and Phrases subtest of the Multilingual Aphasia Examination, second edition (MAE; Benton & Hamsher, 1989). Two performance-level subgroups were composed from the sample of unilaterally lesioned left-hemispheric aphasic cases, based on MAE aural comprehension scores above or below the fifth percentile total score level for the normative reference sample. (This fifth-percentile cutoff value is a standard clinical impairment limit for tests in the Benton-Iowa Neuropsychological Battery.) Forty-two percent (42/100) of the aphasic patients showed intact auditory comprehension; this skill was defective in the remainder of that subgroup. In the aphasic subgroup with intact auditory comprehension on the MAE aural comprehension subtest, 95% of them (40/42) also showed normal-range PDT performance. Among the subjects with defective MAE aural comprehension subtest performance, however, 38% showed normal PDT performance (for cross-tabulated raw score distributions, see Benton et al., 1983, p. 102, Table 10-3).

Because phonemic discrimination presents the most elementary level of auditory comprehension, it seems intuitively logical that disturbance of phonemic hearing also would affect more complex types of linguistic understanding. However, the empirical results reviewed below do not always fully support this proposition. The reason for this paradox may lie in the nature of the multiple-component functional systems that adults may use for linguistic auditory comprehension. If a child (or an older person learning a new language for the first time) were deficient in phonemic comprehension ability, then all of the more complex, syntactically organized sorts of linguistic processing that depend initially on phonemic comprehension for mastery also would be compromised. One originally learns more complex elements of a language such as sentence structure and syntactical relationships only after mastering the lexical, phonemic, syllabic, and single-word linguistic basics. In the case of a linguistically competent adult, however, the great majority of syntactical language processing no longer requires analysis at the phonemic or other elementary level as part of the routine auditory comprehension process. Such piecemeal structural analysis may be necessary, however, if the word or phrase to be understood is unusual or unfamiliar to the individual interpreter. In essence this means that the same behavior, such as auditory comprehension of a word, phrase, or paragraph, may be accomplished by very different cognitive processes (piecemeal and labored for the novice, holistic and overlearned for the expert), which are dependent on differentiable classes of cognitive processes or "functional systems" (Luria, 1973, 1980). Components of these systems may be selectively spared or impaired in patients who were premorbidly linguistically competent but who subsequently have suffered brain disease or trauma that has impaired their auditory comprehension ability.

The nature of the aphasic syndrome can be influenced by the patient's premorbid linguistic competence, the locus and chronicity of the lesion, and the compensatory postmorbid functional system that the patient uses to compensate for the aphasic deficit. A variety of clinical syndromes could emerge across comparable individuals in which phonemic comprehension may or may not be associated with other, more complex auditory comprehension deficits, even if their lesion loci and aphasic subtypes are similar. Key parameters that can account for such differences in the individual case remain to be fully clarified. The reader should bear these syndrome analytic issues in mind while considering the following summaries of research findings about phonemic analysis and its role in auditory comprehension. Theoretical and empirical controversies that have divided linguistic experts over the role of phonemic analysis in auditory comprehension appear to have overlooked systematic application of this functional system approach to syndrome analysis of the problem.

The following overview derives from a more complete discussion of materials, samples, and methods in the PDT test manual (Benton et al., 1983, pp. 102–104). The reader interested in greater detail about these issues should consult the PDT test manual or the original journal sources. The aim here is to summarize psychometric issues rather than to review the methodology of the literature in detail.

Benton et al.'s (1983) concurrent validational study, in which they compared the PDT with the MAE aural comprehension subtest, suggests an inconsistent level-of-performance association between phonemic and semantic auditory comprehension on these two measures. In the aphasic subgroup with defective semantic auditory comprehension, 62% of the patients still showed normal-range phonemic comprehension on the PDT. In the subjects who failed the PDT as well as the MAE Aural Comprehension of Words and Phrases subtest, there was a wide range of performance levels, from chance through mild impairment. Benton et al. (1983, p. 102) concluded that their results showed "a significant association between phonological and semantic levels of auditory information processing." They did not report an empirical measure of independence (chi-square) or nonparametric correlational association (such as Spearman's rho) to test the strength of the relationship between these two categorical variables. They cited previous work by Hécaën (1969) and Luria (1970), which had shown that "the impairment in oral verbal comprehension of some aphasic patients may be based primarily on a failure in phoneme discrimination" (Benton et al., 1983, p. 102). The identification of a subgroup of aphasic patients for whom this is the case certainly jibes with their findings, but this is only part of the clinical syndrome pattern suggested by these data.

The variability patterns are much more impressive than the concordant central tendency trends in the PDT versus MAE validational study of Benton and his colleagues. The modal PDT score is nearly errorless in approximately a third (34%, or 20/58) of the aphasic patient subsample showing syntactical auditory comprehension deficit on the MAE. Agreement between the deficit performance levels of the MAE and PDT auditory comprehension measures emerges in only 38% of cases. An alternative explanation from the viewpoint of Lurian functional system theory might suggest that these data show a spectrum of patterns consistent with sparing and impairment among a variety of auditory comprehension functional system components. This theoretical model aligns with the observed wide and continuous distribution of PDT error scores from errorless through chance levels of PDT performance. Based on these data, it appears that there is no necessary relationship of auditory comprehension ability at the phonemic and semantic levels and that a variety of syndromatic patterns may emerge clinically, as these data suggest.

Tallal and Newcombe (1978) reported a strong association between defective auditory-verbal comprehension on the Token Test (De Renzi & Vignolo, 1962) and phonemic discrimination difficulty in a small group of mildly-to-moderately impaired aphasic patients (6/7 cases, 86% incidence). Varney and Benton (1979) compared performance on the PDT and the aural comprehension subtest of the MAE in a sample of 39 aphasics. A variety of syndrome patterns emerged in a manner similar to the pattern of results for the validational study of the PDT that the test manual reports. Seventy-four percent (29/39) of this aphasic sample scored within normal limits on the PDT. They were nearly evenly divided by their ability to aurally comprehend words and phrases on the MAE subtest (13/29, or 45%, normal MAE aural comprehension; 16/29, or 55%, defective MAE aural comprehension). These researchers reported a nonparametric correlational relationship of .61 between the phonemic and semantic auditory comprehension measures. Although a moderately strong correlation, it explains only 37% of the shared variance in the PDT and MAE measures. Work by Blumstein, Baker, and Goodglass (1977) with different correlational statistical methods and another aphasia battery produced nearly identical quantitative results using dimensionally comparable linguistic measures. Clearly there are many linguistic functional system elements that may be selectively dysfunctional. They appear to account for the unexplained majority of the variance in these auditory comprehension measures. Variable patterns of linkage between phonemic and semantic auditory comprehension deficit measures also were reported by Miceli, Gainotti, Caltagirone, and Masullo (1980).

Benton et al. (1983, pp. 102–103) concluded from their data (reinterpreted above) that "intact phonemic discrimination is a necessary but not sufficient basis for intact oral verbal comprehension in aphasic patients." As noted above, this conclusion is valid only for a subgroup of aphasics in which the phonemic and semantic deficits are correlated; it is not an invariant pattern or a general diagnostic principle. In a comment on the work of Blumstein et al. (1977), Benton et al. (1983, p. 103) noted that the Wernicke aphasics in the sample, who showed more severe impairment in oral verbal comprehension than did the nonfluent aphasics, were superior to the nonfluent aphasics in the phonological tasks. Hence it was concluded that the comprehension deficit of the Wernicke aphasics could not be attributed to a deficit in phonemic discrimination.

Evidence supportive of this conclusion was reported independently by Basso, Casati, and Vignolo (1977).

Preliminary data were collected on 89 normal control subjects who completed the PDT under a "live-voice" condition in which the test items were read to them by the same male examiner who recorded the standard PDT audiotape. Frequency distribution data for this subsample appear in the test manual (Benton et al., 1983, p. 101, Table 10-2). This version of the test apparently was easier than the standard audiotaped version. Twenty-seven percent (8/30) of the control subjects in the PDT normative group scored in the range of 29–30 points, compared to 76% (68/89) of the controls in the "live-voice" condition. Only one control subject (1%) scored below 25 on PDT in the "live-voice" condition, whereas 10% (3/30) of controls in the PDT normative sample (responding to stimuli from the audiotape) scored in this range. As it is unclear whether the two control samples were comparable in age or educational level, the user should consider these results preliminary until they can be replicated with both live and taped forms of the test administered to the same subjects.

In such a study the order of test administration should be counterbalanced (each form given first to a random half of the control sample) to control for practice effect, which may be greater because the "live-voice" form appears easier than the audiotaped version. The audiotaped format allows for standardized administration and requires the subject to rely solely on auditory cues for phonemic discrimination. In contrast, the "live-voice" presentation as investigated by the test authors allows the subject to see the examiner's lips while the items are read, which mediates the task visually as well as aurally and makes it easier for the observant subject. Variants on the "live-voice" version might include having the examiner stand beside or behind the subject so that he or she cannot see the examiner's oral-facial movements while the items are presented. Benton et al. (1983) also suggest videotaping the confronting examiner approach ("live-voice" presentation) as another way to standardize this version of the administration.

Critique

The PDT is a brief, well-operationalized, carefully constructed standardized measure of the most elementary component of auditory comprehension, the ability to accurately recognize the basic phonemic units of speech. The clinical diagnostic role of phonemic comprehension in aphasic syndrome analysis remains a matter of theoretical quandary and some empirical controversy, as discussed above. There is no serious question, however, that accurate evaluation of phonemic hearing represents an important element of a thorough clinical linguistic evaluation. The PDT was designed as a performance-level screening measure to evaluate for the presence or absence of phonemic hearing difficulty. A deficit performance on the PDT suggests the need for a more extensive analysis of the qualitative aspects of the phonemic comprehension deficit, including clinical audiometry to test for hearing impairment. The presence of valid phonemic comprehension deficit may or may not point to the presence of syntactical or semantic speech disorder.

Phonemic discrimination analysis by means of the PDT complements Benton and Hamsher's (1989) Multilingual Aphasia Examination, which does not provide a subtest to evaluate this elementary linguistic skill. Given the current state of knowledge about the relationship of deficit and sparing on the PDT and on the MAE auditory comprehension subtests, the presence of aphasic performance deficit on either of these linguistic measures probably should prompt administration of the other test. Inconsistent linkage exists between these indices in cases of aphasic deficit, but specific patterns are not yet predictable in the individual case based on clinical diagnostic categories. Syndrome analysis is therefore advisable in clinical application of the tests to the individual case. A normal-range score on the MAE or the PDT certainly should not lead one to presume that the results of auditory comprehension measures on the other test necessarily would fall within normal limits.

To date almost all validational and clinical syndrome-analytic work with the PDT has been exploratory. Subsequent work should study an expanded normative database for normal controls and specific aphasic subpopulations. Comparison of the "live-voice," videotaped, and audiotaped versions of test administration would be valuable, particularly with diagnostically specific, demographically equated aphasic subgroups whose linguistic deficits are well understood. Comparison of "live-voice" administration formats where the patient can see the examiner speak might be compared with "live-voice" administration where the examiner was present but out of the patient's visual field, providing only auditory input. Both of these administration formats should be compared with the standard audiotaped method of PDT administration.

Analysis of the PDT in combination with other linguistic tests of known validity such as the MAE would be useful to clarify *patterns of performance* in specific aphasic subgroup syndromes. Contrasted group designs are better set up to detect level-of-performance group differences (test sensitivity) than pattern-of-performance individual syndromatic similarities (test specificity). Although cross-validation of PDT performance-level sensitivity still is needed in larger samples, the more important validational work will involve the specificity of the role of this test in linguistic analysis. Those investigators with access to large PDT data sets also could approach this problem using factor analytic methods to study PDT construct validity. Such an approach might employ rational, theoretically guided marker variables to highlight relationships among linguistic parameters, particularly the relationships of PDT to MAE subtest measures.

The reliability, and hence the psychometric measurement accuracy, of the PDT remains to be demonstrated. This is a commonly neglected issue in clinical neuropsychology, as clinicians typically are interested primarily in decision-making, classification, and treatment-planning information. As a result, validational studies usually take precedence, and the need for preliminary reliability studies tends to be overlooked. This is an important oversight, however, because a test cannot be valid unless it is reliable. As the PDT is scored clerically, no error bias should be attributable to interrater scoring variation. The internal consistency of the items and the temporal stability of the overall scores remain to be demonstrated for the PDT. The importance of these measures and procedures for their estimation will be discussed in turn.

Internal consistency perhaps presents the most crucial element of reliability for an itemized test because it is a statistical measure of the degree to which the test items intercorrelate or coalesce numerically to measure a single construct or dimension. The higher the internal consistency of the items, the more accurate (free from measurement error) the scale will be. Nunnally (1978) has recommended that coefficient alpha, a measure of internal consistency, is the first and foremost measure of reliability to compute for any new itemized test. He suggested an ideal value of .80 for coefficient alpha, as that value reduces the error of measurement due to item sampling to a practical minimum. Reliability will be artifactually reduced if the score range sampled is too small, however (i.e., if the sample is too restricted in range or too homogeneous to show the overall pattern of performance in the population as a whole); therefore, test developers should calculate coefficient alpha for a relatively large sample in a diagnostically and demographically heterogeneous sample that is clinically representative of the referral population to be served. Nunnally (1978) advises that a sample size of 300 or more subjects should give a good estimate of the parametric value of coefficient alpha. Calculation of this statistic in a sample of that size should generalize to a population of essentially any size that is similarly composed.

The other measure of reliability that must be calculated for the PDT is its test-retest reliability, or temporal stability. Typically in such a study the test is given twice, with approximately a 2-week interest interval, and the two scores then are correlated. It would be useful to sample both normal controls and clinically stable, preferably chronic, aphasic patients with the PDT to establish retest reliabilities in a variety of groups. The retest reliability again should approximate .80. Retest reliability demonstration allows one to assert that changes over time in PDT scores are due to actual changes in the patient's phonemic comprehension ability and not due to simple variation in extratest, extraneous variables.

The PDT is potentially a very useful screening measure for assessing a specific, basic linguistic function in patients with acquired language disturbance. It also offers a useful research tool, which deserves careful and intensive study in combination with a variety of other, more comprehensive measures of psycholinguistic function. Its careful, experimentally rigorous use in research and clinical work doubtless will pay rich rewards in theoretical insight and improved, objective, thorough clinical care for aphasic patients.

References

Basso, A., Casati, G., & Vignolo, L.A. (1977). Phonemic identification defect in aphasia. *Cortex, 13,* 85–95.

Benton, A.L., & Hamsher, K. (1989). *Multilingual Aphasia Examination* (2nd ed.). Iowa City: AJA Associates.

Benton, A.L., Hamsher, K.deS., Varney, N.R., & Spreen, O. (1983). *Contributions to neuropsychological assessment: A clinical manual.* New York: Oxford University Press.

Blumstein, S.E., Baker, E., & Goodglass, H. (1977). Phonological factors in auditory comprehension in aphasia. *Neuropsychologia, 15*, 19–30.

De Renzi, E., & Vignolo, L. (1962). The Token Test: A sensitive test to detect receptive disturbances in aphasia. *Brain, 85*, 665–678.

Hécaën, H. (1969). Essai de dissociation du syndrome de l'aphasie sensorielle. *Revue Neurologique, 120*, 229–237.

Luria, A.R. (1970). *Traumatic aphasia.* The Hague: Mouton.

Luria, A.R. (1973). *The working brain: An introduction to neuropsychology.* New York: Basic Books.

Luria, A.R. (1980). *Higher cortical functions in man* (2nd ed.). New York: Basic Books.

Miceli, G., Gainotti, G., Caltagirone, C., & Masullo, C. (1980). Some aspects of phonological impairment in aphasia. *Brain and Language, 11*, 159–169.

Nunnally, J.C. (1978). *Psychometric theory.* New York: McGraw-Hill.

Tallal, P., & Newcombe, F. (1978). Impairment of auditory perception and language comprehension in dysphasia. *Brain and Language, 6*, 13–24.

Varney, N.R., & Benton, A.L. (1979). Phonemic discrimination and aural comprehension among aphasic patients. *Journal of Clinical Neuropsychology, 1*, 65–73.

Timothy D. Orrell, Psy.D.
Neuropsychology Fellow, Department of Psychology, University of North Carolina, Wilmington, North Carolina.

Antonio E. Puente, Ph.D.
Professor of Psychology, University of North Carolina, Wilmington, North Carolina.

THE PIN TEST

Paul Satz and Lou D'Elia. Odessa, Florida: Psychological Assessment Resources, Inc.

Introduction

The Pin Test is a measure of manual dexterity with secondary assessment of fine motor coordination and visual-motor skills. The instrument was developed by Drs. Paul Satz and Lou D'Elia from the University of California at Los Angeles and represents an international collaborative effort with assistance from Dr. Harry van der Vlugt of the Netherlands. The Pin Test evolved from an interest in developing a measure of manual dexterity that was more sensitive and reliable than others available. The first published study using this test (Orsini, Satz, Soper, & Light, 1985) used multiple measures of handedness and laterality. Orsini et al. reported a disconcordance between self-reported handedness and several of the measures. Such findings indicated that existing measures of handedness perhaps were not that accurate, hence the need for a more sensitive measure.

The Pin Test consists of six separate parts: a 16-gauge aluminum holder; a 16-gauge aluminum plate (about 5" × 4") with 101 holes drilled in a sinusoidal pattern across it; a noncoated piece of corrugated (C flute) cardboard with a burst weight of 150 psi (each piece has a log to keep track of the 10 uses printed on it); a numbered trial sheet; a satin straight pin, 1¹⁄₁₆ inches long; and a record form.

Prior to administration of the test, the examiner must prepare the resistance cardboard by inserting it into the aluminum holder, placing the metal plate on top, and then, using the straight pin, piercing each of the 101 holes for both the left- and right-handed administration. Once this is completed, the test is ready for administration. This process must take place for each new piece of resistance cardboard. The authors suggest that the cardboard and the straight pin be replaced after every 10 subjects. The Pin Test kit includes materials for 50 administrations and a test manual (Satz & D'Elia, 1989).

Test administration is quite simple and appropriate for ages 16 through 69. The test may be administered by anyone who has a good grasp of neuropsychological tests, but interpretation requires a thorough understanding of neuropsychological

---

Dr. Timothy Orrell, the first author of this review, is currently Director of Behavioral Medicine at Florida CORF, South Daytona, Florida.

principles. To administer the Pin Test, the examiner sets the testing apparatus in front of the subject, consisting of the resistance cardboard, the trial sheet, and the metal plate inserted into the aluminum holder. A square cutout in the metal plate indicates whether a right- or left-handed administration is being conducted. The examiner administers the test to the subject's dominant hand on the first trial, then alternates between the nondominant and dominant hand until two 30-second trials have been completed for each hand. The manual includes specific administration instructions. It is important first, of course, to determine handedness and whether peripheral damage may affect testing. Once this is ascertained, the subject is given a straight pin and asked to "push the pin into" the cardboard through as many of the holes as he or she can in a 30-second period. The record form allows the administrator to record a) the number of "hits" (i.e., complete holes punched by the pin) for each trial, b) total hits for each hand, c) percentile for each hand, d) standard score for each hand, e) Advantage Index, f) Advantage Index percentile, and g) Advantage Index standard score. The Advantage Index is calculated by dividing the number of hits for the dominant hand by those of the nondominant hand. The manual includes norms based on handedness and age, grouped as follows: 16–19, 20–29, 30–39, 40–49, 50–59, and 60–69.

The results of the Pin Test allow the examiner to determine how a particular subject performs relative to age-clustered peers for each hand, as well as dominant/nondominant performance. The authors' interpretive guide gives suggested causes for three patterns of performance. Pattern 1 occurs when total hits for both hands are below a standard score of 70. Pattern 2 is found with either a high (standard score above 130) or low (standard score below 70) Advantage Index. Pattern 3 is a combination of Patterns 1 and 2.

Practical Applications/Uses

The Pin Test is designed as a multisetting instrument to measure manual dexterity and handedness. To successfully complete the task, a subject must also utilize visual-motor and fine motor coordination. In research settings this would be an excellent task for determining concordance between report of handedness and actual hand preference. Further, the ease of administration and specific instructions make the test ideal for administration by research assistants and/or students. In clinical settings, the Pin Test would provide another measure of handedness as well as a very sophisticated measure of fine motor skills for return to work. This test may also be useful when inconsistent results are found with other tests of manual dexterity. For instance, if the Finger Tapping Test (Reitan & Wolfson, 1984) provides conflicting data, perhaps the Pin Test could serve as an additional measure. If continued discrepancies exist, then motivational or other areas could be explored. The authors suggest that the test be used in rehabilitation settings to assess improvement in fine motor skills. However, they warn that the Pin Test is not designed to be a screening test for brain damage; rather, it is a brief, nonthreatening adjunct to a comprehensive evaluation.

One drawback for its use as a pre/post measure is the test's documented robust practice effect, which may interfere with correct interpretation of results unless the clinician is very familiar with the test and its serial administration. Very fine motor skills are required to hold and manipulate a straight pin. Application of this instrument to lower functioning populations such as moderate to severe traumatic brain injury patients, lower functioning developmentally disabled individuals, or others having difficulty with very fine motor skills would be inappropriate. Although a straight pin is relatively safe for most populations, safety and liability issues may need to be addressed when using this test in some settings.

Administration is straightforward and the manual provides adequate instructions. However, preparing the resistance cardboard requires approximately 5 minutes and is, at the very least, unpleasant. Pushing a pin through 202 holes (for both right- and left-handed administrations) with corrugated cardboard underneath is no easy task. The authors of this review could find no painless solution to this task if the instructions are to be followed carefully. Also, certain holes are more difficult to prepare due to the "spines" or corrugated ridges running throughout the cardboard, and these may affect subjects' performance. Pilot subjects taking the test for these reviewers also complained that it was slightly painful, particularly on the second trial of each hand.

Scoring the Pin Test requires approximately 3 minutes, and the process is easy as long as the scorer remembers two very important details: first, that the norms tables are based on hand dominance, and second, that one must look under the correct age.

Interpretation of the test requires both an objective scoring process as well as clinical judgment. Although norms are provided with which to compare the subject's performance, clinical judgment determines whether motivation can be considered as a contributor to a certain pattern of performance. Analysis of performance can be done at two levels. The first is relatively unsophisticated—a quantitative determination of handedness. This superficial approach still requires an analysis of subject's motivation and ruling out alternative hypotheses if the result is unexpected. At the most sophisticated level, an analysis of the Advantage Index and determining the pattern of performance will require special training in neuropsychological assessment. An understanding of laterality, handedness, plus their relationship (see Henninger, 1992) and its effect on neuropsychological functioning also will be necessary.

Of note, one study found the Pin Test correlated significantly with the Wisconsin Card Sorting Test (Green, Satz, Ganzell, & Vaclav, 1992). Green et al. postulated that neuromotor sequencing, as evidenced by the Pin Test, might be a very basic measure of higher order cerebral activation. Such a hypothesis bears further scrutiny of the precursors of executive functions and the use of such measures as the Pin Test in this issue.

Technical Aspects

Several studies were conducted as part of the standardization project. The first focused on the relationship between reported handedness on the Edinburgh Inventory (a finger-tapping apparatus) and the Pin Test. The results suggested very high concordance between self-reported handedness and the Pin Test for both right- (98%) and left-handed (96%) subjects. In comparison, there was less concordance between self-reported handedness and the finger-tapping apparatus—90% for right-handers and 80% for left-handers.

In the second investigation, practice effects were studied using a repeated-trials protocol. Significant increase in performance was noted across trials (total trials = 3).

Test-retest stability over 5 to 20 days also was explored. Whereas practice effects were again noted, no change was observed with the Advantage Index.

Finally, using a very small sample of right-handed "brain-damaged" subjects, the authors reported defective performance on several of the measures.

Critique

The Pin Test provides a quick and useful assessment of manual dexterity and handedness. The test can be administered in most settings, provided there is sufficient light and a table, and administration does not require a thorough knowledge of assessment principles—it can be accomplished by a competent student or research assistant. The test authors do include interpretive strategies that require a more sophisticated understanding of neuropsychological assessment.

Problems exist, however, that detract from the utility of this test. For instance, the norming process is not well explained in the manual and overrepresents the younger ages while underrepresenting older age groups. Also, although the test was standardized with a large sample of normal subjects, there are actually more left-handed subjects than right-handed ones, which is somewhat unusual. Norms for brain-damaged subjects, both right- and left-handers, with varying neurological conditions would be very useful. Although the test is fairly simple to administer, the preparation of materials is somewhat burdensome for the examiner. The use of straight pins also presents a safety consideration with patients who are either lower functioning or prone to acting out. Both subjects and administrators have remarked that the test is painful, which may result in a motivational problem for a few patients. Finally, the fact that this test is highly sensitive to practice effects makes it less useful for serial testings as a measure of improvement.

However, it is important to recognize that while these limitations exist, the Pin Test still could serve numerous purposes. Overall, the test undoubtedly will provide neuropsychologists with an appreciation for the comprehensive assessment of fine motor activity and visual-motor function. Further, the criticisms outlined in this review would also be applicable to widely accepted measures such as The Finger Tapping Test. Hence, the Pin Test's presumed limitations are based on an absolute reference point rather than a relative one vis-à-vis other neuropsychological instruments and may reflect the status of the field much more than the adequacy of this test.

References

Green, M., Satz, P., Ganzell, S., & Vaclav, J. (1992). Wisconsin Card Sorting Test performance in schizophrenia: Remediation of a stubborn deficit. *American Journal of Psychiatry, 149,* 62–67.

Henninger, P. (1992). Handedness and lateralization. In A.E. Puente & R.J. McCaffrey (Eds.), *Handbook of clinical neuropsychological assessment* (pp. 141–179). New York: Plenum.

Orisini, D.L., Satz, P., Soper, H.V., & Light, R.K. (1985). The role of familial sinistrality in cerebral organization. *Neuropsychologia, 23*(2), 223–232.

Reitan, R., & Wolfson, D. (1984). *The Halstead-Reitan Neuropsychological Battery.* Tucson, AR: Reitan Neuropsychology Press.

Satz, P., & D'Elia, L. (1989). *The Pin Test: Professional manual.* Odessa, FL: Psychological Assessment Resources.

Michael H. Mattei, Psy.D.
Staff Psychologist, Napa State Hospital, Napa, California.

Grant Aram Killian, Ph.D.
Adjunct Professor of Psychology, Nova University, Fort Lauderdale, Florida.

William I. Dorfman, Ph.D.
Associate Professor of Psychology, Nova University, Fort Lauderdale, Florida.

PSYCHOLOGICAL/SOCIAL HISTORY REPORT

Giles D. Rainwater and Debora Silver Coe. Melbourne, Florida: Psychometric Software, Inc.

Introduction

The Psychological/Social History Report (Rainwater & Silver Coe, 1988a, 1988b) is a computer-based structured interview that gathers client information and produces a written narrative report. In addition to the information obtained from the standard structured interview, the user may modify the program to include other questions or topics deemed appropriate or necessary for a particular administration.

The first author, Giles Rainwater, earned his Ph.D. from the University of Oregon in 1978. He is currently in private practice. Diane Silver Coe earned her Psy.D. from the Florida Institute of Technology and also maintains a private practice.

The Psychological/Social History Report was developed in order to facilitate the quick and efficient collection of data required for psychological assessment and diagnosis. Development began in 1982 and took approximately 1 year. Ideas for topics and questions were generated from reviewing textbooks and journal literature related to interviewing. Final topic areas and questions derived in part on their suitability for placement into a multiple-choice question-answer format (G.D. Rainwater, personal communication, July 9, 1991). Prior to its release, a prototype was field tested with four psychologists, all of whom were in general clinical practice. Their feedback resulted in the addition of select questions to the instrument.

The instrument was revised in 1983, 1984, and again in 1988. The first revision added branching logic functions, which increased the program's efficiency. The second revision decreased lag time between questions and also introduced an IBM-compatible version of the software. The last revision added the capacity to modify or add questions and topics to suit the individual user's needs. The last edition, which is the focus of this review, is not available for Apple computer users.

The assessment kit includes a manual and a program disk. Paper-and-pencil questionnaires are available separately. To run the software, users need an IBM PC or compatible system and any version of DOS. An earlier version is also available for Apple and Macintosh systems, but it does not allow the user to edit or add questions and topics.

The examiner's participation in the administration process is minimal. He or she either instructs clients to fill out a paper-and-pencil questionnaire or directs them to the computer for direct input of the data. Once the interview data have been entered into the computer, the examiner can print a copy of the narrative or save the information on disk for future access or word processing. However, should input need to be suspended for any reason, the data cannot be saved and the respondent will have to start from the beginning when ready to resume.

According to the first author, this instrument is suitable for use with adults only (G.D. Rainwater, personal communication, July 9, 1991). The publisher, however, states it can be used to assess both adolescents and adults (J. Redman, personal communication, July 12, 1991). Unfortunately, as the manual does not clarify the issue, ambiguity surrounds this question. Both the publisher and authors concur that anyone with seventh-grade reading ability can complete the assessment, and this apparently was measured by one of the authors, who has a background in assessing reading ability.

The software may be modified by the user in a number of ways that may significantly increase the flexibility and utility of the program. One can alter existing questions, response options, and narrative statements, add new questions, options, and statements, add new topics, and select specific topics to be administered. Users also may add branching sequences to their modifications in order to increase the amount of detailed inquiry and decrease redundant or unnecessary questioning.

The main topics covered in the standard interview are presenting problem, family history, developmental history, education, financial status, employment history, medical history, marital/family status, diet/exercise, and psychological/social stressors. These areas are explored both by the paper-and-pencil version of the interview as well as by the computer-administered procedure. When using the computer to administer the interview, the examiner may elect to alter the order in which topics or questions are presented. Further, the client using the computer may choose to "earmark" particular questions for later discussion or elaboration by pressing a designated key. When computer administration is impractical, the client may complete the written form and the clinician can then enter responses into the computer. The standard printed questionnaire is only suitable for when the program has not been modified. However, the publisher will help in developing and printing customized questionnaires for interested users.

The narrative report presents the data grouped by topics and in the same order that it was acquired. The order of data presentation in the narrative will reflect any changes made from the standard format. The report also identifies "earmarked" and "clinically significant answers." That is, any questions that the client marked for discussion or that the program determined were answered with clinically significant responses are printed along with the client's answer.

Practical Applications/Uses

The Psychological/Social History Report is designed to administer a structured interview, gather basic psychological data, and produce a written narrative from the information obtained. Because the user is free to add or edit questions and topics, the variables assessed by the software can be greatly expanded. However, along with this greatly expanded utility comes a concomitant increase in the potential for misuse by undertrained individuals.

Branching logic functions can be programmed into any of the modifications, which allows for further exploration of a topic and decreases the frequency of redundant questions. For example, it is possible through branching to flag a question such as "Do you use any street drugs?" If the client acknowledges drug use, the program can be set to inquire automatically then about the use of specific drugs. Once that list is narrowed, branching could allow for further probing regarding frequency of use and so forth. If the client denies drug use, the program can be made to skip the rest of the inquiry and proceed to the next topic. Without branching, respondents would have to answer all questions relating to substance abuse regardless of applicability.

This assessment program has been used in both hospital and private practice settings. According to the first author, sales are restricted to psychologists and other qualified mental health professionals such as social workers and psychiatrists (G.D. Rainwater, personal communication, July 9, 1991). The publishers state that the examiner should be a mental health professional or someone under the supervision of a professional (J. Redman, personal communication, July 12, 1991).

Administration procedures are simple and easy to learn. The process begins by instructing the client to follow the directions that appear on the screen. The program offers a short tutorial covering the keyboard functions needed to answer the questions—how to choose a desired answer, how to back up within a topic, how to change an answer, and, when applicable, how to make multiple responses to a question. Once this training module is completed, the program presents the respondent with the first topic and its related questions. Administration proceeds through each topic area until the entire questionnaire has been presented. Throughout the administration, a "help" line appearing at the bottom of the screen gives a brief synopsis of the necessary keyboard commands. When the administration concludes, the program automatically returns to the main menu and one can print a report based on the client's responses.

As noted previously, the Psychological/Social History Report may be modified in various ways to suit the examiner. Prior to administration, for example, a user may alter the sequence of the available topics and present them in any order deemed preferable or convenient. In addition to the basic topics covered in the standard format, the examiner can add up to 28 other topic areas, each of which may contain up to 20 questions. The system also offers the flexibility of deleting unneeded topics or questions. The manual gives clear, step-by-step instructions on the procedures involved in editing the program.

The time required for a standard administration is approximately 30 to 45 minutes. When a client completes the paper-and-pencil questionnaire, the data can be entered into the computer in approximately 10 minutes. Naturally, as topics are added, the time required for each function increases. The computer processes results and has them ready for printing within seconds after data are entered. Another system option, saving the data to disk, allows accessing and editing the report at the examiner's convenience.

Minimal interpretations of the acquired data are made. The client's answers print out in a narrative-form text corresponding to the topic areas covered during the administration. In addition to any questions "earmarked" by the respondent, the program also notes those responses interpreted as clinically significant (based on the test developers' subjective opinion). When the users modify the program, they can then select what responses will be flagged as clinically significant.

Technical Aspects

No attempts have been made to estimate levels of validity and reliability for the Psychological/Social History Report. The lack of available data makes it difficult to evaluate the suitability of this instrument for any particular use. Structured interviews traditionally have been neglected in the research literature (Morgan-stern, 1976). Considering their pervasive use in mental health, though, this lack of attention seems remarkable. Studies have shown that structured interviews typically possess characteristics that make them amenable to psychometric inquiry and study (Haynes & Jensen, 1979). The *Standards for Educational and Psychological Testing* (American Educational Research Association, American Psychological Association, & National Council on Measurement in Education, 1985) state with regard to computerized interviews that "all the standards apply with equal force" (p. 4). As such, an evaluation of the Psychological/Social History Report's technical aspects should include an examination of how well it meets the primary professional standards related to validity and reliability. For a more exhaustive review of which standards this instrument met, the reader is referred to Mattei (1991).

The utility of a structured interview rests in part on evidence of its content-related validity. An examination of how the Psychological/Social History Report was constructed shows that the established procedures for building and demonstrating content validity in an instrument were, for the most part, not followed. To begin with, the developers fail to clearly specify the domain(s) that their instrument represents. The *Standards* (3.3) state that domain definitions and test specifications must be presented in a manner that will allow for evaluating how test items relate to the domains they represent (AERA et al., 1985). Only general content areas are identified, some of which are vague in terms of meaning. For example, the topic area entitled Developmental History implies that the program gathers data on salient aspects of the individual's early development. In fact, little more than basic childhood-related demographic information is gathered.

Another flaw in this construction pertains to the use of subject-matter experts. According to the *Standards* (1.7), when subject-matter experts have been used, their relevant training, experience, and qualifications should be described (AERA et al., 1985, p. 15). Although not mentioned in the manual, the subject-matter experts consisted of four psychologists involved in "general psychological practice" (G.D. Rainwater, personal communication, July 9, 1991). Without this information, one cannot determine whether these individuals were qualified to have served in this capacity.

The *Standards* (3.1) also specify that assessment instruments must be developed in a sound scientific manner. As previously described, the developers consulted textbooks on interviewing to select a preliminary list of topics and questions. Item selection was determined in part by how suitable a given question was for use with a multiple-choice format (G.D. Rainwater, personal communication, July 9, 1991). This type of selection criteria seems to conflict with the goal of building content validity. Further, once the topics and questions were determined, field testing took place using four local psychologists. According to Anastasi (1982), the use of subject-matter experts is an established part of test development, but tapping them should occur before the actual preparation or selection of items, not afterward as is the case with the Psychological/Social History Report.

It appears thus that efforts to build content validity into this instrument were unsystematic and flawed. As such, the developers have failed to demonstrate that the instrument's content is relevant to its proposed use of obtaining social history data. In comparison to established clinical interviews (Korchin, 1976; Sundberg, Tyler, & Taplin, 1973), it becomes more apparent that the Psychological/Social History Report lacks both depth and scope.

One of the primary *Standards* (1.1) states that "evidence of validity should be presented for the major types of inferences for which the use of a test is recommended" (p. 13). Although the manual has a disclaimer stating that the instrument is not recommended for any specific use, the program is promoted as suitable for gathering the background information necessary for clinical assessment and diagnosis (J. Redman, personal communication, July 12, 1991). Therefore, according to standard 1.1 (AERA et al., 1985), without evidence of content validity the use of the instrument for this type of data gathering is unsupported.

Many studies have shown the reliability of self-report interview data to be quite low (Erdman, Klein, & Greist, 1983; Klein, Greist, & Van Cura, 1975; Walsh, 1967; Yarrow, Campbell, & Burton, 1970). Sources of error encountered during the interview, including client bias and selective unwillingness to disclose information, make it difficult to obtain reliable data. The Psychological/Social History Report manual fails to address these issues, which may lead users to assume reliability erroneously where none has been shown.

Another issue regarding reliability concerns the use of alternate forms of an instrument. The *Standards* (4.6) state that if more than one method exists to gather the information, "the manual should report data, references, or a logically developed argument on the degree to which results from these methods are interchangeable" (p. 37). The Psychological/Social History Report allows respondents to record their answers on paper or directly into the computer. No data, references, or arguments appear regarding the interchangeability of these two recording techniques. Not addressing this issue implies parallelism between the two data-gathering methods. Claims of parallelism, as stated by the *Standards* (4.6), must be supported with data (AERA et al., 1985). This issue assumes added importance in light of the literature indicating significant differences in the amount and quality of data obtained from computer-administered interviews as opposed to paper-and-pencil forms (Angle, Johnsen, Grebenkemper, & Ellinwood, 1979; Carr, Ghosh, & Ancill, 1983).

As previously noted, this program has a feature allowing the user to delete topic areas for any given administration. He or she also can alter the order of presentation of topic areas. AERA/APA/NCME standard 3.17 states that if a short form of a test is prepared by reducing the number of items or organizing portions of a test into a separate form, the developer must provide empirical data or a theoretical rationale estimating the reliability for each short form (1985, p. 29). Clearly a developer cannot anticipate the many alterations possible, so the issue becomes the responsibility of the user, who becomes a test developer when making modifications to the original program. However, because the developers have not provided reliability data to begin with, no comparisons can be made between forms.

Critique

The Psychological/Social History Report is a flexible assessment instrument with many potential uses. The ease with which it can be administered and the speed with which it produces a report make it a desirable software package. However, a detailed examination of how it meets or fails other relevant professional standards (AERA et al., 1985) will be useful in evaluating its overall utility.

Standards 5.2 and 5.4 clearly state what the appropriate contents of a test manual should be (AERA et al., 1985). The manual accompanying this instrument provides no information regarding the process of test construction or how the developers attempted to build in content validity. Content-related evidence of validity holds great importance for a social history interview. The lack of documentation included with this assessment makes it impossible for the prospective user to determine whether the instrument was constructed in an acceptably scientific manner.

Another of the primary standards states that test manuals should clearly delineate the recommended uses of an instrument and provide a summary of the evidence supporting these uses. This manual fails to provide any information regarding recommended uses. In fact, a disclaimer of liability appears in the appendices stating that no warranties are made with respect to the program's "fitness for any particular purpose." AERA/APA/NCME standard 5.2 also states that "where particular misuses of a test can be reasonably anticipated, the test manual should provide specific cautions against such misuses" (1985, p. 36). Several of the manual's deficiencies are addressed in this statement. The ability of the computer program to be customized by the user creates the strong potential for misuse. As previously noted, the test user becomes the test developer when modifications are made. The manual makes no mention of how this could create the potential for misuse, nor does it make clear the obligations incurred by the user who chooses to alter the instrument. Further, the manual fails to specify the age groups with which the instrument can be used. One of the test developers states uncategorically that the instrument should be used only for adults (G.D. Rainwater, personal communication, July 9, 1991), while the publishers recommend its use for adolescents as well (J. Redman, personal communication, July 12, 1991). Not addressing this formally in the manual creates the potential for significant misuse.

The *Guidelines for Computer-Based Tests and Interpretation* (American Psychological Association, 1986) state that the manual should report the rationale and evidence supporting any computer-based interpretations (21). The *Guidelines* (27) also add that the extent to which interpretive statements are based on empirical research versus clinical opinion should be made clear. The manual fails to indicate how the program interprets certain answers as clinically significant. This ambiguity furthers the potential for misuse of the instrument.

Another area of concern arises due to fact that the software can inadvertently allow a respondent access to other client files. Once the program has finished administering the interview, the main menu appears. One of the options on this menu is "Quit," which if selected exits the program and accesses the clinician's DOS directory or software management system. Unless the examiner has taken security measures to restrict access to other programs or databases, an unsupervised client may intentionally or inadvertently gain access to unprotected data. Unfortunately, no mention about this possibility appears in the manual. This violates APA (1986) guideline 15, which states that procedures must be established to ensure confidentiality and privacy. Ultimately it is the user of course who is responsible for maintaining confidentiality, but it would appear that marketing a test that presents such a strong potential for misuse seems ill advised.

The *Guidelines* (10) state that automated assessment instruments should allow for the same degree of editorial control as traditional testing formats. The Psychological/Social History Report allows clients to back up to any question within a topic area and change their answers. This provides a great degree of editorial control over responses, but not to the same degree as the paper-and-pencil version, which permits a change in any answer at any point during the administration. However, this program performs better than similar automated social histories in this regard. For example, the Automated Child/Adolescent Social History (ACASH; Rohde, 1988) only allows respondents to back up one question to make corrections. One drawback to the Psychological/Social History Report, however, is the inability to suspend an interview and save the data if the need arises. Unlike the ACASH, the data cannot be stored in such a situation and the respondent must restart the whole process.

The manual presents clear directions, and it is relatively easy for respondents to learn the procedures from the tutorial. In terms of performance, though, this program does not appear to stand up well to similar products. For example, it makes relatively little use of its branching capabilities, which relates to another flaw in the instrument; namely, that inquiry into topics tends to be superficial and incomplete. Questions regarding major medical illnesses and childhood mental difficulties are not followed up if the respondent answers in the affirmative. If a client reports being raised in an institution, inquiries do not follow as to the necessity of these arrangements. (In fact, the program goes on to ask about family life with the parents.) In this regard, the interview is neither thorough or comprehensive. The questioning in the developmental history section is incomplete as compared to the GOLPH Psychosocial History (Giannetti, 1987), which inquires about type of delivery, birth weight, birth defects, and developmental milestones. None of these areas are addressed by the Psychological/Social History Report. As opposed to the ACASH, it does not possess the ability to flag inconsistent response patterns. For example, a client can endorse items indicating he or she was raised as an only child and then go on to answer questions about relationships with siblings.

By allowing for the interview to be customized, this instrument appears to have been based in part on the false assumption that (a) the appropriateness and utility of a structured interview depends on the individual user's needs and (b) by meeting these needs an instrument will possess the necessary validity for its intended uses. The basic interview here is incomplete and lacks thoroughness. Furthermore, it appears that few guidelines were followed to ensure the construction of a content-valid instrument. The feature allowing users to customize the program also creates the potential for serious misuse.

In a review by Mattei (1991), this instrument failed to meet a full 82% of the 17 primary AERA/APA/NCME standards on which it was evaluated. Naturally, not every standard is of equal importance and should not be given equal weight. For example, publishing a manual that does not specify the qualifications needed to administer an interview may not be as important or crucial as failing to develop an instrument in a sound scientific manner. In summary, the Psychological/Social History Report appears to be a seriously flawed instrument. With the absence of reliability or validity estimates, and with the violation of such a significant number of primary professional standards, it would seem that using this program for any specific purpose is inappropriate.

Empirical investigation regarding the use of case history interviews must assume greater importance. One factor that appears to have hampered such efforts is the widespread assumption that self-report measures are inherently invalid and unreliable. Although studies have tended to support this view, certain evidence does suggest that carefully designed interviews may be reliably and validly used to measure specific target behaviors (Linehan, 1977; Lucas, 1977). In addition, Haynes and Jensen (1979) have outlined steps for beginning to estimate the validity of interview-derived information.

The clinical interview must be fully recognized as an assessment instrument and, as such, held to the same standards of reliability and validity required of other assessment tools. Until these standards are accepted as applicable to the clinical interview, instruments of poor quality will continue to be distributed for widespread use. Psychologists should abandon the use of interviews, tests, and procedures that are recommended only by their availability, ease of use, and familiarity. In 1984 Killian, Holzman, Davis, and Gibbon proposed that psychologists had an ethical obligation to use instruments that conformed at least to the original APA standards published in 1966. These reviewers propose now that psychologists have an ethical obligation to use instruments constructed in a sound scientific manner and that conform to the current professional standards (AERA et al., 1985). Given that test users and developers increasingly are being held accountable by the courts for "defective test design" and "defective validation" procedures (Smith, 1991), clearly what once was an exclusively ethical issue has now become a legal one as well.

References

American Educational Research Association, American Psychological Association, & National Council on Measurement in Education. (1985). *Standards for educational and psychological testing.* Washington, DC: American Psychological Association.

American Psychological Association. (1986). *Guidelines for computer-based tests and interpretation.* Washington, DC: Author.

Anastasi, A. (1982). *Psychological testing* (5th ed.). New York: Macmillan.

Angle, H.V., Johnsen, T., Grebenkemper, N.S., & Ellinwood, E.H. (1979). Computer interview support for clinicians. *Professional Psychology, 10,* 49–57.

Carr, A.C., Ghosh, A., & Ancill, R.J. (1983). Can a computer take a psychiatric history? *Psychological Medicine, 13,* 151–158.

Erdman, H.P., Klein, M.H., & Greist, J.H. (1983). The reliability of a computer interview for drug use/abuse information. *Behavior Research Methods and Instrumentation, 15,* 66–68.

Giannetti, R.A. (1987). The GOLPH Psychosocial History: Response-contingent data acquisition and reporting. In J.N. Butcher (Ed.), *Computerized psychological assessment: A practitioner's guide* (pp. 124–144). New York: Basic Books.

Haynes, S.N., & Jensen, B.J. (1979). The interview as a behavioral assessment instrument. *Behavioral Assessment, 1,* 97–106.

Killian, G., Holzman, P., Davis, J., & Gibbon, R. (1984). The effects of psychotropic drugs on cognitive functioning in schizophrenia and depression. *Journal of Abnormal Psychology, 93*(1), 58–70.

Klein, M.H., Greist, J.H., & Van Cura, L.J. (1975). Computers and psychiatry. *Archives of General Psychiatry, 32,* 837–843.

Korchin, S.J. (1976). *Modern clinical psychology: Principles of intervention in the clinic and the community.* New York: Basic Books.

Linehan, M. (1977). Issues in behavioral interviewing. In J.D. Cone & R.P. Hawkins (Eds.), *Behavioral assessment* (pp. 248–277). New York: Brunner/Mazel.

Lucas, R.W. (1977). A study of patients' attitudes to computer interrogation. *International Journal of Man-Machine Studies, 9,* 69–86.

Mattei, M.H. (1991). *Structured clinical interviews: A review and critique of three instruments.* Unpublished professional research project, Nova University, Ft. Lauderdale, FL.

Morganstern, K.P. (1976). Behavioral interviewing: The initial stages of assessment. In M. Hersen & A.S. Bellack (Eds.), *Behavioral assessment* (pp. 51–75). New York: Pergamon.

Rainwater, G.D., & Silver Coe, D.S. (1988a). *Psychological/Social History Report* [Computer program]. Melbourne, FL: Psychometric Software.

Rainwater, G.D., & Silver Coe, D.S. (1988b). *Psychological/Social History Report manual.* Melbourne, FL: Psychometric Software.

Rohde, M. (1988). *Automated Child/Adolescent Social History (ACASH)* [Computer program]. Minnetonka, MN: National Computer Systems.

Sundberg, N.D., Tyler, L.E., & Taplin, J.R. (1973). *Clinical psychology: Expanding horizons* (2nd ed.). Englewood Cliffs, NJ: Prentice-Hall.

Walsh, W.B. (1967). Validity of self-report. *Journal of Counseling Psychology, 14,* 18–23.

Yarrow, M.R., Campbell, J.D., & Burton, R.V. (1970). Recollections of childhood: A study of the retrospective method. *Monographs of the Society for Research in Child Development, 35*(5, Serial No. 138).

Kathleen Chwalisz, Ph.D.
Assistant Professor of Psychology, Southern Illinois University,
Carbondale, Illinois.

PSYCHOSOCIAL ADJUSTMENT TO ILLNESS SCALE

Leonard R. Derogatis. Riderwood, Maryland: Clinical
Psychometric Research, Inc.

Introduction

The Psychosocial Adjustment to Illness Scale (PAIS) is a multidimensional, semistructured interview designed to assess the level of a patient's adjustment to a current medical illness and/or its residual effects. Psychosocial adjustment status is measured with regard to seven domains, which cover functioning in primary life roles, attitudes toward health and health care, and psychological distress. The PAIS is to be completed by a trained health professional or interviewer, or a self-report form (PAIS-SR) may be completed directly by the respondent. The 46-item PAIS interview takes 20 to 30 minutes to complete, and the PAIS-SR takes 15 to 20 minutes. Although the present critique will focus on the PAIS interview, the self-report form is similar in most relevant areas.

The PAIS is one of the many tests distributed by Clinical Psychometric Research, a testing corporation owned by Leonard R. Derogatis and Maureen F. Derogatis. Dr. Leonard Derogatis is well known with regard to the measurement of psychiatric symptomatology and is the primary force behind the well-used Symptom Checklist 90–Revised (SCL-90-R) and its predecessors, the SCL-90 and the Hopkins Symptom Checklist; the Brief Symptom Inventory (BSI), short form of the SCL-90-R; the Affect Balance Scale (ABS); and the Hopkins Psychiatric Rating Scale (HPRS). Clinical Psychometric Research also offers the Derogatis Stress Profile, the Derogatis Sexual Functioning Inventory, the Derogatis Interview for Sexual Functioning, and the Derogatis Symptom Inventory. The PAIS appears to be an attempt to measure "normal" responses to stress, particularly the severe stress associated with medical illness.

The author cites the literature on assessing the psychosocial adjustment of psychiatric patients as the impetus for developing the Psychosocial Adjustment to Illness Scale. He refers users to reviews of that literature by Weissman and colleagues (Weissman, 1975; Weissman & Bothwell, 1976; Weissman, Sholomskas, & John, 1981). These reviews present brief synopses of available instruments, but provide little in the way of theoretical bases for the instruments. It is unclear how, and with what purpose, Derogatis developed the specific items for the PAIS.

A strength of the PAIS is the author's adherence to psychometric measurement techniques in its development and validation. The instrument was normed on four groups of medical patients: lung cancer patients, renal dialysis patients, acute burn patients, and essential hypertensives. In addition, Derogatis notes in the manual that Clinical Psychometric Research is in the process of developing a *normative library* as patient groups with different illnesses become available for study. The author provides traditional reliability and validity data for each of the normative groups.

The materials needed to administer the PAIS include the administration manual, reusable interview booklets, and score sheets. Normed combination score/ profile sheets are available for the four original normative populations (lung cancer patients, renal dialysis patients, burn patients, and essential hypertension patients). To use the PAIS-SR, a booklet must be purchased for each participant. Score sheets and normed profile sheets also are available for the PAIS-SR, with different normative groups (mixed cancer patients, cardiac patients, diabetic patients). An optional microcomputer scoring program is available for both the PAIS and PAIS-SR.

The PAIS interview booklet provides suggested probes to obtain information relevant to a judgment about the patient's status in each of the domains, and it provides sample criteria for making the judgments. The manual further provides interviewers with decision rules regarding what to do in different interviewing situations as well as information on which to base judgment calls (e.g., what to do if the patient is hospitalized at the time of the interview). Sample items, one from each domain, are presented in Derogatis (1986). The PAIS-SR, in contrast, provides specific questions and specific responses for each of the domains.

The PAIS is designed to assess adjustment to medical illness primarily in terms of the individual's ability to function at his or her previous level in various life roles. In other words, one is able to determine how disruptive a given medical illness has been to the patient's life. Psychosocial functioning is measured by 46 items across seven domains:

I. *Health Care Orientation:* patient attitudes, quality of information about the illness, nature of expectancies about the disorder and treatment.

II. *Vocational Environment:* functioning at work, school, or home (as appropriate), covering issues such as perceived job performance, job satisfaction, and lost time from work.

III. *Domestic Environment:* illness-induced difficulties in home or family life, including quality of relationships, family communications, financial effects, and effects of physical disabilities.

IV. *Sexual Relationships:* changes in quality of sexual functioning or relationship associated with the illness, such as sexual interest, frequency, quality of performance, and level of satisfaction with sexual relationships.

V. *Extended Family Relationships:* disruption of relationships with the patient's extended family as a result of the illness, such as quality of relationships, impact on communication, and interest in interacting with family.

VI. *Social Environment:* effects of the current illness on social and leisure time activities, assessing both interest and actual behavior associated with these activities.

VII. *Psychological Distress:* symptoms of psychological difficulties such as depression, anxiety, hostility, reduced self-esteem, and body image problems.

Practical Applications/Uses

The PAIS was designed to be used with anyone who is coping with a medical illness. No mention is made regarding age, but the complexity of the roles presented suggest that the PAIS is appropriate only for adults. The author also suggests that it may be used to assess family members' adjustment to the patient's illness, but no norms exist for family members at this time. The issue of norms is an important one in general for anyone who is considering using the PAIS. As noted previously, the author is in the process of building a normative library of scores for groups of patients with different medical illnesses. However, there are no general medical population norms, so if one is planning to use the instrument with any patient for whose condition norms do not yet exist, one is left with not much better than descriptive information, because there is no appropriate comparison group.

The PAIS is designed to be administered by a trained interviewer. The author does not make it clear, though, how interviewers are expected to obtain training (e.g., Clinical Psychometric Research does not offer training courses). The instrument appears straightforward enough that the manual might provide enough information to conduct the interview or train others to do so. However, the interview is semistructured, it provides *suggested* rather than specific questions to gather information in each of the domain areas, it does not specify an exact order for questions to be asked, and it does not provide the interviewer with specific probes to gather any additional information that is needed. Given all of these areas of flexibility, there are potentially many sources of interview error or other nonrandom effects. This is particularly problematic for an instrument used to judge patient responses compared to norms for similar patient populations. Comparisons with the norms is technically questionable if the interview conditions differ from those used with the normative samples.

The manual is not very specific in describing how the interview is to be conducted. The instrument was designed to be "semistructured," providing a "suggested order" for the PAIS items and a "recommended" form of query to gather information for each item except those in the Psychological Distress domain, which has "required" questions. The interviewer is expected to judge where the patient would be placed on a 4-point Likert scale for each item. Each point on the scale is associated with a stem that reflects four levels a patient might present for a given question, and stems are unique to each question. For example, in response to an attitude question (question omitted for security reasons), the interviewer must judge whether the patient's attitude is "clearly negative with a lack of confidence and mistrust," "somewhat negative with visible cynicism," "generally positive with some reservations," or "very positive with high levels of confidence."

Prior to beginning the semistructured portion of the interview, the interviewer must gather several pieces of information for which there are no cues on the interview form (so inadequately trained, new, or forgetful interviewers may fail to gather the information). Necessary background information encompasses the nature of the present illness, occupation of the individual, marital status, household composition, family composition, geographic location, and typical social and leisure activities. This information apparently is used to aid the interviewer in making judgments, but exactly how is not specified. The time frame for the interview is 30 days; that is, patients are to answer consistent with their thoughts, feelings, and attitudes during the past 30 days. If the patient is hospitalized at the time of the interview, the time frame should be the 30 days immediately prior to entering the hospital. The manual provides very good instructions for how the interviewer is to deal with special cases.

Scoring the PAIS is relatively simple, and the procedures, including those for handling missing data, are clearly described in the manual. Even-numbered items are reverse-coded (or "reflected") by subtracting the obtained score from 3. Domain scores derive simply from the sum of the scores for the items within each domain. The seven domain scores are converted to standardized T-scores by looking them up on the norm table for the appropriate group. The T-scores then are summed to generate the PAIS Total Score. Scoring may be facilitated by using one of the score/ profile forms, which also are useful if records are to be kept in patient files. Profile forms are available for each of the norm groups, with raw score values corresponding to T-scores in each of the domains printed on the form. Although nonnormed scoring forms also are available, it is not clear from the manual how users are expected to determine the standardized T-scores without the benefit of norms.

The use of standardized scores is an advantage of the PAIS (with groups for which norms are available) because it allows for easy comparison between a given patient and others coping with the same illness. Because adjustment is a construct for which no truly objective criteria exist, comparison is about the only method one can use to judge how a patient is doing. T-scores also allow for direct interpretation in terms of percentile scores, so one may determine where the individual stands on a normal distribution.

Interpretation is based on a comparison of the patient's level of functioning with others in a similar situation. The primary method for this comparison is the use of the T-score. Preliminary analyses by the author suggest that patients with a PAIS Total Score equivalent to or greater than a T-score of 62 are positive for clinical levels of psychosocial maladjustment. (Total Scores may also be converted to T-scores by looking them up in a table.) This method of interpretation involves determining "caseness," or the extent to which an individual's symptoms might warrant diagnosis or treatment, rather than considering degrees of maladjustment. With the standardized scores, however, users also should be able to discuss, with reasonable validity, how severe one's level of maladjustment is or how good one's level of adjustment is based on percentile rank within a group of patients with the same medical problem.

The PAIS is designed to be interpreted at three distinct but related levels: a) the global level, reflected by the PAIS Total Score; b) the domain level, reflected by scores in each of the domains; and c) the discrete item level, based on a patient's response to a particular item. The Total Score is an indicator of the patient's overall adjustment, the domain scores identify particular areas of adjustment and/or maladjustment, and the discrete item level provides a more detailed picture to help determine what specific issues underlie areas of successful and unsuccessful adjustment for an individual. The discrete level may particularly benefit members of the helping professions who are developing interventions to assist patients with adjustment to a particular illness.

Technical Aspects

Derogatis provides information in the manual on both internal consistency and interrater reliability for the PAIS. Internal consistency reliability, or the extent to which items in a given subscale consistently measure the same construct, is particularly important for an instrument designed to measure a single construct (in this case, adjustment) via information in a number of domains. Internal consistency reliability (Cronbach's alpha) was calculated for the PAIS on two different samples for the seven domains. The sample of renal dialysis ($N = 269$) yielded reasonably good alphas, ranging from .63 to .80. Internal consistency was lowest for Health Care Orientation (.63), Extended Family Relationships (.66), and Domestic Environment (.67). A sample of lung cancer patients ($N = 89$) yielded quite different alpha coefficients. This sample produced a very poor alpha of .12 for the Extended Family Relationships subscale and a relatively low alpha for the Domestic Environment subscale (.68). The remaining subscales, however, yielded higher alpha coefficients than those found in the renal dialysis sample, ranging from .81 to .93. Alpha coefficients for a sample of cardiac patients on the PAIS-SR ($N = 69$) ranged from .47 (Health Care Orientation) to .85 (Psychological Distress). It should be noted that two of the three samples were quite small. The least reliable of the PAIS and PAIS-SR subscales, consistent across the three patient samples, are Health Care Orientation, Domestic Environment, and Extended Family Relationships. It would seem prudent to present Cronbach's alpha for the PAIS Total Score as well, given that the seven domains are assumed to reflect the patient's overall adjustment to his or her illness, but Derogatis does not do so.

Intraclass correlations are presented as evidence of interrater reliability for two samples, patients with breast cancer ($N = 17$) and patients with Hodgkin's disease ($N = 37$). Judges for the breast cancer sample were a psychologist and a nurse, and the intraclass correlation coefficients for the domains ranged from .56 to .84. The intraclass correlation for the PAIS Total Score was .86. Judges for the Hodgkin's disease sample were a mixed group of interviewers, including physicians, psychologists, and social workers. Intraclass correlation coefficients for the domains ranged from .33 to .82, and the PAIS Total Score yielded an intraclass correlation coefficient of .83. It should be noted that intraclass correlations do not provide the full picture regarding interrater reliability. Intraclass correlations indicate how consistently, proportionally, the raters are using the scale. In other words, intraclass correlations tell whether raters are ranking subjects the same on the scale. This statistic does not, however, give any indication of whether the actual adjustment *ratings* are in agreement. It is quite possible that interviewers are anchoring their ratings on different points of the scale. Furthermore, the author does not describe in detail anything about the interviewers or their training prior to the study. In addition, the samples were quite small. In general, it appears that the author has not adequately demonstrated interrater reliability for the PAIS, and users should test interrater reliability during the course of their studies as a safeguard.

The author provided, as the first piece of evidence for construct validity, a test of the domain-related subscale structure of the PAIS using factor analysis. Traditional (exploratory) factor analysis was used (although the author refers to it as confirming the structure), and it is unclear why confirmatory factor analysis techniques were not used, given the fact that the structure of the instrument already had been determined. The factor analysis was conducted using PAIS data from 120 lung cancer patients. This number of cases violates the rule of thumb that 5 cases per item are needed (230 in this case) in order to produce a reliable factor structure.

In reference to the results of the factor analysis with varimax rotation, the author states that "clearly the hypothesized dimensional structure of the PAIS was confirmed by this analysis" (Derogatis & Derogatis, 1990). This is only partially true. Only four of the seven domains had all items in that domain load on only one factor: Vocational Environment, Sexual Relationships, Extended Family Relationships, and Social Environment. Of the seven empirically derived factors, only four factors contained items from only one of the domain subscales, and only one of those loaded with items from an entire subscale (Sexual Relationships). Two factors loaded with items from two domains, and one factor loaded with items from three domains. In addition, there were two items on the Psychological Distress subscale that loaded significantly on two different factors.

Examination of the specific items that loaded on factors that were different from the hypothesized structure suggests that there might be different configurations of items that should be calculated into a given subscale score. Generally when items from more than one subscale load on a single factor, they appear to "hang together" logically or theoretically. For example, three of the Psychological Distress items (e.g., depression) loaded empirically with both items assessing leisure interest and activity and with physical disability and interference with household activities. These interpretations at the item level, however, are not intended to undermine the domain structure of the instrument. There may be other explanations for these findings, such as the small sample size or interviewer-introduced error. At any rate, further research into the structure of the PAIS is needed, and users should be cautious in basing clinical judgments on domain scores, particularly when dealing with domains that are not as cleanly measured.

Because several items did not load on the hypothesized scale, it is useful to examine the intercorrelations of the domain scores and the PAIS Total Score. The author provides intercorrelations among the domains and the total score for two samples, 120 lung cancer patients and 37 with Hodgkin's disease, and intercorrelations on the PAIS-SR are presented for 148 kidney dialysis patients. Unfortunately the author does not indicate which of the correlation coefficients are considered statistically significant, and the differences in sample sizes make the correlation coefficients difficult to compare in a meaningful way. Correlations ranged from .01 to .70 for the domain subscale scores, and they ranged from .08 to .83 for the domain scores with the total score. Applying a relatively arbitrary criterion of .39 for a correlation coefficient of practical significance, a number of domains are significantly correlated. Social Environment correlates with all of the other domain scores. In addition to Social Environment, Psychological Distress correlates with Domestic Environment and Extended Family Relationships. Extended Family Relationships also correlates with Domestic Environment. In addition to Social Environment, Domestic Environment correlates with Sexual Relationships and Vocational Environment. The fact that so many significant correlations exist between domain scores suggests that these domains may not be as discrete as the author suggests.

Evidence for convergent validity was provided by correlating the PAIS with a number of other measures for a sample of 27 breast cancer patients (Derogatis,

Abeloff, & Melisaratos, 1979). The PAIS correlated .81 with the Global Adjustment to Illness Scale (GAIS), .60 with the SCL-90-R, .69 with the Affect Balance Scale (ABS), and .64 with the Patient's Attitudes Information and Expectancies Scale (PAIES). The GAIS and PAIES, however, are unstandardized measures created by the authors for that study. The use of these measures provides little validity information for the PAIS, because they are also unvalidated. The author suggests that the higher correlation with the GAIS, a measure of general adjustment, compared to correlations with psychological symptom distress (SCL-90-R), positive and negative affect (ABS), and information/expectations (PAIES), indicates that the PAIS is a measure of more global adjustment. Further, the SCL-90-R and the ABS correlate higher with the Psychological Distress domain of the PAIS than with the PAIS Total Score, suggesting convergent validity for the Psychological Distress domain. The other half of this method of construct validation, discriminant validity, was not demonstrated for the PAIS.

As evidence of predictive validity, the author reports a study in which PAIS scores were compared for 120 persons screened positive for lung cancer and 86 persons screened negative. Patients with confirmed diagnoses of lung cancer showed poorer adjustment (higher scores on the PAIS) at 3 months. In this case, having a disease predicted scores on the PAIS.

Other investigators have provided additional evidence for the predictive utility of the PAIS. For example, Lampling (1981) found that PAIS scores could discriminate among dialysis patients in terms of life events, stress, work status, severity of illness, and coping styles. Patients who dropped out of chemotherapy were found to be different than a matched control group on the PAIS and the Brief Symptom Inventory (Gilbar & Kaplan DeNour, 1989).

Critique

The most significant criticism of the PAIS concerns its apparent lack of theoretical basis. Reviews of other adjustment instruments were cited by the author as the source of information about adjustment that led to the development of the PAIS. There is no description of how items were developed, and while they appear "face valid," Derogatis presents no compelling arguments for why these item domains were included and other possible ones were excluded. Further, there is no discussion of how this instrument offers an improvement over other measures of psychosocial adjustment. The manual merely states that "few formal psychometric instruments have been developed to evaluate the psychosocial adjustment of medical patients" (Derogatis & Derogatis, 1990, p. 1). In fact there is a sizeable amount of literature devoted to measuring adjustment and quality of life among medical patients (e.g., Bergner, Bobbitt, Pollard, Martin, & Gilson, 1976; Katz, 1987; Siegrist & Junge, 1990; Stewart, Hays, & Ware, 1988; Wiklund, 1990).

The author provides reasonable psychometric information about the PAIS and PAIS-SR. The instrument shows adequate internal consistency reliability, but the information on interrater reliability is incomplete, so a proper judgment cannot be made. The looseness of the instructions, however, suggest the potential for a number of sources of interviewer error, so users should put a significant amount of effort into training, checking, and retraining interviewers in order to assure reliable results. The author provides some evidence of construct validity and predictive validity. The structure seems generally appropriate, but some of the domains do not appear as unique as they are presented to be. Some care may be warranted if the user is planning to interpret results at the domain level.

The PAIS and PAIS-SR have been used widely; Derogatis (1990) has compiled a bibliography of 52 studies, which appears to be supportive of the instrument's utility. As a general rule, though, one should first look carefully at an instrument rather than merely using what others have used. A particularly important consideration, in the case of the PAIS and PAIS-SR, is the presence of a currently limited number of normative groups on which to gauge comparisons, leaving researchers of nonnormed populations with only descriptive information.

The PAIS appears to do a good job of measuring what it measures, but it is still not clear whether that is "adjustment to illness." Given the lack of theoretical basis for the instrument, one should exercise caution in interpreting PAIS scores as indicating "adjustment." Users should be clear about what they want to know about their subjects in the realm of "adjustment," and choose this test only if they are interested in role functioning, psychological distress, and health care orientation. The PAIS offers a good measure of those domains.

References

Bergner, M., Bobbitt, R.A., Pollard, W.E., Martin, D.P., & Gilson, B.S. (1976). The Sickness Impact Profile: Validation of a health status measure. *Medical Care, 14,* 57.

Derogatis, L.R. (1986). The Psychosocial Adjustment to Illness Scale (PAIS). *Journal of Psychometric Research, 30*(1), 77–91.

Derogatis, L.R. (1990). *PAIS/PAIS-SR: A bibliography of research reports 1975–1990.* Towson, MD: Clinical Psychometric Research.

Derogatis, L.R., Abeloff, M.D., & Melisaratos, N. (1979). Psychological coping mechanisms and survival time in metastic breast cancer. *Journal of the American Medical Association, 242,* 1504–1508.

Derogatis, L.R., & Derogatis, M.F. (1990). *PAIS and PAIS-SR administration, scoring, and procedures manual II.* Towson, MD: Clinical Psychometric Research.

Gilbar, O., & Kaplan DeNour, A. (1989). Adjustment to illness and dropout of chemotherapy. *Journal of Psychosomatic Research, 33*(1), 1–5.

Katz, S. (1987). The science of quality of life. *Journal of Chronic Disease, 40,* 459–463.

Lamping, D.L. (1981). *Psychosocial adaptation and adjustment to the stress of chronic illness.* Unpublished doctoral dissertation, Harvard University, Cambridge, MA.

Siegrist, J., & Junge, A. (1990). Measuring the social dimension of subjective health in chronic illness. *Psychotherapy and Psychosomatics, 54*(2–3), 90–98.

Stewart, A.L., Hays, R.D., & Ware, J.E. (1988). The MOS Short-Form General Health Survey. *Medical Care, 26*(7), 724–734.

Weissman, M.M. (1975). The assessment of social adjustment: A review of techniques. *Archives of General Psychiatry, 32,* 357–365.

Weissman, M.M., & Bothwell, S. (1976). Assessment of social adjustment by patient self-report. *Archives of General Psychiatry, 33,* 1111–1115.

Weissman, M.M., Sholomska, D., & John, K. (1981). The assessment of social adjustment: An update. *Archives of General Psychiatry, 38,* 1250–1258.

Wiklund, I. (1990). Measuring quality of life in medicine. *Scandinavian Journal of Primary Care Supplement, 1,* 11–14.

Rolf A. Peterson, Ph.D.

Professor and Director, Clinical Psychology Training, The George Washington University, Washington, D.C.

QUALITY OF LIFE QUESTIONNAIRE

David R. Evans and Wendy E. Cope. North Tonawanda, New York: Multi-Health Systems, Inc.

Introduction

The Quality of Life Questionnaire (QLQ) was developed as a multifactor measure of behavioral and activity effectiveness in a variety of life situations. The measure covers a wide variety of personal, interpersonal, and environmental dimensions: Material Well-Being, Physical Well-Being, Personal Growth, Marital Relations, Parent-Child Relations, Extended Family Relations, Extramarital Relations, Altruistic Behavior, Political Behavior, Job Characteristics, Occupational Relations, Job Satisfiers, Creative/Aesthetic Behavior, Sports Activity, and Vacation Behavior. As can be seen from this list, the measure provides a person's report of behavior and evaluation of situations for what appear to be the major activities of life. Each scale has been developed to assess quality of activities and perception of situations for each area of life to determine area quality of life and a total picture of the person's reported quality of life. As the authors point out, this is not merely a measure of satisfaction or perceptions, but, from the reviewer's perspective, the measure involves these aspects as well reports of behaviors in given situations and in general.

The development of the QLQ appears to have begun in the late 1970s, with a carefully developed programmed approach to developing a comprehensive quality of life measure. Dr. Evans and his associates reviewed a wide range of articles on quality of life to form a broad, comprehensive listing of areas of personal, interpersonal, vocational, and recreational behaviors to represent the many major (e.g., vocational) and subdomains (e.g., job characteristics, job satisfiers) of what might be called "quality of life domains." After 15 different domains were identified, the authors formulated rationally developed descriptors of someone high and low on each. From these descriptors, two "naive item writers" then wrote items to define the descriptors. For most areas a pool of 30 items (15 positive and 15 negative) were developed to measure each dimension. Additionally a Social Desirability scale was included to determine item–social desirability relationships and identify possible invalid profiles due to a socially desirable response pattern. A representative random sample of 298 adult community members from London, Ontario, Canada, was obtained to assess item quality. A carefully devised, appropriate set of rules was developed to determine item inclusion in a final scale. From the item pool, 6 positive and 6 negative for each of the 15 domains, plus 12 items for a social desirability scale were selected to form the final scale. This item set has remained constant until the present. The authors also developed rules as to number of items answered on a particular scale to score the scale and number of necessary valid scales in order to form a total Quality of Life score. The single-form English version appears to be the only one available at this time.

The questionnaire comes in a booklet form, with all 192 items presented in a true/false format, with instructions on how to indicate items not relevant to the examinee. The answers can be recorded on a regular answer form or the Quik-Score Form. The latter provides an automatic record on a second page that contains a score code plus domain subscores and total score recording spaces. The back of the score form presents the profile form, to which score totals can be easily transferred to a standardized profile system. The profile form provides for a plotting of the scores for all 15 domains, the total score, and a social desirability score. All scores have been standardized with a T-score mean of 50 and standard deviation of 10. Thus, the profile provides a quick view of the variability between scales, high and low points, and any extreme scores.

The QLQ can be administered individually or in groups. The primary role of the examiner is to read the printed instructions on the test form, answer any questions, and check that the answer form has been filled out correctly.

This questionnaire has been developed for use with adults of normal cognitive abilities. Data on possible adaptations (e.g., reading questions to someone visually impaired) are not provided. Such adaptations in administration could be made with relative ease, but whether the normative data would provide an appropriate interpretation would be left for the examiner to determine.

Practical Applications/Uses

As noted previously, this measure was designed to offer a comprehensive assessment of the domains of quality of life. This reviewer's summary of the rationally developed descriptors of high and low scorers on each dimension is provided as an overview of the information obtained from the assessment:

Material Well-Being: High—income and living situation is acceptable/positive; Low—income limits goal achievement and living situation has negative qualities.

Physical Well-Being: High—appropriate health and health behaviors/access; Low—poor health behaviors and poor health service use.

Personal Growth: High—good self-actualization; Low—self-dissatisfaction and the presence of personal problems.

Marital Relations: High—positive, good interactive relationship; Low—difficult interpersonal and sexual relationship.

Parent-Child Relations: High—positive interactions and control; Low—lack of positive interactions and some discipline issues present.

Extended Family Relations: High—good interactions and support; Low—minimal contact and poor interactions.

Extramarital Relations: High—good outside-marriage social support and mutual partner acceptance; Low—poor outside friendships and social support.

Altruistic Behavior: High—active in helping others; Low—does not help others.

Political Behavior: High—interested in and/or involved in activities; Low—not interested in, nor involved in, political/government events.

Job Characteristics: High—positive job and workplace; Low—negative job characteristics and negative workplace.

Occupational Relations: High—good fellow-worker interactions; Low—poor fellow-worker and supervisor interactions.

Job Satisfiers: High—positive monetary and nonmonetary benefits; Low—low job and performance reinforcement.

Creative/Aesthetic Behavior: High—active in such behaviors; Low—uninvolved in creative/aesthetic activities.

Sports Activity: High—interested and/or active; Low—uninvolved in sport/recreation activities.

Vacation Behavior: High—has positive vacation behaviors; Low—few vacations and/or unrelaxing vacations.

From the above domains and brief summaries, one can see that the QLQ undertakes a fairly comprehensive examination of a person's personal, interpersonal, and vocational activities and satisfaction.

The question then becomes, when do we need or want to obtain a comprehensive assessment of quality of life? This instrument does not measure psychopathology or stress reactions per se. Rather, it provides an assessment of quality of life across a broad number of dimensions and allows identification of both the strong and weak areas and the particular problem areas. As an outcome measure it can serve as an assessment of how situations, life environments, personality, stress reaction effects, and particular events such as chronic illness or chronic pain might be impacting quality of life. The areas in which the scale would appear to provide especially important information might be with general stress management and lifestyle change programs as well as assessing the level of adjustment/coping with particularly stressors such as chronic pain, chronic illness, and significant personal losses. In terms of studying variables associated with low quality of life in general, the scale might function to serve as a dependent measure for the study of workplace environments, community environments, or particular groups (e.g., military). Thus, one needs to define when quality of life, as a construct and as a set of life-functioning areas, rather than particular emotional-cognitive (depression, beliefs) or behavioral (drinking behavior) areas, is a major issue or additional issue for individual or group assessment.

The length of the QLQ may be an issue in some settings/projects, but the assessment usually can be administered in 30 minutes according to the manual. Information is not provided on how reliable or valid a scale(s) would be if only one or two scales were used or the scales were taken out of the context of the entire questionnaire. The QLQ is easy to administer, can be administered by a trained nonprofessional and with the QuikScore form, and is easy to score and profile. The Quality of Life Questionnaire manual (Evans & Cope, 1989), score sheet, and profile form are well presented, as are the instructions in the use of these materials. Machine scoring is not available, but the QuikScore form answer sheet in effect provides a very fast (5-minute) scoring and profile entry. On-line computer administration, which provides scoring, profile, and interpretive paragraphs, is available from the publisher. Interpretation requires a professional trained in test use and the limitations/issues associated with reliability and validity information and the application of test results. With the standard scores presented on the profile form, and a quick reading of the reliability data and validity data provided in the manual, a person trained in test administration and interpretation should be able to interpret the results will relative ease. The manual also provides guidelines on individual scale T-score level interpretations. The type of information provided also makes for easy feedback to the subject in lay terms. Subjects should be able to provide their subjective evaluation of quality of life in each area in response to the feedback.

The authors caution that knowledge of cultural, gender, and socioeconomic factors needs to be taken into account when interpreting the scores. Neither separate norms nor guidelines are provided for the above factors, and the person interpreting the results must possess the knowledge of how these factors might influence the score outcome and how the scores might relate to norms within a particular group.

Technical Aspects

The internal and test-retest reliability of the QLQ domains appears quite good. Kuder-Richardson formula 20 coefficients for each subscale range from .61 to .96 on the original sample and .55 to .97 on a cross-validation sample. For the six subscales and total score for which data are provided, 2-week test-retest reliabilities range from .77 to .89.

The normative data on which interpretation is based were developed by combining the original sample and a second, cross-validation sample for a total sample of 437. Some confusion exists here because in the normative sample data, for some scales the N is listed as 446. It is unclear where the additional subjects came from. Because the difference is small, however, this should not have any effects on the properties of the test or the interpretation.

Intercorrelations between scales are generally low (most in the teens or twenties) and all correlate moderately with total score (.41 to .64). The domains tend to function independently, yet factor analysis does suggest relationships and a factor structure similar to what might be expected from a larger domain picture of quality of life (Physical Well-Being, Personal Growth, Marital Relations, and Parent-Child relations load together; Extended Family Relations, Extramarital Relations, Altruistic Behavior, Political Behavior, and Creative/Aesthetic Behavior load together; Material Well-Being, Job Characteristics, Occupational Relations, Job Satisfiers, Sports Activity, and Vacation Behavior load together).

The items, based on the descriptors of high-low scorers, have content validity but have not been directly validated. No study was reported in which high and low scorers were described by others or by scores on a wide range of measures that would fit with high-low score descriptions. Correlations have been obtained with a variety of other measures, and in general the results are supportive of the descriptors for the scales and for expected relationships with other variables and treatment effects. Life satisfaction ratings for a variety of areas are correlated as expected at moderate levels (e.g., Material Well-Being with neighborhood, .48, and friendships with Extramarital Relations, .52; Garrett, 1983). A measure of physical health was most strongly correlated with Physical Well-Being ($r = .58$; Evans, Burns, Lidkea, & Shatford, 1980). A study on alcohol use among a normal population reported in the manual found that alcohol use was significantly but weakly (-.30 to-.39) correlated with Physical Well-Being, Marital Relations, and Parent-Child Relations. The range and direction of the correlations for other domains with alcohol use are in the expected direction. Evans, Hearn, Levy, and Shatford (1989) included the QLQ in the assessment of stress management effects. The QLQ did show a quality of life improvement at 6-month followup but not a posttreatment or 12-month followup. The 6-month followup result suggests some support for the QLQ as a measure of intervention effectiveness. The manual does not report studies regarding intervention with problem groups, where initial quality of life is expected to be negative, at least among some individuals, and change is expected with treatment.

Critique

The Quality of Life Questionnaire is a comprehensive, psychometrically well-developed measure. The item selection process and resulting good internal and test-retest reliability suggest that the QLQ is a sound instrument. For these reasons alone, the questionnaire should be included in studies and evaluated, both as a dependent and independent measure of the role and effects of quality of life. The QLQ also has attractive qualities for a comprehensive assessment of life area problems as part of clinical assessment procedures. Defining quality of life domain functioning adds to the clinical assessment of particular personality, psychopathology, mood state, and stressor–stress reaction in forming a total picture of the person and present level of functioning. We assume a relationship exists between quality of life, as a cause and as an effect, and a variety of life stressors and psychopathology, but rarely is the quality of life formally assessed. For clinical and clinical research purposes, this measure offers an opportunity to further evaluate such relationships and treatment effects.

Some limitations and unanswered questions regarding the value of the QLQ are pointed out in the manual. The authors note that this is a new instrument and it needs evaluation as a measurement instrument in longitudinal and intervention studies. This reviewer agrees with this point but also feels studies are needed to determine if the QLQ is sufficiently sensitive to personal change to function as an intervention evaluation measure. Levels of mood or distress and problem stress reactions may not result in, or when treated, change the rather global level of life functioning (quality) assessed by the QLQ. The validity studies reported in the manual focus primarily on supporting the domains as measures of that domain, and the correlations with other measures suggest they are appropriate domain measures. What is not reported is relationships with outcome variables such as depression or anxiety. Within a chronically ill group, even if the group mean QLQ score is normal (and in some cases it should be), do particular scales on the QLQ correlate highly with adjustment and mood? In a study with chronic renal disease, scores on a measure called the Illness Effects Questionnaire (IEQ; see Peterson & Greenberg, 1989) correlated .67 with the Beck Depression Inventory scores (Sacks, Peterson, & Kimmel, 1990). The IEQ is in some ways a measure of perceived quality of life on a more narrow range of personal and social functioning. It is necessary to determine if the QLQ, or certain domains, are associated with emotional reactions to loss and perceived loss. The effects of chronic illness and coping with chronic illness has a presumed association with quality of life, and this is one area where a comprehensive evaluation of quality of life should be a necessary part of evaluation. If it can be shown that the QLQ provides important and sensitive measurement in this and other special-stressor populations, the QLQ will represent a major contribution to the assessment of quality of life.

Thus, the QLQ is a measure with strong potential, but it is still questionable whether or not the apparent potential exists. This is the most comprehensive assessment of quality of life this reviewer has seen and thus offers the opportunity for a detailed assessment of multidomains quality of life. I personally will look for situations where I can include the QLQ in research and clinical assessment. One hopes others will begin to evaluate the QLQ as a clinical and research instrument so that in a few years a more definitive assessment can be made of the usefulness of this questionnaire.

References

This list includes text citations and suggested additional reading.

Evans, D.R., Burns, S.R., Lidkea, D.L., & Shatford, L.A. (1980). *The development of continuous measures of health behaviors* (Research Bulletin No. 525). London, Ontario: The University of Western Ontario, Department of Psychology.

Evans, D.R., Burns, J.E., Robinson, W.E., & Garrett, O.J. (1985). The Quality of Life Questionnaire: A multidimensional measure. *American Journal of Community Psychology, 13,* 305–322.

Evans, D.R., & Cope, W.E. (1989). *Quality of Life Questionnaire manual.* Toronto: Multi-Health Systems.

Evans, D.R., Hearn, M.T., Levy, L.M.L., & Shatford, L.A. (1989). *Modern health technologies and quality of life: A generalizability study.* Paper submitted for publication in the *Proceedings of the XXIV International Congress of Psychology* (Vol. 8).

Evans, R.W., Manninen, D.L., Garrison, L.P., Hart, L.G., Blagg, C.R., Gutman, R.A., Hull, A.R., & Lowrie, E.G. (1985). The quality of life of patients with end-stage renal disease. *New England Journal of Medicine, 304,* 309–313.

Garrett, O.J. (1983). *The role of cognitive appraisals, coping, life style well-being and magnitude of events as factors mediating the impact of a stressful life event.* Unpublished master's thesis, The University of Western Ontario, London.

Hearn, M.T., Yuzpe, A.A., Brown, S.E., & Casper, R.F. (1987). Psychological characteristics of *in vitro* fertilization participants. *American Journal of Obstetrics and Gynecology, 156,* 269–274.

Peterson, R.A., & Greenberg, G.D. (1989). The role of perception of illness. *The Health Psychologist, 11,* 2–3.

Sacks, C.R., Peterson, R.A., & Kimmel, P.L. (1990). Perception of illness and depression in chronic renal disease. *American Journal of Kidney Diseases, 15,* 31–39.

John H. Rosenbach, Ed.D.
Professor, Department of Educational Psychology and Statistics,
State University of New York at Albany, Albany, New York.

THE RBH TEST OF LEARNING ABILITY

Richardson, Bellows, Henry, and Company, Inc. Washington,
D.C.: Richardson, Bellows, Henry, and Company, Inc.

Introduction

The RBH Test of Learning Ability (TLA) is a 12-minute, 54-item group instrument designed to be used primarily in business and industry for various personnel decisions (e.g., employee selection, placement, or promotion). Its 54 items are arranged in 18 clusters, each including a verbal item (vocabulary), a spatial item (block counting), and a numerical item (arithmetic problem). The test is steeply scaled; that is, items are ordered in sharply increasing levels of difficulty so that, along with the short time limit (according to the manual), few examinees ever attempt to answer the final items. Although not specified, it would appear that a single, total raw score is used most commonly, although one could compute separate scores for the three dimensions (no information is provided in the manual for this breakdown); the manual does provide, however, a norm table using a standard score scale, with a mean of 20 and a standard deviation of 5.

The original version of this test was published in 1947. The item pool was taken from the U.S. Army General Classification Test (AGCT), which was developed and widely used during World War II for a variety of personnel applications. The 150-item AGCT was a successor to the well-known Army Alpha. The TLA items have remained relatively unchanged over the years. In the most recent 1989 revision (Forms S89 and T89), the arithmetic items have been updated or modernized to reflect social changes, particularly those related to economic inflation. The technical information provided in the manual is based on the earlier forms, but the authors argue "there is little reason to believe that Forms S89 and T89 will behave differently in view of the comparability of the various item statistics" (Richardson, Bellows, Henry, & Co., 1989, p. 2).

The test is presented in a simple, eight-page format (including two blank pages), with the items taking up only three pages. The directions are brief and easy to follow. Although scoring can be done via machine, the publishers provide a scoring key card that is used in the customary way (i.e., by lining up the answer circles with the matching question circles, an old-fashioned yet still effective process, especially if one is dealing with a relatively small number of test booklets). The test items are also conventional, with a four-choice format. The vocabulary items are of the type, "(word) means . . ."; the arithmetic questions (although a few involve simple algebra) use the format, "If Susan buys $4.00 worth of candy and gives the clerk a $5 bill, how much change . . . ?" The spatial test involves counting stacked blocks (the easier items use cubes, the more difficult employ

576

rectangular designs). The examiner's role is minimal: simply passing out the materials, taking the examinees through four sample questions, reading aloud five short sentences, and stopping the test session after 12 minutes.

Practical Applications/Uses

The TLA technical manual, which accompanies the test booklets, is unusual in that no effort is made to address such questions as, what does the TLA measure? Or for what purposes is it most appropriate? The reader is left to infer answers to such questions by being told the item pool was drawn from the AGCT and that the TLA has "enjoyed wide usage in business and industrial selection and promotion" (Richardson et al., 1989, p. 1) and by being presented with over 60 tables containing mostly correlations between the TLA and other standardized tests, measures of job performance, and success in training. In a few tables, data regarding gender and racial comparisons also are provided.

With respect to the question of what the TLA measures, one can begin by considering what others have had to say about the AGCT and the TLA. In one widely used text, Anastasi (1961) discusses the AGCT under the section heading "General Intelligence Tests." She points out that the AGCT has been shown to correlate in the low .70s with amount of schooling, about .90 with the Army Alpha, and in the low .80s with the Otis Higher Mental Ability Examination. All of these r's are consistent with what one would expect of a measure of general intelligence. In another well-known source, *The Seventh Mental Measurements Yearbook*, the TLA is reviewed in the section "Intelligence-Group" (Taylor, 1972).

A second line of evidence relating to what the TLA measures can be found in the correlations of the TLA with other tests as presented in the technical manual. The highest r's (mostly in the .60s and .70s) are obtained with tests of educational achievement, as, for example, the California Achievement Test (13 studies) and The Psychological Corporation Test of Industrial Reading (also 13 studies). Substantially lower r's are reported with measures of such variables as shop arithmetic, mechanical comprehension, or classifying speed. These patterns are again consistent with what one would expect of a general intelligence test.

Based on the above, it seems reasonable to conclude that the TLA would be classified as an intelligence test and be used in accordance with what is known about such instruments, noting, however, that it is much shorter than most other similar tests.

Given the paucity of information concerning what the TLA purportedly measures and the fact it contains only 54 items, it is difficult and perhaps risky to recommend how it should be used. The AGCT was designed for adults (military recruits and personnel), and all of the "validity" data included in the manual (to be discussed later) come from business and industrial settings. Any applications with other age groups or in different contexts would be questionable. Perhaps the most interesting and potentially productive use would occur in research, to investigate more fully both its internal properties (e.g., its three dimensions) and how it relates to a range of external variables. A reliable (which it generally is), short, and well-validated instrument could be a valuable research tool.

In the judgment of this reviewer, the user of the TLA should, first, be well-versed in the field of the measurement of intelligence, especially with respect to issues of validity, and, second, possess a good grasp of how to interpret and apply empirical validity coefficients. These points are addressed more fully in the final sections of this review.

Technical Aspects

Of the 34 pages in the technical manual, 25 are devoted to presenting data (mostly validity coefficients) from almost 200 studies, with N's ranging from 33 to 7,146. (It is possible that some of the studies appear more than once, which would reduce the total number.) Most of the studies appear to involve samples from petroleum and chemical industries, and include jobs such as refinery operator, machinist, and pipefitter. A relatively small number deal with such clerical positions as secretary, keypunch operator, and general clerk. Correlations of the TLA with other tests are presented for over 100 studies (discussed above), and over 80 studies are cited that deal with job-related variables (e.g., success in training, promotion, supervisory ratings, and job level attained). According to the manual, the average correlation coefficient of the TLA with these job-related variables is .24, with a standard deviation of .15. In 56% of these studies, the r's were significantly different from zero at the .05 level. The magnitude of these r's is generally in line with the findings of other researchers. For example, Ghiselli (1966) reported average r's of .30 for tests with training success and of .19 for tests with measures of performance. Incidentally, he also noted that the average r between training and performance was .14. These averages were based on 107 correlations.

A major problem in interpreting the validity coefficients pertaining to job-relatedness stems first from the fact that the r's range from .00 to the .50s; second, the samples are so poorly described (and there are no citations as to where the studies could be found) that the potential user is unable to determine which r's would be relevant in any particular setting. This, along with the finding that about half the r's are smaller than .23, should give one pause when considering this test, as well as all others of similar nature, as a tool in making personnel decisions. It is one thing for the military to employ tests with low validity coefficients when dealing with millions of people, where even miniscule improvements over chance can translate into millions of dollars in savings. It is something quite different, however, to use such tests in more typical business and industrial settings where the numbers are relatively small and where the use of the test may contribute little, if anything, to the accuracy of decisions. It is hoped, however, if a company chooses to engage in such testing that it develop its own norms and validity data.

On the issues of reliability and equivalence of forms, the TLA fares well. The reliabilities hover around .90, which is acceptable for group measures and quite impressive given that the TLA is administered in 12 minutes. Evidence also is presented indicating the two forms of the test are equivalent. On the matter of norms, however, the picture is quite different. The reader is presented with a table of raw score–standard score norms based on 63,691 applicants for entry-level jobs. Beyond that no information is provided. Given the lack of specifics, one has to question whether such a table is of any value at all.

In the manual the authors do address, albeit briefly, two other issues of importance, namely race and gender differences. With respect to race, the manual states that minority examinees as a group (apparently referring to African Americans) score lower than whites but that, with the exception of mean differences, the test works the same way for minority and nonminority examinees. The authors conclude that the fairest use of the test is without special consideration of race/ethnic group membership. It should be noted, however, that the authors fail to provide, systematically, data that would support these claims.

With respect to gender differences, the authors present one table containing the results of nine undescribed studies. The composite results, based on *n*'s of 399 for each sex, show a significant mean difference in favor of the males. However, there was a 94% overlap in the distribution of scores, and the authors claim that separate norms do not appear justified unless it could be reliably shown that females overachieve predicted criteria. Unfortunately, data are not presented that could clarify this point.

Critique

The TLA has been in use for over 45 years and owes its technical heritage to the well-known and widely used AGCT. It is somewhat surprising, therefore, that the authors simply disregard the topics of content and construct validity, and treat the use of norms so casually, especially given the stance taken on test standards by the American Psychological Association and the American Educational Research Association. In fact, one of the most serious indictments one can make about the TLA relates to its name. Potential users who are not well versed in the literature of learning and measurement could well believe they are purchasing a measure of a person's ability to learn. It is not uncommon for those naive to this field to equate intelligence with learning ability. However, the question of how intelligence relates to learning has a long and controversial history, so much so that one must question the wisdom of giving any test a title that suggests it measures the ability to learn. The nature of this controversy is well illustrated in comments made by Cronbach (1972, p. 619)—"Such labels as 'learning potential' and 'capacity' are even more objectionable than the term intelligence"—and by Fleishman and Bartlett (1969, p. 355)—"The general misconception of defining intelligence as the 'ability to learn' dies hard, but the evidence against the notion continues to accumulate."

Despite its serious limitations, the TLA, largely because it is so short and easy to administer, probably will continue to be a popular test in business and industry. One can only hope, therefore, that test users become well informed about the measurement of general intelligence, the importance of understanding issues of construct validity, the problems associated with using validity coefficients (especially when they are low), and the significance of developing local norms. As a quick estimate of general intelligence, and used with appropriate restrictions, the TLA has certain assets. Beyond that, its use is fraught with problems.

References

Anastasi, A. (1961). *Psychological testing* (2nd ed). New York: Macmillan.

Cronbach, L.J. (1972). Analysis of Learning Potential. In O.K. Buros (Ed.), *The seventh mental measurements yearbook* (pp. 618–622). Highland Park, NJ: Gryphon Press.

Fleishman, E.A., & Bartlett, C.J. (1969). Human abilities. In P.H. Mussen & M.R. Rosenzweig (Eds.), *Annual review of psychology* (Vol. 20, pp. 349–380). Palo Alto, CA: Annual Reviews.

Ghiselli, E.E. (1966). *The validity of occupational aptitude tests.* New York: Wiley.

Richardson, Bellows, Henry, and Company, Inc. (1989). *Technical manual: Test of Learning Ability.* Washington, DC: Author.

Taylor, E.K. (1972). The RBH Test of Learning Ability. In O.K. Buros (Ed.), *The seventh mental measurements yearbook* (pp. 701–702). Highland Park, NJ: Gryphon Press.

Brian Bolton, Ph.D.
University Professor, Arkansas Research and Training Center in Vocational Rehabilitation, University of Arkansas, Fayetteville, Arkansas.

REHABILITATION INDICATORS

Leonard Diller, Wilbert Fordyce, Durand Jacobs, and Margaret Brown. New York, New York: New York University Medical Center.

Introduction

The Rehabilitation Indicators (RIs) constitute a comprehensive assessment system for describing the functional capabilities of rehabilitation clients. RIs focus on observable elements of client behavior, using lay terminology to characterize a broad range of content (e.g., vocational, educational, self-care, communication, mobility, household, recreation, and transportation) at varying levels of detail from specific to general. There are three types of RIs: Status Indicators (SIs), which describe categorical statuses or roles that are crucial to clients' functioning; Activity Pattern Indicators (APIs), which describe clients' daily-living activities in terms of frequency, duration, social interaction, and assistance needed; and Skill Indicators (SKIs), which describe the behavioral tools that clients need to attain their rehabilitation goals. In summary, RIs are a standardized procedure for quantifying rehabilitation clients' activities of daily living and their independent-living skills.

The Rehabilitation Indicators Project was carried out primarily during the 9-year period from 1974 through 1982; some project activities continued thereafter under the auspices of the NYU Medical Center. The impetus for the project was the legislative and professional concern with accountability in the provision of rehabilitation services embodied in the Rehabilitation Act of 1973. The specific goal of the Rehabilitation Indicators Project was to develop instruments to measure the impact of rehabilitation services on clients and patients and, thereby, document the benefits of rehabilitation services.

The Division on Rehabilitation Psychology of the American Psychological Association appointed three prominent rehabilitation psychologists (Leonard Diller, Wilbert Fordyce, and Durand Jacobs) to a task force charged with developing a research project to construct accountability measures. The Rehabilitation Indicators Project was funded subsequently by the National Institute of Handicapped Research, and the three task force leaders became co-directors of the project, located at the New York University Medical Center.

In addition to the three project co-directors, the principal investigators included Margaret Brown (project coordinator) and Wayne Gordon (research supervisor). These five individuals co-authored most of the products (instruments, reports, conference papers, journal articles, book chapters, and training manuals) generated over the 10-year duration of the project. The Rehabilitation Indicators Project benefited substantially from the advice and recommendations of almost 100 rehabilitation professionals, including academics, administrators, consumers, legislators, researchers, and service providers, who composed the project advisory committee and five specialized task forces on utilization, activities of daily living, environmental assessment, field testing, and social issues.

As indicated above, RIs describe elements of clients' functional capabilities, including what the individual typically does, or behavioral *output* (assessed by the SIs and APIs), and what the client can do, or behavioral *tools* (assessed by the SKIs). Five features of the RIs are especially noteworthy and deserve emphasis. First, RIs are *comprehensive* in that they cover the entire range of individual behavioral functioning relevant to rehabilitation concerns. Second, RIs address only *observable* and inherently meaningful aspects of behavior, such as "reads the newspaper," "walks up and down stairs," and "brushes teeth." Third, RIs are *organized* into hierarchical taxonomic frameworks, with branching systems of general and specific indicators and modules of disability-relevant indicators. Fourth, RIs refer to client behaviors and roles that are potentially *modifiable* through rehabilitation interventions, and thus they can be used to evaluate changes that occur as a result of rehabilitation services. Fifth, RIs materials were devised to provide maximum *flexibility* for users, with each component (SIs, APIs, SKIs) administrable by interviews with the client or a family member, by the independent observation of a professional or family member, or by self-report. Another aspect of flexibility is that with both SIs and SKIs, the user selects only those items relevant to the purpose for which the RIs are being used.

The RIs assessment materials include instrument forms, training manuals, and various supplementary resources. All materials are printed, with "pencil-and-paper" formats; no apparatus or hardware is required. The Status Indicators (SIs) consist of an interviewer form (4 pages; Diller, Fordyce, Jacobs, & Brown, 1982c), a self-administered form (6 pages; Diller, Fordyce, Jacobs, & Brown, 1981e), and a training manual (47 pages; Diller, Fordyce, Jacobs, & Brown, 1981h). Two approaches to the assessment of Activity Pattern Indicators (APIs) are available, an inventory strategy and a timeline strategy. The APIs inventory materials include the inventory diary (6 pages; Diller, Fordyce, Jacobs, & Brown, 1981c), a follow-up to the inventory diary (6 pages; Diller, Fordyce, Jacobs, & Brown, 1981d), a self-administered inventory (6 pages; Diller, Fordyce, Jacobs, & Brown, 1981a), and a training manual (57 pages; Diller, Fordyce, Jacobs, & Brown, 1981f). The APIs timeline materials include the timeline diary (9 pages; Diller, Fordyce, Jacobs, & Brown, 1982d), a training manual (100 pages; Diller, Fordyce, Jacobs, & Brown, 1981g), a reviewer's manual (82 pages; Brown, 1985b), a coding manual (20 pages; Brown, 1985a), and a data entry and reduction computer program (Orazem, Brown, & Gordon, 1985). Two additional APIs instruments are the delegatable activities form (2 pages; Diller, Fordyce, Jacobs, & Brown, 1982a) and the special events form (2 pages; Diller, Fordyce, Jacobs, & Brown, 1982b). Finally, the Skill Indicators (SKIs) consist of a list of skills (21 pages; Diller, Fordyce, Jacobs, & Brown, 1979b), with brief instructions and illustrative recording formats.

Not all RIs materials are used in any particular assessment situation. The three components (SIs, APIs, and SKIs) can be employed separately, of course. But usually only one mode of administration (i.e., interview, observation, or self-report) is used for each of the RIs components.

To better appreciate the detail and comprehensiveness of the RIs, and to provide a concrete context for the discussion in later sections, examples of RIs from each of the three components follow:

The Status Indicators (SIs) consist of 48 indicators that represent six role or status categories. One indicator from the "Self Care" sphere is *Hired Assistance.* The respondent estimates the number of person-hours of service rendered on a typical day by each of the following possible sources of assistance:

Nurse	_____
Attendant	_____
Chore Services	_____
Interpreter	_____
Reader	_____
Companion	_____
Other Assistant	_____

The Activity Pattern Indicators (APIs) include 106 indicators organized into 15 categories of activities. Fourteen specific activities (see below) comprise the category "Active Recreation." In the APIs inventory strategy, the respondent indicates how often the client engaged in each activity during the previous week. (Duration, location, physical assistance required, and social interaction also may be recorded.)

Ambulate for recreation	_____
Participate in sports or exercise	_____
Care for a pet	_____
Dine out	_____
Visit a night club	_____
Go to a movie	_____
Attend clubs or organizations	_____
Visit a museum or library	_____
Go to a theater, concert, or musical event	_____
Attend a sports event as a spectator	_____
Visit a park, beach, or playground	_____
Travel as recreation	_____
Other active recreation activities	_____

The Skill Indicators (SKIs) consist of more than 700 skills that represent 78 skill modules. The modules in turn are organized under 14 categories of functioning. In the "Vocational Skills" category, the module *Reacting to Instruction/Feedback* contains six indicators (see below). The respondent records whether the client performs the skill independently, with assistance, or not at all (other response formats may be used).

Listens carefully to criticism and feedback	_____
Avoids defensive responses to criticism	_____
Acts on suggestions and instructions of supervisor; follows directions	_____
Asks questions if he/she does not understand criticism or feedback	_____
Seeks help or instructions when having difficulty with task	_____
Works toward and maintains desired changes in behavior	_____

These examples constitute only a small fraction of the total number of statuses, activities, and skills that RIs can assess. Every conceivable aspect of clients' functioning relevant to rehabilitation treatment is covered by one or more categories of RIs, as the following list of categories illustrates:

Status Indicators
　　Vocational
　　Income
　　Education
　　Self-care
　　Family Role
　　Transportation
Activity Pattern Indicators
　　Work Activities
　　Education Activities
　　Rehabilitation Activities
　　Quiet Activities
　　Personal Care Activities
　　Housework Activities
　　Household Business Activities
　　Child-centered Activities
　　Quiet Recreation Activities
　　Active Recreation Activities
　　Telephone Activities
　　Letter Writing/Receiving Activities
　　Socializing Activities
　　Travel Activities
　　Other Activities
Skill Indicators
　　Self-care
　　Mobility
　　Cognition
　　Communication
　　Social ADL
　　Household Business and Housework
　　Childcare
　　Political and Community Skills
　　Selecting an Educational Program
　　Attending School
　　Problem Solving, Vocabulary, and Other Basic Skills
　　Seeking Employment
　　Selecting and Advancing Within a Career Ladder
　　Vocational Skills

RIs can be administered most appropriately to adolescent and adult rehabilitation clients, but, with suitable modification, one also may use them with children with disabilities and nonhandicapped elderly persons, too. A trained professional or paraprofessional must conduct the interviews and supervise the administration of self-report forms and observational procedures when the latter approaches are deemed suitable. Most of the raw data collected with RIs numeric; only API diary formats entail the collection of nonnumeric information, and a coding system quantifies this information. Assessment data for the SIs and SKIs typically are reported in a behavioral format, while APIs usually are summarized as a profile of the client's daily activities. Details about the administration and scoring of RIs appear in the next section.

Practical Applications/Uses

RIs were developed for the explicit purpose of describing rehabilitation clients' statuses or life roles, daily-living activities, and behavioral competencies or skills in ways that are especially helpful in the provision and evaluation of rehabilitation services. Specific applications of the RIs are discussed with reference to three classes of activities: case management, program administration, and program evaluation and research.

1. RIs are potentially applicable in all phases of the rehabilitation process, from the initial diagnostic review of the client's problems, assets, and needs, through the formulation of goals and objectives and the design of an individualized treatment plan, to the measurement of improvement in the client's functioning. RIs constitute a systematic approach to assessment that can enable rehabilitation professionals to plan more effective services for their clients, especially by including clients and their families in the service-planning process. Also, having available objective measures of the client's functioning allows practitioners to monitor progress toward treatment goals.

2. RIs can provide rehabilitation administrators and program planners with a functional assessment database that defines the needs of their client populations, thus establishing an empirical foundation for the design and development of treatment programs. RIs can be used to ensure that eligibility determination for needs-based service programs is a fair and objective process. Also, RIs can enhance the supervision and management of the rehabilitation service process by facilitating cross-disciplinary and interagency communication, a benefit of having a common language system for describing clients.

3. RIs are especially suitable for their original purpose, which is to measure client outcomes in functional terms as a basis for assessing the impact that rehabilitation services have on their lives. A variety of evaluation projects have demonstrated RIs' usefulness for documenting the specific benefits that clients receive from rehabilitation programs. Finally, RIs are applicable in most types of rehabilitation research investigations that address the relationships between the functional implications of disablement, treatment programs, and client outcomes.

RIs can be used appropriately in all rehabilitation settings that provide client services and/or support research, including medical institutions, rehabilitation hospitals, comprehensive rehabilitation facilities, independent living centers, state-federal VR agencies, mental health centers, residential treatment programs, vocational adjustment workshops, and homebound programs. Professionals who would find RIs useful in their work include physicians, nurses, physical therapists, speech therapists, occupational therapists, psychologists, social workers, rehabilitation counselors, job placement specialists, vocational evaluators, independent living counselors, special education teachers, program evaluators, and rehabilitation researchers. RIs have been used in assessing the roles, activity patterns, and skills of clients with various types of intellectual, medical, and sensory handicaps.

Depending on the mode of administration (interview, observation, or self-report), one can administer the RIs in almost any setting, ranging from the examiner's office to the client's home. After carefully reviewing the training materials, any of the professionals listed previously could administer the RIs, as could most para-professionals and aides after training and under the supervision of a professional. The training materials contain detailed instructions for administering the RIs, thus virtually guaranteeing adequate test standardization if the guidelines are followed.

Brief descriptions of the various approaches to data collection using the RIs, with times required for test administration, follow:

Because the Status Indicators (SIs) are essentially just facts about the client, completion of the interview form (with the client or a family member) requires only 5 to 10 minutes. This time may be reduced if the user chooses not to include all SI items. The self-administered SIs take about 10 to 15 minutes for the typical respondent (when this form of data collection is judged appropriate).

The inventory form of the APIs, which consists of a structured list of a week's activities that are reviewed in an interview with the client (in person or over the telephone), requires from 10 to 30 minutes to administer, depending upon the complexity of the client's life and upon the number of response dimensions selected (i.e., frequency, duration, location, functional assistance, and social contact). The client may complete the optional inventory diary for the week preceding the interview by recording his or her daily activities, a procedure that takes 5 to 10 minutes each day. The self-administered inventory, which requires 10 to 20 minutes, can substitute for the interview when time is severely limited, when only frequency and duration data are needed, and when the client is capable of this method of inquiry.

In the timeline interview version of the APIs, the client is asked to recall his or her activities for two recent typical days, one weekday and one weekend day. As an optional supplement to the interview, the client may complete a timeline diary for each of the two preselected days. The diary, which facilitates the accuracy and completeness of the timeline interview, requires about 20 minutes per day of the client's time. Administration of the timeline interview without the diary takes between 40 and 90 minutes, depending on the complexity of the client's life and on the number of response dimensions used. Administration of the timeline interview after review of the completed diary, the purpose of which is to clarify responses, requires between 15 and 30 minutes. As with the inventory interview, API data may be collected via personal interview or over the telephone with the client or, alternatively, data may be collected from an informant familiar with the client's daily activities. The coding of information recorded in the timeline version is based on the APIs activity list, which consists of the same activity categories and indicators as the inventory form.

The two supplementary APIs instruments, the Special Events Form and the Delegatable Activities Form, can be used independently or with either the inventory or timeline version of the APIs. The purpose of the Special Events Form is to find out if the client has participated in major activities that occur infrequently, such as registering to vote, buying a car, or getting married. The Special Events Form may be administered by interview or self-report in 10 to 15 minutes. The purpose of the Delegatable Activities Form is to quantify the extent to which the client can function independently in carrying out household activities, such as cooking, doing laundry, caring for pets, shopping, and caring for children. The Delegatable Activities Form may be administered by interview (client or informant) or self-report in 10 to 15 minutes.

To administer the Skill Indicators (SKIs), users must first identify from the skills list the areas and specific skills relevant to their concerns. Then a measurement scale is selected, which may be as simple as "can do" or "cannot do" or may include an assessment of independence, such as "performs skill independently," "performs skill with assistance," or "does not perform skill." More refined scales can be adopted also, which differentiate between degrees of assistance required in performing the task. The SKIs can be administered by interview with the client or an informant, through observation by professionals or family members, or by self-report. The time required depends on the number of skills evaluated as well as the mode of administration.

For many applications of functional assessment instruments, item scores provide the most useful data. For example, the use of SKIs to diagnose specific skill deficits so that remedial training can be initiated is the most common application of item information. Of course, SKIs can be aggregated (summed) within skill modules to assess overall levels of competency at a broader level of functioning. And module scores could be summed within skill areas, but this probably would result in scores with too much content heterogeneity for most applications. The nature of the SIs (i.e., elemental facts about the client) virtually precludes any type of data aggregation. In other words, the SI items are discrete bits of information about individuals that cannot be combined in any manner without destroying the concrete features of the SIs.

With the APIs, the situation with regard to scoring is entirely different. APIs data by definition is incomplete, if not meaningless, without the ability to generate comparative scores across the entire spectrum of daily activities. Thus, either strategy for recording APIs (inventory or timeline) produces a profile of scores on 15 activity categories. The scores may be frequencies or time percentages, and they may include indices of diversity, mobility, social integration, or independence. The most elaborate and time-consuming procedures involve the reduction of APIs timeline data. As suggested by the materials available, timeline data must be reviewed carefully and prepared for coding before the coder records the numeric scores for statistical analysis. Computer programs have been developed for scoring the APIs, for generating recovery curves for the SKIs, and for reporting the SIs, APIs, and SKIs (Brown & Gordon, 1986).

The final topic of direct relevance to users of RIs concerns the interpretation of indicator scores. Despite the accumulation of extensive data files on subject samples with a variety of handicapping conditions (e.g., spinal cord injury, severe mental retardation, traumatic brain damage, post-stroke, and hearing impairments), no published norms exist for the RIs. And though normative data are not essential for the interpretation of behavioral instruments, such information can help to place an individual's protocol in a broader perspective. Because the item scores by themselves are inherently meaningful, the interpretation of RIs data does not require special training—all of the professionals listed previously are qualified to translate RIs into implications for service planning in their specialties.

Technical Aspects

In the final report on the Rehabilitation Indicators Project, the authors (Diller et al., 1983) thoughtfully discussed the problems associated with evaluating the reliability and validity of the RIs. They argued that traditional notions of reliability and validity are of limited utility when applied to functional assessment instruments like the RIs, an assertion only partially true. A variety of studies that provided data supportive of the psychometric adequacy of the RIs are summarized in the final project report. Selected evidence from the report is presented in abbreviated form in this section.

The Status Indicators (SIs), essentially the hard facts about the client, require very little discretionary judgment in the recording process. During the final stage of development, each of the SIs was refined until across-recorder and test-retest consistency were obtained in 10 out of 10 respondents sampled (for both interview and self-report formats). The authors state that the reliability of the SIs has been maximized through item design and by thorough training of data collectors (accomplished via the detailed SIs training materials). The validity of the SIs was assessed by comparing 100 clients' self-reported SIs with data obtained from available records and significant others. Agreement for all items (except questions dealing with income) exceeded 95%. No studies of predictive validity of the SIs have appeared in the literature.

Because of the practical difficulties in evaluating the reliability of the APIs (e.g., fluctuations in activity patterns from day to day and week to week essentially preclude test-retest designs as meaningful reliability assessment), the RI authors made the decision to invest their resources in validity studies, while relying on evidence in the literature that supports the reliability of activity data. Based on Brown's (1982) review, the authors concluded that under optimal assessment conditions the reliability of activity clusters and summary scores can be quite high for individual clients.

The final report describes several validity studies of the APIs, two examples of which will be presented here. Statistical analyses of API inventory data for 75 spinal cord–injured individuals who used wheelchairs as their principal mode of ambulation located numerous within-sample differences that were consistent with clinical experience or commonsense expectations. For instance, paraplegic individuals participated in a greater variety of activities and used transportation more than quadriplegic individuals. Workers spent more time in vocational, educational, and travel activities that nonworkers, while unemployed individuals spent more time engaged in rehabilitation and recreational activities.

Another investigation of spinal cord–injured patients correlated APIs cluster scores with the scales of two self-report adjustment inventories, and the results were consistent with clinical expectations (e.g., the greater the diversity of activities in which an individual participated, the more he or she was satisfied with life). Also, greater activity diversity was correlated with less depression, and more social participation was correlated with less anxiety and depression.

Because both the selection of a specific set of skill items from the 700+ available and the choice of a measurement scale are decided by the user, reliability and validity data are not available for a "standard form" of SKIs. However, their reliability and validity can be inferred from studies of "tailored" instruments. For example, a trained data collector interviewed 10 resident staff members, each of whom reported on one client's functioning twice (with an interval of 2 weeks between reports) with respect to 269 skills in 18 skill areas. The average test-retest correlation for the 18 skill area scores was .92; in only two areas did coefficients fall below .80. A representative SKIs validity study involved comparisons of groups of paraplegic and quadriplegic patients at three points in time (rehabilitation admission, discharge, and 1 year later) on grooming skills (four items) and bathing skills (eight items). Statistical analyses confirmed all predicted differences (e.g., paraplegic individuals performed better than quadriplegic persons on all skills). In contrast to indicators requiring predominantly motor skills, mobility, or physical strength, paraplegic and quadriplegic individuals differed little or not at all in skills involving predominantly social judgment and cognitive abilities.

In addition to the data produced by formal validity investigations, considerable evidence supporting the validity and utility of RIs is embedded in the 35 research and demonstration studies summarized in the final report (Diller et al., 1983, pp. 47–52). Six of these studies have been published in journal articles and books, thus making extended reports available to interested readers. Very brief descriptions follow here for reference. O'Neill, Brown, Gordon, Schonhorn, and Greer (1981) and O'Neill, Brown, Gordon, and Schonhorn (1985) used APIs and SKIs to measure changes in the activity patterns and skills of severely disabled former residents of total-care institutions who were placed in supportive community living arrangements. Brown, Gordon, and Ragnarsson (1987) investigated the impact of financial and educational resources on the activity patterns of persons with severe disabilities by comparing APIs profiles of matched samples of men with spinal cord injury and nondisabled men. Efthimiou, Gordon, Sell, and Stratford (1981) used APIs to document the benefits of electronic assistive devices on the daily living of male quadriplegic individuals. Gordon and Diller (1983) compared the typical daily activities of 29 right brain–damaged stroke patients with those of a matched sample of 85 nondisabled adults using APIs time usage indices, for the purpose of identifying the unmet needs of stroke patients after completion of the in-hospital rehabilitation phase. Gordon et al. (1980) used APIs to describe the effects of a psychosocial intervention on adult cancer patients by comparing participants in the psychosocial rehabilitation program with patients who did not participate in the program.

The authors concluded from their review of the reliability and validity studies pertaining to the RIs that the evidence is "encouraging but not complete." They recommend reasonably that when users have some doubts about the reliability or validity of RIs for their particular purposes, it would be wise to conduct preliminary feasibility studies before actually implementing the RIs on a permanent basis for diagnostic or evaluative applications.

Critique

The conceptual foundation of the RIs is excellent—well thought out, precise and detailed, and highly relevant to assessment goals in rehabilitation. Likewise, the technical development of the RIs was outstanding, from the initial construction of the instruments, through the preliminary tryouts and revisions, to the field tests and demonstrations of the final versions of the SIs, APIs, and SKIs and the writing of the training materials. In essence, the RIs provide rehabilitation professionals with a standardized common-language system for assessing their clients' daily-living activities and the skills required for living independently.

The instruments were carefully designed to ensure maximum user flexibility and application in a wide range of rehabilitation settings. Most of the instrument forms are attractively printed and published in a standard format, but a few are still available only in typed and photocopied draft form. The training manuals for SIs and APIs, including the extensive materials for completing, reviewing, and coding the timeline version of the APIs, were all carefully developed, with detailed instructions for administration and numerous examples and practice exercises. However, none of the manuals has been published in final form. They are distributed in typed and photocopied draft form with updates and corrections inserted on separate pages.

The reliability and validity data supporting the RIs are fairly extensive and generally good. However, as the authors caution, the evidence is not complete. Two omissions are especially noteworthy. First, studies of the convergence of methods (interview, observation, self-report) within each of the components (SIs, APIs, SKIs) using disability-homogeneous samples—a design analogous to parallel form reliability—would contribute greatly to knowledge about the RIs. Second, studies of the psychometric structure of the RIs components based on correlation among items, modules, and clusters, both within and across components, would address the construct validity of the RIs.

Even though the RIs are probably used primarily as behavioral assessment devices for diagnostic and evaluative purposes, some tabled normative data would help professionals establish a framework for understanding a client's functioning, relative to a group of individuals with similar disabilities. For example, publishing distributions (percentages) for SIs and SKIs items, as well as means and standard deviations for APIs cluster scores and SKIs module and area scores, for a half dozen populations of persons with disabilities would provide handy reference points for practitioners. Of course, if the computerized RIs system could incorporate normative information in the reports, this would present the optimal form of usage. In fairness to the authors, however, it should be recognized that 10 years after formal termination of project funding, the records upon which an adequate normative database could be established are probably irretrievable.

The RIs are the result of a large-scale instrument development effort that spanned 9 years and benefited from the expertise of outstanding researchers and the input from knowledgeable advisory groups. The product is a comprehensive, standardized, and flexible assessment system of direct relevance to rehabilitation service provision, especially applicable with clients who have severe disabilities. Yet, despite the substantial investment of time and resources, the RIs probably are not widely used at present in rehabilitation settings. It is certainly safe to say that utilization of the RIs is not commensurate with the instruments' potential to assist service providers and program evaluators in their work.

One can attribute underutilization of the RIs in good part to the premature termination of project funding in 1982. The National Institute of Disability and Rehabilitation Research should allocate sufficient funds for the collection of new normative data and the completion of the RIs project. Then the instruments and manuals that comprise the RIs should be published in final form and disseminated, along with the computerized RIs scoring and reporting programs, as a package to major rehabilitation agencies and facilities in the United States. The package should also include a brief manual containing summaries of the demonstration studies that illustrate concretely the range of feasible applications of RIs in rehabilitation settings.

For further information about the RIs, write to the Rehabilitation Indicators Project, Behavioral Science Department, Institute of Rehabilitation Medicine, New York University Medical Center, 400 East 34th Street, New York, NY 10016.

References

This list includes text citations as well as suggested additional reading.

Brown, M. (1982). *Actual and perceived differences in activity patterns of able-bodied and disabled men.* Unpublished doctoral dissertation, New York University, New York.

Brown, M. (1985a). *Activity Pattern Indicators: Timeline diary: Coding manual.* New York: New York University Medical Center.

Brown, M. (1985b). *Activity Pattern Indicators: Timeline diary: Reviewing manual.* New York: New York University Medical Center.

Brown, M. (1988). The consequences of impairments in daily life activities: Beliefs vs. reality. *Rehabilitation Psychology, 33,* 173–184.

Brown, M., Diller, L., Fordyce, W., Jacobs, D., & Gordon, W. (1980). Rehabilitation Indicators: Their nature and uses for assessment. In B. Bolton & D.W. Cook (Eds.), *Rehabilitation client assessment* (pp. 102–117). Baltimore: University Park Press.

Brown, M., Diller, L., Gordon, W.A., Fordyce, W.F., & Jacobs, D.F. (1984). Rehabilitation Indicators and program evaluation. *Rehabilitation Psychology, 29,* 21–35.

Brown, M., & Gordon, W.A. (1986). Rehabilitation Indicators: A complement to traditional approaches to patient assessment. *Central Nervous System Trauma, 3,* 25–35.

Brown, M., & Gordon, W.A. (1988). The impact of impairment on activity patterns of children. *Archives of Physical Medicine and Rehabilitation, 68,* 878–882.

Brown, M., Gordon, W., & Diller, L. (1983). Functional assessment and outcome measurement: An integrative review. *Annual Review of Rehabilitation, 3,* 93–120.

Brown, M., Gordon, W.A., & Diller, L. (1984). Rehabilitation Indicators. In A.S. Halpern & M.J. Fuhrer (Eds.), *Functional assessment in rehabilitation* (pp. 187–203). Baltimore: Brookes.

Brown, M., Gordon, W.A., & Ragnarsson, K.T. (1987). Unhandicapping the disabled: What is possible? *Archives of Physical Medicine and Rehabilitation, 68,* 206–209, 317.

Diller, L., Fordyce, W., Jacobs, D., & Brown, M. (1979a). *Activity Pattern Indicators: Activity list.* New York: New York University Medical Center.

Diller, L., Fordyce, W., Jacobs, D., & Brown, M. (1979b). *Skill Indicators: Skill list.* New York: New York University Medical Center.

Diller, L., Fordyce, W., Jacobs, D., & Brown, M. (1981a). *Activity Pattern Indicators: Self-administered inventory.* New York: New York University Medical Center.

Diller, L., Fordyce, W., Jacobs, D., & Brown, M. (1981b). *Activity Pattern Indicators: Timeline.* New York: New York University Medical Center.

Diller, L., Fordyce, W., Jacobs, D., & Brown, M. (1981c). *Daily activities diary: Inventory.* New York: New York University Medical Center.

Diller, L., Fordyce, W., Jacobs, D., & Brown, M. (1981d). *Inventory diary follow-up.* New York: New York University Medical Center.

Diller, L., Fordyce, W., Jacobs, D., & Brown, M. (1981e). *Self-administered Status Indicators.* New York: New York University Medical Center.

Diller, L., Fordyce, W., Jacobs, D., & Brown, M. (1981f). *Training materials: Activity Pattern Indicators: Inventory.* New York: New York University Medical Center.

Diller, L., Fordyce, W., Jacobs, D., & Brown, M. (1981g). *Training materials: Activity Pattern Indicators: Timeline.* New York: New York University Medical Center.

Diller, L., Fordyce, W., Jacobs, D., & Brown, M. (1981h). *Training materials: Status Indicators.* New York: New York University Medical Center.

Diller, L., Fordyce, W., Jacobs, D., & Brown, M. (1982a). *Activity Pattern Indicators: Delegatable activities.* New York: New York University Medical Center.

Diller, L., Fordyce, W., Jacobs, D., & Brown, M. (1982b). *Activity Pattern Indicators: Special events.* New York: New York University Medical Center.

Diller, L., Fordyce, W., Jacobs, D., & Brown, M. (1982c). *Status Indicators: Interview format.* New York: New York University Medical Center.

Diller, L., Fordyce, W., Jacobs, D., & Brown, M. (1982d). *Timeline diary (instructions, weekday, weekend day).* New York: New York University Medical Center.

Diller, L., Fordyce, W., Jacobs, D., Brown, M., Gordon, W., Simmens, S., Orazem, J., & Barrett, L. (1983). *Final report: Rehabilitation Indicators Project* (Grant No. G008003039). New York: New York University Medical Center.

Efthimiou, J., Gordon, W.A., Sell, G.H., & Stratford, C. (1981). Electronic assistive devices: Their impact on the quality of life of high level quadriplegic persons. *Archives of Physical Medicine and Rehabilitation, 62,* 131–134.

Gordon, W.A., & Diller, L. (1983). Stroke: Coping with a cognitive deficit. In T.E. Burish & L.A. Bradley (Eds.), *Coping with chronic disease: Research and applications* (pp. 131–135). New York: Academic Press.

Gordon, W.A., Freidenbergs, I., Diller, L., Hibbard, M., Wolf, C., Levine, L., Lipkins, R., Ezrachi, O., & Lucido, D. (1980). Efficacy of psychosocial intervention with cancer patients. *Journal of Consulting and Clinical Psychology, 48,* 743–759.

O'Neill, M., Brown, M., Gordon, W., Orazem, J., Hoffman, C., & Schonhorn, R. (1990). Medicaid versus state funding of community residences: Impact on daily life of people with mental retardation. *Mental Retardation, 28,* 183–188.

O'Neill, J., Brown, M., Gordon, W., & Schonhorn, R. (1985). The impact of deinstitutionalization on activities and skills of severely/profoundly retarded multiply handicapped adults. *Applied Research in Mental Retardation, 6,* 361–371.

O'Neill, J., Brown, M., Gordon, W., Schonhorn, R., & Greer, E. (1981). Activity patterns of retarded adults within institutions and the community: A longitudinal study. *Applied Research in Mental Retardation, 2,* 367–379.

Orazem, J., Brown, M., & Gordon, W. (1985). *Activity Pattern Indicators: Timeline diary: Data entry and reduction program.* New York: New York University Medical Center.

Brian Rabian, Ph.D.
Assistant Professor of Psychology, University of Southern Mississippi, Hattiesburg, Mississippi.

REVISED CHILDREN'S MANIFEST ANXIETY SCALE

Cecil R. Reynolds and Bert O. Richmond. Los Angeles, California: Western Psychological Services.

Introduction

The Revised Children's Manifest Anxiety Scale (RCMAS; Reynolds & Richmond, 1978) is a 37-item self-report questionnaire designed to assess both the degree and nature of trait or chronic anxiety in children and adolescents. The instrument is intended for children aged 6 to 19 and can be administered both individually and to groups.

Items presented to the examinee describe anxious thoughts, feelings, or actions that he or she might experience, such as "I am afraid of a lot of things" (Reynolds & Richmond, 1978). The child responds by circling either "yes," if he or she thinks the item is descriptive, or "no" if it is not descriptive. Although the RCMAS is intended to be completed in a paper-and-pencil format, it also can be administered in an interview format, where items are read aloud by the examiner who circles the response indicated by the child. In either format, the examiner's role is limited almost entirely to explaining the meaning of terms when the child expresses confusion about an item.

Factor analyses on the RCMAS (Reynolds & Paget, 1981; Reynolds & Richmond, 1978) have yielded several factors, each of which corresponds to a scale or subscale score that can be generated from the measure: 1) Total Anxiety, 2) Physiological Anxiety, 3) Worry/Oversensitivity, 4) Social Concerns/Concentration, and 5) a Lie factor. The scoring and interpretation of these factor scores will be discussed in later sections.

The term *manifest anxiety* was coined by Taylor (1951) to describe anxiety as a drive that strengthens or energizes response tendencies in individuals. To measure this drive-level anxiety in adult populations, Taylor developed the Manifest Anxiety Scale (MAS; Taylor, 1953), which used select items from the Minnesota Multiphasic Personality Inventory (MMPI; Hathaway & McKinley, 1942). The MAS was found useful as both an experimental and a clinical measure. In 1956, undoubtedly because of its utility, a children's version of the MAS was developed by Castaneda, McCandless, and Palermo. The Children's Manifest Anxiety Scale (CMAS) used items from the MAS, rewording them when necessary to make them more appropriate for children. Based on a sample of 386 children from Grades 4 through 6, the 53-item CMAS was found to consist of two factors: a general anxiety factor and a lie scale (Castaneda, McCandless, & Palermo, 1956).

Although the CMAS became a popular tool of both clinicians and experimenters, it was criticized for being too narrow in focus, too difficult for young children and slow learners to understand (Reynolds & Richmond, 1978), and for being psychometrically unsound (Flanagan, Peters, & Conry, 1969).

To address these concerns about the CMAS, in 1978 Reynolds and Richmond developed the Revised Children's Manifest Anxiety Scale, subtitled "What I Think and Feel." Test development was based on administration of the measure to 329 school-aged children in Grades 1 through 12. Starting with a total of 73 items (the original 53 items of the CMAS plus 20 more generated by a panel of experienced clinicians and teachers), only those anxiety items with an item-to-total test score correlation of >.40 were retained. This work resulted in the current structure of the RCMAS—28 anxiety items and 9 lie items.

The RCMAS was then standardized on a sample of 4,972 children between the ages of 6 and 19 who represented 13 states and more than 80 school districts across the United States (Reynolds & Richmond, 1985). Normative data for these children, including a complete breakdown of the sample by age, ethnicity (white and black), and gender, are contained in the RCMAS manual.

Although most research using the RCMAS has been on North American samples, the measure has also been translated into German (RCMAS-G; Boehnke, Silbereisen, Reynolds, & Richmond, 1986), Spanish (Richmond, Rodrigo, & de Rodrigo, 1988), and Japanese (Richmond, Sukemune, Ohmoto, Hawamoto, & Hamazaki, 1984). The extent to which North American norms can be generalized to other cultures is unclear. Although the factor structure found in North American samples has been replicated using data from a German sample (Boehnke et al., 1986), a study of Zimbabwean children failed to produce any interpretable anxiety factors (Wilson, Chibaiwa, Majoni, Masukume, & Nkoma, 1990). These findings suggest that caution when employing the RCMAS to previously unstudied samples of children.

Practical Applications/Uses

The RCMAS was designed as an "objective" measure of anxiety experienced by a child. The measure is useful in its provision of a total score of anxiety, a lie scale, and individual factor scores for separate types of anxiety. As a result, it can provide valuable information to clinicians regarding the way in which children experience anxiety and thus may play a role in determining the focus of assessment and/or treatment. For example, a clinician may choose to employ relaxation training for the child whose RCMAS scores indicate that his experience of anxiety is largely physiological in nature. In addition to its application in the clinical setting, the RCMAS generates information that may also be of use to others who work with children, such as teachers or school counselors. For example, information from the RCMAS might help teachers to recognize and address the emotional needs of students as well as their academic needs.

Although some have suggested that high RCMAS scores may indicate clinical anxiety in children, the relationship of RCMAS scoring to the presence of specific anxiety diagnoses has gone virtually unstudied. One investigation, however, based on a sample of 139 children between the ages of 8 and 12, found that the Worry/

Oversensitivity factor significantly distinguished a group of clinically anxious children from a group with other emotional and behavioral disorders (Mattison, Bagnato, & Brubaker, 1988). In this study, however, no other RCMAS factor score was found to differentiate diagnostic groups, and the findings regarding the differentiating abilities of the Worry/Oversensitivity factor have yet to be replicated. One study specifically examining the RCMAS Lie scale found that the Lie factor can be used as a short measure of social desirability (Hagborg, 1991). Again, however, these findings have not yet been replicated.

Optimally, the RCMAS may be useful in the identification of children with anxiety disorders when employed in conjunction with other data-gathering techniques, such as parent- or teacher-completed behavior checklists, interviews, and direct observation.

The RCMAS is intended for children with at least third-grade reading ability, although, as previously mentioned, the items can be read aloud to subjects who experience reading problems. Group administration is recommended only for children who are 9½ years and older. Administration in an individual format is especially recommended for younger children and for those with reading problems.

Because the RCMAS is a self-report measure and is relatively short, there are virtually no constraints on the settings in which it can be administered. Historically its uses have been in the clinician's office, the research facility, and the classroom. As this suggests, the RCMAS usually is administered by clinicians, researchers, and, less often, teachers and school counselors. Although the RCMAS can be used in the classroom, administration should follow the American Psychological Association's ethical principles for test administration. Thus, ideally the administrator should be knowledgable about the measure and its purposes, and should be trained in the procedures for administration.

Instructions for the administrator are outlined in the manual (Reynolds & Richmond, 1985) with great clarity. Directions for the child are printed on the front of the measure itself. Specifically, examinees are instructed to circle, after reading each item, the word "yes" if the item is generally true about them or "no" if the item is not true. When administered to a group, items can be read aloud by the administrator while the children read each silently to themselves. Few other instructions are given to the administrator, except that no interpretation of items should be made for the child.

All five scores yielded by the RCMAS can be generated in a matter of minutes by hand, although a scoring template is also available. Scoring the instrument involves tallying the number of items circled "yes" for each subscale and across all 28 anxiety items in the case of the Total Anxiety score. Thus, the Total Anxiety score may range from 0 to 28. The Physiological subscale consists of 10 items, the Worry/ Oversensitivity scale consists of 11 items, and the Social Concerns/Concentration factor consists of 7 items. The Lie scale, whose items describe ideal behavior (e.g., "I am always kind"), is scored by tallying "yes" responses across its 9 items.

The manual of the RCMAS provides tables for converting raw scores into standardized scores and percentiles, based on the standardization sample described previously. Norms also are provided for the total normative sample, as well as for each ethnic and sex combination for blacks and whites. It is recommended that the clinician or researcher refer to these norms when interpreting RCMAS scores.

The manual offers guidelines for making interpretations, although some discretion is left to the clinical judgment of the examiner. Thus, interpretation of scores and subscores is best reserved for clinicians and other professionals trained in the use of clinical measures, and more specifically, for those who are familiar with the administration, scoring, and interpretation of the RCMAS.

In general it is recommended that one attach significance to scores that fall more than 1 standard deviation above the mean scores of the normative sample. As stated above, these means and standard deviations are supplied in the RCMAS manual. A high score for the Total Anxiety scale suggests that the child's current level of anxiety is significantly elevated compared to other children his or her age. In order to make determinations regarding the nature of the current anxiety experienced by the child, examination of the anxiety subscales is necessary. For example, endorsement of many of the items comprising the Physiological Anxiety subscale likely indicates that the child experiences specific physiological responses when anxious. Further, a high score on the Physiological subscale coupled with little or no endorsement of the Worry/Oversensitivity or Social Concern/Concentration items might suggest that the child's experience of anxiety is primarily physical. An elevated score on the Worry/Oversensitivity subscale suggests nervousness, oversensitivity to environmental pressures, and a tendency to internalize the feelings of anxiety. Reynolds and Richmond (1985) offer that a high score on this subscale may suggest a need to provide the child with skills enabling him or her to express the experience of anxiety more outwardly. Finally, the items making up the Social Concerns/Concentration subscale express concerns about living up to others' expectations, which may interfere with the child's ability to concentrate. Children who show an elevated score on this scale may be concerned that they do not compare favorably to their peers in academics, athletics, and so forth.

Elevated scoring on the Lie subscale can imply a number of interpretations. In general, however, it has been suggested that high scores may indicate a child who has an idealized or inaccurate view of him- or herself. It also may be possible that a child who endorses a significant number of lie items may be trying to "fake good" or present him- or herself in a positive light. This suggested interpretation has some empirical support. As mentioned previously, one investigation has reported that the Lie scale correlates significantly with a measure of social desirability. Before making any interpretations involving the Lie scale, however, administrators should be aware that some age-related differences have been found for this scale. Specifically, young children tend to have higher Lie scores than do adolescents (Reynolds & Richmond, 1985).

The content of individual RCMAS items also may help the clinician gain insight into specific matters of concern to the child, or into specific situations that tend to elicit anxiety. In addition, individual items may be used as tools to make inquiries of the child, giving him or her the opportunity to verbalize feelings further and opening up topics for discussion.

Technical Aspects

The reliability and validity of the RCMAS has been studied rather thoroughly, on a variety of samples. Only a brief overview of the available literature is presented here. For a more detailed discussion of the psychometric properties of the RCMAS, the reader is directed to the manual (Reynolds & Richmond, 1985).

Reliability of the RCMAS has most often been assessed via internal consistency coefficients, such as Cronbach's alpha. On the test development sample of 329 children, Grades 1 through 12, an alpha of .83 was found for the Total Anxiety scale. Reliability alpha coefficients of above .80 for the Total Anxiety scale have also been reported for samples of children in kindergarten (Reynolds, Bradley, & Steele, 1980), children with learning disabilities (Paget & Reynolds, 1984), English-speaking Nigerian children (Pela & Reynolds, 1982), and children of superior intelligence (Reynolds & Scholwinski, 1985). Reynolds and Paget (1982) reported coefficient alpha reliabilities for the standardization sample of 4,972 children. For the overall sample, reliability of the Total Anxiety scale was .82. When this sample was broken down by ethnicity (black and white), age (12 individual age levels), and gender, reliability coefficients remained consistently high (Reynolds & Richmond, 1985). With the exception of black females younger than 12, coefficient alphas were consistently above .80. In sum, sufficiently high internal consistency coefficients have been found on a variety of samples, across a broad age range, and across gender and ethnic groups (with the exception of young black females).

Less information is available regarding the internal reliability of specific RCMAS subscales. The standardization sample produced internal consistency coefficients ranging from .56 to .80 across 11 age groups for the three anxiety subscales (Reynolds & Paget, 1982). Although alpha coefficients for Worry/Oversensitivity were mostly high, reliabilities for the Physiological and the Social Concerns/ Concentration subscales were less consistent across age groups and, therefore, more suspect. However, given the brevity of the individual subscales, their overall reliabilities can be considered satisfactory. The standardization sample also yielded alpha coefficients consistently above .70 across age, gender, and ethnicity groups for the RCMAS Lie factor (Reynolds & Paget, 1982). It appears, however, that this factor may be less reliable with younger children, who in general have alpha coefficients in the range of .50 to .70, than with older children, whose coefficients tend to be above .70 (Reynolds & Richmond, 1985).

Regarding test-retest reliability, thus far studies have focused exclusively on the Total Anxiety score and the Lie subscale. For the Total Anxiety score, a test-retest reliability coefficient of .68 has been reported for a sample of 534 elementary school children tested 9 months apart (Reynolds, 1981). A test-retest coefficient of .98 has been reported for 99 Nigerian children tested 3 weeks apart (Pela & Reynolds, 1982). Thus, the RCMAS Total Anxiety score appears to be stable across both long-term and short-term intervals. One study has also supported the stability of the Lie factor over a short-term interval ($r = .94$; Pela & Reynolds, 1982), but data on its long-term stability are somewhat less impressive ($r = .58$; Reynolds, 1981).

One noticeable limitation to the reliability studies that have been conducted to date on the RCMAS is the lack of reliability data for children above Grade 7. While the manual acknowledges this weakness, a literature search by this reviewer found no recent articles addressing the problem.

Evidence for the construct validity of the RCMAS comes from a number of sources, including factor analytic studies. Examining the items for the standardization sample, Reynolds and Paget (1981) employed the method of principal factors followed by varimax rotation in order to derive those factors with the greatest clinical utility. Reynolds and Paget (1981) found the same five-factor structure that had been reported previously for the CMAS by Finch, Kendall, and Montgomery (1974) and for the RCMAS by Reynolds and Richmond (1979). The consistency of results across studies has been taken as support for good construct validity. Further evidence for the scale's construct validity comes from factor analyses that have replicated the findings of Reynolds and Paget (1981), albeit with much smaller samples (Paget & Reynolds, 1984; Reynolds & Scholwinski, 1985).

Other studies (Reynolds, 1980, 1982, 1985) have examined convergent and divergent validity by comparing RCMAS scores to scores from the State-Trait Anxiety Inventory for Children (STAIC; Spielberger, 1973). Reynolds (1980) reported a significant Pearson product-moment correlation of .85 between the RCMAS and STAIC A-trait scale for 42 children ages 6 to 16. In the same study, no significant correlation was found between the RCMAS and the STAIC A-state scale. Based on these data, Reynolds (1980) concluded that the RCMAS is a valid measure of chronic anxiety. Reynolds reported similar findings (i.e., a strong correlation between the RCMAS and the STAIC A-trait scale coupled with a nonsignificant correlation between the RCMAS and the STAIC A-state scale) in two additional studies, one involving a sample of third- and fourth-graders (Reynolds, 1982) and the second a sample of 465 high-IQ children (Reynolds, 1985). At least one recent study has supported the convergent and discriminant validity of the RCMAS Total Anxiety score with a sample of adolescents (Lee, Piersel, Friedlander, & Collamer, 1988). To date, validity of the RCMAS subscales has not been examined adequately. In one study using behavioral ratings from parents and teachers as measures of comparison (Lee, Piersel, & Unruh, 1989), little evidence was found to support the validity of the Physiological subscale. As the authors noted, however, a better test of the validity of this subscale would come from comparisons with more direct, objective measures of physiological functioning.

At least one study has raised questions regarding the construct validity of the RCMAS. Studying large samples of schoolchildren in England and the United States, Ollendick and Yule (1990) found that the RCMAS was significantly correlated with a self-report measure of depression, suggesting that the scale may not, in fact, be measuring trait anxiety as proposed. However, the authors acknowledge that their findings, rather than indicating poor construct validity of the RCMAS, might simply reflect the high degree of comorbidity between anxiety and depression reported by others (Last, Strauss, & Francis, 1987).

Critique

The Revised Children's Manifest Anxiety Scale is arguably the most widely used self-report measure of children's anxiety. Its value to both clinicians and researchers comes from its relative brevity and from its ability to provide information on the specific nature of anxiety experienced by the child. Unfortunately, the ease of administration and scoring of this measure can sometimes lead to its misuse, especially in clinical settings. Specifically, clinicians may use the RCMAS as an independent measure of clinical anxiety, a practice that has not yet been supported empirically and that may result in the inaccurate and inappropriate labeling of some children. However, when used properly (i.e., in conjunction with other information-gathering techniques, such as diagnostic interviews), the RCMAS can be a constructive asset in helping clinicians better identify and understand the nature of anxious symptomatology experienced by children.

Despite the extensive empirical work that has been conducted on the psychometric properties of the RCMAS, more work in this area is necessary. Overall, studies conducted to date have supported the scale's good reliability and validity. However, data are lacking on the reliability of the measure for older children and on the validity of the anxiety subscales. These limitations need to be addressed through empirical studies before the full value of the measure can be assessed.

References

Boehnke, K., Silbereisen, R.K., Reynolds, C.R., & Richmond, B.O. (1986). What I Think and Feel—German experience with the revised form of the Children's Manifest Anxiety Scale. *Personality and Individual Differences, 7,* 553–560.

Castaneda, A., McCandless, B., & Palermo, D. (1956). The children's form of the Manifest Anxiety Scale. *Child Development, 27,* 317–326.

Finch, A.J., Kendall, P.C., & Montgomery, L.E. (1974). Multidimensionality of anxiety in children: Factor structure of the Children's Manifest Anxiety Scale. *Journal of Abnormal Child Psychology, 2,* 331–336.

Flanagan, P.J., Peters, C.J., & Conry, J.L. (1969). Item analysis of the Children's Manifest Anxiety Scale with the retarded. *Journal of Educational Research, 62*(10), 472–477.

Hagborg, W.J. (1991). The Revised Children's Manifest Anxiety Scale and social desirability. *Educational and Psychological Measurement, 20,* 423–427.

Hathaway, S.R., & McKinley, J.C. (1942). *The Minnesota Multiphasic Personality Inventory.* Minneapolis: University of Minnesota Press.

Last, C.G., Strauss, C.C., & Francis, G. (1987). Comorbidity among childhood anxiety disorders. *Journal of Nervous and Mental Disease, 175,* 726–730.

Lee, S.W., Piersel, W.C., Friedlander, R., & Collamer, W. (1988). Concurrent validity of the Revised Children's Manifest Anxiety Scale (RCMAS) for adolescents. *Educational and Psychological Measurement, 48,* 429–433.

Lee, S.W., Piersel, W.C., & Unruh, L. (1989). Concurrent validity of the physiological subscale of the Revised Children's Manifest Anxiety Scale: A multitrait-multimethod analysis. *Journal of Psychoeducational Assessment, 7,* 246–254.

Mattison, R.E., Bagnato, S.J., & Brubaker, B.H. (1988). Diagnostic utility of the Revised Children's Manifest Anxiety Scale in children with DSM-III anxiety disorders. *Journal of Anxiety Disorders, 2,* 147–155.

Ollendick, T.H., & Yule, W. (1990). Depression in British and American children and its relation to anxiety and fear. *Journal of Consulting and Clinical Psychology, 58,* 126–129.

Paget, K.D., & Reynolds, C.R. (1984). Dimensions, levels, and reliabilities on the Revised Children's Manifest Anxiety Scale with learning disabled children. *Journal of Learning Disabilities, 17,* 137–141.

Pela, O.A., & Reynolds, C.R. (1982). Cross-cultural application of the Revised Children's Manifest Anxiety Scale: Normative and reliability data for Nigerian primary school children. *Psychological Reports, 51,* 1135–1138.

Reynolds, C.R. (1980). Concurrent validity of What I Think and Feel: The Revised Children's Manifest Anxiety Scale. *Journal of Consulting and Clinical Psychology, 48,* 774–775.

Reynolds, C.R. (1981). Long-term stability of scores on the Revised Children's Manifest Anxiety Scale. *Perceptual and Motor Skills, 53,* 702.

Reynolds, C.R. (1982). Convergent and divergent validity of the Revised Children's Manifest Anxiety Scale. *Educational and Psychological Measurement, 42,* 1205–1212.

Reynolds, C.R. (1985). Multitrait validation of the Revised Children's Manifest Anxiety Scale for children of high intelligence. *Psychological Reports, 56,* 402.

Reynolds, C.R., Bradley, M., & Steele, C. (1980). Preliminary norms and technical data for use of the Revised Children's Manifest Anxiety Scale with kindergarten children. *Psychology in the Schools, 17,* 163–167.

Reynolds, C.R., & Paget, K.D. (1981). Factor analysis of the Revised Children's Manifest Anxiety Scale for blacks, whites, males, and females with a national normative sample. *Journal of Consulting and Clinical Psychology, 49,* 352–359.

Reynolds, C.R., & Paget, K.D. (1982, March). *National normative and reliability data for the Revised Children's Manifest Anxiety Scale.* Paper presented at the annual meeting of the National Association of School Psychologists, Toronto.

Reynolds, C.R., & Richmond, B.O. (1978). What I Think and Feel: A revised measure of children's manifest anxiety. *Journal of Abnormal Child Psychology, 6,* 271–280.

Reynolds, C.R., & Richmond, B.O. (1979). Factor structure and construct validity of "What I Think and Feel: The Revised Children's Manifest Anxiety Scale." *Journal of Personality Assessment, 43,* 281–283.

Reynolds, C.R., & Richmond, B.O. (1985). *Revised Children's Manifest Anxiety Scale: Manual.* Los Angeles: Western Psychological Services.

Reynolds, C.R., & Scholwinski, E. (1985). Dimensions of anxiety among high IQ children. *Gifted Child Quarterly, 29,* 125–130.

Richmond, C.R., Rodrigo, G., & de Rodrigo, M. (1988). Factor structure of a Spanish version of the Revised Children's Manifest Anxiety Scale in Uruguay. *Journal of Personality Assessment, 43,* 281–283.

Richmond, B.O., Sukemune, S., Ohmoto, M., Hawamoto, H., & Hamazaki, T. (1984). Anxiety among Canadian, Japanese and American children. *Journal of Psychology, 116,* 3–6.

Spielberger, C.D. (1973). *Preliminary manual for the State-Trait Anxiety Inventory for Children ("How I Feel Questionnaire").* Palo Alto, CA: Consulting Psychologists Press.

Taylor, J.A. (1951). The relationship of anxiety to the conditioned eyelid response. *Journal of Experimental Psychology, 41*(2), 81–92.

Taylor, J.A. (1953). A personality scale of manifest anxiety. *Journal of Abnormal Social Psychology, 48,* 285–290.

Wilson, D., Chibaiwa, D., Majoni, C., Masukume, C., & Nkoma, E. (1990). Reliability and factorial validity of the Revised Children's Manifest Anxiety Scale in Zimbabwe. *Personality and Individual Differences, 11,* 365–369.

Jerry B. Hutton, Ph.D.

Professor of Psychology and Special Education, East Texas State University, Commerce, Texas.

REYNOLDS CHILD DEPRESSION SCALE

William M. Reynolds. Odessa, Florida: Psychological Assessment Resources, Inc.

Introduction

The Reynolds Child Depression Scale (RCDS; Reynolds, 1989) is a recently developed self-report measure of depressive symptomatology for children ages 8 through 12 years (third through sixth grade). Developed for use in schools and clinics, children respond to each of the 30 items by indicating how they have been feeling for the previous 2 weeks. The purpose of the RCDS is to provide a direct way of estimating the severity of depressive symptoms in children and, thus, to contribute to the procedures used for screening and identifying childhood depression.

The author of the RCDS, William M. Reynolds, is a professor in the Department of Educational Psychology at the University of Wisconsin–Madison. Dr. Reynolds also has published two other self-report scales, the Reynolds Adolescent Depression Scale (RADS; Reynolds, 1986) and the Suicidal Ideation Questionnaire (SIQ; Reynolds, 1987), each reviewed in previous volumes of *Test Critiques* (Vols. VII and VIII, respectively). Although the publication of the RCDS was preceded by the RADS, the development the former was initiated in 1981 and the two instruments are quite similar.

The RCDS is packaged in a box that contains the professional manual, 25 hand-scorable answer sheets (Form HS), and the scoring key. An available mail-in scoring service assists in scoring and reporting on large-group administrations. The manual is well organized and easy to understand. A neutral title *(About Me)* appears on the yellow answer sheets. Either individually or in groups, children respond to 29 of the items by marking a 4-point scale to show how they have been feeling within the past 2 weeks, indicating if they have experienced the stated feeling almost never, sometimes, a lot of the time, or all the time. Six of the items consist of positive statements (i.e., feeling happy, feeling important, etc.), and reversed scoring is used for seven of the items. The last item presents five faces (a 5-point scale) that range from an obvious frown (sad face) to an obvious smile (happy face), and the child has to mark the one that shows how she or he feels.

Practical Applications/Uses

The RCDS purports to measure the severity of self-reported symptoms of depression. It is intended to be used for screening depression in large groups of schoolchildren as well as in the individual assessment of depression. Although the RCDS is not promoted as an instrument that diagnoses depression independent of other assessment procedures, self-reported symptoms constitute a very important part of the diagnostic picture when identifying depression in children or adolescents (Kazdin, 1989; Reynolds, 1990). The RCDS may also be used in research to assess treatment outcomes and to study depression in children.

The author recommends and describes the use of the RCDS within a three-stage screening model. The multiple-gate model starts with group screening using Form G of the RCDS. It is noted that 8% to 12% of the children tested at Stage 1 score at or above the cutoff score. These children are readministered the RCDS in small groups of 5 to 10, and those who meet or exceed the cutoffs for depressive symptomatology progress to Stage 3. A psychologist, counselor, or mental health professional administers an individual interview to Stage 3 children, and those who meet the criteria for clinical depression are referred for treatment and intervention.

The RCDS may be employed in schools, clinics, and hospitals, or other settings where children are taken to receive a service. Those who use the RCDS must have professional knowledge of childhood psychopathology, diagnostics, and the professional and ethical guidelines regarding the use and interpretation of psychological tests and information (American Educational Research Association, American Psychological Association, & National Council on Measurement in Education, 1985; American Psychological Association, 1981). Qualified users may include psychologists and other mental health professionals.

As noted earlier, the RCDS is designed for children ages 8 through 12 or Grades 3 through 6. It may be used with children who are gifted or with those who are considered to have disabilities. It is probably not appropriate for children whose cognitive abilities are developmentally younger than 8 years (even if their chronological age falls within the specified range) or for those whose language proficiency is below the expected minimal level of competence (8 years). Examiners can compensate for the presence of a learning or reading disability by administering the RCDS orally. Also, children with Attention Deficit Hyperactivity Disorder (ADHD) may benefit from the pacing inherent in an oral administration of the RCDS.

The test materials recommend that 5 to 10 children be tested in a group, although some intact classrooms may be tested as one group (20 to 30 students). Children below 10 years of age (third and fourth grades) and those with reading problems or learning disabilities should have the RCDS presented orally. As reported by the author, the readability of the RCDS is at the second-grade level. Most examinees can complete the RCDS in about 10 minutes.

The person who administers the RCDS should be aware of the need to present the test in a neutral way, to avoid establishing a negative or positive mental set. The manual provides clear directions for individual and group administration.

Hand scoring is easy using the transparent key. The user places the key over the marked items on each of the two pages of the questionnaire and then totals the point values to reach the raw score. By using the tables in the manual, he or she may convert raw scores to percentile ranks. The tables show the percentile ranks when comparing raw scores to the total sample (1,620), total number of boys (751), or total number of girls (842). Also, the norms are provided for Grades 3 through 6 for the total sample as well as for boys or girls. Similar to the RADS, six of the RCDS items are marked on the answer key as "critical items." Children who endorse four or more of these items at a critical level should be singled out for further assessment regardless of the total score.

The publisher of the RCDS also offers a group scoring service, which may be desirable when screening large groups, evaluating programs, or conducting large research projects. When the group scoring service is appropriate, the administrator should plan to use Form G. The mail-in service provides a report that includes total scores, number of items completed, and percentile ranks for each child. Data for the group are summarized in the report, indicating which children had invalid protocols who met or surpassed stated cutoff levels.

Interpretation of the RCDS results is uncomplicated. First, one inspects the overall raw score to see if it meets or exceeds the cutoff. Next, the percentile ranks may be viewed to see how the child's score compares to the overall normative group and to his or her specific group (e.g., fourth-grade girls). Item analysis may be directed first to the raw scores on the six critical items and then to specific items, which may raise questions concerning endogenous depression (feeling sick, having stomachaches, experiencing sleeping problems or fatigue, etc.) or more cognitive problems (self-depreciation, low self-worth). Finally, the determination may be made to conduct further assessment, to defer to a later review, or to refer to other professionals. Of course, the responses of a child to the RCDS should not be used in isolation but rather integrated into information received from multiple sources.

Technical Aspects

The RCDS was normed on 1,620 U.S. children from schools in Midwestern and Western states. Some of the children were in second ($n = 18$) and seventh ($n = 60$) grades, but the remainder were in third through sixth grades. The sample, with a mean age of 10.45 years ($SD = 1.17$ years), consisted of 52.9% girls. The race/ethnicity percentages were as follows: white 70.9%, black 18.4%, Hispanic 4.8%, Asian 3.7%, and other 2.1%. The socioeconomic status (SES) of the sample, based on teacher ratings for 611 children, was estimated as mostly middle class (85.1% received SES-level ratings of 2,3, or 4 out of a 6-point rating scale).

Reynolds and Graves (1989) report information concerning the internal consistency and stability (test-retest) reliability of the RCDS. California children ($n = 220$) were administered the RCDS in their classrooms two times, with the testing intervals ranging between 3½ to 4½ weeks. The raw score differences for gender, race/ethnicity, and age were reported as nonsignificant. The coefficient alphas of .88 on the first administration and .90 on the second suggest good internal consistency. A moderate to high correlation coefficient of .85 was reported for the total group, suggesting good stability reliability. Separate correlational analyses for racial/ethnic groups found the stability coefficients to range from a low of .72 (Asians, $n = 33$) to .90 (blacks, $n = 73$). The stability coefficients were higher for girls ($r = .86$) than for boys ($r = .83$), and ranged from .81 for third-graders ($n = 55$) to .92 for sixth-graders ($n = 18$). Other studies noted in the manual (Breen, 1987; Lopez, 1985) reported data consistent with the Reynolds and Graves study.

The manual reports good content validity for the RCDS by showing how the items include the symptoms of depression specified by DSM-III-R (American

Psychiatric Association, 1987) as well as from formal interview schedules developed by other authors (Petti, 1978, 1985; Pozanski et al., 1984). In addition, 24 of the 30 RCDS items correlate with the total score at or above the .40 magnitude. Criterion-related validity is supported by a significant correlation coefficient of .76 ($p < .001$) between the RCDS and a structured clinical interview, the Children's Depression Rating Scale–Revised (Posanski et al., 1984). Construct validity is supported by correlational studies between the RCDS and another self-report measure of depression, the Children's Depression Inventory (Baker & Reynolds, 1988; Bartell & Reynolds, 1986; Lopez, 1985; Reynolds, Anderson, & Bartell, 1985; Stark, 1984). The manual reports significant correlations between the RCDS and measures of self-concept and anxiety, as well as data showing factorial validity.

Critique

The RCDS is a brief, self-report measure of the severity of depressive symptomatology in children enrolled in Grades 3 through 6. It may be used for screening or as a part of assessment procedures used to diagnose childhood depression. The instrument RCDS appears both reliable and valid, and it is obvious that much work has been done to support its appropriate use.

The RCDS has one major weakness that practitioners may wish to consider: the norms do not approximate demographic expectations regarding geographic regions. The author selected the standardization group from only the Midwestern and Western states. Further, the percentages of children from these two areas are not reported in the manual. The rationale Reynolds offers for not providing nationally representative norms is based on the observation that children from various locations attain similar RCDS mean scores. In addition, he argues that no data exist to support the contention that depression demonstrates geographic differences. However, the lack of nationally representative norms is a serious shortcoming if one accepts the standards described by Hammill, Brown, and Bryant (1992).

Two other points may interest prospective users. First, percentile ranks and suggested cutoff raw scores provide the major indicators of the severity of depressive symptomatology. Some practitioners may prefer reporting standard scores, and these are not available in the RCDS manual. Second, practitioners sensitive to ethnic representation should be aware of the apparent underrepresentation of Hispanics or Latinos in the standardization group (4.8%).

The weaknesses of the RCDS may not restrict its usefulness as a screening tool. Also, as long as multiple sources of data are used, the RCDS could add meaningfully to the information necessary to make clinical judgments regarding the presence or absence of childhood depression. The author's extensive publications in the area of depression may contribute to the confidence one gives to the clinical utility of the RCDS.

References

American Educational Research Association, American Psychological Association, & National Council on Measurement in Education. (1985). *Standards for educational and psychological testing.* Washington, DC: American Psychological Association

American Psychiatric Association. (1987). *Diagnostic and statistical manual of mental disorders* (3rd ed. rev.). Washington, DC: Author.

American Psychological Association. (1981). Ethical principles of psychologists. *American Psychologist, 36,* 633–638.

Baker, J.A., & Reynolds, W.M. (1988, August). *An examination of the benefits of training teachers to recognize depressed students in their classrooms.* Paper presented at the 96th Annual Convention of the American Psychological Association, Atlanta.

Bartell, N.P., & Reynolds, W.M. (1986). Depression and self-esteem in academically gifted and nongifted children: A comparison study. *Journal of School Psychology, 24,* 55–61.

Breen, D.T. (1987). *Changing family structures: An intervention study in the schools.* Unpublished doctoral dissertation, University of Wisconsin–Madison.

Hammill, D.D., Brown, L., & Bryant, B.R. (1992). *A consumer's guide to tests in print* (2nd ed.). Austin, TX: PRO-ED.

Kazdin, A.E. (1989). Childhood depression. In E.J. Mash & R.A. Barkley (Eds.), *Treatment of childhood disorders* (pp. 135–166). New York: Guilford.

Lopez, N. (1985). *Assessing depressive symptoms using the Child Depression Scale and the Children's Depression Inventory: A cross-cultural comparison of children in Puerto Rico and the United States.* Unpublished doctoral dissertation, University of Wisconsin–Madison.

Petti, T.A. (1978). Depression in hospitalized child psychiatry patients: Approaches to measuring depression. *Journal of the American Academy of Child Psychiatry, 17,* 49–59.

Petti, T.A. (1985). Scales of potential use in the psychopharmacologic treatment of depressed children and adolescents. *Psychopharmacology Bulletin, 21,* 951–977.

Pozanski, E.O., Grossman, J.A., Buchsbaum, Y., Banegas, M., Freeman, L., & Gibbons, R. (1984). Preliminary studies of the reliability and validity of the Children's Depression Rating Scale. *Journal of the American Academy of Child Psychiatry, 23,* 191–197.

Reynolds, W.M. (1986). *Reynolds Adolescent Depression Scale.* Odessa, FL: Psychological Assessment Resources.

Reynolds, W.M. (1987). *Suicidal Ideation Questionnaire.* Odessa, FL: Psychological Assessment Resources.

Reynolds, W.M. (1989). *Reynolds Child Depression Scale.* Odessa, FL: Psychological Assessment Resources.

Reynolds, W.M. (1990). Depression in children and adolescents: Nature, diagnosis, assessment, and treatment. *School Psychology Review, 19,* 158–173.

Reynolds, W.M., Anderson, G., & Bartell, N. (1985). Measuring depression in children: A multimethod assessment investigation. *Journal of Abnormal Child Psychology, 13,* 513–526.

Reynolds, W.M., & Graves, A. (1989). Reliability of children's reports of depressive symptomatology. *Journal of Abnormal Child Psychology, 17,* 647–655.

Stark, K.D. (1984). *A comparison of the relative efficacy of self-control therapy and behavior therapy for the reduction of depression in children.* Unpublished doctoral dissertation, University of Wisconsin–Madison.

James A. Moses, Jr., Ph.D.

*Clinical Associate Professor of Psychiatry and Behavioral Sciences,
Stanford University School of Medicine, and Coordinator,
Psychological Assessment Unit, Department of Veterans Affairs
Medical Center, Palo Alto, California.*

RIGHT-LEFT ORIENTATION TEST

*Arthur L. Benton, Kerry deS. Hamsher, Nils R. Varney, and
Otfried Spreen. New York, New York: Oxford University
Press.*

Introduction

Some patients with syndromes of lateralized brain disease experience difficulty in distinguishing between the right and left sides of the body. This deficit has been recognized as a symptom of neurologic disease for approximately a century, and numerous variants of it have been described (for a literature overview and discussion, see Benton, Hamsher, Varney, & Spreen, 1983, chapter 2). Professionals have realized the need for an objective, standardized assessment procedure to identify and analyze right-left disorientation for many years, and a variety of procedures have been proposed for its evaluation. The Right-Left Orientation Test (RLO) offers a brief procedure, suitable for routine clinical bedside testing, that clearly identifies the nature of the underlying cognitive deficit in the individual case and distinguishes specific laterality orientation deficit from linguistic, motor, or spatial disturbance.

The RLO is a hierarchically organized, 20-item measure that allows one to investigate variants of the ability to identify lateralized body parts. On verbal command, subjects carry out crossed and uncrossed movements with their hands and arms, relative both to their own bodies and to that of the examiner facing them. A frontal view image of a person may be used in place of a live examiner if desired. Benton et al. (1983, p. 12, Table 2-2) note that the human image model should be at least 15 inches high and 6 inches wide for the latter administrative procedure.

Both spatial perception and verbal analysis are necessary to consistently and accurately apply the labels *right* and *left* to one or the other side of the body. The RLO systematically separates these features and provides a basis for analysis of them in right-left disorientation syndrome variants (Benton et al., 1983). RLO tasks are organized in five sequential levels of complexity, outlined by Benton et al. (1983, p. 11, Table 2-1) as follows:

Orientation toward one's own body:

The subject is instructed to

    A. point to single lateral body parts on his or her own body (e.g., the left ear);

    B. execute double uncrossed commands (e.g., touch the *left* ear with the *left* hand); and

C. execute double crossed commands (e.g., touch the *left* ear with the *right* hand.

Orientation toward a confronting person:

With the object of orientation being either the confronting examiner or a front-view representation of a person, the subject is instructed to

D. point to single lateral body parts.

Combined orientation toward one's own body and a confronting person:

The subject is instructed to

E. place either the left or right hand on a specified lateral body part of the confronting person (e.g., his or her *right* hand on the *left* ear of the confronting person).

For a complete listing of RLO items for all forms of the test (A, B, R*, L*), see Benton et al. (1983, pp. 17–20). The RLO is provided commercially for clinical use in two parallel forms (A and B) for examining patients with normal or partial residual motor response capacity in both arms. The two forms differ in that the left and right elements of each item are reversed in the alternate forms. This form parallelism allows for retesting with lessening of practice effect. For patients who are hemiplegic, Benton et al. (1983) present two forms of the RLO specifically designed for examinees who can respond motorically with one hand only: Form R*, for patients with a right body side hemiplegia, and Form L*, for those with a left body side hemiplegia. Note that Forms R* and L* are clinically descriptive, experimental procedures; as yet they have not been normed. Specific items for all RLO forms and samples of the standardized answer sheets appear in Benton et al. (1983, pp. 17–20).

The principal author of the RLO, Arthur L. Benton, received his A.B. (1931) and A.M. (1933) degrees from Oberlin College, followed by his Ph.D. from Columbia University (1935). He began his career as an assistant in psychology, first at Oberlin College (1931–33), then at Columbia University and New York State Psychiatric Institute (1934–36), and finally of Cornell University Medical College (1936–39), where he subsequently served as a staff psychologist. He was appointed as an attending psychologist at New York Hospital–Westchester Division and as a psychologist in the Student Personnel Office of the City College of New York from 1939 to 1941. After serving on active duty in the U.S. Navy during and after the Second World War (1941–46), he was appointed as Associate Professor of Psychology at the University of Louisville Medical School and as chief psychologist at the Louisville Mental Hygiene Clinic and the Louisville General Hospital (1946–48). From 1948 to 1958 he served as Professor of Psychology and Director of the Graduate Training Program in Clinical Psychology at the University of Iowa, and then, for the next two decades, (1958–78) as Professor of Psychology and Neurology. Dr. Benton has continued to coauthor theoretical and research papers and books since 1978, when he became Professor Emeritus at the University of Iowa.

Benton's fundamental contributions to the field of clinical neuropsychology have been acknowledged extensively and internationally. He has received honorary Doctor of Science (Cornell College, 1978) and Doctor of Psychology (University of Rome, 1990) degrees, as well as numerous other honors and awards, including the Distinguished Service Award of the Iowa Psychological Association

(1977), the Distinguished Professional Contribution Award from the American Psychological Association (1978), the Outstanding Scientific Contribution Award of the International Neuropsychological Society (1981), The Samuel Torrey Orton Award from the Orton Dyslexia Society (1982), the Distinguished Service and Outstanding Contributions Award from the American Board of Professional Psychology (1985), and the Distinguished Clinical Neuropsychologist Award from the National Academy of Neuropsychology (1989).

Benton is a past president of both the American Orthopsychiatric Association (1965–66) and the International Neuropsychological Society (1970–71), and he served as secretary-general of the Research Group on Aphasia for the World Federation of Neurology (1971–78). He has been a lecturer or visiting scholar at the University of Milan (1964), Hôpital Sainte-Anne, Paris (1968), Hadassah-Hebrew University Medical School, Jerusalem (1969), Free University of Amsterdam (1971), University of Helsinki (1974), University of Melbourne (1977), University of Minnesota Medical School (Baker Lecturer, 1979), University of Victoria, British Columbia (Lansdowne Scholar, 1980), and the University of Michigan (1986), plus the Directeur d'Études Associé, École des Hautes Études, Paris (1979) and a visiting scientist at the Tokyo Metropolitan Institute of Gerontology (1974).

Benton has authored, coauthored, or edited 12 books and monographs, approximately 150 professional journal articles, and 22 historical reviews in the area of clinical neuropsychology and behavioral neurology. He is recognized as a pioneer and a leading authority in the area of clinical neuropsychology.

The standardized, commercially published version of RLO appears with the clinical manual for this and other tests in the Benton-Iowa Neuropsychological Test Battery (Benton et al., 1983). Coauthors of this clinical manual with Dr. Benton are Kerry deS. Hamsher, Ph.D. (Associate Professor of Neurology, University of Wisconsin Medical School); Nils R. Varney, Ph.D. (staff neuropsychologist, Department of Veterans Affairs Medical Center, Iowa City, Iowa); and Otfried Spreen, Ph.D. (Professor Emeritus, Department of Psychology, University of Victoria, Victoria, British Columbia, Canada).

Practical Applications/Uses

The RLO is not designed to be exhaustive in its treatment of right-left orientation skill deficit. Its procedures were adapted from more extensive inventories designed to investigate right-left orientation and related skills very thoroughly (Benton, 1959; Benton & Kemble, 1960; see also Benton et al., 1983, pp. 10–11, for discussion). On the RLO the patient points rather than speaks to indicate the lateralized response, to avoid confounding the evaluation of right-left orientation with linguistic deficit, particularly anomia. The motor pointing response required is relatively minimal and the specific type of creditable motor response is variable, so that even hemiparetic patients often can be examined with the usual RLO procedure involving the use of both arms alternatively. As noted previously, however, Forms R* and L* are available for nonnormative evaluation of hemiplegic patients.

The administration time for the RLO is approximately 5 minutes. The manual does not suggest the qualifications necessary to administer the RLO, but one would expect that a competent examiner would be a multidisciplinary health care professional with a thorough knowledge of brain-behavior relationships. A trained technician could administer this test to a patient, but a professional such as a neuropsychologist or a neurologist should interpret the results.

The examiner should read each command to the patient slowly and clearly. The *right* or *left* word in each command is underlined on the test form and should be emphasized verbally by the examiner as the item is read to the patient. Each fully correct response receives 1 point; no credit is allowed if any error is made. Possible scores thus range from 0 to 20 points. Once the examiner is sure that the patient is oriented to task, nonresponse should be prompted with repetition of the command. Spontaneous corrections of response errors by the patient are credited as correct.

Response slowness and need for prompting should be noted qualitatively by the examiner. Benton et al. (1983, p. 13), however, report that women and ambidextrous persons generally tend to show relatively slower responses to RLO questions, as many persons in these groups reportedly "lack an intuitive sense of the difference between the right and left sides of the body, and hence experience difficulty in making rapid discriminations (Benton, 1959; Harris & Gitterman, 1978; Wolf, 1973)." Because the RLO questions are untimed, slowness of response would not elevate the error score. These qualitative observations in normal subgroups are of particular value as examples of normal variants, so that relative slowness of response alone is not overinterpreted as a pathognomonic sign in groups without known neurologic disorder.

Benton et al. (1983) recommend recording the patient's incorrect responses to allow for qualitative analysis of errors. Differentiation of a patient's misunderstanding of the body part to be pointed at from true laterality errors may be important for distinguishing true right-left disorientation errors from those due to auditory comprehension deficit or naming difficulty. For example, if a patient is asked to point to his *right* foot with his *left* hand and points to his left foot with his left hand, this error suggests difficulty with right-left orientation but not with understanding the elements of the command (hand, foot). If he points to his right ear instead of his right foot with his left hand, then the laterality of the response would be correct but the patient may have difficulty understanding some of the words said to him. In the example cited, such errors could present indications for further testing of auditory comprehension, naming, or body part identification confusion.

A pattern of "systematic reversal" occurs occasionally in children and in some aphasic adults in which the individual consistently reverses identification of the left and right body sides. When the person with this deficit is asked to use the left hand or arm to point to some structure on the right side of the body, the right hand or arm is used to point to the left body side in almost every instance. The same sort of systematic reversal would occur in this individual if the left and right elements of the example were reversed. In such cases there is confusion over the verbal labels *right* and *left* but not with regard to the spatial aspect of body laterality, as the lateral reversal errors are consistent. A special RLO scoring category is designed to quantify this error pattern objectively. In the case of an RLO protocol containing a sizeable number of right-left reversal responses, the examiner rescores the protocol using a special system: the reversed scores (right for left or vice versa) are scored as correct, and the correct scores are scored as errors. This "reversal score" gives an index of the consistency of reversal of lateralized responses. The consistency with which the reversal score is higher than the conventional score provides a measure of the systematic reversal tendency. A consistent systematic reversal score would fall in the range of 17–20 points when the items were reverse scored for laterality.

RLO Forms A and B were normed jointly on a mixed sample of 234 subjects representing either normal controls or medical patients without past or present evidence of brain disease. The sample consisted of 126 men (53.8%) and 108 women (46.2%). Breakdown of the sample by control group health status is not provided in the manual (Benton et al., 1983, pp. 13–14).

On the average, normal men and women above and below age 50 typically obtain nearly errorless scores on the RLO regardless of whether their educational level exceeds or is below 12 years (for detailed test statistics, see Benton et al., 1983, p. 14, Table 2-3). More than half of the subjects in the normative sample made errorless scores of 20 points, and 96% of them scored in the range of 17–20 points. Scores in the range of 17–20 points are classified as normal; those less than 17 points are classified as defective on a performance level basis. Because no normative sample subjects made two or more errors on the identification of left and right parts of their own bodies, an error score of 2 or more points on the 12 RLO "own body" laterality identification items also is classified as defective.

The following summary classification of RLO score patterns comes from the test manual (Benton et al., 1983, p. 14), illustrating five level and pattern of performance categories that are important for clinical interpretation of RLO results:

A. *Normal:* total score of 17–20, not more than one error on the 12 "own body" items.

B. *Generalized defect:* total score of less than 17, more than one error on the 12 "own body" items.

C. *"Confronting person" defect:* total score of less than 17, not more than one error on the 12 "own body" items.

D. *Specific "own body" defect:* more than one error on the 12 "own body" items, not more than two errors on the eight "confronting person" items.

E. *Systematic reversal:* total score of 17–20 when performance is scored in reverse fashion, not more than one error on the 12 "own body" items.

Technical Aspects

In validational studies of the RLO with neurologic clinical groups, Benton et al. (1983, p. 15) studied patients with bilateral lesions (34 cases), right-hemispheric lesions (20 cases), left-hemispheric lesions with aphasia (20 cases), and left-hemispheric cases without aphasia (20 cases) to evaluate distributional syndrome patterns of the five-part classification schema. In the bilateral lesion group they found 35% incidence of normal RLO performance, 38% incidence of generalized defect, and 27% incidence of "confronting person" defect patterns. In the right-hemispheric group they reported 65% with normal performance on RLO and 35% with a "confronting person" defect. Among the left-hemispheric-lesioned subjects without aphasia, 80% showed normal performance on RLO, 10% had a generalized defect, and 10% had a "confronting person" defect. Among the left-hemispheric subjects with aphasia, only 25% produced a normal performance pattern; 30% had a generalized defect, 40% had a "confronting person" defect, and 5% had a specific "own body" defect. No subject in any of these lesion groups showed the pattern of systematic reversal.

The bilateral brain disease group, most of whom are described in the test manual as "at least moderately demented," showed no consistent pattern of RLO performance as a group. Errors in the right-hemispheric group were confined to the "confronting person" defect, which suggests a deficit associated with spatial-perceptual difficulty. A very high proportion (80%) of the nonaphasic left-hemispheric-lesioned group showed normal RLO performance, probably because of the sparing of linguistic and right-hemisphere-dependent spatial skills. The left-hemispheric-lesioned aphasic group showed a wide variety of RLO performance patterns without a consistent error syndrome trend, as was the case with the bilaterally lesioned group. Benton et al. (1983) go on to note that right-left disorientation for identification of one's own body parts is atypical of patients who are neither demented nor aphasic. The differential diagnostic significance of the RLO for identifying brain disease in cases of aphasia and dementia remained moot at the time they wrote (for discussion, see Benton et al., 1983, p. 16).

Important subsequent work using an abbreviated version of the RLO to clarify these questions in the differential diagnosis of dementia was published recently by Fischer, Marterer, and Danielczyk (1990). They excluded patients with advanced dementia who produced severely defective RLO scores because they could not perform a single body part identification screening task on a confronting human figure. These investigators showed that right-left disorientation with the "confronting person" defect was significantly greater in patients with Alzheimer-type dementia (ATD) than in those with multi-infarct dementia (MID), even when the degree of cognitive deficit was equated across the groups. The "confronting person" defect was present at all severity phases of the ATD syndrome alone. The "own body" right-left disorientation symptom pattern did not differentiate the MID and ATD groups, and this sign was present only in the severely demented cases. In the MID cases with focal brain disease, item analysis showed significant relationships of RLO "own body" and "confronting person" scores to indices of both spatial perception and auditory comprehension. In the ATD group the RLO "own body" items correlated significantly with auditory comprehension score but *not* with visuospatial ability. The "confronting person" RLO items did not correlate with either auditory comprehension difficulty or visuospatial ability in the ATD group.

Fischer et al. (1990) suggest that their preliminary evidence of early appearance of the "confronting person" defect only in ATD, followed by late appearance of the "own body" RLO deficit in both ATD and MID syndromes, might have diagnostic value in the early-phase differential diagnosis of ATD from MID. Their findings should be duplicated and their diagnostic-group-by-experimental-task analytic methods of investigation emulated in subsequent syndrome-analytic work with the RLO.

Approximately one third of right-hemispheric patients show right-left disorientation relative to the body of a confronting examiner. In a supplementary analysis, Benton and his collegues examined the protocols of their right-hemispheric-lesioned patients with significant right-left disorientation for evidence of errors due to failure to respond to stimuli in the patient's left visual field. They found no evidence for this response tendency in their sample. The authors noted that their patients had recovered from the acute phase of brain disease (often stroke), so that the incidence of visual neglect may have been lessened as a result. The possibility of occurrence of this pattern due to left visual field neglect or defect in acute poststroke patients should be borne in mind by clinicians who use the RLO.

Critique

The very low base rate of right-left disorientation in neurologically normal populations makes defective performance on the RLO a useful screening sign of brain dysfunction by itself. Right-left orientation difficulty is a potentially important sign that can contribute to the syndrome analysis of lateralized brain disease, particularly in the presence of aphasia or dementia. Specific trends in RLO deficit patterns are already identifiable within lateralized brain lesion groups. More specific patterns of deficit on the RLO may be elicited with analysis of more circumscribed lesions (e.g., anterior vs. posterior hemispheric lesions) and in analysis of specific disease states, such as various subtypes of aphasic disorder or dementing disorder. The work of Fischer et al. (1990) is particularly instructive in this regard. Their attention to subunits of the RLO rather than to the RLO global score alone, plus their use of visuospatial and linguistic marker variables to highlight the basis of the RLO performance patterns in diagnostic groups, should help future researchers to attempt additionally refined syndrome-pattern analyses of this kind. The RLO's potential to specify symptom patterns in cerebral disease is just beginning to be explored, but preliminary results above suggest which diagnostic groups and loci of cerebral disease are most likely to be initially productive to analyze. Investigation of subcortical versus cortical dementing syndromes also may prove fruitful in clarifying the anatomic and syndromatic aspects of right-left disorientation in cerebral disease.

The relationship of right-left orientation to linguistic and spatial variables as a topic of experimental interest requires more controlled study as well. One way to approach this problem might be to study children with soft neurologic signs that include relatively mild linguistic, visual-spatial, and right-left disorientation difficulty. Those children with specific learning disability would be a particularly useful group to study in this regard. Use of some of the more complex forms of right-left orientation tasks to which Benton et al. (1983) allude in their literature review on the RLO also might be used productively to study the relationship of right-left orientation to linguistic and spatial variables in normals and even gifted subjects, to build a more general theoretical model of this neuropsychological skill.

The RLO is a clinical task, suitable for consulting room and bedside use. It is an inexpensive, well-standardized, objectively scored, clinically rich source of interpretive hypotheses about visual-spatial, linguistic, and cognitive performance-level skills. Results from the RLO can be incorporated easily with neurologic examination findings and usually should be elicitable when more complex, lengthy, formal tests of higher cortical functions are not possible during the phase of acute neurologic illness. As such, the RLO can provide multiple baseline results that are comparable over a wide range of function as the patient recovers from the acute phase of the illness. It provides specific information about an important area of higher cortical functioning that most standardized neuropsychological procedures overlook. Thus it offers an important contribution to the literature and a procedure that should become a standard part of a clinical neuropsychological examination in which personal and extrapersonal spatial orientation is at clinical issue.

References

Benton, A.L. (1959). *Right-left discrimination and finger localization: Development and pathology.* New York: Hoeber-Harper.

Benton, A.L., Hamsher, K.deS., Varney, N.R., & Spreen, O. (1983). *Contributions to neuropsychological assessment.* New York: Oxford University Press.

Benton, A.L., & Kemble, J. (1960). Right-left disorientation and reading difficulty. *Psychiatria and Neurologia* (Basel), *139*, 49–60.

Fischer, P., Marterer, A., & Danielczyk, W. (1990). Right-left disorientation in dementia of the Alzheimer type. *Neurology, 40*, 1619–1620.

Harris, L.J., & Gitterman, S.R. (1978). University professors' self-descriptions of left-right confusability: Sex and handedness differences. *Perceptual and Motor Skills, 47*, 819–823.

Wolf, S.M. (1973). Difficulties in right-left discrimination in a normal population. *Archives of Neurology, 29*, 128–129.

Michael D. Franzen, Ph.D.
Associate Professor of Behavioral Medicine and Psychiatry and Director of Neuropsychology, West Virginia University School of Medicine, Morgantown, West Virginia.

RIVERMEAD BEHAVIOURAL MEMORY TEST

Barbara Wilson, Janet Cockburn, and Alan Baddeley. Bury St. Edmunds, England: Thames Valley Test Company. U.S. Distributor—National Rehabilitation Services.

Introduction

Memory impairment is an extremely common problem in individuals who have acquired brain damage. The prevalence of memory impairment is responsible for the proliferation of clinical memory tests and for the popularity of these tests in both diagnostic and treatment settings. Most memory tests are derived from modifications of paradigms that have been used in experimental investigations of both normal and anomalous memory functions. As such, they are very appropriate for diagnosis; however, they possess limitations when applied in a treatment setting. Individuals with clinical memory impairment may use compensatory strategies in the open environment, which may mask their actual memory impairment while improving the application of the impaired skills to real-life tasks. On the other hand, by using tasks with few real-life correlates, the clinical memory tests may not tap relevant aspects of the patient's memory impairment. In some instances, the use of clinical memory measures is supplemented by questionnaires and observations. However, both of these methods have their limitations, as memory-impaired patients may not have adequate insight into the nature and extent of their problems, and observations may be insufficiently systematic.

The Rivermead Behavioural Memory Test (RBMT; Wilson, Cockburn, Baddeley, & Hiorns, 1991) was designed to provide an assessment of memory with greater similarity to the actual tasks that a memory-impaired person may face in the open environment. The authors did not attempt to model the RMBT after a theoretical model of memory, and they intended that it be used to document improvement in acute cases. Because tests of memory have significant practice effects with repeated administrations, the RBMT exists in four parallel versions.

The authors of the RBMT are well known for their rehabilitative work in treating memory impairment (Barbara Wilson) and for their experience in experimental investigations of abnormal memory processes (Alan Baddeley). The RBMT was meant to provide a bridge between traditional measures of memory and those involving questionnaires and observations (Wilson, Cockburn, Baddeley, & Hiorns, 1989). Additionally, the RBMT was designed so that individuals with normal memory would be able to pass all of the items; that is, ceiling effects were built into the test.

The RMBT materials consist of a few small paper cards (some with line drawings of common objects and some with photographs of people), a set of four larger photographs of individuals, recording forms, a 20-minute timer, instruction manuals, and an instruction tape with an example of an administration. The tape is especially helpful because aside from providing the administration example, a commentary is woven into the recording. There is also a sheet with the short story printed on it. Because of cultural differences, there are both British and American versions of the stories. All of the materials are available in four alternate forms. The RMBT takes approximately 20 minutes to administer.

Practical Applications/Uses

The RMBT can be helpful in rehabilitation settings when the question to be answered is related to the ability of an individual to successfully engage in common tasks that require memory. The manual also states that the RMBT can be used to assess change in memory skill due to recovery. Each type aspect of memory is evaluated using only a few items, and, as noted above, a ceiling effect has been built into the test. These two factors may limit the amount of improvement that can be documented.

The test may be used with patients as young as age 11. Wilson, Forester, Bryant, and Cockburn (1990) present data on 85 normal subjects between the ages of 11 and 14. Norms available for elderly patients extend up to age 94, based on 119 subjects between the ages of 70 and 94. A children's version for 5- to 10-year-olds (RMBT-C) uses a modification of the short story procedure and a set of orientation questions that are more developmentally appropriate. The other procedures remain unchanged (Aldrich & Wilson, 1990).

Administration of the RMBT is accomplished in a face-to-face setting on an individual basis. The first task given to the patient is to remember the name of an individual who is pictured on the card, thereby assessing cross-modality associative memory. Additional procedures that do not require test materials include hiding an object belonging to the patient somewhere in the room, and taking an envelope and tracing a route around the room. The patient also is asked to inquire regarding his or her next appointment when the timer goes off. The line drawings are used to assess recognition memory as the patient is asked to identify the original 10 drawings from a group of 20. Somewhat more complex aspects of recognition memory are assessed by asking the patient to identify a group of 5 individuals in photographs from a group of 10 alternatives. There are both immediate and delayed recall procedures. Additionally, the patient is asked questions regarding orientation to person, date, time, and place.

The manual describes the scoring procedures and contains examples of exact and acceptable answers for the short story recall items. Both a Screening score and a Profile score are available. The Screening score ranges from 0 to 12 points and is used to determine whether a general memory impairment exists. Here each item is scored pass or fail. The Standardised Profile Score is obtained by summing values of 0, 1, or 2, depending on the transformation of raw scores. This second procedure has a summed range of 0 to 24 points and allows comparison across subtests.

Technical Aspects

The original reliability and validation studies on the RMBT are reported both in the manual (Wilson et al., 1991) and in a previous publication (Wilson et al., 1989). The authors of the test investigated interrater reliability by having pairs of raters (10 raters altogether) independently score 40 protocols from the original standardization sample. The report does not specify which form was used, but presumably it was Form A. Both the Screening score and the Profile score were evaluated, and 100% agreement existed between raters (Wilson et al., 1989). Alternate forms reliability was investigated by administering Form A and one other form of the test to a total of 118 patients. Reliability coefficients for the Screening score were .84 for Forms A and B, .80 for Forms A and C, and a somewhat less impressive .67 for Forms A and D. The Profile score investigation resulted in coefficients of .86, .83, and .88. Although the test-retest reliability was not measured directly, investigating the results of administration of the two forms indicates that even using two different forms results in a slight improvement in score the second time; however, this difference is not statistically significant.

Wilson et al. (1989) investigated validity in a number of ways. First, the study showed that the brain-damaged patients exhibited poorer performance than did the normal control subjects. The authors also correlated the results of the RBMT with scores obtained from standardized memory tests such as the Recognition Memory Test, the Corsi blocks, and parts of the Randt Memory Test. The correlation coefficients were modest, ranging from .20 to .63, with the highest correlation coefficients occurring for the Recognition Memory Test. More importantly, the RBMT correlated -.71 for the Screening score and -.75 for the Profile score with a checklist of observed memory problems completed on the patient sample by their therapists. The RBMT correlated modestly with the National Adult Reading Test and with the Raven matrices, indicating minimal influence from intelligence.

Another study (Beardsall & Huppert, 1991) indicated that the RBMT provided greater discriminability of normal elderly from demented elderly than did a standardized memory test. Conference reports have noted modest correlations with the Wechsler Memory Scale–Revised indices (O'Brien & Chiapello, 1990) and greater correlations for the RBMT with observations by staff and family than with the Knox Cube Test and the 15 Words Learning Test (van der Feen, van Balen, & Eling, 1989). Finally, Schwartz and McMillan (1989) found that the RMBT correlated moderately with both the Subjective Memory Questionnaire and the Everyday Memory Questionnaire.

Critique

The RMBT appears to be a reasonably good tool in the assessment of everyday memory. Because it contains only a few items to tap each aspect of memory, it may not be useful, however, in the diagnostic study of memory in an impaired individual. The normative data were derived from use of the British stories, and data are needed specifically for the American stories. There are four alternate forms available in order to obviate the problems attendant upon repeated administration of a memory assessment instrument; however, empirical investigations of the ability of the RMBT to accurately document memory change are lacking. Even with these limitations, the RMBT is still the only way to evaluate everyday aspects of memory in an ecologically valid manner using standardized procedures. As such it is likely to attract a great deal of attention in both clinical and research settings.

References

Aldrich, F.K., & Wilson, B. (1991). Rivermead Behavioural Memory Test for Children (RMBT-C): A preliminary evaluation. *British Journal of Clinical Psychology, 30,* 161–168.

Beardsall, L., & Huppert, F.A. (1991). A comparison of clinical, psychometric, and behavioural memory tests: Findings from a community study of the early detection of dementia. *International Journal of Geriatric Psychiatry, 6,* 295–306.

O'Brien, K.P., & Chiapello, D.A. (1990). *Wechsler Memory Scale–Revised and the Rivermead Behavioural Memory Test: Correlational analysis.* Paper presented at the 19th Annual Meeting of the International Neuropsychological Society, San Antonio, TX.

Schwartz, A.F., & McMillan, T.M. (1989). Assessment of everyday memory after severe head injury. *Cortex, 25,* 665–671.

van der Feen, B., van Balen, E., & Eling, P. (1989). *Assessing everyday memory in rehabilitation: A validation study.* Paper presented at the 12th European Conference of the International Neuropsychological Society, Antwerp, Belgium.

Wilson, B., Cockburn, J., Baddeley, A., & Hiorns, R. (1989). The development and validation of a test battery for detecting and monitoring everyday memory problems. *Journal of Clinical and Experimental Neuropsychology, 11,* 855–870.

Wilson, B., Cockburn, J., Baddeley, A., & Hiorns, R. (1991). *The Rivermead Behavioural Memory Test manual.* Bury St. Edmunds, England: Thames Valley Test Co.

Wilson, B., Forester, S., Bryant, T., & Cockburn, J. (1990). Performance of eleven to fourteen year olds on the Rivermead Behavioural Memory Test. *Clinical Psychology Forum, 30,* 8–10.

Frank M. Bernt, Ph.D.
*Assistant Professor, Department of Education and Health Services,
St. Joseph's University, Philadelphia, Pennsylvania.*

SALAMON-CONTE LIFE SATISFACTION IN THE ELDERLY SCALE

Michael J. Salamon and Vincent A. Conte. Woodmere, New York: Michael Salamon, Ph.D.

Introduction

The Salamon-Conte Life Satisfaction in the Elderly Scale (LSES) is a 40-item self-report inventory designed to measure life satisfaction among older adults. It provides a total score as well as subscores for eight different dimensions relevant to subjective well-being: daily activity, meaning, life goals, positive mood, positive self-concept, perceived health, financial security, and quality of social contacts.

Michael J. Salamon, principal author of the LSES, received his doctorate from Hofstra University in applied psychological research and has worked in the field of adult development in both community and institutional settings for over 15 years. He currently serves as executive director of the Adult Developmental Center of Woodmere, New York, and as clinical supervisor and research director at the New Hope Guild Community Mental Health Center in Brooklyn, New York.

Construction of the LSES began with the identification of eight domains or categories related to life satisfaction among the elderly. The first five listed above were taken from the Life Satisfaction Index scales developed by Neugarten, Havighurst, and Robin (1961); the remaining three categories were drawn from existing literature on life satisfaction among the elderly (Salamon & Conte, 1984). From an initial pool of 80 items, 40 were retained based on having "the highest reliability" (it is not clear whether this refers to items' correlations to their respective subscales or to the entire LSES). The final version of the LSES contains five items for each of the eight scales. The technical manual indicates that a panel of four specialists reviewed the 40 items to establish their face validity.

The subscales are described briefly in the technical manual as follows:

Daily Activities: measures the extent of pleasure and satisfaction one feels with unspecified daily activities and routine tasks.

Meaning: measures one's sense of feeling useful, of having purpose in life, and of having a positive attitude toward one's present life situation.

Goals: measures the perceived goodness of fit between desired and achieved goals; in particular, one's satisfaction with present development relative to past accomplishments.

Mood (or positive mood tone): measures general positive affect, happiness, and optimism.

Self-Concept: measures the degree or extent of one's positive self-regard or self-appraisal.

Health: measures one's perception of overall physical well-being.

Finances (or financial security): measures satisfaction with one's recent and current financial situation.

Social Contacts: measures satisfaction with the number and quality of one's social contacts.

The LSES technical manual was being revised at the time of this writing, changes to include clarification of the process by which the LSES was constructed and discussion of recent studies employing the scale. A conversation with Dr. Salamon revealed that he also plans to include more comprehensive and updated norms. Apparently there is a French version of the LSES currently under study in Quebec, but specific results regarding its psychometric qualities are not yet available.

Practical Applications/Uses

The introduction of the LSES technical manual indicates a need for a tool that professionals can use for research and evaluation as well as for clinical and counseling purposes. The manual's interpretation section offers specific examples of how LSES scores might be useful in a clinical setting; the authors argue that "LSES scores produce diagnostically significant information which is sensitive enough to aid in establishing treatment plans and in monitoring patient progress" (Salamon & Conte, 1984, p. 19). Although such confidence may be somewhat overstated, the scale does show promise as a screening device for identifying areas of potential concern for professionals working with the elderly. Further, the LSES is also appropriate for use in research and evaluation; to date, however, few studies using the scale have been published (Brockett, 1987; Salamon, 1985, 1986, 1987).

The LSES can be administered in either paper-and-pencil or personal interview format, depending on the respondent's functional level and the user's purposes. Individuals are instructed to place an X over the word or phrase (following each item stem) that best represents how he or she feels. The entire scale usually can be completed in 15 to 25 minutes. Nearly all of the items are worded in the first person to facilitate respondents' understanding. In addition, all items are scaled in the same direction to alleviate confusion; although this increases the risk of response bias, the authors point out (correctly, in this reviewer's opinion) that the risk of misunderstanding created by reversing items would create a much more serious difficulty. Test administration instructions are clear as well as sensitive to the unique needs of the elderly respondent; for example, the manual stresses the importance of establishing rapport and of reducing anxiety prior to any interview or written administration.

Scoring the LSES is quite simple. For each item, an X marked above the far left anchor is scored as 1, an X above the anchor to left of center is scored as 2, and so on. A separate scoring sheet provided facilitates the computation of subscale scores. No items are reversed, making the summing of subscale scores straightforward. Scores for each subscale range from 5 to 25; for the total scale, from 40 to 200.

Norms for LSES total scores appear in the technical manual. Unfortunately, the quantile scores provided are rather global and invite further explication. In addition, norms presented in the original technical manual are probably not representative of the elderly population as a whole. One hopes that the forthcoming revised document will provide updated and more comprehensive norms.

Technical Aspects

Initial assessments of the scale's validity and reliability were based on studies of two separate samples: 408 individuals "of reasonable health" aged 55 to 90, and 241 individuals aged 65 to 89 who were affiliated with a variety of health care providers. Internal consistency estimates for the subscales (using Cronbach's alpha) ranged from .47 to .79 for the two samples (mean $r = .70$); estimates were .70 or higher for all except the Goals and Self-Concept subscales, for which estimates ranged from .47 to .61 across the two studies. The test-retest reliability estimate for the LSES total score over a 6-month period was .67, based on a subset of 120 subjects in the first sample. A second study using 50 older adults residing in a housing complex obtained a test-retest coefficient of .90 for the total scale and of .88 or higher for the eight subscales over a 1-month period.

Principal components and cluster analyses served to evaluate the construct validity of the LSES. Although the authors suggest that the eight scales are "factorially distinct," the actual picture is somewhat mixed. The Health and Finance subscales are very clearly supported by factor loadings resulting from a procrustes confirmatory factor analysis and from a principal components factor analysis with varimax rotation; however, factor loadings suggest a substantial degree of overlap among the remaining six subscales. In the absence of any analyses of discriminant validity, it is difficult to determine just how factorially distinct the subscales are. The results of a cluster analysis further support a mixed picture: for five of the eight subscales, four of their five items cluster together, while those of the Self-Concept, Goals, and Daily Activities subscales do not.

Studies of concurrent validity provide preliminary evidence that the LSES Mood subscale is strongly correlated with both the Beck Depression Inventory ($r = .73$) and with the Geriatric Depression Scale ($r = .78$). In addition, the LSES total score was reported to correlate moderately with the Multi-dimensional Observation Scale for Elderly Subjects (MOSES), an instrument for staff assessment of patients' social networking and functional performance (Salamon, 1985). Unfortunately, very small samples were used in both cases, so that further replication is required. Salamon (1988) also reports "significant" correlations between LSES subscale scores and the Health Background Questionnaire (Kopf, Salamon, & Charytan, 1982); however, no details are provided to allow for independent evaluation of these findings. More recently, Perceived Health and Daily Activities subscale scores have been found to relate to self-reported health and monthly activity records, respectively (Meiner, 1991); in addition, total LSES scores were positively correlated with the Hardiness scale and negatively correlated with the Social Readjustment scale (Barry, 1988).

Several studies have assessed the LSES's utility as a tool for discriminating among subpopulations of the elderly. A study of 41 geriatric residents referred for psychotherapeutic intervention obtained an average total LSES score for this group that was lower than that achieved by other groups (Salamon, 1987). In addition, data from the second sample of 241 subjects mentioned above were analyzed to determine whether the LSES could differentiate effectively among subjects from six different health care settings. A series of one-way ANOVAs revealed that the total LSES scale as well as the Daily Activities, Goals, and Health subscales differentiated among subjects from different health care settings, especially between those receiving home care (who scored low on these subscales) and those residing in skilled nursing or health-related facilities.

Critique

The LSES has several qualities that support its use. To begin with, its psychometric qualities, relative to many of its competitors, are more than satisfactory. As the authors note, few of the other available scales report any validity or reliability information. In addition, the LSES's coverage of subcomponents of life satisfaction among the elderly is rather extensive, offering an advantage over earlier unidimensional scales.

A number of areas, however, need further development. Many of the articles, as well as the technical manual itself, are too elliptical and lack sufficient detail to allow for a sufficiently critical analysis of the scale's psychometric properties. For example, although internal consistencies are reported in the technical manual, the authors fail to report intercorrelations among the subscales to allow the potential user to judge their merits and distinctness. Several articles make general statements about the LSES without reporting the types of inferential statistics used (Salamon, 1988). Elsewhere, subscales' abilities to distinguish among different populations are suggested, but more powerful multivariate approaches might have indicated more precisely which subscales or which set of subscales do so more effectively (Salamon, 1987). Finally, relationships between total LSES scores and other scales are reported (Salamon, 1986), but no mention is made of correlations between those scales and the subscales of the LSES. In each of these cases, reanalysis of available data and more detailed discussions of findings would aid the reader in understanding this scale's strengths and weaknesses.

This reviewer was somewhat surprised that, such weaknesses notwithstanding, the LSES has not been cited more widely in studies of life satisfaction in the elderly. Discussion of this matter with Dr. Salamon suggested that the LSES may be used more extensively in clinical practice and that the data generated by such use has not been made available. In light of this, the authors request that current and future users of the LSES report findings or make available any relevant data that would further extend knowledge about the scale's psychometric aspects.

With regard to the paucity of published studies using the LSES, a review of the literature on life satisfaction among the elderly suggests that researchers may be prone to use "mainstream scales" such as Neugarten et al.'s (1961) Life Satisfaction Index or the Philadelphia Geriatric Morale Scale (Lawton, 1975). Both scales seem to operate on the assumption that subjective well-being is best treated as a unidimensional construct and that dichotomous or trichomotous response formats can fairly capture respondent attitudes and beliefs. It is by no means clear that consensus has been reached concerning either of these assumptions (Cohen-Mansfield, 1990; Liang, 1985). Depending on one's purposes, it may be necessary to draw conceptual distinctions among specific subdomains of life satisfaction. Although the exact number or nature of these subdomains cannot be determined based on extant research, the LSES provides a very useful instrument for wrestling with such questions.

In summary, this scale is a very promising, if not yet proven, instrument for use in assessing elements of life satisfaction among the elderly. More detailed descriptions of its psychometric qualities, further revisions of its structure and constitution, and objective comparison to similar instruments may lead to its use by a wider audience of both researchers and clinicians.

References

Barry, B. (1988). *Hardiness as a mediator between stressors and life satisfaction in the elderly: A path analytic study.* Unpublished doctoral dissertation, Hofstra University, Hempstead, NY.

Brockett, R.G. (1987). Life satisfaction and learner self-direction: Enhancing quality of life during the later years. *Educational Gerontology, 12,* 225–237.

Cohen-Mansfield, J. (1990). Perceived control, reinforcement, satisfaction, and depression in community elderly. *Journal of Applied Gerontology, 9*(4), 492–503.

Kopf, R., Salamon, M.J., & Charytan, P. (1982). The Preventive Health History Form: A questionnaire for use with older patient populations. *Journal of Gerontologic Nursing, 8,* 519–523.

Lawton, M.P. (1975). The Philadelphia Geriatric Center Morale Scale: A revision. *Journal of Gerontology, 30,* 85–89.

Liang, J. (1985). A structural integration of the Affect Balance Scale and the Life Satisfaction Index A. *Journal of Gerontology, 40*(5), 552–561.

Meiner, S.E. (1991). *Life satisfaction, perceived health status and activities of young-old and old-old women living in urban and rural settings.* Unpublished doctoral dissertation, Southern Illinois University, Edwardsville.

Neugarten, B.L., Havighust, R.J., & Robin, S.S. (1961). The measurement of life satisfaction. *Journal of Gerontology, 16,* 134–143.

Salamon, M.J. (1985). Sociocultural role theories in the aged: A replication and extension. *Activities Adaptation and Aging, 7,* 111–122.

Salamon, M.J. (1986). Measures for psychotherapy outcome in institutionalized aged. *Clinical Gerontologist, 6*(1), 62–63.

Salamon, M.J. (1987). Health care environment and life satisfaction in the elderly. *Journal of Aging Studies, 1*(3), 287–297.

Salamon, M.J. (1988). Clinical use of the Life Satisfaction in the Elderly Scale. *Clinical Gerontologist, 8*(1), 45–54.

Salamon, M.J., & Conte, V.A. (1984). *The Life Satisfaction in the Elderly Scale.* Odessa, FL: Psychological Assessment Resources.

Andrew G. Bean, Ph.D.
Assistant Professor of Marketing, La Salle University, Philadelphia, Pennsylvania.

Michael J. Roszkowski, Ph.D.
Associate Professor of Psychology and Director of Marketing Research, The American College, Bryn Mawr, Pennsylvania.

SALES ATTITUDE CHECK LIST

Erwin K. Taylor. Rosemont, Illinois: SRA/London House.

Introduction

The Sales Attitude Check List (SACL), a brief instrument designed to predict a salesperson's work performance, consists of 31 forced-choice items. Each item contains four statements (tetrads) describing a salesperson's behavior. For each tetrad, respondents are asked to select the one statement that is most descriptive of them and the one that is least descriptive.

The history of this instrument extends back to the 1950s, where it began as the Sales Personnel Description Form (SPDF; Taylor, Schneider, & Symons, 1953), a forced-choice scale intended for use by sales executives in rating the performance of their sales personnel. The original 28 items were constructed by executives in sales organizations who were enrolled in a seminar on performance appraisal conducted at Western Reserve University. Taylor and Hilton (1960) presented data supporting the validity of the SPDF for predicting a variety of performance criteria in several different types of sales positions.

Given the validity shown by the Sales Personnel Description Form, the authors felt that the instrument perhaps was measuring behaviors characteristic of successful salespeople in a wide variety of occupations. Based on this assumption, they rewrote the original items to be suitable for use in a self-descriptive instrument. This 1960 version was named the Sales Attitudes Check List. Foley reviewed this form of the instrument in 1965.

In 1985, the items of the 1960 SACL were edited to remove any wording that might be sex biased (e.g., items referring to "salesmen"). The revised scale, renamed the Sales Attitude Check List (note the singular *Attitude*), underwent field testing in a heterogeneous group of sales applicants including both men and women (Science Research Associates, 1985).

The SACL was developed by Irwin K. Taylor and his staff. Dr. Taylor, born in 1913, was educated at Northwestern University, earning his B.S. degree in 1935, his M.A. in 1939, and his Ph.D. in 1941. Between 1943 and 1951 he served as a research psychologist for the Adjutant General's office of the U.S. Army, during which time he specialized in test construction, analysis, and interpretation. In 1948 he founded *Personnel Psychology*, a journal of applied research, and served on its editorial board for many years. From 1951 to 1955 he was on the faculty at Western Reserve

University and director of the Personnel Research Institute. In 1955 Taylor left full-time teaching to establish the Personnel Research and Development Corporation, a firm devoted to personnel consulting and research. He was serving as that firm's chairman and director of research at the time of his death in 1975. A eulogy published by two of his colleagues provides an intriguing analysis of his personality (Rubin & Walker, 1976).

The purchaser of the SACL receives a six-page manual along with the three-page test form. As noted previously, each item consists of four statements (tetrads) describing a salesperson's attitudes or behaviors. From each tetrad, respondents must select the one statement that is *most* descriptive of them and the one that is *least* descriptive. Of the 31 items, 27 are actually keyed to yield a single summary score designed to be predictive of on-the-job sales performance. The manual does not explain the purpose of the four unscored items.

An inspection of the item content reveals that persons earning a high score on the SACL describe themselves in ways that would be consistent with good sales performance: being assertive, well organized, sensitive to customer needs, and responsive to administrative needs, and producing a high variety and volume of sales.

Practical Applications/Uses

The SACL is presented as an instrument to be used in the selection of sales personnel for a variety of sales positions. The manual states that the scale can be a useful part of a "sales selection test battery," which implies that the authors do not believe that the SACL should be used as the sole basis for making the selection decision.

Because the instrument requires self-ratings of behaviors in a sales position, one might expect that the author of the scale would view it as appropriate for selecting only experienced salespeople. This is clearly not the case, however, because applicants with no sales experience are instructed to "select the answers that come closest to describing the way you would or would not act in the situations described" (Science Research Associates, 1985, p. 2).

The SACL can be given to a single job applicant or to a group simply by having an examiner read the instructions and then check to make sure that the directions are understood. The test is untimed and typically takes 5 to 15 minutes to complete. All questions must be answered in order for the instrument to be scored because the total score is determined not only by which "most" and "least" choices are marked, but also by which choices are *not* selected as "most" or "least" like the individual.

According to the manual, the scoring key was developed a priori to reflect sales success generally. However, local development of an empirically validated scoring system is encouraged if a sufficient sample size is available.

The mechanics of scoring the SACL are simple, with the scoring key neatly built into the instrument on the back of each of the two pages of questions (through the use of carbon paper). By examining the key, one can determine that 27 of the 31 items are actually scored, with each item yielding a score of 0, 1, or 2. Thus, the total score potentially can range from 0 to 54 points. However, the 1985 percentile norms in the manual show that raw scores of 20 and 43 correspond to the 1st and 99th percentiles, respectively.

Normative data, all in percentile form, are presented for six groups: automobile salespeople (N = 197), utility salespeople (N = 54), office equipment salespeople (N = 141), freight traffic salespeople (N = 95), applicants–sales and managerial positions (N = 180), and sales applicants (N = 86). Only the norms of the last mentioned group, developed in 1985, deal with the revised version of the instrument; the others are for the earlier version of the instrument, the Sales Attitudes Check List. The manual states that given their recency, the norms developed on the 86 sales applicants are preferable to the other norms.

Technical Aspects

No reliability data are presented in the examiner's manual. The text justifies the omission by noting the difficulty of showing empirical reliability in a forced-choice instrument such as the SACL. It further argues that the validity evidence presented indicates that the reliability is sufficiently high. The view seems to be that reliability is only useful in that it allows one to estimate potential validity.

Three concurrent validity studies are reported. In the first, the SACL correlated .31 with the average monthly earnings of 197 new car salespeople. For the 23 office equipment salespeople serving as subjects in the second study, the SACL correlated .23 with average monthly dollar-volume of sales but only .04 with the number of orders written. The third study, involving several groups of railroad traffic salespeople, used a criterion of overall performance as rated by the individual's supervisor. Validities obtained were .15 (n = 50), .44 (n = 30), .11 (n = 40), .37 (n = 16), and .02 (n = 26). Although the manual does not report levels of statistical significance for all the obtained validities, it should be noted that only two of the eight were significant at the .05 level using a one-tailed test.

Correlations between the SACL and several other standardized instruments are reported in the examiner's manual: Kuder Preference Record–Occupational Form D (special key), -.48; Thurstone Test of Mental Alertness, -.35; Kerr Empathy Test, -.28; and Biographical Information Form (special key), -.19. However, the manual indicates that these correlations are not presented as validity data, but rather to illustrate the instrument's relationship to other potential predictors of sales performance.

A technical supplement to the manual presents additional validity data for the SACL (Neuman, Raote, & Jones, 1990). In a study of 82 jewelry store sales associates, validity coefficients were obtained by correlating scores on the SACL with sales performance evaluations. The SACL correlated .21 with overcoming customer objections, .21 with greeting style, and .30 with working independently. All of these correlations were statistically significant (p < .05).

Critique

In order to critically evaluate the SACL, one needs to examine it against the procedures ordinarily used in the development of any forced-choice instrument. The primary advantage claimed for this format is that an acceptable pattern of responses is difficult to falsify; one cannot generate a high score simply by selecting socially desirable responses. This property is particularly advantageous when an instrument is used as part of the selection process.

Because the SACL is a forced-choice instrument used in the selection of salespersons, a resistance to faking would be a desirable property. However, to obtain the advantages of this format, each item in the SACL would need to be constructed in the following way: First, the two positive statements in the tetrad should be equated with each other for social desirability; one of these positive choices should be empirically keyed to correlate with effective sales performance, while the other should not show a significant relationship. The same requirements also should be met for the two negative choices in the tetrad: they should be equal in social desirability, but only one of the two should correlate with sales performance. When an instrument is constructed in this way, a respondent cannot earn a high score simply by answering items in a socially desirable fashion.

Given the forced-choice format of the SACL, these reviewers have several concerns about the procedures used to construct the instrument. First, the manual offers no explanation of any empirical procedure used to equate the statements within an item on social desirability. Second, there is no mention of empirically keying the item choices. In fact, the manual describes the keying as a priori. A priori keying, which typically suggests a rational rather than an empirical approach, constitutes a deviation from the usual procedure for constructing forced-choice scales. Normally data are collected on each statement's social desirability and empirical validity. It is hard to see how one could have confidence in the SACL without such empirical evidence.

A rationally constructed instrument should by its very nature have a high degree of face validity for the keyed choices, yet the keyed responses to several SACL items run counter to what one would expect intuitively. Perhaps the examiner's manual is using the term *a priori* in an unorthodox manner. In any event, the text should clearly explain what is meant by the term, especially if it is being used in an unconventional way.

As noted above, no reliability data appear in the SACL manual. Although internal consistency reliability may be inappropriate for a forced-choice scale, some evidence of temporal stability would be highly desirable. If scores on the SACL are to have any practical value in the prediction of sales performance, they must exhibit adequate test-retest reliability.

In addition, reliability data would be particularly useful given the weak evidence for validity presented in the manual. In the validity data described above, only two of the eight validity coefficients reached conventional levels of statistical significance. If the low reported validities are due to low test reliability, then perhaps the test could be improved by adding more items that would discriminate between high and low sales performers.

These reviewers notice several important deficiencies in the SACL manual. One problem is that the text treats the current and previous versions of this instrument as if they were interchangeable. Most often, the only clue as to which version is being discussed lies in the subtle change from the "Sales Attitude Checklist" (the current version) to the "Sales Attitudes Checklist" (the previous version). Unless the reader remains extremely alert, it is easy to assume that the current version is under discussion when in fact it is not. As far as we can tell, the evidence offered for the scale's validity deals only with the earlier version.

Although the two instruments are in fact quite similar, there are some indications that the scores from each may not be interchangeable. For example, while the manual explicitly states that the *Attitudes* check list has 28 scorable items, the number of scorable items on the *Attitude* check list is not given. These reviewers could find only 27 used in the scoring key of the current version.

A careful inspection of the norms tables reveals that only one of the six was obtained using the latest version of the SACL. The one norm group for the current version consists of only 86 sales applicants, a rather limited sample size for norming purposes. Furthermore, the characteristics of this group are not described adequately.

Quite a bit of variation can be noted across the six groups in the percentile ranks of a given raw score. For instance, while a raw score of 33 is at the 40th percentile for the group of 86 sales applicants, it is at the 91st percentile for the group of automobile salespersons. The examiner's manual, acknowledging this variability, points out the need for local norming and validation. Because the manual generally recommends using the current norms, one wonders why the other norm groups were included, given that they may be outdated and derived from a somewhat different version of the SACL.

We disagree with the author regarding the level of experience necessary to respond meaningfully to the SACL items. Although the manual claims that the instrument can be used to test and select individuals who have not held sales positions previously, we have some concerns about using it for such applicants. In our opinion, the nature of the questions would require inexperienced respondents to guess how they might behave in a situation they have never encountered.

Given the limitations noted above, these reviewers would be cautious in using the SACL to select salespersons without first obtaining some local validation data. Additional reliability and validity data, along with improvements in the examiner's manual, would significantly increase our confidence in this instrument. The Sales Attitude Check List is not so much unpromising as unfinished.

References

Foley, J.P. (1965). SRA Sales Attitudes Check List (1960 version). In O.K. Buros (Ed.), *The sixth mental measurements yearbook* (pp. 1177–1178). Highland Park, NJ: Gryphon Press.

Neuman, G.A., Raote, R.G., & Jones, J.W. (1990). *Validation of the SRA Sales Attitude Check List (SACL) at Elangy Corporation.* Unpublished technical supplement, Science Research Associates, Park Ridge, IL.

Rubin, S.I., & Walker, W.B. (1976). Erwin K. Taylor: 1913–1975. *Personnel Psychology, 29*, 1–4.

Science Research Associates. (1985). *Examiner's manual: Sales Attitude Check List.* Park Ridge, IL: Author.

Taylor, E.K., & Hilton, A. (1960). A sales personnel description form: Summary of validities. *Personnel Psychology, 13*, 173–179.

Taylor, E.K., Schneider, D.E., & Symons, N.A. (1953). A short forced-choice evaluation form for salesmen. *Personnel Psychology, 6*, 393–401.

Robert J. Drummond, Ed.D.

Program Director, Counselor Education, University of North Florida, Jacksonville, Florida.

THE SALIENCE INVENTORY (RESEARCH EDITION)

Donald E. Super and Dorothy D. Nevill. Palo Alto, California: Consulting Psychologists Press, Inc.

Introduction

The Salience Inventory, Research Edition (SI) is a 170-item objective assessment of individuals' participation in, commitment to, and values expectations of their major life roles as students, workers, homemakers, leisurites, and citizens.

The SI was constructed as part of the Work Importance Study by an international consortium of vocational psychologists headed by Donald E. Super. The team collaborated in the literature review, conceptualization, definitions, and item writing. The preliminary edition was tried out on samples in the United States, Canada, Yugoslavia, and Portugal. Dr. Dorothy Nevill from the University of Florida became a coauthor of the SI in 1981. The inventory was used in the Work Importance Study that involved not only the United States but Australia, Canada, Portugal, France, Italy, Yugoslavia, Israel, Czechoslovakia, and India. The purpose of the study was to assess the relative importance of the work role in the context of other life roles, and to better understand the values that individuals seek or hope to find in various life roles.

The 6-page inventory contains a page of directions, a page of items dealing with participation (what the test taker actually does or has done recently), a page of items dealing with commitment (how the test taker feels about what he or she does or has done recently), and a page of items on value expectations (what opportunity the test taker sees now or in the future to . . .). The test taker responds to each item on a 4-point scale, with "1" usually representing "never, rarely, little, or none" and "4" representing "almost always, always, or a great deal." The last page presents a grid of 20 occupational groups to help the respondent select the group in which he or she works, an item asked on the answer sheet. The booklet is reusable.

The SI packet also includes a separate answer sheet. The front side consists of grids on which tests takers record their name, age, level of education, marital status, occupational status, how they feel about some of their roles, where they are or were employed, their occupational group, and the type of work their father, mother, or spouse does. The back side is the answer sheet for the three parts of the test. A separate profile sheet contains on one side the means and standard deviations from the preliminary sample, and on the other side the report form on which individuals can record and graphically plot their scores.

628

A question similar to the type of items found on the SI goes as follows:

Participation

What did I do last week? I have spent time in

A. community service	1	2	3	4
B. home and family	1	2	3	4
C. leisure activity	1	2	3	4
D. studying	1	2	3	4
E. working	1	2	3	4

The test can be administered by the examiner or self-administered. Directions are provided in the test booklet as well as on the profile and answer sheets.

Fifteen scales make up the SI. There are five role scales—Studying, Working, Community Service, Home and Family, and Leisure Activities—for each of the three dimensions—Participation, Commitment, and Value Expectations. Participation is viewed as the behavioral component of the importance of a role. Nevill and Super (1986) state that it denotes action and can be measured by the amount of time given to a particular role (p. 11). Commitment is viewed as the affective component of the importance of a role and provides information on the individual's attitude toward each of the five roles. Value Expectations is also an affective component, assessing the degree to which individuals find major life satisfactions or values in each role. On this scale each role includes 14 values: Ability Utilization, Achievement, Aesthetics, Altruism, Autonomy, Creativity, Economics, Life Style, Physical Activity, Prestige, Risk, Social Interaction, Variety, and Working Conditions.

Practical Applications/Uses

The Salience Inventory can be used as a research instrument to assess the relative importance of the five major life roles among individuals of different gender and culture, to compare differences during different developmental stages, and to study the role commitments of different occupational fields. The instrument also has potential for personal and career counseling, and could be used to identify role and value conflicts. At present the inventory serves primarily in research on Super's theories and on career development and satisfaction.

In addition to measuring the relative importance of five major life roles to the individual, the Salience Inventory is designed to help the respondent understand the impact of each role on the others. Nevill and Super (1986) suggest that the SI provides an instrument to track the commitments and importance of life roles of various populations (p. 13). In Super's (1983) developmental assessment model, work salience is assessed in Step II.

The SI is appropriate for use with high school, college and university students, and adults. Although the authors state that the SI could be used with middle school students, they do not present any evidence of the validity, reliability, and interpretability of the test for this group. The test is for normal populations and requires at least eighth-grade reading ability. No special forms have been developed for handicapped individuals. Forms are available in the languages of the different groups participating in the Work Importance Study, but not from the publisher.

The Salience Inventory can be group or individually administered to most high school, college, or adult subjects in 30 to 45 minutes. Directions are presented in detail in the test booklet, and no special training is needed to administer the measure.

The SI can be hand scored or scored by the publisher. The answer sheet was designed to make hand scoring a simple matter of adding the appropriate role columns for Participation, Commitment, and Value Expectations. The test is easy to score and demands just basic addition skills on the part of the examiner. Instructions are presented in the manual text and through a properly scored sample answer sheet.

The manual provides a discussion of both ipsative and normative systems of interpretation for the SI. The authors provide the user with several case studies and illustrate how other counseling instruments can be interpreted using role salience as a frame of reference. The SI's interpretation does not present major difficulty for counselors and psychologists who have a background in assessment procedures. Much larger samples are necessary across age, gender, and ethnic group, however, if norm-referenced interpretation is to be meaningful.

Technical Aspects

Two types of reliability coefficients are reported: test-retest and alphas. The alpha coefficients, reported for high school (n = 353), college (n = 295), and adult subjects (n = 20), are all above .80; for example, the alphas for the high school group ranged from a low of .85 (Participation/Working) to a high of .93 (Participation/Community Service; Commitment/Home and Family; Commitment/Community Service; and Value Expectations/Community Service). The median coefficient for this group was .90. The test-retest coefficients, based on 85 college students, ranged from .37 (Value Expectations/Leisure Activities) to .83 (Participation/Community Service). Only one of the 15 test-retest coefficients was above .80.

Content, construct, and concurrent validity studies are reported in the test manual. The items on the test underwent elaborate field testing and the feedback was used to refine the definitions and phrasing that appear in the instrument. The authors report that sex and age differences in the commitment to home and family provide some support for the validity of the SI (Nevill & Super, 1988, p. 24). They also indicate that the relative rankings of the five roles for high school, college, and adult samples show the validity of the instrument. The intercorrelations of the Participation, Commitment, and Value Expectations scales are reported. The correlations for the specific roles across Participation, Commitment, and Value Expectations are moderate to high; for example, the correlation is .75 between Participation/Studying and Commitment/Studying, and .52 between Participation/Studying and Value Expectations/Studying.

No factor analytical studies are reported. The authors do not present the standard errors of measurement for the scales across age or educational levels.

Critique

The Salience Inventory has an excellent theoretical base in the career development theory of Donald E. Super. The instrument is one of the assessment tools he proposes for use in his developmental model of assessment. This inventory along with the Values Scale and Adult Career Concerns Inventory present good tools in teaching courses on career development and career counseling. However, this reviewer finds the SI is rather tedious for clients to take, and they find it rather repetitious and fatiguing to complete. Maybe the same information could be gained more easily by asking clients to rank the five major roles rather than complete the 170 inventory items, especially when one primarily uses ipsative interpretation to interpret the results. This reviewer has used the SI in a number of research studies investigating job satisfaction in the helping professions, but has found that the SI's scales do not contribute significant variance in predicting job satisfaction for this group. Outside of some earlier reports on the SI from the Work Importance Study, limited citations appear in the professional literature (Fitzsimmons, 1990; Krau, 1989).

The information on the validity, reliability, and norms of the SI needs to be expanded in future editions. The technical information reported is based primarily on samples (usually relatively small) from high school and college groups; more attention should be directed toward adults and non–college bound youth. Further, more information needs to be focused on the present version of the SI rather than on previous versions. Additional construct validity studies should be conducted. What is the factor structure of this instrument? How does the SI compare with other instruments measuring role preferences?

Although the construct of role salience is an important one in career counseling, this reviewer is not sure that the SI presents the best way to get at it.

References

Fitzsimmons, G. (1990). *Career development instruments* (Monograph No. 5). Edmonton, Canada: Alberta Department of Education.

Krau, E. (1989). The transition in life domain salience and the modification of work values between high school and adult employment. *Journal of Vocational Behavior, 34*(1), 100–116.

Nevill, D.D., & Super, D.E. (1986). *The Salience Inventory: Theory, application, and research manual (research edition)*. Palo Alto, CA: Consulting Psychologists Press.

Super, D.E. (1983). Assessment in career guidance: Toward truly developmental counseling. *Personnel and Guidance Journal, 61,* 555–562.

Gregory J. Boyle, Ph.D. (Delaware), Ph.D. (Melbourne)
Associate Professor of Psychology, Bond University, Gold Coast, Queensland, Australia.

SELF-DESCRIPTION QUESTIONNAIRE II

Herbert W. Marsh. Macarthur, Campbelltown, Australia: SDQ Instruments.

Introduction

The Self-Description Questionnaire II, or SDQII (one of three sets of SDQ instruments—Marsh, 1990b), is a 102-item paper-and-pencil instrument designed to measure and analyze individual and group differences in adolescents' self-concept. The SDQII is suitable for use with junior and senior high school students in Grades 7 through 10 (ages 13–17 years). A subset of items from the SDQII instrument has been included in the large (25,000 students), nationally representative (U.S.), longitudinal (data to be collected in Grades 8, 10, and 12, and 2 years after high school graduation) National Education Longitudinal Study (NELS, 1992). Because of the huge range of variables included in this study and its likely impact (like the earlier High School and Beyond study), it has important implications for the study of self-concept based on responses to the SDQII instrument.

The SDQII manual is extremely comprehensive, with separate chapters on the theoretical model underlying construction of the instrument, administration and scoring procedures, development of norms and interpretation, reliability, construct validity, age and sex effects, self-concept and academic achievement, effects of experimental interventions, sexual identity, and self-concept. In addition, there is a summary and review chapter, as well as a detailed set of appendices and an extensive list of references.

The test author, Herbert W. Marsh, Ph.D., has published extensively in the field of self-concept and psychoeducational assessment. The initial multidimensional instrument and associated background test construction research is described fully in *SDQI: Manual and Research Monograph* (Marsh, 1988). The SDQI instrument was designed for use with elementary school children in Grades 4 through 6, the SDQII was constructed to measure self-concept among junior high school students, and the SDQIII (Marsh, in press) is intended for college students. It is important to consider the SDQII within the broader context of the set of three SDQ instruments because the research findings from each instrument complement each other so well, and the combined results are more important than those based on any one instrument alone. Materials for each SDQ version include a comprehensive test manual, a detailed set of 87 abstracts covering Marsh's extensive publications on self-concept since 1982, an SPSSX computer-scoring program, the relevant SDQ instrument and response sheet, as well as permission to make an unlimited number of copies of the instrument and scoring key. The separate list of abstracts from self-concept and related research provides abundant empirical information pertaining to the psychometric and applied characteristics of the SDQ instruments. Marsh (1990a) has published a major overview in *Educational Psychology Review*—the single most important reference—highlighting especially the emphasis placed on construct validity in developing the three SDQ instruments.

Many educational and clinical psychological efforts have attempted to enhance individuals' positive self-concept. A number of early psychometric studies reported in the self-concept literature suggested limitations in the underlying theoretical model and psychometric adequacy of the then available measurement instruments. In an attempt to resolve these problems, Shavelson, Hubner, and Stanton (1976) postulated a multifaceted hierarchical model of self-concept, which served as the basis and provided the impetus for construction of the three SDS instruments.

The original instrument (SDQI) was designed to index three major aspects of academic self-concept (Reading, Mathematics, and General School), as well as four dimensions of nonacademic self-concept (Physical Abilities, Physical Appearance, Peer Relations, and Parent Relations). The instrument was later revised to include a General Self scale. The SDQII incorporated all seven of the original scales, but the Peer Relations scale was split into Same and Opposite Sex scales. A General Self scale plus two additional scales labeled Emotional Stability and Honesty-Trustworthiness were added, bringing the total number of scales to 11. While early SDQ research investigated the structural dimensionality of self-concept, more recent studies (see Marsh, 1990a) have systematically manipulated self-concept, examining the interrelationships between the dimensions of self-concept and other constructs such as academic achievement.

Several distinct facets of self-concept are measured in the SDQ instruments. The actual scales are labeled as follows: Math, Physical Appearance, General Self, Honesty-Trustworthiness, Physical Abilities, Verbal, Emotional Stability, Parent Relations, General School, Same-Sex Relations, and Opposite-Sex Relations. The Physical Abilities scale relates to skills/interest in sporting/physical activities; Physical Appearance concerns one's physical attractiveness to others; Opposite-Sex Relations involves interactions with members of the opposite sex; Same-Sex Relations concerns interactions with peers of the same sex; Parent Relations focuses on relationships with one's parents; Honesty-Trustworthiness measures one's dependability and truthfulness; Emotional Stability relates to one's freedom from emotional dysfunction; Math measures one's interest and ability in mathematic reasoning; Verbal pertains to interest and ability in reading and English; General School involves one's interest and abilities in schoolwork; and General Self pertains to one's feelings of self-worth, self-confidence, and self-satisfaction. Items in the test booklet are "cycled" (so that each scale is measured by only one item in every 11 sequential items) to avoid spurious contiguity or position effects. Because adolescents' responses vary according to gender, tables of norms are provided in the manual for males and females separately.

The cover sheet of a six-page test booklet gives detailed instructions on and examples of how to respond to the SDQII items. This is followed by five pages of easily understood descriptive statements scored on a 6-point self-rating scale (individuals simply tick the appropriate response option for each item in turn), thereby avoiding the psychometric limitations of categorical data, which are so prevalent with dichotomous response measures. The six response options are labeled as "false," "mostly false," "more false than true," "more true than false," "mostly true," and "true," thereby providing a wide range of possible choices. A separate scoring and profile booklet enables calculation of scores on each of the 11 scales (which reflect an adolescent's self-ratings in various areas of self-concept), as well as a total self-concept score summed across all scales.

Seven of the SDQII scales consist of 10 items each, while four scales (Physical Appearance, Physical Abilities, Parent Relations, and Opposite-Sex Relations) include only 8 items each. The scales with fewer items have only 8 instead of 10 because they have high coefficient alphas (.85 to .90), in accord with the traditional interpretation of "internal consistency." The decision to go with slightly shorter scales in this case was felt to be an appropriate compromise between reliability and length of the instrument. Test-retest reliability estimates for these shorter scales are all adequate (.75, .86, .77, and .79, respectively; mean stability estimate = .80—see "Technical Aspects" section). Mean scores (based on the total normative sample of 5,494 adolescents) also are provided for each scale, and they are substituted for missing scores if five or fewer responses are left blank. Half of the items are reversed in direction of scoring to minimize the impact of possible response sets. The manual clearly indicates directly worded items with a plus (+) sign and negatively worded ones with a minus (–) sign. A separate profile sheet enables quick and convenient comparison of an adolescent's T-scores across each of the scales simultaneously. The scoring and profile booklet also includes a blank page for examiner comments, which is a useful addition.

No specific training is needed to administer the SDQII, as the instrument is self-contained with ample instructions provided on the cover sheets prefacing the SDQ materials. Although professional examiners can be used, the SDQII also could be administered satisfactorily by teaching/research assistants or by classroom teachers with minimal instruction (it has been found in practice that 10 minutes enables sufficient instructions to be provided for successful administration of the SDQ instruments).

Practical Applications/Uses

The SDQII is a multidimensional instrument that measures some of the major aspects of an adolescent's self-concept. Although no restrictions on administration time are specified, the instrument is easy to administer, taking only about 20 to 25 minutes to complete (although is highly likely that many adolescents would easily complete the 102 items in about 15 minutes). Consequently, use of the multifaceted SDQII instrument would be attractive to a range of professionals, including researchers and applied practitioners, particularly in the fields of psychology, psychiatry, social work, and education. It is a useful tool for the educator who wishes to investigate why a particular student is not achieving academically. Junior high school counselors find the SDQII a great practical help in their role of advising adolescents. Efficacy of particular therapeutic/treatment interventions can be monitored progressively throughout a course of counseling or therapy in determining the influence of treatment interventions on an adolescent's self-image.

Private practitioners and clinicians in mental health services find this instrument helpful in monitoring an adolescent's feelings of self-worth and self-esteem and his or her overall psychological adjustment. In addition, the instrument is useful in a wide range of research studies in psychology and education, as self-concept has an important influence on many behavioral and performance outcomes.

Although the item content is directed toward young adolescents, this instrument also may be administered to older adolescents and young adults. At present there are no specific adaptations of the SDQII for special groups such as the blind or intellectually disabled (in the latter instance use of the companion SDQI would be more appropriate, as a reading age of only Grade 4 is required). However, use of the *read-aloud* administration procedure would enable the SDQII to be used with some special groups. The examiner needs to take an active role only when the read-aloud group administration procedure is used. In this situation, the examiner reads aloud the instructions (provided on the test booklet cover sheet) before allowing group members to respond to the items. When administering SDQ instruments to large groups, it is obviously more expedient to have all group members work in accord with directives so that adequate control over the testing procedures is maintained. Also, the individually administered procedure used with the SDQI for children as young as kindergarten-aged could be adapted for use with almost any group (Marsh, Craven, & Debus, 1991).

Administration instructions in the manual include both the "standard administration procedures" as well as the "read-aloud administration procedures." This latter method is useful when adolescents do not have sufficient grasp of written English, or when the instrument is administered to large groups and it is necessary to finish by a set time. Both sets of administration instructions are set out clearly and concisely in the manual. There is little point in departing from the order of items as presented, as all SDQII items are of an approximately equivalent reading level. As the instrument is not a timed one, respondents who leave out any particular items should be encouraged to go back over their answer sheets and complete their responses to any items omitted. Examiners should be vigilant, particularly when the instrument is being administered to large groups, to ensure that missing item responses are minimized.

Instructions for scoring the SDQII are clearly provided in the scoring and profile booklet. These instructions, including details on scoring of reverse-worded items, are fully self-contained and self-explanatory. It is only necessary to read the scoring instructions in order to calculate the raw scores, to convert them into percentiles, and transform them into normalized standard scores with a mean of 50 and standard deviation of 10 (T-scores). Such scores are not encumbered either by decimal points or negative signs.

Scoring the instrument takes only a few minutes. Directions are straightforward, and there are no apparent hidden complications in the scoring procedures. The manual provides detailed instructions on the calculation of raw scores, the total raw score, and conversion of raw scores to scaled scores. A complete worked example is provided for all 11 of the SDQII scales, making scoring virtually foolproof. Tables of percentiles and corresponding T-scores are provided in Appendix A of the manual, so that derivation of the scaled scores is as simple and straightforward as possible.

As no templates are required for scoring (it is only necessary to transcribe the respondent's raw scores for each item onto the scoring sheet), problems due to fragile templates and so forth are avoided. Optical scanning of response sheets was not available at the time of this writing. The preconstructed computer programs operate on a data file that does, however, require keypunching. Nevertheless, it would not be difficult to build optical scanning of response sheets into future editions of the instruments, obviating the need to keypunch respondents' raw scores into a file and thereby alleviating the risk of transcription errors creeping into the data.

A computer disk is provided for scoring and analyzing responses for all three SDQ instruments. Moreover, these programs are very comprehensive, providing extensive and detailed descriptive statistics on the demographic variables of sex, age, school attended, and the student's particular teacher, as well as substituting mean scores for missing values (provided no more than four responses are missing within any particular scale) and automatically computing scale scores for each of the eight basic SDQ scales, for the academic and nonacademic total scores, and for the total self. In addition, the computer program calculates item homogeneity indices (Cronbach alpha coefficients) for each scale, carries out a detailed exploratory factor analysis (with an almost orthogonal, but nevertheless oblique rotation of derived factors), computes factor score coefficients, and provides a number of additional descriptive statistics, including estimates of skewness and kurtosis and also the corresponding Pearson product-moment correlation coefficients. For users interested in research applications, factor scores based on analytically weighted responses for the total normative sample can be calculated by reference to the regressed factor scores presented in Appendix B of the SDQII manual.

Interpretation of the SDQII instrument is based on objective standard scores (percentiles and T-scores). Direct comparison of raw scores to elucidate underlying self-concept differences may be problematic. However, even interpretation of percentiles can present difficulties (slight differences in raw scores at the high end of the range can result in large differences in percentile scores). Use of the profile T-scores (modified standard scores) is relatively straightforward and enables direct comparison of an adolescent's scores across each of the SDQII scales.

Nevertheless, some knowledge of errors of measurement and of the relationships between raw scores, percentiles, and T-scores is required in order to make sensible interpretations of SDQII profiles. It is necessary to bear in mind when interpreting profiles that an adolescent's responses may be biased due to inadequate self-insight, resulting in an unrealistic self-concept score on some of the SDQII scale dimensions. Valid interpretations depend on adolescents providing honest responses. Efforts to facilitate honest responding can be made by reassuring students that their responses will remain confidential and may be helpful to them. It is not possible, however, to incorporate a social desirability scale into the SDQ instruments, as responding in a socially desirable manner coincides with positive self-concept. If there is no reason to suspect dishonest or biased responding, interpretation can proceed by comparing an adolescent's percentiles or T-scores on each scale, using the tables of norms provided in the appendix of the SDQII manual.

As the standard errors of measurement for the SDQII range from 3 to 4 T-score units, scale differences smaller than this should not be interpreted substantively. It is difficult to discriminate between high T-scores, as small differences in raw scores can produce large differences in percentiles and T-scores (at the high end of the range). T-scores above 50 (suggesting better than average development of self-concept) are not readily distinguishable, due to some negative skewness in the responses of young adolescents. Because self-concept dimensions are slightly negatively skewed in the normative data, this suggests that most adolescents tend to experience somewhat favorable self-concepts. On the other hand, low scale scores (T-scores below 30) suggest poor self-concept development, possibly indicative of serious psychopathology. Occurrence of only one or two low scores may not be particularly problematic, but when most or all scores are low, psychological investigation is warranted. To ensure that any low scores are valid, inspection of item responses should be undertaken to rule out the possibility of random or careless responding (there are no quantitative measures of either of these distorting influences built into the existing version of the SDQII instrument, although half the items are reversed in direction of scoring in order to minimize the impact of such distorting influences). As the General Self scale is a global evaluation of an individual's self-esteem, particular attention should be given to scores on this scale. Low General Self scores should be investigated. The manual advises that scores on the Total Self-Concept scale should be interpreted with caution, as the separate components of self-concept do not necessarily adhere closely (for instance, Math and Verbal dimensions are notably distinct).

Technical Aspects

The manual reports Cronbach alpha coefficients ranging from .83 to .91 (.94 for the Total Self-Concept scale), based on results from the total normative sample. Likewise, item homogeneity data from a separate sample ($N = 137$) produced alpha coefficients ranging from .77 to .93. These estimates suggest high levels of interitem correlations within each of the SDQII scales. Although classical itemetrics suggest that alpha coefficients should be maximized (the notion of "internal consistency"), there is, however, controversy over this point as high levels of item homogeneity may also suggest narrow scales with significant item redundancy, where items are virtually paraphrases of each other (cf. Boyle, 1991). Item homogeneity estimates can be either high or low irrespective of actual reliability (test-retest estimates), although classical itemetric opinion equates internal consistency with reliability. Nevertheless, perusal of the item intercorrelations within each of the scales suggests that, in the main, items did not unduly overlap, so that the issue of possible item redundancy does not appear to be particularly problematic for the SDQII instrument.

As for reliability, stability estimates for a 7-week test-retest interval ($N = 137$) ranged from .72 for Emotional Stability to .88 for Math, suggesting moderate stability of the SDQII scales (and also suggesting that the SDQII scales may not be operating as situationally sensitive states as intended by the test author), despite an intervention (physical fitness training program) designed to enhance physical fitness. It would be interesting, however, to compare these stability estimates with the dependability (immediate or short-term retest) reliability coefficients. Regardless of whether self-concept is more trait-like as opposed to state-like, the dependabilities should be high if the SDQII scales are indeed reliable. Within the context of the SDQ research, self-concept is clearly viewed as a trait and therefore high levels of stability (.80 to .90) over time would be predicted (if the SDQ instruments are truly sensitive to situational variability; cf. Boyle, 1987). The test-retest correlations would almost surely be substantially higher during a shorter time interval (1 to 2 weeks vs. 7 weeks) in which no intervention occurred.

Several aspects of construct validity (factor analysis, multitrait-multimethod analysis, developmental changes, associations with other instruments, and effects of experimental manipulations) have been studied. The SDQII was based on the Shavelson et al. (1976) multidimensional model, which has been validated by means of exploratory factor analysis of 51 item pairs on the total normative sample, using an iterative principal factoring procedure, together with direct oblimin oblique rotation to simple structure, even though the factor pattern solution was almost orthogonal (cf. Gorsuch, 1983). Marsh (1990b, p. 33) provided a sound rationale for undertaking the factor analysis on the intercorrelations of item pairs rather than on individual item intercorrelations. To obtain reliable factors, the number of subjects should greatly exceed the number of variables (cf. Boyle, 1988). Use of item pairs (*item parcels* in Cattellian terminology) generally produce highly valid correlations, which therefore provide a sound point of departure for conducting subsequent factor analytic investigations. Use of such item parcels (two items per parcel) doubles the ratio of subjects to variables. Item parcels are more reliable than individual items, thereby producing more accurate factor loadings. A reduced number of variables (51 items pairs instead of 102 items) concomitantly enables a saving in computer time, reducing computer costs. Less important these days are the size limitations of various statistical computing packages, but this may be a consideration with certain software applications of exploratory factor analysis.

In terms of the rotational strategy adopted, the SPSSX delta shift parameter was set at –2.0 (an almost orthogonal rotation), thereby reducing the intercorrelations among the factors as compared with the actual SDQII scale intercorrelations. Nevertheless, the $\pm$ .10 hyperplane count (percentage of factor loadings $\leq$ .10) was 84.14%, indicating a good approximation of the final rotated factor pattern solution to simple structure criteria. Perusal of the hyperplane counts for each of the 11 SDQII factors indicates that the least satisfactory were Factor 10 (General School—74.5%) and Factor 11 (General Self—70.6%). As acceptable hyperplane counts range from 65% upwards (Cattell, 1978), extraction of both these factors seems to have been fully warranted. The empirical factor analytic evidence reported in the manual indicates that overextraction did not occur and that extraction of all 11 factors was justified. This provides strong support for the Shavelson-Marsh (1986) multidimensional model of self-concept.

It would seem useful to consider the SDQII within the broader context of other SDQ research in which a) there is clear support for the SDQ factor structure and its invariance over gender and age using confirmatory factor analytic approaches, and b) considerable research evaluating the construct validity of SDQ responses against a wide variety of other "real-life" constructs. In regard to the former requirement, Marsh (1992a) recently completed a chapter for the Suls and Greenwald monograph series and a confirmatory factor analysis showing the factorial invariance of SDQII responses over eight groups consisting of a 4 × 2 (age × gender) design. As for the latter requirement, relative to most psychological constructs, the SDQ self-concept instruments (including SDQI, SDQII, and SDQIII) have been evaluated experimentally against a wide variety of real-life criteria. A number of experimental attempts to enhance specific components of self-concept have been successful even though they have had limited effects on various global self-concept measures. From a practical perspective, this argues for the use of multidimensional self-concept instruments—including scales most relevant to the content of the intervention—instead of, or in addition to, more global measures.

Separate exploratory factor analyses for different levels of sex and age separately also supported the 11-factor model of self-concept. The results of these validity studies are reported comprehensively in the SDQII manual. Several validity studies also are reported providing further support for the predictive validity of the SDQII, especially in regard to the prediction of academic school achievement. Further, there is good evidence of both concurrent and discriminant validity provided. A number of complex structural models are also included in the manual, thereby providing the starting point for future studies of the "causal" relationships between the various dimensions of self-concept and "real-life" performance criteria (e.g., academic achievement).

The manual also includes an informative chapter on various experimental studies of self-concept. Experimental manipulation was viewed within the desirable context of the construct validation approach, wherein attempts were made to enhance domains likely to be susceptible to such interventions. In general, the specific components of self-concept most relevant to a particular experimental investigation have been enhanced significantly in several studies by Marsh and his colleagues (although some aspects of self-concept seem less tractable). However, the overall finding from several controlled studies is that experimental attempts to enhance self-concept are relatively unsuccessful, especially when global self-esteem is the major outcome variable. These empirical studies, however, provide additional support for the construct validity of the SDQII instrument and for the separate facets of self-concept. A further chapter in the manual deals with the relationship of self-concept to sexual identity. Results suggest little support for interactive and sex-typed models, but they strongly support a differentiated additive androgyny model. These results also suggest a new model of the role of masculinity/femininity in self-concept, which should stimulate further research into sexual identity and self-concept (Marsh & Byrne, 1991).

Critique

The study of self-concept has a long history, spanning the writings of William James in the 19th century to the plethora of empirical research studies in recent years. A greater understanding of self-concept may have important implications for many areas of an adolescent's functioning, not only including academic and physical performance but also social, emotional, and psychological adaptation. The empirical SDQ research to date is based on a strong multidimensional model of self-concept and has resulted in construction of psychometrically sound instruments for measuring several distinct aspects of self-concept. As pointed out in the SDQII manual, test construction and theory building are inextricably intertwined (equivalent to the Cattellian inductive-hypothetico-deductive method of scientific investigation). Moreover, the extremely comprehensive and sophisticated computer scoring programs provided with the SDQ instruments are a bonus, seldom seen with most other psychoeducational assessment instruments. Use of the relevant program enables extensive computer printout information on adolescents' SDQII self-concept responses.

The major limitations center around the drawbacks of self-report questionnaires in general. Although reliance solely on self-report measures undoubtedly has limited the generalizability of results from self-concept research, nevertheless "there are, as yet, few alternative avenues to investigate self-concept. Self-report may be one of the most defensible ways to assess a person's 'conception of self' as the emphasis is upon their 'conception' not their reality" (Hattie, 1992, p. 246). Like any self-report questionnaire, the SDQ instruments are likely to exhibit all the drawbacks of such measures, and responses will be influenced, to some extent at least, depending on the capability and willingness of respondents to provide valid and reliable responses to the SDQ items. One problem is the distorting influence of response sets. Currently available measures of self-concept, such as the SDQ series of instruments, utilize Q-data methods rather than objective test (T-data) measures, so that motivational/response distortion remains potentially problematic. Incorporation of reverse-worded items into the SDQ instruments definitely minimizes the possible influence of response sets, although the effects of social desirability responding cannot be controlled effectively in self-concept measures. Use of reversed and nonreversed items also runs the risk of measuring distinct/separate constructs. Random or careless responding is also potentially problematic. However, the control scores developed for the SDQI could easily be adopted to the SDQII for checks on random or careless responding. Another potential problem (due to item transparency) is that self-report instruments often are plagued by problems associated with response distortion, ranging all the way from inadequate self-insight to deliberate dissimulation. The SDQII is a self-report questionnaire and therefore is subject to these distorting influences. Even so, most of the so-called response biases (such as social desirability) lead to substantially higher correlations among the scales. The finding that the SDQII scales are nearly uncorrelated provides a logical argument that such biases—if they exist at all— must be rather weak.

Having pointed to possible problems, it is nevertheless clearly evident that the SDQ instruments are based on a good theoretical model and that they enable psychometrically sound measurement of the major multidimensional factors of self-concept. One possible difficulty, however, is that the SDQ measures may discriminate inadequately between self-concept and self-esteem (Hattie, 1992, p. 247). Whereas self-concept relates to largely descriptive and nonevaluative aspects, self-esteem is more concerned with evaluative dimensions. Within the context of the Shavelson model, however, Marsh would regard both self-concept and self-esteem as synonymous. Consequently, the reported lack of discrimination between these two constructs may be more apparent than real. Another possible difficulty is that the dimensionality of self-concept may differ for males and females as reported in a study by Byrne (1990). Prompted by this criticism, Marsh (1992c) has investigated the invariance of Math, Verbal, Academic, and General self-concept factor structures across both gender and age, using a sample of 4,000 students administered the SDQII. Marsh concluded that the factor structure of academic self-concept is invariant for males and females. In these more recent SDQ studies, Marsh has placed a greater emphasis on the use of confirmatory factor analysis and complex structural ("causal") modeling (via Lisrel 7—Jöreskog & Sörbom, 1989) than in earlier studies, where the emphasis was more on the use of exploratory factor analysis, at least in terms of the factor analytic information provided in the SDQII manual. For example, Marsh (1989) tested a number of such models, including a structural equation model of the longitudinal panel design relating academic achievement and academic self-concept. Use of such advanced multivariate structural equation modeling techniques combined with experimental designs has greatly enhanced the quality of self-concept research over recent years, as compared with much of the earlier work predating Professor Marsh's endeavors, which was largely correlational in nature and somewhat atheoretical. In contrast, the almost exhaustive and programmatic series of SDQ studies has been well grounded in a clearly multidimensional model of self-concept, for which extensive empirical evidence has supported the postulated structural dimensionality of self-concept.

It is probably fair to say that the SDQII (and its companion scales—SDQI and SDQIII) should be among the instruments of choice for researchers wanting to measure well-defined multiple dimensions of self-concept. Its major competitors in terms of current usage, the Coopersmith scale and the Piers-Harris Children's Self Concept Scale, do not do the best job of measuring multiple dimensions and were really designed for younger children (the age range covered by the SDQI). The other major instrument, the Tennessee Self Concept Scale, also has a factor structure not wholly supported by the literature and was developed for university-aged students and adults. The various SDQ instruments have been compared with each of these scales in numerous empirical studies. Another instrument, the Beck Self-Concept Test, or BST (Beck, Steer, Epstein, & Brown, 1990), has proved useful in assessing self-concept among depressed individuals, and it would be interesting to see what relationships exist in terms of concurrent and discriminant validity between the SDQIII and the BST. Hattie (1992) undertook fairly extensive reviews of major self-concept instruments, including the Coopersmith, Piers-Harris, and SDQ instruments, as well as an instrument of his own. He concluded that

> the SDQ appears to be an excellent measure of the various first-order dimensions of self-concept as proposed by Shavelson et al. The estimates of reliability are consistently high, and the tests are based on a multifaceted nature of self-concept. The set of SDQs are the best set of measures available (see Wylie, 1989, for a further favorable review). (pp. 82–83)

He goes on to say that

> the most promising new tests of self-concept are the Marsh SDQs. The various versions are becoming more widely used, it is based on the Shavelson model, and there is much evidence accumulating from various research teams to support its usefulness and to provide information on its psychometric properties. (p. 175)

It is evident that self-concept plays an important role in influencing individuals' behaviors. According to Beck et al. (1990, p. 191), "The self-concept is the product of input of self-relevant data and relatively stable structures (self-schemata) that serve as information processors . . . data supporting the self-concept will be processed, whereas data not supporting the self-concept will be ignored." Measures of self-concept, which are invariably obtained from self-report questionnaires (Cattellian Q-data), are regarded as essential in assessing various self-perceived attributes pertaining to various aspects of one's life such as marital/family problems, educational performance, occupational success, and even maladaptive personality functioning. Of these areas, academic self-concept is one of the major domains of interest to researchers.

Taken overall, the development of a multidimensional self-concept model has been supported empirically in both exploratory and confirmatory factor analytic research as well as in a number of experimental studies, and the resultant SDQ instruments have been shown generally to exhibit satisfactory reliability and validity, good dimensionality, and sound psychometric scoring properties. Consequently, this reviewer highly recommends use of the SDQ instruments in future research and applied studies.

References

This list includes text citations and suggested additional reading.

Beck, A.T., Steer, R.A., Epstein, N., & Brown, G. (1990). Beck Self-Concept Test. *Psychological Assessment: A Journal of Consulting and Clinical Psychology, 2*, 191–197.

Boyle, G.J. (1987). Use of change scores in redundancy analyses of multivariate psychological inventories. *Personality and Individual Differences, 8*, 845–854.

Boyle, G.J. (1988). Elucidation of motivation structure by dynamic calculus. In J.R. Nesselroade & R.B. Cattell (Eds.), *Handbook of multivariate experimental psychology* (rev. 2nd ed., pp. 737–787). New York: Plenum.

Boyle, G.J. (1991). Does item homogeneity indicate internal consistency or item redundancy in psychometric scales? *Personality and Individual Differences, 12*, 291–294.

Byrne, B.M. (1990). Investigating gender differences in adolescent self-concept: A look beneath the surface. *Applied Measurement in Education, 3*, 255–274.

Cattell, R.B. (1978). *The scientific use of factor analysis in behavioral and life sciences.* New York: Plenum.

Gorsuch, R.L. (1983). *Factor analysis* (2nd ed.). Hillsdale, NJ: Erlbaum.

Hattie, J. (1992). *Self concept.* Hillsdale, NJ: Erlbaum.

Jöreskog, K.G., & Sörbom, D. (1989). *Lisrel 7: A guide to the program and applications* (2nd ed.). Chicago: SPSS.

Marsh, H.W. (1988). *Self-Description Questionnaire I: Manual and research monograph.* San Antonio, TX: Psychological Corporation.

Marsh, H.W. (1989). *The causal ordering of academic self-concept and academic achievement: A multiwave, longitudinal panel analysis.* Sydney, Australia: University of Sydney.

Marsh, H.W. (1990a). A multidimensional, hierarchical self-concept: Theoretical and empirical justification. *Educational Psychology Review, 2*, 77–172.

Marsh, H.W. (1990b). *Self-Description Questionnaire II: A theoretical and empirical basis for the measurement of multiple dimensions of adolescent self-concept: A test manual and research monograph.* San Antonio, TX: Psychological Corporation.

Marsh, H.W. (1990c). The structure of academic self-concept: The Marsh/Shavelson model. *Journal of Educational Psychology, 82,* 623–636.

Marsh, H.W. (in press). *The Self-Description Questionnaire III: Manual and research monograph.* San Antonio, TX: Psychological Corporation.

Marsh, H.W. (1992a). Academic self-concept: Theory, measurement and research. In J. Suls & A.G. Greenwald (Eds.), *Psychological perspectives on the self* (Vol. 4). Hillsdale, NJ: Erlbaum.

Marsh, H.W. (1992b). The content specificity of relations between academic achievement and academic self-concept. *Journal of Educational Psychology, 84,* 43–50.

Marsh, H.W. (1992c). *The multidimensional structure of academic self-concept: Invariance over gender and age.* Manuscript submitted for publication.

Marsh, H.W., & Byrne, B.M. (1991). Differentiated additive androgyny model: Relations between masculinity, femininity and multiple dimensions of self-concept. *Journal of Personality and Social Psychology, 61,* 811–828.

Marsh, H.W., Craven, R., & Debus, R. (1991). Self-concepts of young children aged 5 to 8: Their measurement and multidimensional structure. *Journal of Educational Psychology, 83,* 377–392.

NELS. (1992). *Users' manual: National Education Longitudinal Study of 1988: First follow-up.* Washington, DC: U.S. Department of Education.

Shavelson, R.J., Hubner, J.J., & Stanton, G.C. (1976). Validation of construct interpretations. *Review of Educational Research, 46,* 407–441.

Shavelson, R.J., & Marsh, H.W. (1986). On the structure of self-concept. In R. Schwarzer (Ed.), *Anxiety and cognitions* (pp. 305–330). Hillsdale, NJ: Erlbaum.

Wylie, R.C. (1989). *Measures of self-concept.* Lincoln, NE: University of Nebraska Press.

Frank M. Bernt, Ph.D.
Assistant Professor, Department of Education and Health Services,
St. Joseph's University, Philadelphia, Pennsylvania.

THE SELF-ESTEEM INDEX

Linda Brown and Jacquelyn Alexander. Austin, Texas: PRO-ED, Inc.

Introduction

The Self-Esteem Index (SEI) is an 80-item, norm-referenced, self-report instrument designed to assess children's global self-esteem as well as their perceptions of their personal traits and of their relationships with others. The scale is comprised of four subscales (20 items each): Perception of Familial Acceptance, Perception of Popularity, Perception of Academic Competence, and Perception of Personal Security. The SEI is appropriate for use with children in Grades 3 through 12, in both research and clinical/counseling settings.

Coauthors of the SEI are Linda Brown and Jacquelyn Alexander. Dr. Brown received her Ph.D. from Kansas State University in 1974. In addition to the Self-Esteem Index (1991), she has authored numerous other scales, including the Test of Nonverbal Intelligence, Second Edition (1990), the Behavior Rating Profiles, Second Edition (1990), and the Index of Personality Characteristics (1988). She also coauthored (with Donald Hammill and Brian Bryant) *A Consumer's Guide to Tests in Print*, a reference text that evaluates the psychometric characteristics of over 250 norm-referenced tests. Jacquelyn Alexander, the SEI's coauthor, earned her doctorate at the University of Texas at Austin and currently teaches at Our Lady of the Lake University in San Antonio, Texas.

Steps in the construction of the SEI are laid out in detail in the examiner's manual. An initial pool of over 1,000 items was accumulated through a variety of techniques, including an examination of content-related instruments, a review of the literature, and consultation with mental health professionals. After duplicates and highly similar items were eliminated, a smaller pool of 300 items was submitted to a group of professionals in the fields of psychology, education, and counseling. These reviewers were instructed to identify items they felt would most likely discriminate individuals with healthy self-concepts from those with low self-concepts and/or emotional disturbances.

The resulting subset of 120 items constituted a preliminary version of the SEI, which was administered to 550 students equally distributed from 8:0 through 18:11 years of age. Items were retained for the final version based on two criteria: a) item-to-total correlations between .30 and .80 for both the entire test and for the four subscales; and b) less than 50% of respondents marking "incorrect" answers (viz., "always true" for negative items; "always false" for positive items).

Eighty items meeting the above criteria constituted the final version of the SEI, which was administered to a sample of 2,455 subjects between October 1988 and

October 1989. The normative group consisted of children ranging from 8:0 through 18:11 years of age drawn from a broad cross-section of schoolchildren in 19 different states; as a result, the sample's demographic characteristics closely resembled those of the U.S. population (based on the 1985 *Statistical Abstract of the U.S.*) with regard to gender, domicile, race, geographic area, ethnicity, principal language, and parents' educational attainment.

Materials for the SEI consist of a student response booklet and a profile and record form. The 80 items in the response booklet are structured in a 4-point Likert-type format (always true, usually true, usually false, always false). Students note their responses directly in the booklet. Responses are translated onto the record form for scoring. The profile and record form provides space for subscore and total score computation, examiner comments and recommendations, identifying information, and numerical and graphical presentation of SEI and other test scores.

The four subscales constituting the SEI are clearly described in the examiner's manual. Perception of Familial Acceptance measures components of self-esteem related to home and family. It includes items addressing issues of trust and security, belonging, family activities, and parental expectations and attitudes. Perception of Academic Competence measures the respondent's perceptions of his or her intellectual and academic abilities, interests, and values. It includes items related to teacher interactions, school performance, and academic motivation. Perception of Peer Popularity measures self-esteem in social situations outside the family unit, including relationships with friends, general likability, and comfort in social situations. Perception of Personal Security measures self-esteem as it relates to the individual's physical and psychological well-being. It includes items addressing perceptions of safety, confidence, vulnerability, and anxiety.

Practical Applications/Uses

One of the appealing aspects of the SEI is its "user friendliness." Although the authors appropriately caution against the use of their instrument by professionals who lack any training in the area of personality assessment, this reviewer's impression is that professionals with a basic understanding of psychometric principles and with an appreciation of the limits of such tests would be qualified to use the SEI. The manual is written in layperson's terms, describing the elementary essentials of test construction and of test interpretation. This characteristic, in combination with the inclusion of counselors and educators in the early stages of content validation, results in a test that is intuitively appealing to users in educational and counseling settings. The authors state that the SEI can be used for individual assessment, for evaluation of program effectiveness, for monitoring individual progress over time, and for research purposes. They appropriately caution against the use of the SEI as a "standalone" measure of self-esteem, encouraging users to include the instrument as part of a larger assessment process including observation, interview, family history, and so on.

The SEI is a paper-and-pencil inventory and may be administered in one-on-one or group settings. It requires approximately half an hour to administer (although no time limit should be imposed). Specific instructions are spelled out in the examiner's manual that accompanies the scale. It is worth noting that the authors do not recommend that the SEI be administered orally in a group setting; they feel that doing so "detracts from the privacy of the situation," appealing to the importance of following ethical guidelines for the use of tests. This position contradicts standard administration procedures for similar tests (Marsh, 1988; Piers & Harris, 1984), whose authors instruct administrators to read each item aloud to subjects. There is a philosophical tradeoff between optimizing respondent understanding and preserving a sense of respondent privacy; one's stance on this matter does not reflect directly on the test used. Oral administration remains an option in any case, but the consequences of such differences in administration may be worth noting.

Scoring is done by simply adding the respondent's choices for every fourth item throughout the scale, as items score alternately on the four scales (e.g., items 1, 5, 9, 13, etc. for the first subscale; 2, 6, 10, 14, etc. for the second subscale; and so on). The score summary section on the profile and record form facilitates these computations. Half the items are reverse scored; items are differentiated by squares and circles in the student response booklet to aid in the identification of items to be reverse scored.

Raw scores are easily translated into percentile ranks or into stanine scores using tables in the manual; in addition, a "Self-Esteem Quotient" (SEQ)—based on a normalized distribution with a preset mean of 100 and standard deviation of 15—can be determined for the total SEI score (simply the sum of the four subscale scores) to facilitate comparison with other norm-referenced test scores. The authors discuss using the standard error of measurement for building confidence intervals around the SEQ, and they include a table of standard errors of measurement by age group for the total SEQ score and for each subtest standard score.

Technical Aspects

Internal consistency estimates for the SEI are quite acceptable, with r's from .80 to .90 for the subscales and .93 for the total scale. An examination of estimates for subgroups divided by age reveals somewhat lower reliabilities for younger ages (8 and 9), especially for the Perception of Familial Acceptance subscale; this is consistent with previous results obtained for similar instruments (Marsh, Barnes, Cairns, & Tidman, 1984).

The test authors omit any evaluation of test-retest reliability for the SEI, citing Anastasi's (1988) argument that personality traits are susceptible to random fluctuations over time. Feldt and Brennan (1989) support the authors' contention, suggesting that stability estimates for paper-and-pencil instruments are potentially confounded by respondents' tendency to be "spuriously consistent" with previous responses. Studies of other frequently used self-esteem measures have obtained stability coefficients averaging .69 or higher for intervals of up to 6 months (Epstein, 1985; Marsh & Richards, cited in Marsh, 1988; Wylie, 1974). Though test-retest reliability estimates should be interpreted cautiously (perhaps even skeptically), nonetheless this may be the "only method available" (practically speaking) that reflects day-to-day error factors (Feldt & Brennan, 1989).

The issue, then, is whether an admittedly rough estimate of temporal stability is preferable to no estimate at all.

Separate studies were conducted to determine the relationship of the SEI to several related measures: teachers' estimates of the students' self-esteem; scores on the Piers-Harris Children's Self Concept Scale, Revised (Piers & Harris, 1984); scores on the Self-Esteem Inventories, School Form (Coopersmith, 1984); and scores on the Index of Personality Characteristics (Brown & Coleman, 1988). Small samples of 25 subjects or less were used in these studies (except for the study of teacher ratings); also, narrowly circumscribed age groups were employed in each case.

An examination of correlations between the SEI total score and total scores from other self-esteem measures ranged from .77 to .83, supporting its validity as a measure of global self-esteem. The picture created by correlations among subscale scores is less clear. For example, while the SEI Perception of Peer Popularity subscale scores correlate highly with the Coopersmith Social Self–Peers subscores ($r = .79$), they correlate even more highly with the Coopersmith General Self subscores ($r = .86$) and nearly as highly with the Home-Parents subscores ($r = .71$). With regard to the Piers-Harris scale, the SEI Percentage of Peer Popularity subscores are more highly correlated with every other subtest score (mean $r = .55$) than they are with the Piers-Harris Popularity scale ($r = .29$). Similar inconsistencies appear with regard to the other subscales, providing an initial impression that convergent validity is adequately addressed but that divergent or discriminant validity of subscales is virtually ignored. This difficulty will be discussed in more detail in the next section.

Correlations between SEI subscale scores and teacher global ratings on a 9-point scale ranged from .21 (Perception of Academic Competence) to .44 (Perception of Peer Popularity).

The examiner's manual reports a study done to evaluate the SEI's effectiveness in distinguishing between normative and special population groups; these groups included learning disabled, emotionally disturbed, gifted, and behaviorally disordered students. Results tentatively suggested that the SEI academic competence and personal security subscales might be useful in discriminating among these groups; however, data is presented only in graphic form, and sample sizes are quite small for three of the groups. Further evaluation of this aspect of the SEI's validity would strengthen its credibility as a clinically useful instrument.

Discussion of the factorial structure of the SEI is rather brief. The four subscales were "initially imposed" by the authors for reasons that are not outlined clearly in the manual. The use of principal components analysis to investigate factorial structure yields a fairly convincing picture of the four-factor structure assumed by the scale. Results of the factor analysis indicated a strong general factor, accounting for 51% of the variance, and a subsequent four-factor varimax-rotated solution accounted for 87% of the total variance. The rationale for four factors may be too sparse to convince users with a theoretical bent that four is anything more than a convenient number to choose, especially in the face of extensive and sophisticated discussions surrounding this controversy (Harter, 1982; Marsh, 1988; Wylie, 1974); nonetheless, the description of constructs that the SEI purports to measure and the instructions for interpreting test results are certainly sufficient for the user who is comfortable with the authors' definition of self-esteem.

Critique

Those familiar with the history of self-esteem assessment may wonder whether a new instrument is really necessary, given the abundance of existing scales for assessing this construct. The answer to this question might be come from determining just what is the same and what is different about the SEI.

The SEI is similar to other widely used measures of self-esteem in its length and structure. It especially resembles Coopersmith's Self-Esteem Inventories in its choice of subscales. The available manual provides useful information concerning scoring and administration, concepts essential to test interpretation, and data to support (at least tentatively) the authors' hypotheses concerning what the SEI measures.

What is different about the SEI that may be of interest to potential users is its recent development. Although this may discourage researchers who are looking for an instrument allowing for direct comparison with other studies, this problem will be resolved as the list of studies using the SEI begins to accumulate (the SEI was first published in 1991). An advantage deriving from its recent publication is that normative data are current. In addition, the sample used for standardizing the SEI is broadly representative of the U.S. population. Other widely used scales often have been standardized on non–U.S. samples (Marsh, 1988) or on less than adequate samples (e.g., the Piers-Harris scale used subjects from a single school district in Pennsylvania and has not be renormed since the 1960s).

Although the SEI is of similar overall length and reports internal consistency estimates that equal or surpass those of other self-esteem scales, its 80 items measure only four dimensions of self-esteem; others with no more or with fewer items measure six or more dimensions. Whether this reflects a weakness or not clearly depends on the purposes of the user. If the latter require distinguishing between mathematical and reading self-concepts, or if they require separating physical appearance from physical ability, then other instruments may be more helpful. However, "more" is not necessarily "better." The four dimensions described in the SEI may be quite sufficient for practitioners and for researchers who are investigating self-esteem as an explanatory or as an outcome variable; the measure may be less appropriate for researchers aiming at advancing, extending, or confirming current theories about self-esteem.

The SEI fails to address the issue of divergent or discriminant validity. Subscale scores overlap with each other and with conceptually distinct subscores to such an extent that their "dimensional purity" is highly suspect. This weakness also has been noted in the Coopersmith instrument (Shavelson, Hubner, & Stanton, 1976). The dimensionality of self-esteem has been evaluated more rigorously in some cases, supplementing item analysis and exploratory factor analysis with multitrait-multimethod and confirmatory factor analysis techniques (Marsh, 1988). Such techniques are currently recommended as a means of strengthening the construct validity of many educational and psychological tests (Cronbach, 1988; Messick, 1989). Future revisions of the SEI would do well to incorporate these powerful techniques in the assessment of the instrument's validity.

The SEI lacks any scale to assess social desirability, negative item bias, or response inconsistency. The authors argue that such biases created by "dissemblance" ("faking good" or "faking bad") are adequately accounted for in the test's normative tables. Although response bias in self-report instruments is a problem for which no single solution is satisfactory (see Wylie, 1979, pp. 57 ff. for an enlightening discussion), the authors of the SEI dismiss the problem too readily on the simplistic grounds that "normal dissemblers" will fall in the normal range of SEI scores, while individuals falling in either extremely high or in extremely low ranges will be distinctive enough to warrant closer examination. While this certainly drives home the importance of using multiple indicators of self-esteem, it does not account for the possibility of an extremely low self-esteem individual who "fakes good" only to an extent that places him or her in the normal range, and it also fails to satisfy the researcher who may be looking for a single scale that can separate out a person's self-concept from how that person would like to appear to others. Although extreme dissemblance will not go unnoticed, there is no provision for the wide range of "normal tendencies" to dissemble that will have a negative impact on the validity of self-esteem scores.

It may be that the SEI has appeal to users who are content with fewer subscales or who find the SEI's particular subscales (e.g., Perception of Familial Acceptance) more suitable to their purposes. In such a case, the SEI becomes the scale of choice, with the proviso that there is a good deal of overlap among subtest scores. An examination of specific items on the SEI indicates that the "flavor" of the items may have more "clinically relevant" appeal than items on inventories established with more concern about psychometric purity.

In addition, as mentioned above, the SEI is user friendly and intuitively appealing to a broad group of mental health professionals and educators. The manual is both easily readable and educational for novices of test construction and use; the one drawback is that it may be somewhat too brief and simplistic in its treatment of the finer points of the instrument's psychometric qualities. Perhaps a separate, more sophisticated technical manual providing additional evidence for the SEI's validity and reliability would strengthen its credibility. In addition, a more explicit description of the theoretical assumptions underlying the selection of four (rather than six or seven) subscales seems necessary. Vague remarks about "what theory says" and about "what research studies show" may fail to satisfy students of self-esteem and may be misinterpreted by users unfamiliar with literature in this area.

In summary, the SEI seems to present a satisfactory measure of global self-esteem that will be very useful for professionals whose assessment needs are also global. Although conscientiously and competently constructed, its failure to address critical theoretical developments in the field of self-esteem and to assess discriminant validity and test-retest reliability weaken its position alongside more established instruments. Other aspects of the test make it a promising but not yet proven candidate for measuring self-esteem; perhaps further research and development that more closely analyzes its comparability to conceptually similar instruments will strengthen the SEI's credibility among already-established scales measuring self-esteem.

References

This list includes text citations and suggested additional reading.

Anastasi, A. (1988). *Psychological testing* (6th ed.). New York: Macmillan.

Brown, L., & Coleman, M.C. (1988). *Index of Personality Characteristics*. Austin, TX: PRO-ED.

Coopersmith, S. (1984). *Self-Esteem Inventories, School Form*. Palo Alto, CA: Consulting Psychologists Press.

Cronbach, L.J. (1988). Five perspectives on validation argument. In H. Wainer & H. Braun (Eds.), *Test validity* (pp. 3–17). Hillsdale, NJ: Erlbaum.

Epstein, H. (1985). Piers-Harris Children's Self Concept Scale. In J.V. Mitchell, Jr. (Ed.), *The ninth mental measurements yearbook* (pp. 1168–1170). Lincoln, NE: Buros Institute of Mental Measurements.

Feldt, L.S., & Brennan, R.L. (1989). Reliability. In R.L. Linn (Ed.), *Educational measurement* (3rd ed., pp. 105–146). New York: Macmillan.

Harter, S. (1982). The Perceived Competence Scale for Children. *Child Development, 53*, 87–97.

Marsh, H.W. (1988). *The Self-Description Questionnaire–I*. San Antonio, TX: Psychological Corporation.

Marsh, H.W., Barnes, J., Cairns, L., & Tidman, M. (1984). Self-Description Questionnaire: Age and sex effects in the structure and level of self-concept for preadolescent children. *Journal of Educational Psychology, 76*(5), 940–956.

Marsh, H.W., Parker, J., & Barnes, J. (1985). Multidimensional adolescent self-concepts: Their relations to age, sex, and academic measures. *American Educational Research Journal, 22*, 422–444.

Marsh, H.W., Parker, J.W., & Smith, I.D. (1983). Preadolescent self-concept: Its relation to self-concept as inferred by teachers and to academic ability. *British Journal of Educational Psychology, 53*, 60–78.

Messick, S. (1989). Validity. In R.L. Linn (Ed.), *Educational measurement* (3rd ed., pp. 13–102). New York: Macmillan.

Peterson, C., & Austin, J.T. (1985). Coopersmith Self-Esteem Inventories. In J.V. Mitchell, Jr. (Ed.), *The ninth mental measurements yearbook* (pp. 396–398). Lincoln, NE: Buros Institute of Mental Measurements.

Piers, E.V., & Harris, D.B. (1984). *Piers-Harris Children's Self Concept Scale (The Way I Feel About Myself)*. Los Angeles: Western Psychological Services.

Shavelson, R.J., & Bolus, R. (1982). Self-concept: The interplay of theory and methods. *Journal of Educational Psychology, 74*, 3–17.

Shavelson, R.J., Hubner, J.J., & Stanton, G.C. (1976). Validation of construct interpretations. *Review of Educational Research, 46*, 407–441.

Wylie, R.C. (1974). *The self-concept: Theory and research on selected topics* (Vol. 1). Lincoln, NE: University of Nebraska Press.

Wylie, R.C. (1979). *The self-concept: Theory and research on selected topics* (Vol. 2). Lincoln, NE: University of Nebraska Press.

James A. Moses, Jr., Ph.D.
Clinical Associate Professor of Psychiatry and Behavioral Sciences, Stanford University School of Medicine, and Coordinator, Psychological Assessment Unit, Department of Veterans Affairs Medical Center, Palo Alto, California.

SERIAL DIGIT LEARNING TEST
Arthur L. Benton, Kerry deS. Hamsher, Nils R. Varney, and Otfried Spreen. New York, New York: Oxford University Press.

Introduction

Serial Digit Learning (SDL), or "digit supraspan," is a rote memorial task in which a subject is asked to learn a list of eight or nine nonrecurring digits in serial order from auditory presentation by an examiner. The choice of list length depends on the examinee's demographic characteristics. Pioneering work by Zangwill (1943) showed that amnesic brain-injured patients had normal immediate recall performance on digit span, an attentional measure, usually through a span of six or seven digits. Increasing the span of digits to be recalled beyond the attentional range, to a "supraspan" level of eight or nine digits, however, produced deficits in recall among amnesic patients. Zangwill suggested that rote memory tasks mastered with repeated presentations of the same material would be more sensitive to memorial deficit than would "immediate memory" tasks such as digit span.

Subsequent work has shown that digit span is indeed an attentional and not a memorial task (Zimmerman & Woo-Sam, 1973). The distinction between attentional and memorial processes is an important one to make in clinical assessment. A patient who cannot attend to task normally will not recall normally either. The recall deficit will stem from failure to focus on the task and register the information initially, not from subsequent failure to recall or to retrieve information stored in short-term memory. The ability to attend to task normally, however, will not ensure that an attentive patient will encode or retrieve information effectively. Subsequent work by Drachman and Arbit (1966), Drachman and Hughes (1971), and Schinka (1974) confirmed the initial findings of Zangwill (1943). In addition, the work of Schinka (1974) showed significant relationships of SDL performance to age and educational level variables, which clarified the need for statistical control of these demographic variables in clinical applications of SDL methodology. For a detailed review of these studies, see Benton, Hamsher, Varney, and Spreen (1983, pp. 23–24).

It remained for Hamsher, Benton, and Digre (1980) to develop the first version of SDL for clinical use. Subsequently three parallel forms of the eight-digit and nine-digit SDL sequences were developed (for item listings, see Benton et al., 1983, p. 25). Benton and his colleagues recommend use of the nine-digit SDL task (SD9)

651

for patients under the age of 65 years and for those who have completed 12 or more years of education. They recommend use of the eight-digit SDL task (SD8) for patients aged 65 and older and generally for all patients with less than 12 years of education. However, the test authors recommend flexibility in the application of these demographic guidelines. An outstanding vocational history in a patient with less than 12 years of education and with at least average intellectual ability would suggest SD9 as the better measure to use. College or postgraduate education in a person over the age of 65 or an outstanding performance on the digit span measure (seven or more digits forward) also would suggest that SD9 rather than SD8 would be more appropriate. In the latter case of seven-digit recall on digit span, it would be important to use SD9 to ensure that the patient's short-term rote memorial ability and not attention span was being assessed, as SD8 would be very near to the unusually large seven-digit attentional capacity of that patient.

The principal author of the SDL test, Arthur L. Benton, Ph.D., received his A.B. (1931) and A.M. (1933) degrees from Oberlin College, followed by his Ph.D. from Columbia University (1935). He began his career as an assistant in psychology, first at Oberlin College (1931–33), next at Columbia University and New York State Psychiatric Institute (1934–36), and then at Cornell University Medical College (1936–39), where he subsequently served as a staff psychologist. He was appointed as an attending psychologist at New York Hospital–Westchester Division and as a psychologist in the Student Personnel Office of the City College of New York from 1939 to 1941. After serving on active duty in the U.S. Navy during and after the Second World War (1941–46), he was appointed as Associate Professor of Psychology at the University of Louisville Medical School and as Chief Psychologist at the Louisville Mental Hygiene Clinic and the Louisville General Hospital (1946–48). From 1948 to 1958 he served as Professor of Psychology and director of the Graduate Training Program in Clinical Psychology at the University of Iowa, and then for the next two decades (1958–78) as Professor of Psychology and Neurology. Dr. Benton has continued to coauthor theoretical and research papers and books since 1978, when he became Professor Emeritus at the University of Iowa.

Benton's fundamental contributions to the field of clinical neuropsychology have been acknowledged extensively and internationally. He has received honorary Doctor of Science (Cornell College, 1978) and Doctor of Psychology (University of Rome, 1990) degrees, as well as numerous other honors and awards, including the Distinguished Service Award of the Iowa Psychological Association (1977), the Distinguished Professional Contribution Award from the American Psychological Association (1978), the Outstanding Scientific Contribution Award of the International Neuropsychological Society (1981), The Samuel Torrey Orton Award from the Orton Dyslexia Society (1982), the Distinguished Service and Outstanding Contributions Award from the American Board of Professional Psychology (1985), and the Distinguished Clinical Neuropsychologist Award from the National Academy of Neuropsychology (1989).

Benton is a past president of both the American Orthopsychiatric Association (1965–66) and the International Neuropsychological Society (1970–71), and he served as secretary-general of the Research Group on Aphasia for the World Federation of Neurology from 1971 to 1978. He has been a lecturer or visiting scholar at the University of Milan (1964), Hôpital Sainte-Anne, Paris (1968), Hadassah-

Hebrew University Medical School, Jerusalem (1969), Free University of Amsterdam (1971), University of Helsinki (1974), University of Melbourne (1977), University of Minnesota Medical School (Baker Lecturer, 1979), University of Victoria, British Columbia (Lansdowne Scholar, 1980), and the University of Michigan (1986), plus Directeur d'Études Associé, École des Hautes Études, Paris (1979) and a visiting scientist at the Tokyo Metropolitan Institute of Gerontology (1974).

Benton has authored, coauthored, or edited 12 books and monographs, approximately 150 professional journal articles, and 22 historical reviews in the area of clinical neuropsychology and behavioral neurology. He is recognized as a pioneer and a leading authority in the area of clinical neuropsychology.

The standardized, commercially published versions of SDL appeared with the clinical manual for this and other tests in the Benton-Iowa Neuropsychological Test Battery (Benton et al., 1983). Coauthors of this clinical manual with Dr. Benton are Kerrry deS. Hamsher, Ph.D. (Associate Professor of Neurology, University of Wisconsin Medical School); Nils R. Varney, Ph.D. (staff neuropsychologist, Department of Veterans Affairs Medical Center, Iowa City, Iowa); and Otfried Spreen, Ph.D. (Professor Emeritus, Department of Psychology, University of Victoria, Victoria, British Columbia, Canada).

Practical Applications/Uses

Since Zangwill (1943) first noted the dissociability of attentional and short-term memorial processes, clinicians have recognized the importance of short-term rote memory deficit as a feature of cognitive deficit in many forms of brain dysfunction (for a review, see Benton et al., 1983). SDL thus serves as an important marker variable for analysis of brain dysfunction and more specifically as a key variable in mnestic assessment. The assessment of rote memory typically involves analyzing the span as well as the strategy of encoding and recall. Patients who have no strategy for memorial encoding other than trying to repeat the lengthy number sequence as it is presented almost surely will do poorly on the SDL task, and they are likely to make little progress on it unless they make use of feedback from their previous attempts and their errors. They may benefit, however, from general instruction as to how to approach the task and how to make use of feedback from errors to improve their performance. The instructions for SDL are intentionally detailed and suggestive of how the patient may most successfully approach the task with these issues in mind:

> Now I am going to say a number and I want you to repeat it it after me. It's a very long number; it has 9 (or 8) digits, so you are not expected to be able to repeat it after you have have heard it only once. I will say the number and then you tell me what you can remember; after that I will say the number again and then you will try to repeat it back to me. The best approach is not to try to memorize the whole number all at once. Try to remember the first few numbers and add more numbers on the later trials. You must try to learn this number and you will be given 12 trials to learn it. This may be a hard task and you will have to concentrate very hard. Try not to interrupt the task; if you have any comments we can discuss them after we have finished. Do you understand? Do you have any questions? (Benton et al., 1983, p. 24)

Repetition of all or part of the instructions is allowed, as is elaboration of the explanation. The SDL authors even allow use of a five-digit number, an attentional task, as an unscored sample item to demonstrate the concept of serial digit recall if the patient remains unsure of the procedure. Once the examiner is certain that the patient has understood the task, he or she says, "Fine, here is the number. Listen carefully now." These last few comments are designed to attentionally orient the patient to the task.

The digits in the SDL sequence are spoken to the patient at the rate of one per second. Testing is discontinued and all subsequent unadministered trials are given full credit when the patient achieves the criterion performance of two consecutive errorless repetitions of the digit sequence. Until this criterion is mastered, the task is repeated up to a maximum administration of 12 trials. Because the task is often frustrating to patients who experience difficulty, so that their motivation may lag, the SDL authors (Benton et al., 1983, p. 25) recommend encouraging "successive approximations" to the goal with comments such as "You are doing fine, try again," or "You are getting closer," or "You almost have it now." The first fully correct repetition of the sequence should be acknowledged with the response, "That is right; let's try it once more." If the subsequent trial is incorrect, the recommended response is "No, now listen again." Such comments provide useful feedback as well as encouragement and can help the patient modify faulty encoding and recall strategies. The subject's responses are recorded verbatim. Spontaneous corrections of initial errors are credited as correct, but initial errors should be recorded for later qualitative analysis.

Originally the SDL items were scored only as fully correct or incorrect. Some hospitalized control patients without brain disease, however, were noted to have great difficulty mastering the SDL task at the criterion level when only the fully correct versus incorrect scoring method was employed. Neurologically normal medical patients typically reversed sequential order of two adjacent digits or substituted a single digit in the sequence when they made minor errors. In contrast, patients with brain disease had difficulty when they attempted to learn more digits than they could retain in the span of immediate attention (five to six digits), even after as many as 12 learning trials.

Based on these observations, the SDL scoring system was modified. Full credit (2 points per item) now is assigned for perfect recall of the entire digit sequence on a trial. Partial credit (1 point per item) is assigned when there is a specific minor error on the digit sequence recall that may be attentionally related. Partial credit is assigned to "'near correct' responses, i.e. those characterized by only one simple error, namely, one digit is either omitted, added, or substituted, or there is a simple reversal of two adjacent digits" (Benton et al., 1983, p. 25). This partial credit scoring system was designed to acknowledge approximations to the criterion goal and to extend the range and sensitivity of SDL total score.

Some patients will recall the partial, component digit sequences of the overall SDL series correctly, but they may transpose the component subsequences. For example, they may recall the series 123456789 as 6789-12345. If the patient begins to recall the SDL series with a digit sequence later in the overall series (6789) followed by the preceding digit sequence (12345), he or she is encouraged by the examiner to begin again with the first digit in the original SDL sequence and to recite the entire sequence again. This revised sequence is credited as the scored response. In this case the attempt is made to separate "sequencing" errors from recall errors. Because the span of recall is normal and only the sequence is in error, there is no issue of attentional deficit in this type of erroneous response. In any case it would be advisable for clinicians routinely to administer a standard measure of digit span attentional recall, such as that of the Wechsler Adult Intelligence Scale–Revised, to assess the patient's attentional competence before administering the SDL test.

Technical Aspects

Normative standards for SDL were established by Hamsher et al. (1980), who studied a group of 500 patients ages 16–74 with SDL forms SD8 and SD9. Within the SD8 test group, subjects were dichotomized educationally into subsamples with 6–11 years of education and 12–16 years of education. Each of these educational groups was subdivided further by age into groups aged 65–74 years. In the SD9 normative sample, the group with educational levels in the range 6–11 years were aged 16–44 years, whereas the group with educational levels in the range 12–16 years were aged 16–64 years. No sex differences were found for either form of SDL. The ethnic heritage of the normative sample was predominantly European and Caucasian.

On both forms of the SDL, those subjects with 12 or more years of educational training scored consistently higher than did subjects with 6–11 years of education. The 45- to 64-year-old age group consistently scored higher on SDL than did subjects in the 65- to 74-year-old group. For a detailed percentile distribution of SD8 and SD9 raw score and percentile distributions as a function of age and educational level, see Benton et al. (1983, p. 27, Table 3-1).

Benton et al. (1983, p. 28) recommend "general guidelines" for normative interpretation of SDL relative to the percentile equivalents of raw scores that they report. They also recommend consideration of base-rate issues in using cutoff values for the assessment of memorial impairment in clinical groups. Attention to socioeconomic status as well as ethnic and linguistic differences also may be important when norms based on Caucasians of European descent are employed with other demographic groups. The guidelines Benton and his colleagues tentatively recommend are *mild impairment* for scores in the fourth to seventh percentile range, *moderate impairment* for scores in the second and third percentiles, and *severe impairment* for scores below the second percentile.

Hamsher et al. (1980) cross-classified their sample of 100 brain-damaged, non-aphasic patients into subjects who passed or failed SDL and those who passed or failed digit span (DSP). Forty-six percent of the subjects passed both tests, and 23% of them failed both tests; the pass/fail classification concordance rate across test performance levels thus was 69%. Of the remaining 31% who passed either SDL or DSP, 74% of them failed SDL but passed DSP, while the remaining 26% of them passed SDL but failed DSP. SDL was significantly more sensitive to the presence of brain disease than DSP in this sample, but considerable individual differences were apparent on both measures in the brain dysfunctional group. Comparison of the laterality of brain lesion was not significantly related to differential performance level on SDL and DSP. In a subsequent analysis in which the subjects with lateralized brain lesions were combined into a single group and compared with the bilateral brain lesion group, SDL was found significantly more sensitive to the presence of brain dysfunction than was DSP. In subsequent work of this kind it might prove useful to build upon these exploratory analyses by evaluating the sensitivity of SDL to memorial impairment in various specific types of dementing and amnesic conditions.

An example of such syndrome-specific application appears in the work of Spicer, Roberts, and Lewitt (1988), who studied samples of Parkinsonian patients with predominantly right versus left body motor signs. The two groups of subjects were matched carefully on age, educational level, estimated premorbid intelligence level, motor sign severity, and medication level. Patients with right body motor sign predominance showed greater impairment on SDL, confrontation naming, and verbal fluency tasks, which the authors associated with dominant hemispheric functional integrity. No differences were found on measures of visual form discrimination, line orientation spatial analysis, or facial recognition, which the authors associated with nondominant hemispheric function.

Critique

SDL is a well-standardized, brief, objective measure of rote learning and memorization. It can be compared directly to DSP, the standard index of attention span, to differentiate memorial from attentional deficit. Two versions of SDL (SD8, SD9) provide for demographic adjustment of this rote learning task to the ability of the subject. Three parallel forms of each SDL version allow for retesting of the same patient with minimization of practice effect.

An exceptionally well-crafted psychometric device, SDL should play an important role in memorial assessment. Though it should not be the only memorial measure in a clinical assessment battery, it should be an integral one. While SDL has been shown consistently to be more sensitive to the presence of some forms of brain dysfunction than DSP alone, clearly it is not sufficiently sensitive to the presence of brain dysfunction or damage in unselected cases to be used as a general screening device. Rather, one should use it as part of any detailed investigation of memorial difficulty in cases of amnesia, dementia, or learning difficulty. Qualitative analysis of SDL performance may be particularly useful for discrimination and analysis of difficulties in sequential ordering, encoding strategy, use of feedback, and attentional deficit that may produce rote recall difficulty. As such it is an invaluable addition to clinical memorial assessment methodology.

References

Benton, A.L., Hamsher, K.deS., Varney, N.R., & Spreen, O. (1983). *Contributions to neuropsychological assessment.* New York: Oxford University Press.

Drachman, D.A., & Arbit, J. (1966). Memory and the hippocampal complex: II. Is memory a multiple process? *Archives of Neurology, 15,* 52–61.

Drachman, D.A., & Hughes, J.R. (1971). Memory and the hippocampal complex: III. Aging and temporal EEG abnormalities. *Neurology, 21,* 1–4.

Hamsher, K.deS., Benton, A.L., & Digre, K. (1980). Serial digit learning: Normative and clinical aspects. *Journal of Clinical Neuropsychology, 2*, 39–50.

Schinka, J.A. (1974). *Performances of brain damaged patients on tests of short-term and long-term verbal memory.* Unpublished doctoral dissertation, University of Iowa, Iowa City.

Spicer, K.B., Roberts, R.J., & Lewitt, P.A. (1988). Neuropsychological performance in lateralized Parkinsonism. *Archives of Neurology, 45*, 429–432.

Zangwill, O.L. (1943). Clinical tests of memory impairment. *Proceedings of the Royal Society of Medicine, 36*, 576–580.

Zimmerman, I.L., & Woo-Sam, J.M. (1973). *Clinical interpretation of the Wechsler Adult Intelligence Scale.* New York: Grune & Stratton.

Edward E. Gotts, Ph.D.
Director of Psychology, Madison State Hospital, Madison, Indiana.

SHORT CATEGORY TEST, BOOKLET FORMAT
Linda C. Wetzel and Thomas J. Boll. Los Angeles, California: Western Psychological Services.

Introduction

The Short Category Test, Booklet Format (SCT-B), is a more easily administered and briefer version of the Category Test presented as part of the Halstead-Reitan Neuropsychological Test Battery. As such, the SCT-B is designed to be a sensitive indicator of brain damage, in the tradition of the Halstead-Reitan. It accomplishes its neuropsychological assessment objective by challenging the ability of a respondent to decide, within a test-item format, which of four numbers (i.e., 1–4) may be suggested or implied by way of a visually presented figure. This is carried out under the following special set of conditions: Following each choice made, the respondent receives feedback as to whether the number concept depicted via the figure was or was not correctly identified by the respondent's number choice. Thus, the instrument actually tests the ability to form a concept, as a diminished capacity to do so indicates cerebral impairment. Moreover, the SCT-B uses a second feature of the Halstead-Reitan: It, too, shifts the concept being tested at the end of each subtest. As a result, the respondent not only must learn a concept but further must remain flexible and be capable of setting aside what was previously learned in the interest of forming a different concept just a few minutes later. Flexibility in learning, hence, is also sampled and provides another indication of cerebral integrity.

Thomas J. Boll, coauthor of the SCT-B, received his Ph.D. in clinical psychology from Marquette University in 1967, after which he had the important formative experience of serving as a USPHS postdoctoral fellow in clinical psychology (1968–70) at the Indiana University Medical Center. The IU Medical Center was permeated with the influence of Ralph M. Reitan, Ph.D., who served as Professor and Director of Neuropsychology there from 1951 through 1970. IU Medical Center staff in fact continue their use of the Reitan tests up to the present time. As a result of his experiences there, Boll has devoted his subsequent career to the study and applications of neuropsychological assessment. His partnership with the first author of the SCT-B, Linda Wetzel, Ph.D., commenced during her doctoral program at the University of Health Sciences–Chicago Medical School, where Boll was at the time Professor and Chairman, Department of Psychology. Dr. Wetzel's dissertation (Wetzel, 1982/1983) provided the original research basis for the further development of the SCT-B and its publication by Western Psychological Services (Wetzel & Boll, 1987).

The more remote beginnings of the SCT-B trace back to its predecessor tests the Halstead Category Test (Halstead, 1947) and a shortened version of it, the Halstead-

Reitan Category Test (Reitan, 1959). A confusing issue arises in that persons who work with and publish studies using the neuropsychological tests originating with Halstead and Reitan often fail to make clear which version of the Category Test they have used. For example, when describing this battery of tests, as eminent a group as Golden and his associates refer to the Halstead Category Test, whereas a careful reading of their description reveals they are citing the shortened version derived by Reitan (Golden, Osmon, Moses, & Berg, 1981). For the foregoing reason it remains unclear which version of the Category Test has been used in some published reports of its reliability and validity, although most users seem to prefer the shorter Halstead-Reitan version. The Booklet Category Test (DeFilippis & McCampbell, 1979) represents one of several prior attempts to move away from the cumbersome testing apparatus required for presenting Reitan's 208-slide version. Wetzel and Boll (1987) considered its merits and shortcomings and decided to develop their short version.

The SCT-B testing materials consist of five spiral-bound booklets that stand up like miniature easels when opened. The stimulus side faces the respondent; the opposing side, visible to the examiner, contains all instructions needed for administration and identifies the sequence number of the stimulus currently exposed. Each easel booklet further contains a fold-out response strip containing the numbers, from left to right, "1 2 3 4." The respondent is asked to point to the number on the strip that each card brings to mind. Although pointing to the number is encouraged, the examiner may accept verbal reporting of the respondent's choice. Booklets are called "subtests" in the directions and are administered in serial order, Subtests 1–5. Each subtest's booklet contains 20 stimulus items, making the entire SCT-B 100 items long in contrast to the 208 items of the Halstead-Reitan version (arranged in seven subtests) or to the original Halstead's 360 items (appearing in nine subtests).

In addition to presenting items in the easel booklets, the examiner also works with a single-page, one-sided answer sheet on which answer choices are recorded (as 1, 2, 3, or 4). Each subtest appears in a column, so a new column is recorded as each booklet is given. To the left of each space provided for recording an answer, the keyed choice appears, which facilitates providing feedback to the respondent and makes scoring possible on the answer sheet without searching through any additional reference source. Together with the manual containing information on history, development, administration, scoring, norms, and interpretation of the SCT-B, the foregoing materials comprise the entire test kit.

Each test item typically appears as a white figure on a black background. Colored instead of white figures occur occasionally. Figures may be solid or outlined geometric shapes, widened lines resembling Roman numerals, capital letters from the Roman alphabet, stick-figure people, incomplete geometric forms, forms suggested by bold dots that outline an area, and simple forms made up of combinations of geometric forms.

Following is a facsimile subtest, neither from the actual SCT-B nor based on one of its concepts. Imagine that a clock face appears as the primary stimulus and that the hands together always point to only one of four numbered locations around the face: 2, 5, 8, or 11. Then suppose that "1" is the correct response when the hands point toward 2, "2" is correct when they point to 5, "3" is correct for 8, and "4" goes with 11. The respondent, however, does not know this and must use the tester's feedback to learn how to make the correct choices. Later in the same subtest, the items will shift from a clock face to an arrow-like pointer all by itself, with nothing else on the card. On successive items, the pointer will be oriented in the same directions as were the hands on the clock, but without the numerals or circular perimeter. The response key will follow the same progression as before.

If this seems confusing or difficult to follow, that is often how respondents feel as they are being tested and until they have figured out the concept. Let us now name a concept that could include the preceding variations and from which additional stimulus cards could be constructed. The concept is four quadrants of a circle numbered clockwise such that 0–90 degrees = 1, 91–180 = 2, 181–270 = 3, and 271–360 = 4. The actual concepts used in the SCT-B cannot, of course, be reproduced here, but it can be stated that some are easier to infer than the foregoing example, whereas others may be of comparable difficulty.

During the concept attainment or learning process, the examiner reads directions, presents the successive stimulus cards, records each response, and immediately gives feedback by saying either "right" or "wrong," depending on the accuracy of the answer given. The examiner does not identify the concept nor ask the respondent to do so. Thus, no formal verbal statement of the concept is provided or acknowledged. The ability to apply the concept to recognize correct instances or examples is all that is demanded of the examinee. The examiner sums the errors for each of the five subtests and then sums the error subsets for the entire SCT-B, resulting in a single score for the total errors. Norms are based on this single fact and are applicable to two groups: younger adults (from 15 to 45 years) and older adults (46 and above). Although subtest scores are not used in a normative way, the SCT-B manual provides clinical interpretations that may apply in some instances to variations in particular subtest scores (Wetzel & Boll, 1987, p. 13).

Practical Applications/Uses

In general the SCT-B is not intended to be used alone, but rather as a part of a battery of neuropsychological tests. Low scores on it relate to the ability to learn concepts, apply them in new situations, and to shift point of view when a new subtest begins. Furthermore, a low score suggests that the individual has sufficient emotional control to accept feedback about correct and incorrect performance and use it to improve future performance. Significantly, this is accomplished in a nonverbal response format that is relatively independent of prior accumulated learning. Research has suggested that the longer Halstead-Reitan Category Test is one of the single most sensitive test indicators of cerebral impairment and that it measures general rather than specific adaptive ability. Studies also have shown that the posterior two thirds of the cerebrum more than the anterior one third are involved in successful versus impaired performance on the Category Test (e.g., see studies cited in Wetzel & Boll, 1987). Another way of viewing the Category Test is as a measure of fluid intelligence as opposed to crystallized intelligence. Notably, the capacity to make use of crystallized intelligence (e.g., as measured by a general test of intelligence) is often quite dependent on the abilities measured by this particular test (Wetzel & Boll, 1987). The SCT-B's authors believe that their instrument has many of the essential measurement strengths of the longer Category Test and measures essentially the same functional characteristics.

For the foregoing reasons, the SCT-B is likely to be used in neuropsychological assessments that address impairment following head trauma, toxic exposure, oxygen deprivation, suspected demyelinating disease, CVA, possible dementia, and so forth. In addition to neuropsychologist users, the test's much abbreviated length and the convenience of its booklet format also make it attractive to clinical psychologists who must answer similar questions about cerebral impairment. The SCT-B's ease of administration and scoring enables technicians to complete the testing, leaving interpretation to the psychologist. The instrument also has potential as a screening procedure for organicity due to the low cost of administration.

In addition to clinical issues that might lead to use of the SCT-B, its appropriateness must be considered in terms of other patient characteristics such as visual acuity, ability to concentrate, and motivation to cooperate with testing. Capacity to comprehend directions is a further issue; rather than presenting these orally, adaptations are possible via print instructions and sign language for persons with particular receptive language limits. Testing in other than English could be accomplished readily with only minimal translation. Further, persons with expressive language difficulty are at no disadvantage; pointing is a basic and simple response mode.

The SCT-B is administered to a single examinee in a quiet setting, with minimal distractions of movement and noise. Only one easel-type subtest booklet and answer form are used at a time, no timekeeping is necessary, the answer format is direct and unmistakable, and answers are recorded simply as a check mark or numeral. This ease of administration represents a major advantage of the SCT-B over the Halstead-Reitan Category Test. The latter requires operating a large apparatus that is cumbersome, nonportable, and, in the experience of many users, mechanically unreliable. Moreover, even during stationary office use, with no equipment malfunctions, the operation of the equipment is demanding. These facts plus the greater initial cost of the apparatus and the fatigue-inducing nature of the task have limited the use of the Halstead-Reitan version to better equipped offices and clinics. Estimated time to administer the SCT-B is only 15 to 30 minutes compared to over twice that for the Halstead-Reitan Category Test. The only administration problem arising in this reviewer's experience with the SCT-B is that occasionally a patient will try to give a second response just as soon as the first is called "wrong." The examiner usually can manage this by cautioning the patient that only the first answer can be counted (and therefore to decide carefully before responding) and that no comment or feedback is allowed regarding any additional choice made after the first one (and therefore none will be given). This problem is not unique to the SCT-B and can be even more awkward with the apparatus for the Halstead-Reitan due to its mechanical operating features. Unquestionably the SCT-B is not only easier to administer than the Halstead-Reitan, it is easy to administer from any perspective. Recording answers is also easy. The authors advise doing so by a check mark if the response is correct and by the number chosen if incorrect.

Scoring the SCT-B is simplicity itself. All information needed for scoring appears on the single-page answer form, including a key to the correct answer for each of the 100 items. The examiner has no decisions to make regarding equivocal or ambiguous responses; each answer choice is unmistakably clear. Obtaining the score (i.e., sum of the errors) requires only that the user add 1 point for each item with a number entered (check marks are not counted). On the other hand, it is quicker to count the check marks and subtract them from 100 to obtain the total errors when scoring a record that consists primarily of incorrect answers. The job of scoring should not take more than 2–3 minutes, including a second counting for reliability. Due to the simplicity of scoring, no advantage would exist for machine or computer scoring; hand scoring is the method of choice and, hence, the only method made available.

Interpretation derives from the objective score obtained after transforming the raw error score to a standardized T-score and its corresponding percentile. Separate columns of the table of standard scores are entered depending on the age of the respondent (i.e., for either age 45 and below or 46 and above). Halstead-Reitan users rely on cutoff scores; SCT-B's interpretation chapter omits these. Instead, the task of interpretation considers the individual's performance against that of others on a continuum. Specific case examples appear in the interpretation chapter, yet without exact guidelines for reaching a conclusion that an individual's test performance indicates probable impairment. Cutoff scores also are omitted from the SCT-B's table of norms. In order to find cutoffs, one must search in a separate chapter titled "Psychometric Properties." There cutoffs are identified as follows: a raw score of 41 for persons 45 or younger, and a raw score of 46 for persons "45 [*sic*] years and older" (Wetzel & Boll, 1987, p. 32; should read "46 years" to fit the corresponding tabled values on p. 37). Compared respectively for younger and older normative sample respondents, these cutoffs equate to the following T-score/percentile value pairings: T-64/92nd %ile and T-62/88th %ile. In the absence of more explicit guidance in the chapter on SCB-T interpretation, the above-cited values should likely be used. These cutoffs differentiated effectively (i.e., with 83% accuracy) between cerebrally impaired persons and the normative sample.

Additional guidance provided in the interpretation chapter is likely to prove most helpful to users less familiar with judging the meaning of neuropsychological findings. This reviewer's observations suggest that inexperienced users are inclined to overinterpret neuropsychological results and hence may benefit from that chapter. Someone with only limited specialty training in neuropsychology should take a more descriptive approach, reporting how a patient compares to others of his or her age group in terms of the available norms. They should report above-cutoff scores as probable indicators of learning and adaptive difficulties and as pointing to a need for additional evaluation. Inexperienced nonspecialists should seek quality consultation from those who possess expertise in recommending additional assessment procedures and in assisting with interpretation.

Technical Aspects

Although the SCT-B manual does not report on reliability of scoring, stability is likely quite good due to the simplicity of both recording and scoring. Two types of reliability are reported: split-half and test-retest in relation to practice effects. Many of the reported findings, however, are for the Halstead-Reitan Category Test rather than for the SCT-B. Split-half values for the Halstead-Reitan (HR) are uniformly high in various studies, ranging from .90 to .99 (see citations in Wetzel & Boll, 1987, p. 31). Wetzel and Boll observe correctly that these figures likely are somewhat elevated or inflated due to the interdependency of the items upon what was or was not learned on prior items in a test of this type. The authors mention a study comparing the split-half reliabilities of the HR and the SCT-B (Summers & Boll, 1987). These were corrected by the Spearman-Brown formula for their shortened lengths. The tests' respective coefficients of reliability, based on this study, were .89 and .81, and the researchers found no statistically reliable differences between the mean scores of the even- and odd-numbered items for either test. This is the only study bearing on the SCT's split-half reliability.

Test-retest reliability studies are available for the HR test only. The HR test coefficient was .96; its stability over a 12-month interval was .72 for a group of chronic schizophrenics (Wetzel & Boll, 1987, p. 31). The SCT-B's authors acknowledge a problem, however, with the foregoing figure of .96, which is that practice effects undoubtedly influence the results. That is, someone who retakes the test after a brief interval likely will remember some of what was learned before. Yet, it is not irrelevant to the notion that the SCT-B is a test of learning that the intersession learning would be correlated substantially (i.e., practice effects may relate to the intended criterion).

No internal consistency reliability studies appear in the SCT-B manual for either the HR or the SCT-B.

In summary, only one reliability study is reported for the SCT-B as such, with all others relating to the HR Category Test. Nevertheless, the solitary study relevant to the SCT-B does offer evidence that the latter is almost as reliable as the HR even though less than half its length.

Validity studies are also limited. In the first of these (Summers & Boll, 1987), participants were all aged 18–40 and were enrolled in college coursework; they likely would resemble the more capable members of the younger age group in the normative sample. Surprisingly, in view of the foregoing sample characteristics, the average error rate on the HR Category Test was 58.5 based on calculations from the manual's Table 8 (Wetzel & Boll, 1987, p. 32), which substantially exceeds the established cutoff of 51 errors. Certainly it is puzzling to contemplate how or why such an elevated error score rate may have occurred in the sample just described. One must, accordingly, ask just how representative the sample's performance was of its members' capability; further inquiry into such matters would require going beyond data now available to this reviewer. A further inconsistency was noted between the authors' reference in text to a mean of 27.0 errors for the SCT-B when it was taken first and the mean percentage error rate of 25% for the same finding as reported in Table 8 (Wetzel & Boll, 1987, p. 32). If in fact the mean was 27.0 errors as stated, this would be equal to a mean error rate of 27% instead. This inconsistency in reporting raises a related question about one of the statistical tests reported for the same set of data; that is, whether the correct mean error percent (27%) was used in this computation or if perhaps the tabled mean of 25% was used. In the latter possible event, one of the main conclusions based on this first mentioned validity study may need to be reexamined. Whichever the case, any further clarification or emendation on this matter must be left to the SCT-B's authors.

In the foregoing study, half the sample was assigned randomly to complete the SCT-B and then, after 1 week, the HR. The remainder of the sample completed the two tests in the reverse order (i.e., HR, SCT-B). The actual mean errors for the SCT-B and HR, when expressed in the form of percentages, are not dissimilar: 25% (*sic* 27%) and 28%, respectively, when taken first and 16% and 17%, respectively, when taken after 1 week. It is evident on inspection that the mean percentage errors were lower upon retesting with either alternate test. Wetzel and Boll (1987) found that the errors just noted declined significantly when the HR was completed first, followed by the SCT-B. They interpreted this in terms of a practice effect. A statistical test for a practice effect was nonsignificant, however, for the order SCT-B first, followed by HR. As discussed in the preceding paragraph, this latter finding and the authors' interpretation of it (i.e., "no significant practice effect") for the SCT-B, HR order is all necessarily called in question by the possibility that the incorrect rate of 25% was used in the test rather than the rate of 27%. For the present, hence, the possibility cannot be ruled out that a significant practice effect also may exist for the second experimental order of test administration. The authors present a collateral line of evidence in terms of the strength of relationship or association between the two tests under the differing orders of administration. When HR was given first, it related to SCT-B a week later with a correlation of .92; with SCT-B given first, it related to HR at a lower level ($r = .80$; reduced to .66 if two outliers were deleted). This is the only reported validity study in the manual wherein both SCT-B and HR were administered to the same sample.

The authors cite the standardization study as a second source of validity evidence. Here 120 volunteers comprised the normal sample, which was 55% male, ranged in age from 21 to 79 years (mean = 43.57 years), was predominantly white, and had above-average educational and occupational levels. These subjects were compared in a discriminative validity analysis to a sample of 70 persons affected by neurological and psychiatric disorders. This clinic sample consisted of 55 males and 15 females, with a mean age of 52.67 years and a mean educational level of 11.67 years. These subjects were older and less educated than the normative sample members, and education and age were both found to relate significantly to error scores on the SCT-B. Consequently, the authors used age and education as covariates in all comparisons in order to correct statistically for disparities between the two samples.

In the discriminative validity study mentioned above, the authors accomplished optimum separation of impaired and nonimpaired individuals by setting cutoffs separately for ages 45 and below and 46 and above, and by using the educational-level covariate. When separated as noted by age, 83% of normative and impaired sample members combined were correctly classified. This rate of accurate classification appears to exceed that of all known individual psychometric tests and further of some commonly used neurodiagnostic tests. The SCT-B's authors further report that its accuracy exceeded that of the Halstead-Reitan Impairment Index, which in one representative study correctly classified 80% of brain-damaged persons and 78% of controls. The somewhat lower figures for the Impairment Index, however, may stem from the fact that data had not been adjusted for age and educational level as had the SCT-B. In any event, this 83% correct classification record for the SCT-B is impressive from any perspective.

A third line of validity evidence cited derives from using a standard neuropsychological battery of tests together with the SCT-B and, in a separate sample, the same battery with the HR. This permits comparison of the correlations between the HR and the other measures as a standard and the correlations of the SCT-B with these same measures. The 100 neurological patients who completed the battery with the HR are actually a subset of the sample originally used by Wetzel (1983) to create and evaluate shortened versions of the HR. The larger sample ($N = 300$) had a mean age of 43.76 years and an average 12.13 years of education. This subset of 100 cases is not further described in the SCT-B manual and may differ in some respects from the overall sample of 300. The sample completing the SCT-B with the neuropsychological battery consisted of 51 persons with neurological conditions. These subjects are a subset of the sample of 70 impaired persons described in the second of the validity studies above, after removing 19 cases with psychiatric diagnoses only.

In this study, comparability of the HR and SCT-B versions was tested by performing a statistical analysis for the significance of the difference between two correlations, those between the two respective category tests and the individual tests or indexes within the overall battery. No significant differences existed between the HR and SCT-B's correlations with the following measures: WAIS/WAIS-R Verbal, Performance, and Full Scale IQs; Impairment Index; Trail Making Parts A and B; WMS Memory Quotient; and tapping with the nondominant hand. Correlations were reliably different only for tapping with the dominant hand (i.e., with HR, $r = -.26$; with SCT-B, $r = -.49$; $p < .05$). The authors concluded that the similarity of the two tests' relations with other standard neuropsychological measures suggests they are measuring essentially the same general thing. This is the final line of validity evidence cited.

In addition to the reliability and validity studies just reviewed, the authors have performed an analysis of the difficulty of the respective subtests of the SCT-B in their standardization sample of 120 (see Wetzel & Boll, 1987). This analysis revealed that Subtest 1 was extremely easy for all of seven age groups, yielding a mean error rate of well under 1 error per record ($M = 0.44$). In this reviewer's estimate of mean errors and for those that will follow below, the sample means (i.e., descriptive statistics) for the seven age groups were calculated using the means of the seven groups as unit scores. This method of combining data for the seven groups was followed because they differed greatly in size ($n = 8$–37). To have weighted the data by the size of each age group would have unduly influenced the overall mean by those age groups that were more heavily sampled. This approach treats the sample statistics as if they are satisfactory estimators of their respective population parameters for the group means. The resulting subtest means will be used in the following paragraph.

Based on the foregoing approach, Subtest 2 has an estimated error rate of 11.25; Subtest 3, $M = 5.37$; Subtest 4, $M = 7.16$; and Subtest 5, $M = 4.60$. As the principle or concept embodied in Subtests 4 and 5 is the same, the lower mean error rate for

Subtest 5 probably exemplifies its difficulty level not so much as it indicates transfer of learning from Subtest 4. That is, Subtest 5 would be more difficult if it preceded Subtest 4, while the latter's difficulty would drop if it followed Subtest 5.

The foregoing calculated means reveal that the SCT-B proceeds from very easy to difficult, with all difficulty levels arranged in about the correct order except for Subtest 2, which would appear to be unusually difficult for placement at this early point within the series. Subtest 2 itself accounts for fully 39.57% of all SCT-B errors when gauged against the composite mean rate of 28.53 errors. The high difficulty level of Subtest 2 is the subject of special comments by the authors, who recognize its potential interaction with the subject's emotional disposition in terms of anxiety and frustration. Some subjects, they found, "seem completely unable to recover" from the frustration and sense of failure induced by Subtest 2 (Wetzel & Boll, 1987, p. 34). Accordingly one may ask how wise it is to retain this subtest so early in the evaluation. Their own concerns about this have prompted the SCT-B authors to suggest that future research might focus on revamping the administration procedures, particularly on Subtests 1 and 2 and possibly 3—although to do this would result in an entirely different procedure that would invalidate current norms. These suggestions will be considered below.

Critique

The SCT-B represents an important effort to make the HR Category Test less cumbersome and time-consuming and more portable, while retaining its amply demonstrated validity as an indicator of cerebral impairment. There can be little disagreement that the difficulty and expense of using the machine-administered HR had long invited improvements of the types attempted by Wetzel and Boll.

The authors have followed a test design and development strategy that maintains considerable continuity with the earlier test, while pursuing their changes. They kept identical items in their original sequences. They shortened the HR to the SCT-B by dropping Subtests 1 and 7 and by retaining the first 20 items each of Subtests 2–6. Their rationale for dropping Subtest 1 was that it was unnecessarily redundant of original Subtest 2 (which becomes Subtest 1 of the SCT-B). Subtest 7 involved no concept attainment but was more a measure of the patient's recall of items presented in earlier subtests of the HR, so it measured less of the intended abstraction and new learning ability for which the Category Test is traditionally valued.

The foregoing appear to be supportable grounds for removing Subtests 1 and 7. By next keeping the first 20 items of each of the remaining five subtests, Wetzel and Boll avoided changing the inherent structure and order of the center portion of the HR. On the other hand, it should be noted that shortening the subtests decreases the subject's sense of success and may be more likely to produce frustration and emotional reactions than would the longer version. As Wetzel and Boll (1987) acknowledge, the difficulty level of the SCT-B exceeds that of the HR due to the shortened subtests.

Perhaps in response to such observations as those just offered, the test authors suggest directing future research to an administration method that involves coaching the subject by offering additional informative feedback when items are missed.

The examples of prompting that Wetzel and Boll give, however, would be tantamount in some instances to stepwise direct teaching of the concept or principle that the subject must induce. Once this is done, the test no longer would measure concept attainment but, in some sense, teachability. Thus, the suggested research would lead to more than a need for restandardization. Rather, it would result in an entirely new test. Certainly that could be of value, but it would lead away from the original, more circumscribed objective of producing a better Category Test.

If one is particularly concerned about the SCT-B's difficulty level peaking too soon at Subtest 2, then less momentous changes could be tried first. One strategy would be to study first the relative difficulty of Subtests 4 and 5 administered in two orders following the SCT-B's Subtest 1: Subtest 5 followed by 4 and following 4. This would establish the absolute respective difficulties of these two subtests. Next the entire test would be reordered: Subtest 1, Subtest 3, the less difficult of Subtests 4 and 5, the more difficult of Subtests 4 and 5, and finally Subtest 2. Now the entire test would be ordered from least to most difficult—a progression calculated to minimize loss of confidence, motivation, and emotional control. It would remain an empirical question, of course, whether this reordered instrument would perform as well as has the present SCT-B in detecting organicity. This should not be judged hastily, as perhaps emotional control is an essential part of the criterion variance that not only the SCT-B but also the earlier category tests have measured. In any event, the suggestions made here retain the 100 items of the SCT-B, all from the original HR, keeping them in their original orders within subtests and only reordering the subtests themselves. This minimalist approach would preserve continuity.

Although Wetzel and Boll have emphasized retaining HR items and structure in their revision, one notable design change has occurred without much discussion. Yet it may have resulted in a significantly different test in one respect. Instead of using sounds to signal success or failure, as did the HR, these authors have used verbal feedback. During the HR's administration, the following signals are explained and demonstrated: a correct response is greeted with a bell, and an incorrect one is followed by an unpleasant-sounding buzzer. The SCT-B changes this to utterances of "right" and "wrong" (another booklet test uses "correct" and "incorrect"; DeFilippis & McCampbell, 1979). The HR's method of providing feedback contrasts with the booklet versions by being impersonal and nonverbal. This difference further suggests that one's performance and involvement via the SCT-B might be experienced more as part of an interpersonal situation, which carries with it the possibilities of perceiving support or lack thereof, impersonally versus personally induced frustration, and so forth. These comments are of course hypothetical, but nonetheless the changes have been made without evaluating the possibly differential effects of impersonal versus personal feedback. That is, the psychological equivalence of the two feedback modes needs further study before one can make final judgments about the comparability of the SCT-B and the HR.

After weighing the merits of the SCT-B against the issues considered in this review, this reviewer would judge that Wetzel and Boll have contributed significantly to streamlining the Category Test. The result of their effort is unquestionably a move in the correct direction, but further study and refinement will be needed to address the matters raised here as well as in the authors' suggestions for future research on the SCT-B (Wetzel & Boll, 1987). The substance of their achievement can be summed up in a single finding: The SCT-B appears 83% accurate in distinguishing organically impaired from nonimpaired persons.

References

This list includes text citations and suggested additional reading.

Cullum, M., Steinman, D.R., & Bigler, E.D. (1984). Relationships between fluid and crystallized cognitive function using Category Test and WAIS scores. *International Journal of Clinical Neuropsychology, 6,* 172–174.

DeFilippis, N.A., & McCampbell, E. (1979). *Manual for the Booklet Category Test: Research and clinical form.* Odessa, FL: Psychological Assessment Resources.

Golden, C.J., Osmon, D.C., Moses, J.A., Jr., & Berg, R.A. (1981). *Interpretation of the Halstead-Reitan Neuropsychological Test Battery: A casebook approach.* New York: Grune & Stratton.

Halstead, W.C. (1947). *Brain and intelligence: A quantitative study of the frontal lobes.* Chicago: University of Chicago Press.

Jarvis, P.E., & Barth, J.T. (1984). *Halstead-Reitan Test Battery: An interpretive guide.* Odessa, FL: Psychological Assessment Resources.

Reitan, R.M. (1959). The effects of brain lesions on adaptive abilities in human beings. Indianapolis, IN: Author.

Reitan, R.M., & Wolfson, D. (1985). *The Halstead-Reitan Neuropsychological Test Battery: Theory and clinical interpretation.* Tucson, AZ: Neuropsychological Press.

Rourke, B.P., Bakker, D.J., Fisk, J.L., & Strang, J.D. (1983). *Child neuropsychology: An introduction to theory, research, and clinical practice.* New York: Guilford.

Summers, M., & Boll, T.J. (1987). Comparability of a short booklet version of the traditional form of the Category Test. *International Journal of Clinical Neuropsychology, 9,* 158–161.

Wedding, D., Horton, A.M., Jr., & Webster, J. (Eds.). (1986). *The neuropsychological handbook: Behavioral and clinical perspectives.* New York: Springer.

Wetzel, L. (1983). Development of a short, booklet form of the Category Test: Correlational and validity data (Doctoral dissertation, University of Health Sciences/The Chicago Medical School, 1982). *Dissertation Abstracts International, 42,* 4409A.

Wetzel, L., & Boll, T.J. (1987). *Short Category Test, Booklet Format: Manual.* Los Angeles: Western Psychological Services.

Frank J. Dyer, Ph.D.

Private Practitioner, Montclair, New Jersey.

SHORT IMAGINAL PROCESSES INVENTORY

G.J. Huba, J.L. Singer, C.S. Aneshensel, and J.S. Antrobus.
Port Huron, Michigan: SIGMA Assessment Systems, Inc.,
Research Psychologists Press Division.

Introduction

The Short Imaginal Processes Inventory (SIPI) is a 45-item measure of three factorially derived dimensions of a domain of inner experience that includes daydreaming, fantasy, and nondirected thought. The three factors measured by the SIPI include Positive-Constructive Daydreaming, Guilt and Fear of Failure Daydreaming, and Poor Attentional Control.

The authors of the SIPI are well-known researchers in imagination and daydreaming among other topics in the study of personality. The primary author, George Huba, is also a recognized expert in the field of psychometrics and computer-assisted psychological assessment. The SIPI is an abbreviated version of Singer and Antrobus's (1970, 1972) Imaginal Processes Inventory (IPI), a 344-item instrument for measuring 28 aspects of fantasy, daydreaming, and related mental processes. The sheer length of the IPI made it unsuitable for experiments in which subjects had limited time in which to respond to the experimental procedures. Administration of the IPI takes fully 1 hour with college students and even longer with older or less educated subjects. Thus, the SIPI fulfills the need for a shorter, more conveniently administered instrument for use in research on fantasy. The criteria that the authors specified for the development of the SIPI were that at least three factorially supported dimensions of the longer instrument were represented, that administration time be reduced to a maximum of 10 minutes, that items have an adequate breadth of content to reflect that of the full IPI, and that an adequate number of reverse-worded items be included to counter the effects of an acquiescence response set.

The development of the SIPI was facilitated by the research finding over a number of years that three latent variables accounted for a substantial portion of the variance in IPI scores. These factor analytic results guided the development of an abbreviated form of the test. The test construction model employed was that of Jackson (1971), stressing convergent validity through within-scale homogeneity and discriminant validity through across-scale orthogonality.

This shortened form was developed on a sample of college students from an Ivy League university as part of an extensive study of drug use and daydreaming. The sample was predominantly white, evenly balanced between males and females, and predominantly age 21 years or less. Factor analytic procedures were combined with judgmental procedures to derive a final set of 100 items. This item pool was then factor analyzed using the principal components technique, and three dimensions were retained for rotation according to a normalized varimax procedure. Based on the results of this factor analysis, 35 items were eliminated. Content considerations guided the final stage of development, in which additional items were eliminated as sets drawn from scales of the IPI.

The SIPI is self-administered in booklet form. The 45 individual items are presented in a 5-point Likert scale format, and responses are marked directly on the test booklet.

Practical Applications/Uses

While the authors of the SIPI believe that the instrument provides important information for assessing the totality of the person, they explicitly advise against its use in employment selection. In terms of clinical issues, the SIPI does not provide data that practitioners would find useful in the typical assessment situation. There has been no systematic investigation of the relation of SIPI scores to psychological or personality disorders. The primary value of the instrument at this point is to serve as a factorially pure measure of well-researched constructs of inner experience for use in experimental studies. The authors point out that the SIPI is a theoretical tool undergoing continued development and that the theory itself also is evolving. The inventory may have a good deal of potential utility as a treatment resource for behavior therapists working with clients who present attentional disorders or other pathology involving the inner fantasy life.

The SIPI is appropriate for use with adolescent and adult subjects. Although an "average" reading level is specified, users should remember that the instrument was standardized at an Ivy League university. There is a significant effect for sex on one of the SIPI scales, with females showing a slightly higher tendency to have positive and constructive daydreams. Minority subjects in the standardization pool tended to have a greater frequency of guilty and fear of failure daydreams. Whether this finding can be generalized to minority background test subjects in other than Ivy League university settings is a matter for further research.

This inventory can be group administered by a research assistant, whose function would be to distribute the test, answer questions regarding the mechanical marking of responses, and collect the materials afterward. Administration time is 10 minutes or less. Scoring can be accomplished in less than 5 minutes per record, using cardboard scoring stencils to derive raw scores on each of the three scales. T-scores for the three dimensions are plotted on a nomograph, using separate norms for males and females. The scoring templates are well constructed and easy to use.

Scores on the three scales are interpreted according to descriptions of high scorers given in the test manual (Huba, Singer, Aneshensel, & Antrobus, 1982). These descriptions are essentially restatements of the content of the individual scales, in some instances almost literally repeating the test items. The manual does not provide any information about inferences regarding other psychological characteristics that one could derive from SIPI scores.

Technical Aspects

The test manual presents extensive psychometric data on the SIPI, relating items on this version to those on the parent instrument. Rotated factor loadings are given for each of the 45 items, using both varimax and confirmatory methods. As would be expected, three well-defined orthogonal factors resulted from this analysis, with all retained scale items having very substantial loadings on their respective scales. Means, standard deviations, and Likert response category frequencies and percentages also are given for all of the items. Item-scale correlations are provided, and means and standard deviations for ethnicity-sex groups are listed as well.

The results presented in the manual indicate that the SIPI is a factorially pure test with high internal consistency that achieves its purpose of efficiently measuring core dimensions of the parent instrument. Its use has been restricted to students at selective institutions of higher education. No criterion-related validity statistics are presented. The validity of the SIPI derives from the well-researched validity of the parent instrument. Content validity is demonstrated by relating scale items to findings from extensive prior research into daydreaming and related mental states. Factorial validity is amply demonstrated by the clustering of scale items according to theoretical expectations.

Critique

The SIPI is essentially a finely crafted research instrument at this point in its development. Investigators seeking a brief measure of subjects' capacity for self-regulation of fantasy, extent of guilty or dysphoric fantasy in conscious experience, and extent of constructive, planful, wish-fulfilling fantasy should look no further than this instrument. As noted, there is no evidence at this time to support use of this inventory in clinical or employment selection settings, and practitioners should avoid such use unless they have an independent capability for conducting on-site validation research.

The next stage of evolution of this instrument should concentrate on extending the construct validity research beyond the factorial methods into the realm of systematic criterion-related validity studies. For example, it would be of considerable experimental interest to study the characteristics of high and low scorers on the three SIPI scales as assessed by objective inventories that measure the "big five" factors of personality.

References

Huba, G.J., Singer, J.L., Aneshensel, C.S., & Antrobus, J.S. (1982). *Manual for the Short Imaginal Processes Inventory*. Port Huron, MI: Research Psychologists Press.

Jackson, D.N. (1971). The dynamics of structured personality tests: 1971. *Psychological Review, 78*, 229–248.

Singer, J.L., & Antrobus, J.S. (1970). *Manual for the Imaginal Processes Inventory*. Princeton, NJ: Educational Testing Service.

Singer, J.L., & Antrobus, J.S. (1972). Daydreaming, imaginal processes, and personality: A normative study. In P. Sheehan (Ed.), *The function and nature of imagery*. New York: Academic Press.

Jerry L. Johns, Ph.D.
Professor of Reading, Northern Illinois University, DeKalb, Illinois.

Peggy VanLeirsburg, Ed.D.
Teacher, Elgin Public Schools, Elgin, Illinois.

SLOSSON INTELLIGENCE TEST–REVISED

Charles L. Nicholson and Terry L. Hibpshman. East Aurora, New York: Slosson Educational Publications, Inc.

Introduction

The Slosson Intelligence Test–Revised (SIT-R) is an individually administered screening device intended for situations in which "a quick estimate of general verbal cognitive ability" is needed (Nicholson & Hibpshman, 1991a, p. 1). These situations may include 1) screening in educational, clinical, and vocational settings to aid in determining whether further, more in-depth evaluation is needed; 2) providing a tentative diagnosis of cognitive ability to include strengths and weaknesses of clients or students; and 3) confirming previous test results.

The SIT-R has been designed for use by teachers, principals, guidance counselors, special education personnel, psychologists, psychometrists, social workers, and other responsible professionals who must evaluate a client or student's mental ability. The authors stress that the SIT-R is merely a screening device for estimating the cognitive ability of an individual, public school student, college student, mental patient, or mentally handicapped person, and it is not intended for use in final placement decisions.

Originally authored in 1961 by Richard Slosson, the SIT was produced as a brief, individually administered measure of "intelligence." In 1981, a second edition appeared, evidencing no changes in the directions, items, scoring, or computation of the IQ. The scoring continued to use the ratio method, considered problematic due to nonuniform standard deviations at different age levels (Reynolds, 1985). Also, for both of these editions, items were designed to resemble several found on the Stanford-Binet Intelligence Scale, allowing a claim of congruence with Form L-M.

The SIT-R remains consistent with its two predecessors in that the main purpose is to provide a quick index of verbal intelligence, but its authors have answered most previous criticisms and improved several areas. Item distribution of the number of questions in each classification category is more equal. The revised test includes the following categories: General Information, Similarities and Differences, Vocabulary, Comprehension, Digit Span, Arithmetic, Visual-Motor, and Auditory Memory for Sentences. The standardization sample is larger than before

---

The reviewers wish to thank Cheryl Coseglia for her assistance with parts of this review.

and generally represents the current U.S. population. The Deviation IQ is now referred to as the Total Standard Score (TSS).

For effective administration and score interpretation, SIT-R users are urged to have knowledge in the following areas:

1. Administering, scoring, and interpreting group tests, especially in the area of achievement, ability, aptitude, and intelligence.
2. Application and interpretation of basic statistics, including the concepts of mean, standard deviation, and correlation.
3. Application and interpretation of scores, including mean, standard scores, percentiles, normal curve equivalent, T-scores, [and] Z-scores.
4. Application and interpretation of reliability, including the meaning of reliability, methods of determining reliability, standard error of measurement, and confidence intervals.
5. Application and interpretation of validity, including the meaning of validity, types of validity, standard error of estimate, and confidence intervals.
6. Effectively establishing rapport with clients (Nicholson & Hibpshman, 1991a, p. 2).

The primary SIT-R manual contains the 187 oral questions and tasks arranged in order of difficulty, ranging from age 4 through 16 and above. A second manual includes norms tables and technical information. The answer sheets provided are easy to use for both scoring and interpreting the test. Users also can obtain an item analysis kit containing both manual and scoring sheets, though it was not available for review at the time of this writing.

The SIT-R is an untimed test, requiring "from about 10 to 15 minutes for the average person to 20 or even 30 minutes for the very gifted or the person who is defective in certain areas while normal or high in other areas" (Nicholson & Hibpshman, 1991a, p. 4). The examiner begins the administration reading the items suggested by the subject's age. Individual items are numbered consecutively and no longer given age classifications. Testing is continued to establish a basal of 10 consecutive correct responses and stopped when the examinee produces 10 consecutive incorrect responses.

Scoring is completed directly on the answer sheet. Users obtain the raw score by adding the number of items passed to the ceiling item. The raw score is converted (by consulting a table) to a Total Standard Score (TSS), which has a mean of 100 and standard deviation of 16, very similar to other IQ scores. A second type of score furnished by means of tabular data is the Mean Age Equivalent (MAE), which is "analogous to the mental age produced by the original SIT, except that items were not calibrated by age level" (Nicholson & Hibpshman, 1991b, p. 22). The SIT-R authors urge caution regarding the use of MAE scores due to serious theoretical problems that can produce misleading results. The authors, however, provide such scores because some educational systems use them.

Total Standard Scores (TSS) can be converted easily to standard scores, z-scores, College Entrance Exam Board (CEEB), T-scores, NCEs, stanines, and percentiles by means of a simple chart included in the norms manual. Confidence levels for 95% or 99% can be determined for age levels 4 through adult by looking at Table D. The user can easily obtain many types of normed data for individual raw scores.

Practical Applications/Uses

Nicholson and Hibpshman (1991a) emphasize that the sole purpose of the SIT-R is to obtain a brief estimate of general verbal cognitive ability. Appropriate consumers of this screening instrument are educators, psychologists, and social workers with the basic knowledge often taught in introductory tests and measurements courses. The SIT-R is intended for persons of many abilities and disabilities, age 4 through adult. This test should not be used as a measure of intelligence by itself, but instead as an indication for further in-depth evaluation or as part of a battery to confirm other testing results.

The manual includes specific instructions for administering the SIT-R to persons with handicaps. The standardization sample included subjects who were blind, learning disabled, cerebral palsied, orthopedically handicapped, emotionally disturbed, mentally handicapped, and behavior disordered, but none that were hearing impaired or mute. Users should exercise caution in administering the SIT-R to subjects not included in the norming sample; such scores may be invalid and lead to incorrect interpretation.

Scoring procedures are simple and relatively objective; the examiner enters a "1" for each correct response and a "0" for incorrect responses. The manual offers specific instructions for what to do if subjects provide questionable answers. Further probing may be necessary, and at times the examiner must use informed judgment to determine whether a response should be scored as correct or incorrect. However, the majority of responses (e.g., repeating a number sequence) are easily scored without probing.

Interpretation of raw scores via tables in the technical manual reduces the need for calculations. The SIT-R presents the tables on fewer pages than did earlier versions, thereby streamlining their use. The total variety of score types can be determined quite simply.

In summary, the SIT-R offers an appropriate screening device with which to measure an individual's cognitive verbal ability. Used by informed professionals, the test can be administered and scored quickly and directly.

Technical Aspects

The information and data found in the SIT-R technical manual provided the basis for the following evaluation of the test's technical aspects.

The validity section in the technical manual begins with the rationale for the SIT-R and contains information on construct, content, and criterion-related (concurrent) validity. The framework for this revision was guided by considering how respected authors in the field (e.g., Wechsler, Guilford, Thorndike) viewed intelligence. Construct validity for the SIT-R derives from the theory that intelligence is global, commonly referred to as g. The SIT-R measures crystallized intelligence, which is "reflective of one's cultural exposure and experience, including education," in contrast to fluid intelligence, which often is regarded as "native" ability (Nicholson & Hibpshman, 1991b, p. 2). In essence, the SIT-R is a general measure of intelligence that taps two broad domains (crystallized and memory) within the global *(g)* area. Crystallized intelligence divides into two major components: verbal and quantitative. Four of the six SIT-R item types are found in the verbal area, thereby heavily loading the SIT-R in the verbal intelligence factor. The test's construct validity, then, is based on a global *(g)* view of the nature of intelligence that draws very heavily on the verbal area.

The heavy loading in the verbal area is readily revealed when considering content validity. Although the SIT-R does not contain subtests, four of its six cognitive domains are considered verbal: Vocabulary, General Information, Similarities and Differences, and Comprehension. (The remaining two areas are Quantitative and Auditory Memory.) Items for these six areas were developed with the goal of assuring that examinees would encounter at least one item of each type within every group of 10 items with the exception the "the lower range and one sequence in the upper range of the test" (Nicholson & Hibpshman, 1991b, pp. 3–4). A cursory check of item sequence supports this claim.

The content of the SIT-R retains more than half the items from the original test. Some items were eliminated from the original because "they contained traditional English units of measurement and transformation into metric units would have radically altered the difficulty or meaning of the item"; other items were updated "to reflect current prices and wages" (Nicholson & Hibpshman, 1991b, p. 4). Users should welcome these long overdue content changes.

The technical manual mentions field testing, but no details are given. The new items were selected from a pool of more than 600 items, some of which were in Slosson's original item pool but not used in his original test. One of the most striking changes in the SIT-R is in the content of the new items. Within the category of Comprehension, as described on page 4 of the technical manual, more than 90% of the items are new. Among these, many involve higher level thinking skills not clearly addressed in the original SIT. Several deal with processes such as using social judgment, logical reasoning, and interpreting figurative language. Overall, the new and revised items appear to strengthen the test's content. The lack of information about the field trials is unfortunate, however, and reduces the confidence users can place in the final item selection.

Criterion or concurrent validity in this instance refers to how closely the SIT-R relates to other tests of intelligence (i.e., WAIS-R and WISC-R). Correlation coefficients are reported for five different age groups (6–8, 9–11, 12–14, 15–16, and adult), with sample sizes ranging from 10 for the adults to 78 for the 12–14 age group. Generally, the SIT-R Total Standard Score (TSS) correlates most highly with the Verbal IQ of the Wechsler scales (range = .83–.91). This finding is not unexpected, given the high verbal loading of the SIT-R. TSS correlations with Wechsler Performance IQs are quite low (range = .38–.84) and with Full Scale IQs range from .61 to .92. Almost all the correlations between the two tests are significant. Only three mean scores are significantly different, and two of these involve the Wechsler Performance IQ. The confidence one can place in these data is diminished by each age group's relatively small sample size.

Concerning validity, perhaps the greatest improvements arise in the SIT-R's content. The need to update and replace numerous items was readily apparent to frequent users of the SIT. These changes should help make the SIT-R a more valid measure of crystallized intelligence.

Reliability refers to the consistency or stability of rank scores. A sample of 1,793 subjects ranging in age from 4.0 to 64.9 participated in reliability studies using the Kuder-Richardson formula 20 (KR-20), the Spearman-Brown correction formula, and the Rulon (another split-half procedure). For the total group, the reliability coefficient for each formula was .96, .97, and .97, respectively. The standard error of measurement ranged from 2.88 to 3.37. KR-20 reliability coefficients were calculated for 18 separate age groups, with sample sizes ranging from 41 to 220. Only two coefficients fell below .90 (.88 and .89). The modal coefficient was .96, and the standard error of measurement ranged from 2.88 to 5.50. Overall the internal consistency of the SIT-R appears sufficient for an individual test. The sample sizes on which these coefficients were determined, however, vary considerably and are based on less than 1,800 total subjects.

The only statement related to test-retest reliability appears in a single sentence: "During the norming process, the SIT-R was administered twice, to a sample of 41 individuals with administrations one week apart, producing a stability coefficient of .96" (Nicholson & Hibpshman, 1991b, p. 7). With no further details of this extremely small sample, very little evidence is offered for test-retest reliability. Much larger samples and more specific information about the subjects involved are needed to support test-retest reliability.

In summary, reliability coefficients and standard errors of measurement are based on sample sizes of roughly 100 subjects (41 to 220) at each of five age levels. The SIT-R appears to be most reliable with subjects ages 7 through 34, where KR-20 coefficients are .93 or larger for each age group. Only extremely limited information is presented on test-retest reliability. SIT-R users should keep in mind that no details of the sample are provided and the size of the samples in the various age groups is limited.

The standardization of the SIT-R first tapped test results gathered from more than 2,400 subjects of the original test and other professionals (e.g., psychologists, educational diagnosticians, school assessment personnel). From these a sample of 1,854 individuals was selected "to match the U.S. population as closely as possible (Nicholson & Hibpshman, 1991b, p. 15).

Based upon a visual analysis of data presented in four tables, the present reviewers judged the match between SIT-R sample and the U.S. population to be fair. In regional terms, the SIT-R sample overrepresented the South and underrepresented the North Central area by 4% in each instance. Occupational category comparisons revealed that the SIT-R sample overrepresented the professional and service categories, as well as farm, fishing, and forestry. Production, craft, repair, operators, and fabricators were underrepresented. In terms of educational level, observed differences in the percentages were not significant "between the expected distribution of educational attainment for the U.S. population and the proportionate attainment of any age group" (Nicholson & Hibpshman, 1991b, p. 16).

The gender distribution of the SIT-R sample matched the U.S. population. In terms of race, blacks were slightly underrepresented (by 2%) and whites were overrepresented (by 9%). The 7% underrepresentation in the "Other" category was explained by noting that standardization subjects were required to speak fluent English, and the primary language for many of these individuals was not

English. Despite difficulty in identifying individual items in two charts containing delta values, a visual inspection of data in the charts reveals several items that appear to differ by ethnicity and sex. Analyses of test bias for the "raw score means and standard deviations were calculated by race and gender for the entire normative sample. No significant differences were found between these means" (Nicholson & Hibpshman, 1991b, p. 12). Although no differences were statistically significant, the authors might have discussed individual items where possible bias might exist.

Although these reviewers judge the standardization group match to the U.S. population as just fair, a latent trait analysis using the Rasch model led the authors of the SIT-R to conclude that "meaningful test norms can be produced without creating a painstakingly representative sample of the entire U.S. population" (Nicholson & Hibpshman, 1991b, p. 8). The validity of this claim depends, in large measure, on the strong assumptions often specified in such models; namely, that a single factor accounts for a subject's performance on a test item and that performance on one test item is independent of performance on other test items. Because all 187 SIT-R items "were found to adequately fit the Rasch model," the norms tables were generated "using the results of the latent trait analysis" (Nicholson & Hibpshman, 1991b, pp. 9–10). Users should keep in mind the strong assumptions on which the norms ultimately were based.

Critique

In a review of an earlier edition of the SIT, Oakland (1985) noted that "its theoretical rationale is not clearly stated, and the empirical basis for its concept of intelligence is also uncertain. Its standardization sample is meager [$N = 1,109$], narrow, and unrepresentative of the U.S. Little information on reliability and validity specific to the 1981 version is presented" (p. 1403). Another reviewer (Reynolds, 1985) stated that "the SIT remains a psychometrically poor measure of general intelligence" (p. 1404). The overall tone of these reviews is clearly negative. Although published in the early 1960s, reviewers and users of subsequent revisions or editions found that the test items were basically identical to those of the original test. The major changes involved the price of the test and norms booklets that required "more empirical research" (Wagner, 1987, p. 507).

SIT-R, the 1991 edition by Nicholson and Hibpshman, represents a genuine revision of earlier editions and seems to deal with some of the criticisms raised by previous reviewers. Generally its technical aspects and psychometric properties surpass those of the earlier editions. The greatest improvements lie in the item revisions and replacements along with the discussion of how the six different cognitive domains fit into a theoretical construct of intelligence. The descriptions of field tests used to refine the more than 600 items in the pool, however, are sketchy and incomplete.

Criterion validity coefficients that emerged using the Wechsler scales involve less than 250 subjects in five different age groups. Correlations of Wechsler Full Scale IQs with SIT-R Total Standard Scores range from .61 to .92, with a median value of .82; correlations with the Wechsler Verbal scales are higher (.83 to .91), with a median value of .88. For the total group of younger subjects ($n = 234$), the highest correlation (r = .89) occurred between the SIT-R and the WISC-R Verbal IQ. These correlations are not nearly as high as those reported between the Stanford-Binet Intelligence Scale and the original SIT. Even more noticeable in the SIT-R is the definite move away from comparisons with the Stanford-Binet. A possible reason for this course of action may be the decline of the Stanford-Binet in popularity and the increasingly negative reviews (Spruill, 1987).

KR-20 reliability is very high for the entire sample of 1,793 subjects (r = .96). KR-20 coefficients also are reported for 18 separate age groups and, with two exceptions (.89 and .88), correlations emerged above .90. In earlier SIT manuals, the reliability may have been inflated because of the broad age span that comprised the sample. Reporting separate reliability coefficients in the SIT-R for the various age groups increases the confidence one can place in the test's consistency of measurement, with two reservations: First, sample sizes vary widely among age groups. For example, 41 subjects are in the 45.0 to 54.9 age group while 220 subjects comprise the 18.0 to 24.9 age group. Second, the standardization involved 1,854 subjects; however, reliability coefficients are reported for only 1,793. No explanation for this discrepancy appears in the technical manual.

Two additional points arise regarding reliability. First, test-retest reliability (r = .96), while high, is based on a clearly inadequate sample (N = 41), and the authors offer no details about the ages or abilities of the subjects involved. Second, reporting the standard error of measurement for the various age groups permits users to record confidence intervals for the obtained test score. The test form has space for this welcome addition, and users should find this information helpful in reporting and using the test results.

The standardization sample (N = 1,854) is meager and unrepresentative of various aspects of the U.S. population. A latent trait analysis was used to make "meaningful test norms" (Nicholson & Hibpshman, 1991b, p. 8). If users do not share the strong assumptions for such models, the resulting norms may be open to question.

Overall the SIT-R materials are clear and easy to use. More careful editing would have found both small errors (e.g., *lets* on p. 3 in the manual and an inconsistent reference format) and errors of greater consequence. For example, the technical manual contains two different values for the 99% confidence interval for the oldest age group (compare Table 1, p. 7, and Table D, p. 35). In addition, the sample scoring procedure inside the front cover of the manual (and on p. 5) contains arrows that confuse more than clarify. For example, an arrow points to item 75 as the ceiling item when, in fact, item 74 represents the ceiling. Another error appears in a table on page 5, listing item 73 of the SIT-R as equivalent to item 7-8 in the original SIT, whereas SIT item 7-6 should have been cited instead. Such errors and inconsistencies should be corrected in future printings. The publisher might also reconsider its decision to print the test questions all in capital letters. A conventional upper- and lowercase type treatment would enhance the ease of reading the questions.

The SIT-R represents a definite improvement over earlier editions, but its primary use should continue to be for screening purposes. It is a quick test with stronger evidence of validity and reliability; however, the authors and publisher are encouraged to take steps to make this a more valid and reliable instrument.

References

Nicholson, C.L., & Hibpshman, T.L. (1991a). *Slosson Intelligence Test (SIT-R) manual.* East Aurora, NY: Slosson Educational Publications.

Nicholson, C.L., & Hibpshman, T.L. (1991b). *Slosson Intelligence Test (SIT-R) norms tables/technical manual.* East Aurora, NY: Slosson Educational Publications.

Oakland, T. (1985). Slosson Intelligence Test. In J.V. Mitchell, Jr. (Ed.), *The ninth mental measurements yearbook* (pp. 1401–1403). Lincoln, NE: Buros Institute of Mental Measurements.

Reynolds, W.M. (1985). Slosson Intelligence Test. In J.V. Mitchell, Jr. (Ed.), *The ninth mental measurements yearbook* (pp. 1403–1404). Lincoln, NE: Buros Institute of Mental Measurements.

Spruill, J. (1987). Stanford-Binet Intelligence Scale, Fourth Edition. In D.J. Keyser & R.C. Sweetland (Eds.), *Test critiques* (Vol. VI, pp. 544–559). Austin, TX: PRO-ED.

Wagner, E.E. (1987). Slosson Intelligence Test. In D.J. Keyser & R.C. Sweetland (Eds.), *Test critiques* (Vol. VI, pp. 509–511). Austin, TX: PRO-ED.

Shirley L. Robinson, Ph.D.

Clinical Psychologist and Mental Health Coordinator,
Comprehensive Child Development Program, Civitan International
Research Center, University of Alabama, Birmingham, Alabama.

C. Eugene Walker, Ph.D.

Professor of Psychology and Director of Pediatric Psychology
Internship, Oklahoma Health Sciences Center, Oklahoma City,
Oklahoma.

STRESS AUDIT

Lyle H. Miller and Alma Dell Smith. Brookline,
Massachusetts: Biobehavioral Associates.

Introduction

The Stress Audit is a 238-item measure of perceived stress and relative vulnerability to stress. It yields a composite profile of the magnitude and types of a respondent's experienced stress within the past 6 months, anticipated stress in the future 6 months, and potential vulnerability to stress in general. Similar forms are available for adults and teenagers.

This measure represents its authors' initial attempts to provide a "comprehensive and psychometrically sound" inventory of stress in adults. An undated first revision, the Stress Profile for Teenagers, is also available. The authors are clinicians in an urban stress management clinic in Brookline, Massachusetts. According to the manual (Miller, Smith, & Mehler, 1988), the authors hope that other clinicians and researchers will help to further develop their empirical database by providing additional normative data for regions outside the northeastern United States and for other subject applications. The manual reflects no indication of format revisions beyond collection of initial normative data and the first revision yielding a version for teenagers. Nor is it clear whether treatment outcome studies are planned to address the multicomponent treatment recommendations made by the authors for reducing stress in specific physiological systems.

With the Stress Audit, Miller and Smith have ambitiously attempted to operationalize a complex biobehavioral model of stress. In summary, the model posits that stress is a "dynamic state of tension" between an organism and its environment, created to maintain the integrity of the organism as it responds to the demands of the environment. As such, the model assumes that "stress" is additive, cumulative, and a "relatively enduring" state phenomenon. It assumes that demands are perceived and that in order to respond to demands, the organism must mobilize physiological resources via the sympathetic nervous and endocrine systems. Prolonged mobilization results in "strain." Strain is manifested by any number of physiological "symptoms" endorsed by respondents, and these symptoms are thought to be associated with discrete neurophysiological systems such as the neuromuscular system, the limbic system, the neurohormonal system, and the neuroimmune system.

Intuitively, the model is a provocative one. Although the authors are to be commended for intent, it might be helpful for them to provide references for the theoretical basis of the selected model as well as for empirical research to support such a model. The authors also may wish to clarify potential confounds that likely exist in defining "discrete neurophysiological systems" and symptoms identified within these systems. In addition, these reviewers note that the assumptions of the model initially define physiological "symptoms of strain," while later documentation in the manual refers to the same physiological manifestations as "stress symptoms," two very different concepts as described in other literature on stress and coping. Because of these theoretical confounds and other concerns about the validity of the measure as discussed herein, caution is recommended in making clinical, personal, or work-related decisions based primarily on the results of this questionnaire. For instance, comparisons to normative data are lacking and other claims for validity should be tempered, given the concerns addressed herein. However, this tool may be a useful adjunct to clinical interview and other measures with demonstrated validity and reliability in helping individuals recognize and concretely document stressful situations and associated physiological and emotional responses.

The Stress Audit is available in either a paper-and-pencil booklet format or a personal computer (PC) format. The paper-and-pencil format can be self-scored or scored by an optical mark reader. The paper-and-pencil format is easy to read and follow, and most adults or teenagers who could respond to census forms by filling in appropriate circles could complete the questionnaire. According to the manual, the PC format assumes operating knowledge of IBM or compatible personal computers, including familiarity with DOS commands. A chapter of the manual is devoted to a cookbook guide for use of the PC format. Software for the PC versions of the Stress Audit, the recommended NCS 3000 Optical Mark Reader, and the interpretive software all are available from the publisher.

The paper-and-pencil version for adults contains 238 items in booklet format. A similar version is available for teenagers. The manual states that the latter also contains 238 items, but on inspection, these reviewers observed 263. For both age groups, scale scores are obtained for six domains of stressful events or sources of stress: family, individual roles, social being, environment, finances, and work or school. Item loadings appear different for teenagers. For instance, teens are asked about parental marital stress, and the items appear to presuppose that teen respondents live with their biological families. Thus, those living in step families or foster care, or with a spouse or significant other, may not respond to certain items as stated. Scale scores on both versions are also provided for seven domains of stress symptoms: muscular, parasympathetic, sympathetic, emotional, cognitive, endocrine, and immune. The version for teenagers also includes an item about suicidal thoughts within the cognitive system symptoms. Both the adult and teenaged versions yield summary indices for sources of situational stress, symptoms, and vulnerability to stress. Each is given for past, future, and combined scores. With computerized or optical mark reader scoring, item responses for both versions are also regrouped to offer factor scores for 16 factors (acute stress, chronic stress or strain, work setting, powerlessness, discrimination, social demands, personal uncertainty, marital turmoil, financial pressure, burnout, personal success, personal loss, reproduction, personal isolation, relocation, and housing demands), but no normative data are provided for these factors.

The profile for stress situations, symptoms, and vulnerability can be plotted by the respondent or supervising test administrator directly in the test booklet. Written report summaries also can be generated with appropriate software, as can forms for professional and/or personal use. While the summary report booklets are attractive and professional looking, concerns about the validity of the measure and a bias toward recommending behavior change in the absence of clinical significance warrant caution in the use of this scale. For instance, the sample reports for clinical and personal use generated by the teenager's version suggest that low scores on the vulnerability to stress scale may be independent of high scores on the stress situations and symptoms scales. In both sample reports, a teenager endorsed situational stress higher than 94% of the general population and symptom stress (including thoughts about suicide) greater than 76% of the population, yet her profile suggested her vulnerability to stress was greater than only about 24% of the population. For teens in particular, given the inclusion of the suicidality item, perhaps professional administration and interpretation of the Stress Audit would be clinically preferred over self-administration.

Practical Applications/Uses

The Stress Audit was designed to provide clinicians, employers, and individuals with a profile of stressful situations (past and anticipated) and stress symptoms, plus an index of the respondent's vulnerability to stress. The latter appears to be an attempt to measure stress-moderating variables (Peterson, 1989), such as the individual's social support network and healthy coping strategies.

A telephone conversation with the first author, Lyle Miller, Ph.D., suggests that the inventory has been used primarily by clinicians in private practice and for industrial and organizational applications. For instance, Dr. Miller reported that a large communications firm had purchased copies of the inventory for use with its employees. The authors suggest that the measure may have utility for physicians, psychologists, counselors, and personnel staff at present. The teenage stress profile also contains school-related items of potential interest to guidance and vocational counselors (Miller, Mehler, & Smith, n.d.). Dr. Miller noted that while some purchasers of the measure have indicated a desire for research applications, he is unaware of published data utilizing the measure as of about October 1990. It is not clear whether the authors intend to further revise or update their database in the near future. A computerized search of a psychological abstract database by these reviewers yielded no additional references to other studies using the measure.

The Stress Audit manual (Miller et al., 1988) suggests that the norm sample consisted of nurses at an urban hospital, college freshmen, and a group of psychology graduate students. No breakdown by number, age, or sex is offered other to state that the total N equals 1,450 subjects drawn from an urban population in the northeastern United States. From an appendix to the manual, one infers that 234 (or possibly 237) of these subjects were stress clinic patients, but descriptive data for this subgroup are not offered. Data from this group alone appear to have generated the authors' impressions supporting construct validity of the Stress Audit symptom scales when compared to the "neurotic triad" and other aspects of the MMPI. Taken in conjunction with problems of regional specificity acknowledged by the authors, generalization to clinical and industrial samples as recommended by them warrants considerable caution.

According to the manual, the paper-and-pencil version of the Stress Audit can be self-administered, or an examiner can supervise individual, group, or take-home administration. An inspection of the test booklet suggests that adults or teens with a moderate degree of literacy could understand the clearly stated test items. In general, one could expect the measure to take about 30 minutes to an hour to complete. Individuals with little experience marking computerized score sheets may need the most time.

The paper-and-pencil booklet for adults begins with easy-to-read instructions for completing the questionnaire, followed by a brief demographic section. Then the respondent is asked to identify and rate personally relevant stressful events from a pool of 148 items similar to those on other published life events inventories. For instance, events such as divorce, recent moves, family changes, and so forth are listed. Although the authors clearly state that items are drawn from previous research and their own clinical experience, no references are provided to help other researchers distinguish the sources of particular items generated for this item pool. The respondent rates his or her level of stress on a Likert-type scale ranging from 1 ("not stressful") to 5 ("very stressful"). Separate columns are provided to mark responses for stressful events in the past 6 months versus those anticipated to be stressful in the upcoming 6 months.

The next 70 items have a similar response format but ask the respondent to identify his or her own stress reactions or symptoms. Samples of physical (e.g., muscular, sympathetic and parasympathetic, endocrine, and immune), emotional (e.g., anger, loss of control, and anxiety), and cognitive (e.g., memory, confusion, and preoccupation) responses are offered. Upon completion of these items, an additional 20 items attempt to measure the individual's "vulnerability" to stress symptoms. For instance, the respondent rates items suggestive of coping resources, such as the availability of a social network, financial resources, a healthy diet, and so forth on a scale of 1 ("almost always") to 5 ("never"). Level of readability appears similar to that in other published studies of life events, social support, and coping inventories for teenagers and adults.

Finally, instructions for self-scoring are presented, and the respondent or examiner tallies section scores for past and future stress and plots totals for situational stress, stress symptoms, and stress vulnerability. It is likely that unsupervised respondents might have difficulty understanding the guidelines for scoring and plotting the Stress Audit profile, which is designed to be a graphical representation similar to that of the Minnesota Multiphasic Personality Inventory (Dahlstrom, Welsh, & Dahlstrom, 1975). However, templates are not required to summarize and plot scale scores, and no validity scales are offered. Only the situational stress source scales, the stress symptom scales, the vulnerability scale, and the summary scales for stress situations and symptoms are plotted. The additional scale scores yielded by computer analyses for another 16 factors are not plotted on the profile sheet, nor are scoring instructions or supportive descriptive and validity data presented in the manual.

For the personal computer format of the questionnaire and for paper-and-pencil questionnaires scored by optical mark reader, a Stress Audit report with additional interpretive information can be generated for personal or professional use. The general guidelines for interpreting the questionnaire and the resulting profile appear inadequate. For instance, trained clinicians expecting T-scores of 70 and above to reflect clinical significance may be surprised that the authors of the Stress Audit define T-scores of 50 and above as "not necessarily healthy," with a potential need for behavioral change or stress management strategies. In fact, the language of the sample computerized report for personal use and interpretation may cause clients with T-scores in the 50s to be overly concerned about a need for change. The authors do not cite clinical or empirical assumptions supporting use of T-scores as low as 50 to indicate a need for behavior change. Although their model for biobehavioral stress posits that stress is a "relatively enduring state phenomenon," no attempt is made to verify how long an individual has perceived stress or manifested stress (or strain) symptoms over time before clinical intervention is warranted.

Technical Aspects

The authors have thoughtfully targeted the lack of empirical and theoretical support for the tenets of a comprehensive biobehavioral model of stress in the literature. Indeed, the manual spends considerable time delineating a definition of stress and associated assumptions for the professional user. The resulting format for the Stress Audit asks the respondent to define stressful areas of his or her life on a scale of most to least stressful and not to fill in items that do not apply personally. These reviewers would note, however, that some individuals may consistently deny stress (e.g., teenagers who externalize responsibility, defensive individuals, those who "fake good," etc.). Underreporting of stress also could occur, for example, when an individual in a bad marriage perceives the positive impact of divorce as greater than any temporary discomfort resulting from the process of divorce itself. Perhaps these individuals would be more willing to endorse stress per se if also given an option to endorse whether a situation has a negative or positive impact on their lives. Or they might endorse situational stress if also given an option to rate their perceived efficacy to cope with such stress. Models for such instruments can be found in the life events and coping literature, and Miller and Smith may wish to consider or rule out such options for modifying this instrument. Finally, in the event the present format is maintained, the authors may want to consider in what cases and to what extent a low situational stress summary score taken in conjunction with a high stress symptom score may reflect somatization (and by inference, underreporting of situational stress in the absence of known medical etiology). Indeed, correlational and factorial data supplied by the authors suggest that one of four factors yielded by analysis of the Stress Audit and the MMPI suggests "classic neurotic conversion" of stress into somatic symptoms. Clinicians and lay users of the Stress Audit also should be made aware of how diagnosed illness and associated complaints might inflate stress symptom scale scores in the profile. Personal interpretations of users who self-administer and score their own Stress Audit profile also may be compromised in the case of individuals who tend towards somatization. Concerns about the interpretation of somatization taken with others discussed herein all suggest caution in distributing this measure for purposes of self-administration.

In addition to concerns about interpretation and about the theoretical confounds already mentioned, the following comments about the validity of this scale are offered. The total sample size ($N = 1,450$) appears adequate; however, statistics by age, gender, clinical status, and so forth are not offered. The failure to offer descriptive data such as means or standard deviations renders clinical decision making difficult, in that researchers sampling other regional and application pools cannot compare their data to the norm sample. In addition, these reviewers would concur with the authors when they address concerns for generalizability, given that regional representation was limited to an urban northeastern United States sample.

To demonstrate internal consistency, Hoyt's estimates of reliability are offered for the stress, symptom, and vulnerability subscales. These are generally good for past stress situations and symptoms, ranging from an adequate estimate of .80 for immune system symptoms to a moderately high estimate of .94 for the work/school stress situation scale for adults. Reliability estimates are similarly adequate for future stress situations and symptoms, ranging from a low of .83 for endocrine system symptoms to a high of .95 for the work/school stress situation scale for adults. In general, reliability estimates are higher for future stress and symptoms than for past stress and symptoms, although perhaps not significantly so. Cronbach's alpha estimates for composite stress situation and symptoms scores also are moderately high. The vulnerability scale, which attempts to quantify moderating factors, incurred the lowest estimate, .76.

One-week test-retest reliability coefficients for the group of nurses (*n* unknown) range from .65 for financial stress to .87 for social stress (past and future combined in both cases). Two-week reliability for the group of psychology graduate students ranges from .48 for endocrine system symptoms to .82 for financial stress. In general, this represents more variability and a decline in range over a 2-week period of time. Six-week reliability estimates for the group of college freshmen ranged from .54 for family stress and sympathetic nervous system symptoms to .69 for work/school stress, again suggesting a decline in range over time. Unfortunately, however, within-group differences cannot be ruled out, given that a different subsample of respondents was used for each test-retest interval. These estimates are at least adequate and at best moderately high for certain groups of subjects if, as the authors assume, stress is a relatively enduring state phenomenon. However, other empirically based literature suggests that both perceived stress and physiological indices thought to be associated with stress show diurnal variation in some individuals (e.g., the concepts of "hot reactors" and sympathetic and/or cardiac hyperreactivity). The authors may wish to consider and discuss these findings in light of their own conclusions, and particularly given claims to validity based on test-retest reliability.

Additional claims for validity appear to be based on results suggesting high interscale correlations for stress situation and symptom scales. This follows for the correlations among summary scale scores for stress sources and symptoms (.77 overall) but not for individual subscale scores for stress and symptoms (e.g., $r = .46$ for social sources and sympathetic symptoms to $r = .71$ for individual roles and emotional symptoms). Considerable range of variability is noted for individual symptom scale scores and stress sources.

It is very interesting that the authors cite emotional and cognitive subscales as the most highly related to stress, regardless of stress source. Future research efforts might address these findings with respect to cognitive-behavioral treatments that might affect these systems rather than attempting to target specific physiological systems such as immune, endocrine, sympathetic, and parasympathetic symptoms per se.

According to the authors, interscale correlations for the vulnerability scale and stress sources scales are less robust in general but still statistically significant. Although this may be the case statistically, users should be cautious about relying on this clinically. For instance, consider the sample clinical and personal use reports generated for a teenaged girl. Her vulnerability to stress score ($T = 43$) falls within the average range using conventional standards, with a moderately high summary score for situational stress ($T = 66$) and an average summary score for stress symptoms ($T = 57$). From these summary scores alone, one might infer adequate resources for coping with moderately high situational stress. However, inspection of individual scale scores reveal that she endorsed significant situational stress for school and family scales (T-scores greater than 70), moderately high situational stress for social and individual roles (T-scores greater than 60), and moderately high stress symptoms for the immune and cognitive systems. Further inspection of individual items rated "very stressful" on the social scale reveals the suicide of "someone you know" within the past 6 months. On the cognitive scale, the girl also endorsed very stressful thoughts of death or suicide in the past 6 months and anticipated more in the upcoming 6 months. Reliance on summary scores and the plotted profile alone by individuals not trained to assess suicidal risk or self-administration and interpretation of the measure may not provide opportunities to explore suicidal risk further. For instance, were her thoughts of death or suicide related to her friend's death alone, or might she also be suicidal? Clearly the inclusion of such questions furthers warrants the need for trained professional administration and interpretation of the Stress Audit.

Finally, the authors present results of a correlation matrix and follow-up factor analyses yielded by a principal components method with orthogonal rotations. In these analyses, the relationship of stress source and symptom scale scores with subscale scores from the MMPI were explored, using only the data from 234 (or 237) clinic patients. According to the authors, the first "almost pure stress factor" loads for all Stress Audit situational source scales and symptom scales and the F scale of the MMPI. The psychological distress factor loads for emotional, cognitive, and muscular symptoms of the Stress Audit and assorted MMPI scales. The decomposition factor loads for individual role stress and cognitive system symptoms of the Stress Audit and assorted MMPI scales. It is not clear why this scale should refer to decomposition, or what defines decomposition. The neurotic conversion factor loads for symptom scales of the Stress Audit (excluding immune and endocrine symptoms) and several MMPI scales with somatization interpretations. Thus, the authors conclude that clinic patients rate personal stress levels independent of hypochondriacal or hysterical personality influences that may drive symptom reporting. Although this likely would be the case for many individuals completing the questionnaire, clinical interviews to rule out viable medical symptomatology and/or somatization tendencies appear warranted (given the identification of a neurotic conversion factor). Factor analyses suggest that cognitions are very important to the biobehavioral stress model. Factor 2 (psychological distress) and Factor 3 (decomposition) both yield significant loadings for both cognitive and emotional symptoms on the Stress Audit. Only the cognitive symptom factor of the Stress Audit loads on all four factors, an interesting finding that might be pursued further in terms of the theoretical implications of the biobehavioral stress model.

The manual also notes that correlational and factor analyses of the Stress Audit and the MMPI utilized scale scores, however it is not clear whether these were raw scores or T-scores. These reviewers assume raw scores were used in lieu of MMPI scores with K corrections, given that all three validity scale scores are treated individually in the factor analysis table of the Stress Audit manual. Consequently, we wonder what the effect of using scale scores without K corrections for adults might have on claims for validity, particularly on situational stress factors of the Stress Audit. The authors do report significant negative correlations between the K scale and most situational stress scale scores of the Stress Audit, but more discussion of this matter would be welcomed. Although adolescent MMPI protocols are often uncorrected by K scores (Archer, 1987), one does not know whether scoring protocols for adolescents or adults were used with teenaged students included in the normative sample for the Stress Audit.

In addition, high F scores on the MMPI conventionally suggest socially deviant or atypical responses (Graham, 1987). Were the clinical patients in the norm sample significantly high scorers on the F scale? Did the authors attempt to use the three validity scales of the MMPI to eliminate any questionable protocols (i.e., faking good, faking bad, random responding) prior to analyses? These reviewers would feel more comfortable about accepting validity claims based on analyses using the MMPI had the authors stated what checks, if any, were used in this regard.

Finally, we also note that correlational and factor analyses were based on the scores of stress clinic patients. Given the authors' use of T-scores greater than 50 to define possible clinical populations, these reviewers would have liked to have seen descriptive statistics such as means and standard deviations presented for the norm sample. We do not know whether this group differed significantly from "normals," what the subjects' ages were, or whether nurses, college freshmen, and graduate students constituted this group as in the reliability samples.

Critique

In summary, Miller and Smith have undertaken an ambitious project in the development of the Stress Audit and they are to be commended for attempting to operationalize a biobehavioral stress model. However, formal use of the Stress Audit for assisting in clinical and industrial decision making should not be weighted toward use of this measure in the absence of supportive data from multiple sources. Indeed, at the time of this writing (1991) and at the present stage of its developmental history, it appears that the measure might best be utilized as an adjunct to other previously validated measures and well-documented clinic findings.

Initial normative data are lacking in terms of descriptive statistics for comparison, and it would have been helpful if questions about representative stratification within the norm sample were addressed. For instance, no breakdown is provided for age or sex of respondents, or for numbers of nurses, graduate students, and/or college freshmen whose earlier data yielded reliability estimates. In addition, it appears that analyses reported to support the reliability and validity of the version for teenagers might have been based on data from a subset of college freshman (*n* unknown) participating in the original normative sample of 1,450 subjects.

Concerns about the validity of the measure also are discussed in this review. Most salient are apparent theoretical confounds between the definitions of stress and strain, questions about the assumption that stress is a relatively enduring state phenomenon, and a need for more discussion and data to support claims of construct validity based on relationships (or lack of relationships) with MMPI subscale scores. Clarification of use of the three MMPI validity scales to eliminate questionable protocols and explanations of use of K-corrected scores for adults versus adolescents are warranted. Given the questions raised herein, it is also troublesome that unsupervised individuals may attempt interpretation of the scale, particularly teenagers. For instance, some individuals may overestimate the need for behavior change based on the authors' adoption of T-scores of 50 rather than the conventional cutoff of 70 for clinical significance. In other cases, use of summary scores and plotted profiles only may result in underestimating need for clinical intervention.

Unfortunately, a lack of references to previously published research in the area of stress and coping may hinder other researchers interested in exploring this model theoretically or empirically in the future. It is also unclear as to whether the authors intend to revise the Stress Audit or engage in other applications to further develop their database in the near future. One hopes that, because the measure is intuitively attractive and has been marketed for industrial applications and unsupervised personal use, further studies will be forthcoming.

References

Archer, R.P. (1987). *Using the MMPI with adolescents.* Hillsdale, NJ: Erlbaum.

Dahlstrom, W.G., Welsh, G.S., & Dahlstrom, L.E. (1975). *An MMPI handbook: Vol. II. Research applications.* Minneapolis: University of Minnesota Press.

Graham, J.R. (1987). *The MMPI: A practical guide.* New York: Oxford University Press.

Miller, L.H., Mehler, B.L., & Smith, A.D. (n.d.). *The teenage stress profile manual.* Brookline, MA: Biobehavioral Associates.

Miller, L.H., Smith, A.D., & Mehler, B.L. (1988). *Stress Audit manual.* Brookline, MA: Biobehavioral Associates.

Peterson, R.A. (1989). Stress Audit. In J.C. Conoley & J.J. Kramer (Eds.), *The tenth mental measurements yearbook* (pp. 783–784). Lincoln, NE: Buros Institute of Mental Measurements.

Kathleen Bieschke, Ph.D.
Assistant Professor of Counseling Psychology, The Pennsylvania State University, University Park, Pennsylvania.

STUDENT ADAPTATION TO COLLEGE QUESTIONNAIRE

Robert W. Baker and Bohdan Siryk. Los Angeles, California: Western Psychological Services.

Introduction

The Student Adaptation to College Questionnaire (SACQ; Baker & Siryk, 1989) is a self-report instrument designed to assess student adjustment to college. An underlying assumption of the SACQ is that adjustment to college is multifaceted and requires a range of coping responses that may or may not be effective. Each item of the SACQ represents a demand associated with adjustment to college and how well the student copes with that demand. Thus, the SACQ is not an evaluation of the college environment but rather of a student's adjustment to that environment.

The SACQ was developed by Robert Baker, Ph.D. and Bohdan Siryk, M.A. The first version of the questionnaire included only 52 items. Fifteen items were added later to improve the internal consistency of the subscales, particularly Personal-Emotional Adjustment (Baker & Siryk, 1984).

The SACQ packet consists of three 8½" × 11" pages, printed on both sides, and one carbon, bound by a perforated tab. Questionnaire items appear on the front and back pages; a scoring sheet, profile form, and carbon are inside. Identifying information, directions, and a sample answer are printed on the top of the front page. Directions are clear and concise. A 9-point continuum is used to answer each item, ranging from "applies very closely to me" at the left to "doesn't apply to me at all" to the right. Student responses are transferred by carbon to the scoring sheet inside; later, the administrator removes the perforated tab to tabulate scores and complete the profile form.

Although the SACQ originally was intended for freshmen, the authors have revised it to apply to any college student. Two recent research studies have used the SACQ successfully with a non-freshmen population (Lapsley, Rice, & Shadid, 1989; Rice, 1992). The reading level of the questionnaire is not specified, but the questions are clearly appropriate for any college student. The SACQ can be administered by paraprofessionals. In fact, the authors state that it is not necessary for the examiner to be present and that the instrument is suitable for administration by mail. However, someone with advanced training in psychological assessment must undertake the interpretation.

Four principal subscales are included in the SACQ. Academic Adjustment contains 24 items and reflects the educational demands of the college setting. The item clusters associated with this subscale include motivation, application, performance, and academic environment. Social Adjustment has 20 items and assesses interpersonal-societal demands. There are also four item clusters associated with this subscale: general, other people, nostalgia, and social environment. Personal-Emotional Adjustment contains 15 items that reflect the degree to which a student is experiencing psychological or somatic distress. Goal Commitment/Institutional Attachment, more commonly referred to as the Attachment subscale, also contains 15 items, 8 of which come from the Social Adjustment subscale and 1 of which comes from the Academic Adjustment subscale. The Attachment subscale was derived empirically from the original 52-item version of the SACQ, using items that correlated with attrition in freshmen at Clark University. This subscale explores the feelings a student has about being in college, and in particular the college he or she is currently attending. It focuses on the bond between the student and the institution.

Practical Applications/Uses

The purpose of the SACQ is to "assess how well a student is adapting to the demands of the college experience" (Baker & Siryk, 1989, p. 4), and it is designed to be useful to both counselors and researchers in a university setting. Because it is nonthreatening, brief, and suitable for large-group administration, the SACQ would be helpful in identifying those students in need of assistance. The profile form graphically represents SACQ results for both males and females and allows for comparison among subscales and the full scale. It also may be possible for counselors to use the Attachment subscale to help identify those at risk of being lost to attrition—bearing in mind that the subscale was developed for students at Clark University and may not be predictive of attrition at other schools.

The SACQ has been used primarily in research pertaining to college adjustment. Over 30 studies using the SACQ can be found in the manual's reference section. A perusal of the current literature indicates that this questionnaire continues to be widely used as a measure of college student adjustment. A recent research study by Haemmerlie, Robinson, and Carmen (1991) assessed Type A personality traits and adjustment to college. Rice and his colleagues (Lapsley et al., 1989; Rice, 1992; Rice, Cole, & Lapsley, 1990) used the SACQ as part of their series of studies examining separation-individuation and adjustment to college. Mooney, Sherman, and Lo Presto (1991) attempted to identify predictors related to college adjustment. Their results indicate that college adjustment is not a function of a single variable but instead is better explained by interrelated variables. In another recent study, Lopez (1991) examined patterns of family conflict and their relation to college student adjustment.

The SACQ can be administered and scored either via standard paper-and-pencil procedures or by microcomputer. Mail-in computer scoring also is available. Individual administration and group administration are equally appropriate. The SACQ generally requires no more than 20 minutes to complete. For scoring, responses are assigned points ranging from 1 to 9, with lower points indicating less adaption to college. The sum of the scores for each subscale and the full scale reflects an index of adjustment. Raw scores are converted to T-scores based on a normative sample stratified by sex and semester. The higher the score on the full scale and each subscale, the better the self-described adjustment to college.

Hand scoring is thoroughly explained in the manual and relatively easy to master. The profile form contained in the test packet is appropriate for a college student of either sex and any age. The profile form cross-tabulates raw scores, T-scores, and percentiles to present a pattern of responses for the full scale and subscales. The item clusters for each subscale must be scored separately using information provided in the manual. Computer-scored reports provide a student's score on each item cluster as well as for the full scale and the various subscales. A profile form is also provided for computer-scored reports. Clinical interpretation of the SACQ is straightforward, relying primarily on the normative data, subscales, and item clusters. In the manual, the authors emphasize that one should never interpret questionnaire items in isolation.

Technical Aspects

Because significant differences were found on some SACQ variables, the normative sample is stratified by sex and semester. Although, as noted, norms are based on Clark University students, data collected from other universities are generally consistent, lending support for the use of the SACQ with other university populations.

Reliability has been established by using internal consistency coefficients. The authors have not established test-retest reliability because they expect that a student's score on the SACQ would be impacted by changes in environment, life situation, and personality characteristics. The manual presents internal consistency coefficients established by the author and other researchers. These coefficients range from .89 to .95 for the full scale, .78 to .90 for the Academic Adjustment subscale, .73 to .91 for the Social Adjustment subscale, .73 to .89 for the Personal-Emotional Adjustment subscale, and .81 to .91 for the Attachment subscale. Internal consistency coefficients for the item clusters contained within a subscale are lower, ranging from .56 to .91. Clearly users should interpret item clusters with caution.

Validity was established first by examining the pattern of intercorrelations between the subscales, using data from a variety of universities. With the exception of the Attachment subscale, the median correlations between subscales are moderate, ranging from .39 to .60. The Attachment subscale contains items from the other subscales, and thus these correlations are more substantial. Results of a principal-components analysis using empirical data from several studies are supportive of a general factor of adjustment to college. However, the authors report that in all cases of the maximum likelihood statistical test, a single factor was rejected, supporting the inclusion of subscales in the SACQ.

Criterion-related validity evidence is presented in the manual for each of the four subscales. SACQ subscales correlated in the expected direction with freshman-year GPA, appeals for psychological services, and attrition. In addition, the manual presents numerous studies that report correlations between the SACQ and other tests measuring similar variables. The other tests fall into two primary categories:

those that measure mental health variables and those that measure environment-related experience. Correlations with a number of these tests are supportive of the SACQ.

Critique

The SACQ seems to be a reliable and valid instrument for measuring adjustment to college. Though apparently used most often in research studies, it potentially offers an efficient assessment tool for identifying students having difficulty adjusting to college. The manual for the SACQ is very useful, providing users with clear and concise descriptions of the purpose, administration, and scoring procedures. The authors present a thorough review of the questionnaire's measurement properties, and they describe numerous research studies in which their instrument has been used. The actual administration and scoring of the SACQ is straightforward.

In the manual, Baker and Siryk (1989) discuss three important limitations to the SACQ. First, its purpose is transparent, and thus students can answer questions in a way consistent with whatever image they wish to project. The instrument does not include a means of identifying students who have not been truthful in their responses. Second, the norms for the SACQ are based on students from one university. Though data from other universities are supportive of the norms, establishing local norms would help professionals interpret the questionnaire. Finally, individual items should not be interpreted out of context. Using only the Full Scale score masks meaningful differences in patterns of subscale scores.

It would be helpful to users if the manual provided demographic data for the normative sample beyond sex and age, particularly ethnicity. It is not clear whether the SACQ is appropriate for use with ethnic minorities, although two recent research studies have used it with minority populations. Results of a study by Kaczmarek, Matlock, and Franco (1990) support using the questionnaire with a Hispanic population. The SACQ has also been used successfully with black students. Graham, Barker, and Wapner (1985) examined the impact of prior interracial experience on college adjustment.

Further information on the development and structure of the SACQ is necessary. It is unclear how subscale items were generated and how factor analyses performed on the SACQ supported a four-factor solution. Though maximum likelihood statistical tests seemed unsupportive of a single-factor solution, it is questionable whether a four-factor solution is appropriate. A confirmatory factor analysis of the SACQ would provide useful information regarding the instrument's factor structure.

The SACQ potentially offers an important evaluation tool for student affairs professionals, though a review of the literature reveals only one study in which it has been used for this purpose (Schwitzer, McGovern, & Robbins, 1991). As in that study, student affairs professionals could administer the questionnaire before and after an intervention to assess its impact. Professionals in the field also could utilize the SACQ as a needs assessment tool when planning programming and other interventions. Furthermore, students having a particularly difficult time adjusting could be identified and worked with individually.

Despite some questions regarding factor structure, the SACQ's measurement properties seem sound. And while it seems to be the measure of college student adjustment employed most frequently by researchers, counselors and student affairs professionals also would find this questionnaire useful.

References

Baker, R.W., & Siryk, B. (1984). Measuring adjustment to college. *Journal of Counseling Psychology, 31,* 179–189.

Baker, R.W., & Siryk, B. (1989). *Student Adaptation to College Questionnaire manual.* Los Angeles: Western Psychological Services.

Graham, C., Baker, R.W., & Wapner, S. (1985). Prior interracial experience and black student transition into a predominantly white college. *Journal of Personality and Social Psychology, 47,* 1146–1154.

Haemmerlie, F.M., Robinson, D.A., & Carmen, R.C. (1991). "Type A" personality traits and adjustment to college. *Journal of College Student Development, 32,* 81–82.

Kaczmarek, P.G., Matlock, C.G., & Franco, J.N. (1990). Assessment of college adjustment in three freshman groups. *Psychological Reports, 66,* 1195–1202.

Lapsley, D.K., Rice, K.G., & Shadid, G.E. (1989). Psychological separation and adjustment to college. *Journal of Counseling Psychology, 36,* 286–294.

Lopez, F.G. (1991). Patterns of family conflict and their relation to college student adjustment. *Journal of Counseling and Development, 69,* 257–260.

Mooney, S.P., Sherman, M.F., & Lo Presto, C.T. (1991). Academic locus of control, self-esteem, and perceived distance from home as predictors of college adjustment. *Journal of Counseling and Development, 69,* 445–448.

Rice, K.G. (1992). Separation-individuation and adjustment to college: A longitudinal study. *Journal of Counseling Psychology, 39,* 203–213.

Rice, K.G., Cole, D.A., & Lapsley, D.K. (1990). Separation-individuation, family cohesion, and adjustment to college: Measurement validation and test of a theoretical model. *Journal of Counseling Psychology, 37,* 195–202.

Schwitzer, A.M., McGovern, T.V., & Robbins, S.B. (1991). Adjustment outcomes of a freshman seminar: A utilization-focused approach. *Journal of College Student Development, 32,* 484–489.

James A. Moses, Jr., Ph.D.

*Clinical Associate Professor of Psychiatry and Behavioral Sciences,
Stanford University School of Medicine, and Coordinator,
Psychological Assessment Unit, Department of Veterans Affairs
Medical Center, Palo Alto, California.*

TACTILE FORM RECOGNITION TEST

*Arthur L. Benton, Kerry deS. Hamsher, Nils R. Varney, and
Otfried Spreen. New York, New York: Oxford University
Press.*

Introduction

The Tactile Form Recognition Test (TFRT) provides a detailed, standardized,
quantified measure of nonverbal, "higher order" tactile-kinesthetic or stereognostic sensory information-processing ability with plane stimulus figures. Difficulty with this complex, integrative task can occur independently of disturbance
of basic sensory modalities such as light touch, pain, or temperature sensation,
which are mediated by specific, "hard-wired" anatomical peripheral receptors
and neural pathways. Failure on stereognostic tactile identification tasks also can
occur due to interruption or dysfunction of the relevant sensory pathways anywhere in their course from the peripheral neuronal receptors to the cerebral
cortex, and complex variants of clinical syndromes may occur. TFRT results are
particularly useful for objective and quantitative analysis of specific variants of
these patterns of sensory disturbance.

Benton, Hamsher, Varney, and Spreen (1983) note that neurological and neuropsychological clinicians have not reached a generally accepted consensus on the
nature of stereognostic deficit, even after more than a century of observation,
study, and theoretical analysis since the astereognostic syndrome was first isolated and clinically described by Hoffmann (1885; cited by Benton et al., 1983, p.
70). In part this lack of diagnostic consensus has stemmed from use of nonstandardized examination procedures and test materials that have varied across studies
as well as relative lack of experimental control in case report syndrome analyses.

The findings based on these results are specific to the sensory modality and
sensory analytic complexity level tested, and they should not be generalized
beyond the bounds of the test procedures to other types of complex sensory
ability or deficit. The TFRT was designed to analyze discrete components of the
functional system that underlie tactile form recognition as well as to identify the
presence or absence and deficit level of this type of complex sensory deficit.
Different objective deficit patterns also have been described based on TFRT performance in patients with unilateral versus bilateral cerebral lesions. These patterns, some of which involve a generalized, cross-modal spatial deficit, will be
overviewed in the next section of this critique. For a detailed, integrated analysis

694

of historical trends concerning syndrome-analytic issues with an element of neurologically based spatial deficit, see Benton (1982).

The TFRT test materials consist of two parallel sets of 10 cards, each of which presents a geometric figure made of fine-grade sandpaper. Using the right or left hand, the subject must feel the figure (concealed from view by a box) and identify it while looking at a multiple-choice card that contains 12 line drawings of the figures, slightly reduced in size. The format allows the subject 30 seconds to explore each figure, and then he or she must respond within 45 seconds (Benton et al., 1983, p. 71). A practice card used at the beginning of the test, before the test items are begun, serves to familiarize the subject with the task and the manner of response. The two parallel sets of stimulus cards are comparably difficult and may be used interchangeably to test either of the subject's hands.

The principal author of the TFRT, Arthur L. Benton, Ph.D., received his A.B. (1931) and A.M. (1933) degrees from Oberlin College, followed by his Ph.D. from Columbia University (1935). He began his career as an assistant in psychology, first at Oberlin College (1931–33), then at Columbia University and New York State Psychiatric Institute (1934–36), and finally at Cornell University Medical College (1936–39), where he subsequently served as a staff psychologist. He was appointed as an attending psychologist at New York Hospital–Westchester Division and as a psychologist in the Student Personnel Office of the City College of New York from 1939 to 1941. After active duty in the U.S. Navy both during and after the Second World War (1941–46), he accepted an appointment as Associate Professor of Psychology at the University of Louisville Medical School and as chief psychologist at the Louisville Mental Hygiene Clinic and the Louisville General Hospital (1946–48). From 1948 to 1958 he served as Professor of Psychology and Director of the Graduate Training Program in Clinical Psychology at the University of Iowa, followed by two decades (1958–78) as Professor of Psychology and Neurology. Dr. Benton has continued to coauthor theoretical and research papers and books since 1978, when he became Professor Emeritus at the University of Iowa.

Benton's fundamental contributions to the field of clinical neuropsychology have been acknowledged extensively and internationally. He has received honorary Doctor of Science (Cornell College, 1978) and Doctor of Psychology (University of Rome, 1990) degrees, along with numerous other honors and awards, including the Distinguished Service Award of the Iowa Psychological Association (1977), the Distinguished Professional Contribution Award from the American Psychological Association (1978), the Outstanding Scientific Contribution Award of the International Neuropsychological Society (1981), The Samuel Torrey Orton Award from the Orton Dyslexia Society (1982), the Distinguished Service and Outstanding Contributions Award from the American Board of Professional Psychology (1985), and the Distinguished Clinical Neuropsychologist Award from the National Academy of Neuropsychology (1989).

Benton is a past president of both the American Orthopsychiatric Association (1965–66) and the International Neuropsychological Society (1970–71), and he served as secretary-general of the Research Group on Aphasia for the World Federation of Neurology (1971–78). He has been a lecturer or visiting scholar at the University of Milan (1964), Hôpital Sainte-Anne, Paris (1968), Hadassah-Hebrew

University Medical School, Jerusalem (1969), Free University of Amsterdam (1971), University of Helsinki (1974), University of Melbourne (1977), University of Minnesota Medical School (Baker Lecturer, 1979), University of Victoria, British Columbia (Lansdowne Scholar, 1980), and the University of Michigan (1986), plus as the Directeur d'Études Associé, École des Hautes Études, Paris (1979) and as a visiting scientist at the Tokyo Metropolitan Institute of Gerontology (1974).

Benton has authored, coauthored, or edited 12 books and monographs, approximately 150 professional journal articles, and 22 historical reviews in the area of clinical neuropsychology and behavioral neurology. He is recognized as a pioneer and a leading authority in the area of clinical neuropsychology.

The standardized, commercially published version of the TFRT appeared with the clinical manual for this and other tests in the Benton-Iowa Neuropsychological Test Battery (Benton et al., 1983). Coauthors of this clinical manual with Dr. Benton are Kerry deS. Hamsher, Ph.D. (Associate Professor of Neurology, University of Wisconsin Medical School); Nils R. Varney, Ph.D. (staff neuropsychologist, Department of Veterans Affairs Medical Center, Iowa City, Iowa); and Otfried Spreen, Ph.D. (Professor Emeritus, Department of Psychology, University of Victoria, Victoria, British Columbia, Canada).

Practical Applications/Uses

During administration of the TFRT, the examiner and the subject face each other across the corner of a table so that the examiner can easily see the response card when the patient points to a response alternative. Between them is an open-ended box with a top that slants downward toward the subject. The box is open on the ends toward the subject and the examiner. A drape covers the opening on the subject's side of the box to prevent him or her from seeing the test stimuli inside the box. The subject places one hand under the drape to feel the stimulus figures one at a time. The open end on the examiner's side of the box allows for placement and removal of the stimulus cards as the test trials progress. The test manual illustrates both the apparatus and the recommended seating arrangement (Benton et al., 1983, p. 72, Fig. 8-1). The 10 sandpaper-figure stimulus cards are placed in the box in the order of administration, with the first card positioned on top of the stack before the test begins. The administrative instructions to the examiner and the verbatim instructions to the subject follows:

> "Now I want to see how good you are at finding out what I put in this box by feeling it with your fingers. I will put some sandpaper figures on cards in the box. The figures look like the ones on this card here."
> Examiner places the multiple-choice card on the slanted top of the box. Then he places the practice card in the box and says:
> "Feel around and touch all parts of this card so that you won't miss anything."
> As the subject explores the card, say:
> "Now, can you show me which figure it was? Point to the figure on this card which is the same as the one in the box." (Benton et al., 1983, p. 72)

A subject with grossly adequate motor function should be asked to point to the response alternative with his or her free hand (the one not feeling the stimulus figure). If the subject is more seriously motorically impaired with the free hand, then he or she should remove the functional hand from the box and use it to point to the response alternative after feeling the figure. If the subject makes an error on the sample item, the examiner should repeat the practice procedure and then point to the correct option on the multiple-choice response card. The sample stimulus figure is removed and placed face down on the table by the examiner, followed by these instructions:

> Place your hand in the box and feel the next figure there. Make sure that you have touched all the parts before you make your choice. After you have felt the whole card I want you to point to the figure on this board which is the same shape as the figure you just felt. If you don't know for sure, make a guess. (Benton et al., 1983, p. 73)

Response latency is timed in seconds. The examiner should use a stopwatch to optimize timing accuracy, although a sweep second hand on a wristwatch will suffice in the absence of a stopwatch. During administration the stimulus card is removed as soon as the subject has responded by pointing to a response alternative on the response card. The examiner removes the completed stimulus card from the box and places it face down on the table next to the side of the box. The next stimulus card thus is automatically in place in the box (next in the pile) for the patient's response. As noted previously, the subject is allowed up to 30 seconds to feel the stimulus card. If he or she has not responded by that time, the examiner prompts for a response. If the subject does not respond within another 15 seconds, the examiner prompts him or her to guess. Failure to respond at the second prompt is scored as an item failure; the stimulus card is removed, and the next item is presented. Each succeeding card is introduced with "Here is another figure for you to feel. Once again, feel the whole card" (Benton et al., 1983, p. 73).

Once the set of 10 trials for one hand has been completed, the examiner places the second set of stimulus cards in the box and the corresponding multiple-choice response array on top of the box. Tactile sensory or motor deficit may preclude testing stereognostic function in one hand. Benton and his colleagues advise that moderate sensory deficit may still be compatible with valid TFRT administration. In such cases the nature of the primary sensory deficit should be established by medical or neuropsychological testing, so that peripheral sensory impairment will not be confused with higher order stereognostic or supramodal spatial deficit when the TFRT performance is defective. Moderate motor deficit, however, commonly prevents adequate ability to palpate the stimulus figures and hence may invalidate TFRT administration. Testing is done with only the unaffected hand in such cases. The detailed TFRT scoring and classification system allows for objective, quantified analysis of unimanual and bimanual administration procedures and performance deficit subpatterns within them.

The TFRT originally was designed to measure sensory integration and interpretation independent of naming and bimanual tactile comparison requirements. TFRT administration explicitly requires that the subject only point on the geometric response array to the shape of the stimulus object felt. Anomia should not compromise the accuracy of the response, as the format requires no explicit verbalization to choose or indicate an answer. (The empirical TFRT performance of aphasic patients relative to other diagnostic reference groups will be discussed later in this review.) The TFRT also was designed to assess stereognostic sensory ability in each hand independently. Unimanual TFRT deficit (when both hands are tested) does suggest stereognostic integrative sensory deficit of the contralateral hemisphere. Bilateral impairment on the TFRT, however, may stem from a generalized, supramodal spatial deficit that, if present, will adversely affect all sensory modalities having a spatial-processing component.

Scoring the TFRT responses is straightforward and actuarial. Each correct response receives 1 point of credit, and incorrect responses are entered on the record form with a letter-number code. For example, "A-1" identifies the correct response for Form A, item 1. If the subject incorrectly points to the A-1 shape as the response choice for another Form A item, the examiner would record the incorrect response with the A-1 code on the answer sheet. The shapes of the stimulus figures and their corresponding codes are presented for easy reference on the answer sheet for both forms of the TFRT. A facsimile of the answer sheet appears in the test manual (Benton et al., 1983, p. 74, Table 8-1). Benton and his colleagues encourage examiners to record item response latency, although an optional step and not a formal part of the TFRT scoring system. The number of correct responses are summed for each hand separately and for both hands jointly to provide three TFRT summary accuracy scores.

Forms A and B of TFRT were compared in an elegant, counterbalanced experimental design that took into account the effect of test administration order. Four groups of 14 subjects (each with 4 men and 10 women) were composed and administered the two TFRT forms in all possible combinations: right hand with Form A (RH-FA) followed by left hand with Form B (LH-FB); RH-FB followed by LH-FA; LH-FA followed by RH-FB; and LH-FB followed by RH-FA. The mean scores for the overall sample of 56 subjects were 9.12 for Form A and 8.95 for Form B, which are equivalent within the limits of small psychometric measurement error. Neither handedness (mean RH = 9.00; mean LH = 9.07) nor administration order (mean first trial score = 8.98; mean second trial score = 9.08) exerted any remarkable influence on TFRT performance level or pattern (Benton et al., 1983, pp. 73–74).

Normative standards have been developed for the TFRT in groups of neurologically normal children, adolescents, and adults aged 8–80 years. The manual presents tabular summaries of child (ages 8–14), adolescent and adult (ages 15–70), and geriatric (ages 71–80) subject samples (Benton et al., 1983, pp. 74–80, Tables 8-2 through 8-4, and Tables 8-6 through 8-8). Norms for children are categorized by year of age and by sex for TFRT accuracy scores with the preferred and nonpreferred hands. Childhood TFRT norms present descriptive statistical mean and standard deviation (variability) data at each age level. Normative sample sizes range from 16 to 45 subjects at various ages. Norms for adolescents and adults are presented for the age cohorts 15–50 years (27 men, 15 women), 51–60 years (8 men, 8 women), and 61–70 years (6 men, 26 women). Mean and range data are presented for TFRT accuracy scores for samples of men and women with each hand separately and both hands jointly. Standard deviation statistics do not appear for these samples. In the geriatric sample (8 men, 17 women), the manual reports mean data in frequency distribution format without descriptive statistics.

Descriptive statistical details of the TFRT performance patterns for the sample of children appear in the test manual (Benton et al., 1983, p. 78) and in the original article that reported these results (Spreen & Gaddes, 1969). In a summary of developmental trends, Benton and his colleagues noted no consistent sex, handedness, or test form differences that had significant effects on TFRT performance patterns. Performance accuracy increased with age, as expected, although some sampling variability was noted and this trend was not consistently monotonic. Children below age 12 show considerable individual differences, which makes normative cutoff interpretation of scores inadvisable. For children in the 12–14 age range, the scores are considerably more homogeneous, and the test authors recommend use of the adult interpretive cutoffs (total score of 7 = borderline, total score of 6 or less = defective) to interpret their performance (Benton et al., 1983, p. 78).

Based on analysis of the lower limit of normal performance in adolescent and adult samples, a TFRT total correct score of 7 is rated as borderline impaired, and a score of 6 or less for either hand is categorized as a defective performance. This score ranks at approximately the second percentile of the normal distribution for this age range (15–70 years). A combined accuracy TFRT score for both hands of 15 was rated as borderline impaired, while a total accuracy score of 14 or less for both hands was rated as clearly defective in the 15–70 year age cohort.

Analysis of the performance patterns of elderly subjects showed somewhat greater incidence of errors among them, although these conclusions are tentative due to small sample size (25 cases total). Eight percent (2/25) of the elderly subjects scored as low as 6 correct responses on one hand for TFRT, another 8% of the elderly subjects earned correct unimanual TFRT scores of 7, and 12% of the elderly sample (3/25) earned total TFRT accuracy scores of 14–15. Only one geriatric subject (4%) showed a difference of 3 points between the accuracy scores for the two hands. Greater individual variability among subjects in the geriatric age range typically would be expected.

Based on these normative studies, Benton and his colleagues have explicated a series of "performance patterns" or syndrome groupings with intuitive interpretive labels to aid diagnostic classification based on TFRT performance accuracy. Categories are provided for unimanual and bimanual syndromes, covering the range of normal variation as well as clinical groupings. The subtypes are described as follows (Benton et al., 1983, p. 77):

A. *Normal:* total score = 16–20; difference between single-hand scores = 0–2 points.

B. *Borderline:* total score = 15; difference between single-hand scores = 0–2 points.

C. *Bilateral symmetric defect:* total score = 0–14; difference between single-hand scores = 0–2 points; single-hand scores = 0–7.

D. *Bilateral asymmetric (right hand) defect:* total score = 3–11; single-hand scores = 0–7; right-hand score 3 points lower than left-hand score.

E. *Bilateral asymmetric (left hand) defect:* total score = 3–11; single-hand score = 0–7; left-hand score 3 points lower than right-hand score.

F. *Right unilateral defect:* total score = 8–17; right-hand score 3 or more points lower than left-hand score of 8–10.

G. *Left unilateral defect:* total score 8–17; left-hand score 3 or more points lower than right-hand score of 8–10.

AR. *Normal right hand:* right-hand score = 8–10; left hand not tested.
AL. *Normal left hand:* left-hand score = 8–10; right hand not tested.
BR. *Borderline right:* Right-hand score = 7; left hand not tested.
BL. *Borderline left:* left-hand score = 7; right hand not tested.
(F). *Right-hand defect:* right-hand score = 0–6; left hand not tested.
(G). *Left-hand defect:* left-hand score = 0–6; right hand not tested.

Technical Aspects

The primary validational study of TFRT was carried out by the test authors in a sample of 104 patients (56 men, 48 women) cross-classified by hemispheric lesion locus, presence or absence of aphasia, and presence or absence of sensorimotor deficit. Ages ranged from 18 to 69 years; the test manual does not report descriptive statistics for age. Statistics to describe the educational level of the subjects, an important copredictor of cognitive performance level, do not appear in the demographic description of the sample. Ninety-six percent (100/104) of these patients were right handed. All aphasic patients had confirmed lesions of the left cerebral hemisphere. Fifty-one patients had unilateral right-hemispheric lesions; 55% of them (28/51) also had associated sensorimotor deficit. Forty-one patients had unilateral left-hemispheric lesions; of these, 6 had neither aphasic nor sensorimotor deficit, 23 had sensorimotor deficit without aphasia, 7 had aphasia without sensorimotor deficit, and 5 had both aphasia and sensorimotor deficit. Twelve patients had bilateral cerebral hemispheric disease; none of them were aphasic. These subjects were analyzed as a group without respect to sensorimotor deficit because this sample was too small to allow for generalizable syndrome subtype analysis.

This neurologic sample was diagnostically heterogeneous. Of the 92 patients with unilateral lesions, 2 had degenerative "atrophic" brain disorders; the remainder presented with cerebrovascular disease or brain tumor. In the bilaterally lesioned group were eight cases of degenerative brain disease, two cases of cerebrovascular disorder, one case of brain tumor, and one traumatically brain-injured patient. Seventy-two percent (75/104) of the subjects performed the TFRT with both hands in succession. The other 29 patients were tested on one hand only due to sensorimotor deficit.

Benton et al. (1983, pp. 80–81) note that 56% of the patients who had both of their hands tested and 55% of the sample who had only one hand tested performed defectively on TFRT relative to normative standards. A higher incidence of defective performance occurred among patients with sensorimotor deficit (57%) than among those who were free of such deficit (44%), although failure rates on TFRT were considerable in both groups. Bilateral TFRT deficit was frequent (38%) in patients who had both hands tested. In the sample of subjects who had only one hand tested, more than half (54%) showed TFRT deficit for the hand *ipsilateral* to the brain lesion. Nearly twice as great an incidence of TFRT deficit emerged among nonaphasic patients with right-hemispheric lesions (53%) as among nonaphasic patients with left-hemispheric lesions (28%). The frequency of TFRT deficit in patients with bilateral hemispheric lesions and in those with brain lesions ipsilateral to the body side affected by the sensorimotor deficit was approximately 50%. This incidence resembles that found in nonaphasic patients with lesions of the right hemisphere only (53%). Patients with lesions of both cerebral hemispheres showed the highest incidence of TFRT deficit (83%) among the diagnostic subgroups studied in the validational sample.

Benton and his colleagues emphasize that TFRT deficit patterns that involve isolated stereognostic sensory deficit contralateral to the side of the brain lesion should be distinguished from syndromes that involve bilateral stereognostic deficit and those in which the brain lesion is ipsilateral to the side of the stereognostic deficit. They conclude that

> it is reasonable to interpret contralateral impairment as a higher-level somesthetic defect related to injury of critical areas of the affected cerebral hemisphere and as being comparable in nature to other tactile-spatial defects such as loss of position sense and impaired recognition of the direction of lines drawn on the skin surface. (Benton et al., 1983, p. 81)

Bilateral TFRT impairment or unilateral TFRT in which the stereognostic deficit is ipsilateral to the brain lesion (so that the two deficits cannot be directly related on a sensory deficit basis) require a different explanation. Benton and his colleagues propose that these deficit patterns typically are associated with a cross-modal, generalized, higher order deficit in *spatial* reasoning. They cite considerable descriptive clinical historical information (Benton, 1982) as well as supportive, cross-validated empirical data (Corkin, 1965; De Renzi & Scotti, 1969; Dee & Benton, 1970; Milner, 1965; Semmes, 1965, 1968) in support of their interpretation. They note that all of these investigators have found "significant associations between tactile-spatial and visuospatial performances in brain-injured patients" (Benton et al., 1983, p. 82). The increased frequency of TFRT deficit among patients with unilateral right-hemispheric lesions and the very high incidence of TFRT deficit in patients with bilateral lesions is consistent with the theory that the right cerebral hemisphere is significantly involved in the processing of sensory information with a spatial component.

Critique

The Tactile Form Recognition Test is a standardized, quantified, well-operationalized measure of stereognostic recognition ability that also is relatively brief and easily administered. It provides clear, syndrome-analytic information that is categorized objectively by the formal scoring system according to standard clinical diagnostic criteria. Results of TFRT examination therefore are directly relevant to objective diagnosis and treatment planning. The test is suitable for a standardized examination of patients with sensorimotor deficit affecting one hand, and it can be administered validly to and interpreted for patients with moderate peripheral tactile sensory deficit. Elimination of naming as a response component also makes the TFRT appropriate for examining specific stereognostic deficit and related spatial organization in aphasic patients. TFRT pattern analysis allows for separation of higher order, stereognostic sensory deficit from supramodal spatial orientation deficit by means of objective syndrome analysis. TFRT is normed for a very wide age range of subjects, from childhood to old age, and offers a very wide range of demographic and diagnostic applicability. Economical in both administration time and effort, the TFRT is easily scored and provides a rich source of information to the busy clinician.

Reliability studies are needed to establish the test's measurement accuracy. Examining test-retest reliability with an intertest interval of approximately 2 weeks would establish the temporal stability of the TFRT findings in normal subjects. Test-retest reliability studies of patients with chronic, stable neurologic deficit also would be useful to extend the temporal psychometric stability finding to clinical groups. In this way one could assert more justifiably that TFRT retest change scores relative to baseline performance levels resulted from actual changes in the subject's stereognostic ability and not from random measurement error inherent in the test itself.

The TFRT's internal consistency also should be established. This correlational criterion requires that the items of a test coalesce to measure a single common dimension or construct. Demonstration of internal consistency for the TFRT would provide a psychometric basis for adding the accuracy (or error) scores of the items together to form summary scales or index scores. The best statistical criterion for demonstrating this property is coefficient alpha, which provides the mean of all possible split-half comparisons of the test as a whole (Nunnally, 1978). Although the number of trials for each hand is relatively small for a study of internal consistency, a liberalized criterion value for Cronbach's alpha, perhaps in the region of .70, could be used when this statistic is computed for TFRT performance with each hand. The liberalized value of .70 is recommended in place of the optimal .80 value, which minimizes error variance because a test's reliability is directly proportional to its length. Longer tests that are internally consistent provide a more stable and thorough examination of item content than do briefer measures, and hence are more reliable on the average. A value of .70 for coefficient alpha in a test with only 10 responses per form (hand tested) is suitable for a measure of this length.

This reviewer would encourage expanding the exploratory studies of TFRT patterns of deficit in the normal elderly population that Benton et al. completed as part of the test validation process. Samples of 100 or more subjects equally divided by sex would be desirable as a normative database. Use of TFRT clinically to study patterns of complex sensory stereognostic deficit and sparing in *specific* neurologic disorders is needed to extend and apply the syndrome-analytic studies of Benton and his colleagues reported in the manual. We know that the TFRT is sensitive to stereognostic deficit, but indications for use of the test in the analysis of specific syndromes and the variants of deficit within those syndromes remain to be clarified. To date this potentially rich source of clinical analysis has not been explored systematically in the literature.

References

Benton, A.L. (1982). Spatial thinking in neurological patients: Historical aspects. In M. Potegal (Ed.), *Spatial abilities: Development and physiological foundations.* New York: Academic Press.

Benton, A.L., Hamsher, K.deS., Varney, N.R., & Spreen, O. (1983). *Contributions to neuropsychological assessment.* New York: Oxford University Press.

Corkin, S. (1965). Tactually-guided maze learning in man: Effects of unilateral cortical excisions and bilateral hippocampal lesions. *Neuropsychologia, 3,* 339–351.

De Renzi, E., & Scotti, C. (1969). The influence of spatial disorders in impairing tactual discrimination of shapes. *Cortex, 5,* 53–62.

Dee, H.L., & Benton, A.L. (1970). A cross-modal investigation of spatial performances in patients with unilateral cerebral disease. *Cortex, 6,* 261–272.

Hoffmann, H. (1885). Stereognostiche Versuche, angestellt zur Ermittelung der Elemente des Gefühlssinnes, aus denen die Vorstellungen der Körper im Raume gebildet werden. *Deutsches Archiv fuer Klinischen Medizin, 36,* 398–426.

Milner, B. (1965). Visually-guided maze learning in man: Effects of bilateral hippocampal, bilateral frontal and unilateral cerebral lesions. *Neuropsychologia, 3,* 317–338.

Nunnally, J.C. (1978). *Psychometric theory.* New York: McGraw-Hill.

Semmes, J. (1965). A non-tactual factor in stereognosis. *Neuropsychologia, 3,* 295–315.

Semmes, J. (1968). Hemispheric specialization: A possible clue to mechanism. *Neuropsychologia, 6,* 11–26.

Spreen, O., & Gaddes, W.H. (1969). Developmental norms for 15 neuropsychological tests age 6 to 15. *Cortex, 5,* 171–191.

Karyn Bobkoff Katz, Ph.D.
*Associate Professor, School of Communicative Disorders, The
University of Akron, Akron, Ohio.*

Carol W. Lawrence, Ph.D.
*Associate Professor, School of Communicative Disorders, The
University of Akron, Akron, Ohio.*

TEST FOR EXAMINING EXPRESSIVE MORPHOLOGY

*Kenneth G. Shipley, Terry A. Stone, and Marlene B. Sue.
Tucson, Arizona: Communication Skill Builders, Inc.*

Introduction

The Test for Examining Expressive Morphology (TEEM; Shipley, Stone, & Sue, 1983) is a formal, norm-referenced clinical procedure for the assessment of expressive morphological development in young children. Using a sentence-completion task, the test evaluates children's acquisition of various grammatical morphemes.

The first author of the test, Dr. Kenneth G. Shipley, is an associate professor of communicative disorders at California State University–Fresno. His clinical background as a speech/language pathologist includes public school and educational and medical consultation. Terry A. Stone is a speech/language pathologist working in a public school setting in Nevada. Ms. Stone also has worked as a therapist and consultant in school systems. The third author, Marlene B. Sue, is a speech/language pathologist in a California school district. All of the authors hold the Certificate of Clinical Competence awarded by the American Speech-Language-Hearing Association.

In the TEEM manual, the authors present a discussion of the theoretical foundations on which they based the test. Their explanations include the concepts of language and communication, as well an acknowledgment of the interdependent nature of the areas of language. In viewing the communicative development of children, the authors emphasize their basic goal "to obtain a 'complete picture' of [children's] language abilities. . . . The TEEM is intended to help us view one important area: children's morphologic development" (Shipley et al., 1983, p. 1).

Several considerations formed the foundation on which the TEEM was constructed. A number of these reflect research findings in language development, particularly in the acquisition of morphology. Other considerations involve the authors' specific decisions regarding testing methodology. For example, the TEEM utilizes meaningful stimuli (familiar words in sentences) in contrast to the nonsense-word paradigm occasionally used to assess morphology. The rationale for their test construction decisions was supported by relevant research. Based on clearly stated assumptions, "the TEEM was developed to (a) sample a variety of morphemes and allomorphic variations, (b) use an expressive sentence-completion model, (c) detect differences between age levels, (d) employ a lexical-stimuli test paradigm, and (e) sample various morphologic abilities expeditiously" (Shipley et al., 1983, p. 7).

During the development of the TEEM, prestandardization testing was conducted. Initially stimulus words were chosen for the content of the test items. A pool of words was selected based on specific criteria, then these items were tested to assess their familiarity for "15 normal, three-year-old children in a preschool setting" (Shipley et al., 1983, p. 8). The most familiar words then were used as final test items. The manual reports that the prestandardization was conducted by Stone (1980). Forty children ranging in age from 3 to 7 years were studied. The results of this phase of test development were then used for final standardization. The manual also discusses Sue's (1981) standardization study, conducted on 500 children judged to have normal speech, language, and hearing skills. One hundred children in five age groups (3- through 7-year-olds) were used. The data presented for norm-referenced comparisons were based on the results of this study.

The TEEM is designed for young children aged 3 to 8. Normative data presented for this age range appear in the manual and also on the scoring form. The TEEM consists of three components: the manual, the stimulus pictures or test booklet, and the test protocol. The manual provides theoretical and practical information about the test's construction and administration, as well as descriptions of all procedures, including administration, scoring, and interpretation. The stimulus pictures are black-and-white line drawings arranged in a spiral-bound book. The child looks at a test plate while the examiner reads aloud the stimulus presentation on the opposite page. Five demonstration examples and 54 test items are provided.

The scoring protocol is a comprehensive four-page form. The examiner can record basic descriptive information about the child on the first page, as well as other testing information and comments. The second page of the scoring form is for recording the child's responses to each example and test item. The targeted items are clearly presented, along with the allomorphic variation of each. The age at which 75% and 90% of children responded correctly to each item also appears. The third page of the protocol allows for an analysis of the test results by summarizing the data according to specific morphemes and error clusters. Finally, tables for age level approximations and means and standard deviations are presented on page 4.

The assessment technique utilized by the TEEM is a sentence-completion or cloze procedure. The examiner guides the entire administration by showing the child a picture plate and reading a stimulus sentence specified on the test protocol. Instructions to the examiner suggest pointing to each picture and indicating to the child through a hand gesture or an ending inflection that he or she is to complete the sentence. The examiner continues this administration procedure throughout the test. One of the demonstration items, for example, includes a picture of one boat next to two boats. The presentation of the plate is accompanied by the examiner pointing to each picture and saying, "Here is a boat. Here are two _____."

Practical Applications/Uses

The TEEM is formal sentence-completion test designed to assess the expressive morphological development of young children. Selected grammatical morphemes are assessed in various allomorphic contexts. Although developed to focus on the acquisition of bound morphemes, the test does include several items evaluating irregular forms of plurals and present tense verbs. The 54 TEEM items are distributed as follows: 4 test present progressive forms, 14 test plurals, 7 test possessives, 7 test third-person singular forms, 12 test past tense, and 10 test derived adjectives. Each item is evaluated as it occurs in varying allomorphic contexts, allowing the examiner to study the acquisition of each tested morpheme in many possible forms. An example of the range of items used for each morpheme includes the 14 plural items divided into /z/, /s/, /ʊz/, /əz/, and irregular forms. Only one specific word (unbound plus bound morpheme) is targeted for each item; all other words within the stimulus sentence are presented to the child (e.g., "This boy likes to read. Here he is _____ [reading]."). Therefore, information regarding the development of other grammatical morphemes, such as copula and auxiliary forms (see Brown, 1973), is not available through the use of the TEEM.

The subjects for whom the TEEM was designed are described in the test manual. These include children developing language normally (ages 3 to 8), children displaying delayed or disordered language development, children with hearing loss, and children learning English as a second language. The authors provide several valuable considerations to users regarding appropriate subjects for this test. They specifically caution that the TEEM "was developed using standard English rules of morphology. If the test is used with nonstandard English speakers, careful clinical judgment is necessary with respect to interpreting and reporting the results obtained" (Shipley et al., 1983, p. vii). No recommendations are made in the scoring or interpretation sections of the manual regarding specific modifications for speakers of other dialects. In addition, concern is raised regarding whether children with articulatory problems could take the test successfully.

The authors suggest that some children may need to be taught the particular test paradigm in order to complete the procedures successfully. Further, they offer a caution regarding the assumptions about a child's morphologic development that can be made from any specific item. The authors state that "it is better to look for patterns of correct and incorrect productions within morpheme or allomorph types, rather than to assume that a given stimulus word has been mastered or not mastered" (Shipley et al., 1983, p. vii).

The TEEM is an individually administered test during which the child and examiner sit opposite each other with the test book positioned between them. The picture plate should face the child while the stimulus item to be read faces the adult. The suggested environment is referred to as "distraction free" (Shipley et al., 1983, p. 14). The specific training required for the test administrator includes a familiarity with "children's language development, as well as psychometric, speech and language, or academic achievement procedures" (Shipley et al., 1983, p. 13). Experience with phonetic transcription also is suggested for noting the allomorphic differences in responses.

Basic administration instructions appear in the test manual. The examiner is provided with specific statements to say to the child as the test begins. Suggestions also are made for enhancing test administration, particularly for a child who is not responding to the practice items or whose initial attempts at them yield incorrect responses. Beyond these points, little elaboration is provided for any other testing situation that might occur (e.g., if the wrong word is used, but the bound morpheme is correct, as in *drawing* for *writing*). The examiner reads the items aloud, each of which is presented in clear, easy-to-read print. Test administration continues for all 54 items. The test manual gives an average time of test administration (calculated on 437 children, ages 3 to 8) of 6½ minutes.

On the whole, the instructions for recording responses and scoring each item are helpful, and the scoring form allows adequate space for transcribing each response. The authors recommend that the minimal recorded score include writing the regular allomorph tested by each item. Scoring is made easier by the inclusion of a phonetic notation of the allomorph required for each item. The scoring procedure appears efficient, with limited time needed to learn or to record the necessary response information. Rules for calculating the raw score are included along with specific allomorphic variations that might occur and influence the scoring procedure. After the response form has been completed, the authors suggest transferring the information to the next page of the scoring form, entitled "Analysis of Results." This analysis summarizes the responses according to patterns of performance for each morpheme tested, for the allomorphic variations of each, and for the error clusters displayed. Finally, the raw score is used for comparison with age-level approximations (based on 95% confidence-level intervals for mean scores). The authors caution the test user on the strong limitations of age-level estimates and the greater variability of scores for younger children. The last table used in scoring includes clearly presented means and standard deviations (–2 through +2) for the seven 6-month age ranges. The child's raw score is used on this table. A sample test protocol provided in the manual can serve as a helpful guide for implementing the scoring and analysis procedures and for interpreting the test results.

Two types of test interpretation are available after administration of the TEEM. The first is based on comparison of the child's raw score with the normative data presented (i.e., age equivalents, means and standard deviations). The authors remark, "Children whose scores are from one to two standard deviations from the mean merit consideration of special attention, although this should be considered in combination with other test findings" (Shipley et al., 1983, p. 16).

Perhaps more valuable for clinical purposes, the construction of the test also allows for interpreting the child's performance according to error patterns. The potential intervention program needed for morphological development can be directed by the analysis of specific morpheme errors as well as errors on allomorphic types. The ages at which 75% and 90% of children produced each item correctly also adds important information to planning therapy for young children. The authors do suggest caution by stating "it is probably inadvisable to draw definitive conclusions about these features solely on the basis of a single test administration. Rather, confirmation of these findings is suggested when developing a clinical/remedial program" (Shipley et al., 1983, p. 17).

Technical Aspects

The TEEM authors addressed three forms of validity: content, construct, and concurrent. Content validity, which describes the extent to which individual items and items as a whole measure the behavior they are intended to measure, was "presumed within the test construction" (Shipley et al., 1983, p. 8). In other words, in that the test was designed to assess bound morphemes and tested six major types of bound morphemes developed by normal language learners between 2 and 8, the test was deemed to show content validity.

Construct validity, which addresses the degree to which a test measures the theoretical construct it is intended to measure, also was deemed adequate by the authors. The authors based this conclusion on a significant Pearson r correlation (.87, $p < .05$) between the TEEM scores and ages of the 40 subjects in the prestandardization study. Although this measure does reveal that as children get older their performance on a test for bound morphemes is increased, this is but one perspective in the study of "expressive morpheme development" (Shipley et al., 1983, p. vii). In relevant literature in language assessment, concern has been raised regarding the nature of norm-referenced tests and their ability to reflect construct validity adequately (e.g., Muma, 1983). The basis of this concern lies in the nature of language as a system of communication. Any assessment tool that does not allow for descriptive information on the child's use of the targeted behavior in conversation has been questioned regarding the degree to which construct validity is achieved.

Concurrent validity is established by comparing test scores with one or more criterion variables. The variable is measured at the same time using an already validated instrument that measures the same behavior. The test authors compared TEEM scores with those of the Peabody Picture Vocabulary Test (Dunn, 1965), obtaining a Pearson r of .84 ($p < .05$). The assumption that this procedure measures concurrent validity is suspect. The PPVT measures receptive vocabulary, and the relationship between receptive vocabulary and the use of expressive morphemes is not clearly established. The analysis of concurrent validity would be more appropriate had the TEEM been compared with another measure of expressive morphology.

Inter- and intratester reliability studies are reported in the TEEM manual. For the measure of intertester reliability, 12 subjects randomly selected from the prestandardization test group ($N = 40$) were retested by a second clinician. Although a Pearson r of .95 ($p < .05$) was found, no timeframe for this testing is given. Intratester reliability was established by retesting 12 different randomly selected subjects from the prestandardization group within 7 to 14 days after the initial testing, revealing a Pearson r of .94 ($p < .05$). It should be noted that the reliability measures were conducted during the prestandardization phase of test development, which involved only 40 subjects, whereas the normative data reported for the TEEM (including mean and standard deviations) were collected during final standardization with 500 child subjects.

As noted, TEEM standardization was completed during two phases, the prestandardization and the final standardization. The initial study was conducted by Stone (1980) with subjects who ranged in age from 3 to 7. All subjects were in one of three preschool/day-care centers in Reno, Nevada, and all "exhibited normal speech, language, and hearing abilities," with no further description of methods used to determine normalcy. The authors state that the prestandardization studies were aimed toward estimating test validity and reliability with measures such as evaluating whether children's responses differed at various age levels.

The final standardization study, conducted by Sue (1981), included 500 children, ages 3 to 8. One hundred children were in each 1-year age group. The sex distribution was roughly equal in each 1-year group, ranging from 38 males/62 females to 49 males/51 females. The subjects, all residents of Fresno, California, were selected from seven nursery/preschools and three public schools, the latter selected "for their 'middle class' populations and because their student academic achievement scores were near the national median" (Shipley et al., 1983, p. 9). The preschools were located near the public schools and therefore presumed to contain similar children. All subjects exhibited "normal speech, language, and hearing abilities" (with no description offered of methods used to determine normalcy) and spoke standard English.

Initial analyses of variance demonstrated significant differences in performance between subjects when grouped at 1-year intervals. Only two significant differences between 6-month groupings were found (with nine possible 6-month groups). The significant differences appeared between the 3.0–3.6 versus 3.7–3.12 groups, and between the 4.7–4.12 versus 5.0–5.6 groups. A Scheffe multiple-range test for analysis of variance showed significant differences in performance between the youngest two 6-month groups (3.0–3.6 versus 3.7–3.12), and between the second youngest 6-month group (3.7–3.12) and the 4-year-olds. Only significant differences between the whole-year groupings were found for children older than 3.12. It is important to note the recommendations for analysis of test performance include age-level approximations for all 6-month intervals between 3.0 and 4.12, then whole-year breakdowns after 4.12. These age groupings also were used to report means and standard deviations. For these measures, the raw score means showed an increase for each of the age groups, with standard deviations decreasing regularly as age increased. The authors demonstrated a steady increase in percentage of items responded to correctly with each successive age group. No differences in scoring patterns by sex were found.

Critique

In a recent survey of California speech/language pathologists (Wilson, Blackmon, Hall, & Elcholtz, 1991), respondents were asked to report on frequently used assessment tools for expressive and receptive language. The TEEM was among the 11 expressive tests mentioned by at least 10% of the professionals. One may interpret the frequent use of the TEEM found in this survey in several ways. For those clinicians deciding to use standardized, norm-referenced methods of assessment, the need for evaluating expressive morphologic skills is apparent. The prevalence of language problems that involve the development of language form (e.g., syntax, morphology) is often discussed in the literature of language disorders in children (e.g., Johnston & Kahmi, 1984; Lahey, 1988). Procedures for systematically studying morphologic ability in young children therefore present a valuable clinical tool.

Although the use of descriptive assessment procedures (e.g., language sampling) is typically recommended for a complete, naturalistic evaluation of a child's language abilities (Damico, Secord, & Wiig, 1992; McCauley & Swisher, 1984b; Muma, 1983), the need for formal assessment measures is also apparent for certain clinical needs. Shipley et al. (1983) discuss the use of formal methodologies such as the TEEM versus language sampling, noting that

> Clinicians will realize that such samples may need to be extensive to provide ample opportunities for the occurrence of a variety of morphemes and their allomorphic variations. Probably it is more time-efficient to examine specific words. . . . we can determine the presence, absence, or partial development of the morphologic features in question. (p. 18)

Given that many clinicians will choose to use formal tests in specific work settings (McCauley & Swisher, 1984a; Wilson, Blackmon, Hall, & Elcholtz, 1991), methodology issues regarding the adequacy of the TEEM need to be addressed. The testing procedure employed (i.e., sentence completion) is frequently used for assessing expressive morphology (Channell & Ford, 1991). The use of this technique spans years of research and test construction, from Berko's (1958) study of morphology to recently published instruments such as the Test of Language Development–P:2 (Newcomer & Hammill, 1988). This method of testing is easily administered by an examiner and easily learned by most children. The highly constrained response mode may also prove beneficial for assessing morphology with preschool children of lowered intelligibility as opposed to language sampling, which may result in unanalyzable data (Lawrence & Klingler, 1988).

The sentence-completion technique, however, does have some limitations. Any test that reduces the contextual support of language to individual test items may influence the adequacy and completeness of the assessment results (Damico et al., 1992; Muma, 1983). In addition, the TEEM uses a technique that allows only the final word of each sentence to be produced by the child, which limits the type of grammatical morphemes that one can assess. Several morphemes studied by Brown (1973) and others are not grammatical forms appearing in the final position of sentences (e.g., copular verbs, articles). The importance of also evaluating preschoolers' acquisition of these morphemes would be obvious for most clinicians working with language-disordered children. The TEEM provides extensive data on bound morphemes (and irregulars) and their allomorphic variations, yet other tests, such as the Structured Photographic Expressive Language Test–II (Werner & Kresheck, 1983), may be required for an extensive evaluation of a wider range of morphological expression.

Issues concerning the statistical foundation and breadth of the measure were addressed in the "Technical Aspects" section of this review. Despite the questions raised, the careful design of the TEEM does provide a clinician with comprehensive information on the targeted behaviors. For children not performing adequately on the measure, intervention may be a typical recommendation. The data collected by administering the TEEM appear to successfully sample many examples of the target behaviors and would provide a clinician with helpful information for designing an intervention program.

It is noteworthy that the authors address some valuable concerns that professionals need to consider when selecting the TEEM, such as using the test with speakers of nonstandard English, with children who have articulatory problems, and with those for whom the task of sentence completion is difficult. Although most speech/language pathologists would be aware of these considerations, the authors' acknowledgment of these topics is important.

The present reviewers had not used the TEEM previously in their clinical work. In order to become familiar with the methodology, one reviewer administered it to a preschool child. The test was easy to administer and score. The data were quickly analyzed via the manual's clear directions, and the sample protocols also added to the ease of scoring and analysis. Information regarding ages of acquisition listed on the simple, easy-to-read score form were helpful for understanding test performance. The thin text paper in the picture booklet produced occasional difficulty in turning the pages and also allowed the examinee to see the next stimuli picture through the one being used.

In summary, the TEEM appears to be a well-developed method for studying expressive acquisition of selected grammatical morphemes. Assessment tools addressing morphology serve an important clinical need. With consideration of the TEEM's scope, purpose, and limitations, clinicians may find that it yields extensive data on morphemes and allomorphic variations and aids in planning intervention for the child with morphologic problems.

References

Berko, J. (1958). The child's learning of English morphology. *Word, 14*, 150–170.

Brown, R.A. (1973). *A first language: The early stages.* Cambridge, MA: Harvard University Press.

Channell, R.W., & Ford, C.T. (1991). Four grammatical completion measures of language ability. *Language, Speech, and Hearing Services in Schools, 22*, 211–218.

Damico, J.S., Secord, W.A., & Wiig, E.H. (1992). Descriptive language assessment at school: Characteristics and design. In W.A. Secord & J.S. Damico (Eds.), *Best practices in school speech-language pathology* (pp. 1–8). San Antonio, TX: Psychological Corporation.

Dunn, L. (1965). *Peabody Picture Vocabulary Test.* Circle Pines, MN: American Guidance Service.

Johnston, J.R., & Kahmi, A.G. (1984). Syntactic and semantic aspects of the utterances of language-impaired children: The same can be less. *Merrill-Palmer Quarterly, 30*, 65–86.

Lahey, M. (1988). *Language disorders and language development.* New York: Macmillan.

Lawrence, C.W., & Klingler, M. (1988, November). *Testing expressive language of reduced intelligibility children using SPELT-II.* Paper presented at the annual convention of the American Speech-Language-Hearing Association, Boston.

McCauley, R.J., & Swisher, L. (1984a). Psychometric review of language and articulation tests for preschool children. *Journal of Speech and Hearing Disorders, 49*, 34–42.

McCauley, R.J., & Swisher, L. (1984b). Use and misuse of norm-referenced tests in clinical assessment: A hypothetical case. *Journal of Speech and Hearing Disorders, 49*, 338–348.

Muma, J.R. (1983). Speech-language pathology: Emerging clinical expertise in language. In T.M. Gallagher & C.A. Prutting (Eds.), *Pragmatic assessment and intervention issues in language* (pp. 195–214). San Diego: College-Hill Press.

Newcomer, P.L., & Hammill, D. (1988). *Test of Language Development–Primary* (2nd ed). Austin. TX: PRO-ED.

Shipley, K.G., Stone, T.A., & Sue, M.B. (1983). *Test for Examining Expressive Morphology (TEEM).* Tuscon, AZ: Communication Skill Builders.

Stone, T.A. (1980). *A method of examining expressive morphology.* Unpublished master's thesis, University of Nevada, Reno.

Sue, M.B. (1981). *Standardization of the Test for Examining Expressive Morphology.* Unpublished master's thesis, California State University, Fresno.

Werner, E.O., & Kresheck, J.D. (1983). *Structured Photographic Expressive Language Test–II.* Sandwich, IL: Janelle Publications.

Wilson, K.S., Blackmon, R.C., Hall, R.E., & Elcholtz, G.E. (1991). Methods of language assessment: A survey of California public school clinicians. *Language, Speech, and Hearing Services in Schools, 22,* 236–241.

Jim C. Fortune, Ed.D.
Professor of Educational Research, Virginia Polytechnic Institute, Blacksburg, Virginia.

Abbot L. Packard, M.Ed.
Director, Educational Computing Laboratory, Virginia Polytechnic Institute, Blacksburg, Virginia.

TEST OF ATTITUDE TOWARD SCHOOL
Guy Thibaudeau. Montreal, Quebec, Canada: Institute of Psychological Research, Inc.

Introduction

The Test of Attitude Toward School (TAS) is an individually administered projective test for assessing the scholastic attitude of prereading students.

The measurement of scholastic attitude or attitude toward school of prereading students is compounded by the necessity to save costs, the need for independent, reliable, and valid information, and the absence of the ability to transmit the test stimuli through written media. Attempts to measure the construct include scaling strategies using the "smiley" faces response mode, the Q-sort, the semantic differential, self-report questionnaires administered individually, observation, and projective techniques. Almost all of the strategies appear vulnerable to the "near-fatal" criticism.

Perhaps the strategy that possesses the most potential is that of projective testing combined with the "smiley" faces response mode. Both theoretical and applied conceptual bases can be established for this strategy in either experimental or practical instructional settings. The strategy appears less prescriptive in biasing student responses and appears less susceptible to criticisms of "putting words in the child's mouth." The adoption of a projective technique does, however, raise questions of validity, of the transfer of expressed attitudes to school settings, and of scoring capability by the end user.

In his technical manual, the author of the TAS includes a fairly comprehensive review of prior projective instruments, the theoretical foundation of the instrument, and the history of the technique. He describes one validation study and reports several studies in which the instrument has been used. (Missing, however, from Thibaudeau's review is a similar and competitive scale developed at University of California at Los Angeles by Strickland, Hoepfner, and Klein [1976].)

The TAS contains 14 "rough" drawings of school-related situations and two drawings of a child's face. The student is asked to describe the situation in each of the drawings, indicating their scholastic attitude and their emotional states. The two drawings of a child's face (one happy and one sad) are presented to determine the correct identification with emotional states. The testing of an individual student lasts approximately 30 to 40 minutes. Additional time is required to collect the teacher and parent data. These additional data are necessary to satisfy one advantageous claim for the TAS, that it uses multiple measurements: the projection of the student, the interview, and the direct observation of behavior to assess scholastic attitude.

Practical Applications/Uses

From a review of the technical manual, it is apparent that the author intended the TAS to be used in the study of learning in early elementary school. The manual provides case interpretations and the descriptive power of the test results is discussed. Such a role as a supporting instrument in a basic learning study appears to be very appropriate use of the instrument.

In the evaluation of special programs, such as Chapter I, Even Start, Follow Through, and special education, the measurement of scholastic attitude is often a frequently desired but difficult task for the evaluator. Because of the necessity for individual administration, the apparent desirability of the teacher and parent data, and the requirement for hand scoring, the TAS would not be recommended as a measure to be used in program evaluations at the lower elementary level. The TAS can be group administered to students if they can respond in writing. This would make the scale potentially useful for evaluations of middle and upper elementary school programs.

During development the TAS was used with 90 males in Grades 1, 3, and 5. All levels of school performance were included in the validity test of the instrument. The intent of the validity study was to demonstrate the utility of the instrument in the measurement of the scholastic attitude of prereading students. Males were used to fit with the 14 pictures and to avoid the potential confounding of gender.

Being of the conservative mode, these reviewers believe that a test should be used with the population on which it was normed. Hence, appropriate use would be with elementary school males. However, we also believe that the strategy has greater potential than the limited range of the norming population. Given normative data, the test could be used with both boys and girls in elementary school. We believe that the strategy does not compete well with Thurstone, Likert, and semantic differential techniques for the measurement of scholastic attitude of secondary school students.

The TAS has been designed to be administered individually to prereading students. The exact administration procedures are difficult to discern from the technical manual, but these reviewers were assured by staff of the Institute of Psychological Research, Inc. that the test is packaged in a kit with explicit administration instructions. The administration as we envision it encompasses the following: The student is brought from the classroom to the testing room by the examiner; in the process, attempts are made to reduce the stranger/child effect by planned "chit-chat"; the student is asked a global question about liking to go to school; the examiner shows the student the two faces ("smiley" and "frowny") and the association of happy/sad is established; the students then is shown the pictures in planned sequence and asked to describe the activity depicted and if it is a happy/sad one. Parents and teachers then are asked to fill out the supportive questions.

Scoring is both descriptive and quantitative. The manual is very clear as to scoring procedures. The user should be able to score the scales without difficulty.

The manual is helpful in directing the user to form basic interpretations. Interpretations made using the data from the three sources appear most useful; those made by using only the projective scale results may only involve positive/negative predispositions.

Technical Aspects

In the technical manual, Thibaudeau reports a validity study that these reviewers believe was too limited in scope. The study involved nine male students from each of 10 Catholic schools. The schools were chosen using stratified random selection, taking into account socioeconomic status of the attendance areas. One third of the students came from the first grade, one third from the third grade, and one third from the fifth grade. One third of the students were considered strong students, one third were considered average students, and one third were considered poor students. This study shows that teachers rate the child similarly to the measure obtained using the TAS in 80% of the cases. Teachers rated students as more positive toward school than was shown by the projective instrument. It seems that similar validity information is needed on females, on kindergarten students, on a larger sample of schools, and on a larger sample of students.

These reviewers could not find either reliability or reproducibility of results for the scale in the technical manual. Test-retest reliability appears necessary at the minimum.

Critique

The idea of expanding the number of TAS questions and increasing the reference to school settings is a step in the right direction. These reviewers hope that further standardization will be conducted with the prereading population. It is our understanding that more work is being done at the adult level, and we feel that at the upper grades and adult level, a wider range of established scaling techniques is available than at the prereader level. The contribution that could be made by this scale is at the prereader level, and more standardization, greater student diversity, and a larger norming population are needed at that level.

In preparing the scale for use at the prereader level (kindergarten, first and second grade), better pictures are needed, especially cross-gender pictures. Color may be used to keep the child's interest. Further, users may appreciate a separate set of instructions for administration of the scale. Overall, the TAS represents a beginning with potential, but more work in norming is needed prior to recommending it.

References

Jacobson, M.G. (1986). Attitude to School Questionnaire. In R.C. Sweetland & D.J. Keyer (Eds.), *Test critiques* (Vol. V, pp. 21–25). Austin, TX: PRO-ED.

Strickland, G.P., Hoepfner, R., & Klein, S.P. (1976). *Attitude Toward School Questionnaire manual.* Hollywood, CA: Monitor.

Thibaudeau, G. (1984). *Test of Attitude Toward School (T.A.S.).* Montreal: Institute of Psychological Research.

Selma Hughes, Ph.D.
Professor, Department of Psychology and Special Education, East Texas State University, Commerce, Texas.

TEST OF PRAGMATIC SKILLS–REVISED EDITION

Brian B. Shulman. Tucson, Arizona: Communication Skill Builders, Inc.

Introduction

The Test of Pragmatic Skills (TPS; Shulman, 1986) is an individually administered, standardized test designed to assess the use of language for conversational intent by children aged 3 through 8. The format of the TPS is very different from usual language tests. It consists of four guided-play interactions/scenarios through which the clinician may observe the child's ability to use language to communicate.

The author, Brian B. Shulman, is Professor of Speech Pathology and Audiology at the University of South Alabama and an active researcher and practitioner in the field of child language development and language disorders. He is author of the Pragmatic Development Chart (1983) and coauthor of the *Language Assessment Handbook* (1985), among other publications.

The Test of Pragmatic Skills was first published in 1985, and the revised edition appeared the following year when changes were made to the score sheet to facilitate scoring. The test materials consist of the manual, the manipulatives kit, and the task score booklets. The manipulatives kit contains 2 toy telephones, 10 colored cubes/blocks, and 2 felt puppets (one male and one female). This is all the examiner needs to assess the child (with the addition of a pencil), as the back cover of the task score booklet may be cut off and given to the child as a worksheet for Task 2.

The four tasks involve the child in using language in different contexts or settings:

Task 1: The examiner and the child talk about a favorite television show through the medium of the two puppets.

Task 2: Conversation is initiated about the child copying the three drawings (circle, square, and cross) on the back cover of the booklet.

Task 3: The examiner and the child talk about what the child did that day and explore other aspects of conversation using two toy telephones.

Task 4: The examiner initiates general conversation with the child while getting him or her to play with a set of blocks.

The examiner administers a total of 34 probes during the four TPS tasks with the purpose of eliciting specific pragmatic forms of language. The child's utterances in response to the probes are scored on a scale from 1 to 5, where "0" is no response. An exact description of the criteria for each rating is given. For example, a one-word

716

contextually appropriate response rates a "3," while a response of two or three words rates a "4." The score sheet gives sample utterances adjacent to each probe, which is helpful to the examiner, and a space is provided for writing each response.

The manual suggests in addition that the clinician should video- or audiotape the test administration. This reviewer supports the suggestion for several reasons: 1) it may not be possible to transcribe the utterances and maintain the flow of dialogue, 2) it is not always easy to rate a response immediately, and 3) a recording permits further analysis of what the child said in terms of, for example, semantic and grammatical rules. The author does in fact provide a helpful supplement for interpreting the utterances in terms of verbal turn taking, speaker dominance, topic maintenance, and topic change.

Raw scores are summed and the average of the four raw scores becomes the Mean Composite Score (MCS), which is converted to a percentile rank. A normative data summary sheet provided on each task score sheet shows the data in graphic form.

Practical Applications/Uses

The TPS was designed as a supplement to conventional language tests to assess children's communicative intent. It is not intended to replace instruments that assess language structure, but rather to add to them by providing a standardized instrument for measuring language functions.

Verbal communication results from an interaction between language structures and language functions. Language structures involve word meanings (semantics), word patterns (syntax), word forms (morphology), and speech sounds (phonology). Language functions pertain to the reasons for selecting specific language structures to achieve specific purposes (Berdine & Meyer, 1987).

Communication in the broadest sense is characterized by an exchange of information or ideas. Communication can occur with or without language, through gestures and facial expressions, and through sounds as well as speech (Benner, 1992). The Test of Pragmatic Skills assesses the strategies children use for controlling or influencing the behavior of the listener. It is concerned with nonverbal as well as verbal aspects of language.

The authors of the Tests of Language Development (TOLD-2; Hammill & Newcomer, 1988) acknowledge that their test assesses whether a child has developed the particular language structures around which the measure is designed; it does not assess whether the child uses those structures. In contrast, the TPS does not assess language structures but whether the child uses them appropriately in a conversational/play setting. The design of the Test of Pragmatic Skills allows the clinician to examine how the child interprets conversational stimuli and maintains dyadic communication and interaction.

Information is provided in the TPS on 10 categories of communicative intentions expressed by children aged 3 through 8. These 10 categories, which constitute a rational sampling of the reasons why children use language, are Requesting Information, Requesting Action, Rejection/Denial, Naming/Labelling, Answering/Responding, Informing, Reasoning, Summoning/Calling, Greeting, and Closing Conversation. Although the reasons (functions) in reality can (and do) occur in combination (Simon, 1981), the categories are treated separately. This enables the clinician to compare the child's performance on specific aspects of usage with that of children the same age in the standardization sample.

The TPS is designed for use by speech and language clinicians. The author does not say whether it could be used by professionals other than those who have experience in language evaluation. In the opinion of this reviewer, the test could be used by educational diagnosticians and school personnel who have a background in language testing. The TPS should be given in an informal setting (on the floor for younger children), and in that respect it differs from conventional norm-referenced tests.

The author points out that pragmatic aspects of language are usually assessed through observation of behavior or analysis of spontaneous language samples. Both these methods require trained language professionals and considerable expenditure of time. The TPS is a form of dynamic assessment that may be used relatively easily to provide a norm-referenced score, always recognizing that tests are an aid to clinical judgment and not a substitute for it.

The Test of Pragmatic Skills was standardized on 650 children between the ages of 3 and 8 years, 11 months. The sample contained more than 100 subjects in each 1-year age interval, which meets the criteria of acceptability proposed by Hammill, Brown, and Bryant (1992). The overall sample size is slightly smaller than the size they suggest but comparable with that of other well-known and well-used language tests.

The normative group is representative of the U.S. population (from the 1980 census) with regard to geographical data. There are equal numbers of boys and girls, from Anglo, middle-class backgrounds only. The children were tested to be sure that they had no speech, language, or hearing deficits, and that they were not receiving any special services in school.

The TPS author recognizes that the sample is not linguistically and culturally diverse, and he suggests the development of local norms for special groups of children. Dr. Shulman currently is working on the development of a more culturally sensitive test for black, Hispanic, Vietnamese, and Laotian preschool/primary children for whom some of the pragmatic categories are not discriminating or appropriate.

Few problems should be encountered in the administration of this test because the tasks are well defined and the probes quite specific. The raw score for each task is the total number of points obtained. These scores are summarized in a table on the front cover (which would be simpler to use if a line were inserted for the total score from which the mean is derived). The mean of the raw scores then becomes the Mean Composite Score (MCS), which is converted to a percentile rank (PR) from a table in the manual.

The percentile ranks for the MCS are shown for six age groups; they are not provided for all scores at all age levels. For example, in the age range 6:0 to 6:11, no PR is given for scores between 27 and 33 (27 is at the 25th percentile, 33 is at the 50th). It would be helpful to know how an MCS of 30, for example, should be reported. Is it permissible to interpolate and state that an MCS of 30 is at the 38th percentile and thus that "between a quarter and a half of all children at that age would do better than this child did"?

A normative data summary sheet forms part of the scoring sheet for each student, and the test data are shown graphically on this. (Here again it would be helpful to users if the axis could be repeated the opposite side of the page to aid in plotting the data.) After completing the chart, the examiner can visually compare the results to the normative data for each task to determine how well or how poorly the child performed compared to same-age peers.

Computer scoring is available with a software program developed by Shulman and Fitch (Computerized Test of Pragmatic Skills; 1986). The disk may be used with the Apple II/IIe/IIc/IIG3 computer and provides additional data on the coded responses beyond that obtained by hand scoring.

No indication is given of the amount of time needed to administer the TPS probes, as this would depend on the age and responsiveness of the child as well as the examiner's skill in the particular type of interaction style required by the test. The probes may be repeated only once and must be given verbatim to maintain consistency in test administration, so this would make the amount of time reasonable (i.e., no more than 20 or 30 minutes).

The level of difficulty in interpreting the test results is low because percentile ranks alone are provided. As with all tests, however, interpretation is improved if the examiner has some sophistication in testing, and more so if experienced in language development. The author states that from the TPS results the clinician can ascertain which pragmatic behaviors require clinical treatment. The importance of paying attention to items assigned "0" or "1" is stressed. The interpretation essentially is left to the examiner. What is provided is an objective comparison with children the same age; no indication of degrees of competence or lack of competence (e.g., mild, moderate, severe) appears. Few trained examiners would want to quantify the data further (e.g., by calculating the percentage of items correct in each category), and the author does not suggest doing so.

Technical Aspects

The technical adequacy of a test is determined by its norms, reliability, and validity. Particular attention is paid to the nature of the normative sample and to the various kinds of normative scores that commonly are derived from a test's raw scores (Hammill et al., 1992). The TPS norms were discussed earlier in this review and are adequate.

Reliability is the extent to which a test is consistent in its scores or measurements, and the TPS manual addresses several kinds of reliability. Stability reliability was determined from a sample of 120 children (20 in each age group) and is reported as .96. This indicates that the TPS has good test-retest reliability. Interexaminer reliability is reported as .92, which is substantial (Hammill et al., 1992).

The Test of Pragmatic skills is a stable and consistent instrument in assessing the pragmatic language skills of children ages 3 through 8. However, a test may be reliable without necessarily being valid (Salvia & Ysseldyke, 1991). Validity refers to the extent to which a test measures what is says it measures. Some kinds of validity are only derived over time, and no data are available on the predictive validity of this test other than the author's hypotheses.

Some attempts were made to establish concurrent validity by taking language samples from two children at the age extremes of the standardization sample. These samples then were evaluated by independent clinicians and the scores correlated with the subjects' scores on the TPS. Correlations of .68 and .64 are reported. It is premature to say that this establishes how well test performance on the TPS relates to performance on other tests of language from a sample of two. As clinicians and others use this test, more appropriate data will accrue to support its concurrent validity.

The manual does provide evidence of an appropriate data-based approach to item selection that was made from a pilot study. The content or curricular validity is derived from a review of the literature on pragmatic categories and represents an adequate sampling of skills from several theoretical orientations described by the author.

Construct validity has to do with the extent to which a test measures some type of theoretical characteristic or concept (Taylor, 1989). The establishment of construct validity includes the careful identification and definition of the construct, followed by the derivation and verification of the hypothesis concerning test performance related to the construct (Gronlund, 1987). The author certainly provides the former (definition of construct), and empirical evidence of the latter is provided by the normative data summary sheet. The mean raw scores reported in the tables become larger as the age increases. This shows that test scores are related positively and significantly to age.

At the present time it is difficult to establish a positive correlation between TPS scores and those on other tests that purport to measure the same construct because no other such tests exist. Simon's (1986) Evaluating Communicative Competence (ECC) instrument is the nearest in theoretical orientation, but it is designed for subjects between the ages of 9 and 17 years and is nonnormative (i.e., criterion-referenced). Until TPS users generate more data, the present technical data could be considered adequate.

Critique

The Test of Pragmatic Skills is an evaluative procedure that provides data about a child's skills in both listener and speaker roles. It yields pragmatic information about children's ability to understand and to use language. The TPS presents an innovative combination of the techniques of dynamic assessment with the precision of norm-referenced testing. Unlike norm-referenced testing where the examiner elicits responses to structured questions, the TPS facilitates language through the examiner interacting with the child at the child's level during play. The format is nonthreatening and would encourage participation by children who do not test well and by younger children, too.

The TPS is not intended to replace but rather to augment other measures of language. The author stresses that it is not intended as a sole measure of a child's language; it should be used with additional assessment instruments to determine the adequacy of the child's receptive and expressive language. The test is foremost a measure of communicative intent and as such is an innovative, useful addition to the language clinician's testing library.

As with all new tests, research is needed to support some of the technical aspects that presently are supported by nonempirical data. This no doubt will come as users appreciate the usefulness of the TPS in providing a comprehensive picture of children's cognitive-linguistic skills in use.

References

Benner, S. (1992). *Assessing young children with special needs.* New York: Longman.

Berdine, W.H., & Meyer, S.A. (1987). *Assessment in special education.* Boston: Little, Brown.

Gronlund, N. (1987). *Measurement and evaluation in guidance* (4th ed.). New York: Macmillan.

Hammill, D., Brown, L., & Bryant, B.R. (1992). *A consumer's guide to tests in print* (2nd ed.). Austin, TX: PRO-ED.

Hammill, D., & Newcomer, P. (1988). *Tests of Language Development* (2nd ed.). Austin, TX: PRO-ED.

Salvia, J., & Ysseldyke, J.E. (1991). *Assessment.* Boston: Houghton Mifflin.

Shulman, B. (1983). *Pragmatic development chart.* Salt Lake City: Word Making Productions.

Shulman, B. (1986). *Test of Pragmatic Skills–Revised Edition.* Tucson, AZ: Communication Skill Builders.

Shulman, B., Barrick, M., & Chaney, L. (1985). *Language assessment handbook.* Salt Lake City: Word Making Production.

Shulman, B., & Fitch, J. (1986). *Computerized Test of Pragmatic Skills.* Tucson, AZ: Communication Skill Builders.

Simon, C. (1981). *Communicative competence: A functional pragmatic approach to language therapy.* Tucson, AZ: Communication Skill Builders.

Simon, C. (1986). *Evaluating communicative competence: A functional pragmatic approach to language therapy.* Tucson, AZ: Communication Skill Builders.

Taylor, R. (1989). *Assessment of exceptional students.* Englewood Cliffs, NJ: Prentice-Hall.

James A. Moses, Jr., Ph.D.
*Clinical Associate Professor of Psychiatry and Behavioral Sciences,
Stanford University School of Medicine, and Coordinator,
Psychological Assessment Unit, Department of Veterans Affairs
Medical Center, Palo Alto, California.*

TEST OF TEMPORAL ORIENTATION

*Arthur L. Benton, Kerry deS. Hamsher, Nils R. Varney, and
Otfried Spreen. New York, New York: Oxford University
Press.*

Introduction

The Test of Temporal Orientation (TTO; Benton, 1975; Benton, Hamsher, Varney, & Spreen, 1983; Benton, Van Allen, & Fogel, 1964) is a standardized, five-question interview technique designed to identify, objectify, and quantitatively measure the accuracy of an individual's orientation to time. Temporal orientation evaluation composes an integral part of the standard neuropsychiatric examination of mental status. It may be disturbed in a wide variety of neuropsychiatric conditions. Syndromes of cerebral injury, disease, or psychiatric disorder that can affect the ability to recall or to track serial temporal events accurately include various types of confusional states, psychotic disorders, amnesic states, dementing conditions, and factitious or malingering syndromes (Benton et al., 1983).

The principal author of the TTO, Arthur L. Benton, Ph.D., received his A.B. (1931) and A.M. (1933) degrees from Oberlin College, followed by his Ph.D. from Columbia University (1935). He began his career as an assistant in psychology, first at Oberlin College (1931–33), then at Columbia University and New York State Psychiatric Institute (1934–36), and finally at Cornell University Medical College (1936–39), where subsequently he served as a staff psychologist. He was appointed as an attending psychologist at New York Hospital–Westchester Division and as a psychologist in the Student Personnel Office of the City College of New York from 1939 to 1941. After serving on active duty in the U.S. Navy during and after the Second World War (1941–46), he was appointed as Associate Professor of Psychology at the University of Louisville Medical School and as chief psychologist at the Louisville Mental Hygiene Clinic and the Louisville General Hospital (1946–48). From 1948 to 1958 he served as Professor of Psychology and director of the Graduate Training Program in Clinical Psychology at the University of Iowa, followed by two decades (1958–78) as Professor of Psychology and Neurology. Dr. Benton has continued to coauthor theoretical and research papers and books since 1978, when he became Professor Emeritus at the University of Iowa.

Benton's fundamental contributions to the field of clinical neuropsychology have been acknowledged extensively and internationally. He has received honor-

722

ary Doctor of Science (Cornell College, 1978) and Doctor of Psychology (University of Rome, 1990) degrees, as well as numerous other honors and awards, including the Distinguished Service Award of the Iowa Psychological Association (1977), the Distinguished Professional Contribution Award from the American Psychological Association (1978), the Outstanding Scientific Contribution Award of the International Neuropsychological Society (1981), The Samuel Torrey Orton Award from the Orton Dyslexia Society (1982), the Distinguished Service and Outstanding Contributions Award from the American Board of Professional Psychology (1985), and the Distinguished Clinical Neuropsychologist Award from the National Academy of Neuropsychology (1989).

Benton is a past president of both the American Orthopsychiatric Association (1965–66) and the International Neuropsychological Society (1970–71), and he served as secretary-general of the Research Group on Aphasia for the World Federation of Neurology (1971–78). He has been a lecturer or visiting scholar at the University of Milan (1964), Hôpital Sainte-Anne, Paris (1968), Hadassah-Hebrew University Medical School, Jerusalem (1969), Free University of Amsterdam (1971), University of Helsinki (1974), University of Melbourne (1977), University of Minnesota Medical School (Baker Lecturer, 1979), University of Victoria, British Columbia (Lansdowne Scholar, 1980), and the University of Michigan (1986), as well as Directeur d'Études Associé, École des Hautes Études, Paris (1979) and a visiting scientist at the Tokyo Metropolitan Institute of Gerontology (1974).

Benton has authored, coauthored, or edited 12 books and monographs, approximately 150 professional journal articles, and 22 historical reviews in the area of clinical neuropsychology and behavioral neurology. He is recognized as a pioneer and a leading authority in the area of clinical neuropsychology.

The standardized, commercially published version of the TTO appeared with the clinical manual for this and other tests in the Benton-Iowa Neuropsychological Test Battery (Benton et al., 1983). Coauthors of this clinical manual with Dr. Benton are Kerry deS. Hamsher, Ph.D. (Associate Professor of Neurology, University of Wisconsin Medical School); Nils R. Varney, Ph.D. (staff neuropsychologist, Department of Veterans Affairs Medical Center, Iowa City, Iowa); and Otfried Spreen, Ph.D. (Professor Emeritus, Department of Psychology, University of Victoria, Victoria, British Columbia, Canada).

Practical Applications/Uses

The need to assess temporal orientation in the evaluation of mental status is universally accepted, and clear disorientation to time is easily recognized. A patient who confuses day and night, or morning and afternoon, or who does not know the current month or year clearly is disoriented to time. This pattern presents no difficulty in time orientation deficit assessment. Minor temporal orientation disturbance, however, may be a prodromal or residual symptom of neurologic, psychiatric, or neuropsychiatric disorder. If the temporal disorientation is noted early in the clinical course, the cognitive dysfunction associated with this orientation deficit may be more readily identified and treated. It is therefore important to have a brief, objective, standardized technique for identifying minor but clinically significant degrees of temporal orientation disturbance that can be readily incorporated into the neurologic or psychiatric examination to aid the busy clinician in the evaluation of mental status. The TTO was designed to perform this function, and it has not been revised since its public appearance.

Administration and scoring of the TTO are straightforward. The patient is asked to answer three questions with five responses in all: a) "What is today's date?" (the patient must give month, day, and year); b) "What day of the week is it?"; and c) "What time is it now?" (Benton et al., 1983, p. 4, Table 1-1). Responses are recorded on a Temporal Orientation Record Form (Benton et al., 1983, p. 9), on which the patient's response is compared to the correct response. Discrepancies in terms of the number of half-hour intervals, days of the month, days of the week, months of the year, and years that the patient's responses deviate from the correct answer are calculated on the record form for each of the five questions asked. An error score is assigned to each incorrect response, the various types of which have particular error point weights.

Greater score weights are assigned to errors that are more serious indicators of temporal disorientation. For *day of the week,* 1 error point is assigned for each day the response is separated from the correct day of the week, up to a maximum of 3 points. For *day of the month,* 1 error point is assigned for each day the response is separated from the correct numerical day of the actual date, up to a maximum of 15 points. For *month of the year,* 5 error points are scored for each month the response varies from the correct month at the time of testing. If, however, the subject's response falls within 15 days of the correct date, no error score is assigned for the incorrect month (e.g., March 29 as the patient response with the correct response as April 2 = 4 error points for the day of the month error only). For the *year* response, 10 error points are assigned for each year that the subject deviates from the correct response, up to a maximum of 60 points. As with the month of the year, if the patient's response falls within 15 days of the correct answer (as at the end of one year and the beginning of another), then only the error points for days are penalized. For example, if the respondent says the date is December 27, 1992, when in fact it is January 3, 1993, then 7 error points total accumulate for this response based on the error magnitude in numerical days alone. For the *time of day* item, the respondent is penalized 1 point for each 30-minute period the response deviates from the correct time, up to a maximum of 5 points. The TTO total score is the sum of the five item error scores.

All normative standards are based on the premise that the patient has taken a valid TTO examination. Benton et al. (1983, p. 9, Table 1-5) leave room on the answer sheet for the examiner to note the patient's "cooperation, understanding, and linguistic competence." These qualitative aspects of the performance should be evaluated by the clinician before and during the administration of the TTO to ensure that he or she can give rational, comprehensible, and meaningful responses to the TTO questions.

Total TTO error scores of 0–2 points are classified as normal; 3 points = borderline, 4–7 points = moderately defective, and 8 or more points = severely defective (they rank below the first percentile of normal performance). No demographic correction of the TTO normative standards or clinical interpretive guidelines has been recommended by Benton et al. (1983).

The manual does not detail the appropriate professional qualifications for clinicians who might make use of the TTO, but one would expect a qualified interpreter to be either a multidisciplinary mental health professional with clinical care responsibilities or a trained technician. Any clinician who routinely examines the mental status of patients is a potential user of the TTO as a supplementary technique in clinical practice.

Technical Aspects

The TTO originally was developed and validated on a sample of 110 normal controls and 60 brain dysfunctional patients (Benton et al., 1964), then cross-validated in a follow-up study (Levin & Benton, 1975) with 70 normal controls and 55 brain dysfunctional patients. A large TTO normative sample of 254 normal controls subsequently was studied by Natelson, Haupt, Fleischer, and Grey (1979). Normative standards for the TTO as published by Benton et al. (1983) thus derive from a composite sample of 434 normal controls.

Impairment cutoff scores for the TTO total error score are based on a percentile standard that best separates brain dysfunctional from normal control subjects with an actuarial classification criterion. Ninety-three percent of the control subjects in the composite sample scored in the range of 0–2 total error score points. Scores of 3 or more total error score points are classified as defective because 95% of the subjects in the composite normal control sample exceeded this value. Subsequent analysis of the full range of error scores reported by Benton et al. (1964) and by Levin and Benton (1975) but unfortunately not by Natelson et al. (1979) helped determine the ordinal deficit levels of temporal disorientation for the commercially published form of the TTO.

Benton et al. (1964) compared neurologically dysfunctional and normal control subject groups on TTO total score classification. Between these broad diagnostic groups they found no significant relationship of TTO total score range to age, educational level, verbal intelligence, or sex. Natelson et al. (1979) reported a modestly significant correlation of educational level to TTO total score among their normal sample, but this result may have been a statistical artifact of their relatively large sample size. Benton et al. (1983) note that TTO errors among normals and neurologically impaired patients typically involve the day of the month item, and that the next most common error occurs with the exact time of day item. They also found that errors in identification of the month or the year are "most exceptional" among normals, so that one probably is safe in considering such errors as pathognomonic signs of temporal disorientation. The TTO scoring system error score weights support this inference.

Eslinger, Damasio, Benton, and Van Allen (1985) employed the TTO in combination with measures of verbal and visual recall, visual perception, attention span, and verbal fluency as part of a neuropsychological battery designed to detect the presence of dementia in an elderly population and to discriminate that generic syndrome from the effects of normal aging. Demented subjects showed a greatly elevated mean error score and great variability on the TTO total score ($M = 26.2$ error points; $SD = 34.4$) relative to the scores of controls ($M = 0.3$ error points; $SD = 1.0$) who were matched to the demented sample subjects by age (range = 60–88 years) and sex.

Varney and Shepherd (1991) used the TTO in combination with a series of standardized tests of visual and verbal memory in a sample of 253 alcoholic inpatients with no less than a 15-year history of problem drinking who were intoxicated when admitted to an alcohol rehabilitation unit. All subjects were tested with the TTO, an abbreviated form of the Wechsler Adult Intelligence Scale (WAIS), and memorial measures when they had abstained from alcohol for a period of 3 to 7 days. None of them showed signs of acute alcohol intoxication or withdrawal at the time of testing. None of the subjects showed evidence of neurologic disease or disorder other than what was consistent with the effects of problem drinking alone. Error scores on TTO greater than 8 points were associated with consistent failure on the memorial measures. Temporal disorientation was not a predictable measure of significant cognitive decline on the brief form of the WAIS that was administered. There was no consistent relationship between normal range temporal orientation on TTO total error score and performance on the memorial measures. Varney and Shepherd recommended that temporally disoriented patients with TTO error scores of 8 or more should not be given memorial measures until the TTO score falls below that error level, as memorial performance across measures is prone to be grossly and globally impaired. They specifically recommended use of the TTO to monitor the degree and fluctuation of temporal disorientation in patients with gross cognitive impairment.

Jones, Tranel, Benton, and Paulsen (1992) demonstrated the usefulness of the TTO as one of a battery of brief nonverbal measures that has predictive value for the evaluation of prodromal-phase dementia. They found that patients who subsequently became demented showed moderately defective TTO scores when the diagnosis of dementia initially was in question, during the prodromal phase of the illness (TTO error score baseline $M = 4.9$, $SD = 7.2$), and that these individuals developed severely defective TTO scores at the time of follow-up assessment (TTO error score $M = 15.3$, $SD = 23.9$), when the diagnosis had been established clinically. In each case the large amount of individual variability associated with the large standard deviation value should be noted. It is also remarkable that a comparison group of patients with "pseudo-dementia" who did not progress to a dementing condition at follow-up evaluation also showed borderline-to-mild temporal disorientation (TTO error score $M = 3.86$, $SD = 9.3$ at baseline; $M = 3.1$, $SD = 6.0$ at follow-up). The authors concluded that initial deficits on measures of temporal orientation, visual memory assessed with Benton's Revised Visual Retention Test, and the Block Design subtest of the Wechsler Adult Intelligence Scale–Revised present significant predictors of subsequent dementia onset. They speculated that these measures may have particular value in this differential diagnostic formulation because they are "both novel and multidimensional in their demand on cognitive abilities" (Jones et al., 1992, p. 19).

The use of the TTO in psychotic populations without known brain dysfunction has been little studied or reported in the literature. An exploratory study by Joslyn and Hutzell (1979), however, showed that the incidence of defective temporal orientation in their schizophrenic sample of 45 subjects was relatively low (4/45, 8.8%). This study should be replicated in larger samples and with additional well-diagnosed psychotic and nonpsychotic psychiatric diagnostic patient groups.

Critique

The TTO offers a sensitive, accurate, brief, well-quantified, easily scored and administered, inexpensive, and clinically rich source of mental status information, which also is easily interpreted. It is predictively valid for the evaluation of prodromal-phase dementia. The differential diagnostic value of the TTO in the evaluation of dementia will be enhanced when one combines this test with other visual memorial and visuoconstructional measures that are incrementally sensitive to dementing illness when administered jointly.

The TTO presents an important addition to any standardized mental status examination, and it has wide applicability in neuropsychiatric screening for a wide variety of conditions. Knowledgeable use can alert clinicians to the minor cognitive lapses associated with residual or prodromal temporal disorientation, which may herald the onset of a reversible dementing condition while there still is time for clinical treatment to be optimally effective. The TTO is sensitive to minor lapses of cognitive efficiency, and its exceptionally broad range can document and monitor even gross fluctuations and deficit in temporal orientation as an indicator of mental status efficiency. Benton et al.'s TTO should become an integral part of the standard neurologic and psychiatric examination of mental status.

References

Benton, A.L. (1975). Psychological tests for brain damage. In A.M. Freedman, H.I. Kaplan, & B.J. Sadock (Eds.), *Comprehensive textbook of psychiatry* (Vol. 1, 2nd ed., pp. 757–768). Baltimore: Williams & Wilkins.

Benton, A.L., Hamsher, K.deS., Varney, N.R., & Spreen, O. (1983). *Contributions to neuropsychological assessment.* New York: Oxford University Press.

Benton, A.L., Van Allen, M.W., & Fogel, M.L. (1964). Temporal orientation in cerebral disease. *Journal of Nervous and Mental Disease, 139,* 110–119.

Eslinger, P.J., Damasio, A.R., Benton, A.L., & Van Allen, M. (1985). Neuropsychologic detection of abnormal mental decline in older persons. *Journal of the American Medical Association, 253,* 670–674.

Jones, R.D., Tranel, D., Benton, A., & Paulsen, J. (1992). Differentiating dementia from "pseudodementia" early in the clinical course: Utility of neuropsychological tests. *Neuropsychology, 6,* 13–21.

Joslyn, D., & Hutzell, R.R. (1979). Temporal disorientation in schizophrenia and brain-damaged patients. *American Journal of Psychiatry, 136,* 1220–1222.

Levin, H.S., & Benton, A.L. (1975). Temporal orientation in patients with brain disease. *Applied Neurophysiology, 38,* 56–60.

Natelson, B.H., Haupt, E.J., Fleischer, E.J., & Grey, L. (1979). Temporal orientation and education: A direct relationship in normal people. *Archives of Neurology, 36,* 444–446.

Varney, N.R., & Shepherd, J.S. (1991). Predicting short-term memory on the basis of temporal orientation. *Neuropsychology, 5,* 13–16.

Jennifer Ryan Hsu, Ph.D.
Associate Professor of Communication Disorders, William Paterson College, Wayne, New Jersey.

Louis Michael Hsu, Ph.D.
Professor of Psychology, Fairleigh Dickinson University, Teaneck, New Jersey.

TEST OF WORD FINDING

Diane J. German. Allen, Texas: DLM Teaching Resources.

Introduction

The Test of Word Finding (TWF) is an instrument designed to describe the word-finding skills of elementary school children. The current version of the test consists of five naming task sections and an additional section for assessing comprehension. The TWF yields two formal summary measures (an accuracy score and a response latency score), which classify examinees as belonging to one of the following four profiles: fast and inaccurate namers (Profile A), slow and inaccurate namers (Profile B), fast and accurate namers (Profile C), or slow and accurate namers (Profile D). The comprehension task, which is an informal procedure, is designed to distinguish between those children manifesting naming difficulties with good comprehension of the target words and those manifesting naming difficulties with poor comprehension. The former are considered to have word-finding problems. In addition, the TWF includes procedures for evaluating the frequency of gestures and extra verbalizations accompanying naming responses as well as procedures for analyzing the types of naming substitutions manifested by the examinee. The results of the TWF may be combined with other assessment data to diagnose the presence of a word-finding problem.

The TWF was developed by Dr. Diane German, currently a professor of special education and holder of the Ryan Endowed Chair at National-Louis University. The Ryan Endowed Chair was created to support her research on word finding. As a professor in special education, Dr. German's experience includes directing the Learning Disabilities Teacher Training Program as well as the Diagnostic and Remedial Clinic for Children with language and learning disorders at the College of Racine in Racine, Wisconsin. In addition, she directed the certification program in learning disabilities at the University of Wisconsin–Parkside, Kenosha, Wisconsin. She has an extensive list of published papers and has given numerous presentations in the area of word-finding disorders in children. Her publications have appeared in respected journals such as *Language, Speech, and Hearing Services in*

The reviewers would like to thank Amy Anderson for her comments on the TWF and her assistance in the literature search for this review. We are also grateful to Ann Klunk and the students in the spring 1991 William Paterson College course on language disorders in children for their comments on the test.

Schools; *Journal of Speech and Hearing Research; British Journal of Disorders of Commu-nication;* and *Journal of Learning Disabilities.* Her presentations include miniseminars at annual conventions of the American Speech-Language-Hearing Association as well as short courses at various conferences.

German developed the TWF over an 8-year period between 1976 and 1984. In 1984 a national standardization program was conducted, with a sample consisting of 1,200 normal children residing in 18 states and attending Grades 1 through 6. There were 200 children in each of six grade levels and, with the exception of the youngest age group, over 100 in each of seven age groups. The sample ranged in age from 6:6 to 12:11, with six of the age groups spanning a 12-month interval. The youngest group spanned a 6-month interval (6:6 to 6:11) and included only 93 children. The distribution of the children according to sex, geographic region, parent education level, and ethnicity or race closely matched the percentages reported in the 1980 census (German, 1986a). With respect to geographic region, the children were selected from the Northeastern, North Central, Southern, and Western United States. The subjects represented families classified in terms of three categories of parental education: a high school education or less, 1 to 3 years of college, or 4 or more years of college. The sample also included representative subsamples of children from Caucasian and minority backgrounds.

In addition to the 1,200 normal children, 40 children with word-finding prob-lems (termed *linguistically handicapped*) were tested. Some slight differences existed between the normal and linguistically handicapped children with respect to their distribution on three of the demographic variables. With respect to geographic region, there were no linguistically handicapped children from the Northeast. All children in the standardization group were drawn from either small communities, large urban communities, or rural areas.

The TWF consists of a test booklet, an administration manual, a technical man-ual, and a response booklet. The test booklet uses a convenient easel format with all instructions clearly printed at the beginning of the stimulus materials and on the back of each stimulus item. Color-coded dividers clearly mark the beginning of each section. The administration manual also includes detailed directions for administering the test, as well as instructions for scoring the responses and inter-preting the results. The response booklet provides space for recording and scoring responses to each item in the five naming sections and in the comprehension task. The front page of the booklet summarizes all performance measures, including the child's profile classification, and the back page outlines the procedures for determining a child's profile classification.

The TWF consists of two forms: Primary, for children enrolled in Grades 1 and 2, and Intermediate, for children in Grades 3 through 6. The Primary form con-tains 80 items and the Intermediate contains 90. Among the five naming sections in the TWF, three involve naming items presented in a picture. The titles of these sections indicate the types of words to be named (i.e., Picture Naming: Nouns, Picture Naming: Verbs, and Picture Naming: Categories). A fourth section (Sen-tence Completion Naming) requires naming a word that will complete a sentence (i.e., a cloze procedure), and a fifth (Description Naming) involves naming an item in response to a description that presents three attributes of the target word. The following description illustrates the type of item included in this section:

"What is used to slide on ice, has a blade, and has a top made of leather?" (*Answer:* skate).

German designed the final section, the comprehension task, to assess understanding of all the target words in the naming tasks that elicited an error. A picture selection task is used whereby the child responds to the command "Point to the _____." The stimulus items appear in two rows of four pictures per page. As noted by Donahue (1989), the array of pictures could be confusing to some children. Items in Sentence Completion Naming involve an additional task of selecting the appropriate picture in response to the original sentence stimulus; items in Description Naming involve an additional picture selection response to the original set of descriptions. Because only erred items are given, the examiner must check errors and locate the appropriate set of pictures. Administration could be facilitated by the inclusion of tabs identifying each item.

Practical Applications/Uses

The primary purpose of the TWF is to provide a description of a child's word-finding abilities. According to the manual (German, 1989b), this description may be used in conjunction with other assessment data to confirm the presence of a word-finding difficulty, and the inclusion of normative data in the TWF does support this application. Users also may find the test helpful in documenting a child's progress over time, via the response accuracy and response latency scores; however, clinicians should note McCauley and Swisher's (1984b) cautions regarding the use of norm-referenced tests for this purpose. During intervention, the identification of naming strategies and the count of secondary characteristics could serve to document changes in a child's performance during the course of therapy. German (1989b) also claims that the test results are useful in planning intervention programs for children with word-finding difficulties. Although little guidance is provided in the TWF manuals for this particular application, a teacher's manual for word-finding intervention was being prepared at the time of this writing (D.J. German, personal communication, August 14, 1991). Finally, this test could be used for research purposes (Donahue, 1989; Drum, 1989).

The TWF should be administered to children who range in age from 6 years, 6 months to 12 years, 11 months and are suspected of having word-finding difficulties. One likely will find such children among those considered to have learning disabilities, specific language impairments, neurological or perceptual impairments, dyslexia or other reading difficulties, and fluency disorders. The test is not appropriate for children with visual or hearing impairments.

The TWF may be administered by speech/language pathologists, learning disabilities teachers, school psychologists, reading specialists, special education teachers, and other individuals trained in psycholinguistics and/or language disorders in children. German (1989b) states that the examiner should have knowledge and experience in administering, scoring, and interpreting psychoeducational diagnostic instruments. Preparation should include careful reading of the administration manual and a review of all of the test materials. Although German (1989b) states that the examiner should complete five trial administrations, more practice may be required for a smooth presentation of items, reliable scoring, and reliable interpretation of the results. (Donahue, 1989, makes a similar point.) There is no discussion of the amount of training and practice required for accurate estimation of response times (a latency measure that practitioners may elect to use).

Examiners should administer the TWF on an individual basis in a room with adequate lighting and limited distractions. The student and the examiner should sit across from one another with the test booklet between them. The TWF takes approximately 20 to 30 minutes to administer. The manual (German, 1989b) states that administration should take place in one session and the presentation of the stimuli must be continuous. Valid administration of the test requires that the pictorial stimuli be presented immediately following the child's response without any delay during or between page presentations (German, 1989b).

The test sections and items within each section must be presented in the order the test booklet prescribes. Although the TWF is easy to administer, the examiner must learn to maintain a continuous presentation of the picture stimuli while simultaneously recording incorrect responses and checking items that elicited extra verbalizations, gestures, and excessive response latencies. One of many positive features of the test manual is that the instructions for administration are extremely clear.

Scoring the TWF involves several procedures, among them deriving measures for accuracy and response latency. The scores for accuracy include a Total Raw Score, which is converted to a Accuracy Standard Score and/or percentile rank. With respect to response latency, examiners may choose between two procedures: Estimated Item Response Time (ERT) or Actual Total Item Response Time (TRT). The accuracy and latency scores classify children relative to their speed and accuracy in naming, and this classification is termed a Word Finding Profile. In addition, the TWF yields several informal measures: 1) percent of known words, 2) prorated Accuracy Standard Score, 3) a count of the gestures or extra verbalizations, and 4) an optional measure of completion time based on the time taken to complete three of the naming sections. Finally, substitution errors on the naming tasks may be classified according to type.

German defines the Total Raw Score as the total number of correct responses on the five naming sections. The information is summarized in the Accuracy Score Summary located on the cover page of the response booklet. Using tables with normative statistics for either age or grade level, the user converts the Total Raw Score into the Accuracy Standard Score and percentile rank. According to the manual, only the converted scores are meaningful in evaluating the child's performance.

The response latency measures, Estimated Item Response Time (ERT) and Actual Total Item Response Time (TRT), are based on the child's speed in naming items on Section 1, Picture Naming: Nouns. As noted previously, examiners have the option of choosing between the two procedures. ERT involves estimating whether the time between the presentation of a picture stimulus and the child's first effort to name the target word exceeded 4 seconds. The number of delayed responses on Section 1 are determined and recorded on the cover page of the response booklet. TRT involves measuring and adding the actual times for naming individual items in Section 1. The examiner also records the TRT on the cover page of the response booklet. He or she then calculates a student's average response time (ART) for each item in Section 1 by dividing the TRT by the number

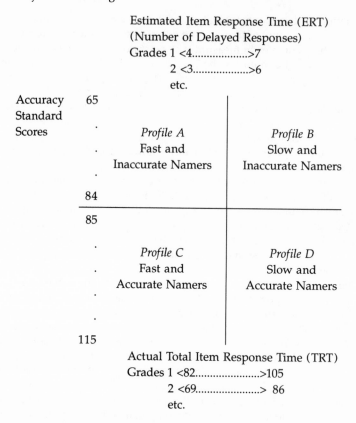

Fig. 1. Diagram of the TWF accuracy and time chart for identifying a child's Word-Finding Profile

of items. The divisor varies depending on the form in use (Primary or Intermediate). The procedure for calculating the ART is clearly outlined on the cover page of the response booklet.

Once the Accuracy Standard Score and response latency score have been determined, the child's word-finding profile is identified. A chart listing the four possible profiles appears on the back of the response booklet. As indicated in Fig. 1, a vertical axis on the left indicates the range of Accuracy Standard Scores and the horizontal axis indicates response latency, with the range of ERT scores at the top and the range of TRT scores at the bottom.

The Accuracy Standard Score of 85 is considered the cutoff for separating accurate namers (i.e., children with scores of 85 and above) from inaccurate namers (i.e., children with scores of 84 and below). The critical response latency score, which varies as a function of grade level, bisects the chart into "slow" and "fast" namers (see Fig. 1).

The examiner circles the child's obtained Accuracy Standard Score (based on either age or grade) and his or her ERT or TRT scores on the chart. The location of the intersection of the two lines in one of the four quadrants indicates the child's word-finding "profile," which is then recorded on the cover page of the response booklet.

Although cutoff scores are identified for both the accuracy and response latency scores, alternative cutoffs also are indicated. German (1989b) states that these alternative scores may be used if the examiner feels they may identify a more appropriate proportion of accurate and inaccurate namers and/or a more appropriate proportion of slow and fast namers. Unfortunately the test materials give little guidance for decisions regarding the use of these alternative scores.

If the child's profile indicates a possible word-finding problem, then responses on the comprehension section are scored. According to the manual (German, 1989b, pp. 97–101), a low accuracy score and/or a long latency score indicate a possible problem. The purpose of the comprehension section is to determine whether the child knows the target words that he or she was unable to name. For the picture naming sections (i.e., naming of nouns, verbs, and categories), the examiner bases this decision on a straightforward count of the items not comprehended; for the sentence completion and description naming sections, items with errors on either the sentence or the word are counted as incorrect. The author states (D.J. German, personal communication, December 23, 1991) that

> In order to assure sentences well as vocabulary comprehension, a yes score on both the sentence and the target word is required. Therefore when scoring, one no (either target word or sentence) is considered a comprehension error. The double scoring of each item helps the examiner determine whether a student's lack of understanding of the sentences could have contributed to the naming errors on those items in Sections 2 and 3. A yes on both suggests that the student understood not only the target word, but the sentence also.

When the number of comprehension errors have been counted to derive the total number of unknown words, this number is then subtracted from the total number of items administered (i.e., 80 for the Primary form and 90 for the Intermediate form) to obtain the number of known words. The examiner then calculates the percentage of words comprehended by the child by dividing the number of known words by the number of items on the test. Cutoff scores provided determine whether the child manifests word-finding difficulties and high comprehension. German (1989b) states that such children would be considered to fit the classical definition of a word-finding disorder. She recommends that children who manifest low comprehension (operationally defined as lower than 90% or 95% on the Primary and Intermediate forms, respectively) should be evaluated for a possible comprehension deficit (German, 1989b).

The TWF materials recommend an additional scoring procedure for those children manifesting low comprehension. This step, a Prorated Accuracy Rescoring, is intended to determine whether a child has word-finding difficulties on words that he or she knows. The examiner first calculates the percentage of known words named correctly. The percentage then is converted to a Prorated Accuracy Score, which in turn is converted to a standard score. The examiner uses the standard score to determine whether the child falls within the normal range of word-finding skills for his or her age or grade level (i.e., the score classifies the child as an accurate or inaccurate namer). In essence, one uses the Prorated Accuracy Score to determine a standard score for word finding that takes into account deficiencies in comprehension. Prorated standard scores that fall above the cutoff of 85 indicate that naming errors occurred for the most part on unknown words. Prorated standard scores falling below the cutoff (i.e., 84 or lower) suggest that naming errors have occurred on both known and unknown words.

The Prorated Accuracy Rescoring procedure is recommended as a means of assessing word-finding skills in children who may have comprehension deficits. German (1989b) suggests that the procedure may help evaluate the word-finding skills of bilingual students with low receptive vocabulary skills in standard English.

The TWF includes three additional informal scoring procedures. First, the examiner may obtain an optional completion time screening measure to determine the child's overall speed in naming. The score represents the combined completion times for three of the naming sections (naming nouns, verbs, and categories). Scores may be compared to standards for each grade level. A second informal procedure involves determining the percentage of items in all sections combined on which the student manifested gestures and/or extra verbalizations. Finally, if the examinee manifested accuracy standard scores below the cutoff but a normal comprehension score, then one can analyze the substitution errors. This procedure involves classifying substitution errors by means of categories specified in the manual and then counting the number of substitutions occurring in each category. The substitution categories for four of the naming sections are further classified in terms of three general categories: semantic, perceptual, and nonspecific words. An additional "other" category is identified that includes circumlocutions and substitutions plus self-corrections. The classification process is facilitated by the manual's clear definitions and multiple examples.

According to the manual (German, 1989b), the TWF should be the first step in the assessment of a child's word-finding abilities, and the results obtained then should guide further testing. Thus, the interpretation of the scores consists of formulating hypotheses, which are evaluated later in follow-up testing (German, 1989b, p. 103). This cautious approach to interpreting results illustrates another positive feature of the TWF. However, only limited recommendations appear regarding follow-up procedures. As it is suggested that the TWF comprise part of an overall assessment, it would be helpful for the manual to suggest specific follow-up tests or procedures and to include guidelines for interpreting the results of the test battery.

Interpreting TWF results involves classifying a child as an inaccurate or accurate namer and as a fast or slow namer. These decisions are a straightforward outcome of using the scoring procedures to identify a child's word-finding profile. As noted in the discussion of scoring, the Accuracy Standard Scores and the percentile ranks may be determined from either age or grade-level norms. Decisions concerning which norms to use (age or grade level) are left to the clinician's judgment. Furthermore, only limited guidelines appear for the interpretation of percentile ranks. The latency data are compared to cut scores for the student's grade level.

Although German (1989b) indicates that a critical cutoff score of 85 generally should apply to distinguish between "accurate" and "inaccurate" namers, she also indicates that this score may be inappropriate for some populations. In populations where this cut score would seem to over- or underestimate the correct proportion of "accurate" (or "inaccurate") namers, German (1989b) suggests using alternative cutoffs. She makes similar recommendations for latency cut scores. These recommendations suggest that the meaning of the same TWF score (e.g., an accuracy score of 85) does not generalize to all populations. This type of meaning does not appear to be consistent with the Rasch model (see below), and it further presents serious problems to the practitioner insofar as the manual does not identify the populations for which the conventional cut scores would be inappropriate.

A critical issue in interpreting the results of the TWF is whether a child's naming and latency performance reflect word-finding difficulties or a comprehension deficit. The TWF includes the comprehension section to enable the differential diagnosis of a word-finding problem. (See the Critique for a discussion of limitations of the comprehension results.) German (1989b) identifies three types of children. *Type 1* fits the classical definition of a word-finding problem; that is, word-finding difficulties in the presence of good comprehension. Children classified as manifesting high comprehension and Profiles A, B, or D are likely Type 1 (German, 1989b). Children with low comprehension scores may have either a comprehension deficit alone (viz., a Type 2 classification) or such a deficit in combination with a word-finding problem (viz., a Type 3 classification). The *Type 2* child manifests word-finding difficulties for the most part on unknown words. The *Type 3* child manifests word-finding difficulties on both known and unknown words.

Although the TWF is not recommended as a tool for diagnosing a comprehension deficit, it does provide some information that may help to differentiate Type 2 and Type 3 children (German, 1989b). The Prorated Accuracy Rescoring procedure for low comprehension is intended to determine if the student also manifested naming errors on known TWF target words. If the prorated accuracy score falls above 85, the results suggest that the child performed on the TWF like one who would be classified in the Type 2 category (i.e., he or she made naming errors, for the most part, on words not known on the TWF). If, on the other hand, the prorated accuracy score is below 85, then the results indicate that the child performed on the TWF like one who would be classified as Type 3 (i.e., manifesting word-finding difficulties on known TWF words in conjunction with naming errors on unknown words).

As noted previously, the scoring procedures provide a count of the number of gestures and extra verbalizations. The manual (German, 1989b) suggests that these behaviors, termed Secondary Characteristics, may provide information related to confirming the existence of a word-finding problem. In particular, the manual states that secondary characteristics on 25% or more of the items, along with a low accuracy score, a high number of delayed responses, and a high comprehension score, suggest word-finding problems on the TWF.

German (1989b) recommends analyzing the substitution errors of students with suspected word-finding difficulties to determine any unique naming patterns. The manual indicates that identifying specific naming patterns may prove useful in establishing goals, remediation programming, and self-advocacy counseling for students manifesting word-finding difficulties on the TWF (German, 1989b, p.

89). However, no examples illustrate how to use the results of the substitution analysis. German indicates (personal communication, December 23, 1991) that this type of information is included in her forthcoming teacher's manual on word-finding intervention.

Technical Aspects

The reliability statistics reported in the technical manual (German, 1986a) include test-retest coefficients and internal consistency coefficients of the TWF scores. Two studies of test-retest reliability are discussed (German, 1986a). In the first, the TWF was administered twice to 30 normally learning students in Grades 1 through 6 by two trained examiners. A period of 10 to 14 days intervened between the two testing sessions. The technical manual reports a partial correlation of .91 between the composite accuracy raw scores (i.e., Total Raw Score for number of correct items), partialling out grade level. The second study involved 20 second-grade and 30 third- and fourth-grade normally learning children who were tested a second time after a 10- to 14-day interval. Test-retest correlations of raw accuracy scores were .85 for the second-grade children and .90 for the third- and fourth-graders.

Examination of Table 4-8 in the technical manual indicates that the difference in the test-retest correlations cannot be attributed to range restriction effects. The test-retest correlation of the Accuracy Standard Scores for the combined groups was .82. In line with Kaplan and Saccuzzo (1982) and McCauley and Swisher's (1984a) suggestion that correlation coefficients of .90 or better indicate adequate test-retest reliability, there appears to be good stability for the raw accuracy scores obtained from children in the third and fourth grades. The author indicates (D.J. German, personal communication, August 14, 1991) that the difference between the partial correlation (.91) of the composite accuracy scores and the correlation (.82) of the standard accuracy score reported for the combined groups can be attributed to three factors: 1) use of different student populations in the two studies, 2) use of different versions of the TWF, and 3) use of different scores.

The stability of two of the latency measures, the average item response time and the composite completion time, was also investigated (German, 1986a). The test-retest correlations for the second-graders were .87 for the average item response time and .63 for the composite completion time. For the third- and fourth-graders, the correlations were .65 for the average item response time and .80 for the composite completion times. The variation in the coefficients across grade levels indicates that test-retest reliabilities are not generalizable across grade levels. Furthermore, because the average item response time is derived from the TRT (total response time), the results also indicate that the TRT varies across grade levels and is unstable for third- and fourth-graders. This suggests that the word-finding profiles, which are based on both Accuracy Standard Scores and either a child's ERT (estimated response time) or TRT, are also likely to be somewhat unstable for these groups.

German (1989b) investigated the relationship between the TRT and ERT measures in a study of 66 children with word-finding difficulties and 66 normally learning children, reporting correlation coefficients for the two scores that ranged from .90 to .94. She concludes that examiners may use the ERT procedure and obtain results that are consistent with the actual item response times. However, it should be recognized that because ERTs are estimated by individual examiners, correlations involving ERTs are examiner-specific. Thus, large differences in these correlations conceivably could occur across examiners for the same set of examinee responses. Recognition of this fact is important, as the manual indicates one can use ERT measures instead of the TRT to identify a child's word-finding profile.

The technical manual does not report any interrater reliability studies. It is important to determine whether practitioners who use the test manifest agreement on scores, classifications of examinees, and diagnostic decisions as well as on goal selection and remedial programming.

German (1986a) reported some classical internal consistency statistics for Primary and Intermediate forms of the TWF: Kuder-Richardson formula 20 values extended from .69 for sixth-grade normally learning children to .83 for third- and fourth-grade normally learning children. The KR-20 value for the combined Grades 1 and 2 was .80, and the coefficient for the combined Grades 3 through 6 was .81. German (1986a) states that these relatively low reliability coefficients resulted from range restriction.

Construction of the TWF involved use of what German (1986a, p. 36) describes as "the Rasch latent trait model" for item selection. As Rasch has proposed more than one latent trait model (see Allen & Yen, 1979; Rasch, 1960, cited in Allen & Yen, 1979), it should be noted that the model used in the development of the TWF was the one-parameter logistic model. A critical assumption of this model is that the measured trait is unidimensional (Gustafsson, 1980; Hambleton & Cook, 1977).

Although the TWF manuals do not discuss the assumption of unidimensionality, the author states (D.J. German, personal communication, August 14, 1991) that "the TWF is designed to test only one dimension of word finding, i.e. convergent, discrete naming, also called constrained naming or single word retrieval." Furthermore, in the same communication she states that one would expect other measures of word finding to assess other dimensions of word finding. In view of these statements, it may be more appropriate to term the significant factor resulting from the factor analysis reported in the manual the "convergent discrete naming factor" rather than the "word finding factor" (see German, 1986a, p. 90). Because item selection procedures connected with the Rasch model eliminate items failing to meet discrimination and goodness-of-fit indices, it is possible that some valid measures of other dimensions of word-finding ability were eliminated. It is also important to note that the issue of the dimensionality of word-finding ability should be distinguished from the operations (or tasks) that have been used to assess word-finding ability.

German could strengthen the manual by clarifying both the dimension of word-finding ability measured by the TWF as well as the dimension(s) of word-finding abilities that the TWF does not measure (if these dimensions exist). Consistent with this comment, information about the characteristics of items deleted because of poor fit to the Rasch model would be desirable, as would information about degree of fit of rationally constructed subsets of these items to the Rasch model. A factor analysis of responses to all items in the original item pool might also provide useful information about the dimensionality of word-finding abilities, as would factor analyses involving the combined items of the TWF and other measures of word-finding ability. As noted by Gustafsson (1980), "factor analytic methods are likely to give much information about the dimensionality and grouping of the items that is impossible to obtain in any other way" (p. 217).

An additional assumption (besides unidimensionality) of the Rasch one-parameter logistic model is that all items selected for the test have the same discriminative power. That is, all the item characteristic curves are parallel. As a result, items are considered to differ only in terms of difficulty. Other latent trait models allow items to differ in terms of more than one parameter. For example, two-parameter logistic models allow items to differ in terms of discriminative power as well as difficulty. Items deleted because of poor fit to a Rasch model may actually be shown to be perfectly good measures of the unidimensional construct when one fits the two-parameter model to the data (see Gustafsson, 1980). If both models appear reasonable, then it would be desirable to compare fits of competing models. It is not unusual for a two-parameter latent trait model to fit a data set better than a one-parameter model (see, e.g., Hambleton & Traub, 1973, cited in Allen & Yen, 1979). It is important to note that in responding to these recommendations, German and her colleagues D. Kistler and F. Schrank assert (personal communication, August 14, 1991) that the one-parameter model is the only one appropriate for the TWF and that there is no practical way to use a two- or three-parameter model in a clinical instrument such as the TWF. In the same personal communication, she states the belief that the work of Wright and his colleagues support that position.

Procedures for selecting items to fit the Rasch model and then "testing" the fit of the retained items have been criticized because these "tests" generally yield spurious fit (see Gustafsson, 1980). It is not surprising (or particularly informative) to report that a set of items, as well as individual items in the set, fit a Rasch model when those items that did not fit the model were systematically discarded from that set. Overall-fit and item-fit mean squares reported in the manual (pp. 37–44) are of this type. More useful would be information that 1) the set of items that were deleted when fitting the Rasch model to the calibration sample ($N = 210$) would also have been deleted had another sample been used; 2) estimates of item difficulties are also independent of the sample tested; and 3) estimates of ability levels of the subjects are independent of the subsets of items in the scale. It is generally this type of information (particularly #2 and #3 above) that provides the strongest evidence of tenability of assumptions of the Rasch model (see Gustafsson, 1980). Empirical evidence relating to #2 would also be welcome, in view of the fact that German's calibration sample consisted of only 210 subjects. According to Kline (1986), a minimum of 1,000 subjects should be included in the calibration sample before Rasch scaling can be expected to be sample free. German states (personal communication, August 14, 1991) that the

> item selection procedures employed in the development of the TWF using Rasch were those recommended by Wright & Stone, 1979. In addition, although additional calibration samples were not used, random split sampling was conducted on the TWF calibration sample. Using Rasch analyses, good agreement was shown between these random split samples.

The two TWF manuals (German, 1986a, 1989b) report findings related to content, concurrent, and construct validity of the TWF. With respect to content validity, there are two important issues: defining the relevant behavioral domain and adequately sampling the domain. (See American Educational Research Association, American Psychological Association, & National Council on Measurement in Education, 1985; Anastasi, 1982; Lieberman & Michael, 1986; and Suen, 1990, for a general discussion of these issues.) In an extensive review of the literature on word-finding difficulties in children and adult aphasics, German (1986a, 1988, 1989a, 1989b) provides a rationale for the structure of the test. A number of studies (see literature reviews in German, 1986a, 1989a, 1989b; Wiig & Becker-Caplan, 1984; Wiig & Semel, 1984) indicate the relevance of naming objects in detecting word-finding difficulties in children and the relevance of using three types of stimulus contexts (i.e., naming pictured objects as well as naming in response to a spoken definition and naming in response to a cloze procedure) as well as both accuracy and response latency measures.

Several studies were conducted to establish the concurrent validity of the TWF. Four tests—the Boston Naming Test, the Expressive One-Word Picture Vocabulary Test (EOWPVT), The Word Test (Synonyms and Antonyms), and the rapid "automatized" naming (R.A.N.) test—were administered to 39 normally learning children ranging from Grades 2 through 4. The tests were selected because they were designed to assess oral production or they had been used as supplemental tests in word-finding assessment batteries (German, 1986a). Among the tests that yielded accuracy scores, the correlation coefficients were .52, .55, .70, and .75 for The Word Test–Antonyms, The Word Test–Synonyms, Boston Naming Test, and EOWPVT, respectively. The R.A.N., which is scored in terms of the number of errors, yielded a correlation coefficient of –.56. German noted (personal communication, August 14, 1991) that this moderate correlation was not surprising, as the R.A.N. uses a continuous format and the TWF is a discrete naming task. The R.A.N. and the TWF also differ with respect to the type of items. For example, the R.A.N. includes the naming of colors, numbers, and letters as well as objects. In contrast, the Boston Naming Test and the EOWPVT, which yielded higher correlations with the TWF, involve the naming of objects. Overall, the results suggest that performance of normally learning children may differ depending on the types of items and types of tasks used in an assessment of naming.

In a second concurrent validity investigation, the TWF as well as two subtests of the Clinical Evaluation of Language Functions (Producing Names on Confrontation and Producing Word Associations) were administered to 20 children with word-finding difficulties. German (1986a) reports that the correlations for the TWF as compared to Producing Names on Confrontation (scored in terms of number of errors) and Producing Word Associations (scored in terms of number of words produced) were –.54 and .64, respectively. The low correlation between the TWF and the Producing Names on Confrontation test may be explained by the fact that the latter requires naming colors and geometric shapes. Producing Word Associations involves naming members of two semantic categories in 60 seconds. The moderate correlation with the TWF suggests that this type of task also taps some different abilities than the TWF tasks. Overall it appears that the items and tasks used by the TWF require some different naming abilities than those tapped by some of the tasks currently used to assess word-finding difficulties. German concurs (personal communication, August 14, 1991) and added that the convergent naming assessed by the TWF is different from the divergent naming assessed by word associations.

In another study, speech/language pathologists rated 20 children with word-finding difficulties on a scale describing behaviors associated with word-finding problems. Pearson product-moment correlations between the TWF standard scores and the number of characteristics identified on the survey were –.57 (German, 1986a).

Investigations related to the the construct validity of the TWF included a study of the relationship between scores on the TWF and age, a factor analysis of the TWF, and studies on the extent to which the TWF differentiates between children with normal word-finding abilities and those with word-finding disorders. German (1986a) reports a correlation of .51 between TWF accuracy scores (scale scores generated by the Rasch analyses and age); a correlation of –.49 between TRT scores and age; and a correlation of .46 between composite completion times and age. These results, which are consistent with other reports (see Denckla & Rudel, 1974; Wiig & Becker-Caplan, 1984) of developmental trends in word-finding abilities, suggest a moderate relationship between age and performance on the TWF. In view of the fact that the Rasch one-parameter logistic model was used for item selection, it is not too surprising that a principal-components analysis with varimax rotation yielded only one factor with an eigenvalue greater than 1, which German (1986a) labeled "word finding." The five sections of the TWF had loadings (i.e., correlations with this factor) ranging from .71 to .81 for the primary grade subjects and .67 to .75 for the intermediate grade subjects (German, 1986a). It is important to note that the factor accounted for less than 50% of the variance in the scales of the TWF.

Several studies have investigated the extent to which the TWF distinguishes between normally learning children and those with word-finding difficulties. In one study (German, 1986a), researchers administered the TWF to 29 children with word-finding difficulties and 29 normal peers matched in terms of sex, age, grade, ethnicity, and geographic region. The children with word-finding difficulties were selected on the basis of several criteria, including an independent diagnosis by a speech/language pathologist and evidence of at least 10 word-finding characteristics on a speech/language pathologist–completed word-finding survey. The subjects, who were selected from the Chicago metropolitan area, ranged in age from 6 years, 6 months to 12 years, 6 months. A one-way analysis of variance indicated that accuracy scores for the children with word-finding problems were significantly lower on each section than those of the matched normals (p values ranged from < .001 to < .01) (German 1986a).

In a second study (German, 1986a), the performance of 33 primary grade children (first- and second-graders) with word-finding difficulties was compared to that of 33 matched normally learning children. The subjects were selected from the standardization sample, and the selection criteria described previously were used. German (1986a) reports that children with word-finding difficulties had significantly lower accuracy scores ($p < .001$), longer composite completion times ($p < .001$), and longer TRT scores ($p < .001$).

In a third study (German, 1986a), the TWF was administered to 33 intermediate grade children (third- through sixth-graders) with word-finding difficulties and 33 matched normal children. The children with word-finding difficulties, also selected using the guidelines described previously, had significantly lower accuracy scores ($p < .001$), significantly longer composite completion times ($p < .001$), and significantly longer TRT scores ($p < .001$) (German, 1986a).

The findings related to the accuracy scores and TRT scores have been confirmed in a recent study by German and Simon (1991). Composite completion times were not measured in this study. These statistics are consistent with the view that the TWF can discriminate between children who have word-finding difficulties and those who do not. Such findings are important as a major purpose of the test is to differentiate between children with and without word-finding difficulties on discrete naming tasks. In addition, a recent study by Wing (1990) indicates that the TWF can detect improvements in word-finding abilities that result from remedial training.

An important consideration is the extent to which results of the TWF accurately identify children with word-finding difficulties. Using an a priori criterion Accuracy Standard Score of 85, German (1986a) reports that 1% (15 subjects) of the normal children in the standardization sample were misclassified (i.e., false positives). This type of misclassification most likely will be corrected with further testing or when the child enrolls in therapy and manifests normal word-finding abilities. A more serious type of misclassification is the false negative. Although the manuals do not explicitly report false negative misclassification rates, there are some relevant statistics reported by German (1986a) from a study that compared the TWF performances of 33 children with word-finding difficulties and 33 normally developing children. Using the accuracy scores to classify the children as inaccurate, accurate, or very accurate namers, the TWF classified 90% of the primary grade and 97% of the intermediate grade children with word-finding problems as inaccurate namers (German, 1986a). These results indicate that between 3% and 10% of these children were classified as accurate namers.

German (1986a) also reports that in the same study, 12% of the normal children were classified as inaccurate namers. Using the TRT latency measure to classify the children as slow namers, average namers and fast namers, German (1986a) reports that among the primary age groups, 39% of the children with word-finding problems were classified as slow namers, whereas 9% of the normal children were classified as slow namers. Among the intermediate grade level children, 61% of the children with word-finding difficulties and 12% of the normal children were classified as slow namers. Finally, using both accuracy scores and TRT latency measures to classify children in terms of the four word-finding problems, German (1986a) reports results summarized in Table 1.

Statistics in Table 1 indicate that 10% of the primary children with word-finding difficulties were classified as not manifesting word finding difficulties in the TWF convergent naming tasks. However, there appear to be no misclassifications among the intermediate group. These statistics also indicate that inaccurate naming responses appear to be characteristic of most children with word-finding difficulties, while long latencies may be characteristic of approximately half of these children.

Table 1

Percentage of Normally Developing Children and Those with Word-Finding Difficulties Classified According to Naming Profiles (German, 1986a)

| | Types of Children | | | |
| | Primary | | Intermediate | |
Profile	Normal	Word-Finding Problems	Normal	Word-Finding Problems
Slow and Inaccurate	12[a]	42	6	58
Fast and Inaccurate		48	6	39
Fast and Accurate	76	10	79	0
Slow and Accurate	12	0	9	3

[a]The manual reports a combined percentage for normal primary children in the Slow and Inaccurate and Fast and Inaccurate categories.

In summary, German has addressed some of the major issues regarding the reliability and validity of the TWF. The amount of research that has been done is a positive feature of the test. However, the results suggest some areas that need further study. With respect to reliability, the author should undertake additional studies to determine test-retest reliabilities for ERT scores and the extent to which correlations involving ERTs are examiner-dependent. Information is also needed on interrater agreement in diagnostic decisions. As mentioned previously, the manual would be strengthened by including data on the dimensionality (factor structure) of word-finding ability. This type of information would be relevant to the content and construct validity of the TWF. Furthermore, difficulty parameter estimates in cross-validation samples, plus stability of ability estimates of subjects across subsets of items, would provide useful information regarding the Rasch-model fit of the TWF items.

Critique

The TWF is a carefully designed instrument whose construction, standardization, and validation conforms closely to APA, AERA, and NCME recommendations (see *Standards for Educational and Psychological Testing*, 1985). As noted by Donahue (1989), "the extensive test development procedures and standardization efforts are described in detail, and represent an excellent model for other test developers to follow" (p. 856). Important features of these efforts are the size of the standardization sample, the clear definition of the nature of the sample, and the use of statistical tests to determine the extent to which the demographic characteristics relate to test performance. The careful design also is reflected in the stimuli, which are for the most part clear, unambiguous, and attractive. Furthermore, all of the materials are convenient to use, due in part to the inclusion of duplicate instructions in the manuals, the test book, and the response booklet.

Finally, the structure and content of the TWF is based on a thorough review of the research on word-finding difficulties in children and adults as well as a variety of studies completed by German. This information is summarized in the test manuals as well as in a journal article (German, 1989a). Donahue (1989) is correct in noting that the technical manual includes "not only a careful research review, but also a discussion of important factors influencing word-finding performance that underlie the design of the test" (p. 856). The variables considered in selecting the target words and the number of words representing each variable are clearly described, as is the rationale for the stimulus contexts included in the test.

Although much care was taken in the selection of the final sets of items, it should be reiterated that the procedure used to control for bias may have eliminated good items. German (1986a) systematically removed items whose proportions of correct responses differed significantly for gender groups (male and female), ethnic groups, and geographic regions. Although this strategy makes sense when groups are equated with respect to word-finding ability, it can lead to the elimination of good items when they are not. For example, if the word-finding ability level of one group falls considerably below that of a second group, one would *expect* the proportion passing a good item to be lower in the first group than in the second. Thus, relying on the presence of a difference between these proportions to delete items, without taking into account differences in ability levels, can lead to the elimination of good items.

In responding to the point (D.J. German, personal communication, August 14, 1991), the author suggests that consistent errors on a particular item by a particular group indicate that the item may not be part of the linguistic culture of the group and therefore not appropriate for the assessment of word-finding. She also notes that data reported in the manual (German, 1986a, pp. 44–47) did not, for the most part, indicate any differences as a function of stratification variables. However, it is difficult to reconcile this statement with the recommendation that practitioners may want to alter cut scores to adjust for differences between the performance of local populations and that of national norms (German, 1989b, pp. 74, 78). The reviewers do agree that it is vital to consider item bias when developing a test.

The exceptional amount of information on reliability and validity is a positive feature of the TWF. Furthermore, the amount of technical information included in the manuals is unusual. The Technical Aspects section of this review has commented on some additional reliability and validity information that would strengthen the TWF manuals. However, some further observations regarding the technical information need to be made. First, although test-retest reliabilities are reported (German, 1986a) for preliminary studies of children with word-finding difficulties, Donahue (1989) notes that the reliabilities for the final version are based only on normal children. It would be desirable if reported information on the standardized version of the TWF included test-retest and interrater reliabilities for children with word-finding difficulties.

Second, Drum (1989) comments that the predictive validity of the TWF has not been established. As suggested by Drum (1989), it would be important to show that the TWF predicts future academic difficulties and that improvement in word-finding abilities relates to improvement in specific areas of academic performance (p. 858).

Finally, German's inclusion of standard errors of measurement (SE_M) should remind practitioners that obtained scores are only estimates of true scores. Detailed information about SE_Ms is useful in the construction of confidence intervals for true scores. Of special interest is the dependence of the standard errors of measurement on the total scores. The reported SE_Ms indicate that precision of estimation of true scores varies with ability levels of the children. Of particular importance, with respect to evaluation of borderline scores, is the fact that precision tends to be good (i.e., SE_Ms tend to be small) in the region surrounding profile cut scores. On the negative side, it should be noted that no information is provided in the manual about regression toward the mean effects or about methods of estimating true scores that take regression effects into account. The manual would be strengthened by a description of these methods and a brief discussion of conditions under which they should be used.

Fried-Oken (1987) identifies two problems with naming tasks: the lack of differentiation between word recall problems and expressive vocabulary problems, and the lack of qualitative information obtained from the diagnostic instruments. The TWF partially addresses both of these issues. With respect to the differential diagnosis of a retrieval problem, the TWF includes a comprehension section to help determine whether the child knows items missed on the naming tasks. Although Fried-Oken (1987) describes an administration procedure for discriminating between comprehension and retrieval problems (viz., the Double Administration Naming Technique), the TWF is unique in its inclusion of the comprehension task as well as the alternative scoring procedures that take knowledge deficits into account. The comprehension task enables differentiation between children who have no knowledge of a word and those who have sufficient knowledge to correctly associate a picture with the word.

There is, however, disagreement on the level of semantic knowledge that can be assumed from correct responses on the comprehension task. German indicates (personal communication, December 23, 1991) that

> during the development of the TWF much attention was paid to the knowledge students had of the TWF target words. In fact, words difficult to comprehend were excluded during test development so that the final TWF target word list was understood by more than 95% of the standardization sample. Documentation of this can be found in Appendix A of the TWF manual where comprehension scores of all TWF items are presented.

In the same communication she also states that because in the TWF the student is presented with words that he or she most likely knows, the examiner can assume that when the child identifies the picture in the comprehension check, he or she knows the word well enough to retrieve it in the picture naming or sentence naming tasks. She further states that it is the student who cannot identify the TWF target words in the comprehension section, in the presence of a standardization sample that could, that needs further study. This student needs deep assessment in the area of semantic knowledge to clarify the nature of his or her word-finding difficulties.

In contrast, Donahue (1989) suggests that a correct response on the comprehension task does not require detailed knowledge of the meaning of the word. This issue is relevant to a more fundamental question regarding the underlying nature of naming difficulties in children. Leonard, Nippold, Kail, and Hale (1983), Kail, Hale, Leonard, and Nippold (1984), Kail and Leonard (1986) and McGregor and Leonard (1989) have argued that naming difficulties may derive either from problems in accessing a word (the retrieval hypothesis) or from deficiencies in the representation of a word in the child's lexicon (the elaboration hypothesis). Although Wing (1990) reports data supporting the retrieval hypothesis, Leonard and his colleagues report findings supporting the elaboration hypothesis. According to Leonard (personal communication, August 20, 1991), a simple picture selection task cannot distinguishing between children with accessing problems and those with limited knowledge of the word. (See Donahue, 1989, for additional discussion of this point.)

Clearly, there is a need for additional research on such issues. In view of these competing claims, it does seem possible that the TWF may not provide an unambiguous diagnosis of a retrieval problem for the child manifesting a low accuracy score and/or slow response latencies in conjunction with high comprehension (i.e., the Type 1 child). Furthermore, it may not unambiguously identify children with mixed knowledge and retrieval deficits (i.e., the Type 3 child). Because therapy procedures differ for knowledge versus retrieval deficits (see, e.g., Kail & Leonard, 1986; McGregor & Leonard, 1989; Wing, 1990), it is important for practitioners to confirm the diagnosis of a retrieval deficit. In view of the elaboration hypothesis, this may require in-depth testing of the child's semantic knowledge.

The TWF addresses the issue of a qualitative analysis of naming abilities by providing a detailed system for classifying substitution responses. Donahue (1989) is correct in noting that this is a valuable feature of the TWF. Clinicians seeking guidance in how to use the information in either the determination of goals or remedial programming may want to refer to articles by Fried-Oken (1987) and German (1982). Fried-Oken (1987) comments that substitutions may indicate the strategies that are not working for the child and that alternative strategies may be needed. A procedure that may help in differentiating between effective and ineffective strategies is outlined. German's (1982) article also suggests intervention strategies based on target-word substitutions.

The general issue of how the TWF's results contribute to classification decisions or to instructional methods is raised by Drum (1989). Some of these issues apparently will be addressed in the forthcoming teacher's manual on word-finding intervention. As this manual is intended to be a comprehensive review that integrates assessment and intervention (D.J. German, personal communication, August 14, 1991), it will be a welcome companion to the TWF.

German's method of combining accuracy and latency information, in relation to classifying children with respect to their word-finding ability, involved dichotomizing both the latency and the accuracy continua. Two of the resulting four quadrants (viz., Profile B, Slow and Inaccurate Namers, and Profile C, Fast and Accurate Namers) are relatively unambiguous. However, the other two quadrants are difficult to interpret. Information about external clinical correlates of membership in these four quadrants would be welcome. Furthermore, German should explore alternative methods of combining accuracy and latency scores, particularly with regard to optimal methods of combining these scores for clinical diagnosis and prognosis. No evidence appears in the manual showing that optimization methods, such as discriminant function, discriminant classification, or multiple regression analyses, have been used to combine latency and accuracy scores for these purposes. It also appears that these methods have not been used to combine scores on the five sections of the TWF for the same purposes.

In conclusion, German must be commended for her objective and scientific approach to test development and for the quality of the manuals. She also should be commended for her cautious approach to the use of the TWF in the diagnosis of word-finding difficulties. Her recommendation that the TWF should be used as the first step in the evaluation of word-finding abilities is underscored by the fact that 1) the test was designed to assess a single dimension of word-finding and 2) the validation results suggest that the dimension assessed differs from dimensions tapped by other informal measures. The design of the TWF, in conjunction with the extensive norms, make it a valuable addition to any comprehensive evaluation of the word-finding abilities of an elementary school–aged child.

References

Allen, M.J., & Yen, W.M. (1979). *Introduction to measurement theory.* Monterey, CA: Brooks/Cole.

American Educational Research Association, American Psychological Association, & National Council on Measurement in Education. (1985). *Standards for educational and psychological testing.* Washington, DC: American Psychological Association.

Anastasi, A. (1982). *Psychological testing* (5th ed.). New York: Macmillan.

Denckla, M.B., & Rudel, R. (1974). Rapid "automatized" naming of pictured objects, colors, letters and numbers by normal children. *Cortex, 10,* 186–202.

Donahue, M. (1989). Test of Word Finding. In J.C. Conoley & J.J. Kramer (Eds.), *The tenth mental measurements yearbook* (pp. 855–857). Lincoln, NE: Buros Institute of Mental Measurements.

Drum, P.A. (1989). Test of Word Finding. In J.C. Conoley & J.J. Kramer (Eds.), *The tenth mental measurements yearbook* (pp. 857–858). Lincoln, NE: Buros Institute of Mental Measurements.

Fried-Oken, M. (1987). Qualitative examination of children's naming skills through test adaptations. *Language, Speech, and Hearing Services in Schools, 18,* 206–216.

German, D.J. (1982). Word-finding substitutions in children with learning disabilities. *Language, Speech, and Hearing Services in Schools, 13,* 223–230.

German, D.J. (1986a). *Test of Word Finding (TWF): Technical manual.* Allen, TX: DLM Teaching Resources.

German, D.J. (1986b). *Test of Word Finding (TWF): Test book.* Allen, TX: DLM Teaching Resources.

German, D.J. (1988, November). *Word finding assessment and intervention for adolescents.* Mini-seminar presented at the annual meeting of the American Speech-Language-Hearing Association, Boston.

German, D.J. (1989a). A diagnostic model and a test to assess word-finding skills in children. *British Journal of Disorders of Communication, 24,* 21–39.

German, D.J. (1989b). *Test of Word Finding (TWF): Administration, scoring and interpretation manual.* Allen, TX: DLM Teaching Resources.

German, D.J. (1989c). *Test of Word Finding (TWF): Response booklet.* Allen, TX: DLM Teaching Resources.

German, D.J., & Simon, E. (1991). Analysis of children's word-finding skills in discourse. *Journal of Speech and Hearing Research, 34,* 309–316.

Gustafsson, J.E. (1980). Testing and obtaining fit of data to the Rasch model. *British Journal of Mathematical and Statistical Psychology, 33,* 205–233.

Hambleton, R.K., & Cook, L.L. (1977). Latent trait models and their use in the analysis of educational test data. *Journal of Educational Measurement, 14*(2), 75–96.

Kail, R., Hale, C.A., Leonard, L.B., & Nippold, M.A. (1984). Lexical storage and retrieval in language-impaired children. *Applied Psycholinguistics, 5,* 37–49.

Kail, R., & Leonard, L.B. (1986). Word-finding abilities in language-impaired children. *ASHA Monographs, 25.*

Kaplan, R.M., & Saccuzzo, D.P. (1982). *Psychological testing: Principles, applications and issues.* Monterey, CA: Brooks/Cole.

Kline, P. (1986). *A handbook of test construction: Introduction to psychometric design.* New York: Methuen.

Lieberman, R.J., & Michael, A. (1986). Content relevance and content coverage in tests of grammatical ability. *Journal of Speech and Hearing Disorders, 51,* 71–81.

Leonard, L.B., Nippold, M.A., Kail, R., & Hale, C.A. (1983). Picture naming in language-impaired children. *Journal of Speech and Hearing Disorders, 26,* 609–615.

McCauley, R.J., & Swisher, L. (1984a). Psychometric review of language and articulation tests for preschool children. *Journal of Speech and Hearing Disorders, 49,* 34–42.

McCauley, R.J., & Swisher, L. (1984b). Use and misuse of norm-referenced tests in clinical assessment: A hypothetical case. *Journal of Speech and Hearing Disorders, 49,* 338–348.

McGregor, K.K., & Leonard, L.B. (1989). Facilitating word-finding skills of language-impaired children. *Journal of Speech and Hearing Disorder, 54,* 141–147.

Suen, H.K. (1990). *Principles of test theories.* Hillsdale, NJ: Erlbaum.

Wiig, E.H., & Becker-Caplan, L. (1984). Linguistic retrieval strategies and word-finding difficulties among children with language disabilities. *Topics in Language Disorders, 4*(3), 1–18.

Wiig, E.H., & Semel, E. (1984). *Language assessment and intervention for the learning disabled* (2nd ed.). Columbus, OH: Merrill.

Wing, C.S. (1990). A preliminary investigation of generalization to untrained words following two treatments of children's word-finding problems. *Language, Speech, and Hearing Services in Schools, 21,* 151–156.

Selma Hughes, Ph.D.

Professor, Department of Psychology and Special Education, East Texas State University, Commerce, Texas.

TESTS OF LANGUAGE DEVELOPMENT: SECOND EDITION

Donald D. Hammill and Phyllis L. Newcomer. Austin, Texas: PRO-ED, Inc.

Introduction

The Tests of Language Development, consisting of Primary (TOLD-P:2) and Intermediate (TOLD-I:2) versions, are individually administered standardized tests designed to assess the receptive and expressive language abilities of children ages 4 through 12 in order to identify those with language problems.

The TOLD was first published in 1977 and covered the age range 4 years, 0 months to 8 years, 11 months. The format resembled that of the present TOLD-P:2. This original test was revised and renamed in 1982 as the Test of Language Development–Primary and the Test of Language Development–Intermediate. The latter was an upward extension of the Primary edition and assessed ages 8:6 to 12:11. The present TOLD-P:2 and TOLD-I:2 are 1988 revisions of the TOLD-P and TOLD-I, respectively.

The purpose of the revision was to include more difficult words on some of the subtests, to delete or reword items found to be ambiguous, and in general to ensure that the language of the test was representative of the language children need in everyday life today. No change was made in the theoretical foundations on which the test was based.

The TOLD-P:2 is designed to assess the comprehension and expression of spoken language in children from 4:0 through 8:11 years of age. The test is built on a linguistic model of language and incorporates the views of many researchers rather than adhering to one theoretical viewpoint about language. The seven TOLD-P:2 subtests are derived from a two-dimensional model of language structure that assesses three features of language (semantics, syntax, and phonology) and the two language systems (speaking and listening). The seven subtests encompass Picture Vocabulary, Oral Vocabulary, Grammatic Understanding, Sentence Imitation, Grammatic Completion, Word Discrimination, and Word Articulation.

Picture Vocabulary assesses receptive language skills and requires the ability to point correctly to the one picture out of four that best represents the stimulus word. There are 35 items on the revised test (instead of 25) and the words added include more difficult words from the list from which the original selection was made (the Thorndike-Lorge list, which is over 40 years old). The words were checked for level of difficulty against a 1979 list.

Oral Vocabulary also was revised to include 30 items instead of 20. The child must say what each stimulus word means, and the examiner follows precise criteria for scoring. As with Picture Vocabulary, the choice of words could be questioned, although the authors state that for this subtest possible items for inclusion were administered to a group of children and the results analyzed statistically. Thus some attempt has been made to justify the revision and the inclusion of those particular words.

The subtest of Grammatic Understanding requires the child to match an oral sentence to a page in the Picture Book. Several confusing or ambiguous items on the early test were deleted or changed. The grammatical forms used in the sentences are complex (as the manual acknowledges), but this was done deliberately to challenge the older children.

No changes occurred on the Sentence Imitation subtest, which still consists of 30 items; these were well selected initially and an excellent rationale is given to justify their inclusion.

The authors made changes on the subtest of Grammatic Completion to minimize the confusion in wording. This subtest assesses the child's knowledge of morphology, and as it relies neither on picture cues nor on nonsense words, it needs to be clear. Some of the oral statements are still capable of misrepresentation because they are given out of context, with no cues.

The last two TOLD-P:2 subtests, Word Discrimination and Word Articulation, assess phonology (knowledge of sounds). As in the TOLD-P, the first subtest requires the child to discriminate 20 pairs of words as being the "same" or "different," while the second requires him or her to pronounce a word when shown a picture of it. There are also 20 items on this subtest.

TOLD-P:2 scoring is done directly on the Profile/Examiner Record Form. There are no materials to manipulate, and the instructions are easy to follow. The examiner also may use the form to record qualitative data (e.g., incorrect answers, verbalizations, etc.). The record of scores shows the standard scores and percentile ranks (derived from the raw scores) and the composites or quotients (explained in a later section). The profile of scores shows these data in graphic form, which is appealing to test users.

The TOLD-I:2 measures the receptive and expressive language skills of children ages 8:6 to 12:11. This test is built on the same model of language as the primary test but uses different subtests to assess the linguistic features of language and the two linguistic systems. The six subtests are Generals, Malapropisms, Vocabulary, Sentence Combining, Word Ordering, and Grammar Comprehension.

Generals assesses knowledge of abstract relationships, and the 25 items are the same as on the 1982 edition. The student must say how groups of three words are alike (e.g., *inch, foot, yard* = measures of distance). One could question whether the relationships expressed are arranged in increasing order of difficulty, as some earlier items are more difficult than later ones. The justification given for the format is that it had previously been used by one of the authors to measure reading vocabulary.

Malapropisms is a new subtest that assesses recognition of ridiculous sentences. In each of 30 sentences a phonetically similar word has been substituted that the student must identify and correct (e.g., "We should brush our feet [teeth] every morning").

The Vocabulary subtest has an original format. Thirty-five word pairs are presented, and the student must say whether they have the same meaning, opposite meanings, or no connection with each other.

Sentence Combining assesses the child's ability to construct a sentence from several smaller ones, and this subtest has not changed from the previous edition.

Word Ordering remains substantially the same as the earlier version. This subtest requires the child to arrange a number of words presented in random order into syntactically correct sentences (e.g., *to, ready, you, go, are* = "You are ready to go/Are you ready to go?").

The sixth subtest, Grammatic Comprehension, requires recognition of sentences as correct or incorrect, and the 40 items remain unchanged from the earlier edition.

TOLD-I:2 answers are scored directly on the Profile/Examiner Record Form and the raw score then is computed from this. As with the Primary version, the record of scores shows the percentile ranks together with the composite scores, and the profile of scores presents these data graphically.

Practical Applications/Uses

According to the test authors, the TOLD-P:2 and TOLD-I:2 serve four principal purposes: a) to identify children who are significantly below their peers in language proficiency, b) to determine children's specific strengths and weaknesses in language skills, c) to document children's progress in language as a consequence of special intervention programs, and d) to measure language in research studies.

Both TOLD-2 tests are designed for use by professionals who have experience in test administration but not necessarily in language evaluation, including teachers, psychologists, language therapists, and counselors. The tests are useful in preschool, school, clinic, hospital, or daycare settings where some objective measure of language ability is needed. The authors caution against using the tests with children who have language characteristics that vary greatly from those of the standardization sample. The TOLD-2 normative tables are based on the scores of children who speak "typical" English.

Verbal communication is the result of an interaction between language structures and language function. Language structures involve word meanings (semantics), word patterns (syntax), word forms (morphology), and speech sounds (phonology). Language functions pertain to the reasons for selecting particular language structures to achieve specific purposes (Berdine & Mayer, 1987). The Tests of Language Development are concerned with the structures of language that make communication possible and not with the purposes of communication.

Children with language impairments typically show disruptions in the onset, progression, and sequence of development of language structures. The subtests of both the Primary and Intermediate version of the TOLD-2 are adequate measures of the structure of language. The TOLD-2 enables the practitioner to narrow down a child's language deficit and identify some of the specific structures that are delayed. Although the authors caution against translating the tests' results into educational programming, nevertheless the results do indicate areas of language that need attention.

Language processing involves receiving, organizing, analyzing, and making sense of incoming sensory data. This process is assessed adequately by the subtests at both levels. The inclusion of a subtest of auditory discrimination on the TOLD-P:2 is appropriate, although, as the examiner's manual points out, most children have mastered these skills by age 7. The subtest is useful for younger children and those with delays in language.

Language formulation or language expression is typically poorer than language reception in children with language problems (Berdine & Mayer, 1987). The expressive language of such children tends to be inaccurate or incompletely organized. What is not clear is whether these children lack the rules for processing and formulating sentences or simply do not use them, and the TOLD-2 cannot make this distinction.

Dynamic approaches to assessment developed in the mid-1970s that considered language as dynamic, relative, complex, and conditional (e.g., Muma, 1978). Assessing language structure without taking into account the functional use of language is not an adequate measure. The authors of the TOLD-2 acknowledge this and point out that the test results specify a performance level at a given time under a particular situation and do not tell why a person performed as he or she did. Test results are aids to clinical judgment (Kirk, 1984), not substitutes for them.

The TOLD-P:2 and TOLD-I:2 are useful for identifying children who lag behind in language skills, as well as for determining current performance level as required by Public Law 94–142. By using these tests, practitioners can document what children actually can do (Taylor, 1989).

The TOLD-P:2 was standardized on 2,436 children in 29 states, and the subjects' characteristics correspond to those of the U.S. population with respect to place of residence, geographic distribution, and parents' socioeconomic status. Slightly more boys and minority children are included than in the national sample, as this is more typical for the age range 4 through 8. The TOLD-I:2 was standardized on 1,214 children in 21 states. The characteristics of these subjects also reflect the population of the United States, with, again, a larger number of boys and minority children included. The authors also recommend the development of local norms and provide guidelines for doing so.

Detailed information is given for general test administration, and the examiner should encounter few problems in using the manual, which is quite comprehensive. About 30 to 60 minutes are needed to give the test, which is individually administered and untimed. The TOLD-I:2 makes use of entry points to establish a basal and ceiling, which speeds up test administration with older students. All items are given with the TOLD-P:2.

Raw scores are converted to standard scores and percentiles based on age tables. The mean of the subtest scores is 10 and the standard deviation 3. These standardized scores are then aggregated and converted to provide the various composite scores or quotients. For example, on the TOLD-P:2 the Listening Quotient (LiQ) is the sum of standard scores on Grammatic Understanding and Word Discrimination. On the TOLD-I:2 the LiQ is the sum of the Vocabulary, Grammatic Comprehension, and Malapropisms subtests.

Each quotient has a mean of 100 and a standard deviation of 15, which allows direct comparison of the TOLD-2 with other tests that use similar scoring (e.g.,

Wechsler Intelligence Scale for Children–Revised, Detroit Tests of Learning Aptitude). An optional software scoring system is available for both tests.

The interpretation of TOLD-2 results is facilitated by precise criteria for the standard scores and quotients, and aided by a comprehensive discussion on each of the quotients. The rationale for each quotient is plausible, and case examples appear in both manuals.

Technical Aspects

A test's technical adequacy is determined by its validity and reliability. Validity refers to the extent to which a test measures what it purports to measure; reliability refers to its consistency. If a test is not reliable, by definition it cannot be valid.

The authors provide considerable evidence related to the TOLD-P:2's content, criterion-related, and construct validity. Content validity was determined by a group of language professionals who rated the subtests as an adequate sampling of the skills of language. Concurrent validity is reported by comparing performance on the subtests with performance on nine published tests of language. The correlations reported are substantial for each of the subtests at each age level, with the exception of Grammatic Understanding.

Construct validity of the TOLD-P:2 is demonstrated by relating raw scores to chronological age and showing that the abilities measured are developmental in nature. The relationships of the subtests to each other, to tests of intelligence, and to tests of school readiness and achievement also were examined, and the results lend support to the theoretical constructs underlying the test.

Reliability is reported in terms of internal consistency, stability, and standard error of measurement, derived from the 1977 or 1988 Test of Language Development–Primary. A study was done to show the equivalency of the two versions. Five studies are cited to support high internal consistency of the test. Some of the studies were cited in the 1982 edition and have been criticized for the small sample size. Test-retest reliability is derived from two studies done on the 1977 edition where the sample size also was small (21 children). The authors point out that the small standard error of measurement is an index of the test's consistency.

Similar technical information is provided for the Intermediate version of the TOLD-2 as for the Primary. Content validity was determined by a group of professionals who rated the subtests as an adequate sampling of the skills of language. Concurrent validity was assessed by correlating scores on the TOLD-I:2 with the Test of Adolescent Language Development (Hammill, Brown, Larsen, & Wiederholt, 1980/1987). The use of a test based on the same model of language and developed by the same author could be questioned, but the examiner's manual addresses this point specifically and reports that the large correlation between the two tests supports the validity of the TOLD-2 Intermediate.

Construct validity is adequately dealt with by identifying several basic questions. One of them relates to age differentiation. The data do not show strong support for the developmental nature of the subtests (as was the case with the Primary version). The authors conclude that this mirrors language development, which "slows down dramatically during the elementary school years." (It could also indicate that the Intermediate test has less validity than the Primary version.)

Reliability data in the form of internal consistency, stability, and standard error of measurement are provided, derived from 150 protocols. Stability was based on two studies, and the reliability coefficients are substantial.

Critique

The TOLD-2 Primary and Intermediate tests are very similar to their predecessors. The tests measure a number of areas of language, both receptive and expressive, including semantics, syntax, and phonology. They are individually administered, intended to identify children with language problems and to ascertain strengths and weaknesses of the child's language structures.

The value of the tests depends on the extent to which the subtests actually measure the various components of language. The authors argue that a group of experts felt that the test items were measuring the appropriate domains but present no evidence that the subtests sample the intended domains systematically or completely (Salvia & Ysseldyke, 1991). Although the authors state that the TOLD-2 tests have the strongest research base of any current available language test, little has been published that supports the tests' validity.

These tests meet a higher number of psychometric criteria than many tests designed to evaluate oral language. In addition, a considerable amount of clinical evidence supports them. In practice the TOLD-P:2 and the TOLD-I:2 do what they say they will do, and consequently they offer a valuable assessment tool.

References

This list includes text citations and suggested additional readings.

Berdine, W.H., & Meyer, S.A. (1987). *Assessment in special education.* Boston: Little, Brown.

Hammill, D.D., & Newcomer, P.L. (1988). *Test of Language Development–2 Intermediate examiner's manual.* Austin, TX: PRO-ED.

Hammill, D.D., Brown, V.L., Larsen, S.C., & Wiederholt, J.L. (1980/1987). *Test of Adolescent Language.* Austin, TX: PRO-ED.

Hammill, D.D. (1985). *Detroit Tests of Learning Aptitude.* Austin, TX: PRO-ED.

Kirk, S.A. (1984). Introspection and prophecy. In B. Blatt & R.J. Morris (Eds.), *Perspectives in special education: Personal orientation.* Glenview IL: Scott Foresman.

Muma, J.R. (1978). *Language handbook: Concepts, assessments, intervention.* Englewood Cliffs, NJ: Prentice-Hall.

Newcomer, P.L., & Hammill, D.D. (1988). *Test of Language Development–2 Primary examiner's manual.* Austin, TX: PRO-ED.

Salvia, J., & Ysseldyke, J.E. (1991). *Assessment.* Boston: Houghton Mifflin.

Smith, C.R. (1991). *Learning disabilities: The interaction of the learner, task and setting.* Boston: Allyn & Bacon.

Taylor, R. (1989). *Assessment of exceptional students.* Englewood Cliffs, NJ: Prentice-Hall.

Wechsler, D. (1974). *Wechsler Intelligence Scale for Children–Revised.* San Antonio, TX: Psychological Corporation.

James A. Moses Jr., Ph.D.
Clinical Associate Professor of Psychiatry and Behavioral Sciences,
Stanford University School of Medicine, and Coordinator,
Psychological Assessment Unit, Department of Veterans Affairs
Medical Center, Palo Alto, California.

THREE-DIMENSIONAL BLOCK CONSTRUCTION TEST

Arthur L. Benton, Kerry deS. Hamsher, Nils R. Varney, and Otfried Spreen. New York, New York: Oxford University Press.

Introduction

The Three-Dimensional Block Construction Test (3DBCT) is a higher order measure of constructional ability that requires the subject to build three-dimensional designs of graded complexity from block or photographic models with a set of 29 loose cubical and rectangularly shaped wooden blocks. Two parallel forms of equal normative difficulty level are available. In different forms of the test each of the three-dimensional block structures may be built from actual block models that have been previously assembled or from photographs of the block structures. The test kit includes 87 blocks (29 blocks for each form and 29 for the tray). It is expected that the purchaser will construct fixed block models with glue for each design (A.L. Benton, personal communication, July 13, 1992).

There are three block models within each version of the 3DBCT. For Form A the three models are "a pyramid made from six one-inch cubes; an eight-block four level construction; and a fifteen-block, four-level construction"; for Form B, the parallel series of models are "a pyramidal structure of six blocks; an eight-block, four-level construction; and a fifteen-block, four-level construction" (Benton, Hamsher, Varney, & Spreen, 1983, p. 107). The test manual graphically displays the geometric models to be built from blocks as well as their component parts, with block dimensions indicated on the figures (Benton et al., 1983, pp. 108–109, Fig. 11-1 through 11-4).

Constructional difficulty was first recognized as a differentiable sign of neurologic disease by Kleist (1923, 1934; cited by Benton, 1989). Kleist conceptualized the syndrome of "constructional apraxia" as a higher order cognitive deficit "in formative activities such as assembling, building, and drawing, in which the spatial form of the product proves to be unsuccessful, without there being an apraxia of single movements" (Benton et al., 1983, p. 105). Several points are very important to note in Kleist's classic description of this syndrome. There is a distinct (visual-) *spatial* component to the constructional defect. By definition there also is no motor deficit associated with function of the hands or arms that would preclude skilled voluntary movement per se. True apraxia is a complex

754

syndrome of higher order voluntary motor deficit in which the patient has difficulty carrying out skilled movements on command despite sparing of muscular
strength, motor coordination, and sensation in the affected body part.

Considerable theoretical controversy has persisted since Kleist's time in attempts to identify the basis of the constructional deficit syndrome, which is
defined by *behavioral* rather than anatomic deficit criteria. Benton et al. (1983) have
contributed a very important dimensional task analysis to this problem, which
helps to operationally define more specifically what is meant by "constructional
apraxia" so that the syndrome is more amenable to scientific investigation. Unstandardized tasks that have been used clinically to investigate constructional
ability commonly require the patient to

> assemble, join, or draw parts to form a single, unitary structure. However
> they differ from each other . . . in complexity, in the type of movement and
> the degree of motor dexterity required in achieving the task, in the demands
> made on the higher intellectual functions, and in whether they involve con-
> struction in two or three spatial dimensions. (Benton et al., 1983, p. 105)

Examples of well-standardized, commonly used, two-dimensional constructional tasks are the copying portion of the Benton Visual Retention Test (Sivan,
1991), the Kohs Block Design Test, and the related Block Design subtests from the
Wechsler intelligence scales for children and adults. The 3DBCT might well be
used to assess higher order constructional difficulty in patients who show impairment on these more routinely administered visual-motor and cognitive measures.
Even patients who perform adequately on plane drawings or other two-dimensional
constructional tasks such as Block Design may show varying degrees of impairment on 3DBCT (Benton et al., 1983).

Drawings of two-dimensional, elementary plane figures such as a circle, trian-
gle, or square generally present the easiest constructional tasks to perform and
are useful as constructional ability screening measures with severely dysfunctional adult patients. The examiner may introduce an element of dimensional
complexity by asking the patient to draw a three-dimensional figure in the plane
projection, such as a house or a cube in perspective, so that the top and two of the
sides of the structure can be seen. Three-dimensional constructions require a
qualitatively different sort of visual-spatial and visual-motor analysis and execution than do two-dimensional projected representations of such figures in the
plane (Benton et al., 1983; Critchley, 1953).

The 3DBCT has been designed to operationally define and quantify aspects of
three-dimensional constructional ability; it is not a measure of constructional
ability in general. The introduction of a third dimension to the constructional task
makes it likely that 3DBCT will be clinically sensitive to higher order, complex
levels of constructional difficulty. Use of other constructional tasks as well as
visual-spatial and visual-motor tests likely will be clinically useful to better define
the nature of the cognitive deficit in patients who show deficit on 3DBCT. Those
patients who do not show basic perceptual or motor deficit but who still experience difficulty with 3DBCT may be said to show one form of higher order "constructional apraxia" in the sense that Kleist originally described this clinical syndrome.

The evolution of the 3DBCT progressed through a number of phases to reach its current form. Benton and Fogel (1962) developed the first standardized form of this test based on the clinical observations and recommendations of Critchley (1953), who reported that such a measure could be diagnostically useful for syndrome analysis of specific three-dimensional constructional difficulty. Benton (1968) refined the psychometric characteristics and standardization of the original 3DBCT and published a revised version of the test. Subsequently he and his colleagues developed a parallel, equivalent difficulty-level form of the 3DBCT, but they had patients complete these block construction designs from photographic models of the designs rather than from actual block models. This experimental procedure controls for the spatial orientation of the viewer, it appears to require a more active sort of visual-spatial processing and depth perception, and it is thought to be normatively more difficult to complete as there are fewer explicit visual-spatial cues to aid the patient when constructing the designs. Benton et al. (1983, p. 124) have noted, however, that empirical results generally have failed to support the hypothesis that the photographic model presentation of 3DBCT might be more sensitive to perceptually mediated three-dimensional constructional deficit among patients with right-hemispheric lesions.

The principal author of the 3DBCT, Arthur L. Benton, Ph.D., received his A.B. (1931) and A.M. (1933) degrees from Oberlin College, followed by his Ph.D. from Columbia University (1935). He began his career as an assistant in psychology, first at Oberlin College (1931–33), then at Columbia University and New York State Psychiatric Institute (1934–36), and finally at Cornell University Medical College (1936–39), where he subsequently served as a staff psychologist. He was appointed as an attending psychologist at New York Hospital–Westchester Division and as a psychologist in the Student Personnel Office of the City College of New York from 1939 to 1941. He served on active duty in the U.S. Navy during and after the Second World War (1941–46), then was appointed as Associate Professor of Psychology at the University of Louisville Medical School and as Chief Psychologist at the Louisville Mental Hygiene Clinic and the Louisville General Hospital (1946–48). From 1948 to 1958 he served as Professor of Psychology and Director of the Graduate Training Program in Clinical Psychology at the University of Iowa, followed by two decades (1958–78) as Professor of Psychology and Neurology. Dr. Benton has continued to coauthor theoretical and research papers and books since 1978 when he became Professor Emeritus at the University of Iowa.

Benton's fundamental contributions to the field of clinical neuropsychology have been acknowledged extensively and internationally. He has received honorary Doctor of Science (Cornell College, 1978) and Doctor of Psychology (University of Rome, 1990) degrees, as well as numerous other honors and awards, including the Distinguished Service Award of the Iowa Psychological Association (1977), the Distinguished Professional Contribution Award from the American Psychological Association (1978), the Outstanding Scientific Contribution Award of the International Neuropsychological Society (1981), The Samuel Torrey Orton Award from the Orton Dyslexia Society (1982), the Distinguished Service and Outstanding Contributions Award from the American Board of Professional Psychology (1985), and the Distinguished Clinical Neuropsychologist Award from the National Academy of Neuropsychology (1989).

Benton is a past president of both the American Orthopsychiatric Association (1965–66) and the International Neuropsychological Society (1970–71). He served as secretary-general of the Research Group on Aphasia for the World Federation of Neurology from 1971 to 1978. He has been a lecturer or visiting scholar at the University of Milan (1964), Hôpital Sainte-Anne, Paris (1968), Hadassah-Hebrew University Medical School, Jerusalem (1969), Free University of Amsterdam (1971), University of Helsinki (1974), University of Melbourne (1977), University of Minnesota Medical School (Baker Lecturer, 1979), University of Victoria, British Columbia (Lansdowne Scholar, 1980), and the University of Michigan (1986), as well as Directeur d'Études Associé, École des Hautes Études, Paris (1979) and a visiting scientist at the Tokyo Metropolitan Institute of Gerontology (1974).

Benton has authored, coauthored, or edited 12 books and monographs, approximately 150 professional journal articles, and 22 historical reviews in the area of clinical neuropsychology and behavioral neurology. He is recognized as a pioneer and a leading authority in the area of clinical neuropsychology.

The standardized, commercially published version of the 3DBCT appeared with the clinical manual for this and other tests in the Benton-Iowa Neuropsychological Test Battery (Benton et al., 1983). Coauthors of this clinical manual with Dr. Benton are Kerry deS. Hamsher, Ph.D. (Associate Professor of Neurology, University of Wisconsin Medical School); Nils R. Varney, Ph.D. (staff neuropsychologist, Department of Veterans Affairs Medical Center, Iowa City, Iowa); and Otfried Spreen, Ph.D. (Professor Emeritus, Department of Psychology, University of Victoria, Victoria, British Columbia, Canada).

Practical Applications/Uses

The 29 loose blocks for the 3DBCT are placed in a standard array that sorts the blocks by size and shape (see Benton, 1983, p. 111, Fig. 11-5 for an illustration) on a tray that the examiner positions to one or the other side of the examinee. If the patient has full visual fields, the block array should be placed on the side that the patient prefers. If the patient has a visual field defect, the block tray should be placed in the patient's sighted visual field. After each block construction has been completed, the blocks are replaced in the standard array before the next design is attempted. The patient is shown only the model to be copied on that trial; the other models are not shown until the blocks have been put back into the standard array and the next design is ready to be assembled.

When a trial of 3DBCT is to begin, the model is placed before the patient and the following verbatim directions are read to him or her:

> Use these blocks and put some of them together so that they look like this model. Make the model as it looks as you face it, as you see it, not as I see it. You will not need all the blocks here and you will have to pick out the ones you need to make a copy of the model. Make your model as carefully as you can. This is more important than how long you take. Place the blocks in the same position and with the same angles as they are in the model. Tell me when you are finished. (Benton et al., 1983, p. 111)

The subject should be allowed to handle and examine the blocks briefly before the test begins.

Benton and his colleagues note that an occasional overly conscientious patient may attempt to match fine perceptual surface features of the blocks such as their "grain and color" in addition to the overall figure modeled. Such detail-preoccupied patients are instructed to disregard such extraneous cues and to concentrate only on reproducing the exact geometric structure of the model as a whole. Aside from obsessional concern with detail, however, such behavior may be a subtle, higher order version of perceptual stimulus-bound "concrete" thinking, which could be related to executive function deficit, particularly if it is not modifiable by instructions from the examiner to disregard such irrelevant visual details. It may be useful to note such idiosyncrasies of task solution parenthetically in the course of test administration for later qualitative analysis to supplement interpretation of the standardized 3DBCT results.

The time required by the patient to complete each of the three 3DBCT models is timed in seconds. A 5-minute maximum is allowed for the patient to complete each of the models for either form of the test. If the model construction is not completed within the time limit, the examiner removes the model design, scores the subject's reproduction of it, rearranges the blocks in the standard pretest array, and presents the next model in the series. The examiner encourages the subject to indicate when he or she has completed the reproduction of the model. At that point the response time is scored and the reproduction is scored for accuracy and error types. Although changes and corrections made after the completion of the task are not formally scored, one may wish to note if the patient makes impulsive errors and then corrects them, as this may be a sign of executive function deficit related to disinhibition of impulse and poor use of self-corrective feedback. Such extratest behavior may provide useful qualitative information about why the patient experiences difficulty on the 3DBCT beyond complex constructional deficit per se.

Benton et al. (1983) note that the original form of the test allowed the patient to use only one hand to complete the task. They initially thought that this procedure would control for the disability of hemiplegic individuals who could motorically control only one hand effectively after stroke. It became clear, however, that the one-handed procedure did not uniformly equate neurologic and control patients for use of the dominant or nondominant hand, as either hand could be impaired in stroke. Normals also found the task more difficult when they could not use the nondominant hand to make fine motor adjustments in the overall design or to position some of the larger blocks bimanually. The one-handed procedure therefore was abandoned as a standardized administration procedure.

Hemiplegic patients who show clear motor difficulty in positioning a block that they know how to arrange spatially may be helped by the examiner to overcome the motor deficit (Benton et al., 1983, p. 112) so that they can continue to work on the construction of the overall figure. This modification of the standard test administration procedure is allowable because the functional system under study involves higher order constructional ability that may be impaired independently of simple motor or even complex apraxic motor deficit. Removal of the motor coordination obstacle allows one to assess more accurately the higher order constructional ability that is of primary interest in 3DBCT evaluation. In the unusual case where a lesion of the corpus callosum has induced a disconnection syndrome between the two cerebral hemispheres, study of the patient's 3DBCT performance with each hand separately is recommended. In such cases, different forms of the test should be completed with the right and left hands independently so that the constructional competence of each cerebral hemisphere can be evaluated and compared independently, and so that practice effects will be minimized.

The alternative administration method in which the 3DBCT is administered to the patient from photographic models of the block constructions is an experimental version of the test and not yet recommended for clinical use. The photographic viewpoint shows these models in a top-corner-angle manner that makes all dimensions and the internal spatial interrelationships of the blocks in the structure clearly visible. The designs are similar to the schematic figures of the models that are presented in the test manual. The photographic models of the designs are presented upright to the subject while they are being reproduced. The size of the photographic reproductions is not specified in the test manual.

The manual does not explicitly state the qualifications of the examiner to competently administer and score the 3DBCT. Given the clinical complexity of the administration, scoring, and interpretation, however, one would expect a competent examiner to be a multidisciplinary professional in clinical neuropsychology, behavioral neurology, or a related clinical neuroscientific field. A thorough knowledge of brain-behavior relationships, constructional deficit syndrome analysis, test standardization, and psychometric principles would be necessary for a clinician to accurately record and validly interpret the patient's deficit performances on this test. Extensive practice with the complex administration and scoring system in particular would be highly desirable to ensure that qualitative and quantitative aspects of errors are recorded readily, accurately, and completely.

Scoring the 3DBCT is a well-standardized but difficult procedure to master expertly. It must be well practiced so that the patient's performance can be scored efficiently and accurately for correct and incorrect details immediately after the structure has been assembled, and so that test administration is not delayed inordinately. One might consider photographing the final reproductions of the initial 5 to 10 3DBCT administrations with low-cost black-and-white film to check on the accuracy of scoring. This method of photographic recording could be extended to analysis of unusual and complex model reproductions. It appears worth the effort and expense involved to accurately record the errors of clinical patients, whose deviant responses often are extraordinarily difficult to quickly sketch freehand or to describe verbally with a task of this visual-spatial complexity and small-component detail.

A facsimile of the record form appears in the test manual. One point is awarded for each correctly placed block in each design. Maximum possible scores for the three 3DBCT models for either form of the test therefore are 6, 8, and 15 points, respectively. In addition to the number of points awarded for correct block placements, the examiner also records qualitative error scores in four descriptive categories. These error types are described in the test manual (Benton et al., 1983, pp. 112–113) as follows:

1. *Omissions:* omission of one or more blocks from the constructed design.

2. *Additions:* placement of one or more blocks beyond the number required. (If the subject produces an unconnected arrangement of loose blocks, the examiner

should ask him or her to indicate which ones he or she intended to constitute the attempted construction.)

3. *Substitutions:* substitution of a block of incorrect size or shape in place of one of the blocks in the model (substitution is counted as one error, including the interchange of two or more blocks).

4. *Displacements:* the following criteria are used to evaluate displacement errors:

A. angular deviations (rotations) of 45 degrees or greater, as estimated by visual inspection (rotation of the whole construction or a minor rotation of an individual block are not counted as errors).

B. separations and misplacements, as when one or more blocks are placed in incorrect parts of the design or outside the design, if one or more blocks of the design are connected with the block model, or if no space is allowed between blocks that are spaced apart in the model (minor displacements, such as poorly centered blocks, blocks that are farther apart than in the model, etc., are *not* counted as errors).

Special qualitative performance errors also have been described and illustrated by the test authors in the test manual (Benton et al., 1983, pp. 119–123). Classical qualitative constructional deficit errors that may appear in 3DBCT performance include "closing-in" and unilateral spatial inattention or visual-spatial neglect. "Closing-in" may be understood as an extreme form of stimulus-bound or "concrete" thinking in which the subject incorporates all or part of the original block model into the reproduction of it. In such errors the subject is unable to separate conceptually and perceptually the perceived block model from its reproduction. 3DBCT reproductions also may be simplified so that although the overall form of the figure is not grossly violated, many of the key details may be omitted. In cases of visual-spatial neglect or inattention, half of the block model (usually the left half) is partially or completely omitted (see Benton, 1983, p. 123, for illustrative examples). Such spatial neglect syndromes may or may not be associated with visual field deficit.

If the patient's reproduction of the model introduces a spatial rotation of the viewing angle that is different from the model as presented, the patient should be reminded to reproduce the model from the viewpoint that is presented. Such rotational perspective changes should be noted qualitatively, but the relationships of the blocks to each other in the model reproduction serve as the basis for the formal scoring.

Benton and his colleagues introduced a useful principle of conservatism to 3DBCT error scoring. To avoid duplicate scoring of multiple categorical errors for a single block misplacement, they recommend that the examiner score the smallest number of errors that, if corrected, would produce a perfect construction. For example, they state that "incorrect angular placement of a block often involves a separation error as well. However, since correct placement of this single block would eliminate both errors, only one point is subtracted from total score and only one displacement error is noted" (Benton et al., 1983, p. 113). If a patient's performance is so defective that only a few blocks are correctly placed and the resultant design is hardly recognizable as a reproduction of the original model, then the examiner should score the number of correctly placed blocks rather than attempting to count the potentially very large number and types of scorable errors.

Several scoring samples are provided in the 3DBCT manual (Benton et al., 1983, pp. 113–114), with a photograph of three defective reproduction designs and explanations of key errors in each of them. Novice examiners may wish to practice the 3DBCT with normal volunteers who can simulate common errors and others who can present difficult scoring examples. Alternatively one could make random or systematically erroneous reproductions of each of the designs and then score them to learn to recognize efficiently the key elements of the blockwise credit system and errorwise scoring features for each design. Given the complexities of the scoring and the permutations and combinations of design errors that examinees can make, it would be wise to carry out such practice extensively before attempting the test with neurologically impaired patients. Clinical variants could be complex and difficult to score, and one would want to ensure that clinical data and important error variants were not misscored or unrecognized.

The total score for the 3DBCT is the sum of the correct points for the three models of the test form administered. Five minutes (300 seconds) maximum are allowed for completing each of the three models. If the total time required to construct *all three* of the designs exceeds 380 seconds, however, the examiner subtracts 2 points from the total correct score as an actuarial penalty for performance slowness. This time-corrected score is the normative standard for overall 3DBCT performance evaluation.

As noted previously, two equivalent forms (A and B) have been developed for the 3DBCT. To compare them for performance-level equivalence, the authors composed four groups of 30 patients each. Ten patients per group had either unilateral left-hemispheric disease, unilateral right-hemispheric disease, or normal brain structure and function by history and current medical findings. Subjects were matched for group mean age (group mean range = 43–48 years), but they were not matched on other demographic variables. The groups received one of the following: Form A–block model, Form B–block model, Form A–photographic model, or Form B–photographic model. The descriptive statistics for mean and standard deviation values are very closely comparable (less than 1 mean point difference) between Forms A and B within block model and photographic model presentations. On average the mean scores of these diagnostically mixed subject groups on the block model presentation were consistently 4 to 5 3DBCT total score points higher than total scores for the photographic model presentation. Variability within and between groups appears to be similar. Clearly the 3DBCT photographic model presentation proved more difficult than the block model presentation for these mixed samples of neurologic patients and controls regardless of their diagnostic category.

Normative standards have been established in samples of 100 subjects for the block model and photographic model presentations of the 3DBCT. Score frequency distributions for each presentation are listed in the manual (Benton et al., 1983, pp. 115–116, Tables 11-2 and 11-3). For the *block model presentation,* the sample consisted of 100 medical control patients without past or present history of brain disease, brain trauma with loss of consciousness, or psychiatric disorder. The sample was predominantly middle aged ($M = 42$; SD and range statistics not reported) and partially high school–educated on the average ($M = 10$ years; SD and range statistics not reported). Seventy-eight percent (78/100) of these medical control patients earned errorless scores of 29 points, 12 other controls (12%) scored 28 points, and the remaining 10 controls (10%) scored in the range of 25 to 27 3DBCT total score points. Most of the controls' constructional errors were omissions of one or more minor blocks from their reproductions of the model figures. The test authors report that substitution errors were rare among their normal sample.

The *photographic model presentation* also was studied in a separate sample of 100 medical control patients (42 men, 58 women; other demographic characteristics unknown) with the same exclusion criteria as described for the previous sample. Forty-three percent (43/100) of the total sample earned a perfect score of 29 points with the photographic model presentation, 12% (12/100) earned a score of 28, and 37% (37/100) scored in the 25–27 range. Eight percent of the control patients (8/100) scored in the 17- to 24-point range. The percentage of male (23/42, 55%) and female (32/58, 55%) medical control patients who earned errorless or nearly errorless scores on 3DBCT with the photographic model presentation was identical. Clearly the photographic model presentation of 3DBCT administration was more difficult for medical control patients than was the block model format. This trend can be seen from the considerably lower percentage of scores in the errorless or near-errorless range of 28 to 29 total points (90% for block model construction, 55% for photographic model construction).

Individual differences among medical controls also were more apparent on the more difficult photographic presentation condition (score range = 17–29) than on the block model condition (score range = 25–29). Inspection of mean score values between the photographic ($M = 27.3$) and block ($M = 28.6$) model total score values alone do not reflect the descriptive data trends clearly. These data illustrate the value of reporting and analyzing variability statistics throughout the data analysis process, as the individual specificity of the test is shown by its variability rather than by its central tendency (sensitivity) distributional characteristics.

The comparability of the demographic characteristics of the two samples also are important to assess when score trend results are compared. Age and particularly educational level of the samples comprise important variables that typically strongly influence performance level on cognitive tasks that are sensitive to brain function integrity. Benton and Ellis (1970) investigated the effects of age and educational level on 3DBCT performance within the photographic model administration format. They dichotomized their sample of 80 patients into those with an educational level greater than or equal to 11 years ($n = 52$) and those with an educational level of 10 years or less ($n = 28$). The higher educational level group had a somewhat greater 3DBCT mean score ($M = 28.0$) and a greater proportion of patients with 0–1 errors (38/52, 73%) than did the lower educational level group ($M = 26.2$; proportion = 9/28, 32%).

Experimental studies of this kind can be improved in several ways. Continuous variables such as educational level (or age) should not be categorically dichotomized for comparison because statistical power is lost by such a procedure and the chance of detecting valid differences present is lessened. Naturally continuous variables generally should be analyzed with parametric statistics, while naturally occurring, disjoint categorical data should be analyzed with nonparametric statistics. Reporting central tendency, variability, and range statistics as well as percentile values for impairment cutoff levels (such as the fifth percentile of normal range performance) is valuable to estimate individual (variability indices) and group (central tendency indices) trends in the data. One sort of information does not substitute for the other in analyses of this kind.

The trends in the normative data for 3DBCT are certainly robust. When these findings are replicated, attention to demographic variables would be an important issue to consider as a basis for recommendations about the generalizability of results. Ideally both administration methods (block model and photographic model) for the 3DBCT would be administered to the same patients so that the results across administration methods would be directly comparable. Based on such refinements in the data analysis, users perhaps could identify the strengths and limitations of this technique more precisely. The value of actuarial adjustments of the total score for age and educational level remains to be investigated. Actuarial corrections for continuous demographic variables might be attempted by means of a weighted variable formula to predict 3DBCT total score from the demographic variables of interest, such as age and educational level. Such a procedure could be developed easily with multiple regression techniques, based on data from the entire score distribution of the normative samples already collected and reported in the test manual.

Developmental trends for Canadian children ages 6 to 12 years on 3DBCT performance have been reported by Spreen and Gaddes (1969). For a detailed summary of central tendency and range statistics with normative values by age level, one may consult the original article or the 3DBCT manual (Benton et al., 1983, p. 117, Table 11-4). A review of trends in these data shows the expected increase in mean 3DBCT total score with age (21.8 at age 6 to 27.2 at age 12) and a gradually decreasing score range with advancing age (14–28 at age 6 years to 23–29 at age 12 years).

Technical Aspects

Benton and Fogel (1962) studied performance impairment patterns on the 3DBCT with block model presentation in a group of 100 neurologic patients with mixed types of brain disease (age range = 16–60 years). They reported that 26% of their heterogeneous sample scored below the first percentile of the normal control distribution on the 3DBCT. Analysis of the data by lesion locus showed that 40% (8/20) of the patients with bilateral brain disease, 14% (6/43) of those with unilateral lesions of the left cerebral hemisphere, and 32% (12/37) of those with unilateral right-hemispheric lesions performed below their first percentile impairment cutoff value. The investigators concluded from this exploratory study that severe three-dimensional constructional ability defect was a relatively common sign in neurologic patients with a variety of brain disease syndromes, and that this sign was most likely to occur in patients with bilateral or right-hemispheric disease.

Keller (1971) administered the 3DBCT with block model presentation to a sample of 40 patients ages 19 to 64 with unilateral neurologic disease of one cerebral hemisphere (20 left hemisphere lesion, 20 right hemisphere lesion cases). It is not clear whether the two lateralized lesion groups were demographically equivalent.

In the sample as a whole, 30% (12/40) of the patients earned perfect scores and an additional 10% (4/40) made only one error. Approximately one third (32.5%, 13/40) of the total sample showed grossly defective 3DBCT total scores of 25 or less, which ranks below the first percentile of the medical control sample distribution.

This relatively high base rate finding of three-dimensional constructional difficulty in a mixed neurologic sample with brain disease reconfirms the relevance of the 3DBCT as a measure of higher cortical function integrity in selected patients. Analysis of deficit patterns showed two distinct subcategories that are clinically important to distinguish. Fifteen percent (6/40) earned 3DBCT scores in the 22- to 25-point range, described as "moderately defective." The other seven patients who performed defectively overall scored in the range of 8 to 15 total points, described as "grossly defective." Qualitative analyses of performances showed that error scores at this level typically indicated that the constructions were so poor they could not be recognized as reproductions of the model figures.

Analysis of the data by hemispheric lesion site showed greater than twice the incidence of 3DBCT overall score performance level failure among patients with lesions of the right cerebral hemisphere (9/20, 45%) than among those with lesions of the left cerebral hemisphere (4/20, 20%). The group comparison was even more clear when the incidence of severe 3DBCT performance level deficit (total score in the 8- to 15-point range) was analyzed. The right-hemispheric lesion group showed a 30% (6/20) incidence of scores in this range, whereas the left-hemispheric lesion group showed only a 5% (1/20) incidence of severe 3DBCT performance deficit.

The *block model presentation* and the *photographic model presentation* of the 3DBCT were compared in a neurologic patient sample as part of Keller's (1971) study. A counterbalanced experimental design was employed that controlled for test form and administration condition. There was a 10-minute distraction task interval between the administration of the two 3DBCT forms. Half of the total sample of 40 mixed diagnosis brain-damaged subjects performed Form A with the block model presentation and Form B with the photographic model presentation. The other half performed Form A with the photographic model presentation and Form B with block model presentation. Analysis of performance level patterns between patients with unilateral left- or unilateral right-hemispheric lesions under these conditions is instructive. Four patients (4/20, 20%) in each lateralized lesion group scored in the normal range of 26 to 30 total score points. The range of 3DBCT total scores ranged widely within the deficient performance range for both lateralized lesion group (range = 5–25 in each group). There were no apparent pattern-of-performance differences as a function of lesion laterality in these lateralized lesion group analyses.

Kawahata, Nagata, and Kawamura (1988) reported a case study of head trauma in an executive who fell down a flight of stairs, was unconscious for 10 days, and complained of object and facial agnosia for familiar objects and people upon recovery from coma. Neurological examination was remarkable only for visual field deficit. The WAIS Verbal IQ was 108; Performance IQ could not be determined due to the visual object agnosia. Linguistic skills were within normal limits. The neuropsychological syndrome included deficits of "an impairment of the recent verbal memory, alexia, agraphia, object agnosia, color naming difficulty, prosopagnosia, and visuospatial constructional difficulty" (Kawahata et al., 1988). On the 3DBCT the patient was significantly more impaired with reproduction of the figures from photographic models than from block models, but both performances were defective. Computerized tomographic brain scanning showed bilateral subcortical hematomas with adjacent focal brain edema in the temporo-occipital zones.

Another analytic study that employed the 3DBCT as part of a thorough diagnostic neuropsychological test battery was reported by Mendez (1988). In two patients with visual agnosia, he reported a syndrome in which the patients performed adequately on "form discrimination, mental rotation, and visuospatial skills," but did poorly on "figure-ground discrimination, visual integration, facial discrimination, and constructional tasks" (Mendez, 1988, p. 1754). The 3DBCT was the constructional measure employed in this study.

An elegant analytic study that clarified the relationship of the laterality of a cerebral lesion to the presence and type of aphasic disturbance and performance level on the 3DBCT was reported by Benton (1973). All aphasic patients had lesions confined to the left cerebral hemisphere. The percentage of failing cases on the 3DBCT (defined as performance level below the first percentile of the normative group; total score of 25 or less) was computed for patients with left- or right-hemispheric lesions. The incidence of 3DBCT failure among all patients with left-hemispheric lesions as a group was 32.4% (11/34), and the incidence of 3DBCT failure among all those with right-hemispheric lesions was 35.7% (5/14).

The left-hemispheric lesion group was subdivided into subgroups of aphasic patients with severe receptive language deficit (nine cases), aphasic patients with moderate receptive language deficit (nine cases), patients with expressive language deficit only (eight cases), and nonaphasic patients (eight cases). The incidence of 3DBCT failure was calculated in each of these subgroups, and error patterns among them were compared. Incidence of 3DBCT failure was twice as high among aphasic patients with severe receptive language deficit (66.7%, 6/9) as among those with moderate receptive language deficit (33.3%, 3/9). The overall rate of 3DBCT failure among all patients with receptive language deficit was 50% (9/18). Among patients with only expressive language deficit, the incidence of 3DBCT failure was only 12.5% (1/8), which equaled the rate of failure among the nonaphasic patients with left-hemispheric lesions (12.5%, 1/8). Clearly there is a robust relationship of the presence and severity of receptive language disturbance to 3DBCT ability, while the relationship of expressive language deficit to 3DBCT performance level appears relatively minimal. Benton et al. (1983, p. 119) concluded from a comparison of the 3DBCT findings for the left- and right-hemispheric lesion groups that "there are two discrete types of visuoconstructive disability which are associated with side of lesion, one being language related and the other not." Confirmatory results have been reported independently by Damasio (1985, pp. 281–282).

This investigation clearly illustrates the need for pattern-of-performance as well as level-of-performance analysis to clarify variability as well as central tendency data trends, respectively. Qualitative syndrome patterns often are reflected quantitatively as disjoint subgroup performance patterns on variability measures. Such patterns can be measured objectively when their underlying dimensions are well understood and when they are operationally defined with standardized psychometric techniques such as the 3DBCT.

Benton et al. (1983, p. 122) raised the important question of the sensitivity versus the specificity of 3DBCT performance deficit to the presence of dementing illness. They dichotomized their sample of 100 neurologic patients with brain disease into subgroups with and without generalized cognitive deficit (dementia). Their criterion of general mental impairment was "a WAIS Verbal Scale IQ score which was 20 or more points below the IQ score to be expected on the basis of the age and education of the patient." Previous work by Fogel (1964) had shown a 2% incidence of such a discrepancy score in a sample of 100 cognitively normal patients. Benton and his colleagues identified a subgroup of 35 cognitively impaired patients who met this cognitive impairment criterion in their neurologic sample. Discrepancy scores for the neurologic group were in the 20- to 49-point range. The remainder of the sample (65 patients with discrepancy scores of 19 or less) comprised the cognitively unimpaired subgroup.

The overall rate of impairment (performance level below the fifth percentile) on 3DBCT total score in the neurologic sample was 37% (37/100). Within the demented neurologic subgroup 3DBCT failure incidence was 60% (21/35), whereas within the nondemented neurologic subgroup the failure rate was 25% (16/65). Although 3DBCT performance level clearly is related to the presence of generalized cognitive impairment, fully 40% of demented patients were not deficient on 3DBCT performance, and 25% of nondemented patients performed deficiently on 3DBCT. It is clear from these findings that three-dimensional constructional difficulty may occur with or without generalized cognitive deficit in clinical neurologic samples. 3DBCT deficit also may occur in a sizeable number of control patients without other evidence of cognitive deficit. One therefore should be cautious to interpret 3DBCT performance only as one source of syndrome-analytic data among many other performance-level and pattern indicators. In particular 3DBCT performance level is sensitive to higher order constructional deficit, but a level of performance total score on the 3DBCT can not be interpreted by itself as a sign of either normal or abnormal neurological or cognitive status.

Critique

The development of 3DBCT as a psychometric measure has operationally defined, standardized, and objectified measurement standards for evaluation of the "higher order" cognitive construct of three-dimensional constructional deficit. One must be cautious, however, not to reify the constructional deficit syndrome as though it were an objectively observed behavior pattern. It is not. Rather, it is a complex theoretical construct that is *inferred* from behavior deficit on certain complex tasks. Originally it was described both by the presence of complex spatial deficit and by the absence of limb apraxia affecting voluntary movements of the hands and arms. Complex, higher order behavioral syndromes of this kind exist only in the sense that they are operationally defined by deficit on some sort of objective instrument that allows one to *measure* discrete behavioral elements that may be deficient. The successful development of the 3DBCT therefore may be said to be definitive for many aspects of the three-dimensional constructional deficit syndrome.

In essence the task of syndrome analysis is one of operationally defining the necessary and sufficient conditions for emergence of the deficit pattern. This is a matter of functional system analysis (Luria, 1973, 1980). Spatial aspects of the constructional deficit syndrome were recognized from the outset by Kleist (1923, 1934) in the original description of the syndrome deficit pattern. The work of Benton (1973) has shown the complementary and intimate relationship of receptive language deficit to the presence and severity of constructional difficulty on the 3DBCT.

Many other aspects of the functional system that underlies 3DBCT performance remain to be investigated. Construct validation of the test requires its comparison to other conceptually related tests of known validity and reliability. Demonstration that the 3DBCT shows convergent validity with other tests of three-dimensional constructional ability and divergent validity with unrelated tests is necessary to show that it is specific as well as sensitive to constructional behavior deficit.

The role of visual perception in the three-dimensional constructional deficit disorder remains to be thoroughly investigated. The relationship of the ordinary visual field defect associated with a unilateral lesion of each cerebral hemisphere with the syndrome of constructional difficulty as measured by the 3DBCT needs study as a basic sensory-processing modality feature. Systematic study of 3DBCT performance by patients with varying degrees of unilateral spatial neglect also would be useful to clarify syndrome subtype patterns. Study of 3DBCT performance in patients with focal brain lesions and in sizeable samples of well-chosen patients with specific neurologic syndromes also would be useful to extend the scope and focus of the test for clinical use.

Benton's (1973) dimensional analysis of the key relationship between receptive language processing and 3DBCT performance level should be replicated. Dimensional refinement of these patterns could be achieved by using available standardized auditory comprehension and other parametric linguistic measures with a number of standard aphasia batteries, such as Benton and Hamsher's Multilingual Aphasia Examination.

The relationship of 3DBCT performance to specific linguistic deficit patterns in homogeneous aphasic syndrome subtypes also should be performed to extend Benton's (1973) work. The role of verbal mediation appears to be as important as the visual-spatial features for performance of the 3DBCT task. Identification of the specific elements of receptive linguistic deficit that are related to 3DBCT performance also are important to determine if these aspects of the syndrome are to be clearly understood in a multidimensional behavioral context.

Analysis of related constructional skills such as *two*-dimensional constructional competence on copying the standardized figures from the Revised Visual Retention Test (Benton, 1974) or construction of the Block Design subtest figures of the Wechsler Adult Intelligence Scale–Revised (Wechsler, 1981) should be investigated in combination with 3DBCT performance to clarify variants in presence, severity, and type of syndrome characteristics as a function of constructional task type. Performance on a battery of simple and complex motor tasks also should be carried out in conjunction with 3DBCT performance in contrasted groups of patients who do and who do not show the three-dimensional constructional deficit in order to better define the motor component of the syndrome.

The sizeable proportion of neurologically impaired patients who do not show 3DBCT performance deficit and the remarkable proportion of medical controls who do show this deficit require much more detailed study. Whether 3DBCT performance difficulty is truly a pathognomonic sign of cognitive deficit by itself or whether it should be clinically interpreted only in the context of other related deficits such as receptive aphasic disorder remains to be determined. It is likely that multiple subsyndromes exist within the three-dimensional constructional deficit syndrome complex. It is clear that at least some of them are related to receptive language ability.

Identification of the features specific to each of these syndrome subtypes remains to be clarified. Mixing syndrome subtypes in the same study could produce apparently conflicting results based on sampling bias so that there could be paradoxical overlap between clinical and control groups, as Benton et al. (1983) have reported. It is also worth considering that our screening measures for neurologic deficit may not be sensitive to "higher order" deficit. Control patients who show only the subtle aspects of the syndrome without disturbance of the elementary functional system components thus actually may represent clinical cases that have gone unrecognized without specialized techniques such as the 3DBCT.

All of the validational investigations suggested above depend on establishing rigorous reliability indices for the 3DBCT. To be an accurate measure of a specific behavior pattern for a theoretical construct, a test must satisfy rigorous psychometric reliability criteria. Three types of reliability indices must be established for the 3DBCT. The first of these, alternate forms reliability, has been well demonstrated and reported in the test manual. The provision of alternate forms for the test allows for accurate retesting without direct practice effect through learning the test tasks per se over trials.

Alternate forms reliability is related to test-retest reliability and enhances its standardized investigation. To establish test-retest reliability, the 3DBCT would be given twice to samples of control patients and to patients with stable, chronic neurologic disease. The intertest interval would be approximately 2 weeks. The two sets of results would be correlated with each other, and ideally the value would approximate .80 or higher. Spearman's rho should be used for such correlational studies because this nonparametric rank-order correlational measure is insensitive to the biasing influence of outlying values. Even one deviant performance in a sample using a parametric correlational method could greatly bias the central tendency and variability measures and hence affect the correlational value inordinately.

The other necessary psychometric accuracy measure to establish for the 3DBCT is interrater reliability. Given the great complexity of the test's scoring system, this is a crucial index to demonstrate, particularly for raters of varying experience levels. One might wish to objectify the scoring criteria by photographing difficult as well as ordinary constructions as criterion measures and then using these stimuli as criteria for reconstructing the criterion three-dimensional structures to be scored from the photographic models. Such a procedure would ensure that the

3DBCT stimuli to be scored are reproduced from standardized materials and that the stimuli are uniform across raters.

Interrater indices should be established separately for each design on both forms of the test. Separate statistics should be reported for interrater agreement on scoring discrete or elementary errors as well as for multiple error categories on a single design and for complex error patterns that present special problems in scoring. The interrater accuracy of objective scoring of the grossly disorganized sort of erroneous performance also should be empirically investigated and reported.

A thorough study of 3DBCT interrater reliability also should serve as a guideline for training raters to recognize and to score accurately and objectively both common and uncommon types of errors that one encounters clinically. The experimenter who conducts such a study should be well experienced clinically with 3DBCT administration and interpretation. Verbal description and photographic illustration of difficult scoring items and refinements in the scoring system to objectify and clarify interrater discrepancies in the analysis of difficult error patterns could be of particular value. Comparison of the 3DBCT scoring accuracy of novice and experienced raters would be useful to establish the necessary and sufficient experience standards typically required to master the complex 3DBCT scoring system. Objective methods of recording the stimulus model reproductions photographically or by other means and the relative benefits and difficulties associated with each of the methods should be evaluated and reported.

3DBCT provides a quantified, standardized, objective measure of complex constructional praxis that potentially may highlight many important aspects of complex functional systems as they relate to each other at superordinate levels. Receptive linguistic, visual-spatial, motor, and executive planning components have been identified as important features of 3DBCT performance. The specific interrelationships of these and other as yet unrecognized features of the multidimensional complex of skills underlying this behavioral syndrome remain to be demonstrated. Careful, parametric studies of 3DBCT reliability and construct validity have the potential to unravel and finally to clarify the nature of the enigmatic syndrome of three-dimensional constructional difficulty first intuitively recognized and described by Kleist (1923) nearly 70 years ago. Current findings suggest that achievement of that solution should bring us to a considerably fuller understanding of a wide range of complex cognitive functional systems that have heretofore appeared disparate and unrelated, but which now have begun to appear integrated and interdependent.

References

Benton, A.L. (1968). *Test de Praxie Constructive Tri-Dimensionnelle*. Paris: Editions du Centre de Psychologie Appliquée.

Benton, A.L. (1973). Visuoconstruction disability in patients with cerebral disease: Its relationship to side of lesion and aphasic disorder. *Documenta Ophthalmologica, 33*, 67–76.

Benton, A.L. (1974). *Revised Visual Retention Test: Clinical and experimental applications*. (4th ed). San Antonio, TX: Psychological Corporation.

Benton, A.L. (1989). Constructional apraxia. In F. Boller & J. Grafman (Eds.), *Handbook of neuropsychology* (Vol. 3, pp. 387–394). Amsterdam: Elsevier Science Publishers, B.V. (Biomedical Division).

Benton, A.L., & Ellis, E. (1970). Test de Praxie Tridimensionnelle: Observations normatives concernant la performance au test lorsque les stimuli sont des photographies de construction modeles. *Revue de Psychologie Appliquée, 20,* 255–258.

Benton, A.L., & Fogel, M.L. (1962). Three-dimensional constructional praxis: A clinical test. *Archives of Neurology, 7,* 347–354.

Benton, A.L., Hamsher, K.DeS., Varney, N.R., & Spreen, O. (1983). *Contributions to neuropsychological assessment: A clinical manual.* New York: Oxford University Press.

Critchley, M. (1953). *The parietal lobes.* London: Edward Arnold.

Damasio, A.R. (1985). Disorders of complex visual processing: Agnosias, achromatopsia, Balint's syndrome, and related difficulties of orientation and construction. In M.-M. Mesulam (Ed.), *Principles of behavioral neurology* (pp. 259–288). Philadelphia: Davis.

Fogel, M.L. (1964). The intelligence quotient as an index of brain damage. *American Journal of Orthopsychiatry, 34,* 555–562.

Kawahata, N., Nagata, K., & Kawamura, M. (1988). Associative visual agnosia—A case report. *No To Shinkei, 40,* 253–260.

Keller, W.K. (1971). *A comparison of two procedures for assessing constructional praxis in patients with unilateral cerebral disease.* Unpublished doctoral dissertation, University of Iowa, Iowa City.

Kleist, K. (1923). Kriegsverletzungen des Gehirns in ihrer Bedeutung fur die Hirnlokalisation und Hirnpathologie. In O. von Schjerning (Ed.), *Handbuch der aerztlichen Erfahrung im Weltkriege 1914/1918, Band IV, Geistes und Nerenkrankheiten.* Leipzig: Barth.

Kleist, K. (1934). *Gehirnpathologie.* Leipzig: Barth.

Luria, A.R. (1973). *The working brain: An introduction to neuropsychology.* New York: Basic Books.

Luria, A.R. (1980). *Higher cortical functions in man* (2nd ed.). New York: Basic Books.

Mendez, M.F. (1988). Visuoperceptual function in visual agnosia. *Neurology, 38,* 1754–1759.

Sivan, A.B. (1991). *Benton Visual Retention Test* (5th ed.). San Antonio, TX: Psychological Corporation.

Spreen, O., & Gaddes, W.H. (1969). Developmental norms for 15 neuropsychological tests age 6 to 15. *Cortex, 5,* 170–191.

Wechsler, D. (1981). *Wechsler Adult Intelligence Scale–Revised manual.* San Antonio, TX: Psychological Corporation.

James A. Moses Jr., Ph.D.

Clinical Associate Professor of Psychiatry and Behavioral Sciences, Stanford University School of Medicine, and Coordinator, Psychological Assessment Unit, Department of Veterans Affairs Medical Center, Palo Alto, California.

VISUAL FORM DISCRIMINATION TEST

Arthur L. Benton, Kerry deS. Hamsher, Nils R. Varney, and Otfried Spreen. New York, New York: Oxford University Press.

Introduction

The Visual Form Discrimination Test (VFDT; Benton & Stone 1970; Benton, Hamsher, & Stone, 1977; Benton, Hamsher, Varney & Spreen, 1983) is a 16-item, multiple-choice, perceptual-matching task that measures the accuracy of a subject's ability to match a three-figure plane-geometric form stimulus array to one of four response alternative arrays. Each tripartite geometric form array is composed of two relatively large, centrally located, "major" figures and a single, smaller peripheral figure to the left or right side of the two central figures. One of the four choice alternatives or "foils" for each VFDT item is identical to the master or criterion array pattern. The other three alternative arrays always involve an error of peripheral detail (PE; different spatial location or peripheral figure rotation), or a single major figure rotation error (MR), or a single major figure distortion error (MD). Only one type of design error occurs on any single incorrect response choice alternative. The correct foil is placed four times in each of the four response alternative positions. The peripheral figure is placed on the right of the major figures in eight of the stimulus arrays and on the left of the major figures in the other eight stimulus arrays. On the PE response card choices, half of the peripheral errors involve displacement errors and the other half involve rotational errors. The subject's ability to match the criterion visual form array to its identical choice alternative and the related ability to discriminate the correct array from the three erroneous response choices for each item operationally defines this measure of complex plane-geometric form discrimination.

The ability to make fine visual-perceptual form discriminations of the kind modeled by VFDT items has been noted as a symptom of some types of regional and focal brain disease, particularly syndromes of dysfunction of the right cerebral hemisphere (Benton et al. 1983; Meier & French, 1965; Newcombe, 1969). In a syndrome-analytic study, Dee (1970) also noted a close association of deficit on visual form discrimination tasks with visually guided constructional difficulty. This symptom complex is particularly common in patients with right parietal lesions.

The principal author of the VFDT, Arthur L. Benton, Ph.D., received his A.B. (1931) and A.M. (1933) degrees from Oberlin College, followed by his Ph.D. from Columbia University (1935). He began his career as an assistant in psychology first at Oberlin College (1931–33), then at Columbia University and New York State

Psychiatric Institute (1934–36), and finally at Cornell University Medical College (1936–39), where he subsequently served as a staff psychologist. He was appointed as an attending psychologist at New York Hospital–Westchester Division and as a psychologist in the Student Personnel Office of the City College of New York from 1939 to 1941. He served on active duty in the U.S. Navy during and after the Second World War (1941–46), then was appointed as Associate Professor of Psychology at the University of Louisville Medical School and as Chief Psychologist at the Louisville Mental Hygiene Clinic and the Louisville General Hospital (1946–48). From 1948 to 1958 he served as Professor of Psychology and director of the graduate training program in clinical psychology at the University of Iowa, then, for the next two decades (1958–78), as Professor of Psychology and Neurology. Dr. Benton has continued to coauthor theoretical and research papers and books since 1978, when he became Professor Emeritus at the University of Iowa.

Benton's fundamental contributions to the field of clinical neuropsychology have been acknowledged extensively and internationally. He has received honorary Doctor of Science (Cornell College, 1978) and Doctor of Psychology (University of Rome, 1990) degrees, as well as numerous other honors and awards, including the Distinguished Service Award of the Iowa Psychological Association (1977), the Distinguished Professional Contribution Award from the American Psychological Association (1978), the Outstanding Scientific Contribution Award of the International Neuropsychological Society (1981), The Samuel Torrey Orton Award from the Orton Dyslexia Society (1982), the Distinguished Service and Outstanding Contributions Award from the American Board of Professional Psychology (1985), and the Distinguished Clinical Neuropsychologist Award from the National Academy of Neuropsychology (1989).

Benton is a past president of both the American Orthopsychiatric Association (1965–66) and the International Neuropsychological Society (1970–71), and he served as secretary-general of the Research Group on Aphasia for the World Federation of Neurology from 1971 to 1978. He has been a lecturer or visiting scholar at the University of Milan (1964), Hôpital Sainte-Anne, Paris (1968), Hadassah-Hebrew University Medical School, Jerusalem (1969), Free University of Amsterdam (1971), University of Helsinki (1974), University of Melbourne (1977), University of Minnesota Medical School (Baker Lecturer, 1979), University of Victoria, British Columbia (Lansdowne Scholar, 1980), and the University of Michigan (1986), as well as Directeur d'Études Associé, École des Hautes Études, Paris (1979) and a visiting scientist at the Tokyo Metropolitan Institute of Gerontology (1974).

Benton has authored, coauthored, or edited 12 books and monographs, approximately 150 professional journal articles, and 22 historical reviews in the area of clinical neuropsychology and behavioral neurology. He is recognized as a pioneer and a leading authority in the area of clinical neuropsychology.

The standardized, commercially published version of the VFDT appeared with the clinical manual for this and other tests in the Benton-Iowa Neuropsychological Test Battery (Benton et al., 1983). Coauthors of this clinical manual with Dr. Benton are Kerry deS. Hamsher, Ph.D. (Associate Professor of Neurology, University of Wisconsin Medical School); Nils R. Varney, Ph.D. (staff neuropsychologist, Department of Veterans Affairs Medical Center, Iowa City, Iowa); and Otfried

Spreen, Ph.D. (Professor Emeritus, Department of Psychology, University of Victoria, Victoria, British Columbia, Canada).

Practical Applications/Uses

Benton and his colleagues began to develop the VFDT item pool from an initial series of 64 multiple-choice complex visual form discrimination items. This item pool was administered to a sample of normal children to determine the relative item difficulty levels based on developmental item response trends (Benton et al., 1983, p. 55). The 16 test items that were chosen for the final form of the VFDT (Benton & Stone, 1970) represent considerable item difficulty variability but exclude the most elementary items that are too easy to have differential diagnostic value. Two of these elementary items are used as demonstration tasks to introduce the test.

The stimulus card and the multiple-choice response alternative card for each item are presented simultaneously. The response alternatives are laid flat on the table top and the stimulus card is held up at an angle of about 45 degrees from the table so that the patient can see the stimulus and response arrays easily. In the case of a patient with a homonymous visual field defect, the examiner should position the stimulus and response figures so that they are completely within the patient's intact visual field. All VFDT items are identified with a letter (demonstration items) or number (test items) in the lower left corner of the stimulus card. Further, each alternative array on the response card is numbered, 1–4.

The administration of the VFDT is straightforward. The process begins with the first practice or demonstration item, "A." The examiner points to the stimulus design of item A and says "See this design? Find it among these four designs" (pointing to the multiple-choice card). "Which one is it? Show me" (Benton et al., 1983, p. 57). If the subject responds by pointing to or calling the number of the correct response alternative, the examiner confirms the correct response and continues with demonstration item "B." If the patient gives an incorrect response to item A, the examiner explains the nature of the error (PE, MR, MD) by describing the difference between the incorrect and correct responses before administering item B. The nature of the errors on the other two incorrect response choices also are explained to the patient. The same procedure is employed for administering item B. Thereafter, on the 16 credited VFDT test items, the examiner provides no feedback on the correctness of responses or the nature of errors made. Answers are recorded on a special VFDT scoring sheet available from the publisher (for a facsimile, see Benton et al., 1983, p. 61). For each item the numbered response alternatives are listed in four columns by response type (correct, PE, MR, MD). A fifth column serves to record item nonresponse.

Although the VFDT is not a speeded test, after 30 seconds of nonresponse the test authors recommend that the examiner coax a response from the patient with the phrase, "Which one do you think is the same, what is your best guess?" (Benton et al., 1983, p. 57). As long as the patient actively works on VFDT alternative evaluation and is task-oriented in an attempt at solution, this effort should not be interrupted. If on the other hand the patient appears confused or clearly cannot discriminate between any of the alternatives, then the "no response" alternative should be marked for that item. A patient may be able to eliminate MR and MD errors but have difficulty choosing between correct and PE alternatives. If he or she cannot distinguish between a fully creditable (correct) and a partially creditable (PE) pair of response choices, the examiner assigns the PE alternative response. The logic of this forced-choice scoring is that because the patient could not distinguish the correct response from the peripheral error alternative, then the nature of the PE response could not be recognized and rejected. If the patient cannot distinguish between a PE response and a MD or MR response, the MD or MR alternative would be listed as the final scored response and no credit could be allowed for that item. The inability to choose among these alternatives indicates that the more serious, uncreditable perceptual error could not be distinguished and eliminated as a response alternative.

The VFDT scoring system is simple, actuarial, and objective. Two points are assigned to each fully correct response because the patient who chooses this alternative has recognized both the major figures and the peripheral figure elements of the design correctly. One point is assigned based on each of these two categorical perceptual features. With 16 creditable items, the maximum possible VFDT score is 32 points, and the score range is 0–32 points. As noted above, correct responses are credited with 2 points per item, PE responses are credited with 1 point per item, and MR or MD responses are not credited. A VFDT total score of 12 is consistent with a chance performance alone. There is a one-in-four chance of choosing the correct response by chance (4 fully correct responses by chance alone = 8 points overall), as well as a one-in-four chance of choosing a PE response by chance (4 PE point responses by chance = 4 points overall). The same chance response probabilities apply to the MR and MD choices, which are not credited and therefore do not contribute to the overall chance-response summary score of 12 points.

VFDT was normed on a mixed sample of 85 subjects who were either medical patients without history or evidence of brain disease or healthy volunteers. The relative proportions of subjects in each group, summary statistics to describe their demographic features, the nature of the illnesses in the medical control group, and variability statistics for VFDT total scores of each of the normative subsamples are not provided in the sample description in the test manual (Benton et al., 1983, p. 58). The four subsamples consisted of two groups of neurologically normal men and women, one aged less than 55 years and one aged greater than 55 years. VFDT mean total score performance on the sample of normal younger men (16–54) was nearly errorless ($n = 28$, VFDT $M = 30.8$, VFDT range = 28–32). The performance on VFDT total score among the sample of normal older men (55–75) showed a similar high mean but considerably more normal range variability ($n = 15$, VFDT $M = 29.3$, VFDT range = 23–32). This normative sample is small, and the possible biasing influence of outliers on the range statistic is unclear. Variability and standard error statistics would be helpful to evaluate group trends. The older VFDT normative samples optimally should be larger if they are to serve as a reference groups rather than only as group performance-level exemplars. The normative sample of medically normal younger women (16–54) also was nearly errorless on the average, but they showed more variability than the younger men on the range statistics ($n = 30$, VFDT $M = 29.9$, VFDT range = 24–32). Again the possible biasing effects of outliers on these range results is uncertain. The small sample of normal older women (n = 12, VFDT M = 30.3, range = 27–32) showed less variability than the younger women, but again the sample size appears far too small to show generalizable group variability trends in the age range sampled.

Benton et al. (1983, p. 58) inspected these data and reported that "since the observed differences among subgroups were small and inconsistent in direction, it was decided that no corrections for age or sex needed to be made." No statistical test of these numerical trends was performed to test this conclusion. Central tendency trends among the normative subsamples of subjects with 12 or more years of education (n = 72, VFDT M = 30.1, range = 24–32) and those with 11 or fewer years of education (n = 13, M = 30.2, range = 23–32) also were similar across subsamples, so that Benton and his colleagues also decided against computation of educational-level corrections for the VFDT. These results should be considered preliminary. Replication of these normative studies with larger samples, completely described demographically and statistically, are advisable.

The possible usefulness of age and educational corrections for optimization of VFDT differential diagnostic sensitivity and the breadth of generalizability of these preliminary results remain moot points to be settled by cross-validational studies. In particular, the possible debilitating effects of nonneurologic medical illness, the differences in performance level and pattern between and among neurologically normal subjects who are in good health versus those who are ill, demographic effects on both normal group types as a function of age, sex, and educational level, and developmental performance trends on VFDT in children have been explored only preliminarily to date. The nature of VFDT error types as a function of demographic characteristics is an important issue in pattern analysis to distinguish clinical syndromes from normal variants. Only after a thorough understanding of normal VFDT performance patterns and their variants has been established can we clearly characterize abnormal VFDT patterns. To recognize the discriminative value of pathological performance signs in cases that are outliers on the normal or neurologic patient score distributions, the limits and variants of each distribution must be well established. When such performance level data are not diagnostic, the item-pattern analysis may be particularly important for VFDT score analysis.

Benton et al. (1983, p. 58) noted that in the overall normative group of 85 subjects, VFDT performance-level total scores of 26 to 32 were attained by 95% of the group. Seventy-four percent (63/85) of the control subjects sampled produced errorless or nearly errorless VFDT total scores (range = 31–32). Ninety-seven percent of the sample earned VFDT total scores of 24 or more. The third-percentile VFDT total score of 23 points was chosen as the actuarial criterion of severe performance deficit.

Technical Aspects

Benton et al. (1983, pp. 59–60) originally validated the VFDT in a sample of 58 patients with medically proven disease of one or both cerebral hemispheres. The age range was 16 to 68 years, but the manual does not report other demographic details and associated descriptive statistics. Diagnostic breakdown of the sample showed 7 patients with bilateral or diffuse lesion syndromes, 32 with left-hemispheric disease, and 19 with right-hemispheric disease. Twenty-three of the left-hemispheric lesion subgroup cases were aphasic.

In a summary of trends, Benton et al. (1983) noted the high frequency of failure on the VFDT in all of the lesion locus syndrome groups. More than half of the patients in the pooled total data sample (31/58, 53%) performed defectively, achieving VFDT total scores of 23 or less. VFDT failure rates for patients with bilateral or diffuse lesions were considerably higher (5/7, 71%) than those for patients with either unilateral left-hemispheric lesions (15/32, 47%) or unilateral right-hemispheric lesions (11/19, 58%). Among patients with left-hemispheric lesions, aphasics failed the task relatively less often (10/23, 43%) than did nonaphasics (5/9, 56%).

Within the *left*-hemispheric lesion group, the failure rate was highest in patients with left anterior lesions (7/12, 58%), intermediate in patients with left posterior lesions (7/15, 47%), and lowest in patients with left anterior-posterior lesions (1/5, 20%). Among patients with *right*-hemispheric lesions, the highest frequency of VFDT failure was seen with right posterior lesions (7/9, 78%), an intermediate failure frequency occurred with right anterior lesions (3/7, 43%), and the lowest rate was seen in patients with right anterior-posterior lesions (1/3, 33%).

Due to the general sensitivity of the VFDT to lesions of both cerebral hemispheres, Benton et al. (1983, p. 60) recommended its inclusion in clinical psychometric batteries designed to screen prodromal and early phase cortical dementia syndromes. Benton et al. (1983, p. 59) acknowledged the sensitivity but questioned the specificity of VFDT total score, performance-level results for analysis of focal brain lesion regional effects. In particular they questioned whether failure on the task measured a specific perceptual skill or alternatively reflected generalized attention and concentration breakdown related to brain dysfunction. They noted, however, that the extreme rate of VFDT failure among patients with right posterior lesions was a syndrome pattern consistent with theoretical expectations. They also cited the work of Varney (1981), who found that "aphasic alexics . . . with severely defective reading comprehension . . ." who could still recognize letters failed the VFDT with 36% frequency, while those who could not recognize letters failed with 85% frequency. The rate of VFDT failure was 13% among patients with mild reading comprehension deficit. Varney also noted that increasing VFDT performance level was related to improvement in letter reading performance during the course of recovery from this aphasic disorder.

Failure on the VFDT also can be associated with defective visual-spatial ability in the syndrome of visual neglect or more generally with inefficient visual-perceptual pattern searching. In the case of visual neglect, the response choices on only one side of the page may be chosen. Consistent failure to note errors in major or peripheral figures on one side of a single item array also might occur in milder cases. A similar pattern may occur with a homonymous central visual field defect. Benton et al. (1983, pp. 59–60) suggest that the VFDT should be supplemented with other special psychometric perceptual measures that are specifically designed to evaluate these visual-spatial and visual search deficiency syndromes. The interested reader should refer to the test manual for primary references to these specialized examination materials.

Mendez, Mendez, Martin, Smyth, and Whitehouse (1990) reported that deficit performance on the VFDT served as a useful marker variable for complex visual-perceptual deficit in patients with Alzheimer-type dementia (ATD). They noted a significant association between the Clinical Dementia Rating Scale and the Blessed Dementia Rating Scale syndrome severity scores with the VFDT total score. The ATD samples also were divided into subgroups with and without "prominent abnormalities in scanning, searching, and hand-eye coordination consistent with Balint's syndrome" (Mendez et al., 1990, p. 442). The ATD subjects with the Balint syndrome visual-scanning abnormalities showed poorer performance on the VFDT than those without this condition, as was predicted by Benton et al. (1983). In a case study presentation, Mendez (1988, p. 1754) showed that two patients who presented at testing with visual agnosia after recovery from cortical blindness "were successful on form discrimination (VFDT), mental rotation, and visuospatial skills, but did poorly on figure-ground discrimination, visual integration, facial discrimination, and constructional tasks." These findings suggest that the VFDT has both convergent and divergent validity with other visual-perceptual measures that are useful in complex visual-perceptual syndrome analysis.

Valdois, Poissant, and Joanette (1989) investigated the qualitative nature of VFDT errors in ATD and control subjects aged 55 to 84 years. Both groups produced significantly more peripheral errors (PE) than major rotation (MR) or major distortion (MD) errors. The frequency of all VFDT error types was significantly increased for the ATD group relative to the controls. Further studies of this kind to determine the value of itemized error analysis in specific clinical syndromes are needed to optimize the usefulness of the VFDT as a pattern-analytic as well as a performance-level measure.

Moses (1986, 1989) showed that the VFDT is factorially related to the Revised Visual Retention Test (Benton, 1974) copy and memory scores. The contribution of attention span (as measured by WAIS-R Digit Span) to VFDT performance was inconsistent across these studies. The convergent validity of the VFDT with measures of visual construction (copy) and visual recall is theoretically predictable. One must be able to accurately perceive the figures, the VFDT task, in order to copy or to recall them. Execution of each of these tasks depends on mastery of the previous elements in the sequence.

Critique

The VFDT is a rigorously designed measure of complex visual form discrimination that is relatively sensitive to focal, lateralized (especially right-hemispheric) and generalized brain disease. To date it has been studied relatively little in the empirical literature, although it is widely used in clinical work. The test is useful for monitoring changes in complex visual-perceptual skills during recovery from alexic aphasic syndromes. Its role in other specific aphasic disorders remains to be clarified.

The VFDT also has proven sensitive to level-of-performance deficit in a variety of dementing conditions, particularly during the diagnostically difficult early syndrome onset period. This measure's sensitivity increases when it is used in combination with other standardized Benton-Iowa battery measures of temporal orientation and verbal fluency. The VFDT also shows impressive convergent and discriminant validity in a syndrome-analytic report of two patients with complex visual agnosic syndromes. More studies of this multidimensional, well-operationalized type are needed to test the syndrome specificity and generality of the VFDT as a diagnostic measure. Its diagnostic specificity seems to be increased when one analyzes specific error patterns within dementia syndrome types in addition to the performance-level summary score.

Theoretical and clinical work that has made use of the VFDT to date primarily has been exploratory. Benton et al. (1983) encourage systematic empirical study in combination with other measures of specific perceptual functions to determine the basis of VFDT errors in clinical cases. This dimensional syndrome-analytic approach also can be encouraged on empirical grounds in normal and clinical groups. The role of the VFDT in the analysis of psychiatric syndromes has been generally neglected and should be systematically investigated. Validity studies to date have been promising with neurologic groups, but much more work is needed to explore the specific patterns and limits of VFDT sensitivity to definition of perceptual syndrome deficit in subgroups of more general diagnostic syndrome categories such as aphasic, dementing, and visual agnosic syndrome groups, all of which have been proven to show performance-level deficit on this measure. Investigators also should include itemized error analysis in the design of all syndromatic studies.

Data on the specificity of the VFDT as a function of perceptual error type, lesion chronicity, lesion locus, and neurologic diagnosis are needed to develop an integrated assessment approach that includes other measures that are sensitive and specific to the syndrome being studied. The work of Eslinger and Benton (1983) is illustrative in this regard. Now that we know that the VFDT is sensitive to the *level* of performance findings in a variety of clinical neurologic groups, subsequent studies are needed to establish its construct validity relative to other measures of known validity. Current evidence suggests that the VFDT is more sensitive and specific when used in conjunction with other rigorous, standardized psychometric measures rather than when used alone. This reviewer recommends using it in theoretically guided, integrated batteries of psychometric measures that are designed for analyzing specific disorders, such as the specific aphasic and dementing subgroup syndromes.

Perhaps the next series studies that should be undertaken before the clinical syndrome analyses are those that most often are neglected in applied clinical work, particularly in clinical neuropsychological research. These are studies to establish test-retest and internal consistency reliability values for the VFDT. No such reports appear in the test manual, and demonstration of reliable findings on these statistics is basic to assertions that VDFT results are accurate and stably reproducible. Test-retest reliability should be established in a sample retested over approximately a 2-week period during which they are clinically stable. The value ideally should approximate .80 in a test of this length. Internal consistency ideally should be calculated in a sample of 300 or more cases of mixed diagnostic and demographic characteristics using Cronbach's coefficient alpha statistic. This result also should approximate .80 if error variance is to be minimized. Internal consistency results based on a sample size of 300 or more cases should generalize to a sample of essentially any size (Nunnally, 1978). The normative samples for VFDT need to be increased, particularly in the elderly groups, and subsequent investigators should reinvestigate the role of demographic variables that may affect performance level. In particular age, sex, and educational level are at issue. Full descriptive statistical and diagnostic characteristics of the samples should be reported to allow for judgment of the results' generalizability.

Preliminary validational studies of the VFDT are most encouraging, but extensive additional investigation is needed to establish its psychometric characteristics more rigorously. Empirical results to date suggest that subsequent syndrome-pattern-analytic studies of the VFDT with refined clinical subgroups will continue to extend its range of application. Such studies also should more clearly define its sensitivity and specificity as a valuable clinical and experimental measure of complex perceptual form discrimination.

References

Benton, A.L. (1974). *Revised Visual Retention Test: Clinical and experimental applications* (4th ed.). San Antonio, TX: Psychological Corporation.

Benton, A.L., Hamsher, K.deS., & Stone, F.B. (1977). *Visual Retention Test: Multiple Choice Form I. Administration F: Visual form discrimination. Administration G: Multiple choice—memory.* Unpublished manuscript, University of Iowa, Department of Neurology, Division of Behavioral Neurology, Iowa City.

Benton, A.L., Hamsher, K.deS., Varney, N.R., & Spreen, O. (1983). *Contributions to neuropsychological assessment: A clinical manual.* New York: Oxford University Press.

Benton, A.L., & Stone, F.B. (1970). *Visual Retention Test: Multiple Choice Form I.* (Stimulus plates). Iowa City: Neurosensory Center and Department of Neurology, The University of Iowa College of Medicine.

Dee, H.L. (1970). Visuoconstructive and visuoperceptive deficits in patients with unilateral cerebral lesions. *Neuropsychologia, 8,* 305–314.

Eslinger, P.J., & Benton, A.L. (1983). Visuoperceptual performances in aging and dementia: Clinical and theoretical implications. *Journal of Clinical Neuropsychology, 5,* 213–220.

Meier, M.J., & French, L.A. (1965). Lateralized deficits in complex visual discrimination and bilateral transfer of reminiscence following unilateral temporal lobectomy. *Neuropsychologia, 3,* 261–272.

Mendez, M.F. (1988). Visuoperceptual function in visual agnosia. *Neurology, 38,* 1754–1759.

Mendez, M.F., Mendez, M.A., Martin, R., Smyth, K.A., & Whitehouse, P.J. (1990). Complex visual disturbances in Alzheimer's disease. *Neurology, 40,* 439–443.

Moses, J.A., Jr. (1986). Factor structure of Benton's tests of visual retention, visual construction, and visual form discrimination. *Archives of Clinical Neuropsychology, 1,* 147–156.

Moses, J.A., Jr. (1989). Replicated factor structure of Benton's tests of visual retention, visual construction, and visual form discrimination. *International Journal of Clinical Neuropsychology, 11,* 30–37.

Newcombe, F. (1969). *Missile wounds of the brain.* London: Oxford University Press.

Nunnally, J.C. (1978). *Psychometric theory* (2nd ed.). New York: McGraw-Hill.

Valdois, S., Poissant, A., & Joanette, Y. (1989). Visual form discrimination in normal aging and dementia of the Alzheimer type. *Journal of Clinical and Experimental Neuropsychology, 11,* 91.

Varney, N.R. (1981). Letter recognition and visual form discrimination in aphasic alexia. *Neuropsychologia, 19,* 795–800.

James A. Moses, Jr., Ph.D.
Clinical Associate Professor of Psychiatry and Behavioral Sciences,
Stanford University School of Medicine, and Coordinator,
Psychological Assessment Unit, Department of Veterans Affairs
Medical Center, Palo Alto, California.

WARD ATMOSPHERE SCALE

Rudolf H. Moos. Palo Alto, California: Consulting
Psychologists Press, Inc.

Introduction

The Ward Atmosphere Scale (WAS; Moos, 1974b, 1974c, 1989) is designed to objectify, clarify, specify, and compare multidimensional, categorically descriptive, and phenomenologically impressionistic information from patients and staff in a wide variety of inpatient psychiatric units about the perceived social climate of their treatment setting. The WAS is a 100-item questionnaire comprised of brief declarative statements to which the respondent answers "true" or "false."

Three forms of the WAS are available for comparison of real, ideal, and expected social environmental characteristics in psychiatric ward treatment settings. Items of the *Real Form* (Form R), stated in the present tense, are to be used by patients and staff familiar enough with the ward environment to rate these qualities of the program. The *Expectations Form* (Form E) items, phrased in the future tense, are applicable to persons either about to enter a new ward setting or about to experience some significant change in their current ward patient population, staff, or setting. The *Ideal Form* (Form I), which phrases items conditionally, describes what an ideal psychiatric ward setting might be like.

A short form (Form S) also is available. Form S adequately meets psychometric criteria for analysis of ward treatment programs, but it has too few items to reliably distinguish among the reports of individuals. Composed of the first 40 items of Form R, it draws 4 items from each of the 10 WAS subscales.

The WAS has been translated and validated in several other countries besides the United States, where it was developed. The WAS test manual refers to adaptations and validational studies that have been completed in several languages: Afrikaans, Dutch (Ejsing, 1980; Verhaest, Pierloot, & Janssens, 1982), Hebrew (De-Nour, 1983; Meier, 1983), Italian (Burti, Glick, & Tansella, 1986), German, French (Dauwalder, Chabloz, & Chappuis, 1978), Finnish (Plosila, 1978), Swedish (Gren, Ared, & Nilsson, 1978), and Norwegian (Friis, 1981a, 1981b, 1986a, 1986b). The WAS also has been widely used in Great Britain (Moos, 1972).

The WAS has not been revised since its commercial appearance (Moos, 1974b, 1974c), but a revised administrative and interpretive manual for the test (Moos, 1989) has been published. The revised manual contains an extensive update of the WAS literature, clinical and research applications of the test, and valuable new psychometric data with new derived scales that are useful in treatment planning and program evaluation. The test author advises that the original manual can be used for WAS administration and basic scale scoring, but that the new document now is the standard work for clinical and research applications.

The author of the WAS, Rudolf H. Moos, received the B.A. with honors (1956) and the Ph.D. (1960) degrees from the University of California, Berkeley. Thereafter he was a postdoctoral fellow at the University of California, San Francisco, for 2 years. He is a diplomate in clinical psychology of the American Board of Professional Psychology (1965), a recipient of the Hofheimer Award for Research of the American Psychiatric Association (1975), a Department of Veterans Affairs career scientist (since 1981), and a fellow of numerous learned societies. He has been a faculty member of the Department of Psychiatry and Behavioral Sciences at Stanford University since 1962 (Professor since 1972), and he serves as the director of the postdoctoral research training program at that institution. At the Department of Veterans Affairs Medical Center in Palo Alto, California, Dr. Moos serves as the chief of psychiatric research and directs both the Center for Health Case Evaluation and the Program Evaluation and Resource Center. He had published 12 books and 270 book chapters, manuals, literature reviews, and professional research articles through January 1988. He is best known for his pioneering work in the development and implementation of the social ecological approach to programmatic classification, description, evaluation, and consultation.

Development of the initial WAS item pool began with observing inpatient psychiatric hospital programs, conducting structured interviews with psychiatric inpatients and staff, and reviewing the popular and professional literature concerning psychiatric inpatient treatment. Based on information gained from these sources, Moos developed a preliminary 206-item Form A of the WAS. Item wording derived from the theoretical model of Moos and his colleagues that social ecological description of treatment settings can be described best according to dimensions of interpersonal relationships, personal growth, and programmatic organizational structure. Each item written reflected a specific aspect of one of these three general content areas.

Form A of the WAS was administered to patients and staff from 14 psychiatric inpatient programs. From those data the researchers selected a reduced set of 130 WAS items according to four psychometric criteria. First, the items chosen for the 130-item form had to discriminate significantly among different inpatient psychiatric treatment programs. Approximately 90% of the items selected met this criterion for patients, and approximately 80% met it for staff. Second, three judges had to agree independently that a WAS item measures one of 12 specific dimensions. Each of these dimensions had 10 items. An additional social desirability response set dimension was included in this phase of the scale development, restricting selection to items endorsed by less than 80% of the respondents. This criterion was added to eliminate items that typified only extreme programs. Finally, each subscale was composed of approximately equal numbers of items answered "true" or "false," to control for acquiescence response bias.

Based on these preliminary item analyses, the 130-item reduced Form B of the WAS was developed. Research participants administered it to patients and treatment staff in 160 psychiatric programs in the United States and Canada. Based on this much larger sample, a final rigorous psychometric analysis of the data was carried out to reduce the item pool to the final 100-item form.

Four subsamples were drawn randomly from the very large database described. Based on each subsample, the developers made calculations of item intercorrelations, item-to-subscale correlations, and intersubscale correlations. They eliminated items with low item-to-subscale correlations, because these items were not strong measures of the overall construct or theoretical dimension measured by that subscale. Items that did not discriminate among qualitatively different programs or were not behaviorally specific also were eliminated from the final form of the WAS.

Similarly, the developers eliminated preliminary items that correlated highly with the social desirability response set (an index of acquiescence) or with each other, or that overlapped substantially with other items in the subscale (indications of item redundancy). One preliminary subscale was eliminated altogether because it had low internal consistency, meaning it did not accurately measure a single behavioral dimension. Two other preliminary subscales were combined because they were highly intercorrelated. The final form of the WAS has 100 items and 10 subscales.

Instructions for Form R are relatively simple, requiring the respondent to mark an item "true" if the statement is definitely or mostly true, or false if definitely or mostly false, as it applies to the individual's current view of the psychiatric inpatient unit.

Form E presents the same statements to respondents, phrased in the future tense. In this case one is asked to describe what a new unit about to be entered "will be like," or what the current unit may be like after some sort of anticipated programmatic change. In the case of Form I, the format asks respondents to describe what an ideal unit "would be like."

The WAS is recommended for self-report group administration, with the assurance of individual anonymity to encourage candor in describing the unit rather than defensive or socially desirable responses (some participants may fear a penalty if they are critical about their unit's program or staff).

The WAS test form consists of a 4-page reuseable question booklet. On a separate answer sheet the individual records the scale name (WAS; the same answer form is also used for another Social Climate Scale), the form of the WAS being taken, the date, and the basic demographic information of name (or code number), age, hospital program, sex, period of hospital residence in the current ward or program (in years, months, and days), lifetime length of experience living or working in mental hospitals (in years, months, and days), and exact professional title (staff only). Worked examples appear for "true" and "false" responses to questions. Numbered boxes corresponding to each question are divided in half. "True" is indicated by marking an "X" in the top half of the box, "false" by marking in the bottom half.

The profile sheet can be used with any of the 10 Social Climate Scales. The form provides spaces for the respondent's name or code number, the Social Climate Scale used, the normative group used to transform raw scores to scaled scores, the date of administration, and miscellaneous supplementary data. The legend of the profile has boxes to indicate the scaled score and the subscale title acronym for the appropriate Social Climate Scale used.

On Form R, the developers have provided several elaborate sets of separate norms for representative samples of individual American and British psychiatric patient and staff respondents. Each of these normative samples and their uses will be considered in turn.

Form R: American normative sample. This sample is drawn from

> 160 programs in 44 hospitals located in 16 states. It includes 55 programs in 10 state hospitals, 55 programs in 14 Veterans Administration hospitals, 28 programs in 14 university and teaching hospitals, and 22 programs in 6 community and private hospitals. A total of 3,575 patients and 1,958 staff was tested. (Moos, 1989, p. 8; see also Moos, 1974c, chapter 3)

The test manual (Moos, 1989, p. 9) provides separate normative means and standard deviations for the WAS Form R subscales for patient and treatment staff respondents in the 160 programs sampled. In addition to the standard deviation for the averaged programmatic data for each WAS subscale, there is a separate standard deviation value based on the individual responses of 982 representative psychiatric patients or 876 representative staff members for the respective samples. The standard deviations based on entire programs are smaller values because the individual response variations were averaged to produce group results. These data should be used to compare a WAS description of an entire program with the normative sample values. When comparing individuals with the normative sample, one should use the standard deviations based on the individual responses.

In the appendices to the test manual (Moos, 1989, pp. 65–66) appear tables to translate the mean raw score (for a whole program) on each WAS scale to a standard score for patient respondents. For staff respondents there are normative tables to translate mean raw scores to standard scores both on patient norms and on staff norms. Analysis of the staff responses plotted on patient norms allows one to directly compare patient and staff evaluations of a program using the same normative standards to test for areas of similarity and difference. Use of the mean staff responses plotted on staff norms allows one to compare modal staff perceptions in one treatment program with those from other programs. Another table in the appendix (Moos, 1989, p. 67) allows one to directly convert raw scores for individual profiles to standard scores. Separate normative values are provided for patients and staff.

In an analysis of trends in these data for mean patient versus staff perceptions of treatment programs, Moos (1989, p. 8) notes that

> staff tend to report more emphasis in most areas than do patients. Specifically, staff see treatment programs as more involving, supportive, and spontaneous and as more strongly oriented toward independence, practical and personal problem orientation, and the open expression of anger. They also report clearer expectations but less order and organization and staff control.

Form R: British normative sample. As reported in the manual,

> the British normative sample is composed of 36 programs drawn from 8 hospitals. It includes 3 psychiatric programs in general medical hospitals, 12 programs in university teaching hospitals, and 21 programs in psychiatric hospitals of varying sizes in urban and rural areas. A total of 450 patients and 290 staff were tested. The sample represents a broad range of treatment orientations and includes an acute admission program, a long-term psychotherapy program, and programs for adolescents, geriatric patients, and chronic patients. (Moos, 1989, pp. 8–10)

Descriptive statistics are provided for the British normative sample in the test manual and are divided into patient and staff normative groups.

The manual provides no tables for translation of raw scores to standard scores for the British patient or staff samples, but this could be accomplished easily with a simple computer program based on the descriptive statistical data provided. Norming of staff responses on patient sample norms is not reported, but this appears to be a useful adjunctive analysis for British users of the WAS. Apparently the WAS target audience has been conceptualized as primarily an American one, and through the time of the writing of the revised manual these analyses had not been completed. The manual also reports no normative numerical data on British samples for WAS Forms E, I, or S.

Form R: Cross-national comparisons. In the manual Moos (1989, p. 10) reports a summary of comparisons of the British and American samples on Form R of the WAS. Thirty-six American psychiatric units were chosen to match the sample of British treatment programs in patient population and unit staff-to-patient ratio. In general the pattern of findings was similar in America and Britain. Differences in emphasis suggested cultural variations. Those noted involved "more involvement, autonomy, practical and personal problem orientation, and staff control" on the part of the Americans relative to the British. For more detailed discussions of these analyses, the reader is referred to the primary sources by Moos (1972; 1974a, chapter 3).

Form S: American normative sample. Mean and standard deviation data on Form S appear separately in the test manual for patient and staff groups. Form S norms derive from the same 160-program sample as in Form R. A table in the manual's appendix provides mean raw scores for the short form of each WAS subscale. Separate norms are provided to translate mean raw scores to standard scores for patients. As with Form R, mean raw scores for staff are normed on both patient and staff norms (the rationale for which appeared previously in this review).

Form I: American normative sample. The normative sample for Form I of the WAS consisted of 2,364 patients and 897 staff members in 68 psychiatric programs (Moos, 1989, p. 11). Normative values in the manual provide separate values for psychiatric patients and staff. Within the patient normative group, mean values appear with standard deviation values both for programs (averaged group data) and for individual respondents. Comparison of mean composite reports on a program as a whole with the normative sample would employ the program standard deviation measure. Comparison of individuals with the normative sample would use the standard deviation for individuals.

Form I: American staff versus patient comparison. Moos (1989) notes that American patients and staff share generally similar concepts of an optimal psychiatric treatment program. Differences between their views show that staff would prefer to enhance interpersonal aspects of the program (relationship and personal growth variables) and relatively de-emphasize staff control relative to patient preferences.

Form I: British sample. Although data were collected from 242 patients and 124 staff members in 23 British programs (Moos, 1989, p. 12), they unfortunately are not presented in the manual for normative use. Their representativeness may not have sufficed for this purpose, but the reason for the omission of this analysis is not given.

Form I: Cross-national comparisons. Comparisons of the British and American samples on Form I showed generally similar patterns. Important differences of emphasis for optimal programs in different cultures, however, are instructive. Relative to their British peers, the American patients emphasized a desire for "a more active treatment program. . . . specifically they want more emphasis on involvement, practical orientation, self-understanding, and staff control" (Moos, 1989, p. 12; see also Moos, 1974a, chapter 3).

Practical Applications/Uses

The WAS is based on a tricategorical social ecological model that has been developed and extensively studied by Moos and his colleagues. Their work derives from the theoretical formulations of Henry Murray (1938), who first emphasized the complementary roles of individual needs and environmental press as codeterminants of complex social perception and behavior. The model on which these researchers developed the WAS postulates three categories of Relationship, Personal Growth or Goal Orientation, and System Maintenance dimensions. On the WAS these three sets of dimensions are measured for inpatient psychiatric programs with 10 subscales. Moos (1989, p. 2) provides the following brief descriptions of the 10 WAS subscales in his revised test manual:

RELATIONSHIP DIMENSIONS

Involvement—how active and energetic patients are in the program
Support—how much patients help and support each other and how supportive the staff is toward patients
Spontaneity—how much the program encourages the open expression of feelings by patients and staff

PERSONAL GROWTH DIMENSIONS

Autonomy—how self-sufficient and independent patients are in decision making
Practical Orientation—the extent to which patients learn practical skills and are prepared for release from the program
Personal Problem Orientation—the extent to which patients seek to understand their feelings and personal problems
Anger and Aggression—the extent to which patients argue with other patients and staff, become openly angry, and display other aggressive behavior
Order and Organization—how important order and organization are in the program

SYSTEM MAINTENANCE DIMENSIONS

Program Clarity—the extent to which patients know what to expect in their day-to-day routine and the explicitness of program rules and procedures
Staff Control—the extent to which the staff uses measures to keep patients under necessary controls

The primary application of the WAS in clinical and consultative settings has remained program description and evaluation at the individual and group levels.

Using various forms of the WAS in combination has proven beneficial in the assessment of individuals and programs. The information gained from a comparison of two forms of the WAS on the same individual or program provides unique information that cannot be gathered from either form alone. The categorical subscale structure of the WAS is particularly well designed to make such comparisons dimensionally clear. Comparing patient and staff perceptions of the treatment program on Form R can clarify areas of similarity and difference between the two groups in such important areas as interpersonal style, perceived behavioral limits and flexibility of roles for patients and staff, and treatment goal setting and implementation. The relative emphases among these factors may influence treatment planning and its effectiveness.

For extensive reviews of the literature on basic and applied work with the WAS, the interested reader should consult the test manual and the articles and reviews by Cronkite, Moos, and Finney (1984), Finney and Moos (1984), Moos (1984, 1985a, 1985b), Moos, Clayton, and Max (1979), and Moos and Spinrad (1984).

Users can study type and degree of desired program change when Forms R and I are administered to the same patient or staff groups. From these two sets of data on each respondent, one can calculate the raw difference scores between the real and ideal program descriptions on each subscale of the WAS. Typically Form R scores are subtracted from Form I scores for each respondent to lessen the frequency of negative values. A difference score of 0 on any subscale indicates no perceived desire for change or attainment of the optimal desired state for that individual. A higher Form I than Form R (positive difference score) value on a subscale indicates a desire for greater expression of that dimension in the program. A lower Form I than Form R (negative difference score) value on a subscale indicates a desire for lesser expression of the pattern in the program.

Judging from the magnitude of the standard deviations for Forms R and I subscales, a raw difference score on the order of 1 to 2 points should fall within the interpretable range. Consideration of the differences between staff and patients in terms of variability of scores by subtest is advisable to adjust for the amount of variability in the respective samples. Differences on the order of a standard deviation should suffice for clinical inference in the light of other behavioral data. The above recommendation for interpretation of difference scores on the order of 1 to 2 points derives from this rough standard. The manual for the WAS does not provide clinical examples of this application, but similar test statistics and interpretive rules are recommended for other social climate scales by Moos and his colleagues.

Patients about to enter a new treatment program, as in a ward transfer, or those about to undergo some change in the established treatment program routine can be evaluated before and after the programmatic change using Form E of the WAS. Comparison of Form E with Form R could highlight differences between the anticipated (Form E) and currently experienced (Form R) treatment programs. The same sort of comparison of profiles within patients and between staff and patients across these forms of the test could be carried out with the difference score analyses as outlined above for comparison of Forms R and I.

Another potential use of the alternate forms of the WAS would involve comparing Forms E and I in the same patient or staff groups who were about to undergo some sort of predictable change in the treatment program milieu. In this case one could compare the expected and the optimal changes and perhaps improve the fit between them. If this is not possible, then one could use the discrepancy information to work with patient and staff groups in a consultant role to help them to reduce cognitive dissonance and to improve adjustment to the real-ideal discrepancy if it falls well short of the optimal desired standard.

Administration of more than one form of the WAS is likely to give considerably richer clinical information than any one form of the WAS used in isolation. The optimal combination of forms to administer will depend on the clinical or consulting question in a given setting. Different forms should be taken at different sittings to minimize fatigue and to keep the descriptions disjoint and objective.

Professional qualifications for program consultants who employ the WAS are not stated explicitly in the test manual, but one would expect a qualified user to have completed graduate-level training in a mental health specialty and to have mastered at least a journeyman's level of working knowledge in psychometric theory and statistics. Nonpsychologists in psychiatric treatment settings who make use of the WAS for program evaluation would do well to seek the assistance of such a professional consultant when WAS profile results are interpreted for their programs.

It is important to note that while the WAS is clearly operationalized and easy to administer and score, its interpretation is by no means simplistic. A professional psychologist would be the preferred consultant to an inpatient treatment program tapping the WAS for programmatic description and evaluation.

The WAS is suitable for administration in a wide variety of inpatient psychiatric treatment settings. Although designed primarily for the evaluation of psychiatric treatment programs, some work has begun to extend its use to other medical inpatient treatment programs as well (Alexy, 1981–82; Amaral, Nehemkis, & Fox, 1981; De-Nour, 1983; Rhodes, 1981; Stuart, 1977).

Common applications of the WAS have involved analysis and comparison of hospital-based psychiatric treatment program models and settings (Archer & Amuso, 1980; Grant & Saslow, 1971), documentation of perceived social climate alteration after significant programmatic change (Eriksen, 1987; Willer, 1977), social climate analysis of social learning programs (Gripp & Magaro, 1971; Jeger, 1977), and perceived effects of program relocation (Kelly, 1983). The role of individualizing treatment goals and methods (Willer, 1977), therapeutic community design (Ingstad & Gotestam, 1979; Verhaest, 1983), and effects on therapeutic milieu of therapeutic training for treatment staff (Leviege, 1970) have been documented with the WAS. The instrument also has been used for treatment program problem identification and remediation (Ejsing, 1980; Milne, 1986; Moos, 1973; Pierce, Trickett, & Moos, 1972).

The WAS normative database is extensive and varied. Key validational studies with the WAS show encouraging levels of individual and group cross-cultural and cross-program-type sensitivity and specificity in a wide range of diagnostic groups. Although the minimal age for WAS administration is not stated explicitly in the test manual, the sixth-grade reading level required for independent completion of the scale as well as the item content suggest that it is not appropriate for use before age 11. It is probably best suited to the evaluation of adolescent and adult psychiatric inpatients.

The WAS typically is self-administered as a self-report measure. Moos recommends anonymity for individual patient and staff respondents on the Social Climate Scales. Comparison of anonymous and identified respondents showed more conservative response trends when respondents identified themselves on the answer sheets (Cox, 1977). A quiet, well-lighted, well-ventilated room with sufficient working space for each respondent should be provided for completion of the scale.

The emotional distress, disinhibition, and judgment deficit that may comprise part of the clinical picture in many psychiatric disorders during the acute phase of the disturbance suggests that a proctor should be present to monitor the WAS administration. The proctor should encourage task orientation and absence of socializing or response comparison between patients during the testing session. Respondents who are unsophisticated or disturbed may require more assistance, particularly with explanation of unfamiliar words. Such persons should be tested individually or in small groups as necessary. Simple restatements of individual word meanings are allowable, but the proctor must not influence the responses of patients or staff.

The proctor should read the directions aloud to the respondents while they read them silently and follow the response examples. Lead pencils with erasers should be provided to the respondents so that they do not use pens. Individuals who have difficulty answering questions as true or false should be advised to answer questions "true" if in their opinion the statement is "true most of the time." Persons still unable to answer decisively should be encouraged to guess as an alternative to nonresponse. Particularly on Form S, respondents should answer every item. Incomplete protocols endanger reliability of measurement and hence compromise validity as well. Answer sheets should be checked for completeness of demographic information and responses to test questions as the forms are collected.

In most situations administration of the WAS is straightforward and poses no difficulty for the proctor or for respondents who can read at a sixth-grade level. For patients without that reading ability, Moos recommends using tape-recorded or computerized instructions (1987, p. 23). In psychiatric treatment settings, the proctor might simply read the questions aloud to the respondents, as the suggested audiovisual devices typically are not available in such settings. For respondents with an especially low intelligence level or a generally impaired level of functioning, personal interviewing by a mental health professional and simplification of the language of some items may be necessary to ensure response validity and item comprehension.

Each form of the WAS typically requires 15 to 20 minutes to complete. Forms I and E are available from the publisher for noncommercial use. If more than one form of the WAS is to be administered to the same person, the two versions of the test should be administered at different sittings to prevent response stereotypy.

Scoring of the WAS is a clerical task. The items of the 10 WAS subscales appear in columns on the answer sheet. One places the clear plastic scoring template over the answer sheet and counts the number of answer marks (X's) that show through the circular marks on the scoring template. These sums become the subscale raw scores that are entered in boxes below the response portion of the sheet. The user translates the raw scores to scaled scores using tables provided for a variety of normative groups. The manual provides norms for standard score equivalents of raw scores based on American sample test data only.

Interpretation of the WAS is norm-referenced. Intergroup comparisons on the same form or interform profile differences for the same group typically are interpreted when they approach 1 standard deviation. To benefit users, future work on the WAS should include statistics for standard error of measurement and standard error of difference statistics. These measures can be used to develop objective empirical criteria for statistical significance of score differences or elevations above the mean of the profile at various probability levels. Such tables would help WAS users to identify profile elevations and differences that differ significantly from chance. As it stands, one must infer significance levels through impressionistic intergroup or interform comparison of individuals and groups to make such decisions on a subjective basis. It is notable that real-ideal difference scores of as little as 1 to 2 raw score points may represent significant differences, given the small standard deviation values for both patients and staff on the WAS subscales.

The interpretations modeled by Moos in the test manual (1989, pp. 22–26) compare patients and staff in four modal psychiatric treatment programs on Form R. Various forms of congruence and dissimilarity are highlighted among programs and between staff and patients in programs that vary in their perceived treatment effectiveness. The similarities and differences of the comparisons are made dimensionally clear through the use of the WAS's multiple content categories.

New users of the WAS should implement the methodology with familiar programs whose dimensional characteristics are known. In this way the novice can gain a better impression of the meaning of elevations and profile patterns of the various WAS scales and their characteristics in describing a known program. Descriptions of prototypical treatment programs in the test manual (Moos, 1989, pp. 39–42) are particularly useful in this regard. Sample profiles appear for therapeutic community, relationship-oriented, action-oriented, insight-oriented, control-oriented, and disturbed behavior types of treatment programs.

Technical Aspects

In order for a test to be accurate and for its results to be reproducible, it must be a reliable measure of a psychological pattern. An important index of reliability is a test's internal consistency, computed with a special correlational statistic, coefficient alpha. This statistic measures the degree to which items measure a common theoretical dimension or construct. When coefficient alpha approaches .80, the practical degree of measurement error is minimized (Nunnally, 1978). Constraints on the value of coefficient alpha include the variability of the respondents' answers and the length of the test itself.

The WAS typically is analyzed for one program at a time and its subscales are relatively brief. As a result one would expect that coefficient alpha values for the WAS probably would be moderate in most instances. In sample of 46 programs, the range of values for coefficient alpha on the WAS subscales for patient raters ranged from moderate (.55 for Spontaneity and Autonomy) to high (.78 for Involvement).

For staff raters in the same programs, the mean reliabilities were slightly higher (.60 for Support to .82 for Involvement and for Order and Organization).

A complementary measure of psychometric accuracy involves the item-to-subscale correlational values. These should be moderate in the case of individual items, as each item should relate to the common construct (scale total score) and yet remain complementary to the other items of the scale. A very high item-to-subscale index would suggest item redundancy, whereas a very low score would suggest lack of a common construct or a vaguely defined criterion measure that had been defined operationally by the test items. The WAS items are appropriately in the moderate range (.43–.53 for patients, .42–.54 for staff).

Another measure of reliability involves the reproducibility of results over a brief time interval, assessed by means of test-retest reliability. Over a 1 week test-retest interval, the WAS showed moderate to high reliability (ranging from .68 for Practical Orientation to .79 for Involvement). Longer term (6 to 12 months) mean profile stability studies across four programs produced comparable results (.78 for patients and .82 for staff). Clearly the WAS can measure enduring programmatic characteristics accurately and stably.

A table of profile stability coefficients based on intraclass correlational analyses summarizes results of test-retest studies in a variety of programs with consistent treatment models. Even though patients frequently were discharged from programs in the longer interval studies (up to 3 years, 4 months), the patient and staff descriptions of the programs were remarkably similar. The range of patient ratings for profile stability statistics ranged from .92 at the 1-week interval to .73 at the 40-month test-retest interval. Different programs rated twice at intervals of 1 month to 28 months averaged in the range of .70 to .76 on patient test-retest profile stability ratings. The range for staff test-retest profile stability ratings were even higher (.91 at 1 week to .96 at 40 months; score range = .78–.96 overall).

Evidence for stability of programmatic perception via the WAS, independent of staff and patient turnover, also has been demonstrated. Kobos, Redmond, and Sterling (1982) showed consistent description of a psychiatric treatment program even though there was rapid staff turnover and complete patient turnover during the 6-month period between baseline and follow-up testing. Similar results were produced by Schmidt, Wakefield, and Anderson (1979), who studied another treatment program at four equal intervals over a 6-month period.

Content validity was introduced into the WAS from the outset of item selection. Specific theoretical dimensions or constructs were formulated as central to the naturalistic understanding of treatment environments based on the tripartite social ecological model. The developers wrote item content to operationalize the constructs as they had been defined. Items were independently evaluated by expert raters as to appropriateness and accuracy of measurement. Reliability analyses described earlier in this section were carried out to test empirically the coherence and accuracy of the item groupings as measures of the subscale constructs. Finally, the researchers placed each item on a unique WAS subscale to keep the scale descriptions separate and behaviorally specific. Available evidence suggests that the WAS has adequate content validity relative to independent expert psychiatric raters (Friis, 1986a, 1986b) and other related psychometric program rating measures (Ellsworth & Maroney, 1972).

Attempts to provide an objective statistical analysis of the dimensional structure of the WAS by means of factor analysis have produced tripartite but inconsistent, sample-specific results (cf. Alden, 1978; Fischer, 1977; Friis, 1986a, 1986b; Manderscheid, Koenig, & Silbergeld, 1978). In a critique of these studies, Moos (1989) rightly emphasized that the factorial solutions are influenced greatly both by the method of factor extraction and rotation and by the diagnostic and demographic composition of the samples analyzed. These criteria varied among the studies. The analyses by Manderscheid et al. (1978) most closely approximated the theoretical Relationship, Personal Growth, and System Maintenance domains postulated by Moos and his co-workers as central to their theory of social ecological analysis.

More important to establishing the construct validity of the WAS is the degree to which the subscale dimensions can discriminate between demonstrably different programs. Several lines of evidence converge to support claims that the WAS subscales meet this criterion. One of the most innovative studies of this kind was carried out by Price and Moos (1975), who identified six different treatment program types based on WAS results: the Therapeutic Community, the Relationship-Oriented Program, the Action-Oriented Program, the Insight-Oriented Program, the Control-Oriented Program, and the Disturbed Behavior Program. The model programs are statistically and descriptively different.

The *Therapeutic Community Program* model emphasizes Relationship and Personal Growth dimensions but de-emphasizes System Maintenance dimensions. These programs emphasize individualized treatment, open anger expression, self-direction, self-responsibility, practical skill learning, and personal problem exploration. Therapeutic community treatment programs typically are found in university-based teaching hospitals with relatively high staff-to-patient ratios. Staff control is minimized.

Relationship-Oriented Programs strongly emphasize the WAS Relationship dimensions, encourage patient autonomy, practical problem solving, and personal problem orientation, and provide clear roles for staff and patients and well-defined treatment goals. Staff control is minimized.

Action-Oriented Programs emphasize patient autonomy primarily and have relatively high staff control. There is relative de-emphasis on the WAS Relationship dimensions as well as a lack of clear programmatic guidelines. Patients in such programs are expected to be self-sufficient and to make specific plans for independent functioning after release from the program.

Insight-Oriented Programs emphasize personal problem orientation and open expression of anger but they de-emphasize WAS Relationship dimensions. There is emphasis on staff control but not program clarity. Staff in such programs tend to stress individualized therapeutic programming, which leads to lack of overall consensus about programmatic goal clarity.

Control-Oriented Programs are essentially custodial in format. They emphasize staff control and high programmatic order and organization, with a de-emphasis on all of the other WAS social climate dimensions.

Disturbed Behavior Programs are average on anger expression and somewhat above average on program clarity variables. All other social climate dimensions are de-emphasized in such programs. Many characteristic programs in this group were state hospital admission units, which had high percentages of patients who were acutely symptomatic, emotionally disturbed, and impulsive.

Moos (1989, pp. 41–42) notes that program size and patient-to-staff ratio varied among the prototypical treatment program types. Control-oriented programs had approximately twice as many patients and half as many staff as the four treatment-oriented program types. The disturbed behavior and therapeutic community programs were approximately equal in size and patient-to-staff ratio.

Moos (1989, pp. 42–45) discusses a more general model of "determinants of program climate." He and his colleagues developed a five-part model to investigate the nature of treatment-setting architectural, interpersonal, and programmatic variables that influence the development and evolution of psychiatric inpatient treatment programs. The domains were identified as 1) physical and 2) architectural features, 3) organizational structure and policies, 4) aggregate patient and staff characteristics, and 5) social climate. Moos and his colleagues then postulated a dynamic social model that interactively relates these variables to each other.

The WAS manual summarizes a body of empirical evidence that explains and evaluates the model. Although a detailed analysis or summary of these findings would extend beyond the scope of this review, Moos (1989, p. 45) provides this succinct overview of findings based on the general model:

> These findings point to relatively strong connections between program and suprapersonal factors and the treatment environment. In general smaller and better staffed programs are more involving and supportive and place more emphasis on self-understanding and the open expression of anger. Such programs tend to downplay the System Maintenance dimensions, especially staff control. In contrast, programs with more disturbed and aggressive patients generally lack emphasis on all the dimensions.

Several rigorous studies of the therapeutic community (TC) model in particular have used the WAS to investigate this treatment modality cross-culturally and to compare it with alternative medical treatment models (cf. Lehman et al., 1982; Trauer, Bouras, & Watson, 1987; Verhaest et al., 1982). Both Lehman and his colleagues and Trauer and associates found therapeutic process differences between model programs on the WAS but no significant treatment outcome differences between the TC model programs and the alternative medical model treatment programs they investigated.

The WAS also has been used to describe (Moffett, 1984), design (Van Stone & Gilbert, 1972), modify (Teasdale et al., 1975), and evaluate therapeutic programs for substance-abusing patients. In each case the WAS results facilitated attempts to understand or improve key features of the treatment program that aided or helped to explain the psychosocial basis of its effectiveness.

The Community-Oriented Programs Environment Scale (COPES; Moos, 1988) has been used in combination with the WAS to compare inpatient and outpatient treatment programs for acute schizophrenic patients (Carpenter & Black, 1983; Mosher & Menn, 1978; Mosher, Menn, & Matthews, 1975; Wendt, Mosher, Matthews, & Menn, 1983). Together the two scales helped highlight aspects of a community-based program that both patients and staff preferred to the usual inpatient treatment program for acutely disturbed schizophrenic patients.

Other innovative applications of the WAS have applied the scale to the evaluation of child and adolescent psychiatric treatment programs. The patient populations have ranged widely, including child psychiatric inpatients (Wolff, Herrin, Scarborough, Wiggins, & Winman, 1972), mildly retarded adolescents (McGee & Woods, 1978), and emotionally disturbed children and adolescents (Feist, Slowiak, & Colligan, 1985). Staff and patient views differed considerably around issues of anger expression, limit setting, independence, and self-responsibility. The WAS highlighted issues that promoted productive programmatic feedback and change.

An increasing number of studies have shown that the WAS is relevant to treatment success and post-discharge community adjustment (for a review, see Moos, 1989, pp. 45–53). In particular, special scales have been developed from the WAS subscales that predict program dropout rate, program release rate, and duration of community tenure after program discharge. Scoring criteria for the Dropout Rate, Release Rate, and Community Tenure scales derived from the WAS subscales appear in the test manual's Appendix B. Norms for patient and staff ratings are provided for each of these three special scales based on the WAS American normative sample of 160 programs (Moos, 1989, pp. 70–73).

Positive outcome predictors of independent self-care and successful community adjustment include practical problem-solving skill mastery, self-direction, and acceptance of personal responsibility. If patients are not seriously disturbed, a program that emphasizes "self-understanding and the open expression of anger in a well-organized context in which patients are expected to be independent and responsible" (Moos, 1989, p. 52) is associated with positive treatment outcome. Therapeutic community settings in particular appear contraindicated in the case of severely disturbed patients, particularly psychotic ones, who require a highly structured setting that modulates interpersonal exchange. Poor program outcome, particularly increased dropout rate, tends to be associated with lack of personal involvement and support, poor treatment plan organization, and lack of well-defined therapeutic goals.

Critique

The WAS represents a multidimensional approach that is accurate, specific, and widely applicable in a growing range of inpatient treatment settings. It also shows remarkably accurate cross-cultural applicability in translated forms other than the original English language version developed for an American population of psychiatric inpatients. Though originally designed as a measure of social climate for psychiatric inpatient treatment programs, the scale also has proven useful in the analysis of medical inpatient ward programs. Research has linked the WAS empirically to a number of perceived environmental variables predictive of social climate experience, development, modifiability, and change. The WAS subscales and their derived subscales help predict specific therapeutic outcome variables, including community tenure, program turnover, and dropout rates.

Use of the treatment program typology based on the WAS profile makes it possible to objectify the specific similarities and differences among prototypical psychiatric treatment programs and to link them to treatment planning models, triage assignment decision making, and evaluation of therapeutic outcome for specific diagnostic groups. It also has become possible to identify which aspects of the treatment program can predict successful therapeutic outcome and which cannot. The WAS psychometric technology makes it possible to individualize treatment, to evaluate treatment program effectiveness, to compare programs objectively and multidimensionally, and to contrast both individuals and groups of patients and staff within and between programs.

The actual and optimal aspects of program structure also can be operationalized. The WAS provides the technology to assess goal-outcome congruence or discrepancy in comparison with the actual program when program change can be anticipated and planned. Such evaluation can serve to prepare patients and staff for change as well as to evaluate its impact and its effectiveness in achieving desired ends.

Moos (1989) notes that the WAS has proven particularly useful for a) developing individualized treatment programs for patients, b) designing treatment programs (particularly therapeutic community models), c) evaluating staff training effectiveness, d) optimizing treatment program effectiveness and monitoring program change, and e) comparing therapeutic program models. The use of the WAS in combination with other scales, particularly other Social Climate Scales, is just beginning. This reviewer would encourage the systematic combined use of the WAS and the COPES to evaluate the same patients as they make the transition from hospital care to community life. Further investigations of the relationships between these measures and their predictive relationships may enhance our understanding of community adjustment success and its facilitation through specific aspects of optimal inpatient care.

Investigation of the WAS in combination with demographic variables such as age, educational level, and social class may enhance our understanding of variables that may modify treatment outcome and generality of adaptive social learning. Effects of chronicity of illness, age at onset, medication status, and work history within and between diagnostic groups may aid understanding of perception of various aspects of the treatment programs. The modifiability of the deficits in these areas remains to be specified.

Cooperative cross-cultural studies with the WAS and the COPES in combination to investigate a single group of patients in similar settings across cultures would enhance our understanding of cultural and linguistic differences in perception of treatment milieus. It also would be useful to study U.S. patients of different ethnic backgrounds with a given psychiatric diagnosis and matched samples of their counterparts in the culture of origin to compare the effects of environmental and social ecological variables on the development and expression of mental illness. The WAS could become particularly useful in the analysis of the generalizability of the treatment program methodology from one culture to another and in attempts to extract the most salient treatment program features from a variety of treatment models in different cultures, particularly those that differ dramatically from U.S. culture. Such studies may help isolate the necessary and sufficient variables for expression and symptomatic amelioration or social control of various forms of mental disorder.

More use of the WAS and the COPES in combination with the Work Environment Scale (WES) would be particularly useful to link inpatient and outpatient treatment effectiveness parameters with adaptive social coping skills. The ability to become gainfully self-employed may prove to be an effective marker variable for adaptive ability in and of itself, and its relevance as an outcome variable should be investigated dimensionally. This reviewer suspects that using the WAS, COPES, and WES together could help contrast groups of psychiatric patients in various diagnostic groups who are competent to work at various levels of sophistication. Sheltered workshop, custodial, clerical, and professional patient samples within diagnostic groups could be compared effectively with the three Social Climate Scales mentioned. With the WAS one could define objectively the perceived social environmental characteristics that foster the return to productive living and monitor the degree of perceived deficits at various stages of the illness and their remission during recovery.

Use of behavioral and psychometric measures of adaptive ability and intelligence in addition to the social climate variables also would help to complete the picture and would show the relationship of demonstrated ability and adaptation levels to perceived social and environmental characteristics. In essence this reviewer recommends a generalization of the expanded model of Moos et al. from the social ecological realm, with the environmental institutional characteristics already included in the model and shown to be relevant to adaptive behavior, to one that includes intrapersonal (diagnostic, intellectual) and behavioral measures. This effort would likely require multidisciplinary coordination of assessment resources that typically already are in place but not yet coordinated to form a comprehensive assessment system of the type suggested.

The descriptive and predictive validity of the WAS subscales and their derived measures provides considerable empirical support for the content and construct validity of the WAS and for Moos et al.'s social ecological model as a whole. The WAS presents an invaluable measure for inpatient psychiatric program description, analysis, comparison, and pre-post program modification assessment. Once having used the WAS in practice, one wonders how he or she functioned effectively as a program consultant without its input. The WAS has received international application, and a growing literature attests to and documents both its sensitivity and its effectiveness in a variety of cultures. Its use in theory testing, theory building, and objective programmatic analysis in the hands of competent professionals doubtless will continue to improve the quality of patient care and treatment program effectiveness.

References

Alden, L. (1978). Factor analysis of the Ward Atmosphere Scale. *Journal of Consulting and Clinical Psychology, 46,* 175–176.

Alexy, W. (1981–82). Perceptions of ward atmosphere on an oncology unit. *International Journal of Psychiatry in Medicine, 11,* 331–340.

Amaral, P., Nehemkis, A., & Fox, L. (1981). Staff support group on a cancer ward: A pilot project. *Death Education, 5,* 267–278.

Archer, R.P., & Amuso, K.F. (1980). Comparison of staff's and patients' perceptions of ward atmosphere. *Psychological Reports, 46,* 959–965.

Burti, L., Glick, I.D., & Tansella, M. (1986). *Is the Italian psychiatric reform changing the treatment milieu?* Verona, Italy: University of Verona Institute of Psychiatry.

Carpenter, M., & Black, B. (1983). *Community placement of chronic schizophrenics.* Orangeburg, NY: Rockland Research Institute.

Cox, G. (1977). *Environmental study of the Memphis Correctional Center.* Memphis, TN: State Technical Institute, Correctional Research Evaluation Center.

Cronkite, R., Moos, R., & Finney, J. (1984). The context of adaptation: An integrative perspective on community and treatment environments. In W.A. O'Connor & B. Lubin (Eds.), *Ecological approaches to clinical and community psychology* (pp. 189–215). New York: Wiley.

Dauwalder, J., Chabloz, D., & Chappuis, J. (1978). L'echelle de l'atmosphere dans les services psychiatriques. *Social Psychiatry, 13,* 175–186.

De-Nour, A.K. (1983). Staff-patient interaction. In N. Levy (Ed.), *Psychonephrology: Psychological problems in kidney failure and their treatment* (Vol. II, pp. 31–41). New York: Plenum.

Ejsing, L.O. (1980). Ward Atmosphere Scale anvendt i arbejdet med at mindske afstanden mellem idealer og oplevede realiteter i et terapeutisk samfund. *Nordisk Psykiatrisk Tidsskrift, 34,* 658–671.

Ellsworth, R., & Maroney, R. (1972). Characteristics of psychiatric programs and their effects on patients' adjustment. *Journal of Consulting and Clinical Psychology, 39,* 436–447.

Eriksen, L. (1987). Ward atmosphere changes during restructuring of an alcoholism treatment center: A quasi-experimental study. *Addictive Behaviors, 12,* 33–42.

Feist, J., Slowiak, C., & Colligan, R. (1985). Beyond good intentions: Applying scientific methods to the art of milieu therapy. *Residential Group Care and Treatment, 3,* 13–32.

Finney, J., & Moos, R. (1984). Environmental assessment and evaluation research: Examples from mental health and substance abuse programs. *Evaluation and Program Planning, 7,* 151–167.

Fischer, J. (1977). Alcoholic patients' perception of treatment milieu using modified versions of the Ward Atmosphere Scale (WAS) and Community-Oriented Programs Environment Scale (COPES). *British Journal of Addiction, 72,* 213–216.

Friis, S. (1981a). From enthusiasm to resignation in a therapeutic community: A process evaluation of a mental hospital ward with the Ward Atmosphere Scale (WAS). *Journal of the Oslo City Hospitals, 31,* 51–54.

Friis, S. (1981b). Hva slags postatmosfaere er terapeutisk for psykotiske og for ikkepsykotiske pasienter? *Journal of the Norwegian Medical Association, 101,* 848–852.

Friis, S. (1986a). Factors influencing the ward atmosphere. *Acta Psychiatrica Scandinavica, 73,* 600–606.

Friis, S. (1986b). Measurements of the perceived ward milieu: A reevaluation of the Ward Atmosphere Scale. *Acta Psychiatrica Scandinavica, 73,* 589–599.

Grant, R., & Saslow, G. (1971). Maximizing responsible decision making, or how do we get out of here? In G. Abroms & N. Greenfield (Eds.), *The new hospital psychiatry* (pp. 27–55). New York: Academic Press.

Gren, B., Ared, K., & Nilsson, S. (1978). *A study of the ward atmosphere and its change in a psychiatric unit for acute psychotic patients.* Göteborg, Sweden: Lillihagens Psychiatric Hospital and University at Göteborg.

Gripp, R., & Magaro, P. (1971). A token economy program evaluation with untreated control ward comparisons. *Behavior Research and Therapy, 9,* 137–139.

Ingstad, J., & Gotestam, K.G. (1979). A three level approach to the evaluation of a therapeutic community system. *World Conference of Therapeutic Communities, 3,* 351–363.

Jeger, A. (1977). The effects of a behavioral consultation program on consultees, clients, and the social environment (Doctoral dissertation, State University of New York, Stony Brook). *Dissertation Abstracts International, 38,* 1405B.

Kelly, G.R. (1983). Minimizing the adverse effects of mass relocation among chronic psychiatric inpatients. *Hospital and Community Psychiatry, 34,* 150–157.

Kobos, J., Redmond, F., & Sterling, J. (1982). Measuring ward milieu and the impact of staff turnover on a psychiatry unit. *Psychological Reports, 50,* 879–885.

Lehman, A.F., Strauss, J.S., Ritzler, B.A., Kokes, R.F., Harder, D.W., & Gift, T.E. (1982). First admission psychiatric ward milieu: Treatment process and outcome. *Archives of General Psychiatry, 39,* 1293–1298.

Leviege, V. (1970). Group relations: Group therapy with mentally ill offenders. *Corrective Psychiatry and Journal of Social Therapy, 16,* 15–25.

Manderscheid, R., Koenig, G., & Silbergeld, S. (1978). Psychosocial factors for classroom, group and ward. *Psychological Reports, 43,* 555–561.

McGee, M., & Woods, D. (1978). Use of Moos' Ward Atmosphere Scale in a residential setting for mentally retarded adolescents. *Psychological Reports, 43,* 580–582.

Meier, R. (1983). The impact of the structural organization of public welfare offices on the psychosocial work and treatment environments. *Journal of Social Service Research, 7,* 1–18.

Milne, D. (1986). Planning and evaluating innovations in nursing practice by measuring the ward atmosphere. *Journal of Advanced Nursing, 11,* 203–210.

Moffett, L. (1984). Assessing the social system of a therapeutic community: Interpersonal orientations, social climate, and norms. *International Journal of Therapeutic Communities, 5,* 110–119.

Moos, R. (1972). British psychiatric ward treatment environments. *British Journal of Psychiatry, 120,* 635–643.

Moos, R. (1973). Changing the social milieus of psychiatric treatment settings. *Journal of Applied Behavioral Science, 9,* 575–593.

Moos, R. (1974a). *Evaluating treatment environments: A social ecological approach.* New York: Wiley.

Moos, R. (1974b). *Ward Atmosphere Scale, Form R answer booklet.* Palo Alto, CA: Consulting Psychologists Press.

Moos, R. (1974c). *Ward Atmosphere Scale manual* (1st ed.). Palo Alto, CA: Consulting Psychologists Press.

Moos, R. (1984). Context and coping: Toward a unifying conceptual framework. *American Journal of Community Psychology, 12,* 5–25.

Moos, R. (1985a). Creating healthy human contexts: Environmental and individual strategies. In J.C. Rosen & L.J. Solomon (Eds.), *Prevention in health psychology* (pp. 366–389). Hanover, NH: University Press of New England.

Moos, R. (1985b). Evaluating social resources in community and health care contexts. In P. Karoly (Ed.), *Measurement strategies in health psychology* (pp. 433–459). New York: Wiley.

Moos, R. (1987). *The Social Climate Scales: A user's guide.* Palo Alto, CA: Consulting Psychologists Press.

Moos, R. (1988). *Community-Oriented Programs Environment Scale manual* (2nd ed.). Palo Alto, CA: Consulting Psychologists Press.

Moos, R. (1989). *Ward Atmosphere Scale manual* (2nd ed.). Palo Alto, CA: Consulting Psychologists Press.

Moos, R., Clayton, J., & Max, W. (1979). *The Social Climate Scales: An annotated bibliography* (2nd ed.). Palo Alto, CA: Consulting Psychologists Press.

Moos, R., & Spinrad, S. (1984). *The Social Climate Scales: An annotated bibliography update.* Palo Alto, CA: Consulting Psychologists Press.

Mosher, L., & Menn, A. (1978). Lower barriers in the community: The Soteria model. In L.I. Stein & M.A. Test (Eds.), *Alternatives to mental hospital treatment* (pp. 75–113). New York: Plenum.

Mosher, L., Menn, A., & Matthews, S. (1975). Soteria: Evaluation of a home-based treatment for schizophrenia. *American Journal of Orthopsychiatry, 45,* 455–467.

Murray, H.A. (1938). *Explorations in personality.* New York: Oxford University Press.

Nunnally, J.C. (1978). *Psychometric theory* (2nd ed.). New York: McGraw-Hill.

Pierce, W., Trickett, E., & Moos, R. (1972). Changing ward atmosphere through staff discussion of the perceived ward environment. *Archives of General Psychiatry, 26,* 35–41.

Plosila, A. (1978). *A cross-cultural application of the Ward Atmosphere Scale.* Mikkeli, Finland: University of Jyvaskyla, Department of Psychology.

Price, R., & Moos, R. (1975). Toward a taxonomy of inpatient treatment environments. *Journal of Abnormal Psychology, 84,* 181–188.

Rhodes, L. (1981). Social climate perception and depression of patients and staff in a chronic hemodialysis unit. *Journal of Nervous and Mental Disease, 169,* 169–175.

Schmidt, J., Wakefield, D., & Andersen, C. (1979). Ward atmosphere: A longitudinal and factorial analysis. *Social Psychiatry, 14,* 119–123.

Stuart, D. (1977). Development of a survey instrument assessing staff and patient perceptions of comprehensive rehabilitation programs (Doctoral dissertation, University of Houston, TX). *Dissertation Abstracts International, 38,* 1907B.

Teasdale, J., Evans, J., Greene, S., Hitchcock, C., Hunt, H., & Connell, P. (1975). Ward environment in an inpatient drug dependence treatment unit: II. Attempts to improve ward environment. *International Journal of the Addictions, 10,* 539–555.

Trauer, T., Bouras, N., & Watson, J.P. (1987). The assessment of ward atmosphere in a psychiatric unit. *Therapeutic Communities, 8,* 199–205.

Van Stone, W., & Gilbert, R. (1972). Peer confrontation groups: What, why and whether. *American Journal of Psychiatry, 129,* 583–589.

Verhaest, S. (1983). The assessment of the maturation of a therapeutic community. *International Journal of Therapeutic Communities, 4,* 183–195.

Verhaest, S., Pierloot, R., & Janssens, G. (1982). Comparative assessment of two different types of therapeutic communities. *International Journal of Social Psychiatry, 28,* 46–52.

Wendt, R., Mosher, L., Matthews, S., & Menn, A. (1983). Comparison of two treatment environments for schizophrenia. In J.L.G. Gunderson, O.A. Will, & L.R. Mosher (Eds.), *Principles and practice of milieu therapy* (pp. 17–33). New York: Aronson.

Willer, B.S. (1977). Patient attitudes toward mental hospitalization: A review of quantitative research. *Journal of Health and Social Behavior, 20,* 237–258.

Wolff, W., Herrin, B., Scarborough, D., Wiggins, K., & Winman, F. (1972). Integration of an instructional program with a psychotherapeutic milieu: Developmental redirection for seriously disturbed children. *Acta Paedopsychiatrica: European Journal of Child and Adolescent Psychiatry, 39,* 83–92.

Vishwa K.H. Bhat, Ph.D.
Assistant Professor of Communication Disorders, William Paterson College, Wayne, New Jersey.

WEPMAN'S AUDITORY DISCRIMINATION TEST, SECOND EDITION
William M. Reynolds. Los Angeles, California: Western Psychological Services.

Introduction

Auditory discrimination is a basic and very important perceptual skill, essential for the normal development of language and articulatory proficiency in children. This special ability helps the listener to differentiate speech sounds. Researchers have determined that the verbal expression of speech sounds, language components, and classroom learning are closely related to auditory discrimination ability (Bountress, 1984; Kavale, 1981). For these reasons the evaluation of auditory discrimination skill is crucial for children with problems in speech/language, learning, and other areas. To assess these abilities, Joseph M. Wepman (1958) developed the Auditory Discrimination Test (ADT) for young children aged 5 through 8 years. Within a simple, easy-to-administer format, word pairs are presented orally to the examinee and he or she is required to identify whether the words are the same or different.

The original 1958 version of the ADT was revised in 1973 and again in 1986. The item content and the test administration procedures, however, remained the same in all versions. In the 1958 version, scoring and assessments were based on incorrect responses to the test items, whereas scoring for the 1973 revision was analyzed on the basis of correct responses. This change was made to express discrimination ability in a positive direction. Jamison (1985) criticized the 1973 version for lack of evidence of usable normative data and of validity. The test was revised again in 1986 to strengthen its clinical utility by providing national norms based on a stratified sample of 1,800 normal children. The standardization sample comprised children residing in 30 states across the United States. The distribution of the sample with regard to age, gender, ethnicity, and geographic location closely reflected the percentages reported in the 1980 census. Two major changes were apparent in the 1986 revision: the inclusion of 4-year-olds and the presentation of extensive data on the test's reliability and validity.

There are two versions of the ADT (Form 1A and Form 2A), each containing 40 pairs of words. Each version consists of 10 same-word pairs and 30 pairs that differ in a single phoneme. In the different-word pair category, comparisons are

---

The reviewer wishes to thank Dr. Elena Chopek, associate professor, for her comments on this critique.

made between 4 medial vowel pairs, 13 initial consonant pairs, and 13 final consonant pairs. A considerable effort was taken in the selection of word pairs whereby phonemes were matched within a specific phonetic category. The words used in the ADT were selected from the 1944 Thorndike-Lorge *Teacher's Word Book of 30,000 Words*. The words within each pair were matched for a) the distribution of consonants and vowels, b) word frequency, and c) word length. This ensures that the child's discrimination ability is not based on these parameters but on his or her auditory discrimination skills.

The same-word pairs serve as control items for checking the validity of the test. The different-word pairs are used to evaluate discrimination ability. The instructions for the test and practice word pairs are presented to a child as he or she faces the examiner. Once the child is trained, the actual test is administered with the child's back toward the examiner so that visual cues are not used in responding to the test items. Each form is printed on two sides of one page. Abbreviated instructions appear on one side, and the test items are presented on the other. The user can find detailed descriptions of the instructions in the ADT manual (Reynolds, 1986).

Practical Applications/Uses

The ADT is a measure of a child's auditory discrimination rather than auditory comprehension ability. It is used as a brief reliable screening measure to identify children with problems in the areas of auditory, cognition, speech, and language abilities. According to the manual, this test may be used in conjunction with larger batteries of psychoeducational tests. The ADT is also a useful tool for assessing the effectiveness of speech, psychological, and educational intervention. It could be used for research purposes that require auditory skills (e.g., Camp, 1977).

The test is appropriately administered to normally developing children from ages 4 to 8 years, 11 months, who are suspected of having difficulty in auditory discrimination. Such children are likely to be found among those considered to have problems in the auditory, speech/language, academic, and cognition areas. The ADT response task does not require visual or reading ability, and the memory demands are minimal. Because the child may respond with a "yes" or "no" (verbal) or with a head nod or eye blink (nonverbal), a physically handicapped child can be evaluated using this test. Although the ADT is designed for younger subjects, older children may be tested to determine an approximate age level at which they are functioning with regard to auditory discrimination ability. The inclusion of normative data in the manual supports this application of the test.

The ADT is to be administered by trained professionals using correct pronunciation of the test items to ensure standard administration procedures. Appropriate users would include speech/language pathologists, audiologists, special education teachers, reading specialists, occupational therapists, and university/college students who are in training programs and supervised by a qualified professional. The manual states that the examiner should become familiar with the test items by reading them aloud several times. The manual presents no discussion of the amount of training and practice required before administering the test. In order to ensure validity and reliability, the child must be tested on an individual basis in a quiet setting. The examiner uses sample items to confirm that the child understands the task demands. Once the child is trained, the test can be completed in less than 15 minutes.

The examiner must be observant to ensure the child (particularly the 4-year-old) is involved in the task. Any deviation during the test, such as talking, inattentiveness, looking around the room, or illness, may significantly affect the score. It is important to report briefly about the child's behavior during the test as well as note the time of day the test was administered to reflect the possible cause of the inattentiveness.

The ADT manual provides clear, simple, concise, and straightforward instructions for scoring. The total score (raw score) is the total number of correct responses on the 30 different-word pair items. The total score is obtained by simply adding up the circled "D" responses that appear in the unshaded boxes of the test form. The responses obtained on the same-word pairs are used to evaluate the validity of the test. The test is considered invalid if a child scores 9 or less in the different-word pairs category or a score of 6 or less in the same-word pairs category. Assessment is based on the correct responses obtained in the different-word items. The possible score range is from 10 to 30. According to the manual, the total scores are not meaningful in evaluating the child's performance. Using tables, the total score is converted into a qualitative score, a standard score, and percentile ranks. The qualitative score is obtained by converting the total score to a 5-point rating scale (see Tables 1 and 2 on p. 9 in the manual): +2 = very good development, +1 = above-average ability, 0 = average ability, –1 = below-average ability, and –2 = below the threshold of adequacy. The qualitative score reflects a child's overall performance of the auditory discrimination ability. The manual provides a qualitative score conversion table delineated by half-year age groups between the ages of 4 years and 8 years, 11 months for each of the two test forms. The standard scores of the test are expressed in the form of normalized T-scores in Appendix B of the manual (see pp. 42–45). These scores enable the examiner to compare a child's performance across time as well as within the same-age group. Percentile ranks are presented in the manual's Appendix C (pp. 46–47). Percentiles indicate a child's performance on a given task in relation to other children. The test materials and scoring procedures have been reviewed favorably (DiCarlo, 1965; Jamison, 1985).

Technical Aspects

The reliability statistics reported in the 1986 manual include internal consistency coefficients, test-retest coefficients, and alternate forms reliability coefficients. These measures are estimated using the Kuder-Richardson (1937) KR-20 procedure. Based on the standardization sample of 1,800 normally developing children, the internal consistency reliability estimates for Form 1A were in the range of .74 to .80; for Form 2A, the range was .76 to .82. These estimates were for the age group 4 years through 6 years, 11 months. A slight decrease in these estimates are seen for ages 7 years through 8 years, 11 months. The decrease in coefficients is attributed to a ceiling effect and decrease in score variability. In general the values determined in this measure appear to be satisfactory.

Three studies of the test-retest reliability are discussed. In two studies, normal first-grade children were tested and retested with reliability results of .91 and .96 (Horn & O'Donnell, 1984, cited in Reynolds, 1986; Reynolds, 1986; Wepman, 1958). The third study involved a sample of 26 mildly retarded children between 10 and 16 years (Dahle & Daly, 1972), yielding a test-retest reliability coefficient of .88. All of the data support high test-retest estimates for the ADT.

A measure of alternate forms reliability was possible because of the availability of two ADT forms. Two studies are reported, with a high alternate forms reliability coefficient of .92.

Although a broad range of variables was considered in the selection of test items, the ADT does not test on some phonemes of American English. Jamison (1985) has criticized the ADT as inadequate on content validity, stating that "the Test of Auditory Discrimination includes 14 consonants and six vowel sounds" (p. 37). It is helpful to know the reasoning for not testing the discrimination ability on some group of speech sounds.

The manual reports numerous investigations associated with criterion-related validity. The ADT is compared with other measures of academic achievement, articulation and language, auditory processes, and cognition. Overall, the correlation coefficients of the ADT with these other measures reflect a moderate degree of relationship.

Critique

The ADT is a well-designed screening tool to measure auditory discrimination ability in children. It is inexpensive, quick, and easy to administer. The manual presents excellent straightforward guidelines for administering and scoring the test. The ADT frequently is used in educational and clinical settings related to speech pathology, audiology, and psychology. After understanding the test instructions, a child can complete the test in less than 15 minutes.

The manual provides clear descriptive test development procedures. The standardization of the test is described in detail. Important features of the standardization procedure are the size of the stratified sample, the clear definition of the nature of the sample, and the use of statistical procedures to evaluate the demographic characteristics. The availability of the stratified norm and standard scores enhances the uses of the test in clinical settings. As children have begun to enter the school atmosphere at an early age, Reynolds should be commended for his objective to include 4-year-olds.

Administration of the test requires standard English pronunciation. Because any regional dialect of the examiner may influence the test score, this reviewer believes it would be preferable if Wepman's ADT were made available with audiocassette recordings of standard pronunciation of the test items. Taped presentations of test materials in quiet settings could eliminate the influence of pronunciation variations among examiners. Furthermore, such presentations may even strengthen the internal consistency reliability estimates.

Although more care was taken in the collection of normative data, an inspection of means and standard deviations *(SD)* for both forms shows smaller samples obtained for 4- to 4½-year-olds with greater standard deviation scores for Form 1A (4.55) and Form 2A (5.57) in comparison with other age groups (see Tables 7 and 8 on p. 18 of the manual). An inclusion of more children in this age group may reflect a better estimation of their performance in auditory discrimination ability.

References

Bountress, N.G. (1984). A second look at the tests of speech-sound discrimination. *Journal of Communication Disorders, 17,* 349–359.

Camp, B.W. (1977). Verbal mediation in young aggressive boys. *Journal of Abnormal Psychology, 86,* 145–153.

Dahle, A.J., & Daly, D.A. (1972). Influence of verbal feedback on Auditory Discrimination Test performance of mentally retarded children. *American Journal of Mental Deficiency, 76,* 586–590.

DiCarlo, L.M. (1965). Auditory Discrimination Test. In O.K. Buros (Ed.), *The sixth mental measurements yearbook.* Highland Park, NJ: Gryphon Press.

Jamison, C.B. (1985). Auditory Discrimination Test. In D.J. Keyser & R.C. Sweetland (Eds.), *Test critiques* (Vol. IV, pp. 33–41). Austin, TX: PRO-ED.

Kavale, K. (1981). The relationship between auditory perceptual skills and reading ability: A meta analysis. *Journal of Learning Disabilities, 14,* 539–546.

Kuder, G.F., & Richardson, M.W. (1937). The theory of estimation of test reliability. *Psychometrika, 2,* 151–160.

Reynolds, W.M. (1986). *Manual for Wepman's Auditory Discrimination Test* (2nd ed.). Los Angeles: Western Psychological Services.

Wepman, J.M. (1958). *Auditory Discrimination Test: Manual of directions.* Chicago: Language Research Associates.

Wepman, J.M. (1975). *Auditory Discrimination Test manual* (rev. 1973). Los Angeles: Western Psychological Services.

Raymond E. Webster, Ph.D.

Professor of Psychology and Director, School Psychology Program, East Carolina University, Greenville, North Carolina.

WOODCOCK-JOHNSON PSYCHO-EDUCATIONAL TEST BATTERY–REVISED

Richard W. Woodcock and Mary Bonner Johnson. Allen, Texas: DLM Teaching Resources.

Introduction

The Woodcock-Johnson Psycho-Educational Battery–Revised (WJ-R; Woodcock & Johnson, 1989/1990) is the most recent version of the original battery published in 1977. The battery was developed as a comprehensive set of individually administered tests purporting to measure "cognitive abilities, scholastic aptitudes, and achievements" (McGrew, Werder, & Woodcock, 1991, p. 1). The WJ-R provides norm-referenced assessments in each of three general areas for children as young as 2 up through adults over 90.

The WJ-R is comprised of the Tests of Cognitive Abilities (WJ-R COG) and the Tests of Achievement (WJ-R ACH), Forms A and B. Each test consists of a standard and supplemental battery. The use of Forms A and B with the WJ-R ACH allows more frequent alternated use of this test to measure achievement while reducing the effects of familiarity with test items on performance.

The WJ-R was developed by Richard W. Woodcock and Mary Bonner Johnson. Woodcock is the director of Measurement/Learning/Consultants, a test development and research group that he organized in 1972. He received his Ed.D. in psychoeducation and statistics from the University of Oregon. Johnson is presently the assistant director for Measurement/Learning/Consultants. The examiner's manuals were coauthored by Nancy Mather, who has a Ph.D. in special education from the University of Arizona and is presently an assistant professor in special education at that university. The technical manual was coauthored by Kevin S. McGrew, Ph.D. (an assistant professor in the Department of Applied Psychology at St. Cloud State University) and Judy K. Werder, Ph.D. (a senior evaluator in the Planning, Education, and Testing Department for the Dallas, Texas, Independent School District).

A number of modifications and additions have been made to the WJ that led to the WJ-R. Ten new tests were added to the WJ-R COG and 4 to the WJ-R ACH to expand specific skill and content areas for assessment. Many of the items in the original 22 achievement and cognitive tests have been revised, with additional sample items provided for several of these tests. The scoring procedures for the Memory for Sentences and Spatial Relations tests were changed to more accurately examine the skills measured in each of these tasks.

Several changes were also made regarding the psychometric and conceptual

804

characteristics for the WJ-R. Age ranges for the normative groups were extended to encompass from 2 to over 90 years of age, two parallel forms for the WJ-R ACH were developed, the WJ-R COG was related directly to Horn and Cattell's (1966) theory of fluid and crystallized intellectual abilities, and specific procedures were added so that test performance discrepancies occurring either between or within the various achievement or cognitive tests could be identified. Finally, the Relative Performance Index (RPI) was renamed the Relative Mastery Index (RMI).

The complete WJ-R is comprised of six easel books containing 39 tests. Each book stands independently on the table and offers an easy mechanism to administer the battery to an individual. The WJ-R COG contains a standard battery easel book with tests 1 to 7 and a supplemental test book easel with tests 8 to 21. The WJ-R ACH has two parallel forms matched for content and designated as Form A and Form B. Each form has a standard battery book with tests 22 to 30 and a supplemental test book with tests 31 to 35 plus Punctuation and Capitalization (P), Spelling (S), Usage (U), and Handwriting (H).

Three examiner's manuals accompany the WJ-R. Two manuals were written for the WJ-R COG and one for the WJ-R ACH. Norm tables for the WJ-R ACH and the WJ-R COG supplemental battery are bound separately, while those for the WJ-R COG standard battery are included in the examiner's manual. Other supplemental materials are cassette tapes for standardized administration of tests 2, 4, 9, 11, 17, 18, and 20 from the WJ-R COG; examiner's record booklets with perforated pages and three-page summary sheets for test W scores, standard scores, percentile ratings, and raw scores; and a CompuScore computer scoring program. The examiner is advised to use a calculator if scoring the test using the manuals.

Test items are presented visually, orally, or with both modalities concurrently, using timed and untimed formats requiring either oral or written responses. Examiners must supply a stopwatch, a good quality cassette tape recorder, and pencils. Each test provides basal and ceiling levels involving the six lowest items passed or six highest items failed, respectively. Several of the tests also have been identified as useful measures of early development and designated with (E DEV). These tests are 1, 2, 4, 5, 6, 22, 25, 26, 28, 29, and 30. At the preschool level, or with low-functioning examinees of any age, tests 1, 2, 4, 5, and 6 make up the Early Development Scale.

The WJ-R COG claims to measure cognitive status in seven factors derived from the research and theory of Horn and Cattell (1966). These seven factors are long-term retrieval (tests 1, 8, 15, and 16), short-term memory (tests 2, 9, and 17), processing speed (tests 3 and 10), auditory processing (tests 4, 11, and 18), visual processing (tests 5, 12, and 19), comprehension-knowledge (tests 6, 13, 20, and 21), and fluid reasoning (tests 7, 14, 19, and 21). Specific tests used in the WJ-R COG are described as follows:

Memory for Names (72 items): This measures the ability to learn visual-auditory associations using pictures of unfamiliar space creatures with unusual names. Association string lengths range from one to nine items.

Memory for Sentences (32 items): Sentences of increasing length and complexity are presented either orally or by using a tape recorder, depending on the needs of the person being evaluated.

Visual Matching (66 items): This 3-minute timed task asks the person to circle the two identical numbers in a row of six, with the length of the numbers presented progressing from one to three digits.

Incomplete Words (40 items): Using a recorded tape, the examinee listens to a word with one or more phonemes missing and is asked to name the complete word. The test purportedly measures auditory closure and processing.

Visual Closure (49 items): Pictures of simple objects altered by either distortion, missing areas, or with a superimposed pattern are shown, and the subject is asked to identify the object.

Picture Vocabulary (58 items): This test of verbal comprehension asks the person to name pictured objects. The first six items are presented in a multiple-choice format and the person merely points to the response selected.

Analysis-Synthesis (35 items): This series of incomplete puzzles involving various colored squares presented in increasing complexity requires the examinee to determine and name the missing component to complete the nonverbal equivalence statement. The examiner gives feedback about the correctness of the response. The task is considered to measure reasoning ability.

Visual-Auditory Learning (7 items): This examines a subject's ability to associate rebuses with words and to translate visual symbols into verbal sentences. Corrective feedback is supplied about responses.

Memory for Words (27 items): This measure tops the person's auditory short-term memory capacity to repeat lists of unrelated words presented via tape recording and ranging in length from one to eight items.

Cross Out (34 items): Here the examinee is asked to scan and compare visually presented drawings to a standard during a 3-minute time period.

Sound Blending (33 items): An audiotape presents parts of words and the person is asked to state the whole word.

Picture Recognition (30 items): A target picture is shown and removed. The person then is asked to identify it either by pointing to or naming the designated letter for the recognized picture, which is presented among an array of similar objects.

Oral Vocabulary (Part A, 20 items; Part B, 24 items): This two-part vocabulary test involves single words presented orally and the subject is asked to reply orally. In Part A he or she replies to the target word with a synonym and in Part B with an antonym.

Concept Formation (35 items): This measures the ability to state the rules for concepts when shown illustrations of the concept. Feedback is offered about the accuracy of responses. The test is assumed to measure reasoning ability.

Delayed Recall–Memory for Names (36 items): The examinee is asked to recall the names of the space creatures presented in the first test after a 1- to 8-day interval following that test. The examiner names each creature and the test taker selects the corresponding creature presented randomly in a pictorial display.

Numbers Reversed (30 items): Series of digits ranging from two to eight items are presented using the audiotape, with the person's task to repeat the series in reverse order. The task is presumed to measure both short-term memory capacity and fluid intelligence.

Sound Patterns (54 items): Pairs of sound patterns are presented via the audiotape. Some of the pairs are identical, while others differ in pitch, rhythm, or sound.

Spatial Relations (33 items): Examinees are presented with a partially completed visual shape and asked to choose the various parts needed to complete the shape. The parts are presented in an array format. Shapes increase in difficulty, complexity, and level of abstractness.

Listening Comprehension (38 items): Brief and incomplete prerecorded passages with a single word missing are presented using the audiotape. The examinee must provide the correct single word at the end of the passage.

Verbal Analogies (35 items): Verbal analogies are presented orally, and the person is required to complete each one with the appropriate word that describes the analogical relationship.

In addition to scores for each of these tests, the WJ-R COG generates scholastic aptitude cluster scores that can be used to make predictions about a person's likely achievement levels. The four aptitude clusters are Reading (tests 2, 3, 11, and 13), Mathematics (tests 3, 7, 13, and 14), Written Language (tests 3, 8, 11, and 13), and Knowledge (tests 2, 5, 11, and 14). Finally, an Oral Language cluster (tests 2, 6, 13, 20, and 21) and an Oral Language aptitude cluster (tests 12, 14, 17, and 18) provide information about a person's overall verbal ability and predicted achievement levels in this area.

The WJ-R ACH, Forms A and B, consists of nine tests in the standard battery and five tests in the supplemental battery. Rather than use all 14 tests with every person, specific tests can be administered based on the purpose for the evaluation. The following tests comprise the WJ-R ACH battery:

Letter-Word Identification (57 items): Beginning with five items involving matching a rebus with the picture of the word represented, this test presents individual letters and words visually to the examinee for oral identification.

Passage Comprehension (43 items): The first four items here use a multiple-choice format to match a picture with a phrase. The remainder of the test uses a modified cloze procedure with short written passages for which the examinee states the important word.

Calculation (58 items): This mathematics computation test examines basic whole number arithmetic computations, geometry, trigonometry, and calculus.

Applied Problems (60 items): Mathematical word problems are presented here that require the examinee to distinguish essential from trivial details and decide about the specific arithmetic procedures required to reach a solution.

Dictation (56 items): The first six items of this test measure prewriting skills, while the remaining items test the ability to write phrases and sentences with correct spelling, punctuation, capitalization, and word usage.

Writing Samples (30 items): Written language competency is assessed by having the person write sentences. Responses are not evaluated according to basic syntax or spelling accuracy.

Science (40 items): This test of knowledge in biology and the physical sciences contains items ranging from preschool to adult levels. The first eight items require pointing to indicate the response choice; the remainder involve oral responses.

Social Studies (49 items): This measure knowledge in history, geography, economics, social studies, and government. The first six items involve pointing to the response choice; the remaining items require oral responses.

Humanities (45 items): Within this survey of knowledge in music, art, and literature, the first five items involve a pointing response and the remainder require oral replies.

Word Attack (30 items): The examinee reads aloud nonsense and low-frequency English words to examine phonics, structural analysis, and pronunciation skills development.

Reading Vocabulary (Part A, 34 items; Part B, 35 items): This two-part test evaluates the ability to read words and provide accurate one-word meanings using either synonyms or antonyms.

Quantitative Concepts (48 items): This test examines a person's knowledge about mathematics vocabulary and concepts without actually performing arithmetic computations or applying this knowledge to mathematics problem-solving situations.

Proofing (36 items): The subject is shown a typed page with errors in capitalization, punctuation, use of words, and/or spelling and then is asked to identify and correct these errors.

Writing Fluency (40 items): After a stimulus picture and set of three words are shown, the individual must write a simple sentence about the picture that incorporates the three-word phrase. This test has a 7-minute time limit.

Punctuation and Capitalization (15 items): The scores for this test are derived from the responses given in the Dictation and Proofing tests. The focus is on the appropriate use of punctuation and capitalization in written language productions.

Spelling (9 items): Scores for this test are based on the person's combined performance in the Dictation and Proofing tests where the accuracy of spelling is evaluated.

Usage (12 items): Using the person's performance in the Dictation and Proofing tests, this measure examines the person's ability to generate correct syntax in written language expressions.

Handwriting: Samples of handwriting produced in the Writing Samples test are compared with a ranked scale of handwriting samples to assess legibility. A checklist also is provided to offer a standard for informally examining various qualities of the person's handwriting. These qualities include slant, spacing, size, horizontal alignment, letter formation, line quality, and overall legibility.

Once scores for the entire battery or for 11 specific tests from the WJ-R ACH are calculated, 10 additional achievement cluster scores can be computed. The 11 specific tests that must be administered to compute these cluster scores are Letter-Word Identification, Passage Comprehension, Word Attack, Reading Vocabulary, Calculation, Applied Problems, Quantitative Concepts, Dictation, Writing Samples, Proofing, and Writing Fluency. Administration of the Science, Social Studies, and Humanities tests allows computation of an 11th cluster, called Broad Knowledge. The 10 clusters are described as follows:

Broad Reading provides an overall assessment of reading achievement based on combined performance in the Letter-Word Identification and Passage Comprehension tests.

Basic Reading Skills presents a measure of the person's functional competency with sight vocabulary and application of phonics to word decoding. It represents the combined performance in the Letter-Word Identification and Word Attack tests.

Reading Comprehension is an index of an individual's comprehension of single words and conceptual information based on performance in the Passage Comprehension and Reading Vocabulary tests.

Broad Mathematics is computed based on scores from the Calculation and Applied Problems tests and can be used as a general measure of mathematics achievement level.

Basic Mathematics Skills offers another measure of mathematics achievement in basic arithmetic computational skills, mathematics vocabulary, and concepts. It is derived from scores achieved in the Calculation and Quantitative Concepts tests.

Mathematics Reasoning is a measure of mathematical reasoning and applied problem-solving skills based on achievement in the Applied Problems test only.

Basic Written Language, which is based on performance in the Dictation and Writing Samples tests, provides an estimate of the person's ability to write one-word responses and sentences in response to oral directions and/or pictorial representations.

Basic Writing Skills describes a person's functional level of performance in basic writing skills, spelling, word usage, and syntax. It represents performance in the Dictation and Proofing tests.

Written Expression, based on achievement in the Writing Samples and Writing Fluency tests, offers an estimate of the ability to write simple and complex sentences.

Finally, the *Skills* cluster is designed as an assessment of early developmental skills status and is derived from the test scores obtained in Letter-Word Identification, Applied Problems, and Dictation.

Practical Applications/Uses

The WJ-R provides the user with several different kinds of qualitative and quantitative information about a person's cognitive and educational achievement characteristics. These data include present levels of functioning, developmental status, level of mastery, relative standing to peers on the basis of chronological age or grade level placement, IQ/achievement discrepancies, content area deficiencies, and psychoeducationally relevant modality-based processing strengths and weaknesses. Because of the variety of scores generated, the WJ-R can be used for screening purposes to assess at-risk learners, for diagnosis to determine special education eligibility or need for remedial education services, or for educational program evaluation. It also may be used to conduct research on the cognitive or achievement-level differences that distinguish various types of cognitively disabled learners. The WJ-R seems to have greatest utility within an educational setting, and this seems to have been the primary focus during its development and revision. Selected portions of the WJ-R COG may be applicable in working with aged populations to determine cognitive functional status.

The entire WJ-R administration will require at least 2 days and possibly part of a third if one administers the Delayed Recall–Memory for Names and Delayed Recall/Visual-Auditory Learning tests from the WJ-R COG. The battery should be administered by a professional with formal graduate training in either school psychology, clinical psychology, or special education. Careful examination, study, and review of the examiner's manuals are necessary before one gives the WJ-R. It is strongly advised that several practice administrations be given before using the battery in a professional diagnostic evaluation.

The test battery requires a good deal of physical space for administration. The test book easel requires a fairly large working space, as does the examiner's record form. A tape recorder is also required.

A computerized scoring package (CompuScore) is available for use with the WJ-R and it greatly simplifies the scoring procedures. Hand scoring the test results is a complicated and onerous process, requiring close scrutiny and frequent rechecking of computations. A hand calculator expedites scoring. Raw scores on each test are equated with W scores, a standard error of measurement for W, age equivalent, and grade equivalent scores. These scores are readily obtained from the record form and are presented in tables at the end of each specific test. W scores are based on the Rasch (1960) model of equal interval scaling and have a central point of 500, which approximates the performance of fifth-grade students. Cluster scores on the WJ-R reflect a mean of the test scores making up that cluster.

The resultant W scores are transcribed to pages 2 and 3 of the record form. The examiner then must locate the REF W score, based on age or grade levels, from the appropriate table in the normative manual. The REF W score is subtracted from the obtained W score. A positive difference indicates that the person's score is higher than the scores for the reference group by that many points. A negative difference means that the person's score is lower by that many points when compared with the reference group.

The examiner then must locate the corresponding column in another set of tables to determine the RMI, the standard score (with a range of 0 to 200) along with its standard error of measurement, and the percentile rank with its standard error of measurement. The RMI provides a measure of expected mastery in comparison with the reference group on tasks similar to those presented in the battery.

Test scores also can be plotted on pages 2 and 3 of the record form to provide developmental level bands and instructional ranges. Each of these bands describes a range of functional instructional levels from easy to difficult based on the person's current test performance levels.

The examiner can use any of these scores to interpret the results from the WJ-R, depending on the specific goal for the evaluation. Each test generates a good deal of psychometric data, which describes a person's present levels of functioning from a variety of perspectives and interpretive frameworks.

Technical Aspects

An extensive and impressive array of statistical and empirical data provided in the technical manual supports the psychometric integrity of the WJ-R. Several pilot studies were used for item development and selection.

Items were chosen using the Rasch model, which assumes that individual items within a given test all measure the same latent traits, that no statistical correlation among individual items exists, and that items will discriminate on the basis of difficulty level across the range of ability purportedly measured by the test. With the Rasch model scores are transformed into a W scale, which adjusts scores relative to difficulty of the items and the person's ability level. In short, the W score will be higher when the item difficulty is higher or the person's ability level is higher. With this knowledge it is presumed that predictions can be made about a person's performance on tasks/items in real-life situations that resemble the test items. Items and test data were analyzed at four points during development, with large subject sizes at each point (sample sizes ranged from 1,000 to over 6,000). Decisions concerning the specific tests comprising each cluster were made on the basis of "judgments guided by the results of statistical analyses including exploratory and confirmatory factor analysis, cluster analysis, and multiple regression analysis" (McGrew et al., 1991, p. 62).

The norm group consisted of 6,359 subjects from "over 100" communities throughout the United States. For the kindergarten to 12th-grade sample, 3,245 subjects were used. The sampling was selected based on 10 specific community and individual variables.

Reliability for each individual test comprising the WJ-R was established using the split-half procedure adjusted for length by the Spearman-Brown correction formula. In this respect, reliability truly reflects the internal consistency for each test and not the replicability of scores across test administrations. Because the Visual Matching, Cross Out, and Writing Fluency tests are timed, the test-retest reliability procedure was used. Alternate forms reliability was used with the Handwriting test. Most reliability coefficients fall in the .80 to .95 range, but there is greater variance in reliability as a function of the specific test and age level. Similar levels of internal consistency exist for the various cluster scores generated on the WJ-R. A study examining the interrater reliability in scoring the Writing Fluency and Handwriting tests for subjects at the third- and seventh-grade, college, and adult levels yielded median estimates of .958 and higher for Writing Fluency and .706 and higher for Handwriting.

Evidence for the validity of the WJ-R is provided for each of the four generally accepted categories—content, concurrent, predictive, and construct. The authors state (McGrew et al., 1991, p. 111) that content and concurrent validities are most important to establish for achievement tests (and thus the WJ-R ACH), while predictive, concurrent, and construct validities are more relevant for cognitive tests such as the WJ-R COG.

Content validity, or the degree to which a test's items adequately represent the ability being measured, was established by consulting with outside experts, curriculum consultants, and experienced teachers to identify the scope and sequence of items making up each test in the WJ-R ACH. For the WJ-R COG, specific test items or tasks chosen were based on those that sampled a range of cognitive processing skills consistent with the Horn-Cattell model of intelligence.

Criterion-related validity refers to the degree to which scores on a given test relate with scores on another independent measure described as the criterion. The criterion can be another test, group membership, and/or ratings on a real-life behavior or skill. Concurrent and predictive validity studies are subsumed under this type of validity and describe the timing relative to the measurements taken.

Data from nine studies are described in the technical manual, correlating performance on various tests and clusters for the WJ-R with other test scores. Specific tests examined in these nine studies were the Boehm Test of Basic Concepts, the Bracken Basic Concepts Scale, the Kaufman Assessment Battery for Children, the McCarthy Scales of Children's Abilities, the Peabody Picture Vocabulary Test–Revised, the Standford-Binet Intelligence Scale–Fourth Edition, the Wechsler Intelligence Scale for Children–Revised, the Peabody Individual Achievement Test, the Kaufman Test of Educational Achievement, the Basic Achievement Skills Individual Screener, the Wide Range Achievement Test–Revised, the Test of Written Language, the Picture Story Language Test, the Writing Test–Metropolitan Achievement Test, and the Test of English as a Foreign Language. Samples in these studies ranged from the preschool to adult years and included average and higher functioning individuals. Only one study, conducted by Mathew, Spodak, and Vogel (cited in McGrew et al., 1991, p. 122), included a sample of 47 students from a private school who had severe learning disabilities. Many of the reported bivariate correlations fell within the moderate and higher range, which the authors view as supporting the concurrent validity of the WJ-R.

Because the authors state that "a major function of the WJ-R is to provide statements regarding a person's expected performance in five areas: oral language, reading, mathematics, written language, and knowledge" (McGrew et al., 1991, p. 141), predictive validity becomes a very important variable to establish for the WJ-R ACH. It should be emphasized that the term *predictive validity* is often used to describe the utility of an instrument to provide information about future behavior on some criterion. The studies conducted to demonstrate the predictive validity of the WJ-R for academic achievement reflect measurements taken concurrently on the same persons. Therefore, these data more accurately describe concurrent validation rather than predictive validity. No data are provided regarding the degree to which the WJ-R relates to real-life performance or predicts future success.

The WJ-R tests were correlated with several intelligence and educational achievement measures at three grade levels: 3, 3/4, and 10/11. In addition to conducting a number of correlational studies on the WJ-R COG with the WJ-R ACH, specific independent tests examined were the PIAT-R, BASIS, K-ABC, K-TEA, WRAT-R, the Full Scale IQ score from the WISC-R or WAIS-R, and the composite score from the Stanford-Binet (fourth edition). Sample sizes ranged from 75 to 94 persons in each analysis.

Bivariate correlations between the Broad Cognitive Ability Scales and scholastic aptitude clusters for the WJ-R with these other instruments generally fall in the low to moderate range. The authors attribute these low correlations to a restricted range in the samples used in these studies (McGrew et al., 1991, pp. 150–151).

The authors further note that the WJ-R COG is more strongly predictive of school achievement than the WISC-R, WAIS-R, SB-IV, or K-ABC, at least in this study. The median correlation for the WJ-R COG was .628, while for the Wechsler scales it was .578, .612 for the SB-IV, and .388 for the K-ABC.

In a discriminant validity study reported on pages 152 to 158 in the technical manual, the utility of the WJ-R in distinguishing among gifted, normal, LD, and mentally retarded students enrolled in Grades 3/4 and 10/11 is described. The discriminant functions analysis indicated an 86.0% correct group membership on the basis of WJ-R for the Grades 10/11 group performance. For the gifted sample the WJ-R showed a 68.4% correct group membership rate, while with the LD group the success rate was 78.1%. For the Grades 3/4 sample, the group classification rate was 88.3%, with individual group placement rates of 56.5% for the gifted, 95.4% for the average, 75.4% for the LD, and 69.2% for the mentally retarded.

Construct validity was established by correlating WJ-R test and cluster scores with each other at age levels 2, 4, 6, 9, 13, 18, 30–39, 50–59, and 70–79 years. Low to moderate between-test correlations exist at each age level, which the authors interpret to support the construct validity of the battery.

Factor analytic study of the WJ-R using one fourth of the final norming sample was conducted "to determine how the newly developed tests loaded in each of the G_f–G_c factors" (McGrew et al., 1991, p. 163). Sixteen tests from the WJ-R COG loaded into eight separate factors, which was consistent with the hypothesized model of the WJ-R factor structure using the Horn-Cattell cognitive processing model. In another factorial study involving 1,425 subjects from kindergarten through adult, each of these eight identified factors was comprised of at least 3 of the 21 cognitive and 8 related achievement tests.

Critique

The WJ-R has a number of very positive qualities. As one of the few intelligence tests developed on the basis of a theory of cognitive processing, this theoretical rationale allows further empirical analysis of both the WJ-R and the theory. The battery has impressive psychometric support using confirmatory factor analysis and Rasch modeling procedures. The standardization process appears sound and adequately representative at the various age levels of the battery. The test highlights the multifaceted and complex nature of intellectual functioning. Finally, it allows for examination of modality-based characteristics of individuals. Although many may see this point as a negative aspect of the WJ-R because of the controversy associated with empirical validation of modality-based learning, experimental psychology dating back to the 1890s (Brooks, 1968; Munsterberg, 1894; Reed, 1988) has consistently established the differential effects of modality-based learning on memory and recall. Further support has come from both cognitive psychological (Paivio, 1975; Sperling, 1963) and human neuropsychological research (Lezak, 1983; Warrington & Shallice, 1969). The WJ-R offers educational researchers the opportunity to examine aptitude-by-treatment interactions (ATI) within the academic learning situation using an instrument specifically designed to measure ATIs.

Several aspects of the WJ-R raise concerns about its utility. The first area relates to the specific psychometric procedures used. The Rasch model is a one-parameter item analysis paradigm that examines items only on the basis of their level of difficulty. It assumes that both differences in item discrimination and guessing are trivial and, therefore, represent real differences associated with a single trait (Anastasi, 1988). The validity of these assumptions remains to be established empirically, as does the position that the Rasch model is more statistically robust to distortion because of nuances in the sample's data set.

Though the use of confirmatory factor analysis is a positive characteristic, it also poses a limitation for the WJ-R. In general, there is more than one solution available when using factor analysis. The specific solution selected often is based on an author's theoretical orientation rather than on a "correct" solution. Using different rotation strategies can generate different results. Further comprehensive research on the underlying factor structure is needed.

Data also are lacking that show the efficacy of the WJ-R to predict, from a time-based perspective, actual functional levels of academic achievement and to iden- tify children at risk for failure early in the educational process. It remains to be determined whether the WJ-R is superior to other achievement and/or intel- ligence tests currently available in distinguishing between competent and less competent learners. Studies are needed in which the numbers of participants in each group are approximately equal rather than having the normal group with more participants than the other three groups combined. In the Evans-Carlsen studies described in the technical manual (pp. 155–157), the correct group classi- fication rates for the gifted, LD, and MR groups at Grades 3/4 is 67.97% and for Grades 10/11 it is 78.85%. These rates are enhanced to 88.3% and 86.0%, respec- tively, because of the large number of average students included in each study.

Finally, the construct validity of the WJ-R must be established more definitely using more than measures of internal consistency. Specifically, convergent and divergent validation studies are necessary.

At a practical level the WJ-R is a bulky and heavy set of equipment to transport if one must carry the test from one setting to the next. The basic test easels are large and do not fit easily into a carrying case. Ancillary material, such as a tape recorder, calculator, and lengthy record forms, further complicate easy transpor- tation. A good deal of time also is needed to score the tests, regardless of whether the protocol is hand or computer scored. The complex scoring procedure lends itself to error.

References

This list includes text citations and suggested additional reading.

Anastasi, A. (1988). *Psychological testing* (6th ed.). New York: Macmillan.
Brooks, L. (1968). Spatial and verbal components of the act of recall. *Canadian Journal of Psychology, 22,* 349–368.
Costenbader, V., & Perry, C. (1990). Test review. *Journal of Psychoeducational Assessment, 8,* 180–184.
Horn, J.L., & Cattell, R.B. (1966). Refinement and test of the theory of fluid and crystallized intelligence. *Journal of Educational Psychology, 57,* 253–270.
Lewis, R.B. (1990). Educational assessment of learning disabilities: A new generation of achievement measures. *Learning Disabilities, 1*(2), 49–55.
Lezak, M. (1983). *Neuropsychological assessment.* New York: Oxford University Press.
Mather, N. (1989). Comparison of the new and existing Woodcock-Johnson writing tests to other writing measures. *Learning Disabilities Focus, 4*(2), 84–95.
Mather, N., & Healey, W. (1990). Deposing aptitude-achievement discrepancy as the empiri- cal criterion for language disabilities. *Learning Disabilities, 1*(2), 40–48.
McGrew, K.S., Werder, J.K., & Woodcock, R.W. (1991). *WJ-R technical manual.* Allen, TX: DLM Teaching Resources.
Munsterberg, H. (1894). Memory. *Psychological Review, 1,* 34–38.
Paivio, A. (1975). Perceptual comparisons through the mind's eyes. *Memory and Cognition, 3*(6), 635–647.
Prewett, P., & Gannuli, M. (1991). The relationship among the reading subtests of the WJ-R, PIAT-R, K-TEA, and WRAT-R. *Journal of Psychoeducational Assessment, 9,* 166–174.
Reed, M. (1988). Speech perception of the discrimination of brief auditory cues in reading disabled children. *Journal of Experimental Child Psychology, 48*(2), 270–292.

Reschly, D.J. (1990). Found: Our intelligences: What do they mean? *Journal of Psychoeducational Assessment, 8,* 259–267.

Sperling, G. (1963). A model for visual memory tasks. *Human Factors, 5,* 19–39.

Warrington, E., & Shallice, T. (1969). The relative impairment of auditory verbal short-term memory. *Brain, 92,* 885–896.

Woodcock, R. (1990). Theoretical foundations of the WJ-R measure of cognitive ability. *Journal of Psychoeducational Assessment, 8,* 231–258.

Woodcock, R., & Johnson, M. (1977). *Woodcock-Johnson Psycho-Educational Battery.* Allen, TX: DLM Teaching Resources.

Woodcock, R., & Johnson, M. (1989/1990). *Woodcock-Johnson Psycho-Educational Battery–Revised.* Allen, TX: DLM Teaching Resources.

Ysseldyke, J.E. (1990). Goodness of fit of the Woodcock-Johnson Psycho-Educational Battery–Revised to the Horn-Cattell G_f–G_c theory. *Journal of Psychoeducational Assessment, 8,* 268–275.

Stanley H. Cohen, Ph.D.
Professor of Psychology, West Virginia University, Morgantown, West Virginia.

Judy Cohen, M.A.
Learning Disabilities Specialist, Monongalia County Board of Education, Morgantown, West Virginia.

WOODCOCK READING MASTERY TESTS– REVISED

Richard W. Woodcock. Circle Pines, Minnesota: American Guidance Service.

Introduction

The Woodcock Reading Mastery Tests–Revised (WRMT-R), the 1987 revision of the original, comprise a comprehensive battery of tests purporting to measure the key areas of reading ability. The WRMT-R structure hierarchically arranges individual items into six tests, three clusters, and a full reading scale. Recommended for persons from kindergarten to age 75, the test results can form the basis for individual program planning, instructional placement, and progress evaluation.

The WRMT-R has two forms, G and H. Form G contains the entire battery of tests: Word Identification, Word Attack, Word Comprehension, and Passage Comprehension comprise the reading achievement battery; Visual-Auditory Learning and Letter Identification are the two readiness tests; and there is a supplementary letter checklist. Form H contains only Word Identification, Word Attack, Word Comprehension, and Passage Comprehension (the reading achievement battery). Although separate test books are provided for Forms G and H, an easel design is used for both forms. This design is meant to facilitate the examiner's view of the examiner and subject pages at the same time; however, examiners may find this setup cumbersome and may need to stand up to look at the student pages or to turn the test book around. Three protocol forms are available (Forms G, H, and G & H) on which the examiner records subject responses.

The examiner's manual contains an introduction to the WRMT-R Forms G and H, directions for administration and scoring, interpretation guidelines, instructional implications, and a technical summary. The pronunciation guide audiocassette is intended for the examiner to utilize prior to administering the Word Attack and Word Identification tests. Finally, the four-page "Report to Parents" booklet includes information on what the individual tests measure, what the clusters measure, what types of scores are yielded, and how to interpret those scores.

The examiner's responsibilities in the test process include administering the tests, scoring each item response as correct or incorrect, converting scores from raw scores into age equivalents, grade equivalents, standard scores, and the like, and evaluating the test results. Woodcock suggests that first-time examiners play the role of subject with the test given by someone competent and familiar with it. After studying the first three chapters of the WRMT-R examiner's manual and the contents of the test books (Forms G and H), there is a practice exercise to complete. The novice examiner should perform two or more trial administrations of the test, followed by another practice exercise and a self-evaluation checklist to complete.

Descriptions of the WRMT-R battery components follow:

Test 1: *Visual-Auditory Learning* (Form G only). The seven test stories contain rebuses (unfamiliar visual symbols) that evaluate how well the subject forms associations between visual stimuli and oral responses.

Test 2: *Letter Identification* (Form G only). The 51 items on this test present upper- or lowercase letters to the subject. Many varied letter forms are used, such as roman, italic, bold, serif, sans serif, cursive, and special type styles. The subject may either say the letter name or give its most common sound.

Supplementary Letter Checklist (Form G only). This test contains upper- and lowercase letters in a sans serif type style only (used in early beginning reading materials). The subject may respond by giving the name or sound of the letters. The uppercase portion has 27 items; the lowercase, 36.

Test 3: *Word Identification* (Forms G and H). Here the subject reads words that he or she must pronounce correctly within 5 seconds. Respondents do not need to know the meaning of the words. There are 106 items on both forms.

Test 4: *Word Attack* (Forms G and H). This 45-item test measures a subject's ability to use phonic and structural analysis skills to pronounce nonsense words or words that appear in the English language with low frequency. This test is not always given if the subject scores 0 or 1 correct on the previous subtest (Word Identification).

Test 5: *Word Comprehension* (Forms G and H). Three subtests compose this test: Antonyms, Synonyms, and Analogies. Word comprehension is also measured in the following areas: general reading, science-math, social studies, and humanities.

Subtest 5A: *Antonyms*. The subject reads a word and responds orally with one that has the opposite meaning. Form G contains 34 items; Form H, 33.

Subtest 5B: *Synonyms*. This measure tests reading vocabulary. The subject reads a word and then responds orally with another word similar in meaning. Form G has 33 items; Form H, 34.

Subtest 5C: *Analogies*. Here the subject first reads a pair of words and determines their relationship. Then he or she reads the first word of a succeeding pair and supplies his or her own word to complete the analogy. Both forms contain 79 items.

Test 6: *Passage Comprehension* (Forms G and H). This test measures the subject's ability to fill in a key word missing from a passage (usually two to three sentences long) using contextual clues. He or she must use comprehension and vocabulary skills. Both forms have 68 items.

The Form G test record is 16 pages long and contains Tests 1 through 6 plus information on the Word Attack Error Inventory, the summary of scores, diagnostic profiles, a percentile rank profile, and an instructional level profile. The Form

H test record, 12 pages long, includes Tests 3–6 as well as the inventory, summary, and profile pages of Form G. The G & H test record includes the Instructional Level Profile, the Word Attack Error Inventory for both Form G and Form H, the summary of scores, diagnostic profiles for both basic skills and comprehension, and the Percentile Rank Profile.

Practical Applications/Uses

The WRMT-R is a thorough battery of tests that measure various components of reading ability. The intended use of these tests is to accurately determine the level at which a subject functions in the components of reading skills, primarily students with reading difficulties. Instructional planning, perhaps through the means of an IEP (Individual Education Plan), can show the student's strengths and weaknesses. Users also can obtain error analysis of the responses.

This useful assessment tool also aids in the placement of students into reading groups by determining what the level of instruction should be. It can help to provide guidance in both short- and long-term career goals. WRMT-R results can prove helpful to teachers, counselors, and social workers.

The WRMT-R is best administered individually in a quiet place. The examiner's manual states the guidelines for the examiner to follow from the *Standards for Educational and Psychological Testing* (American Educational Research Association, American Psychological Association, & National Council on Measurement in Education, 1985). Administration of the WRMT-R does not require formal training beyond the practice that the manual suggests.

The manual describes extensively the procedures for administering the WRMT-R. Specific directions also appear in the test books themselves. The examiner is told exactly what to say, how to sit, how to point, and how to briskly administer the test. Every subtest need not be administered; the examiner determines which subtests should be given and in what order. The examiner's manual describes the starting points on the subtests, the concept of testing by complete pages, and the basal and ceiling rules. A sample appears of a test response page. Specific instructions are given for each particular subtest. Administering the entire battery should take about 45 minutes.

Approximately 20 pages in the examiner's manual deal specifically with scoring instructions. The terminology used in the scoring process may not be familiar to all examiners. The user is told how to find raw scores, W-scores, difference scores, standard errors of measurement, grade equivalent scores, age equivalent scores, relative performance indexes, instructional ranges, percentile ranks, and standard scores. Tables are found in the back of the manual, and the examiner is directed by the manual and the test record booklet which one to use.

Directions also are given for cluster scores and completing various profiles: instructional level, percentile rank, and diagnostic. There is a discussion of aptitude-achievement discrepancy analysis and the Word Attack Error Inventory.

The first-time examiner may need approximately 45 minutes to an hour to score the WMRT-R. Once experienced, 25 minutes probably will suffice. The examiner may find some of the manual's tables confusing to read, both some in the back of the manual and the one on page 55 that deals with the estimated aptitude-achievement correlations.

Computer scoring is available for the WRMT-R, via the Automated System for Scoring and Interpreting Standardized Tests (ASSIST). The use of this program dramatically reduces the time needed to process the scores as well as the possibility of computation mistakes. This method is definitely preferred over hand scoring.

Technical Aspects

The WRMT-R is a revised version of the first Woodcock Reading Mastery Tests (Woodcock, 1973), containing both new and expanded tests. A readiness section taken from the Woodcock-Johnson Psycho-Educational Battery was added in Form G. The Word Comprehension test was expanded to include synonyms and antonyms, plus a reading vocabulary component divided into four content areas: general reading, science-mathematics, social studies, and humanities. A total reading short scale was developed with scores from the Word Identification and Passage Comprehension tests. The Relative Mastery Score (RMS) from the 1973 edition is now expressed as a ratio comparing the subject's mastery level with the 90% mastery level and is renamed the Relative Performance Index (RPI). An analysis of errors is now possible with a Word Attack Error Inventory. Equating studies were conducted on a sample of 600 unspecified persons so that scores on the WRMT-R can be compared with the Goldman-Fristoe-Woodcock Auditory Skills Test Battery and the Woodcock-Johnson Psycho-Educational Battery on three special diagnostic profiles. The test norms have been extended to include college-level and adult groups up to 75 years and beyond.

The revised version of the test attempted to fully satisfy the criteria and technical data reporting in the 1974 APA standards for educational and psychological tests and is consistent with the 1985 revised standards. Item selection and test development relied heavily on concepts of item response theory and analysis of data from the Rasch model (Woodcock, 1982). According to the manual (Woodcock, Mather, & Barnes, 1987, p. 95), "the technical criteria for item selection were stringent; items that were retained had to fit the Rasch model."

The normative sample for the WRMT-R consisted of 6,089 persons living in 60 "geographically diverse" communities in the United States. The sampling plan followed a stratified sampling design using 1980 census information. Strata variables included census region, community size, sex, race, origin (Hispanic or non-Hispanic), college (public, private, type), and adult education, occupational status, and occupational type. Oversampling was performed in low-occurrence strata to increase measurement accuracy. The manual includes a table listing the distribution of these variables in the census data and the WRMT-R norming sample. Of the total sample, 4,201 subjects were K–12; 1,023 were college level; and 865 were community dwellers in the 20–80+ age range. Normative data were gathered continuously over 2 complete school years and permitted the computation of "continuous-year norms" for both grade and age equivalents and percentile rank and standard scores. The manual provides a table of mean and standard deviations by selected grade, adult, and college samples on test and cluster W-scores.

The author reports corrected split-half reliability correlation coefficients. Reliabilities are calculated for the six tests, three clusters, and the total reading full and short scale scores. These reliabilities along with standard errors of measurement are further delineated by selective grade, college, and adult groups for either Form G or H or combined. Nearly all of the reliabilities are .90 or higher; many are .95 or higher. A few exceptions to this result appeared in Grade 11 and samples beyond this age on single tests.

Content validity, or the extent to which a test's items represent the domain it purports to measure, was expected by the author because "items were developed with contributions from outside experts, including experienced teachers and curriculum specialists . . . and designed to be comprehensive in both content and difficulty" (Woodcock et al., 1987, p. 97). Additionally, the manual contains 50%, 75%, and 96% mastery performance on representative items by grade equivalent peers on several tests and subtests. The open-ended or free-response nature of the items is a format that usually reduces any guessing confounds in the scores. Other details about item selection are not specified except that the author utilized classical item selection techniques and the Rasch model in later stages of test refinement.

Items were selected in the special reading vocabularies in Word Comprehension based on expert opinion and item validity coefficients with the WJPEB and WRMT-R vocabulary total scores. Additional items and tests were included from the WRMT-R, the GFW, and the WJPEB to sample a complex range of skills related to the Diagnostic Readiness Profile, the Diagnostic Basic Skills Profile, and the Diagnostic Comprehension Profile.

Concurrent validity indicates the extent to which a test relates to an independent criterion that purports to measure the same domain. The author reports concurrent validity coefficients between the Letter-Word Identification, Word Attack, Passage Comprehension, and total reading scores on the WJPEB reading tests and the Word Identification, Word Attack, Word Comprehension, Passage Comprehension, and full and short scale scores on the WRMT-R by Grade 1 ($N = 85$), Grade 3 ($N = 122$), Grade 5 ($N = 33$), and Grade 8 ($N = 84$). Correlation coefficients ranged from .85 to .91 when comparing total full scale reading correlations. Individual tests on the WJPEB and the WRMT-R with similar name labels range from .55 to .90. However, Passage Comprehension on the WJPEB generally correlated higher with Word Comprehension and not Passage Comprehension on the WRMT-R.

The author presents concurrent validity coefficients for the WRMT and reading scores from the Iowa Tests of Basic Skills, Iowa Tests of Educational Development, Peabody Individual Achievement Test, WJPEB, and Wide Range Achievement Test in a 1978 study with subjects in Grades 3, 5, and 12. The manual states it is "because the psychometric characteristics of the original WRMT (1973) and the WRMT-R are so similar that many generalizations from one to the other can be validly made" (p. 100). No correlations between the two versions are reported in the manual. The correlations between the WRMT and the selected reading measures ranged from .78 to .92, with a median value of .87.

The manual presents correlations computed from the norming sample among the test, cluster, and total reading (full and short scale) scores by grade, college, and adult levels. In general, the correlations show an appropriately positive increase with the skill requirements of each type of test. Because of the hierarchical nature of the cluster and test scales, many of the correlations are artifactually high because they share the same scoring content. The pattern of intercorrelations appears somewhat homogeneous across age-grade levels. There is one exception to this finding in the correlations for Grade 5, where the general magnitude of the correlations is lower. Also, correlations are not reported for the Word Comprehension subtests here or in the other technical section summaries.

Critique

The WRMT-R provides an extremely comprehensive analysis of a individual's reading skills. A thorough levels profile can be generated to compare the examinee's performance in terms of age and grade equivalents, standard scores for aptitude tests, and relative ranges of instructional mastery. The several profiles from the test battery pinpoint areas of the examinee's strengths and weaknesses in the reading domain. The WRMT-R is atheoretical in its development, so its interpretation can be linked with many systems of diagnosis and clinical remediation. It can form the basis of a reading improvement program, and the manual presents many illustrative case studies to exemplify this application.

The improvements made in the revised edition of the WRMT remove or alleviate to some degree several deficiencies previously noted regarding the original test battery. The difficulties of scoring and interpreting the battery (see Sherman & Merschman, 1987) have been reduced through the ASSIST computer program and an expansion of the manual. Indeed, the program could be viewed as a necessity if one wants to avoid scoring tedium that might lead to relying on the more easily calculated age and grade equivalents, and thus obviating the very comprehensive analysis the test battery is capable of producing (Eaves, 1989–90). The revised and expanded manual and the addition of a training audiocassette facilitate the instruction of novice examiners in administering, scoring, and interpreting the tests. The manual does presume some background and familiarity with testing and scoring procedures, which if not present might lead to errors of administration and scoring.

The content and subtests in the WRMT-R have been revised to include an error analysis in word attack skills, identification of sans serif letters, and a major addition to the Word Comprehension test (cf. Laffey & Kelley, 1979). It now allows for examining reading vocabularies, antonyms, and synonyms. This test still uses a completion format that apparently requires reasoning and classification skills on the part of the examinee (Sherman & Merschman, 1987). Eaves (1989–90) and others (Lewandowski & Martens, 1990) have noted that the cloze procedure employed in the Passage Comprehension test has context and picture clues that may not give a direct understanding of the examinee's ability to make inferences from or logically analyze reading text.

The author has continued to follow rigorous test procedures and standards in the development and norming of the revised edition. The psychometric techniques yield a test battery that allows for sophisticated age- and grade-equivalent norms, diagnostic and interpretive profiles, and a variety of precise percentiles and standard scores, especially for prescriptive and comparative purposes. Four levels of interpretive information derive from this battery of tests. The WRMT-R allows for an aptitude-achievement discrepancy analysis that can be useful in educational placement.

In contrast to these descriptions, however, only internal consistency coefficients of reliability are reported. Test-retest or parallel-form reliability correlation coefficients are not available in the manual and would provide additional valuable information about the WRMT-R. In a study by Saltstone, Tayler, and Fraboni (1989), the Word Identification subtests of Forms G and H correlated highly ($r = .86$) but failed to demonstrate classification consistency in a sample of 48 seventh-graders on grade-equivalent reading proficiency.

Several reviewers (Dyer, 1985; Lewandowski & Martens, 1990; Sherman & Merschman, 1987) have criticized the original battery for the lack of content and construct validity, the absence of external criterion-referenced norms, or the fragmented rather than holistic approach to reading diagnosis (Cooter, 1988). Also, factorial validity of the WRMT-R tests and subtests have yet to be analyzed by the author or in any other published reports (Eaves, 1989–90). The manual does include tables that present criterion-referenced performance on selected tests and subtests, but the author argues that the Relative Performance Index describes relative quality of performance and *not* relative standing in a group; thus, it serves to anchor the test results to the demands of the curriculum (Woodcock, 1982). Additionally, Woodcock (1973) evaluated and confirmed the predictive validity of the original WRMT instructional range scores. In samples of 103 second-graders and 102 seventh-graders, item pools in one testing session predicted success on items in another pool of criterion tasks given 1 week later.

Administration, scoring, and interpretation of the WRMT-R are greatly facilitated by the test kit, the detailed manual and chapter on instructional implications within it, the scoring guides and templates, and the computer-scoring software. Interscorer agreement in administering and scoring the tests is not reported, but if this information were available, concerns about starting and stopping points could be addressed (Eaves, 1989–90). As with any testing instrument, the user must weigh and decide between the human cost and time to administer and score the test versus the precision and information requirements of the diagnostic or clinical decision to be made. The WRMT-R is not intended or designed to be a simple screening device; rather, it attempts to identify and assess an individual's reading difficulties for prescriptive remediation. Its comprehensiveness as a clinical tool should predominate concerns about administration convenience. The utility and potential of the WRMT-R for predictive or research purposes awaits further experience and study with the revised battery of tests.

References

American Educational Research Association, American Psychological Association, & National Council on Measurement in Education. (1985). *Standards for educational and psychological testing.* Washington, DC: American Psychological Association.

Cooter, R.B., Jr. (1988). Woodcock Reading Mastery Tests–Revised (Forms G and H) (WRMT-R). *The Reading Teacher, 42,* 154–155.

Dyer, C.O. (1985). Woodcock Reading Mastery Tests. In D.J. Keyser & R.C. Sweetland (Eds.), *Tests critiques* (Vol. IV, pp. 704–715). Austin, TX: PRO-ED.

Eaves, R.C. (1989–90). Woodcock Reading Mastery Tests–Revised (WRMTR). *Diagnostique, 15,* 277–297.

Laffey, J.L., & Kelly, D. (1979). Woodcock Reading Mastery Tests. *The Reading Teacher, 31,* 335–339.

Lewandowski, L.J., & Martens, B.K. (1990). Selecting and evaluating standardized tests. *Journal of Reading, 33,* 384–388.

Saltstone, R., Tayler, S.M., & Fraboni, M. (1989). A note on the word identification subtest of the Woodcock Reading Mastery Tests–Revised: Different classification consequences of Forms G and H. *Journal of Psychoeducational Assessment, 7,* 343–345.

Sherman, T.F., & Merschman, J. (1987). *Reading diagnostic tools: Review of Woodcock Reading Mastery Test.* (Eric Document Reproduction Service No. ED 287 153)

Woodcock, R.W. (1973). *Woodcock Reading Mastery Tests.* Circle Pines, MN: American Guidance Service.

Woodcock, R.W. (1982). *Interpretation of the Rasch ability and difficulty scales for educational purposes.* (ERIC Document Reproduction Service No. ED 223 673)

Woodcock, R.W., Mather, N., & Barnes, E.K. (1987). *Woodcock Reading Mastery Tests–Revised: Examiner's manual, Forms G and H.* Circle Pines, MN: American Guidance Service.

Allan P. Jones, Ph.D.

Professor of Psychology, University of Houston, Houston, Texas.

WORK ATTITUDES QUESTIONNAIRE

Maxene S. Doty and Nancy E. Betz. Columbus, Ohio: Marathon Consulting and Press.

Introduction

The Work Attitudes Questionnaire (WAQ; Doty & Betz, 1980, 1981) was developed in response to a perceived trend in the literature to view high levels of work involvement as unhealthy. The test was designed to distinguish between two types of highly career-committed individuals—those whose commitment is positive versus those whose high level of commitment has adverse effects on their psychological health. The authors sought to differentiate between individuals whose commitment was a result of insecurity, fear, or low self-esteem and those who were motivated by feelings of accomplishment and other more intrinsic or fulfilling factors. The test produces scores on two scales. One scale focuses on work commitment, the other on the degree to which the person's attitudes toward work represent psychologically healthy versus unhealthy responses.

The 16-page manual provides a conceptual overview by presenting a four-celled typology based on scores on the two dimensions. High scores on both the Health scale and the Commitment scale reflect Excessive-Detrimental Commitment, where The Addicted Worker neglects other areas of his or her life. Low scores on these two dimensions reflect Other-Than-Work Commitment, where the Uninvolved Worker focuses on other life domains such as family or leisure. A high Commitment score combined with a low Health score reflects High-Positive Commitment, where The Dedicated Worker places heavy but not exclusive emphasis on work. The final type, with low scores on Commitment and high scores on Health, is Inconsistent Commitment and describes The Confused Worker. The authors suggest that this pattern of scores is highly unlikely.

The WAQ was developed in conjunction with the senior author's master's thesis (Doty, 1980). Maxene S. Doty received both her M.A. (1980) and Ph.D. (1984) in psychology from The Ohio State University. She is a licensed psychologist in Maine and Ohio and is currently employed as a staff psychologist in the Counseling and Testing Center at the University of Maine. Nancy E. Betz received her Ph.D. in psychology from the University of Minnesota (1976) and is a professor in the department of psychology at The Ohio State University. She has authored several articles and chapters on vocational psychology, career assessment, and psychological measurement, and has coauthored two books. She is a fellow of both the American Psychological Association and the American Psychological Society.

Practical Applications/Uses

Normative data presented in the WAQ manual are restricted to a single sample of pharmaceutical managers and include the mean, median, standard deviation, and range of the three scales. Demographic data generally are omitted except to describe the sample as male managers. The authors do not specify any population for which this test is more or less appropriate, although the activities described by some of the items (e.g., work-related entertaining and working at the office on weekends) and the phrasing of others ("One project begets another . . . ad infinitum") suggest that the test was intended primarily for managerial and professional-level, white-collar individuals.

The test consists of a four-page booklet containing 45 statements. The test taker indicates agreement or disagreement with these statements on a 5-point, Likert-format scale (1 = strongly disagree, 5 = strongly agree) by circling the appropriate number. The test is hand scored and requires relatively little sophistication for administering or scoring. The questionnaire nature of the WAQ makes it suitable for either individual or group administration.

To score the test, one sums the responses to the items in each scale, taking into account that some of the items (one in the Commitment scale, four in the Health scale) are reverse scored. This procedure yields three scores—a Commitment score, a Health score, and a total Work Attitudes score. No explicit directions are provided for calculating the Work Attitudes score, but it is presumably a sum of the other two scores. No scoring templates are provided, so most WAQ users would find it easier to transfer the data to a computer and use one of the common statistical or other data manipulation packages to score the test. Other users might prefer to create their own templates if scoring were desired for individual feedback rather than research purposes.

The manual provides relatively little information about the interpretation or use of the scores obtained by administering this test. The authors suggest that a Commitment score above 69 reflects a highly committed worker. If that score is combined with a Health score above 66, it describes a level of commitment to work that "is likely excessive, detrimental, and characteristic of the workaholic" (Doty & Betz, 1981, p. 8). However, these cut scores reflect an average response of 3 or "uncertain" rather than an average response of 4 (agree) or 5 (strongly agree). When this fact is combined with the small and somewhat unique sample, a somewhat more conservative interpretation and a higher cut score seem appropriate, especially in a counseling environment.

A related difficulty lies in the labeling of the Health scale, where a high score denotes an unhealthy level of commitment. Most users would find it more convenient if the direction of the score and the label were in the same direction. Misinterpretation when providing feedback to the respondent also would be less likely.

Technical Aspects

The WAQ was developed by generating 80 items that appeared to be related to the two constructs of health and commitment. These items were generated from the literature and interviews with individuals who reported high levels of commitment or who were self-identified as workaholics. Four vocational psychologists each rated the 80 items in terms of their appropriateness to the two concepts of health and commitment. Appropriateness was rated on a 4-point, Likert-format scale, where 1 indicated "not at all appropriate" and 4 indicated "especially appropriate." Ratings were summed for each item to produce an appropriateness score, which ranged from 4 to 16. Of the 80 items, 68 received scores of 10 points or higher.

The four judges, along with an additional Ph.D. psychologist and two advanced graduate students, also rated the items on the degree to which they represented psychologically healthy or unhealthy responses. The ratings were obtained on a 5-point Likert scale that ranged from "unhealthy" to "healthy." The mid-point of the scale was an "uncertain" response. According to the authors, items were included in the Health scale if they received appropriateness scores of 10 or greater, mean unhealthy/healthy ratings of 2 or less or 4 or greater, and no more than two "uncertain" ratings. The authors also included other items "having particular relevance to the construct but failing to meet one or more of the criteria" (Doty & Betz, 1981, p. 6). Unfortunately, they do not indicate which items or how many of the final set of items fell into this category. The above decision rules produced a preliminary Health scale comprised of 30 items. The Commitment scale consisted of 33 items that had appropriateness scores of 10 or greater but which did not qualify for the Health scale. The authors do not specify how these items differed from those that also failed to qualify but were included in the Health scale.

The resulting set of 63 items was then administered to 93 male managers in a pharmaceutical firm. The 45 items in the published version of the questionnaire were obtained by deleting items with item-total correlations less than $r_{it} = .20$ and items whose deletion resulted in higher indices of internal consistency (calculated as coefficient alpha). Reliability estimates were $\alpha = .80$ for the Commitment scale, .85 for the Health scale, and .90 for the total questionnaire. Data were not provided about the correlation between the two scales, but the reliability coefficient for the total scale suggests that the relationship is relatively high. The manual states that none of the 93 managers reported low Commitment scores in conjunction with high Health scores.

Only a single study of validity was found. Doty (1980) reported correlations between the Commitment, Health, and total WAQ scores and the Career Salience Scale (Greenhaus, 1971) of .58, .55, and .62, respectively. Correlations of the three scores with subject's reports of hours worked per week were .38, .29, and .36.

Critique

This test is essentially in its early stages of development. Some work has been done, but much more is needed before it represents a viable tool for the researcher or counselor. The authors appear aware of this need and label the test as a version for research, although the manual does argue that the WAQ is particularly useful for diagnostic purposes. The greatest need is for a systematic appraisal of test validity and a programmatic collection of normative data that would aid interpretation and application. The authors relied heavily on content validity in the development of the test but were not consistent in the use of the resulting data in decisions about including the items in the scales. The ratings of the expert judges generally were used but were ignored when the authors deemed an item appropriate for inclusion. Further, the manual does not provide an explicit conceptual definition of the two main constructs of health and commitment, nor does it provide the definition the judges used to make decisions about the appropriateness of an item or its healthy/unhealthy effects. The test user is left to infer the definition of the concept from the content of the final item set or from his or her knowledge of the relevant literature. This omission invites misinterpretation or misuse.

A question also exists about the ability of the measure to distinguish between the two dimensions discussed in the manual. No discriminant evidence (such as factor analyses or differential patterns of prediction) was provided. The high internal consistency for the total scale and the similar pattern of correlation with outside measures suggest that the scales are not empirically discrete. A comparison of the items included in the two scales reveals many similarities and makes it even more difficult to decipher the decision rules that led to an item's placement in one scale or the other. For example, the Commitment scale contains the following items: "I would rather stay at work and finish a task than leave something half-done and rush to get home," and "I usually take work home with me." Items in the Health scale include "I worry a great deal about what I haven't gotten done" and "I often work after dinner." Several other items are similarly comparable across the two scales. Thus, in spite of the attempt for a conceptual distinction, the WAQ scale seems to represent a single linear measure. This questionnaire was copyrighted over 10 years ago. A search of the literature revealed no published studies using this test nor was the test publisher aware of any. Given this apparent dearth of interest by the research community and the validity and norming concerns noted above, it is unlikely that the Work Attitudes Questionnaire will offer a useful tool to the counselor.

References

Doty, M.S. (1980). *Extreme and excessive levels of commitment to work: Incunabula.* Unpublished master's thesis, The Ohio State University, Columbus.

Doty, M.S., & Betz, N.E. (1980). *Work Attitudes Questionnaire.* Columbus, OH: Marathon Consulting and Press.

Doty, M.S., & Betz, N.E. (1981). *Manual for the Work Attitudes Questionnaire.* Columbus, OH: Marathon Consulting and Press.

Greenhaus, J.H. (1971). An investigation of the role of career salience in vocational behavior. *Journal of Vocational Behavior, 1,* 209–216.

James A. Moses Jr., Ph.D.
*Clinical Associate Professor of Psychiatry and Behavioral Sciences,
Stanford University School of Medicine, and Coordinator,
Psychological Assessment Unit, Department of Veterans Affairs
Medical Center, Palo Alto, California.*

WORK ENVIRONMENT SCALE

*Rudolf H. Moos. Palo Alto, California: Consulting
Psychologists Press, Inc.*

Introduction

The Work Environment Scale (WES; Moos, 1981, 1986) is designed to elicit specific, theoretically guided, systematic, multidimensional, categorically descriptive information from workers and supervisors about their actual and preferred work settings, as well as anticipated changes in the social context of their work environment. The inventory consists of 90 brief, descriptive, declarative sentences that the respondent answers as "true" or "false."

Three forms of the WES are available for comparison of real, ideal, and expected social environmental features of work settings. Items for the *real* form (Form R) are stated in the present tense and designed to be used by employees and supervisors who are familiar with the work setting to describe personal perceptions of their work environments. The other forms of the WES are modifications of Form R, differing in verb tense but not in item content. The *expected* form (Form E) items are phrased in the future tense and are applicable to persons about to enter a new work setting or about to experience some significant change in the established work environment. The *ideal* form (Form I) phrases the items conditionally and describes what an ideal work setting might be like. A short form of the WES (Form S) was proposed based on the first 40 items of the full scale. Its use in clinical and consulting applications is discouraged because there are too few items on each subscale of the short form to provide reliable scores for individuals or groups (Moos, 1986, p. 34). This form should be considered an experimental or research form only.

The author of the WES, Rudolf H. Moos, received the B.A. degree with honors (1956) and the Ph.D. degree (1960) from the University of California, Berkeley. Thereafter he served as a postdoctoral fellow at the University of California, San Francisco, for 2 years. He is a diplomate in clinical psychology of the American Board of Professional Psychology (1965), a recipient of the Hofheimer Award for Research of the American Psychiatric Association (1975), a Veterans Administration Career Scientist (since 1981), and a fellow of numerous learned societies. He has been a faculty member of the Department of Psychiatry and Behavioral Sciences at Stanford University since 1962 (Professor since 1972) and directs the Postdoctoral Research Training Program at that institution. At the Veterans Administration Medical Center, Palo Alto, California, he serves as the founding

828

director of the Social Ecology Laboratory, as the chief of psychiatric research, and as the director of the Far West Health Services Research and Development Service Field Program. He had published 12 books and 270 book chapters, manuals, literature reviews, and professional research articles through January 1988. He is best known for his pioneering work in the development and implementation of the social ecological approach to programmatic and group classification, description, evaluation, and consultation.

The WES has been translated into Dutch (Lange, 1978a, 1978b), French (Gauthier, 1981), German (Weyer, 1981; Weyer & Hodapp, 1978), Hebrew (Meier, 1983), Japanese, Portuguese, Spanish, and Vietnamese (for an overview, see Moos, 1986, p. 36). The scale also was adapted for an Australian study of teachers (Fisher & Fraser, 1983). The psychometric findings for the Dutch, German, and Australian adaptations of the WES were similar to those of the original American form.

The WES has not been revised since its public appearance (Insel & Moos, 1974; Moos, 1981), although a revised manual (Moos, 1986) for the test has been written. Additional information about clinical and program evaluation applications of the WES as well as an expanded review of its research applications are included in the revised manual. Moos recommends use of the revised manual for experimental and clinical applications, although the original manual (Moos, 1981) could be used for administration and scoring.

Development of the WES initial item pool followed from several convergent procedures. The aim was to understand the social environmental characteristics of work group settings. Moos and his colleagues conducted structured interviews in a variety of work settings to identify an initial item pool that would accurately and thoroughly describe these characteristics. Initial descriptive categories and additional items were adapted from the other Social Climate Scales (for a review, see Moos, 1974). An initial 200-item Form A of the WES was reduced to a subsequent 138-item Form B, which was administered to a sample of 624 workers and supervisors in 44 work groups. Moos (1986, p. 3) describes the sources for the previous sample as representing

> a wide range of work groups: municipal employees in administrative, financial, recreational, and community services; janitors, maintenance workers, plumbers, and security officers; maintenance and production workers at a large factory; drivers, mechanics, and forklift operators at a trucking firm; route salesman, bottlers, and night loaders at a soft-drink bottling plant; and employees at an electronics firm. Also sampled were work groups from several health-care employment settings: faculty members in a university-affiliated nursing school, administrative and staff nurses in a Veterans Administration medical center, and professional and paraprofessional workers in a psychiatric outpatient clinic.

Analysis of the Form B sample outlined above led to selection of the 90 best discriminating items that characterized work environments across a variety of settings. Multiple psychometric criteria were used to select items for inclusion in the final scale. Items selected were required to approximate an overall 50-50 item split to avoid those that were descriptive only of unusual work settings. Each item had to correlate more highly with its own subscale than with any other WES subscale; all 90 of the final WES items met this criterion. Each WES subscale was designed to have approximately equal numbers of items scored true and false to control for response-style acquiescence. The WES scales also were designed to have low to moderate intercorrelations among themselves to prevent dimensional redundancy. Each item and each subscale was required to discriminate between different work settings to further demonstrate specificity of the descriptors. Each of these criteria were successfully approximated at psychometrically acceptable levels by the items chosen for the final Form R.

The WES test booklet (Insel & Moos, 1974) consists of a four-page reusable question pamphlet. On the separate answer sheet the respondent records the form of the WES that is being taken, the date, and basic demographic information: respondent name, age, and sex, name of organization, department, job title, duration of employment with the specific department being rated and the overall organization of which it is a part (in months and years), and optional additional descriptive data. Worked examples are provided for true and false response types. Numbered boxes corresponding to each question are divided in half horizontally. "True" is indicated by marking an X in the top half of the box; "false" is noted by marking an X in the bottom half. The profile sheet can be used with any of the 10 Social Climate Scales. The unit rated is indicated in addition to the scale type, the scale form, the normative group used to convert raw scores to standardized scores, and the date. The legend of the profile has boxes to indicate the scaled score and the subscale title acronym for the appropriate Social Climate Scale, in this case the WES.

Separate norms are provided in the WES test manual for representative general work groups and health-care work groups on Form R. Preliminary norms also are provided for Forms E and I. Each of these normative groups will be discussed in turn.

Form R norms: General work groups. Form R of the WES has been extensively studied among "general" work groups that are distinguished from health-care professional groups. The general work group consists of 1,442 employees from commercial and noncommercial radio stations and a sample of over 400 general citizens drawn at random from stratified census tracts in the San Francisco area (Moos, 1986; Moos, Finney, & Chan, 1981). Moos (1986) notes that the descriptive statistics for Form R of the WES are similar for the general work groups and other subgroups of the Form R normative sample, which supports the generality of these norms across work settings sampled.

Form R norms: Health-care work groups. Moos (1986, p. 4) describes this portion of the WES normative sample as

> employees from four outpatient psychiatric clinics and groups of patient-care personnel; personnel not involved in patient care (such as janitors, maintenance workers, and office clerks); and administrative and supervisory personnel from a community mental health center, a children's residential treatment center, two state hospitals, a Veterans Administration medical center, two long-term care facilities, and four intensive care and general medical hospital units.

This health-care worker sample consisted of 1,607 subjects. The 624 subjects used to develop Form B of the WES were included in this sample as well.

Form I preliminary norms. The ideal form of the WES was completed by 348 subjects from varied general and health-care work groups. Moos cautions that these norms are preliminary and should be used primarily in combination with Form R, to assess differences between perceptions of actual and idealized work environment settings. Specific programs and job titles of respondents are not specified in the manual for this sample, but should be varied and preliminarily generalizable within the categories noted. These findings should be replicated and extended before they are recommended for general clinical and consultative use.

Form E preliminary norms. The expectations form of the WES was completed by a sample of only 81 respondents, which makes application of the norms preliminary and largely experimental at this point. Specifics of the respondent demographic characteristics and the varied work settings were not specified in the test manual. Research should replicate and extend these norms to relatively large samples before they are recommended for consultative application and personnel evaluation.

Practical Applications/Uses

The WES is based on a tricategorical social ecological model that has been developed and extensively studied by Moos and his colleagues through their development of the Social Climate Scales. Their model derives theoretically from the formulations of Henry Murray (1938), who was the first personality theorist to describe the complementary roles of individual needs and environmental press as cofactors that determine complex social perception and consequent behavior. The model on which the WES is based posits three dimensions: Relationship, Personal Growth, and System Maintenance–System Change. On the WES these three dimensions are measured for work settings by means of 10 subscales. Moos (1986, p. 2) provides these brief descriptions of the 10 WES subscales in the revised manual:

RELATIONSHIP DIMENSIONS

Involvement—the extent to which employees are concerned about and committed to their jobs

Peer Cohesion—the extent to which employees are friendly and supportive of one another

Supervisor Support—the extent to which management is supportive of employees and encourages employees to be supportive of one another

PERSONAL GROWTH DIMENSIONS

Autonomy—the extent to which employees are encouraged to be self-sufficient and to make their own decisions

Task Orientation—the degree of emphasis on good planning, efficiency, and getting the job done

Work Pressure—the degree to which the press of work and time urgency dominate the job milieu

SYSTEM MAINTENANCE–SYSTEM CHANGE DIMENSIONS

Clarity—the extent to which employees know what to expect in their daily routine and how explicitly rules and policies are communicated

Control—the extent to which management uses rules and pressures to keep employees under control

Innovation—the degree of emphasis on variety, change, and new approaches

Physical Comfort—the extent to which the physical surroundings contribute to a pleasant work environment

Multiple applications of the WES results to practical decision making are recommended in the manual. Common uses include multidimensional description of single settings, cross-setting descriptive comparison, contrast of perceptions of workers and managers within a work setting, comparison of real and idealized work environments, and both evaluation and facilitation of change in work settings. Work and/or managerial subgroups within a setting or employees with various demographic characteristics, productivity levels, or satisfaction levels could be similarly compared using the WES methodology. Examples of applications of the WES to evaluate gender differences, manager-employee perceptual variations, and patient care versus support staff differences are presented in the manual in addition to illustrative examples drawn from general and health care settings (Moos, 1986, pp. 7–8, 12–15). None of these factors produced large enough differences to warrant separate normative standards as a function of sex of respondent, managerial versus line employee status, or patient- versus non-patient-care job classification. Patient-care personnel, however, tended to see their work environments somewhat more negatively and as more stressful than non-patient-care employees. For extended discussions of applications of the WES and its relationship to the other Social Climate Scales, one may consult the reviews by Moos (1984, 1985a, 1985b, 1986), Moos, Clayton, and Max (1979), and Moos and Spinrad (1984).

The normatively best established application for the WES in clinical and consultative settings remains program description with Form R. This application is primarily recommended by this reviewer because Form R is the best norm-referenced version of the WES and it has wide generalizability and applicability as a result. Moos (1986, pp. 12–15) provides several examples of this application of the WES with analysis of work programs at the unit level. The WES provides specific, quantified, multidimensional and categorical information about the social phenomenology to which workers react in their day-to-day work activities. The WES is particularly useful to identify those aspects of the work setting that promote productivity and job satisfaction as well as to identify those features of the perceived job setting that prevent or impede efficient job performance.

The WES can be used to contrast the views of managers and line employees in the same work setting as well as the perceptions of managerial or subordinate employees across similar or different work settings that are thought to vary systematically on the WES dimensions. In essence the WES provides a method for quantification and objective definition of important behavioral variables that affect job performance and that have been shown to relate significantly to work output and employee efficiency.

Different forms of the WES may be used jointly to evaluate job satisfaction or expectations of management or staff employees and after a change in the work program. These applications should be considered exploratory for the time being because they require comparison of the WES real form with the ideal or expected forms. Although the real form is well normed, the ideal and expected forms have, as yet, only preliminary normative data. One might recommend then that only relatively strong trends in differences between real and ideal or expected forms of the scale should be used for decision modeling in studies of program evaluation.

Comparison of the real (Form R) and ideal (Form I) forms of the WES are useful in evaluating desired program change or, alternatively, present program dissatisfaction. The degree of discrepancy between actual and idealized work environment conditions operationalizes this variable. Moos (1986, pp. 15–16) provides an example of such an application of the WES in a health care setting. The level of profile elevation discrepancy between Form R and Form I shows the degree of desired program change, while the categories on which the differences occur highlight its specific multidimensional nature.

Form E, the WES expected form, probably should be considered a research instrument for the time being, at least until adequate normative data have been assembled. This form has the potential to identify expected areas of change for employees about to undergo change in their work milieu or job assignment. It also would be useful for evaluating job expectations of those about to enter the work force for the first time and those returning to work after an absence. In psychiatric and medical health care settings, where changes in the patient's health status may require a change in the job sought, Form E could prove especially valuable as a potential predictor of job adjustment and satisfaction, and possibly job expectancy accuracy as well. The foregoing comments are offered primarily as potential research applications of Form E rather than as current clinical or consulting applications.

The manual does not explicitly state the professional qualifications for program consultants who use the WES, but one would expect a qualified user to have graduate-level training in a mental health specialty and a working knowledge of psychometric theory and statistics. It is important that the examiner understand the psychometric basis of the WES, its normative database, and its scaling model so that interpretations based on profile analysis will be valid. Understanding the scale's reliability and the normative samples used for its various forms is important to understanding the limits of valid application of WES results. Those users without such academic training who wish to make use of this instrument, such as personnel managers, supervisors, administrative executives, and so forth, are encouraged to consult with a qualified professional to interpret WES results for individuals and work groups. A professional psychologist with organizational consultative experience probably would be the ideal consultant for WES interpretation in a variety of industrial and organizational work settings, although other mental health professionals with related consultative experience also could make effective use of the scale findings. A thorough understanding of both the work setting evaluated and the scale itself is strongly recommended for any vocational consultant who will interpret WES results.

Clinical psychologists working in inpatient, partial hospitalization, or outpatient settings could use the WES effectively to assess the expectations of their clients regarding real and ideal job placement characteristics. In combination with a counseling psychologist or other vocational placement specialist, a tailored fit of the job to the individual could be arranged. Follow-up evaluation of job performance and stability and symptomatic status from various treatment programs that differ in key treatment modalities could be worked out in vocational settings. The WES possibly in combination with other Social Climate Scales could offer a potentially powerful measure of "ecological validity," which could relate adaptive behavior in various inpatient and community social settings to intellectual and personological resources. Another application of the WES might involve matching subjects completing rehabilitation for traumatic brain injury to anticipated post-discharge job placements, to optimize matching subject to task and to minimize foreseeable conflicts.

The WES is suitable for administration to a very wide range of adolescents and adults of working age. Although a minimum respondent age is not specified in the manual, a potential subject would not be of competitive working age until some time during adolescence. The primary consideration is the potential employability of the individual. The scale requires approximately sixth-grade reading ability, which is the level of difficulty encountered in most popular magazines and newspapers. Instructions for Form R are straightforward and require one to mark the answer sheet for each item "true" if the statement is definitely or mostly true and "false" if the statement is definitely or mostly false as it applies to one's current perception of the work setting. For Form E the respondent is asked to answer "true" or "false" to the same item content statements phrased in the future tense. In this case one is asked to describe what one thinks a new work setting about to be entered "will be like." In Form I the respondent is asked to describe what he or she thinks an ideal work setting "would be like."

The WES typically is self-administered as a self-report measure. When administered to work groups, it is advisable to have respondents answer anonymously. This method encourages more candid reporting of dissatisfaction with the program in addition to programmatic strong points and helps to provide a more balanced and objective evaluation standard. Employees who are individually identified may fear administrative censure if they are critical of the program.

A quiet, well-lighted, well-ventilated room with sufficient working space for each respondent should be provided. Unsophisticated subjects may require more assistance, particularly explanation of unfamiliar words, and should be situated in smaller groups as necessary. Simple restatements of individual word meanings are allowable, but the proctor must scrupulously avoid influencing responses.

The proctor should read the WES directions aloud to the examinees while they read them silently and follow the response examples on the answer sheet. Lead pencils with erasers should be provided so that respondents do not use pens. Subjects who have difficulty answering questions as true or false should be advised to respond "true" if in their opinion the statement is "true most of the time." Persons who still are unable to decisively answer should be encouraged to guess as a final alternative to nonresponse. Because the WES is a relatively brief instrument, incomplete protocols endanger reliability of measurement and hence validity of results. Answer sheets should be checked for completeness of demographic information and response to test questions as the forms are collected.

In most situations administration of the WES is straightforward and poses no difficulty for the proctor or for respondents who can read at a sixth-grade level. For individuals who cannot read at that level, Moos (1987, p. 23) recommends the use of tape-recorded or computerized instructions. As these audiovisual materials will not be available in many settings, in such cases the proctor might simply read the questions aloud to the respondent(s). For those physically disabled persons who require an individual administration of the WES, the examiner might read items aloud and/or write the subject's responses as appropriate. This method also would be indicated if the respondent had an especially low or generally impaired level of functioning. In such cases a mental health professional who is familiar with the respondent should interview and administer the test and simplify the language of some items as necessary to ensure response validity and item comprehension.

Each form of the WES typically should take approximately 15 to 20 minutes to complete. If more than one form of the test is to be administered to an individual, it is advisable to do so at different sittings to help to keep the descriptions disjoint and objective.

Scoring the WES is a clerical task. Hand scoring and profile plotting for a single client should take only about 10 minutes for an experienced examiner. The items of the 10 WES subscales are arranged in columns on the answer sheet. One places the clear plastic scoring template over the answer sheet and counts the number of answer marks (Xs) that show through the circular marks on the scoring template. These subscale raw scores are entered in boxes below the response portion of the sheet. Norms are provided for translation of raw scores to standardized T-scores only for Form R. Separate norms appear in the test manual for general and health-care work settings on each of the WES subscales. Preliminary raw score central tendency statistical values are given for each WES subscale for Forms I and E. The norms for Form I should be used primarily in conjunction with Form R values for the same person or work group. Form E norms are based on a sample of only 81 subjects and should be extensively supplemented before one uses them in applied settings. Item analysis of the results is advisable for all forms to clarify and individualize the nature of item endorsement.

The publisher has made a self-scoring edition of the WES available, as well as the automated Work Environment Scale Narrative Report developed by the author. This latter scoring and interpretive service makes use of special answer sheets. The WES Narrative Report provides an overview of work environment assessment in general and the WES in particular. A plot of the client's WES profile with raw, standardized, and percentile equivalent scores is presented in addition to the narrative report. The narrative includes an overview of the performance levels of interpretation and advises reference to the WES manual (Moos, 1986) and the Social Climate Scales user's guide (Moos, 1987) for background information. Each of the Relationship, Personal Growth or Goal Orientation, and System Maintenance–System Change Dimensions is interpreted individually. As suggested in this review, there also is an item analysis of key responses that help to clarify the nature of the description in detail. A summary interpretation of the subscale scores provides an overview of the workplace social climate in general and probable behavioral correlates of these social variables for work productivity and job satisfaction. The advantage of comparing the real and ideal forms of the

WES also is highlighted. A breakdown of item responses by subscale appears as well as an indication of the direction of response scoring for the individual scales for the respondent.

WES profile elevations typically are interpreted as significant at approximately 1 standard deviation above the appropriate normative mean. Profile elevation differences of this magnitude between groups compared on the same form of the WES or between different forms of the test on the same work group generally are interpreted as relevant. As noted in a previous review of a related Social Climate Scale (Moses, 1991), it would be valuable to normative interpreters to have available scalewise WES values for the standard error of measurement and standard error of difference statistics. From these values one can calculate tables of scaled score values for statistically significant score differences or elevations above or below the mean of the profile at various levels of probability. Such standards would objectify the level and pattern of performance standards for WES profile interpretation. Further, this also would set objective rules for evaluating chance interscale differences.

As the manual is currently organized, one must impressionistically compare individual and group profile elevations relative to the normative standards provided. It is difficult to detect the threshold for interpretive significance and to distinguish mild elevations of the profile from chance variants. WES users would be well advised to interpret differences on the order of a standard deviation or more as clinically relevant. Examination of the normative tables, however, shows that for Form R of the WES a difference of only 1 raw score point (on a 9-point scale) is on the order of .5–.9 of a standard deviation unit. Relatively small differences on any of the WES scales thus may have a major influence on the WES profile elevation and pattern. This also suggests the importance of item analysis of the WES profile to determine the basis of the item endorsement. In the case of group administration and program evaluation, automated scoring that included item analysis could be particularly helpful in pinpointing key points of work environment satisfaction and areas of desired change.

Moos (1986, pp. 12–16) models the interpretive strategy for profile interpretation of the WES in the test manual. He provides examples in which Form R WES results are contrasted for general work settings and health care settings. He also provides an example of the real (Form R) and ideal (Form I) health-care work setting characteristics in a high stress intensive care unit and shows how the results can be used for program consultation and change. New users of the WES should study these examples carefully and consult Moos (1987) for additional guidelines for interpreting the Social Climate Scales generally and the WES in particular. Such users also might do well to use the methodology with representative groups from programs that they know well in order to see how the WES measures a known work environment's characteristics.

Technical Aspects

An important aspect of any test's measurement accuracy is its reliability. Unless an instrument is reliable, it cannot be valid. Two aspects of reliability have been established for the WES. The degree to which the items of a test measure a common dimension or construct is called *internal consistency*. A special correlational statistic, Cronbach's alpha, objectively measures this characteristic. Ideally Cronbach's alpha would approximate .80, a value that minimizes measurement error related to internal consistency (Nunnally, 1978). The WES subscales show a high level of internal consistency overall, with a range that varies from .69 (Peer Cohesion) to .86 (Innovation). The mean internal consistency value for the WES subscales is .78, based on a sample of 1,045 subjects. All of the scalewise coefficient alpha values for the WES fall within acceptable psychometric limits. The moderate level of internal consistency on the Peer Cohesion subscale very likely reflects relative lack of variability on that dimension among normal working groups. This range restriction is an artifact that limits the magnitude of the internal consistency correlational measure.

Another aspect of item analysis requires analyzing the correlation of each item to the scale to which it is assigned. These values should be moderate so that the items are complementary rather than redundant in measuring aspects of the theoretical construct or dimension under study. In the sample of 1,045 subjects used for the internal consistency analyses, these item-to-subscale values were calculated. They were "corrected" by eliminating the item correlated with each scale from the total scale score to prevent inflation of the values. The mean item-to-subscale values ranged from .36 on Peer Cohesion to .53 on Innovation. These values are within acceptable psychometric limits, particularly considering the high internal consistency values. Moos (1986, p. 6) analyzed the intercorrelations of the WES subscales and noted that the correlations among the WES subscales explained less than 10% of the variance in the test as a whole. In short the scales were significantly different, complementary measures of work environment characteristics and were minimally redundant with each other. This finding supports the multidimensional structure of the WES.

Temporal stability of the WES is assessed by test-retest reliability. The WES was given with a 1-month intertest interval to a sample of 75 subjects. Retest reliability values ranged from .69 on the Clarity subscale to .83 on Involvement. Long-term retest reliability over a 12-month intertest interval in a sample of 254 subjects ranged from .51 on the Supervisor Support subtest to .63 on Work Pressure. Given the likelihood of routine change in work settings over a year interval, these values are moderately high and within acceptable limits for practical application.

Moos evaluated profile stability by testing 90 people who remained in the same work setting at the beginning and end of a 1-year period. Each of the 10 subscales of the WES was correlated for each individual subject for each of the baseline and followup WES scores. The mean profile stability correlational value across scales was .61. Seventy-five of the 90 mean profile stability coefficients equaled or exceeded .50, and 46 equaled or exceeded .70.

The WES has been used successfully to evaluate and provide feedback for modification and optimization of a wide variety of health care, educational, and social work settings (Fawzy, Wellisch, Pasnau, & Liebowitz, 1983; Fisher & Fraser, 1983; Gauthier, 1981; Lusk, Diserens, Cormier, Geranmayeh, & Neves, 1983; Meier, 1983). It provides a valuable methodology for identification of which specific social environmental factors contribute significantly to employee job satisfaction and work productivity. Comparison of discrepancies between real and ideal WES findings has contributed to administrative planning in clinical and educational settings, evaluation of alternative professional educational programs, identification and reduction of stressors in medical intensive treatment programs, and tenure of staff in stressful treatment programs.

The WES has successfully identified specific areas of programmatic stress and "burnout," which then were remedied by consultation and program development based on the WES findings. This approach was considerably more effective than a stress coping and problem solving workshop alone (Hunnicutt, 1983; Hunnicutt & MacMillan, 1983; MacMillan & Hunnicutt, 1983). The WES also has helped design task-relevant workshops for health care and educational staffs (DePiano, 1980/1984; Hirsch & David, 1983).

Individual clinical case evaluation using the WES was illustrated by Moos and Fuhr (1982) in their analysis of a case of an adolescent girl experiencing school difficulty that was conceptualized as related to the primary personal career commitments of her parents. The role of Form R in the individual clinical evaluation and comparison of two alcoholic patients whose addiction adversely affected their job performance also is illustrated in the test manual (Moos, 1986, pp. 20–21). The interaction of the individual with the work milieu as evaluated by the WES proved important in predicting work and treatment program performance and in noting individualized behavior patterns that may present with the same clinical syndrome.

Military planners also have used the WES to study naval staff morale (Booth, McNally, & Berry, 1979; Hoiberg, 1978). Booth and Lantz (1977) also used the WES to document gender differences in perceived chain-of-command social milieu and supervisory relationships in military health care settings.

Moos and his colleagues also have developed a model of the work environment as "a dynamic system composed of four domains: physical features, organizational structure and policies, suprapersonal and task factors, and social climate" (Moos, 1986, p. 23). Their model theorizes that the planning of the architectural, organizational, and task-role elements of the work environment are influenced in part by the social climate that they help to shape. The relationships are thought to be reciprocal, however, in that the social climate can influence the effect of the nonsocial elements on work performance. A detailed review of the studies investigating the validity of this model appears in the WES manual (Moos, 1986, pp. 23–34). However, in summary, social climate factors as assessed by the WES have been found powerfully related to work efficiency and productivity, vocational category choice, employee morale, job-related stressful illness incidence, and receptiveness to office automation. Work role socialization among students, technical training effectiveness as reflected in subsequent work performance, and the matching of personal with social environmental types has received support from WES-based studies of job performance.

Holahan and Moos (1983) developed a Work Relationships Index based on the WES Involvement, Peer Cohension, and Supervisor Support subscales. They found that this composite measure derived from the WES was a useful predictor of work stress–related symptomatology such as depression and somatization disorders even after nonspecific stressors and lack of social system support had been considered. They reported that such symptoms of stress were related to decreased work and family support for both sexes in experimentally controled studies (see Billings & Moos, 1982; Holahan & Moos, 1981).

An important line of research has extended the WES to the study of groups of workers with psychiatric disorders. Bromet and Moos (1977) investigated adaptive occupational functioning of alcoholic patients who had undergone residential treatment for their disorder. They found a relatively strong relationship between the patients' WES perceptions of their work setting characteristics and their post-treatment adaptation if they were *not* living in a family setting. The relationship between work setting perception and adjustment quality was relatively weak for those posttreatment alcoholics who were living in a family setting. Marriage and family support were thought to be an insulator against stress that led to greater likelihood of a satisfactory social adjustment (see also Finney & Moos, 1981; Finney, Moos, & Mewborn, 1980; Moos, Finney, & Cronkite, 1990). These initial findings have been extended in other process and outcome studies that are summarized in the WES manual.

A study of patients with unipolar depression by Billings, Cronkite, and Moos (1983) found more perceived work stress and less social support at work among the depressed patients relative to controls. Chronicity of the depressive disorder was not related to this finding. An Index of Work Stressors was derived from the WES (based on high work demands and high supervisor control with low autonomy and low clarity) by Billings and Moos (1984). This index related significantly to severity of mood and physical symptoms of depression among male patients and to low self-confidence among depressed patients of both sexes.

A key study of the relationship of work stress and coping ability among medical patients was reported by Feuerstein, Sult, and Houle (1985). Using the WES in their investigation, they evaluated relationships between work and family social climate, emotional conflict, and reported severity of low back pain. The emotional and physical distress related to the pain syndromes also were significantly related to the social climate variables.

Booth, Norton, Webster, and Berry (1976) investigated the factor structure of the WES in a large sample of naval paramedical trainees. Five of the original WES scales were reproduced as separate factors in this analysis: Cohesion, Work Pressure, Control, Innovation, and Physical Comfort. The Clarity and Staff Support subscales loaded on a common dimension that was interpreted as a measure of "Communication," while the Involvement and Task Orientation subscales loaded on a common "Task Involvement" dimension. Moos (1986, p. 35) noted that the reliabilities of the factorial dimensions and their intercorrelations were comparable to those of the original WES subscales. This is predictable, given the relative isomorphism of the original scale structure and the derived factorial solution subscales.

Critique

The WES clearly offers a sensitive, specific, brief, and accurate multidimensional measure of perceived occupational environmental "social climate" characteristics. It has proven value as a descriptive tool, and preliminary evidence shows that it may have significant predictive validity as well. The range of vocational assessment problems to which the scale has been applied successfully is highly varied, but these demonstrations only mark the beginnings of its potential applications to the functional analysis of job settings. The work should advance much more rapidly once the expected and ideal forms of the scale are studied and normed with much larger samples of subjects.

Use of the WES with other psychometric measures of personality style, vocational interest, and vocational aptitude could lead to development of a typology of work environments and a complementary spectrum of personality and ability types who work best in each of them. The WES probably can be used most effectively in a comprehensive assessment program that balances objective evaluation of environmental characteristics, phenomenological social climate variables, vocational interest measures, and vocational aptitude measures jointly. Analysis of individual differences within occupational groupings to identify characteristics of the social, personal, and task environment that lead to job satisfaction and productivity also would be theoretically useful. Analysis of productive and unproductive workers within and between occupational types could prove useful in vocational counseling and guidance. What is suggested here is the outline of a variety of interlocking research projects that would share data cooperatively and evaluate personal, social, and environmental characteristics of the work place to identify their individual and joint effects on work output quantity, quality, job tenure, and employee satisfaction. The WES has an important part to play in this proposed comprehensive vocational assessment process, and it is probably best seen in such a larger context.

The normative development of the WES is complete only for Form R. Extensive development of the norms for Forms E and I is necessary to realize the scale's potential for evaluating anticipated and desired change in the vocational environment. Without such information the statistically reliable, norm-referenced value of the scale is limited primarily to descriptive analysis, and this use limits its potentially greater value as an instrument for the assessment of specific areas of adaptive vocational and environmental change. The potential to systematically, objectively, and reliably identify multiple variables that lead to job satisfaction, job productivity, and job tenure as a (partial) function of specific perceived job environment variables is an important contribution of the WES and not readily available from other sources.

Work to develop composite indices from the WES to measure complex behavioral outcome variables is just beginning, and the preliminary results are quite encouraging. Further work of this kind is certainly in order. Moos and his colleagues have conducted many pioneering studies to illustrate the applicability of the WES to a variety of work settings. Social and vocational counseling psychologists would do well to contact individuals who have supervisory responsibility within a very wide range of vocational programs to initiate studies of the WES along systematic lines illustrated by the pioneering studies of Moos and his colleagues.

Objective rules for statistical WES profile interpretation require considerably more specific, rigorous development and explanation for potential users of the scale. One would want to caution potential users that the WES is not easily interpretable as a face-valid measure. Attention to minor objective differences in reporting nuances about the perceived work setting may significantly influence the WES profile pattern. As such, item analysis should be emphasized as part of the routine clinical interpretive procedure.

The provision of a case book or a supplementary workbook with more worked profile interpretation examples would be helpful to novice interpreters. Ideally one might envision an atlas of profile code types for the Social Climate Scales that would summarize prototypical social climate settings for each scale and provide explicit, objective guidelines for their interpretation. Potential users of the WES are advised that it is an excellent psychometric device, but it can be effective only in the hands of an experienced and sophisticated interpreter. Considerable experience with the methodology and correlation of the test findings with those of the work setting are strongly encouraged to ensure that results will be accurately interpreted in context.

The best use of the WES probably will be made when it is applied systematically to match and evaluate placement of specific, well-understood vocational counselees with specific, task-analyzed programs for which they appear to be well suited. There is much available vocational theory and technology to guide such placement. The WES provides a potentially powerful new methodology for evaluating, modifying, and optimizing the results of such assignments. Its initial findings have been groundbreaking in their importance, their scope, and their effectiveness. Further rigorous use of the WES methodology to study vocational placement and performance across programs and across cultural, linguistic, and national groups promises to be both productive and informative as a test of the generality of initial findings with a primarily American population.

References

Billings, A., Cronkite, R., & Moos, R. (1983). Social-environmental factors in unipolar depression: Comparisons of depressed patients and nondepressed controls. *Journal of Abnormal Psychology, 92*, 119–133.

Billings, A., & Moos, R. (1982). Social support and functioning among community and clinical groups: A panel model. *Journal of Behavioral Medicine, 5*, 295–311.

Billings, A., & Moos, R. (1984). Coping, stress, and social resources among adults with unipolar depression. *Journal of Personality and Social Psychology, 46*, 877–891.

Booth, R., & Lantz, K. (1977). Sex differences in psychosocial perceptions toward naval work environments. *Perceptual and Motor Skills, 44*, 1155–1161.

Booth, R., McNally, M., & Berry, N. (1979). Hospital corpsmen perceptions of working in a fleet Marine force environment. *Military Medicine, 144*, 31–34.

Booth, R., Norton, R., Webster, E., & Berry, N. (1976). Assessing the psychosocial characteristics of occupational training environments. *Journal of Occupational Psychology, 49*, 85–92.

Bromet, E., & Moos, R. (1977). Environmental resources and the posttreatment functioning of alcoholic patients. *Journal of Health and Social Behavior, 18*, 326–335.

DePiano, L. (1984). *Factors related to satisfaction and involvement of school advisory councils.* (Doctoral dissertation, University of South Carolina, Columbia, 1980). *Dissertation Abstracts International, 45*, 346B.

Fawzy, F., Wellisch, D., Pasnau, R., & Leibowitz, B. (1983). Preventing nursing burnout: A challenge for liaison psychiatry. *General Hospital Psychiatry, 5*, 141–149.

Feuerstein, M., Sult, S., & Houle, M. (1985). Environmental stressors and chronic low back pain: Life events, family and work environment. *Pain, 22*, 295–307.

Finney, J., & Moos, R. (1981). Characteristics and prognoses of alcoholics who became moderate drinkers and abstainers after treatment. *Journal of Studies on Alcohol, 42*, 94–105.

Finney, J., Moos, R., & Mewborn, C. (1980). Posttreatment experiences and treatment outcome of alcoholic patients six months and two years after hospitalization. *Journal of Consulting and Clinical Psychology, 48*, 17–29.

Fisher, D., & Fraser, B. (1983). Use of the WES to assess science teachers' perceptions of school environment. *European Journal of Science Education, 5*, 231–233.

Gauthier, P. (1981). *Evaluation eco-sociale de deux unites de réadaptation pour jeunes gens déficients mentaux.* Unpublished master's thesis, University of Quebec.

Hirsch, B., & David, T. (1983). Social networks and work/nonwork life: Action-research with nurse managers. *American Journal of Community Psychology, 11*, 493–507.

Hoiberg, A. (1978). Women in the navy: Morale and attrition. *Armed Forces and Society, 4*, 659–671.

Holahan, C.J., & Moos, R. (1981). Social support and psychological distress: A longitudinal analysis. *Journal of Abnormal Psychology, 90*, 365–370.

Holahan, C.J., & Moos, R. (1983). The quality of social support: Measures of family and work relationships. *British Journal of Clinical Psychology, 22*, 157–162.

Hunnicutt, A.W. (1983). *Identifying and reducing burn-out in mental health settings* (Final Report, National Institute of Mental Health Grant No. MH159122). Ukiah, CA: Center for Education and Manpower Resources.

Hunnicutt, A.W., & MacMillan, T.F. (1983). Beating burn-out: Findings from a three-year study. *Association of Mental Health Administrators Journal, 10*, 7–9.

Insel, P.M., & Moos, R.H. (1974). *Work Environment Scale Form R: Test booklet.* Palo Alto, CA: Consulting Psychologists Press.

Lange, M. (1978a). *Some characteristics of the validity of Dutch translations of the FES and WES.* Nijmegen, The Netherlands: Catholic University, Department of Clinical Psychology.

Lange, M. (1978b). *Some psychometric characteristics of Dutch translations of the FES and WES.* Nijmegen The Netherlands: Catholic University, Department of Clinical Psychology.

Lusk, E., Diserens, D., Cormier, P., & Geranmayeh, A., & Neves, J. (1983). The Work Environment Scale: Baseline data for dental schools. *Psychological Reports, 53*, 1160–1162.

MacMillan, T.F., & Hunnicutt, A.W. (1983). Burn-out intervention in mental health settings: An experimental model. *Human Resource Development: An International Journal, 7*, 9–13.

Meier, R. (1983). *The impact of the structural organization of public welfare offices on the psychosocial work and treatment environments.* Haifa, Israel: University of Haifa, School of Social Work.

Moos, R. (1974). *The Social Climate Scales: An overview.* Palo Alto, CA: Consulting Psychologists Press.

Moos, R. (1981). *Work Environment Scale manual.* Palo Alto, CA: Consulting Psychologists Press.

Moos, R. (1984). Context and coping: Toward a unifying conceptual framework. *American Journal of Community Psychology, 12*, 5–25.

Moos, R. (1985a). Creating healthy human contexts: Environmental and individual strategies. In J.C. Rosen & L.J. Solomon (Eds.), *Prevention in health psychology* (pp. 366–389). Hanover, NH: University Press of New England.

Moos, R. (1985b). Evaluating social resources in community and health care contexts. In P. Karoly (Ed.), *Measurement strategies in health psychology* (pp. 433–459). New York: Wiley.

Moos, R. (1986). *Work Environment Scale manual* (2nd ed.). Palo Alto, CA: Consulting Psychologists Press.

Moos, R. (1987). *The Social Climate Scales: A user's guide.* Palo Alto, CA: Consulting Psychologists Press.

Moos, R., Clayton, J., & Max, W. (1979). *The Social Climate Scales: An annotated bibliography* (2nd ed.). Palo Alto, CA: Consulting Psychologists Press.

Moos, R., Finney, J., & Chan, D. (1981). The process of recovery from alcoholism: I. Comparing alcoholic patients and matched community controls. *Journal of Studies on Alcohol, 42,* 383–402.

Moos, R.H., Finney, J.W., & Cronkite, R.C. (1990). *Alcoholism treatment: Context, process, and outcome.* New York: Oxford University Press.

Moos, R., & Fuhr, K.R. (1982). The clinical use of social ecological concepts: The case of an adolescent girl. *American Journal of Orthopsychiatry, 52,* 111-12-2.

Moos, R., & Spinrad, S. (1984). *The Social Climate Scales: An annotated bibliography* (2nd ed.). Palo Alto, CA: Consulting Psychologists Press.

Moses, J.A., Jr. (1991). Correctional Institutions Environment Scale. In D.J. Keyser & R.C. Sweetland (Eds.), *Test critiques* (Vol. VIII, pp. 118–131). Austin, TX: PRO-ED.

Murray, H.A. (1938). *Explorations in personality.* New York: Oxford University Press.

Nunnally, J.C. (1978). *Psychometric theory* (2nd ed.). New York: McGraw-Hill.

Weyer, G. (1981). Self-report measures in research on job related stress. In W.H. Krohne & L. Laux (Eds.), *Achievement, stress and anxiety* (pp. 333–344). Washington, DC: Hemisphere.

Weyer, G., & Hodapp, V. (1978). Eine Deutsche version der Work Environment Scale (WES): Erste anwendungserfahrungen bei lehrern und vergleich mit den Subjektiven Belastungs und Unzufriedenheitsskalen im vberuflichen bereich. *Diagnostica, 24,* 318–328.

Paul P. Baard, Ph.D.

Associate Professor, Departments of Communication and Management, Graduate School of Business Administration, Fordham University, New York, New York.

WORK MOTIVATION INVENTORY

Jay Hall and Martha S. Williams. The Woodlands, Texas: Teleometrics International.

Introduction

The Work Motivation Inventory (WMI) is a self-report survey designed to assess an individual's personal motivational needs. The instrument is based on Maslow's (1970, 1992) "hierarchy of needs" theory of human motivation and Herzberg's (1966, 1984) "hygiene-motivator" model of job satisfaction. The WMI is intended to identify the types of needs and values a worker sees as important considerations in making decisions about his or her job; that is, which needs are felt most salient and to what degree they are being met in that person's work environment.

The WMI is published by Teleometrics International, a Texas firm that provides a range of services to industry, government, and academe, including training, measurement, and instructional materials. The company also conducts seminars, some of which enable attendees to become "certified" as a trainer in the materials and methods of the firm, according to communications to clients (e.g., Teleometrics International, 1992). The firm offers a range of tests, including ones designed to assess communications and relationships within organizations and others measuring management styles.

Teleometrics International is headed by one of the test's authors, Jay Hall, Ph.D., a psychologist and consultant. Dr. Hall served on the faculty of the University of Texas School of Law and later the graduate school of business. He is president and chief executive officer of Teleometrics International, which he founded in 1967. According to company brochures, Dr. Hall has served as a consultant to major corporations and various government agencies, and has sat on several boards of directors. He has authored several books, including *The Executive Trap* (Hall, 1992), written numerous journal articles, and edited an anthology of business management (Hall, 1988).

The test's coauthor is Martha S. Williams, Ph.D., who has research and teaching interests in management of public services and in promoting workforce quality and diversity. She has published a number of articles concerning women's issues, including studies of women in management, work-family roles, and women's careers. Dr. Williams has conducted a series of studies for government and academe, and serves as a training consultant to such groups. She was Dean of the School of Social Work at the University of Texas at Austin and its Centennial

Professor of Leadership for Community, Professional and Corporate Excellence, and is now Dean of Social Work at the University of Wyoming.

As noted previously, the Work Motivation Inventory integrates two popular theories of worker motivation, one of which is Maslow's hierarchy of needs. Abraham Maslow was a clinical psychologist whose work in motivation was first presented in 1943 as part of a larger theory of human behavior. Operating within the humanistic movement, Maslow was concerned about the dignity and worth of individuals, seeing people as moved over a lifetime by a succession of needs, with the potential of rising from an initial "driven" modality to, ultimately, one characterized by a sense of choosing behaviors. He considered motivational propensities as largely maturational, with an individual moving up the scale over time. Immediate circumstances such as the loss of a job or fear of same could, however, bring a person back lower in the hierarchical chain, at least temporarily.

In Maslow's theory, the primary human needs are seen as the physiological ones necessary for survival, such as for food, sex, and sensory satisfaction. Once relatively satisfied, an individual would then experience the emergence of a need to feel safe and secure, focusing his or her energies on eliminating threats from fear and anxiety. These conditions met, a person would turn to satisfy a need for social belonging or connectedness, for affection and acceptance. When the more basic physiological, safety, and interpersonal needs have been met, Maslow saw a person moving to a fourth level focused on issues related to ego. A desire for self-respect, self-esteem, and the esteem of others appears at this stage of life. The means to satisfying these needs can have either an internal focus through achievement or mastery or an external one, as by gaining recognition or prestige.

Finally, although Maslow felt few satisfied this level of development (Muchinsky, 1987), he believed people seek innately to become self-actualized. He asserted that all individuals desire to realize their unique potentials, to become all that they are capable of being and to be autonomous in their functioning. Maslow felt that all a man can be, he must be (e.g., an artist must paint, a poet must write). This highest need level refers to self-realization and continuous self-development, emphasizing the importance of choice. The individual is seen rising above his or her biological, social, and psychological needs to this greater state where desire rather than need predominates. Altruism is one of the characteristics associated with this highest motivational state.

Maslow contended that behavior would be dominated and determined by those needs that are unfulfilled, and that basic needs will take precedence over those further up in the hierarchy. His first proposition is fundamental: Once a need is fulfilled, it will no longer motivate behavior. A hungry person will seek food, but having eaten to satiety, the pursuit of food will no longer dominate his or her behavior. Maslow's theory continues to enjoy a level of popularity in the business sector, although empirical support has been mixed and limited (Muchinsky, 1987; Saal & Knight, 1988).

Frederick Herzberg presented a theory of motivation proceeding from the concept that people have two sets of needs: "as an animal to avoid pain and . . . as a human to grow psychologically" (Herzberg, 1984, p. 334). This theory has at its focus a categorization of variables impacting motivation, separating those things that are necessary but do not really evoke behavior (they merely satisfy needs) from those believed to induce activity, including work.

Herzberg's seminal research consisted of interviews with engineers and accountants. When attempting to answer a question about what people want from their jobs, Herzberg's respondents reported feeling happy due to factors related to the tasks they execute, duties allowing them the experience of being successful in their performance. When queried about those factors that led to negative feelings about their jobs, the subjects reported a markedly different set of variables, dealing largely with more contemporary issues such as supervisory behaviors and compensation. Further analysis of the data revealed a distinction between a set of factors linked to what a person does and another pertaining to the situation in which he or she does the work. Herzberg identified a group of "satisfiers" that included achievement, recognition for work accomplished, the work itself, responsibility for tasks, and advancement. Included in this category are such matters as involvement, goal setting, problem solving, merit increases, and atmosphere of approval. Only these types of factors are thought to be potential sources of motivation.

Borrowing from the medical profession's term pertaining to preventive and environmental variables, Herzberg named a set of "hygiene" factors or potential dissatisfiers: company policies and administration, supervision, salary, interpersonal relations, and working conditions. Included in this domain would be such variables as automatic wage increases, work rules, job titles, work groups, and lunch facilities. This category is considered only to hold the potential of creating job dissatisfaction, not of truly motivating workers. True "motivators" are thought to include aspects of the job that provide people the opportunity to display their competence and be creative in their work, to satisfy their upper level needs and reap social and professional rewards. Motivation-hygiene theory continues to be a topic of interest in the popular business press (Herzberg, 1992).

With the WMI, Hall and Williams appear to integrate an understanding of individuals' needs with a description of factors that allow for either the frustration or satisfaction of them by a person's current work and working conditions.

The Work Motivation Inventory is presented attractively in an 8½" × by 11" booklet, with the scoring and interpretation section contained within a gold seal, to be broken after taking the test. WMI is direct in its administration and scoring. The instructions take about 3 minutes to read aloud and are reasonably easy to follow. The test is not timed, and it could take an examinee from about 30 minutes to well over an hour to complete the 60 items. About 10 minutes are needed to self-score, and instructions and normative data are provided for interpreting one's score.

The WMI employs a forced-choice, paired comparison format. Each item appears as an incomplete, assertive statement followed by two alternative phrases that would complete the sentence. Selections are drawn from the five Maslowian categories, with each of the five need systems identified by Maslow appearing 24 times, paired 6 times with every other need system. Respondents then reveal the relative importance of each in contrast with every other category in turn. An example follows (reproduced here by the publisher's permission):

25. In deciding whether or not to take a promotion, I would be most concerned with the extent to which:

    D. The job would be a source of personal pride and be viewed with respect by others.   _____

    B. Taking the job would constitute a gamble on my part and possibly undo much of what I have accomplished so far.   _____

Examinees are to assign a number from 0 (if completely uncharacteristic of the individual) to 5 (if completely characteristic) to each alternative. The total point allocation for each item must add up to 5, forcing choices between like characteristics when they appear. In the example above, the examinee who is motivated largely by Security issues would presumably assign a 0 or 1 to the "D" option (which pertains to Ego-Status) and a 4 or 5 to "B." Scoring simply entails summing all A (Basic), B (Safety), C (Belonging), D (Ego-Status), and E (Self-Actualization) responses. Because the 60 items appear across six pages, it would be helpful for the less experienced test taker if the scoring scheme was repeated somewhere on each two-page spread.

Practical Applications/Uses

The Work Motivation Inventory is appealing in its very straightforward design and administration as well in its theoretical assertions. When used in conjunction with managerial training, the WMI provides insights into workers' motivational propensities and enables managers to discover same. The instrument also permits contrasting a group's profile with that of the individual to whom they report. The Work Motivation Inventory has proven useful in such endeavors as examining differences between male and female managers; for example, "compared to males, female managers are more concerned with opportunities for growth, autonomy and challenge, and less concerned with work environment, pay, and strain avoidance. And contrary to popular belief, females do not have a greater need to 'belong' than do males" (Hall, 1988, p. 478).

About half of the 12-page WMI booklet is devoted to an explication of Maslow's need hierarchy and Herzberg's hygiene-motivator theories. The material is generally presented in a manner suitable for those who might be unfamiliar with the topics and is faithful to the respective theories' assertions. At times, however, the authors' writing seems less appropriate for the targeted group (i.e., employees of varying rank and education). For example, in the interpretation of scores section, the test taker is offered the following:

> Most people in our culture are Motivation Seekers. Frequently however, higher level needs are in conflict with a single low level need. This may be due to residual effects of early deprivation or it may signify impending frustration and point toward regressive behaviors. . . . It is particularly distressing and the individual is likely to experience a number of depressing and poorly focused tensions. (Hall & Williams, 1967, p. 8)

This reviewer's experience in dealing with motivational issues and explaining psychological concepts such as those found in the WMI to organizations' employees suggests the typical workforce might have difficulty in readily understanding the aforementioned aspects of the instrument and its findings about the respondent.

Following the section on interpreting scores is one called "Where Do I Go from Here?" In it the authors suggest that test takers consider their profiles in light of goals that might best meet their needs, behaviors they are likely to use when given an opportunity to satisfy those needs, and what alternatives are available in their present situations for optimizing need satisfaction. The authors then offer suggestions for creating a personal profile and plan (a need analysis and planning chart is provided). Examinees are encouraged to consider their three strongest needs in descending order and then to identify alternate ways for satisfying one's needs so that movement up the need hierarchy might occur and, at the same time, the individual might contribute effectively to his or her organization's goals.

A companion instrument to the WMI is the Management of Motives Index (MMI), an "assessment of motivational practices" (Hall, 1973). This instrument, also based on Maslow-Herzberg theorizing, measures the amount of emphasis a manager, in dealing with subordinates, places on lower versus higher order needs. Some managers are thought to create better conditions for "motivated" behavior than others, as revealed by their responses in the MMI. By comparing a manager's motivational concerns (as revealed by the MMI) with those of his or her subordinates (as measured by the WMI), disparities are revealed and addressed in subsequent coaching sessions. While available for purchase independently, the WMI and the MMI often are administered in conjunction with Teleometrics training.

Technical Aspects

The WMI has excellent face validity. Its vignettes describe contemporary concerns of employees across many organization types, and the issues presented are easily identifiable with the respective theoretical assertions. The integration of two popular, complementary approaches to understanding human motivation is probably intuitively appealing to most organizations because both theories continue to appear in business and management journals (e.g., Herzberg, 1992).

There is a one-paragraph reliability/validity section at the end of the WMI. The material reports a median coefficient of stability of .70 over a 6-week span, with the instrument "discriminating among high, average and low achieving managers" (Hall & Williams, 1967, p. 9). Construct validity is reported to be .79 ($p <$ .008) with the California Psychological Inventory (CPI), and .69 ($p <$ .008) with the Minnesota Multiphasic Personality Inventory (MMPI).

Additional validation data provided by the publisher (J. Hall, personal communication, December 14, 1992), which do not appear in any publication, consist of a canonical analysis correlating personality constructs of the California Psychological Inventory (CPI) with the WMI. The CPI is considered one of the best personality inventories available (Anastasi, 1976), similar to the MMPI (drawing about half its items from it) but developed specifically for use with normal adult populations. The analysis provided by the WMI's publisher was based on an undescribed sample ($N = 61$) and reported predicted correlations between a number of salient items, including the following:

CPI Variable	WMI "Need"	r	p
Dominance	Basic	−.27	.05
	Belonging	+.21	.10
	Ego-Status	−.21	.10
Capacity for Status	Ego-Status	−.22	.10
Well-being	Actualization	+.21	.10
Responsibility	Actualization	+.21	.10
Socialization	Ego-Status	−.28	.05
Self-control	Belonging	−.23	.10
Communality	Safety	+.36	.01
	Actualization	−.25	.05
Psychological Mindess	Actualization	+.35	.01

The last revision of the WMI occurred in 1988 and focused mainly on removing sexist language from the instrument. The normative data provided for test takers' interpretation purposes consist of average need scores from 34,279 persons across a range of organizations. These data, compiled earlier than the test's last revision, are presented in a manner permitting the user to compare his or her score on each of the five dimensions with those of persons in the fields of science and technology, manufacturing, semipublic organizations, sales and marketing, finance, human service, government, and law enforcement. There were no data offered to support the WMI's appropriateness across cultures, though the publisher provided assurance that the instrument had been used successfully in many countries (R. Skillman, personal communication, December 29, 1992).

Critique

The use of the WMI seems to occur primarily at the application level, in particular for organizational training. There have not been any professional reviews of the WMI's technical qualities since its debut in 1973, which may account for its limited use in academic research. A review of both business and social research databases from 1987 through June 1992 turned up only one reference to the test (Ratliff, 1988), though one of its authors has made greater use of the instrument in his own research and publications (Hall, 1992).

Another possible cause for the limited academic utilization of the WMI might be the fact that the field of motivation has experienced considerable theoretical development since Maslow and Herzberg made their initial contributions in 1943 and 1966, respectively. Research in intrinsic motivation (e.g., Deci & Ryan, 1985) is particularly salient to the work being done in the total quality management area (e.g., Deming, 1982), a topic addressed in Teleometrics's promotional material. The TQM movement, focusing on continuous improvement in all aspects of a system, has generated great interest in corporate America as well as other organizational sectors. TQM provides both a philosophy and series of practices aimed at allowing workers the opportunity to do excellent work in all of their endeavors, a prerequisite for the occurrence of intrinsic motivation (Deci & Ryan, 1985).

The basic needs identified by Maslow, for example, might be categorized as extrinsic motivation (Gilmer & Deci, 1977), focused on matters outside the activity itself, such as those pertaining to behavior intended to gain a reward or avoid a punishment. Intrinsic motivation, by contrast, is that which is engaged in largely because of the satisfaction inherent in the endeavor itself, such as when one's current skill levels are being optimally challenged by an activity. Intrinsic motivation opportunities appear in Maslow's two upper levels of needs and in Herzberg's Motivator category, but many additional issues impact on work variables being experienced as intrinsically motivating (Deci & Ryan, 1985).

Further, the issue of amotivation, as experienced by workers who feel relatively incapable of affecting a desired outcome (e.g., avoiding a layoff despite their best performance), would seem to be a matter of concern for those addressing motivation in a volatile workplace. Deci and Ryan's (1985) cognitive evaluation theory of motivation is but one contemporary theory that addresses this dimension of increasing concern in light of organizational attempts to "downsize" workforces. For this reason, this reviewer asked the publisher if the normative data provided in the WMI booklet would be reviewed to determine if economic downturns, especially the relatively high number of workers dismissed off in the late '80s and early '90s, had an effect on the motivational patterns revealed by the WMI. Specifically, it was thought the scores on the Safety dimension might have risen, which could potentially lead to a test taker's mistakenly finding him- or herself in a poor light on the maturation hierarchy when compared to the average scores of "historical" others. The publisher indicated that, while there is an ongoing effort to review patterns of scores, no changes seemed to be called for at this time in the normative data provided for examinees' self-evaluation; the tenets of the underlining theories for the WMI were believed to transcend episodic events such as economic downturns (R. Skillman, personal communication, December 29, 1992).

The theories of Maslow and Herzberg have been researched extensively but with mixed results (Betz, 1984; Muchinsky, 1987; Wahba & Bridwell, 1976). Maslow's assertion that the five levels of needs are clearly delineated has been questioned, as has the notion that need importance is directly related to need deficiency. Although Maslow himself did not offer empirical research to support his concepts, drawing greatly from clinical observation, his hierarchy of needs has appeared extensively in the literature of organizational theory. There has also been a concern that Maslow's theory is specific to the United States. Steers and Porter (1991) report numerous studies suggesting similar but not identical rank ordering of needs across cultures, concluding that these human needs may differ in importance and in the way they are expressed.

Herzberg's theory also has received an amount of criticism. His original research presumed that those who were interviewed could and would accurately report the conditions that made them satisfied or dissatisfied with their jobs. This self-report method of data collection is thought to suffer from a tendency to attribute favorable dimensions to that person's own accomplishment and unfavorable experiences to others. Further, a number of research attempts to replicate Herzberg's findings have failed. These studies found that people can get pleasure from salary and work conditions and that failure to receive recognition was not benign but actually a cause of dissatisfaction, putting Herzberg's categorization scheme in question (Muchinsky, 1987; Steers & Porter, 1991). The publisher of the Work Motivation

Inventory, however, reports that use of the instrument across many countries does not reveal any significant differences in the patterns of motivation, as found with the WMI (R. Skillman, personal communication, December 29, 1992).

Given the extensive use of the WMI by Teleometrics in its training and consulting activities, perhaps their publication of additional validation data will lead to expanded utilization of the instrument in research by others. For purposes of organizational intervention, however, the WMI seems useful in introducing motivational concepts to superordinates and subordinates, and perhaps in debunking some mythologies about differences between groups.

References

This list includes text citations and suggested additional reading.

Anastasi, A. (1976). *Psychological testing* (5th ed.). New York: Macmillan.

Betz, E.L. (1984). Two tests of Maslow's theory of need fulfillment. *Journal of Vocational Behavior, 24,* 204–220.

Deci, E.L., & Ryan, R.M. (1985). *Intrinsic motivation and self-determination in human behavior.* New York: Plenum.

Deci, E.L., Connel, J.P., & Ryan, R.M. (1989). Self-determination in a work organization. *Journal of Applied Psychology, 74,* 580–590.

Deming, W.E. (1982). *Out of the crisis.* Cambridge, MA: Massachusetts Institute of Technology, Center for Advanced Engineering Study.

Gilmer, B.H., & Deci, E.L. (1977). *Industrial and organizational psychology* (4th ed.). New York: McGraw-Hill.

Graham, G.H. (1982). *Understanding human relations.* New York: Macmillan.

Hall, J. (1973). *Management of Motives Index.* The Woodlands, TX: Teleometrics International.

Hall, J. (1988). *Models for management: The structure of competence* (2nd ed.). The Woodlands, TX: Woodstead Press.

Hall, J. (1992). *The executive trap.* New York: Simon & Schuster.

Hall, J., & Williams, M.S. (1967). *Work Motivation Inventory.* The Woodlands, TX: Teleometrics International.

Herzberg, F. (1966). *Work and the nature of man.* Cleveland, OH: World Publishing.

Herzberg, F. (1984). The motivation-hygiene theory. In D.S. Pugh (Ed.), *Organization theory: Selected readings* (2nd ed., pp. 334–351). New York: Viking-Penguin.

Herzberg, F. (1992, November/December). "I'm sorry I was right" [Letter to the editor]. *Harvard Business Review,* p. 142.

Landy, F.J. (1985). *Psychology of work behavior* (3rd ed.). Chicago: Dorsey.

Maslow, A.H. (1970). *Motivation and personality* (2nd ed.). New York: Harper & Row.

Maslow, A.H. (1992). A theory of human motivation. In V.H. Vroom & E.L. Deci (Eds.), *Management and motivation* (pp. 39–52). London: Penguin.

Muchinsky, P.M. (1987). *Psychology applied to work* (2nd ed.). Chicago: Dorsey.

Saal, F.E., & Knight, P.A. (1988). *Industrial/organizational psychology: Science and practice.* Pacific Grove, CA: Brooks/Cole.

Ratliff, J.D. (1988). *High School Journal, 72*(1), 8–16.

Steers, R.M., & Porter, L.W. (1991). *Motivation and work behavior* (5th ed.). New York: McGraw-Hill.

Teleometrics International. (1992, October). Don't miss out! *Teleometrics International Management Training and Organizational Development Newsletter.*

Wahba, M.A., & Bridwell, L.B. (1976). Maslow reconsidered: A review of research on the need hierarchy theory. *Organizational Behavior and Human Performance, 15,* 212–240.

INDEX OF TEST TITLES

INDEX OF TEST PUBLISHERS

Clinical Psychology Publishing Company, Inc., 4 Conant Square, Brandon, Vermont 05733; (802)247-6871—[III:461; VIII:692; IX:414, 534, 561]

Clinical Psychometric Research, P.O. Box 619, Riderwood, Maryland 21139; (800)245-0277 or (410)321-6165—[II:32; III:583; X:562]

Coddington, R. Dean, P.O. Box 307, St. Clairsville, Ohio 43950; (614)695-4805—[III:383, 388]

College Board, The, 45 Columbus Avenue, New York, New York 10023; (212)713-8000—[VI:120, 609; VII:10; X:128, 136]

College-Hill Press, Inc., 34 Beacon Street, Boston, Massachusetts 02108; (617)859-5504—[III:293]

Communication Research Associates, Inc., P.O. Box 11012, Salt Lake City, Utah 84147; (801) 295-8046; III:669; VII:290]

Communication Skill Builders, Inc., 3830 East Bellevue, P.O. Box 42050, Tucson, Arizona 85733; (602)323-7500 or FAX (602)325-0306—[II:191, 562; V:118; VII:202; VIII:34; X:704, 716]

Consulting Psychologists Press, Inc., 3803 Bayshore Road, P.O. Box 10096, Palo Alto, California 94303; (415)969-8901—[I:34, 41, 146, 226, 259, 284, 380, 482, 623, 626, 663, 673; II:23, 56, 113, 263, 293, 509, 594, 697, 729; III:35, 51, 125, 133, 349, 392, 419; IV:42, 58, 132, 162, 570; V:141, 189, 226, 303, 556; VI:29, 87, 97; VII:20, 55, 59, 66, 87, 446; VIII:111, 115, 118, 241, 251, 384, 436, 516, 563, 574, 630, 734; IX:132, 500, 625, 643, 664; X:143, 388, 628, 780, 828]

C.P.S., Inc., P.O. Box 83, Larchmont, New York 10538; (914)833- 1633—[I:185; III:604; IX:210]

Creative Learning Press, Inc., P.O. Box 320, Mansfield Center, Connecticut 06250; (203) 423-8120—[II:402; VII:110]

Croft, Inc., 2936 Remington Avenue, Baltimore, Maryland 21211-2891; (301)235-1700—[III:198]

CTB/Macmillan/McGraw-Hill. *See* CTB/McGraw-Hill

CTB/McGraw-Hill, 20 Ryan Ranch Road, Monterey, California 93940; (800)538-9547, (408) 393-0700, or FAX (408)3937825—[I:3, 164, 578; II:517, 584, 780; III:186; IV:79, 238; V:406, 494; VI:149, 615; VII:102, 144, 189; VIII:521, 652; IX:591; X:110]

Curriculum Associates, Inc., 5 Esquire Road, North Billerica, Massachusetts 01862-2589; (800)225-0248, in Massachusetts (617)667-8000—[III:79]

Dean, Raymond S., Ph.D., Ball State University, TC 521, Muncie, Indiana 47306; (317) 285-8500—[VI:297]

Delis, Dean, Ph.D., 3753 Canyon Way, Martinez, California 94553—[I:158]

Denver Developmental Materials, Inc., P.O. Box 6919, Denver, Colorado 80206-0919; (303) 355-4729—[VII:234]

Devereux Foundation Press, The, 19 South Waterloo Road, P.O. Box 400, Devon, Pennsylvania 19333; (215)296-6905—[II:231; III:221; V:104]

Diagnostic Specialists, Inc., 1170 North 660 West, Orem, Utah 84057; (801)224-8492—[II:95]

DLM Teaching Resources, One DLM Park, Allen, Texas 75002; (800)527- 4747, in Texas (800)442-4711—[II:72; III:68, 521, 551, 726; IV:376, 493, 683; V:310; VI:80, 586; VII:49; VIII:77, 319; IX:290, 648; X:728, 804]

DMI Associates, 615 Clark Avenue, Owosso, Michigan 48867; (517)723- 3523—[VI:115]

D.O.K. Publishers, Inc., P.O. Box 605, East Aurora, New York 14052; (800)458-7900—[II:211; VI:303, 582; VIII:708; IX:391]

Eagleville Hospital, 100 Eagleville Road, Eagleville, Pennsylvania 19408; (215)539-6000—[VII:561]

Economy Company, The, P.O. Box 25308, 1901 North Walnut Street, Oklahoma City, Oklahoma 73125; (405)528- 8444—[IV:458]

Educational Activities, Inc., 1937 Grand Avenue, Baldwin, New York 11520; (800)645-2796, in Alaska, Hawaii, and New York (516)223-4666—[V:290; VI: 249]

Educational and Industrial Testing Service (EdITS), P.O. Box 7234, San Diego, California 92107; (619)222-1666—[I:279, 522, 555; II:3, 104, 258; III:3, 215; IV:199, 387, 449; V:76]

Educational Assessment Service, Inc., 6050 Apple Road, Watertown, Wisconsin 53094; (414) 261-1118—[II:332, VI:415; VIII:235]

Educational Development Corporation, P.O. Box 470663, Tulsa, Oklahoma 74147; (800) 331-4418, in Oklahoma (800)722-9113—[III:367;VI:244]

Educational Evaluation Enterprises, Awre, Newnham, Gloucestershire GL14 1ET England; (0594)510503—[VIII:308]

Educational Performance Associates, 600 Broad Avenue, Ridgefield, New Jersey 07657; (201)941-1425—[VIII:713; X:318]

Educational Studies and Development, 1428 Norton, Muskegon, Michigan 49441; (616) 780-2053 or 755-1041—[IX:3]

Educational Testing Service (ETS), Rosedale Road, Princeton, New Jersey 08541; (609) 921-9000—[III:655; VI:404; VIII:44, 717; IX:411]

Educators/Employers' Tests & Services Associates (ETSA), 341 Garfield Street, Chambersburg, Pennsylvania 17201; (717)264-9509—[IX:219]

Educators Publishing Service, Inc., 75 Moulton Street, Cambridge, Massachusetts 02238-9101; (800)225-5750, in Massachusetts (617)547-6706 or FAX (617)547-0412—[IV:195, 611; VI:188, 392; VIII:22; IX:385; X:528]

El Paso Rehabilitation Center, 1101 E. Schuster Avenue, El Paso, Texas 79902; (915) 566-2956—[III:171, 628]

Elbern Publications, P.O. Box 09497, Columbus, Ohio 43209; (614)235-2643—[II:627]

Elsevier Science Publishing Company, Inc., 52 Vanderbilt Avenue, New York, New York 10017; (212)867-9040—[III:358]

English Language Institute, Test Publications, University of Michigan, 3004 North University Building, Ann Arbor, Michigan 48109-1057; (313)747-0456 or 747-0476—[IX:214]

Epidemiology and Psychology, Research Branch, Division of Clinical Research, NIMH, 5600 Fishers Lane, Room 10C-05, Rockville, Maryland 20857; (301)443-4513—[II:144]

Essay Press, P.O. Box 2323, La Jolla, California 92307; (619)565- 6603—[II:646; IV:553]

Evaluation Research Associates. *See* FAAX Corporation

FAAX Corporation, 770 James Street, Suite 216, Syracuse, New York 13203; (315)422-0064—[II:551; III:158]

Fairleigh Dickinson University, Division of Psychological Services, Teaneck, New Jersey 07666; no business phone—[IX:496]

Family Social Science, University of Minnesota, 290 McNeal Hall, St. Paul, Minnesota 55108; (612)625-5289—[VII:209, 417; X:244, 261, 268]

Family Stress, Coping and Health Project, School of Family Resources and Consumer Sciences, University of Wisconsin, 1300 Linden Drive, Madison, Wisconsin 53706; (608) 262-5712—[VI:10, 16]

Foreworks, P.O. Box 9747, North Hollywood, California 91609; (818)982-0467—[III:647]

Foundation for Knowledge in Development, The—[I:443 *See* Psychological Corporation, The]

George Washington University, Department of Human Services, Rehabilitation Counselor Education Program, 2021 K Street, N.W., Washington, D.C. 20052; (202)994-7204—[X:8]

G.I.A. Publications, 7404 South Mason Avenue, Chicago, Illinois 60638; (312)496-3800—[V:216, 351]

Grune & Stratton, Inc.—[I:189; II:819; III:447, 526; IV:523; V:537; VI:52, 431 *See* Psychological Corporation, The]

Guidance Centre, Faculty of Education, University of Toronto, 10 Alcorn Avenue, Toronto, Ontario M4V 2Z8, Canada; (416)978-3211/3210—[III:271]

H&H Publishing Company, 1231 Kapp Drive, Clearwater, Florida 34625; (813)442-7760—[X:355]

Halgren Tests, 873 Persimmon Avenue, Sunnyvale, California 94087; (408)738-1342—[I:549]

Hanson, Silver, Strong and Associates, Inc., 10 West Main Street, Moorestown, New Jersey 08057; (609)234-2610—[VII:589; IX:620]

Harding Tests, P.O. Box 5271, Rockhampton Mail Centre, Queensland 4702, Australia; no business phone—[IV:334]

Harvard University Press, 79 Garden Street, Cambridge, Massachusetts 02138; (617) 495-2600—[II:799]

Hawthorne Educational Services, Inc., 800 Gray Oak Drive, Columbia, Missouri 65201; (800)542-1673 for ordering, or (314)874-1710 for information—[X:363]

Hilson Research Inc., 82-28 Abingdon Road, P.O. Box 239, Kew Gardens, New York 11415; (718)805-0063—[VI:265; IX:261; X:282]

Hiskey, Marshall S., 5640 Baldwin, Lincoln, Nebraska 68507; (402)466-6145—[III:331]

Hodder & Stoughton Educational, A Division of Hodder & Stoughton Ltd., P.O. Box 702, Mill Road, Dunton Green, Sevenoaks, Kent TN13 2YD England; (0732)450111—[IV:256; VII:646; VIII:544, 647, 749; IX:204]

Hodges, Kay, Ph.D., 801 Duluth Street, Durham, North Carolina 27710; (919)684-6691—[VI:91]

Humanics Limited, 1389 Peachtree Street, P.O. Box 7447, Atlanta, Georgia 30309; (404) 874-2176—[II:161, 426]

Humanics Media—[V:522, 524; VI:76 *See* Western Psychological Services]

Industrial Psychology Incorporated (IPI), 111 North Market Street, Champaign, Illinois 61820; (800)747-1119—[II:363]

Institute for Child Behavior Research, 4182 Adams Avenue, San Diego, California 92116; (619)281-7165—[VII:185]

Institute for Educational Research and Development, Memorial University of Newfoundland, St. John's, Newfoundland A1B 3X8, Canada; (709)737-8625—[IX:579]

Institute for Personality and Ability Testing, Inc. (IPAT), 1801 Woodfield Drive, Savoy, Illinois 61874-9505; (217)352-4739 or FAX (217)352-9674—[I:195, 202, 214, 233, 377; II:357; III:139, 246, 251, 319, 567; IV:595; V:283; VI:21, 359, 560; VII:374; VIII:190, 278, 289, 294; X:188]

Institute for Psycho-Imagination Therapy, 179 South Burrington Place, Los Angeles, California 90049; (213)652-2922—[I:593]

Institute for Psychosomatic & Psychiatric Research & Training/Daniel Offer. *See* Center for the Study of Adolescence

Institute for the Advancement of Philosophy for Children, Montclair State College, Upper Montclair, New Jersey 07043; (201)893-4277—[VII:365]

Institute of Psychological Research, Inc., 34 Fleury Street West, Montreal, Quebec H3L 1S9, Canada; (514)382-3000 or FAX (514)382-3007—[II:530; VI:601; X:713]

Instructional Materials & Equipment Distributors (IMED), 1520 Cotner Avenue, Los Angeles, California 90025; (213)879- 0377—[V:109]

International Association for the Study of Pain, 909 N.E. 43rd Street, Room 306, Seattle, Washington 98105-6020; (206)547- 6409—[VIII:402]

International Universities Press, Inc., 315 Fifth Avenue, New York, New York 10016; (212) 684-7900—[III:736]

INTREX Interpersonal Institute, P.O. Box 55218, Madison, Wisconsin 53705; (801) 363-6236—[VII:541]

Irwin, Richard D., Inc., 578 Arcade Avenue, Seekonk, Massachusetts 02771; (800)285-2564—[X:515]

ISU Research Foundation, Iowa State University, Ames, Iowa 50011; no business phone—[X:164]

Jamestown Publishers, P.O. Box 9168, 544 Douglass Avenue, Providence, Rhode Island 02940; (800)USA-READ or (401)351-1915—[V:212]

Jastak Associates, Inc., P.O. Box 4460, Wilmington, Delaware 19807; (800)221-9278—[I:758, 762; IV:673; VI:135; IX:653]

Johnson, Suzanne Bennett, Ph.D., Childrens's Mental Health Unit, Box J-234, J. Hillis Miller Health Sciences Center, University of Florida, Gainesville, Florida 32610—[VI:594]

Jossey-Bass, Inc., Publishers, 433 California Street, San Francisco, California 94104; (415) 433-1740—[III:395]

Keegan, Warren, and Associates Press, 210 Stuyvescent Avenue, Rye, New York 10580; (914)967-9421—[IX:335]

Kent Developmental Metrics, 1325 South Water Street, P.O. Box 845, Kent, Ohio 44240-3178; (216)678-3589—[III:380]

Khavari, Khalil A., Ph.D., Midwest Institute on Drug Use, University of Wisconsin-Milwaukee, Vogel Hall, Milwaukee, Wisconsin 53201; (414)963-4747—[VII:193]

Kovacs, Maria, Ph.D., 3811 O'Hara Street, Pittsburgh, Pennsylvania 15213-2593; (412) 624-2043—[V:65]

Krieger, Robert E., Publishing Company, Inc., P.O. Box 9542, Melbourne, Florida 32901; (305)724-9542—[III:30]

Ladoca Publishing Foundation—[I:239 *See* Denver Developmental Materials, Inc.]

Lafayette Instrument Company, Inc., P.O. Box 5729, Lafayette, Indiana 47903; (317) 423-1505—[V:534; VIII:337]

Lake, David S., Publishers, 19 Davis Drive, Belmont, California 94002; (415)592-7810—[II:241]

Lea and Febiger, P.O Box 3024, Malvern, Pennsylvania 19355-0799; (215)251-2230—[I:117; X:91]

Learning House, distributed exclusively by Guidance Centre, Faculty of Education, University of Toronto, 10 Alcorn Avenue, Ontario, Canada M4V 2Z8—[VI:66, 70, 73]

Lefkowitz, Monroe M., Ph.D., P.O. Box 1685, Lenox, Massachusetts 01240; (413)637-2113—[VII:432]

Lewis, H.K., & Co. Ltd., 136 Gower Street, London WC1E 6BS, England; (01)387-4282—[I:47, 206, 595; IV:408]

Libraries Unlimited, P.O. Box 3988, Englewood, Colorado 80155-3988; (303)770-1220—[VII:505]

LinguiSystems, Inc., 716 17th Street, Moline, Illinois 61265; (800)ALL-TIME, in Illinois (309) 762-5112—[II:831; V:221; VII:282, 600]

Lippincott, J.B., Company, 12107 Insurance Way, Hagerstown, Maryland 21740; (800) 638-3030—[X:457]

London House Press, 9701 West Higgins Road, Rosemont, Illinois 60018; (800)323-5923, in Illinois (312)298-7311—[III:510; IV:463; V:565; VI:529; VII:570; VIII:173; IX:18, 363]

MacKeith Press, 5A Netherhall Gardens, London NW3 5RN, England; (01)794-9859—[X:457]

Macmillan Education Ltd., Houndmills, Basingstoke, Hampshire RG21 2XS, England; (0256)29242—[VII:40; VIII:163, 374]

Marathon Consulting and Press, P.O. Box 09189, Columbus, Ohio 43209-0189; no business phone—[II:138, 535; VI:640; VII:159; X:824]

Martinus Nijhoff—[III:288 *See* SWETS and Zeitlinger, B.V.]

McCarron-Dial Systems, P.O. Box 45628, Dallas, Texas 75245; (214)247-5945—[IX:526]

Medical Research Council—[V:314 *See* Elithorn & Levander]

Psychological Services, Inc., Test Publication Division, 100 West Broadway, Suite 1100, Glendale, California 91210; (818)244-0033—[I:266; VIII:583, 589]

Psychological Test Specialists, P.O. Box 9229, Missoula, Montana 59807; no business phone—[I:530; II:299, 376, 451, 603; III:375; V:128]

Psychologistics, Inc., P.O. Box 033896, Indiatlantic, Florida 32903; (305)259-7811—[VIII:7]

Psychologists and Educators, Inc., P.O. Box 513, St. Louis, Missouri 63006; (314)576-9127—[I:568; III:206; V:323, 483; VI:412; VII:381; VIII:347, 394]

Psychometric Affiliates, P.O. Box 807, Murfreesboro, Tennessee 37133; (615)890-6296 or 898-2565—[IV:519; V:367; VI:437, 486; X:195]

Psychometric Software, Inc., P.O. Box 1677, 2210 South Front Street, Suite 208, Melbourne, Florida 32902-1677; (407)729-6390—[X:553]

Psychonomic Society, Inc., *Psychonomic Science,* 2904 Guadalupe, Austin, Texas 78705; (512) 476-9687—[V:513]

Psytec, Inc., P.O. Box 300, Webster, North Carolina 28788; (704)227-7361—[V:55]

Pumroy, Donald K., Ph.D., CAPS, College of Education, University of Maryland, College Park, Maryland 20742; (301)454- 2026—[VII:328]

Purdue University Bookstore, Division of Sponsored Programs, Patents and Copyright Office, Room 328, Building ENAD, West Lafayette, Indiana 47907; (317)494-2610—[V:326]

Quay, Herbert C., Ph.D., P.O. Box 248074, University of Miami, Coral Gables, Florida 33124; (305)284-5208—[V:371]

Reason House, 204 East Joppa Road, Suite 10, Towson, Maryland 21204; (301)321-9101 or 321-7270—[IX:154]

Reddin, W.J., and Associates, Station Road, Motspur Park, New Malden, Surrey KT3 6JH, England—[VII:321]

Reid Psychological Systems, 233 North Michigan Avenue, Chicago, Illinois 60601; (312) 938-9200—[I:631]

Reitan Neuropsychology Laboratory, 1338 East Edison Street, Tucson, Arizona 85719; (602) 795-3717—[I:305, 536; II:637; III:640]

Renovex, 1421 Jersey Avenue North, Minneapolis, Minnesota 55427; (612)333-9179—[IX:13]

Research Press Company, 2612 North Mattis Avenue, Champaign, Illinois 61821; (217) 352-3273—[VIII:132]

Research Psychologists Press, Inc. *See* SIGMA Assessment Systems, Inc.

Richardson, Bellows, Henry, and Company, Inc., 1140 Connecticut Avenue, N.W., Suite 610, Washington, D.C. 20036; (202)659- 3755—[VIII:67, 381, 674; X:576]

Riverside Publishing Company, The, 8420 Bryn Mawr Avenue, Chicago, Illinois 60631; (800)323-9540, in Alaska, Hawaii, or Illinois call collect (312)693-0040—[I:421, 603, 641; II:416, 674, 835; III:475; IV:11, 310, 453; V:517; VI:277, 397, 544; VII:228, 255, 610; VIII:216, 506; IX:105, 139]

Rocky Mountain Behavioral Science Institute, Inc. (RMBSI), P.O. Box 1066, Fort Collins, Colorado 80526; (303)221-0602—[I:436, 682; V:266]

Roll, Samuel, Ph.D., 5712 Osuna N.E., Albuquerque, New Mexico 87109; (505)881-1464—[II:559]

Salamon, Michael, Ph.D., Adult Developmental Center, 920 Broadway, Suite 1-A, Woodmere, New York 11598; (516)374-5360—[X:618]

SCAN-TRON Corporation, Reading Test Division, 2021 East Del Amo Boulevard, Rancho Dominguez, California 90220; (213)638-0520—[VII:499]

Scholastic Testing Service, Inc. (STS), 480 Meyer Road, Bensenville, Illinois 60106-1617; (708)766-7150 or FAX (708)766-8054—[I:300; II:45; III:75, 344; IV:245, 264, 666; V:90, 505; VI:239; VII:427, 619; VIII:138, 613; IX:340; X:521]

Treatment Research Institute, 3600 Market Street, Suite 846, Philadelphia, Pennsylvania 19104-2648; (215)349-8982 or FAX (215)349-8984—[X:20]

Union College, Character Research Project. *See* Personality Research Services Ltd.

United Educational Services, Inc., P.O. Box 1099, Buffalo, New York 14224; (800)458-7900 or (716)668-7691—[V:26; VII:595; VIII:183; X:102]

United States Department of Defense, Testing Directorate, Headquarters, Military Entrance Processing Command, Attn: MEPCT, 2500 Green Bay Road, North Chicago, IL 60064; (800)323-0513, in Illinois call collect (312)688-6908—[I:61]

United States Department of Labor, 200 Constitution Avenue N.W., Room N-4460, Washington, D.C. 20213; (202)535-0192—[I:83; III:673; V:150; VII:240; IX:503]

University Associates, Inc., Learning Resources Corporation, 8517 Production Avenue, P.O. Box 26240, San Diego, California 92121; (619)578-5900—[I:559; II:765; VI:109; VIII:603]

University of Denver, Department of Psychology, Attn: Dr. Susan Harter, Denver, Colorado 80208; no business phone—[IX:472]

University of Florida, Department of Psychiatry, Attn: Dr. Suzanne Bennett Johnson, Gainesville, Florida 32610; no business phone—[IX:149]

University of Illinois Press, 54 East Gregory Drive, Champaign, Illinois 61820; (217) 333-0950—[I:354; II:543; V:32]

University of Minnesota Press—[I:466 *See* National Computer Systems/PAS Division]

University of Missouri, Career Planning and Placement Center, Columbia, Missouri 65201; (314)882-6801—[VIII:498]

University of New Hampshire, Family Research Laboratory, Durham, New Hampshire 03824; (603)862-1888—[VIII:98]

University of Vermont, College of Medicine, Department of Psychiatry, Section of Child, Adolescent, and Family Psychiatry, 1 South Prospect Street, Burlington, Vermont 05401; (802)656-4563—[I:168]

University of Washington Press, P.O. Box 50096, Seattle, Washington 98145; (206)543-4050, business department (206)543- 8870—[II:661, 714]

University of Wisconsin–Stout, Stout Vocational Rehabilitation Institute, Materials Development Center, Menomonie, Wisconsin 54751; no business phone—[VIII:209]

Valett, Robert E., Department of Advanced Studies, California State University at Fresno, Fresno, California 93740; no business phone—[II:68]

Variety Pre-Schooler's Workshop, 47 Humphrey Drive, Syosset, New York 11791; (516) 921-7171—[III:261]

Vocational Psychology Research, University of Minnesota, N620 Elliott Hall, 75 East River Road, Minneapolis, Minnesota 55455-0344; (612)625-1367—[II:481; IV:434; V:255; VI:350]

Vocational Research Institute, 2100 Arch Street, 6th Floor, Philadelphia, Pennsylvania 19103; (215)496-9674—[VII:623]

Walker Educational Book Corporation, 720 Fifth Avenue, New York, New York 10019; (212)265-3632—[II:689]

West Virginia Rehabilitation Research and Training Center, #1 Dunbar Plaza, Suite E, Dunbar, West Virginia 25064; (304)766- 7138—[VIII:301; IX:405]

Western Psychological Services, A Division of Manson Western Corporation, 12031 Wilshire Boulevard, Los Angeles, California 90025; (310)478-2061 or FAX (310)478-7838—[I:315, 338, 511, 543, 663; II:108, 430, 570, 607, 723, 826; III:145, 255, 282, 340, 402, 415, 615, 714, 717; IV:15, 33, 39, 259, 274, 300, 351, 382, 440, 501, 565, 606, 649; V:9, 73, 83, 378, 382, 425, 458, 549; VI:60, 260, 505, 519, 576, 629; VII:277, 301, 313, 404, 463, 480; VIII:358, 668; IX:10, 51, 99, 358, 431, 465, 490, 545, 611, 660; X:13, 39, 120, 124, 251, 383, 409, 593, 658, 689, 799]

Westwood Press, Inc., 251 Park Avenue South, 14th Floor, New York, New York 10010; (212)420-8008—[VII:466]

Wilmington Press, The, 13315 Wilmington Drive, Dallas, Texas 75234; (214)620-8531—[VI:383; IX:145]

Wolfe Personnel Testing and Training Systems, Inc., P.O. Box 319, Oradell, New Jersey 07649; (201)265-5393—[VIII:741]

Wonderlic, E.F., & Associates, Inc., Frontage Road, Northfield, Illinois 60093; (312)446-8900—[I:769]

World of Work, Inc., 2923 North 67th Place, Scottsdale, Arizona 85251; (602)946-1884—[VI:644]

Wyeth Laboratories, P.O. Box 8616, Philadelphia, Pennsylvania 19101; (215)688-4400—[V:499]

York Press, Inc., 2712 Mount Carmel Road, Parkton, Maryland 21120; (301)343-1417—[VII:163]

Zung, William W.K., M.D., Veterans Administration Medical Center, 508 Fulton Street, Durham, North Carolina 27705; (919)286-0411—[III:595]

INDEX OF TEST AUTHORS/REVIEWERS

885

SUBJECT INDEX

Marriage and Family: Family

Personality: Adolescent and Adult

Personality: Child

Personality: Multilevel

Education Development and School Readiness

Reading: Elementary

Reading: High School and Above

Reading: Multilevel

School and Institutional Environments

Speech, Hearing, and Visual: Visual

Student Evaluation and Counseling: Behavior Problems and Counseling Tools

Teacher Evaluation

BUSINESS AND INDUSTRY

Aptitude and Skills Screening

Clerical

Management and Supervision

Mechanical Abilities and Manual Dexterity

Sales